THE JEW IN THE MODERN WORLD

THE JEW IN THE MODERN WORLD

A DOCUMENTARY HISTORY

Third Edition

Compiled and Edited by

Paul Mendes-Flohr
THE UNIVERSITY OF CHICAGO

Jehuda Reinharz
BRANDEIS UNIVERSITY

NEW YORK   OXFORD
OXFORD UNIVERSITY PRESS

Oxford University Press, Inc., publishes works that further Oxford University's
objective of excellence in research, scholarship, and education.

Oxford   New York
Auckland   Cape Town   Dar es Salaam   Hong Kong   Karachi
Kuala Lumpur   Madrid   Melbourne   Mexico City   Nairobi
New Delhi   Shanghai   Taipei   Toronto

With offices in
Argentina   Austria   Brazil   Chile   Czech Republic   France   Greece
Guatemala   Hungary   Italy   Japan   Poland   Portugal   Singapore
South Korea   Switzerland   Thailand   Turkey   Ukraine   Vietnam

For titles covered by Section 112 of the US Higher Education
Opportunity Act, please visit www.oup.com/us/he for the latest
information about pricing and alternate formats.

Published by Oxford University Press, Inc.
198 Madison Avenue, New York, New York 10016
http://www.oup.com

Oxford is a registered trademark of Oxford University Press

Library of Congress Cataloging-in-Publication Data

   The Jew in the modern world : a documentary history /
compiled and edited by Paul Mendes-Flohr, Jehuda Reinharz.—3rd ed.
      p. cm.
   ISBN 978-0-19-538906-7
   1. Jews—History—17th century—Sources. 2. Jews—History—18th century—Sources.
3. Jews—History—1789–1945—Sources. 4. Judaism—History—Modern period, 1750—Sources.
I. Mendes-Flohr, Paul R. II. Reinharz, Jehuda.
DS102.J43 2011
909'.04924—dc22   2010046010

Printing number: 9 8 7 6 5 4 3 2 1

Printed in the United States of America
on acid-free paper

To Inbal, Yael,
Itamar, and Naomi

CONTENTS

PREFACE TO THE THIRD EDITION

NEW TO THE THIRD EDITION

- Over 100 new documents address important issues to understanding modern Jewish history, including the status of women, and debates between traditional and secular Jews and the role of Zionism in modern Jewish life.
- One new chapter—Chapter 8, "Sephardi and Middle Eastern Jewry,"—enhances the book's scope and chronology.
- Four new maps show the concentration of Jews throughout the Mediterranean and Middle East.
- The Appendix has been completely updated with the latest population figures.

During the thirty years since the first edition of this book appeared, Jewish historiography has undergone significant changes. The postmodern critique of the guiding presumptions of how history is to be constructed and told has led to a methodological self-awareness regarding the metanarratives that historians adopt. The first two editions of this documentary history followed by and large a narrative trajectory that culminated in the twin events of the Holocaust and the establishment of the State of Israel and the enactment of the Law of Return. This metanarrative, the prefix "meta" underscoring that there is an overarching dialectic *logos* to modern Jewish history, is now questioned. Historians now tend to honor a plurality of narratives that constitute the modern Jewish experience. We have sought to accommodate this historiographical shift by placing the chapter on the renegotiations of Jewish identity characteristics of modernity at the end of the volume. In this chapter we have extended the *terminus ad quem* beyond 1948, which set the chronological end point of the first two editions of this volume. Moreover, we have included in this chapter voices that had hardly been represented in the previous editions, namely, the voices of Sephardi Jews and those of women with a feminist perspective. The underrepresentation of Sephardi and Oriental Jewry has been corrected by the inclusion of a chapter that is entirely devoted to the encounter of the Jewries of the Balkans and the Near East—from North Africa to Persia—with modernity, largely through the auspices of Western colonialism. We like to take this opportunity to thank Jonathan P. Decter of Brandeis University, who prepared this chapter on our behalf.

Sephardi and female voices are more amply represented in other chapters of this edition to resonate with the multiple and often contrasting Jewish encounters with the modern world. Similarly we have given greater attention to diverse perceptions of the challenges facing Jewry, with their passage from their sequestered existence prior to their emancipation to the culturally and socially open terrain beyond the political boundaries of the ghetto. Michael Silber, of the Hebrew University, was particularly helpful in identifying for us expressions of ultra-Orthodox opposition to the allure of integration into non-Jewish cultures and political structures. Yaacov Shavit, of the University of Tel Aviv, provided us, as is his wont, with sage advice on the chapter on Zionism. Sergio DellaPergola, of the Hebrew University of Jerusalem, and Benjamin Phillips and Leonard Saxe, both of the Steinhardt Social Research Institute, Brandeis University, reviewed our appendix on demography and offered constructive advice, particularly with respect to the calculation of contemporary Jewish populations. Sylvia Barack Fishman, codirector of the Hadassah-Brandeis Institute on Jewish Women, Brandeis University, brought our attention to the most recent statistical study on Jewish education in the United States. We are most obliged to Irene Eber for providing us with a document from her research on the Jewish refugee community of Shanghai, and to Antony Polonsky for providing documents on twentieth century Polish Jewry. Elizabeth Gallas provided and annotated a hitherto unpublished report by Hannah Arendt on efforts to recover and redistribute cultural treasures looted by the Nazis. Rachel Seelig, Adam Stern and Dov Weiss translated and annotated difficult but seminal documents.

The following colleagues shared with us their experience of teaching *The Jew in the Modern World*, alerting us to typographical and occasional factual errors, as well as making suggestions about how we may enhance the pedagogical value of the book: Marc D. Angel, Allan Arkush, David Berger, Menachem Brinker, Irene Eber, David Ellenson, Sylvia Barack Fishman, Rachel Freudenthal, Sylvia Fuks Fried, (who was very helpful in many other ways as well), David Graizbord, Brian J. Horowitz, Shulamit Magnus, Pamela S. Nadell, Ben Phillips, Yehiel Poupko, Shalom Ratzabi, Ben Ravid, Marsha L. Rozenblit, Michael W. Rubinoff, Jonathan Sarna, Adam Shear, and Martina Urban. Michael Silber offered sapient advice on Hungarian Jewry.

Various individuals assisted us with technical tasks that were attendant to preparing this volume for publication. We would also like to thank the following people for reviewing the Second Edition: Robin Judd, The Ohio State University; Rebecca Lesses, Ithaca College; James Loeffler, University of Virginia; Avinoam J. Patt, American University. Under the pressure of meeting a pressing deadline, Joanna Gould, Jennifer Kullas, and Emily Spero Smith graciously pitched in to help us with typing the lengthy manuscript that we delivered to the publisher. Tracy Guy, Sarah Imhoff, and David Lyons read through the second edition and with an eagle eye spotted typographical errors and occasional inconsistencies. Sarah Imhoff also offered sapient advice regarding the chapter on American Jewry and the inclusion of representative women. With exemplary resourcefulness and dedication, Caroline Young Friedman was of invaluable assistance in arranging copyright permissions and proofreading. The index was ably prepared by Virginia Ling. We are very grateful to Bob Grogg who copyedited the manuscript with great care and expertise. We also wish to acknowledge Shay Rabineau's contribution as a very dedicated and exacting proofreader; we are grateful for his hard work.

Finally we wish to express our gratitude to the editorial staff of Oxford University Press, Charles Cavaliere, Marianne Paul, Keith Faivre and Lauren Aylward, for their cordial collaboration in seeing this book to press.

Erev Pessach 5770 — Paul Mendes-Flohr

April 2010 — Jehuda Reinharz

PREFACE TO THE SECOND EDITION

The Psalmist exults that he has "gained insight from all my teachers" (Ps. 119:99), from all who have taught him. Indeed, in the preparation of this second edition of *The Jew in the Modern World* we have gained insight from our many "teachers," our colleagues and students. Since the publication of the first edition some fifteen years ago, colleagues and students have graciously shared with us their responses to our documentary history, bringing to our attention documents offering greater nuance or different perspectives or addressing aspects we had overlooked. We have kept a careful record of all their comments and have endeavored to incorporate many of their suggestions in our revisions.

Accordingly, we have amended the chapter introductions and notes, eliminated some documents, and added many more. Thanks to the support provided by Oxford University Press—and especially our editor, Nancy Lane, whom we profoundly thank—the result has been a greatly expanded volume. Nonetheless, we readily acknowledge that no book of this nature could ever claim to be exhaustive.

Nor can the list of individuals to whom we are gratefully indebted be exhaustive. Nevertheless, we feel obliged to express our gratitude to the following colleagues who have offered helpful comments, often based on their personal experience utilizing our text in the classroom: Howard Adelman, Phyllis Albert, Gershon Bacon, David Bankier, Sergio DellaPergola, Jonathan Frankel, Gregory Freeze, the late Ben Halpern, Deborah Hertz, Marion Kaplan, Lionel Kochan, Otto Dov Kulka, Steven Lowenstein, Frances Malino, Michael A. Meyer, Antony Polonsky, Aviezer Ravitzky, Yosef Salmon, Anita Shapira, Uziel Schmelz, David Sorkin, Shaul Stampfer, and Ellen M. Umansky. Several colleagues have been particularly giving of their knowledge and time, exemplifying academic collegiality at its best. It is with great pleasure that we thank Israel Bartal, Evyatar Friesel, Yisrael Gutman, Zeev Gries, Jonathan D. Sarna, Michael Silber, and Leni Yahil.

Finally, we wish to thank Sylvia Fuks Fried and Janet Webber of the Tauber Institute for the Study of European Jewry, Brandeis University, for their unstinting administrative and secretarial assistance. We acknowledge with thanks the generous support of the Cyrene and Andrew Weiner Tauber Institute Research Fund. We are grateful to Brandeis University and to the Hebrew University of Jerusalem for providing funds for translation and technical assistance. Gila Svirsky intelligently rendered translations from the Hebrew of new documents included in this volume. Virginia Perrin helped with technical aspects of the book. Special thanks are due Mark A. Raider, who took time away from his graduate studies at Brandeis University to provide invaluable editorial assistance.

We conclude with heartfelt expressions of gratitude to our respective families for their support and indulgence.

Jerusalem   P.M.F.
Waltham, Mass.   J.R.
March 1994

PREFACE TO THE FIRST EDITION

Peoples of the past, it has been ironically observed, did not live as self-consciously as we do—they did not even know whether they were living in the fifth or fourth century B.C.E. In contrast, we are distinctly conscious of our place in history, and undoubtedly this consciousness derives from a profound sense of being witness to a radically new era in human history. Heralded first in Western Europe, this new or modern period is marked by far-reaching transformations in almost every aspect of human culture. For the modern Jew this consciousness of history is perhaps even more pronounced than it is for others—if for no other reason than that the Jew's entry into the modern world was marked by a radical, sudden break with the past. Western Jews "did not enter modern European [and American] society in a long process of 'endogenous' gestation and growth, but they plunged into it as the ghetto walls were breached, with a bang, though not without prolonged whimpers."[1]

These whimpers express the modern Jew's bewilderment. Beyond the walls of the ghetto and the precincts of the Pale, the Jews found horizons that led them far from the world of their fathers. The modern, secular world has granted the Jews equality and has opened before them undreamt of opportunities for intellectual and personal development—opportunities that have immeasurably enriched them. Moreover, the modern world has encouraged the development of new and rewarding forms of Jewish self-expression and collective organization. Yet this same new era has been for many Jews a veritable purgatory: in the Jews' passage through modernity their religion, culture and identity have suffered severely, and, tragically, they have borne the brunt of the most demonic enemies of modernity, the antisemites, who, eventually, leading an apocalyptic war to dismantle the modern world—or at least what in their eyes were its most egregious features, democracy and Jewish emancipation—unleashed a Holocaust that devoured a third of the Jewish people. This trauma, in consonance with the contradictory rhythms of modern Jewish history, was quickly followed by the rebirth of the State of Israel and a renewal of Jewish pride and sense of community.

In light of the ambiguous quality of their recent history, the Jews of the modern age are profoundly perplexed. This perplexity has intrigued us, the editors, and many others, and has encouraged us to study, and, we hope, to understand, modern Jewish history. This

---

[1] R. J. Zwi Werblowsky, *Beyond Tradition and Modernity: Changing Religions in a Changing World* (London: University of London, The Athlone Press, 1976), p. 42.

book, the product of our study, is not, however, a "Guide to the Perplexed": it offers no release from the contradictions; but, rather, offers a guide through the dynamic forces that shape the modern Jewish experience.

The study of modern Jewish history is encumbered by many of the same processes that produced that history: rapid changes in Jewish life have pushed and pulled the Jews across numerous linguistic, cultural and political boundaries. The examination of modern Jewish history thus requires the knowledge of the many languages that have affected Jewish destiny in the recent past. Also required is an understanding of the dialectical tension between religious tradition and secularity. Likewise the comprehension of Jewish history rests on a knowledge of European, Near Eastern and American political, economic, cultural and social history, particularly of the Enlightenment, the formation of the modern nation-state, the development of democracy, liberalism, capitalism, socialism and the conservative and romantic reactions to these processes.

As teachers of modern Jewish history, our task is encumbered by the inaccessibility of many of the primary documents that illustrate the various processes at work in modern Jewish history. Hitherto no comprehensive attempt has been made to gather—either in the original languages or in translation—the relevant primary documents. For this reason we have selected over two hundred French, German, Hebrew, Portuguese, Russian and Yiddish documents—most of them especially translated for this volume—which we consider central and illuminating. The length of the documents varies: some briefly illustrate a point, others delve into the intricacies of a debate or process. Generally, a document speaks for itself, but when arcane references make it unintelligible, we have added explanatory numbered notes following the document. Notes original to the document are marked by symbols and appear at the bottom of the page. We have also woven the documents into a conceptual and narrative apparatus—explained in the introduction— which helps articulate their meanings. Although our selection and organization of the documents reveal a certain perspective, we do not propose a specific thesis. Rather, we seek to encourage a creative interplay between the documents and the reader. Thus, while not presuming to relieve the "perplexity" of readers, this volume is intended to aid them in understanding the experience of the Jew in the modern world.

We have adopted two technical guidelines in the selection of the documents in this reader. First, we have sought to minimize duplicating material found in volumes that are readily available.[2] Second, we have made an effort to include documents which, although frequently referred to in scholarly discussions of modern Jewish history, are not generally available in English translation.

Although scholars' lives are said to be solitary, they also participate in a special sharing, both with the subject of inquiry and with fellow scholars. The scholarly community bridges time and space and includes persons not personally known by the individual scholar. Our indebtedness to the community of scholars is recorded in the text. In the preparation of this book we also enjoyed the personal encouragement and generosity of many colleagues and friends in the academic community: Lloyd P. Gartner, Arthur A. Goren, Michael

---

[2] See Robert Chazan and Marc Lee Raphael, eds., *Modern Jewish History: A Source Reader* (New York: Schocken, 1974); Lucy Dawidowicz, ed., *The Golden Tradition: Jewish Life and Thought in Eastern Europe* (Boston: Beacon Press, 1967); Nahum N. Glatzer, ed., *The Judaic Tradition* (Boston: Beacon Press, 1967), pt. 3; Arthur Hertzberg, ed., *Readings in Modern Jewish History: From the American Revolution to the Present* (New York: Ktav Publishing House, 1977); Walter Ackerman, ed., *Out of Our People's Past: Sources for the Study of Jewish History* (New York: The United Synagogue Commission on Jewish Education, 1977).

Heymann, Jacob Katz, Otto Dov Kulka, Walter Z. Laqueur, Ezra Mendelsohn and George L. Mosse. We are most grateful for their assistance and sincere interest in our project.

We also wish to acknowledge the competent translations by Saul Fischer, Sylvia Fuks, Mark Gelber, Deborah Goldman, Jeffrey Green, Jacob Hessing, Rita Mendes-Flohr, Jeffrey Rubin, Laura Sachs, Arnold Schwartz, Saul Stampler, Stephen Weinstein and Rachel Weiss. We are grateful to Ann Joachim and Carole Wolkan for their help in preparing the first draft of the index, to Ann Hofstra Grogg for preparing the final version of the index and to Regina Alkalai for typing the manuscript. We particularly appreciate the intelligent, resourceful and devoted assistance of Stephen Weinstein.

Thanks are due also to the Horace H. Rackham School of Graduate Studies of the University of Michigan for financial assistance in the final stages of the preparation of the manuscript.

Finally, we would like to express our deepest gratitude to our former teachers at the Department of Near Eastern and Judaic Studies of Brandeis University: Professors Alexander Altmann, Nahum N. Glatzer and Ben Halpern. With scholarly eminence, sensitivity and wisdom they taught us that genuine scholarship is a moral and spiritual endeavor. We hope that this book will prove a worthy tribute to them.

THE JEW IN THE MODERN WORLD

INTRODUCTION

According to most empirical indices contemporary Jewish life in the West is markedly different from that which the Jews traditionally led. The overarching role of religion is no longer a self-evident feature of Jewish life. Integrated in western, secular culture, many, if not the majority of contemporary Jews do not, as their forbears did, conduct their lives according to norms and criteria exclusively derived from Judaism and the Jewish experience. Economically and vocationally the Jews' activity now has an immeasurably wider range and variety than formerly. Politically, the Jews have left the ghetto, and they legally enjoy either civic parity in the counties of their residence or political independence in the newly sovereign State of Israel. These transformations in Jewish life are structurally parallel to the process generally called modernization that has affected any number of traditional societies in recent times.[1]

Scholars differ, of course, regarding the exact definition of modernization with varying components of the process being alternately emphasized. Dating the process is related to the question of definition, and it is thus no less controversial. Periodization in history is inevitably problematic, for history as a fluid, dynamic process is never uniform and unidimensional. A "period" is not intrinsic to history; it is imposed by the historian to bracket years that give witness to a process he or she deems salient. For example, Heinrich Graetz, one of the pioneers of Jewish historiography in the nineteenth century, characterized the "latest epoch"[2] in Jewish history as an intellectual-spiritual process that brought the Jews to a new level of historical self-awareness (*Selbstbewusstsein*).[3] This epochal leap beyond the preceding period of spiritual "exhaustion"[4] was quickened by an intense, but at its most genuine moments never self-abnegating, contact with liberal

---

[1] For a most illuminating discussion of modern Jewish history within the framework of a comparative analysis of the dialectical encounter of traditional cultures with modernization, see R. J. Zwi Werblowsky, *Beyond Tradition and Modernity: Changing Religions in a Changing World* (London: University of London, The Athlone Press, 1976), ch. 3, "Sacral Particularity: The Jewish Case, with a Digression on Japan."

[2] H. Graetz, *Geschichte der Juden*, 2nd ed. rev. (Leipzig, 1900), vol. 2, p. 3.

[3] Ibid., p. 1.

[4] H. Graetz, "Die Construction der juedischen Geschichte," *Zeilschrift fuer die religioesen Interessen des Judentums* 3 (1846).

European culture. Graetz associated the beginnings of the modern epoch in Jewish history with Moses Mendelssohn—the son of a Torah scribe who without forfeiting his Jewish self-esteem enjoyed the friendship and intellectual fellowship of Gotthold Ephraim Lessing and other prominent figures of the German Enlightenment.[5] For the Russian Jewish historian Simon Dubnow, on the other hand, Mendelssohn and the Jewish Enlightenment (*haskalah*) in general were merely of transitional significance.[6] Dubnow held that "the principal processes of the most modern history of the Jews" were political and social, and not cultural.[7] The fact that Mendelssohn served as the prototype for "Nathan the Wise"—the literary figure that Lessing hoped would inspire political tolerance for the Jews and for all dissenters[8]—was thus eminently more important, in Dubnow's view, than was Mendelssohn's cultural activity. Mendelssohn *qua* Nathan the Wise is a precursor, according to Dubnow, of the era of Jewish political emancipation (and the antisemitic reaction to it) ushered in by the French Revolution of 1789. The late Israeli historian Ben-Zion Dinur had yet another conception of modern Jewish history.[9] The modern era, as he understood it, began in 1700 when Rabbi Judah Hasid led a band of some thousand pious Jews on a march to settle the Holy Land. Most of Rabbi Judah Hasid's followers did not complete the then difficult journey, but for Dinur their effort at "organized immigration" to the ancestral homeland signified the beginnings of the revolt against Jewry's millennial Exile—a revolt which steadily gained momentum, ineluctably culminating in the 1948 reestablishment of the Jewish commonwealth in the land of Israel.

There are other conceptions of Jewish modernity, of course, many of which we will make reference to in the course of the volume.[10] What is, however, manifest in all of these conceptions, despite their often extreme variation, is the conviction that the last two hundred years or so have witnessed a radical transformation of Jewish life. If we emphasize the aspect of transformation, it is to underscore that the process of modernization in Jewish Diaspora history is neither chronologically nor geographically uniform. Not all of Mendelssohn's contemporary German Jews were "modern," nor were most nineteenth-century East European Jews. Middle Eastern Jewry encountered modernity largely through the auspices of colonial powers, which sought to secure their political influence in the Muslim world by disseminating the "blessings" of European culture. Accordingly, as Jonathan P. Decter notes in the introduction to chapter VIII, "Sephardi and Middle Eastern Jewry," which he prepared especially for the third edition of this volume, "for Sephardi and Middle Eastern Jewry, modernization was largely tantamount to westernization." From the late eighteenth century onward, European ideas and values slowly spread throughout the Middle East and North Africa. Although colonialism was the dominant agent of this process, the process was also facilitated by internal developments and, for Jews, by "the cultural

---

[5] H. Graetz. *Geschichte der Juden*, vol. 11, pp. 1–36. On the Friendship of Mendelssohn and Lessing, see chapter 2 of this volume.

[6] S. Dubnow, *History of the Jews*, ed. and trans. Moshe Spiegel, 4th definitive rev. ed. (New York: Thomas Yoseloff, 1971), vol. 4, pp. 325–47.

[7] Ibid., pp. 493–501.

[8] On the history and significance of Lessing's "Nathan the Wise," see chap. 2, documents 4 and 5.

[9] Ben-Zion Dinur, *Israel and the Diaspora* (Philadelphia: Jewish Publication Society, 1969), pp. 79–161.

[10] For a fine survey of the leading trends in the historiography of modern Jewish history, see Michael A. Meyer, "Where Does the Modern Period of Jewish History Begin?" *Judaism* 24, no. 3 (Summer 1975), pp. 329–38.

and educational reforms that were introduced by European Jews."[11] This uneven pattern of Jewish modernization explains the selection of the documents we have included in this volume. While the documents, arranged according to themes, illustrate the various dimensions—political, social, intellectual—of Jewish modernity which are generally considered significant, we have emphasized those aspects that point to a break with, or at least a weakening of, traditional values, institutions and socioeconomic patterns of Jewish life. To understand the nature of this eclipse of tradition (in both its specific religious and its broad cultural

---

[11] For a comprehensive review of the issues concerning the modernization of Oriental Jewry, see Harvey E. Goldberg, "Religious Responses [to Modernization] in the Nineteenth and Twentieth Centuries," in Jack Wertheimer, ed. *The Uses of Tradition: Jewish Continuity in the Modern Era* (Cambridge, Mass.: Harvard University Press, 1992), pp. 121–46. Also see Shalom Bar-Asher, Yaakov Barnaea, Yaakov Tubi, *The History of the Jews in Islamic Lands* (in Hebrew) 3 vols., ed. Shmuel Ettinger (Jerusalem: Israel Historical Society and the Zalman Shazar Center, 1981); the third volume also includes articles by Michel Abitboul; Doris Besimon-Donath, *Evolution du judïsme marocain sous le protectorat français, 1912–1956* (Paris: Mouton, 1968): André N. Chouraqui, *Marche vers l'Occident: Les Juifs d'Afrique du Nord* (Paris: Presses Universitaires de France, 1951); ibid., *Between East and West: A History of the Jews of North Africa* (Philadelphia: Jewish Publication Society of America, 1968), pt. 3; Mordechai Hacohen, *The Book of Mordechai. A Study of the Jews of Libya*, ed. and trans, with an introduction and commentaries by Harvey E. Goldberg (Philadelphia: Institute for the Study of Human Issues, 1980); Shlomo Deshen and Moshe Shokeid, *The Predicament of Homecoming* (Ithaca, N.Y.: Cornell University Press, 1974); Shlomo Deshen and Walter P. Zenner, eds., *Jewish Societies in the Middle East* (Washington, D.C.: University Press of America, 1982); Shmuel Eisenstadt, *Israeli Society* (New York: Basic Books, 1967); Renzo De Felice, *Jews in an Arab Land: Libya, 1835–1970*, trans. Judith Roumani (Austin: University of Texas Press, 1985); Harvey E. Goldberg, *Cave Dwellers and Citrusgrowers: A Jewish Community in Libya and Israel* (Cambridge: Cambridge University Press, 1972); Haim Zeev Hirschberg, *A History of the Jews of North Africa*. Vol. 2: *From the Ottoman Conquests to the Present Time* (Leiden: Brill, 1981); Haim Zeev Hirschberg and Eliezer Bashan, *East and Maghreb: A Volume of Researches*, 2 vols. (Ramat Gan: Bar-Ilan University, 1974); Shimon Schwarzfuchs, *Les Juifs d'Algérie et la France, 1830–1855* (Jerusalem: Ben-Zvi Institute, 1981); Shimon Shamir, ed., *The Jews of Egypt: A Mediterranean Society in Modern Times* (Boulder, Colo.: Westview Press, 1987); Norman Stillman, *The Jews of Arab Lands: A History and Source Book* (Philadelphia: Jewish Publication Society of America, 1979); idem, *The Jews of Arab Lands in Modern Times* (Philadelphia: Jewish Publication Society, 1991); Zvi Zohar, "Halakhic Responses of Syrian and Egyptian Rabbinical Authorities to Social and Technological Change," in *Studies in Contemporary Jewry* 2 (1986), pp. 18–51; Zvi Zohar, *Tradition and Change* (in Hebrew) (Jerusalem: Ben-Zvi Institute, 1993); Zvi Zohar, "Un grand decisionnaire sepharade défend les droits de la femme," *Pardes* 2 (1985), pp. 128–148; Zvi Zohar, "Halakhah and Modernization in Egypt, 1882–1918" (in Hebrew), ed. Jacob M. Landau, *The Jews in Ottoman Egypt, 1517–1914* (Jerusalem: Misgav Yerushalayim, 1983), pp. 577–608; Zvi Zohar, "A 'Maskil' in Aleppo: The Torah of Israel and the People of Israel' by Rabbi Yitzhak Dayyan (Aleppo, 5683/1923)," in Yedida K. Stillman and George K. Zucker, eds., *New Horizons in Sephardic Studies* (Albany: State University of New York Press, 1993), pp. 93–107.

For the seminal role of the Alliance Israélite Universelle, founded in 1860 in Paris, as a purveyor of French culture and as an instrument of modernization among Jews of the Orient, see Michael Laskier, *The Alliance Israélite Universelle and the Jewish Community of Morocco, 1862–1962* (Albany: State University of New York Press, 1983); and Aaron Rodrique, *De l'instruction à émancipation: Les Enseignants de l' Alliance Israélite Universelle et les Juifs d'Orient* (Paris: Calmann-Lévy, 1989). Since the second edition of this volume the scholarly study of Oriental and Sephardi Jewry in the modern period has flourished. See Amiel Alcalay, *After Jews and Arabs: Remaking Levantine Culture* (Minneapolis: University of Minnesota Press, 1993); Mordecai Arbel, *The Jewish Nation of the Caribbean: The Spanish-Portuguese Jewish Settlement in the Caribbean and the Guianas* (Jerusalem: Gefen); Marc D. Angel, *Voices in Exile: A Study in Sephardic Intellectual*

sense),[12] it is necessary to note that it is not fortuitous that Jewish modernity, regardless of which periodization is employed, roughly coincides with what are generally considered to be the temporal delimitations of the modern period in Europe. Indeed, the transformations in Jewish life are synchronized with and informed by the intellectual criteria and institutional patterns that regulated the changes in European culture and polity. This implies that both ideationally and institutionally, Jewish modernity derives its primary energy and legitimation from sources other than the sacred authority of Jewish tradition. With this in mind, the documents we have selected make little reference, for instance, to Hasidism, a movement of popular mysticism that emerged among eighteenth-century East European Jewry.[13] To be sure, the custodians of Jewish tradition—and the Hasidim were among the most forceful— did respond to modernity and were quick to note its "dangers," often with an impressive understanding of its radical nature. We have included some illustrations of their arguments.

The conception of modernization that guided our selection of documents should explain what might seem to be an inordinate emphasis on the German and Central European

---

History (New York: Ktav, in association with Sephardic House, 1991); Shlomo Deshen and Walter P. Zenner, eds., *Jews Among Muslims: Communities in the Precolonial Middle East* (New York: New York University Press, 1996); Harvey Goldberg, *Sephardi and Middle Eastern Jewries: History and Culture in the Modern Era* (Bloomington: Indiana University Press, 1996); Hagar Hillel, *"Yisra'el" in Cairo: A Zionist Newspaper in Nationalist Egypt, 1920–39* (Tel Aviv: Am Oved, 2005); Lev Hakkak, *The Budding of Modern Hebrew Creativity in Babylon* (Or Yehuda Israel: Babylonian Jewry Heritage Center, 2004) (Hebrew); Yosef Kaplan, *An Alternative Path to Modernity: The Sephardi Diaspora in Western Europe* (Leiden: Brill, 2000); Matthias Lehmann, *Ladino Rabbinic Literature and Ottoman Sephardic Culture* (Bloomington: Indiana University Press, 2005); Lital Levy, "Jewish Writers in the Arab East: Literature, History, and the Politics of Enlightenment, 1863–1914" (Ph.D. dissertation, University of California at Berkeley, 2007); Lital Levy, "Historicizing the Concept of Arab Jews in the *Mashriq*," *Jewish Quarterly Review*, 98 (2008), 452–69; Susan Gilson Miller, "Inscribing Minority Space in the Islamic City: the Jewish Quarter of Fez (1438–1912)," *Journal of the Society of Architectural Historians* 60 (2001), 310–27; Shmuel Moreh and Philip Sadgrove, *Jewish Contributions to Nineteenth Century Arabic Theatre: Plays from Algeria and Syria* (Oxford: Oxford University Press, 1996); Aron Rodrigue, *Images of Sephardi and Eastern Jewries in Transition: The Teachers of the Alliance Israélite Universelle, 1860–1939* (Seattle: University of Washington Press, 1993); Daniel J. Schroeter and Josef Chetrit, "The Transformation of the Jewish Community of Essaouira (Mogador) in the Nineteenth and Twentieth Centuries," in *Sephardi and Middle Eastern Jewries: History and Culture in the Modern Era*, ed. Harvey Goldberg (Bloomington: Indiana University Press, 1996), pp. 99–116; Yehouda A. Shenhav, *The Arab Jew: A Postcolonial Reading of Nationalism, Religion and Ethnicity* (Stanford, Calif.: Stanford University Press, 2006); Reeva Spector Simon, Michael Menachem Laskier, and Sara Reguer, *The Jews of the Middle East and North Africa in Modern Times* (New York: Columbia University Press, 2003); Reuven Snir, "Arabic Literature by Iraqi Jews in the Twentieth Century: The Case of Ishaq Bar-Moshe (1927–2003)," *Middle Eastern Studies* 41:1 (January 2005): 7–29; Sasson Somekh, "Lost Voices: Jewish Authors in Modern Arabic Literature," in *Jews Among Arabs: Contacts and Boundaries*, ed. Mark Cohen and Abraham Udovitch (Princeton, N.J.: Darwin Press, 1989), pp. 9–20; Sarah Abrevaya Stein, *Making Jews Modern: The Yiddish and Ladino Press in the Russian and Ottoman Empires* (Bloomington: Indiana University Press, 2004).

[12] For a discussion of the meaning of tradition in the Jewish context, see Nathan Rotenstreich, *Tradition and Reality: The Impact of History on Modern Jewish Thought* (New York: Random House, 1972), pp. 7–18; ibid. "Tradition," *Contemporary Jewish Religious Thought*, ed. Arthur A. Cohen and Paul Mendes-Flohr (New York: The Free Press, 1987), pp. 1007–16; and Gershom Scholem, "Revelation and Tradition as Religious Categories in Judaism," in Gershom Scholem, *The Messianic Idea in Judaism and Other Essays on Jewish Spirituality* (New York: Schocken, 1971), pp. 281–303.

[13] Although historians generally agree that Hasidism had no direct impact on the shaping of Jewish modernity, it has been argued that Hasidism challenged, often quite effectively, traditional

Jewish experience. The transformations in traditional Jewish life occurred in a comprehensive way among the Jews of the Germanic lands first and in a particularly intense manner.[14] Hence the dynamic of Jewish modernization—with all its passion, ambiguity, promise and contradictions—is viewed in an especially clarion fashion in Germany and Central Europe. Moreover, the Jewry of these regions—the so-called *deutscher Kulturbereich*[15]—established many of the intellectual and institutional forms that were paradigmatic for Jewish modernity in general. We may mention, at random, Reform, Historical (or Conservative) and Neo-Orthodox Judaism; the academic study of Judaism (*Wissenschaft des Judentums*); political Zionism. Nonetheless, we have allotted separate sections for both American and East European Jewry, because of their special experience and response to modernity. Undoubtedly the most universal feature of the Jewish experience of modernity is antisemitism. As they sought integration in the cultural, economic and political life of modern society, the Jews met resistance. To be sure, this resistance was in part engendered by traditional Christian antipathy toward the alleged nation of deicides, but antisemitism in the modern period received a unique stamp. Again Germany provides the most intense and voluble expression of our subject. The selections on antisemitism are thus perforce largely German. Whether or not antisemitism inhered logically in the process of modernization is an immensely complex question. However pertinent and interesting the question is methodologically and philosophically, the historical fact is that in their encounter with modernity the Jews experienced antisemitism and, worse, the Shoah.

---

rabbinic institutions of authority and models of religious virtuosity. Hence, it is said that Hasidism indirectly—dialectically—prepared the way to the secularization of East European Jewish life if by secularization is meant the weakening and eclipse of religious authority and traditions. See Jacob Katz, *Tradition and Crisis: Jewish Society at the End of the Middle Ages* trans., with afterword and bibliography by Bernard Dov Cooperman (New York: New York University Press, 1990), ch. 22; Gershom Scholem, *Major Trends in Jewish Mysticism*, 3rd ed. (New York: Schocken, 1961, 1995), pp. 299ff. Both Katz and Scholem also attribute great significance to Sabbatianism—the messianic movement engendered by Shabbetai Zevi (1626–1676) and the concomitant antinomian mood that affected wide circles of Jewry—as a factor weakening traditional Jewish authority and religious practice. In that the alleged impact of Hasidism (and Sabbatianism) on Jewish modernity is largely social-psychological, its significance is admittedly difficult to measure. On the other hand, Hasidism created institutions that manifestly served to reinforce traditional Judaism in the modern period. "However much Hasidism challenged some of the norms of rabbinic Judaism, it surely did not create the characteristics of Jewish modernity. On the contrary, it soon became the most vociferous opponent of Jewish modernity." Meyer, "Where Does the Modern Period of Jewish History Begin?" (see note above), p. 336.

[14] In this regard, see Gerson D. Cohen's pertinent observations in his "German Jewry as Mirror of Modernity," introduction to *Leo Baeck Institute Year Book* 20 (1975), pp. ix–xxxi. Salo Baron traces the emergence of certain aspects of Jewish modernity to sixteenth-century Italy and eighteenth-century Holland. See S. Baron, *A Social and Religious History of the Jews* (New York: Columbia University Press, 1937), vol. 2, pp. 205–12; see also Isaac E. Barzilay, "The Italian and Berlin Haskalah," *Proceedings of the American Academy for Jewish Research*, 29 (1960–61), pp. 17–54.

[15] The term *deutscher Kulturbereich* refers to the regions of Europe in which the German language predominated as the arbiter of middle-class culture. The term thus has primarily sociological and cultural connotations. One need only mention such urban centers as Budapest (at least until the latter part of the nineteenth century), Prague and Vienna—all of which are included in the *deutscher Kulturbereich*. It is important to note that in the process of modernization many middle-class Jews in such East European cities as Lemberg, Czernowitz and Posen sought to identify with German language and culture.

I

HARBINGERS OF POLITICAL AND ECONOMIC CHANGE

The emergence in Europe of the centralized state—the so-called Absolute State—from the sixteenth to the eighteenth centuries marked the transition from the medieval, feudal era to what is called the modern period. This transformation of the European political structure is associated with the concentration of political, legal, and economic authority in the hands of a single ruler independent of the nobility and the church. In this process two elements were crucial: the ruler's ready access to liquid assets and a bureaucracy controlled by him. In consonance with these requirements, the centralized state facilitated the development of mercantilism or early capitalism. The Jews, particularly in central Europe, were in a unique position to benefit from this process. Bereft of political power, thus not a threat to the ruler, yet possessing the requisite skills to assist the "absolute monarch" to develop his treasury and economy, certain *individual* Jews acquired a new status as "court Jews." This unique institution flourished especially in the seventeenth century, after the conclusion of the Thirty Years' War (1648), when each of the 240 territories that formerly constituted the Holy Roman Empire of the German Nation sought to consolidate their newly gained autonomy in the spirit of absolutism and mercantilism. Most German princes had their court Jews. Because of their *utility* these Jews enjoyed privileges—such as those delineated in the bill of patent by Emperor Leopold to the court Jew Samson Wertheimer (1658–1724).

The institution of the court Jews—there were several hundred of them—introduced a radically new and explicit criterion for determining the legal status of the Jew in Europe: utility rather than theology. The privileged status of the court Jew, however, was a matter of exception. Most of his brethren remained despised and *dis*-privileged. But the mercantilism of the absolute state had an inner logic that led to a more "enlightened" policy. The commitment of the centralized state to economic independence eventually included a program of economic expansion, of increased industry and commerce and, as a corollary, of an increase of population. This program encouraged the augmentation of the number of "useful" subjects, including Jews. The policy of "enlightened absolutism" is illustrated by the declaration of the Estates General of the United Netherlands in 1657 and the charter concerning the Jews issued by King Frederick the Great of Prussia in 1750. Indicating an acute understanding of the new economic and political ethos, Rabbi Menasseh ben Israel based his appeal for the readmission of the Jews into England, "The Humble Addresses" (1655), on mercantilist arguments. John Toland (1670–1722), Irish Deist and political philosopher, echoed remarkably similar views when he argued that England would immeasurably benefit from attracting Jews to its shores. In his pamphlet, "Reasons for Naturalizing the Jews in Great Britain and Ireland" (1714), he maintained that the manifest faults of the Jew were not innate but circumstantial. Granted equal opportunity and dignity they would prove to be resourceful and loyal subjects.

The ideological rationale of this policy was refined by the German scholar Christian Wilhelm von Dohm. In his treatise, "Concerning the Amelioration of the Civil Status of the Jews" (1781), written at the behest of his friend Moses Mendelssohn, Dohm argues that the Jew is not inherently "evil," for the faults in the character of the Jew can be ascribed to the deleterious effects of repression and economic restrictions. He thus concludes that the removal of these negative conditions would render the Jews less "harmful" and, moreover, prepare them for a gradual increase of rights and improved conditions "if and when they may deserve them." The Edict of Tolerance (1782), issued by Joseph II, the Holy Roman Emperor, emphasizes Dohm's proposition that civic betterment of the Jews requires that in exchange the Jews reform many of their cultural values and institutions. This quid pro quo exacted of the Jews indicates how far the policy of enlightened absolutism was from the democratic principles of civic parity as an intrinsic right to be granted the Jew as a human being. The remaining selections, which record the debate surrounding Dohm's treatise, underscore this point.

1. HOW PROFITABLE THE NATION OF THE JEWS ARE (1655)

MENASSEH BEN ISRAEL[1]

Three things, if it please your Highnesse, there are that make a strange *Nation* well-beloved amongst the Natives of a land where they dwell: (as the defect of those *three* things make them hateful) viz. *Profit*, they may receive from them; *Fidelity* they hold towards their Princes; and the *Noblenes* and purity of their blood. Now when I shall have made good, that all *these three* things are found in the *Jewish* Nation, I shall certainly persuade your Highnesse, that with a favorable eye (Monarchy being changed into a Republicq), you shall be pleased to receive again the Nation of the Jews, who in time past lived in that Island: but, I know not by what false Informations, were cruelly handled and banished.

Profit is a most powerfull motive, and which all the World preferres before all other things: and therefore we shall handle that point first.

It is a thing confirmed, that merchandizing is, as it were, the proper profession of the Nation of the Jews. I attribute this in the first place, to the particular Providence and mercy of God towards his people: for having banished them from their own Country, yet not from his Protection, he hath given them, as it were, a natural instinct, by which they might not only gain what is necessary for their need, but that they should also thrive in Riches and possessions; whereby they should not onely become gracious to their Princes and Lords, but that they should be invited by others to come and dwell in their Lands.

Moreover, it cannot be denyed, but that necessity stirrs up a man's ability and industry; and that it gives him great incitement, by all means to try the favour of Providence.

Besides, seeing it is no wisedome for them to endeavour the gaining of Lands and other immovable goods, and so to imprison their possessions here, where their persons are subject to so many casualties, banishments and peregrinations; they are forced to use merchandizing until that time, when they shall return to their own Country, that then as God hath promised by the Prophet Zachary. *There shall be found no more any merchant amongst them in the House of the Lord.*

From that very thing we have said, there riseth an infallible Profit, commodity and gain to all those Princes in whose Lands they dwell above all other strange Nations whatsoever, as experience by divers *Reasons* doth confirm.

I. The Jews, have no opportunity to live in their own Country, to till the Lands or other like employments, give themselves wholy unto merchandizing, and for contriving new Inventions, no Nation almost going beyond them. And so 'tis observed, that where so ever they go to dwell, there presently the Traficq begins to flourish. Which may be seen in divers places, especially in Lighorne, which having been but a very ignoble and inconsiderable City, is at this time, by the great concourse of people, one of the most famous places of Trafiq of whole Italy....

II. The Nation of the Jews is dispersed throughout the whole World, it being a chastisement that God hath layd upon them for their Idolatries, Deut. 28:69, Ezech. 20:23, Nehem. 1:8, Ps. 107:27. and by their other sinnes their families suffer the same shipwrack.

Now in this dispersion our Fore-fathers flying from the Spanish Inquisition, some of them

Source: Menasseh ben Israel, "To His Highness the Lord Protector of the Commonwealth of England, Scotland and Ireland, "*The Humble Addresses of Menasseh ben Israel* (1655), in *Menasseh ben Israel's Mission to Oliver Cromwell: Being a Reprint of the Pamphlets published by Menasseh ben Israel to promote the Re-admission of the Jews to England, 1649–1645*, ed. Lucien Wolf (London: Macmillan, 1901), pp. 81–89. The original orthography has been retained.

came in Holland, others got into Italy, and others betooke themselves into Asia; and so easily they credit one another; and by that means they draw the Negotiation where-ever they are, where with all of them merchandizing and having perfect knowledge of all the kinds of Moneys, Diamonds, Cochinil, Indigo, Wines, Oyle, and other Commodities, that serve from place to place; especially holding correspondence with their friends and kinds-folk, whose language they understand; they do abundantly enrich the Lands and Countrys of Strangers, where they live, not only with what is requisite and necessary for the life of man; but also what may serve for ornament to his civill condition. Of which *Traficq*, there ariseth ordinarily *Five* important benefits.

1. The augmentation of the Publiq Tolls and Customes, at their coming and going out of the place.
2. The transporting and bringing in of merchandises from remote Countries.
3. The affording of Materials in great plenty for all Mechaniqs; as Wooll, Leather, Wines, Jewels, as Diamants, Pearles, and such like Merchandize.
4. The venting and exportation of so many kinds of Manifactures.
5. The Commerce and reciprocall Negoation at Sea, which is the ground for Peace between neighbour Nations, and of great profit to their own Fellow-citizens.

III. This reason is the more strengthened, when we see, that not onely the Jewish Nation dwelling in Holland and Italy, trafficqs with their own stocks but also with the riches of many others of their own Nation, friends, kinds-men and acquaintance, which notwithstanding live in Spain, and send unto them their moneys and goods, which they hold in their hands, and content themselves with a very small portion of their estate, to the end they may be secure and free from danger that might happen unto them, in case they should fall under the yoke of the Inquisition; whence not onely their goods, but oftentimes also their lives are endangered.

IV. The love that men ordinarily beare to their own Country and the desire they have to end their lives, where they had their beginning, is the cause, that most strangers having gotten riches where they are in a forain land, are commonly taken in a desire to returne to their native soil, and there peaceably to enjoy their estate; so that as they were a help to the places where they lived, and negotiated while they remained there; so when they depart from thence, they carry all away, and spoile them of their wealth; transporting all into their own native Country: But with the Jews the case is farre different; for where the Jews are once kindly received, they make a firm resolution never to depart from thence, seeing they have no proper place of their own: and so they are always with their goods in the Cities where they live, a perpetuall benefit to all payments. Which reasons do dearly proove, that it being the property of Citizens in populous and rich countries, to seeke their rest and ease with buying lands and faire possession of which they live; many of them hating commerce, aspire to Titles and Dignities: therefore of all strangers, in whose hands ordinarily Trafique is found, there are none so profitable and beneficiall to the place where they trade and live, as is the Nation of the Jews. And seeing amongst the people of Europe, the chiefest riches they possess, from Spain, those neighbour Nations, where the Jews shall find liberty to live according to their own Judaicall Laws, they shall most easily draw that benefit to themselves by means of the industry of our Nation, and their mutual correspondence.

From hence (if it please your Highness) it results, that the Jewish Nation, though scattered through the whole World, are not therefore a despisable people, but as a Plant worthy to be planted in the whole world, and received into Populous Cities: who ought to plant them in those places, which are most secure from danger; being trees of most savory fruit and profit to be always most favoured with Laws and Privileges, or Prerogatives, secured and defended by Armes.

…The chiefest place where the Jews live, is the Turkish Empire, where some of them live in great estate, even in the Court of the Grande Turke at Constantinople, by reason there is no Viceroy or Governor, or Bassa,[2] which hath not a Jew to manage his affaires, and to take care for his estate: Hence it cometh that in short time they grow up to be Lords of great revenues, and they most frequently bend the minds of Great ones to most weighty affaires in government.

The greatest Viceroy of whole Europe is the Bassa of Egypt; this Bassa always takes to him, by order of the Kingdom, a Jew with the title of Zarf-Bassa (*Thresurer*) viz. of all the Revenues of that government, who receives purses full of money, seals them, and then sends them to the King. This man in a short time grows very rich, for that by his hands as being next to the Bassa, the 24 Governments of that Empire are sould and given, and all other businesses managed. At present he that possesseth this place, is called Sr. Abraham Alhula. The number of Jews living in this Kingdome of the Great Turke, is very great, and amounts to many Millions. In Constantinople alone there are 48 Synagogues, and in Salaminque 36, and more than four score thousand souls in these two Cities alone.

The first King gave them great privileges which they enjoy untill this day: for besides the liberty, they have every-where, of trading with open shops, of bearing any Office and possessing of any goods, both moveable and immoveable, he yet granted them power to judge all Civil causes according to their own Laws amongst themselves. Moreover they are exempted from going to Wars, and that souldiers should be quartered in their houses, and that Justice should take no place upon the death of any one that left no heir to his Estate....

In Germany, there live also a great multitude of Jews, especially at Prague, Vienna and Franckfurt, very much favoured by the most mild and most gracious Emperors, but despised of the people, being a Nation not very finely garnished by reason of their vile cloathing: yet notwithstanding there is not wanting amongst them persons of great quality.

...But yet a greater number of Jews are found in the Kingdome of Poland, Prussia and Lethuania, under which Monarchy they have the Jurisdiction to judge amongst themselves all causes, both Criminal and Civil; and also great and famous Academies of their own. The chief Cities where the Nation liveth, are Lublin and Cracow, where there is a Jew, called Isaac Iecells, who built a Synagogue, which stood him in one hundred thousand Francs, and is worth many tons of gold. There is in this place such infinite number of Jews; that although the Cosaques in the late warres have killed of them above one hundred and four score thousand; yet it is sustained that they are yet at this day as innumerable as those were that came out of Egypt. In that Kingdome the whole Negotiation is in the hand of the Jews, the rest of the Christians are either all Noble-men, or Rustiques [peasants] and kept as slaves.

In Italy they are generally protected by all the Princes: their principall residence is in the most famous City of Venice; so that in that same City alone they possesse about 1400 Houses; and are used there with much courtesy and clemency. Many also live in Padoa and Verona; others in Mantua, and also many in Rome it self. Finally they are scattered here and there in the chief places of Italy, and do live there with many special privileges...

In all these places the Jews live (in a manner) all of them Merchants, and that without any prejudice at all to the Natives: For the Natives, and those especially that are most rich, they build themselves houses and Palaces, buy Lands and firme goods, aime at Titles and Dignities, and so seek their rest and contentment that way: But as for the Jews they aspire at nothing, but to preferre themselves in their way of Merchandize; and so employing their Capitals, they send forth the benefit of their labour amongst many and sundry of the Natives, which they, by the trafick of their Negotiation, do enrich. From whence it's easy to judge of the profit that Princes and Commonwealths do reap, by giving liberty of Religion to the Jews, and gathering them by some special privileges into their Countries: as Trees that bring forth such excellent fruits.

So that if one Prince, ill advised, driveth them out of this Land, yet another invites them to his; and shews them favour. Wherein we may see the prophecy of Jacob fulfilled in the letter: *The staffe (to support him) shall not depart from Jacob, untill Messias shall come*. And this shall suffice concerning the Profit of the Jewish Nation.

NOTES

1. Menasseh (also Manasseh) ben Israel (c. 1604–1657), Dutch rabbi of Marrano parentage, that is, of Spanish and Portuguese Jews who had converted to Christianity under coercion but secretly preserved their Jewish identity. He energetically sought to persuade the English to permit the return of the Jews to their country, from which they were expelled in 1290. He went to London in 1655 and presented a petition to Oliver Cromwell, Lord Protector of Great Britain. Although his mission was ostensibly unsuccessful, it did prepare the way for the resettlement of the Jews in England.
2. Early English for the Turkish word "Pasha."

2. REASONS FOR NATURALIZING THE JEWS IN GREAT BRITAIN AND IRELAND (1714)[1]

JOHN TOLAND

Tis manifest almost at first sight, that the common reasons for a GENERAL NATURALIZATION, are as strong in behalf of the *Jews,* as of any other people whatsoever. They encrease the number of hands for labor and defence, of bellies and backs for consumption of food and raiment, and of brains for invention and contrivance, no less than any other nation. We all know that numbers of people are the true riches and power of any country, and we have been often told, that this is the reason, why *Spain* (since the expulsion of the *Jews* and *Moors*) being continually drained of her inhabitants by the colonies in *America,* and all other Nations being in a manner kept out by the rigor of the *Inquisition,* is grown so prodigiously weak and poor: whereas, tho *Holland has comparatively but few native Inhabitants, and sends great numbers yearly to the East-Indies;* yet allowing an unlimited LIBERTY OF CONSCIENCE, and receiving all nations to the right of citizens, the country is ever well stockt with people, and consequently both rich and powerful to an eminent degree....

My purpose at present then, is to prove, that the *Jews* are so farr from being an Excrescence or Spunge (as some wou'd have it) and useless members in the Commonwealth, or being ill subjects, and a dangerous people on any account, that they are obedient, peaceable, useful, and advantageous as any; and even more so than many others: which last point, as seeming the least-probable, I shall briefly demonstrate in two or three respects. And, in the first place, it is evident, that by receiving of the *Jews,* no body needs be afraid that any religious Party in the nation will thereby be weaken'd or enforc'd. The *Protestant Dissenters* have no reason to be jealous, that they should join with the *National Church* to oppress them, since they have an equal Interest to preserve LIBERTY OF CONSCIENCE; and that the example of *Spain* and *Portugal* has taught 'em how dangerous a thing it is, that one sett of *Clergy-men* shou'd dispose and influence all things at their pleasure in any country. The *National Church* on the other hand, has no reason to be jealous that the *Jews* should come in for snacks with them in sharing the Ecclesiastical Benefites; so that no candidate or expectant from the *University* needs shew his zeal on this occasion, to keep the *Jews* out of the nation (as has been done once on a time to keep the *Dissenters* out of the *Church*) lest he should be shoulder'd out of a Parish by some *Levite,* or be kept from a fat Bishoprick by a *Rabbi.* There's as little danger they shou'd ever join with any particular Body of *Dissenters* against the *National Church,* since they can expect no more favor from the one, than from the other; and that it is always their interest to preserve the legal Establishment, on which their own Security is grounded. For this reason likewise, they'll never join with any Party in civill Affairs, but that which patronizes LIBERTY OF CONSCIENCE and the NATURALIZATION, which will ever be the side of Liberty and the Constitution. But otherwise they are wholly devested of those engagements to WHIG and TORY, which are become hereditary in so many Families: and this holds as true of other Factions; which shou'd consequently recommend them to the favor of all Parties, would people but think for themselves; and not, like so many Brutes, be led or driven by a few self-interested Demagogues.

ANOTHER Consideration that makes the *Jews* preferable to several sorts of People, is, their having no

---

Source: John Toland, *Reasons for Naturalizing the Jews in Great Britain and Ireland, On the same foot with all other Nations. Containing also, A Defence of the Jews against all Vulgar Prejudices in all Countries* (London, 1714), pp. 6, 10–15, 17, 20, 39–46. Original orthography and emphases are retained.

Country of their own, to which they might retire, after having got Estates here; or in favor of which, they might trade under the umbrage of our NATURALIZATION, which I am certain will be done by many, unless prevented by proper Laws: for I have known several get themselves naturaliz'd before the late *Act*, yet without ever designing to live in *England*, or to become a part of the *English* Government; but to avoid in their Factorship paying Aliens duties, and for other reasons well known to the Merchants. But the *Jews* having no such Country, to which they are ty'd by inclination or interest as their own, will never likewise enter into any political engagements, which might be prejudicial to ours, as we have known (for Example) certain *French* Refugees to have done, notwithstanding their protection; nay, and to be ever pleas'd with any successes against us (which I say, without Prejudice to the more honest and more numerous part) as making for the greatness of their nation, wherein they still took a sort of pride, and to which, some of 'em are gone back again, after failing of their expectations here. The *Jews* therefore being better us'd with us, than any where else in the world, are sure to be ours for ever; which is more than we dare reasonably promise from any other nation, whatever may be expected from their posterity.

To ascend from these particular to more general Reasons, we may observe that Trade is by certain circumstances shar'd in such a manner, and parcell'd out among the inhabitants of the earth, that some, by way of eminence, may be call'd the Factors, some the Carriers, some the Miners, others the Manufactorers, and others yet the Store-keepers of the world. Thus the *Jews* may properly be said to be the Brokers of it, who, whithersoever they come, create business as well as manage it. Yet it is neither by any National Institution of Inclination (as many ignorantly believe) that they do now almost entirely betake themselves to business of Exchange, Insurances, and improving of money upon Security; but they are driven to this way of Livelihood by mere Necessity: for being excluded every where in *Europe*, from publick Employments in the State, as they are from following Handycraft-trades in most places, and in almost all, from purchasing immovable Inheritances, this does no less naturally, than necessarily, force 'em to Trade and Usury, since otherwise they cou'd not possibly live. Yet let 'em once be put upon an equal foot with others, not only for buying and selling, for security

and protection to their Goods and Persons; but likewise for Arts and Handycraft-trades, for purchasing and inheriting of estates in Lands and Houses (with which they may as well be trusted as with Shares in the *publick Funds*) and then I doubt not, but they'll insensibly betake themselves to Building, Farming, and all sorts of Improvement like other people.... I envy not those whole streets of magnificent buildings, that the *Jews* have erected at *Amsterdam* and the *Hague*: but there are other *Jews* enow in the World to adorn *London* or *Bristol* with the like, the fifth part of the People in *Poland* (to name no other Country) being of this Nation. Nay, the very Original of their present numerous Settlement at *Prague* in *Bohemia*, is a Privilege granted them in the tenth Century, to build a Synagogue there, as a recompence for the valiant assistance they lent the inhabitants, in expelling the invading and depopulating Barbarians: And I fancy they could kill the enemies of our British Islands, when they become their own with equal alacrity....

There are among the *Jews*, to be sure, sordid wretches, sharpers, extortioners, villains of all sorts and degrees: and where is that happy nation, where is that religious profession, of which the same may not be as truly affirm'd? They have likewise their men of probity and worth, persons of courage and conduct, of liberal and generous spirits. But one rule of life, which is willingly admitted, nay, and eagerly pleaded by all Societies in their own case (tho miserably neglected in that of others) is, *not to impute the faults of a few to the whole number*; which, considering the unavoidable mixture of good and bad in all communities, wou'd be no less want of charity, than want of justice. The *Jews* therefore are both in their origine and progress, not otherwise to be regarded, than under the common circumstances of human nature. The *Romans* were not less esteem'd for being descended from Shepherds and Fugitives (which originally they had in common with the *Jews*), than are the *English* for being the progeny of barbarous pyrates.... The vulgar, I confess, are seldom pleas'd in any country with the coming in of Foreners among 'em: which proceeds first, from their ignorance, that at the beginning they were such themselves; secondly, from their grudging at more persons sharing the same trades or business with them, which they call *taking the bread out of their mouths*; and thirdly, from their being deluded to this aversion by the artifice of those who design any change in the Government. But as wise Magistrates will prevent the last, and are sensible of the first: so they know the second cause of the people's hatred, to be the true cause of the land's felicity; and therefore, not minding those, who mind nothing but their selfish projects, they'll ever highly encourage a confluence of strangers. We deny not that there will thus be more taylors and shoo-makers; but there will also be more suits and shoos made than before. If there be more weavers, watchmakers, and other artificers, we can for this reason export more cloth, watches, and more of all other commodities than formerly: and not only have 'em better made by the emulation of so many workmen, of such different Nations; but likewise have 'em quicker sold off, for being cheaper wrought than those of others, who come to the same market. This one Rule of MORE, and BETTER, and CHEAPER, will ever carry the market against all expedients and devices.

That the encrease of people encreases import and export, garrisons and armies, with the tillage that feeds, and the revenues that pay 'em, is, I hope, no longer a doubt or secret to any. But this only in order the more speedily and effectually to bring these things to pass, that I plead at present for the NATURALIZATION OF THE JEWS. This once accomplish'd, I have reason not only to believe that they'll fall to building, husbandry, navigation, and purchasing (as I hinted before) but that they'll come in greater numbers than other people from all countries hither. In several places they are still very hardly treated, tho their throats are not so familiarly cut as formerly. They are generally expos'd to the affronts and rapine of the Soldiery with impunity; whereas they wou'd be safe from all such rude Insults m the peaceable arms of *Brittania*. I have been in several Cities, where they are infamously lock'd up every night, in a quarter by themselves, under a peculiar guard, as at *Prague*; and in others, as at *Colen*, they are not permitted to dwell within the City, but whenever they come over from *Deuts*, on t'other side of the *Rhine*, they must pay so much for every hour they continue in the town, which they must also leave before Sun-set: whereas, if the Citizens of *Colen* understood their own interest, they shou'd rather give 'em immunities and privileges, with a *Synagogue* into the bargain, in order to inhabit among 'em. What a paltry fishertown was *Leghorn*,[2] before the admission of the *Jews*? What a loser is *Lisbon*,[3] since they have been lost to it? I name these cities only for example-sake, having

been a witness to such preposterous politics in many others. They are in most places forc'd to wear a distinct habit, and they do yellow hats at *Rome*, and red ones at *Venice*; they are often taxt for their passage, and lie under a great many other partial regulations. Tis true, that in *Turky* they enjoy immoveable property, and exercise mechanic arts; they have likewise numerous Academies in *Poland*, where they study in the *Civil* and *Canon* Laws of their nation, being privileg'd to determine even certain criminal Causes among themselves: yet they are treated little better than Dogs in the first place, and are often exposed in the last to unspeakable Calamities.

Now the worse they are us'd on the foresaid and the like accounts in any country, the more they'll be dispos'd to transport themselves hither, where already they live promiscuously with the other Citizens, and without any distinction of habit, or imposition of tribute. They have neither many lucrative employments, nor immoveable possessions to quit in other places, excepting the latter in *Holland*; whereas here they may hope for both, and being once with us, will never leave us: since they cannot be allur'd by ampler privileges from any nation besides; or at least if they be, it must needs be solely our fault. Let no man mistake what I have said of employments: for in the *Church* as I have shewn above, they'll accept of none; and they are as much excluded from most preferments in the *State*, by reason of certain forms of oaths, and some other conditions, which consistently with their religion they cannot perform. But there are offices, where such qualifications are not required; and which may indifferently be held by men of all religions, as many in the *Exchequer*, *Customs*, and *Excise*: nor can I see any reason, why the *Jews* may not be employ'd in several Affairs in the city, as to be Directors of the *Bank*, of the *East India Company*, or the like; and we know the nature of mankind to be such, as not seldom to be ambitious of even expensive employments, for the credit of the honor or the trust. In how many places, since their dispersion (tho not so frequently of late) have they enjoy'd considerable posts and offices? They have in some been *first Ministers*, high *Treasurers* in many, and *Envoys* in most. In a word they ought to be so naturaliz'd in *Great Britain* and *Ireland*, as, like the *Quakers*, to be incapacitated in nothing, but where they incapacitate themselves. A General Naturalization, and a Total Incapacity from Offices, are perfect inconsistencies: for as one, who understood this matter very well, says, *If few have been found ever since mankind existed, that wou'd for their own native country, without the expectation of any reward, expose their bodies to the weapons of their enemies; do you think there may be such a person found, that will undergo dangers for another Government, where not only he receives no reward, but that he is absolutely excluded from any?*[4] But the privilege of purchasing alone (especially since Titles are like to be generally secured by the gradual Introduction of Registers) will be the most powerful motive to bring the richest of the *Jews* hither: for it may be easily demonstrated, that the want of immoveable property is the true Reason, and not any pretended Curse or other ridiculous fancy, why none of the vast estates they so frequently acquire, seldom or ever descends to the third Generation; but are always floating and unfixed, which hinders their families from growing considerable, and consequently deprives them of the credit and authority, whereof all men of worth may be laudably ambitious.

NOTES

1. Influenced by Thomas Hobbes, Baruch Spinoza and John Locke, Toland (1670–1722) was one of the most radical followers of the Enlightenment in Great Britain. His pamphlet, published anonymously, was written during the public debate regarding the naturalization of foreign-born Protestants in Great Britain. Although it elicited little but derisive comment, Toland's essay was the earliest plea for the comprehensive toleration of the Jews, thus initiating the protracted literary struggle for Jewish civic equality.

2. Leghorn (Livorno), a port on the west coast of Italy. Toward the end of the sixteenth century, the ruler of the city encouraged Jewish merchants, mostly former Marranos, (see note 1 of the previous document) to settle in Leghorn. They quickly became a dominant factor in transforming the city into a vibrant, prosperous center of trade.

3. The reference is to Lisbon, Portugal. With their increasing persecution by the Inquisition, many Jewish conversos (Marranos) left Portugal and settled in more liberal communities, such as Leghorn, where they were able to reaffirm their ancestral faith. Toland ascribes the economic decline of Portugal to the departure of the Marrano merchants.

4. Cicero, *Pro L. Cornelius, Balbo Ocatio*, ch. 10.

3. DECLARATION PROTECTING THE INTEREST OF JEWS RESIDING IN THE NETHERLANDS (JULY 13, 1657)[1]

THE ESTATES GENERAL OF THE REPUBLIC OF THE UNITED PROVINCES

Upon the request of the elders of the Jewish nation, residing within the United Provinces, as well as those in the Province of Holland, also of those in the city of Amsterdam presented to Their Very Puissant [the Estates General] containing complaints about unjust and severe procedures applied to them for some time, by the King of Spain and his subjects with regard to their traffic and navigation as well as in other respects; the officials after deliberation do understand and declare that it should be understood and declared herewith that those of the aforementioned Jewish nation are truly subjects and residents of the United Netherlands, and

Source: H. J. Koenen, *Geschiedenis der Joden in Nederland* (Utrecht, 1843), pp. 487–88, in Raphael Mahler, ed. and trans., *Jewish Emancipation, A Selection of Documents by R. Mahler*, Pamphlet Series, Jews and the Postwar World, no. 1 (New York: American Jewish Committee, 1941), pp. 10–11. Reprinted by permission of the American Jewish Committee.

that they also therefore must enjoy, possess and profit by the conditions, rights and advantages, provided by the Treaties of Peace and Navigation concluded with the aforementioned King of Spain, or other Treaties, Agreements, Alliances and Engagements with other Kings, Republics, Princes, Potentates, States, Towns, Cities, demanded and obtained in favor of the inhabitants of the State. Therefore, the rights and advantages of those of this nation will, in the aforementioned cases, as well as in other similar situations, be maintained, and wherever the contrary should be done or undertaken, it shall be prevented as it has been agreed.

NOTE

1. Since 1477, the Netherlands were under Spanish rule. In 1581, the northern Dutch provinces declared independence, their principal motive being the desire to practice Protestant Christianity, which was forbidden by the Spanish crown. Accordingly, religious tolerance was of overarching constitutional importance for the newly independent Republic of the United Provinces. The prospect of religious freedom drew crypto-Jews of Spain and Portugal in ever increasing numbers to the Netherlands, where they formally returned to Judaism and made a singular contribution to the commercial life of the country, especially in Amsterdam. But it was only in 1608 that they were allowed to establish a community and a synagogue, and then with restrictions. In fact, until their emancipation in 1796 (see chapter 3, document 8), the legal status of Dutch Jewry remained ill defined, since local, and provincial authorities retained the right to adopt their own policies toward the Jews. A milestone in the evolving religious freedom that was extended to the Jews of the Netherlands was the Peace of Muenster (1648), according to which Spain was obliged to permit the subjects of the Netherlands to reside and engage in Spain and Portugal. But the Spanish monarch adamantly contended that the provisions of the treaty did not apply to the Jewish residents of the Netherlands. In response, the Estates General or parliament of the Netherlands, promulgated on July 13, 1657, the declaration presented here. Historians have usually regarded the declaration as the first such statement on the part of any government. It should be noted, however, that the declaration sought to secure the commercial rights of the Jews as residents of the Netherlands, but did not entail a confirmation of citizenship; indeed, the concept of citizenship had yet to exist. Moreover, similar declarations of protection had been made earlier in the century (initially with regard to the "Portuguese," that is, Marranos, residing in the Netherlands). See Daniel M. Swetschinksi, *Reluctant Cosmopolitans. The Portuguese Jews of Seventeenth Amsterdam* (London and Portland, Ore.: Littman Library, 2000), pp. 39–47.

4. ACT OF SURINAME (AUGUST 17, 1665)[1]

BRITISH COLONIAL COMMISSIONER

Whereas it is good and sound policy to encourage as much as possible whatever may tend to the increase of a new colony, and to invite persons of whatsoever country and religion, to come and reside here and traffic with us; and whereas we have found that the Hebrew nation now already resident here, have, with their persons and property proved themselves useful and beneficial to this colony, and being desirous to encourage them to continue their residence, and trade here; we have with the authority of the governor, his council and assembly, passed the following act:

Every person belonging to the Hebrew nation now resident here, or who may come hereafter to reside

---

Source: Elias Haim Lindo, *The History of the Jews of Spain* and *Portugal* (London: Brown, Green and Longmans, 1848), pp. 381–83.

and trade here, or in any place or district within the limit of this colony, shall possess and enjoy every liberty and privilege possessed by and granted to the citizens and inhabitants of the colony, and shall be considered as English-born, and they and their heirs shall in this manner possess their property, whether real or personal.

It is also hereby declared that they shall not be compelled to serve any public office in this colony, and that we receive them under the protection and safeguard of our government with all the property they now hold or shall hereafter possess, and import from any foreign place or kingdom abroad. We also grant them every liberty and privilege which we enjoy ourselves, whether derived from laws, acts, or customs, either regarding our lands, our persons, or other property, promising them that nothing of what they now possess, or shall hereafter acquire, shall be taken from them or be appropriated among ourselves by any person of whatever rank; but that on the contrary they shall have full liberty to plant, trade, and do whatsoever they may consider conducive to their advantage and profit, on condition that they shall be true subjects of our Sovereign Lord, the King of England, and shall obey all orders already issued by him, or which he may hereafter promulgate. It is, however, to be well understood, that none of these orders shall be contrary to what is herein contained.

It is also hereby granted and permitted, in the most ample manner possible, to the Hebrew nation, to practice and perform all ceremonies and customs of their religion, according to their usages; also those relating to their marriages and last wills or testaments, and that the acts of marriage, made according to their rites and customs, shall be held valid in every respect. It is also hereby declared that they shall not suffer any let [obstacle] or hindrance in the observance of their Sabbath or festivals, and those who shall trouble them on that account shall be considered disturbers of the public peace, and shall be punished accordingly. Also that they shall not be bound to appear on the said days before any court or magistrate, and that all summonses and citations for the said days shall be null and void. Neither shall their refusal of payment of any claim made against them on these days prejudice them in any way, or diminish any claim they may have.

The possession of ten acres of land at Thoxarica[2] is also hereby granted to them that they may build thereon places of worship and schools, and for the burial of their dead.

They shall, moreover, not be compelled to do personal duty, but shall be permitted to send a substitute, except in case of war, when they also shall be bound to come forward with the other inhabitants. Permission is also hereby granted them to have a tribunal of their own; and that in cases so litigated, the deputies of their nation may pronounce sentence in all cases not exceeding ten thousand pounds of sugar.

Upon which sentence pronounced by the said deputies, the judge of our court shall grant execution to issue, and they shall keep registers and records of the same according to custom. When an oath shall be required, it shall be administered according to the custom of the Hebrew nation, and such oath shall be deemed valid, and have all the force and effect of a judicial oath, notwithstanding any law to the contrary....

NOTES

1. The first Jews to settle in the Americas were largely former conversos. The colonization of the Americas by Protestant countries, particularly the Dutch and English, occasioned new, decidedly pragmatic attitudes toward the Jews. The Dutch and English were the first to grant them extensive rights in their colonial possessions. These practices, together with the growing importance of Jews in commerce, were precedents for the later removal of legal restrictions on Jews in England and the Netherlands. Conversos first settled in relatively large numbers in Dutch Brazil, where many formally returned to Judaism. Upon the conquest of the Dutch colonies in Brazil in 1653 by Portugal, Jews fled to the Dutch and British possessions in the West Indies and the Guianas: Barbados, Jamaica, Curacao, Surinam, and later to the North American continent: New Amsterdam (New York) and Newport. The first permanent settlement of Surinam, located on the northeastern coast of South America, was founded in 1652 by the British. Jews were among the first settlers; by 1694 the Jewish community of Surinam numbered 2,000, constituting the majority white population of the colony. In 1667, the Dutch occupied the colony and confirmed and amplified the privileges granted the Jews by the English authorities in the Act of Surinam of August 17, 1665. Large-scale Jewish immigration to Spanish Latin America, particularly to Argentina, Brazil, and Mexico, began only in the 1880s.

2. Thoxarica was then the administrative capital of Surinam.

5. THE APPOINTMENT OF SAMSON WERTHEIMER AS IMPERIAL COURT FACTOR (AUGUST 29, 1703)

LEOPOLD I[1]

We, Leopold, elected Roman Emperor by the grace of God, in the name [of the House of Habsburg], the name of our heirs and our descendants, with this letter proclaim publicly that we have graciously looked upon the industrious, indefatigable, efficacious, loyal and selfless services that have been rendered to the Holy Roman Empire and to our, the Imperial House of Austria—and especially on behalf of our Court Chamber and other princes and estates of the Roman Empire—by the Court Factor [*Ober Factor*][2] Samson Wertheimer,[3] chief rabbi of the Jews in our countries, throughout the last seventeen years. He has proven himself on various and important missions, here as well as in other places to which he was sent—especially in former Turkey, the Rhineland, France and Italy. When heavy fighting broke out over the issue of the succession to the Spanish Crown,[4] he came to the aid of the Roman Empire greatly expediting the military operations. He took care of expenses incurred by our Emperor, our beloved son, the King of Rome and Hungary, the Archduke Carl and the rest of the court. Further, in order to meet the innumerable and extraordinary expenses of the Imperial Court during the war, he not only spent in a wise and prudent manner the many millions provided him in cash by the War Treasury and the Court, but he also advanced [the Empire] several loans at [a low] interest. The loans were advanced partly by his personal credit, and partly with our principalities as collateral, such as our Archduchy of Silesia and others, but especially the salt-mines of Siebenbuergen. For the lease of these mines he immediately received a million ducats. To our great pleasure, he has managed to perform all these deeds by the allocation of subsidies, money, and work. Even today, he and his son are constantly busy serving us and the public; his only wish is the permission to continue his services. In the light of his well-known qualities, his high intelligence and his considerable skill this permission will gladly be granted. In grateful recognition of all this we have not only presented Samson Wertheimer and his son Wolff with our Imperial chain of grace and our portrait; we have also honored him with a gift of one thousand ducats for the acquisition of some silver or golden dishes for his successful negotiations [in raising a dowry] on behalf of our beloved cousin and brother-in-law, the Count Palatini, Charles Philip. Furthermore, we have decreed that Samson Wertheimer be designated as our Imperial Court Factor, in which capacity he shall remain forever, and which title he shall hold before every man and authority, our heirs and descendants included. But in order that our Court Factor Samson Wertheimer may enjoy our Imperial grace more fully, in order that he may accomplish his tasks with minimal hindrance and may peacefully travel, he and the members of his family, both in our Empire and in foreign lands, we have bestowed still another grace upon him: We have not only confirmed and ratified the protective privileges issued on June 1, 1683, and on May 28, 1695, including all clauses, articles, interpretations and terms contained therein, but have extended their validity for another twenty years beyond the time specified therein. This extension is granted within our rights as Roman Emperor and King and within our rights as a territorial prince: We wish our Court Factor Samson Wertheimer to be successful in all further service which he will render us and the electors of the Empire. We are cognizant that his indefatigable services during the last seventeen years

Source: David Kaufmann, *Samson Wertheimer, Der Oberhoffactor und Landesrabbiner, und seine Kinder* (Wien, 1888), pp. 29–33. Trans. by J. Hessing.

have diminished his bodily strength, and we therefore allow him to dwell in our Roman lands and the lands of our crown—together with his son, daughter-in-law, grandchildren and whoever may dwell with him presently, and also all members of his family of either sex, wherever they may be, grandchildren, servants and others included—for another twenty years, starting on May 18, 1715. During this time he will be exempt from all tithes and taxes. He will have to pay neither protection-money [*Schutzgeld*] nor tolerance-money [*Toleranzgeld*].[5] Nor will he have to pay any duties, whether they be regular or irregular, or however they may be designated. In all the above-mentioned places he will enjoy our Imperial and Royal protection, or the protection extended to him in our capacity as a territorial prince, and everywhere we will guarantee his personal security and the freedom of his movement, be it in Vienna, the city of our Imperial residence, or in any other place. And wherever he may be, whether in the Empire or in our crown lands, whether with the members of his family or without them, their sojourn will be legal; they shall have the right to stay there with their people, their horses, their cattle, their wagons and the rest of their property. They shall be entitled to pay with their own money for room and board wherever they will find it convenient to do so. All this they shall be able to do in peace and security, in freedom and without fear, and no further and special decree from our Court shall be necessary to confirm their rights. Furthermore, they shall not be disturbed in the observance of their religious rites and the Mosaic laws as they appertain to their daily life as well as in matters of death; this right is in accordance with the custom laid down in the constitution of the Empire where similar rights are granted to the Jewish communities which he, Wertheimer, serves as our privileged rabbi. These rights, however, do not affect any other Jews outside these communities....On acquisition of property, they shall have to pay the same duties as Christians do, and no more. In addition, we allow them to move about from place to place, on land or on water, with horse and carriage, without interference or disturbance, taking along their goods and cash assets in order to serve the Court or our military camps. They shall also be entitled to possess, without any restriction, any Hebrew books which he, Wertheimer, needs for the performance of his rabbinical duties...In case any member of the Wertheimer family [men of age]

dies before this privilege and letter of grace expires, all clauses and articles contained therein will remain in force for the widow, children and servants until the specified date. It is understood that you, Wertheimer, will be personally responsible for the conduct of the members of your family and the integrity of their commercial transactions. We hereby order all authorities under our jurisdiction, ecclesiastical and secular, of both the higher and lower echelons, and especially the magistrate and the Lord Mayor of Vienna, the city of our Imperial residence, to protect our Court Factor and Court Jew Samson Wertheimer as well as his sons-in-law, grandchildren and anybody else who may happen to be in his company, their wives and children included, until the date specified in this privilege, issued by our Imperial grace and within our capacity as a territorial prince: that they shall not be troubled, interfered with or harmed in any way, and that anybody who dares to do them any harm shall be punished by the withdrawal of our grace and a penal fine of thirty gold marks. We consider this to be a matter of great seriousness and put our Imperial seal to this document, issued in Vienna, our Imperial capital and city of residence, on August 29, 1703; the forty-sixth year of our Roman reign; the forty-ninth year of our Hungarian reign; the forty-seventh year of our Bohemian reign.

NOTES

1. Leopold I (1640–1705), Holy Roman emperor (1658–1705), King of Bohemia (1656–1705) and King of Hungary (1655–1705). His hostility toward the Jews (whom he expelled from Vienna in 1670) was tempered by his sincere appreciation of court Jews in his service. Samson Wertheimer (1658–1724) was a court Jew, rabbi, scholar and patron of scholars. This document not only delineates his privileges (to be seen in light of the disprivileged status of the Jewish masses) but also describes his varied activities on behalf of the crown—financial, commercial and even diplomatic.

2. A great variety of titles were used to designate court Jews, e.g., *Hofjude, Hoffactor, Hofprovedieteur, Hofagent, Kabinettfactor* and *Kommerzienrat*.

3. The original text consistently has Simsson Wertheimber.

4. The War of the Spanish Succession pitted the Holy Roman Empire in a protracted conflict with France. The immediate background to the war concerned the question of who would inherit the immense

possessions of King Charles II (1630–1700) when the childless and ailing monarch of Spain died. King Louis XIV of France had negotiated with the Holy Roman Emperor to partition Spain and its far-flung dominions. But the grandees of Spain objected and persuaded King Charles, shortly before his death, to name as his heir a Bourbon, Philip Duke of Anjou, the second grandson of Louis XIV, who would maintain the integrity of the Spanish empire. Reluctantly Louis XIV accepted this last act of King Charles II, who died on November 1, 1700. But since the Holy Roman Emperor had already claimed the throne of Spain for his son, the Archduke Charles, war was inevitable. A Grand Alliance was formed by the Holy Roman Empire, together with England, the Dutch Republic, Denmark, and most of the German princes. In 1713 and 1714 the Treaties of Utrecht and Rastadt, respectively, put an end to thirteen years of war between the Grand Alliance and the combined forces of France and Spain.

5. In Austrian usage "protection money" was an annual tax exacted collectively on the Jewish community; "tolerance money" was a tax that individual Jews paid for the right of residence.

6. THE PLANTATION ACT (MARCH 19, 1740)[1]

THE HOUSES OF PARLIAMENT OF GREAT BRITAIN

Whereas the increase of people is a means of advancing the wealth and strength of any nation or country: and whereas many foreigners and strangers from the lenity of our government, the purity of our religion, the benefit of our laws, the advantage of our trade, and the security of our property, might be induced to come and to settle in some of his Majesty's colonies in America, if they were made partakers of the advantages and privileges which the natural born subjects of this realm do enjoy; be it therefore enacted by the King's most excellent majesty, by and with the advice and consent of the lords spiritual and temporal, and commons, in this present parliament assembled, and by the authority of the same, That from and after the first day of June, in the year of our Lord one thousand seven hundred and forty, all persons born out of the ligeance of his Majesty, his heirs or successors, who have inhabited and resided, or shall inhabit or reside, for the space of seven years or more, in any of his Majesty's colonies in America, and shall not have been absent out of some of the said colonies for a longer space than two months at any one time during the said seven years, and shall take and subscribe the oaths, and make, repeat, and subscribe the declaration appointed by an act made in the first year of the reign of his late Majesty King George the First[2] … before the chief judge, or other judge of the colony wherein such persons respectively have so inhabited and resided, or shall so inhabit and reside, shall be deemed, adjudged and taken to be his Majesty's natural born subjects of this kingdom, to all intents, constructions, and purposes, as if they, and every of them had been or were born within this kingdom. …

And whereas the following words are contained in the latter part of the oath of abjuration, Videlicet (upon the true faith of a Christian)[3] and whereas the people professing the Jewish religion may thereby be prevented from receiving the benefit of this act; be it further enacted by the authority aforesaid, That

---

Source: "An Act for Naturalizing Such Foreign Protestants, and Others Therein Mentioned, As Are Settled, or Shall Settle, in Any of His Majesty's Colonies in America," *Collection of Public Statutes* (London, 1740), vol. 13, pp. 167–71. The original orthography has been retained.

whenever any person professing the Jewish religion shall present himself to take the said oath or abjuration in pursuance of this act, the said words (upon the true faith of a Christian) shall be omitted out of the said oath in administering the same to such person and the taking and subscribing the said oath by such person professing the Jewish religion, without the words aforesaid, and the other oaths appointed by the said act in like manner as Jews were permitted to take the oath of abjuration, by an act made in the tenth year of the reign of his late Majesty King George the First, intituled, An act for explaining and amending an act of the last session of parliament intituled, An act to oblige all persons, being papists, in that part of Great Britain called Scotland, and all persons in Great Britain refusing or neglecting to take the oaths appointed for the security of his Majesty's person and government, by several acts herein mentioned, to register their names and real estates; and for enlarging the time for taking the said oaths, and making such registers, and for allowing further time for the inrolment of deeds or wills made by papists, which have been omitted to be inrolled pursuant to an act of the third year of his Majesty's reign; and also for giving relief to the Protestant lessees, shall be deemed a sufficient taking of the said oaths, in order to intitle such persons to the benefit of being naturalized by virtue of this act.

NOTES

1. The passage of the Plantation Act by both Houses of Parliament, without opposition, can be attributed to the desire to increase the wealth and population of Great Britain's colonies, as expressly stated in the preamble to the act. The Plantation Act, which in effect naturalized the Jews of the colonies as equal subjects of Great Britain, was based on earlier precedents that recognized the residents of the crown's colonies as "natural born subjects of the kingdom" and that freed Jewish landowners in the kingdom from the obligation of taking the Christian oath.

2. George I (1660–1727) reigned as king of Great Britain and Ireland from 1714 until his death.

3. The removal of the required Christian oath in effect permitted the naturalization of Jewish landowners of Great Britain's American colonies, who at the time numbered about 190, of whom 151 resided on the island of Jamaica, the rest in New York, Pennsylvania, Maryland, and South Carolina.

7. THE CHARTER DECREED FOR THE JEWS OF PRUSSIA (APRIL 17, 1750)

FREDERICK II[1]

Revised General-Patent and Regulations of April 17, 1750 for Jewry of the Kingdom of Prussia, Electoral and Mark Brandenburg, the Duchies and Principalities of Magdeburg, Cleves, Farther-Pomerania, Krossen, Halberstadt, Minden, Camin, Moers, as well as the Counties and Territories of Mark, Ravensburg, Hohenstein, Tecklenburg, Lingen, Lauenburg, and Buetau—Explanation of the Causes for the further Regulation of Jewry: We, Frederick, by God's grace, King of Prussia, Margrave of Brandenburg, Chancellor and Electoral Prince of the Holy Roman Empire, sovereign and supreme Duke of Silesia, etc., etc., etc.

Source: Jacob R. Marcus, ed. and trans., *The Jew in the Medieval World* (New York: Harper Torchbooks, 1965), pp. 84–97. Reprinted by permission of Dr. Jacob R. Marcus.

Make known and order to be made known: We have noticed in our kingdom of Prussia...and particularly also in this capital [Berlin] various faults and abuses among the licensed and tolerated Jews, and have particularly observed that the rampant increase of these abuses has caused enormous damage and hardship, not only to the public, particularly to the Christian inhabitants and merchants, but also to Jewry itself. For this reason and because of the surreptitious entry of unlicensed Jews—foreigners [non-Prussian] and those who are all but without any country—many complaints and difficulties have arisen.

We, however, out of a feeling of most gracious paternal provision wish to establish and maintain, as far as possible, the livelihood and trades of each and every loyal subject under our protection, Christians as well as Jews, in a continually good and flourishing state.

For this reason we have found it necessary to make such provision that this, our most gracious purpose, may be attained, so that a proportion may be maintained between Christian and Jewish business opportunities and trades, and especially that neither [Jew or Christian] may be injured through a prohibited expansion of Jewish business activity. For this purpose we have again made an exact investigation of the condition, in our kingdom and in the other above mentioned imperial lands, of all Jewry, of their families, their means of subsistence, and their business activity. We have considered certain feasible proposals which have as their basis justice, fairness, and common safety, and have also deemed them useful for the attainment of our ultimate object and the attendant welfare of all inhabitants of the country who live by means of business activity. As a result of these proposals we wish to prepare and to put into effect a special regulation and constitution for all Jewry. Therefore we establish, regulate, and order, herewith and by virtue of this, that...

I. No other Jews are to be tolerated except those named in the lists that are attached to the end of these regulations.

II. List of the tolerated communal Jewish officials in Berlin: The following list of communal officials for the capital here in Berlin has been fixed:

1. One rabbi or a vice-rabbi.
2. Four assistant-judges.
3. A chief and assistant cantor with his basses and his sopranos. These latter must not be married.
4. Four criers, one of whom must report daily to the police office the arrival of foreign Jews. [These criers, or "knockers," used to call people to services at dawn by "knocking" on their doors.]
5. Two employees in the synagogal-school.
6. Six grave diggers who also do other work for the Jewish community.
7. One cemetery guard.
8. Three slaughterers.
9. Three butchers.
10. One secretary of the meat-market and his supervisor.
11. Three bakers and one restaurant-keeper.
12. A communal scribe.
13. Two doorkeepers and one assistant. [The doorkeepers at the city gates examined the papers of immigrant Jews.]
14. Two hospital attendants.
15. One physician.
16. One male and one female bath attendant.
17. A fattener of fowl and cattle.
18. Eight attendants for the sick.
19. Two Hebrew printers.
20. Two teachers for girls. Both must be married....

V. Principles that are to be observed in the settlement of Jews. The following principles respecting the settlement of Jews shall be established and observed in the future....

A distinction is to be made between Regular Protected-Jews and Special Protected-Jews who are merely tolerated during their life time.[2]...

Only those are to be considered Regular Protected-Jews who have the right to settle a child....

The above mentioned Special Protected-Jews, however, are not authorized to settle a child [in business] nor are they to marry off a child by virtue of their privilege....

In accordance with our most graciously issued cabinet-order of May 23, 1749, the fixed number of Jewish families at present is not to be exceeded except by our royal command....

The Regular Protected-Jews, however, are allowed by virtue of their Letter of Protection to settle one child, a son or daughter, during their life time, but once they have made their decision they will not be authorized to change it in the future. This child may marry if it can first establish its identity legally....

Foreign [non-Prussian] Jews are not allowed to settle in our lands at all. However, if one should really have a fortune of ten thousand Reichsthaler, and bring the same into the country and furnish authentic evidence of the fact, then we are to be asked about this and concerning the fee he is to pay....

In order that in the future all fraud, cheating, and secret and forbidden increase of the number of families may be more carefully avoided, no Jew shall be allowed to marry, nor will he receive permission to settle, in any manner, nor will he be believed, until a careful investigation has been made by the War and Domains Offices together with the aid of the Treasury.

Male and female servants and other domestics, however, are not allowed to marry. Should they attempt to do this they are not to be tolerated any longer....

The children of [all] licensed Jews, whose fathers have died or have been impoverished, or are in such a condition that they, the children, have no right of "settlement," or do not possess the required fortune, are to be tolerated, even as are the widows of such people. However, when they come of age, they shall in no wise dare, under penalty of expulsion, to set up a business for themselves but they must either work for other licensed Jews, or go away and seek to be accepted somewhere else. They may, indeed, prepare themselves so that they take the place of Jewish communal officials who leave. Thus it will not be necessary to accept so many foreigners for this purpose....

VII. No Protected-Jew can stay away from home for more than a Year without authorization; otherwise his place will be given to another....

VIII. The Jews must pay their taxes quarterly and all the Jews are responsible as a body for the payment of the taxes....

XI. The Jews must not pursue any manual trade. ... We herewith establish, regulate, and order earnestly that in the future no Jew shall presume to engage in any manual trade, nor venture upon any except seal-engraving, [art] painting, the grinding of optical glasses, diamonds, and jewels, gold and silver embroidery, fine cloth needlework, the collecting of gold dust by a sieving process, and other similar trades in which vocational associations and privileged guilds are not found. Particularly are they enjoined not to brew beer nor to distill spirits. However, they are allowed to undertake the distilling of spirits for the nobility, government officials, and others, with the understanding that only licensed Jews and their sons are to be taken for this task....However, those Jews who have received or may receive special concessions for the establishment of particular types of factories or for the sale of goods of Christian manufacturers are to be protected in the future as in the past.

XII. Jews are forbidden the smelting of gold and silver....

XIV. The Jews in Berlin are not allowed to have dealings in raw wool or woolen yarns or to manufacture woolen goods....[They were allowed, however, to sell the domestic finished product.]

XV. Jews are further allowed to sell one another beer and spirits...[but] with the exception of kosher wines they are not allowed to do any business in wines....[Jews] must not, however, sell strong drink [to non-Jews.]

XVI. Jews are not allowed to deal in raw cattle-and-horse hides, plain or dyed leathers, and foreign woolen wares except those which are specifically permitted in [paragraph XVIII]....[Cheap raw materials were to be reserved for Prussian manufacturers.]

XVII. Under special conditions they may sell choice groceries and spices to other Jews....The Jews are forbidden to trade in raw tobacco, to manufacture tobacco, and to carry a line of [staple] groceries....

XVIII. Precisely the kind of goods with which the Protected-Jews are allowed to do business: In order that all Jews under our protection may be informed and instructed precisely in the business opportunities and trades allowed them, they are allowed to trade and to do business with the following, namely:

With gold-cloth, silver-cloth, fine fabrics and ribbons, native and foreign embroidered goods, domestic gold and silver laces manufactured in the Berlin Royal Gold and Silver Factory, neck bands of lace, Spanish lace, gold and silver thread and purl; likewise with jewels, broken gold and silver, ingots, all sorts of old pocket-watches, and similar things. Furthermore they are permitted to deal in money-exchange and pledges, money-brokerage, and the buying and selling of houses and estates for other people. They are also permitted to do business in all sorts of Brabant, Dutch, Silesian and Electoral-Saxonian fine cloth and silk textiles, in laces, muslin, and all-white domestic coarse linings, domestic linens, white linen thread, and tablecloths of linen and half-linen. They are also specially allowed to deal with domestic silk goods, also with foreign and native undyed, dressed leather, and with domestic velvet.[3] They are also allowed to deal in all sorts of all-wool and half-wool goods and cotton goods—by whatever name they may be called—manufactured here in this country, as well as with cotton and chintz goods made in our lands.

Furthermore they are permitted to deal in horses, in undressed calf and sheep hides, feathers, wigs, hair, also camel and horsehair, tallow, wax, and honey, Polish wares [pelts, potash, hemp, etc.], undressed and unfinished pelts, but not finished furriers' wares in those cities where furriers live, unless they can without hesitation give the name of the furriers from whom they bought the finished product for further sale. [Jews must not compete with the craft-guilds, such as the furriers.] They are also allowed to trade in tea, coffee, chocolate, and foreign and domestic manufactured snuff and smoking tobacco. They are also free to trade, exchange, and do business in all sorts of old clothes, old or used furniture, house and kitchen utensils; to sum up, with everything which is not generally and specifically forbidden in the above paragraphs, even though it is neither specified or mentioned in this special paragraph. But all this is permitted them only in their own homes and in those shops and booths that have been regularly assigned them.

However, with respect to foreign and domestic Jewish trade in our Kingdom of Prussia, the special constitution that has been made there will remain in force, in as much as the Polish and Russian business there is still dependent on both Christian and Jewish commerce....

XIX. The Jews must not trade in anything herein forbidden them, under threat of confiscation of their wares....They may not peddle in cities except at the time of the fairs....

XX. No foreign [non-Prussian] Jews and Jewish boys shall do business in Berlin. Outside of exceptional cases herein specified, those who remain over

twenty-four hours in Berlin must pay one specie-ducat to the Potsdam Orphan Home....

Now it has been noticed that many Jews and Jewish boys from other cities and provinces that are subject to us have tarried in Berlin, year in and year out, and almost daily, constantly coming and going, and, as it were, relieving one another. Through private and public trading they have done tremendous damage, not only to the entire public, but particularly to the entire Christian and authorized Jewish trade, and have at the same time deceived and duped our treasures through all sorts of fraud and malicious practices. Therefore, we establish, regulate, and order herewith by virtue of this, that except for the local fairs no Jew who does not belong to Berlin—whether he is otherwise licensed or non-licensed within our land—shall be allowed to come into the city with any wares except broken gold and silver. Also no foreign [non-Prussian] Jew, male or female, shall be allowed in except at the time of the fairs....

XXI. All foreign [non-Prussian Jews] who do not arrive with the post-carriage or their own vehicles may enter into and leave Berlin by only two gates....

XXII. What is to be done with Jewish beggars: It has already been decreed many times that Jewish beggars are nowhere to be allowed to cross our borders. We not only repeat this, but order that in the event such Jewish beggars nevertheless reach our capital surreptitiously, they shall be brought at once to the Poor-Jews House at the Prenzlau Gate. There they are to be given alms and on the following day evicted through the gate without being allowed to enter the city....

XXIV. The Jews are allowed to lend out money on proper pledges. Inasmuch as the money-business is a particular source of Jewish support, Jews are therefore allowed to lend money on pledges now as in the past. They must not, however, accept pledges from any non-commissioned officer or soldier, or buy anything where they are not sufficiently assured that this is their lawful property and no part of their soldiers' equipment. And in every case they must demand a note from the company commander with respect to these things. Furthermore, the Jews must be very sure in all pawning and selling that the pledges were not stolen or secretly removed and then pledged, either by young folks from their parents, or by unfaithful servants from their employers. On each occasion therefore, the pawnbrokers must make enquiries from the parents or the employers.

Furthermore, those Jews, their wives, or employees must not only surrender such pledges to the owner without compensation, but in case that they knew that the pledge was stolen or secretly removed, and shall be legally convicted of this, then, in accordance with the edict of January 15, 1747, the possessors of such pledges shall be regarded just like those who have wittingly purchased stolen goods. Such a pawnbroker shall lose all rights of protection, not only for himself, but also for his children if some of them have already been settled in business, for their Letters of Protection shall be annulled, and he and his family shall be removed from the country. Furthermore, no one else is to be settled in the vacancy created by that family, and, besides this, the transgressor is to be compelled to pay the full worth of the stolen or illegally received things to the lawful owner, who, if necessary, wall take an oath as to their value.

If the offender cannot pay this because his Letter of Protection has been cancelled and his family already expelled, then the entire Jewry of the town is officially to be held responsible for the payment in cash—and without any protest—to the robbed owner of the value of the stolen or illegally received things. For this reason the Jews must watch one another and pay attention carefully when they find any of their people on the wrong road and immediately report such a person to the proper authorities. Jewry, therefore, and particularly the elders are required to anticipate any annoyance and damage by ridding the country of those receivers of stolen goods and the other rascally crew among them whenever they discover them. And when they submit their information they will be given all assistance....

XXXIII. Concerning the observance of the general-patent for the Jews: in order that this general-patent for the Jews shall be contravened as little as possible, the War and Domains Offices of their respective Departments and local commissaries [the tax-councils] shall watch Jewry very carefully in the cities of the provinces and see to it that the said general-patent is everywhere exactly followed. They are particularly to see that the fixed number of families, communal officials, and Jewish-owned homes in every town is not increased, that no one is admitted without our royal concession, and least of all that no unlicensed Jew be tolerated. For this reason nothing is to be undertaken or conceded by the magistrates on their own authority; nor shall any Jew be permitted to live in the rural districts or in open towns where there is no excise office.

So done and given at Berlin, the seventeenth of April 1750.

NOTES

1. Frederick II (1712–1786), Frederick the Great, king of Prussia (1740–1786). Jacob R. Marcus observes in his *The Jew in the Medieval World* (New York, 1969) that the charter "is a curious combination of medieval and modern elements. It is modern in the sense that the Jew is thought to be no longer a ward of the king, but instead a subject of the state—albeit second class. The former Jewish autonomy is broken down and the Jew is brought closer to the state economically, politically, and culturally. The charter is medieval, however, in the sense that it is filled with a spirit of distrust of and contempt for the Jew, limiting him almost exclusively to commerce and industry" (p. 81).

2. This division of Jews according to their economic value to the state constitutes the unique feature of the charter. In 1763 Moses Mendelssohn became a Special-Protected Jew; despite his fame he was never able to acquire the status of Regular Protected-Jew (see documents 11 and 12 in this chapter).

3. Moses Mendelssohn was employed by a domestic silk firm.

8. "THE JEW BILL" (1753)[1]

THE HOUSES OF PARLIAMENT OF GREAT BRITAIN

Whereas by an Act made in the Seventh year of the reign of King James the First, intituled, An Act that all such as are to be naturalized or restored in Blood, shall first receive the Sacrament of the Lord's Supper, and the Oath of Allegiance, and the Oath of Supremacy, every person who shall apply to be naturalized by Act of Parliament, being of the Age of Eighteen Years or upwards, is required to receive the Sacrament of the Lord's Supper, within One Month before such Naturalization is exhibited, whereby many Persons of considerable Substance professing the Jewish Religion, are prevented from being naturalized by Bill to be exhibited in Parliament for that Purpose: And whereas by an Act made in the Thirteenth Year of his present Majesty's Reign,[2] intituled, An Act for Naturalizing such Foreign Protestants, and others therein mentioned, as are settled, or shall settle in any of his Majesty's Colonies in America, Persons professing the Jewish Religion, who have inhabited and resided or shall inhabit and reside for the Space of Seven years or more, in any of his Majesty's Colonies in America, and shall not have been absent out of some of the said Colonies, for a longer space than two months at any One Time during the said Seven Years, are naturalized upon their complying with the terms therein mentioned, without their receiving the Sacrament of the Lord's Supper; Be it therefore enacted by the King's most excellent Majesty, by and with the Advice and consent of the Lords Spiritual and Temporal, and Commons, in this present Parliament assembled, and by the Authority of the same, That Persons professing the Jewish Religion may, upon Application for that Purpose, be naturalized by Parliament, without receiving the Sacrament of the Lord's Supper, the said Act of the Seventh Year of the Reign of King James the First, or any other Law, Statute, Matter or Thing to the contrary in any ways notwithstanding....

Provided also, and it is hereby further enacted, That no Person shall be naturalized by virtue of any Act to be made or passed in pursuance of this Act, unless Proof shall be made by two credible Witnesses, that such Person professeth the Jewish Religion, and hath for Three Years past professed the same, the Proof in both cases before mentioned to be made in such Manner as is now practised in both Houses of Parliament respectively, when Proof is made that any Person hath received the Holy Sacrament, in order to [be naturalized].

And it is hereby further enacted by the Authority aforesaid,[3] That from and after the First Day of June, one thousand seven hundred and fifty-three, every Person professing the Jewish Religion shall be disabled, and is hereby made incapable to purchase, either in his or her own name, or in the Name of any other Person or Persons, to his or her Use, or in Trust for him or her, or to inherit or take by Descent, Devise, or Limitation, in Possession, Reversion, or Remainder, any advowson or Right of Patronage, or Presentation, or other Right or interest whatsoever of, in, or to any Benefice, Prebend,[4] or other Ecclesiastical Living or Promotion, School, Hospital, or Donative whatsoever, or any Grant of any Avoidance thereof; and all and singular Estates, Terms, and other Interests whatsoever of, in, or any Benefice, Prebend, or other Ecclesiastical Living or Promotion, School, Hospital, or Donative, which, from and after the said First Day of June, shall be made, suffered or done, to or for the Use or Behoof of any such Person or Persons, or upon any Trust or Confidence, mediately or immediately, to or for the benefit or Behoof of any such Person or Persons,

---

Source: "The Jewish Naturalization Act. An Act To Permit Persons Professing the Jewish Religion, To Be Naturalized by Parliament and for Other Purposes Therein Mentioned," *Collection of the Public General Statutes* (London, 1753), vol. 26, pp. 407–11.

shall be utterly void and of none Effect, to all Intents, Construction, and Purposes whatsoever.

NOTES

1. Enacted by Parliament in May 1753, this act, in face of the energetic opposition by Christian merchants of London, was repealed a year later.

2. The reference is to the Plantation Act. See document 6 in this chapter.
3. This paragraph was intended to allay fears that the granting to Jews of civil rights would obscure the social boundaries separating Jew and Christian.
4. Part of revenue of a cathedral or collegiate church granted to canons as a stipend.

9. CONCERNING THE AMELIORATION OF THE CIVIL STATUS OF THE JEWS (1781)

CHRISTIAN WILHELM VON DOHM[1]

What might be the reasons that induced the governments of almost all European states unanimously to deal so harshly with the Jewish nation? What has induced them (even the wisest) to make this one exception from the laws of an otherwise enlightened policy according to which all citizens should be incited by uniform justice, support of trade and the greatest possible freedom of action so as to contribute to the general welfare? Should a number of industrious and law-abiding citizens be less useful to the state because they stem from Asia and differ from others by beard, circumcision, and a special way—transmitted to them from their ancient forefathers—of worshiping the Supreme Being? This latter would certainly disqualify them from full rights of citizenship, and justify all restrictive measures, if it contained principles which would keep the Jews from fulfilling their duties to the state, and from keeping faith in their actions within the community and with single members of the community; and if hatred against those who do not belong to their faith would make them feel an obligation to deal crookedly with others and to disregard their rights.

It would have to be clearly proved that the religion of the Jews contains such antisocial principles, that their divine laws are contrary to the laws of justice and charity, if one were to justify before the eyes of reason that the rights of citizenship should be withheld entirely only from the Jew, and that he should be permitted only partially to enjoy the rights of man. According to what has become known about the Jewish religion so far, it does not contain such harmful principles. The most important book of the Jews, the Law of Moses, is looked upon by Christians with reverence and it is ascribed by them to divine revelation. This belief in its divine origin alone must banish every thought that this law could prescribe any vicious thing, or that its followers must be bad citizens. But even those who did not start from this assumption have found after investigation that the Mosaic law contains the most correct principle of moral law, justice and order....

Source: Christian Wilhelm von Dohm, *Ueber die buergerliche Verbesserung der Juden* (Berlin, 1781); a sequel appeared in 1783. In *Readings in Modern Jewish History*, ed. Ellis Rivkin and trans. Helen Lederer (Cincinnati, Ohio: Hebrew Union College-Jewish Institute of Religion, 1957), pp. 5–7, 9–22, 50–81. Reprinted by permission of Dr. Ellis Rivkin.

It is natural that in the Jews of our time the sense of oppression under which they live mixes with the hostile feelings of their ancestors against other nations whose lands they were to conquer, feelings which were hallowed by their Law. It may be that some of them hold to the belief that it is permitted to hate as they hated the Canaanites those who, in their societies, scarcely give them permission to live. But these feelings are obviously derived from their old laws; and the natural reactions of the offended and oppressed seem to justify these. It is certain, however, that the present faith of the Jews contains no commandment to hate and offend adherents of other religions. Murder, theft, felony, even when committed by a non-Jew, still remains, according to their law, the same crime.* Conclusions of the kind I mentioned above are possible in all religions and, in fact, do occur in all religions. Each one boasts of being the only, or at least the safest and straightest, way to please God, to reach the goal of a blissful life in the hereafter. Each one boasts that its truth is founded on such clear, irrefutable proofs that only wilful shutting of the eyes could deny its shining light. So every religion instils in its adherents a kind of antipathy against adherents of other faiths, an antipathy which borders sometimes on hatred, sometimes more on contempt, and which manifests itself sometimes more, sometimes less, as political conditions influence the sentiments of the various religious groups toward each other and as the cultural level, the influence of philosophy and the sciences strengthen or weaken the impact of religious convictions. If therefore every religion severs the bond between man and man and makes men withhold affection and justice from those who are not of the same faith, if this is a natural consequence of the boasted superiority of every faith, then this phenomenon cannot be a valid reason for withholding the rights of citizenship from the adherents of any one faith....

So, even if actually in the faith of today's Jews there should be some principles which would restrict them too strongly to their special group and exclude them from the other groups of the great civil society; this would still not justify their persecution—which can only serve to confirm them in their opinions—so long as their laws are not contrary to the general principles of morality and do not permit antisocial vices. The only prerogative of the government in this case would be (1) to have an exact knowledge of those principles, or indeed only the conclusions drawn from religious principles, and the actual influence of these on their actions, and (2) endeavor to weaken the influence of these principles, by general enlightenment of the nation, by furthering and advancing its morals independently of religion, and, in general, further the refinement of their sentiments.

More than anything else a life of normal civil happiness in a well-ordered state, enjoying the long withheld freedom, would tend to do away with clannish religious opinions. The Jew is even more man than Jew, and how would it be possible for him not to love a state where he could freely acquire property and freely enjoy it, where his taxes would be not heavier than those of the other citizens, where he could reach positions of honor and enjoy general esteem? Why should he hate people who are no longer distinguished from him by offensive prerogatives, who share with him equal rights and duties? The novelty of this happiness, and unfortunately, the probability that this will not in the near future happen in all states, would make it even more precious to the Jew, and gratitude alone would make him the most patriotic citizen. He would look at his country with the eyes of a long misjudged, and finally after long banishment, re-instated son. These human emotions would talk louder in his heart than the sophistic sayings of his rabbis.

Our knowledge of human nature tells us that conditions of this our actual life here have a stronger

---

*One finds perhaps in the Talmud places where some rabbis endeavored to prove by sophistic conclusion that it is a minor misdeameanor to defraud a non-Jew. An example of such a kind is the statement that expounds the law to "love thy neighbor and not offend him" meaning only the Israelite. Some writers who are very prejudiced against the Jews have collected these items with many reproaches against the Jewish nation, intending to justify thereby the hatred and persecution of Jews. If, however, as is undoubtedly true, these sayings of some single rabbis were never accepted by the nation; if the Mosaic law as well as the greatest Jewish rabbis make no difference at all between vices and crimes, committed against Jews or non-Jews; then it would be grossly unfair to make the whole nation responsible for the prejudices of some single rabbis and to judge their whole religious system by such sayings; just as it would be wrong to judge Christianity and the moral principles of today's Christians from the sayings of some Fathers of the Church (which often are quite unreasonable and misanthropic). [Dohm's note]

influence on men than those referring to life after death. History proves also that good government and the prosperity all subjects enjoy under such a government weaken the influence of religious principles and abolish the mutual antipathy which is only nourished by persecution....

Certainly, the Jew will not be prevented by his religion from being a good citizen, if only the government will give him a citizen's rights. Either his religion contains nothing contrary to the duties of a citizen, or such tenets can easily be abolished by political and legal regulations.

One might oppose to all these reasons the general experience of our states of the political harmfulness of the Jews, intending to justify the harsh way our governments are dealing with them by the assertion that the character and spirit of this nation is so unfortunately formed that on this ground they cannot be accepted with quite equal rights in any civil society. Indeed, quite often in life one hears this assertion that the character of the Jews is so corrupt that only the most restricting and severest regimentation can render them harmless. To these unfortunates, it is said, has been transmitted from their ancestors, if not through their most ancient law, then through their oral tradition and the later sophistic conclusions of the rabbis, such a bitter hatred of all who do not belong to their tribe, that they are unable to get used to looking at them as members of a common civil society with equal rights. The fanatic hatred with which the ancestors of the Jews persecuted the founder of Christianity has been transmitted to their late posterity and they hate all followers of this faith. Outbreaks of this hatred have often shown themselves clearly unless held in check by force. Especially have the Jews been reproached by all nations with lack of fairness and honesty in the one field in which they were allowed to make a living—commerce. Every little dishonest practice in commerce is said to be invented by Jews, the coin of any state is suspect if Jews took part in the minting, or if it went frequently through Jewish hands. One hears also in all places where they were allowed to multiply in numbers, the accusation that they monopolize almost entirely the branches of trade permitted to them and that Christians are unable to compete with them in these. For this reason, it is further said, the governments of nearly all states have adopted the policy, in an unanimity from which alone it can be concluded that it is justified to

issue restrictive laws against this nation and to deviate, in its case alone, from the principle of furthering a continuous rise in population. They could not concede to these people who are harmful to the welfare of the rest of the citizens the same rights, and had to adopt the stipulation of a certain amount of property for those permitted to settle down, as guarantee for compliance with the laws and abstinence from criminal activities.

If I am not entirely mistaken there is one error in this reasoning, namely, that one states as cause what in reality is the effect, quoting the evil wrought by the past erroneous policy as an excuse for it. Let us concede that the Jews may be more morally corrupt than other nations; that they are guilty of a proportionately greater number of crimes than the Christians; that their character in general inclines more toward usury and fraud in commerce, that their religious prejudice is more antisocial and clannish; but I must add that this supposed greater moral corruption of the Jews is a necessary and natural consequence of the oppressed condition in which they have been living for so many centuries. A calm and impartial consideration will prove the correctness of this assertion.

The hard and oppressive conditions under which the Jews live almost everywhere would explain, although not justify, an even worse corruption than they actually can be accused of. It is very natural that these conditions cause the spirit of the Jew to lose the habit of noble feelings, to be submerged in the base routine of earning a precarious livelihood. The varied kinds of oppression and contempt he experiences are bound to debase him in his activities, to choke every sense of honor in his heart. As there are almost no honest means of earning a living left to him it is natural that he falls into criminal practices and fraud, especially since commerce more than other trades seduces people to such practices. Has one a right to be surprised if a Jew feels himself bound by laws which scarcely permit him to breathe, yet he cannot break them without being punished? How can we demand willing obedience and affection for the state from him, who sees that he is tolerated only to the extent that he is a means of revenue? Can one be surprised at his hatred for a nation which gives him so many and so stinging proofs of its hatred for him? How can one expect virtue from him if one does not trust him? How can one reproach him with crimes he is forced to commit because no honest means of earning a livelihood are open to him; for he is oppressed by taxes and nothing is left him to care for the education and moral training of his children?

Everything the Jews are blamed for is caused by the political conditions under which they now live, and any other group of men, under such conditions, would be guilty of identical errors....

If, therefore, those prejudices today prevent the Jew from being a good citizen, a social human being, if he feels antipathy and hatred against the Christian, if he feels himself in his dealings with him not so much bound by his moral code, then all this is our own doing. His religion does not commend him to commit these dishonesties, but the prejudices which we have instilled and which are still nourished by us in him are stronger than his religion. We ourselves are guilty of the crimes we accuse him of; and the moral turpitude in which that unfortunate nation is sunk—thanks to a mistaken policy—cannot be a reason that would justify a continuation of that policy. That policy is a remnant of the barbarism of past centuries, a consequence of a fanatical religious hatred. It is unworthy of our enlightened times and should have been abolished long ago. A look at the history and the origin of the present regulations concerning the Jews will make this clear....

If this reasoning is correct, then we have found in the oppression and in the restricted occupation of the Jews the true source of their corruption. Then we have discovered also at the same time the means of healing this corruption and of making the Jews better men and useful citizens. With the elimination of the unjust and unpolitical treatment of the Jews will also disappear the consequences of it; and when we cease to limit them to one kind of occupation, then the detrimental influence of that occupation will no longer be so noticeable. With the modesty that a private citizen should always show when expressing his thoughts about public affairs, and with the certain conviction that general proposals should always be tailored, if they should be useful to the special local conditions in every state, I dare now, after these remarks, to submit my ideas as to the manner in which the Jews could become happier and better members of civil societies.

To make them such it is first necessary to give them equal rights with all other subjects. Since they are able to fulfill the duties they should be allowed to claim the equal impartial love and care of the state.

No humiliating discrimination should be tolerated, no way of earning a living should be closed to them, none other than the regular taxes demanded from them. They would have to pay all the usual taxes in the state, but they would not have to pay protection money for the mere right to exist, no special fee for the permission to earn a living. It is obvious that in accordance with the principle of equal rights, also special privileges favoring the Jews—which exist in some states—would have to be abolished. These sometimes owed their existence to a feeling of pity which would be without basis under more just conditions. When no occupation will be closed to Jews, then they should, in all fairness, not have a monopoly on any occupation in preference to other citizens. When the government will decide to fix the rate of interest by law, the Jew will not be able to ask for any more than the legal rate of interest. If it will be prohibited to private citizens to lend money on pawns, or do so only under certain conditions, the Jews will have to observe these rules.

Since it is primarily the limitation of the Jews to commerce which has had a detrimental influence on their moral and political character, a perfect freedom in the choice of a livelihood would serve justice, as well as representing a humanitarian policy which would make of the Jews more useful and happier members of society.

It might even be useful, in order to achieve this great purpose, if the government would first try to dissuade the Jews from the occupation of commerce, and endeavor to weaken its influence by encouraging them to prefer such kinds of earning a living as are the most apt to create a diametrically opposed spirit and character—I mean artisan occupations....

The Jews should not be excluded from agriculture. Unless the purchase of landed property is restricted in a country to certain classes of the inhabitants, the Jews should not be excluded, and they should have equal rights to lease land. But I do not expect very great advantages from this occupation in respect to the improvement of the nation, because, as remarked above, it is too similar to commerce, it nourishes the spirit of speculation and profit-seeking. I do not wish to see the Jews encouraged to become owners of big estates or tenants (few of them have the necessary capital) but peasants working their own land. The funds which many states provide for colonists could in many cases be used to better advantage by settling the

Jews of the country on vacant pieces of land, and by providing houses and money for agricultural implements. Perhaps it would help to reawaken the love for such work in the nation if the big Jewish tenants or owners of estates would be required to employ a number of Jewish farmhands.

From several sides the proposal has been made that the Jews should be allotted separate districts for settlement and be kept isolated there from the rest of the subjects. In my opinion it would not be advisable to make the religious difference more noticeable and probably more permanent by this step. The Jews, left entirely to themselves, would be strengthened in their prejudices against Christians, and vice versa. Frequent intercourse and sharing the burdens and advantages of the state equally is the most certain way to dull the edge of the hostile prejudices on both sides. The *Judengasse* (*Juiveries* in France) [ghetto] and restricted districts of Jewish residence in many cities are remnants of the old harsh principles. In many places (for instance, Frankfurt on the Main, where the *Judengasse* is locked up every night) the evil consequence is that the Jews are forced to build their houses many stories high and live under very crowded conditions resulting in uncleanliness, diseases, and bad policing, and greater danger of fire.

No kind of commerce should be closed to the Jews, but none should be left to them exclusively and they should not be encouraged by privileges. On the contrary, by encouraging skilled crafts and agriculture they should be drawn away from commerce, and in the intention of weakening the influence of this one occupation which for such a long time was their only one, it would even be permissible at least in the beginning, to restrict the number of Jews active in commerce, or subject them to special taxes and so establish a fund to encourage other occupations among the nation.

A useful new regulation, which has already been introduced in various states, would be to obligate the Jews to keep their books in the language of the land and not in Hebrew. This would facilitate communication with Christian merchants and in cases of litigation over these books the judges would have less difficulties, fraud and crooked dealings in commerce should be represented to the Jews as the most heinous crime against the state which now embraces them with equal affection, and these crimes should be subjected to the harshest penalties—perhaps exclusion

from the newly granted freedoms for a period of time or permanently.

Every art, every science should be open to the Jew as to every other free man. He, too, should educate his mind as far as he is able; he, too, must be able to rise to promotion, honor, and rewards by developing his talents. The scientific institutions of the State should be for his use, too, and he should be as free as other citizens to utilize his talents in any way.

Another question is whether in our states Jews should be admitted to public office immediately. It seems, in fact, that if they are granted all civil rights, they could not be excluded from applying for the honor to serve the government, and if they are found to be capable, from being employed by the state. I think, however, that in the next generation this capability will not yet appear frequently, and the state should make no special effort to develop it. In most countries there is no lack of skilled civil servants, and without any efforts on the part of the government there are enough applicants for public office. For some of these jobs early education and scholarship, which are hard to come by in the present educational setup for Jews, is required. Other jobs require that the applicant be far removed from any suspicion of misdemeanors due to greed, and this will probably not always be the case in the Jews of today and of the next generation. The too mercantile spirit of most Jews will probably be broken more easily by heavy physical labor than by the sedentary work of the public servant; and for the state as well as for himself it will be better in most cases if the Jew works in the shops and behind the plow than in the state chancelleries. The best middle way would probably be to allow the Jews, without especially encouraging them, to acquire the education necessary for public service, even to employ them in cases where they show special capability, if only to overcome the prejudice which will no doubt endure for a long time. But impartiality would demand that if a Jewish and a Christian applicant show equal capability, the latter deserves preference. This seems to be an obvious right of the majority in the nation—at least until the Jews by wiser treatment are changed into entirely equal citizens and all differences polished off.

It should be a special endeavor of a wise government to care for the moral education and enlightenment of the Jews, in order to make at least the coming generations more receptive to a milder treatment and the enjoyment of all advantage of our society. The state should not look further into their religious education than would perhaps be necessary to prevent the teaching of antisocial opinions against men of other persuasions. But the government should take care that, besides the holy teachings of his fathers, the Jew is taught to develop his reason by the clear light of knowledge, the science of nature and its great creator, and that his heart is warmed by the principles of order, honesty, love for all men and the great society in which he lives; that the Jew, too, is led at an early age to the sciences required more or less for his future profession. This would have to be done either in the Jewish schools, or if teachers and funds are for the time being lacking, the Jews should be permitted to send their children to the Christian schools (except for the hours reserved for religious instruction). As some Jews perhaps would be kept from making use of this permission by prejudice, they should even be required to send their children to certain classes in accordance with their future vocations. That department of the government which is in charge of public education (an office which should always belong to the state, not to a religious party) should extend its supervision over the education of the Jews, except only for their religious instruction. Regarding all other subjects Jewish schools should be organized just like the best Christian schools, or the Department should order the Jewish children to be admitted to these latter and take care to make sure that Jewish parents need not be afraid that their children might be lured away from the religion of their fathers. No doubt it would be useful for the education of the moral and civil character of the Jew if the government would arrange that in the synagogues, besides the religious instruction which is not to be interfered with, instruction be given sometimes in the pure and holy truths of reason, and especially on the relationship of all citizens to the state and their duties to it. An institution which would, in fact, be highly desirable also for the Christians!

With the moral improvement of the Jews there should go hand in hand efforts of the Christians to get rid of their prejudices and uncharitable opinions. In early childhood they should be taught to regard the Jews as their brothers and fellow men who seek to find favor with God in a different way; a way they think erroneously to be the right one, yet which, if they follow in sincerity of heart, God looks at with favor. Other men should not quarrel with them

about it, but try to lead them by love to still higher truths. The preachers should be required to repeat frequently these principles so much in accord with real Christianity, and they will do it easily if the spirit of love which rules in the parable of the Good Samaritan fills their hearts, if they, like the apostles of Christ, teach that any man of any nation who does right finds favor with God.

An important part of civil rights would be the right for Jews in all places of free worship, to build synagogues and employ teachers at their own expense. This freedom should be limited only in special cases, for instance for the reason that a synagogue would be too much of a financial burden on a very small Jewish community or that the support of too many teachers would cause too great a hardship; just like Christian communities have often to get along without their own teachers and churches. The care of the poor could either be left to the Jews alone, as until now, without help of the government, or the Jews should contribute proportionately to the general fund of these institutions and partake in their advantages. At any rate, government supervision of the Jewish poorhouses and hospitals would be useful, in order to assure the healthiest and best organization and the best utilization of the money appropriated for them. The Jewish community, just as any other organized religious society, should have the right to excommunicate for a period of time or permanently, and in case of resistance the judgment of the rabbis should be supported by the authorities. Regarding the execution of this ban, the state should interfere less when it does not go beyond a religious society and has no effect on the political society, for the excommunicated member of any church can be a very useful and respected citizen. This is a principle of general church jurisprudence which should no longer be doubtful in out times.

The written law of Moses, which does not refer to Palestine and the old judicial and ritual organization, as the oral law, are regarded by the Jews as permanently binding divine commandments. Besides, various commentaries to these laws and argumentations from them by famous Jewish scholars are held in the same respects as laws. Therefore, if they are to be granted full human rights, one has to permit them to live and be judged according to these laws. This will no more isolate them from the rest of the citizens of the state than a city or community living according to their own statutes; and the experience made with Jewish autonomy during the first centuries in the Roman Empire as also in some modern states has shown that no inconvenient or detrimental consequences are to be feared. Although this does not necessarily mean that the laws should be administered by Jewish judges, this would always be more agreeable to them and would avoid many difficulties arising from ignorance of the complicated Jewish jurisprudence in Christian judges which requires the knowledge of the Hebrew language and Rabbinics. It would therefore be better to leave litigation between Jew and Jew in civil cases to their own judges in the first instance, but also to permit the Jews to start court proceedings at the court of the regular Christian judges. These courts as well as the higher instances to which Jews might appeal from the decision of the Jewish judge, would of course have to decide according to Jewish laws; for if they would decide according to the common law great confusion would be unavoidable, and besides the litigants would have the unfair advantage that he could file his claim with the Judge whose decision he would expect to be favorable to him. I think, Jewish judges could also (like in Anspach and Baireuth, in Alsace and other countries) take care of the business of notaries and, under supervision of the authorities decide on inheritances, appoint guardians, etc....

A constitution shaped according to these principles would, it seems to me, bring the Jews into society as useful members and at the same time would abolish the many ills that have been done to them and of which they were forced to make themselves guilty. Men of higher insight will decide if my assertions are correct, my proposals feasible....

Now I want to touch upon some objections which might be made to my proposals.... The most serious reason for asserting that the Jews cannot obtain equal rights with the rest of the citizens is the belief "that the Jews are prohibited by their religion from serving in the army, because their Sabbath regulations forbid them to fight on the Sabbath, to make extended marches, and because they would not be able to fulfill their religious obligations and customs when in the army...." [However,] there is not the slightest indication of this in the Mosaic law, and up to the destruction of the First Temple we do not find anywhere a remark that the Jews, in their numerous wars, refrained on the Sabbath from defense against their enemies or attack upon enemy armies....

[Further,] just as usual were the military service of this nation under the Pagan and the first Christian emperors, until in 418, the emperor Honorius ruled the Jews to be incapable of serving in war, and so founded a prejudice which he himself uttered not without some doubts, but which in later times took root and will now be quite hard to destroy.... As they fought in Greek and Roman armies they will fight in ours, and just as in ancient times they will again learn to reconcile the observance of the Sabbath and other religious commands and customs [of Judaism] with military service.

Certainly the unnatural oppression under which the Jews have been living for so many centuries contributed to the deterioration of their religious laws from their original goodness and utility, as well as to their general moral corruption. Moses intended to found a permanent, thriving state, and his law contains nothing to the contrary. Governed by this law the state had its golden age, and up until the fifth century the Jews were good citizens of the Roman Empire. Only when they were excluded from all the civil societies of the earth did they forget the relation of their law to the state. As their only occupation, commerce, gave them leisure and at the same time inclination to sophistic speculation, they wove speculations around their religious laws; and lacking better occupations, they strove by anxious observance of certain customs and holidays to achieve special holiness and greater rights to heaven, because civil happiness on earth was so limited. This timid and petty spirit of ceremony which has sneaked into the present day Jewish religion is sure to disappear again as soon as wider horizons are opened to the Jews, as soon as they [are] accepted as members of the political society and can make its interests their own. They will then reform their religious laws and regulations according to the demands of society. They will go back to the freer and nobler ancient Mosaic Law, will explain and adapt it according to the changed times and conditions, and will find authorizations to do so alone in their Talmud.[2]

It is therefore not to be doubted that the Jews, too, will fulfill the obligation to defend the society which has given them equal rights. Of course, this improvement of the Jews in general must not be expected immediately in the coming generation. It is natural that a nation estranged to carrying firearms for fifteen centuries will not be able to acquire immediately along with the good will, also the soldierly courage and physical fitness required for military service. The last named quality will be furthered by more extended physical labor in farming and crafts, and more nourishing food. Personal courage is in today's kind of warfare no longer so very essential in the soldiers of the rank and file as it used to be in ancient times, when the Jews made good soldiers. The same discipline and training which daily transforms the clumsiest young peasant lad into a worthy soldier will certainly effect the same transformation in the Jew.

For all these reasons, and trusting that human nature is the same in all people, I am convinced that in a few generations the Jews will be just like all other citizens in those states which will give them equal rights, and they will defend the state just like the others....

NOTES

1. Christian Wilhelm von Dohm (1751–1820), German scholar in constitutional law, statistics and modern history; active in the Enlightenment circles of Berlin, where he befriended Moses Mendelssohn. (See documents 11 and 12 in this chapter.) In 1779 he assumed a position in the Prussian government, serving as the registrar of the secret archives and as councillor in the Department of Foreign Affairs. The title of Dohm's essay may also be translated as "On the Civil Improvement of the Jews." This translation underscores Dohm's argument that an amelioration of the Jews' civil status would bring about the "desired" improvement in their public morality. Dohm's plea for admitting the Jews to citizenship; which he wrote at the behest of Mendelssohn, coincided with the reforms of Joseph II, the emperor of Austria, and thus helped give focus to the ensuing debate throughout Europe on the desirability of granting the Jews civil parity.

2. Dohm's note: A great Jewish scholar [presumably Moses Mendelssohn] whom I questioned about this matter did not hesitate to give his opinion that military service is allowed to his co-religionists today just as it was in old times. He quoted the following supporting passages: "According to Maimonides (*Hilchot Shabbat*, chapter 2, par. 23–25) it is the duty of the Jew to participate in the defense of a city under siege by the enemy on the Sabbath, even if there is only human life in danger, and delay is not permitted. It is also the duty of every Jew to do any kind of work on the Sabbath, without exception, if a human life can be saved by it" (Talmud, Tractate *Eruvin*, pp. 19, 45).

10. ARGUMENTS AGAINST DOHM (1782)

JOHANN DAVID MICHAELIS[1]

Herr Dohm admits candidly that the Jewish brain is more harmful and more corrupted than that of other Europeans, an admission which several defenders of the Jews were hitherto unwilling to make. He seeks the reason for this, however, in the condition in which the Jew lives, reviled, oppressed, and forced to support himself almost exclusively from trade. Herr Dohm has probably no idea to what extent I agree with him in this matter; I wrote exactly the same thing thirty years ago in a piece in the *Goettingische gelehrte Anzeigen*. I would like to express my opinion as it was then and as it still is

Source: Johann David Michaelis, "Herr Ritter Michaelis Beurtheilung." In Christian Wilhelm von Dohm, *Ueber die buergerliche Verbesserung der Juden* (Berlin & Stettin, 1783), vol. 2, pp. 33–51. Originally appeared in *Orientalische und Exegetische Bibliothek*, 19 (1782). Trans. by L. Sachs.

today. Mine goes one step further, however, than does that of Herr Dohm in that it takes account of the deceitfulness of the Jews.

We can see, principally from reports of investigations of thieves, that the Jews are more harmful than at least we Germans are. Almost half of those belonging to gangs of thieves, at least those of whose existence is known to us, are Jews, while the Jews are scarcely 1/25th of the total population of Germany. If this 1/25th part supplies the same number of riff-raff as the whole German people, or even more, then one must conclude that at least in respect to thievery, which I consider to be the lowest of vices, the Jews are twenty-five times as harmful or more than the other inhabitants of Germany.

I also agree with what Herr Dohm says about the praiseworthy aspects of the national character of the Jews and I would add only one comment: The Jews have a great deal of national pride, and not the least reason for this is their conception of themselves as God's Chosen People. It seems to me, however, that this pride has deleterious effects on their nation, preventing them from mingling with other peoples.

It is clear from several of Herr Dohm's remarks that he does not seek, as others do, to obtain special privileges for those who are Jews only in name or in origin and who do not believe in the Jewish religion, those who are known as Deists, or who are perhaps not even that. I agree with this completely. When I see a Jew eating pork, in order no doubt to offend his religion, then I find it impossible to rely on his word, since I cannot understand his heart.

After so much argument with Herr Dohm on basic issues it undoubtedly appears to my readers that I agree with him about granting citizenship to the Jews. But this is not the case and I must now express my reservations.

In mentioning the Law of Moses Herr Dohm considers that religion to be superior to mine. He sees nothing inimical in it, nothing that could incite the hatred of the Jews towards other people. No one could agree with him about this more than I; permit me nevertheless to raise a different question: Does the Law of Moses make citizenship, and the full integration of the Jew into other peoples, difficult or impossible? I think it does! The purpose of this Law is to maintain the Jews as a people almost completely separate from other peoples, and this

purpose is an integral part of all the laws, down to those concerning kosher and non-kosher food, with the result that the Jews have lived as a separate group during 1700 years of dispersion. As long as the Jews continue to observe the Mosaic Laws, as long as they refuse, for example, to eat together with us and to form sincere friendship at the table, they will never become fully integrated in the way that Catholics, Lutherans, Germans, Wends, and French live together in one state. (I am not discussing isolated cases, but rather the Jews as a collective entity.) Such a people could be useful to the state in agricultural work or in various crafts, if the matter be handled wisely. But it will be impossible to consider the Jew as an equal of our citizens, and it is therefore impossible to grant him the same freedoms. For he will never be a full citizen with respect to love for and pride in his country (as Herr Dohm, for example, takes pride in his Prussian citizenship) and he will never be fully reliable in an hour of danger....

One must mention something in addition to the Law of Moses which Herr Dohm seems not to have considered, and which casts doubt on the full and steadfast loyalty of the Jews to the state and the possibility of their full integration, namely their messianic expectation of a return to Palestine. The Jews will always see the state as a temporary home, which they will leave in the hour of their greatest happiness to return to Palestine. For similar reasons their forefathers were suspect in the eyes of the Egyptians (Ex. 1:10). Passages in the sayings of the Prophets, even in those of Moses himself, seem to promise the Israelites a future return to Palestine, and the Jews at least hope for this return on the authority of those passages. And this is true not only for the simple masses, but also for the great commentators on the Bible who have been universally admired for many hundreds of years, men such as Rashi,[2] and others who are more objective such as Ibn Ezra[3] and David Kimchi,[4] whose names I cannot mention but to honor them. It is true that our Lutheran commentators often deny this (not all, not the wise Phillip Jakob Spener[5] for example, whose arguments have almost the force of legal authority among jurists), and so do several others of different religions. But it is doubtful whether they will convince the Jews, particularly when philosophers of the greatest eminence (not necessarily

Newton, who is too apocalyptic, but rather Locke) interpret these passages in exactly the same way. A people which nurses these hopes will lack, at the very least, a patriotic love for the fields [*Ackers*] of their fathers. There is even the danger that if the Jewish people lives separately (for it will be necessary to provide special villages for Jewish agricultural settlers and to avoid placing them among the Christians) it may at some time be inflamed by a febrile vision, or led to destruction by some latter-day Pied Piper of Hamlyn.

And now I must state my principal objection. Herr Dohm's proposal to give the Jews rights of citizenship equal to our own, even to the poor Jew who does not bring money into the state, and to open to them all the professions such as agriculture, crafts, etc., would indeed be a blessing for them. But it would gravely weaken the state, even in the unlikely case that the Jews would bring wealth and money directly into the state, or attract them in the course of time. For the power of a state does not depend on gold alone, but rather, in large part, on the strength of its soldiers. And the Jews will not contribute soldiers to the state as long as they do not change their religious views. There are several reasons for this. First, the Jews will not fight on the Sabbath, for they are forbidden to do so if not attacked....As long as they observe the laws about kosher and non-kosher food it will be almost impossible to integrate them into our ranks. No one would recommend forming special units for them, especially since the oath of the Jews is one of the most complicated matters in the world. Eisenmenger[6] is justified in complaining that it is highly doubtful whether the Jew respects an oath

as we do. One must add to this a further physical argument, albeit a hypothetical one, which Herr Dohm seems not to have considered. It is held that the conduct of modern warfare requires a specific minimum height for the soldiers. Whether this claim is justified I am not qualified to judge. At any event this is accepted practice in the two most militarily powerful German states. If this claim be true, very few Jews of the necessary height will be found who will be eligible for the army.

NOTES

1. Johann David Michaelis (1717–1791), German Bible scholar and professor of Oriental languages at the University of Goettingen.
2. Rashi (acronym of *Rabbi Solomon Yitzhak* [1040–1105], French rabbinical scholar and biblical exegete.
3. Abraham Ibn Ezra (1098–1164), Spanish Jewish scholar and poet.
4. David Kimchi (c. 1160–1235), Spanish Jewish grammarian, philologist and biblical exegete.
5. Phillip Jakob Spener (1635–1705), Protestant theologian. His *Pia desideria oder herzliches Verlangen nach gottgefaelliger Besserung der wahren evangel. Kirche* (1675) is a classic statement of Pietism, which he subsequently defended against the objections of orthodox theologians.
6. Johann Andreas Eisenmenger (1654–1704) author of *Entdecktes Judenthum* [Judaism Unmasked], a work denouncing Judaism, including charges of using Christian blood for ritual purposes and of poisoning of wells. Eisenmenger supported his argument with citations from talmudic literature, which he had studied with rabbis for nineteen years under the pretence of becoming a proselyte.

11. RESPONSE TO DOHM (1782)

MOSES MENDELSSOHN[1]

While reasonable arguments are unanimous in adjudging also to the Jews a participation in the rights of man, it is not thereby understood that even in their present debased condition, they may not be useful to the state, or that their increase might possibly become injurious to it. On this too, Rabbi Menasseh's reasoning in this tract, well deserves attention, since in his days, he would seek for none but a very qualified admission of his brethren to England. Holland alone affords an example which may remove all doubts on that head. There, the increase of the Jews has never yet been complained of; although the means of getting a living are almost as scantily doled out to them, and their privileges are almost as stunted as in many a province of Germany. "Ay," it is said, "but Holland is a commercial country; and therefore cannot have too many trading inhabitants." Agreed. But I should like to know, whether it was commerce which drew people thither; or whether commerce was not rather drawn there by the people? How is it, that so many a city in Brabant and the Netherlands, with equal or perhaps superior commercial accommodations, comes so much behind the city of Amsterdam? What makes people crowd together on a barren soil, ill marshes not intended by Nature to be inhabited; and by industry and art metamorphose lone fens into a garden of God, and invent resources for a comfortable existence, which excites our admiration? What else but liberty, mild government, equitable laws and the hospitable manner in which men of all complexions, garbs, opinions, manners, customs and creeds, are admitted, protected and quietly allowed to follow their business? Nothing else but these advantages have produced, in Holland, the almost superabundant blessings and exuberance of prosperity, for which that country is so much envied.

Generally speaking, "Men superfluous to the state, men, of whom a country can make no use at all," seem to me terms which no statesman should make use of. Men are all more or less useful: they may be employed in this or that way; and more or less promote the happiness of their fellow creatures and their own. But no country can, without serious injury to itself, dispense with the humblest, the seemingly most useless of its inhabitants, and to a wise government, not even a pauper is one too many—not even a cripple altogether useless. Mr. Dohm, in the introduction to his work, has, indeed, tried to determine the quantity which population may not exceed, without overfilling the country and becoming injurious to it. But I think that, with any proviso whatever, no legislator should give this the least consideration; there is no arrangement to oppose the accumulation of souls, no measure to put a stop to increase, that does not tend far more to injure the improvement of the inhabitants, the destination of man and his happiness, than is done by the alleged superfluity. In this, let them depend upon the wise ordering of Nature. Let it quietly take its course, and on no account place impediments in its way, by unreasonable officiousness. Men will flock to places where they can get a living; they multiply and crowd together where their activity has free play. Population increases as long as genius can discover new means of earning. When the sources become exhausted, it instantly stops, of course; and if you make a vessel too full on one side, it will, of itself, discharge the superfluity on the other. Nay, I venture to assert, that such an instance never occurs; and that there never has been a thinning or emigration of the people, which was not the fault of the laws or the management of them. As often as, under any government whatsoever, men become a

Source: Moses Mendelssohn's Preface of 1782 to the German translation of Menasseh ben Israel's *Vindiciae Judaeorum*, in Mendelssohn's *Jerusalem* (a two-volume collection of Mendelssohn's Jewish writings), trans. M. Samuels (London, 1838), vol. 1, pp. 90–99.

nuisance to men, it is owing to nothing but the laws of their administrators.

In some modern publications, there is an echo of the objection—"The Jews are an unproductive people; they neither till the ground, cultivate the arts, nor exercise mechanical trades; and, therefore, do not assist Nature in bringing forth, nor give her produce another form, but only carry and transport the raw or wrought commodities of various countries one to another. They are therefore, mere consumers, who cannot but be a tax upon the producer." Nay, an eminent, and, in other respects, a very acute author, the other day, loudly complained about the hardship of the producer having to maintain so many consumers, to fill so many useless stomachs. Mere common sense, thinks he, shows that the price of the products of nature, and of the arts, must be run up the greater the number of intermediate buyers and sellers, who themselves add nothing to the stock, yet will have them. Accordingly he gives the State this advice and friendly admonition, either not to tolerate Jews at all, or to allow them to exercise agricultural and mechanical trades.

The conclusion may be heartily well meant, but so much weaker are the premises, which appear so plain and irrefutable to the author. According to his ideas, who are precisely called *producers* and *consumers*? If he alone produces who co-operates in the composing of some tangible thing, or improves it by the labour of his hands, the largest and most valuable portion of the state consists of mere consumers. According to these principles, both the learned and military professions produce nothing, unless the books written by the former may be said to form an exception. From the trading and working classes, there are first to be deducted, merchants, porters, carriers by hand and by water, etc., and at the upshot, the class of producers, as they are called, will consist chiefly of ploughboys and journeymen mechanics. For landholders and master-manufacturers, now-a-days, rarely put their hands to the work themselves. Thus, with the exception of that carefully useful, but considerably minor portion of the population, the state would be composed of individuals who neither cultivate the productions of nature, nor improve them by the labour of their hands—that is, of mere consumers; and will it be therefore said also, of useless stomachs which are a burden to the producers?

Here the absurdity is palpable: and as the conclusion is just, the error must lodge somewhere in the antecedents. And so it does. Not only *making something* but *doing something* also, is called *producing*. Not he alone who labours with his hands, but, generally, whoever does, promotes, occasions, or facilitates anything that may tend to the benefit or comfort of his fellow-creatures, deserves to be called a producer; and, at times, he deserves it the more, the less you see him move his hands or feet. Many a merchant, while quietly engaged at his desk in forming commercial speculations, or pondering, while lolling on his sofa, on distant adventures, produces, in the main, more than the most active and noisy mechanic or tradesman. The soldier too produces; for it is he who procures the country peace and security. So does the scholar produce, it is true, rarely anything palpable to the senses, yet matters, at least, equally valuable, such as wholesome advice, information, pastime and pleasure. The expression, "that there is more produced by any Paris pastrycook, than by the whole Academy of Science," could have escaped a man like Rousseau, only in a fit of spleen. The well-being of a country, at large, as well as of every individual in it, requires many things both sensual and intellectual, many goods both material and spiritual; and he who, more or less directly or indirectly, contributes towards them, cannot be called a mere consumer; he does not eat his bread for nothing; he produces something in return.

This, I should think, places the matter in a far clearer light to common sense. And as to immediate buyers or sellers, in particular, I will undertake to maintain, that they are not only far from prejudicial, either to the producer or consumer, provided abuses be prevented, but very beneficial and almost indispensable to both; nay, that through their agency, commodities become more useful, more in demand, and also, cheaper; while the producer gains more, and is thereby enabled to live better and happier without any extraordinary exertion of his strength.

I imagine a workman who is obliged to go himself to the farmer for the raw material, and also to take the manufactured product to the wholesaler himself; who has to mind that he lays in, at a certain season of the year, an adequate stock of the former, and takes the latter, as often as he has occasion, to one who may just have a demand for it, and will become a purchaser. Compare to him, the workman to whom the intermediate dealer brings the raw material into his house, sells it for him for ready money or on credit, according to his present exigency and circumstances. At times he also takes the wrought articles off his hands, and disposes of them to the shopkeeper, at convenient opportunities. What a deal of time and trouble must not the former save, which he may devote to his in-door business, and which the latter is obliged to waste in chance travelling and tarrying about the country, in ever so many avocations, or convivialities, which either he dare not or cannot prevail upon himself to decline. How much more, then, will the former, with the same degree of exertion, work and produce; and thus be able to afford higher prices, and live comfortably notwithstanding? Will not real industry be promoted thereby, and does the intermediate dealer still deserve to be called a useless consumer? This argument in favour of the petty buyer and seller becomes still more forcible when applied to the wholesale dealer, to the merchant proper, who removes and transports the productions of nature and the arts from one country to another, from one hemisphere to another. He is a real benefactor to the state, to the human race at large, and therefore, every thing but a useless stomach living at the producer's charge.

I said, "provided abuses be prevented." These principally consist in the manoeuvres and tricks resorted to by the intermediate dealers in raw materials, to get the grower's fate into their power, and become the rulers of the prices of things, by depressing them in the hands of the first holder, and driving them up in their own. These are great evils, which crush the producer's industry and the consumer's enterprise, and which should be counteracted by laws and by policy regulations. Not indeed summarily, by prohibiting, excluding, or stopping; and least of all, by granted or winked-at monopoly or forestalling. Such measures either aggravate the evils which it is intended to avert by them, or bringing on others still more ruinous. Rather let them seek to abate, as much as possible, all restrictions, abolish all chartered companies, abrogate all preferring and excluding exceptions, grant the humblest dealer and jobber in raw materials, equal rights and privileges, with the first house of commerce; in one word, let them every way promote competition, and excite rivalry, and, amongst the intermediate dealers,

whereby the prices of commodities will be kept in equilibrium, arts and manufacturing encouraged on the one hand, and on the other, every one enabled to enjoy the industry of his fellow-creatures without excessive exertion. The consumer may live comfortably without luxury, and the artist yet maintain himself respectably. It is by competition only, by unlimited liberty, arid equality of the laws of buying and selling, that those ends can be obtained; and, therefore, the commonest salesman or buyer-up, who takes the raw material from the grower to the workman, or the wrought from him to the grower, is of very considerable utility to the prosperity of the arts, industry, and commerce in general. He causes the raw material to maintain its price to the advantage of the grower, while, for the benefit of the workman, and the prosperity of trades, he seeks to spread the products of industry about in all directions, and to render the comforts of life more known, and more generally serviceable. On this consideration, the pettiest trafficking Jew is not a mere consumer, but a useful inhabitant (citizen, I must say) of the state—a real producer.

Let it not be said, that I am a partial advocate of my brethren; that I am magnifying everything which may go in their favour, or tend to their recommendation. Once more I quote Holland. And when the subjects treated of industry and commerce, what country in the world can be more aptly quoted? It is merely through competition and rivalry, through unlimited liberty and equality of the privileges of buyers and sellers, of whatsoever station, quality, or religious persuasion they be, that all commodities have their price there, but with a moderate difference as to buying and selling; while rivals and competitors bring both the parties to a mean, which tends to their mutual advantage. Hence, with a small sacrifice, you can buy or sell any article whatsoever, at all seasons of the year, and at all times of the day, nowhere better, and with greater ease, than at Amsterdam.

NOTE

1. Moses Mendelssohn (1729–1786), the central personality of the German Jewish Enlightenment. To strengthen the impact of Dohm's treatise, Mendelssohn induced Markus Herz (1747–1803) to translate Menasseh ben Israel's *Vindiciae Judaeorum*, the Dutch rabbi's 1656 refutation of objections advanced by British clergy against

Jewish readmission to England (see document 1 in this chapter). Mendelssohn's lengthy preface, intended as a supplement to Dohm's essay, also gave him the opportunity to correct some of Dohm's views. Mendelssohn, as we see from this excerpt, was particularly perturbed by Dohm's endorsement of the popular view of Jewish commercial and moral corruption—a corruption, Dohm contended, that would be eliminated with the Jews' admission to citizenship. Mendelssohn, of course, objected to this type of argument. Indicatively, he also rejected the term *buergerliche Verbesserung* (the civil amelioration or betterment), preferring the term *buergerliche Aufruhme* (civil admission). See chapter 3, introduction, note. 1.

12. REMARKS CONCERNING MICHAELIS'S RESPONSE TO DOHM (1783)

MOSES MENDELSSOHN

Ritter Michaelis does not seem to know any other vice besides fraud and roguery. I think, however, that where the wickedness of a people is to be evaluated one should not entirely overlook murderers, robbers, traitors, arsonists, adulterers, whores, killers of infants, etc.

But even if one where to judge [a people's] wickedness only by the quantity of thieves and receivers of stolen goods among them, this number should not be viewed in terms of that people's proportion of the entire population. The comparison should rather be made between traders and pedlars among the Jews on the one hand, and among other peoples on the other. I am sure that such a comparison would yield very different proportions. The same statistics, I do not hesitate to maintain, will also show that there are twenty-five times as many thieves and receivers of stolen goods among German pedlars as among Jewish. This is aside from the fact that the Jew is forced to take up such a calling, while the others could have become field marshals or ministers. They freely choose their profession, be it a trader, pedlar, seller of mouse traps, performer of shadow plays or vendor of curios.

It is true that quite a number of Jewish pedlars deal in stolen goods; but few of them are outright thieves, and those, mostly, are people without refuge or sanctuary anywhere on earth. As soon as they have made some fortune they acquire a patent of protection from their territorial prince and change their profession. This is public knowledge; when I was younger I personally met a number of men [Jews] who were esteemed in my native country after they had elsewhere made enough dubious money to purchase a patent of protection. This injustice is directly created by that fine policy which denies the poor Jews protection and residence, but receives with open arms those very same Jews as soon as they have "thieved their way to wealth."Although he is inspired by Scripture, Herr Ritter Michaelis seems to

---

Source: Moses Mendelssohn, "Anmerkung zu des Ritters Michaelis Beurtheilung des ersten Theils von Dohm, ueber die buergerliche Verbesserung der Juden" (1783), in *Moses Mendelsohns gesammelte Schriften*, ed. G. B. Mendelssohn (Leipzig, 1843), vol. 3, pp. 365–67. Trans. by J. Hessing.

have a bias against poverty. Among the Jews, however, I have found comparatively more virtue in the quarters of the poor than in the houses of the wealthy.

The hoped-for return to Palestine, which troubles Herr M. so much, has no influence on our conduct as citizens. This is confirmed by experience wherever Jews are tolerated. In part, human nature accounts for it—only the enthusiast would not love the soil on which he thrives. And he who holds contradictory religious opinions reserves them for church and prayer. In part, also, the precaution of our sages accounts for it—the Talmud forbids us *even to think* of a return [to Palestine] by force [i.e., to attempt to effect Redemption through human effort]. Without the miracles and signs mentioned in the Scripture, we must not take the smallest step in the direction of forcing a return and a restoration of our nation. The Song of Songs expresses this prohibition in a somewhat mystical and yet captivating verse (Song of Songs, 2:7 and 3:5):

> I charge you, O daughters of Jerusalem,
> By the gazelles, and by the hinds of the field,
> That you stir not up, nor awake my love,
> Till it please.

...I doubt the validity of Herr Michaelis' view that we are unfit for army service. Does he wish to say that religion should sanction wars of aggression? Let him name the one religion which is cursed enough to do so. Christianity, to be sure, does not. And are not Quakers and Mennonites tolerated and allowed many more privileges and rights than we are?

Herr Michaelis never speaks of Christians and Jews, but always of *Germans* and *Jews*. He does not content himself with establishing the religious differences between us; he prefers to see us as strangers who will have to agree to all conditions which the owners of the land are ready to concede to us. But this, in the first place, is a question to be decided: would it not be better for the owners of the land to accept those they now merely tolerate as citizens rather than bringing strangers at great cost, into their country[?] Secondly, we should also consider the following problem: for how long, for how many millennia, must this distinction between the owners of the land and the stranger continue? Would it not be better for mankind and culture to obliterate this distinction?

I think, moreover, that laws should not be influenced by personal convictions at all. Laws should take their inevitable course, proscribing whatever is not beneficial to the general good. When personal convictions conflict with the laws it is up to the individual to resolve this problem on his own. If then the fatherland is to be defended, everybody who is called upon to do so must comply. In such cases, men usually know how to modify their convictions and to adjust them to their civic duty. One merely has to avoid excessively emphasizing the conflict between the two. In a few centuries the problem will disappear or be forgotten. In this way, Christians have neglected the doctrines of their founders and have become conquerors, oppressors and slave-traders, and in this way, Jews too could be made fit for military service. But it is obvious that they will have to be of the proper height, as Herr Michaelis wisely reminds us, unless they are merely to be used against hostile pygmies and fellow Jews.

13. EDICT OF TOLERANCE (JANUARY 2, 1782)[1]

JOSEPH II[2]

We, Joseph the Second by the Grace of God, elected Roman Emperor, at all times the Enlarger of the Empire, King of Germany, Hungary and Bohemia, etc.. Archduke in Austria, Duke of Burgundy and Lorraine, send our Grace to all and graciously make known the following:

From the ascension to Our reign We have directed Our most preeminent attention to the end that all Our subjects without distinction of nationality and religion, once they have been admitted and tolerated (*aufgenommen und geduldet*) in Our States, shall participate in common in public welfare, the increase of which is Our care, shall enjoy legal freedom and not find any obstacles in any honest ways of gaining their livelihood and increasing general industriousness.

Since, however, the laws and the so-called Jewish Regulations [*Judenordnungen*] pertaining to the Jewish nation [*Nation*] prevailing in Our hereditary countries in general and particularly in Vienna and Lower Austria[3] are not always compatible with these Our most gracious intentions, We hereby will amend them by the virtue of this present edict in so far as the difference in times and conditions necessitates it.

The favors granted to the Jewish nation by this present amendment, whereby the latest Jewish Regulation of May 5, 1764, is fully repealed consist of the following:

As it is our goal to make the Jewish nation useful and serviceable to the State, mainly through better education and enlightenment of its youth as well as by directing them to the sciences, the arts and the crafts, We hereby grant and order....

1. It certainly is not at all our supreme wish herewith to grant the Jews residing in Vienna an expansion [of rights] with respect to external tolerance [*Duldung*]. On the contrary, in the future it will remain that they do not constitute an actual community under a designated leader from their own nation, but as hitherto each family, considered separately, will serenely enjoy the protection of the laws of the land in accordance with the tolerance [*Duldung*] specifically given it by Our government of Lower Austria. Further, as hitherto they will not be allowed public religious worship or public synagogues; they will not be permitted to establish their own press for the printing of prayer books and other Hebrew books, but when necessary they are to turn to available printing presses in Bohemia; should they wish to import Jewish books from foreign lands, which in general is forbidden, they are accordingly obligated in each such instance, to apply for permission and, like all other subjects, to submit imported books to the censor.

2. Likewise, We have no intention by virtue of these new ordinances to increase the number of the members of the Jewish religion in Vienna or in general elsewhere in Our states; nor do we wish to bring foreign [Jews] here without important cause and special merits recommending them. Rather we expressly wish that the number of Jews, and the manner with which they are tolerated, currently in Lower Austria will remain unchanged; and in the places where Jews never resided they will not in the future be granted the right of residence. Only in accordance with specific circumstances and for good cause, We will find it tolerable to make one or two exceptions.

3. In consonance with these limitations to tolerance [*Duldung*], which remains valid, Jews from other lands of Our Inheritance will therefore also not be

Source: Alfred Pribram, *Urkunden und Akten zur Geschichte der Juden in Wien* (Vienna, 1918), vol. 1, pp. 494–500, in Raphael Mahler, ed. and trans., *Jewish Emancipation: A Selection of Documents by R. Mahler*, Pamphlet Series, Jews and the Post-War World, no. 1 (New York: American Jewish Commitee, 1941), pp. 18–20 Reprinted by permission of the American Jewish Committee. Paras. 1–8, 11,13, 14–17, 20–23; trans. by P. Mendes-Flohr.

allowed in the future to come to Vienna in order to stay here permanently, unless they have received a permit from Our government of Lower Austria. And should foreign Jews wish to seek such permission, they would have to apply directly to Us.

4. In order to receive such permission, each and every applicant must indicate without deceit that trade he intends to engage in, or the means of livelihood he wishes to pursue; he must also indicate that he has the assets necessary to support his occupation and to securing the local tolerance [*Toleranz*]. At the same time, he is to indicate to the government of Lower Austria what he believes he can pay for the tolerance to be granted him. The government will then determine the actual sum of the protection money [*Schutzgeld*] or the so-called tolerance, and in such a manner that after due consideration the government could increase or lower the sum should the circumstances of, the tolerated [Jew][4] improve or worsen.

5. In exchange for payment of the protection money, one will be allowed together with his wife and his children who do not have a trade of their own and who do not independently conduct any commerce, but are still dependent on him, to live in Vienna, to enjoy Our protection and to conduct the activities allowed to his nation, or to engage the means of livelihood opened to him.

6. This protection, however, does not apply to the son of the tolerated head of a household, who is married and has begun to maintain his own household, nor to a daughter who is married to a Jew who is not yet *tolerated*, or is married to a foreign Jew. The father is obliged forthwith to announce such marriages, and should the son-in-law choose to stay here, he must pay a special tolerance [fee] or, if he should receive permission to leave, pay an exit fee. A son-in-law who is yet tolerated but who contemplates living here, must seek to attain permission—should he be a foreigner, from Us, and should he be a subject of one of the states of Our Empire, from the government of Lower Austria. In such cases in which permission was granted the daughter to marry a foreigner, the bridegroom must pay an exit fee from the dowry that he will take with him.

7. As in the past, it is forbidden for Jews to live in rural regions of Lower Austria, except if they wish to establish a factory or pursue a useful trade in some village, in one of the market towns, in a provincial city, or perhaps in a desolate area. In such an instance,

they must request permission of the government, but after they receive it their rights and freedoms will be the same as their co-religionists in the capital city [Vienna].

The favors granted to the Jewish nation by this present amendment, whereby the latest Jewish Regulation of May 5, 1764, is fully repealed consist of the following:

As it is Our goal to make the Jewish nation useful and serviceable to the State, mainly through better education and enlightenment of its youth as well as by directing them to the sciences, the arts and the crafts, We hereby grant and order:

8. Graciously, that the tolerated Jews may send their children to the Christian primary and secondary schools so that they have at least the opportunity to learn reading, writing, and arithmetic. And although they do not have in Our capital a real synagogue, We nonetheless allow them to establish for their children and at their own expense a school of their own, organized in the standard fashion with teachers of their own religion. Toward this end, they are to select three suitable young people to be instructed by the administration of local primary schools in the acceptable pedagogical practice. Their future primary school will be under the aforementioned administration like all local German primary schools, and with respect to the specific equipment, particularly as regards books of a moral content, the most fundamental will be legislated as soon as possible. In the meantime, it is Our wish to announce to them that in order to remove any worry regarding matters of religion and opinion, that we are inclined to leave it to them to compose these books, on the one condition that they must submit them to the superintendent of schools for inspection and approval.

9. With regard to schools of higher degrees which were never forbidden to Jewish co-religionists. We hereby merely renew and confirm this permission.

10. In order to facilitate their future means of support and to prepare the necessary ways of gaining a livelihood We hereby most graciously permit them from now to learn all kinds of crafts or trades here as well as elsewhere from Christian masters, certainly also amongst themselves, and to this end to apprentice themselves to Christian masters to work as their journeymen, and the latter [the Christian craftsmen] may accept them without hesitation. This, however, should not be interpreted as if We wish to exercise any

compulsion on Jews and Christians. We merely grant both sides full freedom to come to an understanding about this amongst themselves to their satisfaction.

11. We hereby further grant to the Jewish nation the general license to carry on all kinds of trade, without however the right of citizenship and mastership from which they remain excluded, to be carried on by them freely, only consequently as it is usual here and even then not before having obtained, same as Christians do, the consent of the *Magistrate* in the city, and the government of Lower Austria.

12. These authorities will grant or decline this consent in accordance with the circumstances. The final decision will be in the hands of the bureau of Our royal court in the same manner that matters of the freedoms requested by Christians are. Painting, sculpture and the practice of the other free arts are granted them as to Christians; and We further grant to the Jewish co-religionists the completely free choice of all non-civic branches of commerce and authorize them to apply for the right of wholesale trade under the same conditions and with the same liberties as are obtained by Our Christian subjects....

13. Since the investment in factories and manufacture has always been permitted them, We only use this opportunity to renew this permission in order to encourage them openly to such undertakings that benefit the public.

14. Furthermore, in order to allow them to invest their capital and to secure it, they will be permitted to borrow against real estate, although they do not have the right to assess the latter themselves.

15. Considering the numerous openings in trades and manifold contacts with Christians resulting therefrom, the care for maintaining common confidence requires that the Hebrew and the so-called Jewish language and writing of Hebrew intermixed with German be abolished....We therefore explicitly forbid their use in all public transactions in and out of the courts; in the future the vernacular of the land is to be used instead. In order to obviate all excuses or objections that such a hasty transition would be impossible, We will allow a period of two years, to be calculated from the day of the promulgation of this decree, in which it should be possible to carry out all the necessary changes and arrangements. We, accordingly herewith announce that after this period all legal instruments written in Hebrew or written only in the Hebrew and Jewish letters will be invalid and null and void.

16. In order to facilitate the tolerated Jews in their trades also with regard to the question of servants, it shall be permitted to them from now on to employ as many Jewish as well as Christian servants as their business requires....Nonetheless, they will be required, not as in the past every quarter of a year but once a year, to submit to the government a trustworthy testimony noting together with the children and other family members beholden to their care and fatherly charge also their servants, their names, ages and religion. Every head of a [Jewish] household is required not only to lodge in their homes their Jewish servants but also to ensure that they will not engage in any trade of their own, which is prohibited to Jews who are not tolerated. Moreover, We expect that they [the heads of Jewish households] will not allow foreign Jews residence [in their homes] on the pretext that they are servants and through such a ruse violate Our commandment. Should such violations be discovered, they will be severely punished.

17. It is self-evident that these Jewish servants must be unmarried, and should they have a family, their wives, husbands, or adult children must also be in the service of the same household or in that of another [tolerated] Jew or have the right to engage in a trade, otherwise they will not have the right to reside here [in Vienna] without being tolerated or servants.

18. By the present Decree We hereby permit the existing restrictions with regard to definite Jewish houses to lapse and allow tolerated Jews to lease at their choice their own residences in the city as well as in the suburbs.

19. No less do We hereby completely abolish the head toll hitherto levied on foreign Jews and permit them to enter Our residence [Vienna] from time to time in order to carry on their business.

20. Since we have already announced that We do not wish to increase the number of Jewish families residing here, any foreign Jew who comes here, must immediately upon his arrival register with the government of Lower Austria, and indicate the business [that has brought him to Vienna] and the time required in order to complete it, to wait for the approval, or in any case an answer from the appropriate office. When this period of time is over, they must either leave [Vienna] or request from the government an extension. All those who hide or stay here without the required license or stay beyond the time allotted them, will be sought out, arrested and evicted from

here. We, therefore, impose upon Our government in Lower Austria the explicit task constantly to keep a watchful eye through the police that these foreign Jews will depart [at the appointed time]. To facilitate this surveillance, We also order those Christians and [tolerated] Jews at whose homes alien Jews may be lodging to report this to the authorities, which they are in any case required to do, immediately.

21. With respect to such arrivals [*Ankömmlinge*] it is self-evident that they cannot be treated equally with the local tolerated Jews in transactions and in the management of food shops. Accordingly, they do not have the license to deal in such goods for which only authorized merchants and tolerated Jews have been granted permission. Similarly, the general prohibition, applying to them as well as all others, against peddling (that is, the selling of goods from house to house in the city and also in the country) still remains and with the [threat of] confiscation of these goods.

22. On the other hand, foreign Jews are permitted during the period of fairs to deal in all goods that one is generally allowed to import; at other times, however, they are only permitted to deal in those goods that foreign merchants are permitted to sell. Similarly, like all others, they are permitted to buy goods in order to export them abroad; likewise, they are permitted to take orders from factories and licensed merchants and craftsmen for raw and uncorked materials, and equipment that they have imported here. They are, however, warned to take care not to buy or even help conceal stolen goods and moveable property, a [crime] for which they will be punished with all severity in accordance with the law.

23. In addition, the special double court and notary taxes incumbent upon Jews that hitherto existed are herewith cancelled and [We remove].

24. In general all hitherto customary distinctive marks and distinctions, such as the wearing of beards, the prohibition of leaving their homes before twelve o'clock on Sundays and holidays, the frequenting of public places and the like; on the contrary, it shall be permitted to wholesale merchants and their sons as well as to people of such rank to carry swords.

25. Since by these favors We almost place the Jewish nation on an equal level with adherents of other religious associations in respect to trade and employment of civil and domestic facilities, We hereby earnestly advise them to observe scrupulously all political, civil and judicial laws of the country to which they are bound as all other inhabitants, just as they remain subject with respect to all political and legal matters to the provincial and municipal authorities within their jurisdiction and pertinent activities.

Done in our City of Royal Residence Vienna, the second day of January, 1782, in the eighteenth year of Our reign in the Holy Roman Empire and in the second year of reign in Our hereditary lands.

NOTES

1. Promulgated on January 2, 1782, by Joseph II, this edict—pertaining initially only to Lower Austria—reflects his policy of enlightened absolutism. This was the first of a series of imperial edicts that were designed to end the social and economic isolation of the Jews and render them "useful" to the state. A year after he promulgated the Edict of Tolerance, Joseph II issued yet another decree pertaining to the Jews. This 3,500-page document, entitled Systematic Regulation of the Jewish Nation, granted the Jews further rights, such as the right to rent land and engage in almost all forms of commerce and crafts. The regulation also contained certain restrictions. The prohibition of the use of Yiddish or Hebrew in public and commercial documents was extended to all Jewish cultural activities. The regulation stipulated that "in the interest of expediting the extirpation of Jewish languages" and at the same time facilitating the use of the languages of the realm, the printing or import of books in Hebrew or Yiddish, except for purely liturgical reasons, was forbidden.

2. Joseph II (1741–1790), was the son of Maria Theresa and Holy Roman Emperor Francis I, whom he succeeded. From the death of his father in 1765 to that of his mother in 1780, he ruled the Habsburg lands jointly with her, but had little power. Upon the assumption of full power, he immediately instituted far-reaching reforms toward the creation of a centralized, rationally organized bureaucratic state; essential correlates to this policy were religious tolerance, unrestricted trade, and universal, secular education, and the reduction of the power of the Church.

3. Lower Austria, which included the city of Vienna, was one of the provinces (*Lande*) of the Habsburg monarchy.

4. The edict confirmed the category of "tolerated Jew" and indeed maintained the restrictions regarding their number. The "tolerated Jews," however, were now granted new cultural and economic opportunities.

14. EDICT OF TOLERANCE FOR THE JEWS OF GALICIA (MAY 7, 1789)[1]

JOSEPH II

We, Joseph the Second, Roman Emperor by the grace of God etc having instituted provisional measures to do with the Jews, find it appropriate to the accepted principles of tolerance (*Duldung*)[2] and also in contributing to the general good, to abolish the differences that have until now been enforced by law between Christian subjects (*Untertanen*) and the Jews, and confer on the Jews living in Galicia all benefits and rights that the rest of our subjects enjoy.

And so in general terms from now on the Jews of Galicia will have the same rights and duties as other subjects. Detailed instructions bearing on religious practice, educational instruction, the legal constitution of the community, population registry, means of earning a living (*Nahrungswege*), juridical and civic authorities, and obligations to the state, will be implemented in the following manner:

RELIGION

1. The whole of Jewry will be totally free and without hindrance in observance of the religion of the forefathers and traditional customs, in as much as they do not oppose existing laws and the general principles of the state.

2. Instead of local rabbis serving in different communities from now on only one rabbi will be appointed in every district, either in district capital, or when the district capital does not have a Jewish community then in a community with the largest number of Jews. The remaining communities of the district will only be allowed to have so-called religious teachers and cantors (*Schulsinger*).[3]...

4. The following duties will be imposed on the district rabbi in his community as well as on the religious teachers and cantors: (1) to administer a list of births, marriages and deaths, and (2) to supervise the community's ritual slaughterers.

5. ... Six years after the district rabbi has first been chosen in accordance with the instructions of this patent, knowledge at the level of [a graduate of] a German primary school will be absolutely required in order to hold the post of a rabbi....

EDUCATIONAL INSTRUCTION

11. In order to render the Jews through the cultivation of their rational understanding (*Verstand*) and ethical conduct, able to comply with the salutary intentions of the state, a German school will be established for Jewish children in every community on the model of the German primary schools. In addition, the teachers of these schools will take oaths of allegiance [to the state] as translators for the community.

12. And since according to the law as it now stands, written and spoken knowledge of the German language, for a number of reasons, is compulsory for Jews, no youth will be allowed Talmud study, wherever there is a German school, unless he can prove with a certificate from a German teacher that he attends the German school on a regular basis and has taken advantage of the instruction he receives there....

13. No Jew will be married unless he can prove with a certificate according to clause 12 above that he has studied the German language in a public school or at home....

Source: *Edicta et mandata in Regnis Galicae et Lonomeriae* (Lemberg 1789), pp. 90–100. Reprinted in Joseph Karniel, "Das Toleranzpatent Kaiser Josephs II. für die Juden Galizens und Lodomeriens," *Jahrbuch des Instituts fuer deutsche Geschichte* (Tel Aviv 1982), pp. 75–89. Translated by Mark Jacobs.

LEGAL CONSTITUTION OF THE COMMUNITY

15. Galician Jewry is presently divided into 141, or with Bukovina, 143 communities; this division will remain as it is in the future.

16. The reason for the Jews' being organized into communities is for no other reason than to serve their special interests as Jews. They must then be seen only as guilds, and with anything that doesn't relate to the purposes of the organization as defined above, there isn't any difference between the guild members and other citizens. It follows that every Jewish resident as a citizen belongs to the same local authority as the rest of the local residents, whether Jews or Christians, and he can be chosen as head of his local authority. To qualify for participation in such an election, he must be registered as a Jew in one of the 143 communities, and belong to it, according to the above mentioned division....

19. The obligations of the leaders of the community are: to represent their communities whenever necessary. To speak there, to protect their rights, to be concerned for the economic state of poor Jews, to collect taxes, that are set to cover the activities of the community, and if there is an unexpected and unplanned for large expenditure, to turn to the local government, and generally to be concerned with and manage all matters connected with the good of the community. In all these matters and in all matters of the community and its accounts, only the German language may be used....

22. Every head of family must participate in covering the expenses and meeting the needs of the community according to his professional rank. There are three professional ranks:

To the first rank belong those who work their land or rented land, who earn a living from manual labour, or supplying services for a wage, for example artisans, print shop supervisors, scrap dealers, carters, innkeepers.

In the second rank are those serving society or the community, such as doctors, medical assistants, rabbis, cantors, and artists.

And finally, the third rank belongs to all those who earn a living from industry and trade, such as leaseholders, factory owners, merchants, money changers and capitalists.

POPULATION REGISTRY

23. In order to get the required information to the state about the Jewish population, and about the changes applying to it, a census of the population will be taken of the Jews, by the army, in the same way that it is taken of Christian citizens, and this procedure will be implemented regarding them from now on.

24. The restriction on Jewish families to a fixed number in a certain place of domicile will be completely abolished. The Jews are consequently free to enter a marriage contract without payment of marriage license fees in exactly the same circumstances where the law allows Christian citizens, and to the extent that this edict doesn't include any restriction relating to the Jews. Regarding the wedding contract they must act according to general civic law and according to the regulations enacted for Galicia.

25. After the end of the year 1790 living in villages will not be authorized except to those Jews earning a living from working the land or from trade. A heavy fine will be imposed on Jews found after this date in the villages earning a living from business other than these two, and on the village heads, who welcomed them or allowed their presence....

29. To maintain order in the registers of inhabitants and civic transactions, the instruction has already been issued that every head of family shall bear a fixed name....

MEANS OF EARNING A LIVING

31. Permission is given to the Jews to work at any occupation and administrative business allowed by law. From now on all restrictions that existed until now and were imposed only on the Jews will be completely abolished.

32. The Jews will be forbidden to lease more than what encourages that diligence that the state means to instill in the Jews, beyond that which only increases idleness, and until activity and diligence in other occupations has become widespread among them. Therefore an absolute restriction on renting inns to Jews either in villages or towns will remain.

33. An inherited business is maintained only in the case of those inns established by Jews in their own houses and at their own expense.

Where the validity of the regulation allowing those Jews who earn a living as described above is renewed from November 5, 1784, they can continue.

34. For the same reasons, from which stem the necessity, from the point of view of the good of the citizens of Galicia, to keep Jews from buying inns, they are also prevented from leasing;

(1) separate building plots belonging to those paying mortgage taxes.
(2) Flour mills.
(3) Market stall franchises, places of sale, pasture and footpaths. Renting of whole estates in perpetuity or temporarily is not prohibited.

35. In addition to manual labor, inherited occupations and leases are allowed to Galician Jews in all trades and all manner of goods, as long as they keep the general laws of commerce and manage their register book according to the directives and in the language of the state. This permit applies to foreign Jews as well as to the Jewish residents of Brody, wherever a trade is permitted to foreign Christian traders in Galicia....

36. Even begging or what is known as peddling is permitted to Jews in towns, markets and villages, according to the general orders already in force in regard to these activities.

37. In order to move the Jews into agriculture and give poor Jewish families an opportunity to find their livelihood from the land each Jewish community will settle a specific number of families and contribute money according to professional status.

The district authorities will inform the communities of the number of families to be settled and how their settlement is to be carried out....

JUDICIAL AND CIVIC AUTHORITIES

41. In civic matters the Jews fall under the ordinary authority of the national government according to the existing provisions. Therefore a Jew must, just like the rest of the citizens of the land, make a complaint or a request in a civic matter first to local government, then to the district authorities, and finally at national level, and always in German.

42. Only local government shall be involved in resolving conflicts in the community and the district offices are not to be bothered with such matters....

44. Just as civic matters to do with Galician Jewry are under the authority of national government, so in judicial matters it will depend on the ordinary courts now in existence. Therefore the rabbis, most of whose judicial authority has already been annulled, are forbidden to declare what is called major or minor excommunication, to impose a fine or the stocks or other act of atonement or to take a judicial action; and if they do so, a fine of 50 ducats will be imposed on them....

46. Every legal conflict the Jews have with Christians and amongst themselves about some matter will be judged and decided by the first court, that is to say by the local authorities (the magistrate) or by whom the matter belongs with, in accordance with the general laws of the land and according to due legal process. Additional petitions will be directed to the local appeals court.

47. Because according to all this the Jews are thought of by the state, according to the existing general laws, as equals to the rest of the citizens, from the beginning of the year 1791, external signs of difference in clothing, both those that were followed at one time by order and those that were followed out of custom, will be completely abolished, and only rabbis will be permitted the clothing that was accepted until now.

DUTIES TOWARD THE STATE

48. That good equally enjoyed, that the Jews derive with the Christian citizens under the auspices of the state, is imposed on them along with duties towards it. These duties are divided between the provision of public services and taxes.

They therefore must provide for dispatches and repairs to roads—that can bear pack-animals and military transports—just the same as Christian inhabitants. In places where road paving is imposed on Jewish home owners, they must see to providing manual labor on set days, either themselves or with tenants of Jewish houses or with Jewish workers.

Where they are serfs of local lords they must behave according to the new urbarium order.

49. Likewise Jewish citizens are fit for military service just the same as Christian citizens, and therefore all instructions relating to conscription apply to them.

But so that they don't get dispersed among different military units, they will all go exclusively to the transport corps, where they will be able to eat together according to the concepts and customs of their religion.

It will further be taken into account that no work will be imposed on them on the Sabbath except for necessary works and which the Christians are also required to do on Sundays and festivals.

50. The taxes on Jews are protection tax and the tax on consumption of kosher meat.

51. Every Jewish head of family must pay the four "Kaiser-Gulden" every year as a protection tax. Exempt from this tax are those heads of family who currently earn their livelihood from working the land and those who plan on working it in the future....

We hope that Galician Jewry will appreciate, as is appropriate, the attention we devote to all matters relating to their status, and our concerns for their true and enduring welfare, and that they will make efforts to be worthy of the protection of the authorities, that the present law promises them, by the precise fulfillment of the duties that this law imposes on them.

Done in the City of [Royal] Residence Vienna on the 7th of May in the year Seventeen Hundred and Eighty Nine, in the twenty fifth year of Our reign in the Holy Roman Empire and in the ninth year of reign in Our hereditary lands.

NOTES

1. The Edict or Patent of Tolerance for Galicia—a crown land of the Habsburg Empire, which now is part of southeastern Poland and northwestern Ukraine—culminated the series of regulations that Joseph II promulgated appertaining to the Jews of his realm. It was also the most comprehensive of the edicts and as such served, as Michael Silber has noted, as a model—"in truncated fashion—that is, divested of all its truly liberal clauses" for the Jewish legislation that followed in Central and Eastern Europe. (Cf. M. Silber, "Josephinian Reforms," *Yivo Encyclopedia of Jews in Eastern Europe*, ed. G.D. Hundert, New Haven, 2008, vol. 1: 833.) The Edict addressed two overarching questions: "Were Jews to continue their existence within the state as a separate corporate entity with special privileges and liabilities, or were they to be set on equal footing with other citizens and all that implied as rights and duties were concerned?" (ibid.) The implicit premise of this twofold question was articulated by Count Stanislas Clermont-Tonnere in his speech of December 23, 1789, before the French National Assembly, when with allusion to the Galician Edict of Tolerance, he declared "Everything must be refused to the Jews as a nation; everything must be granted to them as individuals.... There cannot be a nation within a nation." (cf. chapter 3, document 2.)

2. The employment of *Duldung*, which is best translated as "sufferance," as a synonym for *Toleranz*, by Emperor Joseph attests to the fact that his attitude toward the Jews was prompted more by pragmatic considerations than an enlightened ethical affirmation of their humanity and inherent dignity.

3. The cantors (in Hebrew: *shaliach Tzibbur*), who led the community in prayer, were to perform the additional tasks of religious instruction, attending to the rite of circumcision, and the ritual slaughter of animals.

15. PETITION TO THE HUNGARIAN DIET (JUNE 1790)[1]

THE COMMUNITY OF JEWS LIVING IN HUNGARY

Now that the Estates of the Realm, with the mutual will of the Emperor and King Leopold II,[2] after a cessation of twenty-five years, again hold a national assembly, and the desire, endeavor, and activity of all of them is directed to making the much troubled Hungary strong, based on a safe system, happy, and fortunate, and to let all inhabitants equally, without distinction of station and class, have a share in the public welfare, let it be permitted also to us, the seed of Abraham, who because of the various misfortunes

Source: Translated from the Latin by Raphael Patai, *The Jews of Hungary. History, Culture, Psychology* (Detroit: Wayne State University, 1996), pp. 219–23.

of adversity have been suffering for many years, to come before you and to hope for a minute share in the happiness that the whole fatherland now expects from you and from our new king. To our greatest pain, we have been despised until now, but not because of our own fault; here and there they treated us not as is customary to treat humans and the inhabitants of the same country but like slaves, not to say draft oxen. We have been driven from city to city, from village to village, often exposed to the ridicule, derision, and the insult of the mob; even on the highways and the crossroads, though it is necessary that every traveler should have secure and safe journey on them, the mischievous youths not infrequently threw stones at us, unpunished.

But now, the happy sun of Europe has arisen, so to speak, so that there is no longer anyone so savage and uneducated as not to know those duties that man naturally owes to man. Now already, everywhere the more sober philosophy has raised its head, to so speak, that philosophy which, with clear and understandable words, teaches everybody that no single inhabitant of the state, whatever his religion, status, and manner, can be insulted unpunished, and that among all the inhabitants of the state there is not a single one who should not be able to obtain the proper right of sustaining life and body, of acquiring fame and fortune. Christian faith itself, whose followers in former centuries had not shrunk from persecuting with fire and iron those who did not belong to the Roman Church, now lets the mild spirit of Christian charity trickle into everybody, and either privately or openly proclaims that all men are brothers, and therefore it is forbidden to leave unpunished lawlessness, the persecution of anybody, the deprivation of anybody of his fortune, and what is more valuable than anything else, of his faith. In this enlightened century, should we not be allowed to give room to the certain and undoubted hope that, through the generosity of our most excellent King and the noble Hungarian Estates of the Realm, we should gain that for which in those dark centuries we barely dared to hope?

Ever since the beginning the Jewish people have lived in the Hungarian kingdom. This is amply attested by the old annals of events, as well as the Hungarian laws, whether they were enacted in favor of the Jews or for their restriction, according to the views of the people in a certain century. And if at times it happened as old memories tell us that it did under Lajos I,[3] that religious hatred forced our people to emigrate from the country, shortly thereafter, with a change of

The Habsburg Empire in the late eighteenth century

circumstances, they not only obtained the freedom to return but were showered with greater favors than previously. And truly, if the Jew does differ in custom and religion from the multitude of the people it is certain, experience confirms it, that throughout those many centuries he did not fall behind the citizens in faithfulness and reliability toward the kings and the fatherland. Moreover, if one examines the Hungarian annals, the undoubted documents of past events, there is scarcely an age in which our ancestors had not courteously helped the Hungarian state, which suffered the greatest need, with great amounts of cereals, often purchased with money, or had not straightened out and restored, with tremendous effort, advice, and useful collaboration, the royal treasury itself, which in various cases was completely exhausted by cruel fate. Who does not know what a sorry state the treasury was in under Endre II,[4] Béla IV,[5] Sigismund,[6] Ulázló II,[7] Lajos II[8]? In the extreme peril of the shaky state, what else did those kings of superior wisdom consider the best remedy but to vest in the Jews various positions of the chamber, and to entrust the treasury of the king and the country to their fidelity and fervor. We do not deny that our ancestors often suffered persecution, visited upon their heads by envy or by the fanaticism of the defense of religion, and at times—we are convinced of this also by too intense greed, of which many of our ancestors were not free. But meanwhile most Hungarian kings who saw at close quarters the outstanding services the Jews rendered to the state, which often struggled against the greatest disturbances—and how indeed, could they have observed with an indifferent soul how great a profit was derived from their intelligence, fervor, astonishing adroitness, for the entire country and the royal house?—not infrequently adorned the Jews with grace, favor, and privileges and accorded them permanent protection. The memory still exists of those privileges, which Béla IV and Sigismund, those two fervent champions of Christian faith, granted to the Jews, and which Albert,[9] László V,[10] and Matthias Corvinus[11] did not hesitate to reconfirm with solemn documents. Well known to us also are the various decrees of the later kings, and mainly those who descended from the Austrian house, which were given at various times, repeated, and more than once broadened by various additions.

But our endeavor on this occasion is not to demand the resuscitation of the old privileges of our people, which are buried in our archives and are no longer suited to the changed conditions of today. We request of the King and the states only that which one is entitled by holy nature and the law of the nations to demand. Since the grace of the King and the favor of the Estates of the Realm have permitted us to live in Hungary, as a result of which we can count on being considered, and must be considered, the oldest inhabitants of Hungary and, in addition, an incorporated nation; since the experience of years, even centuries, teaches that we do not take abroad the fortune accumulated in the country as well as in the external provinces but consume it in the country or keep it in constant circulation; since we and our families belong in the ranks of the taxpayers and, beyond that, must pay, in addition to the public burdens, also a royal census, that is, a toleration tax; since we are obliged to carry a *subsidum* for all the needs of the kingdom, the supply of food, and all kinds of burdens; since we comport ourselves always and everywhere with due obedience to then authorities and superiors, and pay promptly and without complaints or resistance the taxes to the landlords, which often are heavy and exceed our ability; since we live peacefully and quietly in the midst of the Hungarian nation, offend nobody, tolerate nobody, tolerate everything peacefully, do not decline any burden—therefore, why should we not be able to demand of the most gracious King and the Estates of the Realm at least the right to live in the confidence that we, too, should be given the same kinds of subsistence as the other inhabitants of Hungary, and that every obstacle that either restricts our livelihood or impedes the customary practice of our faith according to the Laws of Moses should cease? Animated by this hope, we present a few of our requests to the King and the Estates, with proper humility, begging that they should graciously include our just requests with approval among the provisions of the country in legal form.

1. The Jews should be allowed to practice their religion freely, and nobody should be forced to convert to Christianity.
2. They should be allowed to settle everywhere and purchase or rent houses and lots.
3. They should be allowed to transact business undisturbed at the national and weekly markets.
4. They should be free to practice handicrafts and to purchase or rent land.

5. The source of income of the free royal cities, [through an onerous taxation] of Jewish restaurants, should cease.

6. They should be able to attend lower and higher educational institutions without being hindered in the practice of their religion.

7. In lawsuits between Jews and Christians, not the city or the village judge should be competent to pass judgment but only the manorial or county court.

8. In lawsuits among Jews, the rabbis, the experts in Jewish law, should decide.

9. The rabbis should be given the power to prevent acts contrary to Jewish religion.

These are our humble desires, these are the questions which we have the temerity to bring before the Diet. We do not belong among those who request exception from the law, privileges, extraordinary favors. We only wish that those rights that are the dues of every man in general, that can in no cultured state be denied to any citizen, should be given to us as well, wholly, soundly. In conclusion we also request that we should be treated humanely, that we should be considered brothers, the descendants of Adam, of one and the same tribe, believers in the same Supreme Being who is adored by the Christians as well; at long last let it be permitted to us, too, to be citizens, useful citizens of the fatherland. In the whole world we have outside Hungary no fatherland, no other father than the King, to whose rule the Lord of the Universe entrusted Hungary and its people; we have no other protectors than the public authorities and our landowners, no other brothers than those with whom we live and in one society; we have no other protection than the laws of the fatherland, no other refuge than the duties of humanity that man owes to man without exception.

After all, we are but those kinds of vine tendrils which, because of their very nature, creep along the ground, and cannot rise up unless a neighboring tree gives them support, or the beneficent hand of man places a stick next to them on which they can raise themselves. To whom should we appeal in our need if not to the common father of all of us, the King, and to those who are entrusted with governing the state? From where should we not find support if not in you, to whom the will of the ruler and the mindful disposition of your ancestors have entrusted

the power of legislation and of making the peoples happy? Do strive, therefore, Your Majesty the King, your illustrious magnates and emissaries of the provinces, to clear away the fog of prejudices with which many of the people do not shrink to persecute the Jews, so that the obstacles suppressing the efforts of the Jews should disappear, so that security be given to our persons, freedom of commerce, and the ability of decently earning a living to everybody. Do strive that we should be treated no worse than other inhabitants of the country, that people should not be able to insult, beat, oppress us unpunished, that access to the free royal cities, the country towns, the villages not be restricted for us, that we should not be exposed to derision on the highways and public places. Do strive to place us in a position where we do not have to neglect ourselves, our wives, our children, that we should not collapse under the weight of public and private burdens, or that the state should not be able to say with justification that we are not as useful for it as we should be and as we ourselves desire to be.

And as for us, we shall always consider it our task to direct our endeavors, our strength and our work to making everybody recognize that we are worthy of the grace that we expect today from you, and the hope of attaining it that fills us. Our task will be to request in our unceasing prayer of the Supreme Judge of all beings, Jehova, who unites peoples and disperses them, and whose will makes all kingdoms of the world stand and fall, that he keep our most gracious King to the longest age, in health, glory, and good fortune, together with his imperial house, and grant the Hungarian kingdom peace, tranquility, concord, splendor, and all happiness. Our task will be finally everywhere and always to prove with deeds that we have no other desire than to live and die in eternal devotion.

NOTES

1. Joseph II, who in 1780 was also named king of Bohemia and Hungary, was bent on extending his reforms to all realms of his empire, the integration of the Jews into the public educational system being one of his paramount objectives. In 1786, following a decree already introduced in Austria, he issued a law that required all Hungarian Jews, male and female, who wished to marry to provide proof that they had successfully completed public primary school. To induce compliance, the law stipulated that Jewish pupils would not

be discriminated against in any form whatsoever, and, moreover, would be exempt from attending school on the Sabbath and Jewish holidays. Furthermore, all passages in the textbooks deemed offensive to Jews would be deleted. Needless to say, the Hungarian Jewish community was ambivalent about these regulations and, in general, about the reforms, which had failed to remove many of the obstacles to civic equality. In June 1790, a few months after the death of Joseph II, the community presented a petition to the Hungarian Diet or parliament, which had not convened during the twenty years of the deceased emperor's reign. The Latin petition "is a remarkable document, not so much because for the reforms [it requests] as for its description of the conditions of Jewish life in Hungary in the latter part of the eighteenth century and, even more, for the feelings of the Jewish community it reveals" regarding their sorry situation in Hungary (Raphael Patai, *The Jews of Hungary*, p. 218).

2. Leopold II (1747–1792), Holy Roman Emperor (1790–92), king of Bohemia and Hungary (1790–92).

As the third son of Maria Theresa, he succeeded his brother Joseph II as ruler of the Hapsburg lands and Hungary. He repealed most of Joseph's reforms.

3. King of Hungary (1326–1382), he reigned from 1342.
4. King of Hungary (1175–1235), he ascended the throne in 1205. In 1222 he issued the Golden Bull, which has been called the Hungarian Magna Carta.
5. King of Hungary (1206–1270), he ascended the throne at age seven as the junior king (*rex iunior*).
6. King of Hungary (1387–1437).
7. Also known as Vladislaus II (1456–1516), king of Hungary from 1490 until his death.
8. Also known as Louis Jagiellon (1506–1526), he was king of Hungary, Croatia, and Bohemia from 1516 to 1526, when he was killed in battle.
9. Albert II (1397–1439) was king of Hungary from 1437 until his death.
10. Also known as Ladislas V (1440–1457), he was "boy" king of Hungary from 1453 until his early death.
11. Matthias the Just (1443–1490) was king of Hungary from 1458 until his death.

16. *DE JUDAEIS*: LAW GOVERNING THE STATUS OF THE JEWS OF HUNGARY (1791)[1]

LEOPOLD II[2]

So that the situation of the Jews should be taken care of even before their affairs and several of their privileges of the royal free cities pertaining to them will be discussed by a national commission that will report to the next Diet, and the joint will of His Majesty and of the Realm will decide on the position of the Jews, the Estates of the Realm have decided with the approval of His Majesty that the Jews who are living within the borders of Hungary and the attached Parts should be maintained in all

the free royal cities and the other places (not including the royal mining towns) in the same condition in which they were on January 1, 1790, and if by any chance they were expelled, they should be reinstated in them.

NOTES

1. The Petition of the Jewish Community of Hungary was presented to the Diet on its behalf by Baron Ferenc Splényi, Bishop of Vàc. It was enacted December 2,

Source: Raphael Patai, The Jews of Hungary. History, Culture, Psychology (Detroit: Wayne State University Press, 1996), p. 230.

1790. The law, known as *De Judaeis*, passed by the Diet and duly confirmed by the emperor on January 10, 1791, hardly addressed the grievances and proposals of the Jewish community. The substantial issues were deferred to a "national commission," which eventually presented its findings to the Diet, and noted: "Jewry does have its faults, because until now it was despised; bad manners are general, but this does not prove anything against them, since formerly even the belief that the sun revolved around the earth was general; one cannot support that the true God, whom they worship, would have commanded them to commit crimes." The commission's report proceeded to recommend that *all* the proposals of the Jewish community to improve their lot be adopted by the Diet. The recommendation was not accepted, and *De Judaeis* set the legal position of Hungarian Jewry until the liberal reforms of 1840.

2. Emperor Leopold II (1747–1792), Joseph's brother, served as emperor of the Holy Roman Empire and king of Hungary from 1790 until his death two years later.

17. AN ESSAY ON THE PHYSICAL, MORAL AND POLITICAL REFORMATION OF THE JEWS (1789)

ABBÉ GRÉGOIRE[1]

But the Jews, I shall be told, are incapable of being reformed, because they are absolutely worthless. I reply, that we see few of them commit murder, or other enormous crimes, that call forth public vengeance; but their abominable meanness produces base actions. Mr. Michaelis[2] assures us, that in Germany, of twenty-five criminals imprisoned or condemned, twenty-four are always Jews. This is the assertion of Mr. Michaelis—but, in the first place, an assertion is no proof. The truth of this, however, might have been easily ascertained, by examining and producing the criminals. Secondly, supposing the circumstances to be as true as it is doubtful, this would prove nothing but against the German Jews; and lastly, it would still be necessary to establish as a certainty that this perversity proceeds immediately from their religion, or their natural disposition. That it is not inspired by the Torah, is evident; shall we believe, then, that it is innate? Some peevish philosophers, indeed, have pretended, that man is born wicked; but happily for the honor and comfort of humanity, this system has been banished to the class of absurd and mortifying hypotheses. So many laws made against the Jews, always suppose in them a natural and indelible worthlessness; but these laws, which are the fruit of hatred or prejudice, have no other foundation but the motive which gives rise to them. This perversity is not so inherent in their character as to affect every individual. We see talents and virtues shine forth in them wherever they begin to be treated as men, especially in the territories of the Pope, which have so long been their terrestrial paradise; in Holland, Prussia, and even among us. Hertz[3] and Bloch[4] render the Jewish nation illustrious at present in Germany; and the Hague is honored by a Pinto.[5] We must, therefore, believe these people susceptible of morality, until we are shown, that they have invincible obstacles in their physical organization, and in their religious and moral constitution.

Let us cherish morality, but let us not be so unreasonable as to require it of those whom we have

---

Source: Abbé Grégoire, *Essai sur la régénération physique, morale et politique des juifs* (Metz, 1789), in Abbé Grégoire, *An Essay on the Physical, Moral and Political Reformation of the Jews,* translator not indicated (London, 1791), pp. 134–44.

compelled to become vicious. Let us reform their education to reform their hearts; it has long been observed, that they are men as well as we, and they are so before they are Jews.

Mr. Michaelis objects also, that this nation being in constant opposition to general manners, will never become patriotic. We allow that it will be difficult to incorporate them into universal society; but between difficulty and impossibility, there is the same difference as between impossibility and possibility. I have myself remarked, and even proved, that hitherto the Jews have been invariable in their manners and customs; but the greater part of their customs are not contrary to civil functions; and with regard to those which may appear to be incompatible with the duties of the citizen, they are preserved only by the uniformity of that conduct, which all nations observe towards them. If we do not maintain, with Helvetius,[6] that the character and disposition of man depend altogether on his education, we at least allow, that in a great measure they are the result of circumstances. Can the Jews ever become patriots? This is a question proposed by those who reproach them with not loving a country that drove them from its bosom; and with not cherishing people who exercised their fury against them—that is to say, who were their executioners.

Flatterers, in every country, extol the attachment of the people to their sovereigns, and to their country; thus gratifying the vanity of the master at the expense of truth. Study the characters of men, in different countries, and you will find, that pleasure and interest are the grand springs by which they are actuated; provided the people sleep securely in their habitations, and enjoy there in peace, the fruits of their fields, which they cultivate at their ease, and provided they are not subjected to the scourge of the law, nor oppressed by the iron hand of despotism, they are satisfied; but under any other circumstances, they show something more than indifference with regard to their government, as well as to their sovereign: they even offer up secret vows for a revolution, because they imagine that a new order of things will procure them happiness; and they know nothing of patriotism but the name, except, perhaps, in places where they have a share, though at a distance, in the legislative or executive authority. We may, therefore, lay it down as a fact, that the character of the French, for two years past, has acquired more energy

and displayed more patriotism than in the two last centuries.

The Jews, everywhere dispersed, yet no where established, have only had the spirit of a body which is entirely different from the spirit of a nation; for this reason, as has been observed, it is neither that of the English at London, nor that of the Dutch at the Hague, nor that of the French at Metz; they form always a state within a state,[7] because they are never treated as children of the country. In republics even, where the people taking an active part in the legislation, are subject only to themselves, the Jews are always passive, and counted as nothing; they possess no landed property; though commerce, which generally renders men citizens of the world, procures them portable riches, that afford them a small consolation for the opprobrium thrown upon them, and the load of oppressive laws under which they groan. You require that they should love their country—first give them one.

But, says Mr. Michaelis, they will always look towards Palestine, as the seat of their repose; and will never consider other countries but as places of passage, without ever attaching themselves to them. Whom must we believe, him or Boulanger?[8] The latter assures us, that the fanaticism of the Jews begins to cool; and that, in the process of time, it may be totally extinguished. They hope to return to Palestine, but they hope at the same time to conquer the whole world, which will secure to them the possession of other countries. Besides, this return is fixed at an uncertain epoch; the Talmud forbids them to think of it; and to take any step on consequence of their expectations, until prodigies announce the arrival of their deliverer.

At the moment when the weight of misfortune oppresses the Jew, and when he eats with trembling the bread of sorrow, he sights, perhaps the arrival of the Messiah. I say, perhaps, for all do not consider that event as a very favourable prospect; since, according to some Rabbis, a severe judgment must previously try those who are to be made partakers of the felicity that will thence arise to men. The exclamation of a certain doctor is well known, "let him come, provided I do not see him!" However this may be, his coming will appear less desirous to our Israelite, when the humanity of the world shall suffer him to breathe in peace under his paternal roof, become the abode of tranquility and happiness, which to him will possess all the charms of novelty. The comforts of the present life make people too often forget those promised in the next; the Jew has his sensations as well as we, and his hopes will never induce him to abandon present enjoyments, when he can obtain them. When he is once become a member of the state, attached to it by the ties of pleasure, security, liberty, and ease, the spirit of the body will become diminished in him; he will not be tempted to transport his riches elsewhere, when his landed property has fixed him in that country where he has acquired it and he will cherish his mother, that is to say his country, and interests of which will be confounded with his own.

…Clenard,[9] in his letters, speaks of the Jewish beauties of Fez and Morocco. These all of Avignon have been extolled; and Le Roque,[10] the traveller, describes the Hebrew women of Moka[11] as being extremely well made [sic]. Perhaps, even in our own countries, fewer faults will be found in their conformation than among us. However, if we can believe Michaelis, and our own eyes, the greater part of the Jewish visages are seldom adorned with beautiful features or the bloom of health. Besides, they are marked with shades of difference, which are as striking as difficult to be accounted for. Lavater[12] the philosopher, who may be considered as a legislator in whatever relates to physiognomy, told me, that according to his observations, the Jews in general had sallow complexions, hooked noses, hollow eyes, prominent chins, and the constrictory muscles of the mouth are very apparent.…

It is added, that the Jews abound with bad humours; are very much subject to those disorders which indicate that the general mass of the blood is corrupted, as appears from their being formerly troubled with the leprosy, and at present with the scurvy, which has so much affinity to it, and with the scrophula, bloody-flux, etc. If to the testimony of those who make the above assertion, we join the acknowledgement of Abrabanel,[13] we shall be tempted to believe, that the hemorrhoides are endemic among them; and as this malady has sometimes periodical returns, several writers have seriously concluded, that the Jews are subject to menstrual evacuations. Cardoso[14] quotes and refutes various authors, who have propagated these ridiculous notions.

It is contended also, that the Jews constantly exhale a bad smell. This, indeed, is not a new opinion; for we find frequent mention made of it in old authors; and this accusation, repeated in all ages, has perpetuated the same prejudice. Ramazzini,[15] in his *Treatise on the Diseases of Tradesmen*, has inserted a chapter on those of the Jews. He has no doubt, that the Jews exhaled a very fetid smell, when they lived amidst the splendor of Jerusalem; and he assigns as the cause of this pretended stink, and of their paleness, which is more real, their occupations, (such as that of selling old clothes) and their poverty. Others ascribe these effects to the frequent use of herbs, such as onions and garlic, the smell of which is penetrating; and some to their eating the flesh of he-goats; while others pretend, that the flesh of geese, which they are remarkably fond of, renders them melancholy and livid, as this food abounds with viscous and gross juices.

I admit the influence of these particular causes upon the constitution, but the inductions thence drawn are not satisfactory. Who will believe, for example, that selling old clothes is sufficient to render the complexion dark? Are the inhabitants of the street Tirechape at Paris, or the Ray-fair at Strasbourg, less blooming than those of other streets in the neighbourhood? Besides, the Jews are neither all poor, nor sellers of old clothes; and the custom of Metz, already mentioned, is not general. Mr. Venel,[16] after remarking that epilepsy is common among the Jews, that the greater part of them soon appear old, and that they seldom attain to a great age, pretends that their ablutions [ritual baths] contribute much to enervate their constitutions. In answer to this it may be said, that the continual use of the bath did not enervate the Romans; that the Turks, subjected in this respect to more legal ceremonies than the Jews, are not effeminated; and that besides, cold ablutions, such as those used by the latter, instead of relaxing the body, ought to strengthen the muscles, and give them more elasticity.

We shall, perhaps, approach nearer each other, if we assign different causes, the united effects of which may disfigure the person, and impress on it the marks of degeneration. Such as,

First, dirtiness, which in certain respects is legal in the time of mourning, and which is constantly the source of cutaneous disorders, so common among the Jews. Their ablutions, however, as we are told, ought to produce a contrary effect. This we allow; but it is to be observed, that these ablutions, which are less frequent than is supposed, are a yoke to which the Jews have been subjected, and not a precaution taken for the preservation of health: seldom are they employed in such a manner as to be useful; and they are attended with no effect, when cleanliness in furniture, linen, food, and the renewal of fresh air, etc., are not made to conspire towards the same end.

Second, their nourishment is more suited to the climate of Palestine than to ours; for, independent of religious and moral reasons, abstinence from certain kinds of food, such as is prescribed by Moses, is often justified by a knowledge of the climate....

Third, the use of ill-chosen and ill-prepared food. It is certain from experience, that this cause makes the human race soon degenerate; and the authority of Buffon[17] gives an additional weight to this assertion; but it is certain, that from a fear of eating blood, the Jews squeeze it almost entirely from their meat, and by these means deprive it of much of its nutritive juice. We are assured, that in certain countries, they salt very little flesh; and on this account it must have a noxious quality, and become difficult to be digested; for it is well-known what a happy effect salt has over the animal economy.

Fourth, the want of a mixture in the breed, which causes a race to degenerate, and lessens the beauty of individuals....

Fifth, another cause is the general practice of marrying very young. This custom, prejudicial to both sexes, whom it enervates, causes women to be with child prematurely; which, according to Mr. Venel, weakens the mother, and the fruits of her womb. This truth, of which we have repeated examples in the present day, refutes the opinion of those who believe that the epoch of puberty, and being marriageable, are the same; and that early unions are according to the order of Nature.... Let me add, that their women are continually enervated by a sedentary life; that the greater part of the men are in the same situation; and that some, following a wandering life, which affords no exercise but to the legs, never have the vigorous arms of our rustics....

NOTES

1. Abbé Henri Baptiste Grégoire (1750–1831), Jesuit priest, who despite his negative views of Judaism and "Jewish" commercial behavior, consistently advocated the granting of equal rights to Jews (and to other minorities). As a delegate to the French National Assembly he placed a motion for Jewish emancipation. (See "Motion en Faveur des Juifs par M. Grégoire, curé d'Embermenil, député de Nancy, précédée d'une notice historique sur les persécutions qu'ils viennent d'essuyer en divers lieux…" [Paris, 1789]). On the day on which his motion was considered by the Assembly, Grégoire exclaimed before the Assembly: "Fifty thousand Frenchmen arose this morning as slaves; it depends on you whether they shall go to bed as free men." Although Grégoire's arguments on behalf of Jewish civil parity are not original, they are significant because he advanced them as a professing Catholic and priest. Grégoire's essay was first submitted in a 1785 competition held by the Société Royale des Arts et Sciences at Metz on the question: "Are there possibilities of making the Jews more useful and happier in France?"

2. Johann David Michaelis, see document 10, note 1, in this chapter.

3. The reference is apparently to Markus Herz (1747–1803), German-Jewish physician, friend and disciple of Kant. See chapter 2, document 6.

4. The reference is apparently to Markus (Mordecai) Eliezer Bloch (1723–1797), German-Jewish physician, famed zoologist, friend of Mendelssohn.

5. Isaac de Pinto (1717–1787), philosopher and economist of Portuguese-Jewish descent; born in France, but lived most of his life in Holland. See chapter 6, document 2.

6. Claude Adrien Helvetius (1715–1771), French philosopher, one of the Encyclopedists.

7. This was a frequent charge of opponents of Jewish emancipation See chapter 6 document 4.

8. The reference is apparently to Nicholas Antoine Boulanger (1722–1759), French philosopher and scholar. See his controversial *L'Antiquite dévoilée par ses usages, ou Examen critique des principales, opinions, cérémonies et institutions religieuses et politiques des differens peuples de la terre*, 3 vols. (Amsterdam, 1766).

9. Nicholaus Clenard (Clendarus), c. 1495–1542, Christian Hebraist from Flanders.

10. Jacques Le Roque, fifteenth-century traveler.

11. Moka or Mocha, a small port in South West Yemen, which until the nineteenth century was a well-known harbor for the export of the coffee to which it gave its name.

12. Johann Caspar Lavater (1741–1801), Swiss clergyman and theologian. Lavater was the author of the influential study *Physiognomische Fragmente zur Befoerderung der Menschenkenntnis und Menschenliebe* (1775–1778).

13. Judah Abrabanel (c. 1460–1523), Jewish physician and poet and one of the foremost philosophers of the Italian Renaissance.

14. Isaac (Fernando) Cardoso (1604–1685), Marrano physician and scientist.

15. Bernardino Ramazzini (1633–1714), Italian physician.

16. Gabriel Venel (1723–1775), French chemist, surgeon and physiologist.

17. George-Louis Leclerc, Comte de Buffon (1707–1788), French naturalist.

II

HARBINGERS OF CULTURAL AND IDEOLOGICAL CHANGE

On the cultural and ideological level, a departure from the regnant medieval and theological attitudes toward the Jew was evident in the Enlightenment, the seventeenth- and eighteenth-century intellectual movement that held that reason, not religion or tradition, is the ultimate arbiter of truth, both epistemological and moral. The Enlightenment celebrated reason as a universal attribute of human beings that transcends differences of religion and of national and social origin. Reason, accordingly, constitutes a universal bond among all people. In adopting this premise the Enlightenment adumbrated the liberal and democratic values that would eventually embrace the Jew as a fellow human being. The selections from Gotthold Ephraim Lessing (1729–1781) are representative of the Enlightenment as it relates to the Jew.

Parallel to the Enlightenment there was a shift in the attitudes of Jews toward their own religious tradition and the outside world. One may refer to this shift as a secularization of consciousness, or a disengagement of the consciousness of the individual from the authority of religious tradition. Perhaps the first instance of this process was the circle of Daniel (Juan) de Prado (c. 1615–c. 1672) and Baruch Spinoza, or, as he is also known, Benedict de Spinoza (1632–1677), in the Jewish community of Amsterdam. These men questioned some of the basic tenets of Jewish faith, for example, the divine authorship of the Scripture, rabbinic authority and, most significantly, the relevance of ritual as divine service. In expressing these heretical views Prado and Spinoza revealed— and thus met violent opposition from the elders of their community—the spiritual turmoil of a community of former Marranos. Having lived for generations as Christians, they found the process of reconstructing their lives in accordance with the traditional patterns of Judaism not simply an organizational but a complex cognitive process involving the acceptance of a new source of religious authority. Cognitively, Prado and Spinoza were marginal Jews and thus apparently receptive to the Deism and rationalism of the early Enlightenment. The text of the ban of excommunication (*herem*) of Spinoza, presented herein, reflects this situation. Prado recurrently sought to have the *herem* repealed and to be readmitted to the House of Israel. Spinoza, on the other hand, apparently accepted his banishment from Judaism without regret. He steadfastly refused, however, to adopt another positive religion. His rejection of Albert Burgh's appeal to embrace Catholicism illustrates both his Deistic rationalism and his insistence that a person of reason need not belong to a church. (See the second edition of this book, pp. 58–60.) In that Spinoza left Judaism without adopting another faith he is said to be the first modern, secular Jew.[1]

The selection "The Right To Be Different" from Moses Mendelssohn's *Jerusalem* (1783) illustrates an attempt to argue that participation in the secular culture of the Enlightenment need not involve a rejection of Judaism. In consonance with the proposition that the community forged by reason—the so-called *Gelehrterrepublik* (the republic of the learned, viz., those who developed their reason)—was ideally neutral to one's religious faith and background, Mendelssohn proudly pointed to his friendship with the leading personalities of the Enlightenment. "I have the good fortune to include among my friends," Mendelssohn wrote, "quite a number of fine men who are not of my faith. We have a genuine affection for each other, although we take it for granted that in matters of religion we have very different beliefs. I enjoy their company and feel enriched by it" (Letter to J. C. Lavater, December 12, 1769).[2] As is indicated by Immanuel Kant's letter to Markus Herz (document 6), these individuals just as enthusiastically esteemed their relationship with Mendelssohn. The reading from Naphtali Herz Wessely (1725–1805), who was like Mendelssohn an observant Jew, expresses ideas similar to Mendelssohn's in a programmatic fashion, emphasizing the need for a reform in Jewish education to encourage participation in the universal and secular learning of Europe. *Hameasef* [The Gatherer], a journal published intermittently from 1784 to 1811, was founded by disciples of Mendelssohn and Wessely to propagate among Jewry the *Weltanschauung* of the Enlightenment. Specifically, *Hameasef*, written in Hebrew, sought to re-orient the axis of Jewish concern from Talmud and halakhah (Jewish law) to the Bible and the Hebrew language—aspects of Judaism deemed more amenable to the values of the Enlightenment. Included herein are the prospectus of *Hameasef* and the lead article, "We Shall Not Be Deterred," of the fourth volume of the journal. The custodians of traditional Judaism for the most part responded to the efforts of Mendelssohn and his followers with vehemence, for they feared that these new trends would undermine the integrity of the traditional Jewish way of life. The reading from Rabbi David (Tevele) ben Nathan of Lissa (d. 1792) is one of the milder responses on behalf of traditional Judaism.

With the rapid acculturation of German Jewry, not only was the commitment to Talmud and halakhah eclipsed but so was the interest in the Hebrew Scripture and language. The Jewish votaries of Enlightenment quickly adapted to the situation and began to use German as a medium of expression. In that the exigent need was no longer to encourage Jewish adaptation to the spirit of the age, the message, of course, changed somewhat: the focus was now on how Judaism could be adapted and integrated into the secular life of the modern Jew (documents 11 and 12). *Sulamith*, issued from 1806 to 1833 in Dessau, Germany, became a major organ of the Jewish Enlightenment. Not surprisingly, *Sulamith* also became a forum advocating religious reformation, as the "Preface" from its first issue (1806) indicates.

---

[1] Daniel Swetschinski, *Reluctant Cosmopolitans: The Portuguese Jews of Seventeenth-Century Amsterdam* (London: Littman Library of Jewish Civilization, 2000); Yirmiyahu Yovel, *Spinoza and Other Heretics* (Princeton: Princeton University Press, 1989); Yosef Kaplan, *From Christianity to Judaism: The Story of Orobio de Castro* (New York: Oxford University Press, 1989).

[2] See Jacob Katz, *Exclusiveness and Tolerance* (New York: Schocken, 1962), p. 173.

From the second issue (1808) the selection "Call for Religious Enlightenment," a proto-Reform proposal for a Judaism based exclusively on moral precepts, represents a weakening of tradition and the demand for a redefinition of Judaism compatible with the new cultural orientation of "enlightened" Jewry.

The passages from the writings of Saul Ascher (1767–1822) and Lazarus Bendavid (1762–1832), antedating those from *Sulamith*, represent early appeals to minimize the "ceremonial laws" of Judaism, which, they contended, obstructed the Jew's integration in the modern world. They differed sharply with Mendelssohn, who had previously argued (see document 21 in this chapter) that fidelity to halakhah was not incompatible with Enlightenment. Mendelssohn did, however, urge the dissolution of the legal autonomy enjoyed by the Jewish community since the Middle Ages in order to underscore the Jew's commitment to the separation of church and state and to facilitate the Jew's integration in the unitary legal structure of the modern state.

This chapter concludes with David Friedlaender's (1750–1834) petition to the religious authorities of Berlin for a "dry baptism." Despairing of inner reform and of political emancipation, Friedlaender in the name of some of Berlin's leading Jewish families sought admission to the Church without the confessional obligation to affirm Christian dogma.

1. THE WRIT OF EXCOMMUNICATION AGAINST BARUCH SPINOZA (JULY 27, 1656)[1]

THE SEPHARDI COMMUNITY OF AMSTERDAM

The Senhores of the Mahamad[2] make it known that they have long since been cognizant of the wrong opinions and behavior of Baruch d'Espinoza, and tried various means and promises to dissuade him from his evil ways. But as they effected no improvement, obtaining on the contrary more information every day of the horrible heresies which he practised and taught, and of the monstrous actions which he performed, and as they had many trustworthy witnesses who in the presence of the same Espinoza reported and testified against him and convicted him; and after all this had been investigated in the presence of the rabbis, they decided with the consent of these that the same Espinoza should be excommunicated and separated from the people of Israel, as they now excommunicate him with the following ban:

> After the judgment of the Angels, and with that of the Saints, we excommunicate, expel and curse and damn Baruch d'Espinoza with the consent of God, Blessed be He, and with the consent of this holy congregation [*kahal kadosh*] in front of the holy Scrolls with the 613 precepts which are written therein, with the anathema with which Joshua banned Jericho, with the curse with which Elisha cursed the youths, and with all the curses which are written in the Law. Cursed be he by day, and cursed be he by night; cursed be he when he lies down, and cursed be he when he rises up; cursed be he when he goes out, and cursed be he when he comes in. The Lord will not pardon him; the anger and wrath of the Lord will rage against this man, and bring him all the curses which are written in the Book of the Law, and the Lord will destroy his name from under the Heavens, and the Lord will separate him to his injury from all the tribes of Israel with all the curses of the firmament, which are written in the Book of the Law. But you who cleave to the Lord your God are blessed.

We order that nobody should communicate with him orally or in writing, or show him any favor, or stay with him under the same roof, or come within four ells of him, or read anything composed or written by him.

NOTES

1. After several warnings, the writ of excommunication against Spinoza was proclaimed on July 27, 1656. The extant copy of the document does not include the signatories of the writ.
2. The term used by the Spanish-Portuguese Jewish (Sephardi) community to designate the governing council of the synagogue.

Source: J. Freudenthal, ed., *Die Lebensgeschichte Spinoza's in Quellenshcriften, Urkunden und nichtamtlichen Nachrichten* (Leipzig: Veit & Co., 1899), pp. 114–16. Trans. from the Portuguese by Rita Mendes-Flohr.

2. ON THE ELECTION OF THE JEWS[1]

BARUCH SPINOZA

Every man's true happiness and blessedness consist solely in the enjoyment of what is good, not in the pride that he alone is enjoying it, to the exclusion of others. He who thinks himself the more blessed because he is enjoying benefits which others are not, or because he is more blessed or more fortunate than his fellows, is ignorant of true happiness and blessedness, and the joy which he feels is either childish or envious and malicious....Whoever, therefore, rejoices for such reasons, rejoices in another's misfortune, and is, so far, malicious and bad, knowing neither true happiness nor the peace of the true life....The Hebrews did not surpass other nations in knowledge, or in piety, but evidently in some attribute different than these....The Hebrews were not chosen by God before others for the sake of the true life and sublime ideas....

Before I begin [to show what was the nature of the Hebrews' election], I wish in a few words to explain what I mean by the guidance of God, by the help of God, external and inward, and, lastly, what I understand by fortune.

By the help of God, I mean the fixed and unchangeable order of nature or the chain of natural events: for I have said before and shown elsewhere that the universal laws of nature, according to which all things exist and are determined, are only another name for the eternal decrees of God, which always involve eternal truth and necessity.[2]

So that to say that everything happens according to natural laws, and to say that everything is ordained by the decree and ordinance of God, is the same thing. Now since the power in nature is identical with the power of God, by which alone all things happen and are determined, it follows that whatsoever man, as part of nature, provides himself with to aid and preserve his existence, or whatsoever nature affords him without his help, is given to him solely by the Divine power, acting either through human nature or through external circumstances. So whatever human nature can furnish itself with by its own efforts to preserve its existence, may be fitly called the inward aid of God, whereas whatever else accrues to man's profit from outward causes may be called the external aid of God.

We can now easily understand what is meant by the election of God. For since no one can do anything save the predetermined order of nature, that is by God's eternal ordinance and decree, it follows that no one can choose a plan of life for himself, or accomplish any work save by God's vocation choosing him for the work or the plan of life in question, rather than any other. Lastly, by fortune, I mean the ordinance of God in so far as it directs human life through external and unexpected means. With these preliminaries I return to my purpose of discovering the reason why the Hebrews were said to be elected by God before other nations, and, with the demonstration I thus proceed....

The Hebrew nation was not chosen by God in respect to its wisdom nor its tranquility of mind, but in respect to its social organization and the good fortune with which it obtained supremacy and kept it for many years. This is abundantly clear from Scripture. Even a cursory perusal will show us that the only respects in which the Hebrews surpassed other nations, are in their successful conduct of matters relating to government, and in their surmounting great perils solely by God's external aid; in other ways they were on a par with their fellows, and God was equally gracious to all. For in respect to intellect....they held very ordinary ideas about God and

Source: B. Spinoza, "A Theologico-Political Treatise," in *The Chief Works of Benedict de Spinoza,* trans. R. H. M. Elwes (New York, 1951), vol. 1. The section is from chapter 3 of the Treatise, pp. 43–47, 49, 52, 54–56.

nature, so that they cannot have been God's chosen in this respect; nor were they so chosen in respect of virtue and the true life, for here again they, with the exception of a very few elect, were on an equality with other nations: therefore their choice and vocation consisted on the temporal happiness and advantages of independent rule.[3] ...

We conclude, therefore (inasmuch as God is to all men equally gracious, and the Hebrews were only chosen by Him in respect to their social organization and government), that the individual Jew, taken apart from his social organization and government, possessed no gift of God above other men, and there was no difference between Jew and Gentile. As it is a fact that God is equally gracious, merciful, and the rest to all men.... The prophetic gift was not peculiar to the Jews....

It now only remains to us to answer the arguments of those who would persuade themselves that the election of the Jews was not temporal, and merely in respect of their commonwealth, but eternal; for, the way we see the Jews after the loss of their commonwealth, and after being scattered so many years and separated from all other nations, still surviving, which is without parallel among other peoples, and further the Scriptures seem to teach that God has chosen for Himself the Jews for ever, so that though they have lost their commonwealth, they still nevertheless remain God's elect....

As to their continuance so long after dispersion and the loss of empire, there is nothing marvelous in it, for they so separated themselves from every other nation as to draw down upon themselves hate, not only by their outward rites, rites conflicting with those of other nations, but also by the sign of circumcision which they most scrupulously observe.

That they have been preserved in great measure by Gentile hatred, experience demonstrates. When the king of Spain formerly compelled the Jews to embrace the state religion or to go into exile, a large number of Jews accepted Catholicism. Now, as these renegades were admitted to all the native privileges of Spaniards, and deemed worthy of filling all honorable offices, it came to pass that they straightway became so intermingled with the Spaniards as to leave of themselves no relic or remembrance [of Judaism]. But exactly the opposite happened to those whom the king of Portugal compelled to become Christians, for they always though converted, lived

apart, inasmuch they were considered unworthy of any civic honors.[4]

The sign of circumcision is, as I think, so important, that I could persuade myself that it alone would preserve the nation for ever. Nay, I would go so far as to believe that if the foundations of their religion have not emasculated their minds they may even, if occasion offers, so changeable are human affairs, raise up their empire afresh, and that God may a second time elect them.[5]

NOTES

1. Spinoza seems to have detached himself from Judaism—and the Jewish people—even before his excommunication; he certainly expressed no regret that he was banished from his ancestral faith and community. Yet paradoxically he has retained a place in Jewish history and consciousness. As "the first Jew to separate himself from his religion and people without a formal religious conversion" (Y. Baer, *Galut* [New York 1947], p. 105), he was a pioneer in forging the path to a distinctive modern "secular" identity, which an ever increasing number of Jews would follow. Of equal significance was his "secular" view of Judaism, which questioned the theological presuppositions of traditional Jewish self-understanding. In his Latin monograph *Tractatus theologico-politicus*, published anonymously in 1670, he offered an analysis of biblical Judaism "in the light of natural reason" alone. In chapter three of this work, he presented a purely naturalistic explanation of Israel's election and thereby dismissed two overarching, interrelated principles of traditional Judaism, namely, that Israel is blessed through its covenantal and thus providential relationship with God.

2. These are views he would develop more extensively in his *Ethics* (1674).

3. Spinoza argued that the objective of the Torah was in essence to establish the social order and government of the sovereign state of the Hebrews. Furthermore, he argued, when that political entity ceased to exist, its "constitution" was rendered null and void. Hence, by equating Israel's election with the "Mosaic constitution," Spinoza implied that with the Jews' dispersion, the election was devoid of all meaning. Israel's election is historically conditioned and thus not eternal.

4. From different theological perspectives, Jews and Christians had traditionally viewed Jewish historical destiny as guided by divine Providence. By arguing that Jewish unity in the Diaspora was sustained by a defensive response to the prejudice and animosity that

Jews encountered, Spinoza challenged this view. In advancing this argument, he reversed the Roman historian Tacitus' judgment that Jewish religious separation, expressing a disdain for non-Jews, provoked antipathy; rather, Spinoza contended, it was the nigh-universal hatred toward them that prompted Jews to withdraw and band together. The historian Joseph Haim Yerushalmi discerns in this argument a vengeful note. "I dare say that if one reads between the lines this passage reflects Spinoza's resentment and even contempt of his former co-religionists who excommunicated him....In determining that hatred sustained Jewish identity, he did not say so in a vacuum....The thesis that the existence of Israel is not in the hands of God is not new. What renders it offensive, of course, is that it attributes Israel's existence to its enemies. The offense, of course, affects all Jews, but given the actual background [of Spinoza's remarks], it is directed especially to the Sephardic community, in which he was raised. Most of the community's members were survivors of the Inquisition, who took pride in their success to preserve their Judaism in the Iberian Peninsula despite the hatred of the gentiles, not because of it." Moreover, Yerushalmi questions the accuracy of the historical evidence that Spinoza marshals to anchor his thesis—namely, that in contrast to Portugal, where racial laws—barring those lacking "pure [Portuguese] blood" from privileged civic and ecclesiastical positions—kept Jewish converts to Christianity apart, whereas the absence of such restrictions in Spain allowed the former Jews in that country to assimilate fully. See Y. H. Yerushalmi, "Spinoza's Statements on Jewish Existence," *Proceedings of the Israel National Academy of the Sciences,* 6:6 (1982), pp.10, 11–14 (Hebrew).

5. This passage is often interpreted as an expression of Spinoza's proto-Zionism. In assessing the accuracy of this interpretation, one must recall that Zionism is not simply defined by a longing to reclaim Israel's patrimony in the Land of Israel. As is attested by the documents in chapter X, Zionism is first and foremost an ideology that offers a program to solve the Jewish problem, however that problem may be conceived by various streams of that movement.

3. MOSES MENDELSSOHN VISITS THE SEER OF KOENIGSBERG (1777)[1]

Without paying particular attention to those present, but nonetheless with anxious, quiet steps, a small, physically deformed Jew with a goatee entered the lecture hall and stood standing not far from the entrance. As was to be expected there began sneering and jeering that eventually turned into clicking, whistling and stamping, but to the general astonishment of everyone the stranger stood with an ice-like silence as if tied to his place. For the sake of showing clearly his interest in waiting for the Professor [Immanuel Kant] he took an empty chair and sat. Someone approached him, and inquired [why he was there], and he replied succinctly but courteously that he wanted to stay in order to make the acquaintance of Kant. Only Kant's appearance could finally quiet the uproar. His lecture drew the attention of everyone to other matters, and one became so enraptured, so immersed in a sea of new ideas, that one long forgot about the presence of the Jew.

At the conclusion of the lecture, the Jew pushed himself forward with an intensity, which starkly

Source: Simon Dubnow, *Weltgeschichte des jüdischen Volkes* (Berlin: Juedischer Verlag, 1929), vol. 10, pp. 24–25. Trans. by P. Mendes-Flohr.

contrasted with his previous composure, through the crowd in order to reach the Professor. The students hardly noticed him, when suddenly there again resounded a scornful laughter, which immediately gave way to wonder as Kant, after briefly looking at the stranger pensively and exchanging with him a few words, heartily shook his hand and then embraced him. Like a brushfire there went through the crowd, "Moses Mendelssohn. It is the Jewish philosopher from Berlin." Deferentially the students made way as the two sages left the lecture hall hand in hand.

NOTE

1. In July 1777 Mendelssohn made a business trip to Memel and en route went to Koenigsberg, where he made the acquaintance of Kant. The renowned philosopher received him cordially, and a warm friendship quickly developed between them. In August, on his way home to Berlin, Mendelssohn once again visited Kant, who invited his guest to attend his lectures at the university. This account by one of the students in attendance at one of the lectures illustrates the vision of the Enlightenment as a "neutral society" in which Jew and non-Jew could meet as equals and on the basis of mutual respect. See document 6 in this chapter.

4. THE JEWS (1754)

GOTTHOLD EPHRAIM LESSING[1]

Scene 21. (Baron, Traveller)

. . . .

BARON: But how should I, my dear friend, acknowledge my gratitude to you? Now, for yet a second time you saved me from danger—a danger as great as the first. I am indebted to you for my very life. I never would have discovered this near tragedy without you. My steward, a man whom I totally trusted with my property, was a godless accomplice [of the highway robbers]. I would have never suspected it. Had you departed today without....

TRAVELLER: It is true—but then the help I provided yesterday would have remained incomplete. I deem myself extremely fortunate that heaven brought me to this unexpected discovery [of the steward's complicity]. At this moment I am so overjoyed that I am trembling, just as before when I feared I made a mistake.

BARON: As much as I esteem your generosity of spirit I admire your love of man.(*Aside*) I may say that what [my housemaid] Lisette reported is true![2]

Scene 22. ([Baron's daughter's maid] Lisette, Baron, Baron's Daughter, Traveller, [Traveller's servant] Christophe)

LISETTE: And why shouldn't it be true?

BARON: Come my daughter, come! Join your plea to mine. Entreat my saviour to take your hand, and together with your hand to accept my good fortune. What could be more precious to him as a token of my gratitude, than you, whom I love so very dearly. (*To the Traveller*) Aren't you surprised that I can make such a proposal to you? Your servant revealed your identity to us. Grant me the boundless joy of expressing my gratitude. My good

Source: Gotthold Ephraim Lessing, "Die Juden," in *Saemmtliche Schriften*, ed. Karl Lachmann (Leipzig, 1853), vol. 1, pp. 381–84. Trans. by M. Gelber.

fortune, as yours, is my [high] social standing. Here [under the protection of my family], you will be safe from your enemies. You will be with friends who will cherish you. Alone, you will surely be vanquished.

BARON'S DAUGHTER: Are you in doubt on my account? I assure you that I will gladly obey my father in this matter.

TRAVELLER: Your generosity astounds me. By the magnitude of the remuneration you offer me, I first realize how trifling my deed was. But how should I tell you? My servant did not speak the truth. And I...

BARON: Would to heaven that you aren't what he made you out to be! Would to heaven that your position be less than mine. Then, at least, my offer should seem all the more precious and you would be more disposed to accept it.

TRAVELLER: (*Aside*) Should I not disclose my true identity?—Dear Sir, your magnanimity touches me profoundly. Ascribe it to fate alone, not to me, that your offer is in vain. I am...

BARON: Perhaps already married?

TRAVELLER: No—

BARON: What then?

TRAVELLER: I am a Jew.

BARON: A Jew? Cruel misfortune!

CHRISTOPHE: A Jew?

BARON'S DAUGHTER: But, what difference does it.make?[3]

LISETTE: Shush, Fraülein, shush. I'll tell you later what difference it makes.[4]

BARON: So, there are times when heaven itself prevents us from being grateful?

TRAVELLER: You are already more than grateful, just by your desire to be so.

BARON: Then I will do at least as much as fate allows me. Take my entire wealth, I prefer to be poor but grateful, than rich and ungrateful.

TRAVELLER: This offer, too, is in vain, since the God of my fathers has granted me more than I need. I ask for no recompense, except perhaps that in the future you judge my people somewhat more leniently and with fewer generalizations. I didn't conceal my identity from you because I am ashamed of my religion. No! I saw that although you indicated hostility toward my nation, you were favorably disposed towards me. And, a man's friendship,

whoever he be, shall always be invaluable to me.

BARON: I am ashamed of my conduct.

CHRISTOPHE: Only now after my initial astonishment, am I regaining my wits. How? Your are a Jew and had the heart to take an upright Christian into your service? You should have served me. Then it would have been right according to the Bible. Good Heavens! You've insulted through me all of Christianity.— Hmm, I didn't know why the man wouldn't eat pork during our travels, for which he made a hundred silly excuses. —Don't think that I'll accompany you any further. And, moreover, I'll bring a suit against you.

TRAVELLER: I can't expect more from you than I can from the other Christian rabble. And, I'll not remind you of the pitiful circumstances from which I removed you in Hamburg. I don't wish to force you to remain with me any longer. Still, because I have been rather satisfied with your services and also for a time suspected you unfairly [of theft], take for recompense that which aroused my suspicions in the first place. (*He gives Christophe a snuff-box.*) You may also have your wages. Go then where you will!

CHRISTOPHE: No! The deuce! Certainly there are also Jews who aren't Jews.[5] You're an upright man. By God, I'm staying with you! A Christian would have given me a kick in the ribs, not a [valuable] snuff-box.

BARON: All of your deeds enchant me. Come, let's make certain that those guilty are brought into custody. Oh, how commendable the Jews would be, if they were all like you!

TRAVELLER: And how worthy of love the Christians, if they all possessed your qualities! (*The Baron, his Daughter and the Traveller exit*)

Last Scene. (Lisette, Christophe)

LISETTE: Now then, did my friend lie to me before?

CHRISTOPHE: Yes, and for two reasons. First, because I didn't know the truth, and second, because you can't speak much truth for a bribe that you have to give back in the end.

LISETTE: For that matter, how can he be considered a Jew if he conceals his identity?

CHRISTOPHE: For a maid, that's too curiously put! Come let's go. (*He takes her under the arm and they exit*)

NOTES

1. Gotthold Ephraim Lessing (1729–1781), dramatist, critic and philosopher. Aside from Immanuel Kant, Lessing is probably the best-known representative of the Enlightenment in German-speaking Europe. This play was written in 1749 but first published in 1754; this translation is based on the revised edition of 1770. In addition to its dramaturgical innovations, the significance of the play lies in its unambiguous portrayal of a Jew as a virtuous individual. These excerpts are taken from the play's denouement. The anonymous traveller, who on the previous day rescued the Baron and his entourage from the hands of highway robbers, initially assumed to be "damned Jews," now identifies the scoundrels as none other than the steward and the administrator of the Baron's own estate. Finally, the chivalrous traveller discloses his own identity.

2. At the Baron's behest, Lisette had solicited from the anonymous traveller's servant, Christophe, his master's identity. Although equally ignorant of his master's identity, Christophe was enticed by a promise of a bribe (the snuff box) and told Lisette that his master was a nobleman who had fled his native Holland after having killed an opponent in a duel.

3. The 1754 text reads: "What does that mean? You can certainly still marry me."

4. The 1754 text reads: "Be quiet, Fraülein. I will explain later what that means."

5. "Es gibt doch wohl auch Juden, die keine Juden sind." The 1754 text reads. "No the deuce! The Jews are generous people."

5. A PARABLE OF TOLERATION (1779)[1]

GOTTHOLD EPHRAIM LESSING

NATHAN: In days of yore a man lived in the East,
Who owned a ring of marvellous worth,
Given to him by a hand beloved.
The stone was opal, and shed a hundred lovely rays.
But chiefly it possessed the secret power
To make the owner loved of God and man
If he but wore it in this faith and confidence;
What wonder then that this man in the East
Ne'er from his finger took the ring.
And so arranged it should forever with his house remain,
Namely, thus: He bequeathed it to
The most beloved of his sons,
Firmly prescribing that he in turn
Should leave it to the dearest of his sons;
And always thus the dearest, without respect to birth,

Source: Gotthold Ephraim Lessing, *Nathan the Wise*, trans. Williams Jacks (Glasgow, 1894), act 3, scene 7.

Became the head and chieftain of the house
By virtue of the ring alone.
You understand me, Sultan?

SALADIN: I understand. Proceed.

NATHAN: The ring, descending from son to son,
Came to the father of three sons at last,
All three of whom obeyed him equally,
And all of whom he therefore loved alike.
From time to time indeed, now one seemed worthiest of the ring,
And now another, now the third,
Just as it happened one or other with him were alone,
And his o'erflowing heart was not divided with the other two;
And so to each one of the three he gave
The promise—in pious weakness alone—
He should possess this wondrous ring.
This then went on as long as it could;
But then at last it came to dying,
Which brings the father into sore perplexity.
It pains him much to practise such deceit
Upon two sons who rested so upon his word.
What can be done? In secret
He seeks out a skilful artist,
And from him orders two other rings,
Just to the pattern of his own.
And urges him to spare neither pains nor gold.
To make a perfect match.
The artist so succeeded in his task,
That, when he brought the jewels home,
The father even failed to tell which was the pattern ring.
Now, glad and joyous, he calls his sons—
But separately of course—gives each
A special blessing with his ring, and died,
You hear me, Sultan?

SALADIN: (*Somewhat moved, turns from him*)
I hear, I hear;
But pray get ended with your tale.
You soon will be?

NATHAN: I'm at the end,
For what follows is self-understood.
Scarce was the father dead,
When each one with his ring appears
Claiming each the leadership of the house.
Inspections, quarrelling, and complaints ensue;
But all in vain, the veritable ring
Was not distinguishable—
(*After a pause, during which he expects the Sultan's answer*)
Almost as indistinguishable as to us,
Is now—the true religion.

SALADIN: What? Is that meant as answer to my question?

NATHAN: This meant but to excuse myself, because
 I lack the boldness to discriminate between the rings,
 Which the father by express intent had made
 So that they might not be distinguished.
SALADIN: The rings! Don't play with me.
 I thought the faiths which I have named
 Were easily distinguishable.
 Even to their raiment, even to meat and drink.
NATHAN: But not yet as regards their proofs;
 For do not all rest upon history, written or traditional?
 And history can also be accepted
 Only on faith and trust. Is it not so?
 Now, whose faith and confidence do we least misdoubt?
 That of our relatives? Of those whose flesh and blood we are,
 Of those who from our childhood
 Have lavished on us proofs of love,
 Who ne'er deceived us, unless 'twere wholesome for us so?
 How can I place less faith in my forefathers
 Than in yours? or the reverse?
 Can I desire of you to load your ancestors with lies,
 So that you contradict not mine? Or the reverse?
 And to the Christian the same applies.
SALADIN: By the living God, the man is right, I must be dumb.
NATHAN: Let us return unto our rings.
 As said, the sons accused each other,
 And each one swore before the judge
 He had received his ring directly
 From his father's hand—which was quite true—
 And that, indeed, after having long his promise held,
 To enjoy eventually the ring's prerogative,
 Which was no less the truth.
 Each one insisted that it was impossible
 His father could play false with him.
 And ere he could suspect so dear and true a father,
 He was compelled, howe'er inclined to think
 The best of them, to accuse his brothers
 Of this treacherous act, to unmask the traitors,
 And avenge himself.
SALADIN: Well, and the judge? I'm curious to hear what you will give
 The judge to say, Go on.
NATHAN: The judge said this; Produce your father here
 At once, or I'll dismiss you from this court.
 Think you I'm here but to solve riddles?
 Or would you wait till the true ring itself will speak?
 But stop; I've just been told that the right ring
 Contains the wondrous gift to make its wearer beloved,
 Agreeable alike to God and man.

That must decide, for the false rings will not have the power.
Now which one do the other two love most?
Come, speak out; you're silent?
Do the rings work only backwards and not outwardly?
Does each one love himself the best?
Then you're all three deceived deceivers;
None of your rings are genuine.
The genuine ring is no doubt lost.
To hide the loss and to supply its place
The father ordered the other three.

SALADIN: Splendid, splendid!

NATHAN: The judge went further on to say;
If you will have my judgment, not my advice,
Then go. But my advice is this;
You take the matter as it stands.
If each one had his ring straight from his father,
So let each believe his ring the true one.
T'is possible your father would no longer tolerate
The tyranny of this one ring in his family.
And surely loved you all—and all alike,
And that he would not two oppress
By favouring the third.
Now then, let each one emulate in affection
Untouched by prejudice. Let each one strive
To gain the prize of proving by results
The virtue of his ring, and aid its powers
With gentleness and heartiest friendliness,
With benevolence and true devotedness to God;
And if the virtue of the ring will then
Have proved itself among your children's children,
I summon them to appear again
Before this judgment seat,
After a thousand thousand years.
Here then will sit a judge more wise than I,
Who will pronounce. Go you.
So said the modest judge.

SALADIN: God, oh God!

NATHAN: Saladin, if now you feel yourself to be
That promised sage—

SALADIN: (*Rushes to him and seizes his hand, which
to the end he does not let go*)
I, dust? I, nothing? Oh God!

NATHAN: What ails thee, Sultan?

SALADIN: Nathan, dear Nathan, your judge's thousand
Thousand years have not yet fled,
His judgment seat's not become mine.
Go, Go; but be my friend.

NOTE

1. This play, first published in 1779, is based on the para-
    ble of the three rings, a story from Giovanni Boccaccio's
    Decameron (composed between 1348 and 1353). The
    play presents Judaism, Christianity and Islam as three
    sons of a benevolent father who gave each an identical
    ring, although each claims that his alone is authentic.
    Nathan, a Jew, is made the spokesman for the ideals
    of the Enlightenment: tolerance, brotherhood and love
    of humanity. Lessing regarded his close friendship with
    Mendelssohn as a testimony to these ideals. It is thus
    believed that Nathan was modeled after Mendelssohn.

6. LETTER TO MARKUS HERZ (1777)

IMMANUEL KANT[1]

Dearest Friend,

Today Herr Mendelssohn, your and my honorable friend—as I take pride in calling him—departed from here. Having a man of such gentle disposition, and good spirits and intelligence for a constant and intimate companion in Koenigsberg would be the kind of spiritual nourishment which is completely lacking here, and which, as I grow older, I increasingly miss. I did not (I must admit) know how to enjoy the company of such a rare person, or how to avail myself sufficiently of [his presence in Koenigsberg] in part because I was afraid to interfere with the business that had brought him here. The day before yesterday, he honored me by attending two of my lectures—*à la fortune du pot*, as one might say, since the table was not prepared for such a distinguished guest. The lecture, this time, must have seemed rather tumultuous to him; vacations had interrupted the previous one and most of the time, therefore, was spent on summarizing its content. The summary, naturally, lacked all the clarity and order of the lecture itself, I beg you to help me retain the friendship of this venerable man. ...

NOTE

1. Immanuel Kant (1724–1804), German philosopher who articulated in a systematic manner the precepts of the Enlightenment. Despite his negative views of Judaism, he had many Jewish disciples and friends.

    Markus Herz (1747–1803) was a German-Jewish physician, disciple of Kant, friend of Moses Mendelssohn and advocate of the Enlightenment among his fellow Jews. In August 1777, Mendelssohn (see chapter 1, document 11, note 1) had made a business trip to Koenigsberg, the East Prussian city where Kant taught. Mendelssohn met Kant, with whom he quickly developed a friendship (see document 3 in this chapter). This letter is dated August 20, 1777.

Source: Immanuel Kants Werke, ed. E. Cassirer (Berlin: Bruno Cassirer, 1918), vol. 9, pp. 158–59. Trans, by J. Hessing.

7. THE RIGHT TO BE DIFFERENT (1783)[1]

MOSES MENDELSSOHN

Brothers, if you care for true piety, let us not feign agreement where diversity is evidently the plan and purpose of Providence. None of us thinks and feels exactly like his fellow man; why then do we wish to deceive each other with delusive words? We already do this, unfortunately, in our daily intercourse, in our conversations, which are of no particular importance; why then also in matters that have to do with our temporal and eternal welfare, our whole destiny? Why should we make ourselves unrecognizable to each other in the most important concerns of our life by masquerading, since God has stamped everyone, not without reason, with his own facial features? Does this not amount to doing our very best to resist Providence, to frustrate, if it be possible, the purpose of creation? Is this not deliberately to contravene our calling, our destiny in this life and the next?—Rulers of the earth! If it be permitted to an insignificant fellow inhabitant thereof to lift up his voice to you: do not trust the counselors who wish to mislead you by smooth words to so harmful an undertaking. They are either blind themselves, and do not see the enemy of mankind lurking in the ambush, or they seek to blind you. Our noblest treasure, the liberty to think, will be forfeited if you listen to them. For the sake of your felicity and ours, *a union of faiths is not tolerance*; it is diametrically opposed to true tolerance! For the sake of your felicity and ours, do not use your powerful authority to transform some *eternal truth*, without which civil felicity can exist, into a *law*, some *religious opinion*, which is a matter of indifference to the state, into an *ordinance of the land*! Pay heed to the right *conduct* of men; upon this bring to bear the tribunal of wise laws, and leave us *thought and speech* which the Father of us all assigned to us as an inalienable heritage and granted to us as an immutable right. Should, perhaps, the link between *right* and *opinion* be too prescriptive, and should the time not yet be ripe for abolishing it completely without courting damage, try, at least, to mitigate as much as you can its pernicious influence, and to put wise limits to prejudice that has grown gray with age.[2] At least pave the way for a happy posterity toward that height of culture, toward that universal tolerance of man for which reason still sighs in vain! Reward and punish no doctrine, tempt and bribe no one to adopt any religious opinion! Let everyone be permitted to speak as he thinks, to invoke God after his own manner or that of his fathers, and to seek eternal salvation where he thinks he may find it, as long as he does not disturb public felicity and acts honestly toward the civil laws, toward you and his fellow citizens. Let no one in your states be a searcher of hearts and a judge of thoughts; let no one assume a right that the Omniscient has reserved to himself alone! If we render unto *Caesar* what is *Caesar's*, then do you yourselves render unto *God what is God's! Love truth! Love peace*!

NOTES

1. This call for religious tolerance and pluralism served as the peroration of Mendelssohn's *Jerusalem* (1783), his systematic demonstration of the compatability of traditional Judaism with the precepts of the Enlightenment.
2. Alas, we already hear the Congress in America striking up the old tune and speaking of a *dominant religion*. [Mendelssohn's note.]

Source: Moses Mendelssohn, *Jerusalem, or, on Religious Power and Judaism*, trans. Allan Arkush, with an introduction and commentary by Alexander Altmann (Hanover: University Press of New England, 1983), pp. 138–39. Reprinted by permission of the University Press of New England.

8. WORDS OF PEACE AND TRUTH (1782)

NAPHTALI HERZ (HARTWIG) WESSELY[1]

Said the wisest of men: "Educate a youth in the path he is to take [literally: "according to his way"], and even when he is old he will not depart from it" (Prov. 22:6). This statement has two parts. The first—"educate a youth," that is, one should be educated in his youth, when his heart is unsullied by the vanities of the world and by the perversities of strange ideas. For when his heart is like clean and smooth paper it shall be easiest to write words of truth upon it, and they shall be well inscribed. The second part—"according to his way," that is, according to his qualities and potential. For the disposition of men and their spiritual faculties are not the same; what is easy for one to receive and retain will be difficult for another, while other matters will be easy for the latter and difficult for the former.... And if he shall be educated in his youth, and the education will be according to his way, then "when he is old he will not depart from it."

Now, in order to educate the youths of Israel in the proper manner, two types of studies should be established. The first type is the study of "human knowledge" [*Torat haadam*], that is, those matters which earn for their possessors the title "human" [*adam*], since he who lacks this knowledge hardly deserves this title, as shall be explained. The second type is the study of the Torah of God, that is, God's laws and teachings, matters that are above human reason and that were made known to Moses through prophetic revelation. Had the Torah not come to us in this divine fashion, it would have remained hidden from even the most sagacious of men, for its contents cannot be deduced from the fixed laws of nature. Moreover, only the seed of Israel is obligated by the laws of the Torah....

In general, human knowledge as opposed to revealed knowledge is comprised of etiquette, the ways of morality and good character, civility and clear, graceful expression; these matters and their like are implanted in man's reason. He who possesses human knowledge will gain much from the poetic expression of the divine Torah and from the ways of God that are written therein.... Similarly, history, geography, astronomy and the like—which are inscribed in the mind of man as innate "primary ideas" whose foundation is reason—produce truths in every matter of wisdom. Included in this category of knowledge are the natural sciences, which provide genuine knowledge about all things: animals, plants, minerals, the elements, meteorology (clouds and their effects), botany, anatomy, medicine, chemistry, etc. It is in man's power to study all of these phenomena by means of his senses and reason; he does not need anything divine to comprehend them.

Now, human knowledge is anterior to the exalted divine laws. Hence it is proper that in his youth man should crown himself with the fear of God, with the rules of etiquette and with knowledge to which the appellation "human" is appropriate. With this knowledge he will prepare his heart to learn the laws and teachings of God.... From Adam to Moses twenty-six generations elapsed and during this time men acted according to human knowledge alone, that is according to the seven Noachide laws[2] and their details as they have been affirmed by the majority of sages, as well as the etiquette, to the arts and to the sciences, all of which are included in "wordly affairs." This "human knowledge" benefits the commonweal, as it teaches how to avail oneself of all things under the sun. It is responsible for man's success in all his worldly endeavors and provides a means for every man to be an aid to his fellow through his affairs and actions. Therefore he who lacks human knowledge, even though he has learned the laws and teachings of God and lives according to them, gives no

Source: Naphtali Herz Wessely, *Divrei shalom veemet* (Berlin, 1782), chaps. 1, 3, 4 and 5. Trans. by S. Weinstein and S. Fischer.

pleasure to others and this for two reasons. First, his fellowship is burdensome to other people. He will constantly err in the manners of men, his speech in worldly affairs will not be in conformity with reason, and his actions worse than useless, for they will be of no benefit and no service to other people. Second, even though the laws and teachings of God are far superior to human knowledge they are closely correlated to it; where human knowledge ends, the divine teaching begins, instructing us on what is beyond man's power of reason. Therefore he who is ignorant of the laws of God, but is versed in human knowledge, even though the sages of Israel will not benefit from his light in the study of Torah, he will benefit the remainder of humanity. But he who is ignorant of human knowledge, though he knows the laws of God, gladdens neither the wise of his own people nor the remainder of humanity. Thus our sages have said (Midrash Rabba on the first *Parashah* of Leviticus [i.e., Lev.1–5]: A ritually unclean carcass is more worthy than a scholar who knows the laws of God and His teachings but is void of knowledge (of manners and etiquette.)[3] . . .

There is one people in the world alone who are not sufficiently concerned with human knowledge and who have neglected the public instruction of their youth in the laws of etiquette, the sciences and the arts. We, the children of Israel, who are dispersed throughout all of Europe and who live in most of its states, have turned our backs on these studies. Those among us who dwell in Germany and Poland have been especially negligent in this regard. Many among them are men of intelligence and great understanding, and many are also men of faith and piety, but from childhood their exclusive preoccupation has been God's laws and teachings. They have not heard of or studied human knowledge. They are ignorant even of the grammar of the holy tongue, and they do not discern the beauty of its diction, the rules of its syntax and the purity of its style—which are wells from which spring wisdom and moral instruction. It goes without saying that they lack proper knowledge of the language of the peoples among whom they live. Many of them do not even know how to read or write the native language. Knowledge of the structure of the earth and the events of history are hidden from them, as are matters of civility, the sciences and the arts. They do not know or understand, for from the start nothing of all this was told to them, neither

by their fathers nor by their teachers, who themselves were ignorant of these subjects. Even the fundamental principles of their faith were not taught systematically, so that all the youth might become conversant with them in an orderly fashion. Similarly, our youth were not taught ethics and psychology. Only some of the more outstanding students of God's Torah as they grew older perceived deficiency in matters of human knowledge, and accordingly endeavoured to correct the fault committed by their teachers by gleaning knowledge either from books or from conversation, "here a little, there a little," but, alas, unsystematically and ineffectively. Their knowledge is like a lightweight coat on a cold day. Indeed, a clear knowledge in these subjects is not found except among individuals whose hearts and spirits moved them to listen to wisdom and pay heed to reason. They learned languages and read books with understanding and thus became like a fountain which replenishes and augments itself. They acquired this knowledge unassisted by their fathers and their superiors. They were driven solely by their love of truth. Such superior men, however, are few. . . .

Let it be understood, however, that we ourselves are not responsible for this state of affairs. We should not pour out our anger upon ourselves or direct our complaints against ourselves. Rather, it is the nations who have hosted us for more than a thousand years who are to blame for our misfortune, for they have terribly wronged us by the command of their kings and ministers. Inspired by many evil motives they have risen against us to destroy us and to humble us to the dust, for which purpose they subjected us to irrational decrees. They thereby acted contrary to human knowledge, for they thrust our bodies to the dust and depressed the spirit within us.

The hearts of our community subsequently have grown dark. Seeing that we are treated with a heavy hand and that in the eyes of our oppressors we are beneath the rank of man, we have lost the inclination to pursue the study of human knowledge. When our brethren saw that they had no share in all the good that God had provided for all his creatures from one end of the world to the other, they despised all worldly things. In their bitterness they disregarded and entirely neglected the laws and sciences concerning the administration of world affairs: knowledge of the movement of celestial bodies, of the cultivation of the earth, of the crossing of the seas, of the construction of cities and fortifications, of the governance of kings. For they said: "What have we to do with all this? The inhabitants of the land are our enemies, to our counsel they will not listen, to our valor they pay no heed; moreover, we do not possess fields and vineyards. Let us abandon these studies and occupy ourselves with trade and commerce to enable ourselves to live and feed our children, for only this have they left us. And even of this they have left us only in small measure and in a reduced way. Our Father in Heaven shall be our support and we will engage chiefly in those things which bring eternal life—the laws and teachings of God which we were commanded to obey and upon which God made a covenant with our fathers." The few superior individuals among them ceased to teach the people human knowledge for they knew that even the sweetest wisdom is bitter to the embittered soul. Were they to teach them the duty of loving all men, the crown of etiquette, the people would not heed them, since they live among peoples who daily conspire to do evil against them, who slander them in a mendacious and cruel fashion and who in return for their love give forth hate. Were they to teach linguistics so that they may marshal their words according to the rules of speech, to be pleasing to both kings and common men, the people would refuse to listen to them. For their enemies despise the logic of their words and cover them with shame. Were they to teach the people the arts and sciences they would abhor these, because they receive no advantage from them. They cannot work in field or vineyard, or in the construction of towers, fortresses and cities. These nations have not permitted them to work in any practical crafts. Once all these studies and disciplines were forgotten by our community with the passage of time, we have been unable to acquire them again even in those kingdoms ruled by generous kings, who lifted the iron yoke from upon our necks, for we had become alienated from these matters. We did not have books in the Hebrew language and we were not conversant in the language of the Gentiles, for in the times of great troubles...we had become estranged from the Gentiles and their languages. Thus we did not learn to read their books, and, it goes without saying, we did not learn to speak their language accurately. When, out of our great distress, we went from nation to nation and from kingdom to kingdom, we learned a bit of the language of one people and a bit of the language of another so that our speech became a jumble.

It is thus a source of thorough amazement how in spite of all the evil that has befallen us we have remained a people and how, notwithstanding the flow of mighty waters, we have nevertheless retained our humanity. It is the power of the divine Torah that is responsible for this. Despite our lack of all the above mentioned knowledge, the Torah stood by us and assured us of a human heart, protecting us thereby from the trait of cruelty and from truly evil actions, far be these sins from us! From the days of yore until now we were never in a rebellious association or in a wicked band who devises evil against men. In every generation we were faithful to the kings ruling over us and to the inhabitants of the land, and we besought God for the well-being of the monarchy of the land. If we found ourselves in the humblest of stations we consoled ourselves with the thought of our innocence and we said: "These are prejudices in the hearts of the people and their rulers, who are acting in the tradition of their fathers," and we hoped that God would change their hearts toward us for good, and have us find mercy in their eyes.

So matters developed generation after generation, and such remains the state of affairs today. To be sure, generous kings reigned in several kingdoms, and in this generation also there are kings of Europe who are wise, philanthropic and kind, treating us with kindness and mercy, may God remember them for good. Nevertheless, many of the iron laws that their cruel predecessors have decreed against us, laws which were intended to remove us from the society of men and which prevented us from performing those acts by means of which man aids his fellow man,...have not been abrogated. Rather, they have taken root in the hearts of the peoples and their leaders, and have become venerable to them with the passage of time. Therefore it is difficult for mercy to counteract them and for reason to become strong enough to argue with them and to overcome this perversion. Even if for one moment the heart sees that these are rash laws, habit will quietly extinguish the light of reason. No one has compassion for the many righteous and unfortunate souls who seek only peace and whose sole fault is that they were born Jewish and maintain the faith they had nursed from their mother's breast. We believe in one God who is the same God for all men; the same for our brothers, the men of Europe, and for our brothers, the men of Africa and Asia. Our Torah teaches the love of mankind and the way of life and peace which is the foundation and cornerstone of the religion of Europe and the religion of the Arabs. Nevertheless we were treated unkindly, and thus we despaired, imagining that for the rest of the Exile we would be oppressed.

However, it was not as man envisioned, for to everything there is a season, and a time for every purpose under the heaven. From the time the Creator, blessed be He, established heaven and earth, He ordered in His superior wisdom the appointed times of the universe, times of good and times of evil, for He proclaims the generations from the beginning and sees to the end of all existence. From generation to generation, knowledge that was hidden was revealed by wise men in the arts, sciences and crafts, such as the discovery of America, the inventions of printing, gunpowder, spectacles and so forth. In similar fashion, the Creator ordered every generation and its leaders from the beginning, raising kings to their thrones to be instruments of His craft and to work His decrees and designs. For behold, the prophet Isaiah lived about three hundred years before the destruction of Babylon, yet prophesied Israel's conqueror and named him, as he said. "Thus says the Lord to his anointed, to Cyrus" (Is. 45:1); so, too, the man of God Jeroboam said two hundred years before the event: "Behold a child shall be born in the House of David, Josiah by name" (1 Kings 13:2). King Solomon enumerated times of good and evil that encompass all the inhabitants of the earth. Among these, he observed, there is "a time to love and a time to hate" (Eccles. 3:9). And so now, perhaps the time has come to remove hatred from the hearts of men, an unfounded hatred based on a quarrel which is not theirs and whose source lies in differences of faith and worship. O Generation! You have seen that God is good. He has raised up a great man, a saviour to mankind, the exalted emperor, His Majesty Joseph II. Aside from the tidings of his wisdom, his counsel and his military might, imperial statements that have recently issued from him have brought us tidings of even more heroic deeds. These statements—words of peace and truth to all his subjects—have been tried in the crucible of reason and are founded on the love of mankind. Moreover, in his many good works he has not forgotten a poor

people, long abused, the Jews. He gave us many good and consoling commands, as a father does to his son, a teacher to his pupils and a [benign] ruler to his people. He has unshackled the disabling bonds by permitting the Jews to engage in all forms of cultivation of the land, to work in all crafts and to trade in all merchandise. In his interest he has also observed that few among us speak the German language accurately…and as a result cannot read German books, neither history books nor books on etiquette, science and the arts. Neither can we speak in a clear fashion with the inhabitants of the land and their ministers. Taking this into consideration he has commanded us upon a righteous path. He has instructed the Jews to establish schools in which to teach their children to read and write the German language. He has also instructed them to write edifying books according to the Torah, to teach the children understanding and the rules of behavior in society. Arithmetic, geometry, astronomy, history and geography, however, are to be studied from existing books used by the children of the kingdom, for these sciences do not impinge upon faith, and the ideas of all men concerning these subjects are identical. Knowledge of these subjects can only strengthen the House of Israel and mend the breaches made by the preceding rulers.…And thus, the children of Israel will also be men who accomplish worthy things, assisting the king's country in their actions, labor and wisdom.

NOTES

1. Naphtali Herz Wessely (1725–1805) was a poet, linguist, biblical exegete, pioneer of the revival of biblical Hebrew, and advocate of the Enlightenment among his fellow Jews. In this controversial work Wessely sought to marshal Jewry's support of the Edict of Tolerance issued by Emperor Joseph II of Austria in 1782 (chapter 1, document 13).

2. Injunctions traditionally given to Noah and therefore binding upon Jew and Gentile alike. According to the Talmud there were seven such laws derived from the early chapters of Genesis.

3. This parenthetical reference to manners and etiquette is Wessely's interpolations. The text of the Midrash speaks of the sacrificial procedures delineated in Leviticus as elaborated by the Talmudic sages.

9. A SERMON CONTRA WESSELY (1782)

DAVID (TEVELE) BEN NATHAN OF LISSA[1]

We speak of an act by a sycophant, an evil man, a man poor in understanding, the most mediocre of mediocre of men. This man, Herz Wessely of Berlin, has addressed an epistle to those of the House of Israel who dwell in the land of His Majesty the Emperor.[2] This epistle, called "Words of Peace and Truth," makes one's heart heavy. It consists of eight chapters of bootlicking. And, deeming himself unique in his generation, he offers his rash advice to wise, understanding, perfect and flawless men. The gist of his [insolent] remarks is that since His Majesty the Emperor commanded the Israelites to establish schools to teach their youths the German language and to educate them to do mighty deeds in all areas of knowledge, that he, this worthless man, will extend counsel to fulfill His Majesty the Emperor's wishes. I am thoroughly amazed and my heart skips many beats when I contemplate the audacity of this evil man. Aside from the fundamentals of the Hebrew language and a simple rudimentary knowledge of Scripture and the commentaries, this man is bereft of the sublime wisdom of Torah. He manifestly lacks an understanding of the profundities of the Talmud, the early commentaries and the Oral Torah—the testament of God, His laws and statutes. These sources of wisdom are obviously beyond the grasp of this fool. How dare he say, "I shall extend counsel to men of wisdom, understanding and knowledge"? How can one who does not possess any of the foundations of knowledge presume to teach the correct manner of study, proper conduct and the way of God to this people of God? Can one who is weak claim he is strong? Can a blind man say, "Hearken to me and I will teach you to read"? Or can a poor and ill man, whose house is empty of bread, say, "Come eat my bread"?

Beware! This man, Wessely, is an impious man. Beware, do not draw near to him! God, the Lord of Hosts, knows that for the sake of the glory of your Holy Torah I have come this day to hew down he who tramples upon the heads of your Holy People, and to make known to You the evil machinations of this man. In my perusal of his small book I have noted that the spirit of sin animates it. This book seeks to lead the masses astray and to mislead children just out of the womb so that they will not know the paths of Torah and piety. Wessely's counsel is that of a renegade. So that the people should heed him, this imposter associates his sacrilegious ideas with the great and majestic thoughts of His Majesty the Emperor.

What the Emperor actually commanded and what never occurred to Wessely I shall now explain: in His infinite mercy the Lord, the God of Israel, has rendered our people pleasing to His Majesty the Emperor, who now urges each of us to cross the threshold of science and knowledge, [promising] us a place among the royal servants and ministers. The Emperor has commanded all his subjects the following: Every child shall be taught to speak and write the German language so that he will know the language of the land. Everyone shall [also] remain true to the rites and principles of his faith; no part of his faith shall be made alien to him. No Jew will be prevented from fulfilling the fundamentals of our faith, the Written and Oral Torah. (One Torah was spoken by God, although we heard two— may the Lord be blessed that He gave us both of them!).... His Majesty the Emperor wishes to teach our children an hour or two a day to speak and read the German language. [But he also wishes] to educate all who spring from the loins of Jacob in

---

Source: Hebrew manuscript published by Louis Lewin, "Aus dem juedischem Kulturkampfe," *Jahrbuch der juedisch-Literarischen Gesellschaft* 12 (1918), pp. 182–94. Trans. by S. Fischer and P. Mendes-Flohr.

the manner of their traditions, for what is primary remains primary and what is secondary remains secondary. How great are his [the Emperor's] works and how precious is his kindness, for indeed all parents wish to provide their children with an education in every type of wisdom, science and craft.... But this imposter, Wessely, perverts and distorts the counsel of His Majesty, the Emperor, claiming that he commanded that Jewish children shall no longer attend schools [which teach a traditional Jewish curriculum].... This is a prevarication. Far be it from any intelligent man to think this of the righteous and sincere lover of mankind and leader of nations, his most pious Majesty the Emperor. In the abundance of his righteousness he actually wishes to strengthen the fortress of religion, each man according to his faith.

Our children shall study the sciences as an adornment; however, the foundations of their education will be in accordance with the command of our ancient sages of the Talmud. Our children shall be taught Torah, ethics, Mishnah and Talmud. Wessely, a foolish and wicked man of coarse spirit, is the one who lacks civility. A carcass is better than he! Whom does he seek to defame and abuse? He has interpreted the thoughts of His Mighty and wise Majesty, the Emperor in the light of his own schemes. Moreover, he has distorted the teachings of our holy sages.... Can his behavior be construed as proper etiquette or any other virtue?...

Wessely is a cunning man. He gives the impression that he is well versed [in the teachings of Judaism] and thus he is treated with the honor that befits a scholar. He has falsified the words of the Holy Torah. In chapter one [of his book] he glibly writes: "...he who lacks 'human knowledge,' even though he has learned God's laws and teachings and acts according to them, he does not please God, because he is certain to sin in the ways of man." May God punish this ever so glib tongue—a tongue that renders its master as disgusting as a creeping reptile.... Who of the pious students of God's laws—assuming that he is an intelligent, honest and understanding student of the Torah—is not a tribute to humanity, even if he has not learned etiquette and languages? Can such a man be lacking in "human knowledge"? The moral instruction of Scripture and the words of the holy sages of the Talmud teach [one] how to behave and converse [with his fellow men]. Indeed, does not the

student of Torah study the words of Maimonides in the *Book of Knowledge*[3] and the codes of other masters which teach the path of righteous conduct, the path which is a holy path? Does not the student of Torah also study *Duties of the Heart*[4] and other books of ethical teaching? The roots of these works extend from the Prophets and the talmudic sages. [The ethical relevance of traditional Jewish studies is especially manifest if one considers] the divine statutes such as the prohibitions against theft, financial manipulations and the like. Even if one knows but a fraction of these laws one is awed by the depth of their ethical wisdom. How great are thy works O Lord, Your statutes are of great depth....

Could it be that Wessely is directing his calumny against those who are immersed in spiritual meditation, and who have set themselves apart from the vanities of the world? If he has raised his hand against these individuals who have consecrated their lives to the service of God, let his hand wither! He has chosen to blaspheme God and those whom He has hallowed merely because they err in the customs of men [and do not] adorn themselves and paint their eyes. And the fool has said that God does not derive any pleasure from these men. You, Wessely, are a despicable man. Shame on you! May you be mocked by man! Woe to him who does not reprove you! Wessely has shorn his beard and therefore all who have beards and sidecurls are deemed by him to lack "human knowledge" and to deviate from the ways of humanity. This prattler thoroughly disgusts me.... It is a source of great consolation to learn from a reliable report that in Vilna, the great city of God,[5] they have burned Wessely's book in the streets. Before doing so they hung his book from an iron chain in the courtyard of the synagogue. Even though the Emperor's name and praises are mentioned numerous times therein, justice, in my opinion, was served in Vilna.

NOTES

1. David ben Nathan (d. 1792) was Rabbi of Lissa (Polish Leszno), center of rabbinic learning in Western Poland, from 1774 to 1792. In 1774, he gave his approbation to Wessely's *Yein levanon*, a commentary on the Mishnaic tractate *Avot*. Later when he perceived Wessely's program of Enlightenment to be a threat to the integrity of traditional Judaism, he became his bitter opponent.

2. Joseph II, emperor of Austria.

3. *Sefer hamada*, the first part of Maimonides' (1135–1204) *Mishneh Torah*, which is devoted, among other matters, to ethics.
4. *Hovot halevavot* (Duties of the Heart) by Bahya ben Joseph ibn Pakuda, an eleventh-century Spanish moral

philosopher. This work discusses the duties of Jews to cultivate their inner spiritual and ethical life.

5. Because of its preeminence in rabbinical study, Vilna was reverently called by East European Jewry the Jerusalem of Lithuania.

10. SERMON ON WESSELY AND THE EDICT OF TOLERANCE (1782)

EZEKIEL LANDAU[1]

"We were slaves to Pharaoh in Egypt."

A careful reading might suggest that the Passover Haggadah should have said only "We were slaves in Egypt," for what difference did it make whether we were slaves to Pharaoh or to someone else? The essence of the miracle was that we emerged from slavery to freedom. Furthermore, all this commotion in celebrating the holiday of Passover at the present time may seem strange. Now, too, we are in exile, outside our land. Why then such great joy at the Exodus from Egypt?[2]

However, the one to whom you are enslaved does indeed make a difference. We about whom Ezra said, *For bondsmen are we, though even in our bondage God has not forsaken us, but has disposed the king of Persia favorably toward us, to furnish us with sustenance* (Ezra 9:9). The tax paid to such a king is fair. He is the lord of the land, and it is fitting and proper that all who enjoy protection should pay a tax. The gracious king does not make the burden of taxes too heavy. What he takes is collected legally and fairly for our own welfare. When a person leases out a room in a house, the rent he demands is not intended to cause grief to the tenant; it is a proper return for the room. In fact,

if the landlord sees the tenant prospering in his quarters, he is happy.[3]

Pharaoh, by contrast, was by nature an evil king, a cruel man filled with hate for those who found refuge in his realm. His intention in subjugating the children of Israel was not to improve his own lot but rather to degrade the Israelites, to cause them sorrow, and to embitter their lives. This is what the Bible says: the Egyptians *embittered their lives ... with all the work that they ruthlessly imposed upon them* (Exodus 1:14): "Why were the slave girls stricken? Because they made Israel subservient."

... That bitter Egyptian exile was unlike the experience in Persia. Although we were in exile there, we were considered important and respected. Cyrus[4] and Darius[5] were compassionate and merciful toward us. This is also the case in our own time, when our lord His Majesty the emperor has decided to help us and to raise us from our degradation.[6] May God reward him for his good deed and raise his glory ever higher! How abundant is his gracious beneficence!

We Jews should not for this reason become insolent and begin to behave with haughtiness and arrogance. We should act respectfully toward the inhabitants

---

Source: Ezekiel Landau, "Sermon for the Sabbath Preceding Passover, 1782, Prague" (in Hebrew), in Marc Saperstein, ed. and trans., *Jewish Preaching*, 1200–1800: *An Anthology* (New Haven: Yale University Press, 1989), pp. 361–73. Notes 2–4 and 6–21 are adapted from Saperstein's commentary. Reprinted by permission of Yale University Press.

of this kingdom. It is their own land, while we are only guests. A sense of submissiveness is good when it comes from within.[7] It is enough that His Majesty the emperor has extended his protection over us, so that no one will use force to harm or degrade us. That is what Ezra said: "We *consider ourselves* to be bondsmen; even though God has not forsaken us in our bondage and has disposed the king of Persia favorably toward us,"[8] nevertheless, we consider ourselves to be bondsmen.

This is what may have been intended by the author of the [Passover] Haggadah in the passage beginning, "This is like the bread of affliction." That passage ends, "Now we are here, next year may we be in the land of Israel. Now we are slaves, next year may we be free."...

The author of the Haggadah was warning us not to become insolent and arrogant. Even if there should be a gracious and compassionate king who abundantly helps us, we should inwardly know that we are in a land not our own, and that we should remain submissive to the peoples of that land....

Therefore he said: "Even if you know that the year of redemption is definitely near, even if you are certain that this will be your last year here and that in the future years you will be in the land of Israel, still you should not become arrogant, for now you are still slaves, and you should continue to behave submissively.[9] Only next year, when you are in the land of Israel, our own ancestral estate, will you be truly free."

This is therefore followed by a question: since it is that we are still slaves, why is this night of Egyptian exile different from all other nights of exile under other kingdoms? Why all this commotion on the night when we went from Egypt, if we are still slaves? The answer is that there is a great difference, for then in Egypt we were slaves to Pharaoh, a cruel king, a king who made us suffer without benefit of himself, solely in order to humiliate us. But now there is a gracious and compassionate king. Even though we are slaves, he has removed from us the stigma of bondage, removed all externally recognizable signs of servitude. If we inwardly take it upon ourselves to be submissive, this is as it should be.

Therefore, my brothers and friends, be careful to avoid an arrogant disposition. If a Jew hears himself being insulted, he should remain silent, for *starting a quarrel is like opening a sluice* (Prov. 17:14). Our father Abraham was considered extremely important by

both God and men, yet he prostrated himself before the people of the land, the children of Heth, and spoke submissively: *I am a resident alien among you* (Gen. 23:4).

Three times each day we ask in prayer, "May my soul be like dust to all." How then can we possibly be arrogant? But because of our many sins, our prayer has become mere empty words, unaccompanied by a contrite and humble heart. And then we ask, "Open my heart to Your Torah, and let my soul pursue Your commandments," while there is no true desire for Torah or commandments.

In my opinion, these two requests are linked together because at times there is some good in feeling pride. An example is the envy leading to emulation of the great leaders of Israel who excel in Torah, learning and in good deeds. Although this is not ultimately a worthy motive—for the ultimate motive must be only to act purely out of love, leading to communion with God—nevertheless, such communion is not achieved at the beginning. This is why the rabbis said, "One should always engage in Torah and commandments, even for impure reasons, for what begins with impure motivation may end with pure motivation."[10] In any case, there is some need for envy and pride, for it may lead to the service of God.

But all this applies only to the religious realm. Envy of worldly things, such as the wealth of a rich man, or arrogance because of them, is reprehensible. Nothing good results from it....

But now, because of our many sins, I have seen everything overturned. How can one envy the study of Torah, when an evil man[11] has arisen from our own people and brazenly asserted that the Torah is not all important, that an animal carcass is worth more than talmudic scholars, that etiquette is more vital than the Torah?[12] This man is certainly blind to his own faults. He is worse than an animal carcass, and in the end his corpse will lie like dung upon the field!

Now as to the substance of the matter—the value of etiquette and of grammatical knowledge of the languages spoken by our neighbors—I too esteem these things. The government has done a great favor in deciding to teach our children to speak [German] correctly. Even in the Bible we were criticized for not knowing how to speak the various languages of one's neighbors.[13] Do not think that you know how to speak the German language. No one can be said to know a language unless he can speak it grammatically....

Therefore, His Majesty the emperor has done us a great favor in commanding us to learn the language grammatically so that we can speak it properly, as I stated in a sermon last winter. Even in the time of the last prophets, the king commanded that Daniel, Hananiah, Mishael and Azariah be taught the literature and language of the Chaldeans, and they distinguished themselves both in this area and in their knowledge of Torah and their performance of good deeds.

Those who fear the Lord have eyes to see, and they will be able to master both, making Torah the basis, yet also learning to speak correctly and behave according to the patterns that guide a person on the right path.[14] "Torah unaccompanied by labor will eventually come to naught," but most of our labor is in the area of trade and commerce, which requires the ability to write and to speak the language of the country. Likewise, the members of the Sanhedrin, the pillars of the Torah faith, were required to understand the languages of other peoples.[15]

Do not mix with those who are "unstable"— those who follow arbitrary whims, who cogitate and ponder with their confused intellects, darkening the religion of the Torah, whether they be Jews or from any other people, those who deny individual providence over the affairs of men, who deny the revelation of the Torah and supernatural miracles, who say that religion was not given by the Creator. Now because of our many sins, various strange sects have multiplied among our people, each different from the other—except in their common proclivity to undermine the perfect faith. It was about such sects that Solomon warned: *Do not mix with the unstable, for disaster comes from them suddenly, the doom of them both who can foreknow?* (Prov. 24:21–22). He was alluding to those sects that are alike in their capacity for evil.

But we, God's people, are obliged to sacrifice our lives for our sacred Torah, both the written Torah and the oral one. Whatever we are admonished in the Talmud must be equivalent in our minds to what is written in the Ten Commandments. What do we care if these sects mock us? We shall walk in the name of the Lord, in the path trodden by Alfasi[16] and Maimonides[17] and Rabbenu Asher[18] and the Tosafists,[19] who found bright light as they walked in the path of the Talmud, who had no interest in esoteric doctrines, yet were deemed worthy of eternal life. The foundation of all is faith!...

Now in our times there are many Jews who reject the words of the sages and set out intentionally to keep their children from the oral Torah. I warn you, children: do not consent to hear of such a thing from anyone.

I do not suspect that the *Normallehrer*[20] would do such an evil thing and utter such falsehoods, God forbid! This would be against the desire of the exalted government, which established the position solely for the purpose of teaching children German, writing, mathematics, ethical behavior and etiquette, and not to speak calumnies against our religion. If in any town or city such a teacher should be found transgressing in this matter and acting with duplicity, pay him no heed whatsoever.

Hear me, my fine children: take what is good from them, but if you should discover in them something not good, do not follow in their path. *Shelach bekhor*, "send away the firstborn," namely, the evil impulse, which is the firstborn, present in each person in varying degrees from birth, while the good impulse arrives only at the age of bar mitzvah. Send away the firstborn, and bring near that impoverished child, the impulse toward good.[21]

NOTES

1. Ezekiel Landau (1713–1793) was an outstanding halakhic authority and a highly revered rabbi. In 1754 he was named chief rabbi of Prague, one of the most prestigious positions in European Jewry. By virtue of this appointment he was recognized by the Austrian crown to be the leader of the Jewish community of Bohemia. Rabbi Landau took an active part in contemporary Jewish affairs, regarding it as his duty to secure the integrity of traditional Judaism. He thus opposed the remnants of Sabbateanism and Frankism, heresies that he attributed to the deleterious affects of Kabbalah; he likewise vigorously objected to Hasidism, a movement that began to crystallize in his day and that drew great inspiration from the Kabbalah. He was not opposed in principle to *haskalah* to the extent that it promoted good relations with non-Jews and strengthened patriotic feelings for the country in which one resided. Nor did he object to the introduction of a general education for Jews. He did, however, take offense at the often aggressively antirabbinic tendency of the *maskilim*, and the tendency to assign supreme moral and even religious significance to a general

education (see this chapter, document 8) elicited Rabbi Landau's ire. In this sermon, given on the Sabbath preceding Passover, 1782, and which proceeds from an exegetical problem in the Passover Haggadah—which in his judgment calls upon Israel to differentiate between various degrees of enslavement in the Exile—Rabbi Landau obliquely but pointedly castigates Wessely. It is also manifest that he regarded the Edict of Tolerance to be what Jewish tradition decries as a *gezerah*, a disastrous decree. On the other hand, it is also palpable that he was keen not to offend the emperor and undermine the emergence of a more tolerant attitude toward the Jews.

2. The sermon addresses two questions arising from the Passover Haggadah: (a) an apparently superfluous word and (b) the relevance of Passover observance in exile.

3. The rabbinic tradition has long upheld the right of the authorities of the respective countries of the diaspora to exact taxes from the Jews.

4. Cyrus II (d. 529 B.C.E.) was king of Persia. In the course of his battles, he conquered Babylonia and its empire. In consonance with his enlightened policies, in 538 B.C.E. he granted the Jewish exiles permission to return to Judea and rebuild the Temple (Ezra 1:1–44; Chron. 36:22–73). Cyrus was, accordingly, hailed as a divine agent (cf. Isaiah 44:28; 45:1).

5. Darius I inherited the throne from Cyrus I. Reigning from 522–486 B.C.E., he removed all remaining obstacles to the rebuilding of the Temple (cf. Ezra 6:12).

6. This is a reference to the Austrian emperor Joseph II and the Edict of Tolerance (see chapter 1, document 13.

7. Cf. Babylonian Talmud, Berakhot, 7a. "Although this submissiveness should not be imposed upon the Jews by others, Landau maintains that it must be retained despite the new spirit of tolerance." Saperstein, *Jewish Preaching*, p. 302f., n. 4.

8. Babylonian Talmud, tractate Pesahim, 50b.

9. The emphasis on the obligation of Jewish submissiveness, even if messianic redemption is deemed imminent, is to be viewed in light of one of the arguments against Emancipation, namely, that Jewish loyalty to the countries of their residence was tenuous because of messianic longing to be redeemed from exile, cf. chapter 1, document 12.

10. Babylonian Talmud, tractate Pesahim, 50c.

11. The reference was patently to Naphtali Herz Wessely (see note 1 in this selection and document 8 in this chapter).

12. In characterizing the rabbinic scholar bereft of worldly knowledge and social etiquette, Wessely had cited a famous rabbinic midrash, "As for a scholar who lacks sense (*deah*), a carcass is better than he" (Lev. Rabbah 1:15). See this chapter, document 8, note 3.

13. Landau cites Nehemia's admonishment of his fellow Jews for not knowing how to speak the languages of their neighbors (cf. Neh. 13:24). Landau also marshals Maimonides in support of the need to know well the foreign languages one speaks.

14. *Mishnah avot* ("Chapters of the Fathers"), 2:22.

15. Babylonian Talmud, tractate Sanhedrin, 17a.

16. Isaac ben Joseph Alfasi (1013–1103) was a talmudic scholar who lived and taught in Fez, North Africa. His compendium of the legal discussion of the Babylonian Talmud, *Sefer halakhot* [Book of Legal Decisions) was superseded only by Maimonides, *Mishneh Torah*, known in English as the Code of Law.

17. Maimonides (Moses ben Maimon, also known by the acronym Rambam, 1135–1204), is the most celebrated philosopher and halakhic scholar of medieval Jewry.

18. Asher ben Yehiel (1250–1327 popularly known as the Rosh) was regarded as the spiritual leader of German Jewry; he later emigrated to Spain, where he was soon recognized as the supreme rabbinic authority. He vigorously opposed the tendency of some Spanish rabbis to place secular studies above traditional religious learning.

19. Tosafists were French and German rabbinic scholars of the twelfth and thirteenth centuries who wrote important critical and explanatory notes to the Talmud. (*Tosafist* is derived from the Hebrew term for addenda.)

20. *Normallehrer* were the teachers for the standard, secular education to be introduced in the schools established in accordance with the Edict of Tolerance.

21. Landau is alluding to a midrash in *Avot derabbi Natan*, recension A, 16.

11. THE STREAM OF BESOR (APRIL 1783)

HAMEASEF[1]

This prospectus brings good tidings and greetings to every enlightened member of the congregation of Yeshurun [Israel] who seeks the truth and loves natural science. May the Lord be gracious unto him, now and forevermore, Amen.

The truly wise man, who yearns to know the nature and purpose of every thing from all its aspects, will divide his examination into five principal questions: What? Who? For whom? Why? How?

And now, gentle reader! When you see that a new journal is being published abroad, one that has never existed before, you will undoubtedly be eager to know its nature and curious to ask more about it; What is this new thing? Is it about the Law [halakhah], or is it a collection of tales? Does it deal with matters of worldly knowledge [hokhmah],[2] with civility and etiquette and such matters? In order to explain our objectives in such a way that you will have no further doubts, we will answer our five principal questions one by one.

In answer to the question: What?

The article you have before you is an introduction and a preface to a journal which will make its first appearance in a few days, God willing, and will thereafter appear monthly. This journal will be called *Hameasef* because it will gather a variety of different articles from all branches of natural science and ethics, articles which will be instructive to the soul that yearns for wisdom. It will have five sections:

In this section we will have poems in the Holy Tongue by select poets whose work has never before appeared in print and who, with God's help, will continue to write. These poems will be about worldly knowledge, ethics, beauty, friendship, and the blessings of love. Poems of passion and lust, however, are an abomination and will not be accepted. Also alien and unacceptable to us are the poems of a few new poets who chose the way of the Gentiles and write hymns to idols and appeal to pagan gods. This will be explained further in the letter of the eloquent Rabbi Hirsch Weisel,[3] may his light shine!

Essays and disquisitions. This section will separate into four streams.

At the source will be the words of men who are learned in languages in general and in the wisdom and character of the Hebrew language in particular. This section will illuminate subjects in Hebrew grammar, clarify problems of phraseology and rhetoric, chart a path in Hebrew poetry, and teach the reader to recognize the meaning of the individual root words.

The tributaries of this section will divide into interpretations of difficult passages in the Scripture. The opinions of ancient commentators will be examined, and where these are insufficient different interpretations will be offered. The understanding and honest reader must judge and decide whether the simple, true solution has been found. And in order to teach students to pay attention to the purpose of an article, and to demonstrate the way in which articles are analyzed and composed...we have chosen the method of question and answer as will be seen below in the answers to the questions. For whom?, and Why?

The springs of this section will pour forth short, clear, pleasant, and elegant studies, either from ancient wise men or from wise men of our generation, on those subjects of natural science and ethics that seem appropriate for presentation to enlightened Jews. There will also be translations from the languages of the Gentiles.

The streams of this section will flow into the sea of the Talmud in order to remove obstacles which have deterred many teachers of our people who are unacquainted with the Talmud and its problems and have never applied themselves to the study of the sources

---

Source: "Nahal Besor" [Prospectus of *Hameasef*, April 13, 1783], *Hameasef* 1 (1784), pp. 1–4, 11–14. Trans. by L. Sachs.

of wisdom, but rather stumble in the Talmud like the blind groping in the dark. Since they are ignorant of the source of halakhah, these teachers have no profound understanding of the ideas of our sages of blessed memory. Moreover, in their teaching to their students they have yet to discuss this source.

And through the tributaries of this section will flow the rest of the things necessary to moral education. Nor will we avoid discussing physical education, for many of our artisans are sedentary and unaware of the importance of physical education. They do not know that the preservation of the body and its powers is an excellent way of preserving the soul and its powers.

Biographies of the great men of Israel. This will include biographies of rabbis, geniuses of the land, those who are great and famous for their worldly knowledge, honored scholars and wealthy men of the people who support the House of Israel and who present themselves before kings to speak for the good of their people. We shall describe the place and time of their births, the events of their lives, and the good that they have done for their fellowmen. And an enlightened man will understand of what great benefit this will be to enlightened youths, quite apart from the pleasure the soul takes in hearing about the events which occurred to famous men in different times and various circumstances.

News. Accounts of the events occurring among us in these days, the days of the first fruits of natural science and love in all the kingdoms of Europe. And the reader who is unable to read the language of the Gentiles will yet know the state of God's people in his times and the things which occur among them. The reader will hear in what way God will move the heart of kings for the good of the people. All these matters will be included in the journal.

Announcement of new books, which will be published for our edification and benefit, both in the Holy Tongue and in the languages of other peoples. Occasionally there will be critical reviews of these books, discussing their virtues and faults and whether or not they are beneficial. Each matter will be treated in its proper place, God willing, as regards its relevance for our actions.

And now, dear reader, you will certainly be curious to know who is putting out this journal and bringing these matters to print. Is it a famous man, or not? Is it one man or many? Is he young or old?

Be assured that this journal is not the work of one man or even of two, but rather of a community of enlightened men who have spent their lives in diligent study of the Torah and the sources of worldly knowledge. These include masters of the Talmud who know how to discuss the profundities of halakhah in a clear and truthful manner, and wise men learned in foreign languages. Each one of them has spent long periods investigating and studying the characteristics of our Holy Tongue as it is used in the Holy Scriptures and in the writings of ancient authors. Each of these has written a book about the interpretations of Scripture, about its grammar, the language, rhetoric and poetry, and about the clarity of its stories and the gracefulness of its syntax and diction. These scholars have joined forces to master the Torah and worldly knowledge, as those of blessed memory said in the verses: "Listen and give ear Israel; today you have become a nation."[4] They formed groups and studied the Torah, for it can be mastered only in a group. And each man will bring the findings of his study to the daily meetings of the group, in order that the group may pursue its work in an orderly fashion.

Answer to the question: How?

And now, enlightened reader! In order to answer the question How?, we will disclose to you the rules and conditions which were established in our councils.

The Society of the Friends of the Hebrew Language was founded on Sunday the seventh of the Hebrew month of Teveth, in the presence of all its members, and this was the gist of their decision:

Four men, whose signatures appear below, were chosen as chairmen and charged with a sacred duty; two will examine the articles to be printed, removing any impurity or blasphemy which may not be admitted to the House of God. The other two will oversee income and expenditures and the other needs of the group.

If a member of our congregation (may the Lord grace it with strength!) wishes to join us and become one of our group, he should announce his intention in writing to our confidential secretary, the enlightened Zanvil Friedlaender[5] and address the application to the Society of Friends of the Hebrew Language. At its next meeting he will be summoned to discuss the amount that will be fixed as his contribution to the Society's treasury.

Hameasef will appear monthly after the publication of this prospectus, "The Stream of Besor." For although matters of Torah and worldly knowledge are like a flowing spring—its waters may be drawn every day for they are unlimited and inexhaustible—nevertheless we cannot publish more than this, for the expenses are very heavy. This is particularly true in our area where there are no Hebrew type-setters and the printers raise their prices at whim. Also the font of type we have is not attractive and properly arranged, and we have been obliged to bring new type from Berlin in order to put out a work of finished craftsmanship. At the end of every three months a frontispiece on colored paper will appear with the names of all members of the Society and any noteworthy events which have occurred among them. Whenever it becomes possible to enlarge the scope of our publication we will do so....

And now, dear reader! be you artisan or metalworker among the Sons of Israel! We depend on you! We know that you have works of worldly knowledge and ethics which shine forth like the brightness of the firmament to those who walk in darkness. Each one of you should search in his desk and send us what he finds there, and thus crown our efforts with success. Please strengthen and encourage our hearts with your friendship and learning. We shall listen to what you say and take you to our bosom that you may never leave us. We will applaud you with thanks, and God, He who is honored by men of wisdom, will grant you immortality.

These are the words of your servants who stand at the watch for the Society of Friends of the Hebrew Language, Tuesday the thirteenth of Nisan, 5544, in Koenigsberg, Friesen.

Mendel Breslav,[6] Zanvil Friedlaender, Isaac Euchel,[7] and Simon Friedlaender.

NOTES

1. *Hameasef* [the collector or the gatherer], a Hebrew magazine published intermittently from 1784 to 1811 by the Society of Friends of the Hebrew Language (*Doreshei leshon ever*) founded in Koenigsberg, East Prussia, in 1783. In 1787 the Society was renamed Friends of Goodness and Virtue and the Friends of the Hebrew Language (*Shoharei hatlov vehaltushiyah vedorshei leshon ever*). An occasional German supplement was also included. This little magazine, containing on the average twenty pages, served as the forum of German-Jewish followers of the Enlightenment. Specifically, *Hameasef* sought to revive biblical Hebrew, esteemed for its linguistic refinement, as a means of elevating the aesthetic sensibility of the Jews and as a vehicle for introducing its readers to the value of the Enlightenment and to secular knowledge. Published in the midst of the debate concerning the Edict of Tolerance, *Hameasef* urged its readers to respond favorably to the edict, particularly the provision for the reform of the traditional Jewish educational system. Significantly, a portrait of Wessely graced the frontispiece of one of the first volumes of the magazine. *Hameasef* quickly became the symbol of the movement of Jewish Enlightenment (in Hebrew, *haskalah*), whose votaries became known as "the generation of Measfim."

   Stream of Besor is the name of a river in the Negev Desert in Israel, mentioned in 1 Sam. 30; it is here used as a pun on the Hebrew word *besorah* "good tidings."

2. Cf. "Wisdom [*hokhmah*] includes every occupation, study, activity, deportment that brings one closer to human perfection." "Preface," *Hameasef* (1787–1788), p. 5 (see document 12 of this chapter). See Wessely's concept of human knowledge (*Torat haadam*), document 8 of this chapter.

3. I.e., Naphtali Herz Wessely.

4. Deut. 27:5.

5. Zanvil (Samuel) Friedlaender and his brother Simon—brothers of David Friedlaender (cf. document 12 of this chapter) and sons of the wealthy Protected Jew Joachim Moses Friedlaender of Koenigsberg—gave *Hameasef* financial and administrative support.

6. Mendel Breslav (1786–1829), tutor in the Friedlaender family, Hebrew publicist, dramatist and co-editor of *Hameasef*.

7. Isaac Euchel (1756–1804), tutor in the Friedlaender family, Hebrew writer and biblical exegete. Co-editor of *Hameasef* until 1790; published therein the first biography of Moses Mendelssohn, *Toldot rabenu hehakham Moshe ben Menahem* [The history of our teacher, the sage Moses son of Menahem]

12. WE SHALL NOT BE DETERRED (1787)[1]

HAMEASEF

Sons of Israel who march to the forefront of worldly knowledge [hokhmah] without a guide to show you a path, incline your ear and listen to members of a Society who desire your well-being and take pleasure in your peace of mind. Examine the statements of your friends, draw your conclusions, and "Be Men!"[2]

We have seen many novices who start out on the path in search of worldly knowledge fall into the pit of doubt, not knowing where to turn. For they listened to the talk of some pretenders to wisdom [hokhmah], different factions which conspire together and make speeches. The first faction says: "Why should you bother about vacuous knowledge of men, and the nonsense of the toil of the flesh. Do you not know the sayings of the wisest man: 'He who increases in knowledge [daat] increases in suffering.'"[3] And the listener, in ignorance of the real intention of this wise king, and the real truth of his words, retreats backwards and stands before wisdom like a man stunned and terrified of jackals. This faction drives many away from "cleaving to the inheritance of wisdom"[4] and we shall call them the tormentors of the enlightened man.

The second faction is a group of men who have retained only a portion of what they learned as youths. They think that one can see at a glance all the branches of worldly wisdom and its secrets, for a few limited words from the books of worldly knowledge were sufficient for them. They say: "Now we know the path of wisdom [hokhmah] and its ways; it is sufficient. We will no longer seek to question and investigate through study, for such is an artifice. And in less time than a single day or a single night we can find anything that a scholar might find in long days and nights of study." When they are in doubt about matters of belief, the force of this worldly knowledge leads them to invent things which are untrue about God and His creation. And in the absence of any instruction or introduction to the natural sciences and worldly knowledge (for only the enlightened man who applies himself daily to the study of these subjects will know and understand them) they will mistake their random musings and fantasies for reality. Their sloth numbs their souls so that they no longer follow the path of disciplined inquiry and do not seek to correct distortions in their understanding. Every enlightened man who persists in learning and scholarship is contemptible in their eyes, for he is diligent about a matter they regard as trivial, and they consider him ignorant and simple-minded. These are the people we will call "the disparagers of the enlightened man."

The third group is composed of those for whom wisdom is alien and who have no knowledge or understanding of it. When they see a wise man who is preeminent among his people and honored by large numbers, the fire of jealousy is ignited in their breast. They become quarrelsome and contentious towards him because his nature is alien to them, and they will hate him and insult him, saying: "He is strange, and he must be forbidden to take part in the Holy, for he has looked to treacherous men, and cast away belief."[5] And they will talk about him and make false accusations against him, until they humiliate him and drive him from the community of the righteous. These are the despisers of the enlightened man.

The factions we have discussed have led many of our youths astray, youths of clean heart and innocent of the concept of wisdom [hokhmah] which will become alien and an anathema to them. In the course of time the number of enlightened men dwindled and that of the ignorant and the wanton and the vacuous increased. We became like a widower in

Source: "Preface," Hameasef 4 (1787–88), pp. 1–8. Trans. by S. Weinstein.

the eyes of our neighbors who said of us: "They have lost their wisdom and none of them knows to what extent."

These are the reasons which aroused us to speak in this introduction about man and his creations, about wisdom and its concerns, and about the value of worldly knowledge to man, in order that beginning students may find a straight path to the temple and sanctuary of wisdom, and turn their backs on its slanderers.

From the substance of this introduction the enlightened reader will see what principles a man must obey if he desires life and wishes to sit securely in the tent of wisdom without slander or abuse. We, the collectors of the articles and notes which appear in this journal, published by us with God's help for the past three years, have adhered to these principles. And although *Hameasef* has not reached perfection, or attained freedom from blemish—for we are young in years and most of the members of our group are busy at their labors to earn their daily bread, some engaged in teaching youth, others in trade—yet the enlightened reader is aware of the extent of *Hameasef's* activity to date. It has elucidated difficult passages in the Bible and in the works of our sages of blessed memory, and has published clear and eloquent articles in the Hebrew language. These will give young men thorough knowledge of the language. Questions about the customs of Israel were solved in consonance with the words of ancient sages. Biographies of the great men of our people were presented as an example for the enlightened man. And since the journal is published in its entirety every month, young men look forward to its appearance. In addition, we have shown the community of Israel that we have not labored so hard to issue the journal for the profit that is to be found in publishing (as unfortunately is apparently the case with most authors), for it will be sold at a fair price. From now on thirty pages a year will cost 2 Reichsthalers, and we will include articles on natural science. Concerning natural science, history, etc., the kind reader is referred to the article entitled "The Program of the Society of the Friends of Goodness and Virtue," which will be published on the first day of Tamuz of the Hebrew year 5548.[6] Thus every sincere man will know that we have performed this labor for the public good; we have taken this burden on our shoulders in order to spread Torah and wisdom *[hokhmah]*. The intention of our hearts is clear—we wish to light the path for the sons of our nation, who yearn to hear about ethics and knowledge *[daat]*. Therefore we will not pay attention to the gossip which has been circulated by many in the camp of our fellow Jews to slander and abuse us. We shall not fight with them, and shall not sully our lips with their names....And we shall never fight anyone except on a matter of truth....

NOTES

1. Title given by the editors of this book. *Hameasef* met with bitter opposition from traditional elements within the Jewish community. While following Wessely's advice to avoid open conflict with their opponents, the editors of *Hameasef* nonetheless resolutely maintained their commitment to bring Enlightenment to the Jewish public.
2. *"Hay leanashim!"* The authors of this article evidently have in mind the German word *Menschen*, which in the parlance of the Enlightenment meant not simply a human being but human existence defined by that quality—viz. reason—that assures our inherent humanity and our bond with all human beings irrespective of religion and national origin.
3. Eccles. 1:18.
4. An allusion to 1 Sam. 26:19: "cleaving to the inheritance of the Lord." Note the replacement of "inheritance" with " wisdom."
5. An allusion to Ps. 40:5: "Happy is the man who makes the Lord his trust and does not look to brutal and treacherous men."
6. July 1788.

13. PREFACE TO VOLUME ONE OF
SULAMITH (1806)[1]

JOSEPH WOLF

Religion is the essential intellectual and moral need of a cultured man. It is the purpose of *Sulamith* to expose this religion to the highest light. *Sulamith* desires to arouse the nation to a respect of religion, that is, of those truths which alone are worthy of the name of religion. It wants to revitalize the urgent need for religious sentiment and concepts, but at the same time it wants to point up the truth that the concepts and commands contained in the Jewish religion are in no wise harmful, either to the individual or to society. Further it desires to bring the Jewish nation back to its native level of education. It will demonstrate thereby that this education is entirely pure and that our religious concepts and teachings, as long as they have not been disfigured through superstitious additions, would never be an obstacle to any political constitution, but would rather be part of it, and that in those countries where total integration is not taking place, at least brotherly integration is possible. Finally, *Sulamith* wants to sort out truth from falsehood, reality from illusion, the useful from the corrupt. *It wants to enlighten the Jewish nation about itself.* It wants to strike the dry and hard rock and bring forth from it a spring of goodness which will then, by its own power, flow forth in its pristine clearness and purify the sap of the tree. In no wise do we desire, by vain artifices to graft foreign fruit upon this tree which could not grow by itself. Only in this manner do we believe that we can utilize for the best purposes the happy atmosphere which enlightenment and education have brought the souls of men and spread blessing and well-being on the whole Jewish nation.

Therefore, we issue an invitation to all those who want to take part in the spread of useful truths, in the advancement of general human welfare, in a pleasant and tasteful conversation amongst the readers; and we hope that they will participate with fitting contributions to this magazine in a manner adequate to its plan. Every truth, every inquiry which stems from pure intention, regardless from which pen it comes, will be welcome to *Sulamith*.

NOTE

1. Full title: *Sulamith, Eine Zeitschrift zur Befoerderung der Kultur und Humanitaet unter der juedischen Nation* [A periodical for the promotion of culture and humanism among the Jewish nation]. In 1810 the words *Jewish nation* were replaced by the word *Israelites*. This first German-language periodical for Jews appeared intermittently from 1806 to 1833. It explicitly viewed itself as a continuation of *Hameasef*. While supporting Enlightenment among Jews, it also placed special emphasis on synagogal reform. The co-founders and first co-editors were David Frankel (1779–1865), director of a modern Jewish primary school in Dessau, and Joseph Wolf (1762–1826), scholar and translator of various books of Hebrew Scripture into German. The latter was a collaborator in nine volumes of *Sulamith* and ten of *Hameasef*.

Source: Joseph Wolf, "Inhalt, Zweck und Titel dieser Zeitschrift," *Sulamith* 1 (Leipzig, 1806), p. 9. W. Gunther Plaut, *The Rise of Reform Judaism: A Sourcebook of Its European Origins* (New York: World Union for Progressive Judaism, 1963), p. 13. Reprinted by permission of the World Union for Progressive Judaism.

14. CALL FOR RELIGIOUS ENLIGHTENMENT (1808)

SULAMITH

Now we wish to define the concept of *religious* enlightenment....

The task of *religious* enlightenment is to illuminate and elucidate the concept of man regarding religious truths, the existence of the Creator, providence, immortality, etc., and to clarify man's religious creed and free it from the additions and abuses of harmful fanaticism and foolish prejudices. Enlightenment teaches us that the essence of religion is not mere ceremony, not a mere matter of remembrance. Enlightenment banishes the low, slavish fear of the world's Ruler from our hearts. It shows us the true purpose of our existence; it also shows the proper relationship to the Invisible One, and to those who share with us a common origin, the same priorities and common destiny.[1] Enlightenment offers us the correct vantage point from which we must view our obligations, which originate from these relationships. It teaches us that serving one's fellow also means serving God, that loving him also means loving God....Enlightenment teaches us that we must think liberally and act humanely, not offend anyone who thinks differently or worships differently than we; but, rather follow the example of the Creator, who embraces and preserves the entire host of Creation with the eternal bonds of love. Finally, it instructs us concerning the brevity of our existence; however, at the same time, enlightenment indicates that our future life stands in the closest connection to the present one, indeed, that it is a consequence of this one; it also indicates that the degree of perfection which we have attained here in this life will determine the degree of perfection which we will be capable of in future life. Accordingly, good care should be taken for our present and eternal well-being, which are one and the same.

NOTE

1. This is the only reference in the article, an indirect one at that, to Jews or Judaism.

Source: Anonymous, *Sulamith* 2 (Leipzig, 1808), pp. 221–22. Trans. By M. Gelber.

15. ON THE NEED FOR A GERMAN TRANSLATION OF SCRIPTURE (1782)[1]

MOSES MENDELSSOHN

The Holy Tongue in which the 24 books of Scripture that we presently possess is the language in which the Holy One, Blessed be He, spoke to the first human being, to Cain, Noah, and the holy Patriarchs; it is the language in which He gave the Ten Commandments on Mt. Sinai, in which the Tablets of the Law were written, and in which God spoke to Moses and the prophets. And by virtue of this it is exalted above all other languages, indeed, is called the Holy Tongue. . . . And as long as the Children of Israel did not change their vernacular, the old and young were conversant and fluent in the language of the Holy Land, there was no need for a translation of the Torah. Everyone properly understood the reader as he intoned and chanted the Torah, and comprehended the intention of the words in accordance with their literal meaning (*'al pi pshuto*),[2] for [the Torah's] metaphors and inflections are familiar to those who use them in their everyday activities and needs. And when they did not grasp the intention of what was written, they had recourse to a commentary (*Bi'ur*), which explained the term with other figures of speech in the Holy Tongue itself, and not in a translation to a foreign language. If one is able to draw from the Fountain of Life, why should one hew worthless wells?

But when Israel was exiled to Babylon and mixed with the gentiles and married foreign women, they forgot their [mother] tongue. As is attested in Scripture, "In those days I also saw Jews who had married wives of Ashdod, of Ammon, and Moav, and their children spoke half in the speech of Ashdod, and could not speak the language of Judah, but according to the language of various other peoples" (Nehemiah 13, 24). . . . And when Ezra and his faction saw that the masses of Israel had forgotten the Holy Tongue, they set about to translate for them the Torah in the Aramaic, with which they had grown accustomed to conduct all their affairs. . . . And they explicitly said that this was a translation, the intention of which was that they [the Children of Israel] would understand Scripture, and will be taught in the language with which they were conversant, and resume to study Torah. In this manner, one will learn to understand another language [namely, Hebrew] which they no longer knew. And they composed for them prayers in the Holy Tongue so that it would be established in the mouths of all. . . .

When the Greeks gained hegemony, [the Jews] quickly abandoned Aramaic, for they always learn the language of the nation that has sway over them, and some even confounded the languages, and did not master properly any of them. As a consequence they were no longer capable of reading the translation that Ezra and his faction prepared for them. . . .

In 1544 the great grammarian Rabbi Elijah Bachur (Elijah Levita)[3] translated the Torah and the Five Scrolls word by word into German.[4] His translation was published in Constance, Switzerland. A later German translation, printed in Hebrew letters, was published by Rabbi Josel Witzenhausen in Amsterdam in 1679 (second edition in 1687).[5] In the same year, still another German translation by Rabbi Yekutiel Blitz, of Witmund, appeared in Amsterdam, containing appropriations as well as admonitions [against unauthorized reprintings] by several eminent rabbis of his time.[6] In his preface, Rabbi Yekutiel vehemently criticizes the Constance translation, and said he was convinced that it could not possibly have

Source: Moses Mendelssohn, *Or li-Netiva*. Introduction to *Netivot ha-Shalom*. German translation of the Pentateuch (Berlin 1778); Reprinted in Moses Mendelssohn, *Hebraeische Schriften*. Gesammelte Schriften. Jubilaeumsausgabe, vol. 14 , ed. Haim Borodianski, trans. By P. Mendes-Flohr (Stuttgart/Bad Cannstatt: Verlag Guenther Holyboog, 1972), pp. 214ff., 232–34, 242–44.

been the work of the illustrious grammarian Elijah Bachur. I myself have never seen the translation attributed to Rabbi Elijah, since copies are not available in this country [Germany]. However, I have seen Rabbi Yekutiel's translation and [noted his criticism of other translations of faults that he himself also makes]. His ability is very limited. He neither understands the spirit of the Hebrew language nor masters its use; and whatever little he did understand, he rendered into a language so corrupt and garbled that any reader who is accustomed to precise usage must find it repugnant.

Since that time, no one has attempted to improve what had been corrupted and to translate the Holy Torah into the kind of language that would be appropriate for our time. The Jewish boys who are able to understand and probe its wisdom must acquire their knowledge of God's word from the translations prepared by Christian scholars. Christians have translated the Torah repeatedly and into various languages, in accordance with the needs of the time and changes in style and linguistic usage. Sometimes they translated literally, sometimes in paraphrases; sometimes they were faithful to the text, and sometimes they rendered its general meaning in order to satisfy the needs and desires of every reader....

This procedure is hardly appropriate for the people of Israel. For the Torah is, indeed must be considered, as the source of law. To make sure that our life's purpose and direction should not be dependent on subtle and frequently changing interpretations and speculations, our wise ancestors have established the *Masorah*,[7] thereby erecting a fence around the Torah and the law,[8] so that we would not have to tap around in darkness like blind human beings. From this established path we may not turn right or left, nor may we follow the opinions or hypotheses of this or that grammarian or critic of the text. Our sole guiding principle must be the text itself that the Masoretes have established for us....

When God in his grace gave me sons and the time arrived to teach them diligently in the words of the living God, as Scripture bids us to do,[9] I took it upon myself to translate the Five Books of the Torah into pure and refined German such as that spoken in our time, and I did this for the benefit of the children. I put the translation into their mouth[s] when teaching them in the [Hebrew] text, rending it sometimes word by word, sometimes according to its meaning[10]

or sometimes according to context,[11] so as to introduce them to the intent of Scripture, its idiomatic figures of speech, and the fine points of its teaching, all in the hope that as they grew older they would by themselves achieve the right understanding.

The Lord then sent me our teacher and master Rabbi Solomon of Dubno (may his light shine forth),[12] to teach my only remaining son,[13] the only one left me at the time (may God strengthen his heart for serving and revering Him), the science of [Hebrew] grammar one hour every day. When he [Rabbi Solomon] saw my translation of the Torah, he liked it and considered it adequate. He urged me to have it printed for the benefit of other students whom God had endowed with linguistic interest and talent. I agreed, but only under the condition that he himself would put his heart and mind to the task of preparing a commentary *(Bi'ur)* in order to explain and justify [the] translation—e.g., why, in certain instances, I had preferred the views of an older commentator to some other commentators altogether and had instead provided an explanation of my own, which in my judgment, is in accord with the semantic significance and theme, and presuppositions [of a given phrase or term]. This required interpretation and research. For it was incumbent upon me to provide a commentary on Scripture that was in an accessible language and readily understood by every reader.

NOTES

1. Mendelssohn initiated a translation of the Hebrew Bible into High German. He solicited the collaboration of rabbinic scholars, among them, Solomon Dubno, Hartwig Wessely, Naphtali Herz Homberg, and Aaron Jaroslaw. The translation was printed in Hebrew characters under the title *Netivot ha-Shalom* (Paths of Peace; cf. "Her ways are ways of pleasantness, and all her ways are peace" Proverbs 3:17). The translation appeared alongside the original Hebrew and with a commentary *(Bi'ur)*. Mendelssohn himself translated the Pentateuch, the Psalms, Ecclesiastes, and Song of Songs. In the introduction to the translation of the Pentateuch, Mendelssohn explained the origin of the project and its guiding principles. In the Introduction—*Or li-Netiva* (A Light unto the Path), written in Hebrew—he indicated that he initially undertook the translation for the sake of his children and that he consented to its publication only at the insistence of Solomon Dubno. In a letter to his friend August von Hennings, dated June 29, 1779,

he noted that in addition to rendering "a service to my children," the translation and the *Bi'ur* were meant for Jewry at large: The translation was thus envisioned as "the first step to culture from which, alas, my nation has held itself so aloof that one might almost despair of any possibility of improvement." Cited in Meyer Kayserling, *Moses Mendelssohn: Sein Leben und seine Werke*, 2nd ed.(Leipzig, 1888), p. 543. It has been noted that Mendelssohn adumbrated in his commentaries many of the ideas that he would later elaborate in *Jerusalem* (see this chapter, document 21).

2. As Mendelssohn explains, the guiding principle of the translation was to provide a simple and lucid rendering of the Scripture into standard German. Hence, primacy was given to the plain-sense meaning (*pshat*) of the Hebrew text, as explicated principally by the four leading rabbinic exegetes: Rashi, Rashbam, Ibe Ezra, and the Rambam.

3. Elijah Bachur (1468–1549), better know as Elijah Levita, was a scholar of Hebrew grammar and a poet. He published a Judeo-German (Yiddish) translation of the Pentateuch and other books of the Bible.

4. The translation was actually in Judeo-German (Yiddish) with many Dutch expressions.

5. Josel (Joseph) Witzenhausen was employed as a typesetter by the famed Amsterdam printer and publisher of Hebrew books Joseph b. Abraham Athias (d. 1700), who published Witzenhausen's translation of the Bible. He came from Witzenhausen in Hessen, Germany. A fine Hebrew stylist and a *maskil*, he was a contributor to *Hameasef*.

6. Isaac Yekutiel ben Isaac Blitz lived in the second half of the seventeenth century in Amsterdam. A rabbi, he hailed from Wittmund in northern Germany. His Yiddish translation of the complete Bible was published in Amsterdam in 1679 by the printer and publisher Uri Fayvesh. His and Witzenhausen's two rival translations were the first renderings into Yiddish of the entire Hebrew Bible. They were intended for an East European readership. See Marion Aptroot, "'*In galkhes they do not say, so, but the taytsh is as it stands here:*' Notes on the Amsterdam Yiddish Bible Translations by Blitz and Witzenhausen." *Studia Rosenthaliana*, 27: 1–2, 136–58.

7. *Masorah* or *mesorah* is the Hebrew term for the transmission or tradition. Here it refers specifically to the so-called Masoretic Text, the version of the Hebrew Bible that was sanctioned as authentic by rabbinic scholars, the Masoretes, who from the sixth to the tenth centuries C.E. examined diverse manuscripts to determine the most accurate text. The canonic version of the Hebrew text was established in 930 C.E. by Aaron ben Moses Ben-Asher, who was the last of a family of Masoretes who were active for five generations in Tiberias, Palestine.

8. This phrase is an allusion to the dictum of Rabbi Akiva that the "*masoret* is a fence for the Torah (Avot 3:13), or that the written text as handed down is a fence to protect the integrity of God's word."

9. Cf. Deuteronomy 6:7.

10. Namely, by substituting idiomatic German terms and phrases for idiomatic Hebrew.

11. Mendelssohn and his colleagues would depart from the traditional interpretation of a given passage when they deemed that the context required another reading. See Edward Breuer, *The Limits of Enlightenment: Jews, Germans, and the Eighteenth-Century Study of Scripture* (Cambridge, Mass.: Harvard University Press, 1996), pp. 177ff.

12. Salomon ben Joel of Dubno (1738–1813); Dubno was a town in the Ukraine, from which he took his family name. A Bible scholar and Hebrew poet, Dubno was engaged by Mendelssohn as a tutor for his son Joseph. He also served as Mendelssohn's first collaborator in the *Bi'ur*, having completed a commentary on Genesis (except for chap. 1) and part of Exodus before he departed for Vilna in 1781.

13. Mendelssohn's son Mendel died at the age of six in September 1775; his son Abraham was born in December 1776. At that time, Mendelssohn's only remaining son was Joseph (1770–1848).

16. ON THE CURTAILMENT OF JEWISH JURIDICAL AUTONOMY (1782)[1]

MOSES MENDELSSOHN

I can scarcely conceive how a writer of Herr Dohm's great judgment could say: "As all other religious societies have a right of expelling members, either for a limited time or for ever; the Jewish should have it too; and, in case of resistance of the Rabbi's sentence, be supported by the civil authorities." All societies have a right of expelling members; religious ones only have not: for it runs diametrically contrary to their principle and object, which is joint edification and participating in the outpouring of the heart, by which we evince our thankfulness to God for the many bounties he bestows on us, and our filial trust in his sovereign goodness and mercy. Then, with what conscience can "we deny entrance to dissenters, separatists, misbelievers, or sectarians, and deprive them of the benefit of that edification? For rioters and disturbers there is the law and the police; disorders of that kind may, nay must, be restrained by the secular arm. But a quiet and inoffensive attendance at the meeting may not be forbidden even to an offender, unless we purposely want to bar him from every road to reformation. The doors of the house of rational devotion require neither bars nor bolts. There is nothing locked up within, and, therefore, no occasion to be particular in admitting from without. Whoever chooses to be a tranquil spectator, or even to join in the worship, is right welcome to every pious man, at the hour of his own devotions.

Herr Dohm, on this occasion, has perhaps taken things as they are, and not as they should be. Mankind seems to have agreed to regard the external form of divine worship, that is the church, as a moral being, who has her own rights and claims or duties; and to grant to her more or less authority to assert those rights, and enforce them by external power. It is not thought contrary to common sense, to style, in every country, one of those beings, the *Dominant*, who treats her sisters just as the whim takes her, at times using, to oppress them, the power delegated to herself, and, at others, generous enough to *tolerate* them, and concede to them as much of her own prerogative, of her own pretensions and consequence, as she thinks proper. Now as anathematizing and excommunicating is always the first right with which a dominant church enfolds tolerated ones, Herr Dohm claims, for the Jewish religion, the same privileges which are granted to all other religious societies. As long as these still possess the right of expelling, he deems it an inconsistency, to put the Jewish under greater restrictions in that respect. But if, as it does evidently appear to me, religious claims to worldly things, religious power, and religious compulsory law, are words without a meaning—and if generally expelling must be called irreligious—then let us still be consistent, rather than heap abuses.

I do not find that the wisest of our forefathers ever did pretend to any such right as excluding individuals from religious exercises.

When King Solomon had finished the building of the Temple, he included in his sublime dedication prayer even strangers, a denomination in his days, of course, synonymous with idolators. He spread forth his hands towards heaven, saying: "Moreover concerning a stranger that is not of thy people Israel, but cometh out of a far country for thy name's sake (for they shall hear of thy great name, and of thy strong hand, and of thy stretched-out arm); when he shall come and pray toward this house; hear thou in heaven thy dwelling-place, and do according to all that the stranger calleth to thee for: that all people of the earth

Source: Moses Mendelssohn's Preface of 1782 to the German translation of Menasseh ben Israel's *Vindiciae Judaeorum*, in *Writings Related to Mendelssohn "Jerusalem,"* trans. M. Samuels (London, 1838), vol. 1, pp. 108–16.

may know thy name, as thy people of Israel; and that they may know that this house which I have built, is called by thy name."[2] In the same manner our Rabbis directed the voluntary gifts and votive offerings of idolators to be accepted in the Temple, and not turn away the sacrifice of even an offender belonging to the nation itself, as long as he had not positively abjured his religion; in order, said they, that he may have an opportunity and inducement to amend.[3] So *they* thought at a period, when they had a little more power and authority to be exclusive in religious matters: and yet shall we presume to shut out dissenters from our barely *tolerated* religious meetings?

I shall forbear speaking of the danger there is in entrusting *any one* with the power of excommunicating—with the abuse inseparable from the right of anathema, as indeed with every other form of church discipline, or ecclesiastical power. Alas! it will require ages yet, before the human race shall have recovered from the blows which those monsters inflicted on it. I can imagine no possibility of bridling false religious zeal; as long as it sees that road open before it; for a spur will never be wanting. Herr Dohm fancies he is offering us an ample guarantee from all the abuses, by taking for granted, that the right of anathema, entrusted to the colony, "will never reach beyond religious society, and have no effect at all on the civil; and this, because an expelled member of any church whatsoever may be a very valuable and estimable citizen notwithstanding: a principle in universal ecclesiastical law . . . which should be no longer questioned in our days."

But if universal ecclesiastical law, as it is called, at last acknowledges the important principle, in which I concur with all my heart, "that the expelled member of any and every church, may be a very useful and respected citizen notwithstanding," the evil is far from being remedied by that weak reservation. For, in the first place, this very estimable and useful citizen, who, perhaps, is also internally a very religious man, may not like to be debarred from all meetings for worship, from all religious solemnities; and may not like to be entirely without external religion. Now, if he have the misfortune to be thought a dissenter by the congregation he belongs to, and his conscience forbids him to join any other religious party established or tolerated in the state; must not this very useful and estimable citizen be exceedingly unhappy when his own congregation is allowed to exclude him, and

he finds the doors of their religious assemblies shut against him? And it is possible, that he finds them so everywhere; for every religious community would perhaps turn him away by the same right. But how can the state allow any one of its useful and estimable citizens to be made unhappy by the laws? Secondly, what church excommunication, what anathema is entirely without secular consequences, without any influence whatever on, at least, the civil respectability, on the fair reputation of the excommunicated, on the confidence of his fellow citizens, without which no one can exercise his calling and be useful to the state? As the boundary-laws of this nice distinction between the civil and the ecclesiastical are barely perceptible to the keenest eye, it becomes truly impossible to draw them so firmly and precisely, in any state, as to make them obvious to every citizen, and cause them to have the desired effect in common civil life. They will remain dubious and undefined, and very frequently expose innocence itself to the sting of persecution, and blind religious zeal.

To introduce church-discipline, and yet not impair civil happiness, seems to me a problem, which yet remains for politics to solve. It is the answer of the Most High Judge to Satan: "He is in thine hand but save his life,"[4] or, as the commentators add; *Demolish the cask, but let not the wine run out . . .*

I have that confidence in the more enlightened amongst the Rabbis, and elders of my nation, that they will be glad to relinquish so pernicious a prerogative, that they will cheerfully do away with all church and synagogue discipline, and let their flock enjoy, at their hands, even that kindness and forbearance, which they themselves have been so long panting for. Ah, my brethren, you have hitherto felt too hard the yoke of intolerance, and perhaps thought it a sort of satisfaction, if the power of bending those under you to such another yoke were allowed you. Revenge will be seeking an object; and if it cannot wreak itself on strangers, it even tortures its own flesh and blood. Perhaps, too, you let yourselves be seduced by the general example. All the nations of the earth, hitherto, appear to have been infatuated by the error, that religion can be maintained by iron force—doctrines of blessedness inculcated by unblest persecution—and true notions of God, who, as we all acknowledge, is love itself, communicated by the workings of hatred and ill-will only. You, perhaps, let yourselves be seduced to adopt the same system; and the power of persecuting was to you the most important prerogative which your own persecutors could bestow upon you. Thank the God of your forefathers, thank the God who is all love and mercy, that that error appears to be gradually vanishing. The nations are now tolerating and bearing with one another, while to you also they are showing kindness and forbearance, which, with the help of Him who disposes the hearts of men, may grow to true brotherly love. O, my brethren, follow the example of love, the same as you have hitherto followed that of hatred. Imitate the virtues of the nations whose vices you hitherto thought you must imitate. If you would be protected, tolerated and indulged, protect, tolerate and indulge one another. *Love, and ye will be beloved.*

NOTES

1. In his essay on Jewish civil rights, Christian Wilhelm von Dohm favored the retention of Jewish juridical autonomy, particularly the right of excommunication.

Mendelssohn objected, for he strongly felt that Jewish Enlightenment and the liberalization of society in general required the relinquishment of traditional ecclesiastical juridical prerogatives such as that of excommunication. He elaborated this position in his preface to the German translation of Menasseh ben Israel's *Vindiciae Judaeorum*. Mendelssohn initiated the translation of the Dutch rabbi's 1656 refutation of objections advanced by British clergy against Jewish readmission to England, and he used the occasion of writing a preface to the volume, which he felt would strengthen the impact of Dohm's treatise, as an opportunity to both supplement and correct aspects of Dohm's argument. Some of Mendelssohn's readers, for example, the author of "Search for Light and Right" (see document 18 in this chapter), interpreted his argument for the annulment of Jewish juridical autonomy to be an implicit admission that Judaism was an anachronistic religion.

2. 1 Kings 8:41–43.
3. Talmud, tractate *Hulin*, 5a.
4. Job 2:6.

17. ON SELF-DEVELOPMENT AND THE ABOLISHMENT OF JEWISH AUTONOMY (MARCH 19, 1792)

DAVID FRIEDLAENDER[1]

I need not have to tell you about the conception of God which the rabbis define as religion. Three thousand years after the granting of the Torah, [these rabbis] are still busy pondering the question whether on consumption of less than a morsel, one must recite the grace after meals or not. He who does [recite the grace] belongs to the Jewish religion, and he who does not make such a blessing, does not belong. It can easily be imagined what such masters of the Torah consider to be truth. The most noble gift of God, reason, is treated as a base handmaid; they are even impertinent enough to say that after the removal of the Torah from the Temple, a cloud of darkness and of fog descended upon the

---

Source: David Friedlaender to Meir Eger, March 19, 1792, in J. Meisl [Letters of David Friedlaender], *Historishe shriftn* (Vilna: Yidisher Visnshaftlekher Institut, 1937), vol. 2, p. 402. Trans. by J. Hessing.

world. If this is what is taught by the "judges and the leaders" of the nation, what do you expect the masses to believe? Imagine all of Jewry assembled in one room and you and I standing at the threshold, asking everyone. Who exists? What is God? What is Judaism? What is virtue?! What is truth? Faith?! Only a few will be able to give a clear answer to any of these questions. We have here [in Berlin] a so-called *Torani,* one who studies [Torah] every day, day in, day out. He would give his life for the Jewish religion and would never taste [a morsel of food] without a blessing before and a blessing after eating. He is wealthy, possessing abundant assets and money, and, yet, a few years ago, this very man allowed his own brother to go begging. In short, we do not know anymore what religion is, and what is virtue. When we stand in front of the throne to be weighed on the scales of the Creator, it will be found that we have lived by the principles of cannibals. We speak the language of the [primitive] Hottentot, not that of the Torah of the living God which was given to us in glory and in honor!

The consequence of all this is obvious. We are living among the Gentiles, all of whom daily probe into their religions in order to eliminate the chaff, to purify their morals and to improve their faith. We, on the other hand, who have started out on the highest level, constantly deteriorate. The ignorance of our people accumulates in a most frightful manner, and in twenty years you will hardly find a man who is able to read the Torah. The Talmud is kept in dire contempt, and daily something is lost from the treasures of our Torah. The natural consequence of all this must be—my hairs bristle at the thought of it!—that our sons will first abandon Judaism and then convert to Christianity. Were our rabbis not completely blind, were they not

confined within the four walls of the halakhah—where they know as much about the things of the world as I know about the doings of the Nabob in Sanghar—they would think of repairing the breach. But nobody seems to notice. They think that by writing, "ours is a lost generation, may the Lord forgive us," they have done their duty. But, alas, what can they do, utterly ignorant as they are, superstitious and bent on closing their eyes to the facts? I have been watching all this for the last twenty years, and I have found only one possible solution: to throw off the heavy yoke under which the king and the judges of this country, who are not of our people, have harnessed us; to throw off, furthermore, that other yoke which we have taken upon us with the rule of our own rabbis and communal leaders. Only if we are free, neither afraid of the ruling party nor intimidated in our enlightenment, by the threat of excommunication and the refusal of burial rites, will it be possible to raise Israel's prestige, our Torah and the teachings of Moses from the dust.

NOTE

1. David Friedlaender (1750–1834), a wealthy and respected entrepreneur. He was also widely held to have inherited from his close friend Moses Mendelssohn the leadership of the movement of Enlightenment among German Jewry. His interest in this area was expressed in his activities on behalf of the religious reform of Judaism and his unflagging efforts in the protracted struggle of German Jewry for emancipation. These interests are reflected in this document, a letter Friedlaender wrote to his business associate Meir Eger, an Orthodox Jew. Aside from a few select Hebrew expressions, the letter is written in German transliterated into Hebrew script.

18. SEARCH FOR LIGHT AND RIGHT: AN EPISTLE TO MOSES MENDELSSOHN (1782)[1]

Estimable Sir,

There was a time, when I could not help blaming Lavater's[2] obtrusion, in calling upon you in so singularly solemn a manner to embrace his faith; or, in the event of declining the proposal, demonstrate the unsoundness of the Christian religion. That step having been made in consequence of what fell from you in the course of a friendly conversation, which, probably, was not meant to go forth to the public, is what I shall never cease to think unjustifiable.

Now, however, I scarcely can resist the temptation of wishing that Lavater would make another attack on you, with all the force of his emphatic adjuration, so as actually to make a convert of you, or provoke you to refute a religion, which it seems, you are neither willing, nor (from conviction) able to embrace.

At all events, certain candid expressions, in your excellent "Preface" to Rabbi Menasseh Ben Israel's *Vindication of the Jews*, give every searcher for truth a right to expect of you some further explanation; lest you should appear unintelligible on a comparison with former statements....

In your former reply to Lavater, you all along insist on your adherence to the *Faith of your Forefathers*. But you never tell us what you properly mean by the *Faith of your Forefathers*. The substance of the Christian religion, too, is the Faith of your Forefathers, transferred to us, weeded of rabbinical institutions, and improved by additions, new, indeed; but nevertheless derived from the Faith of your Forefathers, and, interpreted as the consummation of Old-Testamentary prophecies.

In a wider sense of the term, the *Faith of your Forefathers* is that which the Christians profess; namely, the adoration of an only God; the keeping of the divine Ten Commandments delivered by Moses; and a belief in the gathering of all the nations of the earth, in one flock, under the universal sceptre of a Messiah announced by the prophets.

In a narrower sense, the expression, *Faith of your Forefathers*, comprises only the proper Jewish ecclesiastical system, together with all scriptural appointments, rabbinical interpretations thereof, and statutory laws thereon, the whole constituting the proper distinctive doctrine, which separates the Jews from the faith of all other nations, and also from Christians.

From that latter particular faith, my dear Mr. Mendelssohn, you have, in your remarkable preface, wrenched the corner-stone, by stripping, in dry words, the synagogue of its original power; by denying it the right of expelling from the congregation of the holy, the backslider from the Faith of your Forefathers, curtailing anathema and malediction on the heretic, and cutting him off from the people of Israel. It may consist with reason, that ecclesiastical law, in general, and the authority of spiritual courts to enforce or restrict opinion, is an inconceivable thing....

In common sense, religion without conviction is not possible at all; and every forced religious act is no longer such. The keeping of the divine commandments from fear of the ecclesiastical penalties annexed to them is servile compliance, which, according to refined notions, cannot be acceptable to God. Still, it will not be denied, that Moses puts prohibitions and positive punishments on the neglect of religious observances. His statutes ordain that the Sabbath-breaker, the reviler of the divine name, and other infringers of his law shall be stoned, and their souls exterminated from amongst his people.

Source: Anonymous, "Das Forschen nach Licht und Recht in einem Schreiben an Herrn Moses Mendelssohn auf Veranlassung seiner merkwuerdigen Vorrede zu Menasseh Ben Israel, 1782" [Search for light and right, an epistle to Moses Mendelssohn, occasioned by his remarkable "Preface" to Rabbi Menasseh ben Israel's *Vindiciae Judaeorum*], in *Writings Related to Mendelssohn "Jerusalem,"* trans. M. Samuels (London, 1838), vol. 1, pp. 119–20, 122–41.

That rule, it is true, could be carried into practice, only so long as the Jews had an empire of their own; so long as their Pontiffs were princes, or such sovereign heads of the people, as created princes, and governed them. But cease it must, as did the sacrifices, upon the Jews having lost territory and power, and, depending on foreign laws, found their jurisdiction circumscribed by very narrow limits. Still, that circumscription is merely the consequence of external and altered political relations, whereby the value of laws and privileges, consigned to quiescence, cannot be diminished. The ecclesiastical law is still there, although it be not allowed to be put into execution. Your law-giver, Moses, is still the drover, with the cudgel, who leads his people with a rod of iron, and would be sharp after any one who had the least opinion of his own, and dared to express it by word or deed....

Agreed and most unqualifiedly granted, that the foundation of such an ecclesiastical law is the most inconceivable thing in the world; that it does not answer the purpose of bringing the strayed back into the bosom of the church; but, on the contrary, removes them from it; that its object cannot be to reclaim but to undo them; that the rigour of ecclesiastical law, excommunication, and anathema, cannot be exercised without the most serious injury to civil happiness; that true worship ought to be a spontaneous homage, founded on one's own conviction, and practised out of love to the Father of all beings, and with perfect filial confidence in the mercy and goodness with which he lets his sun shine even for the erring, and his dew fertilise also the fields of the dissenter from religious dogmas; that servile awe, extorted by penalties, cannot be an acceptable offering on the altar of the God of Love. Granting and admitting all this, it certainly is very true, that the church has no need either of sword or scourge to bind the sceptic beneath a yoke—repugnant to the standard of his intellect—to reconcile the dissenter to articles of faith, or to ruin the rebellious. But then, what becomes of the rabbinical statutes, passed into laws which Judaism is strictly bound to obey? What becomes of even the Mosaic law, and of its authority derived immediately from God himself? Armed ecclesiastical law still remains the firmest groundwork of the Jewish polity, and the master-spring of the whole machinery. Then good Mr. Mendelssohn, how can you profess attachment to the religion of your forefathers, while you are shaking its fabric, by impugning the ecclesiastical code established by Moses in consequence of divine revelation? The public, whose attention you have excited, is entitled to both an explanation of—and instruction in—so important a point.

Or are we to presume that the present very remarkable step of yours is really one toward complying with the wishes formerly expressed to you by Lavater? No doubt but that affair induced you to give Christianity a further consideration; and more nicely to weigh, with your peculiar penetration, and the impartiality of an incorruptible searcher after truth, the merits of its theology, as you had it before you in all its forms and modifications. By this time, perhaps, you approximate to Christianity, by shaking off the trammels of an oppressive church [Judaism], and by now preaching the refined theory of a more liberal religion, which is impressed with the stamp of proper divine adoration; whereby we are to be emancipated from restraints and burdensome observances, and which limits true worship, neither to Jerusalem nor to Samaria, by which, as our Savior said, recognizes the essence of religion in the creature's worship of his Creator and God in spirit and truth.[3]

Allow me, good Sir, to submit to your opinion a few remarks, which appear to me of importance in the present age, when a great revolution in favour of your nation is dawning forth. You yourself speak, in your preface, of the unjust persecutions which have hung over the whole of your race ever since the destruction of their Capital, and the dispersion of the Jews amongst all the nations of the world. The Christian's silly hatred and absurd contempt of them [the Jews] has, during many ages, denied them all pretensions to the universal rights of man.... [But in our own times] the wise and reasonable amongst the Christians are willing to love as brethren the good amongst your nation. This your own experience must tell you, Mr. Mendelssohn. Do not Christian men, superior to nursery, schoolboy, or popularly vulgar impressions, come forward at this time, and openly plead with frankness and energy, the cause of humanity on behalf of your nation; men, who make it their business to couch the Christian rabble, both high and low, for the cataract of old and inveterate infection, in order to enable them to recognise Jews as God's goodly and rational creatures? Are there not now sovereigns who listen to such appeals of humanity, and give fair hopes that they will not let all pious wishes remain unfulfilled, in their dominions.

To what may it be owing, that brotherly love does not more generally unite two nations, both of the same nature and substance, both worshipping the same God, and both coinciding in the fundamental points of their religion?

The civil disabilities, the exclusion from common privileges, and from a participation in the reciprocal offices of men and brethren—those hardships, Mr. Mendelssohn, about which your nation can feel only in a certain measure, justly aggrieved, are not the fault of Christians. In the religion of your forefathers itself, there is a tremendous breach which keeps your nation far removed from an unqualified sharing in both the public and private advantages of social life, which, in a state, are enjoyed by all citizens alike.

I shall say nothing about your excessively strict keeping of the Sabbath, which is not the Sabbath of the nations amongst whom you dwell. That inconvenience, perhaps, may not be the one that least admits of mitigation, yet it will always be found impossible entirely to remove the difficulties which would attend the measure of employing Jews in those capacities, whereby the state and the public service must necessarily be sufferers, as long as the duties thereof remain incompatible with the uncompromising Sabbath Laws. It may, however, be asked, whether the solemnisation of the Rabbinical Sabbath, with all its nervous niceties and shivering scruples, should not be referred exclusively to the former territory and polity of the Jews; and amidst different relations, and under foreign dominion, be subordinate to the circumstances in which Providence itself has placed them since the abolition of their empire? The laws of sacrifices, I should think, were no less sacred and inviolable than those of the Sabbath; and yet they were discontinued on the breaking up of the Jewish State, because the practice could not be carried on under foreign governments. Then, why may not those of the Sabbath be equally subject to some modification, at least, when times, circumstances, and local situations, do not admit their full observance?

But of still greater importance is the obstacle which the Jewish law places in the way of a more general intermixture with Christians. The very scorn and contumely which furnish the Jew no unjust grounds of complaint against the Christian, form an article of faith of the Jewish religion; according to which all other nations are deemed unclean creatures, by a social intercourse with whom the people of God would be defiled. All victuals and certain drink prepared by the hands of a Christian, are, by law, an abomination to a Jew.

Those laws, no doubt in former times, were the offspring of pure precaution, to keep a people so prone to idolatry from associating with their pagan neighbours, and from being ensnared by them into the worship of idols. But that precaution has become quite supererogatory at present....

If it be possible to suppress, without any detriment to pure Judaism, ecclesiastical law, founded as it is on express Mosaic Statutes, why then should mere rabbinical reservations, subsequently devised, and opening so injurious a breach between Jew and Christian, not be set aside as well, for the good of the nation? But if the ecclesiastical laws, assumed to have been given by revelation, form a part of the Jewish religion, we must admit those Rabbinisms also to do so: and, in that case, you, good Mr. Mendelssohn, have renounced the religion of your forefathers. One step more, and you will become one of us.

As long as you forbear taking the other step now that you have taken the first, the public is most justly entitled to expect of you, either a reason for so glaring a discrepancy from the religion of your forefathers, or the statement of any cause you may have to show why you should not publicly embrace Christianity, or the production of an argument against Christianity.... This whole truth-loving public expect of every inquirer, "Light and Right," and long to hear an approved thinker speak, in the evening of his life, without reserve, of the most important human concerns. By a more particular explanation, you either will use your endeavours to relieve your nation from many an antiquated and paralysing constraint, and to regenerate them into freer, and less abashed beings, who will unite themselves by mutual ties more closely to their fellowmen of another persuasion—men who already evince a strong and cordial disposition to regard them too as men and brethren, in a greater degree than heretofore—or you will draw your brethren nearer to us, or, by removing our errors, ourselves to them....

At the present remarkable juncture, there is nothing whatsoever to deter you from unfolding to us your sincere and real conviction. Now that you have so heroically battered down the once impregnable steel gate of ecclesiastical authority, what should keep you from celebrating your ovation in the very essence of truth, which has been so long inaccessible to us? You have put your hand to the plough, as the saying is; and a man, firm in his conviction, as you are, and, on account of his extraordinary talents, called by Providence itself to the service and promulgation of truth, cannot possibly withdraw it again, and deprive the world of the final result of the long exercise of his mental energies, after having already given it, in his preface to Rabbi Menasseh Ben Israel's works, so beautiful a specimen, as one of the most elegant and valuable presents from the vast museum of his learning and information.

Your sincere admirer,

S.

Vienna, June 12, 1782

NOTES

1. The authorship of this anonymous epistle was until recently in doubt. The latest research, however, indicates that the epistle was written by August Friedrich Cranz (1732–1801), a German author of satirical essays. This epistle and the postscript by D. E. Moerschel (see document 19 in this chapter) prompted Moses Mendelssohn to break his resolve to eschew public debate on religious issues and to write his famous treatise, "Jerusalem, or On Religious Power and Judaism" (1783).

2. In 1769 Johann Caspar Lavater (1741–1801), a Swiss clergyman and theologian, publicly challenged Mendelssohn to defend the superiority of Judaism. In his published reply to Lavater, Mendelssohn politely declined to accept the challenge, indicating that polemics on religious questions were contrary to the spirit of tolerance and, moreover, imprudent for a Jew. "I am a member of an oppressed people," he reminded Lavater, "which must appeal to the benevolence of the government for protection and shelter....Should [the Jews] therefore attack their protectors on an issue to which men of virtue are particularly sensitive? Or would it not be more fitting if they abstained from religious disputes with the dominant creed?" (Mendelssohn, *Jerusalem and Other Jewish Writings*, trans, and ed. A. Jospe [New York: Schocken, 1969], pp. 119–20.)

3. Cf. "And Jesus saith unto to her, 'Woman [of Samaria] believe me, the hour cometh, you shall neither in this mountain, nor yet at Jerusalem, worship the Father....The hour cometh when the true worshippers shall worship the Father in spirit and in truth...'" (Gospel of John 4:21, 23) Alexander Altmann suggests that this assertion that faith was no longer tied to Jerusalem prompted Mendelssohn to entitle his book *Jerusalem*. "Mendelssohn chose the name in order to indicate that Jerusalem, though destroyed and bereft of power, was still the symbol of the true worship of God." Altmann, *Moses Mendelssohn: A Biographical Study* (University: University of Alabama Press, 1963), p. 514.

19. POSTSCRIPT TO "SEARCH FOR LIGHT AND RIGHT" (1782)

DAVID ERNST MOERSCHEL[1]

I think I have discovered in your preface [to Menasseh ben Israel's *Vindication of the Jews*] certain characteristic remarks by which I feel myself perfectly warranted to regard you as removed from the religion in which you were born and educated, as you are from the one which has been transmitted to me by my own forefathers: and, having done so, I shall not charge you with untruthfulness for replying that you are equally as little inclined to Judaism as you are to Christianity, being as you are, an opponent of revealed religion in general. In order to show what grounds I have for my assertion,

Source: David Ernst Moerschel, "Postscript to 'Search for Light and Right,'" in Moses Mendelssohn, *Jerusalem*, trans. M. Samuels (London, 1838), vol. 1, pp. 144–45.

I shall refer you to the first paragraph of your preface, where you say: "The doors of the house of rational devotion require neither bars nor bolts. There is nothing locked up within, and, therefore, no occasion to be particular in admitting from without. Whoever chooses to be a tranquil spectator, or even to join in the worship, is right welcome to every pious man, at the hour of his own devotions." Let me add, that, on account of your personal merits, such an explanation as I beg of you, may become the occasion of meditations which speculative men cannot make too often. I say meditations, because, in religion, the infallible word of God can alone be admitted as a rule.

What is there, worthy man, to deter you from at once openly acknowledging to the world that you are a Jew or a Christian, or neither one nor the other? My request, indeed, is not important enough to betray you into confession; still I flatter myself, you will render to the call of truth, that homage, to which myself, simply an honest man, may not pretend.

Forgive my boldness, and be assured that it is with the sincere consent of my heart, that I call myself your reverer, although I have never yet intruded upon you, to declare by word of mouth, the esteem with which I am Cordially yours,

D. E. Moerschel

Berlin, September 3, 1782

NOTE

1. David Ernst Moerschel, a military chaplain from Berlin, took the occasion of the publication of "Search for Light and Right" to voice his opinion that Mendelssohn's endorsement of a universal, rational religion implied a rejection of divine revelation and *a fortiori* Judaism, a revealed, particularistic religion. Accordingly, Moerschel felt he detected an inconsistency in Mendelssohn's devotion to rational religion and his abiding loyalty to Judaism.

20. JUDAISM IS THE CORNERSTONE OF CHRISTIANITY (1783)[1]

MOSES MENDELSSOHN

This objection [of the author of the "Search for Light and Right"] cuts me to the heart. I must admit that the notions given here of Judaism, except for some indiscretion in the terms used, are taken to be correct even by many of my co-religionists. Now if this were true, and I were convinced of it, I would, indeed, shamefully retract my propositions and bring reason into captivity under the yoke of—but no! Why should I dissimulate? Authority can humble but not instruct; it can suppress reason but not put it in fetters. Were it true that the word of God so manifestly contradicted my reason, the most I could do would be to impose silence upon my reason. But my unrefuted arguments would, nevertheless, reappear in the most secret recesses of my heart, be transformed into disquieting doubts, and the doubts would resolve

---

Source: Moses Mendelssohn, *Jerusalem, or, on Religious Power and Judaism,* trans. Allan Arkush, with an introduction and commentary by Alexander Altmann (Hanover, N.H.: University Press of New England, 1983), pp. 85–87. Reprinted by permission of the University Press of New England.

themselves into childlike prayers, into fervent supplications for illumination. I would call out with the Psalmist:

> Lord, send me Thy Light, Thy truth,
> that they may guide and bring me
> unto Thy holy mountains, unto Thy
> dwelling place!
>
> [Ps. 43:3]

It is, in any event, harsh and offensive to impute to me—as do the anonymous *Searcher for Light and Right* and Mr. Moerschel, the non-anonymous author of a postscript to the work of the "Searcher"—the odious intention of overthrowing the religion I profess and of renouncing it surreptitiously, as it were, though not expressly. Imputative inferences like these ought to be banished forever from the intercourse of learned men. Not everyone who holds a certain opinion is prepared to accept, at the same time, all the consequences flowing from it, even if they are ever so correctly deduced. Imputations of this kind are hateful and lead only to bitterness and strife, by which truth rarely gains anything.

Indeed, the Searcher goes so far as to address me in the following manner: "Is it possible that the remarkable step you have now taken could actually be a step toward the fulfillment of the wishes which Lavater formerly addressed to you? After that appeal, you most undoubtedly have reflected further on the subject of Christianity and, with the impartiality of an incorruptible searcher after truth, weighed more exactly the value of the Christian systems of religion which lie before your eyes in manifold forms and modifications. Perhaps you have now come closer to the faith of the Christians, having torn yourself from the servitude of iron churchly bonds, and having commenced teaching the liberal system of a more rational worship of God, which constitutes the true character of the Christian religion, thanks to which we have escaped coercion and burdensome ceremonies,

and thanks to which we no longer link the true worship of God either to Samaria or Jerusalem, but see the essence of religion, in the words of our teacher, wherever the true adorers of God pray in spirit and in truth."

This suggestion is advanced with sufficient solemnity and pathos. But, my dear sir, shall I take this step without first deliberating whether it will indeed extricate me from the confusion in which you think I find myself? If it be true that the cornerstones of my house are dislodged, and the structure threatens to collapse, do I act wisely if I remove my belongings from the lower to the upper floor for safety? Am I more secure there? Now Christianity, as you know, is built upon Judaism, and if the latter falls, it must necessarily collapse with it into one heap of ruins. You say that my conclusions undermine the foundation of Judaism, and you offer me the safety of your upper floor; must I not suppose that you mock me? Surely, the Christian who is in earnest about *light and truth* will not challenge the Jew to a fight when there seems to be contradiction between truth and truth, between Scripture and reason. He will rather join him in a effort to discover the groundlessness of the contradiction. For this is their common concern. Whatever else they have to settle between themselves may be postponed to a later time. For the present, they must join forces to avert the danger, and either discover the paralogism or show that it is only a seeming contradiction that has frightened them.

I could, in this way, avoid the trap, without engaging in any further discussion with the Searcher. But what advantage would I derive from such a subterfuge? . . .

NOTE

1. This excerpt from *Jerusalem* is Mendelssohn's explicit reply to the author of "Search for Light and Right" (see document 18 in this chapter).

21. JUDAISM AS REVEALED LEGISLATION (1783)[1]

MOSES MENDELSSOHN

I must, however, also do justice to his [Herr Moerschel's] searching eye. What he saw was, in part, not wrong. It is true that *I recognize no eternal truths other than those that are not merely comprehensible to human reason but can also be demonstrated and verified by human powers*. Yet Mr. Moerschel is misled by an incorrect conception of Judaism when he supposes that I cannot maintain this without departing from the religion of my fathers. On the contrary, I consider this an essential point of the Jewish religion and believe that this doctrine constitutes a characteristic difference between it and the Christian one. To say it briefly: I believe that Judaism knows of no revealed religion in the sense in which Christians understand this term. The Israelites possess a divine *legislation*—laws, commandments, ordinances, rules of life, instruction in the will of God as to how they should conduct themselves in order to attain temporal and eternal felicity. Propositions and prescriptions of this kind were revealed to them by Moses in a miraculous and supernatural manner, but no doctrinal opinions, no saving truths, no universal propositions of reason. These the Eternal reveals to us and to all other men, at all times, through *nature* and *thing*, but never through *word* and *script*....

Now I can summarize briefly my conceptions of the Judaism of former times and bring them into a single focus. Judaism consisted, or, according to the intention of the founder, was to consist of:

1. Religious doctrines and propositions or *eternal truths* about God and his government and providence, without which man cannot be enlightened and happy. These are not forced upon the faith of the nation under the threat of eternal or temporal punishments, but, in accordance with the nature and evidence of eternal truths, recommended to rational acknowledgement. They did not have to be given by direct revelation, or made known through *word* and *script*, which are intelligible only here and now. The Supreme Being has revealed them to all rational creatures through *things* and *concepts* and inscribed them in the soul with a script that is legible and comprehensible at all times and in all places. For this reason our much-quoted poet sings [Ps. 103:2–4]:

> The heavens declare the majesty of God,
> And the firmament announceth the work of His hands,
> From one day this doctrine floweth into another;
> And night giveth instruction to night.
> No teaching, no words,
> Without their voice being heard.
> Their choral resoundeth over all the earth.
> Their message goeth forth to the ends of the world,
> To the place where He hath set a tent for the sun, etc.

Their effect is as universal as the beneficent influence of the sun, which, as it hurries through its orbit, sheds light and warmth over the whole globe. As the same poet explains still more clearly in another place:

> From sunrise to sundown
> The name of the Lord is praised.

Or, as the prophet says in the name of the Lord: From the rising of the sun to its setting, My name is great among the heathens, and in every place frankincense is presented unto My name, even pure oblations, for My name is great among the heathens. [Malachi 1:11]:

Source: Moses Mendelssohn, *Jerusalem, or, on Religious Power and Judaism*, trans. Allan Arkush, with an introduction and commentary by Alexander Altmann (Hanover, N.H.: University Press of New England, 1983), pp. 89–90, 126–30. Reprinted by permission of the University Press of New England.

2. Historical truths, or records of the vicissitudes of former ages, especially of the circumstances in the lives of the nation's forefathers; of their having come to know the true God, of their way of life before God; even of their transgressions and the paternal chastisement that followed them; of the covenant which God concluded with them; and of the promise, which He so often repeated to them, to make of their descendants, in the days to come, a nation consecrated to Him. These historical records contained the foundation for the national cohesion; and as historical truths they can, according to their nature, not be accepted in any other manner than on *faith*. Authority alone gives them the required evidence; these records were also confirmed to the nation by miracles, and supported by an authority which was sufficient to place the *faith* beyond all doubt and hesitance.

3. Laws, precepts, commandments and rules of life, which were to be peculiar to this nation and through the observance of which it should arrive at national felicity, as well as personal felicity for each of its individual members. The lawgiver was God, that is to say, God not in his relation as Creator and Preserver of the universe, but God as Patron and Friend by covenant of their ancestors, as Liberator, Founder and Leader, as King and Head of this people; and He gave his laws the most solemn sanction, publicly and in a never heard-of, miraculous manner, by which they were imposed upon the nation and all their descendants as an unalterable duty and obligation.

These laws were *revealed*, that is, they were made known by God, through *words* and *script*. Yet only the most essential part of them was entrusted to letters; and without the unwritten explanations, delimitations, and more precise determinations, transmitted orally and propagated through oral, living instruction, even these written laws are mostly incomprehensible, or inevitably became so in the course of time. For no words or written signs preserve their meaning unchanged throughout a generation.

The written as well as the unwritten laws have directly, as *prescriptions for action* and rules of life, public and private felicity as their ultimate aim. But they are also, in large part, to be regarded as a kind of script, and they have significance and meaning as ceremonial laws. They guide the inquiring intelligence to divine truths, partly to eternal and partly to historical truths upon which the religion of this people

was founded. The ceremonial law was the bond which was to connect action with contemplation, life with theory. The ceremonial law was to induce personal converse and social contact between school and teacher, inquirer and instructor, and to stimulate and encourage rivalry and emulation; and it actually fulfilled this mission in the early period, before the constitution degenerated and human folly again interfaced to change, through misunderstanding and misdirection, the good into evil and the useful into the harmful.

In this original constitution, state and religion were not conjoined, but *one*; not connected, but identical. Man's relation to society and his relation to God coincided and could never come into conflict. God, the Creator and Preserver of the world, was at the same time the King and Regent of this nation; and his oneness is such as not to admit the least division or plurality in either the political or the metaphysical sense. Nor does this monarch have any needs, He demands nothing from the nation but what serves its own welfare and advances the felicity of the state; just as the state, for its part, could not demand anything that was opposed to the duties toward God, that was not rather commanded by God, the Lawgiver and Regent of the nation. Hence, in this nation, civil matters acquired a sacred and religious aspect, and every civil service was at the same time a true service of God. The community was a community of God, its affairs were God's; the public taxes were an offering to God; and everything down to the least police measure was part of the *divine service*. The Levites, who lived off the public revenue, received their livelihood from God. They were to have no property in the land, for *God is their property*. He who must sojourn outside the land *serves foreign* gods. This [statement which occurs] in several places in Scripture cannot be taken in a literal sense. It actually means no more *than that he is subject to alien political laws which, unlike those of his own country, are not at the same time a part of the divine service.*

The same can be said of the crimes. Every sacrilege against the authority of God, as the lawgiver of the nation, was a crime against the Majesty, and therefore a crime of state. Whoever blasphemed God committed *lese majesty*; whoever sacrilegiously desecrated the Sabbath implicitly abrogated a fundamental law of civil society, for an essential part of the constitution; was based on the establishment of this day. "*Let the*

Sabbath be an eternal covenant between Me and the children of Israel," said the Lord, *"a perpetual sign that in six days the Eternal, etc...."* Under this constitution these crimes could and, indeed, had to be punished civilly, not as erroneous opinion, not as *unbelief*, but as *misdeeds*, as sacrilegious crimes aimed at abolishing or weakening the authority of the lawgiver and thereby undermining the state itself. Yet, nevertheless, with what leniency were even these capital crimes punished. With what superabundant indulgence for human weakness. According to an unwritten law, corporal and capital punishment could not be inflicted unless the *criminal had been warned by two unsuspected witnesses with the citation of the law and the threat of the prescribed punishment;* indeed, where corporal or capital punishment were concerned, the criminal had to *have acknowledged the punishment in express words, accepted it and committed the crime immediately afterwards in the presence of the same witnesses.* How rare must executions have been under such stipulations, and how many an opportunity must the judges have had of avoiding the sad necessity of pronouncing a sentence of death over their fellow creature and fellow image of God. *An executed man is,* according to the expression of Scripture, *a reproach to God.* How much the judges must have hesitated, investigated, and considered excuses before they signed a sentence of death! Indeed, as the rabbis say, any court competent to deal with capital offenses and concerned for its good name must see to it that in a period of *seventy years* not more than one person is sentenced to death.

This clearly shows how little one must be acquainted with the Mosaic law and the constitution of Judaism to believe that according to them ecclesiastical power, are authorized, or that temporal punishments are to be inflicted for unbelief or erring belief. *The Searcher for Light and Right,* as well as Mr. Moerschel, are therefore far removed from, the truth when they believe I have abolished Judaism by my rational arguments against ecclesiastical right and ecclesiastical power. Truth cannot be in conflict with truth. What divine law commands, reason, which is no less divine, cannot abolish.

Not unbelief, not false doctrine and error, but sacrilegious offenses against the majesty of the lawgiver, impudent misdeeds against the fundamental laws of the state and civil constitution were punished; and these were punished only when the sacrilege exceeded all bounds in its unruliness, and came close to rebellion; when the criminal was not afraid to have the law quoted to him by two fellow citizens, to be threatened with punishment and, indeed, to take the punishment upon himself and commit the crime in their presence. Here the religious villain becomes a sacrilegious desecrator of majesty, a state criminal. Moreover, as the rabbis expressly state, *with the destruction of the Temple, all corporal and capital punishments and, indeed, even monetary fines, insofar as they are only national, have ceased to be legal.* Perfectly in accordance with my principles, and inexplicable without them! The civil bonds of the nation were dissolved; religious offenses were no longer crimes against the state; and the religion, as religion, knows of no punishment, no other penalty than the one the remorseful sinner voluntarily imposes on himself. It knows of no *coercion*, uses only the staff [called] *gentleness*, and affects only mind and heart. Let one try to explain rationally, without my "principles, this assertion of the rabbis! ...

NOTE

1. This passage from Mendelssohn's *Jerusalem* is in direct response to David Ernst Moerschel's "Postscript to 'Search for Light and Right'" (see document 18 in this chapter). This response occasioned Mendelssohn's famous and controversial definition of Judaism as a divine legislation of ceremonial laws, as opposed to a revelation of truths which either supersedes or superflously duplicates the judgments of reason. Mendelssohn thus held that Judaism in no way interferes with the free use of one's reason, and, contrary to, Moerschel's assertion, one can be both an observant Jew and a consistent votary of Enlightenment.

22. A TIME WILL COME WHEN NO PERSON WILL INQUIRE WHO IS A JEW OR A CHRISTIAN (1789)

JOHANN GOTTFRIED VON HERDER[1]

The *Jews* we shall consider here only as parasitical plants, having fixed themselves on almost all the nations of Europe, and sucked more or less of their juices. After the downfall of Rome, there were yet comparatively few of them in Europe; but from the persecution of the Arabs they fled thither in great multitudes and divided themselves nationally. That the leprosy was brought into Europe by them is improbable: but it was a still worse scab, that in all barbarous ages they were the base implements of usury, as bankers, brokers, and servants of the empire, and thus hardened the proud barbarian ignorance of the Europeans in trade against their own profit. They were often treated with great cruelty; and what they had acquired by avarice and deceit, or by industry, prudence, and order, was tyrannically extorted from them: but being accustomed to such treatment, and forced to reckon upon it, they carried their artifice and extortion to greater lengths. Still to many countries they were indispensable at that time, and are even now: it cannot be denied, likewise, that by them Hebrew literature was preserved; by them the sciences acquired from the Arabs, physics and philosophy, were propagated in the dark ages; and much other good was performed, for which no one but a Jew was adapted. A time will come, when no person in Europe will inquire whether a man be a Jew or a Christian; as the Jews will equally live according to European laws, and contribute to the welfare of the state. Nothing but a barbarous constitution could have been such an obstacle as to have prevented this, or rendered their abilities injurious.

NOTE

1. Johann Gottfried von Herder (1744–1803) was a German Protestant theologian, literary critic, and philosopher of history. Regarded as the father of the ideas of "nationalism, historicism, and the *Volksgeist*" (Isaiah Berlin), he wrote extensively on the Hebrew Bible. In *Vom Geist der Ebraeischen Poesie (On the Spirit of Hebrew Poetry, 1782–83)*, he presented the Bible as the greatest poetry given to humankind. His admiration of the poetic and religious genius of the "Old Testament" is tempered by a measure of contempt for the Jews of the Diaspora, as is evidenced in this passage from his *Ideen zur Philosophie der Geschichte der Menschheit*, First Part (Riga and Leipzig: Johann Friedrich Hartknoch, 1784). The concluding passage of the present selection has been often cited as evidence that Herder supported the emancipation of the Jews. It has also been argued that he expresses here but a Utopian wish and that he did not believe that the Jews would abandon their "barbarian constitution," namely, rabbinic Judaism, anytime in the near future.

Source: Johann Gottfried v. Herder, *Outlines of a Philosophy of the History of Man,* trans. of *Ideen zur Philosophic der Geschichte der Menschheit* by T. Churchill (London 1800), p. 486.

23. LEVIATHAN (1792)

SAUL ASCHER[1]

Finally, we will discuss Judaism in our era. Fortuitous circumstances compelled Mendelssohn to write his *Jerusalem* and declare his views on Judaism. This great spirit took a path that was absolutely different from his predecessors [e.g., Maimonides and Spinoza]. He placed—who can believe it?—reason in the shadow of faith. He neither explicated faith by means of the principles of reason, nor did he differentiate between faith and reason, rather he placed reason in the captivity of faith. He esteems only a faith which masters reason.

The path that he took is understandable. Mendelssohn had to be cautious. He had an adversary that set a trap for him. Consequently, he could not pursue a subtly reasoned argument, lest he forget to circumvent this trap. His opponent appealed to [creedal and scriptural] authority, obliging Mendelssohn to counter with similar arguments. Thus, already in the first round the debate came to an end over marginal issues.... [Mendelssohn] permitted extraneous issues to lead him to adopt extreme positions.

...And in order to save Judaism from the politicians, Mendelssohn dared to present it in such a manner that neither the politician, nor the philosopher, much less the common man, know what to make of it. Even if we assume that Judaism is indeed based on [divine] legislation, the question remains to be asked: To what end was the Law [of Moses] given? If as this sage, Mendelssohn, himself keenly argues the Jews were given the Law in order to preserve the nation in the knowledge [of the eternal, rational truths] possessed by their forefathers on the one hand, and, as one may assume, to maintain the memory of certain historical truths on the other, then fine. It would indeed be laudatory if reason, apprehending through the Law eternal truths and faith, offering the historical truths, would free the nation from the Law.

In order to prove the assumption that Judaism has no Canon law [*Kirchenrecht*] Mendelssohn seeks to demonstrate that Judaism is essentially based on knowledge and on obedience. Does not he himself admit, however, the possibility of faith founded on historical truths? And could not this fact lead him to conclude that the laws [of Judaism] are also largely based on historical truths? The error lies in that Mendelssohn considered these laws strictly as statutory duties [*constituirte Pflichten*], and failed to differentiate correctly between the essence of law [*Gesetz*] and the essence of rule [*Anordnung*].[2] To be sure [given this error], he was right in his presentation of Judaism as revealed legislation and in his designation of what is merely a means to an end to be essential.

In general, as a psychologist, Mendelssohn should have clarified the nature of obedience and not confined the entire purpose of revelation in Judaism to the Mosaic constitution. Had he done so he would have had to reach—as he most certainly would have—a different conclusion. One may assume, however, that he would have tried to evade this conclusion, as may be anticipated from the limited goal he set for himself.

If the politician does not know what to do with [Mendelssohn's thesis], even less so does the philosopher. Mendelssohn contends that Judaism contains religious doctrines of eternal truths. According to his system, and in consonance with the purpose he assigns to the Law, it must be assumed that the eternal truths are made known to man through the Law. Are these eternal truths then only determined by what is arbitrary and revealed? Can reason even deduce anything necessary from something contingent? Is

Source: Saul Ascher, *Leviathan, oder ueber Religion in Ruecksicht des Judenthums* (Berlin, 1792), pp. 149–50, 157–60, 226–28, 232, 235–38. Trans. by S. Fischer and P. Mendes-Flohr.

not the meaning of this [proposition] to forsake the truths of reason to fortuity?

As may be assumed from Mendelssohn's argument, the Law, however, is also a symbol for eternal truths—again I do not understand how it is possible to identify eternal truths with the Law. Contingent as well as historical and moral truths can be expressed in various ways. However, to present eternal truths, which are imprinted in all men, in a symbolic manner has yet to appeal to any nation. The common man is totally confused. If the Law has a purpose, it is completely self-evident that when the purpose becomes obsolete the Law is rendered superfluous. If the purpose of the Law in Judaism, as might be assumed from Mendelssohn, is to establish a Mosaic constitution, Judaism must cease the moment that this constitution no longer exists.[3] If the intention of the Law, however, is to bring men to faith and to knowledge of historical and religious or eternal truths, then the Law is only a method to guide men upon a certain path. If they are already walking upon this path, then it undoubtedly follows that they can forego this method, and nevertheless their descendants will remain on the same path.

How then did Herr Mendelssohn reach a conclusion which does not at all follow from his own system, and which, as it seems, he drew under duress: Whoever is born to the House of Jacob cannot in good conscience rid himself of the Law.

...Where do we find today a systematic doctrine of the essence of Judaism [from which] it may be learned how far one may go [to free himself from the Law]? Indeed, such a doctrine is precisely that which was missing until now. Transgression of the Law is deemed as an absolute abandonment of Judaism, and because those who have dared to transgress [the law] publicly were despised by their co-religionists, the significant aspects of Judaism have ceased to concern them. This process, which grows greater with each day, threatens us with a total disintegration of our faith, a faith whose *form* so bestows felicity and so uplifts the heart and which can render men so happy. This disintegration cannot be prevented unless we do away with the present constitution of Judaism and permit men unlimited use of their rational faculties, so that they may—without acting in opposition to the constitution of our religion—choose a position [*ein Beruf*] for themselves in society.

In overthrowing the old constitution we must establish a new one which will maintain us in the faith of our fathers, teach us the true essence of Judaism, present in a vital way its objectives and guide us in the path upon which we can, at the same time, be good human beings and good citizens.

...I therefore ask whether I may be regarded a heretic or an enemy of our faith because I argue that morally our nation cannot hope for a genuine amelioration [of this situation] unless we begin a positive reformation in the area of the Law. How may this reformation be brought about? What should be the limits of this reformation? The theologian, i.e., the rabbi, must answer these questions.

I believe I have already adumbrated several replies to these questions in this essay in which I surveyed the entire scope of Judaism. I would like to summarize here the thoughts which I expressed because I believe that some of my suggestions may lead us upon the correct course. First, I contend that the only possible object of Judaism was to make men as happy as possible, and with this in mind to establish a society. Second, in Judaism the only component of revelation is faith. Third, as a result [Judaism] is not based on obedience to the Law, rather this obedience required by the Almighty under certain circumstances is only a means to attain the higher aims of Judaism. Fourth, Judaism posits the true autonomy of the will. Fifth, the intention of the Almighty was not to reveal laws to the Jews so as to undermine their autonomy. Sixth, the Law only establishes [the framework] of religion, but it does not constitute its essence. Seventh, the laws came into effect only as statutes for the sake of maintaining a society and as rules intended to preserve certain deeds and [the memory of certain] events.

If it were my intention to support these theses with authority, I would illustrate them with numerous references to the writing of the prophets and other authors. But the matter must speak for itself.... We do not understand the deep intention of the Almighty which He made manifest to us in the word that was recorded by our fathers, which at the same time He inscribed in our souls and hearts. We fail to understand, however, that if our faith is strong we do not need symbols and if we make a genuine effort to achieve earthly happiness we can liberate ourselves from the Law. We do not understand that we are united among ourselves in faith alone, but in law [i.e., natural law] with all men.

Why did we not understand the intention of the Almighty? Why? Because we considered the legal constitution of our faith to be its essence: because by keeping the Law we neglected the entire form of our faith...; because those who received the constitution of our faith from the Eternal were not capable of achieving true faith and of establishing its true purpose.

Those who dared penetrate into the Holy of Holies of our faith are left to stand on its outer boundary only. They call to us: "Your religion is no longer good for our time, deny it and become men." Come to us, they intimate, and an abundance of bliss will be yours.

But no! Children of Israel, remain on the path of your fathers. Our religion is for every individual and is valid at all times. Show that your religion is capable of turning you into true human beings, and soon you will be capable of developing yourselves into citizens, that is, if only the constitution of your religion were reformed. If we persist [in effecting such a reformation] we will become, in all corners of the earth and among all men, a people worthy of divinity....

[Reformation will not undermine the essence of the religion.] What, in fact, does this essence consist of? What distinguishes it? And how far must the new constitution go?...Judaism, like every revealed religion, is given to man in its entirety, as an undefined compendium of principles, doctrines and laws. It is incumbent upon us to develop certain disciplines to create some other therein. The designated task must first delineate systematically the sources, the principles of Judaism and the history of their development; from this will emerge Theoretical Dogmatics, or the science of the sources of our faith. Second, it is necessary to learn the skills to teach the truth of our religion.... From this will emerge Practical Dogmatics, or the science of the constitutive faith of our religion.... Through this type of constitution.... our faith will stand pure and ennobled and no adversary will dare to deny its sanctity. Moreover, the adherents of this constitution will not dare to violate it.

Our form of faith must be open before the world and coming generations like the Book of Nature.... Let the witness of faith step forward:

1. I believe in one God.
2. I believe in a unique God that revealed Himself to our forefathers, Abraham, Isaac and Jacob and promised our salvation.
3. I believe in a God who chose Moses and others who were pleasing to Him and gave them the gift of prophecy.
4. I believe in a God who at Mount Sinai gave to our forefathers laws.
5. We accordingly believe that the observance of these laws was sacred to our fathers, and by their observance they were maintained on the same path upon which we march today solely through faith in God and His prophets.
6. We believe that this God is a God of Love.
7. We believe that He rewards good and punishes evil.
8. We believe that He guides the world through providence and omnipotence.
9. We believe that He will turn our misfortune to good.
10. We hope for redemption through the agency of His Messiah, in this world or after our death, with those whom He will deem worthy of resurrection.
11. We are obliged to continue and maintain the covenant that the Eternal One made with our fathers through the rite of circumcision.
12. We are obliged to celebrate the Sabbath as a day that is sanctified to God.
13. We are obliged to renew through the holidays the memory of His acts of grace.
14. We are obliged to seek through repentance God's grace and purification.

This is the pristine constitution [*Organon*] of Judaism. It must be explicated clearly with the aid of Scripture and Tradition. Faith, trust and obedience—these constitute the bond that binds us and holds us together. True as long as we are under the yoke of the present [rabbinic] constitution, our actions contrary to it are indeed improper. Therefore, I have shown the ways which we may, in a lawful manner, discard this constitution and introduce a new one, so that we will not be attacked as children who have forgotten their duties and violate the faith of their fathers. Thus we will not be placed in a position of being rebels against God, and of being mutineers who rely solely on their own arbitrary judgment, and further, we shall not be despised for forgetting all that has happened to our people, nor shall we be deemed—because of a lack of faith—the cause of the covenant's disintegration.

NOTES

1. Saul Ascher (1767–1822), a Berlin bookdealer who wrote widely on Jewish political and literary subjects. In so far as he regarded Judaism to be constituted by essential principles of faith (*Glaubenslehre*) and denied the eternal value of the *mizvot*, Ascher is considered a forerunner of Reform Judaism. The point of departure of Ascher's view on Judaism was his rejection of Moses Mendelssohn's definition of Judaism as essentially a religion of ceremonial laws.

2. Asher wishes to suggest that there is a categorical distinction between law, which is fixed by legislation, and rules, which are determined by custom drawn from historical experience. As such, rules are adaptable to new circumstances and even ultimately dispensable.

3. This judgement is drawn from Spinoza's *Theological-Political Treatise* in which he held that the Law of Moses was essentially the political constitution of the Hebrew commonwealth, and hence with the demise of the ancient Jewish state, the law was defunct. On Spinoza's views see this chapter, document 2.

24. NOTES REGARDING THE CHARACTERISTICS OF THE JEWS (1793)

LAZARUS BENDAVID[1]

I wish, then, to describe the four classes to which Jews today belong in order to derive therefrom the principal claim of this discussion, namely: to the extent that the Jews do not take advantage of [the opportunity] to abrogate the ceremonial law, which are meaningless and inappropriate for our time; to the extent that they do not establish a purer religion, more worthy of God—the pure teaching of Moses—they will perforce remain, even if baptized, apathetic citizens who are harmful to the states [they inhabit].

The four classes are the following: The first class, which is still the largest, is that which retains its loyalty to and its belief in the entire immense conglomeration of Jewish traditions. This class considers it to be a sin if it is doubted that the distance between the heel and the ankle of the foot of Og, King of Bashan, is less than thirty cubits or that Moses received on Mount Sinai from God Himself the melody of several of the hymns sung on the Day of Atonement. This class will remain forever irredeemable and its extinction is the only hope for the coming generations. For this class of Jews baptism and the acknowledgment of the Christian faith are of value only in that the zeal for bread is no more injurious to their existence than it is to the Christian who wants to be accepted into a particular guild. Aside from this, they pray with the rosary with the heart of a superstitious Jew, harboring resentment toward the Jews and contempt for the Christians. One rich fellow belonging to this gang who was baptized—for what reason I know not—recently wrote to another baptized Jew and invited him, although he was poor, to marry his daughter since he did not want her to marry a Christian.

Among those who remain steadfast in the faith of their forefathers, they are not infrequently to be found—in spite of their superstitions—exceedingly worthy men who, with respect to their sincerity and to the ardent zeal of their efforts for the good of their co-religionists truly embellish this class. I knew a

---

Source: Lazarus Bendavid, *Etwas zur Characteristick der Juden* (Leipzig, 1793), pp. 45–53. Trans. by S. Fischer and S. Weinstein.

director of a hospital in Berlin who was willing to share his last shirt with anyone who needed it. I knew another, a very poor man, who made it his business to collect donations for people even poorer than himself and who would have thought it the greatest sin to have taken even a penny of the money placed in his hands for his own use, even at the time of his greatest need.

The second class of Jews is that dissolute mob who have abandoned the ceremonial laws[2] because they were too much of a burden and because they prevented them from following unhindered their unbridled passions. Unfortunately, their number is still very great and will increase from day to day if a change does not soon take place. These, who in most cases were born to rich parents of the first class, were raised without a proper education and were led astray by love and wine. They consider themselves to be enlightened, but they merely arouse contempt. Their fathers are least at peace with themselves, while they must suppress the voice of conscience at every moment. They simulate enlightenment, but are incorrigible, uninformed vagabonds. These are the ones who, for the most part, are responsible for the bad opinion the Christians have of the Jews. These are the ones who through their immoral way of life cause the best of the first and third classes to abhor enlightenment in any form. The majority go over to Christianity the moment they meet a Christian maiden who is more cunning and more beautiful than she is clever and eloquent. After baptism, were it possible, they would be prepared to undergo a second circumcision were the acceptance of the Jewish religion to confer as many advantages as those attained through the acceptance of the Christian religion.

The third class seems to me to be always worthy of respect, even though my outlook in religion is far removed from theirs, for they are good men. Their intellect has not been cultivated by proper education, but their hearts are without blemish. [Consequently] their intellect is not sufficiently strong to elevate them to that level of enlightenment that makes a man moral even without such a religion that constantly reminds him of his [moral] duties. They are, however, cognizant of this weakness. Through fear of immorality, they remain [embedded] in an unrefined Judaism. With respect to themselves, they are suspicious of every innovation, but do not in principle

disallow innovation for others. They are deemed to be stubborn and unbending Jews, but if the Jews of the first class could read what is in their hearts they would accuse them of heresy. For the most part they have a system entirely their own in matters of religion. They persecute no one and act charitably toward everyone. They are faithful husbands, loving parents, true friends and good citizens. The countries of Prussia and Austria benefit greatly from their devoted and indefatigable industry. In the majority of cases—though not without exception—the state can rely on the sons of these noble men to be loyal, useful men.

The fourth class is composed either of the sons of the third class or of men who, owing to fortunate circumstances, have been equipped by heaven with adequate mental powers and who have met with men of the better sort. This class, which combined all the virtues of the previous class with true enlightenment, is as removed from Judaism as it is from apathy [*Indifferentismus*]. They are disciples of the genuine natural religion. Sensing the necessity of the duty of believing with all the ardor that this religion instils in men of reason, they are nonetheless aware of the precarious pillars upon which civic security would rest and the superficial foundations upon which human happiness would lie were man prevented from believing in God, immortality or the advance toward further perfection after death. Their words are holy to them. A member of this class would be ashamed of himself were he to make a profession of faith—even if only *pro forma*—of that of which in his heart he was not convinced. He would think that such a profession of faith, such a mockery of man's most important possession, implies a different kind of belief, one which every upright man would abhor. He would in effect be saying: "Citizens and compatriots! I hereby betray my conscience for the sake of ephemeral happiness; I avow with my lips that which is not in my heart! Trust me not! Do not charge me with public office, for I have committed perjury and I could easily do so again were I to be prompted by equally powerful inducements!"

The men of this class cannot be very happy as long as they are considered by the Christians to be Jews because they are not Christians and they are considered by the Jews to be apostates because they are men [*Menschen*]. They cannot be very happy as long as their solicitude for the integrity of their own mode of life and for the upbringing of their children is beset by obstacle after obstacle. On the one hand they have no access to any branch of livelihood other than that open to the ordinary Jew, namely, to make money through money. Their demands for civic respectability, which, in spite of all philosophizing, are motivated by a strong and sincere uprighteousness, are either rejected, as in the case of the ordinary Jew, or are granted solely out of charity. Moreover, the state forces them to be wicked men who must act contrary to their convictions before it permits them (according to present regulations) to engage in even the lowest of occupations of the civil service. On the other hand, those who support the meaningless ceremonial laws still bind them with iron chains. The vagabonds who have also abandoned the ceremonial laws consider themselves to be like the members of this class, while the better Jews of the third class consider them to be apathetic and even wicked men who are willing to separate themselves from Judaism because of its obligations.

NOTES

1. Lazarus Bendavid (1762–1832), German-Jewish mathematician, philosopher and educator. Despite his love of philosophy (in 1801, the Royal Academy of Sciences in Berlin awarded him a prize for a study on Immanuel Kant's epistemology), he devoted himself largely to Jewish problems. He regarded a religious reform of Judaism as the only feasible means of stemming the growing tide of conversions.

2. In this work Bendavid advocates the abolition of the ritual or "ceremonial laws" of Judaism. Here he demonstrates a sensitivity to Kant's criticism of Judaism as a "heteronomous" system of morally and spiritually vacuous ritual obligations: (Cf. Immanuel Kant, *Religion Within the Limits of Reason Alone* [1793], trans. T. M. Greene and H. H. Hudson [New York: Harper Torchbooks, 1960], pp. 115–90.) Kant misunderstood Bendavid's call for the reform of Judaism as intimating the desirability of conversion. He accordingly urged Bendavid to abandon the "pseudo-religion" of his forefathers and openly embrace Christianity. (See the following document.)

25. THE EUTHANASIA OF JUDAISM (1798)[1]

IMMANUEL KANT

On the subject of sectarianism (which, as in Protestantism, goes so far as to multiply churches), we are accustomed to say that it is desirable for many kinds of religions (properly speaking, kinds of ecclesiastical faith) to exist in a state. And this is, in fact, desirable to the extent that it is a good sign—a sign, namely, that the people are allowed freedom of belief. But it is only the government that is to be commended here. In itself, such a public state of affairs in religion is not a good thing unless the principle underlying it is of such a nature as to bring with it universal agreement on the essential maxims of belief, as the concept of religion requires, and to distinguish this agreement from conflicts arising from its nonessentials. Differences of opinion about the relative efficacy of the vehicle of religion in promoting its final aim, religion itself (that is, the moral improvement of human beings) may therefore produce, at most, different church sects, but not

Source: Immanuel Kant, "The Conflict of the Faculties," in idem, *Religion and Rational Theology,* trans. Allen W. Wood and George di Giovanni (Cambridge, England; New York: Cambridge University Press, 1996), p. 274ff.

different religious sects; for this is directly opposed to the unity and universality of religion (and so the invisible church).[2] Enlightened Catholics and Protestants, while still holding to their own dogmas, could thus look upon each other as brothers in faith, in expectation (and striving toward this end): that, with the government's favor, time will gradually bring the formalities of faith closer to the dignity of their end, religion itself (and for this reason the faith in question cannot be faith that we obtain God's favor or pardon by anything other than pure moral attitude of will)....With dreaming of a conversion of all Jews[3] (to Christianity in the sense of a *messianic* faith), we can consider it possible even in their case if, as is now happening, purified religious concepts awaken among them and throw off the garb of the ancient cult, which now serves no purpose and even suppresses any true religious attitude. Since they have long had *garments without a man* in them (a church without religion) and since moreover, a *man without garments* (religion without a church) is not well protected, they need certain formalities of a church—the church best able to lead them, in their present state, to the final end. So we can consider the proposal by Ben David,[4] a highly intelligent Jew, to adopt publicly the religion of *Jesus* (presumably with its vehicle, the *Gospel)*, a most fortunate one. Moreover, it is the only plan, which, if carried out, would leave the Jews a distinctive faith, and yet quickly call attention to them as an educated and civilized people who are ready for all the rights of citizenship and whose faith could also be sanctioned by the government. If this were to happen, the Jews would have to be left free, in their interpretation of the Scriptures (the Torah and the Gospels), to distinguish the way in which Jesus spoke as a Jew to Jews, from the way he spoke as a moral teacher to human beings in general.—The euthanasia of Judaism is pure moral religion, free from all the ancient statutory teachings, some of which were bound to be retained in Christianity (as a messianic faith). But this division of sects, too, must disappear in time, leading, at least in spirit, to what we call the conclusion of the great drama of religious change on earth (the restoration of all things), where there will be only one shepherd and one flock.

NOTES

1. *The Conflict of Faculties* (1798) is one of the last works that Kant published in his lifetime. The work, comprised of three essays written on different occasions, constitutes a milestone in the struggle for unfettered academic freedom and the liberation of the university from subservience to state authorities. The first essay addressed "The Conflict of the Philosophy Faculty with the Theology Faculty." Within the then regnant university system, the latter was defined as a "higher faculty," for it served the interest of the state to train priests who would be loyal both to the ecclesiastical and temporal authorities. Kant sought to defend the right of the "lower" faculty of philosophy to scrutinize theological issues from the independent perspective of reason alone. In the excerpt from this essay that is presented here, Kant considers the state's attitude toward contending Christian sects and Judaism. In accord with his view that true service to God must be the promotion of individual moral perfection, he calls for the "euthanasia of Judaism," urging Jews to free their ancestral faith of ritual and liturgical practices that, to his mind, hinder the development of proper moral attitudes.

2. Kant envisioned the "invisible church" as the realization of the ethical commonwealth, in which the most effective forms of service to God would be to mediate moral reason alone. Positive or historical religions are to be adjudged according to the degree to which they serve to promote this ideal.

3. Kant's note: "Moses Mendelssohn rejects this demand in a way that does credit to his cleverness (by *argumentatio ad hominen*). Until (he says) God, from Mount Sinai, revokes our law as solemnly as He gave it (in thunder and lightning)—that is, until the end of time—we are bound by it. By this he apparently meant to say: Christians, first get rid of the Judaism in *your own* faith, and then we give up ours. But it is for his co-religionists to decide whether this does credit to his good will; for by this stern challenge he cut off their hope for any relief whatsoever from the burden that oppresses them, though he apparently considered only the smallest part of it [that is, rabbinic law] essential to his faith." (Italics in the original.)

4. On Lazarus Bendavid, see document 24 of this chapter.

26. OPEN LETTER TO HIS REVERENCE, PROBST TELLER (1799)[1]

DAVID FRIEDLAENDER

In light of the wisdom of He who gave the Torah we may assume, even if this cannot be proved in detail in every instance, that each custom and each commandment had its own meaning, which went hand in hand with the welfare of the nation and its moral stature. From those [customs and commandments] whose purpose has been stated or is clearly discernible to the eye, it is reasonable to infer concerning all the others [that they too have purposes], which are likely to appear to us as aimless, trivial or even entirely ridiculous. Even those whose membership in that society obligated them to fulfill the commandments did not always have a clear knowledge of their purpose. It is sufficient for the lawgiver that for the present the fulfillment of the commandments contributed something to the happiness either of the group or of the individual. He who inquires [into these matters], however, was given cause for reflection or was provided with the opportunity to be enlightened by the sages and the leaders of the people. This is not an hypothesis that has been fabricated in order to save these laws. The very spirit of the entire system clearly demonstrates this. The written laws were few, and even these were for the most part unintelligible without oral commentary. It was axiomatic that it was forbidden to write down anything concerning the Law. [Indeed] it was explicitly stated: "The words transmitted orally thou art not at liberty to recite from writing."[2] The unwritten laws were thus learned only through oral transmission; for understandable and judicious reasons these laws remained vague. The teacher of the people in every generation was thereby given a free hand to alter and to adapt the commandments to the conditions of the time. No one could take a book of laws and contradict the teacher, for in this respect there were no written laws. "Even though these prohibit and these permit"—it is explicitly stated concerning the ceremonial laws [*Ceremonialgesetze*]—"these and these are the words of the living God."[3] This statement and many others in the Talmud demonstrate beyond any doubt that it was the intention of the first lawgiver that the sages of each generation would remain free to expand or limit the laws linked to time and place, to give them a more precise interpretation or to cancel them completely, all according to the needs of the time and to the moral behavior and the general progress of the nation. Not only is the cancellation of the laws linked to time and place grounded in the nature of the Law and evident throughout all of the Holy Scriptures, but even teachers of the people from such later periods, from whom the respect, spirit and authority of the first lawgiver had long since been withdrawn, acknowledged this as being fundamental. How else could they have cancelled and altered on their own authority many laws the fulfilment of which in foreign lands and in different climates either was of no use or subjected them to great difficulties?...The [Jewish] people, dispersed throughout the world and completely abandoned, with no permanent abode, no political sovereign and no spiritual leader, finally lost all touch with the values of reason and all inclination for the higher truths, which had constituted the foundation of their original religion. Instead, they fulfilled the ceremonial laws with a scrupulous exactness. The beautiful edifice of their religion was destroyed. Those who escaped the collapse embraced the ruins not of the Temple

Source: David Friedlaender, *Sendschreiben an seine Hochwuerdigen, Herrn Oberconsistorialrat und Probst Teller zu Berlin, von einigen Hausvaetern juedischer Religion* (Berlin, 1799), pp. 25–27, 30–34, 48–49. Trans. by S. Weinstein.

but of its scaffolding, that is, the external customs, the only thing which they saved. Had their spirit not been so profoundly distorted and their psychic powers so paralyzed, they would have learned in other lands and under other conditions to cancel the ceremonial laws as something that had become completely superfluous. Because of their state of mind at the time, however, their adherence to these laws grew increasingly stronger. The greater the persecutions were, the more anxiously their teachers, who lacked spiritual inspiration, urged the fulfillment of meaningless actions.

To all this the idea of a messiah was added, which completely clouded their minds and made all independent thought impossible. This idea arose quite early as a result of the mistaken interpretation of [certain] passages containing the inspired words of their prophets. In all these prophetic utterances the messiah, or the redeemer [of the people] from prevailing hardship and distress, appears as the customary figure of consolation. When the people repent of their sins—so proclaimed the prophets in all their oracles—they will be freed of the yoke of oppression and will return to the land of their fathers. This idea became ever more deeply rooted [in the minds of the people]. As the likelihood that redemption would take place by natural means decreased, the hope for a return to Jerusalem occurring by miraculous means grew stronger. If the people of God are to dwell once again in the land of their fathers, their return must be bound to the restoration of the ancient political order, to service in the Temple and to sacrifices. This delusion was much beloved by the people and was entirely in keeping with the spirit of the slogans of their seers and demagogues who in their vision of the future could not imagine—because of the situation at the time—the liberation of their nation by any other means. Accordingly, the strict fulfillment of the ceremonial laws was necessary for two reasons: first, in order to be worthy of the miraculous redemption through meritorious conduct and second, in order to be able, upon arriving in Jerusalem, to live according to the ancient political order and to fulfill the will of God.

This anticipation of [the coming of] the messiah and the return to the promised land fortified the inclination to direct all efforts and all thoughts to ancient history, service in the Temple, sacrifice and ceremonial laws. All faculties of the soul were devoted to these studies, all ingenuity was focused on hairsplitting musings. Their scholars multiplied and perverted [the obligations], increasing the yoke of the ceremonial laws, which in any case had been heavy. The separation from other peoples and from other subjects of human knowledge was thereby accentuated. The more meticulous [the fulfillment of] the ceremonial laws became, the more deserving became the people's demand for speedy redemption, for miraculous deliverance from misfortune. They overworked their brains and those of their contemporaries with responses to hairsplitting questions concerning the laws that will come into effect upon their return to Jerusalem or with the solution of the most trifling problems, which inclined to childishness and quixotry.

Given this frame of mind it is easy to perceive not only how the intellect and most likely the manners of the people were increasingly corrupted but also how even their external appearance took on a one-sidedness bordering on caricature. Accompanying this was an ever more rapidly increasing ignorance of their primordial language, Hebrew. That which was known [of Hebrew] through exegesis, together with the scarcely comprehensible translations [of Scripture] contributed to the dissemination of even more erroneous concepts. Moreover, the power of imagination [of the people], which in any case had been unrestrained, was provided with a new opportunity to generate fantastic notions and extravagant expectations. Under the circumstances in which the people found themselves, it was hardly to be expected that the teachers would cancel those ceremonial laws which had become inapplicable and replace them with other laws better suited to the spirit of the times. It was even less likely that these leaders, who were no longer capable of spiritual elevation and who had a scant knowledge of Hebrew, could extract the religious concepts and moral teachings expounded in the Holy Scriptures, order them systematically and present them to the best of their ability—even, if need be, in the adulterated language of the people—for the enlightenment and moral edification of the people.

Finally, what strengthened the yearning for Jerusalem and the hope for [the coming of] the messiah, and turned this into the most fervent wish of the people, was the fact that this yearning and this wish were transposed into the liturgy, becoming thereby an integral part of the worship of God and the prayer service.... [However, with the passing of time] the Jews' greatest gain lies no doubt in the fact that the yearning for the messiah and for Jerusalem has become removed ever further from their hearts in so far as reason has increasingly rejected these expectations as chimerical. It is always possible that certain isolated individuals, confined to their cloisters or in other respects alienated from worldly affairs, still preserve such wishes within their souls. [However,] with regard to the majority of Jews, at least those in Germany, Holland and France, this notion receives no support and the last traces of it will ultimately be eradicated....

If the authority of the lawgiver and one's own discernment, wisdom and duty, if the innermost conviction of the rightness of the action all point toward a single aim, namely, toward the cancellation of the ceremonial laws, then one may ask [us]: Wherefore do you procrastinate? Wherefore do you hesitate to declare that these laws are no longer binding on you, that you are ready to abandon the religion of your fathers (insofar as it is understood as the fulfillment of these laws and customs) and to convert to Christianity?

Here, our worthy, virtuous friend, our conscience bids us pause. Here we face the abyss which we know neither how to circumvent nor how to leap over. In short, here is the point at which we seek your counsel, your assistance and your instruction.

With the same audacious candor with which we have presented the results of our investigations into the Law of Moses and the foundations of the Mosaic religion, with the same love of truth, we must confess that which is surely sufficiently clear from our presentation. To abandon the religion of our fathers, that is to say, the ceremonial laws, and to accept the Christian religion are to us two entirely different matters.

... [Beyond the ceremonial laws Judaism contains at its core principles] which we deem to be the foundation of every religion, the principles upon which the religion of Moses is built have for us the highest certainty. We do not doubt that the creed of the Church corresponds to the principles of our faith in spirit, if not in wording, and we would [be ready to] embrace it. [Moreover,] we would [be ready to] make a public confession of that which the Christian teacher [Jesus] has taught, for we do not [merely] believe in his teachings as an aggregate of truths but

rather are convinced of their correctness. From this direction, therefore, there is no obstacle facing us and we need not fear that we would be repulsed [by the Church]. These [universal] principles are not all that we will bring with us from Judaism, however. In addition to them we shall bring other principles of the utmost significance, the truth of which is equally clear to us and which we are obligated to accept with equal conviction.[4] Will these principles conform to the teachings of the religious society that we are choosing? Will the teachers of the Christian Church be prepared if not to accept these principles then at least to display tolerance toward them, allowing us to publicly acknowledge these other principles which for us are convincing and beyond doubt? We do not venture to answer this question in the affirmative. At the very least we must not make a decision regarding this without the consent of a teacher of religion as respected, learned and noble as you, worthy Sir.

... That which we wish to do, with full conviction of the rightness of our action, our descendants—and perhaps even our contemporaries—will be forced to decide to do. Therefore why should we conceal the true condition of the great part of our brethren, above all those who reside in the large cities? The study of Hebrew and the Talmud declines among us day by day. The authority of the rabbis is diminishing, and with the neglect of the ceremonial ritual laws it must continue to diminish. In every country the government, with great justice, has taken from these rabbis all power to make binding judgments and enforce the halakhah. For the application of the civil laws of Judaism in our time is no longer to be tolerated and the retention of the power of excommunication and similar punishments in the hands of the scholars and theologians would seriously retard the progress of the members of the [Jewish] community. At a time when all religious factions are complaining that the bonds of religion are becoming weaker, it is to be expected that the Jews, who have no genuine religious instruction and no worship of God aimed at increasing piety, would relate to these matters with ever-increasing thoughtlessness. The contact and the social ties with the Christians, which are becoming more numerous, together with the willingness of the Christians to accept Jews in their temples as fellow believers should have sufficed to have aroused the oppressed, abandoned and on occasion even despised Jew to cross over to the Christian religion without further scruples. By this means, through the recital of a few words, he could secure for himself all the advantages of life, all the civil liberties which even the most upright Jew could not attain through a lifetime of faultless behavior. This consideration is extremely depressing for every thinking man and perhaps even the ruling authorities are not indifferent to it.

[On the one hand] the thinking man dare not assume that his descendants will possess the unselfishness and the strength of character to persevere in the face of the powerful enticement of such great, and so easily attainable benefits. [On the other hand] the ruler cannot view as desirable the increase of such families who were either tempted out of rashness or forced by need to break all family ties and who without shame and solely out of self-interest took a step against which at one time there had been a general bias.

In this labyrinth, into which we have fallen because of the time and circumstances, we might almost say because of our very virtues we have recourse to you, worthy and venerable Sir. Instruct us how we can find our way out [of this impasse]. Tell us, noble lover of virtue, should we decide to choose the great Protestant Christian community as a place of refuge, what kind of public declaration would you, and the men who sit with you on the venerable council, demand of us?...

The number of people who, full of trust, are sending this epistle to you is quite small. However, unless we are mistaken there must be a sizable number of heads of families who find themselves in a similar position and who perhaps lack only an initial example to arrive at a similar decision. This is also demonstrated by the numerous attempts of individuals of our religion to outline proposals concerning how religious reform is to be instituted. Although we doubt the feasibility of these attempts, they nevertheless make manifestly clear the need felt by our heads of families to do away with the fetters of the ceremonial laws as well as their desire to be incorporated, one way or another, into the wider society of the state.

A positive pronouncement by a man of your stature and authority in the Christian Church can thus have the most auspicious consequences for a multitude of upright, truth-loving men. By your pronouncement, noble Sir, you can establish and promote the prosperity and well-being of creatures yet unborn who will be able to enjoy a life of happiness and for whom your name will remain an eternal blessing.

The very fact that we are not taking this step merely out of consideration for ourselves helps us meet the objections that can be raised against us....We can be asked, for instance: Why are you not satisfied with disseminating morality and virtue among your brethren and leaving the future in the hands of Providence? The step that you are taking is astonishing. Would it not be more advisable to walk upon the slow path and to wait for time to unite all those who serve God in spirit and in truth? Further, we might be asked: Do you have such little trust in your wise and noble government and in the truly praiseworthy councillors of the consistory [Lutheran clerical board]? Will they not provide you with protection and assure you of tolerance once you declare your views in public? Why expose yourselves to the accusation that will inevitably be raised against you, namely, that you find fault with your fellow human beings?

We shall answer these questions frankly. Our circle of influence is small. However clear and pure the fundamental truths that we have made our own might be, however great and earnest our efforts to establish and spread these truths among our families might be, we nevertheless cannot help but fear that the purity and wholeness of these truths would not be preserved were they to be transmitted to future generations solely by oral means. In addition, we have never denied that our aim is to attain the rights of the citizen by means of our declaration and that it is our ardent wish that in this way we may see our descendants develop their intellectual and physical powers. Therefore, even if we concede that the assumption that the state will preserve and protect us is well grounded, we nevertheless will always exist merely as an intermediary body between Christians and Jews. We will be regarded and treated as an isolated sect without disciples which can offer [to its adherents] no more than a wretched existence. It would be far too much to hope that under these circumstances we could be accepted as citizens, attain [civil] liberties and enter society at large through matrimonial ties.

Finally, the history of all periods teaches that those principles which we have called eternal truths are indeed the religion of individual men, but cannot serve as the religion of the people, and certainly not for a prolonged period of time. In order to perpetuate them and preserve their salutary influence these delicate flowers of the power of thought require a vessel, the vessel of ways and means. These flowers wither easily, and the noblest creation of reason can in its decay be fatal for the spirit. Or, to use less figurative language, when sophistry and self-interest take possession of a person, our system, like every other, is subject to corruption and falsification. It therefore degenerates either into superstition and fanaticism or into heresy and atheism.

Without in the least seeking to forestall your opinion [of our proposal], venerable Sir, we [nevertheless] expect that within the wide circle of the true spirit of Protestantism we and our system can also find shelter and protection. In this way we will be able to attain the goal we have set for ourselves.

If the Protestant religion does indeed prescribe certain ceremonies, we can certainly resign ourselves to their performance as mere forms necessary for [our] acceptance as members of this society. Let it be understood that we are presupposing as a matter of principle that these ceremonies are required merely as actions, as customs that attest to the fact that the newly admitted member accepts the eternal truths out of conviction and that he submits to all the duties that result from this as a man and as a citizen. We do not regard this demand as a sign that he who performs the ceremonies is tacitly acknowledging that he accepts out of faith the dogmas of the Church. Should the demands of the Church be confined to formal ceremonies, we could accept these demands with a quiet conscience and fulfill them with total peace of mind.

The words of the prophet Zephania will thereby surely be consummated: "For then I will convert the peoples to a purer language that they may all call upon the name of the Lord, to serve Him with one consent."[5]

NOTES

1. David Friedlaender published this open letter to Wilhelm Abraham Teller (1734–1804), Protestant philosopher and scholar identified with the Enlightenment, anonymously in the name of an unspecified number of heads of Jewish households in Berlin. The circumstances of the letter are not clear.

Historians suggest that the letter indicates *inter alia* the despair of some German Jews in the struggle for civil equality, or that it perhaps bespeaks an attempt of well-to-do Jews to separate themselves from the Jewish masses and so improve their image and socioeconomic position. Whatever the motive behind the letter, it clearly reflects the frustrations and dilemmas of a generation of acculturated Jews prior to full emancipation. Friedlaender proposed to accept Christianity, if he and his colleagues were freed from the confession of certain dogmas (e.g., the divinity of Jesus) and the acceptance of sacraments. His proposal assumes a Deistic conception of reason as a self-sufficient means both to know God's will and to serve him. Accordingly, he not only rejected the ritual precepts of Judaism, but also the dogmas Christianity deemed as saving truths; even they conflicted with reason. The eternal, principally moral, truths that are accessible to reason and that can serve as a basis for unifying enlightened Jews and Christians are, according to Friedlaender, identical with the original teachings of Moses. This argument indicates an ambivalence toward Judaism. On the one hand, he is critical of the ritualism of Rabbinic Judaism; on the other, he is enthusiastic in his presentation of biblical faith or "pristine Judaism." As much as a proposal for conversion, the letter is then to be understood as an apologia for Judaism.

Teller was appointed dean (*Probst*) in the German Protestant Church, with a seat in the supreme consistory of Berlin, in 1767. In 1792 he issued his work *Die Religion der Volkommenen*, an exposition of his theological position, in which he advocated at length the idea of the "perfectability of Christianity"—that is, of the ultimate transformation of Christianity into a scheme of simple morality with a complete rejection of all specifically Christian ideas and methods. Friedlaender thus apparently felt that Teller would respond favorably to his proposal for a "dry baptism." With the eyes of Berlin upon him, Teller, however, proclaimed that conversion to the Church required a confession of the superiority of Christianity to Judaism, and the acceptance of baptism and the sacraments as the indispensable symbols of the religion founded by Christ. The Jew entering the Church would have to become a Christian! See David Friedlaender, Friedrich Schleiermacher, and William Abraham Teller, *A Debate on Jewish Emancipation and Christian Theology in Old Berlin*, eds. and trans., Richard Crouter, Julie Klassen (Indianapolis: Hackett, 2004).

2. Babylonian Talmud, *Gittin* 60b.

3. The citation is a composite of a midrash on Eccles. 12:11, in *Fathers of Rabbi Nathan*, version A, ch. 18,

and passages from the Jerusalem Talmud, *Berakhot*, Mishnah 7:1, p. 3a.

4. Friedlaender is referring here to principles of Judaism that cannot be verified by reason. In the succeeding paragraphs he calls these principles, which must be affirmed by belief alone, historical truths, following the distinction made by Mendelssohn in *Jerusalem* between eternal (or rational) and historical truths, e.g., the story of the exodus from Egypt. This discussion is part of Friedlaender's attempt to justify his proposal for a qualified conversion to Christianity.

5. Zeph. 3:9.

III

THE PROCESS OF POLITICAL EMANCIPATION IN WESTERN EUROPE, 1789–1871

The process of legal emancipation[1] of the Jews was ambiguous. The granting of citizenship—or full equality of each individual before the law—did not necessarily signify a basic and widespread change in attitudes toward the Jew. The modern, democratic state of France, established in 1789 on the principles of equality before the law, initiated the ambiguous process of the emancipation of Jewry. After an initial hesitation to extend to the Jews "the Rights of Man and of the Citizen," the National Assembly of France decided that its founding principles would be seriously vitiated should the Jews be excluded from citizenship. Despite legislators' personal and moral reservations regarding the Jews, the constitution of the Republic made it de rigueur for the Assembly to grant the Jews citizenship (see documents 1–5). Indicative of the disparity between principle and personal attitudes toward the Jews was the emphasis made in the Assembly's deliberations on the obvious fact that the rights of the citizen granted to the Jews appertain to the Jew *qua* individual and not to the Jews *qua* nation (see document 2). Presumably, it is the Jew *qua* member of the Jewish nation who bears all the egregious qualities that evoke the Frenchman's fears.

---

[1] In Jewish historiography and social philosophy the term *emancipation* is generally used to designate the legal process, which began in Europe with the French Revolution, of granting to the Jews equal civic rights in the countries in which they reside. The term *emancipation,* however, is somewhat of a linguistic anachronism, for it first emerged with specific reference to the Jewish struggle for civic rights only in 1828. The term was borrowed from the great debate of that year regarding the Catholics' accession to Parliament in England. (See Jacob Katz, "The Term *Jewish Emancipation:* Its Origin and Historical Impact," in Alexander Altmann, ed., *Studies in Nineteenth-Century Jewish Intellectual History* [Cambridge, Mass.: Harvard University Press, 1964], pp. 1–25.) Some historians use the term *emancipation* to describe the whole cultural and social movement promoting directly and indirectly Jewish integration; here the historical anachronism of the term is even greater.

The difference between legal emancipation and the basic acceptance of the Jew is underscored by the manner in which the Jews were emancipated in the rest of French-"liberated" continental Europe. Here citizenship was granted the Jews by the decree or suasion of the conquering armies of revolutionary France (see document 10). The French emperor Napoleon, (1769–1821), who fancied himself the custodian of the French Revolution, pointed to this disparity when he called 112 Jewish "notables" to the plush Hôtel de Ville in Paris on July 29, 1806 (see document 11). Through a series of pointed questions, he requested that this Assembly of Jewish Notables affirm that Judaism—the *national* religion of the Jews—does not undermine the civic morality and responsibility expected of the Jew as citizen (see documents 12 and 13). In their carefully worded reply, the notables indicated that Judaism does not interfere with the obligations of citizenship (see document 14). The reply of the notables was given the sanctity of binding religious law by the Sanhedrin—the supreme political, religious, and judicial body in Palestine during the Roman period until the fifth century C.E.—convened by Napoleonic decree. (According to Jewish lore, the reconstitution of the Sanhedrin is associated with the coming of the Messiah, of which Napoleon was well aware.) Meeting from February to March 1807, the Sanhedrin endorsed the answers of the notables (see document 16).

As Napoleon marched east to Poland and to Russia, he had undoubtedly hoped that this dramatic "messianic" gesture of convening the Sanhedrin would earn him the enthusiastic support of the millions of traditional Jews of the region. Indeed many greeted him as a latter-day Cyrus, an eschatological liberator; others thought that he covertly sought to subvert traditional Judaism (see document 17).

The Congress of Vienna, held in 1814 and 1815 for the reorganization of Europe after the defeat of Napoleon at Waterloo, marked the return of the conservatives (see document 21). For the lands formerly under French influence, the *Vormaerz*, the period between the Congress of Vienna and the liberal revolutions that began in March 1848, witnessed the erosion of the reforms inspired by the French Revolution. In France, however, the legal and economic achievements of the Revolution were respected. The revolutions of 1830 renewed the process of liberalization throughout Europe, redounding to more favorable legislation on behalf of the Jews. The liberal democratic mood was rekindled more forcefully with the revolutions of 1848. The struggle for liberal and democratic government was accompanied by a demand for the full emancipation of the Jews (see document 24). The resolutions were soon suppressed, and much of the legislation that they inspired was repealed. What the liberals were unable to achieve at the barricades was attained through the economic and social revolution that was slowly affecting Europe. This socioeconomic transformation of Europe led to a greater support of the "bourgeois" principle of legal equality, to which the remaining or renewed disabilities were an offense. The process of legal emancipation of the Jews in Central Europe was completed only with the unification of Germany between 1869 and 1871 and even then was not truly consummated until after World War I (see documents 26 and 27).

1. DECLARATION OF THE RIGHTS OF MAN AND OF THE CITIZEN (AUGUST 26, 1789)[1]

THE FRENCH NATIONAL ASSEMBLY

Article I. All men are born and remain, free and equal in rights: social distinctions cannot be found but on common utility....

10. No person shall be molested for his opinions even such as are religious, provided that the manifestation of these opinions does not disturb the public order established by the law.

NOTE

1. After the fall of the Bastille on July 14, 1789, a revolutionary national assembly set out to dismantle France's feudal monarchy and to establish a constitutional democracy. With the declaration of the rights of man and of the citizen, inspired by the Declaration of Independence of the United States, the National Assembly transcribed the slogan of the French Revolution—"liberty, equality and fraternity"—into law. It became the basic law of the French constitution.

Source: Benjamin Flower, ed. and trans., *The French Constitution* (London, 1792), pp. 17–18.

2. DEBATE ON THE ELIGIBILITY OF JEWS FOR CITIZENSHIP (DECEMBER 23, 1789)[1]

THE FRENCH NATIONAL ASSEMBLY

MONSIEUR THE COUNT OF CLERMONT TONNERRE:[2] You have, by the Declaration of Rights, secured the rights of men and of citizens. You have irrevocably established the conditions of eligibility for the administrative assemblies. It seemed that there was nothing further to do in this regard. One honorable member has in the meantime informed us that non-Catholic inhabitants of several parts of the provinces have been seeing their rights challenged by motives drawn from the very laws made in their behalf. Another has called your attention to citizens who find in their professions obstacles to their enjoyment of the same rights.

Source: Achille-Edmond Halphen, *Recueil des Lois, Décrets, Ordonnances, avis du conseil d'état, Arrêtés et Règlements concernant les Israélites depuis la Révolution de 1789* (Paris, 1851), pp. 184–89. Trans. by J. Rubin.

I have thus two issues to examine: exclusion related to profession and exclusion related to religion....

I will deal now with religion. You have already addressed this point in stating in the Declaration of Rights that no one shall be persecuted for his religious beliefs. Is it not profound persecution of the citizen to want to deprive him of his dearest right because of his opinions? The law cannot affect the religion of a man. It can take no hold over his soul; it can affect only his actions, and it must protect those actions when they do no harm to society. God wanted us to reach agreement among ourselves on issues of morality, and he has permitted us to make moral laws, but he has given to no one but himself the right to legislate dogmas and to rule over [religious] conscience. So leave man's conscience free, that sentiments or thoughts guided in one manner or another toward the heavens will not be crimes that society punishes by the loss of social rights. Or else create a national religion, arm yourself with a sword, and tear up your Declaration of Rights. [But] there is justice, there is reason....

Every religion must prove but one thing—that it is moral. If there is a religion that commands theft and arson, it is necessary not only to refuse eligibility to those who profess it, but further to outlaw them. This consideration cannot be applied to the Jews. The reproaches that one makes of them are many. The gravest are unjust, the others are merely wrong. Usury, one says, is permitted them. This assertion is founded on nothing but a false interpretation of a principle of charity and brotherhood which forbids them to lend at interest among themselves.... Men who possess nothing but money cannot live but by making that money valuable, and you have always prevented them from possessing anything else.... This people is insatiable, one says. This insatiability is [however] not certain.

The Jews should be denied everything as a nation, but granted everything as individuals.[3] They must be citizens. It is claimed that they do not want to be citizens, that they say this and that they are [thus] excluded; there cannot be one nation within another nation. The Jews in the [Habsburg Empire] enjoy not only the rights of citizens but [even] the possibility of attaining the honorific distinction [of ennoblement] that we have destroyed and still survives there in all its vigor[4].... It is intolerable that the Jews should become a separate political formation or class in

nationalism

the country. Every one of them must individually become a citizen; if they do not want this, they must inform us and we shall then be compelled to expel them. The existence of a nation within a nation is unacceptable to our country.... The emperor admitted the Jews to all ranks, to all duties. They exercised in France the most important public functions. One of our colleagues has authorized me to say that several Jews contributed to his election. They are admitted to the military corps; when I was chairman, a patriotic gift was brought to me by a Jew, a national soldier....

The Jews must be assumed to be citizens as long as it is not proven that they are not citizens, as long as they do not refuse to be citizens. By their petition,[5] they demand to be considered as such; the law must recognize a right that prejudice alone refuses. But, one says, the law does not rule over prejudice. That was true when the law was the work of one man only; when it is the work of all, that is false.

It is necessary to explain oneself clearly on the position of the Jews. For you to keep silent would be the worst of evils. It would be to have seen the good and not to have wanted to do it; to have known the truth and not to have dared to speak it; finally it would be to place on the same throne prejudice and law, error and reason....

MONSIEUR DE LA FARE, bishop of Nancy:[6] My arguments and my evidence could not add anything to what M. l'abbé Maury[7] has said. Placed close to a great number of Jews by the functions with which I am honored, I must present to you my observations of them, and I will limit myself to that.

The Jews certainly have grievances which require redress. Rights enacted by this legislature should be revoked without forgetting that the Jews are men and are unhappy. It is necessary to grant them protection, security, liberty; but must one admit into the family a tribe that is a stranger to oneself, that constantly turns its eyes toward [another] homeland, that aspires to abandon the land that supports it; a tribe that, to be faithful to its law, must forbid to the individuals who constitute it its entrance into armies, the mechanical and the liberal arts, and into the employ of the civil courts and municipalities; a tribe that, in obeying both its own law and the national law, has 108 valueless days in the year?

In all fairness, I must say that the Jews have rendered great service to Lorraine, and especially to the city of Nancy; but we are faced with a pressing situation. My evaluation [of the situation] obliges me to stand against the motion that has been put before you.

The interest of the Jews themselves demands this stance. The people detest them; in Alsace the Jews are often the victims of popular uprisings. In Nancy, four months ago, people wanted to pillage their homes. I went to the site of the agitation and I asked what complaint they had to make. Some claimed that the Jews had cornered the wheat market; others, that the Jews banded together too much, that they bought the most beautiful houses and that soon they would own the whole city. One of the protesters added: "Yes, Monsieur, if we were to lose you, we would see a Jew become our bishop, they are so clever at taking possession of everything."

A decree that would give the Jews the rights of citizenship could spark an enormous fire. Once they obtained a similar favor from the parliament of England, but immediately the bakers refused them bread, and these unfortunate Jews very soon demanded the repeal of the bill.

I propose to establish a committee which will be charged with the revision of all the legislation concerning the Jews.

NOTES

1. It would have been logical for the Declaration of the Rights of Man and of the Citizen to have embraced all the denizens of France regardless of religion. Abbé Grégoire for one, assumed that it would be sufficient to assure equal rights for the Jews and that no special legislation would thus be necessary (cf. chapter 1, document 17). But the French National Assembly hesitated, continually postponing the decision as to whether the Jews of France were indeed included within the purview of the declaration. The issue of Jewish citizenship was immediately prompted by reports from the province of Alsace that the peasants, riding on the crest of revolutionary enthusiasm, had rioted against the Jews.

The Jews of Alsace and of the neighboring province of Lorraine, (numbering about 30,000 or eighty percent of the Jewish population of France), were Yiddish-speaking and traditional. With few exceptions they earned their livelihood through peddling, grain and cattle trading and petty money lending—pursuits that recurrently brought them into conflict with the local peasantry. The speeches in this document are from the debate in the Assembly on December 23, 1789. On the following day the debate was adjourned, and as was typical no decision had been reached.

2. Count Stanislas de Clermont-Tonnerre (1757–1792), French revolutionary, deputy to the national assembly and consistent advocate of equal rights for the Jews as individuals.

3. That is, citizenship would require that the Jews relinquish their national distinctiveness and communal autonomy and implicity cultural separateness.

4. This is a reference to the approval of the legislation by Joseph II in 1789. See chapter 1, documents 13 and 14.

5. The count is referring either to the address of the Jews of Paris to the Assembly or to that of the community of Alsace and Lorraine in which they petitioned for full citizenship. (See *Adresse présentée a l'Assemblé Nationale le 26 août 1789, par les Juifs résidant à Paris* [*près 1789*]; *Adresse présentée à l'Assemblée Nationale, 31 août 1789, par les députés réunis des Juifs établis à Metz, dans les Trios Evêchés, en Alsace et en Lorraine* [1789].) He may also be referring to Berr Isaac Berr's speech before the Assembly on behalf of the Jews of Alsace-Lorraine on October 14, 1789.

6. Anne-Louis-Henri de la Fare (1752–1829) was bishop of Nancy, Lorraine, and a vigorous opponent of Jewish civil rights. His speech before the Assembly was reprinted and widely read. See *Opinion de M. l'évêque de Nancy, député de Lorraine sur l'admissibilité de Juifs à la plénitude de l'état civil et des droits de citoyens actifs* (Paris, 1790).

7. Abbé Jean Sieflein Maury (1746–1817), delegate from Peronne near Lyons. In opposing an increase of Jewish rights, he argued that by virtue of their religion the Jews were alien to France and that, moreover, their malevolence was incorrigible.

3. DECREE RECOGNIZING THE SEPHARDIM AS CITIZENS (JANUARY 28, 1790)[1]

THE FRENCH NATIONAL ASSEMBLY

All of the Jews known in France, under the name of Portuguese, Spanish, and Avignonese Jews, shall continue to enjoy the same rights they have hitherto enjoyed, and which have been granted to them by letters of patent.

In consequence thereof, they shall enjoy the rights of active citizens, if they possess the other requisite qualifications, as enumerated in the decrees of the National Assembly.

NOTE

1. The equivocation of the Assembly regarding Jewish civil equality especially aggrieved the Sephardim (Jews of Spanish and Portuguese origin) of Bordeaux and Bayonne. Residing in France (initially as "New Christians") since the sixteenth century, these Jews were highly acculturated Frenchmen. Moreover, by virtue of letters of patent issued by several French monarchs, these Jews had tacitly enjoyed extensive civil rights for some two hundred years. They thus argued that their eligibility for citizenship was not to be considered in connection with the Ashkenazi of Alsace and Lorraine. The Sephardim emphasized that the two communities were quite distinct socially, culturally and legally. This argument prevailed, and, together with the Jews of Avignon, who had also obtained letters of patent from the *ancien régime*, their "civil rights" were confirmed by the Assembly. This recognition of Jews, even if only of a specific category of Jews, served as an important precedent.

Source: M. Diogène Tama. *Transactions of the Parisian Sanhedrin,* trans. F. D. Kirwan (London, 1807), pp. 3–4.

4. THE CONSTITUTION OF FRANCE (SEPTEMBER 3, 1791)[1]

THE FRENCH NATIONAL ASSEMBLY

Title 1. Fundamental Regulations Guaranteed by the Constitution. The Constitution guarantees, as national and civil rights, (1) That all the citizens are admissible to places and employments, without any other distinction than that of VIRTUE and TALENTS.... (3) Liberty to every man to...exercise the religious worship to which he is attached.

NOTE

1. These provisions of the new constitution set the stage for the extension of rights of the citizen to all Jewish residents of France.

Source: Benjamin Flower, ed. and trans., *The French Constitution* (London, 1792), pp. 20–23.

5. THE EMANCIPATION OF THE JEWS OF FRANCE (SEPTEMBER 28, 1791)[1]

THE FRENCH NATIONAL ASSEMBLY

The National Assembly, considering that the conditions requisite to be a French citizen, and to become an active citizen, are fixed by the constitution, and that every man who, being duly qualified, takes the civic oath, and engages to fulfill all the duties prescribed by the constitution, has a right to all the advantages it insures;

Annuls all adjournments, restrictions, and exceptions contained in the preceding decrees, affecting individuals of the Jewish persuasion, who shall take the civic oath, which shall be considered as a renunciation of all privileges in their favor.[2]

NOTES

1. All remaining reservations regarding the applicability of the Declaration of the Rights of Man and of the Citizen to the Jews were removed in this resolution of the National Assembly, which explicitly recognized the Jews as full citizens of France. Adrien Duport, a member of the Jacobin Club, who presented the resolution

Source: M. Diogène Tama, *Transactions of the Parisian Sanhedrin*, trans. F. D. Kirwan (London, 1807), pp. 6–7.

for adoption by the Assembly, argued that the inviolability of the principle of religious freedom, and indirectly all the principles of the constitution, would be assured only if it was consistently applied. "I believe that freedom of worship," he concluded, "does not permit any distinction in the political rights of citizens on account of [the Jews'] creed. The question of the political existence of the Jews has been [repeatedly] postponed. Still the Muslims and the men of all sects are admitted to enjoy political rights in France. I demand that the motion of postponement be withdrawn, and a decree passed that the Jews in France enjoy the privileges of full citizens [*citizens actifs*]" (Achille-Edmond Halphen, *Recueil des Louis*, p. 229).

2. The reference is to the communal autonomy that the European Jews enjoyed in the Middle Ages. Such autonomy was deemed to be incompatible with the principles of the modern state.

6. LETTER OF A CITIZEN TO HIS FELLOW JEWS (1791)

BERR ISAAC BERR[1]

Gentlemen and dear brethren,

At length the day has come when the veil, by which we were kept in a state of humiliation, is rent; at length we recover those rights which have been taken from us more than eighteen centuries ago. How much are we at this moment indebted to the clemency of the God of our forefathers!

We are now, thanks to the Supreme Being, and to the sovereignty of the nation, not only Men and Citizens, but we are Frenchmen! What a happy change thou hast worked in us, merciful God! So late as the twenty-seventh of September last, we were the only inhabitants of this vast empire who seemed doomed to remain forever in bondage and abasement; and on the following day, on the twenty-eighth, a day for ever sacred among us, thou inspirest the immortal legislators of France. They pronounce, and more than sixty thousand unfortunate beings, mourning over their sad fate, are awakened to a sense of their happiness by the liveliest emotions of the purest joy. Let it be acknowledged, dearest brethren, that we have not deserved this wonderful change by our repentence, or by the reformation of our manners: we can attribute it to nothing but to the everlasting goodness of God: He never forsook us entirely: but, finding that we were not yet worthy of seeing the accomplishment of his promises of a perfect and lasting redemption, he has not, however thought proper still to aggravate our sufferings: and surely our chains had became the more galling from the contemplation of the rights of man, so sublimely held forth to public view. Therefore, our God, who reads the heart of man, seeing that all our resignation would have proved unequal to the task, and that supernatural strength was wanting to enable us to support these new torments, has thought of applying the remedy: He has chosen the generous French nation to reinstate us in our rights, and to effect our regeneration, as, in other times, he had chosen Antiochus, Pompey, and others, to humiliate and enslave us. How glorious it is for that nation, who have, in so short a time, made so many people happy! And surely, if Frenchmen are

---

Source: Berr Isaac Berr, "Lettre d'un Citoyen" (Nancy, 1791), in M. Diogène Tama, *Transactions of the Parisian Sanhedrin,* trans. F. D. Kirwan (London, 1807), pp. 11–29.

to become so themselves, by the additional rights and the additional liberty they have just acquired, how much the more are we, in particular, gainers by the change! And what bounds can there be to our gratitude for the happy event. From being vile slaves, mere serfs, a species of men merely tolerated and suffered in the empire, liable to heavy and arbitrary taxes, we are, of a sudden, become the children of the country, to bear its common charges, and share in its common rights.

What orator could presume to express to the French nation and to its king, all the extent of our gratitude, and of our unalterable submission? But neither the king nor the representatives of the nation seek praise or acknowledgment; their only wish is to behold people happy. In that they expect and they will find their reward. Let us then, dear brethren, let us conform to their wishes; let us examine with attention what remains to be done, on our part, to become truly happy, and how we may be able to show, in some measure, our grateful sense for all the favors heaped upon us. On this subject, gentlemen and dear brethren, give me leave to submit to your judgment the result of some reflections, which our change of condition has suggested to me.

The name of active citizen, which we have just obtained, is, without a doubt, the most precious title a man can possess in a free empire; but this title alone is not sufficient; we should possess also the necessary qualifications to fulfill the duties annexed to it: we know ourselves how very deficient we are in that respect; we have been in a manner compelled to abandon the pursuit of all moral and physical sciences, of all sciences, in short which tend to the improvement of the mind, in order to give ourselves up entirely to commerce, to be enabled to gather as much money as would insure protection, and satisfy the rapacity of our persecutors....

I cannot too often repeat to you how absolutely necessary it is for us to divest ourselves entirely of that narrow spirit, of Corporation and Congregation, in all civil and political matters, not immediately connected with our spiritual laws; in these things we must absolutely appear simply as individuals, as Frenchmen, guided only by a true patriotism and by the general good of the nation; to know how to risk our lives and fortunes for the defence of the country, to make ourselves useful to our fellow citizens, to deserve their esteem and their friendship, to join our

efforts to theirs in maintaining public tranquility, on which that of individuals depends.

Let us do for the present what is within our power, let us take the civic oath of being faithful to the nation, to the law and to the king. This oath contains only the sentiments we have always professed. We have never been accused of being breakers of the law, or of having rebelled even against those who domineered over us; we have always respected and obeyed even those by whom we were ill-treated: we shall then, upon much stronger grounds, remain faithful to laws which reinstate us in our rights, and place us on the same footing with all Frenchmen, leaving us at the same time, at full liberty to profess our religion, and to follow our mode of worship. This oath, I say, which, on our side, is nothing but a renunciation of those presented privileges and immunities which we enjoyed, cannot, under any point of view, wound the conscience of the most observant and the most scrupulous of our brethen; our privileges and our immunities were only relative to our state of slavery.

This oath once taken, let us exert ourselves to fulfil the duties within our reach, but let us avoid grasping at our rights; let us not rush headlong against the opinions of some of our fellow citizens who, rendered callous by prejudice, will reject the idea of Jews being fellow men, fellow creatures. Let it be sufficient for us, at present, to have acquired the invaluable right of assisting at all assemblies of French citizens; but let us not attend them, till we have acquired knowledge sufficient to make ourselves useful members; till we know how to discuss and defend the interests of the country; in short, till our most bitter enemies are convinced, and acknowledge the gross misconceptions they had entertained of us....

Our education has been defective in many points of view. Already the famous Rabbi Hartwig Wessely, of Berlin, has rendered us an eminent service, by publishing several works in Hebrew on this subject. One of his productions, entitled [*Words of Peace and Truth*][2] has been translated into French, in the year 1792. It details the causes of our present ignorance, and the means by which we may deserve once more the appellation of the learned and intelligent nation, which God himself gave us. I shall not report here what you find in these useful publications; but I entreat you, dear brethren, to follow this author in his meditations; and you will easily remark that our fate, and the fate of our posterity, depends solely on the change we shall effect in our mode of education....

French ought to be the Jews' mother tongue, since they are reared with and among Frenchmen; it has always been the language in which they have made the least proficiency, and which very often they scarcely understand. It is only when compelled by necessity to speak to and to be understood by their neighbours that they begin to blunder some inarticulate words; from hence proceeds this other inconvenience, that those among us who have felt early enough the usefulness of the French language, and have acquired the habit of speaking it with facility, cannot, however, get rid of a German or other foreign accents. Their diction, too, is generally incorrect. I even must say myself, that while I am thus addressing you in French, I feel my want of experience and of proficiency in that language, which I have however chosen in preference, to prove to you, that Jews may commune together and confer with one another in that language, on all topics even on religious matters, and that it is entirely in our powers to avoid encumbering the minds of our youth with the useless study of foreign languages.[3] Have we not the example of the Jews of Asia, the most devout and the most scrupulous of our brethren, who read and write only Hebrew and the language of their country? Why should we continue to bear the name of German or Polish Jews, while we are happily French Jews?...

Let us establish charitable houses of industry, in which the children of poor people and those who are not born to a higher rank, shall learn all the trades and mechanical occupations necessary to society. Let us form among us carpenters, smiths, tailors, etc. And if we can succeed in having a man in each profession, able to work as a master, he will soon form apprentices; and gradually we shall see Jewish workmen who will strive to deserve esteem by earning honourably their livelihood. Thus shall we banish sloth and indolence, occasioned by the idleness of our youth....

If we have been reproached at one time with want of industry, indolence and aversion to labour, let us now avoid such reproaches, which might be unjust formerly, but which we should now deserve. Let us exert all our influence to accustom our poor, who, till now, have been fed by our alms, to prefer the gains of labour, even at the sweat of their brows.

In thus imparting to you my humble ideas of our personal situation, I am, dear brethren, fulfilling a duty the most congenial to my feelings. My thoughts, as you may see, are presented to you in a crude state: it is by your attention and by your meditations, should you deem [my thoughts] worthy, that they are to be matured and quickened into action. Whatever success may attend them, I hope, at least, that you shall do justice to the fraternal sentiments, which unmixed with any other motives, have urged me to exhort and press you, dear brethren, not to lose one moment in taking our situation into your consideration.

I have the honour to be most fraternally, your most obedient and very humble servant,

Berr Isaac Berr

NOTES

1. Berr Isaac Berr (1744–1828), a successful merchant and banker from Nancy. He was prominent in efforts against the defamation of Jewry and in the Jewish struggle for civil equality. In 1789 he was one of six delegated by the Jewish community of Alsace and Lorraine to present its case for civil protection and rights before the National Assembly. He later served successively as a member of the Assembly of Jewish Notables and the Parisian Sanhedrin. Among his literary works is a translation into French of Naphtali Herz Wessely's *Words of Peace and Truth* (see chapter 2, document 8) under the title *Instructions Salutaires Addressées aux Communautés Juives de l'Empire de Joseph II* (Paris, 1792).

   On the morning of the resolution of the National Assembly emancipating all the Jews of France, Berr dispatched this letter to the Jewish congregations of Alsace and Lorraine.
2. See chapter 2, document 8.
3. The reference is to Yiddish.

7. THE DEBATE ON JEWISH EMANCIPATION (AUGUST 22–31, 1796)[1]

NATIONAL ASSEMBLY OF BATAVIA[2]

Van Hamelsfeld:[3]

Is it true that this Assembly presently discusses the question whether 50,000 people will be free or slaves? Why, if this were the case, does one need to search for an answer? If the question "will he be free or a slave?" were to be asked even concerning one single man, those who recognize freedom as an innate and inalienable right of man will not be in doubt for one moment, and they will declare that man is free. How, then, could we doubt when the question "will they be free or not?" concerns 50,000 people?

The question which we are presently discussing is not whether 50,000 people will be free or slaves, since we are talking about Jews. The question is: will the Jewish people be recognized among the Dutch and will it be treated on equal terms with all Dutch citizens in such a way that the Jewish people will be totally equal to the Dutch, without any distinction whatsoever.

This changes the nature of the question entirely, Citizens Representatives! Now it can, it must be a subject for discussions in this Assembly.

It can be a subject for discussions in this Assembly. The Jews are not slaves among us. They may be aliens and, as aliens, be excluded from the special privileges which belong to citizens of the Netherlands, the Dutch people, and which are rights of the citizen in the Netherlands. But no one disputes their rights of man (and these two, rights of man and rights of the citizen, should not be confused).

As superstition in other countries caused inhumane persecutions, the Jewish people were received here, as aliens, with all hospitality. Our wise and fair ancestors granted them the freedom to live among us in safety, not only for their person, but also for their property.... In short, our ancestors allowed to the Jewish people the protection of the laws, which also protect the alien against every form of maltreatment and unjust oppression.

The question, therefore, is only: Will we continue to regard the Jewish people as alien residents, or will we go further and regard them, as Dutchmen, as members of the Batavian people— in other words, not only as our fellow human beings, but also as our fellow-citizens—on an equal footing with Dutchmen?

This question becomes all the more important with regard to the Jews, the more their manners, laws, and customs distinguish them from all other peoples so that a fraternization of this nation with other nations even seems impossible. I merely request that one keep in mind that in this discourse I am not speaking about a few individuals but about the bulk of the Jewish nation living among us.

I may be permitted, Citizen Representatives, to express freely and candidly my feelings about this subject which is not entirely strange to me.

In the first place, I must remark that I do not consider the Jews as a religious faith or a mere brotherhood.... Likewise, I think we must not consider the Jews, in this case, merely as men and, as such, as our natural fellows, our brothers.

Thus, it will not be sufficient to prove that the Jews among us should enjoy all of what men are entitled to as human beings. We must especially consider whether they can be regarded as Dutch and Batavian human beings, that is, as citizens of the Batavian Commonwealth, and consequently whether they can enjoy the same rights as citizens with the Dutch citizens.

However, before I come to the principal and proper question, I will have to say that I am not unfavorably

Source: *Dagverhaal der handelingen van de Nationaale Vergadering,* (The Hague: Swart, 1796), Part 2, pp. 647–736, trans. Daniel M. Swetschiniski.

disposed toward the Jews. If any one thinks so, I will assure him now that I have a deep regard for the Jews for the sake of their forefathers, and because he whom I recognize as the greatest benefactor and enlightener of the world was a Jew [Jesus].

When I consult the chronicles of the Jews and the spirit of their laws, they show me a nation which, however full of shortcomings—attributable partly to the oriental climate, partly to the uncivilized state of those days, partly to their circumstances, partly to the power of prejudices—is conspicuous for its great men, excellent laws, illustrious deeds, and glorious virtues.

Liberty has always been dear to the Jewish people; so dear that they dared boast: "Never have we served any one!" Equality, Citizen Representatives, was nowhere more esteemed by any people than by the Jews. Equality and true liberty are the soul of Moses's laws. However, with regard to Fraternity, Citizen Representatives, we have to be more specific. The Jews have always considered, and still consider themselves the people which the Godhead favored most on earth. They have always had a very high opinion of themselves and held other peoples in contempt. Among themselves they greet and treat each other like brothers. However, their laws—in their origin, spirit and meaning are fit to make and keep them a separate people. Their circumcision serves that purpose, as well as so many laws which regulate their religious ceremonies, such as their marriage and dietary laws.

However, the Jews so far extended their essential privileges by conceit and prejudices, they behaved toward other peoples with such pride, that they incurred the hatred of all of mankind, as Tacitus expressed it.[4]

Will we have to regard the Jews as members of our Dutch citizens-society? Are they entitled to the rights of Dutch citizens? Or are the Jews part of a separate nation which, living among us as aliens, consequently, cannot be regarded as Dutch citizens and can claim the rights of man, but not the rights of Dutch citizens? In other words, can I say equally "Dutch Jews, Portuguese, German and Polish Jews" as well as "Jewish Dutchmen?" I can say, without distinction, "Reformed, Roman Catholic (etc.) Dutchmen" and "Dutch Reformed, Dutch Roman Catholics," etc. But can I say the same of Jewish without differentiation?

It seems to me, Citizen Representatives, that, as soon as someone hears the question and understands the words in which it is phrased, he will have no doubts about the answer. He will say: The name itself "Jewish Nation," nation par excellence, which we and the Jews themselves customarily give to them, indicates sufficiently that they are a separate nation and not Dutchmen.

These, Citizens, are the reasons which confirm this assertion indisputably. The Jews came to us as aliens and were received as such. No one can deny this. They have and keep their own laws. I do not mean the laws of their religion but their civil laws which, as I said, are of such a nature that they create a separation between the people of the Jews and all other peoples… The emigrants or so-called Refugiés [i.e., the Huguenots] are, in my opinion, a less felicitous comparison. These were individuals who did not come as a people or as part of the French people and who did not want to continue to adhere to and respect French laws. They not only subjected themselves to the Dutch laws but accepted them as theirs; in one word, they became Dutchmen.

The [Hahn][5] report asks whether the Jews are and remain a people, even though they have been expelled from their own land for almost 2,000 years. What, it asks, constitutes the distinctive characteristic of a people: the possession of a specific land or a community of faith?

I answer: certainly not a community of faith, but also not the actual possession of a specific land, since it is possible that a people is expelled from its land but retains, as a people, a claim on it and, eventually, restores itself…. Today they are still Jews; that is the peculiar thing about this nation. They retain their claim on their fatherland of old. It is immaterial whether their expectation will ever be fulfilled….

I think to have shown convincingly that the Jews are a separate nation and I add assuredly that they will remain one until those happy days when, finally, all of mankind will constitute one family, one household of brothers and sisters.

Certainly, Citizen Representatives, the Jews themselves do not desire to be incorporated into the Batavian people. A few individuals may desire it, but it is very far from certain that the [Jewish] nation, as a nation, even if we were to offer them everything, would accept it or would like to be regarded as Dutch citizens. They have too high an opinion of themselves to humble themselves in order to become Dutchmen….

Likewise, I do not take into consideration the natural and moral state of the Jewish People, this may have been caused by the circumstances in which this people finds itself. A people which lives in exile, which is exposed—through its own fault or through the fault of others—to contempt and maligning, will adopt all the shortcomings, both natural and moral, which accompany humiliated human beings. Many moral failings may also be attributed to the way of life of the Jews who engage in trade to provide for their livelihood. Whenever they will nobly rise above their prejudices, they will also conquer the shortcomings of humiliation and recapture the virtues which commonly adorn a free and enlightened people.

Among the 50,000 Jews, at the least, who live in the Netherlands, there are certainly a few genuine and very enlightened Patriots but, for the rest, the Jews are generally filled with a blind love for the government and regime of the House of Orange.[6]

On the one hand, I completely agree with the rule that every government maintains itself best by moderation, fairness and benevolence. I am equally convinced that this rule is especially appropriate at times when a country experiences dissensions, smoldering beneath the ashes of resentful discontent. On the other hand, I believe that we ought to be careful with regard to the Jewish nation as a nation. They have publicly acted criminally; all the more criminally because they are merely aliens who have no business mixing in our domestic affairs. Can we incorporate such persons as a nation, in the hope that they will be liable to gratitude and hold the citizenship of the Dutch People in such high esteem that they will prefer it over their self-interest, of which they have shown themselves to be slaves?

I consider it, Citizen Representatives, a serious crime when an alien who has enjoyed many benefits of hospitality interferes in the affairs of the people among whom he resides and shows himself a supporter of rebellion and oppression. Furthermore, I do not need many words to demonstrate that true statecraft does not tolerate that aliens be admitted to governmental posts as long as they keep their own laws which differ from ours in many respects.

But why, Citizen Representatives, do we need to discuss at length whether we will recognize the Jews as Dutch citizens? Have they asked us for it? Are they asking us? Did the Jewish nation truly speak and give some of them the authority to speak for them? I believe not. Will this Assembly, then, compromise itself and decree something in favor of the Jewish nation which they who did not request it will refuse? ...

Our discussions must be regarded as totally superfluous if anyone thinks that it concerns the question whether individual Jews (who want to declare themselves Dutch citizens and who want to abandon their Jewish civil laws) will be treated as citizens and will enjoy the privileges of society.

I come to the conclusion and infer the following from what I have said: Collectively speaking, the Jews cannot share in our Batavian social rights as citizens as long as they are Jews. If they want to share in them, they will have to abandon their civil laws (I do not speak of the religious) and accept our Constitution alone.

On this occasion, I only have to add that I find repugnant the impudence of some who, as happened in this case, seek to disturb this Assembly by speaking of wisdom, justice, courage and, what is more, by telling us that the French Minister Noel[7] has expressed an interest, etc. As a representative of the Batavian people, I find such insinuations indecent. We should consider only our duty and nothing but the good of the Batavian people should be our motive and goal.

Lublinck:[8]

The Jews are men. Jews and non-Jews are, in the fullest sense of the word, our natural fellows. Who can, who will deny this? Consequently, they have the same rights as we in all those respects in which they are equal to us as people, as natural fellows. Let us never forget our adopted principle "Equality and Fraternity." But let us also be careful not to draw a conclusion prematurely and wish to infer and prove from this proposition more than it contains. There is a difference whether the Jews have to share with us in equal advantages or in all advantages equally. They may and must certainly do so in all those advantages of which they are equally as susceptible as we, and in the way of which they themselves do not put any obstacles. In the latter case, circumstances change the relations. The Jews are people; but does it follow from that they might not be prevented, because of their special religious-political principles, from fulfilling the same duties as do Christians even though they enjoy the same rights? Women are also people, are also our natural fellows; but are they, therefore, with these equal rights, also capable in all cases to fulfill the same duties as we men?

May I be permitted to make one general remark. When we carefully peruse the pamphlets which, from time to time, appear both for and against our Jewish fellow brothers, we will soon notice that their authors are often drawn to a biased opinion by their respective principles. Their opponents have heard a lot of talk of guile, deceit, usury, thievery, and whatever else I do not know, which they attribute to the Jews as characteristic features, because of which the entire nation is depicted as unsuitable, as absolutely dangerous to society and to social intercourse. I do not have to say how wrong, how false, how malicious, how un-Christian this is, and how the genuine philosopher must hold all similar, general charges in abhorrence. The same applies to the opposite case. Most supporters allow themselves to be seduced by another, nobler, but not less uncertain, principle. Naturally innate compassion, tender-heartedness, aversion to pressure and misery (all stemming purely from general and praiseworthy love of mankind) easily place us in a position from which we view things in the wrong light. We like so much to preach the pleasant phrase "Equality and Fraternity" that we shrink from the bogey of intolerance with such a shudder as to easily lose the trail of impartial and cool reasoning. May we try to beware of these obstacles in our further examination of this subject....

The Report rightly represents as chimerical the fear for an overcrowding, an overflowing of Jews, in case they are allowed to become Dutch citizens. History and experience tend to disprove that fear. The Report continues by saying: "the increase of good citizens, of whatever conviction they may be, is most beneficial for the state." We must remark here that everything depends on the expression good citizens. The general term good, in its relative application, is liable to many interpretations. Thus, we may ask ourselves the question: to what extent are the Jews suited to be good citizens of this commonwealth? Surely, the mere populousness of a land, without qualification or condition, does not determine its happiness. Only useful, industrious, healthy members are suited to foster the well-being of the body of society. Every increase of the population not founded on these grounds is extremely disadvantageous to the state. The required qualifications of such citizens are not a little motivated by the local circumstances and temporal needs of a state or land.... Now we ask: How do matters stand with the Jews in this regard? The bulk, the majority of this nation supplies us with an abundance of obliging buyers and sellers, money-changers, wheedlers, traders, peddlers, bargain hunters for whatever one can imagine, masters of all these instruments in petty trade. Because of this abundance, they become a source of poverty to themselves. However, agrarians, in the real sense, ploughmen, diggers, scythers, people we lack so conspicuously, where are they to be found among them? Nowhere in our fatherland, as far as I know, are the Jews, the common Jews, really farmers. There are among the more prosperous ones some who possess landed property, but then only as merchants, as speculators, and not in order to make this useful branch of our fatherland's existence flourish by trial or energetic support. It used to be the reverse with the ancient Israelites....

We dislike raising these objections. It grieves us that we cannot be more optimistic on the issue of marriages between Jews and Christians, especially since this would be the most certain, the most adequate way of successfully working toward the reform of the national character of the Jews. This is quite apparent from the Spanish and Portuguese Jews in so far as they are the result of the mixing of Jewish and Christian parents and who, consequently, are very different in morals and thinking from the Polish and German Jews....

The dogmatic lies outside the scope of politics as long as it is restricted to thought. But as soon as the thought stops, as soon as the thought passes on to action, then begins the authority of civil society to judge and restrict, not the feelings, but the actions produced. At that moment, it ceases to be a decision about truth or error and becomes one about the good or evil that result there from. This is the important issue to which I wanted to draw your attention. This is what matters to me most, namely the question: can we imagine a Jew as citizen, apart from what is his religion? In other words, are not his political and religious relations united so inseparably, do not his religious and political systems interlock in such a way, that the one cannot be conceived without the other? We do not have a single doubt that the latter indeed is the case. In the case of the Jews, Citizen Representatives, not the religious prescriptions, not their special concepts and feelings, make the Jews unfit for citizenship, but their special laws, commandments, orders which have the validity of instructions of the Divine will for them....

May I be permitted, Citizen Representatives, to infer briefly a few consequences from what I have adduced.

One may ascribe more or less force to this connection of politics and religion, but one thing is indisputable: that it always contains the basis of a certain separatism which, indeed, makes the union with the Jews difficult with regard to all civil rights.

This separatism is inevitably connected with a certain assembly, a special association, an esprit de corps, or whatever one wants to call it, which can lead to harmful developments for an emerging state and new form of government, if badly directed. Far be it from us to condemn such an esprit de corps. We praise it to the utmost where it can be put to the use of the common good. Only, we have to consider whether a nation which is so completely dedicated to commerce, which thinks so intently of all that could bring damage or gain, which cherishes such a real Jewish patriotism, whether such cosmopolitans (who will not easily choose sides, except where it concerns personal interests) are true patriots, patriots of the stamp we would like....

I would like to conclude by expressing my approval of the statement of Dohm: That which distinguishes the Jews from their Christian brothers, which prevents the Jews from joining the Christians, will first have to be leveled, and the Jews will have to become a less heterogeneous people before they can claim completely homogeneous rights.

Floh:[9]

[Floh begins by expressing his agreement with many of the arguments of the Report.]

Without considering the Jew from the point of view of his special feelings, I may be permitted to ask: can the Jew as Jew really be proclaimed a citizen of the Netherlands?

If one wishes to regard, as the honored writers of the Report do, the Jewish residents of the Netherlands to be a part or section of the Dutch people, the question raised would be superfluous. However, I venture to differ with the Report's writers.

Ask a Jew himself whether he wants to be regarded as belonging to the people of the Netherlands or to the people of Israel? If I am not deceiving myself, the sincere and genuine Jew (I am only speaking of true Jews, not of circumcised philosophers, less of circumcised free-thinkers or Naturalists), I say, the genuine Jew, if sincere and honest and without fear

of insulting someone, will proudly answer: "No, I do not belong to the people of the Netherlands. I am and will remain a resident, an inhabitant of the Netherlands as long as it pleases Jehovah, during our exile. I have the honor of belonging to the chosen People of Israel," sadly suffering from the punishment deserved by their ancestors. Nowhere on earth, it is true, does it exist as a nation, for it does not have a state nor an authoritative government. However, it does live in the hope of and looks eagerly forward to that happy moment, when all its dispersed parts will be assembled together. Then, under the wise and happy rule of the messiah, it will again raise its head courageously, as a formidable people, above all the peoples of the earth.

If what I think is true, it seems to me that the Dutch Jews cannot be regarded but as a part of a scattered, alien nation which lives and resides among us for a while and which only waits and longs for that happy moment of union into one whole. Consequently, they cannot be regarded as a real part of the Dutch people, for they themselves do not even wish to be considered as such....

Does not the sincere Jew expect an earthly king in the literal sense? However beautiful some philosophical Jews may depict the rule of that king, he will nevertheless be a real absolute earthly sovereign who will regulate and arrange, according to his wisdom, everything arbitrarily, without consulting the people, according to his will and pleasure. Then I ask: What, if such a form of government is desired, remains of the supreme power of the people which we respect so much?

[F. would like active Dutch citizenship to be given only to persons who declare themselves patriots, i.e., republicans.]

The Jew is also, as Jew and as a human being, our brother. When he shares all the burdens equally with all the inhabitants of the Netherlands, when he carries the burdens of the country in equal proportion and pays the same scot and lot, when he cherishes the same patriotic sentiments with regard to the civil state and social happiness—what reasons can there be to exclude such a man, such a brother, such an inhabitant of the Netherlands, such a patriot even though he is circumcised, even though he invokes God in Hebrew, from the social privileges and advantages, and refuse him the full citizen's right in the Netherlands?

[F. believes that it is not the task of the National Assembly to decide whether it is possible for a Jew to be a republican.]

I conclude, therefore, that this Assembly may not let the admittance or non-admittance of the circumcised inhabitants of the Netherlands depend on general, popular Jewish concepts, but on the solemn making of a fitting statement. I would like to take the liberty to propose:

1) that the National Assembly solemnly declare that it recognizes all Jews on earth to be fellow human beings and, in the fullest sense, our natural fellows;

2) that it holds out the hand of fraternity especially to all the Jews in the Netherlands, that it grants them the fullest enjoyment of the Rights of Man, that it places them under the general Protection of the laws of the land, and that it opens to them the free entrance to the local assemblies, on condition of their making the common civic declaration;

3) and finally, that it grants all Jewish inhabitants of the Netherlands, who have resided in the Republic for more than one year, the full right of Dutch Citizenship, on condition that they make the following declaration:

"I, so-and-so, declare that I do not belong to any other people, nor any part of a people, but solely and only to the people of the Netherlands, whose supreme power I acknowledge and respect, without expecting any other supreme rule on earth. And I promise to conduct myself, always and in everything, conforming to its principles, as a good and faithful citizen of the Netherlands."

Zubli:[10]

[Zubli begins by expressing his agreement with the arguments of the Report. He admits that the Jews themselves are partly to blame for the contempt they experience, but he refuses to exonerate the Christians. He argues that the past behavior of Christians was clearly in contradiction to the teachings of Jesus.]

O my brothers, let us not widen the gap which separates us from the Jews with further sophistries, but let us try to fill it with benevolent means! Let us not waste time in a loveless investigation as to whether their religion forbids them to accept benefactions which our religion enjoins us to extend to all! Jews who imagine they lack the freedom to do so

will not accept our Christian offer and those among them who believe the opposite will gratefully do so. It is not up to us to judge the principles from which both operate. The judgment of man's heart and his innermost intention concerns only the Divinity. . . .

Who knows what changes we will shortly witness in the thinking and the character of the Jews and to what extent the changes we are making in their situation will be a contributing factor?

As far as we are concerned, we are representatives of Jews and of Christians. We are indebted to both. We have to do justice to both. Are we going to be children now in our decision concerning the Jews, whereas we were men for the Christians on the eternally memorable day of 5 August? (cf. next document, note 2.) Let us set the world another example of justice and let us not just partly triumph over prejudice! Let us decree the rights of citizenship of the Jews!

Breekpot:[11]

[B. is of the opinion that the Jews should fully enjoy the rights of man, but definitely not the rights of the Dutch citizen.]

Because of the following reasons. First, because I am not at all certain that the Jewish nation desires it. [B. is convinced that the Jews prefer their own civil laws over those of the Netherlands.]

Colmschate[12]

[C. begins by defending the Dutch Christians against the complaints of Friedrichsfeld and other Jews against Christians in general. He refrains from expressing his opinion over the religious concepts of th e Jews. Similarly, he will not examine the degree of patriotism, i.e., republicanism, among the Jews, but reminds his listeners of their affection for the House of Orange. C. suggests that the decision be referred to the constitutional committee.]

Metelerkamp:[13]

[M. refers to the arguments expressed by Van Hamelsveld. M. would deny the Jews the rights of citizenship because of their contempt for Jesus and because only very few Jews are animated by genuine republican feelings. M. wants the matter referred to the constitutional committee.]

Van Hoorn:[14]

. . . I would be ashamed for myself and for the spirit of my era and would consider it slanderous to my compatriots if I deemed it necessary to declare the humanity of the Jews or to prove that the Jews are our natural fellows. Never, in whatever century, among whatever people, have they been refused the title of human being. But, unfortunately, they themselves used to be the only ones on this earth who ventured to call other people dogs, and who denied them equal natural rights, which they appropriated to themselves as privileges of a partial Godhead.

In my eyes, the Jews are members of another civil state and as such they are unqualified to become citizens of our commonwealth.

The Jews never constituted a mere religious association. Their legislator, Moses, was the founder of a theocracy in which politics and civil laws are combined with religious concepts and customs, in such a way that what later came to be called the complete fusion of Church and state forms the real basis of the entire constitution of the Jewish state.[15]

[This fusion, Van Hoorn argues, was maintained even after the dispersion of the Jews.]

Because of this attachment to the old spirit of the theocratic legislation, Judaism was, remained, and is always, a religious-political body. However much dismembered, it did not cease to keep itself unadulterated, free from all forms of foreign corruption. Its separate parts maintained a universal attachment, parts whose complete reunion depends, in their own eyes, on future events.

I refrain intentionally from imagining all that society may have to fear if the Jews were ever to consider their messianic ideas fulfilled....

It is nevertheless possible that some Jews and, after their example, all Jews would show themselves ready and would immediately be thought capable (both of which I find equally improbable) to separate church and state and to change their political body into a mere association of faith. But, even in such a case, political forethought calls for mature reflection.

I am of the opinion that we would not be obliged to incorporate all these thousands at once into all the relations of our hitherto completely distinct society, just as we are not required to accept every other alien immediately in all civil rights. [Van Hoorn mentions the example of the emancipation of the slaves of Santo Domingo, which led to the ruin of this French colony. He also mentions usury, dishonesty, attachment to the House of Orange and to England, and corruptibility, as characteristics disqualifying Jews from citizenship.]

This total unfitness of the majority of the Jews (even in case of their general transformation into a mere religious association) would require a slow transition to fullfledged citizenship of a free state. The rights of the citizen should only be awarded at the moment that our society can be certain of their satisfactory enlightenment and improvement. To this end, the lot of the Jews as mere inhabitants ought to be softened as much as possible by making them equal, immediately following that transformation (into a mere religious association), to our passive citizens. The national schools ought to be opened to their children for a certain number of years, after which this rising generation, properly educated in all civic virtues and all the fundamental truths of republicanism, could be admitted to the status of active citizens, even with all rights. At the same time, this condition of a change of Jewish society and of the preparation of the Jewish youth in the general schools would serve to ward off that overflowing influx of foreign Jews which is always to be apprehended....

On all these grounds, I arrive at a conclusion of disagreement with the opinion of the authors of the Report. I propose that this Assembly decree: "As members of a theocratic state, the Jews can only be inhabitants of the Netherlands on the condition to be permitted by the Constitution. But, if they renounce all political and civil laws and institutions, they will become, as members of a mere religious faith, passive citizens of the state, whereas their children will share in all the rights of civil society as active citizens, upon completion of six years of education in Dutch citizens' schools."

Bicker:[16]

I have always pictured the Jewish nation, and have heard it defined thus, as a separate nation dispersed over the entire earth, which is not mixed with the Dutch people and which properly belongs in Palestine. Their national longing extends to Palestine, where they hope to return, led by a triumphant king. I have always heard it said that a sincere Jew considers himself in alliance with all the Jews spread over the entire earth, and that they expect a messiah who will restore them in Canaan, who will raise them again above all peoples as God's favored people, after so many centuries of oppression, and who will revenge them on their enemies.

If we consult history, we see that they have always separated themselves from those nations among which they settled. [B. refers to the corporate autonomy granted Jewish communities, and mentions the example of Amsterdam.]

If it is true (and, according to my information, it admits of no contradiction) that a sincere Jew considers himself a member of a separate nation that is dispersed over the entire earth, it means that as an individual he is a fellow member, fellow citizen, brother, part of a nation which finds itself in Asia, Europe, Africa and America. It also means that he cannot be at the same time a separate, individual member of a nation which calls itself the Dutch nation. It also follows that, if I as a citizen "fraternize" with the Jewish nation, I simultaneously "fraternize" insofar as I am a citizen, with a Jew in Ispahan, Algiers, Tunis, and Boston. The consequences of such a "fraternization," of a recognition of co-membership in one and the same relationship as citizens, would be so incalculable that I need not expound on them....

Let us consult the Jewish nation itself. When I say Jewish nation, I mean those who are truly Jews, who faithfully adhere and will adhere to the principles of the religion, ethics and customs, by which one recognizes a Jew and may call them Jews. I dare say definitely—and these are not guesses, are not based on rumors, but opinions gathered by me *e professio*—I dare say that the great mass of the Jews disapproves of the requests made by some of them to grant them full citizens' rights. Except for a small number of Jews, almost all of them wish that the request will not be granted. Those who consider the matter calmly state that, were the request granted, it would cause interminable discord between Jews and Jews, and between Jews and Christians. I have been assured that, if one were to inquire after their own opinions, at best one out of ten would vote in favor of the request. The others would respond that they await their prophet who has to liberate them and that they must remain as they are until his arrival.

[B. says that he is ready to assist them in improving their lot, in fighting their poverty, in bettering their education, in combating the denigration to which they are subjected, because the Jews are his fellow men and even ought to be respected as a nation. He longs for the day when they will repudiate their political ideas.]

We recently removed the principle by which a certain church and the state were one, but among the Jews church and state are most certainly connected, are most closely intertwined, according to their pure doctrine. How is it possible, then, since they differ so widely from us in this important respect, that we could declare the Jewish nation qua Jewish nation united with the Dutch nation and equal with it. If there are, meanwhile, some among them who cast off these political principles, which, I have been told, are interconnected with their religious principles, then my arguments are not applicable to these.

The request itself, insofar as it was made by members of the Jewish nation on behalf of, and for the benefit of, the entire Jewish nation, ought, I think, to be kept in deliberation or referred to the Committee for the Constitution.

Van Lokhorst:[17]

I am an enemy, Citizen Representatives, of defending or censuring religious sentiments in this council-room. The Dutch people have not appointed us for that. Therefore, I will make no mention whatsoever of the belief of the Jews regarding their messiah....

Indeed, Citizen Representatives, I am surprised that we discuss here whether the Jews will be admitted to partnership in the citizens' society of the Netherlands. We could as well, I think, discuss whether the Roman Catholic, the Calvinists, the Remonstrant, the Lutheran, and all others who belong to this or the other denomination will be citizens....

Shall we, Citizen Representatives, decide this issue? And shall we decree their admittance or non-admittance into the Civil State of the Netherlands on the basis of whether we consider the sentiment of the Jews either religious or political? Are we infallible judges in this matter? Do we have the authority to be able or to be allowed to do this? We cannot, we may not hesitate for one moment, faithful as we are to the principles of Liberty, Equality and Fraternity, to refuse their application to anyone. The true Republican knows no Jew, no Malabar, no Calvinist, no Catholic; he knows only men and insofar as they live in the same country as he, he considers them all as his fellow citizens. Thus the Jews are men, they are our compatriots. I beseech you, what else can that mean than this? They can claim, just as we, the Rights of Man and the Citizen; but also, they are equally bound to fulfill the duties of Men and Citizens. They must obey the law and defend the fatherland. They have to do everything to which the duty of an upright citizen calls them. One must no longer be able to distinguish a Jew from a Christian. The beards, the oriental tabards[18] of the Parnassim[19] must no longer be seen in public, just as little as the robes and bands, as the surplices of the Christian preachers.

Perhaps, someone thinks: yes, but that is just the trouble; what you propose is indeed something the Jews never can nor will do. But I ask you: How does one know this? Am I, are you competent to decide this?

…I conclude, therefore, that this assembly decide one of two things:

1) either to let the Jews, by solemn summons, decide themselves whether they want to be citizens of the Netherlands or not. In my opinion, this could best be done by clearly presenting to them the Rights and Duties of the Citizen in the name of the Dutch people and inviting them to partake of them by making and signing this declaration: that they consider themselves as Dutchmen, who differ from the other inhabitants only in religious conceptions, and that they are thus ready to cast off every national distinctiveness in clothing and the like and to act according to those laws which are binding on every Dutchman.

2) or to refer the entire matter to the Committee for the Constitution of whose wisdom we may expect that they will determine who belongs to that people for which they are drafting a Constitution.

Kantelaar:[20]

[When the request of the Jews was submitted, K. was of the opinion that it could not become a subject of discussion.]

It seemed to me that, in a society in which liberty exists and equality is respected, the rights of the citizen cannot be refused to any independent inhabitant who carries his share of the burden of the state, be he Jew, Christian, heathen or Turk [i.e., Muslim]: When these rights were solemnly proclaimed in our fatherland, the Jew was not excluded. And at the election of the members of this Assembly the Jew already made use of these rights. As far as these issues were concerned, the matter was no longer open to doubt or debate.

[However, K. says, the Assembly decided differently and asked for a report. This report unexpectedly changed the course of the deliberations.]

For it seems now not so much to be the question whether the Jews will be granted immediately civil rights, but whether they are really entitled to these rights. Thus, what I already considered indisputable, what I thought that the representatives of the Batavian people had already recognized, in speech and action, seems still to be considered doubtful.…

The writers of the report can never have intended, and the Assembly can never make it its goal, to proclaim the entire brotherhood of the Jews collectively, by one single decision, Dutch citizens at once. One can force no one to make use of his rights. Society only has to be careful not to impede anyone's exercise of his rights. The decree can and must not contain anything else than that no Jew will be excluded from the enjoyment of these rights, supposing that he desires to enjoy them. Only when there will no longer be any law in the Netherlands which excludes the Jews as Jews from the enjoyment of civil rights will the aim of the report be attained, and the demands of justice be fulfilled.

[K. thinks that the newly accepted political principles make an exclusion of the Jews impossible. The separation of state and church enacted on 5 August 1796 removes the argument based on the difference in religious and theological ideas. But, K. continues, some argue that certain religious ideas of the Jews could be harmful to the state.]

And chiefly, some think to have found a strong proof against the spirit of the report in the Jewish belief in a messiah whom they are still awaiting and in the nature of his reign. "The Jew," they say, "preserves throughout all the vicissitudes of his fate his original character. Conquered, dispersed, hated, despised, he remains ever a Jew. In whatever country he dwells, he lives with the expectation of a redeemer and dies with his eyes fixed on his ancient temple. And do you think such people can become useful citizens of the state?" Yes, Citizen Representatives! I can see in this belief in a future redeemer no obstacle whatsoever for the state and I hope that the following remarks will justify my contention.

1) If you carefully observe the mass of men, you will discover that their speculative ideas about theological doctrines generally have very little influence on their actions. The latter mostly stem from other sources.…

2) If this is true in general, how much more must one concede this with regard to the ideas of the Jews concerning their messiah. According to the testimony of their own writers, most

ordinary Jews rarely think about this matter, and even fewer correctly understand the doctrine of their church concerning the messiah's future reign.

3) Let us, however, assume that all the Jews know and understand this doctrine; that, contrary to our experience, all regard it with the same mind; that this doctrine forms the daily subject of their speculations; and that it has all the effects on their behavior which it can have. Even then this effect could only be the patient awaiting of an event which the Christians consider as already present, and which they regard, not as detrimental, but as highly beneficial for the happiness of mankind and the prosperity of civil societies. The Jews, meanwhile, must, if only in their own interest, collaborate diligently in the promotion of the welfare of the country in which they, perhaps, as so many generations of their ancestors, will have to the end of their days....

It is strange to hear some of you still call thousands of people, who have been settled in a country for several centuries; who have begotten children into the sixth degree; who have built houses, constructed pleasant homes and founded rich commercial firms; who, not like travelers paying only a few taxes on consumed goods but, like all citizens, paid all ordinary and extraordinary taxes whatever their designation....

All ancient legislators sanctioned their laws with the authority of the gods. But there was never a people whose religion and politics were so much interwoven into one whole as the Jews, as long as they constituted a separate nation....

This was, in fact, the spirit of the political organization of the Jews, so long as they constituted a separate nation. However, everyone will easily perceive that this should have ceased as soon as their state was destroyed and they were dispersed among the peoples. They should have immediately made a separation between their purely religious institutions and their civil laws. Whereas they could continue to adhere to the former, as long as they themselves were convinced of their necessity or usefulness, they should naturally have regarded the latter as terminated since, in that respect, they were no longer Jews, but became Portuguese, Germans, French, Dutch, in a word, inhabitants of the countries in which they settled and where they had to subject themselves undoubtedly to the civic institutions which existed here.

However, the bulk of the nation was too ignorant to sense that distinction. And those who did perceive it had generally too large a stake in the intertwining of the civil and the religious to disclose the absurdity of its continuation to their brethren. Consequently, in all countries where the Jews enjoyed considerable liberties, they preserved as many of their ancient civil laws as they were allowed. The Jews blessed the toleration of the government which seemed to allow them great freedoms in matters of religion, but which in fact forged more tightly the fetters which their imperious clerics had thrown around their neck.

At first sight it seems indeed surprising that the government could allow such a community to exist in their country, a community which to a large extent lived according to its own civil laws, and which stood under the coercion of a few persons who were nominally humble servants, but in reality civil rulers. But this surprise gives way if we take into account that arbitrary governments are used to seize upon anything that may confirm their illegal authority; that they will readily make smaller sacrifices in return for greater services; and that for that reason they have always stimulated the clergy's lust for power, although they hated and despised them at heart.

[K. then gives the example of Amsterdam's government sanctioning the Jews' communal ordinances, which contain also nonreligious provisions.]

As the proverb says, one good turn deserves another. The government slackened the reins in favor of the Parnassim, and the Parnassim in turn inspired in the Jews a blind zeal for the old constitution on which the government's arbitrary authority was founded. And the poor Jew willingly carried the yoke of the Parnassim, and was a zealous advocate of the government on whose behalf he raved and rebelled. This poor Jew became the sport of both and reveled in the delusion, inspired by the hypocrisy of his superiors, that his ancient religion was preserved in this manner.

I dare indulge the belief that experts will agree that this sketch is quite accurate and I think I can safely draw the following conclusions: First, the union of church and state is not a natural outcome of the Jewish religion.

Second, the former government allowed the Jews the union of church and state on the basis of false fundamental principles only. This union, presupposing two peoples in one country, was therefore one of the abominations of our country.

Third, the union of church and state will thus also no longer prevent the Jews' admittance to the enjoyment of the rights of citizens of the Netherlands. For this union must and will no longer exist and what no longer exists can have no effect.

Fourth, the foregoing argumentation revealed the reasons why the Jewish Parnassim so little desire this important change. But just as we will not force anyone, even if we were begged, to exercise the rights nature gave him, we will yet be wise enough, even if we were begged a thousand times, not to refuse any Jew the enjoyment of these rights....

Blok:[21]

From the discussions, it seems that doubts have arisen as to whether the solemn proclamation of the rights of man and the citizen is also applicable to the Jewish inhabitants of the Netherlands. Therefore, the National Assembly, interpreting insofar as it may be necessary its proclamation of 4 March 1796, should solemnly declare that no Jew shall be excluded from any rights or privileges attaching to Batavian civil laws which the Jew may wish to enjoy. The governments in the respective provinces should be informed thereof by means of a circular missive and should be admonished to allow every Jew, who so desires, to enjoy the rights pertaining to the proclamation of 4 March 1796, insofar as this is possible before the adoption of the Constitution.

[Bicker states that he had been convinced of the justice of the request from the outset. The Jews had already been recognized as fellow citizens by having been allowed to vote for the National Assembly, The granting of full civil rights is merely a logical consequence of that recognition. The speeches of Van Hamelsveld, Bicker, and Lublink, however, had persuaded him that citizenship ought to be granted the Jews with due caution.]

So as not to fight shadows, I have to delineate the status of the dispute a bit more carefully. I have never thought that it could ever be discussed and intended here to grant Dutch citizenship to a Jew just because he is a Jew, and consequently to all Jews, or as some say to the Jewish people as a people. This would be too blatant an absurdity. In that case all

Jews dispersed over all the four continents would have to be considered as Dutch citizens; or, at least, all Jews in the Netherlands. This no one will argue, as little with regard to them as to others, when all the requirements of an enfranchised Dutch citizen are also added. We are only considering such Jews. And the question is whether, presupposing the above, such a Jew cannot be a citizen, but has to be excluded from citizenship merely because he is a Jew; in one word, whether the requirements of a Dutch citizen, must or can include that one is not a Jew.

[B. feels that thus formulated the problem concerning granting civil rights to a collective body must disappear. He agrees with others that the extent to which a Jew can remain a Jew when accepting Dutch citizenship is none of the concern of the representatives but only of the individual Jews. He speaks in terms of natural religion, common to all men.]

For the essence of this (natural) general and, as it were, supreme religion consists only in the respectful exercise of these natural moral laws or, if you wish, of the rights and duties of Man which beneficent and supreme Wisdom dictates to us, as endowed with reason, through our essence itself and through our mutual relations. This religion of obligation and reason which ought to be respected by everyone, as man, of whatever persuasion he may be, is offended, degraded and violated in its demands when the sacred precepts of a universally equal fairness, the neutral balance of rights, are trodden under foot.

[B. continues his rather verbose and philosophical argument by demonstrating that on the basis of this natural religion whose tenets are dictated by nature a natural state must be founded which allows only one distinction, the difference between the sexes. And no man, thus also no Jew, can be excluded from this natural state. He also counters the arguments that Jews hate all uncircumcised gentiles by saying that if this were true the non-Jews can still not hate them in return but can merely pity them. But B. does not believe this argument to be true.

He notes that Jesus commanded the Christians to love the Jews as their brothers. He feels that Christians have a duty to enlighten the Jews and points to the examples of Mendelssohn, Pinto and others (in Italy and in Bohemia) to demonstrate their capacity for enlightenment. He concurs with the arguments of Kantelaar presented against the objection to Jewish citizenship due to their messianic expectations, their observance of the Sabbath, etc. and emphasizes that there are still many Millenarians among Christians.

With regard to the alienhood of the Jews, he states:] Not being admitted to any people, but only left to themselves as aliens, the Jews were forced, since they could not bear the name of another people, to retain that of the Jewish people or the Jewish nation and call themselves by that name; Polish Jews yes, but not Jewish Poles. It thus seems to me a mere playing with words, or an unsuspected deception to want to conclude from this customary appellation concerning their essential status as a people or as citizens. For that reason, it would be unintentional, entrapping ambiguities to ask them to relinquish their belonging to the Jewish people. For it could only be understood to mean to relinquish their feelings or Jewish faith. This they would certainly answer negatively and it would also bear the semblance of a restraint of conscience. The ambiguity will disappear if one only asks them whether they consider themselves members of any other existing civil state, or whether they want to obey and be loyal to the structure and laws of our state.

[B. repeats his argument that the compatibility of Jewish doctrines with citizenship can only be decided by the Jews themselves. If the Assembly decided this issue for them that would be pure oppression.]

I will pass over the objection based on the ignorance, jargon, lowly nature, deceitfulness, usurious spirit, ill manners and plain dirtiness of most Jews. Although often greatly exaggerated and all too worthy of compassion, this is often true and will for a long time prevent closer relations with them. But precisely for this reason one should allow them so much less to suffer in this lowly state, which sadly and largely produced all these characteristics.

I also think that they whose ancestors, though accustomed to the nomadic life of oriental shepherds, learned to cultivate wheat and olive and fig trees once they had come to rest, may also here one day, with firmer incorporation and ampler freedom, engage themselves in agriculture. But although that class is undoubtedly most attached to the soil of the fatherland, not all citizens should be farmers. I do not think that one would like to throw suspicion on our merchants and craftsmen of substance, as if they could only be indifferent citizens uninspired by any warm patriotism.

[B. considers the question of the admission of the Jews into the guilds though least discussed, to be one of the most important. He feels that every man should have the right to earn his living in the profession in which he is most able. If the coming constitution is going to abolish the guilds, the problem will be solved. If it does not, one may have to be cautious and not create too many disturbances at once. One may somehow slowly work toward a satisfaction of the rights of the Jews and the self-interest of the guilds.

Although he praises the tolerance of his ancestors, he agrees with Kantelaar that the power of the Parnassim will have to be curtailed.

In conclusion, he expresses his basic agreement with the report, but prefers the formulation of Kantelaar. He also feels that the committee which drafted the report may be asked, for the sake of greater reassurance, to examine what should precede the ultimate equality of the Jews, as e.g., a declaration containing not ideas but an acceptance of duties; and also whether it would not be useful to wait for the draft constitution to determine such issues as admission into the guilds and voting rights.]

Stoffenberg:[22]

You, my natural fellows, who are called Jews, tell me, is it your special case over which we will judge, or is it the case of truth and thus of mankind in general? Spare me your answer. Sound reason convinces me, and a pleasant feeling in my heart shares that conviction, that the entire case of mankind is comprised in yours. Therefore, do you not thank me for choosing your side in this dispute? No, I believe to have chosen that of truth and of sound philosophy. He who thus advocates the case does not merely plead the case of the Jews, but the case of mankind in general....

The question with which we are now dealing confronts us, in my opinion, again with the same problem. Your wisdom and justice, Citizen Representatives, is being tested severely. And the outcome will teach all of Europe whether we in the Netherlands honor the rights of man or only of Christian man; the rights of citizens or only the rights of Christian citizens.

[S. responds to the arguments of Van Hamelsveld by saying that the report never intended to grant citizens' rights to the Jews as a collective body. The report addressed itself only to the question of individual Jews. Thus, S. concludes, in essence Van Hamelsveld and the report agree.]

The inhabitants of the Netherlands forming themselves into a people will draft a constitution, i.e., a social contract. This constitution will to each and every one prescribe equal duties, offer equal rights, promise equal protection. He who does not wish to subject himself to the prescription of that social contract can also not be considered as a real member of the greater Dutch society. But then Jacob, David, Benjamin, etc., belonging to the Jewish church (etc.), offer to participate in this social contract and to subject themselves to all the duties arising from it. Does the legislator now, in this case (if they otherwise satisfied the requirements of residence, payment of taxes, good conduct, etc.) have to concern himself with the question whether this can be reconciled with the Jewish religious system? No, the legislator as such only knows Jacob, David and Benjamin as men, as inhabitants [of the country], but not as Jews. As regards their being Jews, they are not members of the civil state but of a special religious association. As such they have to take counsel with their own conscience and decide to what degree their faith, as Jews, should have prevented them from becoming members of the civil state of the Netherlands. They may square this with their conscience and their coreligionists. It is not the business of the legislators.

It is by no means the task of the people to make the constitution subordinate to the different ideas of one or another brotherhood. It is the duty of the latter either to adapt its thinking to the social contract or to relinquish any claim to the rights of any active fellow member of that contract.

[S. then counters some other arguments. The messianic expectations of the Jews can be punished and acted upon only when they are put into action and not so long as they are mere speculations.]

But I will go a step further and ask whether you truly believe that the Jewish faith makes such an impression on the hearts of the Jews that it produced of necessity a constant spirit of conspiracy against the constitution of a commonwealth and that consequently the fatherland would harbor, as it were, constant enemies in its midst by granting them civil rights? If this were true, it would prove too much. For it would mean that their faith contained totally antisocial principles, i.e., principles which are resolutely destructive to human society. And if that were true, it would be equally as absurd to tolerate such an antisocial horde as fixed inhabitants, as it would be foolish to admit them to the civil state. The measure against this supposed evil should then not be half-hearted, but total and complete.

[Regarding the immorality of the Jews,] look for the cause, Christians, and blush with shame! Or do you want the oppressed to retain their original manly and honest character after centuries of oppression? Do you want that they, who for many centuries have been the object of derision and contempt, should not in fact become contemptible? The same cause has always and everywhere the same effects. Christians, look at your own brothers living here and there, under the Turks or other oriental scepters. You will find them oppressed and despised, but at the same time and in the same proportion you will find them truly despicable. The gap between the loftiness and honesty of the character of the proud Moslem and that of the degraded Christian is certainly not smaller than that between Jew and Christian.

[As far as the hatred of the Jews toward the Christians is concerned, S. retorts that the pyres of the Inquisition and the centuries of oppression could hardly be expected to have instilled very warm feelings for Christians in the hearts of the Jews.]

I conclude therefore in favor of the report. I will leave it to the wisdom of the Assembly whether the decree (if one is necessary) should clearly and explicitly state that it does not concern the Jews collectively as an association, but only such individuals among them who are ready to subject themselves to all the prescriptions of the larger social contract of the Dutch people and in return also to claim all its rights.

I have not come to enlighten you, colleagues (of that I am incapable), but to share in the honor of our liberation.

I am all too aware that I am not free of prejudice in this matter. I have tried to resist it as much as possible and have tried to regard everything that was put forth on behalf of the Jews or rather on behalf of their request in the most unfavorable light. But after ample consideration, I am totally convinced that justice, sound politics, philosophy and Christ's teaching, all equally dictate that he who helps carry the burden must also enjoy the amenities; that no one who fulfills the general duties of the Batavian citizen can be excluded from the general enjoyment arising from this obligation.

NOTES

1. Soon after the establishment of the Batavian Republic, the opponents of the House of Orange, known as the party of the Patriots, convened a General Assembly

constituted by "citizen representatives." Among the first items discussed was a report prepared by Jacob George Hieronymous Hahn (1761–1822), the secretary ("Reporter") of a committee that had been appointed by the Assembly to study the petition by members of a club of predominantly Jewish "Patriots," *Felix Libertate*, requesting equal rights for the Jews.

2. Following their defeat in January 1795 by the French Revolutionary armies, the United Provinces of the Netherlands were reconstituted as the Batavian Republic. The day prior to the proclamation of the republic, the head of state, the Stadtholder William V of the House of Orange, fled to England. Despite the institution of democratic principles of government, the country remained under French occupation and tutelage. *Batavi* is the name of the ancient German tribe that gallantly fought for its freedom against imperial Rome, which occupied its land. Their struggle for liberation plays a seminal role in Dutch collective memory. In 1806 Napoleon disbanded the Batavian Republic and installed his brother Louis Bonaparte as ruler of the Kingdom of Holland.

3. Ysbrand van Hamelsveld (1743–1812).

4. Cornelius Tacitus (c. 56–117 C.E.), Roman senator and historian. His *The Histories* (c. 110 C.E), book 5:2–5, contains an excursus on the Jews, in which Jewish religious practices and attitudes are described.

5. See note 2.

6. The vast majority of the Jews were fervent supporters of the House of Orange, which consistently honored Jewish communal autonomy and steadfastly opposed calls for anti-Jewish measures.

7. A strong supporter of Jewish emancipation, François Noel was France's first ambassador to the Batavian Republic.

8. Johannes Lublink, de Jonge (1736–1816).

9. Jacob Hendrik Floh (1758–1830).

10. Ambrosius Justus Zubli (1751–1820).

11. François Breekpot (1756–1801).

12. Hendrik Jan Colmschate (1754–1829).

13. Eisso Metelerkamp (1756–1813).

14. Hendrik Daniel van Hoorn (1731–1802).

15. This is the thesis first articulated by Spinoza. See chapter two, document two.

16. Jan Bernd Bicker (1746–1812).

17. Johannes van Lokhorst (1761–1826).

18. A tabard is a short coat, usually sleeveless or with half sleeves or shoulder pieces.

19. Parnassim (Hebrew) are the wardens of the Jewish community.

20. Jacobus Kantelaar (1759–1821).

21. Bernardus Blok (1753–1818).

22. Jan Hendrick Stoffenberg (1749–1838).

8. EMANCIPATION OF DUTCH JEWRY (SEPTEMBER 2, 1796)[1]

NATIONAL ASSEMBLY OF BATAVIA

The National Assembly having repeatedly deliberated on the petition of several Jewish citizens, presented on the 29th of March of this year, "that this Assembly should see fit to declare that the Jews being now citizens of the Batavian Republic with the right to vote, and having exercised this right of citizens, shall also be granted the full possession of and the right to further exercise their rights of citizenship and that they shall enjoy this right to its full extent"; as [after due consideration] of the [Hahn] Report on that petition presented to us on August 1st..., and considering that the right to vote and of citizenship belongs only to individuals and that it would be an absurdity to grant the same to any collectivity, since society is

Source: H. J. Koenen, *Geshiedenis der Joden in Nederland,* (Utrecht: C. van der Post Jr., 1843), pp. 489–91, trans. Rita Mendes-Flohr.

not a collection of *corpora* but only of individuals, Decrees:

1. No Jew shall be excluded from exercising any rights or advantages which are attached to the rights of Batavian citizens and which he might wish to enjoy, under the condition that he meets the requirements and fulfills all the conditions demanded by the Constitution from every active citizen of the Netherlands.

2. The highest constituted powers of the provinces [of the Batavian Republic] shall be notified of this Decree by a circular letter and are thereby beseeched to allow any Jew who might so desire to enjoy the effects of the basic principles on which the said [Decree] rests, insofar as this can be done before the introduction of the Constitution, and immediately declare as null and void the sanction granted by previous provincial and municipal governments to the so-called Church Regulations on the Jews, which have been declared already null and void in view of the adoption of the presently recognized basic principles and which directly contradict the Decree passed by the Assembly on August 5, of this year.[2]

NOTES

1. Officially called the "Decree on the Equal Status of the Jews with All Other Citizens," it was passed unanimously by the National Assembly on September 2, 1796. The Decree was based on the Hahn Report, which was approved only three days earlier with more than one-third of the representatives opposed. The turnabout is explained by the intervention of the French ambassador François Noel. (Cf. Jozeph Michman, *Dutch Jewry during the Emancipation Period. 1787–1815* [Amsterdam: Amsterdam University Press, 1995, p. 24.]) The wording of the Decree reflects the spirit of Count Clermont-Tonnere's dictum: "The Jews should be denied everything as a nation, but granted everything as individuals." (Cf. this chapter, document 2.) The implementation of the Decree was inconsistent; there were quite a few towns of the Republic, which considerably delayed enacting the principles of the Decree (Michman, p. 24ff.)

2. On August 5, 1796, the National Assembly adopted a law separating church and state.

9. FIRST EMANCIPATION IN ROME (FEBRUARY 1799)[1]

THE ROMAN REPUBLIC

Whereas in accordance with the principles sanctified by the Constitutional Act of the Roman Republic all laws must be common and equal for all Roman citizens, the following Law is hereby decreed: Jews who meet all conditions prescribed for the acquisition of Roman citizenship shall be subject solely to the laws common to all citizens of the Roman Republic. Accordingly, all laws and particular regulations concerning Jews shall be null and void forthwith.

NOTE

1. France's armies, fighting under the banner of the principles of the Revolution, introduced democratic government and Jewish emancipation to the lands of their conquest (e.g., Belgium, the Netherlands, southern Germany, Italy).

Source: Raphael Mahler ed. and trans., *Jewish Emancipation, A Selection of Documents*, Pamphlet Series, Jews and the Post-War World, no. 1 (New York: American Jewish Committee, 1941), p. 28. Reprinted by permission of the American Jewish Committee.

10. TEARING DOWN THE GATES OF THE VENETIAN GHETTO (JULY 10, 1797)[1]

PIER GIAN MARIA DE FERRARI

Early on the 22nd [of Messidor or 10 July 1797], I went to fetch the three deputies of the Jews, the Citizens Daniel Levi Polacco, Vidal d'Angeli, and Moise di David Sullam, with whom I worked out all possible measures to make the ordered demolition of the gates of the Ghetto that was to take place that day both dignified and peaceful. At five in the afternoon, the officers of my battalion, number 3, Second Bucchia Brigade, left the square where they customarily drilled and then, accompanied by beating of tambourines and a band, went with me to the Ghetto gate that faces the paved walkway of San Gerolamo,[2] which was lined with French and Italian troops, as were the other three [Ghetto] gates of Cannaregio, Calleselle and Aggui.[3] An adequate number of French sentinels was already present in the square of the Ghetto Nuovo, and my battalion of officers took up its post in the middle of the square, accompanied by many other officers of other battalions of the National Guard and by numerous assembled members of the Patriotic Society, in addition to a large number of people of both genders who emerged out of every door. The three Citizen Deputies of the Hebrew Nation presented themselves, and immediately the order [to abolish the Ghetto] was read aloud to them by my Adjunct Major Goldoni.

Having heard [the] order, the Jewish Deputies delivered all the keys of the four aforementioned gates of the Ghetto and gave them into my hands, and I passed them on to the workmen, including many arsenal workers, who were ready to demolish those gates. One cannot express the satisfaction and happiness of all the populace present who, with jubilant cries of "freedom," never tired of dragging those keys on the ground, blessing the hour and moment of regeneration. The echo of these spirited "Vivas" and of the pulling down of the four gates, one by one, under the direction of Adjunct Goldoni, who distinguished himself with the zeal of a patriot, combined into almost one sound.

In the moment in which the gates were knocked down, joyous dances by people of both genders without any distinction wove around the middle of the square..., and it must be noted that also the rabbis danced, dressed in Mosaic garb, producing still greater energy.

Meanwhile, the two parish priests of San Geremia and San Marculoa[4] came, and their presence was applauded by their parishioners, who in this manner acknowledged the removal of the prejudices of a strict segregation that was not reconcilable with the sacred principles of pure democracy.

Several popular speeches certainly worthy of mention followed. Meanwhile, the broken gates were carried triumphantly by the crowd that had come to take the gates from the citizens and the workers and smashed them into pieces on the square of the Ghetto Nuovo in front of the National Guard, where, in the sight of all and with shouts of joy, they were delivered to the fire that rapidly consumed them. Then when a motion was made by Citizens Goldoni and Momolo Greco out of sentiments of patriotism that it would be good to plant a Liberty Tree in the square, it was enough for such words to be heard that all eagerly responded with the desired effect. The National Guard then departed, and passing through a neighborhood garden, in a moment cut down a tree that

---

Source: *Roccolta di decreti, processi, verbali e discorsi concernenti li cittandini ebrei di Venezia dopo la loro felice rigenerazione* (Venice, 1797). Translation and annotations by Benjamin Ravid.

was carried triumphantly with patriotic hymns right to the middle of the said square where it was planted, and a virtuous female citizen [took] the ornament of [the] National Beret off her head to crown the Tree of Liberty. Those gathered resumed the patriotic dances with a democratic disposition.

Finally, the day came to a close with the sudden splendid illumination of the Spanish synagogue where the worthy Citizen Massa, President of the Patriotic Society, addressed the numerous people assembled there with a discourse worthy of his talent.

Here are the most detailed and exact minutes that I give you, O citizens, and for the completion of your work it only remains to give a new name to the Ghetto in order to destroy this ignominious mark whose name still serves as a representation of the former separation, and I would suggest the substitution of the name Contrada delle Reunione.

Greetings and fraternity!

Venice, the 24th of Messidor, the first year of the Freedom of Italy [12 July 1797]

Pia Gian Maria de Ferrari

Head of the Third Battalion, Second Bucchia Brigade

NOTES

1. In 1516, the Venetian Senate segregated the Jews as a compromise between the alternative either to grant them freedom of residence in the city or to expel them. All Jews were required to move to the island known as the Ghetto Nuovo (the New Ghetto), which was walled up and provided with four gates, which were initially locked from sunset to sunrise. The word "ghetto," of Venetian origin, referred to the municipal copper foundry (*il geto*) that was active until 1413 in the area known as the Ghetto Vecchio (the Old Ghetto), to differentiate it from the later adjacent dumping ground for waste on the island across the canal from the Ghetto Nuovo. The original area of the Jewish ghetto

of Venice was expanded in 1541 by the addition of the Ghetto Nuovo and again in 1633 by the addition of another area that came to be known as the Ghetto Nuovissimo.

From Venice, the word "ghetto" spread throughout the Italian peninsula to refer to the many compulsory segregated and enclosed Jewish quarters that were established during the Counter Reformation and then later, in an extended sense, first to any area densely inhabited by Jews and eventually to the residential area of any clearly identifiable ethnic group.

In May 1797 the Venetian government (Venice was at the time an independent city-state) dissolved itself in favor of a municipal council as Napoleon's armies of liberation stood poised across the lagoons at the outskirts of the city. The municipal council ordered that the ghetto gates be removed and the restrictions on the Jews of Venice be abolished.

When Austria took control of Venice, later that year, it reinstituted some of the restrictions, but did not reestablish the ghetto. Then, when Venice became a part of the Napoleonic Kingdom of Italy from 1805 to 1814, the rights of the Jews were fully restored. After the Austrians returned in 1815, they again revoked many of the rights accorded the Jews. Only when Venice became part of the emerging sovereign Kingdom of Italy in 1866 did the Jews receive complete emancipation. The eyewitness account of the demolition of the gates of the Venetian ghetto, presented here, was provided by the individual responsible for the action, Pier Gian Maria de Ferrari, leader of the Third Battalion, Second Bucchia Brigade of the National Guard of Venice.

2. The gate of the Ghetto Nuovo, near the Old Age Home of contemporary Venice.

3. The gates of the Ghetto Vecchio at the paved walkway along the canal of Cannareigio, of the Ghetto Nuovissimo, coming from outside the ghetto, and over the Aggui canal between the Ghetto Vecchio and the Ghetto Nuovo, respectively.

4 Two parishes near the ghetto.

11. IMPERIAL DECREE CALLING FOR AN ASSEMBLY OF JEWISH NOTABLES (MAY 30, 1806)[1]

NAPOLEON BONAPARTE

On the report, which has been made to us, that in many of the northern departments of our empire, certain Jews, following no other profession than that of usurers, have, by the accumulation of the most enormous interests, reduced many husbandmen of these districts to the greatest distress:

We have thought it incumbent on us to lend our assistance to those of our subjects whom rapacity may have reduced to these hard extremities.

These circumstances have, at the same time, pointed out to us the urgent necessity of reviving, among individuals of the Jewish persuasion residing in our dominions, sentiments of civil morality, which, unfortunately, have been stifled in many of them by the abject state in which they have long languished, and which it is not our intention either to maintain, or to renew.

To carry this design into execution, we have determined to call together an assembly of the principal Jews, and to make our intentions known to them by commissioners whom we shall name for that purpose, and who shall, at the same time, collect their opinions as to the means they deem the fittest, to re-establish among their brethren exercise of mechanical acts and useful professions, in order to replace, by an honest industry, the shameful resources to which many of them resorted, from generation to generation, these many centuries.

To this end, on the report of our Grand Judge, Minister of Justice, of our Minister for the Interior, our Council of State being heard, we have decreed, and do decree as follows:

1. There is a suspension for a year, from the date of the present decree, of all executions of judgment and bond-obligations, except so far as to prevent limitation, obtained against husbandmen, not traders, of the departments of La Sarre, La Roer, Mon Terrible, Upper and Lower Rhine, Rhine and Moselle and Vosges whenever the bonds entered into by these husbandmen are in favour of Jews.

2. There shall be formed, on the fifteenth of July next, in our good city of Paris, an assembly of individuals professing the Jewish religion and residing in the French territory.[2]

3. The members of this assembly, of the number fixed in the annexed List, shall be chosen in the departments therein named, and nominated by the prefects from among the rabbis, the land-holders, and other Jews, the most distinguished by their integrity and their knowledge.[3]

4. In all the other departments of our empire, not mentioned in the aforesaid table, and where men of the Jewish persuasion should reside to the number of one hundred, and less than five hundred, the prefect may name a deputy for every five hundred, and for a higher number, up to one thousand, he may name four deputies, and so on.

5. The deputies thus named shall be in Paris before the tenth of July, and shall send notice of their arrival, and of their place of residence, to the secretary's office of our Minister for the Interior, who shall acquaint them of the place, day, and hour of the meeting.

6. Our Minister for the Interior is charged with the execution of the present decree.

NOTES

1. In January 1806, on his return from the victory at Austerlitz, Napoleon stopped at Strasbourg and received

Source: M. Diogène Tama, *Transactions of the Parisian Sanhedrin*, trans. F D. Kirwan (London, 1807), pp. 105–8.

several local delegations' complaints about the "usurious" activities of Jewish moneylenders in Alsace and Lorraine. Inclined to believe these complaints, Napoleon brought the issue before his Council of State, and his imperial decree was the result of these consultations.

2. The Assembly actually was convened on July 29, 1806.
3. The Assembly of Jewish Notables comprised 112 prominent businessmen, financiers, rabbis, and scholars—all handpicked by the prefects of various government departments of France and Italy.

12. INSTRUCTIONS TO THE ASSEMBLY OF JEWISH NOTABLES (JULY 29, 1806)

COUNT MOLÉ[1]

His Majesty, the Emperor and King, having named us Commissioners to transact whatever relates to you, has this day sent us to this assembly to acquaint you with his intentions. Called together from the extremities of this vast empire, no one among you is ignorant of the object for which His Majesty has convened this assembly. You know it. The conduct of many among those of your persuasion has excited complaints, which have found their way to the foot of the throne: these complaints were founded on truth; and nevertheless, His Majesty has been satisfied with stopping the progress of the evil, and he has wished to hear you on the means of providing a remedy. You will, no doubt, prove worthy of so tender, so paternal a conduct, and you will feel all the importance of the trust, thus reposed in you. Far from considering the government under which you live as a power against which you should be on your guard, you will assist it with your experience and cooperate with it in all the good it intends; thus you will prove that, following the example of all Frenchmen, you do not seclude yourselves from the rest of mankind.

The laws which have been imposed on individuals of your religion, have been different in the several parts of the world: often they have been dictated by the interest of the day. But, as an assembly like the present one has no precedent in the annals of Christianity, so will you be judged, for the first time, with justice, and you will see your fate irrevocably fixed by a Christian Prince. The wish of His Majesty is, that you should be Frenchmen; it remains with you to accept the proffered title, without forgetting that, to prove unworthy of it, would be renouncing it altogether.

You will hear the questions submitted to you, your duty is to answer the whole truth on every one of them. Attend, and never lose sight of that which we are going to tell you; that, when a monarch equally firm and just, who knows every thing, and who punishes or recompenses every action, puts questions to his subjects, these would be equally guilty and blind to their true interests, if they were to disguise the truth in the least.

The intention of His Majesty is, Gentlemen, that you should enjoy the greatest freedom in your deliberations, your answers will be transmitted to us by your President, when they have been put in regular form.

As to us, our most ardent wish is to be able to report to the Emperor, that, among individuals of the Jewish persuasion, he can reckon as many faithful subjects, determined to conform in every thing to the

---

Source: M. Diogène Tama, *Transactions of the Parisian Sanhedrin,* trans. F. D. Kirwan (London, 1807), pp. 130–34.

laws and to the morality, which ought to regulate the conduct of all Frenchmen.

(One of the secretaries [proceeded to read the following] questions proposed to the Assembly of the Jews by the Commissioners named by His Majesty the Emperor and King)....

Is it lawful for Jews to marry more than one wife?

Is divorce allowed by the Jewish religion? Is divorce valid, when not pronounced by courts of justice, and by virtue of laws in contradiction with the French code?

Can a Jewess marry a Christian, or a Jew a Christian woman? Or has the [Jewish] law ordered that the Jews should only intermarry among themselves?

In the eyes of Jews are Frenchmen considered as brethren or as strangers?

In either case what conduct does their law prescribe towards Frenchmen not of their religion?

Do the Jews born in France, and treated by the law as French citizens, consider France as their country? Are they bound to defend it?[2] Are they bound to obey the laws [of France], and to follow the directions of the civil code?

What kind of police-jurisdiction have the Rabbis among the Jews? What judicial power do they exercise among them?[3]

Are the forms of the elections of the Rabbis and their police-jurisdiction regulated by [Jewish] law, or are they only sanctioned by custom?

Are there professions from which the Jews are excluded by their law?

Does [rabbinic] law forbid the Jews from taking usury from their brethren?

Does it forbid or does it allow usury toward strangers?...

NOTES

1. Count Louis Mathieu Molé (1781–1855), a member of the Council of State, served as one of Napoleon's three commissioners to the Assembly of Notables. As Napoleon's informal adviser on Jewish affairs, he advocated the recision of Jewish emancipation.

2. According to the protocol of this session of the Assembly, the delegates were "not able to conceal the emotions caused by [this] question.... The whole Assembly unanimously exclaimed—Even unto death!" (M. Diogène Tama, *Transactions of the Parisian Sanhedrin*, trans. F. D. Kirwin [London, 1807], pp. 134ff.).

3. The seventh question, "Who names the rabbis?" is missing in M. Diogène Tama's text, *Transactions of the Parisian Sanhedrin*.

13. REPLY ON BEHALF OF THE ASSEMBLY TO COUNT MOLÉ (JULY 29, 1806)

ABRAHAM FURTADO[1]

Gentlemen Commissioners,

We have listened with all the attention we could command to the intentions of His Majesty the Emperor, which you have just communicated to us.

Chosen by this assembly as the interpreter of its sentiments, I must assure you, in the name of all those who compose it, that, when His Majesty determined to call us together in his capital, in order to further the accomplishment of his glorious designs, we saw, with inexpressible joy, [the] occasion of doing, away [with] many errors and putting an end to many prejudices.

Source: M. Diogène Tama, *Transactions of the Parisian Sanhedrin,* trans. F. D. Kirwan (London, 1807), pp. 135–38.

The benevolent intentions of His Majesty have offered us an opportunity, most fervently desired this great [occasion], by all honest and enlightened men of the Jewish persuasion, residing in France.

We had, however, but a distant prospect of the epoch which would completely reform habits occasioned by a long state of oppression. Now the moment seems almost at hand, and we owe this precious advantage to the paternal goodness of His Majesty. It was impossible that his exalted mind could, even for an instant, entertain a thought on our situation, without its being materially improved.

We shared, in common with all Frenchmen, the sentiments inspired by that protecting genius which had saved this empire from the rage of factional spirit, from the horrors of a bloody anarchy, and from the ambitious designs of its external enemies.

We could not suppose that after so many benefits, it could be still possible for him to acquire new rights to our gratitude, or to increase our love for his sacred person. Times of ignorance and of anarchy had always been, for us, days of trials and of misfortune. His Majesty had freed us from any apprehension as to the return of the first of these scourges, the other was chained by his powerful hand. His laws, the establishment of his dynasty, and the return of order, had calmed all the fears we might have entertained of a retrograde motion in the progress of the great science of social economy in France; we flattered ourselves with the hope of progressively enjoying the sweets of so many blessings. The slow but sure regenerations of some of our brethren would have been the result of our new condition. His Majesty wishes to hasten the precious moments, and, through his protecting goodness, we shall enjoy, under his reign, social advantages, which we could expect only from centuries of perseverance.

It is thus that the greatest of heroes becomes the common father of all his subjects; whatever religion they follow, he only sees in them children of the same family.

The enterprise His Majesty undertakes is such as might have been expected from the most astonishing man whose deeds were ever recorded by history. Methinks I see the muse holding her immortal burin,

and tracing on her adamant tablets, amidst so many deeds, which make this reign so conspicuous, that which the hero of the age has done to destroy utterly the barrier raised between nations and the scattered remains of the most ancient people.

Such is, Gentlemen Commissioners, the point of view under which we consider, with satisfaction, the communications we have received from you. It confirms us in the idea that no practicable good escapes the penetration of His Majesty, which can be equalled only by his goodness, and by the generosity of his heart.

The choice, which His Majesty has been pleased to make of you, Gentlemen Commissioners, to convey to us his intentions, adds a new value to the favour he intends for the Jews. The most unlimited confidence will reign between us, in the course of our communications.

While this confidence pleads some excuse for our involuntary errors, it will be a pledge of the purity of our intentions.

Have the goodness, Gentlemen Commissioners, to convey our sentiments to His Majesty, and to assure him that he does not reign over subjects more faithful, or more devoted to his sacred person, than we are.[2]

NOTES

1. Abraham Furtado (1756–1817), a member of the Portuguese-Jewish community of France. He was elected president of the Assembly of Notables; later he served as secretary of the Parisian Sanhedrin. In his capacity as president of the Assembly, Furtado delivered these remarks in response to Count Molé's address (document 12 in this chapter).

2. According to the records of the Assembly, upon the conclusion of Furtado's speech "the hall resounded with repeated cries of 'Long Live the Emperor!'... The Commissioners of His Majesty requested an official receipt for the questions they laid on the table. It was given by the President. Many members manifested their intention of delivering their sentiments [personally] before the Commissioner. But they left the assembly amidst the cries of 'Long Live the Emperor!'" (M. Diogène Tama, *Transactions of the Parisian Sanhedrin*, trans. F. D. Kirwin [London, 1807], p. 138.)

14. ANSWERS TO NAPOLEON (1806)

THE ASSEMBLY OF JEWISH NOTABLES[1]

Resolved, by the French deputies professing the religion of Moses, that the following Declaration shall precede the answers returned to the questions proposed by the Commissioners of His Imperial and Royal Majesty.

The assembly, impressed with a deep sense of gratitude, love, respect, and admiration, for the sacred person of His Imperial and Royal Majesty, declares, in the name of all Frenchmen professing the religion of Moses, that they are fully determined to prove worthy of the favours His Majesty intends for them, by scrupulously conforming to his paternal intentions; that their religion makes it their duty to consider the law of the prince as the supreme law in civil and political matters; that consequently, should their religious code, or its various interpretations, contain civil or political commands, at variance with those of the French code, those commands would, of course, cease to influence and govern them, since they must, above all, acknowledge and obey the laws of the prince.

That, in consequence of this principle, the Jews have, at all times, considered it their duty to obey the laws of the state, and that, since the revolution, they, like all Frenchmen, have acknowledged no others.

First Question: *Is it lawful for Jews to marry more than one wife?*

Answer: It is not lawful for Jews to marry more than one wife: in all European countries they conform to the general practice marrying only one.

Moses does not command expressly to take several, but he does not forbid it. He seems even to adopt that custom as generally prevailing [at the time], since he settles the rights of inheritance between children of different wives. Although this practice still prevails in the East, yet their ancient sages have enjoined them to restrain from taking more than one wife, except when the man is enabled by his fortune to maintain several.

The case has been different in the West; the wish of adopting the customs of the inhabitants of this part of the world has induced the Jews to renounce polygamy. But as several individuals still indulged in that practice, a synod was convened at Worms in the eleventh century, composed of one hundred Rabbis, with Gershom at their head.[2] This assembly pronounced an anathema against every Israelite who should, in future, take more than one wife.

Although this prohibition was not to last forever, the influence of European manners has universally prevailed.

Second Question: *Is divorce allowed by the Jewish religion? Is divorce valid when not pronounced by courts of justice by virtue of laws in contradiction with those of the French Code?*

Answer: Repudiation is allowed by the law of Moses; but it is not valid if not previously pronounced by the French code.

In the eyes of every Israelite, without exception, submission to the prince is the first of duties. It is a principle generally acknowledged among them, that, in every thing relating to civil or political interests, the law of the state is the supreme law. Before they were admitted in France to share the rights of all citizens, and when they lived under a particular legislation which set them at liberty to follow their religious customs, they had the ability to divorce their wives; but it was extremely rare to see it put into practice.

Since the revolution, they have acknowledged no other laws on this matter but those of the empire. At the epoch when they were admitted to the rank of citizens, the Rabbis and the principal Jewish leaders appeared before the municipalities of their respective

---

Source: M. Diogène Tama, *Transactions of the Parisian Sanhedrin*, trans. F. D. Kirwan (London, 1807) pp. 149–56, 176–95, 201–7.

places of abode, and took an oath to conform, in every thing to the laws, and to acknowledge no other rules in all civil matters....

Third Question: *Can a Jewess marry a Christian, and a Jew a Christian woman? Or does the law allow the Jews to marry only among themselves?*

Answer: The law does not say that a Jewess cannot marry a Christian, nor a Jew a Christian woman; nor does it state that the Jews can only marry among themselves.

The only marriages expressly forbidden by the law, are those with the seven Canaanite nations, with Amon and Moab, and with the Egyptians. The prohibition is absolute concerning the seven Canaanite nations: with regard to Amon and Moab, it is limited, according to many Talmudists, to the men of those nations, and does not extend to the women; it is even thought that these last would have embraced the Jewish religion. As to Egyptians, the prohibition is limited to the third generation. The prohibition in general applies only to nations in idolatry. The Talmud declares formally that modern nations are not to be considered as such, since they worship, like us, the God of heaven and earth. And, accordingly, there have been, at several periods, intermarriages between Jews and Christians in France, in Spain, and in Germany: these marriages were sometimes tolerated, and sometimes forbidden by the laws of those sovereigns, who had received Jews into their dominions.

Unions of this kind are still found in France; but we cannot deny that the opinion of the Rabbis is against these marriages. According to their doctrine, although the religion of Moses has not forbidden the Jews from intermarrying with nations not of their religion, yet, as marriage, according to the Talmud, requires religious ceremonies called Kiduschin, with the benediction used in such cases; no marriage can be religiously valid unless these ceremonies have been performed. This could not be done towards persons who would not both of them consider these ceremonies as sacred; and in that case the married couple could separate without the religious divorce; they would then be considered as married civilly but not religiously.

Such is the opinion of the Rabbis, members of this assembly. In general, they would be no more inclined to bless the union of Jewess with a Christian, or of a Jew with a Christian woman, than Catholic priests themselves would be disposed to sanction unions of

this kind. The Rabbis acknowledge, however, that a Jew, who marries a Christian woman, does not cease on that account, to be considered as a Jew by his brethren, any more than if he had married a Jewess civilly and not religiously.

Fourth Question: *In the eyes of Jews, are Frenchmen considered as their brethren? Or are they considered as strangers?*

Answer: In the eyes of Jews Frenchmen are their brethren, and are not strangers.

The true spirit of the law of Moses is consonant with this mode of considering Frenchmen.

When the Israelites formed a settled and independent nation, their law made it a rule for them to consider strangers as their brethren.

With the most tender care for their welfare, their lawgiver commands to love them, "Love ye therefore the strangers," says he to the Israelites, "for ye were strangers in the land of Egypt."[3] Respect and benevolence towards strangers are enforced by Moses, not as an exhortation to the practice of social morality only, but as an obligation imposed by God himself.[4]

A religion whose fundamental maxims are such—a religion which makes a duty of loving the stranger—which enforces the practice of social virtues, must surely require that its followers should consider their fellow-citizens as brethren.

And how could they consider them otherwise when they inhabit the same land, when they are ruled and protected by the same government, and by the same laws? When they enjoy the same rights, and have the same duties to fulfill? There exists, even between the Jew and Christian, a tie which abundantly compensates for religion—it is the tie of gratitude. This sentiment was at first excited in us by the mere grant of toleration. It has been increased, these eighteen years, by new favours from government, to such a degree of energy, that now our fate is irrevocably linked with the common fate of all Frenchmen. Yes, France is our country; all Frenchmen are our brethren, and this glorious title, by raising us in our own esteem, becomes a sure pledge that we shall never cease to be worthy of it.

Fifth Question: *In either case, what line of conduct does their law prescribe towards Frenchmen not of their religion?*

Answer: The line of conduct prescribed towards Frenchmen not of our religion, is the same as that prescribed between Jews themselves; we admit of no difference but that of worshipping the Supreme Being, every one in his own way.

The answer to the preceding question has explained the line of conduct which the law of Moses and the Talmud prescribe towards Frenchmen not of our religion. At the present time, when the Jews no longer form a separate people, but enjoy the advantage of being incorporated with the Great Nation (which privilege they consider as a kind of political redemption), it is impossible that a Jew should treat a Frenchman, not of his religion, in any other manner than he would treat one of his Israelite brethren.

Sixth Question: *Do Jews born in France, and treated by the laws as French citizens, consider France their country? Are they bound to defend it? Are they bound to obey the laws and to conform to the dispositions of the civil code?*

Answer: Men who have adopted a country, who have resided in it these many generations—who, even under the restraint of particular laws which abridged their civil rights, were so attached to it that they preferred being debarred from the advantages common to all other citizens, rather than leave it—cannot but consider themselves Frenchmen in France, and they consider as equally sacred and honourable the bounden duty of defending their country.

Jeremiah (chapter 29) exhorts the Jews to consider Babylon as their country, although they were to remain in it only for seventy years. He exhorts them to till the ground, to build houses, to sow, and to plant. His recommendation was so much attended to, that Ezra (chapter 2) says, that when Cyrus allowed them to return to Jerusalem to rebuild the Temple, 42,360 only, left Babylon; and that this number was mostly composed of the poor people, the wealthy having remained in that city.

The love of the country is in the heart of Jews a sentiment so natural, so powerful, and so consonant to their religious opinions, that a French Jew considers himself in England as among strangers, although he may be among Jews; and the case is the same with English Jews in France.

To such a pitch is this sentiment carried among them, that during the last war, French Jews, have been seen fighting desperately against other Jews, the subjects of countries then at war with France.

Many of them are covered with honourable wounds, and others have obtained, in the field of honour, the noble rewards of bravery.

Seventh Question: *Who names the Rabbis?*

Answer: Since the revolution, the majority of the chiefs of families names the Rabbi, wherever there is a sufficient number of Jews to maintain one, after previous inquiries as to the morality and learning of the candidate. This mode of election is not, however, uniform: it varies according to place, and, to this day, whatever concerns the elections of Rabbis is still in a state of uncertainty.

Eighth Question: *What police jurisdiction do Rabbis exercise among the Jews? What judicial power do they enjoy among them?*

Answer: The Rabbis exercise no manner of Police Jurisdiction among the Jews.

It is only in the Mishnah and in the Talmud that the word Rabbi is found for the first time applied to a doctor in the law; and he was commonly indebted for this qualification to his reputation, and to the opinion generally entertained of his learning.

When the Israelites were totally dispersed, they formed small communities in those places where they were allowed to settle in certain numbers.

Sometimes, in these circumstances, a Rabbi and two other sages formed a kind of tribunal, named Beth Din, that is, House of Justice; the Rabbi fulfilled the functions of judge, and the other two those of his assessors.

The attributes, and even the existence of these tribunals, have, to this day, always depended on the will of governments under which the Jews have lived, and on the degree of tolerance they have enjoyed. Since the revolution those rabbinical tribunals are totally suppressed in France, and in Italy. The Jews, raised to the rank of citizens, have conformed in every thing to the laws of the state; and, accordingly, the functions of Rabbis, wherever any are established, are limited to preaching morality in the temples, blessing marriages, and pronouncing divorces....

Ninth Question: *Are these forms of Election, and their police-jurisdiction, regulated by [Jewish] law, or are they only sanctioned by custom?*

Answer: The answer to the preceding questions makes it useless to say much on this, only it may be remarked, that, even supposing that Rabbis should have, to this day preserved some kind of police-judicial-jurisdiction among us, which is not the case, neither such jurisdiction, nor the forms of the elections, could be said to be sanctioned by the law; they should be attributed solely to custom.

Tenth Question: *Are there professions which the law of the Jews forbids them from exercising?*

Answer: There are none: on the contrary, the Talmud (vide Kiduschin, chapter 1) expressly declares that "the father who does not teach a profession to his child, rears him up to be a villain."

Eleventh Question: *Does the law forbid the Jews from taking usury from their brethren?*

Answer: Deuteronomy says, "thou shalt not lend upon interest to thy brother, interest of money, interest of victuals, interest of any thing that is lent upon interest."[5]

The Hebrew word *neshekh* has been improperly translated by the word usury: in the Hebrew language it means interest of any kind, and not usurious interest. It cannot then be taken in the meaning now given the word usury.

Twelfth Question: *Does it forbid or does it allow to take usury from strangers?*

Answer: We have seen, in the answer to the foregoing question, that the prohibition of usury, considered as the smallest interest, was a maxim of charity and of benevolence, rather than a commercial regulation. In this point of view it is equally condemned by the law of Moses and by the Talmud: we are generally forbidden, always on the score of charity, to lend upon interest to our fellow-citizens of different persuasions, as well as to our fellow-Jews.

The disposition of the law, which allows us to take interest from the stranger, evidently refers only to nations in commercial intercourse with us; otherwise there would be an evident contradiction between this passage and twenty others of the sacred writings.[6]

Thus the prohibition extended to the stranger who dealt in Israel; the Holy Writ places them under the safe-guard of God; he is a sacred guest, and God orders us to treat him like the widow and like the orphan.

Can Moses be considered as the lawgiver of the universe, because he was the lawgiver of the Jews? Were the laws he gave to the people, which God had entrusted to his care, likely to become the general laws of mankind? Thou shalt not lend upon interest to thy brother. What security had he, that, in the intercourse which would be naturally established between the Jews and foreign nations, these last would renounce customs generally prevailing in trade, and lend to the Jews without requiring any interest? Was he then bound to sacrifice the interest of

his people, and to impoverish the Jews to enrich foreign nations? Is it not absolutely absurd to reproach him with having put a restriction to the precept contained in Deuteronomy? What a lawgiver would not have considered such a restriction as a natural principle of reciprocity?

How far superior in simplicity, generosity, justice, and humanity, is the law of Moses, on this matter, to those of the Greeks and of the Romans! Can we find, in the history of the ancient Israelites, those scandalous scenes of rebellion excited by the harshness of creditors towards their debtors, those frequent abolitions of debts to prevent the multitude, impoverished by the extortions of lenders, from being driven to despair?

The law of Moses and its interpreters have distinguished, with a praiseworthy humanity, the different uses of borrowed money. Is it to maintain a family? Interest is forbidden. Is it to undertake a commercial speculation, by which the principal is put at risk? Interest is allowed, even between Jews. Lend to the poor, says Moses. Here the tribute of gratitude is the only kind of interest allowed; the satisfaction of obliging is the sole recompense of the conferred benefit. The case is different in regard to capitals employed in extensive commerce: there, Moses allows the lender to come in for a share of the profits of the borrower; and as commerce was scarcely known among the Israelites, who were exclusively addicted to agricultural pursuits, and as it was carried on only with strangers, that is with neighbouring nations, it was allowed to share its profits with them....

It is an incontrovertible point, according to the Talmud, that interest, even among Israelites, is lawful in commercial operations, where the lender, running some of the risk of the borrower, becomes a sharer in his profits. This is the opinion of all our sages.

It is evident that opinions, teeming with absurdities, and contrary to all rules of social morality, although advanced by a Rabbi, can no more be imputed to the general doctrine of the Jews, than similar notions, if advanced by Catholic theologians, could be attributed to the evangelical doctrine. The same may be said of the general charge made against the Hebrews, that they are naturally inclined to usury: it cannot be denied that some of them are to be found, though not so many as is generally supposed, who follow that nefarious traffic condemned by their religion.

But if there are some not over-nice in this particular practice, is it just to accuse one hundred thousand individuals of this vice? Would it not be deemed an injustice to lay the same imputation on all Christians because some of them are guilty of usury?[7]

NOTES

1. The Assembly's replies were entrusted to a committee of twelve, headed by the halakhic scholar Rabbi David Sinzheim (1745–1812). The committee's answers were adopted by the Assembly at three successive sittings, on the fourth, the seventh and the twelfth of August 1806.
2. Although theoretically permissible, polygamy was discouraged by the sages of the Talmud, and it was explicitly prohibited among Ashkenazi Jewry by a ban popularly attributed to Rabbi (Rabbenu) Gershom ben Jehuda (c. 960–1028), German Talmudic scholar and spiritual leader.
3. Deut. 10:19.
4. The following passages from Scripture are cited: Exod. 22:21 and 23:9; Lev. 19:34 and 23:22; Deut. 10:18–19 and 24:19; Psalms 145:9; and several Talmudic texts.
5. Deut. 23:19.
6. The following passages from Scripture are cited: Exod. 12:49ff.; Deut. 1:16 and 10:18–19; Lev. 19:33; Exod. 22:21; Lev. 25:15.
7. The Assembly, after concluding the adoption of the answers to the questions posed by Napoleon, declared the fifteenth of August, the Emperor's birthday, as a day Jewry would celebrate with "prayers, thanksgiving, and all the demonstrations of a pure and lively joy" (M. Diogène Tama, *Transactions of the Parisian Sanhedrin*, trans. F. D. Kirwan [London, 1807], p. 212).

15. SUMMONS FOR CONVENING THE PARISIAN SANHEDRIN (SEPTEMBER 18, 1806)[1]

COUNT MOLÉ

His Majesty the Emperor and King is satisfied with your answers; we are commanded by him to say, that he has approved the sense in which they are written; but the communication we are going to make in his name will prove, much better than our words, to what extent this assembly may depend on his powerful protection.

In entering this hall for the second time, Gentlemen, we are impressed with the same sentiments, and the same ideas which occurred to us when we were first admitted into it. And who could behold without astonishment such a society of enlightened men, chosen among the descendants of the most ancient people the world? If one of those, who lived in former years, could again visit this world, and were to be introduced into such an assembly, would he not think himself brought into the middle of the Holy City, or would he not suppose that a terrible revolution had renewed, from the very foundations, the state of all human things? In this he would not be mistaken, Gentlemen. It is after a revolution which threatened to swallow up all nations, thrones, and empires, that altars and thrones are raised everywhere from their ruins to protect the earth; a furious multitude attempted to destroy everything: a man has appeared, and has restored everything; his eye embraces the whole world and past centuries even, to their very origin; he has the wandering remnants of a

---

Source: M. Diogène Tama, *Transactions of the Parisian Sanhedrin*, trans. F. D. Kirwan (London, 1807), pp. 242–47.

nation, rendered as famous by its fall as others are by their greatness, scattered over the face of the earth: it was just that he should consider their situation, and it was right to expect that these same Jews, who hold such a distinguished place in the memory of mankind, should fix the attention of the man who is to occupy it eternally.

The Jews, exposed to the contempt of nations, and not unfrequently to the avarice of princes, have never, as yet, been treated with Justice. Their customs and their practices kept them afar from society, by which they were rejected in their turn; they have always attributed the ill-conduct and the vices, laid to their charge, to the humiliating laws which oppressed them. Even to this day they attribute the backwardness for agricultural pursuits and useful employments, manifested by some of them to the little reliance which they can place on futurity, after having been, for so many centuries, the sport of circumstances, and seeing their very existence depend on the whim of men in power: they will have no cause to complain in the future, and this ground of defence will be taken from them.

His Majesty's intention is, that no plea shall be left to those who may refuse to become citizens; the free exercise of your religious worship and the full enjoyment of your political rights, are secured to you. But, in return for his gracious protection, His Majesty requires a religious pledge for the strict adherence to the principles contained in your answers. This assembly, constituted as it is now, could not of itself give such a security. Its answers, converted into decisions by another assembly, of a nature still more dignified and more religious, must find a place near the Talmud, and thus acquire, in the eyes of the Jews of all countries and of all ages, the greatest possible authority. It is also the only means left to you to meet the grand and generous views of His Majesty, and to impart, to all of your persuasion, the blessings of this new era.

The purity of your law has, no doubt, been altered by the crowd of commentators, and the diversity of their opinions must have thrown doubts in the minds of those who read them. It will be then a most important service, conferred on the whole Jewish community, to fix their belief on those points which have been submitted to you. To find in the history of Israel, an assembly capable of attaining the object now in view, we must go back to the Great Sanhedrin,[2] and it is the Great Sanhedrin, which His Majesty this day intends to convene. This senate, destroyed together with the

Temple, will rise again to enlighten the people it formerly governed: although dispersed throughout the whole world, it will bring back the Jews to the true meaning of the law, by giving interpretations, which shall set aside the corrupted glosses of commentators; it will teach them to love and to defend the country they inhabit; but will convince them that the land, where, for the first time since their dispersion, they have been able to raise their voice, is entitled to all those sentiments which rendered their ancient country so dear to them.

Lastly, the Great Sanhedrin, according to ancient custom, will be composed of seventy members, exclusive of the President. Two thirds, or thereabout, shall be Rabbis, and among them, in the first place, those who sit among you, and who have approved the answers. The other third shall be chosen, by this assembly itself, among its members, by ballot. The duties of the Great Sanhedrin shall be to convert into religious doctrines the answers already given by this assembly, and likewise those which may result from the continuation of your sittings.

For you will observe, Gentlemen, your mission is not yet fulfilled; it will last as long as that of the Great Sanhedrin, which will only ratify your answers and give them a greater weight; His Majesty is, besides, too well satisfied with your zeal and with the purity of your intentions, to dissolve this assembly before the accomplishment of the great work in which you were called to assist.

In the first instance it is fit that you should name by ballot a committee of nine members to prepare, with us, the ground-work of your future discussions and of the decisions of the Sanhedrin. You will observe that the Portuguese, German, and Italian Jews, are equally represented in this committee. We also invite you to acquaint the several synagogues of Europe of the meeting of the Great Sanhedrin, without delay, that they may send deputies able to give the government additional information, and worthy of communicating with you.

NOTES

1. This statement was read before the Assembly of Notables.
2. The Great Sanhedrin in Palestine was the supreme religious and juridical body of Jewry during the Roman period, both before and after the destruction of the Temple, until the abolishment of the patriarchate by

the Romans. (c. 425 C.E.). No institution in Judaism has since possessed its authority. The announcement of the revival of this ancient symbol of Jewish sovereignty naturally evoked, as Napoleon intended, awe, messianic presentiments and spontaneous feelings of gratitude toward the French emperor. Like the ancient Sanhedrin, the Parisian counsel was to be composed of seventy-one members, two-thirds rabbis, one-third laity. The Assembly of Notables was charged with appointing the Sanhedrin.

16. DOCTRINAL DECISIONS (APRIL 1807)[1]

THE PARISIAN SANHEDRIN

Blessed for ever be the name of the Lord, God of Israel, who has placed upon the thrones of France and of the Kingdom of Italy a prince after His heart. God has seen the humiliation of the descendants of Jacob of old, and He has chosen Napoleon the Great as the instrument of His compassion. The Lord judges the thoughts of men, and He alone commands their conscience, and His anointed one permits all men to worship Him according to their belief and faith. Under the shadow of his name security has come into our hearts and our dwellings and from this time on we are permitted to build, to sow, to reap, to cultivate all human knowledge, to be one with the great family of the State, to serve him and to be glorified in his lofty destiny. His high wisdom permits this assembly, which shall be illustrious in our annals, and the wisdom and virtue of which shall dictate decisions, to reconvene after the lapse of fifteen centuries, and to contribute to the welfare of Israel. Gathered this day under his mighty protection, in the good city of Paris, we, learned men and leaders of Israel, to the number of seventy-one, constitute ourselves the Grand Sanhedrin to the end that we may find the means and the strength to promulgate religious decrees which shall conform to the principles of our sacred laws and which shall serve as a standard to all Israelites. These decrees shall teach the nations that our dogmas are in keeping with the civil laws under which we live, and that we are in no wise separated from the society of men.

We therefore declare that the divine Law, the precious heritage of our ancestors, contains within itself dispositions which are political and dispositions which are religious: that the religious dispositions are, by their nature, absolute and independent of circumstances and of the age; that this does not hold true of the political dispositions, that is to say, of the dispositions which were taken for the government of the people of Israel in Palestine when it possessed its own kings, pontiffs and magistrates; that these political dispositions are no longer applicable, since Israel no longer forms a nation; that in consecrating a distinction which has already been established by tradition, the Grand Sanhedrin lays down an incontestible truth; that an assembly of Doctors of the Law, convened as a Grand Sanhedrin, is alone competent to determine the results of this distinction: that, if the Sanhedrin of old did not establish this distinction, it is because the political situation did not at that time call for it, and that, since the dispersion of Israel, no Sanhedrin has ever been assembled until the present one.

Engaged in this holy enterprise, we invoke the divine light, from which all good emanates, and we feel ourselves called upon to contribute, as far as in

Source: Edmond Fleg, ed., *The Jewish Anthology*, trans. from the French by M. Samuel (New York: Harcourt, Brace and Co., 1925), pp. 255–56. Reprinted by permission of Behrman House.

our power lies, to the completion of the moral regeneration of Israel. Thus, by virtue of the right vested in us by our ancient usage and by our sacred laws, which have determined that the assembly of the learned of the age shall possess the inalienable right to legislate according to the needs of the situation, and which impose upon Israel the observance of these laws—be they written or contained in tradition—we hereby religiously enjoin on all obedience to the State in all matters civil and political.

NOTE

1. The opening of the Sanhedrin was delayed until February 9, 1807, four days after the adjournment of the Assembly of Notables. The presiding officer, appointed by the Minister of the Interior, was Rabbi David Sinzheim (cf. this chapter, document 14, note 1.) After a solemn religious service at a Parisian synagogue, the members of the Sanhedrin assembled at the elegant Hôtel de Ville. In accord with the practice of the ancient Sanhedrin, they took their seats in a semicircle, according to age, on both sides of the presiding officers, the laity sitting behind the rabbis. The members wore black attire, with silk capes and three-cornered hats. The first meeting was opened with a prayer in Hebrew written for the occasion by Rabbi Sinzheim. Convening for five additional sessions, the last being on March 2, 1807, the Sanhedrin ceremoniously voted on separate paragraphs without debate and passed them, giving the "spiritual" sanction desired by Napoleon. The Assembly of Notables convened for a final time on March 25; prepared an official report, which included this statement by the Sanhedrin; and presented it to Count Molé on April 6, 1807.

17. REACTION TO NAPOLEON (C. 1814)[1]

THE HASIDIM OF POLAND

In the time of Napoleon's campaign against the tsar, Rabbi Menahem Mendel of Rymanov[2] sought to see the war as the messianic struggle of Gog and Magog,[3] and in order to hasten the redemption, he prayed that Napoleon should be victorious. Should the battle, he contended, entail the spilling of the blood of Israel until one would wade in it up to the knees from Przytyk[4] to Rymanov it would be good so long as the end of days would come and thus our redemption. The *zadikim* of Koznitz[5] and Lublin[6] did not agree with him, however.[7] They prayed that Napoleon would fall in battle, for in their revelations the end of days had not yet come. The story is told that when passing through the town of Koznitz, Napoleon disguised himself as a simple man and went to the house of the *zadik*. But the *zadik* recognized him, and raising the Scroll of Esther, uttered: "You will surely fall Napoleon, you will surely fall!"[8]

The saintly Rabbi of Ropshits[9]—who was at the time still in his youth and lived in the town of Dukla[10]—agreed with the *zadikim* of Koznitz and Lublin. He thus journeyed to Rymanov in order to persuade Rabbi Mendel to withdraw his support of Napoleon. He arrived in Koznitz on the eve of Passover—a day when a great and fierce battle was taking place, Rabbi Mendel was in his house,

Source: Naphtali Horowitz of Ropshits, *Ohel Naphtali*, ed. Avraham Haim Simha Bunam (Lemberg, 1912), p. 13b; and Rabbi Menahem Mendel of Rymanov, *Ateret Menahem*, ed. Avraham Haim Simha Bunam (Lublin, 1910), p. 38b. Trans. by P. Mendes-Flohr. The first two paragraphs of the document are from the former volume; the last paragraph is from the latter. Both these volumes are collections of talks, stories, and teachings by and about Hasidic masters (*zadikim*).

standing before the oven holding *matzos* ready to be baked, and repeatedly saying, "another five hundred Russians will fall." And so it was in battle.... And suddenly the Rabbi of Ropshits entered Rabbi Mendel's house and shouted, "But Rabbi, Napoleon is ritually unclean, and the unclean must defer the celebration of the Jews' redemption from bondage!"[11] Then he fled from the house. Rabbi Mendel commanded that the Rabbi of Ropshits be brought before him, but he was not to be found, for he had already escaped on a wagon which had been waiting to take him home to Dukla.

At the beginning of the year 5574 (1813), on the Day of Atonement before the afternoon prayer, Rabbi Mendel of Rymanov told the Rabbi of Ropshits, who was the cantor, to pray that Napoleon might be victorious. But the Rabbi of Ropshits of Blessed Memory did not wish for Napoleon's victory, and after the Day of Atonement he travelled to the Seer of Lublin to learn how he might work for Napoleon's defeat. The Seer of Lublin refused to assist him, declaring [he was no longer opposed to Napoleon]![12] The Rabbi of Ropshits then travelled to Koznitz, arriving for the Holy Sabbath on which the portion of the Scripture concerning Jethro is read.[13] The Rabbi of Koznitz was at the time in the *mikveh* [ritual bath], so that the Rabbi of Ropshits went and lay on his bed. When the Rabbi of Koznitz came home form the *mikveh* and desired to lie on his bed, the Rabbi of Ropshits did not allow him to do so until he, the Rabbi of Koznitz, promised [to entreat God against Napoleon]. On the eve of the Holy Sabbath, when the hymn for the Sabbath was recited the Rabbi of Koznitz uttered a prayer: "It is said that the French have retreated from Moscow to the river Berezina.[14] We beseech Thee that they may be destroyed for ever and ever. Thou art above the world, O Lord..." The next day, at the reading of the Torah he cried: "You will wither, Napoleon, you will fall." And thus the Rabbi of Ropshits forced the Rabbi of Koznitz to adopt his view [concerning Napoleon], although he initially held the opinion of Rabbi Mendel of Rymanov.

NOTES

1. As Napoleon's armies moved eastward, the vast traditional Jewish community of East Europe was undecided as to whether to regard Napoleon as a latter-day Cyrus, as an agent of divine redemption, or as a diabolical source of secularism.

2. Rabbi Menahem Mendel of Rymanov (d. 1815), a leading Hasidic master in Galicia. Rymanov is a town in the Rzeszow province of southeast Poland; Galicia embraced what is today southeast Poland and northwest Ukraine. With the various partitions of Poland at the end of the eighteenth century, Galicia became a province within the Habsburg Empire.

3. See Ezek. 38 and 39, in which the prophet relates his vision that the end of days will be heralded by a war of the Lord against "Gog of the land of Magog." In rabbinic literature Gog and Magog are parallel names for the enemies of Israel who are to be vanquished at the end of days.

4. Town in east central Poland where Rabbi Mendel was born.

5. Rabbi Israel ben Shabbetai Hapstein (1733–1814). Because of his eloquence he was also known as the *magid* (the preacher) of Koznitz. Koznitz (Koznienicie, Kozenitsy) is a town in Kielce province, of east central Poland.

6. Rabbi Jacob Isaac, the "Seer" of Lublin (1745–1815). A renowned *zadik* and master of theurgic mysticism, he was one of the founders of Hasidim in Poland and Galicia. Lublin is a city in eastern Poland. Although like many *zadikim* he saw the Napoleonic wars in a messianic perspective, he initially withheld his "support" for Napoleon. In 1813, after the retreat of the French army from Moscow, he reversed his position and began to employ his theurgic powers on behalf of Napoleon.

7. In a letter to Moses Meisels, Rabbi Shneur Zalman of Liady speculated about the consequences of Napoleon's possible defeat or victory: "On the first day of the New Year before the Additional Prayers (*Musaf*) I was shown that if Bonaparte is victorious the wealth of the Jewish people will be increased and the dignity of Israel will be restored; the hearts of Israel, however, will become more distant from their Father in heaven. If our lord Alexander triumphs, even though the poverty of the Jews will be increased and indignity will continue to be their lot, the hearts of Israel will be gathered together and united with their father in Heaven.... For the sake of the Name [i.e., God] burn this letter" (M. Teitelbaum, *Harav Milady*, vol. I [Warsaw: 1910], p. 156).

8. The incantation is from Esther 6:13.

9. Rabbi Naphtali Horowitz of Ropshits (1760–1827), a disciple of both Rabbi Menahem Mendel of Rymanov and the *magid* of Koznitz. According to legend, the Rabbi of Ropshits feared that Napoleon would bring evil upon the Jews of Poland, viz., he would conscript the Jews into military service, oblige their attendance at Gentile schools, and induce unbelief. Ropshits

(Ropszyc) is a town in Rzeszow province, southeast Poland.

10. Town near Rymanov in the province of Rzeszow, southeast Poland.

11. "And there were certain men who were unclean through touching the dead body of a man, so they would not keep the Passover on that day…. The Lord said to Moses, 'Say to the people of Israel, if any man of you or of your descendants is unclean through the touching of a dead body … he shall keep the Passover to the Lord a month later'" (Num. 9:6ff.). By referring to this injunction, the Rabbi of Ropshits sought to indicate that Napoleon did not fulfill the religious prescriptions required of a messianic agent.

12. See note 6. On the Feast of Tabernacles 5475 (1814) the Seer met with the *magid* of Koznitz and the *zadik* of Rymanov in order to hasten the war of Gog and Magog by the means of prayer. All three of these *zadikim* died that very year [5475]. According to Hasidic legend, it was the hand of God that brought their death as punishment for their endeavor "to force the end."

13. Exod. 18–20. The passage is read in the Hebrew month Shevat, which falls in early winter.

14. A tributary of the river Dnieper in Belorussia. At Borisov, a major town on the Berezina, Napoleon incurred heavy casualties during his 1812 retreat from Moscow when he was forced to cross the river.

18. THE "INFAMOUS DECREE" (1808)[1]

NAPOLEON BONAPARTE

Decree on the Regulation of Commercial Transactions and Residence of Jews
(March 17, 1808)

Napoleon, Emperor of the French, etc., etc.; On the report of our Minister of the Interior; Our Council of State in agreement, We have decreed and do decree that which follows:

TITLE I

Article 1. From the date of the publication of this decree, the moratorium declared by our decree of May 30, 1806,[2] on the payment of debts to Jews is cancelled.

2. The aforesaid debts, however, shall be subject to the following provisions.

3. Any transaction for a loan made by Jews: to minors without the consent of their guardians; to women without the consent of their husbands; to the lower ranks of military personnel without consent of their officers, or to the higher ranks, without the consent of superiors; shall be considered void so that the holder of the debt cannot take unfair advantage. And our courts may not authorize any suits for the recovery of such loans.

4. No bill of exchange, no promissory note, and no obligation nor promise signed by one of our non-commercial subjects in favor of a Jew shall be collectable unless the holder of the debt can prove that the complete value of the note has been rendered to the debtor without any fraud.

5. Any debt, the capital of which shall be increased as a matter of course or the capital of which shall

Source: Patrick Gireud, *Les Juifs de France, de 1789 à 1860: De l'émancipation à légalité* (Paris: Calmann-Lévyi, 1976), pp. 282–84. English translation by Simeon J. Maslin, "Selected Documents of Napoleonic Jewry" (Hebrew Union College, 1957). Reprinted by permission of Simeon J. Maslin.

become entirely hidden by the accumulation of interest in excess of five per cent, shall be reduced by our courts. If the interest attached to the capital exceeds ten per cent, the debt shall be declared usurious and, thus, cancelled.

6. For legitimate and non-usurious debts, our courts are authorized to grant extensions to the debtors in conformity with equity.

TITLE II

7. From the first day of the coming July and thenceforth, no Jew shall be permitted to devote himself to any business, negotiation, or any type of commerce without having received a specific license from the prefect of the department in which he resides. This license will only be granted on the receipt of precise information and of certification: a) from the municipal council stating that the said Jew does not devote himself to any illicit business; b) from the consistory of the district in which he lives attesting to his good conduct and his integrity.

8. This license shall be renewed annually.

9. The attorneys-general of our courts are specifically instructed to revoke these licenses on the decision of the court whenever it comes to their attention that a licensed Jew is engaging in usury or devoting himself to fraudulent business.

10. Any commercial action undertaken by an unlicensed Jew shall be null and of no value.

11. The preceding shall also apply to any mortgage taken on property by an unlicensed Jew, whenever it can be proven that the said mortgage was taken in payment of a debt resulting from a bill of exchange or from any commercial enterprise whatsoever.

12. All contracts or obligations endorsed for the profit of an unlicensed Jew, in matters foreign to regular commerce, may be annulled after an inquiry by our courts. The debtor shall be allowed to prove that there was usury or some fraudulent transaction, and, if the proof is valid, these debts shall be liable either to arbitrary reduction by the courts or to annulment if the usury exceeds ten per cent.

13. The provisions of article 4, title 1, of this decree, concerning bills of exchange, promissory notes, etc., are applicable for the future as well as the past.

14. No Jew shall be allowed to lend money on collateral to servants or hired people nor to lend money on collateral to any other persons unless the document be drawn up by a notary who will certify in the document that the items were counted in his presence and in the presence of witnesses. Otherwise he shall forfeit all rights to the debtor's wages, and our courts will, in such a case, be able to order free restitution.

15. Jews may not be allowed, under the same penalties, to receive the tools, utensils, implements, or clothing of day workers or servants in lieu of payment of debts.

TITLE III

16. No Jew not actually now living in our departments of Haut and Bas-Rhin[3] shall be hereafter admitted to take up residence there.

In the other departments of the Empire, no Jew not actually now living in them shall be admitted to take up residence except in a case where he acquires a rural property and devotes himself to agriculture, without entering into any commercial or business transactions. It shall be possible to make exceptions to the provisions of this article by means of a special dispensation from us.

17. The Jewish population in our departments shall never be allowed to supply replacements for conscription; consequently, every Jewish conscript shall be subject to personal service.[4]

GENERAL PROVISIONS

18. The provisions included in this decree shall remain in effect for ten years in the hope that, at the end of this period and as a result of these various measures made necessary because of the Jews, there will no longer be any difference between them and the other citizens of our Empire. But, nevertheless, if our hope is disappointed these provisions shall be extended until whatever time shall be judged convenient.

19. The Jews living in Bordeaux and in the departments of Gironde and Landes,[5] not having caused any complaints and not ever having devoted themselves to illicit business, are not included under the provisions of this decree.

Signed, Napoleon
For the Emperor:
The Minister Secretary of State,
signed, Hugues B. Maret[6]

NOTES

1. In the wake of the Parisian Sanhedrin, Napoleon's government promulgated in March 1808 two edicts in order to hasten the integration of the Jews into French society. The first, an "Organic Regulation of the Mosaic

Religion," while recognizing Judaism as one of the "official religions" of France, stipulated the establishment of a state-supervised consistorial system to regulate Jewish religious life as well as to help the authorities to monitor the conduct of each individual Jew. The decree charged the officials of the Jewish community with promoting among their co-religionists patriotism and respect for the laws of France; the consistories were assigned the task of ensuring that young Jews reported for military conscription. The second decree was even more demeaning and soon was dubbed by the Jews the *Décret Infâme*. Imposing restrictions on the economic activities and the right of residence of Jews, the "Infamous Decree" was unabashedly discriminatory. As such it constituted a grave retreat from the principles of the French Revolution and the emancipation. This decree, presented here, was not renewed after its expiration in 1818.

2. In response to recurrent complaints about the allegedly usurious practices of Jewish moneylenders in Alsace, Napoleon issued in May 1806 an order declaring a one-year moratorium on all debts held by Jewish creditors against farmers in the eastern departments of France.

3. These were departments in the areas of Alsace-Lorraine, in which the vast majority of the Ashkenazi Jews of France lived.

4. French law allowed one called up for military service to arrange for someone else to serve in one's stead.

5. In these departments in southwest France, Jews of predominantly Sephardic origin resided. In contrast to the Ashkenazi Jews of Alsace-Lorraine, they were less observant of Jewish traditions and more integrated into French culture and society. Accordingly, they were by and large regarded with far less suspicion than their more insulated Ashkenazi brethren.

6. Hugues-Bernard Maret, Due de Bassano (1763–1839), was one of Napoleon's closest and most trusted associates.

19. EMANCIPATION IN PRUSSIA (MARCH 11, 1812)[1]

FREDERICK WILLIAM III

We, Frederick William, by the grace of God, King of Prussia, etc., have resolved to grant the adherents of the Jewish faith in Our monarchy a new constitution suitable to the general welfare, and declare all laws and regulations concerning Jews (issued) hitherto, which are not confirmed by the present Edict as abolished, and decree as follows:

1. Jews and their families domiciled at present in Our States, provided with general privileges, patent letters of naturalization, letters of protection and concessions, are to be considered as natives [*Einlaender*] and as Prussian state citizens.

2. The continuance of this qualification as natives and state citizens conferred upon them shall however be permitted only under the following obligation: that they bear strictly fixed family names, and that they use German or another living language not only in keeping their commercial books but also upon drawing their contracts and declaratory acts, and that they should use no other than German or Latin characters for their signatures....

4. After having declared and determined his family name, everyone shall receive a certificate from the Provincial Government of his domicile that he is a native and a citizen of the state, which certificate shall

Source: Raphael Mahler, ed. and trans., *Jewish Emancipation, A Selection of Documents*, Pamphlet Series, Jews and the Post-War World, no. 1 (New York: American Jewish Committee, 1941), pp. 32–35. Reprinted by permission of the American Jewish Committee.

be used in the future for himself and his descendants in place of the letter of protection....

7. Jews considered as natives...shall enjoy equal civil rights and liberties with Christians, in so far as this Order does not contain anything to the contrary.

8. They may therefore administer academic school teaching and municipal offices for which they have qualified themselves.

9. As far as the admission of Jews to other public services and government offices is concerned, We leave to Ourselves its regulation by law in course of time.

10. They are at liberty to settle in the towns as well as in the open country.

11. They may acquire real estate of any kind, just the same as the Christian inhabitants and they may carry on any permitted trade, with the provision that they observe the general legal regulations.

12. Freedom of trade ensuing from the right of state citizenship also includes commerce....

14. Native Jews as such must not be burdened with special taxes.

15. They are, however, bound to fulfill all civic duties towards the State and the community of their domicile which Christians are obliged [to carry out] and to bear imposts equal to those of other citizens, with the exception of surplice fees.[2]

16. Native Jews are also subject to military conscription or to the duty of serving in their cantons as well as to all other special regulations in connection therewith. The way and manner, in which this obligation shall be applied to them, shall be determined in a more detailed manner by the regulation on military conscription.

17. Native Jews may contract marriages among themselves without a special permit for it, or without having to take out a marriage license in so far as no previous consent or permission to contract a marriage depending on others is at all required under the general rules....

20. The civil legal relations of Jews shall be judged by the same laws which serve as the rule for other Prussian state citizens....

29. With regard to competence of a court and to administration by guardianship connected therewith, likewise no difference between Christians and Jews shall take place. Only in Berlin shall the special competence of a court assigned to Jews remain in force for the time being.

30. Under no conditions are Rabbis or Jewish Elders permitted to assume any court jurisdiction nor to institute or direct guardianship proceedings.

31. Foreign Jews are not permitted to take up residence in these States as long as they have not acquired Prussian state citizenship....

36. Foreign Jews may enter the country in transit or for the purpose of carrying on permissible commerce and other business. The Police authorities will be provided with a special instruction concerning the procedure to be observed by them and against them.

37. Concerning the prohibition of peddling in general, police laws shall remain the same also with respect to Jews.

38. In Koenigsberg, Breslau and Frankfurt on the Oder, foreign Jews may stay for the duration of the fairs with the permission of the authorities.

39. The necessary regulations concerning the church conditions and the improvement in the education of Jews shall be reserved [for later issue], and when these will be considered, men of the Jewish persuasion who enjoy public confidence because of their knowledge and righteousness shall be called in and their judgment consulted.

All Our Government authorities and subjects shall be guided accordingly.

NOTES

1. The establishment of constitutional governments after the French model in the countries conquered by Napolean induced those states, e.g., Prussia, which remained free of French rule, to consider liberal reforms. This decree, signed by the Prussian monarch, grants the Jews full civil rights; paragraphs 8 and 9 of the decree, however, were sufficiently vague to exclude Jews from judgeships, the officer corps and administrative positions. In 1822 an amendment to the decree explicitly repealed paragraph 8. After the fall of Napolean, this decree was the most liberal legislation concerning the Jews in a German state until the stillborn constitutions of 1848. The states of southern Germany (e.g., Wuerttemberg, Baden and Bavaria) did not grant their Jews full civil rights; noticeably excluded were the rights to full freedom of trade and to free movement and residence. In the Kingdom of Saxony the Jews did not enjoy equality of rights in trade and industry; they were also forbidden to worship in public.

2. Payment to clergy for marriage and funeral services.

20. ARTICLE 16 OF THE CONSTITUTION OF THE GERMAN CONFEDERATION (JUNE 8, 1815)[1]

THE CONGRESS OF VIENNA

In the name of the most Holy and Indivisible Trinity.

The difference among Christian religious parties shall not form the basis of any distinction in the enjoyment of civil and political rights in the lands and areas of the German Confederation.

The Diet of the Confederation shall take into consideration the means of effecting, in the most uniform manner, an amelioration in the civil status of the confessors of the Jewish faith by Germany, as well as the means for providing and guaranteeing for the same the enjoyment of civil rights in the Confederated States in return for their assumption of all the obligations of citizens. Until then, however, the rights of the adherents of this creed already granted to them by the individual Confederated States shall be maintained.

NOTE

1. The Congress of Vienna (from September 1814 to June 1815), a conference of European leaders that was called to discuss the political structure of Europe after the defeat of Napoleon; the congress also gave witness to the formation of the German Confederation.

Although the defunct Holy Roman Empire's several hundred principalities were replaced by a thirty-six-state Confederation, the states were hardly more interested in a strong centralized Germany than were the principalities. They jealously guarded their sovereignty and their local institutions and practices. Thus the firm rejection of Prussia's proposal (suggested by Austria and Hanover) that the Prussian decree of 1812 concerning the Jews serve as the basis of policy toward the Jews throughout the Confederation. Federal legislation concerning the Jews was postponed to the envisaged Federal Diet, which, in turn, ignored the matter. The only immediately effective measure was a guarantee of the rights accorded the Jews previously "*by* the individual Confederated States." At the last moment, the latter phrase was hastily substituted for the original formula: "*in* the individual Confederated States." The individual states were thus obliged to affirm only legislation enacted *by* their sovereign institutions and, accordingly, they were permitted to rescind the emancipation of the Jews decreed by foreign powers. As finally adopted, Article 16 constituted a serious setback in the struggle for Jewish emancipation in Central Europe.

Source: Acten des Wiener Congresses in den Jahren 1814 and 1815, ed. D. J. L. Klueber (Erlangen, 1815), vol. 2, p. 610f., in Raphael Mahler, ed. and trans., *Jewish Emancipation, A Selection of Documents,* Pamphlet series, Jews and the post-World War, no. 1 (New York: American Jewish Commitee, 1941), P. 38. Reprinted by permission of the American Jewish Committee.

21. THE PAULUS-RIESSER DEBATE (1831)[1]

HEINRICH PAULUS AND GABRIEL RIESSER

PROFESSOR HEINRICH PAULUS:[2] The main point is this.... As long as the Jews believe that their continued existence as Jews must be in accordance with the Rabbinic-Mosaic spirit [*Gesinnung*], no nation could grant them civil rights. Civil rights [are to be denied the Jews] because they apparently wish to remain a nation apart, for they conceive of their religious objectives in such a way that they perforce remain a nation apart from those nations which have provided them with shelter.... One cannot seek or obtain civil rights from any nation if one wishes to continue to belong to a different nation and believes one should persist in this adherence. Clearly, granting civil rights presupposes that [the recipient] belongs to the nation which grants these rights and not to any other nation. Jewry, however, dispersed over the entire earth, aspires to preserve through [endogamous] marriage customs and its many particularistic and exclusive laws its nationhood and apartness.

Therefore, it is only possible to grant the Jews (as one specific association in our society) no more than the status of "tolerated residents" [*Untertanenschutz*] or at best that of "protected residents" [*Schutzbuergerschaft*]. And notwithstanding their egregious religion, they should have no reason or desire to insist upon their own national identity. This renunciation must be emphatic and tangible. The Jews must demonstrate that they belong solely to the country of their residence and accept the national identity of that country. They must demonstrate that they no longer consider themselves as members of a necessarily separate, self-sufficient people of God.

DR. GABRIEL RIESSER:[3] To be sure, the Jews were once a nation. But they ceased to be one some two thousand years ago as have most other nations whose descendants constitute the states of present-day Europe. [When the Jews ceased to be a nation], they were dispersed throughout all the provinces of the Roman Empire and were subject to the same legal provisions that applied to other peoples subjugated by the Romans. After the Peregrinic reforms[4] they enjoyed equal rights as Roman citizens. Their creed was not an obstacle here. Although Roman law did preserve the purity of the Roman cult, it is known that the rule of conduct in and out of Rome allowed non-Romans the rights to preserve their own cult, and did not see this as a basis for the exclusion of non-Romans from civil rights.

The charge that our forefathers immigrated here centuries or millennia ago is as fiendish as it is absurd. We are not immigrants; we are native born. And, since that is the case, we have no claim to a home someplace else. We are either German or we are homeless. Does someone seriously wish to use our original, foreign descent against us? Does someone with that civilized status revert back to the barbarous principle of indigenous rights?...

Religion has its creed; the state its laws. The confession of a creed constitutes a religious affiliation; obedience to laws determines citizenship in a state. The confusion of these principles leads to misunderstanding, thoughtlessness and falsehood.... There is only one baptism that can initiate one into a nationality, and that is the baptism of blood in the common struggle for a fatherland and for freedom. "Your blood

Source: H. E. G. Paulus, *Die juedische Nationalabsonderung nach Ursprung, Folgen und Besserungsmitteln, oder ueber Pflichten, Rechte und Verordnungen zur Verbesserung der juedischen Schutzbuergerschaft in Deutschland* (Heidelberg, 1831), pp. 2–3; and Gabriel Riesser, "Verteidigung der buergerlichen Glueckstellung der Juden gegen die Einwuerfe des Herrn Dr. H. E. G. Paulus" (May 1831), in Gabriel Riesser, *Gesammelte Schriften,* published for Das Comite der Riesser-Stiftung, ed. Z. Isler (Leipzig, 1867), vol. 2, pp. 131, 133, 150, 152, 183ff. Trans. by M. Gelber and P. Mendes-Flohr.

was mixed with ours on the battlefield," this was that cry which put an end to the last feeble stirrings of intolerance and antipathy in France.[5] The German Jews also have earned this valid claim to nationality. The Jews in Germany fulfill their military obligations in all instances. They did so even before the Wars of Liberation. They have fought both as conscripts and volunteers in proportionate numbers within the ranks of the German forces....

We, the Jews of Germany might indeed enjoy a degree of freedom. But we conceive of freedom differently. We struggle and strive with all of our might to obtain a higher freedom than that which we presently enjoy; we are committed to struggle and to strive [to obtain this freedom] until the very last breath of our lives—this is what we believe makes us worthy to be *German* and to be called *German*. The vigorous tones of the German language and the songs of German poets ignite and nurture the holy fire of freedom in our breast. The breath of freedom which wafts over Germany awakens our dormant hopes for freedom, of which many happy prospects have already been fulfilled. We wish to belong to the German fatherland. We can, and should, and may be required by the German state [to do] all that it justly requires of its citizens. We will readily sacrifice everything for this state: not, however, belief and loyalty, truth and honor, for Germany's heroes and Germany's sages have not taught us that one becomes a German through such sacrifices.

NOTES

1. After the Congress of Vienna the Jewish question became a major issue in Germany. The debate between Professor Heinrich E. G. Paulus and the young Jewish jurist Gabriel Riesser gave a particularly poignant focus to the issues of the debate. Riesser added a new twist to the debate when he published a pamphlet entitled "On the position of the adherents [*Bekenner*] of the Mosaic faith in Germany" in 1831. Eschewing all apologetics, and in the name of honor and justice alone, he demanded civil equality for Jews. Among the many responses evoked by his pamphlet was that of Professor Paulus, who issued a pamphlet of his own severely criticizing his younger colleague. Excerpts of his critique and of Riesser's reply are presented here.

2. Heinrich Paulus (1761–1851), professor of Oriental languages and theology at the University of Heidelberg.

3. Gabriel Riesser (1806–1863). After trying in vain to secure a university lectureship in jurisprudence and after being barred from practice as a notary in his native Hamburg because of his Judaism, Riesser devoted his life to the struggle for Jewish emancipation. He propagated his views in the journal *Der Jude: Periodische Blaetter der Religion und Gewissensfreiheit*, which he founded in 1831 and published until 1833.

4. The reference is to the *Constitutio Antoniniana* of 212 C.E. This decree extended Roman citizenship to all free inhabitants of the empire, thus obliterating the distinction between Romans and provincials, between conquerors and conquered, between urban and rural dwellers, and between those who possessed Graeco-Roman culture and those who did not. Promulgated by Caracalla, emperor from 211 to 217 C.E., this legislation culminated a process initiated by Julius Caesar.

5. Even prior to their emancipation, the Jews of France—especially in Bordeaux and Paris—volunteered for the various militias formed during the revolution. This fact was raised and regarded favorably during the debates in the National Assembly concerning the eligibility of Jews for citizenship. See document 2 in this chapter.

22. CIVIL DISABILITIES OF THE JEWS (1831)

THOMAS MACAULAY[1]

In order to contribute our share to the success of just principles, we propose to pass in review, as rapidly as possible, some of the arguments, or phrases claiming to be arguments, which have been employed to vindicate a system full of absurdity and injustice.

The constitution—it is said—is essentially Christian; and therefore to admit Jews to office is to destroy the constitution. Nor is the Jew injured by being excluded from political power. For no man has any right to power. A man has a right to his property; a man has a right to be protected from personal injury. These rights the law allows to the Jew, and with these rights it would be atrocious to interfere. But it is a mere matter of favour to admit any man to political power; and no man can justly complain that he is shut out from it.

We cannot but admire the ingenuity of this contrivance for shifting the burden of the proof from off those to whom it properly belongs, and who would, we suspect, find it rather cumbersome. Surely no Christian can deny that every human being has a right to be allowed every gratification which produces no harm to others, and to be spared every mortification which produces no good to others. Is it not a source of mortification to any class of men that they are excluded from political power? They have on Christian principles, a right to be freed from that mortification, unless it can be shown that their exclusion is necessary for the averting of some greater evil. The presumption is evidently in favour of toleration. It is for the persecutor to make out his case....

It is because men are not in the habit of considering what the end of government is, that Catholic disabilities and Jewish disabilities have been suffered to exist so long. We hear of essentially Protestant governments and essentially Christian governments—words which mean just as much as essentially Protestant cookery, or essentially Christian horsemanship. Government exists for the purpose of keeping the peace, for the purpose of compelling us to settle our disputes by arbitration, instead of settling them by blows, for the purpose of compelling us to supply our wants by industry, instead of supplying them by rapine. This is the only operation for which the machinery of government is fit, the only operation which wise governments ever attempt to perform. If there is any class of people who are not interested, or who do not think themselves interested, in the security of property and the maintenance of order, that class ought to have no share of the powers which exist for the purpose of securing property and maintaining order. But why a man should be less fit to exercise that power because he wears a beard, because he does not eat ham, because he goes to the synagogue on Saturdays instead of going to the church on Sundays, we cannot conceive.

The points of difference between Christianity and Judaism have very much to do with a man's fitness to be a bishop or a rabbi. But they have no more to do with his fitness to be a magistrate, a legislator, or a minister of finance, than with his fitness to be a cobbler. Nobody has ever thought of compelling cobblers to make any declaration on the true faith of a Christian. Any man would rather have his shoes mended by a heretical cobbler, than by a person who had subscribed to all the thirty-nine articles, but had never handled an awl. Men act thus, not because they are indifferent to religion, but because they do not see what religion has to do with the mending of their shoes. Yet religion has as much to do with the mending of shoes, as with the budget and the army estimates....

But it would be monstrous, say the persecutors, that a Jew should legislate for a Christian community.

Source: Maurice Cross, ed., *Selections from the Edinburgh Review* (London: Longman, 1833), vol. 3, pp. 667–75.

That is a palpable misrepresentation. What is proposed is not that Jews should legislate for a Christian community, but that a legislature composed of Christians and Jews should legislate for a community composed of Christians and Jews. On nine hundred and ninety-nine questions, out of a thousand, on all questions of police, of finance, of civil and criminal law, of foreign policy the Jew, as a Jew, has no interest hostile to that of the Christian or even of the Churchman. On questions relating to the ecclesiastical establishment, the Jew and the Churchman may differ. But they cannot differ more widely than the Catholic and the Churchman, or the Independent and the Churchman. The principle, that Churchmen ought to monopolise the whole power of the state, would at least have an intelligible meaning. The principle, that Christians ought to monopolise it, has no meaning at all. For no question connected with the ecclesiastical institutions of the country can possibly come before Parliament, with respect to which there will not be as wide a difference between Christians as there can be between any Christian and any Jew.

In fact, the Jews are not now excluded from political power. They possess it; and as long as they are allowed to accumulate property, they must possess it. The distinction which is sometimes made between civil privileges and political power, is a distinction without a difference. Privileges are power.

That a Jew should be a judge in a Christian country, would be most shocking. But he may be a juryman. He may try issues of fact; and no harm is done. But if he should be suffered to try issues of law, there is an end of the constitution....

What power in civilised society is so great as that of the creditor over the debtor? If we take this away from the Jew, we take away from him the security of his property. If we leave it to him, we leave to him a power more despotic by far, than that of the King and all his cabinet.

It would be impious to let a Jew sit in Parliament. But a Jew may make money, and money may make members of Parliament....

That a Jew should be privy-councillor to a Christian king, would be an eternal disgrace to the nation. But the Jew may govern the money market, and the money market may govern the world....A congress of sovereigns may be forced to summon the Jew to their assistance. The scrawl of the Jew on the back of a piece of paper may be worth more than the royal word of three kings, or the national faith of three new American republics. But that he should put Right Honourable before his name, would be the most frightful of national calamities....

It is our duty as Christians to exclude the Jews from political power, it must be our duty to treat them as our ancestors treated them—to murder them, and banish them, and rob them. For in that way, and in that way alone, can we really deprive them of political power. If we do not adopt this course, we may take away the shadow, but we must leave them the substance. We may do enough to pain and irritate them; but we shall not do enough to secure ourselves from danger, if danger really exists. Where wealth is, there power must inevitably be.

The English Jews, we are told, are not Englishmen. They are a separate people, living locally in this island, but living morally and politically in communion with their brethren, who are scattered over all the world. An English Jew looks on a Dutch or a Portuguese Jew as his countryman, and on an English Christian as a stranger. This want of patriotic feeling, it is said, renders a Jew unfit to exercise political functions.

The argument has in it something plausible; but a close examination shows it to be quite unsound. Even if the alleged facts are admitted, still the Jews are not the only people who have preferred their sect to their country. The feeling of patriotism, when society is in a healthful state, springs up, by a natural and inevitable association, in the minds of citizens who know that they owe all their comforts and pleasures to the bond which unites them in one community. But under partial and oppressive governments, these associations cannot acquire that strength which they have in a better state of things. Men are compelled to seek from their party that protection which they ought to receive from their country, and they, by a natural consequence, transfer to their party that affection which they would otherwise have felt for their country....It has always been the trick of bigots to make their subjects miserable at home, and then complain that they look for relief abroad; to divide society, and to wonder that it is not united; to govern as if a section of the state were the whole, and to censure the other sections of the state for their want of patriotic spirit. If the Jews have not felt towards England like children, it is because she has treated them like a stepmother.

Rulers must not be suffered thus to absolve themselves of their solemn responsibility. It does not lie in their mouths to say that a sect is not patriotic: it is their business to make it patriotic. History and reason clearly indicate the means. The English Jews are, as far as we can see, precisely what our government has made them. They are precisely what any sect—what any class of men selected on any principle from the community, and treated as they have been treated—would have been. If all the red-haired people in Europe had, for centuries, been outraged and oppressed, banished from this place, imprisoned in that, deprived of their money, deprived of their teeth, convicted of the most improbable crimes on the feeblest evidence, dragged at horses' tails, hanged, tortured, burned alive, if, when manners became milder, they had still remained subject to debasing restrictions, and exposed to vulgar insults, locked up in particular streets in some countries, pelted and ducked by the rabble in others, excluded everywhere from magistracies and honours, what would be the patriotism of gentlemen with red hair? And if, under such circumstances, a proposition were made for admitting red-haired men to office, how striking a speech might an eloquent admirer of our old institutions deliver against so revolutionary a measure! "These men," he might say, "scarcely consider themselves as Englishmen. They think a red-haired Frenchman or a red-haired German more closely connected with them than a man with brown hair born in their own parish. If a foreign sovereign patronises red hair, they love him better than their own native king. They are not Englishmen—they cannot be Englishmen—nature has forbidden it—experience proved it to be impossible. Right to political power they have none; for no man has a right to political power. Let them enjoy personal security; let their property be under the protection of the law. But if they ask for leave to exercise power over a community of which they are only half members—a community, the constitution of which is essentially dark-haired—let us answer them in the words of our wise ancestors, *Nolumus leges Angliae mutari* [We are not willing to change the laws of England]."

But, it is said, the Scriptures declare that the Jews are to be restored to their own country; and the whole nation looks forward to that restoration. They are, therefore, not so deeply interested as others in the prosperity of England. It is not their home, but merely the place of their sojourn—the house of their bondage....

A man who should act, for one day, on the supposition that all the people about him were influenced by the religion which they professed, would find himself ruined before night: and no man ever does act on that supposition, in any of the ordinary concerns of life, in borrowing, in lending, in buying, or in selling. But when any of our fellow-creatures are to be oppressed, the case is different. Then we represent those motives which we know to be so feeble for good as omnipotent for evil. Then we lay to the charge of our victims all the vices and follies to which their doctrines, however remotely, seem to tend....

People are now reasoning about the Jews, as our fathers reasoned about the Papists. The law which is inscribed on the walls of the synagogues prohibits covetousness. But if we were to say that a Jew mortgagee would not foreclose because God had commanded him not to covet his neighbour's house, everybody would think us out of our wits. Yet it passes for an argument to say, that a Jew will take no interest in the prosperity of the country in which he lives, that he will not care how bad its laws and police may be, how heavily it may be taxed, how often it may be conquered and given up to spoil, because God has pronounced, that by some unknown means, and at some undetermined time, perhaps a thousand years hence, the Jews shall migrate to Palestine. Is not this the most profound ignorance of human nature? Do we not know that what is remote and indefinite affects men far less than what is near and certain? Besides, the argument applies to Christians as strongly as to Jews. The Christian believes, as well as the Jew, that at some future period the present order of things will come to an end. Nay, many Christians believe that the Messiah will shortly establish a kingdom on the earth, and reign visibly over all its inhabitants. Whether this doctrine be orthodox or not, we shall not here enquire. The number of people who hold it is very much greater than the number of Jews residing in England. Many of those who hold it are distinguished by rank, wealth, and talent. It is preached from pulpits, both of the Scottish and of the English Church. Noblemen and members of Parliament have written in defence of it. Now, wherein does this doctrine differ, as far as its political tendency is concerned, from the doctrine of the Jews? If a Jew is unfit to legislate for us, because he believes that he or his remote descendants will be removed to Palestine, can we safely open the House of Commons to a fifth-monarchy man, who expects that, before this generation' shall pass away, all the kingdoms of the earth will be swallowed up in one divine empire?

Does a Jew engage less eagerly than a Christian in any competition which the law leaves open to him? Is he less active and regular in business than his neighbors? Does he furnish his house meanly, because he is a pilgrim and sojourner in the land? Does the expectation of being restored to the country of his fathers render him insensible to the fluctuations of the Stock Exchange? Does he, in arranging his private affairs, ever take into account the chance of his returning to Palestine? If not, why are we to suppose that feelings which never influence his dealings as a merchant, or his dispositions as a testator, will acquire a boundless influence over him as soon as he becomes a magistrate or a legislator?

There is another argument which we would not willingly treat with levity, and which yet we scarcely know how to treat seriously. The Scriptures, it is said, are full of terrible denunciations against the Jews. It is foretold, that they are to be wanderers. Is it, then, right to give them a home? It is foretold, that they are to be oppressed. Can we with propriety suffer them to be rulers? To admit them too the rights of citizens, is manifestly to insult the Divine oracles.

We allow, that to falsify a prophecy inspired by Divine Wisdom would be a most atrocious crime. It is, therefore, a happy circumstance for our frail species, that it is a crime which no man can possibly commit. If we admit the Jews to seats in Parliament, we shall, by so doing, prove that the prophecies in question, whatever they may mean, do not mean that the Jews shall be excluded from Parliament....

But we protest altogether against the practice of confounding prophecy with precept—of setting up predictions which are often obscure against a morality which is always clear. If actions are to be considered as just and good merely because they have been predicted, what action was ever more laudable than that crime which our bigots are now, at the end of eighteen centuries, urging us to avenge on the Jews—that crime which made the earth shake, and blotted out the sun from heaven? If this argument justifies the laws now existing against the Jews, it justifies equally all the cruelties which have ever been committed against them—the sweeping edicts of banishment and confiscation, the dungeon, the rack, and the slow fire....

We have not so learned the doctrines of Him who commanded us to love our neighbour as ourselves, and who, when He was called upon to explain what He meant by a neighbour, selected as an example a heretic and an alien. Last year, we remember, it was represented by a pious writer in a *John Bull*[2] newspaper, and by some other equally fervid Christians, as a monstrous indecency, that the measure for the relief of the Jews should be brought forward in Passion week. One of these humourists ironically recommended, that it should be read a second time on Good Friday. We should have had no objection; nor do we believe that the day could be commemorated in a more worthy manner. We know of no day fitter for terminating long hostilities, and repairing cruel wrongs, than the day on which the religion of mercy was founded. We know of no day fitter for blotting out from the statute book, the last traces of intolerance, than the day on which the spirit of intolerance produced the foulest of all judicial murderers; the day on which the list of victims of intolerance—that noble list in which Socrates and more are enrolled—was glorified by a yet more awful and sacred name.

NOTES

1. Thomas Macaulay (1800–1859), English historian, essayist and politician. Elected to Parliament in 1830, he made his first speech at the second reading of the bill for the Removal of Jewish Disabilities in April of that year. In an article in the *Edinburgh Review* of January 1831, excerpts of which appear here, he argued the same cause. This support expressed by one of England's leading men of letters had a significant effect on public opinion.
2. John Bull is a literary figure who personifies England.

23. EMANCIPATION ACT (1832)[1]

ASSEMBLY OF LOWER CANADA[2]

Whereas doubts have arisen whether persons professing the Jewish religion are by law entitled to many of the privileges enjoyed by the other subjects of His Majesty within the province, be it therefore declared and enacted by the King's most excellent Majesty, by and with the advice and consent of the Legislative Council and Assembly of the province of Lower Canada, constituted and assembled by virtue of and under the authority of an act passed in the Parliament of Great Britain, intituled (*sic*), "An Act to repeal certain parts of an Act passed in the four-teenth year of His Majesty's reign,[3] intituled, 'An Act for making more effectual provision for the government of the province of Quebec, in North America,' and to make further provision for the government of the said province of Quebec in North America," and it is hereby declared and enacted by the authority aforesaid, that all persons professing the Jewish religion being natural-born British subjects inhabiting and residing in this province, are entitled and shall be deemed, adjudged and taken to be entitled to the full rights and privileges of the other subjects of His Majesty, his heirs or successors, to all intents, constructions and purposes, whatsoever, and capable of taking, having or enjoying any office or place of trust whatsoever within this province.

NOTES

1. In 1804 Ezekiel Hart (1767–1843), a Jew, was elected to the Assembly of Lower Canada. His election raised the question of the civil status of the Jews in Canada, which hitherto had not been defined. At the ceremony inducting new members to the legislature Hart declined to be sworn in according to the established formula "on the true faith of a Christian," but took the oath according to Jewish tradition on the Hebrew Bible and with his head covered. This occasioned a heated debate that led to the formation of special committee to discuss Hart's eligibility as a Jew to serve in the Assembly. The committee ruled that due to his refusal to take the Christian oath Hart was disqualified from elected office. In a subsequent by-election he was elected once again, and once again the Assembly barred him for assuming his office. The ban in practice was extended to civil, judicial and military office. Consequent to a struggle between reformers, largely affiliated with the English community, against the French population, the Assembly unanimously approved on June 5, 1832, the so-called Emancipation Act. Although the legislation refers only to Quebec, the sole province where Jews resided at the time, the civil equality of the Jews in effect appertained to the entire dominion of Canada.

2. The Constitutional Act of 1791, enacted by the Parliament of Great Britain, partitioned the British Colony of Quebec into the Province of Lower Canada and the Province of Upper Canada. Lower Canada was constituted by parts of the former French colony of New France, which was ceded to Great Britain in the wake of France's defeat in the French and Indian wars, known in Canada as the War of Conquest (1754–63). The province consisted largely of French Canadians. Whereas Upper Canada, with a predominantly English population, received English law and institutions, Lower Canada was allowed to retain French law and institutions, including privileges accorded to the Roman Catholic Church. The small Jewish community of Lower Canada was allied with the English, thus finding themselves in the middle of the abiding tension between the country's French and English populations.

3. George III of Great Britain reigned from 1760 to his death in 1820.

Source: The Provincial Statues of Lower Canada (1832), Vol. XIV, cap. LVII, p. 82.

24. THE LAW CONCERNING THE FUNDAMENTAL RIGHTS OF THE GERMAN PEOPLE: RELIGIOUS EQUALITY (1848)[1]

THE FRANKFURT PARLIAMENT

The Imperial Regent [*Reichsverweser*] in execution of the resolution of the National Assembly of December 21, 1848, proclaims as law:

I. The Fundamental Rights of the German People. The following rights shall be granted to the German people. They shall serve as a norm for the Constitution of the individual German states and no constitution or legislation of an individual German state may abolish or restrict them....

Article 5.... Paragraph 14. Every German has full freedom of faith and conscience. Nobody shall be forced to disclose his religious creed....

Paragraph 16. The enjoyment of civil or political rights shall be neither conditioned nor limited by religious confession.

The same religious confession should not impair civil duties.

Paragraph 17.... No religious association shall benefit from any state prerogatives before others. No state church shall exist henceforth.

NOTE

1. The revolutions of 1848 that spread throughout Europe were inspired by liberal democratic principles, among them full civil and political equality for the Jews. The Frankfurt National Parliament, which superseded the Diet of the Germanic Confederation, established a provisional government, headed by Archduke John of Austria. Lacking material power (e.g., an army), this government never established its authority, and the attempt to unite Germany under a liberal, parliamentary system soon failed. The constitution, promulgated by the Assembly in March 1849 and incorporating the Fundamental Rights, became obsolete in a few months. Nonetheless, it established important moral and legislative precedents that made it difficult to return to the prerevolutionary situation. Aside from southern Germany, where Jewish civil disabilities generally persisted, the right to vote and to be elected, although frequently questioned, was preserved. Moreover, the cause of Jewish emancipation won the strong support of liberals. Until 1869 the Jews were still restricted by law from holding administrative and juridical positions. See document 26 in this chapter.

Source: "Law Concerning the Fundamental Rights of the German People (December 27, 1848)," in Raphael Mahler, ed. and trans., *Jewish Emancipation, A Selection of Documents*, Pamphlet Series, Jews and the Post-War World, no. 1 (New York: American Jewish Committee, 1941), p. 49. Reprinted by permission of the American Jewish Committee.

25. THE JEWISH RELIEF ACT (JULY 23, 1858)[1]

THE HOUSES OF PARLIAMENT OF GREAT BRITAIN

Be it enacted by the Queen's Most Excellent Majesty, by and with the Advice and Consent of the Lords Spiritual and Temporal, and Commons, in this present Parliament assembled, and by the Authority of the same, as follows:

1. Where it should appear to either House of Parliament that a Person professing the Jewish Religion otherwise entitled to sit and vote in such House, is prevented from so sitting and voting by his conscientious objection to take the Oath which by an Act passed or [is] to be passed in the present Session of Parliament has been or may be substituted for the Oaths of Allegiance, Supremacy, and Abjuration in the Form therein required, such House if it think fit, may resolve that thenceforth any Person professing the Jewish Religion, in taking the said oath to entitle him to sit and vote as aforesaid, may omit the words "and I make this Declaration upon the true Faith of a Christian," and so long as such Resolution shall continue in force the said Oath, when taken and subscribed by any Person professing the Jewish Religion to entitle him to sit and vote in that House of Parliament may be modified accordingly, and the taking and subscribing by any Person professing the Jewish Religion of the Oath so modified shall, so far as respects the Title to sit and vote in such House, have the same Force and Effect as the taking and subscribing by other Persons of the said Oath in the Form required by the said Act.

2. In all other Cases, except for sitting in Parliament as aforesaid, or in qualifying to exercise the Right of Presentation to any Ecclesiastical Benefice in Scotland, whenever any of Her Majesty's Subjects professing the Jewish Religion shall be required to take the said Oath, the words "and I make this Declaration upon the true Faith of a Christian" shall be omitted.

3. Nothing herein contained shall extend or be construed to extend to enable any Person or Persons professing the Jewish Religion to hold or exercise the office of Guardians and Justices of the United Kingdom, or of Regent of the United Kingdom, under whatever Name, Style, or Title such office may be constituted, or of Lord High Chancellor, Lord Keeper or Lord Commissioner of the Great Seal of Great Britain, or Ireland, or the office of Lord Lieutenant or Deputy or other Chief Governor or Governors of Ireland, or Her Majesty's High Commissioner to the General Assembly of the Church of Scotland.

4. Where any Right of Presentation to any Ecclesiastical Benefice shall belong to any office in the Gift or Appointment of Her Majesty, Her Heirs or Successors, and such office shall be held by a Person professing the Jewish Religion, the Right of Presentation shall devolve upon and be exercised by the Archbishop of Canterbury for the time being and it shall not be lawful for any Person professing the Jewish Religion, directly or indirectly, to advise Her Majesty, Her Heirs or Successors, or any Person or Persons holding or exercising the Office of Guardians of the United Kingdom, or of Regent of the United Kingdom, under whatever Name, Style, or Title such office may be constituted or the Lord Lieutenant or Lord Deputy, or any other Chief Governor or Governors of Ireland, touching or concerning the Appointment to or Disposal of any Office of Preferment in the United Church of England and Ireland, or in the Church of Scotland, and if such Person shall offend in the Premises, he shall, being thereof convicted by due course of Law, be deemed guilty of a high Misdemeanor, and disabled for ever from holding any Office, Civil or Military under the Crown.

Source: *A Collection of the Public General Statutes* (London, 1858), pp. 258–59.

NOTE

1. In Great Britain the process of emancipation occurred gradually through a series of separate legislative acts. The elimination of the Christian oath as a prerequisite for legislative office removed a serious obstacle to the attainment of political rights for Jews. The wording of the parliamentary oath "prevented" professing Jews from serving in the Houses of Parliament of Great Britain. In 1858 the House of Lords passed a bill eliminating the clause "on the true faith of a Christian," but the House of Commons rejected the proposed legislation. A compromise was finally reached, the so-called Jewish Relief Act of July 23, 1858, allowing each House to admit Jews by ad hoc vote. Three days later Baron Lionel de Rothschild (1808–1879), representing the City of London, was sworn into the House of Commons, while covering his head, took an oath with the formula "so help me, Jehovah." He thereupon assumed his office as the first Jewish member of Parliament.

26. NORTH GERMAN CONFEDERATION AND JEWISH EMANCIPATION (JULY 3, 1869)[1]

WILHELM I

We, Wilhelm, by the Grace of God, King of Prussia, etc., with the approval of the Bundesrath and of the Reichstag decree in the name of the North German Confederation as follows:

All still existent restrictions on civil and political rights derived from the difference in religious confession are hereby repealed. In particular, the qualification for participation in communal and provincial representative bodies and for holding public offices shall be independent of religious confession.

Authentically under Our Most High Signature and with the Seal of the Confederation affixed.

Done at the Castle of Babelsberg, July 3, 1869.

NOTE

1. Under the leadership of Chancellor Otto von Bismarck (1815–1898), Prussia led the fragmented states of Germany to a genuine unification. To facilitate this program, Bismarck sought the cooperation of the National Liberal party and, in turn, made economic and political concessions to liberalism, including the removal of all remaining civil and political disabilities due to differences of religious affiliation.

Source: "Law Concerning the Equality of All Confessions in Respect to Civil Rights and Political Rights," in Raphael Mahler, ed. and trans., *Jewish Emancipation, A Selection of Documents,* Pamphlet Series, Jews and the Post-War World, no. 1 (New York; American Jewish Committee, 1941), pp. 57–58. Reprinted by permission of the American Jewish Committee.

27. EMANCIPATION IN BAVARIA (APRIL 22, 1871)[1]

WILHELM I

We, Wilhelm, by the grace of God, German Emperor, King of Prussia, etc., decree, in the name of the German Reich, following the approval of the Bundesrath and the Reichstag, as follows:

1. The laws of the North German Confederation cited in the following paragraphs shall be introduced in the Kingdom of Bavaria as laws of the Reich, according to the detailed stipulations contained in these paragraphs.

2. From the day on which the present law goes into effect the following shall be in force: ... (10) the law of July 3, 1869, concerning the equality of confessions with respect to civil and political rights.

Authentically under Our Most High Signature and with the Imperial Seal affixed.

Done in Berlin, April 22, 1871.

NOTE

1. The three South German states of Baden, Wuerttemberg and Bavaria joined the North German Confederation in 1871, establishing the Second German Reich. Baden and Wuerttemberg had already accorded full rights to the Jews in 1861 and 1864, respectively. These rights were extended to the Jews in Bavaria through this act. Legally the process of emancipation in Germany was thereby completed. In practice, however, Jews remained with few exceptions excluded from the officer corps, administrative posts with prestige and authority, foreign service and teaching positions below the university.

Source: "Law Concerning the Introduction in Bavaria of the Laws of the North German Confederation," in Raphael Mahler, ed. and trans., *Jewish Emancipation, A Selection of Documents*, Pamphlet Series, Jews and the Post-War World, no. 1 (New York: American Jewish Committee, 1941), pp. 58–59. Reprinted by permission of the American Jewish Committee.

IV

EMERGING PATTERNS OF RELIGIOUS ADJUSTMENT: REFORM, CONSERVATIVE, NEO-ORTHODOX, AND ULTRA-ORTHODOX JUDAISM

Emancipation, or at least the promise of emancipation, stimulated a process of acculturation among the Jews. Emancipation implied the breakdown of the Jews' millennial social and cultural isolation; indeed, this was often the explicit expectation of the Gentile advocates of Jewish emancipation. Traditionally, the adoption of non-Jewish culture was frowned upon by Jews as a dangerous act, necessarily involving, especially in the Christian world, religious apostasy. But the "Gentile" culture sponsored by the liberal votaries of the Enlightenment was presumably different. This culture, it was emphasized, was predicated on a resolve to create both a universe of discourse and a structure of social bonds that were open to all persons regardless of class, national origin, or religious affiliation. It was said that for the first time in European history the Jews could participate in non-Jewish culture without the stigma of apostasy.

Observant Jews, such as Moses Mendelssohn, Naphtali Herz Wessely, and other *maskilim* (enlightened Jews), evinced little hesitation in appropriating the philosophical, aesthetic, educational, and political values of the Enlightenment. They vigorously maintained that the integrity of traditional Judaism was not compromised by their adoption of the "neutral" culture of the Enlightenment. To be sure, there were many Jews who were not as sanguine, for they feared that the cultural and social integration recommended by the *maskilim* would inexorably weaken the bonds of the Jews to their ancestral faith. Raising a Cassandran cry, they warned that under the aegis of the Enlightenment, Judaism would lose its exclusive claim on the soul and the mind of the Jew and would thus cease to be the bedrock of the Jew's social and spiritual identity; moreover, they maintained, social integration would lead to a relaxation of religious observance. These premonitions were confirmed by the increasingly lax observance of many "enlightened" Jews and the concomitant call to legitimate this "laxity" by the reform of the traditional ritual practices of Judaism.

The ritual practices of traditional Judaism are comprehensive, and, as is often said, they involve the whole life of the Jew. These practices are supported by unique customs, language, memories, hopes and, until the modern period, legal autonomy. Jewry thus enjoyed a distinctive way of life. Theologically, the divine authority sanctioning this way of life was derived from the Oral Law (*Torah shebeal peh*) given to Moses along with the written Torah. The Oral Law provided the hermeneutics to interpret God's Word, both ritual and juridical, as found in the written Torah, and thus served to guide Jewry in its observance of the divine Will in the ever-protean situations and circumstances of life. The Oral Law was eventually recorded in the second century C.E. in the Mishnah and later elaborated upon in the Gemara (Talmud) and in ongoing commentaries: the consensus regarding the norms of Jewish behavior that emerges from the Oral Law and the commentaries is known as the halakhah. Sociologically, the way of life of halakhic Judaism endowed Jewry with an unambiguously distinct ethnic, indeed national, identity—an identity that was a source of profound discomfort to those Jews who sought cultural, social and political integration in the Gentile community in which they lived.

The reformation of Judaism sought by the enlightened Jews was not simply a diminution of the ritual burdens of the Jew but also an elimination or, at least, a blurring of the ethnic and national features of traditional Judaism. For these Jews, the urgent issue was to challenge the preeminence in Jewish life of the halakhah (or "rabbinism," as it was disparagingly called by Jew and non-Jew alike). The halakhah, it was felt, prevented the necessary adaptations facilitating the Jew's integration in the non-Jewish world. Hence, it was concluded that the halakhah would have to be replaced as the supreme authority governing Jewish life. But this demand presented enormous theological and practical problems. Halakhah, after all, derived its authority as the Word of God. Moreover, halakhah provided the dispersed nation of Israel with a common religious framework that assured an enduring commonality and continuity to Jewish life despite the geographical and cultural diversity among the respective communities of the nation. What authority other than halakhah would both command the universal fidelity of all Jews and ensure the institutional consensus within the Jewish world?

The publication of *Eleh divrei habrit* (see document 3) and the opposition to the nascent Reform movement was the occasion for the crystallization of what was soon to be known as Orthodox Judaism. The leading figure in the struggle of traditional rabbis against Reform was the highly esteemed Talmudic scholar Moses Sofer (popularly known as Hatam Sofer; see document 4). The opposition to Reform was soon extended to all attempts to integrate the Jews and Judaism into the modern world. To preserve the integrity of their ancient faith, Jews were urged to maintain not only the halakhah but a distinctive, even segregative style of life. Hatam Sofer spoke of *shalem*, the Hebrew for "whole," which he presented as an acronym for *shem* (name; one should not use non-Jewish first names), *lashon* (language; one should not learn non-Jewish languages other than for purely instrumental reasons), *malbush* (dress; one should not dress in the current fashion of the gentiles). The revered rabbi presented these views most forcefully in his widely read "ethical testament" (see document 6). Rabbi Akiba Joseph Schlesinger wrote a running commentary on the testament, *Lev haivri* ([The Heart of the Hebrew], 1865), which still serves as a quintessential statement of what is now called Ultra-Orthodoxy in order to differentiate it from the position of traditional Jews who feel that some degree of accommodation to the modern world is permissible (see second edition of this volume, document 14). His views were halakhic sanctions by the rabbinical court of Michalowce (document 16).

Aside from Saul Ascher's purely academic exercise to redefine Judaism as a religion of dogma as opposed to a religion of revealed law, i.e., halakhah (see chapter 2, document 23), early Reform in Germany made little more than desultory aesthetic innovations in Jewish ritual, innovations that were intended to make Jewish liturgical services more decorous and becoming. Undoubtedly, these early Reformers (who were almost exclusively laymen) had in mind such comments as those made by J. H. Campe. In his much acclaimed *Dictionary of the German Language* (1808) Campe urged that German be expunged of foreignisms and that *inter alia* the term *Synagogue*, borrowed from the Greek, be replaced by the German word *Judenschule* (Jew School), for like a school of unruly pupils, the Jews' house of worship is "a place where people gather and mumble in an unlovely manner."[1]

The first comprehensive, systematic reform of Judaism was instituted by the New Israelite Temple Association, founded in Hamburg in December 1817. The Hamburg Temple incorporated the aesthetic innovations of earlier Reformers: strict decorum; emphasis on the Saturday morning service (with the implied neglect of the thrice daily prayers of the weekdays); an abridged liturgy and the inclusion of prayers in German; choral and organ music; the abolition of the "oriental" cantillation traditionally employed in chanting of the weekly Torah portion; and sermons in German on edificatory themes as opposed to the traditional homily (*drashah*) on the weekly Torah portion. For this service the Hamburg Reformers also prepared a new prayer book. Based on the traditional liturgy, the main innovations of this prayer-book were the inclusion of German prayers and the omission or modification of traditional prayers for the coming of the personal Messiah and "national" prayers that expressed the Jews' longing to be redeemed from Exile and to be restored to their ancestral homeland in Zion. In anticipation of rabbinic objection to these reforms, albeit relatively moderate, the Reformers solicited the service of a Talmudic scholar, Eliezer Liebermann, to prepare a halakhic defense of Reform. Liebermann issued two volumes; the first, *Nogah hazedek* ([The Light of Righteousness], 1818) contained the approbations of four rabbis—two Italian and two Hungarian—of the reforms. The second, *Or nogah* ([The Light of Splendor], 1818), an appendix to the first volume but also published separately, presented his detailed apologia for the Hamburg reforms based on halakhah and classical rabbinic opinion (see document 2).[2]

In response, the rabbinic court of Hamburg published a volume entitled *Eleh divrei habrit* ([These Are the Words of the Covenant], 1819). The publication presented statements by twenty-two of Europe's leading rabbis condemning the Hamburg reforms as based on a specious reading of halakhah and as constituting a schismatic threat to the unity of the Jewish people (see document 3). They conspicuously ignored the Reformers' contention that halakhic Judaism itself was in effect schismatic by its failure to acknowledge and adapt to the fact that an ever-increasing number of Jews were abandoning Judaism because they found it incompatible with their new sensibilities and priorities.

---

[1] Joachim Heinrich Campe, *Woerterbuch der deutschen Sprache* (Braunschweig, 1808, 1811), vol. 2, p. 852.

[2] *Reform* is used here and throughout this chapter anachronistically. This term, as well as the term *Liberal*, emerged as a designation only as the movement crystallized. Liebermann's treatises were actually written in defense of the reforms instituted earlier in Berlin; however, because of the timing of their publication, *Nogah hazedek/Or nogah* in fact served as a defense for the Hamburg Temple.

The advocates of Reform Judaism had difficulty determining those principles that would hold an authority similar to that of halakhah. The quest for such principles gained momentum as a new generation of secularly educated rabbis desiring to accommodate Judaism to the "spirit of the age" emerged in the 1830s and 1840s in Germany. These rabbis gathered at various conferences (Brunswick, 1844; Frankfurt, 1845; and Breslau, 1846) to deliberate and to effect a consensus among the attending rabbis regarding the authoritative principles of Reform. Rabbi Samuel Holdheim spoke for the majority of these rabbis when he unequivocally stated that these principles could no longer be based on "rabbinism" as were the earlier lame attempts of Liebermann:

> All the talk about a Talmudical Judaism is an illusion. Science has decided that the Talmud has no authority dogmatically or practically. Even those who will not acknowledge this go beyond the Talmud. The question is, who gives us the right to change the liturgy? This question requires an unequivocal answer. [The rabbis who during the Second Temple period established the traditional liturgy] have authority only in their age; what they ordained was timely, and on this the sanction of their ordinances rested. We have the same authority for our age, [but] even though the Talmud is not authoritative for us we do not wish to disregard the intellectual activity of two thousand years. We say merely this: Anything which upon unbiased, careful criticism contradicts the religious consciousness of the present age has no authority for us.[3]

In their search for an alternative to the Talmudic-halakhic tradition as an authoritative basis for reform, Holdheim and his colleagues were rather eclectic basing their arguments on selective philosophical, biblical and, when deemed appropriate, even Talmudic references (see documents 8–12).

This apparent "lack of principles" alarmed Rabbi Zecharias Frankel, who was aligned with the minority advocating moderate reforms. In an address before the Frankfurt conference of 1845, Frankel held that in their enthusiasm for Reform his more radical colleagues brazenly and irresponsibly sponsored an abstract ideal of Reform that was perhaps compatible with the needs and wishes of some acculturated German Jews but that ignored the existent needs and wishes of the Jewish people as a whole. Frankel, however, agreed with the radical Reformers that halakhah was no longer unquestionably the sole basis of Judaism. As an alternative to both radical Reform and to halakhic Judaism, Frankel presented his conception of a "positive, historical Judaism" that was based on a respect of the patterns of religious community and ritual established by halakhah not as law but as an intrinsic part of the people's evolving historical experience. This conception of Judaism, Frankel maintained, provided the guidelines for reforms that were "organically" part of the nation's experience and thus should be able to command wide adherence (see document 14). Frankel's conception of Judaism constituted the platform for what later became known in the United States as Conservative Judaism.

Traditional or, as they were now called, Orthodox Jews who followed the Reform conferences condemned the deliberations as heretical, and they reasserted that the halakhah

---

[3] Protocol of the Brunsick conference of 1844, cited in David Philipson, *The Reform Movement in Judaism*, ed. S. B. Freehof, rev. ed. (New York: Ktav Publishing House,1967), p. 145. Holdheim, the principal exponent of the most radial wing of Reform in Germany, set forth to demonstrate the time-bound qualities of the Talmud and the halakhah: "The Talmud speaks with the standpoint of its time [*Zeitbewusstsein*], and for that time it was right. I speak from the higher level of consciousness of my time, and for this age I am right" (*Ceremonialgesetz im Gottesreich*, [Schwerin, 1845], trans. in Philipson, op.cit., p.50).

is the unimpeachable standard for Israel as the people of God (see document 15). While assuredly endorsing this position, Samson Raphael Hirsch, the founder of the movement of Neo-Orthodoxy,[4] held that halakhic Judaism need not be totally unresponsive to the "spirit of the times." *Torah im derekh eretz* was his slogan: Torah, Jewish law, should be accommodated to *derekh eretz*, the general norms of the non-Jewish world. In practice, this meant that the halakhic Jew was able to pursue a secular education, to adopt the dress and language of the country in which he resided and to institute some revisions in the external trappings of ritual. These revisions, interestingly, were similar to those aesthetic changes introduced by early Reform: decorum; a choir under the direction of a professional musical director; the participation of the congregation in the singing; and a sermon in the vernacular. In opposition to Reform, however, Hirsch defended the traditional liturgy as sacrosanct and the use of Hebrew as the sole language of prayer (see document 15). According to Hirsch, while appreciating modern secular culture, the Jews had to maintain their apartness and distinctiveness as the servants of God and the guardians of His Torah. To justify this distinction, Hirsch ironically turned to Reform Judaism, which viewed Jewry's abiding singularity with even greater ambivalence, and borrowed its concept of "mission." Israel's particularity, Reformers affirmed, implies not indifference and withdrawal from the community of their fellow human beings but a divine "mission" of universal significance (see documents 11 and 15).

Enlightenment and emancipation created new social and cultural conditions for Judaism. The documents presented in this chapter adumbrate the emerging institutional and theological patterns of religious adjustments to these new conditions: Reform, Conservative, Neo-Orthodox and Ultra-Orthodox Judaism.

---

[4] The term *Neo-Orthodoxy* was never used by Hirsch or his followers but was introduced by scholars to characterize Hirsch's distinctive attempt to combine traditional Torah observance with modern secular culture. For a critical analysis of the term *Neo-Orthodoxy*, see Julius Carlebach, "The Foundations of German Jewish Orthodoxy. An Interpretation, " *Leo Baeck Institute Year Book* 33 (1988), pp. 67–97. See also document 13 in this chapter, pp.198ff.

1. CONSTITUTION OF THE HAMBURG TEMPLE (DECEMBER 11, 1817)[1]

THE NEW ISRAELITE TEMPLE ASSOCIATION

Since public worship has for some time been neglected by so many, because of the ever decreasing knowledge of the language in which alone it has until now been conducted, and also because of many other shortcomings which have crept in at the same time—the undersigned, convinced of the necessity to restore public worship to its deserving dignity and importance, have joined together to follow the example of several Israelite congregations, especially the one in Berlin.[2] They plan to arrange in this city also, for themselves as well as others who think as they do, a dignified and well-ordered ritual according to which the worship service shall be conducted on the Sabbath and holy days and on other solemn occasions, and which shall be observed in their own temple, to be erected especially for this purpose. Specifically, there shall be introduced at such services a German sermon, and choral singing to the accompaniment of an organ.

Incidentally, the above-mentioned ritual shall not be confined to services in the temple; rather it shall apply to all those religious customs and acts of daily life which are sanctified by the church[3] or by their own nature. Outstanding amongst these are the entrance of the newly-born into the covenant of the fathers, weddings, and the like. Also, a religious ceremony shall be introduced in which the children of both sexes, after having received adequate schooling in the teachings of the faith, shall be accepted as confirmants of the Mosaic religion.

NOTES

1. The New Israelite Temple Association of Hamburg instituted the first systematic Reform worship services; it was founded by sixty-six Jews, led by Eduard Kley (1789–1867), Meyer Israel Bresselau (1785–1839) and Seckel Isaak Fraenkel (1765–1835)—all of them laymen. The Hamburg Temple was dedicated on October 18, 1818, the anniversary of the Battle of Leipzig, which marked the liberation of Germany from Napoleonic rule. Some historians see an ideological motive not only in this gesture but also behind the Reformers' naming their synagogue a "temple." That is, that by adopting the designation traditionally reserved for the fallen Temple of Jerusalem, the Reformers symbolically relinquished the hope of Israel's restoration and declared Hamburg their Jerusalem. Other historians ascribe to the Reformers the more innocent motive of simply wishing to distinguish their house of worship from, the traditional synagogue of Hamburg.

2. On the Feast of Weeks (*Shavuot*) in the year 1815, Israel Jacobson (1768–1828)—the father of German Reform, the founder of a Reform temple in Sessen, Westphalia—inaugurated a "private" Reform worship service in his Berlin home. Later the services moved to the home of Jacob Herz-Beer, a wealthy Berlin banker. Due to the opposition of the conservative Prussian govemment, the Reform synagogue of Berlin was closed down in 1817. Eduard Kley had served as a preacher in Beer's synagogue.

3. This word was intended to underscore the purely religious character of the Hamburg Temple.

Source: W. Gunther Plaut, *The Rise of Reform Judaism: A Sourcebook of Its European Origins* (New York: World Union for Progressive Judaism, 1963), pp. 31ff. Reprinted by permission of the World Union for Progressive Judaism.

2. THE LIGHT OF SPLENDOR (1818)[1]

ELIEZER LIEBERMANN

Why should we not draw a lesson from the peoples among whom we live? Look at the Gentiles and see how they stand in awe and reverence and with good manners in their house of prayer. No one utters a word, no one moves a limb. Their ears and all their senses are directed to the words of the preacher and to [the recitation of] their prayers. Now judge please, you blessed of God, people of the Lord, seedlings of the faithful, how very much more there is for us to do. Are we not obligated to be most discreet and to guard our steps and the utterances of our lips when we go to the House of God? Will someone say "that it is prohibited [to learn from our neighbors] for "ye shall not abide by their statutes?"[2] Will it occur to a man of intelligence that we should distance ourselves from a good and righteous act because we do not esteem he who performs it or that a just cause should be invalidated because of the ill-repute of its votaries? Indeed, such opinion is shallow and fatuous. Such an opinion could but evoke derisive laughter.

Pay heed my brethren and my people [so that you might understand]: Who among us is as great in wisdom and works as King Solomon, may he rest in peace, and did he not charge us to receive instruction from animals of a low order of creation when he said: "Go to the ant, thou sluggard, consider her ways and be wise."[3] [In a similar fashion] Job said: "But ask now the beasts and they shall teach thee, the birds of the sky and they shall tell thee... and the fishes of the sea shall declare to thee."[4] And our sages of blessed memory have said: "If the Torah had not been given we could have learned modesty from the cat, manners from the cock, honesty [literally, the (objection) to robbery] from the ant and chastity [literally, forbidden intercourse] from the dove."[5] It is also written: The Lord teaches us by the beasts of the earth and makes us wiser by the birds of the sky."[6]

Understand this, all ye of upright heart: If our holy sages of blessed memory have obligated us to receive moral instruction concerning justice and the straight path from the lowliest orders of creation, how can we avoid receiving edification from the very work of God's hands, blessed be He, [that is] from men possessing reason just as we do. Why should we not learn from them and from their correct actions that which is also good and becoming for us, the children of Israel, and which is proper according to our holy Torah? Regarding this matter the prophet has already admonished: "Has a nation exchanged its gods...?"[7] It is also said: "In every place incense is burnt and sacrifices are offered to my name, and a pure offering."[8] And these are the words of the learned Rabbenu Tam, of blessed memory, in the *Book of Righteousness*:

> One should be envious of the pious and more than these of the penitents, and more than these of those who are younger [than oneself] and who from their youth have been diligent in the service of the Lord, blessed be He....And one should be envious of the nations of the world who serve God in awe, fear and submission. How much more must he who serves the Lord of the world do. Should he not envy them and do all in his power to surpass their works many times over?[9]

[We may also cite] the words of the pious rabbi [Bahya ibn Pakuda], who in the introduction to his book, *Duties of the Heart* states:

> I added [as support for my arguments] Scriptural texts and maxims culled from the writings of our teachers of blessed memory. I quoted also the

Source: Eliezer Liebermann, *Or nogah* (Dessau, 1818), pp. 22–25. Trans. by S. Fischer and S. Weinstein. The language, style, and format of this treatise in defense of Reform are typical of traditional rabbinic literature.

saints and sages of other nations whose words have come to us, hoping that my readers' hearts would incline to them, and give heed to their wisdom. I quote for example the dicta of the philosophers, the ethical teachings of the ascetics and their praiseworthy customs. In this connection our Rabbis of blessed memory already remarked (Sanhedrin 39b): In one verse it is said "After the ordinances of the nations that are round about you, have ye done" (Ezek. 11:12); while in another, it is said "After the ordinances of the nations that are round about you, ye have not done" (Ezek. 5:7). How is this contradiction to be reconciled? As follows: "Their good ordinances ye have not copied; their evil ones ye have followed." The Rabbis further said (*Megillah* 16a): "Whoever utters a wise word, even if he belongs to the gentiles, is called a sage."[10]

And here are the words of Maimonides, of blessed memory:

> As regards the logic for all these calculations [concerning the position of the moon at the time of the new crescent]—why we have to add a particular figure or deduct it, how all these rules originated, and how they were discovered and proved—all this is a part of the science of astronomy and mathematics, about which many books have been composed by Greek sages—books that are still available to the scholars of our time. But the books which had been composed by the Sages of Israel, of the tribe of Issachar, who lived in the time of the Prophets, have not come down to us. But since all these rules have been established by sound and clear proofs, free from any flaw and irrefutable, we need not be concerned about the identity of their authors, whether they were Hebrew Prophets or gentile sages. For when we have to do with rules and propositions which have been demonstrated by sound and flawless proofs, we rely upon the author who has discovered them or has transmitted them only because of his demonstrated proofs and verified reasoning.[11]

All the passages mentioned here are in addition to that which can be found [concerning this matter] in the rest of the books of the great among our ancestors, may they rest in paradise. Space does not permit us to include these texts, which are known to all the educated and learned men of our people, may they be granted long life. . . .

Behold, my brethren, my people know that the Lord has opened the eyes of our brothers [the founders of the Hamburg Temple], men of understanding who are devoted to God, blessed be He. They have cleared the path of stumbling blocks and hailstones and have removed all obstacles from the way of our people by establishing a house of prayer in which they can pour out their hearts before His Great Name, blessed be He. They utter their prayers in an intelligible and lucid manner. They have chosen for an advocate between them and their Father in heaven an upright man, a rabbi eminent in Torah and wisdom and an accomplished orator.[12] His prayer is pleasant and becoming to every one that hears it. All join together with him to praise and glorify in a pleasant and becoming fashion, verse by verse and word by word. No one speaks nor are any words exchanged; the irreverent voices of frivolous conversation are not heard. Would that this be the case in all our houses of worship. For this [manner of prayer] would not dishonor us among the Gentiles, as we have indicated in the passage from Maimonides quoted above. [The present situation] in several of our synagogues is truly a matter of jest and ridicule, fulfilling the words of the prophet: "Has this house become a den of robbers?"[13] Alas for the eyes that witness this.

How much good has [the Hamburg Temple] done by setting up men of wisdom, who walk the upright path and seek the good of their people. These men preach the word of God every Sabbath and festival.[14] They inform the congregation of ways of the Lord and His statutes according to the righteous law of our holy Torah, so that they may fulfill all that is contained in the Written and Oral Torah. The preachers inflame their hearts with the fear of God, blessed be He, so that they may observe His commandments, laws and statutes and befriend the poor, have mercy upon the destitute and revive the downhearted. The preachers even instruct them regarding the unity of His name, blessed be He, and also teach that there is no unity comparable to His. They implant the faith of our God in the hearts of small and great, women and children, so that all know the Lord, from their great unto their small. Regarding other righteous matters, my heart rejoiced and I was filled with exultation to hear worthy, straightforward and sincere words flowing from their lips like sap, words which are sweeter to my palate than honey or the choicest nectar. Who will not acknowledge that these are the words of the living God, restoring the soul and strengthening the faith of the weak?

The preacher firmly implants the love of our Creator, blessed be His name, in the heart of every man. They even arouse love of His Majesty, our pious and merciful king, as well as love of the king's household, a delightful offshoot, and of his loyal ministers and counselors. Similarly they inflame the hearts [of their listeners] with the love of our brethren, the children of Israel, including those who oppose [our views]. For we have one God and one Torah; their portion is our portion, their inheritance is our inheritance. They also arouse the love of our brethren, the inhabitants of our land, even if they not be Jewish, and instill love of the land of our birth, so that we should give our lives for it and always pray for its safety. For the prayer for the land of our birth precedes in time the prayer for the land of our fathers, the land of Israel.[15]...

These are the words of the Talmud [regarding this subject]:

> Rabbi Jose says, "I was once travelling on the road, and I entered into one of the ruins of Jerusalem in order to pray. Elijah of blessed memory appeared and waited for me at the door till I finished my prayer. After I finished my prayer, he said to me: 'Peace be with you, my master!' and I replied: 'Peace be with you, my master and teacher!' And he said to me: 'My son, why did you go into the ruin?' I replied: To pray.' He said to me: 'You ought to have prayed on the road.' I replied: 'I feared lest passers-by interrupt me.' He said to me: 'You ought to have said an abbreviated prayer.' Thus I then learned from him three things: one must not go into a ruin; one may say the prayer on the road; and if one does say his prayer on the road, he recites an abbreviated prayer" [*Berakhot* 3a].

This has been interpreted as follows: It is known that Rabbi Jose lived after the destruction of the Temple. He once entered into prayer to enquire concerning the destruction of Jerusalem. Elijah, who exemplifies the attributes of thought and comprehension, came to him and said: "My son, why did you go into this ruin," that is to say, why do you complain about the destruction of the Temple? Rabbi Jose replied that he was not complaining, but only praying for the Temple to be rebuilt. Elijah said to him: "You ought to have prayed on the road," that is to say, you ought to have

prayed for the preservation and survival of Israel in every place where they may be. Rabbi Jose replied, "I feared lest passers-by interrupt me," that is to say, I am grieved by those who oppress us in the Exile. Elijah replied: "You ought to have said an abbreviated prayer," that is to say, the essence of the prayer is for the present salvation of Israel from the nations. This is what Rabbi Jose then said: "Then I learned three things: One must not go into a ruin," that is to say, one must not make the essence of one's prayer the destruction of the Temple; "one may say the prayer on the road," that is to say, [pray] that God render good upon our people in the Exile. Concerning this the men of the Great Assembly[16] established the benediction [beginning] "Look upon our affliction" and concluding [with the words] "Redeemer of Israel." What is referred to here is not actual redemption, but merely our deliverance from the troubles of Exile. The commentators have offered a similar explanation in the tractate *Megillah* of the Talmud.

To be sure, my brethren and compatriots, tears well up in the eyes of every man of feeling when he remembers that our holy city is burnt and its gates desolate, and we must say along with the exiles, "If I forget thee, O Jerusalem."[17] Nevertheless, the prayer for the land of our birth, our present dwelling place, must take precedence in our time and we should always pray for its safety and for the well-being of its people....

O that it would be in the hearts of our brethren, the children of Israel, to appoint for themselves in every city men such as these [preachers of the Hamburg Temple], who seek the good of their people and teach the upright way. Were this to come to pass, I know that we would glory in the stock of the Lord and [our] sons would be the blessed of God, faithful in spirit to God and to their king. If in former times there had been teachers of righteousness to our people, the children of Israel, who had illuminated the good and beneficial path as contained in our holy Torah and had preached the word of God mingled with sap and nectar, then we would not be an object of ridicule and scorn for the peoples and a figure of strife and contention among the nations. Moreover, many of our people who have left our religion in this generation because of our numerous iniquities would not have done so. For what profit have the people from the sermons of preachers who build fortresses for them, hewn stones and columns, which they ascend by means of homiletics to the heights of sharp-wittedness and erudition. Through casuistry they weave complicated and finespun embroideries. All the people (including the women and children) hear the voices, but they do not understand one word uttered by the man standing on the pulpit. When the ministers and sages [of the Gentiles] come to our places of worship to observe our customs and to hear the words of our teachers, who instruct the people regarding the path they are to follow, they hear merely the sound of noise in the camp of the Hebrews and do not understand anything. Instead of saying, "They are a wise and understanding nation,"[18] they say "They are a misguided and confused people, an impetuous nation." [On this point] my brethren and friends, consult Maimonides *Commentary on the Mishnah*, Sanhedrin, chapter 8.[19] My pleasant brethren, may you enjoy long life, listen to my upright words and be preserved.

NOTES

1. Little is known about Eliezer Liebermann, other than that he was the son of Ze'ev Wolf, rabbi of Hennegau (probably Hagenau, Alsace). Liebermann's services were solicited by Israel Jacobson (1768–1828), the father of Reform in Germany. According to the historian Heinrich Graetz, Liebermann converted to Catholicism, but this assertion has not been corroborated by subsequent research. The name of his pamplet is an allusion to Isaiah 9:1, "The people that walked in darkness have seen a bright light."

2. Lev. 18:3.

3. Prov. 6:6.

4. Job 12:7–8.

5. Talmud, tractate *Erubin* 100b.

6. Job 35:11.

7. Jer. 2:11. The full passage reads: "Has any nation changed its gods even though they are yet no gods? But my people has exchanged its glory for what can do no good." By implication each nation has its own way to the truth.

8. Mal. 1:11.

9. Rabbenu Tam ("our perfect rabbi")—Jacob ben Meir (c. 1000–1171)—grandson of Rashi, was a leading rabbinic scholar from France and one of the principal compilers of the *Tosafot*, commentaries on the Babylonian Talmud. Many of his *tosafot* and corrections to textual corruptions in the Talmud were collected in his *The Book of Righteousness* (*Sefer hayashar*). The work cited here, bearing the same name, however, is

another volume altogether. It is an ethical treatise that was popularly—but according to contemporary scholars falsely—ascribed to Rabbenu Tam (or, alternatively, other medieval authors). For the present citation, see the ethical treatise *Sefer hayashar* (Jerusalem: Eshkol, 1967), pp. 42–43.

10. Bahya ben Joseph ibn Pakuda (second half of eleventh century), moral philosopher who lived in Muslim Spain. *Duties of the Heart* (*Hovot halevavot*), which greatly influenced all subsequent Jewish pietistic literature, contains directions for the development of man's inner life. It is a complement to halakhic books, which concentrate on "the duties of the members of the body," i.e., on religious actions. This passage is found in *Duties of the Heart*, Hebrew-English texts, trans. Moses Hyamson (Jerusalem: Boys Town, 1962), vol. 1, pp. 43–44.

11. "Sanctification of the New Moon," *The Code of Maimonides*, book 3, treatise 8, trans. Solomon Grandz (New Haven: Yale University Press, 1956), ch. 18, par. 25, p. 73.

12. Liebermann apparently is referring to Rabbi Gotthold Salomon (1789–1862), who was appointed preacher of the Hamburg Temple in October 1818. Of the early leaders of the temple, he was the only one to hold a rabbinic title, which at the time meant halakhic ordination. Salomon was an editor of *Sulamith* and evinced even before his appointment to the Hamburg Temple interest in Reform. He was renowned for his eloquence as a preacher; he had studied the sermons and style of famous contemporary Christian preachers for many years.

13. Jer. 7:11.

14. As a preacher Salomon was assisted by Eduard Kley (1789–1867), a disciple of Israel Jacobson and the founding spirit behind the Hamburg Temple. The sermon (*Predigt*) became one of the distinctive features of German Reform. "The nineteenth century saw the rise and development of a new type of Jewish preaching, replacing the traditional *drashah*. The changes involved in this innovation concerned not only the outward form and structure of the sermon but also its substance. The very concept of the purpose of preaching as well as the theology behind it underwent a radical transformation. Obviously, the impact of contemporary trends in the Christian pulpit and in the philosophical thinking of the period accounts for a great deal in this connection" (Alexander Altmann, "The New Style of Preaching in Nineteenth Century German Jewry," *in Studies in Nineteenth Century*

Jewish Intellectual History, ed. A. Altmann, Philip W. Lown Institute of Advanced Judaic Studies, Brandeis University [Cambridge, Mass.: Harvard University Press, 1964], vol. 2, p. 65).

15. The author supports this position by citing a long passage from the Babylonian Talmud, tractate *Berakhot* 3a.

16. The Great Assembly is the *knesset hagdolah*—the institution that embodied the spiritual leadership of the Jewish people at the beginning of the Second Temple period. Constituting the supreme authority in matters of religious practice and law, it was considered the link between the prophets and the first of the rabbis. This body is said to have established the main text of the traditional liturgy.

17. Psalms 137:5.

18. Deut. 4:6.

19. See Maimonides, *Commentary on the* Mishnah, Sanhedrin 1:11. See also Maimonides, *Guide to the Perplexed*, 2:11; 3:31.

3. THESE ARE THE WORDS OF THE COVENANT (1819)[1]

THE HAMBURG RABBINICAL COURT

These are the words of the covenant with Jacob, a law unto Israel, an eternal covenant; the word of God is one forever and ever. [These words are uttered] in accordance with the Torah and by judgment of the rabbinical court of the holy community of Hamburg—may the Lord bless it well—with the support of the leading men of learning in Germany, Poland, France, Italy, Bohemia, Moravia and Hungary. All of them join together, in an edict decreed by the angels and a judgment proclaimed by the holy ones, to abolish a *new law* (which was fabricated by several ignorant individuals unversed in the Torah) instituting practices which are not in keeping with the Law of Moses and of Israel. Therefore these pious, learned, holy and distinguished rabbis have risen to render the Law secure [against such infractions]. They have discovered a breach [of the Law] and have sought to contain it with prescriptions forbidding the three cardinal sins [of Reform]:

1. It is forbidden to change the worship that is customary in Israel from Morning Benedictions to "It is our duty to praise [the Lord of all]";[2] and all the more so [is it prohibited] to make any deletions in the traditional liturgy.

2. It is forbidden to pray in any language other than the Holy Tongue. Every prayer-book that is printed improperly and not in accordance with our [traditional] practice is invalid, and it is forbidden to pray from it.

3. It is prohibited to play a musical instrument in the synagogue on the Sabbath and on the festivals even when it is played by a non-Jew.

Happy is the man who heeds the decree of the sages of the court of justice and the words of the learned, pious and holy. Happy is the man who does not remove himself from the congregation, in order that he may walk in the way of the good. He who desires the integrity of his soul will take utmost care lest he transgress, Heaven forbid, the words of the learned contained in this volume, as the sages of the Talmud, may their memory be blessed, said: "Pay heed to their

---

Source: Eleh divrei habrit (Altona, 1819), pp. 1, 3–5. Trans. by S. Fischer and S. Weinstein.

legacy." Who is the man who fears the Lord and will not fear the words of the forty pious, exalted and holy men who have affixed their signatures to this book, sparing [thereby] himself and his household?

By Order of the Court of Justice of the Holy Community of Hamburg.

…Behold, we had hoped that these men [who have introduced Reform] would have attended to our words and listened to the voice of their teachers, who alone are fit to express an opinion on matters concerning what is permitted and what is prohibited. In former times the men of our proud city have listened to the voice of their teachers, who told them the path they were to take. We had thought that our judgment would be honored and that they would not dare to disobey our utterance, for our strength now is as it was formerly.

But we hoped in vain, for these men disobeyed the counsel [of their teachers] and sank into sin. They quickly built for themselves a house of prayer, which they called a temple, and published a prayer-book for Sabbaths and festivals, which has caused great sorrow and brought tears to our eyes over the destruction of our people. For they have added to and deleted from the text of the prayers according to their hearts' desires. They have eliminated the Morning Benedictions and the blessing for the Torah and have discarded Psalm 145, as well as other psalms from the morning prayers. They have set their hands upon the text of the recitation of "Hear, O Israel," and in the wickedness of their hearts have deleted the texts of "To God who rested," "God the Lord," "True and firm" and "There is none to be compared to Thee."[3] Moreover, they have printed most of the prayers in German rather than in Hebrew. Worst of all, they have perpetrated a sore evil by removing all references to the belief in the Ingathering of the Exiles. [Their deletions include] the text "Lead us with an upright bearing to our land" in the benediction "With great love,"[4] the text "Who will raise us up in joy to our land?" in the Additional Service [*Musaf*] for the Sabbath and the texts "Bring us in jubilation to Zion your city" and "Gather our scattered ones from among the nations" in the Additional Service for festivals. They have thereby testified concerning themselves that they do not believe at all in the promise of our teacher Moses, may he rest in peace: "If any of thine that are dispersed be in the uttermost parts of heaven, from thence will the Lord thy God gather thee, and from thence will He fetch thee."[5] This belief is one of the major tenets of our holy Torah. All the prophets have been unanimous in affirming that the God of our fathers would gather our scattered ones, and this is our hope throughout our Exile. This belief in no way detracts from the honor of Their Majesties the kings and ministers under whom we find protection, for it is common knowledge that we believe in the coming of the messiah and the ingathering of the exiles. No one has ever dared to object to this belief of ours, because they know that we are obligated to seek the well-being of the peoples who have brought us under their protection. They have bestowed much good and kindness upon us, may God grant them success in all their actions and works. Our opinion here corresponds to that which the learned men of our time, may their light shine, have elaborated in their letters. He who rejects this belief denies [one of] the fundamental tenets of our religion. Woe to the ears that have heard that men have arisen in Israel to do violence to the foundations of our holy faith.

Yet with all this they are not content, for their hands are still outstretched and they continue to do evil. At the dedication of their house of prayer men and women sang together at the opening of the ark, in contradiction to the law set out in the Talmud and in the Codes: "a woman's voice is indecent."[6] Such [an abomination] is not done in our house of prayer, which has replaced the Temple, throughout the entire Diaspora of the sanctified ones of Israel. Who has heard or seen such a thing? In addition, they play a musical instrument (an organ) on the holy Sabbath and have abolished the silent prayer. They have even abolished the reading of a selection from the Prophets on the Sabbath [after the reading of the weekly portion from the Pentateuch] as well as the reading of the four portions [of the Pentateuch read in addition to the weekly portion on the four Sabbaths preceding Passover]. On Purim the congregation recited the prayer "Grant us discernment" instead of the Eighteen Benedictions, and in the evening they read the Book of Esther in German from a printed text [rather than from a handwritten Hebrew scroll]. Lack of space prevents the inclusion of all their pernicious customs and practices by means of which they have chosen to disobey the Holy One of Israel and to defy the holy sages of blessed memory, the court of their city and the vast majority of our community who are God-fearing and faithful and fulfill the commandments of God.

Thus we have resolved that this is not the time to place our hands over our mouths and to be silent. Were we to remain silent we would be commiting a sin, for [the Reformers] would say the rabbis are silent and [their] silence [is to be construed] as consent. With honeyed words they would lead astray the God-fearing and the faithful who in their innocence would follow them. [The Reformers] would say to them: "Behold, the path upon which we walk is good. Come, let us join together and be one people." And so the Torah, Heaven forbid, would disappear. Brethren, the Children of Israel, it shall not be; Israel has not yet been abandoned. There are still judges in the land who are zealous for God's sake and who will rend the arm, and even crack the skull, of him who pursues the sin [of Reformers]. To these judges we shall hasten for aid. They will rise up and help us abolish the [wicked] counsel [of the Reformers] and strengthen our religion. Accordingly, we have girded our loins and written to the famous learned men of the holy communities of Germany, Poland, Bohemia, Moravia and Italy. We have sent them our legal judgment, which we mentioned above, and we asked them if after close and careful study by means of their clear and pure reason they would confirm all that is in our judgment as being proper. In this way we can make public the abomination that has been committed in Israel. Every pious man who fears the word of God will pay heed to the words of the learned men of our time, may their light shine, and to our words. He shall not follow the counsels of the perverse who walk upon a crooked path.

NOTES

1. In response to Liebermann's *Nogah hazedek* and *Or nogah*, the rabbinic court of Hamburg published this volume of *responsa* (halakhic opinions) on the admissibility of Reform, solicited from Europe's foremost rabbis, including *inter alios* Rabbi Eger of Posen, Prussia (1761–1837), Moses Sofer of Pressburg, Hungary (1763–1839) and Mordecai Benet, chief rabbi of Moravia (1753–1829). The appearance of this volume, which comprised twenty-two *responsa*, "may be said to mark the beginning coalescence of an Orthodox party opposed to all tampering with tradition" (W. Gunther Plaut, *The Rise of Reform Judaism: A Sourcebook of Its European Origins* [New York: World Union for Progressive Judaism, 1963], p. 34).

2. Prayer appearing at the end of the evening services as well as the morning services.

3. These prayers are part of the morning service for Sabbaths and festivals.

4. Prayer appearing before the recitation of "Hear, O Israel…" in the morning service for weekdays, Sabbaths and festivals.

5. Deut. 30:4.

6. Talmud, tractate *Berakhot* 24a and tractate *Kiddushin* 70a.

4. A REPLY CONCERNING THE QUESTION OF REFORM (1819)[1]

HATAM SOFER

Letter from the Rabbi of Great Learning and Renown, Our Venerable Teacher Rabbi Moses Sofer, May God preserve him, President of the [Rabbinic] Court of Pressburg to the [Rabbinic] Court of the Holy Community of Hamburg.

Your [letter] has reached me and has shocked and overwhelmed me with its bitter tidings. For it brings the news that men who do not submit to the yoke of heaven have lately appeared, seeking to nullify the covenant through devious schemes against the

Source: Eleh divrei habrit (Altona, 1819), pp. 32ff. Trans. by S. Fischer and S. Weinstein.

religion of our forefathers. One of their innovations is that their house of prayer should be tightly closed on weekdays and only open on the Sabbath. Would that even then its doors would be closed, for they have altered the text of the prayers which we have received from the men of the Great Assembly,[2] the sages of the Talmud, and our hallowed fathers. They have added to and deleted from the liturgy, substituting texts of their own invention. [For example,] they have eliminated the Morning Benedictions, which are explained in chapter 3 of the tractate *Berakhot* [of the Mishnah], and they have also discarded [the benediction for] the flourishing of the House of David, our messiah, and for the rebuilding of Jerusalem the Holy City. Moreover, they have appointed a non-Jew to play a musical instrument in their presence on the holy Sabbath, [a matter] which is forbidden us, and significantly the majority of their prayers are in German.

This is a concise summary of the letter which I have received this evening from your glorious excellencies. You have requested me to affiliate myself with the lions, the learned men of our time, who repair the breaches of our generation, and to express my opinion whether the truth is with you or not. What shall I reply? Is it not well known that in exile the delightful Daniel "kneeled upon his knees three times a day, and prayed, and gave thanks before his God, as he did aforetime."[3] From this it is explained that even "aforetime," [that is to say] before the Chaldeans decreed their edict [forbidding Jewish prayer], he would pray three times daily and not only on the Sabbath.[4] In the tractate *Berakhot* our sages of blessed memory interpreted "aforetime" to mean even when the Temple was in existence, as is stated there, "Was it only in captivity [that this began]?"[5]

...It is known that in the days of the Second Commonwealth Israel dwelt in its land, wielding the ruler's scepter with greatness and honor for several hundred years. [During that period] there were among them great sages, whose sole occupation was with the Torah. They and their students numbered tens of thousands. They had great and excellent academies similar to [universities] now being established by all the rulers in their big cities. They also had a Sanhedrin[6] which set up protective fences [around the Law], enacted decrees and maintained everything in good order. After them came tens of thousands of their disciples and the disciples of their disciples, who preceded our hallowed rabbi [Judah

Hanasi], the compiler of the Mishnah.[7] Not one of these sages is mentioned either in the Mishnah or in the Beraita.[8] Only a very few of them were mentioned in Maimonides' introduction to his commentary on the tractate *Zeraim* of the Talmud.[9] Moreover, out of all their sayings only a small number of the shorter ones have been mentioned. Without doubt it would have been possible to make a great book out of the sayings of each of the sages and their disciples, in comparison with which the Mishnah as well as both the Babylonian and Jerusalem Talmuds would appear to be minor works containing only a small amount of wisdom. The reason [for the limited number of extant sayings] is that the sages winnowed and sifted their words to extract the choicest wheat. Concerning this Rabbi Simon stated at the end of chapter 6 of the Talmudic tractate *Gittin*: "My sons, learn my rules [literally "measures"], for they are the cream of the cream of Rabbi Akiba."[10] Afterwards, the choicest statements were set down in the Mishnah and the Talmud.

Now these statements issued from the mouths of wise and discerning men, whose minds were full of knowledge and ideas and who possessed a profound understanding of all the sciences. Over the centuries these ideas have been recurrently clarified by thousands of sages. For nearly two thousand years they have been established in Israel and no one has dared to open his mouth to protest [against them]. But now insignificant foxes have risen up to breach the walls and destroy the fence [that has been erected around the Law]. They seek to change the texts [of the prayers] and the benedictions and to alter the hours and times that have been appointed [for their recitation].

Regarding matters of judgment, one court cannot abolish the ruling of another court unless it is greater in numbers and wisdom. Even if the reason [for the ruling] is invalid the regulation is not voided. This is especially so in the case of the liturgy that is in usage throughout Israel. Even though variant texts exist in several places, [the liturgy] is nevertheless considered to be widespread throughout Israel, since from the beginning one version was established solely for the Ashkenazim, and disseminated among them without dissent, while another version was established among the Sephardim and disseminated among them without dissent....

Therefore let them [the Reformers] stand up and be counted with the sages of our generation; may the grace of the Lord be upon them! These men cannot make the choice to remove themselves from the congregation. If they will say: "we do not accept the sages of the Talmud and their authority," they shall bear the burden of the words of Maimonides: "He who repudiates the Oral Law ... is classed with atheists [whom any person has a right to put to death]."[11] Nothing more [need be said].

[What] if someone will claim that the reason for praying for the flourishing of the glory of the Messiah Son of David and for the restoration of worship [in the Temple] is in any case invalid, since we are dwelling in peace and tranquility among Their Majesties the kings of the nations? This is not so, for as I have already written above, even in the days of the kings of the Second Commonwealth prayers were recited for the rule of the House of David, for when that comes to pass we [all humanity] will all be around to behold the goodness of the Lord. We do not need to eat the fruits and be sated with the goodness [of an easy and tranquil life among the nations. Were this so] one could then make the blasphemous claim: "Have we not found tranquility and goodness among the Gentiles, so what need have we for the land of Israel?" Heaven forbid! We do not pour out our hearts and wait in anticipation all our days for an illusory material tranquility. Rather our hope is to dwell in the presence of God there [in the land of Israel], the place designated for His service and for the observance of His Torah. This does not deprecate the king and ministers under whose protection we live. Nehemia the son of Hakhaliyah was viceroy to the king, enjoying honor and riches. [Yet] he was saddened by the fact that the city, the place of the tombs of his fathers [Jerusalem], lay in waste, its gates consumed with fire.[12] The king [granted his request to return to Jerusalem] and did not do evil by replying, "Have you not riches and all good things in my service? Why do you make this request?" for each people follows the service of its God.

Behold, we are as prisoners of the war of the destruction [of the Second Temple]. In the abundance of His mercy and the righteousness of our dispersion, the Lord had us find favor in the eyes of the kings and ministers of the nations, for whose well-being we are obligated to entreat and for whose safety we are to pray. [We do so] not that we might repay them with evil, Heaven forbid, for they have bestowed many great kindnesses upon us in the past two thousand years. Their reward will surely be great,

for the Lord repays with kindness those who do good. Nevertheless, no harm is done if we long to return to our patrimony. From this good that the Lord bestows upon us the nations of the world will also benefit....

The nations [knew all this regarding our beliefs] and were never vexed. But perhaps these men [the Reformers] neither anticipate nor believe at all in the words of our prophets concerning the building of the Third Temple and the coming of the messiah. Nor do they seem to believe all that is said by our sages of blessed memory regarding these matters. If this is so, then return to the words of Maimonides mentioned above....

With respect to the fact that [the Reformers'] communal prayer is [conducted] in a language other than the Holy Tongue, this is completely reprehensible.... If the reason for this [practice] is that the common people do not understand the Holy Tongue, it would be better if it were arranged to have each one learn the meaning of the prayers and recite them in Hebrew than to arrange for them to pray in another language. One does act in such a fashion before a king of flesh and blood. He who speaks with the king must speak the language of the king; it is not proper that the king speak the language of the [common] people, even though he understands it. Nachmanides writes in the beginning of his commentary to the portion *Ki tisah*[13] that the Holy One, Blessed be He, speaks with His prophets in Hebrew. Our sages of blessed memory said that the world was created in Hebrew....

If this is so, then this is the language of the Holy One, Blessed be He, in which He gave us His Torah and it is inconceivable to speak before Him in our everyday language. Rather, we should speak the special language befitting His holy words. This is the opinion of the men of the Great Assembly who established the texts of the prayers and benedictions in the Holy Tongue. He who deviates [from this practice] is in the wrong, while he who upholds the words of our sages of blessed memory and the customs of our forefathers, has the advantage. He shall perform the will of his Creator and be blessed by God.

Therefore you have acted in accordance with the Torah when you declared in your holy synagogue that it is forbidden to pray from the German prayerbooks of the Reformers and that one may pray [only] in Hebrew according to the versions contained in traditional prayerbooks. Your prohibition of the playing of a musical instrument (organ) in the holy synagogue, especially on the holy Sabbath, is also proper. May our hands be strengthened and may God be with you. There is no doubt that all the learned men, the sages of our time, will concur with this prohibition. They agree and I agree in forbidding every soul in Israel to change even one detail of all that is said above. We will thus be saved from all evil and so merit the rebuilding of the Temple.

Tuesday, Second day of the New Moon of the month of Tevet, Hannukah 1819 (5579).

NOTES

1. Moses Sofer (1762–1839). Popularly known as Hatam Sofer, he was born in Frankfurt am Main. In 1806 he was appointed rabbi of Pressburg, at the time the most important Jewish community in Hungary, where he remained for the rest of his life. Celebrated for his Talmudic erudition and his religious virtue, he was the recognized leader of traditional Jewry in Central Europe. His famed Talmudic academy (*yeshivah*) served as the center of Orthodoxy's struggle against the Reform movement. His adamant opposition to modernism in any form is eloquently expressed in his ethical testament, published numerous times and still popular among the ultra-Orthodox. See this chapter, document 6.

2. See document 2, note 16 in this chapter.

3. Dan. 6:11.

4. In the Book of Daniel, chapter 6, it is related that the plotters against Daniel persuaded the Chaldean king to promulgate a decree forbidding anyone to address a petition to anyone but himself for thirty days, thus effectively, they thought, proscribing Jewish prayer.

5. See Talmud, tractate *Berakhot* 31a.

6. An assembly of seventy-one ordained rabbinic sages functioning both as supreme court and legislature. See chapter 3, document 15.

7. Collection of oral laws compiled by Judah Hanasi in the third century C.E. These laws together with commentaries on them, the Gemara, form the Talmud.

8. "External teaching"; oral laws of the Mishnaic period which were not included in the Mishnah.

9. In this introduction, the famed philosopher and scholar Maimonides (1135–1204) actually presents a history of the Oral Law from Moses until his own day.

10. Talmud, tractate *Gittin* 67a.

11. "Book of Judges," *The Code of Maimonides*, book 14, trans. Abraham Hershman (New Haven: Yale University press, 1949), ch. 3, par. 1, p. 143.

12. See Neh. 2:5.

13. The reference is Exod. 31. Nachmanides or Moses ben Nachman (1194–1270), a Spanish rabbi *inter alia* noted for his halakhic and biblical commentaries.

5. THE SWORD WHICH AVENGES THE COVENANT (1819)[1]

MEYER ISRAEL BRESSELAU

Those who spread slander[2] [the authors of "These Are the Words of the Covenant"] have recounted that which they have neither seen nor heard. The Lord hath not spoken to them yet they presume to speak in His name, not for help or for benefit, but for shame and reproach also. They see false visions and divine lies; they have gathered unto them worthless and reckless people, brutish men, skillful to destroy, every man that is mad and maketh himself a prophet.[3] . . . These are the words of the covenant

Source: M. I. Bresselau, *Herev nokemet nekam berit* (Hamburg, 1819). Trans. in Donald B. Rossoff, *An Annotated Translation of Herev nokemet nekam berit* (rabbinical ordination dissertation, Hebrew Union College—Jewish Institute of Religion, 1981). Reprinted by permission of Donald B. Rossoff.

which they distributed amongst Jacob and dispersed in Israel—a congregation of blind men whose works are done in darkness and for each matter of transgression, they come out and take their stance. This is the way of them that are foolish; darkness, cloud and thick darkness. They bend the bow; they have made ready their arrows upon the string, that they might shoot in darkness at the upright in heart. Their bow they have set in the cloud,[4] and it has been a sign of a covenant. This is the sign of the covenant which they established in the creed of the book which is prescribed against us. The words of the covenant are the words of controversy. By pride cometh contention. All of this hath come unto us written in name and sealed with a ring.... I will not take their names on my lips; they call themselves wise.[5]...Woe unto them that are wise in their own eyes: They commit evil wisely, yet whence then cometh wisdom? How shall ye say, "We are wise?" What wisdom do you possess? Your wisdom is spoiled!...[H]ear now, O House of Israel all! Turn unto me and be astonished, and lay your hand upon your mouth! It has been many years since the plague was begun among the people![6] The Torah has perished from the priest and counsel from the elders. We have no leadership as in the days of yore.[7] Each man doeth what is correct in his own eyes and many Israelites have gone down crooked paths, have forsaken God who made them, and have forgotten both the Festivals and Sabbath. They asked not counsel at the mouth of the Lord and did not call in His name nor appear before Him. And these three men who are in our midst,[8] they have eyes, yet do not see. They go about in darkness. They sleep a perpetual sleep and do not wake. They are stretched out on their couches and are not grieved for the hurt of the daughters of my people. The land hath become corrupt before them and mourning and moaning have multiplied amongst the daughters of Judah. For broken is the covenant with our God which He sealed in our flesh, which He made with Abraham and established with Jacob as a law—to Israel as a perpetual covenant.[9] And there is no one who layeth it to heart. Every man hath his hands on his loins, as a woman in travail, and all faces are turned pale. There is no speech, there are no words, neither is their voice heard....Look now and see![10] Our sons and daughters are grown—a generation that set not their heart and whose spirit is not steadfast with

God. They have known not the God of Jacob, the Holy One of Israel, and it hath been a reproach and a taunt; it is both instructive and amazing for the Gentiles.—Who has caused this evil? It hath come from your hands, for ye have not gone up into the breaches, neither made up the hedge for the House of Israel. Why have ye brought the congregation of the Lord into this wilderness? If the word of the Lord is with you, entreat the Lord of Hosts so that the watered be not swept away with the thirsty. Hear, ye deaf; look, ye blind, that ye may see! Our sons and our daughters are given to another people before they know to refuse the evil and choose the good. Behold, the heavenly hosts cry without, and the angels of peace weep bitterly....Woe to the worthless shepherds! They that forsake the flock! Entreat the favor of the Most High that my people be not scattered, every man from his possession, and the congregation of the Lord be not like sheep who have no shepherd....Do not let your heart be seduced in that you are the majority and that because of your numbers, the Lord loves you. For it is not the numerous who are wise;[11] [w]hat know ye that we know not? What understand ye which we do not understand? With us are both the grey-headed and the very aged men. Can ye not deviate to the right or to the left from the path which our ancestors of old—men of renown—walked?[12] Your ancestors, where are they? Shall the prophets live forever?—How can ye speak so rashly saying that custom liveth a thousand years twice told,[13] therefore its reason still stands and its sense has not departed, and it should be observed as the Torah. No doubt, but ye are only human beings, and wisdom shall die with you! Know ye not? Hear ye not? Have ye not understood that time and happenstance affect them all, and custom, when its reason changes, is observed in madness. It taketh away the heart of the chiefs of the common people and guides like a flock in the wilderness. Has it not fed you and caused you to walk in darkness and not in light? Know now and see, the sheep and the cattle they guided in new customs that came up of late of which our fathers had not imagined.—Certainly, our way is not your way, for the Lord is our judge, the Lord is our lawgiver. Such is God, our God, for ever and ever; He will guide us....Without vision, the people perish. Their fear of the Lord is a commandment of men learned by rote.[14]—This, too, is an iniquity calling for judgment which the wise have told and should not hide from their fathers. . . . Certainly, O ye our brethren.[15] Israel is not yet widowed. Behold, they have arisen and taken their stand, they who offer themselves willingly among the people. They make a sure covenant and subscribe to it. Our princes, our Levites, and our priests set their seal unto it. All they that had set themselves apart unto the Torah of God and put the stumbling block of their iniquity before their face, gave themselves willingly for the service of the House of God, and with a whole heart offered themselves to the Lord. And a house was built for the name of the Lord,[16] the God of Israel. Those who had been distant came and built the Temple of the Lord.[17] And from Sabbath to Sabbath and during the Festivals of the Lord, the holy convocations, the people go up to the House of God; with our youth and our elders we go, with our sons and our daughters. And they read in the scroll of the Torah for a fourth part of the day and another fourth they praise and prostrate themselves before the Lord our God, with thanksgiving and the voice of song. And they rejoice at the sound of the organ. And when the musician plays, they surely come in joy. And the spirit of the Lord cometh mightily upon them to sing in choirs and to sound the voice of His praise. And they respond in praise and in thanks to the Lord, for He is good, for His loving-kindness is great toward us. And we established shepherds for us, who teach the people Torah. And the people standing in their place, their wives, their sons and daughters, understand the words that are declared unto them.[18] And there is great happiness. The time will yet come when it shall be said to us that it is too cramped for us in this place, for the house is filled to the brink. We accepted the obligation to teach our children Hebrew Bible and language and to bring our sons and daughters into the covenant of the Lord,[19] to teach them the path which they should follow and the works which one should perform in order thereby to live. There hath not failed one word of all His good promise which He promised by the hand of Moses, His servant. And sons who had not known listen and learn to fear the Lord our God. They put their confidence in God, not forgetting the works of God, but keeping His commandments. They shall not be as their fathers, a stubborn and rebellious generation. . . . And concerning the changes of the prayers, our many songs and the musical accompaniment of the song which

is sung in the House of our God, and concerning our use of the vernacular, the three are all of the same nature.[20] Also, do not pay attention to all the things which they say and of which they accuse us, for not out of wisdom did they question concerning this. Were they wise, they would see and know, consider and understand that it was the hand of the Lord which has done this to revive many people.[21] Therefore, the prudent should keep silent in such a time. . . .

NOTES

1. Meyer Israel Bresselau (1785–1839) was one of the founders of the Hamburg Temple and a lay leader of the first generation of Reform Judaism in Germany. A notary by profession, he edited and adapted with Seckel I. Frankel (1765–1835) the prayerbook used by the Hamburg Temple. As is evidenced by his sixteen-page pamphlet *The Sword Which Avenges the Covenant*, he had sound traditional Jewish education. Published anonymously in response to *These Are the Words of the Covenant*, the pamphlet is written in uncommonly elegant and stylistically sophisticated Hebrew and parodies the earlier collection of rabbinic opinions opposing religious reform. (The title is taken from Leviticus 26:25. The "covenant" to be avenged, of course, was *These Are the Words of the Covenant*.) With a biting sarcasm, Bresselau ridicules the obscurantism of the rabbis and portrays them—especially the three judges of the Hamburg rabbinical court who solicited their *responsa*—as errant "shepherds" who have allowed their flock to stray so that "our sons and daughters are lost to another people." The young, exposed as they are to refreshingly new aesthetic and intellectual sensibilities, he argues, are increasingly alienated from the cacophonous, unruly traditional service. In contrast, with its decorous and melodious service, the Hamburg Temple is filled with youth who joyously gather as Jews to worship the God of Israel. Clearly, he concludes, the changes introduced by the Hamburg Temple are urgently needed to stem the tide of assimilation. Indicatively, Bresselau eschews the ponderous style of rabbinic Hebrew and adopts the "*melizah*"— the euphuistic biblical Hebrew propagated by the early *maskilim*. Skillfully weaving scriptural phrases and even whole verses into his inspired defense of reform, he obviously felt that a sarcastically witty exposure of the alleged folly of the rabbis would be a more effective defense than marshalling, as Liebermann had, proof texts from the tradition. (In fact, in a separate pamphlet

in German, he presented rabbinic sources supporting prayer in the vernacular (*Ueber die Gebete der Israeliten in der Landsprache* [n.p., 1819]). He also seems to have had in mind as much as the rabbis the members of the Temple who, faced with the assault by an impressive array of learned critics, needed an encouraging word.

2. Bresselau derives the word *slander* by constructing an acronym from the second and the third words of the Hebrew title of *These Are the Words of the Covenant*, namely, *"divrei habrit"*: *d-v[b]-h*, which are the letters for the Hebrew word for slander (*dibah*). So he refers to the work throughout his pamphlet. See Rossoff, op. cit., p. 126.

3. That is, the rabbis who contributed the *responsa* in *These Are the Words of the Covenant*.

4. Cf. Genesis 9:13. Bresselau uses the image of the "bow" of the covenant as that which shoots arrows at "the upright in heart"; the "cloud" points to the darkness in the minds of the rabbis. Thus, he suggests, the rabbis pervert the covenant. See Rossoff, op. cit., p. 128.

5. Following the Sephardic tradition, the Jews of Hamburg often called their rabbis the "wise" ones (*hahamim*).

6. The "plague" alluded to is the ever-increasing alienation of Jewish youth from Judaism. Cf. Rossoff, op. cit., p. 129.

7. Bresselau is referring to the rabbis' loss of authority and the resulting anarchy and religious indifference of contemporary Jewry.

8. The reference is to the three judges of the Hamburg rabbinic court who solicited the *responsa* collected in *These Are the Words of the Covenant*.

9. The covenant "sealed in our flesh" is that of the circumcision, the "sign" of Abraham's covenant with God.

10. "In this section, Bresselau bemoans the state of the Jewish youth who, because of the neglect of those who were responsible for the religious life of the community, have received no Jewish education, have forsaken Judaism, and have embraced Christianity." Rossoff, op. cit., p. 132f.

11. This is an illusion to a rabbinic dictum cited in *These Are the Words of the Covenant*: "No rabbinic court may annul the decree of another court unless the former is greater in number or in wisdom." Purposefully ignoring the "or" of this statement, Bresselau suggests that just because the Reformers were in the minority, this was not a warrant to assume that the rabbis were wiser. See Rossoff, op. cit., pp. 132ff.

12. Here Bresselau challenges the argument of the rabbis that tradition and customs sanctioned by ancient practice preclude all change. Even should the Prophet Elijah suddenly reappear, the rabbis claimed, he would have no authority to change the traditional customs and practice of Israel. Boldly rejecting this dictum, Bresselau insists that customs are as mortal as their authors.

13. This is a citation from *These Are the Words of the Covenant*.

14. Here Bresselau is articulating a recurrent criticism by the reformers of traditional religious practice, namely, that worship is often a mere mechanical observance bereft of genuine religious sentiments and understanding.

15. Bresselau now describes the achievements of the Hamburg Temple.

16. That is, the Hamburg Temple.

17. "Those who had been distant," namely, those Jews who were estranged from the traditional synagogue.

18. Acknowledging the decline in the knowledge of Hebrew, the Hamburg Temple introduced into the worship service prayers translated into German as well as a sermon in the vernacular.

19. The reference is to a confirmation ceremony.

20. Bresselau adds a note here: "The rabbis declared that these three matters were alike in that they were laws without scriptural basis."

21. "To revive many people," that is, to restore them to Jewish religious life.

6. LAST WILL AND TESTAMENT (1839)[1]

HATAM SOFER

I. With the help of God, may He be blessed, Thursday, 15 Kislev 5597 [1837]

"*A man cannot even know his time of [death]*" (Ecclesiastes 9:12)—"*it is a time to act for the Lord*" (Psalms 119:126) [and] "*intensify your Teaching*" (ibid.)[2] [and] "*to raise again the House of God, repairing its ruins*" (Ezra 9:9).

You—my sons and daughters, son-in-laws, and grandchildren, and their children—listen to me and flourish.

Be not inclined to do a wrong thing, to dispute with the wicked "*men who are evildoers*" (Psalms 141:4), "*the new ones, who came but lately*" (Deuteronomy 32:17).

Do not live in their vicinity[3] and do not associate with them at all, and never occupy yourselves with the writings of R.M.D (Reb [Mr.] Moses of Dessau)—then your foot will never stumble.[4]

You shall meditate upon the Bible with Rashi's commentary and the Torah [the Pentateuch] with Ramban's commentary,[5] and teach it to your children, for he [Ramban] is foremost in "*steadfast faithfulness*" (Isaiah 25:1). And through it you will become wiser than "*Kalko, Darda and Heman*" (1 Kings 5:11).[6]

And if, God forbid, you will be tested with the test of hunger and thirst and poverty, may God save you. Survive that test and "*do not turn to idols*" (Leviticus 19:4)—[which the rabbis understand to mean]—"*do not turn to that which comes from your minds*" (Babylonia Talmud, Shabbat 149a).[7]

And [your] daughters may occupy themselves with books [in the language] of Ashkenaz (that is, Germany), published in our font [i.e., Judeo-German, or Yiddish in Hebrew characters], that are based on rabbinic *aggadot*[8] and nothing else. And you should

not set foot into theaters, heaven forbid. I completely forbid you [to do so]. [And by obeying this prohibition] you will merit to "*gaze upon the beauty of the Lord*" (Psalm 27:4) when He will rejoice with His children, soon in our day, Amen.

And if God will raise your prestige and spare you—to have mercy upon you—which I hope, with God's help, do not raise your heads "*in arrogance and haughtiness*" (Isaiah 9:8) against any proper person, heaven forbid.

Know that we are the children of Abraham, disciples of Moses our teacher, servants of King David. Our father said "*I who am but dust and ashes*" (Genesis 18:27), our teacher said "*who are we that you grumble against us?*" (Exodus 16:7), our king said, "*I am a worm, less than human*" (Psalm 22:7). And the hoped-for king [the Messiah] will be revealed in the image of a "*humble [man], riding on an ass*" (Zechariah 9:9). If this is so, from whence our "*arrogance and haughtiness*" (Isaiah 9:8)?

Have strength and courage through assiduousness and great learning in God's Torah. Gather, disseminate, and act for the sake of Torah in public. And if you have at your disposal a little, from the little that God has bestowed upon you, teach in public with all your strength, and in such a way that you will know in your heart that God knows you possess no mixed intentions—but only for the sake of honoring His great name alone, [as it says] "*that no impious man can come into His presence*" (Job 13:16).

Be careful not to change your Jewish name, language, and dress, heaven forbid, and the sign is [the verse] "*and Jacob arrived intact (ShaLem)*" (Genesis 33:18).[9]

Do not worry if I am not leaving you riches since the "*Father of the Orphans*" (i.e. God)[10] will have pity

---

Source: Hatam Sofer, *Moshe 'alah le-Marom*, compiled and edited by Judah ha-Cohen Strasser and Aaron ha-Cohen (Brooklyn: Meshmuel, 1933), pp. 214–216. Translated and annotated by Dov Weiss.

and mercy on children bereft of [both] a father and a mother. And He will not abandon you, [as it says] *"for nothing prevents the Lord from winning a victory by many or a few"* (1 Samuel 14:6). And from God's Torah *"do not make a crown [with which to magnify yourself], nor a spade [with which to dig]"* (Mishna Avot 4:5).[11] God forbid, [and] certainly, heaven forbid, to travel from place to place preaching for a fee or begging to be hired, since *"by your name shall they call you, and in your place shall they seat you, and from your own [portion] shall they provide you"* (Babylonian Talmud, Yoma 38a).

And you shall not say that the times have changed, for we have an Ancient Father, may His name be Blessed, Who has not changed and will not change. And [thus] no evil shall befall [you],[12] and *"His dwelling place has been eternally blessed"* (Deuteronomy 33:27).

[Signed] Moshe Hakatan [i.e., the insignificant] Sofer of Frankfurt-am-Main

II. [*To the Jewish Community of Pressburg*]

With the help of God, May He be Blessed, may your fear of the Lord prolong your life and years (see Proverbs 10:27), you whom I love as my own soul, a magnificent community, the distinguished community of the city of Pressburg, which is majestic in the fear of God and His Torah. May God bless you from the source of [His] blessings.

You have sustained me for Torah and worship since Tishrei, the year of *"miracles"* [1806],[13] to raise up many disciples, *"our leaders of substance"* (Psalm 144:14)[14] [who] *"will cover the face of the world with fruit"* (see Isaiah 27:6)—and wisdom.[15]

And the community is filled with wise people and scribes—[both] young and old—[where] *"all its fruit shall be set aside for jubilation before the Lord"* (Leviticus 19:24). You have sustained a *yeshivah* with intelligence, wisdom, and knowledge, and with a *"designer's craft"* (Exodus 35:33). *"Theirs was the service of the most sacred objects, their porterage was by shoulder"* (Numbers 7:9)—[that is] the yoke of my sustenance.

And you provided for the students, and you raised most of your children to the study of Torah. They (the children) succeeded and also produced fruit [for which] *"He will set you, in fame and renown and glory high above all the nations"* (Deuteronomy. 26:19). And no *"breacher of fences"* (Ecclesiastes 10:8) shall ever rise against you.

And please, the seat of the rabbinate should not be vacant for more than two years; and only a renowned man of learning should fill the position, [one] who shall not seek to make his voice heard from the pulpit but only one whose praises you shall say for his righteousness and fear of God and [who has obtained] the Torah of Moses, Ravina and Rav Ashi from childhood.[16] And [also] one who has not delved into heretical works.

And he shall not preach in the language of the nations, for then like the shadow, *"he will not live long, because he does not revere God"* (Ecclesiastes 8:13), but rather [deliver] sermons of rabbinic *aggadah* in the manner you heard from me.

[Choose someone who] *"shows no favor and takes no bribe"* (Deuteronomy 10:17) of words, nor bribe of honor and pride, but rather, is modest and humble, and disseminates Torah to the masses.

And the fund [to support] the study of Torah and the arrangement of studies should not be changed or replaced. And the one who wants to destroy this [i.e., the curriculum of the *yeshivah*] will be destroyed. And the one who maintains it firmly will be strengthened and encouraged.

The reader's stand[17] and in the arrangements of the synagogue [service] as they were until this very day shall be upheld for eternity. God forbid that anyone will introduce changes, either with regard to the structure [of the synagogue], or the prayer book, and the persons leading the service should continue [in the same manner] as in the past. And anyone who *"alters his visage"* (Job 14:20)—he himself will be changed, but *"no harm befalls the righteous"* (Proverbs 12:21). And you, O God, uplift the prestige of your people in general, and of those in Pressburg specifically, with wealth, assets, honor, and long life, through the fear of God and His Torah *"until Shilo comes"* (Genesis 49:10)[18]—Amen.

My daughters and daughters-in-law, beware lest, God forbid and heaven forbid, you reveal a handbreadth of your flesh by shortening the customary clothing.

God forbid there be any of [such conduct] among those who have grown up in my home. And all the more you shall beware of the evilness of the evil women who let even a single hair be revealed. And even a wig I forbid you [to wear] with absolute prohibition.

And God shall grant you favor, mercy, grace, and compassion. And you shall raise your children and descendants upon Torah and religious worship as the

Lord, our God, has commanded us. God, our Lord, shall be with us and with our children forever.

These are the words of Moses Hakatan mentioned above.

III. My dear children and beloved disciples who are present,

Do not suspend the *yeshivah* and the public daily learning of Torah. At any rate, [for] twelve months, that is, on the appropriate day to deliver a lecture and the time of Halachah and Torah, how great would it be if my beloved son Avraham Shmuel Binyamin would deliver the public lecture and that you will listen to him as it has been til now.

May it be Your will before You, God the giver of Torah, may His name be blessed, that the fruit of the living everlasting tree shall not be cut.

These are the words of Moshe Sofer mentioned above.

[On his deathbed, Hatam Sofer added the following addendum:][19]

And I will conclude, addressing the *dayyanim* of Israel, the distinguished rabbis of the rabbinical courts, May His light shine [upon them], to them know that I have already ordained my son, the great Rabbi, our teacher Rabbi Avraham Shmuel Binyamin, and he is worthy to make [halakhic] decisions and to judge in [this] fine community as [the community] is great and well-known in Israel.

And if they consent to agree with me [to ordain him, then] God will protect him (see Zechariah 12:8), and God will be with him—for his rulings shall prevail in every place in which the fear of God is manifest.

Signed here in Pressburg, Wednesday, the day after Sukkot, 5540.

NOTES

1. Hatam Sofer's ethical testament, composed in 1837 and read at his funeral in 1839, is addressed to his family with an addendum in which he turns to the Jewish community of Pressburg, Hungary, (today Bratislava, Slovakia) where he established the largest rabbinic academy since the Babylonian *yeshivah*, and his children. Although he left the city of his birth at the age of nineteen, he would sign his name as "Moses ha-Katan [the insignificant one] of Frankfurt am Main." The testament gives succinct expression to his uncompromising opposition to modernity.

2. Hatam Sofer cites Psalm 119:126 but replaces the phrase "they violated" with "they increase (or intensify)."

3. See the Babylonian Talmud, tractate Shabbat 63a, where a similar phrase is used.

4. The reference here is to Moses Mendlessohn, who epitomized for Hatam Sofer the dangers that Enlightenment and secular culture posed to Judaism, especially since the philosopher sought to adjust Israel's ancient faith to the modern world. In the eyes of Hatam Sofer, the threat to the integrity of Jewish religious tradition gained subtle expression—and was, therefore, all the more insidious—in Mendelssohn's German translation of the Hebrew Bible and commentary. (See chapter 2, document 15.) All translations of Scripture, Hatam Sofer averred, "remove the dress of pious stones, the allusions and the secrets contained in Torah, and the rabbinic traditions emanating from it...." Cited in Jacob Katz, "Towards a Biography of Hatam Sofer," trans. David Ellenson, in *From East and West: Jews in a Changing World, 1750–1870*, eds., Francis Malino and David Sorkin (Oxford, Blackwell Publisher, 1991), p. 256.

5. The commentary to the Bible by Rashi (Rabbi Shlomo Yitzhak, 1040–1105) is the prime guide of the study of the Torah. While Rashi conveys the plain meaning of the text, he also incorporates midrashic interpretations. Ramban (Rabbi Moshe ben Nahman or Nachmanides, 1194–1270) took a similar conservative approach, although in his commentary he also sought to disclose its inner, mystical teachings. Among other objections that were raised against Mendelssohn was that the Biur commentary, which accompanied his German translation of the Bible, aimed to limit the interpretation of the text to its plain meaning.

6. Scripture claims that Solomon was smarter than these "sons of Mahol," who here represent the Jewish enlighteners (*maskilim*).

7. This is how Rashi reads the Talmudic text. Other Talmudic commentators interpret this phrase to mean "do not remove God from your minds."

8. *Aggadot* (plural of *aggadah*) are the nonlegal sections of rabbinic literature, which treat history, ethics, folklore, pious tales, and the like.

9. The three radical Hebrew letters of the word *Shalem*—Sh, L, and M—are read by the rabbis as an acronym: *Shem* (name), *Lashon* (language), and *Malbush*. Jews must maintain distinctive names, language, and dress in order to resist the allure of modernity—acculturation and assimilation—and remain *shalem*—complete, perfect, authentic Jews. According to midrash, this is one of the strategies that helped the Israelites to preserve their identity during their sojourn in Egypt.

10. See Psalm 68:6.

11. This is the classical rabbinic proof-text prohibiting making a livelihood from teaching Torah.

12. See Proverbs 12:21.

13. "Miracles" in Hebrew (*niflaot*) in gematria is the equivalent of [5]567, the year of the Hebrew calendar corresponding to 1806, when Hatam Sofer was installed as the head of the rabbinical academy (*yeshivah*) in Pressburg.

14. In the context of the Psalm, this phrase should be translated as "our cattle are well cared for."

15. Hatam Sofer here adduces the word *intelligence* (*tevunah*) from fruit (*tenuvah*). One needs only to switch the order of two letters.

16. Rav Ashi and Ravina were the last of the *Amoraim*, the sages of the Talmud. By evoking their names, Hatam Sofer wishes to underscore the need to appoint as his successor an eminent Torah scholar.

17. The reader's stand or *bimah* is the elevated platform in the synagogue at which the reading of the Torah takes place. Many Reform congregations placed the *bimah* at the eastern end of the synagogue adjacent to the ark of the Torah. Hatam Sofer viewed this innovation as a reprehensible imitation of Christian churches in which the altar is at the eastern side of the sanctuary.

18. Midrash Genesis Rabbah (Vayechi, 98, 8) understands this phrase as referring to the coming of the Messiah. *Midrash Rabbah*, trans., H. Friedman (London and New York: Soncino, 1983), vol. 2, p. 8.

19. In this deathbed addendum, Hatam Sofer strongly hints that his son, who was at the time but twenty-five years old, was worthy of inheriting his position as chief rabbi of Pressburg. At the time, the succession of rabbinical posts from father to son was not yet a given practice, hence the oblique wording. In fact, Hatam Sofer himself had argued against the practice in 1820, only to reverse himself a decade later. The naming of his son as the rabbi of Pressburg, at the graveside where Hatam Sofer's will was read, by acclamation instead of conducting the usual "rational" electoral procedure, established a strong precedent in the history of the Orthodox rabbinate.

7. MENDELSSOHN'S *BIUR* IS HERETICAL (1865)

RABBI MOSES SCHICK[1]

Warmest regards to your son-in-law, and my student, the learned and erudite Rabbi Akiva Joseph, who asked that I inform him whether or not it is true that I testified before some Jews in Pressburg regarding the casting to the ground of Mendelssohn's *Biur*. In fact, I never received an inquiry from anyone about such a matter, nor did I ever mention it to anyone. When I saw the story in print, I said to myself, "It is not true, the reporter has exaggerated." Even in private I never mentioned such a matter; thus, even the birds of heaven could not have overheard and spread the story. Indeed, I never heard or witnessed such a matter regarding our Rabbi, the *Gaon*[2] [Hatam Sofer] of blessed memory. Moreover, I suspect that the reporter had in mind an event that did involve me, and this is what really happened.

It was a custom of the Hatam Sofer, when visiting a Jewish community outside of Pressburg, to attend services on Sabbath morning in the community synagogue, after which he would accompany the Rabbi to his home. There he would "order" the Rabbi to deliver an aggadic sermon, after which the

Source: E. Stern, ed., *Liqqutei Teshuvot Hatam Sofer* (London: 1965), p. 75, translated by Shnayer Z. Leiman. "R. Moses Schick: The Hatam Sofer's Attitude Toward Mendelssohn's *Biur*" *Tradition* 24:3, Spring 1989:84–85.

Hatam Sofer would also preach. Now it was his practice never to recite a verse from Scripture by heart, and [when he visited my community] he requested a printed *Humash*[3] containing the appropriate weekly reading. At the time, I owned three printed editions of the Torah. One was an Amsterdam edition with the standard Targums[4] and commentaries. That edition I used to keep in the synagogue over the Sabbath, so that it would not be necessary for me to carry it on the Sabbath. [It, therefore, was not available in my home.] Another edition—printed in Vienna—belonged to my wife, the Rebbetzin,[5] and it, too, was kept in the synagogue over the Sabbath for her use. The third edition, the only one I kept in the house, contained Mendelssohn's translation and *Biur*. When the Hatam Sofer requested a printed *Humash*, and those who were providing for his needs knew that it was his practice not to use the edition with Mendelssohn's *Biur*, he was informed that they could not locate a printed *Humash*. Given the circumstances, he proceeded to preach and cited the verses [the Torah] by heart. He was astounded, however, that a *Humash* could not be located in the Rabbi's house! After the exchange of words of Torah in my home, the pious and righteous Rabbi Hirsch Tyrnau, who was treated as a member of the Hatam Sofer's family, went to visit him at the home where he was staying. The Hatam Sofer queried him about the shortage of *Humashim* in the Rabbi's house. Rabbi Hirsch Tyrnau then explained to the Hatam Sofer what had really occurred.

When I arrived for the Minhah service[6] at the home where the Hatam Sofer was staying, he rebuked me for reading and studying from Mendelssohn's *Biur*. I informed him that a respected colleague, who was considered a righteous Jew even by the Hatam Sofer, testified before me that the well-known *Gaon* used to study the *Biur*, especially the book of Leviticus. The Hatam Sofer responded that, in truth, the *Gaon* did not do well in this matter. I also excused myself by informing him that I had read through the entire *Biur*, and did not find anything that even smacked of heresy or a passage that was suspect in any way! The Hatam Sofer responded: "See the *Biur* to Deuteronomy, chapter so and so,[7] and you will find a heretical comment." Although the passage he cited is not necessarily decisive, nonetheless, the Hatam Sofer has ruled [that the *Biur* is heretical] and who would

contravene his ruling? In any event, it is evident that he considered Mendelssohn a heretic, and his book a heretical work. That is why he had no compunctions about Heidenheim's translation of the Torah; [8] it was specifically Mendelssohn's translation and commentaries that he interdicted. He would not touch them, he kept them at a distance, for they had the status of heretical works (see Babylonian Talmud, Sabbath 116a–b). But we never heard that, if perchance a volume of Mendelssohn's *Biur* came into his hands, he cast it to the ground.[9]

NOTES

1. Rabbi Moses Schick (d. 1879), known as the Maharam, was a close disciple of Hatam Sofer and rabbi and headmaster of the rabbinical academy (*yeshivah*) of Vergin, a town near Pressburg, then called Hust. This document is a postscript to a *responsum* (on a matter of rabbinic law) addressed to Rabbi Hillel Lichtenstein (d. 1891). Dated 1865, the postscript is a reply to a query by Lichentstein's son-in-law, Rabbi Akiva Joseph Schlesinger (d. 1922) as to whether it is true that Hatam Sofer so despised Mendelssohn's *Biur* that he once tossed a copy of it to the ground. The significance of Rabbi Schick's reply is that it confirms the vehement objection to the Mendelssohn *Biur* as embodying to his mind the assimilatory ethos of the *Haskalah*.

2. *Gaon*, Hebrew meaning "excellency" or "pride," is based on such biblical passages as Psalm 47:5: "He chose our heritage for us, the pride (*Gaon*) of Jacob whom He loved." This purely honorific title is given to Talmudic scholars by their disciples.

3. Derived from the Hebrew word for five, *Humash* is one of the Hebrew terms for the Five Books of Moses, also known as the Pentateuch or Torah.

4. *Targum* is the Hebrew for translation; here the reference is to translations of the Bible from Hebrew into another language, especially Aramaic. One of these, Targum Onkelos from the 2nd century C.E., is deemed most authentic and is printed in most editions of the *Humash*.

5. Rebbetzin is the Yiddish title given to the wife of a rabbi.

6. Minhah is the second of three sessions of daily prayers.

7. "The exact reference in Deuteronomy is lacking in the published version of R. Schick's *responsum*. The original text, however, referred to Mendelssohn's translation [of] and [commentary] to Deuteronomy 2:10–21" (translator's note).

8. Wolf Heidenheim (1757–1832) was a Judaica scholar and publisher, especially known for his elegant and scholarly editions of the Hebrew liturgy. His German translation of the Pentateuch, with a commentary, appeared in 1818–1821.

9. "Rabbi Moses Schick's denial was to no avail. Schlesinger found other witnesses who testified that the Hatam Sofer had at least on one occasion cast Mendelssohn's *Biur* to the ground" (translator's note).

8. THE QUESTION OF PATRIOTISM (JUNE 1844)[1]

THE REFORM RABBINICAL CONFERENCE AT BRUNSWICK

Tenth Session, June 18, 1844. Continuation of the committee report regarding Philippson's[2] proposal [to endorse the position of the French Sanhedrin on Jewish patriotism].

Question 4 [addressed to the Sanhedrin]: Do the Jews consider Frenchmen as their brethren or as strangers? Answer [of the Sanhedrin]: French Jews are the brethren of Frenchmen.

The committee recommended that [the present assembly adopt the following statement]: The Jew considers members of the people with whom he lives his brethren.

Plenum discussion. A. Adler:[3] He wants it to be said that the Jews consider not only the people with whom they live as brethren, but all mankind. Do not all men, according to the prophets, have but one Father? . . .

Frankfurter:[4] This is quite right. It is, however, not a question of ethics, but of politics. For Judaism, the principle of human dignity is cosmopolitan, but I would like to put proper emphasis on the love for the particular people [among whom we live] and its individual members. As men, we love all mankind, but as Germans, we love the Germans as the children of our fatherland. We are, and ought to be, patriots, not merely cosmopolitans . . . .

Hirsch:[5] Differentiating between love for the fatherland and love for mankind, he proposes an answer analogous to that of the Parisian notables.

Holdheim:[6] He traces the commandment of recognition and love for fellow countrymen back to the Pentateuch, where the love of the Israelite for the Israelite does not refer to their common religion, but to their common peoplehood. What was once a commandment for the Israelite *with regard to his fellow Israelite*, must also oblige us with regard to our contemporary compatriots—to the Germans. The doctrine of Judaism is thus, first your compatriots [*Vaterlandsgenosse*] then your co-religionists [*Glaubensgenosse*].

A. Adler, therefore, suggests the following proposal: *The Jew acknowledges every man as his brother.* But he acknowledges *his fellow countryman to be one with whom he is connected by a particular bond*, a bond forged by the effort to realize common political purposes [*Staatszwecke*] . . . .

NOTES

1. It was gradually realized that unless the nascent movement of Reform ceased to be merely the desultory effort of isolated congregations it would never obtain the authority to challenge the supremacy of Orthodox-Judaism. Abraham

---

Source: Protokolle der ersten Rabbiner-Versammlung . . . (Braunschweig, 1844), pp. 74–76. Trans. by J. Hessing.

Geiger, the most eminent figure in early Reform, argued that the necessary authority could be obtained only if rabbis supporting religious change would confer and establish common principles and a common program for Reform. In August 1837 Geiger initiated a largely stillborn conference of like-minded rabbis in Wiesbaden, Germany. The first organizationally successful rabbinical conference on Reform took place from the twelfth to the nineteenth of June 1844. Twenty-five rabbis from throughout Germany attended. The above document is extracted from the protocol of the conference.

At the session of June fourteenth, Ludwig Philippson moved that the conference endorse the patriotism expressed by the Parisian Sanhedrin in response to the fourth question posed by Napoleon regarding the Jews' sentiments toward their fellow countrymen. Philippson's motion was referred to a committee, which, at the session of June eighteenth, submitted its recommendation to accept the motion. "By basing itself upon the French Sanhedrin, the first gathering of Jewish representatives resulting from the changes superinduced by the political emancipation of the Jews..., the conference, whether consciously or unconsciously, declared itself the official voice of the modern spirit" (D. Philippson, *The Reform Movement in Judaism*, rev. ed. [New York: Ktav Publishing House, 1967], pp. 159ff.). See chapter 3, documents 15 and 16.

2. Ludwig Philippson (1811–1889), rabbi and preacher at Magdeburg. Supporting a program of moderate Reform, he tried to steer a middle course between radical Reform and Orthodoxy. He was founder and editor of the most widely circulated Jewish publication of the time, *Allgemeine Zeitung des Judentums*; the newspaper was prominent in the struggle for Jewish emancipation and in the fight against antisemitism.

3. Abraham Jacob Adler (1813–1856), rabbi at Worms; he was an exponent of radical Reform.

4. Naphtali Frankfurter (1810–1866), from 1840 to 1866 preacher at the Reform temple in Hamburg; identified with the most radical wing of Reform.

5. Samuel Hirsch (1815–1889), chief rabbi in Luxembourg from 1843 to 1866; he then emigrated to the United States, where he was rabbi of Congregation Keneseth Israel in Philadelphia until 1888. Opposed to the unsystematic reforms by radical lay groups, he upheld the rite of circumcision and the use of Hebrew in the public prayer service; yet, he was the first rabbi to advocate the transfer of the Sabbath to Sunday, and he carried this out in the United States.

6. Samuel Holdheim (1806–1860), rabbi of the province of Mecklenburg-Schwerin from 1840 to 1846. In 1847 he accepted an invitation to serve as the rabbi of the newly founded Reform congregation of Berlin, which under his guidance became a center of radical Reform.

9. HEBREW AS THE LANGUAGE OF JEWISH PRAYER (1845)[1]

THE REFORM RABBINICAL CONFERENCE AT FRANKFURT

Third Session, morning, July 16, 1845.... The President moves that it would seem desirable to discuss the report [of the Commission on Liturgy] immediately.

Question 1: To what degree is the Hebrew language necessary for the public prayer service and, if not necessary, is its retention advisable for the time being?

Report of the committee: With respect to question one, the Hebrew language is not in every instance *objectively* necessary for the service, nor does the Talmud, with very minor exceptions, prescribe it. But

Source: Protokolle und Aktenstuecke der zweiten Rabbiner-Versammlung... (Frankfurt am Main, 1845), pp. 18ff, 32ff. Trans. by J. Hessing.

since a large part of the Israelites in contemporary Germany seem to feel a subjective necessity for it, the committee considers the use of the Hebrew language advisable for typical parts of the liturgy: the *barechu*,[2] the *parshat shema*,[3] the three first and three last benedictions of the liturgy and the blessings upon reading of the Torah, should be recited in Hebrew; all other parts of the liturgy may be recited in a German adaptation.

The PRESIDENT, in accordance with the proposal of the committee, now poses the question: Is praying in the Hebrew language *objectively, legally necessary* [*objektiv gesetzlich notwendig*]?

FRANKEL[4] takes the floor. He deems the occasion important enough to begin with a few general observations. This rabbinical conference consists of the guides and teachers of the people. They are familiar with the people's needs and sorrow; it is their duty to satisfy these needs, to alleviate these sorrows, and to prevent any discord [among the people]. It is the duty of the rabbinical conference to show and to attest that it is moved by serious and sacred aspirations. Its spokesmen, therefore, have to begin by stating their *principles*. It is the pride of Judaism that no person, and no social class, may presume authority, but that every decision must evolve organically from principles and derive its validity therefrom. Points of view may be stated and put to the vote, but without principles they are merely private opinions. First of all, therefore, the people are entitled to an exposition of our principles....

The speaker now explains his principles: He stands for a positive, historical Judaism. [This approach posits that] in order to understand Judaism in the present one must look back and investigate its past.

The positive forms of Judaism are deeply rooted within its innermost being and must not be discarded coldly and heartlessly. Where would we be if we were to tear apart our inner life and let a new life spring forth from our head as Minerva sprang forth from the head of Jupiter. We cannot return to the *letter of Scripture*. The gap [between it and us] is too wide to be bridged. Even a new exegesis of the Bible is subject to changing phases of scholarship and could not serve as a foundation of a firm edifice. Should we allow any influence of the *Zeitgeist*, of the spirit of the time? But the *Zeitgeist* is as fickle as the times. Besides, it is cold. It may seem reasonable, but it will never satisfy, console and calm the soul; Judaism, on the other hand, always inspires and fills the soul with bliss.

The reform of Judaism, moreover, is not a reform of faith, but one of religious commandments. These still live within the people and exert their influence. We are not called upon to weaken, but rather to strengthen this influence. We must not consider the individuals who do not abide by them; we are not a party and must therefore take care of the whole. Now it is necessary to conserve the things which are truly sacred to the entire people, to prevent any schism in Israel. Rather than creating new parties, we must make peace between the existing ones....

Fourth Session, afternoon, July 16, 1845.... GEIGER[5] demands a strict adherence to the expression of the problem as consisting of the following two questions:

1. Is the complete exclusion of the Hebrew language from the liturgy in general desirable?
2. Are there momentary considerations in favour of a provisional solution?

Both questions, however, overlap and cannot be strictly separated in the debate. The speaker considers it desirable to pray in the mother tongue, which is the language of the soul. Our deepest emotions and feelings, our most sacred relationships, our most sublime thoughts find their expression in it. He feels compelled to admit that as regards himself— although Hebrew is his first mother tongue which he has learnt before other languages, and a language he knows thoroughly—a German prayer strikes a deeper chord than a Hebrew prayer.

The Hebrew language, he continues, has ceased to be alive for the people, and the language of [Jewish] prayer is certainly not the language of the Scripture any more. It is obvious, moreover, that even a reading from the Torah tires a large part of the community.

The introduction of the vernacular into the service, it is claimed, effects the disappearance of the Hebrew language and thus undermines the foundations of Judaism. To this objection the speaker replies that anyone who imagines Judaism to be walking on the crutches of a language deeply offends it. By considering Hebrew as being of central importance to Judaism, moreover, one would define it as a national religion, because a separate language is a characteristic element of a separate nation. But no member of this conference, the speaker concluded, would wish to link Judaism to a particular nation....

Fifth Session, morning, July 17, 1845.... FRANKEL [takes the floor]. The ongoing debate, far from offering new ideas, has rather confirmed [Frankel's] point of view. Geiger considers a language to be the mark of a separate nationality and claims that the retention of Hebrew would testify to our national aspirations; this point, however, is not essential to the question under consideration. The cause of emancipation has nothing to do with religion, and no religious aspect should be sacrificed for it. Everything pertaining to religion must be retained, and if our nationality were religious, then we should openly confess to it.

In countries [that have granted the Jews full] emancipation,[6] such as Holland and France, he continues, experience has fortunately shown that the Hebrew language does not prevent the Jews from being genuine patriots and from fulfilling all duties towards the state. One has to be very careful with such expressions; our meetings are public, therefore "O Sages, be careful with your words."[7]

If Geiger goes on to claim that a German prayer strikes a deeper chord in him than a Hebrew one, he makes a purely subjective statement. Most speakers of Hebrew will feel differently, because this language is a stronger expression of religious emotions; as witnesses, the speaker calls upon the majority of Rabbis assembled here, who are familiar with the Hebrew language.

Hebrew, the speaker argues, is the language of our Scripture which contains every ingredient of our religion. Religion must provide not only an abstract but also an external bond between us and the deity, this being the reason for precepts such as the *tefilin*[8] and the *mezuzah*;[9] in like manner, the use of Hebrew in the prayers serves as an external bond. The language of the Scripture is a constant reminder of our Covenant with God. These various bonds and reminders resemble the sheaf of arrows in the following parable: As long as they remain bound together a sheaf of arrows is unbreakable, but as soon as single arrows are removed from the sheaf it will quickly fall apart. Many characteristic elements of Judaism have been effaced by now, it is time to halt the process.

There is another aspect to be considered as well. The Bible has been given to the Jews as a pledge to be safeguarded; they were called upon to carry it through the world for thousands of years. Mind you, not the priests of Israel alone were called upon to do so, but all of Israel. Samuel already, by establishing schools for prophets, undermined the hierarchy; it is therefore written of him, "Moses and Aaron among his

priests, and Samuel among them that call upon His name..." [Ps. 99:6; cited in Hebrew], and the Talmud rightly remarks, "Samuel is equivalent to Moses and Aaron."[10] If the original texts of the Scripture were to become the exclusive property of a separate class of rabbis we should soon have a separation of priests and laymen again. But all of us object to the establishment of a caste of priests and wish to obliterate all memory of it. That is why our youth has to be instructed in the Hebrew language so that it may understand the service and the Scripture.

The speaker adds, however, that it is necessary to conduct part of the service in German; but Hebrew must prevail. The language of revelation, in which God has spoken to Moses, must act as an edifying stimulus. Hebrew, in fact, is so essential to our service *that its use should have been secured by* [halakhic] *law*; had anyone ever thought of abandoning the Hebrew language, such a law would certainly have been passed. The sages allowed another language besides Hebrew in the service [i.e., Aramaic][11] merely out of consideration for the weak who could not find their peace of mind in a Hebrew prayer. They never thought of excluding the Hebrew language from the Temple....

PHILIPPSON: All extremes are to be avoided, and according to the general consensus neither Hebrew nor German should be excluded from the service. The question, then, is one of proportions. We do not work for the moment and for individual communities; we work for the future and for the whole [of Jewry]. The Hebrew and the German elements must be organically melted into one another.

We shall have to distinguish between *prayer* and public *services*. A prayer is the expression of the particular states and emotions of the soul, of happiness and unhappiness, of joy and of suffering, of sorrow, repentance and penance; here, a full understanding is necessary, and a foreign language utterly useless. The public prayer services, on the other hand, do not refer to the individual [*per se*]; public prayer is intended to stimulate, to teach and to express the confession.

The Hebrew language certainly serves as a stimulus. In it, for the first time, the *shema* ["Hear, O Israel," Deut. 6:4], the *unity of God* was expressed; the principle of pure love for mankind, "Thou shalt love thy neighbor as thyself" [Lev. 19:18; cited in Hebrew]; the sentence of the equality of all men before the law, "one law and one ordinance" [Num. 15:16; cited in Hebrew]; Moses spoke to God in Hebrew, "O Lord God, Thou has begun to show Thy servant Thy greatness ..." [Deut. 3:24]. God had *begun* to reveal Himself to him. By using the original expressions, therefore, the public prayer service acts as a powerful stimulus.

When the Torah is read the Hebrew language will also act as a teacher. This reading must not be abolished, otherwise the people would lose all contact with the Scripture...

As a *center of the confessions* the Hebrew language is indispensable. The German Jews are Germans, they feel and think in German and wish to live and act as patriots. But *Judaism* is not German, it is universal. The Diaspora of the Jews is not tantamount to the Diaspora of Judaism; the latter, on the contrary, must keep its unified character. The content of this character is the *confession*; its form is represented in the *Hebrew language.*

As citizens, we all strive towards *unity* with our fellow countrymen; as members of a religion, however, we are allowed, and even obliged, to retain that which distinguishes us. Facing an immense majority, the minority needs some distinguishing features. The Hebrew language fulfills this purpose.

The Hebrew language, moreover, is neither *poor* nor *dead*, as it is claimed. Masterpieces of unperishable value have been written in it, and as a language of religion it has remained fully alive. To repeat, the Hebrew language must be retained, but at the same time it must be organically united with the German element.

KAHN:[12] I am only speaking from an objective point of view. I certainly wish to retain the Hebrew language for the time being, but we must gratefully acknowledge that its use for our prayers is nowhere prescribed. Our ideal, therefore, should be the establishment of a purely *German* service, because language by itself does not constitute a religious element.

Our *schools* ought to teach in Hebrew; the service, however, aims at edification, elevation, instruction; it should not be turned into a means for the preservation of the Hebrew language.

It is claimed that the Hebrew expression *Adonai* (i.e., God) sounds more solemn than the German word *Gott*. To this, differentiation I must seriously object, because it would cast a heavy doubt on our civil oath.[13] The name *Gott* is as sacred to me as *Adonai*, and I hope that everybody, here will agree with me on this. (*General and loud consent.*)

We should not have any religious element wrested from us. Granted. But we must first concur regarding the nature of religious elements. Language is not one of them. The *shema* ["Hear, O Israel"] sounds much more religious to the German when spoken in German, and much more edifying to the Englishman when spoken in English, than when spoken in unintelligible Hebrew. With the elimination of the Hebrew language [from the liturgy], then, nothing would really be lost.... I vote for the introduction of a purely German service...

LOEWENGARD:[14] It was said: "We are Germans and want to be Germans!" If this statement has any political implications I should like to remind you that we are not yet emancipated. (*Disapproval from all sides. The speaker explains that he merely wants to keep all political aspects out of the debate, because their introduction only causes misunderstanding.*) From the religious point of view, a distinction was made between prayer and service; this was correct. The reading from the Torah, for instance, is meant to demonstrate the unity of Israel established by the Torah, as it is expressed in "And this is the law which Moses set before the children of Israel."[15] Instruction [in the Torah] could be managed without this public reading, because [printed] Bibles are available in sufficient numbers now. As a demonstration [of Jewish unity], however, it should be sufficient to read selections from the Hebrew Pentateuch [at the public service but not also the traditional passages from the prophets].

NOTES

1. With thirty rabbis in attendance, this conference took place in Frankfurt am Main July 15–18, 1845. The Frankfurt conference was devoted to the consideration of the report of the Commission on Liturgy established at the previous conference at Brunswick.

   As a consequence of the new cultural and political situation of the Jews, two distinct problems emerged with regard to the continued use of Hebrew as the language of Jewish public worship: First, with the neglect of traditional Jewish learning, Hebrew was increasingly unintelligible to many Jews, and second, it was feared that the use of the "national language of the ancient commonwealth of Israel" would seem to vitiate the Jews' patriotic affiliation to the country of their residence. Accordingly, the Commission on Liturgy was requested to reevaluate the place of Hebrew in the liturgy.

2. Part of the daily service, the *barechu* ("Praise the Lord who is to be praised...") calls the congregation to prayer and affirms the belief in Creation as divine providence. It is followed by *parshat shema* (see note 3).

3. Consisting of the *shema* (Deut. 6:4–9) and accompanying blessings (largely drawn from Deut. 11:13–21, and Num. 15:37–41), the *parshat shema*, recited daily, proclaims Israel's acceptance of God's sovereignty and the yoke of His Commandments; it links this proclamation with the doctrines of Creation, Revelation and Redemption.

4. Zecharias Frankel (1801–1875). At the time of the conference he was the chief rabbi of Dresden and the founding editor of the *Zeitschrift fuer die religioesen Interessen des Judenthums* [Journal for the Religious Interests of Judaism], published from 1844 to 1847. An exponent of "moderate Reform," as he put it, Frankel criticized the Brunswick conference (which he declined to attend) for appropriating the authority of an ecclesiastical synod, when in fact it was no more than a consultative body. Further, he charged that the conference demonstrated a single lack of deference to the regnant sentiments of the Jewish people. He decided to attend the Frankfurt conference in order to assure that his colleagues would not exceed their prerogatives.

5. Abraham Geiger (1810–1874). At the time of the conference he was chief rabbi of Breslau and the founding editor of the *Wissenschaftliche Zeitschrift fuer juedische Theologie* [Scientific Journal for Jewish Theology], 6 vols., 1835–1847. Considered the guiding spirit of the first rabbinical conferences, Geiger emerged as the leading theoretician and spokesman of Reform in Germany. He sought to ground the study of Judaism in a scholarly, historical approach (see chapter 5, document 8) that would validate Reform's conception of Judaism as an ongoing evolutionary process.

6. The Jews of Germany, of course, did not at this time enjoy full civil and political rights.

7. Mishnah, Ethics of the Fathers 1:11, cited in Hebrew.

8. Phylacteries, two small black boxes containing four portions of the Pentateuch written on parchment (Exod. 13:1–16; Deut. 6:4–9 and 11:13–21). Fastened to leather straps, they are bound ("laid") on the arm and the head of the male Jew during the morning prayers.

9. Parchment scroll placed in a container and fixed to the doorpost of the Jew's abode. On the scroll are inscribed portions from Deut. 6:4–9 and 11:13–21.

10. Mishna, tractate *Berakhot* 31b; cited in Hebrew.

11. Aramaic: a cognate of Hebrew that was for many centuries the vernacular of Palestine. Biblical readings were translated into Aramaic in the synagogue for the benefit of congregants who did not understand Hebrew. Some of the prayers of the traditional liturgy are still in Aramaic, most notably the doxology known as the *kaddish*.

12. Joseph Kahn (1809–1875). He was the chief rabbi of Trier, where he officiated for more than thirty years.

13. In the Middle Ages a practice was instituted that required the Jews to make a special oath (*More Judaico*) when testifying before a non-Jewish court. Assuming that the Jews did not respect Christian jurisprudence, these oaths bound the Jew's testimony under rabbinic law. The oaths were accompanied by self-imposed curses, delineating the punishment, often in gruesome detail, if the testimony was falsely made; sometimes they were accompanied by humiliating rites, such as standing on a sow's skin, In France the *more judaico* was abolished only in 1846, in parts of Germany not until the second half of the nineteenth century; it was still administered in Rumania as late as 1904. The Duchy of Brunswick abrogated the practice in 1845.

14. Joseph Loewengard, rabbi of Lehren Steinfels.

15. Deut. 4:44; cited in Hebrew.

10. THE QUESTION OF MESSIANISM (1845)[1]

THE REFORM RABBINICAL CONFERENCE AT FRANKFURT

Eighth Session, July 20, 1845. Agenda: Discussion of questions pertaining to cult. Question 2: To what degree must the dogma of the Messiah, and anything pertaining to it, be taken into consideration in the liturgy?

Before opening the debate, the President[2] considers it necessary to remark that we are not concerned with the establishment of a certain doctrine of the Messiah, and that such doctrines will not be put to the vote; we are only concerned with how the existing liturgy should be evaluated in this respect, or perhaps conveniently changed. Points of view may differ subjectively, but it is hoped that a version acceptable to all will emerge. The numerous speakers, especially those who are ardent believers in traditional messianism, should beware of creating any doubt concerning their allegiance to the state. Such contrasts and seeming contradictions are easily resolved within the mind of the believer. Here we are only concerned with the demands of truthfulness, lest we pray for something that does not coincide with our convictions.

The committee report reads as follows: The concept of the Messiah must continue to occupy a prominent place in the liturgy, but all political and national implications should be avoided.

EINHORN:[3] The concept of the Messiah is closely linked to the entire ceremonial law. The believer in the Talmud finds his salvation only in the reconstitution of the state, the return of the people, the resumption of sacrifices, etc. Here lies the cause for all our lamentations over the destruction of the Temple, and our yearnings for the ruins of the altar. Ardent belief and unshakable courage were expressed in these hopes, uttered forth from the dark caves of our miserable streets.

But now our concepts have changed. There is no need any more for an extended ceremonial law. The earlier approach restricted divine guidance to the land [of Israel] and the people; the deity, it was believed, enjoyed bloody sacrifices, and priests were needed for penance. With increasing zeal, the prophets spoke up against this restricted view. Everybody knows the passage: "It hath been told thee, O man, what is good, and what the Lord doth require of thee; only to do justly, and to love mercy, and to walk humbly with thy God" [Micah 6:8, cited in Hebrew]. The decline of Israel's political independence was at one time deplored, but in reality it was not a misfortune, but a mark of progress; not a degradation, but an elevation of our religion, through which Israel has come closer to fulfilling its vocation. The place of the sacrifices has been taken by sacred devotion. From the land of Israel, the word of God had to be carried to the four corners of the earth, and new religions have helped in carrying out the task. Only the Talmud moves in circles; we, however, favor progress.

At one time I took the concept of the Messiah to be a substitute for the idea of immortality, but now I no longer think so. I rather consider it as a hope of both worldly and heavenly salvation. Neither this idea nor the concept of the Chosen People contain anything reprehensible. The concept of the Chosen People, in fact, offers the undeniable advantage, for it creates a beneficial self-consciousness in the face of the ruling church.

I vote for the renunciation of all petitions for the restoration of the sacrifices and our political independence. I should prefer our prayers for the Messiah to express a hope for a *spiritual renaissance and the unification of all human beings* in faith and in love through the agency of Israel.

HESS:[4] In discussing the concept of the Messiah we run the greatest risk of losing ourselves in diffuse theories. The question is simply whether one wishes to

Source: Protokolle und Aktenstuecke der zweiten Rabbiner-Versammlung...(Frankfurt am Main, 1845), pp 37–77, 81ff. Trans. by J. Hessing.

interpret the Scripture in spirit, or literally; whether one conceives of messianism as an ideal, or as the idea of our religious independence, unattainable without the full political equality of the Israelites; whether, moreover, one sees it as a bond with our brethren living under oppressive rulers. Let us therefore hold on to the fact that the concept of a personal and political Messiah is dead for German Jewry, and that we must not petition God for that which we no longer believe....

HOLDHEIM:[5] Two points of misunderstanding must be clarified:

1. The hope for a national restoration contradicts our feeling for the fatherland; some speakers have claimed, on the other hand, that the two may coexist.

2. We are warned not to emphasize the national element, lest there be misinterpretations; but it was rightly remarked, on the other hand, that we should not pay attention to misinterpretations.

The main point, however, is this: We merely represent the religious, not the political interest of the community. The latter is sufficiently represented by other spokesmen. Our nationality is now only expressed in religious concepts and institutions. It is said: Our original nationality has developed towards religion. But this is erroneous; such a development is unnatural. One must not mistake a national for a religious phenomenon, otherwise many abuses could be justified.

The wish to return to Palestine in order to create there a political empire for those who are still oppressed because of their religion is superfluous. The wish should rather be for a termination of the oppression; which would improve their lot as it has improved ours. The wish, moreover, is inadmissible. It turns the messianic hope from a religious into a secular one, which is gladly given up as soon as the political situation changes for the better. But messianic hope, truly understood, is religious. It expresses either a hope for redemption and liberation from spiritual deprivation and the realization of a Kingdom of God on earth, or for a political restoration of the Mosaic theocracy where Jews could live according to the law of Moses. This latter religious hope can be renounced only by those who have a more sublime conception of Judaism, and who believe that the fulfillment of Judaism's mission is not dependent on the establishment of a Jewish state, but rather by a merging of

Jewry into the political constellations of the fatherland. Only an enlightened conception of religion can displace a dulled one. Those, however, who believe that religion demands a political restoration must not renounce this belief even under the best of circumstances [in the Diaspora], because religion will content itself with nothing less than the complete satisfaction of its demands. This is the difference between strict Orthodoxy and Reform: Both approach Judaism from a religious standpoint; but while the former aims at a restoration of the old political order [in the interest of religion], the latter aims at the closest possible union with the political and national constellations of their times [as the demand of religion]....

WECHSLER:[6] As soon as we try to pin down the "how" of our hope, the hope immediately disappears. We ought not to vivisect our messianism, but to shape the existing prayers in accordance with our consciousness. We must not disregard the masses. If we had to compose new prayers, the situation would be different.

Therefore, everything already in existence should be admitted as long as it does not run counter to commonly accepted truth. *Political* and *national* do not seem to be the right expressions, anyway. Is the *People of Israel* a national or a political term? If it were so the word *People* should not be used, and all passages in the liturgy containing the word should be deleted.

The question only concerns the prayer for our return to Palestine and all its consequences.

In all contemporary additions to the prayerbook our modern conception of the Messiah may clearly be stated, including the confession that our newly gained status as citizens constitutes a partial fulfillment of our messianic hopes....

Resolution adopted by the majority: The messianic idea should receive prominent mention in the prayers, but all petitions for our return to the land of our fathers and for the restoration of a Jewish state should be eliminated from the liturgy....[7]

NOTES

1. The traditional Jewish liturgy gives prominent expression to the millennial yearning for a personal Messiah from the royal House of David who will herald "the ingathering of the exiles" of Israel to their ancestral homeland. The national sentiments of these prayers were considered by some reformers to cast doubt on the Jews' identification with the country of their

residence and citizenship. The Commission on Liturgy was charged with reevaluating the place of messianism within the prayerbook.

2. Leopold Stein (1810–1882). From 1844 to 1862 he was a rabbi at Frankfurt am Main.

3. David Einhorn (1809–1879). In 1842 he was appointed rabbi of Hoppstaedten and chief rabbi of the principality of Birkenfeld. In 1855 he emigrated to the United States, where he became a leader of the radical wing of the Reform movement there.

4. Michael Hess (1782–1860). An advocate of thoroughgoing reform, from 1806 to 1855 he served as headmaster of the Philanthropin in Frankfurt, a Jewish elementary and high school fashioned in the spirit of the *haskalah*.

5. Samuel Holdheim, see documents 8 and 11 in this chapter.

6. Bernhard Wechsler (d. 1874). In 1841 he succeeded Samson Raphael Hirsch as chief rabbi of Oldenburg.

7. The conference unanimously approved the removal of the traditional petitions for the restoration of the sacrificial cult from the liturgy. The majority of the conference, however, voted that provided they were recited only in Hebrew, the Torah passages concerning the sacrifice should remain in the liturgy.

11. THIS IS OUR TASK (1853)[1]

SAMUEL HOLDHEIM

It is the destiny of Judaism to pour the light of its thoughts, the fire of its sentiments, the fervor of its feelings upon all souls and hearts on earth. Then all of these peoples and nations, each according to its soil and historic characteristics, will, by accepting our teachings, kindle their own lights, which will then shine independently and warm their souls. Judaism shall be the seed-bed of the nations filled with the blessing and promise, but not a fully grown matured tree with roots and trunk, crowned with branches and twigs, with blossoms and fruit—a tree which is merely to be transplanted into a foreign soil.

Already 2000 years ago Judaism began to face its historic task and in this manner it must continue to face it. All these unnumbered peoples and nations which were once governed by paganism were converted to ways of thinking which are based—who can deny it—upon the principles of ancient Judaism, which gave them their singular color and form. A forced egalitarianism, which desires that all peoples of the earth should express their innermost thoughts and feelings with the same words, is neither the task nor the content of Judaism. From the beginning it expressed its decisive disapproval of the building of the tower of Babel, that is to say, of the desire to bind men to a single tongue and a single mode of speech and to extinguish their individuality and singularity. Judaism wants to purify the languages of the nations, but leave to each people its own tongue. It wishes for one heart and one soul, but not for one sound and one tone. It does not desire to destroy the particular characteristics of the nations. It does not wish to stultify the directions of spirit and sentiment which their history has brought forth. It does not wish that all should be absorbed and encompassed by the characteristics of the Jewish people. Least of all does it wish to extinguish the characteristics of the Jewish people and to eliminate those expressions of the living spirit which were created through the union and spirit of the Jewish faith.

Source: W. Gunther Plaut, *The Rise of Reform Judaism: A Sourcebook of Its European Origins* (New York: World Union for Progressive Judaism, 1963), pp. 138ff. Reprinted by permission of the World Union for Progressive Judaism.

As a mere philosophical idea, denuded of its historic characteristics and forms, Judaism can never become the common property of mankind. Our ancient Jewish sages correctly understood this important question of the relationship of Judaism to mankind and expressed it felicitously, even though they had a much more limited view concerning that which should be the norm for the internal aspects of our faith. Regarding the peoples of the earth, they spoke of the seven *Noachide* duties,[2] the fundamental rules of faith and morals, but reserved the whole Mosaic law for Israel exclusively. We must spread the *Noachide* laws to all nations, but we must safeguard the Torah as our exclusive possession. To be sure, we do not follow the letter of our sages' pronouncements slavishly, yet we must not fail to acknowledge their spiritual meaning and substance. Translating their words into our more purified expression, we would say: "It is the Messianic task of Israel to make the pure knowledge of God and the pure law of morality of Judaism the common possession of blessing of all the peoples of the earth. We do not expect of the nations that, by accepting these teachings, they would give up their historic characteristics in order to accept those of our people; and, similarly, we shall not permit the Jewish people to give up its innate holy powers and sentiments so that it might be assimilated amongst the nations."

Thus, my friends, we shall safeguard our position internally and externally. What the ancient sages called the seven *Noachide* duties in their universal human application, we now call the Jewish idea of God and the Jewish ethical *Weltanschauung*. What they considered the whole Mosaic ceremonial law as the eternal and exclusive heritage of Israel, we call the inextinguishable historic characteristic of the Jewish people, the singular spiritual life of Judaism.

This, then, is our task: to maintain Judaism within the Jewish people and at the same time to spread Judaism amongst the nations; to protect the sense of Jewish unity and life and faith without diminishing the sense of unity with all men; to nourish the love for Judaism without diminishing the love of man. We pray that God may give us further strength to search out the way of truth and not to stray from the path of love!

NOTES

1. Samuel Holdheim (1806–1860). This sermon is from 1853. The national, particularistic aspects of traditional Judaism, as we have noted, were problematic to the Reform movement. To soften these aspects the universal task or mission of Israel was emphasized; here inspiration was drawn from prophets like Isaiah (42:6–7): "I the Lord have called thee in righteousness....For a light of the nations...." The "mission theory" viewed the diaspora not as a tragic exile but rather as a sublime occasion to transcend the concerns of political existence and thereby illumine spiritual and moral ideals relevant to all mankind. Israel, according to this theory, was a faith community defined mainly by this universal mission. See also document 8, note 6.

2. The Seven Commandments of the Sons of Noah, which the Talmud holds to be binding upon all mankind, are derived from the early chapters of Genesis (e.g., 9:4–7). Six of these Commandments are negative: the prohibition of idolatry, blasphemy, murder, adultery, robbery and the eating of flesh taken from a living animal. The establishment of courts of justice is the only positive Commandment. Maimonides gave these Commandments a decidedly liberal emphasis when he related them to the Talmudic dictum that the "righteous people of all nations [Gentiles] have a part in the world to come" (*Hilkhot melakhim* 8:11). This interpretation, which became the authoritative view of Judaism, was frequently cited by Mendelssohn and other Jewish thinkers in the modern period as evidence of a tolerant and benign attitude toward non-Jews.

12. THE RATIONALE OF REFORM (1844)[1]

AARON CHORIN

The permanent elements of religion must be expressed in terms that appeal to the people and are consonant with the needs of life. If our religion and life appear to conflict with one another this is due either to the defacement of the sanctuary by foreign additions or to the license of the sinning will which desires to make its unbridled greed and its false tendency authoritative guides for life. If we show ourselves as ready to strip off these unessential additions which often forced themselves upon our noble faith as the spawn of obscure and dark ages, as we are determined to sacrifice our very lives for the upholding of the essential, we will be able to resist successfully with the help of God all wanton, thoughtless and presumptuous attacks which license or ignorance may direct against our sacred cause; the seeming conflict will then disappear and we will have accomplished something lasting for God. I need not tell you that of all the external institutions the public service demands our immediate and undivided attention. He who is faithful to his God, and is earnestly concerned for the welfare of his religion, must exert himself to rescue our liturgical service from the ruin into which it has fallen and to give it once again that inspiring form which is worthy of a pious and devout worship of the one true God. For it is not only the excrescences of dark ages which cover it with disgrace, but thoughtlessness, lack of taste, absence of devotion, and caprice that have disfigured its noble outlines.

NOTE

1. Aaron Chorin (1766–1844). From 1789 until his death Chorin was the rabbi in Arad, Hungary. The first traditional rabbi to write on behalf of Reform, in his congregation he abolished the *kol nidrei* prayer. *Kol nidrei* is Aramaic for "all vows"; the prayer opens the evening service commencing the Day of Atonement. He also permitted prayer in the vernacular with an uncovered head, approved of the use of an organ on the Sabbath, curtailed the seven-day period of mourning, and allowed riding and writing on the Sabbath. Chorin was one of the four rabbis who contributed to Liebermann's *Nogah hazedek*. See this chapter, document 2.

   In July 1844, during the last weeks of his life, Chorin wrote from his sickbed a declaration expressing his full accord with the prevailing spirit of the deliberations at the Rabbinical Conference at Brunswick. "The Rationale of Reform" is a similar statement addressed to a conference of Hungarian rabbis that met in August 1844. It is presented here as a concise summary of the rationale of early Reform.

Source: David Philipson, *The Reform Movement in Judaism*, ed. S. B. Freehov, rev. ed. (New York: Ktav Publishing House, 1967), p. 442, n. 112. Reprinted by permission of Ktav Publishing House.

13. OPEN REBUKE (1845)[1]

SALOMON JEHUDA LEIB RAPPOPORT

Under what circumstances did Luther seek to renew the foundations of his religion? [Luther initiated the Reformation] as a result of his dispute with the Christian hierarchy over several serious matters [regarding abuse of power]. But what have the rabbis, the religious leaders in Israel done at present? What harm have they done and to whom have they sought to do evil? Are there still to be found in their houses ram's horns [to pronounce excommunication] or whips [to flog transgressors]? Were they even to have such authority would they desire to make use of it? What has led [the Reformers] to rise up suddenly against congregation and community? Nothing but malice. They are instigating strife and contention in Israel and stirring up immense hatred and animosity, of the kind we have seen with the growth of sects in the Second Temple period and later in the rift with the Karaites[2] and the followers of Shabbetai Zevi.[3]

...He who says that some small benefit will nonetheless sprout from the actions of these men of destruction is wrong; even were there to be some benefit it would be nothing compared to the great damage [caused by their reforms]. But in truth there is not the smallest trace of benefit. Were there some matter among our customs or laws that stood in need of reform or renewal, it would be reformed or renewed with [the passing of] time. Should the process of Reform proceed gradually and its consummation be delayed, we could not accelerate the process by force. [In the meantime] that which remains [unchanged] will continue to be firmly established. This is part of the ways of the wondrous Providence governing the people of God, and there are many passages in the Talmud attesting to this.... [Mere] mortals, however, even were they to number a hundred rabbis and a thousand philosophers, cannot alter that which has become widespread throughout Israel, even if

the matter in question were of little value. No one will heed these reforms [elsewhere] in the Jewish Diaspora, for one quarter or even one half of the Jews in Germany does not constitute the entire [Jewish] world. The obstinate rabbis [who support Reform] are not even as one against a hundred when compared to the rabbis throughout the world who are loyal to the tradition.... Neither will they succeed in reforming themselves, for they have abandoned the Torah and discarded [its] laws long before they gathered together for selfish reasons in their conference [in Frankfurt]. And if they pretend that they are acting for the sake of their descendants, they are either committing an error or are deceitful. We have no doubt that their descendants will prefer to embrace the religions of the gentiles rather than to remain members of an inferior, emasculated religion which contains no trace of feeling or spirit—of a religion which can neither inspire nor direct them heavenwards.... Moreover, it is not in the power of such an empty and impoverished religion to resist the worldly pleasures that will surely entice their descendants. The women of the gentiles will help them leave the Valley of Tears [i.e., the exile] and to mingle with the merry and prosperous gentiles. [Moreover,] the rulers and the gentiles will not be tempted to allow them political liberty in their countries simply because they have abandoned the religious customs and beliefs of their ancestors. The intention and aim of the gentiles, and of the missionary societies that have been established in Rome, Britain and Prussia to convert us,[4] is not to reform our religion but to have us embrace their religion. As long as we do not do so, we are contemptible in their eyes, and perhaps the more despicable are those among us who put on wise airs and stand in our midst, "neither Jewish nor Aramean."[5]...The hostility and the vengefulness [showered upon us] by the gentiles during

---

Source: Tokhahat megulah (Frankfurt am Main, 1845), pp. 1–4, 6, 8, 12, 21, 26–28. Trans. by S. Weinstein.

the Middle Ages was not really due to our observance of the Sabbath and the festivals, or to our recitation of lamentations on the Ninth of Av.[6] Rather, it was due to their burning resentment of us for remaining steadfast to our beliefs, refusing to follow their ways, against which we had been cautioned by the words of our living God. For this reason, hatred has not yet disappeared from the [hearts of the] resentful among them. They are merely too embarrassed to act against us now, as they did in the days of darkness and obscurity....After the anxieties and fears aroused by the oppressive and destructive wrath have passed, and after we have withstood this wrath through all the evil times without relinquishing our faith, are we now suddenly to abandon this faith for the sake of imaginary honor and fabricated pleasures?

Are we to flatter the gentiles, thinking that we can thereby move closer and closer to them until, heaven forbid, there will be no difference between us, when [in reality] they are as distant from us now as they have always been? Woe to such a disgrace!...

To be sure, we have heard more than once the claim made in our generation that the ancient sages, the guardians of the tradition, permitted themselves on several occasions to make some innovations and changes in the halakhah with regard to what was written or accepted as tradition, such as the *prosbul*[7] enacted by Hillel....Let us briefly examine this claim:

...[In the time of the *geonim*[8]] there was one law and one Torah for the entire community, from Egypt to Persia, from one end of the world to the other. The judgments regarding God's Word contained in the Talmud as well as in the words of the *geonim* were thus treated with esteem and respect, for their teachings and rulings were received and propagated through all the borders of Israel and their words were accepted without dispute. It is not surprising therefore that with the passing of time the presidents [of the rabbinic courts] and the heads of the academies [yeshivah] allowed themselves on occasion to enact some religious reform when they perceived that this was necessary for the strengthening and the preservation of the Torah....But even in such cases they did not allow themselves to make even the smallest correction of any part of the Written or Oral Law. They introduced changes only in matters between man and his fellow,...or in matters between man and his Maker relating to negative proscriptions, so that no commandment would be transgressed....

These changes were possible only because there was one great and well-established rabbinic court, to which all the courts in the remaining countries were subordinate, accepting all of its statutes, regulations and teachings. From the time that such a court no longer existed, that is, since the end of the rule of the *geonim* and their *yeshivah*, the nation has ceased to have leaders.[9] The teachers have multiplied and departed to their countries and cities in Asia Minor, Egypt and Cyrene, in the Greek Isles and Italy, in Spain, France and Germany. With the multiplication of communities, each appointed its own teachers and rabbis, and not one of them seeks to raise himself above the others saying, I and my court will rule and from us will come forth Torah. From that time on not one of them dared to alter the teachings and customs of our rabbis of blessed memory—the *tanaim*[10] and the *amoraim*[11] as well as the *geonim*. They did not enact any restrictions or preventive measures, for they could not prohibit for the entire nation what had been explicitly permitted by our rabbis of blessed memory and so much the more did they refrain from permitting even for one state or community that which had been explicitly prohibited. Where [in our day] is the rabbinic court that can say it is greater in wisdom and in the number of people obeying its promulgations than the great court that existed in the times of the Talmud and the *geonim*, a court which was heeded by all the people?...Moreover, it is inconceivable that [the rabbis of the great court] would have made any changes that would divide Israel into factions. Otherwise, that which was held to be prohibited in one place would be held to be permitted in another place and *vice versa*. Jews would not be able to eat the bread and meat of other Jews, for what was fit for some would be an abomination for others. That which was called a house of prayer in one place would not be considered so by those who came from another place, for many would refuse [to acknowledge] alterations in the order and text of the prayers made in opposition to the regulations and customs of the men of the Great Assembly. Differences would also arise among the men of the Great Assembly. Differences would also arise in the laws of marriage and divorce, and families would be separated one from another, so that the nation of Jeshurun[12] would cease to be whole and united as it was in the past.

...If you will say that you no longer wish to follow in the path of the Talmud but rather to free yourselves from its yoke, because this is the only way you can make any reforms in keeping with your views, and if you claim to be able to strengthen the Jewish religion, as you call it, by means of the written Torah alone, then I shall ask you, what you have accomplished by this?... We shall turn our attention not only to the long existence [of the Talmud] but also to the mighty and wondrous divine power that is visible in the Torah and in those who have sustained and transmitted the tradition from generation to generation. Know that it is this power which has carried us on the broad wings of time [through good periods and bad].... How, I ask you, could we have continued to be a nation until the present, and how could we have been able to walk such a great distance along the path of history without losing our unity or having our provisions run out, if we did not have the support to sustain us on the path and to breathe a pure and refreshing spirit into the weary? This support comes from the Sabbaths and holy festivals, the *zitzit*[13] and the phylacteries, the house of prayer and the houses of religious study and together with all these the hope and solace of a better future. And so they have preserved us, guarding us from the danger that we might become too lazy to proceed forward, preferring instead to lie with our mouths open, becoming drunk upon the wine of the time and its pleasures and upon the delicacies of the land and its people. The guardians [of our unity] have isolated us and placed restrictions on all matters of food and marriage, militating against our assimilation among the peoples of the world.... All this you wish suddenly to annul and cast aside, and [yet you] still imagine that the name of Jeshurun will endure? These [customs and laws] that have sustained and guarded us have been tried out and have passed the test of time immemorial. Do you think that you can proceed without them and try a new course, without knowing what results it will bring?...

What has brought you to deny Israel the comfort of the hope for a future redemption? This is due merely to the cry of few reformers who, like a willing slave,[14] say "I love my master, I will not go free." The negation of the hope for redemption has, in turn, led you to seek to change the texts of the blessings, a matter which, in any event, is not within your authority. [Besides] such a step can be of no benefit with regard either to our temporal welfare or to the strengthening of the spirit of Israel. Those among the gentiles who have considered the sons of Jacob to be loyal servants and lovers of their present homeland have done so knowing of [the Jews'] yearning for the holy land of their forefathers. They never rejected, nor will they ever reject, the Jews for seeking comfort in their prayers and pouring out their hearts over past troubles and future good fortune. In contrast, those who have hated Israel in the past will not change their attitudes to the Jews now and love or respect them because they have made themselves desperate and forlorn, without any hope for the future....

Consider also the claim of the reformers that the Jewish nation or Judaism is sick and requires new counsel to make it healthy and to breathe into its midst a new spirit that will cure and sustain it. Let us assume that there is an element of truth in this claim. Even so, the remedy that some of you wish to offer far exceeds the disease. We may compare this matter to a man who received written instructions from distinguished and experienced doctors concerning how he is to behave regarding his diet, bodily activity and repose, bathing and all other similar matters. This man repeatedly ignored the directions of the doctors, eating that which they had warned him not to eat, and in general doing the opposite of what they had suggested. As a result his body grew weaker and weaker and he lost more and more weight becoming so sick that he had to be confined to bed. [Nevertheless] he did not change his mind and continued to do that which he had been cautioned against doing. In his sickness he thought that it was simply his first doctors who had caused him all this trouble by always deterring him from that which he craved, [for] although he violated their instructions he did so in fear and sorrow. Therefore he sought new doctors, and his first demand from them was to give him the opposite advice of all that the first doctors had prescribed, namely to make permissible every food and activity that formerly had been forbidden, so that he longer needed to be grieved in all his actions. The new doctors listened to this fool, flattering him and allowing him everything. As a result they nearly brought him to the gates of death. This is the situation at present among a small number of our brethren. They shout, Judaism is weak and sick. What is the sickness and what caused it? It is due to the fact that many have transgressed the advice of the ancient doctors, the counsellors of the nation; [consequently] the youth have no religion for they no longer know the Torah.... You flatter the side and wish to permit that which the distinguished doctors have cautioned against. Instead of strengthening and preserving our religion, as you seek to do, you will cause it to grow weaker and weaker.

…In my humble opinion, this should be our answer [to the reformers]: Our brethren, children of Abraham, Isaac and Jacob, you are demanding from us things that we cannot give you.…We teachers have been charged to instruct the people according to all that which has been written and transmitted to us for thousands of years. If you have made for yourself a new way either in thought or action we [nevertheless] will not separate you from our midst as long as you do not cease to consider yourselves as one of us and do not cleave to others. In our opinion, if your actions and thoughts will be in accordance with what you say, you will transgress some of the commandments of the Torah. But we will not on this account cease to consider you as being part of our nation.…We are all the children of one father; we share one Torah and even if you do not observe it in a proper and fitting fashion we cannot, nor do we wish to, compel you to accept our view. There is no domination in religion and no compulsion in faith. But from our side, neither can we, nor do we wish to, break down long-lasting barriers and permit you [to do] anything that has been prohibited by our ancient sages or free you from any principle of faith regarding either the past or the future.…

[When it becomes time to determine who is responsible for the decline in observance of the customs of our fathers and for the destructive split among our people] all the rhetorical language and visionary dreams which you repeatedly employ, words of untruth, such as "a step forward," "a new spirit in dry bones," and "a fresh wind over still waters," will be of no avail. The coming generation will know how to make a judgment that is exactly the opposite. The people of Israel have always followed the Oral Law, which gave, and will [continue to] give their religion a new and increasingly life-preserving spirit. The wearing of *zitzit* and the laying of phylacteries every day, [the observance of the Sabbath and sacred festivals, especially the Day of Atonement, as they have been traditionally celebrated by the God-fearing in Jeshurun, [the devotion to] the Torah and prayer and the sanctification of the soul every day, the abstinence from the food and all the lusts of the gentiles, the hope for future redemption—these are

what have renewed, and will always renew, at every time and on every occasion, the spirit of life within our nation. These have been the life of the people and the source of its long life, in former times and forever more. The small sect of reformers will remain with their abbreviated Sabbaths and festivals. Their labor and endeavors on the Sabbath and festivals will be no different from what it is on weekdays. They shall exist without the hope for good times, without the Torah and without feeling. Their life will become like a flat plain and desolate wilderness, lacking flowers and all traces of beauty that could arouse the spirit. Their worship, with the ensemble of singers, will quickly become habitual and insipid, and the house of prayer will appear to the few who visit it as a theatrical stage. Every Sabbath the youth will sing without inner feeling what has already been written down for them. The preacher will demonstrate his proficiency in the movement of his eyes and the twisting of his lips. His eyes will be directed upward and his heart downward; he will set his mouth heavenward and his tongue will crawl along the earth. The few who hear the singers and the preacher will laugh to themselves, and from the house of prayer they will quickly proceed to [pursue] the cravings of their heart or to resume their labors.…[This folly will continue] until those Israelites who within their souls feel attached to heaven shall abhor them.…Not even all of your current expertise in language will enable you to avoid the names that will be given you by future generations, who will recognize you to be sinners, tempters, men who fan the flame of strife in Israel, men who love material things and hate matters of the spirit.

NOTES

1. Salomon Jehuda Leib Rappoport (1790–1867), also known by his acronym *Shir*. In 1840 he was appointed chief rabbi of Prague. Notwithstanding his commitment to halakhah, he had a broad interest in secular learning. Indeed, he was a pioneer in the critical, historical approach to the study of Judaism known as *Wissenschaft des Judentums* (see chapter 5). In this endeavor he cooperated with leading exponents of Reform, for example, Leopold Zunz, Abraham Geiger, and Zecharias Frankel.

The title is taken from Prov. 27:5: "Better open rebuke than hidden love." This pamphlet was written in response to the Frankfurt rabbinical conference of 1845.

2. A still extant sect that first appeared in the eighth century C.E. Rejecting the Oral Law and the Talmudic-rabbinical tradition, the Karaites rely on the Bible as the sole source of creed and law, claiming that they thus represent the pristine Mosaic faith.

3. Shabbetai Zevi (1626–1676), central figure in the messianic movement that swept through the Jewish world of the period: In spite of certain excesses of behavior, Shabbetai Zevi, couching his claims in the symbolism of the Kabbalah, appealed to the people's deeply rooted longings for redemption. Although his apostasy to Islam in 1666 created a profound crisis, the movement continued to have adherents until well into the eighteenth century.

4. In the early nineteenth century missionary efforts directed toward the Jews were intensified; it was assumed that the increasing acculturation of the Jews rendered them susceptible to conversion. Rappoport is apparently referring to the following organizations: House of Catechumens in Rome, London Society for Promoting Christianity among the Jews, and the Berlin Society for Promoting Christianity among the Jews.

5. Palestinian Talmud, tractate *Sheviit*, ch. 4, 35b. The passage actually reads: "If you are a Jew be a Jew, if you are an Aramean [i.e., a Gentile] be an Aramean."

6. Ninth of Av, day of mourning and fasting commemorating the destruction of the First and Second Temples, both on approximately this date. It is also the traditional anniversary of the fall of Betar in 135 C.E., the expulsion from Spain in 1492 and other national calamities.

7. A legal formula whereby a creditor could still claim his debts after the Sabbatical Year despite the biblical injunction against doing so. Rabbi Hillel (first century B.C.E.) instituted the *prosbul* when he saw that people refrained from giving loans to one another before the Sabbatical Year.

8. *Geonim*, formal title of the heads of the Talmudical academies of Sura and Pumbedita in Babylonia. These academies were recognized by the Jews as the highest authority of instruction from the end of the sixth century C.E. to the middle of the eleventh. In the tenth and eleventh centuries the title was also used by the heads of academies in Palestine.

9. The Great Sanhedrin retained its position as the central ecclesiastical authority in Jewry until the middle of the third century C.E., when the Talmudical academies of Babylonia became the center of halakhic scholarship. For the greater part of the period between the sixth and eleventh centuries, the preeminence of the Babylonian academies, with authority alternating between the *geonim* of Sura and of Pumbedita, was acknowledged by Jewry throughout the world.

10. *Tanaim*, the Aramaic word for "teachers." Designation for the sages from the period of Hillel to the compilation of the Mishnah, i.e., from the first and second centuries C.E.

11. *Amoraim*, the Aramaic word for "spokesman." Originally used for the "interpreters" who communicated audibly to the assembled pupils, the term was used genetically from the post-Mishnaic period to the compilation of the Talmud (i.e., from the second to fifth centuries C.E.) to designate the rabbis.

12. Jeshurun, symbolic name for Israel (Deut. 13:25; 33:5, 26).

13. *Zitzit*, the Hebrew word for "fringes." According to the biblical injunction fringes are to be appended to each of the four corners of a garment (see Deut. 22:12). To fulfill this commandment the observant Jew wears a small four-cornered prayer shawl beneath his outer clothing.

14. Literally a "pierced slave." According to biblical law Hebrew slaves are to be freed after six years of service. If the slave refuses to go free and wishes to stay in his master's service, then the master pierces his ear with an awl and in this way the slave is bonded to him forever (see Exod. 21:5–6 and Deut. 15:16–17). The master here, of course, exemplifies temporal life and its pleasures.

14. ON CHANGES IN JUDAISM (1845)[1]

ZECHARIAS FRANKEL

Maintaining the integrity of Judaism simultaneously with progress, this is the essential problem of the present. Can we deny the difficulty of a satisfactory solution? Where is the point where the two apparent contraries can meet? What ought to be our point of departure in the attempt to reconcile essential Judaism and progress and what type of opposition may we expect to encounter? How can we assure rest for the soul so that it shall not be torn apart or be numbed by severe doubts while searching for the warm ray of faith, and yet allot to reason its right, and enable it to lend strength and lucidity to the religious feeling which springs from the emotions? The opposing elements which so seldom are in balance must be united and this is our task....

Judaism is a religion which has a direct influence on life's activity. It is a religion of action, demanding the performance of precepts which either directly aim at ennobling man or, by reminding man of the divine, strengthen his feelings of dependence on God. And because of this trait neither pure abstract contemplation nor dark mysticism could ever strike root in Judaism. This, in turn, guaranteed that the lofty religious ideas were maintained in their purity, with the result that even today the divine light shines in Judaism.

By emphasizing religious activity, Judaism is completely tied to life and becomes the property of every individual Jew. A religion of pure ideas belongs primarily to the theologians; the masses who are not adapted to such conceptions concern themselves little with the particulars of such religions because they have little relationship to life. On the other hand, a religion of action is always present, demanding practice in activity and an expression of will, and its demands are reflected in the manifold life of the individual, with the result that the faith becomes the common property of every follower.

Thus we have reached the starting point for the consideration of the current parties in Judaism. The viewpoint of the Orthodox party is clear. It has grown up in pious activity; to it the performance of precepts is inseparable from faith, for to it, the two are closely and inwardly connected. Were it to tear itself away from observance and give up the precepts, then it would find itself estranged from its own self and feel as though plunged into an abyss. Given this viewpoint, the direction and emphasis of the Orthodox party is clear. Where else, save in the combination of faith and meticulous observance of the precepts, can it find that complete satisfaction which it has enjoyed in the heritage of the fathers? When it will reject that which it has so long kept holy and inviolable? No—that is unthinkable.

Against this party there has arisen of late another one [Reform] which finds its aim in the opposite direction. This party sees salvation in overcoming the past, in carrying progress to the limit, in rejecting religious forms and returning merely to the simple original idea. In fact, we can hardly call it a party in Judaism, though its adherents still bear the name Jew, and are considered as such in social and political life, and do not belong to another faith. They do not, however, belong wholly to Judaism, for by limiting Judaism to some principles of faith, they place themselves partly outside the limits of Judaism.

We will now turn to a third party which has arisen from, the first party, and not only stands within the bound of Judaism, but is also filled with real zeal for its preservation and endeavors to hand it over to the descendants and make it the common good of all times.

Source: "Die Symptome der Zeit," *Zeitschrift fuer juedische religioese Interessen* 2 (1845), pp. 1–21. Mordecai Waxman, ed. and trans., *Tradition and Change: The Development of Conservative Judaism* (New York: Burning Bush Press, 1958), pp. 44, 46–50. Reprinted by permission of the Rabbinical Assembly of America.

This party bases itself upon rational faith and recognizes that the task of Judaism is religious action, but it demands that this action shall not be empty of spirit and that it shall not become merely mechanical, expressing itself mainly in the form. It has also reached the view that religious activity itself must be brought up to a higher level through giving weight to the many meanings with which it should be endowed. Furthermore, it holds that we must omit certain unimportant actions which are not inherently connected either with the high ideas or with the religious forms delineated by the revealed laws. We must, it feels, take into consideration the opposition between faith and conditions of the time. True faith, due to its divine nature, is above time, and just as the nobler part of man is not subjected to time, so does faith rise above all time, and the word which issued from the mouth of God is rooted in eternity. But time has a force and might which must be taken account of. There is then created a dualism in which faith and time face each other, and man chooses either to live beyond time or to be subjected to it. It is in this situation that the Jew finds himself today; he cannot escape the influence of the conditions of the time and yet when the demands of faith bring him to opposition with the spirit of the time, it is hoped that he will heed its call—find the power to resist the blandishments of the times. This third party, then, declares that Judaism must be saved for all time. It affirms both the divine value and historical basis of Judaism and, therefore, believes that by introducing some changes it may achieve some agreement with the concepts and conditions of the time.

In order to have a conception of what changes should and can be introduced, we must ask ourselves the question—does Judaism allow any changes in any of its religious forms? Does it consider all of them immutable, or can they be altered? Without entering into the citation of authorities pro and con, we may point out that Judaism does indeed allow changes. The early teachers, by interpretation, changed the literal meaning of the Scriptures; later scholars that of the Mishnah, and the post-Talmudic scholars that of the Talmud. All these interpretations were not intended as speculation. They addressed themselves to life precepts. Thanks to such studies, Judaism achieved stabilization and avoided estrangement from the conditions of the time in various periods....[The rabbis] established a rule which was

intended as a guardian and protector against undue changes. It reads as follows: That which was adopted by the entire community of Israel and was accepted by the people and became a part of its life, cannot be changed by any authority.[2]

In this fundamental statement there lies a living truth. Through it there speaks a profound view of Judaism which can serve for all times as a formula for needed changes and can be employed both against destructive reform and against stagnation.

This fundamental statement helps to make clear to us what changes in Judaism are justified and how they can be realized. True, Judaism demands religious activity, but the people is not altogether mere clay to be molded by the will of theologians and scholars. In religious activities, as in those of ordinary life, it decides for itself. This right was conceded by Judaism to the people. At such times as an earlier religious ordinance was not accepted by the entire community of Israel, it was given up. Consequently, when a new ordinance was about to be enacted it was necessary to see whether it would find acceptance by the people. When the people allows certain practices to fall into disuse, then the practices cease to exist. There is in such cases no danger for faith. A people used to activity will not hurt itself and will not destroy its practices. Its own sense of religiosity warns against it. Only those practices from which it is entirely estranged and which yield it no satisfaction will be abandoned and will thus die of themselves. On the whole there is always a great fund of faith and religious activity to afford security against negation and destruction.

We have, then, reached a decisive point in regard to moderate changes, namely, that they must come from the people and that the will of the entire community must decide. Still, this rule alone may accomplish little. The whole community is a heavy unharmonious body and its will is difficult to recognize. It comes to expression only after many years. We must find a way to carry on such changes in the proper manner, and this can be done by the help of the scholars.[3] Judaism has no priests as representatives of faith nor does it require special spiritual sanctimoniousness in its spokesmen. The power to represent it is not the share of any one family, nor does it pass from father to son. Knowledge and mastery of the law supply the sanctity, and these can be attained by everybody. In Jewish life, spiritual and intellectual ability ultimately took the place of the former priesthood which, even in early times, was limited in its function primarily to the sacrificial cult. Even in early days, Judaism recognized the will of the people as a great force and because of this recognition a great religious activity came into being. But this activity, in turn was translated into a living force by the teachers of the people through the use of original ordinances and through interpretation of the Scriptures. At times these actions of the sages lightened the amount of observance; at times they increased it. That the results of the studies and research of the teachers found acceptance among the people proves, on the one hand, that the teachers knew the character of their time, and, on the other hand, that the people had confidence in them and that they considered them true representatives of their faith.

Should Jewish theologians and scholars of our time succeed in acquiring such a confidence, then they will attain influence with the introduction of whatever changes may be necessary. The will of the community of Israel will then find its representatives and knowledge will be its proper exercise.

The scholars thus have an important duty in order to make their work effective. It is to guard the sense of piety of the people and to raise their spirit to the height of the great ideas. For this they need the confidence of the people. Opposition to the views of the people, such as some reformers display, is unholy and fruitless. The teacher thereby loses the power to make the essence of faith effective, for in place of that confidence which is the basis in correct relations between teacher and community there comes mistrust and an unwillingness to follow. The truths of faith must be brought nearer to the people so that they may learn to understand the divine content within them and thus come to understand the spiritual nature and inner worth of the forms which embody these truths. Once the people are saturated with an awareness of the essential truths and the forms which embody them, a firm ground will have been established for adhering to Jewish practices. And if the people then cease to practice some unimportant customs and forms of observances it will not be a matter of great concern. And it will not as recent changes have, lead some Jews into shock and hopelessness. They will no longer see all such changes as leading to the disappearance of our faith and language, [and] as their pusillanimity leads them to believe, the end of the existence of Judaism.

NOTES

1. Zecharias Frankel (1801–1875). He attended the Reform Rabbinical Conference at Frankfurt with grave doubts regarding his colleagues' commitment to the place of Hebrew in the liturgy. On the third day of the deliberations he submitted a letter of resignation from the conference in which he stated: "The preservation of Judaism is the innermost core of my life and the aim of all my endeavors. I am ready to make any sacrifice for this cause and shall always resist any tendency to the contrary." To his profound distress the attitude of the conference to Hebrew was indicative of such a tendency. Subsequently, he endeavored without success, to call a conference of all rabbis committed both to the adjustment of Judaism to the spirit of the times and to the preservation of "positive historical Judaism." In his attempt to develop a middle position—articulated in the essay presented here—Frankel was opposed from both Reform and Orthodox quarters. The pain at this failure was assuaged when in 1854 he was named the director of the Juedisch-Theologisches Seminar at Breslau; a position that Geiger, who was instrumental in establishing the institution, desired. Under Frankel's directorship the seminar became the prototype of the modern rabbinical seminary. The seminary's curriculum aimed to teach a "positive historical Judaism," which in this context meant a positive attitude to the practical precepts of Judaism and a critical "historical" inquiry into the Jewish past, including biblical criticism.
2. Talmud, tractate *Avodah zarah* 36a.
3. Here Frankel means the scholar of the modern mode to be developed at the Breslau seminary.

15. RELIGION ALLIED TO PROGRESS (1854)[1]

SAMSON RAPHAEL HIRSCH

"Religion allied to progress": [the leaders of Reform have] with undaunted courage embroidered [this slogan] in scintillating colours on to the banner of our present-day religious struggles, that the educated "progressive" sons and daughters of the new age might rally to this new flag of the prophet and advance with it unhindered. How leaderless was this new congregation of prophets before this new messenger with this new message of salvation appeared among them! Since the beginning of the century the ancient religion had been to them—ancient; it no longer fitted into the society of the sons and daughters of the new age with their frock coats and evening dresses. In club and fraternity, at the ball and supper party, at concerts and in salons—everywhere the old Judaism was in the way and seemed so completely out of place. And even in the counting-house and in the office, in the courtroom and at the easel, on board ship and in the train—throughout the steam-driven lightning activity of the new age the old Judaism acted as a brake on the hurrying march of progress. Above all it seemed to be the only obstacle in the race for emancipation. No wonder then that without hesitation they shook off the old obstructive religion and hurried into the arms of "progress." And in the political market-place where emancipation was to be purchased, the modern sons of Judah could be seen in every corner offering to exchange the old Judaism for something else, since in any case it had lost all its value for their own use.

For many a decade modern Jewry thus soared aloft like dust on the wings of a butterfly and tasted freedom in the unwonted airy heights; and yet they felt a pain in their hearts where the absence of religion had left a void, and at the end they were ashamed while enjoying the brilliance of modern life to be walking the earth without religion; they felt restless and miserable.

But behold! The prophet of the new message came into their midst with the cry of "religion allied to progress"; he filled the blank, pacified their conscience and wiped out their shame. With this magic word he turned irreligion into Godliness, apostasy into priesthood, sin into merit, frivolity into virtue, weakness into strength, thoughtlessness into profundity. By this one magic phrase he distilled the ancient world-ranging spirit of the Torah into a single aromatic drop of perfume so fragrant that in the most elegant party dress they could carry it round with them in their waistcoat pockets without being ashamed. By means of it, he carved out of the ponderous old rock-hewn Tablets of the Law ornamental figures so tiny that people gladly found room for them on smart dressing tables, in drawing-rooms and ballrooms. By means of this one magic phrase he so skilfully loosened the rigid bonds of the old law with its 613 locks and chains[2] that the Divine Word which until then had inflexibly prohibited many a desire and demanded many a sacrifice, henceforth became the heavenly manna which merely reflected everybody's own desires, echoed their own thoughts, sanctified their own aspirations and said to each one: "Be what you are, enjoy what you fancy, aspire to what you will, whatever you may be you are always religious, whatever you may do—all is religion; continue to progress, for the more you progress the further you move from the ancient way, and the more you cast off old Jewish customs the more religious and acceptable to God will you be...."

Source: Samson Raphael Hirsch, "Die Religion im Bunde mit dem Fortschritt" (1854). *Judaism Eternal: Selected* Essays *from the Writings of Rabbi Samson Raphael Hirsch,* ed. and trans. I. Grunfeld (London: Soncino Press, 1956), vol. 2, pp. 224–38. Copyright 1956 by the Soncino Press. Reprinted by permission.

All this would of itself worry us who are of different mind very little. We allow everyone his own peace and bliss and also his fame, if only he would be fair enough to leave us—not indeed our "fame" (to which we lay no claim), nor indeed our "bliss" (which cannot be impaired by human opinion)—but at least our peace and quiet.

But the eulogist of "religion allied to progress" and its prophet has found it necessary to enhance the brightness of his cause by painting its opposite in the blackest colours. He therefore describes us, [we the so-called proponents of Orthodoxy] who do not believe in the mission of the new prophet, as the "black opponents of progress and civilisation."...

May one of these "fools and obscurantists" be permitted in the face of such provocation, a few carefully considered and objective remarks, for the purpose of stating fully and placing in their true light the facts which certain people are so glad to call "religious confusions" (because they fear lest they might be cleared up) and so take the first step towards resolving them?...

[First] a point of fact, it was not "Orthodox" Jews who introduced the word "orthodoxy" into Jewish discussion. It was the modern "progressive" Jews who first applied this name to "old," "backward" Jews as a derogatory term. This name was at first resented by "old" Jews. And rightly so. "Orthodox" Judaism does not know any varieties of Judaism. It conceives Judaism as one and indivisible. It does not know a Mosaic, prophetic and rabbinic Judaism, nor Orthodox and Liberal Judaism. It only knows Judaism and non-Judaism. It does not know Orthodox and liberal Jews. It does indeed know conscientious and indifferent Jews, good Jews, bad Jews or baptised Jews; all, nevertheless, Jews with a mission which they cannot cast off. They are only distinguished accordingly as they fulfill or reject their mission....

Now what about the principle, the much-vaunted, world-redeeming principle of "religion allied to progress"? If it is to be a principle—something more than an empty phrase meant for show—it must have a definable content and we must be permitted to try to clarify it. In the expression "religion allied to progress," progress is evidently intended to qualify religion. Indeed, this is the very essence of the "idea," not religion by itself, but religion only to the extent and in so far as it can co-exist with progress, in so far as one does not have to sacrifice progress to religion.

The claim of religion is therefore not absolute but is valid only by permission of "progress." What, then, is this higher authority to which religion is therefore not absolute but is valid only by permission of "progress"? What, then, is this higher authority to which religion has to appeal in order to gain admission? What is this "progress"? Evidently not progress in the sphere of religion, for then the expression would amount to "religion allied to itself" which is nonsense. It means, then, progress in every sphere other than religion. Speaking frankly, therefore, it means: religion as long as it does not hinder progress, religion as long as it is not onerous or inconvenient....

The subordination of religion to any other factor means the denial of religion: for if the Torah is to you the Law of God how dare you place another law above it and go along with God and His Law only as long as you thereby "progress" in other respects at the same time? You must admit it: it is only because "religion" does not mean to you the word of God, because in your heart you deny Divine Revelation, because you believe not in Revelation given *to* man but in Revelation *from* man, that you can give man the right to lay down conditions to religion.

"Religion allied to progress"—do you know, dear reader, what that means? Virtue allied to sensual enjoyment, rectitude allied to advancement, uprightness allied to success. It means a religion and a morality which can be preached also in the haunts of vice and iniquity. It means sacrificing religion and morality to every man's momentary whim. It allows every man to fix his own goal and progress in any direction he pleases and to accept from religion only that part which does not hinder his "progress" or even assist it. It is the cardinal sin which Moses of old described as "a casual walking with God."[3]

Civilisation and culture—we all treasure those glorious and inalienable possessions of mankind. We all desire that the good and the true, all that is attainable by human thought and human willpower, should be the common heritage of all men. But to make religion—which is the mother and father of all civilisation and culture—dependent upon the progress of this same civilisation and culture would mean throwing it into the melting-pot of civilisation; it would mean turning the root into the blossom; it would mean crowning the human edifice with that which should be its foundation and cornerstone....

Now what is it that *we* want? Are the only alternatives either to abandon religion or to renounce all progress with all the glorious and noble gifts which civilisation and education offer mankind? Is the Jewish religion really of such a nature that its faithful adherents must be the enemies of civilisation and progress?...We declare before heaven and earth that if our religion demanded that we should renounce what is called civilisation and progress we would obey unquestioningly, because our religion is for us truly religion, the word of God before which every other consideration has to give way. We declare, equally, that we would prefer to be branded as fools and do without all the honour and glory that civilisation and progress might confer on us rather than be guilty of the conceited mock-wisdom which the spokesman of a religion allied to progress here displays.

For behold whither a religion allied to progress leads! Behold how void it is of all piety and humanity and into what blunders the conceited, Torah-criticising spirit leads. Here you have a protagonist of this religion of progress. See how he dances on the graves of your forefathers, how he drags out their corpses from their graves, laughs in their faces and exclaims to you: "Your fathers were crude and uncivilised; they deserved the contempt in which they were held. Follow me, so that you may become civilised and deserve respect!"

Such is the craziness which grows on the tree of knowledge of this "religion allied to progress"!

If our choice were only between such craziness and simple ignorance, again we say we would remain ignorant all our life-long rather than be thus godlessly educated even for one moment.

There is, however, no such dilemma. Judaism never remained aloof from true civilisation and progress; in almost every era its adherents were fully abreast of contemporary learning and very often excelled their contemporaries. If in recent centuries German Jews remained more or less aloof from European civilisation the fault lay not in their religion but in the tyranny which confined them by force within the walls of their ghettoes and denied them intercourse with the outside world. And, thank goodness, even now our sons and daughters can compare favourably in cultural and moral worth with the children of those families who have forsaken the religion of their forefathers for the sake of imagined progress. They need not shun the light of publicity or the critical eye of their contemporaries. They have lost nothing

in culture or refinement, even though they do not smoke their cigars on the Sabbath, even though they do not seek the pleasures of the table in foods forbidden by God, even though they do not desecrate the Sabbath for the sake of profit and enjoyment.

Indeed, we are short-sighted enough to believe that the Jew who remains steadfast amidst the scoffing and the enticements of the easy-going world around him, who remains strong enough to sacrifice to God's will profit, inclination and the respect and applause of his fellows, displays far greater moral strength and thus a higher degree of real culture than the frivolous "modern Jew" whose principles melt away before the first contemptuous glance or at the slightest prospect of profit, and who is unfaithful to the word of God and the teachings of his fathers in order to satisfy the whim of the moment....

Our aims also include the conscientious promotion of education and culture, and we have clearly expressed this in the motto of our Congregation: An excellent thing is the study of the Torah combined with the ways of the world [*Yafeh Talmud torah im derekh erez*][4]—thereby building on the same foundations as those which were laid by our sages of old—[then] what is it that separates us from the adherents of "religion allied to progress"?

A mere trifle! They aim at religion allied to progress—and we have seen that this principle negates the truth of what they call religion—while we aim at progress allied to religion. To them, progress is the absolute and religion is governed by it; to us, religion is the absolute. For them, religion is valid only to the extent that it does not interfere with progress; for us, progress is valid only to the extent that it does not interfere with religion. That is all the difference. But this difference is abysmal.

Judaism as it has come down to us from our forefathers is for us the gift and the word of God, an untouchable sanctuary which must not be subjected to human judgment nor subordinated to human considerations. It is the ideal given by God to all the generations of the House of Jacob, never yet attained and to be striven for unto the distant future. It is the great edifice for which all Jews and Jewesses are born to live and die, at all times and in every situation. It is the great Divine revelation which should infuse all our sentiments, justify all our resolutions and give all our actions their strength and stability, foundation and direction.

Comparisons are futile. Judaism is not a religion, the synagogue is not a church, and the rabbi is not a priest. Judaism is not a mere adjunct to life: it comprises all of life. To be a Jew is not a mere part, it is the sum total of our task in life. To be a Jew in the synagogue and the kitchen, in the field and the warehouse, in the office and the pulpit, as father and mother, as servant and master, as man and as citizen, with one's thoughts, in word and in deed, in enjoyment and privation, with the needle and the graving-tool, with the pen and the chisel—that is what it means to be a Jew. An entire life supported by the Divine Idea and lived and brought to fulfilment according to the Divine Will.

It is foolish, therefore, to believe—or to pretend to believe—that it is the wording of a prayer, the notes of a synagogue tune, or the order of a special service, which form the abyss between us. It is not the so-called Divine Service which separates us. It is the theory—"the principle" as you call it—which throws Judaism into a corner for use only on Sabbaths and Festivals, and by removing from Jewish souls that have strayed from their Divine Destiny the consciousness of their guilt robs them also of their last hope of penitence.

The more, indeed, Judaism comprises the whole of man and extends its declared mission to the salvation of the whole of mankind,[5] the less it is possible to confine its outlook to the four cubits of a synagogue and the four walls of a study. The more the Jew is a Jew, the more universalist will his views and aspirations be, the less aloof will he be from anything that is noble and good, true and upright, in art or science, in culture or education; the more joyfully will he applaud whenever he sees truth and justice and peace and the ennoblement of man prevail and become dominant in human society: the more joyfully will he seize every opportunity to give proof of his mission as a Jew, the task of his Judaism, on new and untrodden ground; the more joyfully will he devote himself to all true progress in civilisation and culture—provided, that is, that he will not only not have to sacrifice his Judaism but will also be able to bring it to more perfect fulfilment. He will ever desire progress, but only in alliance with religion. He will not want to accomplish anything that he cannot accomplish as a Jew. Any step which takes him away from Judaism is not for him a step forward, is not progress. He exercises this self-control without a pang, for he does not wish to accomplish his own will on earth but labours in the service of God. He knows that wherever the Ark of his God does not march ahead of him he is not accompanied by the pillar of the fire of His light or the pillar of the cloud of His grace.

In truth, if only most Jews were truly Jews, most of the factors would disappear which today bar many an avenue of activity to them.

If only all Jews who travel or who are engaged in business observed their Jewish duties, the need would—as always—produce its own remedy. The Jew would everywhere find the food demanded by his religion; it would be but little sacrifice for him to refrain from business on the Sabbath; and even in the regulations laid down by state and public bodies enlightened governments would gladly pay respect to a display of conscientiousness which would in itself be a not inconsiderable contribution made by Jewish citizens to the society in which they live.

It is only through unfaithfulness of the majority that the loyalty of the minority becomes a duty demanding so much sacrifice, though the crown which it wins is all the more glorious for the thorns which our brethren strew in our path....

NOTES

1. Samson Raphael Hirsch (1808–1888). Hirsch was born in Hamburg where his family belonged to the traditionalist opponents of the Reform temple of that city. After completing his rabbinic studies he attended the University of Bonn where he befriended his future adversary, Abraham Geiger. From 1830 to 1841 he served as the chief rabbi of the principality of Oldenburg. During this period he published his two most famous works: *Nineteen Letters on Judaism* (1836) and *Horeb: Essays on Israel's Duties in the Diaspora* (1837). Addressed to the perplexed Jewry of his day, both these works seek to demonstrate the viability of traditional Judaism in the modern world. Hirsch did, however, recognize the need to revise certain "external" aspects of Judaism—viz., aesthetic forms of the public worship service—in order to facilitate the Jew's adjustment to the modern sensibility. On the other hand, he emphatically rejected Reform and any changes affecting the principles and content of halakhic Judaism. Hirsch's response to Reform may be summarized as agreeing to revision of the externals but allowing no reform of the principles of Judaism. He added to this formula an endorsement of secular education and patriotic affection to the country of one's citizenship. In 1851 he was called to serve as the rabbi of the traditional congregation of Frankfurt am Main, Adas Yeshurun—a position he

held for thirty-seven years. Under Hirsch's guidance this congregation and its allied educational institutions became the paradigm of his vision of a "Neo-Orthodox Judaism," or halakhic Judaism in harmony with the modern world.

This essay was prompted by the argument of Reform that the rabbinic tradition prevents Jews from finding their place in contemporary German society, not only because of the traditional Jew's distinctive dress and manner of prayer—which Hirsch agreed must be revised—but also because of the practical precepts of halakhah which were allegedly difficult to perform in a secular environment.

2. According to the Talmud (tractate *Makot* 23b), there are 613 divine *mizvot* or precepts in the Pentateuch. Popularly, obedience to the "613 *mizvot*" refers to adherence to the halakhah.

3. In his interpretation of Lev. 26:21ff.—"and if ye walk contrary unto Me…"—Hirsch substitutes "casually" for "contrary."

4. Mishnah, Ethics of the Fathers 2:2.

5. This mission, which Hirsch contends has become more urgent in modern times, is concisely stated in one of his previous works:

> Because men had eliminated God from life, nay, even from nature, and found the basis of life in possessions and its aim in enjoyment, deeming life the product of the multitude of human desires, just as they looked upon nature as the product of a multitude of gods, therefore it became necessary that a people be introduced into the ranks of the nations which, through its history and life, should declare God the only creative cause of existence, fulfillment of His will the only aim of life; and which should bear the revelation of His will, rejuvenated and renewed for its sake, unto all parts of the world as the motive and incentive of its coherence (*The Nineteen Letters on Judaism*, trans. S. Drachman [New York, 1899], seventh letter, pp. 66–67).

16. THE MANIFESTO OF ULTRA-ORTHODOXY (1865)[1]

THE RABBINICAL DECISION OF THE MICHALOWCE ASSEMBLY[2]

The Torah says, "I appoint you watchman for the House of Israel" (Ezekiel 3:17). "If I say to a wicked man, 'You shall die [for your iniquity],' and you do not warn him—you do not speak to warn the wicked man of his wicked course in order to save his life—he, the wicked man, shall die for iniquity, but I will require a reckoning for his blood from you" (Ezekiel 3:18).

"[With no one pursuing them,] they shall stumble over one another [as before the sword]" (Leviticus

---

Source: Pesaq Beit Din (Ungvár: Karl Jaeger, 1866). Translated and annotated by Dov Weiss. The rabbis who composed this rabbinic decree often cited biblical and rabbinical texts in a partial and fragmentary fashion, on the assumption that the readers would know the full text and its extensive meaning. The translator has provided in square brackets the omitted portions of the original text. Similarly, the sources for most of the citations are not given in the document. They are given by the translator in parentheses, as are occasional phrases added to enhance the conceptual clarity of the document.

26:37)—the rabbis expound this to mean "a man will stumble because of the sins of his brother" (Babylonian Talmud, Sanhedrin 27b).

"The Lord will bring this charge against the elders and officers of His peoples" (Isaiah 3:14)—the rabbis expound this to mean "elders who did not protest [the sinful actions of] the officers" (Babylonian Talmud, Shabbat 54b, 55a).

"And I will appoint them as your heads" (Deuteronomy 1:13) should be read as "and their sin shall be on your heads"[3]—the sins of Israel hang upon the heads of the judges (Sifre to Deuteronomy, Piska 13).

"Cursed be he who does not uphold [the terms of this teaching and observe them]" (Deuteronomy 27:26). As the Jerusalem Talmud explains, if one has learned to teach (the precepts of the Torah), and he is able to do so, but does not, such a person is deemed "cursed" (Jerusalem Talmud, Sotah 7:4).

And if this is how the Torah warns an individual person (who has committed) a personal transgression, which causes and brings about a breach and a destruction of the Torah in its totality—and one which has become known to the Jewish public—then one should not stay in the shadows and sit idly by. But rather anyone who has the fear of truth in his heart should gird his hips like a warrior "and gird his loins" (1 Kings 18:46), and say "whoever is for the Lord (and His Torah), come here. [And all Levites rallied to him] (Exodus 32:26)"—as the Midrash (claims)—those (Levites) who earnestly wanted to escort the children (of God) to God (Genesis Rabbah 71:4).[4] And who are they? Those who say, for the sake of loving God and acting for Him, "to his father and mother 'I consider them not,' his brothers he disregarded [and] ignored his children" (Deuteronomy 33:9).

To repair the breaches of Torah and to build a fence around its ruins—lest there will arise another transgressor—we find ourselves obligated in this matter.

Due to our great sins, we see that these are the times, that "new ones, who come but lately" (Deuteronomy 32:17), and "new ones with old ones" (Song of Songs 7:14), who "ruin the vineyards" (Song of Songs 2:15)—vineyards of God, "in time of tumultuous strife in Israel" (Judges 5:2),[5] [and] those who know their creator have breached and transgressed the law and intend to rebel against Him.[6]

And they built and are building altars to uproot and to destroy, to replace and to change the form and image of the synagogue building by making of a tower[7] (by changing the position) of the *bimah*,[8] by [modifying] the *mechitzah* (partition) between the women's and men's section,[9] by placing the wedding *chupah* [in the synagogue],[10] by donning the cantor with a robe, by a notoriously vacuous youth choir, by changing synagogue ritual and prayer melodies that have been practiced amongst the entire Jewish Diaspora since ancient times.

It undoubtedly appears that the intention of the evil inclination and its messengers, "a band of deadly messengers" (Psalms 78:49), is only to imitate, join and intermingle with other religious practices of the nations of the world, and to weaken and uproot, God forbid, the Jewish religion—as one can see from what happened in several places (in Central Europe[11]) some years ago. What they were and what they are now: How have they descended ten degrees lower!

"Defying His majestic glance" (Isaiah 3:8) and the warning of the Torah in regard to all of these things (formulated) with a few "do not dos" (that is, negative commandments): "You shall not copy their practices" (Leviticus 18:3) [or] "beware of being lured [into their ways]...! Do not inquire about their gods, saying "How did those nations worship their gods[?]" (Deuteronomy 12:30). For by [violating these injunctions] the existence of Torah, Heaven forbid, will be destroyed. "And afterwards he afflicted her more grievously" (Isaiah 8:23)—for they conducted themselves such that the name and language of Israel would no longer be remembered.

Woe to their eyes, the eyes of the enlightened, for they see how far this "malignant leprosy" (Leviticus 13:51) and "great fire" (Deuteronomy 5:21) have spread to several countries.

What [good is it] for us to mention (these countries[12]) by name? Our hearts [ache] for the victims who "before them the land was like the Garden of Eden, after them, a desolate waste" (Joel 2:3), (they) who burned and uprooted the foundations of Torah and awe [of God]. And even in Hungary in several places, [their destructive ways] have left their mark. Who knows to what extent will [the destruction] reach?

And there is nothing left for us but to arouse and excite the hearts of the masses towards God and the Words of Torah taught in the sermons—and [yet] even these are given over to the hand of the evil inclination to be dressed in a gentile dress and to be transformed from being the defender into the prosecutor [of Israel], Heaven forbid![13]

"[Such are the ways of an adulteress]. She eats, wipes her mouth, and says, I have done no wrong" (Proverbs 30:20) and in any case many from the multitude of righteous people are ensnared in their control and say "to the guilty, you are innocent" (Proverbs 24:24).

The Torah warns [us] against [these assimilatory ways], and commands us to become there (in the lands of the gentiles) "a great and populous nation" (Deuteronomy 26:5)—thus we learn that Israel maintained there its distinctiveness[14]—and only this prevented them from not being lost amongst the nations in Egypt.

And He called out a cry "I have separated you from the nations" (Lev. 20:26) and "there is a people that dwells apart" (Numbers 23:9)—as [Targum] Jonathan translates, there "they are not conversant in the practices of the nations." [Alas] "they mingled with the nations and learned their ways" (Psalm 106:35).

If we are now idle, and "a future generation, children yet born" (Psalm 78:6) will arise and say "the Pharisees (the Orthodox authorities) have permitted this matter" (Jerusalem Talmud Sanhedrin, chapter 10, 28:4:2). We are, therefore, obligated to legislate with an iron and lead pen—as a memorial for future generations—the following:

1. It is forbidden to deliver sermons in a language of the nations of the world. It is also prohibited to listen to a sermon delivered in the language of the nations of the world. Therefore, every Israelite who hears that a rabbi or someone else is giving a sermon in a foreign language should leave the synagogue forthwith. And the preacher must preach in the Yiddish language, one that is spoken by kosher (sic) Jews of this country.
2. It is forbidden to enter and pray in a synagogue [that] does not have a *bimah* in the middle.
3. It is forbidden to construct a synagogue with a tower.
4. It is forbidden to make special clothes for the cantor and other singers in a manner that resembles the customs of other religions.
5. It is forbidden to make a *mechitzah*, which separates the women's and men's sections,

in a way that enables the men to look at the women. But rather, you shall make it as was practiced in the days of yore. And, moreover, if it was already built in this way, one should not enter the synagogue.
6. It is forbidden to listen to the prayers of a choir, and it is certainly forbidden to pray along with them or respond "Amen," even if by consequence one will be compelled to "*sit alone and keep silent*" (Lamentations 3:28).
7. One is forbidden to enter so-called "choir-synagogues," since they are houses of *apikorsut* (heresy), for as it is stated in [the Babylonian Talmud], Shabbat 116a, "even if someone is in pursuit of him in order to kill him or a snake was running [after him] to bite him, he should enter a house of idolatry[15] to save one's self rather than to enter the houses of these [Jewish heretics] etc."
8. It is forbidden to place a *chuppah* in a synagogue. Rather, it should be under the heavens.
9. It is forbidden to change any Jewish custom or practice in the synagogue, since it has already been accepted by our fathers and our fathers' fathers.

The prohibition on entering the synagogues we have noted above holds for both regular days of the year as well as Shabbat, Rosh Hashanah or Yom Kippur, and even if this means that because of this one is to pray alone.

[We enact this prohibition] in order to repair the breach in the Torah by the multitude of God's nation whose hearts are still close to Him and the embers of Abraham still burns in them, [and] so that they will [now] know clearly that all of the customs and ordinances of Israel have their "foundation on the holy mountains" (Psalms 87:1) and stand at the pinnacle of the world.

And who is [so] important or respected in this orphaned generation to [have the right to] change what is already established? Did not our rabbis of blessed memory say: "If the earliest generations [of sages] were sons of angels, we are [mere] human beings, and if the later generations merited the appellation of human beings, we are like donkeys, and not even like the donkeys of Rabbi Pinchas ben Yair" (Babylonia Talmud, Shabbat 112b).[16] And now, "if sinners entice you, do not yield" (Proverbs 1:10). This is the first [point].

Second, you should know that everything they are doing to change the customs of Israel, to imitate [the gentiles]—"*How did those nations worship their gods*" (Deuteronomy 12:30)—transgresses a few "do not dos" (negative Torah commandments). It is worse than eating pork, both in terms of quantity and quality.

Quantitatively: Eating an olive-size piece of pork is but a [violation] of one negative commandment, while in changing and substituting customs in order to imitate [the gentiles], one violates many negative commandments.

And qualitatively: these prohibitions pertain to the "accessories" of idolatry and [thus] there is a question whether they fall within the category of "[rather] be killed than transgress [them]" (Babylonian Talmud, Sanhedrin 74a).

In truth, because of the severity of the issue, it would have been appropriate to issue bans of excommunications or to proclaim a curse of snakes for which there is no remedy. But we did only this for the sake of masses of God's people who believe in His Torah and desire its fulfillment, and yet there are some [who] imagine and reason "so what" concerning the matters mentioned above, and [that] perhaps [they deem the changes] as merely "pious acts," and that it is not advisable to create a difference of opinion over this, and, all the more so, conflict.

Now, please know, that these [prohibitions] are the fundamentals of Torah and are included under the category of accessories of idolatry, and [the prohibition against] changing one's language is included in the "eighteen matters"[17] that were established with the sword (Jerusalem Talmud Shabbat 1:4), and even Elijah, if he would come to nullify them—we will not listen to him (see Babylonian Talmud, Avodah Zarah 36a).

And the great guide, the Rabbi of Israel in the last generation, the light of the Diaspora, our master and teacher, the author of the Hatam Sofer, of blessed memory—may he abide in paradise, commanded his congregation [in his last will and testament] "that they should not have a preacher who preaches in the language of the nations, but only in the manner as you have heard from me."

And he (Rabbi Sofer) repeated it again in his *responsa* to *Hoshen Mishpat* (no. 196)[18] where he states, that a "[prospective rabbi] should not [deliver sermons in] foreign languages, because it is forbidden to receive Torah from such a rabbi's mouth. [Appointing such a person as rabbi] is like setting up an *asherah* [a tree for idol worship] in the sanctuary of the Lord." For one way or another, they will hear the sermon.

And we made this [proclamation] openly and publicly in a gathering and meeting of the great Sages so that it will be heard. And now, the fearers of God in many communities will no longer need to solicit [rabbinic] *responsa*, [that is], to send off letters to the rabbis [asking them] what to do in the aforementioned matters.

And all the aforementioned [regulations] keeping a distance, [that is], that one is forbidden to imitate [the gentiles] and to practice their customs and to walk in their ways, is only in relation to religion and issues of faith. Because the preservation of our Torah and our religion is very far from other religions and since our Torah beseeches only us with regard to the 613 *mitzvot* (commandments)—unlike the other nations who are not so commanded. But aside from religion, we are beseeched by the Torah, Prophets and the Writings [that is, all three books of the Hebrew Scriptures] to honor the gentiles and seek their peace.

The Torah states "you shall not abhor an Egyptian, for you were a stranger in his land" (Deuteronomy 23:8) and our rabbis say "do not throw a clod of earth into a well from which you drank" (Babylonian Talmud Bava Kamma 92b).

Now we can make an *a fortiori* (*kal vachomer*) argument—if the Egyptians drew Israel close to them only for their own purposes and, [moreover], they [the Israelites] experienced painful afflictions there, as the Torah says, "I have marked well the plight of my people in Egypt" (Exodus 3:7) [or] "and their cry for help from bondage rose up to God" (Exodus 2:23) and yet, with all of this, the Torah, whose "ways are pleasant ways" (Proverbs 3:17) still tells us and commands us that since you had there a safe haven at a time of difficulty "you shall not abhor an Egyptian" (Deuteronomy 23:8).

[Then] these nations, among whom we dwell and are sheltered by their shade, and gain our livelihood amongst them, and, [moreover], they, their kings, officers, nobles, representatives, and judges, and all of the inhabitants of the land are upstanding, kind and just people, and they are at peace with us and do not prevent us or cause us to neglect the observance of our Torah and our religion, then all the more so we are commanded from the perspective of the Holy Torah not to be ungrateful.

And whoever does not do so, he should be afraid of the curse of Solomon "evil will never depart

from the house of him who repays good with evil."
(Proverbs 17:13); [or] in the prophets, "[and] seek
the welfare of the city [to which I have exiled you]
(Jeremiah 29:7), and in the Writings, "I do obey the
king's orders" (Ecclesiastes 8:2) [or] "Fear the Lord,
my son, and the king" (Proverbs 24:21).

This [ruling] emerged from us, the undersigned,
at a conference where we conferred and deliberated
on the matter according to religion[19] and, moreover,
these are matters that are patently clear according to
our Holy Torah without any alteration.

And on this we have signed here in the holy community of Michalowce, God should protect it, on Tuesday
of the Shabbat [where we read] the portion of *Vayishlach*
(Genesis 32:4–36:43), 5625 [28 November 1865].

Do not place significance to the order of the
signatories.

Menachem E[isen]s[taedter], Rabbi of Ungvár
Shlomo Ganzfried, Judge
Shmuel Moskowitz, Judge
Haim Yosef [Gottlieb], Rabbi of Sztropkov
Avraham Schönfeld, Rabbi of Kurame
Naftali Teckman, Judge
Shmuel Shmelke [Klein], Rabbi of Szöllös
Yosef, son of Zalman, Judge
Zeev Wolf Tannebaum, Rabbi of Verpelet
Hillel L[ichten]s[tein], [Rabbi of Szikszó]
Avraham Yehuda Schwartz, Rabbi of Beregszáz
Moshe Heimlich, Judge
Shmuel Aryeh Lichtenstein, Judge
Yehuda E[isen]s[tädter], Rabbi of Szobránc
Zvi Hirsh Weiss, Rabbi of Lapos
Yosef Grünwald, Rabbi of Czeczowitz with his
    rabbinic court
Yehoshua Aharon Zvi Weinberger, Rabbi of
    Margareten
Leibish Jolles, Rabbi of Sebes
Yehuda Leib [Spiro], Rabbi of Hummene
Abish Shapiro, Rabbi of Hummene
Aharon Greenberg, Rabbi of Michalowse
Asher, son of Moshe, Judge
Moshe David Eichenbaum, Judge
Haim [Sofer], Rabbi of Sz[ent] Pét[er]

NOTES

1. Gradually Liberal and modern Orthodox expressions of Judaism began to take root in the Habsburg
   Empire, not only in the German-speaking territories, but also in the Kingdom of Hungary. Alarmed
   by these developments, disciples of Hatam Sofer,
   led by Hillel Lichtenstein (1814–91), Haim Sofer
   (1821–86) and Lichtenstein's son-in-law Akiva
   Yosef Schlesinger 1837–1922) gathered in 1865 in
   Michalowce (Mihalowitz, Nagy Mihály), a town in
   northeastern Hungary (today, Slovakia), and issued
   a *pesaq din* (a rabbinic decision) reiterating Hatam
   Sofer's unyielding opposition to all changes in Jewish
   religious practice and custom, even relatively mild
   adjustments in accord with contemporary sensibilities introduced by the Neo-Orthodox. Indeed, as
   Michael Silber points out, their animus was directed
   not so much to the liberal reformers as it was to the
   neo-Orthodox and their intent to embolden the
   vacillating Orthodox who contemplated introducing merely minor concessions in order to maintain
   communal harmony. "It would be a mistake…to
   view the *pesaq din* [of Michalowce] as primarily an
   attack on Reforms….[In fact], several of the prohibitions were veiled references to innovations
   which had only recently been introduced in none
   other than the bastion of Orthodoxy, Pressburg, the
   seat of the late Hatam Sofer." Michael Silber, "The
   Emergence of Ultra-Orthodoxy: The Invention of a
   Tradition," in *The Uses of Tradition: Jewish Continuity
   in the Modern Era*, ed., Jack Wertheimer (New York:
   Jewish Theological Seminary of America, 1992),
   p. 40. The *pesaq din* was signed by twenty-five rabbis; a few months later, the number of signatories
   had reached seventy, the size of the Sanhedrin (see
   chapter 3, document 15), and received the added
   authority of Hasidic leaders. Because the document
   purported to be a *pesaq din*, that is a decision based
   on *halakhah* (rabbinic law), many of the most prominent Orthodox authorities in Hungary refused to
   sign it. Nevertheless, the *pesaq din* of Michalowce
   served not only to crystallize the Ultra-Orthodox
   movement, but prompted Hungarian Orthodoxy
   in general to move more to the right and reject any
   accommodation to modernity.

2. See Silber, "The Emergence of Ultra-Orthodoxy,"
   pp. 39ff.

3. This reading is based on the linguistic similarity of the
   Hebrew word that opens the biblical passage (*sim*—to
   place, appoint) to the Hebrew term for guilt or sin
   (*ashem*).

4. The rabbis are associating the Hebrew name Levi with
   the term to escort (*livah*).

5. The Jewish Publication Society of America's translation of the Hebrew Scriptures renders this phrase in an utterly different spirit as a dedication, "when locks go untrimmed," although it is traditionally understood as the authors of the *pesaq din* did.

6. See *Midrash Aggadah*, ed., Shlomo Buber, Numbers 11:18.

7. The suggestion is that by the "building of a tower," these synagogues seek to imitate the architecture of Christian churches.

8. See this chapter, document 6, note 16.

9. A *mechitzah* (Hebrew for partition or division; plural *mechitzot*) is a partition that is used to separate men and women during prayer. The signatories of the rabbinic decree deemed the *mechitzot* of the modern Orthodox synagogues to provide an insufficient separation between the sexes.

10. Jewish weddings traditionally take place under a *chuppah* (Hebrew for covering or canopy), which consists of a cloth or sheet and occasionally also a prayer shawl (*tallit*). Traditional practice is to conduct a wedding outdoors under the heavenly canopy. Hence, the tendency of some modern Orthodox (and Liberal) congregations to place the wedding canopy inside the synagogue was frowned upon as yet another deviation from tradition.

11. Specifically, the reference is to the founding of Modern Orthodox congregations in Germany, Bohemia, and nearby Moravia.

12. The reference is to places that were previously great centers of traditional Judaism and the study of Torah.

13. This is an allusion to the increasing practice of even Orthodox rabbis to dress in ceremonial robes and to deliver their sermons in either German or Hungarian.

14. Although there are several variations of this midrash, the authors of the *pesaq din* repeatedly referred to a variant in *Tana Devrei Eliahu* 23:4, wherein the Israelites consciously decided to preserve their identity in "Egypt's Land" by entering into a covenant to maintain distinctive names, language, and dress. In preferring this variant reading of the midrash, the *pesaq din* in effect emphasized the covenantal obligation of the Israelites to enter a sort of social contract to maintain their distinctive religious identity.

15. In this context, houses of idolatry refer to Christian churches.

16. Rabbi Pinchas ben Yair's donkeys were said to have instinctively known not to eat food that was not properly tithed according to biblical law.

17. The reference is to eighteen abiding prohibitions (*gezerot*) that were legislated just after the destruction of the Temple. They were meant to reinforce social and cultural distance from the gentile world. The list in the two Talmuds is not at all identical (compare the Babylonian Talmud, Shabbat 13b-17b, and the Jerusalem Talmud, Shabbat 1:4). The prohibition on "their languages" appears only in the less authoritative Jerusalem Talmud.

18. *Hoshen Mishpat* (the title means "lights of perfection"; cf. Exodus 28:30) is one of the books of the *Shulhan 'Arukh*, the standard Code of Jewish Law by Joseph Karo of the sixteenth century. See *The Responsa of Hatam Sofer*, volume 5, no. 197 (not no. 196 as is erroneously stated in the *pesaq din*).

19. "Religion" (*dat*) in this context is a vague term, apparently employed to avoid explicitly attaching to these "regulations" the authority of rabbinic law (*halakhah*).

17. THE SECESSION OF THE ORTHODOX (1877)[1]

SAMSON RAPHAEL HIRSCH[2]

The issue is not the separation between individuals, a withdrawal from friendly intercourse with brethren of differing religious convictions....The issue is secession from all ties with *minut*,[3] from all ties with acknowledgment of opposition-in-principle to Torah and *mizvot*,[4]—not the secession from social ties with *minim*,[5] with individuals who acknowledge, such opposition-in-principle. Thank God, there are in our days no more *minim* in the sense of our codices, concerning whom they teach us to avoid even mere contact. We are taught that gentiles outside *Eretz Israel* [Hebrew: Land of Israel] are not to be considered idolaters and that there are no *minim* among the nations[6] and that, therefore, what we are commanded concerning the avoidance of contact with pagans does not apply to such gentiles because *minhag avotehem biydehem*[7]—their religious views and ways are habits acquired through parental influence. The same applies to our Jewish contemporaries who have adopted *minut* in attitude and practice. They too are already the second and third generation of those who first thought up the defection and then executed it by means of propaganda....

But, the more we must remain in peaceful and friendly intercourse with our contemporaries who grew up in the ideas and ways of *minut*—the more demanding for us the necessity to remain distant from the *minut*-system [i.e., *minut*-organizations] in whose confession they were raised.... Otherwise this intercourse could have exactly the opposite effect on us and our children. That *minut* is more seductive than idolatry, That *minut maskha*,[8] as our sages put it, we have, unfortunately been shown by the.... experience of our time....

[In support of his position, Rabbi Hirsch cites a just-published *responsum* of Rabbi Moses Sofer,[9] the *Hatam Sofer*—universally recognized as one of the greatest rabbinic authorities of his time—who wrote concerning the reformers]:

"If their judgment were in our hands, it would be my opinion to separate them from our domain, not to give our daughters to their sons [or to take their daughters for our sons] so that we should not come to be drawn after them, so that their congregation should be like the congregation of Zadok and Boethus,[10] Anan and Saul,[11] they for themselves and we for ourselves. All this appears to me as *halakhah*, but not in practice in the absence of permission and authorization of the government—without this [permission] my words should be void and accounted as nonexisting."

This government permission and authorization is now given, and thus this decision, which the *Hatam Sofer* could state only as theoretical, becomes fully valid in practice.[12]

NOTES

1. In 1873 the Prussian legislature (*Landtag*) passed a bill granting every citizen the right to withdraw formally from his or her "religious community," to which previously one was obliged by law to belong. The law came to acknowledge the existence of "those without religion." In July 1876 an amendment was passed specifically permitting Jews, for religious reasons, to leave their local congregation without leaving Judaism. The amendment, the Law of Secession (*Austrittsgesetz*), allowed Hirsch and his followers to leave the "Jewish

Source: Samson Raphael Hirsch, "Die offene Antwort an Herrn Distr. Rabbiner S.B. Bamberger" (1877), in S. R. Hirsch, *Gesammelte Schriften*, ed. Naphtali Hirsch (Frankfurt am Main: Sanger & Friedberg, 1922), vol. 4, pp. 331–60, 361–426. Translated in Leo Levi, "The Relationship of the Orthodox to Heterodox Organizations," *Tradition Journal of Orthodox Jewish Thought* 9, no. 3 (Fall 1967), pp. 97–102. Reprinted by permission of the Rabbinical Council of America.

community" and to establish their own "religious community," called the Israelite Religious Society (*Israelitische Religionsgesellschaft*). Hirsch's congregation in Frankfurt am Main was joined by smaller groups of Orthodox in Berlin, Koenigsberg, Wiesbaden, Cologne and Giessen. But the vast majority of Orthodox Jews in Germany chose to remain within the general community.

2. Initially Rabbi Samson Raphael Hirsch (for his biography, see document 15, note 1, in this chapter) vigorously opposed any tendency allowing the conflict with Reform to lead to a schism within the Jewish people. In contradistinction to some Reform leaders, such as Geiger, who regarded separation as a kind of surgical amputation necessary to save the body of Judaism, Hirsch was eager to maintain the unity of the Jewish people. As long as Reform exercised discretion and modified its demands, he was prepared to maintain the shared communal framework and institutions. In the wake of the Reform rabbinical synods (cf. documents 6–8 in this chapter), which decided to annul some of the basic dietary and matrimonial laws, his attitude changed dramatically. Prussian law, however, did not allow for the organizational separation that Hirsch desired. It was only in 1876, when the Law of Secession was passed, that this was possible (see note 1). In these letters—addressed to the esteemed German Talmudic scholar Rabbi Seligmann Baer Bamberger (1807–1878), who opposed the Secession—Hirsch gives halakhic and theological reasons for the separation. He is careful to underscore that he still affirms the principle of Jewish unity, while seeking to ostracize "heretical" organizations. All Jews, even heretics, are still part of the people of Israel and

are to be loved as such; only heretical institutions are to be condemned and shunned.

3. *Minut* means heresy.

4. In German original: *"Juedisches Gesetz und Wahrheit."*

5. *Minim* is the plural form of the Hebrew term used in rabbinical literature to designate heretics and sectarians.

6. Cf. Babylonian Talmud, tractate Hulin 13b.

7. Meaning "they act according to ways of their fathers," this oft-cited Hebrew phrase is also from the Babylonian Talmud, tractate Hulin, 13b.

8. Hebrew: "Heresy or sectarianism draws [one to idolatry]." Babylonian Talmud, tractate Avodah zarah, 27b.

9. See document 4 in this chapter.

10. Zaddok and Boethus were disciples of the Jewish sage Antigonus of Sokho (early second century B.C.E.) who are said to have misinterpreted his teaching that God should be served without any hope of reward as meaning that there is no recompense for our deeds, either good or evil, in the world to come. The denial of this cardinal principle of Judaism, the rabbis held, led Zaddok and Boethus to found the heretical sects known as the Sadducees and Boethusians, respectively. Cf. Avot de-Rabbi Nathan, recension A, 5; and *ibid.*, recension B, 10.

11. Anan ben David (second half of the eighth century) was the founder of the Karaites, a Jewish sect that denies the validity of the Oral Law upon which the Talmudic and rabbinic traditions are based. The reference to Saul is apparently Saul of Tarsus, the Apostle Paul whom the rabbis regarded as a heretic.

12. Moses Sofer, *The Reponsa of Hatam Sofer*, Part 6, no. 89. This particular *responsum* is from the year 1819/20.

V

MODERN JEWISH STUDIES

One of the distinctive features of the modern sensibility is a critical historical conscious-ness, or what may be briefly defined as the heuristic assumption that social and cultural reality can be adequately explained in terms of its historical antecedents. This assumption, according to the German social historian Ernst Troeltsch (1866–1923), constituted a veri-table revolution in the consciousness of Western humanity.[1] To be sure, a sense of history is not entirely modern; it can be traced to classical antiquity. What is innovative in the modern approach to history is the comprehensiveness of its purview, the emphasis on critical meth-ods, and the proposition that the historical perspective demonstrates the manifest diver-sity of human culture and society.[2] Beginning with the seventeenth century,[3] the historians understand that their task is, in the words of Leopold von Ranke (1795–1886), to record "what really happened" ("*wie es eigentlich gewesen ist*"[4]): to isolate fact from fiction. So con-ceived, historiography was deemed an important supplement to the Enlightenment and the liberation of humanity from prejudice.[5] Ignorance and misinformation were held to be primary sources of prejudice: in the face of historical facts all prejudice would dissipate.

---

[1] Ernst Troeltsch, *Die Absolutheit des Christentums* (Tuebingen: J.C.B. Mohr, 1902); p. 1.

[2] See Johann Gottfried von Herder, *Reflections on the Philosophy of the History of Mankind*, trans. T. O. Churchill, abridged and ed. Frank E. Manuel (Chicago: University of Chicago Press, 1968), pp. 3–78; see also Georg G. Iggers, *The German Conception of History* (Middletown, Conn.: Wesleyan University Press, 1968), pp. 5, 29–43, 289ff.

[3] See Friedrich Meinecke, *Historicism: The Rise of New Historical Outlook*, trans. J. E. Anderson (London: Routledge & Kegan Paul, 1972), pp. 3ff. Meinecke correlates the beginnings of the new historiography with the breakdown of "natural law and its belief in the unvariability of the highest human ideals and an unchanging human nature" (ibid., p. 3).

[4] Leopold von Ranke, *Geschichte der romanischen und germanischen Voelker von 1494 bis 1535* (Leipzig, Berlin, 1823), p. x.

[5] Van Austin Harvey, *The Historian and the Believer: The Morality of Historical Knowledge and Christian Belief* (New York: Macmillan, 1966), pp. 38–44. Paradoxically, as it developed in the nineteenth cen-tury, historicism, the most common term for the new historiography, can also be viewed as an aspect of a European-wide "reaction and revolt of national traditions against the French Revolution and the Age of Reason" (Carlo Antoni, *L'Historisme* [Geneva: Librairie D'roz, 1963], p. 9).

It is the sublime and urgent task of the historian, August Wilhelm Schlegel (1767–1845) wrote, to discern "whether or not something actually happened; whether it happened in the way it is told or in some other way...."[6] To facilitate the isolation of fact from fiction, it was incumbent upon the historian to assume a strictly scientific (*wissenschaftlich*) method of utter objectivity and detachment.[7] This emphasis on the scientific method required not only the suspension of all preconceptions, but also the suspension of one's metaphysical and religious belief systems, namely, those values and ideas one holds to be eternal and absolute. This latter requirement, in turn, reinforced the new historiography's initial assumption that all human institutions—be they social, cultural, or religious—are time-bound and occupy a relative position in the context of history. From this perspective, the alleged absolute status of religious norms and values is radically challenged. The critical, historical consciousness thus leads to relativism. For historians confronting their own cultural and religious tradition, the relativistic premise of the new historiography is especially problematic. In their implicit questioning of the epistemological and ontological status of their subject matter, they court the danger of attenuating their fidelity to the norms and values of their tradition.[8] On the other hand, a historical consciousness may deepen one's identification with and affection for a given facet of human culture, for as the Italian philosopher of history, Benedetto Croce (1866–1952) observed, the study of history may have a synthetic function of molding the sensibilities and personal values of the historian. Refracted and re-animated through the consciousness and writings of the historian, history, as Croce put it, is rendered contemporary.[9]

This contradictory tendency of the new historiography is manifest from the very beginning of modern Jewish scholarship, or, as it is called in German, *Wissenschaft des Judentums* (the Science of Judaism). This contradiction was reinforced by ideological motives—independent of the methodological premises of the new historiography—that initially prompted the introduction of modern historical methods into the study of Judaism.

In 1819 the *Verein fuer Cultur und Wissenschaft der Juden* (the Jewish student circle in Berlin responsible for the beginnings of the Science of Judaism) was founded. At this time in Germany, mounting antisemitism, endorsed by many supposed liberals, followed in the wake of Napoleon's defeat and gained violent expression in the "Hep! Hep!" anti-Jewish riots of 1819.[10] In response, Jewish university students, largely assimilated, joined with a few older *maskilim* of Mendelssohn's generation to establish a sort of anti-defamation project. The new historiography—based on the respectable and objective methodology of *Wissenschaft*—would be their principal weapon to battle the venomous calumny against

---

[6] Cited in Ernst Cassirer, *The Problem of Knowledge*, trans. Willian H. Woglom and Charles W. Hendel (New Haven: Yale University Press, 1950), p. 228.

[7] On the ideal of *Wissenschaft*, see Fritz K. Ringer, *The Decline of the German Mandarins: The German Academic Community, 1890–1933* (Cambridge, Mass.: Harvard University Press, 1969), pp. 102–13; see also L. Wallach, "The Beginnings of the Science of Judaism," *Historia Judaica* 8 (1946), pp. 33–60

[8] Nathan Rotenstreich, *Tradition and Reality: The Impact of History on Modern Jewish Thought* (New York: Random House, 1972), pp. 24–35. Troeltsch contended that historicism presented Christianity (and all positive religions) with a grave challenge, for "once the historical method is applied to biblical science and church history it is leaven that alters everything, and finally, bursts apart the entire structure of theological methods employed until the present" (cited in Harvey, op. cit., p. 5).

[9] Benedetto Croce, *History as the Story of Liberty*, trans. Sylvia Sprigge (London: George Allen and Unwin, 1941), pp. 19–22.

[10] In August 1819, under the rallying cry "Hep! Hep!" a series of vicious anti-Jewish riots broke out in Germany and spread to neighboring countries. Opinions differ as to the origin of the cry; most likely it was originally a shepherd's exhortatory call to drive goats and cattle. The immediate cause of the riots was mounting tensions engendered by the struggle for Jewish commercial and civil rights. (See document 3, note 6.)

Judaism. The "scientific" correction of misinformation regarding the Jews, it was believed, would dispel prejudice. Moreover, this information would restore the acculturated Jews' self-respect and pride that had been undermined by regnant misinformation and accusations. The over-arching desire of the *Verein*, which was reflected in its program and in the scholarship that it sponsored, was to justify the Jews' membership in European culture and politics. *Wissenschaft des Judentums*, in other words, would facilitate Jewry's integration and honorable assimilation into Europe. After the dissolution of the *Verein* in 1825, this objective would remain a dominant feature of modern Jewish scholarship, at least in its first generation.

Concomitant to this objective were subsidiary motives, such as the cause of religious reform and political emancipation, which revealed the contradiction between the desire for a neutral *Wissenschaft* and the ideological motive for a reform of the Jews' place in society. This contradiction engendered a basic tension within the nineteenth-century Science of Judaism, which is traced in the selections presented in this chapter. The selections also illuminate the methodological tension—the dialectic between relativism and a synthetic function—inherent within the new historiography.[11] In the twentieth century both the conception and the methodology of *Wissenschaft des Judentums* underwent far-reaching revisions, as exemplified in the selections from Buber and from the YIVO Institute (documents 12 to 14).

A word about the term *Wissenschaft des Judentums*, which we have translated as "the Science of Judaism." It has been argued by several scholars that "science" is an inappropriate, misleading translation of the German term *Wissenschaft* when it is applied to humanistic studies. Accordingly, *Wissenschaft des Judentums* has been rendered as "modern Jewish studies," "Jewish research," "Judaica" and "Judaistic." These translations, however, obscure the methodological and philosophical nuance that the term originally bore in German. *Wissenschaft* unambiguously meant "science" in the fullest sense of the term: a devotion to factual accuracy, normative neutrality and the quest for empirically grounded truth. To be sure, German scholars were aware of the difference in subject matter and epistemological status between the humanistic and social sciences on the one` hand and the natural sciences on the other. This awareness is witnessed by the protracted debates in Germany regarding the differences between the so-called *Geisteswissenschaften* (literally, "the sciences of the spirit") and the *Naturwissenschaften* ("the sciences of nature").[12] It is significant that proponents of the former, while acknowledging that their respective disciplines do not possess the precision and measurability of the natural sciences, nonetheless insisted on viewing their effort as *Wissenschaft:* as value-free, rigorous research. This was particularly true in the nineteenth century, when it was held that *Wissenschaft* should be the basis of high culture and the bedrock of true humanity. Thus, at least at its inception, "the esoteric purpose" of *Wissenschaft des Judentums* was, as Heinrich Heine, a member of the *Verein*, noted, "none other than the reconciliation of historical Judaism with modern science which, one supposed, in the course of time would gain world dominion."[13]

---

[11] For an appraisal of the *Wissenschaft des Judentums*, both in terms of its methodology and ideology, see the illuminating essay by Gershorn Scholem, "Science of Judaism, its Achievements and Prospects" (document 15).

[12] See Ringer, op. cit., *passim.*

[13] Cited in Michael A. Meyer, *The Origins of the Modern Jew* (Detroit: Wayne State University Press, 1967), p. 173. Ismar Elbogen has highlighted an interesting anomaly concerning *Wissenschaft des Judentums*, which underscores its "esoteric motive," by noting that parallel disciplines did not use *Wissenschaft* as a designation: one did not speak of a *Wissenschaft des Christentums* but rather *christliche Theologie*; nor was there a *Wissenschaft des Deutschtums*, but *Germanistik*. See Ismar Elbogen, "Ein Jahrhundert Wissenschaft des Judentums," *Festschrift zum 50-jaehrigen Bestehen der Hochschule fuer die Wissenschaft des Judentums* (Berlin, 1922), p. 139

1. A SOCIETY FOR THE PRESERVATION OF THE JEWISH PEOPLE (1819)

JOEL ABRAHAM LIST[1]

Behind our decision to found a society for Jews seems to have been an apprehensiveness that in the future we, as individuals, will not be able to continue to live as Jews, or at least not in the way we would like to. Assuming that this is indeed our concern, the immediate question should be: How, then, have we Jews survived until now? To this question, it would be difficult to answer anything but that, even after our banishment from our ancestral home we continue to be a united people—that is, until recent times when a process of dissolution set in. The analysis of what has hitherto constituted the bond and unity of our nation should therefore be our first and foremost priority. There were three reasons for our former unity, which I shall state as generally and as briefly as possible:

1. The avoidance of everything which was likely to undermine our unity. We stuck together like a huddled flock.
2. The instinct for community, a purely human element, which develops when people are faced with a common plight. We clung together like people in a besieged fortress.
3. Religion. We all looked toward a common Heaven and did not lose ourselves in the multifarious activities of earthly life.

If it is evident from all this that we have never been a unity held together by some idea, and even less so, a society dedicated to the achievement of a common goal, we must at least admit that we have had a single-heartedness of sorts.... Even this singleness of purpose, however, is now profoundly shaken. Jews one after another are detaching themselves from the community. Jewry is on the verge of complete disintegration. We no longer isolate ourselves [from non-Jews], nor are we excluded to the degree we were formerly. Our personal affiliations, once mainly restricted to our fellow Jews, have greatly expanded, partly as a result of the Enlightenment which generally tends to distinguish human rights from matters of confession, partly because of natural sympathies developing on closer acquaintance with friendly Gentiles, and partly because of an obvious decrease in pressures and oppression from the outside. Increasingly, we are dedicating ourselves to the needy masses of society in general, rather than exclusively to the needs of our fellow Jews. Our humanity no longer recognizes external boundaries, and therefore it does not wish to be internally restricted to merely national objectives....

Our venerable religion must cease to constitute the bond of our nation, not only because of its aforementioned mistaken goal—which it shares with all other religions—but also because of the severity of its [heteronomous] laws.[2] For many years now, a single-minded adherence to the law on the one hand, and a frivolous indifference to the law on the other, have brought about a division within the nation and even the defection of many, which in time is bound to grow and reach quite dangerous proportions. The divine, which the daughter of Heaven carries inside her breasts, does not feed us any more, and we are the victims of either hunger or surfeit. Everywhere, then, Israel rushes toward its decline which, other things being equal, sooner or later will inevitably have to occur. I say "other things being equal," meaning "things" created by time; everything born of time,

Source: J. A. List, Unpublished Lecture of November 7, 1819, in S. Ucko, "Geistesgeschichtliche Grundlagen der Wissenschaft des Judenthums," *Zeitschrift fuer Geschichte der Juden in Deutschland* 5 (1934), pp. 10–12. Trans. by J. Hessing and P. Mendes-Flohr.

however, carries within itself the germ of its own destruction. And yet my friends, we feel and realize that that which is unique to our nation, our natural essence,[3] is not merely a product of time, not merely a passing phenomenon. The ephemeral features of our external life can by no means vitiate the eternal values we bear deeply within us, and of which we are acutely conscious. We are aware of a substance within us, an essence of timeless existence. In that we are conscious of our existence as Jews, we wish to preserve our Jewishness, and since we *wish* to preserve our Jewishness, we *must* preserve it. We therefore have a clear conception of our being, of our common being, for otherwise we would no longer be ourselves and hence nothing at all. It is the most characteristic feature of an idea, however, that that which is necessary within it is at the same time possible, and the possible, at the same time, necessary. If we feel an inner necessity of our continued existence [as Jews], then we cannot deny its inherent feasibility. And, my dear friends, do we not ourselves constitute the most irrefutable proof of this truth? What is true for us who have convened here must be true for thousands of our brethren as well. And thus we have perceived a true idea of our inner unity. The dissemination of this perception and the realization [of this unity] should be the ultimate objective of our society. We should never lose sight of this objective, even though we may at times stray from it. The intellectual, vocational and civic improvement of the Jews, although it will be beneficial in itself, can therefore be nothing but a necessary consequence and a by-product of this wider objective. The amelioration of Jewish life in these areas is and should be a matter of concern for all mankind and the duty of the governments under which the Jews happen to be living. For us, however, there must be no greater concern than the integrity of our nation, and we must not shy away from any sacrifice to preserve it. With respect to the Jewish nation, we should regard as meritorious only those deeds which further the realization of this goal. All other deeds, from a Jewish point of view, would be unimportant, because I could just as well do them for any needy Gentile. As Jews, however, our national value

must be more important to us than anything else, otherwise it would not be worth twopence that we be called Jews. Why then, this stubborn adherence to something we do not esteem and on account of which we suffer so much?...

If we are convinced of the truth [of these observations] and if it is in the name of our essential nationality that we feel called upon to form a society, then its purpose must be national—otherwise it would be something outlandish....This task, surely, is the most difficult one that we can set for ourselves as Jews. It demands a great devotion to the community, both extensively and intensively. After having formed a society for the aforementioned purpose it should therefore be our first concern (a) to give it the widest possible scope, and (b) to do everything in our power to restore to our nationality all its dignity, a first step in this direction being the complete abolition of rabbinism which has disfigured and debased our nation....

NOTES

1. Joel Abraham List (1780–c.1848). One of the seven founding members of the society for the Culture and Science of the Jews (*Verein fuer Cultur und Wissenschaft der Juden*), he served as its president from March 1820 to March 1821. He was the founder and director of a private elementary school for Jews.

   On November 7, 1819, six Jews—Joseph Hilmar, Isaac Levin Auerbach, Isaac Marcus Jost, Leopold Zunz, Eduard Gans, Moses Moser—accepted List's invitation to meet at his Berlin home. At this meeting they founded the society from which the Society for the Culture and Science of the Jews emerged in 1821. Aside from the desire to work for "the improvement of the situation of the Jews in the German federated states," the initial aims of the society were unclear. In this lecture, given at the first meeting, List sought to outline his understanding of what the society's purpose should be.

2. The members of the society—many of whom were associated with the nascent Reform movement—shared a hostility to rabbinism, or the dominance of Talmudic Judaism in Jewish life.

3. This definition of the essence of Judaism as a nationality, as opposed to a religion, was novel for the time.

2. STATUTES (1822)[1]

THE SOCIETY FOR THE CULTURE AND SCIENCE OF THE JEWS

Introduction: Paragraph 1. The discrepancy between the inner state of the Jews and their outward position among the nations has existed for many centuries. In modern times, however, this contradiction has become more apparent than before. A powerful change in intellectual orientation, among Jews as well as other peoples, has engendered new [cultural and social] patterns which daily enhance the anguish generated by this contradiction. This situation necessitates a complete reform of the distinctive education and self-definition thus far prevalent among the Jews; they will have to be brought to the same point of development reached by the rest of Europe.

Paragraph 2. If this reform can essentially be undertaken only by the Jews themselves, it nevertheless cannot be the work of all of them but solely that of an intellectually congenial elite of educated Jews. To work toward the realization of these goals, in accordance with these statutes, is the purpose of this society, namely: the society is an association of individuals who feel they have the ability and the calling to harmonize, by way of educational work, the Jews with the present age and with the states wherever they live.

Paragraph 3....In order to fulfill its aims, the society should work from above by promoting significant and rigorous projects, assuring their accessibility and interest to the largest possible audience. Moreover, the society must not fail to secure a firm basis for [Jews] of the lower social strata who may have elevated themselves to the ranks of the educated. At the same time, working from below, the society should endeavor to influence the world-view of different social classes [among the Jews] through the dissemination of a clear, objective knowledge. On the one hand, then, everything that can serve to enlarge the intellect will be made use of, such as the establishment of schools, seminaries, academies and the active encouragement of literary and other public activities of every description; on the other hand, the young generation [of Jews] will be directed to crafts, agriculture and practical sciences, in order to suppress the one-sided preference [of the Jews] for petty-trade and to improve the general tone of their social intercourse [with non-Jews]. Thus, gradually, every peculiarity that distinguishes [the Jews] from the rest of the population will be overcome.

Paragraph 4.... In view of the fact that the society, in its nascent stages, will have limited resources at its disposal; in view of the fact that groping about in all directions may dissipate its energies and endanger its future existence; in view of these facts the society feels obliged, albeit in keeping with its basic concepts, to narrow the scope of its activities for the near future. The scope of these activities will be detailed in the following statutes; the broadening of this scope will depend on the degree to which the society manages to increase its strength.

First Section: Activities of the Society.... Paragraph 2. The society limits its activities for the time being to the purely scholarly *[wissenschaftliche]* aspects of its objectives, and to the practical matters immediately arising therefrom.

Paragraph 3. To achieve its objectives, the society will establish several institutes, the central one being: (a) A scientific institute....

Paragraph 4. In order to provide this institute with all the necessary means and in order to increase

---

Source: Entwurf von Statuten des Vereins fuer Cultur und Wissenschaft der Juden (Berlin, 1822), Zunz Archives, Jewish National and University Library, Jerusalem. Trans. by J. Hessing and P. Mendes-Flohr.

as much as possible its effectiveness the society will establish: (b) Archives....

Paragraph 5. In order to bring the more important results obtained through the activities of these institutes to the knowledge of the public, as well as to increase the general interest in the society's endeavors, the society will initiate: (c) The publication of a journal.[2]...

Paragraph 6. Finally, the society will seek to promote and to supervise in a more direct fashion the scientific development of the Jews in general. Accordingly, the society will oblige its members to help the more gifted individuals of the Jewish religion by giving lessons, in accordance with a general plan, in the society's: (d) School.

Paragraph 7. All institutes named above will be maintained by the society, which delegates the special supervision thereof to commissions appointed by it for this purpose; the commissions will keep the society regularly informed about the current affairs of the respective institutes under their supervision....

NOTES

1. Although the society was founded in November 1819, the formulation of the statutes began only at the end of 1820. Drafted by Eduard Gans, Moses Moser and Leopold Zunz, the statutes were passed by the society's membership—which numbered some fifteen at the time—on August 19, 1821. The official name of the society was suggested by Gans and had been adopted the previous month. Gans explained that the concept of "the Science of the Jews" in the name connoted the goal of "rendering the Jewish world [history] part of one's consciousness." "The culture of the Jews" conveyed, according to Immanuel Wolf, who shared Gans's intellectual perspective, "the essence of all circumstances, characteristics, and achievements of the Jews in relation to religion, philosophy, history, law, literature in general, civil life and all the affairs of man" (cited in H. G. Reissner, *Eduard Gans: Ein Leben im Vormaerz* [Tuebingen: J.C.B. Mohr, 1965], pp. 64ff.). The name of the society should be read as having a double meaning, namely, Society for Culture and Science *among/of* the Jews; for as Gans emphasized, "the Jews were to be both the scholars and objects of their scholarship" (cited in Michael A. Meyer, *The Origin of the Modern Jew* [Detroit: Wayne State University Press, 1967], p. 217, n. 69).

2. The journal, titled *Zeitschrift fuer die Wissenschaft des Judentums* (Periodical for the Science of Judaism) and edited by Leopold Zunz, appeared for one year only. The phrase *Wissenschaft des Judentums* occurred for the first time during the course of the debate on the statutes (see Meyer, op. cit., p. 165). The first volume of the journal contained *inter alia* the following articles: "Legislation Concerning the Jews in Rome, According to the Sources of Roman Law," by Eduard Gans; "On the Belief of the Jews in the Coming of the Messiah," by Lazarus Bendavid; "Solomon ben Isaac, called Rashi," by Leopold Zunz; "On the Natural Aspect of the Jewish State," by Ludwig Marcus; "Basic Outlines of a Future Statistic [i.e., sociology] of the Jews," by Leopold Zunz.

3. A SOCIETY TO FURTHER JEWISH INTEGRATION (1822)

EDUARD GANS[1]

If the idea of our society is to be successfully real- ized, one must go back to the more profound preliminary questions, without which the basis for our future effectiveness cannot be assured. The pre- liminary questions, then, are two. What is today's Europe? And what are the Jews? *What* are they I am asking deliberately. Those who have previously dealt with the subject tried to answer the question: *how* are they? Their question was false, and so, by necessity, were their solutions. Who among you, gentlemen and friends, does not remember the stale "pro" and "con" with which, during the last five years—since the end of the War of Liberation—one-sided ratio- nalizers have played their games. They labored under the delusion that all wisdom was to be found in one of the two.... While wrath and impetuosity were the mainstay of the opponents [of Jewish emancipation], the supporters indulged in exaggerated circumspec- tion and attempted, with calculating exactitude, to spell out the alleged virtues of the Jewish race; large tables were prepared in which the advantages of the Jews over the rest of mankind were conveniently listed. The fallacy underlying both tendencies stems from the idea that world history moves as freely as the individual, and that it too must perform good and avoid evil—the fallacy of common sense which cannot be convinced that there may be another form of judgment, which involves neither approval nor disapproval....

This is the situation: today's Europe, in our view, is not the work or the outcome of chance which could have been different, better or worse, but the inevitable result of the effort made, through many millennia, by that Spirit of Reason which manifests itself in world history. The meaning of this process, abstractly speak- ing, lies within the plurality whose unity can only be found in the whole. This we shall now have to work out in detail. As we behold the particular structure of today's Europe, we shall discern it mainly in the blossoming wealth of its many-limbed organism. There is no thought in this organism which has not yet come into being or found its shape; there is no tendency in this organism, and no activity, which has not yet bloomed into fullness. Everywhere one finds the most fertile variety of social classes and condi- tions, the work of the Spirit which gradually achieves its perfection. Each of these classes is a self-contained unit, complete in itself, and yet it does not gain its meaning from within, but only from another class; each limb has its own particular life, and yet it only lives in the organic whole. The essence of one social class is determined by all; the essence of all social classes is determined by the whole. Therefore no social class, and no social condition, is divided from any of the others by sharply drawn lines, but rather by a series of smooth transitions, which bespeak dif- ference and unity at one and the same time. To this totality, the Orient has contributed monotheism; Hellas the ideal of beauty and freedom; the Roman world the importance of the state vis-à-vis the indi- vidual; Christianity the concept of the preciousness of human existence as a whole; the Middle Ages con- tributed the sharp delineation of the states and other groups; and the modern world has added its philo- sophical efforts, so that all these contributions may reappear as moving forces after they have abdicated their temporary single rule. Today, Europe has given to the other [Western] hemisphere, as its legacy, the

Source: Eduard Gans, "Halbjaehriger Bericht im Verein fuer Cultur und Wissenschaft der Juden (April 28, 1822)," in S. Rubaschoff, "Erstlinge der Entjudung. Drei Reden von Eduard Gans im 'Kulturverein,'" *Der juedische Wille* 2 (1919), pp. 109–15. Trans. by J. Hessing.

total product of its life of many thousands of years, without the scaffold of its history, however, and while in Asia the contrast [between the classes] ripens into perfection, Europe, a happy old man, may once again remember its cradle. This is the happiness, and the greatness, of the European: that he may freely choose among the manifold classes [*Staende*] of his bourgeois society and yet, within his chosen class, remain in touch with all other classes of society. Take this freedom away from him, and you have deprived him of his foundations and of his meaning. Thus is the [significance of] European life.

In contrast, let us now consider the Jews and the Jewish life. If one defines Europe as the plurality whose unity can only be found in the whole, one may now define the Jews as follows: they are the unity which has not yet become a plurality. In their earliest days, they were appointed to guard the idea of the oneness of God; but even without this idea, state, ethics, law and religion appeared as one indivisible substance. In this, the Jews did not differ from any other people in the Orient. What set them apart was their fertile creativity by which they gave birth to a new world without being themselves part of this world. When their state went down in ruins they wanted to cling to their concept of unity and therefore took hold of one single social class, the class of the merchants. This class granted the Jews their coveted unity, but at the same time it should have allowed their integration with all other social classes. That such development had been delayed for thousands of years may in part be explained by the fact that society itself had not yet completely developed; as long as numerous groups had not been integrated into a totality, this one particularity—Jewry—hardly seemed to be exceptional. Kept apart, and keeping themselves apart, the Jews lived their own history side by side with world history, held together by the artful convergence of their domestic, political and religious life on the one hand and by the disunion of the other classes [*Staende*] of society on the other.

In recent times, however, the Jews' particularity has become problematic due to the previously described developments in contemporary Europe. We have found Europe's strength and vitality to reside within its luxurious wealth of [socio-cultural] particularities and formations, which nevertheless find their unity in the harmony of the whole. The fewer the remaining number of unintegrated details, however, the more disturbing these details will seem; the pressure of the age to integrate these remnants cannot be rebuffed any longer. Where the organism wants a wavy line, the straight line becomes a Horror. This, then, is the demand of present-day Europe: the Jews must completely incorporate themselves into [the social and cultural fabric of Europe]. This demand, the logical consequence of the European principle, must be put to the Jews. Europe would be untrue to itself and to its essential nature if it did not put forth this demand. Now the time for this demand, and its fulfillment, has come. What to many observers, who do not go beyond the surface of daily phenomena, may look like an age of recurrent, incomprehensible hatred and reawakened barbarism,[2] is nothing but the symptom of the struggle that must precede unification. For precisely this struggle is the full triumph of world history's necessary development: those who think that they can stand in its way, or even destroy it, serve the inevitable progress of events no less than its so-called supporters....

The way in which the Jewish world will merge into the European follows from the above-mentioned principle. To merge does not mean to perish [*aufgehen ist nicht untergehen*].[3] Only the obstinate, self-centered independence of the Jews will be destroyed, not that element which becomes a part of the whole; serving the totality, this element shall lose nothing of its independence or substance. The larger entity [which will embrace all Judaism] shall be the richer for the new ingredient, not the poorer for the lost contrast.[4]

...The wealth of its particularities is the very source of Europe's strength, and it can neither scorn it nor ever have too much of it. No particularity will ever harm Europe; only the single [autonomous] rule of this particularity, its exclusive self-righteousness, must be abolished; it must become a dependent particle among the many. They who see no third alternative between destruction and conspicuous distinction; who consider the eternal substrate of the idea to be its transitory rather than its material [embodiment]; who do not recognize the truth of the whole in every particularity and the truth of every particularity in the whole; who accept their respective viewpoint as the absolute, and reject another as a lie: they have neither understood their age nor the question at hand. This, however, is the consoling lesson of history properly understood: that everything passes without perishing, and yet persists, although it has long been consigned to the past. That is why neither the Jews will perish nor Judaism dissolve; in the larger movement of the whole they will seem to have disappeared, and yet they will live on as the river lives on in the ocean. Remember, gentlemen and friends, remember on this occasion the words of one of the most noble men of the German fatherland, one of its greatest theologians and poets. His words express the intention of my thoughts more concisely: "There will be a time when no one in Europe will ask any longer, who is a Jew and who is a Christian?"[5]

To hasten the coming of this day, to bring it about with all the power at our disposal, and by concentrated effort: this is the task, gentlemen, which we have set for ourselves in establishing our society. What I have said thus far is nothing but an elaboration upon the first paragraph of our statutes. To recapitulate: we wish to help in pulling down the barrier which still exists between the Jew and the Christian, between the Jewish world and Europe; we want to reconcile that which, for thousands of years, has been moving along side by side without so much as touching each other....

We met for the first time toward the end of the year 1819. In many places of the German fatherland those horrible acts had occurred which to many seemed as the harbinger of an unforeseen return of the darkest Middle Ages.[6] We met with a view to help where it was necessary, and in order to consult with one another as to the means by which the deeply rooted malignancy could best be eradicated. At that time we did not have a more detailed purpose. We were then at the beginning of our efforts, sharing in all the wealth and all the poverty which every beginning offers simultaneously: wealth, because all further developments lay still before us, and poverty, because none of these developments had yet come into being. As befits all periods of childhood, a long time of contemplation had to pass before we could begin to work. We should have gladly encompassed all aspects of life; it hurt us to concentrate on a given detail, because in doing so we seemed to be missing so much. Only deeper insight taught us that he who cares for a detail is the most powerful protagonist of the whole. But as soon as we restricted ourselves we gained the certainty, which hitherto eluded us. Only

through this restriction did our society come into being.

In this restriction, however, we have been guided by a truly philosophical conception. Although we felt that, with the limited strength and means at our disposal, we could, for the time being, only deal with the scientific aspects of our project, we nevertheless did not yield to any one-sidedness, forgetting the many other directions of life. We have never failed to cling to the totality of all phenomena of life as our constant basis. No landowner will turn over a part of his ground just because he cannot be at all parts at one and the same time; in like manner, we have never neglected any single activity just because we could not start with all of them simultaneously. Here I am only recapitulating what has been laid down in the introduction to our statutes. May I now proceed to develop the major themes of our scientific activity in their natural order, and briefly characterize each one of them.

The scientific study of Jewish religion, history and philosophy has so far been either bereft of freedom or of independence. The studies of ignorant, prejudiced rabbis, who conceived of Judaism not as a part of the whole, but as exclusive and isolated from other branches of knowledge, did not produce any faithful or credible results—nor could they have done so, innocent as they were of any knowledge beyond their own narrow field. Any credible results [in the field of Jewish scholarship] are mainly due to the efforts of Christian scholars. But while the rabbis lacked the necessary freedom in their studies, the Christian approach to Judaism lacked independence: much too often it was turned it into a discipline secondary, and merely ancillary, to Christian theology. Our first priority, therefore, ought to be the establishment of an unbiased and completely independent study of the Science of Judaism which will be integrated into the whole of human knowledge....

NOTES

1. Eduard Gans (1798–1839), a descendant of court Jews. Gans was a jurist and historian. One of the seven founding members of the Society for the Culture and Science of the Jews, he served as its president from March 1821 until November 1823. Some four years earlier, on December 9, 1819, a month after the inaugural meeting

of the society, Gans submitted an application to the Prussian minister of education for an academic appointment at the Law Faculty of the University of Berlin. The minister unabashedly indicated his doubts as to whether a professing Jew, no matter how qualified, possessed the requisite spiritual aptitude to serve as a custodian of the German-Christian heritage, especially of such a subject as jurisprudence. Chagrined, Gans wrote to the minister, "I belong to that unfortunate class of human beings, which is hated because it is uneducated, and persecuted because it tries to educate itself." After repeated appeals, in August 1822, the Prussian cabinet responded by amending the law to explicity ban members of the Jewish faith from academic teaching positions. Gans subsequently went to Belgium, England, and France in search of a possible appointment. He was unsuccessful. In exasperation, he was baptized in Paris on December 12, 1825. As a Christian he returned to Berlin and was immediately granted the position he was previously denied as a Jew.

In this semiannual presidential address, delivered before the society in April 1822, Gans seeks to clarify the philosophical basis of the society. An outstanding student of Hegel, he was naturally influenced by his mentor.

2. Gans is referring to the 1819 outbreak of anti-Jewish literature and riots (see note 6).

3. The locution here suggests Hegel's concept of *Aufhebung*—connoting both abrogation and preservation—to designate the dialectic process in which a lower stage of history is both cancelled and preserved in a higher one.

4. Cf. "Philosophy, as occupying itself with the True, has to do with the *eternally present*. Nothing in the past is lost for it, for the Idea is ever present; Spirit is immortal; with it there is no past, no future, but an essential *now*. This necessarily implies that the present form of Spirit comprehends within it all earlier steps. The grades which Spirit seems to have left behind it, it still possesses in the depths of its present" (Georg Wilhelm Friedrich Hegel, *The Philosophy of History*, trans. J. Sibree [New York: Dover Publications, 1956], p. 79). This book, based on Hegel's lectures, was first edited and published by Gans.

5. The citation is from Johann Gottfried von Herder, *Reflections on the Philosophy of the History of Mankind*, trans. T. O. Churchill, abridged and ed. Frank E. Manuel (Chicago: The University of Chicago Press, 1968), p. 15.

6. Gans is referring to the anti-Jewish riots—the so-called Hep! Hep! riots—that broke out in August 1819 in Germany and spread to Denmark. The authorities exploited the riots to argue against the wisdom of emancipation since it obviously engendered untoward social tensions. In light of Gans' and his friends' concern about the riots, it should be noted that the Jewish establishment sought to play down the riots' significance.

"Hep! Hep!" was an anti-Jewish slogan used during the riots of 1819. The cry was then said to be of Crusader origin, formed from the initials of words *Hierosolyma est perdita* ("Jerusalem is lost").

4. ON THE CONCEPT OF A SCIENCE OF JUDAISM (1822)

IMMANUEL WOLF[1]

Judaism, based on its own inner principle and embodied, on the one hand, in a comprehensive literature, and, on the other, in the life of a large number of human beings, both can be and needs to be treated scientifically. Hitherto, however, it has never been described scientifically and comprehensively from a wholly independent standpoint. What Jewish scholars have achieved, especially in earlier times, is mostly theological in character. In particular, they have almost completely neglected the study of history. But Christian scholars, however great their merit in the development of individual aspects of Judaism, have almost always treated Judaism for the sake of a historical understanding of Christian theology, even if it was not their intention to place Judaism itself in a hateful light, or, as they put it, to confute Judaism. Even though some important scholarly works written from a general literary standpoint and interest have emerged, not merely as vehicles or propaedeutics for Christian theology (which is admittedly difficult to separate from Jewish theology), these achievements apply only to individual aspects of the whole. But if Judaism is to become an object of science in its own right and if a science of Judaism is to be formed, then it is obvious that quite a different method of treatment is under discussion. But any object, no matter of what type, that in its essence is of interest to the human spirit, and comprehensive in its diverse formation and development, can become the object of a special science.

The content of this special science is the systematic unfolding and representation of its object in its whole sweep, for its own sake and not for any ulterior purpose. If we apply this to the science of Judaism, then the following characteristics emerge:

1. The Science of Judaism comprehends Judaism in its fullest scope;
2. It unfolds Judaism in accordance with its essence and describes it systematically, always relating individual features back to the fundamental principle of the whole;
3. It treats the object of study in and for itself, for its own sake, and not for any special purpose of definite intention. It begins without any preconceived opinion and is not concerned with the final result. Its aim is neither to put its object in a favorable, nor in an unfavorable light, in relation to prevailing views, but to show it as it is. Science is self-sufficient and is in itself an essential need of the human spirit. It, therefore, needs to serve no other purpose than its own. But it is for that reason no less true that each science not only exercises its most important influence on other sciences but also on life. This can easily be shown to be true of the Science of Judaism....

The aim will be to depict Judaism, first from a historical standpoint, as it has gradually developed and taken shape, and then philosophically, according to its inner essence and idea. The textual knowledge of the literature of Judaism must precede both methods of study. Thus we have, first, the textual study of Judaism; second, a history of Judaism; third, a philosophy of Judaism....

Source: Immanuel Wolf, "Ueber den Begriff einer Wissenschaft des Judentums," *Zeitschrift fuer die Wissenschtaft des Judentums* 1, no. 1 (1822), pp. 1ff. Trans. Lionel E. Kochan, *Leo Baeck Institute Year Book* 2 (1957), pp. 201–3. Reprinted by permission of the Leo Baeck Institute.

This would be, in general outline, the framework, of the science of Judaism. A vast field embracing literary researches, compilations, and developments. But if the object, as such, is important in science and the human spirit in general, its progressive development is bound to follow. The truly scientific spirit, therefore, cannot on account of the multifariousness and the vast scope of the field doubt the possibility that such a science might be established. The essence of science is universality, infinity; and therein lies the spur and the attraction which it has for the human spirit whose nobler nature rejects any limitations, any rest, any standing still....

It remains to indicate in a few words that aspect in the light of which establishment of a science of Judaism seems to be a necessity of our age. This is the inner world of the Jews themselves. This world, too, has in many ways been disturbed and shaken by the unrelenting progress of the spirit and the associated changes in the life of the nations. It is manifest everywhere that the fundamental principle of Judaism is again in a state of inner ferment, striving to assume a shape in harmony with the spirit of the times. But in accordance with the age, this development can only take place through the medium of science. For the scientific attitude is the characteristic attitude of our time. But as the formation of a science of Judaism is an *essential need* of the Jews themselves, it is clear that, although the field of science is open to all men, it is primarily the Jews who are called upon to devote themselves to it. The Jews must once again show their mettle as doughty fellow workers in a common task of mankind. They must raise themselves and their principle to the level of a science, for this is the attitude of the European world. On this level the relationship of strangeness in which Jews and Judaism have hitherto stood to the outside world must vanish. And if one day a bond is to join the whole of humanity, then it is *the bond of science, the bond of pure rationality, the bond of truth.*[2]

NOTES

1. Immanuel Wohlwill (pseudonym, Immanuel Wolf, 1799–1829). A student of philosophy at the University of Berlin, he served as secretary of the Society for the Culture and Science of the Jews from 1821 to 1822. This essay served to introduce the society's journal and to define the concept of the Science of Judaism. Like that of his friend Gans, Wolf's thought has a strong Hegelian bent.

2. This dogmatic valuation of science betrays a basic flaw in the society's ideology. "Though the leaders [of the society] were concerned with giving expression to their consciousness of themselves as Jews, they failed to develop a rationale for a continued Jewish identification. Their conception of the future did not provide any incentive for the Jew to remain a Jew. The goal was integration into Europe without specification as to how it was to differ from total absorption. Their primary concern was the Jew as human being, not as Jew; they wanted only to lift him to a higher level of self-understanding" (Michael Meyer, *The Origins of the Modern Jew* [Detroit: Wayne State University press, 1967], p. 180). This ideological flaw may explain why the society so quickly collapsed in the wake of the resignation of its president, Gans. After a Royal Cabinet Order of August 1822 legally proscribed Jews from teaching in Prussia, Gans, in dire economic straits, accepted a government travel grant as "compensation." This act of acquiescence to the powers of reaction irreparably undermined Gans' moral authority within the society, obliging him to withdraw. Dispirited, the society formally dissolved in May 1824. Gans' baptism in December 1825 only added an ironic and tragic coda to the story of a society that was to restore Jewish pride. Gans was not the only member of the society to permit the dictates of career to compromise his integrity and to accept baptism, It is, however, an exaggeration to speak of a mass conversion of the society's members. Of a total of eighty-one regular and honorary members, only six converted (see H. G. Reissner, *Eduard Gans: Ein Leben im Vormaerz* [Tuebingen: J.C.B. Mohr, 1965], pp. 174–85). In addition to the loss of their president and driving spirit, the demise of the society can be attributed to the lack of support from the Jewish community. Yet, in the last analysis, the society was not a total debacle, for emerging from its ruins was the Science of Judaism, thanks largely to the Promethean efforts of its vice president and the editor of its journal, Leopold Zunz.

5. ON RABBINIC LITERATURE (1818)

LEOPOLD ZUNZ[1]

"Anyone can praise," says Nuschirvan, "but well-reasoned censure in a spirit of humility is much more difficult." Now since I esteem this essay above self-love, and science (*Wissenschaft*) above both, I trust that one who truly knows will tell me in his review in what way, my review—for so I see this essay—may be lacking.

The use of the first person "I" in this foreword and of the plural "we" in the essay proper is not intended to satisfy [simultaneously] the captious partisans of both forms. I am of the opinion that an author appears personally only in documents, travelogues, on checks, in prefaces, law suits, laundry slips, receipts, replies to critics, restaurant bills and the like. In humorous pieces the author may use the first person singular but nonetheless, he goes beyond himself; in theoretical speculations he prefers the more modest "we" since he is then part of an entire battalion doing battle for mute science.... *"Primum hoc statuo esse virtutis conciliare animos hominum"* ["The conciliation of the minds of men is deemed the highest virtue"] (Cicero)....

Beyond the interest they arouse, their antiquity and their content, the venerable literary remains from the efflorescence of the ancient Hebrews owe their importance to chance. The revolutions which began among the Jewish people, and which influenced them no less than the entire world, cast these ruins, called the Hebrew canon, as the foundation of Christian states; the constant advance of science [*Wissenschaft*], adding its own embellishments, transformed these several books into a structure of spiritual industry more wondrous even than the Greek, for its richness was created from scantier matter.

Such an appreciation was never granted to the later productions of the Hebrew nation. One had the impression that after Israel's intellectual and political decline her creative energies had been lost for some considerable time and she was content with exegesis, now more, now less successful, of the few works remaining from better days. When the shades of barbarism began to recede slowly from the darkened earth and the light from Jews dispersed everywhere perforce struck everywhere, a new and alien learning [*Bildung*] intermingled with the remains of the ancient Hebrew and was molded by minds and centuries into a literature we call, rabbinic.*

With the Reformation, a necessary consequence of the flourishing of classical learning, great interest was aroused in the study of biblical literature, complemented by what we may call a curious zeal to ransack the Orient. As a result, just as the fatherland's richest and most endearing spiritual creations began to occupy and exhilarate us, we have witnessed this last century a heated assault on rabbinical wisdom which itself had collapsed and had, perhaps, been extinguished forever. But as rabbinic literature was on the decline, European literature was on the rise, and Jews began to be drawn to it. What remains of the former in these last fifty years is nothing but a language borrowed as an accessible and familiar garment for clothing ideas which are to prepare the way for the utter disappearance of rabbinic literature.

Precisely because Jews in our times—limiting our attention to the Jews of Germany—are seizing upon German language and German learning [*Bildung*] with such earnestness and are thus, perhaps unwittingly, carrying the neo-Hebraic literature [i.e., rabbinic

---

* [Asterisks indicate Zunz's note:] Accordingly, one should include under this rubric only those writings which are either by content or by authorship rabbinic. But actually, the title *rabbi* is but a polite honorific and its significance is less than the title *Dr.* Why not then talk of neo-Hebrew or simply Jewish literature?

Source: Leopold Zunz, "Etwas ueber die rabbinische Literatur," *Gesammelte Schriften* (Berlin, 1875), vol. 1, pp. 1–31. Trans. by A. Schwartz.

literature] to its grave, science steps in demanding an account of what has already been sealed away.[2] Now, when no new significant development is likely to disturb our survey, when we have access to tools greater than those available to scholars of the sixteenth and seventeenth centuries, when a higher culture permits a more illuminating treatment, when Hebrew books are more readily available than they will likely be in 1919—now, so we think, the development of our science in a grand style is a duty, one whose weight increases because of the fact that the complex problem of the fate of the Jews may derive a solution, if only in part, from this science. External legal and religious pressures are insufficient to bring forth harmony if one does not know the nature of the instrument or how to handle it. A theoretical—or legal, theological and economic—knowledge of today's Jew is necessarily one-sided; Spirit [*Geist*] can be apprehended only with determinate ideas and by knowledge of customs and of will.[3] An improper point of departure will avenge what goes by the name of amelioration [*Verbesserung*]; hasty innovations grant the old, and what is worse the outworn, too great a value. In order to recognize and distinguish among the old and useful, the obsolete and harmful, the new and desirable, we must embark upon a considered study of the people and its political and moral history. But herein there is a serious problem: that Jewish affairs will be dealt with in the same manner that Jewish literature, if highly esteemed or not, is treated—in the heat of bias.

We have not digressed from literature to the civil existence of the Jews in order to leave behind a tangled skein which more adroit fingers may attempt to unravel. We have traded their mutual influence in broad strokes in order to return to an examination of literature, its origins, its contents, its relations with its elder and contemporary sisters, its current stock, its unique qualities. Here and there we do encounter occasional small lamps but their oil is often poor and insufficient; a search for genuine sunlight would be in vain. How is it possible, one may ask, that at a time when all science and all of man's doings have been illumined in brilliant rays, when the most remote corners of the earth have been reached, the most obscure languages studied and nothing seems too insignificant to assist in the construction of wisdom, how is it possible that our science [i.e., the academic study of rabbinic literature] alone lies neglected? What hinders us from fully knowing the contents of

rabbinic literature, from understanding it, from properly interpreting it, from estimating its proper worth, from surveying it at ease? (We have no fear of being misunderstood in this matter. The entire literature of the Jews, in its widest scope, is presented here as the object of scholarly research; in this context it is not at all our concern whether the context of this entire literature should, or could, also be the *norm for our own judgment.*)[4]

We will reach this height only with the aid of sundry and good preliminary works. The question, therefore, recurs: why are they lacking? In response we must clarify what we understand by preliminary literary works and establish that at present they are in fact lacking. After our attempt to account for this phenomenon it will be apparent that as long as this lack persists we will achieve neither clarity nor completeness in our subject.

By preliminary literary works we mean either studies which deal partially with an entire subject or exhaustively with a limited aspect of a specific subject. In the latter type, each individual subject, each scientific problem—even if it does not admit of a total solution—every noteworthy discovery for the advance of knowledge should be illuminated in a critical light. Critical editions of manuscripts, good translations, accurate reference works, biographies and the like, all can properly make claim to the title of preliminary literary works.

Ranking higher in our estimation are those works which encompass an entire science, enriching knowledge with important discoveries or transforming outlooks with new ideas, which take upon themselves to describe the literature of hundreds, even thousands, of years, leaving behind traces broad enough for another century to follow. These include accounts of philosophical systems, histories of individual doctrines, [ideational] parallels, literary collections, etc.

However laudable and useful these efforts, they will never be able singly to attain to the loftier goal if their authors, in wrapping the small stone they have taken for polishing, disregard the mighty alabaster mountain from whence it came, and having completed their labors, fold their arms, content with themselves and their fine work, another gem among the wonders of nature. Only by considering the literature of a nation as a gateway to a comprehensive knowledge of the course of its culture throughout the ages, by noting how at every moment the essence of the given and the supplementary, i.e., the inner and the external, array themselves; how fate, climate, customs, religion and chance seize one another in friendly or hostile spirit; how, finally, the present is the necessary result of all that preceded it—only thus will one tread with true reverence before this divine temple and humbly enter this hallway, later to regard the panorama spread out below with deserving pleasure.

This honor will be attained only by one who has taken upon himself the pain of scaling this mountain, but even he will be able to give a satisfactory accounting of the entire prospect only if he grasps each part with the perceptive eye of art. In this lofty view our science is transformed into a series of sciences, each of which in all its parts is to be cultivated, lest the whole be distorted by substantial error. If we now turn attention to the vast quantity of material to be investigated, sorted and worked under the aegis of critical scholarship we will discover a three-part path which will assist us in discerning and assessing the given idea [under investigation] as well as our way of knowing it. Theoretically, then, we divide critical scholarship into three aspects: ideational, philological and historical analysis. The latter considers the history of ideas from the time of their transmission to the present in which we have arrived at our knowledge.

Proceeding now to the literary products of the Jewish people, the first question to be asked is: What do they include?...

Beginning with theology, it must immediately be acknowledged that the Jews have never fully nor clearly set out their theological system; nevertheless in worthy fragments they are expressed more clearly than by Bartolocci[5] who from myths and legends has concocted the "contradiction of rabbinical blasphemies." Concerning the mythology of the Jews, with the exception of several valuable works on ancient mythology, we still lag far behind—this is all the more surprising when we recall that like dogmatology the mythology of the Jews is related to the Christians', as Roeder claims.[6] In the realm of religion the sin has been perpetrated intentionally and systematically! Nothing more distorted, more damaging, more dishonest has ever anywhere been written than that which has been written on the religion of Israel. The art of inciting malice has here reached its pinnacle. No distinctions have been made between custom and liturgy, nor between these and fundamental religious principles; in this manner ten blameless matters have shared in the condemnation of one deserving of scorn. To embark on a history of synagogue ritual based on the sources* would at the present time be a worthwhile, although a difficult, undertaking.

Leaving behind the ecclesiastical realm and turning to the political, we come upon the field of legislation and jurisprudence in which several important works by Jews are available for our scholarly scrutiny. Works on the subject of state constitution are interesting, if only in having been written under conditions of subjugation. Nor would it be unrewarding to study the *Poskim*, halakhic decisions in which the rabbis established the authority of their decisions by citing the words of eminent sages as proof-texts. Even more interesting is the task of systematically comparing criminal theory (*culpa*), so acutely presented in the three Talmudic *Babbot*,[7] with Roman law. Hebrew legal terminology will certainly gain clarity from being set parallel to the Roman and Greek. The gradual change of Jewish law and its ultimate submergence in the European could be described only after much arduous preliminary work of this sort.

Religion, legal principles and also ethics should be examined essentially within the context of the sources; and it is high time to present matter-of-factly** the splendid writings on these subjects found in the

---

* This research, it seems to us, should be conducted according to the following topics: (a) The nature of Jewish worship and its position, in the *halakhah*; its influence on the consciousness (*Gesinnung*) and character of the Jews, (b) The form and content of the liturgy; the writings of Jewish authors on this subject...(c) The manner of Jewish prayer; the opinion of non-Jewish authors on this subject. Should the research on this subject, which will, of course, take into cognizance the differences of country and time, be conducted by competent individuals it will be a source of joy. Moreover, much of pragmatic value will be derived from this research, such as the correction of errors that fell into the liturgy and the identification of patterns of change in the liturgy [as a result of the interests of the Reform movement].

** A basic moral sensibility exists in every individual and despite the great variation man is man [*bleibt der Mensch—Mensch*]. The latest innovation in ethical literature is thus but a renewal of the old, pristine Mosaic ethics. It seems to us then that a compendium of the cardinal moral teachings of the Old Testament would be a worthwhile project, one that a beginning scholar could undertake.

Talmud and in the writings of later sages. Similarly, whatever in the works of well-known authors is or appears to be in conflict with these writings should be illuminated—a conflict which could have kept Eisenmenger[8] from publishing his [denunciations of the Talmud]....

We should [now] consider man as a denizen of Earth: how he, from the vantage point of this planet, is an investigator of nature, an astronomer measuring the heavenly bodies, a geographer sailing the seas. If we give attention for a moment to the common basis of these sciences, mathematics, we will note the large number of [Hebrew] works in this field. It will thus seem worthwhile to prepare an explanatory dictionary [of Hebrew mathematical terms], especially since each mathematician frequently employs his own terminology. We would also welcome a presentation of the first traces of mathematics in the Talmud, as well as a history of Hebrew mathematical writings to recent times. A still greater yield awaits the student of Jewish astronomy. Beginning with an etymological study of the most ancient [Hebrew astronomical] terms and a collection of relevant sections from some eighty Hebrew books, it would then be possible to approach this literature proper, which first appears around the year 1100. It also seems to us necessary to add to the foregoing an inventory of Hebrew chronological studies.... Jewish travel and geographic works are less numerous and less interesting, nevertheless it is possible to extract language-enriching topographical notes from them....

The stock of natural science knowledge in the Talmud and in later works is a field which has been completely overlooked. A treasure-house of information addressed specifically to this subject is to be found here. Secular rabbinic literature includes no hiero-botany, hiero-zoology, sacred physics or sacred medical theory, even though it would have been easy to oppose superstition without calling upon its rival, physics. Close by is the theory of medicine, based on a knowledge of nature and man (i.e., psychology, anthropology and physiology and the proper application of this knowledge). Until now no learned physician has taken upon himself the trouble to describe and discuss schools of medical knowledge, discoveries, the biographies and works of ancient Jewish physicians, while Imbonati's[9] catalog of Latin translations from Hebrew mentions only three medical works.

Only one step separates the knowledge of nature from the utilization of this knowledge. But rarely have scholars taken the trouble to penetrate the thickets of technology and industrial arts, nor have the authorities taken the trouble to initiate archeological digs in Palestine and Babylonia. Many references to these matters in the Mishnah, therefore, especially in the sixth order, still remain to be clarified. Industry and commerce also belong here. The study of the ancient histories of [Jewish] industry and commerce compared to the opinions of esteemed authors would be an important work bringing to light significant findings. This field, it is true, is somewhat foreign to us but it seems possible that aspects of the paper money system have been developed by Jews. We have several works concerning not only the use of materials but also their embellishment by art.... Excepting poetry, about which something will be said later, it seems that only [Jewish] architecture has attracted any attention. For some reason we are unable to recall any Hebrew work on the art of printing among the Jews. And why have [Hebrew] calligraphic masterpieces never been collected? Works on [Jewish] music have for the most part yet to be published. The chapter on [Jewish] inventions is still rather thin, but it is hoped that in an age when we enjoy greater liberty and freer activity, something will be done to enrich it.

We have now arrived at the universal life of the nation in which we will have to distinguish between the ephemeral and the lasting, that is, between history and archeology. But from whence will we bring to Jewish history its impartial Paul Sarpi?[10] For a full account of the fate of the Jews in all the lands in which they dwelled, the Hebrew works do not suffice (they have already been drained dry) nor do the well-known studies of modern scholars such as Basnage,[11] Holberg,[12] Prideaux[13] and others. The most neglected books are a possible source of some fragmentary information; just as the Jewish people are dispersed so is their history....

Turning now to the lever for lifting this mass of material we come upon language, which will remain adamantly obscure to whomever does not wholeheartedly devote himself to the lofty treasures ... of this the most dispersed and abject of peoples. For language is the first friend leading us unto the road to science and the last to which we shall long to return. It alone is capable of removing the veil of the past; it alone can prepare minds for the future; the researcher, therefore, must beat its obstinacy—for what has taken hundreds of years to be produced requires hundreds of years to be refined.

Of the entire linguistic creation we begin first with poetry. Whereas the ancient has been the subject of some clarification, the more recent has been totally neglected. There are problems, which have not at all been raised. For example: Did the ancient Jews not write any drama? What poetry was produced during the first thousand years of the Christian era? When were the *piyutim*[14] composed? What is their relation to Chaldean poetry and the like? The situation of rhetorics, or rather the art of style, is worse yet. As Hebrew works on this subject are rare, its rules should be bared with greater diligence, especially in light of the fact that for a hundred years or so Hebrew style has achieved pure and beautiful form. Many special studies can be undertaken in this as yet untended field, such as on the generally misunderstood nature of hyperbole, the use of *remez*[15] in the Talmud, later philosophical style, the differences between prosaic poetry and poetic prose, satiric literature, etc. A two-fold task is called for regarding grammar: to fill in lacunae in the neglected historical account of Jewish grammarians and to establish a system for the structure of modern Hebrew [i.e., post-biblical Hebrew]. This must be preceded, however, by a learned study of the Chaldean language; only afterwards would it be possible to make any claims for a basic history of the Hebrew language, followed by an examination of philosophical parallels between biblical and rabbinic Hebrew. The required auxiliary tools for that, however, are still in short supply; there is as yet no lexicon, like Forcellini's,[16] nor will there be except as a result of the combined efforts of many, each of whom will prepare lists, or rather, concordances of single works. That the old Hebrew dictionaries stuck in the libraries are of no lexicological use as long as they remain in isolation needs no proof. The state of synonymy is even worse: there are hardly any studies of synonyms found which treat the Jewish authors, even less those which concern ancient Hebrew. Meanwhile, etymology is impoverished by the fact that most of our rabbis neglect Oriental studies, and that the Orientalists neglect Hebrew.

And so we are finally presented with a survey of the large stock of writings about which much useful and excellent, even great things, are to be found in the works of scholars; much, however, yet remains to be done. The account of Jewish diplomacy can be completed; once signatures are confirmed, the chronological order of facsimiles can be established, and the order of undated manuscripts be fixed. To this can be added a history of manuscripts, as well as a long-awaited historical account of Hebrew typography. We will still be lacking good catalogs of public and private library holdings, like the Dibdin Catalog of the Spencer Library,[17] without which the necessary listing of Hebrew literature cannot be completed, and with which we can proceed with greater passion to the critical examination of currently, and formerly, available works.

If we want to comprehend the reasons for the absence of research in rabbinic literature, we must first encounter those [representatives of traditional Judaism] who charge us with degrading what took place in "rabbinic obscurity," to use Schickard's[18] expression. To us it appears that the assaults on and dismissals [such as Schickard's] of the glorious and useful work of our ancestors and contemporaries are signs of a fashionable ignorance, or in more refined language, lack of understanding. We have only sought to point out gaps, to encourage a renewal of study which previously had flourished, not always in the proper direction perhaps, but more vigorously than today when this field is neglected by all. Bearing down on our science is the misfortune common to all science—the misfortune of human fallibility; here, however, further damage has been caused as a consequence of those defects [viz., lack of objectivity] which have brought about this decline of scholarship.

The indifference to rabbinic literature is of two sorts. Either it is directed against all scholarship, in which case it is without remedy, or it is directed exclusively against rabbinic scholarship—on the assumption perhaps that it is not useful, or that it contains no wisdom, or that it is damaging to good taste, or that it is not possible to make much of it, or that it is godless, or because it is nowhere well received. Usually this indifference dissolves into contempt, and not infrequently men of science line up against our science rather than against its authors. More objectionable than the indifference, more shocking than the contempt is the partisanship, not of love but of hatred, with which this study is approached. Anything in it which can be used against the Jews or Judaism has been a welcome find. These scholars have gathered half-understood expressions from every corner in order with their aid to pillory their eternal rival; up until a hundred years ago there was not a single case of a learned doctor taking upon himself to collect the good and beautiful in Jewish writings so that for once the Jews would be described in a charitable light.

Thank you, Eternal God! Those times are past. Daring and honest pens spread enlightened learning among the people while greater rulers support the work of those pens with their own honor and might.

Today, when many Jews are lost to the study of rabbinic literature, it is simply because of ignorance, the consequence of an ever-increasing decline in the study of the Hebrew language. This, in turn, is a consequence in part of the poor prospects for advancement in the profession of Jewish scholarship, the easier paths leading to other sciences, the praiseworthy move into arts, crafts, agriculture and military service, but also in part because of the contemporary coldness toward religion in general and toward our ancestral literature in particular, and because of the foolish notion that this history of Judaism does not befit the honor of an educated man and finally because of an amiable modern superficiality about which we will want to say more.

True, there are inherent obstacles which repel even Hebraists from the profession—the paucity of manuscripts, the small hope for advancement and livelihood, the difficulties of the Jewish book trade and certainly the need to acquire skill in various allied disciplines when the mastery of Hebrew alone is often difficult enough to achieve. But the contrary error is also widespread, that a few glances in German books can make one learned, not to mention the concomitant writing fury rampant today. A type of person has been created occupying a middling position, hesitant, going about his studies without zeal, analyzing Hebrew works without sufficient preparation, damaging the science and piling up useless material. One sins against interpretation, criticism and particularly against method; another treats his subject cursorily, without due respect, with so little regard for truth and thoroughness that a contempt for both science and reader is revealed. A third makes his work easier still, knowing in advance what he wants to, and will, find, and then swelling with delight when he finds it; yet another recoils from even putting his hand to the task, since his predecessors did not pave

a way for him. And so the words of the fathers are confirmed: one error leads to another.

In light of these phenomena it is obvious why we have not had satisfactory studies of Hebrew literature until now, nor can we expect any in the near future. Even if we be equipped with all the requisite tools, with knowledge and auxiliary aids, we will ourselves, by working the ideas, be creating new ideas and material; thus is bibliography, criticism and the history not only of the science but of history itself produced. The material we weave into the fabric of objective science, but which originates in the subjective treatment of a preconceived idea, is converted by the art by which we acquire science into new matter to be worked by us and by future generations.

Above all these realms of science, above all this tumult of human activity, ruling in exclusive majesty, is philosophy, omnipresent but invisible, devoted with unassailable independence to all human cognition. Therefore, we preferred not to see it as a special science nor as the essence of Jewish wisdom. It is as well the higher historical knowledge, which this wisdom has traversed over hundreds of years, and which has been set out properly and poorly, in Jewish and non-Jewish works. When we take upon ourselves to learn and transmit the intellectual greatness of this people, it is, therefore, the supreme guide. In this way every historical datum which diligence has uncovered, equity has deciphered, philosophy has utilized and good taste has put in its proper place will be a contribution to human knowledge, the only worthwhile goal of all research. Only this higher view suits a science elevated above human pettiness, lands and nations; it alone can lead us to a true history of Jewish philosophy in which mental processes can be presented and understood while pursuing with all historical rigor the parallel learning embracing the world.

Let not philosophical subalterns hinder this flight to the kingdom of hope by their questions of utility. To whomever does not grasp the highest relations of science, its most estimable greatness, to whomever does not see every detail as an integral part of spiritual creation—to him we have nothing to say. Better that we turn to finer feelings, to noble souls who known that man never ceases his forward motion—those who pay less heed to what has already been done but look instead to what remains to be done. Many fields still covered with thistle and thorn promise a rich harvest to whoever will tend them; many noxious seeds will yet be sown, damaging the fit crop nearby. Much ripened crop will be laid low by the hail of passion, malice and pigheadedness; but much good fruit has been spared lying somewhere in the ground or has been crushed callously by haughtiness.

We conclude this survey of universals with a note on a single unknown and unpublished Hebrew work, on which we are now working. … It is entitled *Sefer hamaalot*[19] by Shemtov ben Joseph ibn Falaquera, a famous rabbi of the thirteenth century. In part because of the solid thoughtfulness of the author it unfolds in a lucid, concise and fluent style a theory of the degrees of intellectual perfection. This work establishes its author as a praiseworthy thinker, a wise reader whose ideas though sometimes daring are presented with restraint.…

In accord with the rigor with which we recommend that science be treated generally, we have in the present case attempted to set the task which this work is to fulfill: to present in this critique not only the theoretical skeleton but also to impart all in pleasing form such that nothing, not even what is veiled, is overlooked. But beyond this desired completeness we hope that our effort will beckon others, more worthy of the subject and closer to the goal, to follow in our footsteps. Our intention has not been only to snatch from oblivion a work venerable by virtue of its age, outstanding by virtue of its content and because of its rarity destined for oblivion. More pleasing hopes have sweetened our labors! The hope that it will awake the passion for more thorough and fruitful studies, with gaze ever fixed on completeness, of the outstanding creations of the Jewish nation; the hope that the light so cast on the better parts of rabbinic literature will assist in dispelling the prejudices usually held against it. Truly, when we so boldly break into the midst of the author's world, it is not our talents but our burning desire to strive for the good and the beautiful which will justify us in the critical and indulgent eyes of the reader.

NOTES

1. Leopold Zunz (1794–1886). Among the active members of the Society for the Culture and Science of the Jews, he was the only one to maintain a commitment to Jewish studies. This is partly explained by the fact that he considered the Science of Judaism to be his professional calling; even before the establishment of the society he engaged in Jewish scholarship. He was uniquely equipped to do so, having received a sound traditional education and possessing the disposition for assiduous and meticulous scholarship. As the Science of Judaism was not recognized as a legitimate and autonomous academic discipline and therefore not included in the university curriculum, Zunz pursued his research in this field as a private scholar. He made his living variously as a preacher in Reform synagogues, as an editor of a Berlin newspaper, as a headmaster of a primary school and as a director of a Jewish teachers' seminary. He refused to support the establishment of an independent institute of Jewish studies for fear that this would sever the discipline from general academic and cultural life. His scholarship was prodigious, the larger portion being devoted to research in synagogal liturgy and practices. Modern Jewish studies are immeasurably indebted to his pioneering effort.

   In this essay, published in 1818, a year prior to the founding of the Society for the Culture and Science of the Jews, Zunz presented a program for the scientific study of Judaism. The essay is permeated with a youthful enthusiasm for the ideal of *Wissenschaft*. Specifically, it provided a new, indeed secular, definition of Jewish intellectual activity. Aside from Scripture, Zunz observed, Jewish literature was almost totally neglected by modern scholarship. This neglect he ascribed to Christian bias against post-biblical Jewish spirituality. As a bias this attitude was by definition unscientific, and it had led to a total ignorance of the wide range of Jewish intellectual activity in the post-biblical period. This activity, he maintained, was not confined to scriptural exegesis and Talmudic legalism, but embraced all aspects of human culture. Zunz felt that it would thus be more proper to place *all* post-biblical Jewish literature under the rubric of "neo-Hebrew" literature. He preferred this term because it underscored the methodological necessity to expand the conception of Jewish literature from a specific genre of religious literature, bearing as it did great stigma, to a broad chronological designation for all post-biblical Jewish literary endeavor.

2. Hegel summarized this historicist premise when he epigrammatically said that the owl of Minerva—the goddess of the sciences—only takes flight at dusk. Contemplation—philosophy and *Wissenschaft*—is *after* the event.

3. The language here is Hegelian. Hegel—whose *Phenomenology of Spirit* (1807) was widely discussed at that time in Berlin academic circles—traces the spiritual history of humanity, namely, the historical

development of humanity's consciousness and rational self-awareness of itself and of his position in the universe. Language, art, religion and philosophy—which develop as humanity's rational consciousness of itself grows—are humanity's vehicles for understanding *Geist*, that is, the cosmic spirit which is the source of truth and rationality and which underlies and manifests itself in all reality. *Geist* is manifest in the world in accordance with a rational and historical plan. In that humanity's rational consciousness of itself is also the consciousness of *Geist*, humanity's cultural history is also the history of *Geist*. The rational plan by which *Geist* unfolds itself is "the universal and one Idea" that determines the inner reason of all external reality. The expression of the idea relevant to an aspect of reality is "the determinate Idea," which is made conscious through conceptual thought. Thus, as Zunz wishes to argue, the essence of a particular cultural group, such as the Jews, is ascertained by its determinate ideas and modes of consciousness. The influence of Hegel is not otherwise marked in Zunz's thought. See A. Altmann, "Zur Fruehgeschichte der juedischen Predigt in Deutschland: Leopold Zunz als Prediger," *Leo Baeck Institute Year Book 6* (1961), pp. 21, 25.

4. In the original text this parenthetical statement appears in a footnote.

5. Giulio Bartolocci (1613–1687), Italian Christian Hebraist and bibliographer. He taught Hebrew and rabbinic literature at the Collegium Neophytorum (for Jewish converts) in Rome. His four-volume *Bibliotheca Magna Rabbinica*...(1657–1693) was the first systematic, comprehensive bibliography of Jewish literature.

6. Johann Ulrich Roeder, *Archaeologie der Kirchendogmen* (1812).

7. Reference is to *Baba kama, Baba mezia* and *Baba batra*—three sections of the Mishnaic tractate *Nezikin*.

8. Johann Andreas Eisenmenger (1654–1704), author of a pseudoscholarly work, *Entdecktes Judenthum* [Judaism Unmasked], denouncing Talmudic Judaism.

9. Carlo Guiseppe Imbonati(-tus) (1650?–1696), Italian Hebraist.

10. Paolo Sarpi (pseudonym, *Pietro Soave Polano*, 1552–1623), Venetian patriot, church reformer and scholar. His chief literary work, *History of the Council of Trent* (1619)—a critique of the papal attempt at a Counter-Reformation—was considered in Zunz's day to be a milestone in scholarly archival research. Leopold von Ranke was later to demonstrate Sarpi's tendentious reading of manuscripts. See Ranke, *History of the Popes* (Berlin, 1834–36), appendix three.

11. Jacques Christian Basnage (1653–1725), French Protestant and historian. His five-volume *L'histoire et la religion des Juifs depuis Jésus Christ jusqu'à present* (1706–1711) marks the first attempt to understand Judaism in terms of history.

12. Ludvig Holberg (1684–1754), Danish writer and dramatist. He published a sympathetic history of the Jews, *Den jødiske historie* (1742).

13. Humphrey Prideaux (1648–1724), English orientalist. He lectured in Hebrew at Christ Church College, Oxford University.

14. As a genre the term *piyutim* ("synagogal poetry") refers specifically to those liturgical poems added to the prayers prescribed by halakhah.

15. Hebrew *remez* ("veiled allusion") is a type of scriptural exegesis.

16. Egidio Forcellini (1688–1768), Italian lexicographer. His monumental *Totius latinilalis lexicon* appeared posthumously in 1771.

17. The Spencer Library was founded by the English bibliophile George John Spencer, second Earl Spencer (1758–1834). His priceless library of over 40,000 volumes is today part of the John Rylands Library in Manchester. Spencer's librarian was Thomas Frognall Dibdin, who prepared the four-volume catalog, *Bibliotheca Spenceriana* (London, 1814).

18. Wilhelm Schickard (also Schickhardt, 1592–1635), professor of biblical languages at the University of Tuebingen.

19. Zunz later wrote a Latin dissertation on this book, for which he was awarded a doctorate from the University of Halle in 1821.

6. SCHOLARSHIP AND EMANCIPATION (1832)[1]

LEOPOLD ZUNZ

Permit me to preface the necessary information about the contents and the meaning of the book, which is herewith presented to my readers with a few remarks about Jewish affairs in general and the problems to whose solution I should like to contribute in particular. In doing so I appeal the judgments of authorities which recognize prejudice and abuses to places where the verdict pronounced is truth and justice. For when all around us freedom, scholarship, and civilization are fighting for and gaining new ground, the Jews too are entitled to make claim to serious interest and untrammeled justice. Or shall the arbitrariness of club-law and medieval medicine retain a foothold only in the laws applying to Jews, at a time when clericalism and Inquisition, despotism and slavery, torture and censorship are on their way out?

It is high time that the Jews of Europe, particularly those of Germany, be granted right and liberty rather than rights and liberties—not some paltry, humiliating privileges, but complete and uplifting civil rights. We have no desire for stingy apportioned rights, which are balanced by an equal number of wrongs; we derive no pleasure from concessions born of pity; we are revolted by privileges obtained in an underhanded manner. Any man should blush with shame, whom a patent of nobility from the powers-that-be raises him above his *brothers in faith*, while the law, with stigmatizing exclusion, assigns to him a place below the lowest of his *brothers in fatherland*. Only in lawful, mutual recognition can we find satisfaction, only irrevocable equality can bring our suffering to an end. However, I see no love or justice in a freedom which removes the shackles from the hand only to apply them to the tongue, in a tolerance which takes pleasure in our decline rather than our progress, in a citizenship which offers protection without honor, burdens without prospects. Such noxious elements can only produce serious sickness in the body politic, harming the individual as well as the community....

The neglect of Jewish scholarship goes hand in hand with civil discrimination against the Jews. Through a higher intellectual level and a more thorough knowledge of their own affairs the Jews could have achieved a greater degree of recognition and thus more justice. Furthermore, much bad legislation, many a prejudice against Jewish antiquity, and much condemnation of new endeavors are a direct consequence of the state of neglect in which Jewish literature and Jewish scholarship have been for about seventy years, particularly in Germany. And even though writings about the Talmud and against the Jews mushroomed overnight and several dozen Solons[2] offered themselves to us as reformers, there was no book of any consequence which the statesmen could have consulted, no professor lectured about Judaism and Jewish literature, no German learned society offered prizes in this field, no philanthropist went traveling for this purpose. Legislators and scholars, not to mention the rabble among writers, had to follow in the footsteps of the 17th-century authorities. Eisenmenger,[3] Schudt,[4] Buxtorf,[5] and others acted like beggars, or had to borrow from the dubious wisdom of modern informants. Indeed, most people frankly admitted their ignorance of this area or betrayed it with their very first words. The [supposed] knowledge of Judaism has not progressed beyond the point where Eisenmenger left off 135 years ago, and philological studies have made almost no progress in 200 years. This explains the fact that even estimable writers assume an entirely different character—one

Source: Leopold Zunz, *Die gottesdienstlichen Vorträge der Juden historisch entwickelt [The liturgical addresses of the Jews].* (Berlin: A. Asher, 1832), pp. iii–v, vii, ix–xi, xii. Trans., Harry Zohn, in Nahum N. Glatzer, *Modern Jewish Thought: A Source Reader* (New York: Schocken Books, 1977), pp. 12–15.

is tempted to call it specter-like—when the subject of the Jews comes around: all quotations from the sources are from the subsidized works of the 16th and 17th centuries; statements that were successfully refuted long ago are served up like durable old chestnuts; and given the lack of any scholarly activity, or any up-to-date apparatus, the oracle of the wretches is consulted. Out of ignorance or malice, some people have blended an imaginary Judaism and their own Christianity into a sort of conversion or concluded that regressive laws were necessary. Although excellent men have already spoken out in favor of Jewish studies and worked for them, on the whole there has been little improvement in this regard....

In the meantime, however, the Jews have not been completely idle. Since the days of Mendelssohn, they have worked and written on behalf of civil rights, culture and reform, as well as their trampled-upon ancient heritage. A new era has revealed its strength in life and scholarship, in education and faith, in ideas, needs, and hopes; good seeds have been sown, excellent forces have been developed. But what is still needed is a protective institution, which can serve as a support for progress and scholarship and as a religious center for the community. The physical needs and public safety of Jewish communities are being met by hospitals and orphanages, poorhouses and burial grounds. However, religion and scholarship, civil liberty, and intellectual progress require schools, seminaries, and synagogues; they must enlist the efforts of capable community leaders, competent teachers, well-trained rabbis. If emancipation and scholarship are not to be mere words, not some tawdry bit of fancy goods for sale, but the fountainhead of morality which we have found again after a long period of wandering in the wilderness, then they must fecundate institutions—high-ranking educational institutions, religious instruction for everyone, dignified religious services, suitable sermons. Such institutions are indispensable for the needs of the congregational totality of the Jews; but to establish them we need religious zeal and scholarly activity, enthusiastic participation in the entire project, benevolent recognition from the outside.

Free instructive words are something not to be denied. Mankind has acquired all its possessions through oral instruction, through an education, which lasts a lifetime. In Israel, too, the words of teaching have passed from mouth to mouth in all ages, and any future flourishing of Jewish institutions may derive only from the words that diffuse knowledge and understanding....

Apart from all present-day efforts in this field and any personal connections I may have with them, the institution of the liturgical addresses of the Jews seemed to me to deserve and require a strictly historical investigation. The substance of my research on the origin, development, and fortunes of this institution, from the time of Ezra[5] to the present, is now presented in this book....I hope that in addition to their main purpose, the recognition of the right and the scholarship of the Jews, my investigations will stimulate interest in related studies and win for the nobler endeavors of our time the favor of the mighty, the benevolence of the prudent, the zeal of the pious. Such a reward will be sweeter to me than any literary acclamation.

NOTES

1. Leopold Zunz devoted his first major book to a study of Jewish homiletic literature and its historical development. The selection presented here is from the preface to this work, which traces through the Midrash, the Haggadah, the traditional prayer book, the gradual growth of what Zunz called "liturgical addresses" (after the Hebrew *drashot*). The intention was to demonstrate that the sermon, which became a pillar of Liberal and Reform congregations, was a Jewish institution of long standing. In the preface, he voices the guiding presupposition of the first generation of modern Jewish Studies that opposition to granting Jews full civil rights was due, in part, to misconceptions about the nature of Judaism, that prejudice toward the Jews was a function of ignorance. In the face of a scholarly presentation, which appeals to reason, prejudice would dissipate. To further this objective, the academic study of Judaism should be regarded as an integral part of the intellectual and spiritual heritage of Europe. Accordingly, Jewish Studies should be integrated into the curriculum of the German universities and given institutional support. The cause of Jewish scholarship and emancipation thus go hand and hand. The governmental authorities took offense at Zunz's preface and duly suppressed it, removing it from most copies of the first edition.
2. The reference is to the Greek law maker, Solon (c.638–558 B.C.E.), whose reforms laid the foundation for Athenian democracy.
3. Johann Andreas Eisenmenger (1654–1704), see chapter 1, document 40, note 6, and this chapter, document 5, note 8.

4. Johann Jacob Schudt (1664–1722), a Protestant theologian who wrote extensively on contemporary Jewish folklore in Germany.

5. Johannes Buxtorf (1564–1629) was a renowed scholar of Judaism. Celebrated as the "Master of the Rabbis," his *De Synagoga Judaica* (1603), meticulously documents in great detail the customs and social structure of German Jewry in the early modern period. Buxtorf served as a professor of Hebrew for thirty-nine years at the University of Basel, Switzerland.

6. Ezra the Scribe led the Israelites who returned to Jerusalem from the Babylonian Exile in 458 B.C.E.

7. THE FUTURE OF JEWISH STUDIES (1869)

MORITZ STEINSCHNEIDER[1]

During the last half century, greater and lesser results have been achieved by Jewish science. For a long time, this endeavor was influenced, externally, by the so-called "question of Jewish emancipation," and, internally, by the various attempts at religious reform. Jewish science has gained from both, and— where it has deepened and clarified the understanding [of Judaism]—it, in turn, has had a salutary influence on the external position of the Jews and on their religious situation as well. (But the findings of science can only serve pragmatic ends; they cannot solve questions of principle.) And the question of Jewish civil equality is no longer a matter of expedience, nor, indeed, merely a *Jewish* question. The religious question, too, is now one of more general interest and its determination no longer depends on the opinions of a narrow circle; religious reform is now a question of principles which perforce demand a broader framework.

At first, the schismatic process [implied by the Science of Judaism and Reform] prompted an opposition to the official representatives of Judaism, namely, the rabbis. A number of scholars refused to accept an office which necessitated considerations extraneous to science. But a new generation of rabbis adopted the new science, and a need was soon felt for institutions in which Jewish clergy [*Cultusbeamten*] could be trained. Halfway through the period under consideration, the establishment of a Jewish theological faculty at a German university, was discussed, but this project had to be dropped for a lack of funds.[2] Moreover, it was by no means sure that German universities at the time would not have interfered with the independent work of lecturers and Jewish science. Since 1848, however, Germany has been working toward the implementation of the postulate: "Science and instruction must enjoy freedom." Yet Jewish history and literature can almost nowhere be studied at the universities.

In the meantime, due to a generous legacy, a rabbinical seminary had been founded. Its curriculum includes a general, preliminary education and is thus especially suited for students without such a background.[3] Aside from this element of secular studies, the seminary has maintained at least the outer appearance of a certain religious direction. Upon graduation, the younger rabbis take up their practical tasks, especially those of giving sermons and religious instruction. The few Jewish Talmudic scholars, who in the big cities make their living from various occupations,

Source: Moritz Steinschneider, "Die Zukunft der juedischen Wissenschaft," *Hebraeische Bibliographie* 9 (1869), pp. 76–78. Trans. by J. Hessing and P. Mendes-Flohr.

are gradually dying out. Most candidates for a rabbinate in Germany attend universities. The majority have graduated from the traditional Talmudic academies of East Europe, where they had no formal secular education. Without these students, the classes on Semitic literature would be almost empty. As a rule, the students base their claim to a doctorate—an indispensable title, in their eyes—on a knowledge of "Semitic literature." The examiners, meanwhile, have to face all kinds of embarrassments.

These students condescendingly still attend the old-style lessons on the Talmud and *Shulkhan arukh*,[4] mainly because of the scholarships that go along with them, or because of the ordination certificate, which can rather easily be attained from the rabbis who conduct these lessons. A talent to preach has become the main requirement of a rabbi, *everything* else has become secondary. Now and again, an attempt is made to give one of these traditional Talmudic academies—the yeshivot—a more modern character. Universally, the amorphous situation with regard to organization and pedagogy that prevails in the *yeshivot* arouses the desire to revamp their methods totally; on the other hand, there is an inhibiting fear that such changes would undermine the inalienable liberties of the traditional manner of Talmudic study.

First and foremost, the debates over the establishment of new, modern institutes refer to the training of rabbis and teachers of religion; opinions differ according to religious affiliations. In this context, the Science of Judaism is largely considered in terms of its pertinence to [religious] cult and pedagogy. This practical point of view is certainly justified, but is it the only feasible approach? What about Jewish history as a link and source of cultural history in general? Is the Science of Judaism a part of theology? What will become of it if the universities, according to the Dutch example, leave theology, as a practical science, to the care of the various religious communities?[5]

It could be argued that the Jews, as a religious community, have no particular reason to take care of a science which goes beyond their religious needs, unless this science is created by Jews and can thus only be transmitted by Jews. The state and its scientific institutions must undertake and foster scientific investigations of the Jewish works contained in their libraries, just as they are investigating the pyramids, the ruins of Pompeii and of Nineveh. They should do

this all the more so since the spirit which has created these works has not yet died out, but is still alive in citizens of their state! If the Jews, so would the argument go, take over this task which rightfully belongs to the state, they would perpetuate the old mistake that Jewish literature is nothing but a subsidiary science to theology. Jewish institutions would also fail to carry their science beyond a narrow circle and thus miss their target—a mistake which could not be easily remedied, even if the Jews restricted themselves to their own theology and consigned everything else to oblivion. But oblivion will be the inescapable future of the new-born science, if it is not soon given the appropriate spiritual nourishment to assure its prosperous growth....

These are some of the questions and doubts concerning the conditions and tendencies of the Science of Judaism as pursued in Germany. If our description has been one-sided or false, we would gladly accept corrections and additions. In Eastern Europe, they are already shouting: German Jewry no longer represents authentic Judaism, as Alexandrian Jewry did not in ancient times.... Are not then the German Jews at least [authentic] representatives of the Jewish science? Can the most urgent needs of this science only be fulfilled at the expense of the Jewish religion or vice versa?...

NOTES

1. Moritz Steinschneider (1816–1907). Having a thorough grounding in traditional Jewish learning, he was introduced to the academic study of Jewish sources by several non-Jewish scholars. Like Zunz, he pursued Jewish science as a "private scholar," supporting himself by officiating as a rabbi at weddings, delivering sermons, teaching, translating and writing textbooks for the study of elementary Hebrew. In 1869 he was named to the important post of assistant in the Royal Library of Berlin. Steinschneider's approach to Jewish studies is usually cited as an extreme example of historicism, of a cold, objective scholarship that posited the demise of Judaism as a living faith and as creative culture. His attitude to Judaism, however, was more complex. Although favoring religious reform, he was actually quite conservative in religious matters, particularly in the earlier part of his career. He insisted, for instance, upon the use of Hebrew in the service as necessary for the integrity of Judaism and Jewry. Also indicative of his attitude was his consistent treatment of the Jews

as a nation and not simply as a religious confession. He was equally concerned with the integrity of Jewish scholarship, and believed that the Science of Judaism, to be credible and true to its calling, must maintain a jealous regard for the standards of objectivity. Thus it must eschew all extraneous concerns, such as religious reform or political emancipation. To be sure, he recognized that these issues were legitimate and exigent, but they could not become the charge of the Science of Judaism, for such concerns inevitably rendered scholarship selective and tendentious. Moreover, although recognizing the desire for a synoptic treatment and presentation of Judaism—a desire related to the drive for religious reform and political emancipation—Steinschneider emphatically opposed such projects. At this early stage of scholarship, such summary treatment of Judaism would perforce be based on hasty, superficial research, which would at best be platitudinous, at worst fraudulent. At this juncture, Jewish science must suffice with laborious, patient groundwork, particularly in philology and bibliography. His scholarship became a paradigm of this type of research, devoted to a thorough and scientific recording of all available printed and manuscript materials in Judaica—work he deemed to be indispensable before scholarship could proceed. He applied himself to this type of research, devoting his efforts to cataloging, with annotations of awe-inspiring erudition, the Judaica collections of Europe's leading libraries: the Bodleian Library in Oxford and the libraries in Leiden, Munich, Hamburg and Berlin. In these catalogs, which represented many years of research, he disclosed hitherto unknown treasures of Jewish literature and culture. The "father of Jewish bibliography," as he is now reverently called, also contributed studies on Jewish literature, especially on the interaction between Hebrew and Arabic literature in the Middle Ages. The bibliography of his own writings, containing more than 1,400 items, constitutes a veritable library. This article was first published in *Hebraeische Bibliographie*, a journal edited by Steinschneider from 1858 to 1882.

2. In 1838 a committee and fund were created to promote the establishment of a Jewish theological faculty at a German university. Steinschneider opposed the idea of such a faculty. He consistently strove, however, to have Jewish science included within the curriculum of German universities. At the height of the Revolution of 1848 he submitted a memorandum to the University of Berlin, suggesting that the triumph of liberalism made it imperative to introduce Jewish studies into the curriculum. His proposal was rejected. It was not until after the First World War that a place was allocated in a German university for the Science of Judaism.

3. The reference is to the Juedisch-Theologisches Seminar in Breslau, Germany, established in 1854 with funds bequeathed by Jonas Fraenkel, a prominent Breslau businessman. The seminary, headed for its first twenty years by Zecharias Frankel, was the first institution that made it possible for scholars to devote themselves entirely to the Science of Judaism. The seminary's principal objective, however, was to train rabbis along the lines of "positive historical Judaism." The seminary, which functioned until 1939, served as a model for similar institutions (e.g., Hochschule fuer die Wissenschaft des Judentums, founded by Abraham Geiger in 1871, and associated with the Reform movement).

4. The standard code of Jewish law and practice compiled by Joseph Caro was first published in 1565. Joseph Caro (1488–1575), was a codifier and kabbalist. In 1536 he went to Palestine and settled in Safed where he was acknowledged as a distinguished scholar and mystic.

5. In Germany, sectarian theological faculties were part of the university structure.

8. JEWISH SCHOLARSHIP AND RELIGIOUS REFORM (1836)

ABRAHAM GEIGER[1]

Alas, we still cleave so horribly fast to the exterior works, and when the blow that will strike the religious world falls...we shall have to fling ourselves into the arms of the new era without having had any significant part in bringing it about....There is one basic thought: *the establishment of proof, just like anything else that exists, is something that has come to be and has no binding force.* Every single piece of research, even if it should amount merely to a scholarly trifle, has worth and retains that worth....But all this does not set the course for us to follow; it is just material, and who knows what its use will be, or whether we, or anyone else, will use it or will be able to put it to use? But the course to be taken, my dear fellow, is that of critical study; the critical study of individual laws, the critical examination of individual documents—this is what we must strive for. The Talmud, and the Bible, too, that collection of books, most of them so splendid and uplifting, perhaps the most exalting of all literature of *human* authorship, can no longer be viewed as of Divine origin. Of course, all this will not come to pass today, or even tomorrow, but it should be our goal, and will continue to be so, and in this fashion we are working closely with every true endeavor and movement of our day, and we will accomplish more by study than we could by means of a hundred sermons and widespread religious instruction. For the love of Heaven, how much longer can we continue this deceit, to expound the stories of the Bible from the pulpits over and over again as actual historical happenings, to accept as supernatural events of world import stories which we ourselves have relegated to the realm of legend, and to derive teachings from them or, at least, to use them as the basis for sermons and texts? How much longer will we continue to pervert the spirit of the child with these tales that distort the natural good sense of tender youth? But how can this be changed? By driving such falsehoods into a corner, of course; by clearly revealing this paradox both to ourselves and to others; by pursuing into their secret hiding places all those who could seek to evade the issue, and thus eventually helping to bring about the great cave-in which will bury an old world beneath its ruins and open a new world for us in its place....

NOTE

1. Abraham Geiger (1810–1871) was one of the leaders of the Reform movement in German Judaism and one of the outstanding scholars of the second generation of *Wissenschaft des Judentums.* He was the founding editor of the journal *Wissenschaftliche Zeitschrift fuer juedische Theologie* (appearing 1835–1839, 1842–1847), which became the most important forum in its day for modern Jewish studies. He also saw the journal as an ally in the movement of religious reform in Judaism. "Jewish theology" based on critical historical scholarship, he held, would validate Reform's conception of Judaism as a continually evolving religion.

   Serving as a rabbi first in Wiesbaden (1836–1840), Breslau (1840–1863), and then in the city of his birth, Frankfurt am Main (1863–1870), in 1870 Geiger moved to Berlin, where he was instrumental in establishing the *Hochschule fuer Wissenschaft des Judentums*, a college for Jewish scholarship and the training of Liberal rabbis and religious school teachers.

   His own wide-ranging scholarship was highly regarded for its erudition and sophistication. Like most

Source: Abraham Geiger, Letter to J. Derenbourg, dated November 8, 1836, translated from the German in *Abraham Geiger and Liberal Judaism. The Challenge of the Nineteenth Century,* trans. Ernst J. Schlochauer (Philadelphia: Jewish Publication Society of America, 1962), p. 86f. Reprinted by permission of the Jewish Publication Society.

earlier scholars of *Wissenschaft des Judentums,* Geiger endeavored to demonstrate the inseparable and ever-fruitful link between Judaism and European culture and to point to the dynamic, developmental aspect of Jewish thought. In stern opposition to Orthodoxy, which he rejected as ossified by an anachronistic legalism and as lacking in aesthetic sensibilities appropriate to cultured Europeans, he emphasized the prophetic dimension of biblical faith and the corresponding universal mission of Judaism.

In this letter to the French Jewish educator and Orientalist Joseph Naphtali Derenbourg (1811–1895), Geiger argues that religious reform must be grounded in critical historical scholarship. He unapologetically emphasizes the historicist presupposition of such scholarship, namely, the methodological requirement of positing a human authorship to the sacred texts of the tradition. Only such an approach, Geiger explains, will effectively serve to free Judaism of its anachronistic elements.

9. A SERMON ON THE SCIENCE OF JUDAISM (1855)

SAMSON RAPHAEL HIRSCH[1]

We who have fully imbibed the spirit of modern Judaism, we do not fast, do not pray *Selihot,*[2] do not say *Kinot*[3] on *Tisha beav* [the ninth of Av][4] anymore. We would be ashamed of the tear in our eye or the sigh in our breast for the fallen Temple; we would be ashamed to feel the slightest longing for this scene of "bloody sacrificial rites." For us, alas, all this has become a myth. With our feelings "refined" by a cool reality, and with our unbiased scientific insights, we understand and evaluate all this very differently. Moses and Hesiod, David and Sappho, Deborah and Tyrtaeus, Isaiah and Homer, Delphi and Jerusalem, the Pythian tripod and the Sanctuary of the Cherubim, prophets and oracle, psalm and elegy—for us, all this has been peacefully encased and buried in our mind, reduced to one and the same human origin. For us, all this has received an identical meaning, human and transitory and of a by-gone age. The fog has lifted; the tears and sighs of our fathers do not fill our breasts

anymore. They fill our libraries. The warmly pulsating heart of our fathers has become our national literature, their ardent life-breath has turned into the dust of letters. On *Tisha beav,* we let the old Jews pray *Selihot* and cry *Kinot;* we, however, know much better than they do in which centuries these "poets" flourished, in what meter they wrote their "verse," at whose breast they fed when they were sucklings. We adore Jewish antiquity so much that we raise all the dust in the libraries and collections in order to verify the dates of birth and death of these authors and to register correctly the inscriptions on their tombstones. We take care that now, as the old Judaism is carried to its grave, at least its memory is kept alive in histories of literature, and that now and then the evergreen around its grave sheds a few of its needles upon our scholarly temple. Our simple-minded fathers did not believe in the death of these authors at all. They—their song, their lamentation, their solace, their prayer—lived

---

Source: Samson Raphael Hirsch, "Die Trauer des 9. Av," *Gesammelte Schriften* (Frankfurt am Main, 1902), vol. 1, pp. 130–31. Trans. by J. Hessing.

on in the breasts of thousands of Jews. While their weather-worn tombstones were crumbling in the graveyards, every Jewish heart was their mausoleum and ensured them the only kind of immortality they desired, that the song might obliterate the poet, the prayer its author and the thought the man who had given expression to it. What they had thought and felt and sung and lamented became the living property of the nation; its origin—the mortal individual, the accidental organ by which these national feelings and thoughts had been voiced—could now step back into the shadow of oblivion.

Will these deceased spirits delight in the literary gratitude of our generation? Whom will they recognize as their true inheritors? Those who prayed their prayers and forgot their names, or those who forget their prayers, but remember their names?

NOTES

1. Samson Raphael Hirsch (1808–1888), foremost exponent of Neo-Orthodoxy in Germany. He looked askance at the Science of Judaism which, because of its historicism, failed, in his view, to contribute to the preservation and strengthening of Jewish life. On Hirsch's concept of Judaism, see chapter 4, document 15. This selection is taken from a sermon Hirsch delivered on *Tisha beav* (see note 4) in 1855.

2. Penitential prayers recited on the days of fast in the Jewish liturgical calendar, especially in the month preceding the Day of Atonement.

3. "Dirges" is the Talmudic designation of the biblical book of Lamentations, which is read in the synagogue during the evening and morning services of *Tisha beav* (See note 4 below).

4. The fast-day commemorating the destruction of the first and second Temples.

10. LEARNING BASED ON FAITH (1860)

SAMUEL DAVID LUZZATTO[1]

Padua, Sivan 15, 5620

To the glory of the rabbis and the crown of the priests, preeminent among scholars and leader among wise men, [Rabbi Rappoport, chief rabbi of Prague],[2]

May the Lord who has brought you to ripe old age prolong your life in goodness and serenity, and may you continue to be a light unto the diaspora…may you strengthen the righteous…may the wicked bow down before you and bite the dust of your feet, Amen.

I am like a mouse, half flesh, half earth; half rotten and worn out like a garment that has been eaten by moths and worms, and half strengthened in the Lord and in the labor of the Torah, to bring its mysteries to the light and to silence those who speak evil.

And now, friend of my soul, hearken and let your servant speak a word before you….Why do you refrain from spreading your wisdom in Israel?

And why should two or three wicked men prevent you from doing justice and goodness with the Torah and with the many who love the Torah and love you, who honor the Torah and honor you? By your silence you give pleasure to your enemies and the enemies of the Torah, for their one aim is to silence a righteous man and slacken the hand of a valiant warrior, that they may behave arrogantly and entrap souls….

For surely you know that a people living in its own country can exist even without faith, but the Sons of Israel, dispersed to the four corners of the earth, have

---

Source: Samuel David Luzzatto to Salomon J. Rappoport, June 5, 1860, in *Igrot Shadal* (Premsl, 1882), pp. 1366–67. Trans. by L. Sachs.

survived to this day only because they have adhered to their faith. And if, God forbid! they should one day cease to believe in the Heavenly Torah, then they will necessarily cease to be a people, the name of Israel will be forgotten, and they will suffer the fate of the streams that run into the sea.[3] For some this would be the final salvation; such men call it fusion. The Wisdom of Israel[4] as it is studied in Germany by several Jewish scholars of this generation cannot continue to exist. It is not studied for its own sake; in the last analysis these scholars respect Goethe and Schiller more than all the prophets and the *tanaim*[5] and *amoraim*.[6] They study ancient Israel the way other scholars study ancient Egypt, Assyria, Babylon and Persia—that is, for the love of science or the love of fame. And they intend, in addition, to increase the honor of Israel in the eyes of the gentiles; they exalt the role of some of our ancient sages in order to hasten the first step toward salvation which is, in their eyes, emancipation. But this kind of wisdom cannot endure; it will cease to exist as soon as salvation is achieved or when those men die who learned Torah as children and who believed in God and Moses before they went to study with Professor so-and-so and his pupils.

But the Wisdom of Israel which will endure forever is learning grounded in faith;[7] it is the wisdom that seeks to understand the Torah and the prophets as the Word of God, that attempts to understand the unique history of our unique people. This Wisdom strives to comprehend how, throughout our history, the spirit of God, which is our nation's inheritance, warred with the human spirit...and how in each generation the divine aspect prevailed over the human. For if at any time the human aspect should prevail in Israel (as some think it now does) then our people would cease to exist and be utterly lost.

This true Wisdom of Israel, which, like the stars, will stand forever, is the very Wisdom you study. It will immortalize those who master it and will make your name blessed unto the furthest generations.

Therefore be strong and of good courage, my dear and illustrious friend! Be not frightened, neither be you dismayed.[8] Do not hasten to the call of the foxes, the small and the great. Collect your ideas and thoughts and make of them a profound little book. You will then carry your head high.[9] Righteous men will revere and praise you, and the honest man will

rejoice and exalt your name, and injustice will be utterly silenced.

And now may God bless you and your house and all that belongs to you. As you have arrived at old age may you continue to live long in full health and happiness. Your honored friend and servant,

Shadal

NOTES

1. Samuel David Luzzatto (1800–1865). Often referred to by his acronym, *Shadal*, he was an Italian-Jewish scholar, philosopher, bible commentator, and translator. He was the only member of the first generation of the Science of Judaism to earn his livelihood as a scholar. In 1829 he was appointed a professor in the modern, albeit traditionalist, rabbinical college of Padua. His scholarship had a wide scope, including Scripture, Hebrew philology, medieval Hebrew poetry and philosophy. His most significant contribution to Jewish studies is probably the discovery and publication of numerous Hebrew manuscripts found in Italian archives and libraries. He shared many of the fruits of his research in a voluminous correspondence with his fellow scholars in the fledgling discipline of Jewish studies. For him critical research was a way of deepening his understanding of and commitment to traditional Judaism. He therefore was profoundly disturbed by the detached scholarship and the historical relativism of his German colleagues.

2. Salomon J. Rappoport (1790–1867). He was perhaps as well known by his acronym, *Shir*; he was an Orthodox rabbi and one of the founders of the Science of Judaism. Within his native Galicia he was esteemed as a brilliant Talmudist and served as the rabbi of Tarnopol; in 1840 he was appointed the chief rabbi of Prague. Although he lacked a university education, he acquired a knowledge of classical, Semitic and modern languages. He published critical, scholarly articles in various Hebrew journals sponsored by the *maskilim*. Known as the father of modern Jewish historiography, Rappoport was the first to realize the value of using traditional Jewish sources to reconstruct Jewish history. Like Luzzatto, Rappoport exercised self-restraint and avoided issues that were liable to affect the essential beliefs of the Jewish people; thus, for example, the Pentateuch was considered too sacred to be profaned by the irreverent scrutiny of critical scholarship. See chapter 4, document 13.

3. An apparent allusion to Eduard Gans's famous simile regarding the type of integration of Jewry into Europe

to be fostered by Jewish science. See document 3 in this chapter, note 3.

4. In Hebrew the Science of Judaism is referred to as *Hokhmat Israel*, "the Wisdom of Israel."

5. Rabbinic teachers mentioned in the Mishnah.

6. Interpreters of the Mishnah noted in the Gemara, the second part of the Talmud.

7. *Hahokhmah hameyusedet al haemunah.*

8. See Josh. 1:7.

9. See Lev. 26:13.

11. *MEKIZE NIRDAMIM* (1861)[1]

ELIEZER LIPMANN SILBERMANN[2]

For many years I have wanted to do something worthy in honor of Jewish scholarship and wisdom, in honor of our sages and our elders, may their memory be blessed, and for the good of our Jewish brethren in all countries, and that is to found a society to publish the many valuable and excellent manuscripts that have reposed for years in large libraries and have not been in print to this day, as well as valuable books that were printed only once and that are now only found in libraries, and to distribute them to the members of the Society and to disseminate them among the Jewish people at a low price. However, the great and demanding work of the periodical *Hamagid*[3] did not allow me to attend also to that work which I would have liked to do. The tasks were many; and I labored totally alone. And even after I found an assistant in my wise friend, our teacher and rabbi, David Gordon,[4] may God watch over and protect him, there was much for us both to do and improve so that the periodical would be glorious from within and without. And now with God's mercy I reached this point to hear the opinions of my great and wise brethren and the opinions of most of the innocent *Hamagid* readers, that it should improve its ways on earth, and after the Lord calmed my sadness and anger, which greatly cast

their weight on me, and I was somewhat relieved, now I will keep my promises to my people, and that which was often written in *Hamagid* shall be carried out with God's help. In this periodical I have taken up the cause of the holy language, to revive it and glorify it for the benefit of my Jewish brethren who are alive; and now my soul wishes to do something also to honor Jewish scholarship in particular and to do well by those who have died and to revive them in their words, may they rest in peace: the righteous even in their death are considered alive. And when I was in the city of Berlin in the early summer, I spoke with the rabbi, the wise man, Dr. Yechiel Michael Sachs,[5] may God watch over and protect him, and in the course of our talk the wise rabbi encouraged me to found a Society like this. As I heard the pleasant words coming from his heart, I told him that for many years I was thinking of doing such a thing. And the wise rabbi pressed me vigorously and said that now is the time to do it, and he agreed to be one of the heads of the Society and promised to write even to the honorable rabbi, the wise man, our honorable teacher, Nathan Adler,[6] may God watch over and protect him, in London and to speak to his heart that he also become one of the heads of the Society. Recently the aforementioned honorable

Source: Hamagid (5 Tishrei 5622 [September 12, 1861]). Trans. by G. Svirsky.

Rabbi also expressed to me his consent. I also wrote to some well-known people, sages of the generation, that I knew would certainly come to assist in this great deed and be directors of the Society, and soon I shall publicly announce their names. And so that this good thing not be delayed for many more days, we the undersigned hereby declare to our Jewish brethren in all countries that we have founded a Society by the name of *Mekize nirdamim* ("rousers of those who slumber"), and its initial goals are as follows:

(a) To publish valuable manuscripts that repose in libraries and have never before been published, and in particular from the sages of Spain, may their memory be blessed, who are famed for their erudition and wisdom and their obvious fear of God, and to distribute these books among members of this Society.

(b) If God is generous to us and increases the number of Society members, we shall also publish valuable books that have already been published but are rare.

(c) And if God desires our success and we can arouse those [books and manuscripts that] slumber, then we shall turn our attention to manuscripts of the wise who are living, although the priority will always be on old manuscripts as mentioned above.

And behold we knew there are people who would say: But there are already publishing houses in many countries that have begun to print old manuscripts as well as rare books, so why establish this Society? To these speakers, we respond in brief: Publishers primarily print books used by many people—and those who tried to publish old manuscripts were not rewarded for their efforts, because there are few buyers and they must increase the price and still they work for nought. And indeed what is the great benefit from such a Society?

(a) It is much easier for a big Society to publish something than for one person to do the work.

(b) The directors of the Society will appoint agents in all the countries, which will make it easier for people in each and every country to obtain the book at a low price.

(c) The directors of the Society will carefully choose only the best and the most useful and will supervise carefully the printing and the proofreading and many other important things known to those who are familiar with publishing.

And after these words, we hereby announce to our brethren the ways of the Society that we plan to found:

(a) Every Jew in any country who kindly agrees to become a member of this Society shall give to the treasury of the Society the amount of two Prussian thalers a year (or the equivalent value for people in other countries).

(b) Generous and wealthy fellow Jews who are happy to do good deeds and desire to increase the honor of Jewish scholarship can add to the above sum through the treasury of the Society, either to the endowment or an annual sum as the spirit moves them, and their name shall be inscribed in the book for eternal memory.

(c) From the total money collected each year we shall print, God willing, as many valuable essays as income will allow and as many books as the number of members of the Society; and every member will receive a copy of each book that is printed in return for the annual subscription. From this it will be understood that if the number of Society members increases, then everyone will receive valuable books that are worth more than double the low annual price.

(d) Every person is entitled to become a member in our Society for at least one year or more.

(e) The directorate of the Society, never less than three nor more than seven, will be public figures, knowledgeable in Jewish scholarship, wise, God-fearing, and from various countries; and they shall take decisions according to the majority and will do everything for the good of and to bring honor to the Society.

(f) From among the directors of the Society, one will be elected treasurer and another, secretary.

(g) At the end of each year, the directors will issue a special report of activities, a true and accurate account of the income and expenditures, numbers and names of the members of the Society, numbers and names of the books printed, and anything that should be known to members of the Society.

And now, honorable brethren, give your attention to this great project and awaken, awaken to join our Society in honor of Jewish scholarship and in honor of our sages, may they rest in paradise, and for your benefit, and hurry each of you to send the small yearly dues to one of the undersigned, now free of delivery fees, and clearly write your names, addresses, and the names of your cities.

And you, honorable brethren, who have written periodicals in Hebrew for Jewish people, we ask that you publish these words in your periodicals and awaken the hearts of your brethren in words that come from the heart; and also publishers of periodicals in Yiddish for Jewish people, copy these words and do your share to assist this great deed as inspired by God; and you rabbis, preachers, teachers and all you wise ones, awaken also to this great thing and awaken the hearts of your brethren who heed your words and true counsel. And we shall ask every good-hearted person to work for the good of the Society and to seek members of the Society, and if someone wishes a reward for his efforts, he may obtain a discount as the directors of the Society so determine.

Be aware, my honorable brethren, that it is not for the sake of profit that we are doing this, so remove all jealousy or animosity from your hearts and look only to the good deed, and hasten to join our Society, and every person can now send the annual dues to one of the undersigned. Very soon, God willing, we shall inform you about everything, and we hope that we shall have good and comforting tidings.

The Lord aid us and bless all our deeds to increase and enhance Jewish scholarship, and bless His people with peace, as pleaded by those who seek the good of his people and plead their cause.

Eliezer Lipmann Silbermann, son of my master, my father, my teacher and my rabbi, Rabbi Yehuda Leib, may his memory be blessed.

Yehiel Michael Sachs, Rabbi and Teacher for the congregation of Israel in Berlin the capital [of Prussia].

Nathan M. Adler, Rabbi of the *Koleil* [Torah Academy] in London and in all the countries of Britain.

Lyck, the Days of Awe, Year of 5622.

NOTES

1. Hebrew: "Rousers of that which Slumbers." This name was given to the Society by Silbermann, for the publication of scholarly editions of medieval Hebrew manuscripts and out-of-print books. Subsidiary aims of the society were to disseminate the fruits of modern Jewish scholarship and to establish personal contact between scholars. As cosignatories to this manifesto calling the Society into existence, Silbermann solicited Yehiel Michael Sachs and Nathan M. Adler (see notes 5 and 6). In contrast to the German *Wissenschaft des Judentums,* the Society gave clear expression to a belief in the renaissance of Jewish culture, one expression of which was its exclusive use of Hebrew. Support for its publications came largely from East European scholars and also from some traditional rabbis. By 1864 the number of subscribers, from many countries, reached 1,200. In the same year the first four publications were issued, among them the initial installment of S. D. Luzzatto's scholarly edition of Judah Halevi's *Diwan.* In 1934 the seat of the Society moved from Lyck to Jerusalem. By 2000 some 150 works had been published by the Society. S. Y. Agnon (1888–1970) served as the Society's director from 1954 to his death in 1970; he was succeeded by Greshom Sibolem (1898–1982), Ephraim E. Urbach (1912–1991), Shraga Abramson (1915–1998), and Ezra Fleischer (1922–2006). Yonah Frankel, professor emeritus of Talmud at the Hebrew University, is the current director

2. Eliezer Lipmann Silbermann (1819–1862) was a Hebrew writer and editor. Born in Koeningsberg (East Prussia) to a traditional family, he remained observant. Nonetheless, he was an advocate of moderate *haskalah*, feeling that it was necessary for Jews to participate in modern culture. In 1856 he began in Lyck (East Prussia) the first Hebrew newspaper, *Hamagid* (The Declarer), which appeared weekly until it ceased publication in 1903. From the beginning *Hamagid* contained a section devoted to modern Jewish studies.

3. See note 2.

4. David Gordon (1831–1886) was a Hebrew journalist and editor. Born in Podmerecz, near Vilna, he accepted Silbermann's invitation to become the assistant editor of *Hamagid* in 1858; in 1880 he was officially named the editor of the newspaper, a position that he had

already *de facto* filled for many years. His articles in *Hamagid* calling for a Jewish national revival are said to be first of their kind in Hebrew. When the *Hibbat Zion* (cf. chapter 10, document 5, note 4) was founded in the early 1880s, he became one of its leading members and lent the pages of *Hamagid* to serve as the voice of the movement.

5. Yechiel Michael Sachs (1808–1864) was a German rabbi and scholar. Famed for his oratory, he was in 1844 appointed a preacher by the Berlin Jewish community, in which he also served as a judge on the rabbinical court (*bet din*). A strong traditionalist, he vigorously opposed the radical Reformers of Berlin, led by Holdheim (cf. chapter 4, document 11). To the disappointment of both the Orthodox and the Reformers, he adopted a unique middle-of-the-road position. His vast knowledge of secular culture and traditional Jewish texts commended him to Zunz, who invited him to work with him on a German translation of the Hebrew Bible. Sachs also joined Zunz in the emerging *Wissenschaft des Judentums* and contributed *inter alia* scholarly studies on the medieval Spanish-Hebrew poets, the liturgy of German and Polish Jewry and Talmudic philology.

6. Nathan Marcus Adler (1803–1890) was the chief rabbi of the British Empire. He was born in Hanover, Germany, then under the British crown, and in 1844 was elected to his prestigious and powerful position, in which he was distinguished for his firm but enlightened Orthodoxy.

12. JEWISH SCHOLARSHIP: NEW PERSPECTIVES (1901)[1]

MARTIN BUBER

What is Jewish science? To what purpose and how, does one engage in it? Where does it exist? What does it have to do with Zionism? And what about the questions concerning the spiritual furtherance of the Jewish people? All this is not self-evident. We must try to clarify the meaning of a Jewish science and its pertinence to our endeavors.

A Jewish science may fulfill a threefold purpose. According to its point of departure, it may either be the Science of Judaism, the Science of the Jewish question, or the Science of Zionism. In the first case, its point of departure would be the historical and present reality of the Jewish people; it would aim to describe and to explain the actual situation; it would pursue no other practical aspect than that of tracing consistent developments through a maze of complex phenomena. In the second case, it would have to deal with an eminently practical problem, with the "pathology" of contemporary Jewry and the anomaly of its relations to other peoples; this science would find it more difficult to remain objective than the science of the Jewish people, for even the choice of its material would already be determined by its purpose. The Science of Zionism, finally, could hardly be objective at all; its point of departure would not be a question, but an answer, which in most cases was not found by a scientific method, but by intuition, or in any case subjectively,

Source: Martin Buber, "Juedische Wissenschaft," *Die Welt*, nos. 41–43 (October 11 and 25, 1901); reprinted in Buber, *Die juedische Bewegung: Gesammelte Aufsaetze und Ansprachen, 1900–1915* (Berlin: Juedischer Verlag, 1916), pp. 45–51. Reprinted by permission of Mr. Rafael Buber. Trans. by J. Hessing.

and must now be justified; the purpose would thus not merely determine the choice of the factual material, but also its arrangement, its interpretation and evaluation....

In truth, there can only be *one* Jewish science: the Science of Judaism [*Wissenshaft des Judentums*]. It would partly result in a scientific treatment of the Jewish question and of Zionism (since it would adumbrate a historical and sociological explanation of contemporary conditions), and would partly be complemented by them, just as the theory of political economy is complemented by economic policy. But where is this Science of Judaism?

One might answer: It does not exist....

This is true. It does not exist. And it cannot be created. It does not exist, because no circumscribed field belongs to it, nor does it have one specific methodology which it systematically pursues. And it cannot be created because no proper science evolves from plans, schemes and programs, however well-intentioned they might be, but from the far-sighted and yet narrowly circumscribed research by the man of knowledge. Plans and programs can never be its foundation, but only its roof.

And yet, we not only speak of a scientifically pursued Zionism, but also of a Jewish science. Admittedly, this expression is not quite correct; it is to be retained for merely practical reasons. But if one accepts our definition of it (I shall presently try to prove its relative justification), then the answers to the questions as to where this science might be found will turn out not to be quite correct, either.

For, if you wish, this science does exist: Its smaller part is embodied in what is presently called the Science of Judaism; its greater part is in various other disciplines. And it is not a matter of creating, but one of tracing and linkage. This process of tracing and linkage, however, does not take place in order to create an independent science, valid according to the principles of the philosophy of science—no independent subject matter without a valid methodology will suffice to establish a particular science—but rather in order to collect that which belongs to us, to build up a continuously developing inventory of Judaism, to see what we are, what we have and what we are able to do. This, too, like the other disciplines I have mentioned above may possess a practical aspect, but it does not diminish the objectivity and completeness of the scientific complex under consideration.

The parts pertaining to Judaism should therefore be traced in the relevant disciplines and then linked to the so-called Science of Judaism. It is to be hoped that through these efforts and the consequent organizational work, as well as through the development and deepening of the Jewish national movement, the interest in the new material will be enhanced, and that Jewish scholars will study the relevant problems in their respective fields.

But what about the so-called Science of Judaism, around which the nascent complex is to crystallize?

It is not entitled to its proud name. That much is certain. It is true that outstanding men have always been dedicated to it. It is true that it has developed its method with critical finesse and heuristic acumen. It is also true that it has researched and analyzed with utmost zeal. But inevitably, it has always remained what it was from the beginning: a species of philology. Its object was ancient Jewish literature; its method of research was philological. It is not entitled to the name Science of Judaism, much less so than German philology to the name Science of Germanism.

Laymen may have grouped other scientific creations under this heading as well. But the history of the Jewish people is certainly a part of the science of history, the legislation in the Bible or the Talmud part of a general history of law, studies of Jewish legends and customs part of folklore, the research of ancient Jewish monuments part of archeology and the history of art. The studies of the Jewish people as an ethnic group, of their alleged psychophysical attributes, of ancient Jewish economy, of our social stratification, of the evolution of specific customs and morals, of Jewish spirit and Jewish culture—all these studies, which we are looking forward to, will not belong to that science which depends on the philological method, but to anthropology, ethnology and economic, social, moral and cultural history—disciplines of different purposes and, therefore, of different methods.[2]...

I have tried to prove that there can be no valid Jewish science in a strictly methodological sense, but merely a scientific complex of Jewish matters. It could be organized by tracing the areas pertaining to Judaism in the various disciplines and by linking them to philological Judaica of a modern type. It is this complex which I shall now, for reasons of expediency, call Jewish science.

This largely answers our first question, "What is Jewish science?" And therefore we already know its purpose as well. We ought to engage in Jewish science in order to learn about the Jewish people—its origins, development and present conditions. This would serve a double purpose. To understand, first of all, what one loves. But then we should go further and learn from the given situation what is needed for our people, and what may be expected from it; in other words, our people's requirements and possibilities. The former and the latter are needed in order to create the scientific foundation for the grand design of a Jewish policy, i.e., in order to approach that which we have called the science of the Jewish question. The purpose is, then, at one and the same time theoretical and practical...

NOTES

1. Martin Buber (1878–1965), German-Jewish social and religious philosopher. After the publication of his book *I and Thou* in 1923, he was best known for his philosophy of dialogue. While a student at the University of Breslau he joined the Zionist movement. He was appointed by Theodor Herzl in 1901 to edit the central weekly organ of the movement, *Die Welt*, in which Buber called for a renaissance of Jewish cultural activity.

In this essay, which first appears in *Die Welt*, Buber criticized nineteenth-century "Jewish science" precisely because it lacked, in his view, a commitment to Judaism as a living cultural reality. In this criticism—and in the related demand that Jewish science expand its thematic horizons from an antiquarian interest in Jewish literature to include all aspects of Jewish life—Buber anticipated the new scope and conception that would characterize Jewish studies in the twentieth century. While perhaps not fully overcoming the historicist bias, the Jewish scholar no longer feels that scientific objectivity is compromised by recognizing, in the words of Julius Gutmann, "the creative energies of present-day Judaism." Methodologically, Jewish scholarship is no longer restricted to philology and the philological study of texts, but employs broad conceptual and phenomenological tools for the study of Jewish literature and civilization; moreover, it incorporates the focus and methods of various disciplines to facilitate the effort, as Buber said, "to explore and know what one loves."

2. In consonance with such considerations, it is now customary to underscore the multidisciplinary character of academic Jewish scholarship by speaking of the sciences of Judaism or, more felicitiously, Jewish studies.

13. DOCUMENTING JEWISH HISTORY IN EASTERN EUROPE (FEBRUARY 25, 1927)

SIMON DUBNOW ET AL.

Yidisher Visnshaftlekher Institut[1] (YIVO Institute for Jewish Research), Historical Section, First Questionnaire, February 25, 1927, TC, 142434.

The history of the Jewish settlement in Eastern Europe is still far from completely studied, and a whole series of materials that could have primary significance for Jewish history are lying around neglected and scattered, inaccessible to the Jewish historian and cultural researcher. During the last tempestuous period,[2] a trove of documents was destroyed that would have helped illumine whole epochs of Jewish life. It is the obligation of Jewish people to

Source: Offprint from *Literarishe bleter*, February 25, 1927, no. 8, p. 149. Drukarnia B-ci Wojcikiewicz, Warsawa, Pawia 10. Cited in Lucian Dobroszycki. "YIVO in Interwar Poland: Work in the Historical Sciences," in Yisrael Gutman, Ezra Mendelsohn, Jehuda Reinharz, and Chone Shmeruk, eds., *The Jews of Poland Between Two World Wars* (Hanover and London: University Press of New England, 1989), pp. 512–13. Trans. Chana Mlotek. Reprinted by permission of Lucjan Dobroszycki.

gather and preserve from destruction whatever has remained.

In order to determine our holdings, YIVO is issuing a series of questionnaires. The present questionnaire is the first. All institutions and individuals for whom Jewish culture is dear are requested to reply to the following questions; in so doing they will be making an important contribution to Jewish scholarship.

1. How large is your city? How many Jews live there, and is there any information as to when Jews first settled there?
2. Does your community have an archive?
3. Do you have a municipal or state archive, museum, etc., and does it house Jewish materials, and what kinds? Give the address of the pertinent institution.
4. Do you have a burial society, care-of-the-sick society, free-loan society, society for dowries for poor girls, consoling mourners society, and is there any information as to whether such societies ever existed in your community?
5. How long has each of these societies existed?
6. Have there remained any written materials about these societies: minute books, statutes, etc.? Indicate the years that each of these documents covers, and copy at least the title page of the document.
7. In whose possession is each of these documents? Indicate an exact address of the individuals or societies where the record books or other materials are located.
8. Does your city have archives of parties, cultural societies, trade unions, etc.?
9. Are there historical materials in the possession of private individuals, such as genealogical papers, memoirs, old volumes, etc.? Indicate their names and addresses and as far as possible at least a short summary of these documents.
10. Did you have documents that were lost or removed? How long ago and under what circumstances were they lost or removed?
11. Are there any information and written materials about former artisans' societies? Have houses of worship for artisans remained, and what are their names?

12. Do you have old synagogues? What are their names, and how old are they? Are they wooden or brick? Do they have any old books, holy ark curtains, candelabra, and other objects, and how old are they?
13. Do you have other old communal buildings?
14. How many cemeteries are there in your city? What are their names? What well-known deceased are interred there (martyrs, saints, communal leaders, writers)? Are there interesting tombstones? As far as possible, send us photographs of them or else precise descriptions.
15. Give us information about the surrounding *shtetlekh* [villages] that were entirely destroyed (in the Poznan region; during the recent catastrophe in the Ukraine, etc.) and have ceased to exist as Jewish settlements. In which of them were the record books and private archives saved, and where are they [now] located?
16. Was your city ever written about, and where was this printed? Indicate the exact author, title of book, city, publisher, and year of publication, or the name and year of the periodical, in which the materials about your city were published.
17. What can you add to the aforementioned questions? If you have anything to add, you are requested to do so.

The Historical Section of the Jewish Scientific Institute

Professor S. Dubnow,[3] Chairman;
E. Tcherikower,[4] I. Chernikov,[5]
E. Ringelblum,[6] Dr. J. Szacki,[7]
Dr. I. Schiper.[8]

Addresses for all shipments: Towarzystwo Przyjaciol Zydowskiego Instytutu Naukowego, Wilno. W[ielka] Puhulanka 18

NOTES

1. Founded at a conference of Jewish scholars and social scientists that took place in Berlin, August 7–12, 1925, the *Yidisher Visnshaftlekher Institut* (YIVO), or Institute for Jewish Research, sought to promote the scholarly study of Jewish culture and history in the Yiddish language. From its inception YIVO endeavored to collect and preserve material reflecting all aspects of Jewish life, religious and secular, and was particularly bent on the central

direction of rescuing Jewish folklore from oblivion. The primary focus of its efforts was East European Jewry and the centers to which large numbers of Yiddish-speaking Jews had immigrated since the late nineteenth century. At the founding conference, Vilna was chosen as the principal seat of YIVO, with subsidiary bureaus in Berlin, Warsaw and New York. By the beginning of World War II there were more than thirty branches of YIVO throughout the world. When Vilna was occupied by the Nazis in 1940, the American office assumed the central direction of YIVO's ramified activities. Cf. chapter 5, document 16, note 6, and chapter 7, document 35, note 1.

2. The Russian Revolution of 1917 and ensuing Civil War engendered numerous pogroms throughout the former Russian Empire, especially in the Ukraine. An estimated 70,000 to 250,000 Jews were killed; the number of Jewish orphans exceeded 300,000.

3. Simon Dubnow (1860–1941), Russian Jewish historian distinguished for introducing a sociological approach to the study of Jewish history. Cf. chapter 7, document 32.

4. Elias Tcherikower (1881–1943), Ukrainian-born historian of the Jewish labor movement in East Europe and of modern antisemitism.

5. I. Chernikov [Joseph Chernikov] (1882–1941), one of the founders of the Folkspartei and the Territorialist Party. See chapter 10, document 8 and document 46, note 2.

6. Emanuel Ringelblum (1900–1944), scholar of the economic and social history of the Jews in East Europe. He was among the founders in Warsaw of the "Circle of Young Historians," which published the Yiddish periodical *Der Yunger Historiker*. During World War II he was active in the Warsaw ghetto's underground movement, where he also coordinated elaborate efforts to document the atrocities. His own notes, summaries and essays written at the time were published posthumously after the war as *Notes from the Warsaw Ghetto* (English trans. 1958). Cf. chapter 11, document 30.

7. Jacob Szacki (also Shatzky; 1893–1956), Warsaw-born scholar of East European Jewish history. In 1922 he settled in New York, where he established the U.S. branch of YIVO.

8. Ignacy (Yitzhak) Schiper (1884–1943), a Galician-born historian of East European Jewish economic life and popular culture. At the time he was a deputy in the Polish parliament, or Sejm. He later taught at the Institute of Jewish Sciences, founded in Warsaw in 1928.

14. JUST WHAT IS JEWISH ETHNOGRAPHY? (1929)

KHAYIM KHAYES AND NAFTULI VAYNIG[1]

When it comes to things whose sense or value is familiar, we are usually inclined to think little of them, or we overlook them completely. To this day, most intellectuals do not understand the importance of collecting and preserving Jewish folk creativity and look with contempt on such efforts. Likewise, the common folk [Yiddish: *folksmentshn*] express a similar response of suspicion or lack of trust. To this day peasants feel uneasy about the botanist who gathers flowers in their fields, or the geologist who scrambles up a mountain to collect pebbles in a little bag. For the same reason, the common folk are reluctant to tell us stories or sing for us. Old wives' tales are only fit for children,

Source: Khayim Khayes and Naftuli Vaynig. *Vos is azoyns yidishe ethnografye?: hantbiklh farn zamler* [Just What is Jewish Ethnography? Handbook for Fieldworkers] Vilna: YIVO, 1929. Published anonymously. Excerpts translated by Jeffrey Shandler and here published with his kind permission.

they know; the kind of person who reads books wouldn't want to listen to them, except perhaps to make fun of them. And why would anyone want to write them down? Don't we have anything better to do? No doubt we just want to laugh at them and make them look foolish before all the world. Often we collectors are left at a loss for an answer, when we are asked: "What do you want with all this foolishness?"

Massive volumes have been written about life in the big cities, their culture and their amusements. But what do the common folk do, the ones who live in some remote little town or some dark back alley, who don't read books or the newspapers, who don't go to the theater or to the concerts? We know very little about this.

The field of ethnography (a word of Greek origin that means "study of the people") seeks to breach this gap. We know that the common folk, cut off from modern life, living in remote little towns and villages, have created their own distinctive cultures. They haven't studied medicine, but they have their own cures and remedies, and their own explanations for natural phenomena. They don't read novels, but they have their own storytellers and folksingers. They don't go to the theater, but they have their own entertainments, folk plays, etc.

Where did they get all this?

When we ask about the meaning of a custom, the answer is frequently: "That's how my father did it." Often a story is told as having happened to a parent or a grandparent, in order to substantiate the belief or the custom. To put it simply, the common folk have lived and live to this day with a tradition that is maintained and passed on from one generation to the next. For these people, tradition is the book, the school, from which they get their information, a great source of life experience that their grandparents left them as a legacy; they enrich it with their own ideas and pass it on to their children.

Tradition is holy. It changes very slowly and lives its own existence for hundreds of years. The silk caftan [Yiddish: *zhupitse*] that Polish intellectuals often make fun of is nothing more than an old-fashioned Polish garment that Jews have adopted and maintained to this day. And so it is with other customs. They often tell us more, and in a livelier fashion, than do the old documents that have come down to us. Thus, for example, there still remains in a number of Polish towns the custom of heating the ovens before the *seder* on the first night of Passover; this serves as a reminder of the blood libels that used to take place on that night.

Thus customs, songs and tales that continue to live to this day among the people clearly transmit the sounds of long forgotten echoes to us. And that is precisely why we must research the life of our people, to learn everything that has come down to us thanks to the strength of our tradition.

Other peoples have already done a great deal in this area of study. Enormous buildings have been devoted to the preservation of the smallest remnants that can tell them something about their past (and what doesn't have something to say to the serious scholar?): old-fashioned garments; examples of houses both inside and out; domestic objects, vessels, ornaments, examples of the food of the past, etc., etc. Extensive collections of folk-melodies, songs, tales, plays, dances, and so on, have been published. Scholars look for years to find a forgotten motif or verse of a song.

A great deal of work awaits us. Much has already been disrupted by modern culture, much has been driven out to the most remote towns, where it is on the verge of disappearing. We must collect what can still be saved.

How to Collect

1. Every collector should carry a pad of paper and a pencil, not only when going out to collect, but always. You might hear something of value just walking down the street or visiting someone at home. It's better not to rely on your memory, but to write things down then and there. If you can't write everything down make notes of characteristic words, style, etc. When you come home, you should write down the story. . . .

2. Usually, if you ask someone to tell you a story, you will get as an answer: "I don't know what to tell you." You can help someone remember be asking careful questions—"do you know anything about a certain custom" or "did you ever hear of anything like it," etc. Such leading questions can be found in our questionnaires, but it is better not to show the questionnaire to the people from whom you are collecting material. If something comes up in your conversation that is not germane to your question, don't lose sight of the opportunity, and write that down as well.

3. Everyone can lend a hand; whoever has even a little bit of interest and understanding can be of great help in this study of the Jewish people. Of special value are:

  a. Those who live near the common folk, who have their trust, who are familiar with their lives.

  b. Teachers, who can reach children, their parents and acquaintances in the course of their work.

  c. Cultural organizations, youth organizations, clubs, etc.

4. The work will be more intensive and more comprehensive if you organize a collector's group (it doesn't have to be big).

. . .

Rules for Collectors

1. You must never think that it is a waste of time to write something down, because "everybody knows that already." It's better to collect too much than too little. It is also important for scholars to know how widespread certain phenomena are, and what variants exist.

2. If you're not sure about what somebody tells you, write down "people say that…" or "it seems that…" or "so-and-so says that…"

. . .

4. Write things down as best as you can according to the local dialect; don't make it "literary;" even if it's not grammatically correct….

5. Don't ever prompt or correct the storyteller or singer.

6. Things that are vulgar and crude should also be written down. Ethnography has no aesthetic criteria and records everything that is a part of the lives of the folk.

7. Write down everything that someone tells you, even words that seem unimportant (like "for example," "well," "how do you say it," etc.). Don't leave anything out, don't put anything in.

NOTE

1. Khyaim Khayes (d. 1941) and Naftuli Vaynig (1897–1943) were, together with Max Weinreich (1894–1969), the founding members of the Ethnographic Commission established by YIVO in 1925. The Commission, renamed in 1930 Folklore Commission, established a network of *zamlers* (collectors) and collectors' clubs to research and record the folk beliefs, folktales, folk songs, popular customs and practices of the Yiddish-speaking masses. To facilitate the fieldwork of the *zamlers* Khayes and Vaynig published anonymously a 32-page handbook, which quickly became the *vade mecum* of YIVO folklorists. On Khayes and Vaynig's authorship of this booklet, see Itzik Nakhmen Gottesman, *Defining the Yiddish Nation: The Jewish Folklorists of Poland* (Detroit: Wayne State University Press, 2003), p. 137. The polemical, apologetic tone of the opening paragraph served to highlight the significance of folklore—although the term itself was carefully avoided in the pamphlet—for the expanded conception of Jewish Studies sponsored by YIVO. Accordingly, the handbook defined the scope of the ethnographical study of the Yiddish-speaking population as embracing all aspects of life as expressed in the popular culture of all strata of society, from shoemakers and *yeshivah* students to the underworld.

15. SCIENCE OF JUDAISM, ITS ACHIEVEMENTS AND PROSPECTS (1971)

GERSHOM SCHOLEM[1]

Jewish Studies (*Wissenschaft des Judentums*) had evolved from a bitter controversy with traditional Judaism, whose opponents showed evident signs of wanting to put an end to Jewish existence. The dialectics of this paradoxical predicament, which has had no equal in any other nation or culture, gave rise to serious problems and contradictions.

For about one hundred years the people actively interested and engaged in Jewish studies were rabbis and teachers in Jewish schools [rabbinic seminaries], not because of the inherent requirements of this discipline but for the simple practical reason that the Jewish community at that time had no place for institutions designed for pure scientific or academic research [on Judaism]. Besides the advantages of this enforced practice, it also had obvious disadvantages, both in the choice of subjects and in the quality of the research. The first attempt to establish a research institute that was not rabbinically [or] theologically oriented were the "academic courses" established by Baron David Guensburg[2] in St. Petersburg, and a little later by Dropsie College[3] in Philadelphia. After World War I, the Society for the Establishment and Promotion of an Academy of Jewish Studies[4] was founded in Berlin. Historically, the decisive step was the foundation [in 1925] of the Institute of Jewish Studies at the Hebrew University of Jerusalem.

Another limiting factor was that the exponents of Jewish studies, while professing an objective approach, had internal and external nonacademic objects in mind. Geiger,[5] for instance, wanted in an academic manner to carry out the antirabbinical program promulgated by some of the founders of the discipline. For others, Jewish studies were a weapon in the fight for internal and external emancipation. Internally they were a means for throwing off the yoke of a fossilized religion and for modifying and adjusting it to the environment. Externally they were used to strengthen the fight for political emancipation. The fact that for about three generations Jewish studies figured extensively in these internal and external struggles affected the choice of research topics. Whatever was not in accord with this nonscientific object was neglected or suppressed.

On examining the effect of Jewish studies on these internal and external struggles, a surprising conclusion is reached. Outwardly they had a certain measure of success: the authorities sometimes took their findings into account. Their impact on the Jewish community, however, was limited, mainly because of its indifference and the strong opposition put up by the Orthodox camp.

Despite all these shortcomings, it must be admitted, however, that an enormous amount of plodding, meticulous work was done in that period. To this day scholars of Judaism profit from these early labors, despite the altered perspective from which historical developments are viewed.

The historical perspective was revolutionized as a result of the national revival movement, which caused a general change of values in Jewish studies. The national-Zionist interpretation evolved only one generation after the Zionist movement had come into being, just as it took one generation from Mendelssohn's time for Jewish studies to emerge. The new discipline that developed some fifty years back was oriented towards secularization and "Zionisation." Besides its advantages, it too had

Source: Symposium, "'Wissenschaft des Judentums' and Its Influence on Modern Research," in *Perspectives on German-Jewish History in the Nineteenth and Twentieth Century*, ed. and trans. from the Hebrew by Meir Golan (Jerusalem: Jerusalem Academic Press, 1971), pp. 42–46. Reprinted by permission of the Leo Baeck Institute, Jerusalem.

its shortcomings. The exponents of Jewish studies in their new conception regarded Judaism as a living body and directed their attention to all aspects of Jewish life. Among their achievements we may list the fact that they, unlike their predecessors who had wittingly or unwittingly ignored the problems of the diaspora, delved into this subject, unearthed its problems and dealt with them extensively. Their endeavors resulted in such important achievements as the works of Ben-Zion Dinur[6] and Salo Baron.[7] Yet the Zionist approach to Jewish history also carried the risk of some bias being introduced by the evaluation of every event according to this pro- or anti-Zionist significance. Bialik's hope that the return of the scholars engaged in Jewish studies to the use of the Hebrew language would in itself suffice to offer a constructive solution was not fulfilled.[8]

Two central problems of Jewish historiography preoccupy scholars to this day:

(a) There is an inherent contradiction in Jewish studies between the perception of Judaism as a conceptual system and the evaluation of Jewish history according to its criteria and looking upon the Jewish community as a living organism with an evolutionary history. These two trends coexisted in Jewish studies since their inception, as may be seen from the very first program drawn up by Zunz.[9] Some scholars who aligned themselves with the first school, nevertheless, unintentionally produced studies corresponding to the second conception because in the course of their work they fell in love with the Jewish historic phenomenon in all its manifestation.

(b) The issue whether Jewish history should be regarded as a single whole or not has not been finally resolved to this day. It is still a moot point whether all Jewish history is subject to the same determinant dynamics or is merely a collection of different fragments or episodes, each explicable by specific circumstances of general history. From our understanding and personal experience we are rather inclined to the holistic view.

The two outstanding events of our period, the Holocaust and the establishment of the State of Israel, will no doubt have tremendous [impact] on scientific developments, since the work of scholars is essentially based on living contemporary experience. For research is being carried out against the background of this experience, which is moreover due to be transmuted into a decisive intellectual-emotional factor whose impact will become apparent only in the future.

NOTES

1. Gershom Scholem (1897–1982) was born in Berlin, Germany, to an assimilated Jewish family. He settled in Palestine in 1923, where he joined the faculty of the fledgling Hebrew University of Jerusalem. At this institution he pursued his pioneering labors in the academic study of Kabbalah and Jewish mysticism. Precisely because of its objective, nonapologetic character, he regarded academic scholarship as a vehicle allowing modern students of Judaism to disclose hidden and long-forgotten expressions of Jewish spirituality. Illuminating these dormant sources, modern Jewish studies thus may contribute to releasing the dynamic of Jewish creativity pinioned, paradoxically, by both Orthodoxy and the ethos of assimilation. Each of these otherwise diametrically opposed forces in modern Jewish life, Scholem contended, assumed a defensive and rigidifying posture regarding its respective conception of Judaism. Hence, he deemed modern Jewish studies to be integral to the Zionist project of renewing Jewish cultural and spiritual life. Accordingly, in various essays he trenchantly criticized the tendency—which, he held, had dominated *Wissenschaft des Judentums* from its very beginnings—to introduce extraneous ideological and theological motives into modern Jewish studies. (See, for example "The Science of Judaism—Then and Now," translated by Michael A. Meyer, in Gershom Scholem, *The Messianic Idea in Judaism and other Essays on Jewish Spirituality* (New York: Schocken, 1971), pp. 304–44.) Turning specifically to his colleagues who identify with Zionism, he contended that not only does a tendentious ideological use of scholarship mark a transgression against the objective standards of academic research, it also constitutes a betrayal of the supreme task assigned modern Jewish studies. The statement printed here was first presented at a colloquium sponsored by the Leo Baeck Institute in Jerusalem in the summer of 1970.

2. A scion of a distinguished Russian-Jewish family of bankers and philanthropists, Baron David Guensburg (1857–1910) was a scholar of Semitic languages. In 1908 he created a Jewish Academy, officially called Higher Courses on Oriental Studies, in St. Petersburg.

The Academy had access to his vast personal library, containing one of the most valuable collections of Judaica in the world. In 1916, with the closing of the Academy, the library was nationalized and transferred to the Lenin State Library in Moscow. Many future scholars of distinction in Jewish studies attended Guensburg's Academy.

3. Dropsie College for Hebrew and Cognate Learning was founded in Philadelphia through the bequest of Moses Aaron Dropsie (1821–1905), who was a lawyer in that city. A postgraduate institute in all branches of Jewish studies and Semitica, it opened its doors in 1909. In 1986 Dropsie College for Hebrew and Cognate Learning became the Annenberg Research Institute, primarily a postdoctoral research center for Judaic and Near Eastern studies.

4. *Verein zur Gruendung und Forderung einer Akademie fuer die Wissenschaft des Judentums* was founded in 1918 at the initiative of Hermann Cohen (cf. chapter 10, document 29) to promote the establishment of an Academy of Jewish Studies for the furtherance of Jewish scholarship and the support of younger scholars. The idea of the Academy was first envisioned by Franz Rosenzweig in his brochure *Zeit Ist's* (1917) ("It is Time," in Rosenzweig, *On Jewish Learning*, ed. N. N. Glatzer [New York: Schocken, 1965], pp. 27–54). In 1919 the research institute of the envisioned academy was founded in Berlin; its activities came to a sudden halt in 1934.

5. See this chapter, document 8.

6. On the faculty of the Hebrew University since 1936, Ben-Zion Dinur (formerly Dinaburg; 1884–1973) was the founder of what has been called the Israeli school of Jewish historiography. He introduced an explicitly Zionist perspective to the study of Jewish history, emphasizing the basic unity of the Jewish people grounded in the abiding centrality of the Land of Israel to the people's religious and secular imagination and hope.

7. Salo Wittmayer Baron (1895–1990) taught at Columbia University from 1930 to 1963 and was the first member of an American history faculty to teach Jewish studies. Eschewing what he called "lachrymose history"—the tale of Jewish persecution and suffering—he focused on the social and religious history of the Jewish people and on the cross-fertilization between Jewish experience and the surrounding cultures. He regarded the diaspora and the Land of Israel as two equally vibrant centers of Jewish creativity.

8. Cf. H. N. Bialik, "On Modern Jewish Studies. A Letter to the Editors of *Dvir*, 29 Iyyar 5683 [May 27, 1922]"; reprinted in the *Collected Works of Bialik* (Tel Aviv: Dvir, 1938), pp. 228–31 (in Hebrew).

9. See document 5 in this chapter.

VI

POLITICAL AND RACIAL ANTISEMITISM

Modern antisemitism, as distinct from Christian medieval contempt toward Jewry, is prompted, at least at the ideological level, by secular motives. As already indicated in our discussion of emancipation, the civil and socioeconomic integration of the Jews into a modern state was not a simple legal process. Emancipation of the Jews met much opposition. We have seen that emancipation was an intrinsic feature in the formation of a modern democratic, liberal state. Correspondingly the antagonism toward the modern, "emancipated" Jew is related to the tensions and ideological responses that surrounded the formation of a modern state. A delineation of some of the principal themes of modern antisemitism readily illustrates this correlation.

1. The modern state requires cultural and national integration. The Jews, possessing distinct cultural and national aspirations of their own, are hence fundamentally incompatible with the modern state that hosts them. Indeed, they form "a state within a state." (See document 4 by Johann Gottlieb Fichte. See also chapter 3, document 23.)

2. The modern state has witnessed the emergence of an aggressive capitalism; its most egregious features, variously defined, were frequently attributed to Jewry. (See the following: document 5 by Jakob Friedrich Fries; document 6 by K. B. A. Sessa; document 13 by Karl Marx; document 18 by Alphonse Toussenel; and document 20 by Edouard-Adolphe Drumont.)

3. The democratic, parliamentary character of the modern state encouraged the politicization of antisemitism. Antisemitism became an aspect of political propaganda, either instrumentally—pandering to popular antisemitic attitudes in order to strengthen a political party's electoral support—or ideologically, the party's principal motive being to check what was perceived to be the excesses of Jewish influence in certain areas of public life. (See document 21 by Adolf Stoecker.)

4. The rise of the modern state wrought many social and economic dislocations, which engendered a profound discontentment with the very fabric and texture of modern life. Those who were discontented with modernity frequently directed their anger at the Jews who seemed to be the most obvious beneficiaries of—and thus somehow responsible

for—modernity. (See the following: document 14 by Richard Wagner; document 15 by Wilhelm Marr; and document 27 by Houston Stewart Chamberlain.) The nexus between modern, secular theories of the Jewish conspiracy and medieval Christian views of Jewry's evil schemes is illustrated by the persistence of the blood libel in enlightened Europe. (See document 30.)

5. Antimodernity developed into a comprehensive Weltanschauung. Joined by antisemitism, it fostered the view that Jewry was secretly conspiring through the manipulation of the various forces of modernity—from capitalism to socialism—to subvert the idyllic world of the Gentiles. (See the following: document 15 by Wilhelm Marr; document 20 by Edouard-Adolphe Drumont; and document 29, the *Protocols.*)

6. The conspiratorial view of the world led to a Manichaean bifurcation of humanity into the opposing forces of good and evil. Racial theories, which associated specific moral and intellectual characteristics with somatic, anatomical, and chromosomal factors of a given "race," helped "explain" the moral and spiritual division of humanity. Peoples, such as the Jews, affiliated with the forces of evil, were members of a distinct race. Hence, the Jews were incorrigibly Jewish. The sublime program (viz., tolerance and education) of the liberals and democrats for the moral "betterment" of the Jews was not only platitudinous but would dangerously mislead the Gentile world. Hence, the warning that appeared on the title page of the *Protocols of the Elders of Zion,* "Gentiles, Beware! The Jews are an alien bacillus that must be urgently contained and isolated." (See the following: document 16 by Karl Eugen Duehring and document 27 by Houston Stewart Chamberlain.)

Whether the political and racial antisemitism that evolved in nineteenth-century Europe led ineluctably to the Holocaust, or even contributed to it, is a complex methodological and historical question. What is certain is that Nazi antisemitism did not arise *ex nihilo.*

1. JEWS (1756)

FRANÇOIS-MARIE AROUET (VOLTAIRE)[1]

You order me to draw you a faithful picture of the spirit of the Jews, and of their history, and—without entering into the ineffable ways of Providence, which are not our ways—you seek in the manners of this people the source of the events which Providence prepared.

It is certain that the Jewish nation is the most singular that the world has ever seen; and although, in a political view, the most contemptible of all, yet in the eyes of a philosopher, it is on various accounts, worthy of consideration.

The Guebers, the Banyans and the Jews are the only nations which exist dispersed, having no alliance with any people, are perpetuated among foreign nations, and continue apart from the rest of the world.... From [a] short summary of their history it results that the Hebrews have always been vagrants or robbers, or slaves, or seditious. They are still vagabonds upon the earth, abhorred by men....

It is commonly said that the abhorrence in which the Jews held other nations proceeded from their horror of idolatry; but it is much more likely that the manner in which they at the first exterminated some of the tribes of Canaan, and the hatred which the neighboring nation conceived for them, was the cause of this invincible aversion. As they knew no nations but their neighbors, they thought that in abhorring them they detested the whole earth, and thus accustomed themselves to be the enemies of all men.

One proof that this hatred was not caused by the idolatry of the nations is that we find in the history of the Jews that they were very often idolaters. Solomon himself sacrificed to strange gods. After him, we find scarcely any king in the little province of Judah that does not permit the worship of these gods and offer them incense. The province of Israel kept its two calves and its sacred groves, or adored other divinities....

You ask, what was the philosophy of the Hebrews? The answer will be a short one—they had none. You then ask whether the ancient philosophers and lawgivers borrowed from the Jews, or the Jews from them? We must refer the question to Philo,[2] he admits that before the translation of the Septuagint[3] the books of his nation were unknown to the Gentiles. A great people cannot have received their laws and their knowledge from a small, obscure and enslaved people. In the time of Osias,[4] indeed, the Jews had no books; in his reign was accidentally found the only copy of the law then in existence. This people, after their captivity at Babylon, had no other alphabet than the Chaldean; they were not famed for any art, any manufacture whatsoever; and even in the time of Solomon they were obliged to pay dear for foreign artisans. To say that the Egyptians, the Persians and the Greeks were instructed by the Jews is as if one were to say that the Romans learned the crafts from the people of Brittany. The Jews never were natural philosophers, nor geometricians, nor astronomers. So far were they from having public schools for the instruction of youth, that they had not even a term in their language to express such an institution. The people of Peru and Mexico measured their year much better than the Jews. Their stay in Babylon and in Alexandria during which individuals might acquire wisdom and knowledge trained the [Jewish] people as a whole in no art save that of usury.... In short, we find in them only an ignorant and barbarous people, who have long united the most sordid avarice with the most detestable superstition and the most invincible hatred for every people by whom they are tolerated and enriched. Still, we ought not to burn them.

Source: *The Works of Voltaire*, trans. William F. Fleming (Akron, Ohio: Werner Co., 1904), vol. 10, pp. 266, 278, 280, 281, 283–84.

NOTES

1. François-Marie Arouet (Voltaire) (1694–1778), perhaps France's most popular and ardent advocate of free thought and of political as well as religious liberty. In his attack on the church—an institution which he deemed to be a major source of humanity's intellectual and spiritual bondage—Voltaire preferred to concentrate his criticism on the precursors of the church, the Old Testament and its protagonists, the Jews. Scholars debate whether Voltaire's venemous comments on Judaism and Jewry were merely a tactical strategem to attack the church or an uncritical hatred of the Jews that contradicted his teaching of tolerance and brotherhood. In any event, in the antisemitic campaigns of the following centuries, he was used as an authority and frequently cited. Thus, paradoxically, he both helped prepare the mental climate that led to the emancipation of the Jews and contributed to the formation of the ideology of modern secular antisemitism. This article first appeared in the fifth edition of Voltaire's *Oeuvres Complètes* (Geneva, 1756), vol. 7, ch. 1; it later appeared in his *Dictionnaire Philosophique* (Basle, 1764), vol. 14, from which it is most frequently quoted.

2. Philo Judaeus (c. 20 B.C.E.–c. 40 C.E.), Jewish philosopher in Alexandria, Egypt, who used a wide but eclectic knowledge of Hellenistic philosophy and culture to illuminate the teachings of Judaism.

3. A Greek translation of the Hebrew Bible, so named because its oldest part, the Pentateuch, was—according to legend—translated at the command of Ptolemy II (d. 246 B.C.E.) by seventy (septuagint is Latin for "the seventy") Jewish scholars, each working independently, whose translations agreed in every word.

4. Osias refers to Josiah, king of Judah (640–609 B.C.E.). It is widely believed by scholars that during Josiah's reign, the book of Deuteronomy—the fifth and last book of the Pentateuch—was found by the prophet Hilkiah in the Temple in 621 B.C.E. This discovery provided an impetus for religious reform in Judah (see Kings 2:22–23).

2. AN APOLOGY FOR THE JEWISH NATION (1762)

ISAAC DE PINTO[1]

Are there any imputations which can be laid on a people in general? Can a whole nation be accessory to a crime? Can the murder of Charles I, be with justice imputed to the whole English nation? Or the massacre of St. Bartholomew to the French in the reign of Charles IX? Every universal proposition is suspicious and liable to error, more especially when we speak of the general character of a nation, the shades of which are always much diversified, according to the station, rank, temper, and profession of every individual. Each province of an empire is as different from the next, as either of these differ from the capital, and the capital from the court, where also each family has a particular tint by which the individuals of it are divided into various characters. If in a wood there are not two leaves which bear a strict resemblance, in the world there are not two faces perfectly alike, nor two men exactly of the same

---

Source: Isaac de Pinto, Apologie pour la nation juive, ou reflexions critiques sur le premier chapitre du VIIᵉ tome des oeuores de M. de Voltaire au sujet des Juifs (Amsterdam, 1762), in Letters of Certain Jews to Monsieur Voltaire, Concerning an Apology for Their Own People and for the Old Testament, 2nd ed., trans. Philip Lefanu (Covington, Kentucky, 1845), pp. 23–35, 37–42.

way of thinking on every subject, how is it possible to give the moral picture of a nation with one dash of the pen?

If this be true with regard to nations in general, it is much more so with respect to the Jews in particular. They have been scattered through so many nations, that they have, we may say, adopted in each country, after a certain time, the characters of the inhabitants; a Jew in London bears as little resemblance to a Jew in Constantinople, as this last resembles a Chinese Mandarin! A Portuguese Jew of Bordeaux and a German Jew of Metz appear two beings of a different nature! It is therefore impossible to speak of the manners of the Jews in general without entering into very long detail, and into particular distinctions; the Jew is a chameleon that assumes all the colors of the different climates he inhabits, of the different peoples he frequents, and of the different governments under which he lives.

Notwithstanding this, M. Voltaire has melted them all down to the same substance, and has given us a shocking picture of them which bears no resemblance....

If M. Voltaire had acted according to that principle of sound reason which he affects to do, he would have begun by distinguishing from the other Jews the Spanish and the Portuguese, who never have been mixed or incorporated with the crowd of the other sons of Jacob; he would have made this great distinction evident. I am aware that it is little known in France, and that the want of proper information on this head has been detrimental on many occasions to the Portuguese [Jewish] nation of Bordeaux. M. Voltaire cannot be ignorant of the scrupulous exactness of the Portuguese and Spanish Jews not to intermix in marriage, alliance, or any other way, with the Jews of other nations. He has been in Holland, and knows that they have separate synagogues, and that, although they profess the same religion and the same articles of faith, yet their ceremonies have often no resemblance. The manners of the Portuguese Jews are also very different from those of the rest: the former have no beards, nor anything peculiar in their dress. The rich among them vie with the other nations of Europe in refinement, elegance and show, and differ from them in worship only. Their variance with their other brethren is at such a height that if a Portuguese Jew in England or Holland married a German Jewess, he would of course lose all his prerogatives, be no longer reckoned a member of their Synagogue, forfeit all civil and ecclesiastical preferments, be absolutely divorced from the body of the nation and not even buried with his Portuguese brethren. They think in general that they are descended from the tribe of Judah, and they hold that the chief families of it were sent into Spain at the time of Babylonian captivity. This is the cause of those distinctions and of that elevation of mind which is observed among them, and which even their brethren of other nations seem to acknowledge.

By this wise policy they have preserved purer morals, and have acquired a certain importance, which helps even Christians to distinguish them from the other Jews. They do not, then, deserve those epithets which M. Voltaire lavishes on them. The Jews of Holland brought thither great riches at the end of the fifteenth century; and with manners irreproachable, greatly improved the trade of that commonwealth. Their Synagogue was like an assembly of senators, and, when German noblemen went into it, they could not be persuaded that those there present were of the same nation with those of Germany. They have been of greater use to Holland, at the beginning of the seventeenth century, than the French refugees were at the end of it. These latter, after the repeal of the edict of Nantes[2] brought into Holland much industry and little wealth, [however] the Portuguese, besides much wealth, drew into Holland the trade of Spain, and excited the industry [of Holland]. Their descendants have been rather dupes than knaves; they have often been the prey of usurers; rarely, if ever, usurers themselves. Scarcely can one instance be given of a Portuguese Jew executed at Amsterdam or the Hague, during two centuries. It would be hard to find in the annals of mankind so numerous a body of people as that of the Portuguese and Spanish Jews settled in Holland and England, among whom so few crimes punishable by law have been committed; and to this I call to witness all well-informed Christians of those nations....

Let us say a word of the German and Polish Jews. Is it surprising that a people who are deprived of all the privileges of society, who increase and multiply by the laws of nature and religion, who are despised and reviled on all sides, who are often persecuted, always insulted, is it surprising, I say, that among them human nature, debased and degraded, should seem to have no acquaintance with any thing but worldly want? The sharp stings of want inspire these martyrs to it with every means of banishing or lessening it. That contempt which is heaped on them chokes up all the seeds of virtue and honour; there can be no sense of shame, where undeserved contempt precedes guilt; to cover the innocent with ignominy is to pave the way to it. And is it wrong to continue firmly attached to a religion which was formerly looked on as sacred by these very persons who now condemn it? We ought to pity them if they err; but it would be ungenerous not to admire the constancy, resolution, courage, steadiness, and disinterestedness with which they give up so many worldly advantages. Who would not praise a son who gives up his right to a great estate, because he thinks, perhaps without just grounds, that he cannot take possession of it without acting in opposition to his father's will by the act required of him? Ought so delicate, so praise-worthy, so noble and so uncommon a feeling to draw on him from his younger brothers, who enjoy the estate, contempt, insults and abuse? It is not sufficient to abstain from burning people with faggots; they may be burned with the pen; and this fire is so much more to be dreaded, because it lasts to future generations. What can be expected from the ignorant, savage [and] vulgar, when the destruction of an unfortunate nation is determined [as by Voltaire], if these horrid prejudices are authorized by the greatest genius of the most enlightened age? Let him consult his reason and his heart, and I am confident he will employ all his talents in recanting his errors: he will show in a masterly way that the mean characters of certain Polish and German Jews are not to be laid to the charge of that ancient, divine, and sacred religion.

NOTES

1. Isaac de Pinto (1717–1787), philosopher and economist of Portuguese-Jewish origin who spent most of his life in Holland. De Pinto earned his reputation as a genuine innovator in economic theory by opposing the Physiocrats and advocating the economically productive role of the national debt as well as of modern credit and commerce.

   In this refutation of Voltaire; de Pinto anticipates a new genre of Jewish apologetic literature. In this literature, self-consciously acculturated Jews seek to parry the accusations of antisemites claiming that the criticism leveled is true only of those Jews who have yet to leave the ghetto. Antisemites would often use such statements as evidence corroborating their charges. De Pinto sent his pamphlet to Voltaire, whose reply is presented in document 3.

2. Edict of Nantes. The law was promulgated in 1598 by the French king Henry IV, and it secured a large measure of religious liberty to his Protestant subjects, the Huguenots. It was repealed in 1685.

3. REPLY TO DE PINTO (c. 1762)

FRANÇOIS-MARIE AROUET (VOLTAIRE)

The lines you complain of are cruel and unjust. There are among you very learned and respectable persons. Your letter is a sufficient evidence of this. I shall take care to insert a cancel-leaf in the new edition. When a man is in the wrong he should make reparation for it and I was wrong in attributing to a whole nation the vices of some individuals.

I shall tell you frankly, that there are many who cannot endure your laws, your books, or your superstitions. They say that your nation has done,

Source: Letters of Certain Jews to Monsieur Voltaire, Concerning an Apology for Their Own People and for the Old Testament, 2nd ed., trans. Philip Lefanu (Covington, Kentucky, 1845), pp. 54–56.

in every age, much harm to itself and to the human race. If you are a philosopher, as you seem to be, you will think as those gentlemen do, but you will not say it. Superstition is the most dreadful scourge of the earth; it is superstition that in every age has caused so many Jews and Christians to be slaughtered; it is superstition that still sends you Jews to the stake among nations praise-worthy in other respects.... But perhaps I should provoke you to anger, and you seem to be too worthy a man to deserve provocation. As you are a Jew remain so. But be a philosopher.[1] This is my best wish to you in this short life.

I have the honor of remaining, Sir, with all the sentiments of respect due to you,

Voltaire

Christian gentleman in Ordinary to the most Christian King [Voltaire, chrétien gentilhomme de la chambre du Roi très-chrétien].[2]

NOTES

1. For Voltaire, to be a philosopher meant the adoption of the rational Deistic culture of the Enlightenment and

assimilation. On the latter point Voltaire was explicit. With his characteristic sarcasm, he contended that the acceptance of the Jew by enlightened society was contingent on the Jew's rejection of his people's dietary laws and alleged misanthropy. "But what shall I say to my brother the Jew?" he wrote.

Shall I give him dinner? Yes, provided that during the meal Balaam's ass doesn't take it into its head to bray; that Ezekiel doesn't come to swallow one of the guests and keep him in his belly for three days; that a serpent doesn't mix into the conversation to seduce my wife; that a prophet doesn't take it into his head to sleep with her after dinner, as that good fellow Hoseah did for fifteen francs and a bushel of barley; above all that no Jew make a tour around my house sounding a trumpet, making the walls come down, killing me, my father, my mother, my wife, my children, my cat and my dog, in accord with the former usage of the Jews. [From "Tolerance," *Questions sur l'Encyclopédie*, cited in P. Gay, *The Party of Humanity* (New York: W. W. Norton, 1971), pp. 101ff.]

2. Voltaire ordinarily signed his correspondence "Down with infamy!"

4. A STATE WITHIN A STATE (1793)

JOHANN GOTTLIEB FICHTE[1]

A powerful, hostilely disposed nation is infiltrating almost every country in Europe. This nation is in a state of perpetual war with all these countries, severely afflicting their citizenry. I am referring to the Jewish Nation [*das Judentum*]. I believe, and hope to demonstrate subsequently, that the Jewish Nation is so dreadful not because it is isolated and closely knit, but rather because it is founded on the hatred of mankind. It is a people whose most humble member elevates his ancestors higher than we exalt our entire history. Jewry sees as its ancestor a patriarch older than itself—a legend we ourselves have incorporated into our creed. It perceives all peoples as the descendants of those it drove out of its fervently loved fatherland. It condemned itself and is condemned to petty trade, which debilitates

Source: Johann Gottlieb Fichte, "Beitrag zur Berichtung der Urteile des Publicums ueber die Franzoesische Revolution" [1793], in *Saemtliche Werke*, ed. J. H. Fichte (Berlin: Verlag von Veit; 1845), vol. 6, pp. 149–50, trans. M. Gelber.

the body and deadens any tendency for noble feelings. The Jewish nation excluded itself from our meals, from our festive toasts, and from sweet, heart-to-heart exchanges of happiness with us by the most binding element of mankind—religion. It separates itself from all others in its duties and rights, from here until eternity. One would expect something different from such a people than what we see, namely, that in a state where the absolute monarch may not take away my ancestral dwelling and where I retain my rights before the all-powerful minister, the first Jew whom it so pleases pillages that which is mine and goes unpunished. You see all this; it cannot be denied. Yet, you speak sugar-sweet words about toleration and human rights and civic rights, by which you infringe upon our basic human rights. Your loving toleration of those who do not believe in Jesus Christ [expressed] by all the titles, honors and high positions you grant [the Jews], brings no satisfaction, for you are openly denouncing those who believe in Christ just as you do, depriving them of their civic honor and their honestly earned bread. Does this not recall to you the notion of a state within a state? Does the obvious idea not occur to you, that the Jews alone are citizens of a state which is more secure and powerful than any of yours? If you also give them civic rights in your states, will not your other citizens be completely trod under foot?*

NOTE

1. Johann Gottlieb Fichte (1762–1814), German philosopher and founder of ethical idealism. Fichte's attitude toward Jews and Judaism was complex. He manifested a reverent attitude toward the Bible but completely rejected the Jewish religion. He fought against the Jews' citizenship rights but declared that human rights must be given to the Jews, "for, they *are* human, [although] their malevolence does not justify our becoming like them.... "

---

*Let the poisonous air of intolerance stay as far from these pages as it is from my heart. The Jew who overcomes the difficult, one may say insurmountable, barriers which lie before him, and attains a love of justice, mankind, and truth—that Jew is a hero and a saint. I do not know whether such Jews ever existed or exist today. I shall believe it as soon as I meet such Jews. But dare you not sell me beautiful appearances for the real thing. Let the Jews never believe in Jesus Christ. Let them never even believe in God. If only they did not believe in a misanthropic God and in a double ethical standard [one applicable to Jews alone, another for their dealings with Gentiles]. They must have human rights, even if they will not grant them to us. For, they *are* human, [although] their malevolence does not justify our becoming like them. Do not force these rights on the Jew against his will—do not allow that to happen when you are present and able to prevent it.... If you have eaten yesterday, but are hungry and only have enough bread for today, then give it to the Jew. He hungers for it, since he did not eat yesterday. You will be doing a good deed. Still, I see absolutely no way of giving them civic rights; except perhaps, if one night we chop off all of their heads and replace them with new ones, in which there would not be one single Jewish idea. And then, I see no other way to protect ourselves from the Jews, except if we conquer their promised land for them and send all of them there. [Fichte's Note]

5. ON THE DANGER TO THE WELL-BEING AND CHARACTER OF THE GERMANS PRESENTED BY THE JEWS (1816)

JAKOB FRIEDRICH FRIES[1]

For about forty years now Prussian scholars, in particular, have defended the Jews in face of the antipathy shown them by the common people. Some were motivated by friendship for noble individuals belonging to this people; others, by their fervor for enlightenment and against narrow-minded attachment in particular, positive forms of religion; still others, because they had become dependent on rich, individual Jews. Yet, the spirit of this debate was cosmopolitan and characterized by a general love of man, whereby each individual held his fellow to be his equal. But precisely because of this last, very noble motivation, many misunderstandings continue to be debated, two of which we wish to mention here.

The first concerns the prejudice that the Jews were persecuted by us with blind rage and unjust religious zeal during the Middle Ages as well as down to the present. This, Herr Ruehs[2] has incontrovertibly disproved. To be sure, due to the more coarse manners of an earlier age, people alternated between rash, superstitious patronage and cruel excesses in their behavior toward the Jews. Princes almost always favored them too much, while cruelty originated from the common people. This cruelty, however, was not due to an inexplicable hatred for those who lived by deceit—those insidious, second-hand dealers and exploiters of the common people. The idea that the Jews were excessively oppressed in civic matters derives from this [erroneous belief that the Jews were treated with blind hatred]. If they were only to receive more civic rights, it is held, they would thus improve themselves. Ruehs has clearly shown that the opposite is true by using examples from history. Both in Germany and abroad the Jews dwelt in free states where they enjoyed every right, and even countries where they reigned—but their sordidness, their mania for deceitful, second-hand dealing always remained the same. They shy away from industrious occupations not because they are hindered from pursuing them but simply because they do not want to.

The second prejudice is the kind that can easily deceive human understanding with regard to the most important things. An abstract, general expression is replaced with the reality of a particular one. In this case, the [terms] Jews, Jewry and Judaism are interchangeable. We declare war not against the Jews, our brothers, but against Judaism. Should one we love be stricken by the plague, is it not proper that we wish him deliverance from it? Should we abuse those who, stricken by the plague, lament its horrors and conjecture how to free themselves from it? Judaism is a residue from the uncultured past, which instead of being restricted should be completely extirpated. In fact, improving the condition of the Jews in society means rooting out Judaism, destroying the whole lot of deceitful, second-hand pedlars and hawkers. Judaism is the sickness of a people who are rapidly multiplying. Jewry will acquire power through money wherever despotism or distress engenders oppressive taxation; wherever oppressive, public ransoms become necessary; wherever the well-being of the citizen is so endangered that indebtedness on a small scale grows ever worse. Finally, the Jews also gain power where many unproductive countries are wasteful. The idle, stagnant capital of these countries is devoured by the Jews like worms gnawing on rotting matter.

Source: Jakob Friedrich Fries, *Ueber die Gefaehrdung des Wohlstandes und Charakters der Deutschen durch die Juden* (Heidelberg: Mahr und Winter, 1816), pp. 9–11, trans. M. Gelber.

NOTES

1. Jakob Friedrich Fries (1773–1843), German philosopher. He lectured in both Jena and Heidelberg and published authoritative works on philosophy and psychology. His popularity with the students contributed to the success of his anti-Jewish writings. Under his influence, the *Burschenschaften* ("students' associations") decided not to accept Jews as members.
2. Christian Friedrich Ruehs (1781–1820), nationalist professor of history in Berlin who opposed Jewish emancipation in a pamphlet entitled *Ueber die Ansprueche der Juden an das deutsche Buergerrecht* (1815). In this work Ruehs maintained that Jewry already constitutes a nation complete with its own laws and aristocracy and therefore cannot be granted citizenship in a Christian state. Because of the unbridgeable gap existing between Germans and Jews, stemming from their inherently opposing natures, Jews may be tolerated only as a subject nation and the medieval restrictions must be reapplied.

6. OUR VISITORS (1816)

K. B. A. SESSA[1]

ABRAHAM: A new perzon you'll become! Avay from Egypt, an from da flesh-pots of mama, you'll go avay! In da vilderness, you'll look around, vere you'll not get da tiniest zip of water for noting! You'll see der da promized lant of da rich goyim! Your inheritenz you'll take avay from dem however you can, if you'll be a true zon of the children of Izrael!...

Geh! Geh! Step on you, let dem! Trow you out, let dem! Sue you in courtz, let dem! You'll go to da dogs, they'll bind you mit rope an chainz. Let dem whip you, martyr you till you're half dead! But (*threateningly*) Rich you *must* become!...

My Yankele! My sonnie! Listen t'me, vat I'll tell you. Not from greed do I vant it. It's da pleasure an joy at havin' muney dat's da reazon. Ven I count muney, my heart's ad ease. Ven I count muney, I need no oder pleasure. Ven I count muney, I need no docta, no medecine. I'm totally vell. Sonnie, von't you do just a little somting for da healt of your papa? Von't you give your old papa some relief in his old age?...

NOTE

1. Karl Barromaeus Alexander Sessa (1766–1813), physician in Breslau. *Unser Verkehr*, a comedy, was first presented on the Breslau stage (under the title *Die Judeuschule*) in 1813. It was performed in Berlin and elsewhere, until it was banned by the police. However, the play was published anonymously in numerous editions, and it inspired many of the antisemitic caricatures found in German literature. Sessa's play emphasizes the putative greed, vulgarity, and pernicious immorality of all Jews. The play's great popularity was due to its parody of the poor German spoken by the Jews who had only recently been liberated from the ghetto.

Source: K.B.A. Sessa, *Unser Verkehr, Eine Posse in einem Aufzug* (Leipzig, 1816), pp. 34ff., trans. M. Gelber.

7. FEATURES OF THE JEWS TO BE CORRECTED (1819)[1]

LEOPOLD ZUNZ

In one of our previous meetings we considered the sources of the so-called Jewish evil, which we initially divided into two categories:

A) Those evils that are to be ascribed primarily to the inner world of the Jews; and
B) Those evils that are to be ascribed largely to the situation of Jews among Christians.

The evils of "A" derive from

1) Ideas
2) Cult
3) The internal state of affairs prevailing in the [Jewish] community
4) Education

A. The inner world

1. Ideas

a) Concepts of Religion, especially God's preferential love of Israel;
b) Conceit;
c) Superstition;
d) The Jews' attitude toward other peoples;
e) Neglect of work for the sake of change in favor of ascetic idleness or meticulous observance of ceremonies;
f) The spirit of petty trade;[2]
g) Avarice;
h) Reduction of all values to money;
i) Contempt of Science;
j) All of the above together amount to maintaining in violation of the law the illusion that one may deceive non-Jews.

2. Cult

a) Divine service;
b) Liturgical Formulations;
c) Outdated, destructive, and meaningless customs;
d) Excessive ceremonial laws.

3. Internal State of Affairs prevailing in the [Jewish] Community

a) The rabbis, their rule, fanaticism, and uselessness;
b) The community's governing council's lack of authority, and as a consequence anarchy, [resulting in] abuses such as;
c) The wasting of charitable funds on good-for-nothings; and hasty burials;
d) Poor or no schooling whatsoever.

4. Education

a) Enfeeblement of the children, and as a consequence;
b) Cowardice;
c) Harmful examples in the parental home;
d) Ignorance, immorality, coarseness of the *yeshivah* students;
e) Rift between the instruction of the laws of the Torah and their observance at home;
f) Inadequate and useless study in school; Talmud, [but] no knowledge of languages and practical subjects;
g) An appreciation of knowledge is not aroused among the pupils;

Source: Leopold Zunz, "Entwurf der an den Juden zu verbessernden Gegenstaende" (15 Dezember 1819). Leopold Zunz Archives, Mappe B10–8. National and University Library, Jerusalem, Israel.

h) Poorly paid and poorly trained teachers;

i) Neglect of the mother tongue;

j) Neglect of the female sex.

B. The Situation of Jews among Christians

a) The exclusion [of Jews] from commerce, and small business; no craftsmen;

b) [The Jews are] work-shy [that is, they are reluctant to engage in manual work]; no Jewish farmers;

c) [Jews are] self-dismissive;

d) [Jews are] physically [indolent];

e) [Jews have] no will to improve [their] situation;

f) No classification [of Jews] according to social class;

g) [Jews tend to] superficially angle for a joke and an effect, [a] consequence of [their] poor upbringing;

h) [The Jews pursue] ungrounded, non-focused study;

i) Sophomoric learning;

j) Defection [from Judaism];

k) [Jews] either seclude themselves from or impose themselves on the Christians;

l) [Jews exhibit a] coarseness in speech, comportment, mores, and manners.

NOTES

1. This "Outline of Features of the Jews to Be Corrected" was an address that Zunz delivered before the Society for the Science and Culture of the Jews (see chapter 5, documents 1–3) and reflects how deeply antisemitic images and stereotypes affected Jewish self-understanding. The list of "Jewish evils" (*Judenübel*) or faults as they are manifest in the Jews' relationships with "Christians" that Zunz delineates are divided between reprehensible traits that are to be traced to the internal life of the Jews and those that are to be attributed to the dynamic of their relations with non-Jews. Although he does not expressly say so, these situations appear under conditions in which the Jews do not enjoy civil rights.

2. The term that Zunz uses, *Schachergeist*, is derived from the Hebrew, (via Yiddish) *sechar* (trade, commerce) and denotes "petty trade, especially of peddlers seeking a quick profit, and is generally employed by Jews in a contemptuous sense." *Grimms Deutscher Wörterbuch*, vol. 14, p. 1959.

8. THE JEWISH MIRROR (1819)

HARTWIG VON HUNDT-RADOWSKY[1]

I do not deny in the least that Jews are able to acquire scholarly knowledge. But such knowledge never ennobles their spirit or feelings. For them, gaining knowledge is like gaining a profit. They deal dishonestly and accumulate their wealth, with no intention of benefiting mankind....The Jew's inherited nature is well disposed to usury and haggling, greed for money, falsehood and deceit, in much the same way that it is disposed to scabies. It is impossible for the Jews to become good. An emperor or king can indeed elevate [a Jew] to nobility, but he can never make him noble; the depravity of this people is too enormous and it increases with every day by its more than one-thousand-year-old hatred and resentment of other peoples....

To be sure, there might be now and then a Jew who seems less wicked than the others. Still, these are

---

Source: Hartwig von Hundt-Radowsky, *Judenspiegel: Ein Schand-und Sittengemaelde alter und neuer Zeit* (Wuerzburg, 1819; Reutlingen, 1821), pp. 45–47, 51, 57–58, 78–79, 106, 109, trans. by M. Gelber.

highly rare, and singular exceptions can never provide the standard for judging a significant and numerous people. An old coincidence of circumstances and a fortunate occurrence of peculiarities can perhaps cause an exception from time to time. However, this never invalidates the rule. If there are also instances where white parents give birth to black children, so can one Jew be born accidentally of an Israelite, lacking the Jewish facial characteristics, odor and haggler's disposition.

Further, granting civic rights to Jews was an injustice perpetrated by the government against the non-Jewish inhabitants. The latter and their ancestors founded the state, defended and preserved it with their wealth, blood, and lives, against both internal and external enemies. Now, however, a class of morally and spiritually degenerate people (whom we shelter, and who have benefited from the state but never benefit it at all) is treated in exactly the same manner that we are. . . .

Certainly they will gain the upper hand in many European countries very soon unless strict laws are introduced against them and circumcision is replaced by castration. . . .

I claim that the Jew is incapable of becoming a scholar: that is a man who benefits the world through his spirit and learning and is instrumental in the further education of his contemporaries for posterity. . . .

[Reflections concerning the betterment, "destruction" (*Ausrottung*) and "expulsion" (*Vertreibung*) of the Jews:] It would not be advisable to gather the Jews together (since they have few admirers left in Germany) and expel them to the promised land, where milk and honey flow and great clusters of grapes grow. Cannot we as easily shove the vermin across Turkey? At any rate, Abraham's other descendants, the Ishmaelites, would push their circumcised half-brothers, the Israelites, even further on. Then, we will have reconquered Constantinople without spilling a drop of Christian blood.

NOTE

1. Hartwig von Hundt-Radowsky (1780–1835), German political writer and journalist. The title of his antisemitic treatise, "The Jewish Mirror," seems to be an allusion to Johannes Pfefferkorn's (1469–1521) similarly titled pamphlet in which he held that Jewish literature was inimical to Christianity. In a later work, *Neuer Judenspiegel oder Apologie der Kinder Israels* (1828), Hundt-Radowsky executed a complete about-face, acknowledging the moral and social perfectibility of the Jews through re-education (albeit after they had repudiated their religion) and recognized the responsibility of the Christian states for what he saw as the Jews' present state of corruption. Not surprisingly, this apology was not as popular as his earlier works.

9. NOTABLES OF THE JEWISH COMMUNITY OF DAMASCUS (1840)[1]

Expressing our best wishes for your health, to our deep regret I address you these few lines, to inform you of the continued state of misery to which our brethren, inhabitants of Damascus, remain, as communicated to you our last letter of the 17th of *Adar* (February).

We had hoped to advise you in this letter that the circumstances of the murder respecting which the Jewish community was calumniated had been ascertained, but in this hope we have been sadly disappointed; we will therefore repeat everything in detail, and it is thus:

Source: Letter by the Elders of the Jewish Community of Damascus to the Elders of the Jewish Community of Constantinople. March 1840. Translated from the Hebrew in *The Times* (London) June 23, 1840, p. 3.

On Wednesday, the 1st day of the month of *Adar* (February) there disappeared from Damascus a priest, who, with his servant, had dwelt for 40 years in this city; he exercised the profession of a physician, and visited the houses of Catholics, Jews, and Armenians, for the purposes of vaccination.

The day following (Thursday) there came people into the quarter of the Jews to look for him, stating that they had seen both him and his servant on the previous day (Wednesday) in that quarter. In order to put in execution their conspiracy, they seized a Jewish barber, telling him he must know all about the matter, and thence they immediately carried him before the governor, before whom they accused him, and he instantly received 500 stripes, and he was also subjected to other cruelties. During the intervals between these inflictions he was urged to accuse all the Jews as accomplices, and he, thinking by these means to relieve himself, accused Messrs. David Arari, Isaac Arari, Aaron Arari, Joseph Laguado, Moses Aboulafis, Moses Benar…Judah and Joseph Arari, as instigating accomplices, who had offered him 300 piasters to murder the above-mentioned priest, inasmuch as, the Passover holy days approaching, they required blood for their cakes; he did not, however, give ear to their instigations, while at the same time he knew not what might have happened to the priest and his servant. Upon this the Pasha caused the aforesaid traduced persons to be arrested as instigators, and punished with blows and other torments of the most cruel nature; but, as they were innocent, they could not confirm as true that which was a calumny, and therefore, in contradictions, they asserted their innocence, appealing to the sacred writings, which strictly prohibit the Jews feeding upon blood, much more that of a fellow-creature, a thing totally repugnant to nature. Nevertheless they were imprisoned and daily, with chains around their necks, there were inflicted on them the most severe beatings and cruelties, and they were compelled to stand without food of any kind for 50 hours together.

Subsequently to this the Hebrew butchers were cited to appear; they were put in chains, together with the rabbis, Messrs. Jacob Antier, Solomon Arari and Asaria Jalfon; and they, too, were beaten to such an extreme that their flesh hung in pieces upon them; and these atrocities were perpetrated in order to induce them to confess whether or not they used blood in the Passover cakes, to which they replied, that if such had been the case, many Jewish proselytes would have published the fact. This, however, was not sufficient. Subsequently to this the same governor went to the college of the boys; he had them carried to prison, loaded them with chains, and forbade the mothers to visit their imprisoned children, to whom only 10 drachmas of bread and a cup-of water per day were allowed, the governors expecting that the fathers, for the sake of liberating their children, would confess the truth of the matter.

After this, the Jew, who was still at liberty, presented himself before the governor, stating that the calumny, that we make use of blood for our Passover cakes, had been discussed before all the powers, who after consulting their devises, had declared the falsehood of such a calumny; and he added, that either others had killed the priest and his servant, or that they had clandestinely absented themselves from the country, and that the barber, to save himself from persecutions, had stated that which was not true.

Upon this the Governor replied, that as he had accused other persons of killing them, he must know who were the murderers; and in order that he should confess, he was beaten to such an extreme that he expired under the blows.

After this the Governor, with a body of 600 men, proceeded to demolish the houses of his Jewish subjects, hoping to find the bodies of the dead; but, not finding anything, he returned, and again inflicted on his victims further castigation and torments, some of them too cruel and disgusting to be described. Incapable of bearing further anguish they preferred death and confessed that calumny was true.

The Governor, hearing the confession, asked them where they had secreted the blood of the murdered man, to which one of them replied that it had been put into a bottle and delivered to Mr. Moses Aboulafis, who declared he knew nothing of it, and in order that he should confess he received 1,000 stripes; but this infliction not extorting his confession, he was subjected to other insupportable torments, which at length compelled him to declare that the bottle was at home in a chest of drawers. Upon this the governor ordered that he should be carried on the Shoulders of four men (for he could not walk), that he might open the bureau. This was opened, but nothing was found in it, except a quantity of money, which the Governor seized, asking him, at the same time, where was the blood; whereupon the said Aboulafis replied, that he made the statement in order that the Governor should see the money in the bureau, trusting by these means to save himself from the calumny. Upon this the torments were repeated and Aboulafis embraced Mahametanism.

It is thus that they treated the whole, and they have now been for one month in this misery. In Beirut, and much more in Damascus, the Jews are not at liberty to get out.

After this, an individual came forward and stated that, by means of astrology, he had discovered and ascertained that the seven individuals above named assassinated the priest, and that the servant was killed by Raphael Farki, Nathan Levi, Aaron Levi, Mordecai Farul and Asser of Lisbon. The first two of these were immediately arrested, the others, it appears, sought safety in flight.

You will judge from this, dear friends, what sort of justice is administered by means of astrology, and how such justice is administered. And there is no one who is moved to compassion in favour of the unfortunate victims of oppression. Even Mr. Bekor Negri, the Governor's banker, unable to bear these afflictions, became a Muslim....

NOTE

1. In February 1840 a Capuchin friar in Damascus vanished without a trace. Given the approach of the Passover holiday, his fellow monks immediately accused the Jews of killing him for their religious ritual. Eager to consolidate his government's influence in the volatile region, the French consul in Damascus actively intervened in support of the monks and their charge against the Jews. The letter presented here from the Jewish notables of Damascus to their colleagues in Constantinople gives the details of the affair—the arrests, torture, exacted confessions, even conversions of those Jews charged with the murder.

The coup de grace was undoubtedly the adamant support of the French government for its representatives in the East.

The so-called Damascus Affair marked the recrudescence of the blood libel, the canard—thought buried with the Middle Ages—according to which Jews murder Christian children to obtain fresh human blood for the Passover rite. Despite the expectation that enlightened opinion would relegate this accusation to the prejudices of the past, the nineteenth and early twentieth centuries actually witnessed a revival of the blood libel (see this chapter, document 30). To be sure, Syria, then under the rule of Muhammad Ali of Egypt, was still largely untouched by the Western Enlightenment and its liberal values, but the very fact that the local representative of France, the cradle of the Enlightenment, supported—and actually supervised jointly with the governor-general of Syria—the investigation of the Jews accused of the crime aroused the concern of world Jewry.

The collusion of European Christians and secular authorities with Muslim mobs alarmed Jewish leaders, in particular those in Western Europe, who, together with enlightened non-Jews, launched protests through the press and mass meetings. A delegation of Jewish dignitaries from France and Great Britain—namely, Moses Montefiore, his secretary Louis Loewe, Adolph Cremieux and Solomon Munk—left for Egypt and was received by Muhammad Ali. Ultimately they succeeded in securing the release (in August 1840) of their co-religionists in Damascus. They then left for Constantinople, where they prevailed upon the Sultan to issue a *firman* proclaiming the blood libel fallacious and prohibiting the trial of Jews on the basis of such an accusation.

The Damascus Affair stimulated the political consciousness of Western Jews, alerting them to the need for intercommunal solidarity and cooperation on behalf of general Jewish interests, and led to the establishment of the first international Jewish organization, the Alliance Israélite Universelle. See document 9 in this chapter.

10. APPEAL TO ALL ISRAELITES (1860)

ALLIANCE ISRAÉLITE UNIVERSELLE[1]

Israelites! If, scattered over the whole surface of the earth and intermingled with all nations, you remain attached to the old religion of your ancestors, however weak be the bond that unites you therewith:

If you do not deny your religion, if you do not hide your worship, if you do not blush at being Israelites;

If you abhor the prejudices still entertained against us; the reproaches raised against us; the slanders, continually repeated, the lies, perpetually renewed; the injustice done us; the persecutions, which are either tolerated or excused;

If you hold, that the oldest and most simple of spiritual religions ought to maintain its place, fulfil its mission, proclaim its right, and manifest its vitality amid the new theories that agitate modern society;

If you believe, that the sublime idea and the vigorous worship of the One and Indivisible God, of which we are the oldest heirs and persistent defenders, ought to be guarded against the insinuations of doubt or indifference;

If you maintain, that religious liberty, this life of the soul, is nowhere better guarded, for the common good of all, than in those countries in which the Jews enjoy it fully and without any restriction whatsoever;

If you believe, that the creed, inherited from his ancestors, is for every one a sacred patrimony, that our firesides and our consciences are inviolable sanctuaries, which ought not to be invaded again as they lately have been;

If you hold, that unity is strength: that, although we are members of various nations, we may still be one nationality in sentiments, hopes and expectations;

If you think, that by legal means, by the invincible power of right and reason—without exciting any trouble, without frightening any power, without raising the indignation of any party, except that of ignorance, bigotry and fanaticism—you would obtain much and impart much by your zealous and intelligent action;

If you agree, that a large number of your co-religionists, still under the yoke of the sufferings, proscriptions and insults of twenty centuries, could regain their dignity as human beings, their rights as citizens;

If you believe, that those who are blind, ought to be enlightened, and not forsaken; and that those who are afflicted, ought to be assisted, and not merely pitied; that we should defend those who are calumniated, and not look on with silent compassion; that we ought to give material aid to those who are persecuted, and not simply cry and lament at their persecution;

If you hold, that the resources, hitherto isolated; the good intentions, one detached from the other; the aspirations, started without any definite object—could be united for higher purposes, so that the united action may be felt all over the globe;

If you hold, that it would be an honor to your religion, a lesson to the nations, a progress of humanity, a triumph of truth and reason, to see concentrated all the forces of Judaism, though small in number, but great by the innate love for the common good;

If you hold, that the influence, which the principles of 1789 exercise all over the world, is paramount; that the law taught by these principles is a law of justice, that it is desirable that this spirit may pervade all nations and that the example of religious liberty is an absolute power;

If you hold all these points to be true and correct, then, Israelites of the whole world, come listen to our appeal and grant us your aid and your assistance. The work is a great and blissful one. We are establishing the Alliance Israélite Universelle!

Source: Constitution of the Universal Israelitish Alliance (New York: Davis Job Printing Office, 1864), pp. 1–2.

NOTE

1. Founded in Paris in June 1860, the Alliance Israélite Universelle was the first modern international Jewish organization. It was an expression of the tendency toward intercommunal Jewish solidarity that had supposedly weakened with the Emancipation and the integration of West European Jewry into the cultural and social fabric of the respective countries of their residence; but this solidarity in fact quickened in the wake of the Damascus Affair. This tendency was reinforced by the Jewish press in various European languages— German, French, English and Dutch—which since its appearance in the 1830s had focused on social and political problems faced by Jews everywhere. (The *Allgemeine Zeitung des Judentums* in Leipzig and the *Jewish Chronicle* in London, founded in 1837 and 1841, respectively, were probably the most influential papers.) The Damascus Affair in particular aroused the Jewish press to an extensive discussion of general Jewish problems. The French-language weekly *Archives Israélites,* which began to appear in Paris in 1840, advocated the establishment of a society of enlightened Jews i.e., of secular, Western culture and in 1853 proposed a Jewish "parliament"—a permanent body to be situated in Paris—made up of representatives from all Jewish communities to consider problems of common interest.

The immediate impetus for the founding of the proposed organization was the Mortara affair in 1858. In that year, a six-year-old Jewish child, Edgardo Mortara, was kidnapped by the Papal guard from his parents' home in Bologna, Italy. Under the pretext that the child's Catholic nurse, believing him to be mortally ill, had him secretly baptized, the Church claimed the right to take custody of him and ensure his proper education. (Mortara later became a priest.) The universal indignation in liberal and Jewish circles led to the convening in Paris in May 1860 of a group of French Jewish leaders. In June they issued an appeal *(Exposé),* presented here, calling for the founding of a worldwide alliance of Jews. The character and ethos of the organization are perhaps best captured by its Hebrew name: *kiyach,* the acronym for *kol israel chaverim,* "all of Israel are friends," i.e., responsible for one another (Babylonian Talmud, Tractate *Hagigah,* 26a). Although an international organization, its administration and character remained decisively French. According to its constitution, two-thirds of its thirty-member central committee had to reside in Paris; and all Alliance presidents except one were French.

11. OUR FIRST THIRTY-FIVE YEARS (1895)

THE ALLIANCE ISRAÉLITE UNIVERSELLE[1]

What was the object of this association about which so many errors and falsehoods have been uttered and printed? It is clearly set forth in the statement which was issued with the first appeal to the public in 1860: "To defend the honour of the Jewish name whenever it is attacked; to use all possible means for the encouragement of arduous and useful professions, to battle, wherever it is necessary, against the ignorance and vice engendered by servitude; to contribute, by persuasion and the moral influence it will be able to exert, to the emancipation of those of our brethren who still suffer from exceptional laws; to hasten and strengthen the complete enfranchisement of all through intellectual and moral regeneration; such is, under its principal aspects, the work to which the Alliance Israélite Universelle has devoted itself."

Source: The Alliance Israélite Universelle, 1860–1895 (Paris: Siège de la Société, 1895), pp. 5–7, 14–17, 25–27, 33–35.

To this program, the Society has remained absolutely and constantly faithful; it has and never had any object but the propagation of human fraternity, it never acted otherwise than by persuasion, and [it] has no other standard than justice, no other adversaries but those of truth and tolerance.

Pursuing a work of pure philanthropy, it never took a part in politics, and has likewise always remained neutral in theological and religious controversies. It has no more to deal with religious sects than with political parties. Ever acting openly, and publicly proclaiming all that it thinks and does, the Society has always made its members acquainted with its deeds and efforts. The publications of the Alliance which all may peruse, state most fairly and minutely the task undertaken and the results obtained.

I

The object of the Alliance is summed up in the first article of its statutes:

1. To promote, everywhere, the emancipation and moral progress of the Jews;
2. To assist efficaciously those who suffer as Israelites;
3. To encourage any publication which might bring about this result.

It is the mission of the Alliance to encourage every effort, every act, every publication, whatever be their origin, which tend to enlighten public opinion with regard to the true object of antisemitism and which destroy calumny or make war on prejudice. That task is still great, and the Alliance is conscious that, while achieving it, the Society struggles, not only for the interests of Judaism, but also for truth and civilization.

II

This part of its mission has not for one instant diverted the thoughts of the Society from the work it undertook from its very outset: that of raising the moral and intellectual status of the Jews. The results obtained at the schools and with apprenticeships become more important every year.

The travelers who, during the first half of this century, journeyed through Morocco, Turkey and Tunis were shocked at the very wretched condition of the Jews in those countries, but still more, perhaps, at their intellectual condition, and at the absence of all modern culture.

Children scarcely learnt to read and write Hebrew. In Russia and Rumania, the Jews were perhaps more miserable, but among them the latent taste for religious studies, with which most of them were acquainted, was preserved, and, in the very midst of darkness, gave birth to eminent scholars, philosophers, divines and exegetists. In the degraded Jews of Mahometan countries, one could hardly recognize the descendants of the Spanish and Babylonian Jews, who, in spite of persecutions, offered the spectacle of a choice bouquet of poetry, literature and sciences. Despotism had achieved its deadly work more than a century before. All who were grieved and preoccupied by that decay were unanimous in their desire. It was only by schools that this population, which had become a stranger to all ideas of progress and was entirely given up to ignorance and weakness, could be raised.

Under the slowly depressing influence of a life imprisoned within narrow ghettos, even the physical strength of the race had decreased; the bodies gave way like the souls. As their mode of living excluded most of them from all handicrafts, the Jews in Mahometan countries are restricted to small trading, peddling and the most miserable professions. No time was to be lost if we wished to rescue those populations from utter degradation. Therefore, the earliest funds of which the Alliance could make use were applied to the creation of a school at Tetuan, in Morocco, and every increase of the Society's means has corresponded to the opening of a new school. The Alliance was founded in 1860; the boys' school of Tetuan was opened in 1862; that of Tangier in 1864; that of Bagdad in 1865; thus by degrees was established that group of institutions which now numbers 57 schools all well organized and prosperous.

The rapid development of the schools, which still continues, is greatly owing to the generosity of Baron de Hirsch. Jewish communities, understanding the value of the instrument of progress placed within their reach, soon began to help the Alliance very efficaciously by contributing to the maintenance of the schools.

The following figures will show the importance of the work: In 1895, 12,050 children attended the schools of the Alliance. The expenses for those institutions amount to 625,000 francs (25,000 pounds), out of which about 300,000 (12,000 pounds) are supplied by the communities.

In Mahometan countries, more than anywhere else, the education of women had to be attended to as carefully as that of men. In order to enable women to acquire the authority, the legitimate rank which belongs to them in the family and which is refused to them by local customs, to let them have in the intellectual and moral guidance of their children a share which they could not possess on account of their social inferiority, it was necessary to make them the equals of their husbands and brothers in knowledge and education. It was on this account that the Alliance, at the very outset, contemplated creating girls' as well as boys' schools; and, at the present time, out of 59 schools, 22 are girls' schools, and 4,900 pupils, out of the 12,050, are girls. The reader will see below that the Alliance has not limited its task to teaching girls; the Society has also added to the girls' schools work-shops, where the pupils, after leaving school, may learn some profession....

The Alliance has also endeavoured to develop among the Jews a taste for agricultural pursuits. This apprenticeship was created or rather revived by the Society at Jaffa.

No race was more averse to commercial enterprises and to what has been called the genius for [worldly] affairs than the Jewish race before the ruin of its nationality and its dispersion among the other nations of the world. Carried away to Assyria or the Roman colonies, they went on, for a long time, living their pastoral life; the persecution of the Roman emperors and the laws of the Church alone compelled the Jews to turn to commerce. If, until the dawn of modern times, they confined themselves to that kind of employment, it was that, being oppressed to an extent unequaled in history, they were allowed to do nothing else. And when they were permitted to possess land and cultivate it, after so many centuries of estrangement, not only had old habits to be altered, but agriculture had to be taught to them.

As early as 1865, one of the founders of the Alliance, Mr. Charles Netter,[2] while traveling in the East, and having a close view of the indescribable misery of the Jews in Palestine, thought that agriculture alone could raise the status of that unfortunate population. He contemplated the creation, at the gates of the Holy Land, of a school, where children should be fitted for agricultural life.

The school was founded in 1870, on an estate of 240 hectares (592 acres) generously granted by the Ottoman government. Mr. Netter devoted several years to its organization; it succeeded, in spite of the slight resources of the Alliance and of all the difficulties encountered in recruiting pupils and masters. It is now attended by a hundred boarders and is administered by professional men trained by the Alliance in European technical schools. All kinds of plants which can be cultivated in the country are grown: olive trees, orange trees, vines, various sorts of corn, fruits and vegetables; the breeding of cattle has been undertaken, as well as that of silk-worms, which has only just begun. In short, the establishment is considered by all professional men as a model of installation and management. The pupils come from Palestine, Egypt, Turkey, Russia, Rumania and even Greece. Whereas, at the outset, we wondered if we should not have to give up the undertaking for want of pupils willing to learn agriculture, now the number of candidates is such, that it is possible to make a serious choice, and to admit only boys who seem apt to become really good farmers....

Though it is an easy task to give a brief account of the schools and of the technical and agricultural establishments created and supported by the Alliance, it is difficult to show all their beneficial effects. It is evidenced by the attachment of the Jewish populations to all these foundations. What is still more precious and evident is the assistance they lend the Society. Does this mean that we are nearing the time when they will no longer need the support of the Alliance? Their poverty and lack of experience will for a long time to come render the action of the Alliance still necessary in the East and in Africa. For there are communities for which so much remains undone, and others for which nothing has yet been done! The Society's resources are not sufficient to provide them with schools and with establishments for technical and agricultural apprenticeship. In order to perform its whole task, the Alliance must have the help of every Jew. There are 30,000 members; their number has not increased for several years; the subscriptions of the members do not yield as much as 200,000 francs (8,000 pounds), whereas the expenses amount to 700,000 (28,000 pounds). And yet, is any Jewish institution more deserving of the assistance of our co-religionists? Undoubtedly, scarcely a Jew is to be found who does not acknowledge the usefulness and importance of the Alliance; but this is not sufficient. We need the adhesion of all: number gives power and strength. The Society appeals to that spirit of solidarity which at all times united the Jews and enabled them to live through the trials of the past. This solidarity will also enable them to overcome the difficulties and perils of the present.

The Alliance is most violently hated by the antisemites. As the acts of the Society supply them with no pretext for attacking it, they invent all kinds of absurd charges and shrink from no falsehood or forgery to ensure their acceptance. Such are their usual tactics against Judaism.

The Alliance can face its adversaries; it is defended by what it has achieved.

To struggle against them is the necessity of the moment; to rescue the Jews from ignorance and misery is the permanent task of the Society. This task has been pursued for thirty-five years and has been regarded favorably by all civilized governments and approved by all honourable men; it deserves the cooperation of all who care for the honour of the Jewish name.

NOTES

1. The Alliance Israélite Universelle sought to realize its aims (see document 10) in a threefold manner. The first tactic was diplomacy on behalf of persecuted Jewish communities. During its first two decades the Alliance's main efforts were devoted to improving the lot of the Jews of Rumania and Serbia; it also interceded on behalf of the Jews of Belgium, Russia and Switzerland. From the 1880s its attention was increasingly directed to the Jewish communities of the Near East. The second tactic was the provision of assistance to emigrants; with the ever-increasing mass emigration of Jews from East Europe beginning in the 1870s, the Alliance saw among its tasks the provision to the migrants of organizational and legal assistance. The third tactic was education. In the 1890s the Alliance began to focus its efforts in this area, especially in the Balkans and in the Near East, where an impressive network of schools and vocational training centers was established. The curriculum and pedagogical orientation of these educational institutions strongly reflected the paternalism and French orientation of the Alliance. Explicitly dedicated to the "moral and cultural elevation" of the less fortunate Jews of the East, the educational programs of the Alliance were meant to propagate French language and culture. Despite the resentment that the Alliance often engendered among the local Jewish population, the Alliance was clearly an important instrument in the modernization of Near Eastern Jewry. Excerpts presented here from the report of the first thirty-five years of the Alliance indicate the scope and nature of its educational activities, which, as the report explains, it saw as an integral aspect of its struggle against antisemitism.

2. Charles Netter (1826–1882) was a French philanthropist and one of the pillars of the Alliance; indeed, it was at his home in Paris that the meeting leading to the establishment of the organization took place. In 1870 he founded *Mikveh Israel* Agricultural School near Jaffa, the pioneer Palestinian colonization institution. The land for the school, which still exists, was purchased through his personal intervention at the court of the Ottoman sultan, and he served as the school's first director from 1870 to 1873.

12. THE JEWISH PROBLEM (1843)

BRUNO BAUER[1]

The advocates of Jewish emancipation are...in the strange position that they fight against privilege and at the same time grant to Judaism the privilege of unchangeability, immunity, and irresponsibility. They fight for the Jews with the best of intentions, but lack true enthusiasm, for they treat the Jewish problem as a matter foreign to them. If they are partisans of progress and the higher development of humanity, the Jews are excluded from their party. They demand that the Christians and the Christian state give up prejudices which not only have grown into their hearts but which are an essential part of their heart and being, and yet they demand no such thing from the Jews. The heart of Judaism must not be touched.

The birth of the new epoch which is now emerging will cost the Christian world great pains: are the Jews to suffer no pain, are they to have equal rights with those who fought and suffered for the new world? As if that could be! As if they could feel at home in a world which they did not make; did not help to make, which is contrary to their unchanged nature!

Those people who want to spare them the pains of criticism are the worst enemies of the Jews. Nobody who has not gone through the flames of criticism will be able to enter the new world which will soon come....

Of the Jews it will at least be admitted that they suffered for their law, for their way of life and for their nationality, that they were martyred. They were thus themselves to blame for the oppression they suffered, because they provoked it by their adherence to their law, their language, to their whole way of life. A nothing cannot be oppressed. Wherever there is pressure something must have caused it by its existence, by its nature.

In history nothing stands outside the law of causality, least of all the Jews. With a stubbornness which their advocates themselves praise and admire they have clung to their nationality and resisted the movements and changes of history. The will of history is evolution, new forms, progress, change; the Jews want to stay forever what they are, therefore they fight against the first law of history—does this not prove that by pressing against this mighty spring they provoke counter-pressure? They were oppressed because they first pressed by placing themselves against the wheel of history.

Had the Jews been outside this action of the law of causality, had they been entirely passive, had they not from their side strained against the Christian world, there would not be any tie to connect them with history. They could never have entered into the new development of history and have influenced it. Then their cause would be quite lost.

Therefore, give the Jews the honor that they were to blame for the oppression which they suffered, that the hardening of their character caused by this oppression was their own fault. Then you admit them to a place in a two-thousand-year-old history, although a subordinate one; then you make them members who are capable, and finally have the duty to take part in history's progress....

Instead of praising the tenacity of the Jewish national spirit and regarding it as an advantage, one should ask what its basis is and where it comes from.

Its base is lack of ability to develop with history, it is the reason of the quite unhistorical character of that nation, and this again is due to its oriental nature. Such stationary nations exist in the Orient because

Source: Bruno Bauer, *The Jewish Problem* [*Die Judenfrage, 1843*], ed. Ellis Rivkin and trans. Helen Lederer (Cincinnati: Hebrew Union College—Jewish Institute of Religion, 1958), pp. 2–3, 5–6, 11–16, 18, 22–26, 39, 41, 45, 57, 61–64. Reprinted by permission of Dr. Ellis Rivkin.

compare to Asians *degrading*

★ what are human rights?

there human liberty and the possibility of progress are still limited. In the Orient and in India, we still find Parsees living in dispersion and worshipping the holy fire of Ormuzd....

The hostility of the Christian world towards the Jews is therefore quite understandable and is caused by these circumstances. Neither of the two parties can acknowledge the other and allow it to remain in existence. The existence of the one excludes the existence of the other; each one believes itself to be the representative of absolute truth. It would mean denying that it is the truth if it were to acknowledge the other.

Jews and Christians can consider each other and treat each other as *men* only when they have given up the special nature which separates them and enjoins them to "eternal segregation"—when they acknowledge the common nature of man and consider humanity as their true nature.

The idea of human rights was discovered for the Christian world in the last century only. It is not innate in man, it has rather been won in battle against historical traditions which determined the education of men until now. So human rights are not a gift of nature or of history, but a prize which was won in the fight against the accident of birth and against privilege which came down through history from generation to generation. Human rights are the result of education, and they can be possessed only by those who acquire and deserve them.

Can the Jew really possess them as long as he lives as a Jew in perpetual segregation from others, as long as he therefore must declare that the others are not really his fellowmen? As long as he is a Jew, his Jewishness must be stronger in him than his humanity, and keep him apart from non-Jews. He declares by this segregation that this, his Jewishness, is his true, highest nature, which has to have precedence over his humanity.

In the same manner the Christian as a Christian cannot grant human rights.

What neither of the two parties possesses it cannot give to or accept from the other.

But surely citizens' rights could be granted the Jews? They cannot be deprived of civil rights.

The question is, rather, whether in a Christian state as such there are such universal rights, whether there are not exclusively special rights; that is, a greater or smaller sum of privileges which are a right for some and a non-right, but not as such a wrong, for the other; for the other will have his own special privileges, unless one would want to assert that the sum of special rights is at the same time the sum total of wrongs, or that the lack of universal civil rights is the universal wrong.

Do the Jews want to become "citizens" in the Christian state? Ask first whether this state knows "citizens" or only subjects; whether the Jewish quarter is a contradiction if the subjects are divided into special estates according to privilege; whether it would even be remarkable if the Jews were commanded to wear special attire or special badges, if even the estates when formally represented must wear different clothes....

If the opposition is no longer religious, if it is scientific and has assumed the form of criticism, if the Jew shows the Christian that his religious view is only the historical product of certain factors, then a solution has been given, because now the opposition is really not even scientific anymore. As soon, namely, as the Jew directs scientific, and not merely crude, religious criticism against Christianity, he must have looked critically at Judaism at the same time, because he must conceive of Christianity as a necessary product of Judaism. As soon, however, as both parties direct scientific criticism against each other, therefore also each against itself, there will be no religious hostility any more, and scientific differences of opinion are solved by science itself.

This is the solution of the contrast, that it dissolves into nothing. The Jews cease to be Jews without the necessity of becoming Christians, or rather, they must cease being Jews and must not become Christians....

All right! The Jew wants to see his religion preserved, it is his real nature, his totality. He wants to make the acknowledgment of human rights dependent upon the acknowledgment and preservation of his religion. The Christian state therefore, is only doing what he himself wishes; it acts according to his words....It declares religion as the foundation and essential characteristic of the state; only this religion is Christianity, the successor of Judaism....

The most universal, therefore, also the most exclusive privilege, is faith....Man cannot acquire it by himself, he cannot develop it from reason, he cannot manipulate it according to his will. It is, rather, a gift of grace, given to the chosen....

Like the community of the believers, Israel boasts of a special privilege. Therefore, one privilege confronts another: one excludes the other. The Christian state is under the obligation to respect privileges, to protect them, to base its organization upon them. The Jew regards his special character as a privilege. Therefore, his only possible position in the Christian state is that of a privileged one, the Jews can only exist as a special corporation....

It had to happen, this epoch had to become a time of general suffering. The error had been that one thought emancipation possible while the privileges of the religious barriers remained standing, even acknowledged in the emancipation itself. The Jew received concessions as a Jew, was allowed to continue to exist as a being segregated from all others, and this in itself made true emancipation impossible. Everybody still lacked courage to be simply a human being. Some privileges were sacrificed at that time, but the main privilege, the heavenly, god-given, supernatural privilege remained in force and this in turn must always generate all the others.

The emancipation of the Jews in a thoroughgoing, successful, safe manner will only be possible when they are emancipated not as Jews, that is as forever alien to the Christians, but as human beings who are no longer separated from their fellowmen by barriers which they wrongly consider to be all-important.

Therefore, the emancipation can also not be made dependent upon their conversion to Christianity, for by this they would only exchange one privilege against another. It would remain a privilege, even if expanded to everybody, to all mankind.

The emancipation problem has until now been treated in a basically wrong manner by considering it one-sidedly as the Jewish problem. Neither was it possible to find a theoretical solution in this manner, nor will it be possible to find a practical solution. Without being free oneself, one cannot help another to freedom. The serf cannot emancipate. The minor cannot help another to get rid of his guardians. One privilege can limit another, that is, by the very act [of] limitation [the privilege] recognizes and designates [itself] as a privilege but it can never replace [itself with] universal human rights without abolishing itself.

The problem of emancipation is a general problem, it is *the* problem of our age. Not only the Jews, but we, also, want to be emancipated. Only because nobody was free, because privilege was the ruling power, the Jews could not have freedom either. We all were surrounded by barriers; the Jewish quarter is right next to the police-supervised quarters where all of us are registered.

Not the Jews only; we, too, are no longer content with the chimera. We want to be real nations.

If the Jews want to become real—they cannot achieve it in their chimerical nationality, only in the real nations of our time living in history—then they have to give up the chimerical prerogative which will always alienate them from the other nations and history. They have to sacrifice their disbelief in the other nations and their exclusive belief in their own nationality. Only then will they be able to participate sincerely in national and state affairs.

We, however, have to give up our skepticism regarding the world and the rights of man, the exclusive belief in monopoly, and our immaturity, before we can think of becoming real nations and within the life of the nation, real human beings....

NOTE

1. Bruno Bauer (1809–1882), German Protestant theologian, philosopher and historian who, as a student in Berlin, came under the influence of Hegel. His radical criticism of the New Testament led to his dismissal as a lecturer at Bonn in 1842. Returning to Berlin, he devoted himself to writing historical works and critical studies of the rise of Christianity. He also wrote on contemporary political issues, defending Prussian conservatism and strongly opposing the granting of emancipation to the Jews in Germany. The essay *Die Judenfrage*, from which these excerpts are taken, argues that the Jew's desire to preserve his identity as a Jew is incompatible with the modern spirit and thus also with the requirements of genuine emancipation. The essay sparked a sharp controversy in which Abraham Geiger, Gabriel Riesser, Samuel Hirsch and Karl Marx (see the following document) took part.

13. ON THE JEWISH PROBLEM (1844)

KARL MARX[1]

Bauer reveals his one-sided conception of the Jewish problem. It is not at all sufficient to investigate: Who shall emancipate? Who shall be emancipated? The critic has to put a third question. He must ask: What kind of emancipation is in question? What conditions are caused by the nature of the demanded emancipation? The critique of political emancipation itself was the final critique of the Jewish Problem and its true solution, dissolving it into the "general problem of the age." Because Bauer does not raise the problem to this level, he falls into contradictions. He poses conditions which are not founded in the nature of political emancipation itself. He brings up questions which are not germane to his subject, and he solves problems, the solution of which leaves his question unanswered. When Bauer says of the enemies of emancipation of the Jews: "Their only mistake was that they presumed the Christian state to be the only true state, and they did not subject it to the same criticism that they applied to Judaism," we hold that Bauer himself makes the mistake of subjecting only the "Christian state" to his criticism, not the "state in itself," that he does not examine the relation of political emancipation to human emancipation, and that he therefore poses conditions which are explicable only by an uncritical confusion of political with universal human emancipation. If Bauer asks the Jews: "Have you, from your point of view, the right to demand political emancipation?" then we rejoin with the question: Has the protagonist of political emancipation the right to demand that the Jew abolish Judaism, that men in general abolish religion?...

The political emancipation of the Jew, the Christian, the religious man in general is the emancipation of the state from Judaism, from Christianity, from religion in general. In its own manner, according to its nature, the state emancipates itself from religion, by emancipating itself from the state religion; that means that the state as such does not profess a religion, but professes itself as a state. The political emancipation from religion is not the accomplished, unresisted emancipation from religion for the reason that the political emancipation is not the accomplished, unresisted manner of human emancipation. The limit of political emancipation is revealed by the fact that the state can free itself of an impediment without the individual becoming really free, that the state can be a free state without the citizens being free men.

We have demonstrated how that political emancipation from religion allows religion to stand, although it tolerates no privileged religion. The contradiction in which the adherent of a particular religion finds himself with his status as a citizen, is only a part of the general contradiction between the political state and bourgeois society. The perfection of the Christian state is that state which proclaims itself a state and ignores the religion of its citizens. *The emancipation of the state from religion is not the emancipation of the individual from religion.*

Therefore we do not tell the Jews as Bauer does: You cannot be emancipated politically without emancipating yourselves radically from Judaism. On the contrary, we tell them: Because it is possible to emancipate you politically without your giving up Judaism completely and absolutely, therefore political emancipation itself is not human emancipation. If you Jews want to be emancipated politically without emancipating yourselves as men, the incompleteness and contradiction is not only to you, it is in the nature and category of political emancipation....

The problem of the capability of the Jews for emancipation becomes in our eyes the question of which

Source: Karl Marx, *On the Jewish Problem* [*Zur Judenfrage, 1844*], ed. Ellis Rivkin and trans. Helen Lederer (Cincinnati: Hebrew Union College, n.d.), pp. 6–10, 34–42. Reprinted by permission of Dr. Ellis Rivkin.

particular social element has to be abolished in order to abolish Judaism. For the capability of today's Jew to be emancipated is the relationship of Judaism to the emancipation of today's world. This relationship is the logical result of the special position of Judaism in our present world of slavery.

Let us observe the real worldly Jew, not the Sabbath Jew as Bauer does, but the everyday Jew. Let us not look for the mystery of the Jew in his religion, let us look for the mystery of the religion in the actual Jew.

What is the worldly basis of Judaism? Practical necessity, selfishness. What is the worldly culture of the Jew? Commerce. What is his worldly God? Money. All right! The emancipation from commerce and from money, from the practical real Judaism, would be the self-emancipation of our age.

An organization of society which would make commerce impossible by abolishing its presuppositions would have made the existence of the Jew impossible. His religious consciousness would dissolve like a thin vapor in the real life atmosphere of society. On the other hand, if the Jew does recognize this, his real nature, as worthless, and works for its annihilation, then he is working for the emancipation of man and turns against the highest practical expression of human self-estrangement.

We recognize therefore in Judaism a generally present anti-social element which has been raised to its present peak by historical development, in which the Jews eagerly assisted, and now it has of necessity to dissolve itself. *In its final meaning the emancipation of the Jews is the emancipation of humanity from Judaism.*[2]

The Jew has emancipated himself in a Jewish manner not only by gaining financial power, but because through him and without him money has become a world power and the practical Jewish spirit has become the practical spirit of the Christian nations. The self-emancipation of the Jews has gone so far that the Christians have become Jews....

Yes, the practical dominion of Judaism over the Christian world has reached its normal, unambiguous expression in North America....

Judaism has survived alongside Christianity not only as religious criticism of Christianity, but just as much because the practical Jewish spirit has survived within the Christian society and even reached its highest development there. The Jew who stands out as a specific member in civil society is only the specific phenomenon of Judaism within civil society.

Out of its own body civil society creates continuously the Jew.

What was the real basis of the Jewish religion? Practical need, egotism.

Jewish monotheism is therefore in reality the polytheism of the varied needs, a polytheism which makes even the privy an object of divine ordinance. Practical need, egotism is the principle of civil society and emerges in its pure form as soon as civil society has given birth to the political state. The God of practical need and egotism is money.

Money is the jealous God of Israel before whom no other God may endure. Money debases all gods of men—and transforms them into commodities. Money is the common value of all things constituted for itself. So it robbed the whole universe, the world of men, of nature, of their specific values. Money is the essence of man's labor and existence, alienated from man, and this alien being rules him and he adores it.

The God of the Jews has become the God of the universe. The real God of the Jews is money. Their God is only an illusory bill of exchange....

Judaism reaches its climax in the perfection of bourgeois society; but bourgeois society reaches its perfect development in the Christian world only. Only under the rule of Christianity, which externalizes all national, natural, moral, and theoretical aspects of man, could civil society separate itself completely from the life of the state, tear all ties to the human race and replace them by egotism and self-interest, dissolving the world of man into a world of atomistic individuals regarding each other with hostility....

The Christian egotism of salvation becomes in practice necessarily the personal egotism of the Jew, the longing for heaven becomes earthly desire, the wish for individual salvation becomes self-interest. We explain the tenacity of the Jew not by his religion, but by the human basis of his religion, the practical need, egotism.

Because in bourgeois society the real nature of the Jew has found universal realization; therefore that society cannot convince the Jew of the non-reality of his religion, which is nothing other than the ideal concept of practical need. Not only in the Pentateuch or Talmud, but in our present society we find the nature of the Jew, not in the abstract, but in a highly empirical being, not in the narrow-mindedness of the Jew but in the Jewish narrow-mindedness of society.

As soon as society will succeed in abolishing the empirical nature of Judaism, commerce and its presuppositions, the existence of the Jew will be impossible, because his consciousness will have lost its object, the subjective basis of Judaism, the practical need, will be humanized, the conflict of the individual-material existence with the existence of humanity as a species will have ceased to exist.

The social emancipation of the Jew is the emancipation of society from Judaism.

NOTES

1. Karl Marx (1818–1883), German social philosopher. His parents were Jewish, but his father had converted before his birth and had him baptized at the age of six. Like Bauer, he was a student of Hegel, but unlike Bauer, he developed the master's thought in a radical, leftist direction. The foregoing selection is taken from a review of two of Bauer's essays, "Die Judenfrage" and "Die Faehigkeit der heutigen Juden und Christen, frei zu werden" [The Jewish Question and the Capacity of the present-day Jews, and Christians to Become Free]. Marx's critique of Bauer's position on Jewish emancipation is a key work in his development toward dialectical materialism and "scientific" socialism. Although it should not be overlooked that in this essay Marx supports Jewish emancipation, he nonetheless unhesitatingly employs derogatory stereotypes of the Jews. The essay has thus been considered by many a *locus classicus* of both Jewish self-hatred and leftist antisemitism.

2. Cf. "The German word *Judentum* had, in the language of the time, the secondary meaning of commerce, and in this and other passages Marx exploits the two senses of the word" (T. B. Bottomore, ed., *Karl Marx: Early Writings* [New York: McGraw-Hill, 1963], p. 36, n. 3).

14. JEWRY IN MUSIC (1850)

RICHARD WAGNER[1]

Since it is here merely in respect of art, and specially of music, that we want to explain to ourselves the popular dislike of the Jewish nature, even at the present day, we may completely pass over any dealing with this same phenomenon in the field of religion and politics.... When we strove for emancipation of the Jews, however, we virtually were more the champions of an abstract principle, than of a concrete case: just as all our Liberalism was a not very lucid mental sport—since we went for freedom of the Folk without knowledge of that Folk itself, nay, with a dislike of any genuine contact with it—so our eagerness to level up the rights of Jews was far rather stimulated by a general idea, than by any real sympathy; for, with all our speaking and writing in favour of the Jews' emancipation, we always felt instinctively repelled by any actual, operative contact with them.

Here, then, we touch the point that brings us closer to our main inquiry: We have to explain to ourselves the *involuntary repellence* possessed for us by the nature and personality of the Jews, so as to vindicate that instinctive dislike which we plainly recognize as stronger and more overpowering than our conscious zeal to rid ourselves thereof. Even to-day we

Source: Richard Wagner [K. Freigedank], "Das Judenthum in der Musik." *Neue Zeitschrift fuer Musik* 33, no. 19 (September 3, 1850), and 33, no. 20 (September 6, 1850). Reprinted in *Richard Wagner's Prose Works*, ed. and trans. W. A. Ellis (London, 1897), pp. 79–84, 87f., 93, 99–106.

only purposely believe ourselves, in this regard, when we think it necessary to hold immoral and taboo all open proclamation of our natural repugnance against the Jewish nature.

We have no need to first substantiate the be-Jewing of modern art; if it springs to the eye, and thrusts upon the senses, of itself. Much too far afield, again, should we have to fare, did we undertake to explain this phenomenon by a demonstration of the character of our art-history itself. But if emancipation from the yoke of Judaism appears to us the greatest of necessities, we must hold it weighty above all to prove our forces for this war of liberation. Now we shall never win these forces from an abstract definition of that phenomenon per se, but only from an accurate acquaintance with the nature of that involuntary feeling of ours which utters itself as an instinctive repugnance against the Jew's prime essence. Through it, through this unconquerable feeling—if we avow it quite without ado—must there become plain to us what we hate in that essence; what we then know definitely, we can make head against; nay, through his [the Jew's] very laying bare, may we even hope to rout the demon from the field, whereon he has only been able to maintain his stand beneath the shelter of a twilight darkness—darkness we good-natured humanists ourselves have cast upon him, to make his look less loathsome.

Only in quite the latest times do we seem to have reached an insight, that it is more rational [*vernuenftiger*] to rid ourselves of that strenuous self-deception, so as quite soberly instead to view the object of our violent sympathy and bring ourselves to understand a repugnance still abiding with us in spite of all our Liberal bedazzlements. To our astonishment, we perceive that in our liberal battles we have been floating in the air and fighting clouds, whereas the whole fair soil of material reality has found an appropriator whom our aerial flights have very much amused, no doubt, yet who holds us far too foolish to reward us by relaxing one iota of his usurpation of that material soil. Quite imperceptibly the "Creditor of Kings" has become the King of Creeds, and we really cannot take this monarch's pleading for emancipation as otherwise than uncommonly naive, seeing that it is much rather we who are shifted into the necessity of fighting for emancipation from the Jews. According to the present constitution of this world, the Jew in truth is already more than emancipated: he rules, and will rule, so long as Money remains the power before which all our doings and our dealings lose their force. That the historical adversity of the Jews and the rapacious rawness of Christian-German potentates have brought this power within the hands of Israel's sons—this needs no argument of ours to prove. That the impossibility of carrying farther any natural, any "necessary" and truly beauteous thing, upon the basis of that stage whereat the evolution of our arts has now arrived, and without a total alteration of that basis— that this has also brought the public art-taste of our time between the busy fingers of the Jew, however, is the matter whose grounds we here have to consider somewhat closer. What their slaves had toiled and moiled to pay the liege-lords of the Roman and the Medieval world, to-day is turned into money by the Jew: who thinks of noticing that the guileless-looking scrap of paper is slimy with the blood of countless generations? What the heroes of the arts, with untold strain consuming belief and life, have wrested from the art-fiend of two millenia of misery, to-day the Jew converts into art-bazaar [*Kunstwarenwechsel*]: who sees it in the mannered bric-a-brac, that it is glued together by the hallowed brow-sweat of the genius of two thousand years?

The Jew—who, as everyone knows, has a God all to himself—in ordinary life strikes us primarily by his outward appearance, which, no matter to what European nationality we belong, has something disagreeably foreign to that nationality; instinctively we wish to have nothing in common with a man who looks like that; a man whose appearance we must hold unfitted for artistic treatment—not merely in this or that personality, but according to his kind in general—neither can we hold him capable of any sort of artistic utterance of purely human essence....

This must heretofore have passed as a misfortune for the Jew: in more recent times, however, we perceive that in the midst of this misfortune he feels entirely well; after all his successes, he needs must deem his difference from us a pure distinction. Passing over the moral side, in the effect of this in itself unpleasant freak of Nature, and coming to its bearings upon art, we here will merely observe that to us this exterior can never be thinkable as a subject for the art of representation: if plastic art wants to present us with a Jew, it mostly takes its model from sheer phantasy, with a prudent ennobling, or entire omission, of just everything that characterizes for us in common life the Jew's appearance. But the Jew never wanders on to the theatrical stage: the exceptions are so rare and special, that they only confirm the general rule. We can conceive no representation of an antique or modern state-character by a Jew, be it as hero or lover, without feeling instinctively the incongruity of such a notion.[2] This is of great weight.

The Jew, who is innately incapable of announcing himself to us artistically through either his outward appearance or his speech, and least of all through his singing, has nevertheless been able in the widest-spread of modern art varieties, to wit in Music, to reach the rulership of public taste. To explain to ourselves this phenomenon, let us first consider how it grew possible for the Jew to become a musician.

From that turning-point in our social evolution where Money, with less and less disguise, was raised to the virtual patent of nobility, the Jews—to whom money-making without actual labour, i.e., Usury, had been left as their only trade—the Jews not merely could no longer be denied the diploma of a new society that needed naught but gold, but they brought it with them in their pockets. Wherefore our modern Culture, accessible to no one but the well-to-do, remained the less a closed book to them, as it had sunk into a venal article of Luxury. Henceforward, then, the cultured Jew appears in our Society; his distinction from the uncultured, the common Jew, we now have closely to observe. The cultured Jew has taken the most inducible pains to strip off all the obvious tokens of his lower co-religionists: in many a case he has even held it wise to make a Christian baptism wash away the traces of his origin. This zeal, however, has never got so far as to let him reap the hoped-for fruits: It has conducted only to his utter isolation, and to making him the most heartless of all human beings; to such a pitch, that we have been bound to lose even our earlier sympathy for the tragic history of his stock. His connection with the former comrades in his suffering, which he arrogantly tore asunder, it has stayed impossible for him to replace by a new connection with that society whereto he had soared up. He stands in correlation with none but those who need his money: and never yet has money thriven to the point of knitting a goodly bond 'twixt man and man. Alien and apathetic stands the educated Jew in midst of a society he does not understand, with whose tastes and aspirations he does not

sympathize, whose history and evolution have always been indifferent to him.

By what example will this all grow clearer to us—ay, well nigh what other single case could make us so alive to it, as the works of a musician of Jewish birth whom nature had endowed with specific musical gifts as very few before him? All that offered itself to our gaze, in the inquiry into our antipathy against the Jewish nature; all the contradictoriness of this nature, both in itself and as touching us; all its inability, while outside our footing, to have intercourse with us upon that footing, nay, even to form a wish to further develop the things which had sprung from out of our soil: all these are intensified to a positively tragic conflict in the nature, life, and art-career of the early deceased Felix Mendelssohn Bartholdy.[3]…

I said above, the Jews had brought forth no true poet. We here must give a moment's mention, then, to Heinrich Heine.[4] At the time when Goethe and Schiller sang among us, we certainly knew nothing of a poetizing Jew. At the time, however, when our poetry became a lie when every possible thing might flourish from the wholly unpoetic element of our life, but no true poet—then was it the office of a highly gifted poet-Jew to bare with fascinating taunts that lie, that bottomless aridity and Jesuitical hypocrisy of our Versifying which still would give itself the airs of true poesìs. His famous musical congeners, too, he mercilessly lashed for their pretence to pass as artists; no make-believe could hold its ground before him: by the remorseless demon of denial of all that seemed worth denying was he driven on without a rest, through all the mirage of our modern self-deception, till he reached the point where in turn he duped himself into a poet and was rewarded by his versified lies being set to music by our own composers. He was the conscience of Judaism, just as Judaism is the evil conscience of our modern Civilization.

Yet another Jew have we to name, who appeared among us as a writer. From out of his isolation as a Jew, he came among us seeking for redemption. He found it not, and had to learn that only with our redemption, too, into genuine Manhood, would he ever find it. To become Man at once with us, however, means firstly for the Jew as much as ceasing to be Jew. And this had Boerne done.[5] Yet Boerne, of all others, teaches us that this redemption cannot be reached in ease and cold, indifferent complacence, but costs—as cost it must for us—sweat, anguish, want and all the dregs of suffering and sorrow. Without once looking back, take ye your part in this regenerative work of deliverance through self-annulment; then are we one and un-dissevered! But bethink ye, that *only one thing can redeem you from the burden of your curse: the redemption of Ahasuerus*[6]—Going under!

NOTES

1. Richard Wagner (1813–1883), German composer who sought to achieve a union of music and dramatic poetry, utilizing a wide range of symbols, with special emphasis on national and romantic themes. He hoped that his music would give expression to, and foster the rebirth of, what he called the Germanic hero-spirit, a "racial characteristic" he believed to be possessed only by the "pure-bred Germanic branches of the Aryan race." His essay "Jewry in Music," first published under a pseudonym and later, in 1869, under his own name, is considered to be one of the first formulations of racial antisemitism. Wagner's works, which enjoyed a large audience among the educated class of his day, made antisemitism culturally respectable and generally facilitated the diffusion of racist doctrines. His political essays were greatly admired by Adolf Hitler, and his operas were regularly performed at Bayreuth in connection with Nazi party conventions.

2. Note to the 1869 and later editions: "To be sure, our later experiences of the work done by Jewish actors would afford food for many a dissertation, as to which I here can give a passing hint. Since the above was written not only have the Jews succeeded in capturing the stage itself, but even in kidnapping the poet's dramatic progeny: a famous Jewish 'character player' not merely has done away with any representation of the poetic figures bred by Shakespeare, Schiller, and so forth, but substitutes the offspring of his own effectfull and not quite untendentious fancy, a thing which gives one the impression as though the Saviour had been cut out from a painting of the crucifixion and a demagogic Jew stuck-in instead. On the stage the falsification of our Art has thriven to complete deception; for which reason, also, Shakespeare & Co. are now spoken of merely in the light of their qualified adaptability for the stage—The Editor [Richard Wagner]."

3. Jakob Ludwig Felix Mendelssohn-Bartholdy (1809–1847), German composer. A grandson of Moses Mendelssohn, he was baptized early in life.

4. Heinrich Heine (1797–1856), one of the greatest lyric poets in the German language and Germany's most famous Jewish writer. Heine's later poems and especially his prose works established him as a satirist of barbed wit and as an astute critic of romanticism, jingoistic patriotism and current and political affairs.

5. Ludwig Boerne (1786–1837), German liberal political essayist. He used wit and irony to inject subversive political allusions into writings on the most harmless of subjects. Born into a prominent Jewish banking family in Frankfurt, he converted to Lutheranism in 1818. The idea that the freedom of humanity as a whole is inextricably bound up with freedom for the Jews recurs consistently in his writings.

6. Ahasuerus is the name given to the wandering Jew, who, according to legend, is doomed to wander eternally without hope of rest until the second coming as punishment for taunting Jesus on the way to his crucifixion. The legend first appeared in a German pamphlet in 1602 and quickly spread in a variety of forms. It was also accorded numerous literary adaptations.

15. THE VICTORY OF JUDAISM OVER GERMANDOM (1879)

WILHELM MARR[1]

There is no stopping them….

Are there no clear signs that the twilight of the Jews [*juedische Goetterdaemmerung*] is setting in?

No.

Jewry's control of society and politics, as well as its practical domination of religious and ecclesiastical thought, is still in the prime of its development, heading toward the realization of Jehovah's promise: "I will hand all peoples over to thee."

By now, a sudden reversal of this process is fundamentally impossible, for if it were, the entire social structure, which has been so thoroughly Judaized, would collapse. And there is no viable alternative to this social structure which could take its place.

Further, we cannot count on the help of the "Christian" state. The Jews are the "best citizens" of this modern, Christian state, as it is in perfect harmony with their interests.…

It is not a pretentious prophecy but the deepest inner conviction which I here utter. Your generation will not pass before there will be absolutely no public office, even the highest one, which the Jews will not have usurped.

Yes, through the Jewish nation, Germany will become a world power, a western New Palestine. And this will happen, not through violent revolutions, but through the compliance of the [German] people.…

We should not reproach the Jewish nation. It fought against the western world for 1,800 years, and finally conquered and subjugated it. We were vanquished and it is entirely proper that the victor shouts "Vae Victis!"[2]

German culture has proved itself ineffective and powerless against this foreign power. This is a fact; a brute inexorable fact. State, Church, Catholicism, Protestantism, Creed and Dogma, all are brought low before the Jewish tribunal, that is, the [irreverent] daily press [which the Jews control].

The Jews were late in their assault on Germany, but once they started there was no stopping them.

Gambetta,[3] Simon[4] and Crémieux[5] were the dictators of France in 1870–1871. During the war, they drove thousands upon thousands of Frenchmen to their senseless deaths. After Sedan, the whole world believed in peace. But, no! Bismarck was lured by the rhetoric of a Jules Favre.[6] "Blood and Iron" had to continue because of the frivolous, worthless, fanatical action of the Semites in Tours.

Poor, Judaized France!

In England, the Semite Disraeli,[7] a German-hater (*comme il faut*), holds in his vest pocket the key to war and peace in the Orient.

Who derived the real benefit at the Congress of Berlin from the spilled blood of the Orient? Jewry. The Alliance Israélite Universelle[8] was first in line. Rumania was forced to open officially its doors and gates to destructive Semitism. Jewry did not yet dare to make the same demand of Russia. But, this demand, too, will soon come.

Dear reader, while you are allowing the German to be skinned alive I bow my head in admiration and amazement before this Semitic people, which has us under heel. Resigned to subjugation to Jewry, I am marshalling my last remaining strength in order to die peacefully, as one who will not surrender and who will not ask forgiveness.

Can we deny the historical fact?

No!

The historical fact that Israel became the leading social-political superpower in the nineteenth century,

---

Source: Wilhelm Marr, *Der Sieg des Judenthums ueber das Germanenthum vom nicht confessionellen Standpunkt ausbetrachtet* (Bern: Rudolph Costenoble, 1879), pp. 30–35, trans. P. Mendes-Flohr and J. Reinharz.

lies before us. It is already notorious to what extent we lack the physical and intellectual strength to de-Judaize ourselves. The raw, brutal, but completely unconscious protest against the real Judaization of society was Social Democracy. It sided, however, with the Jews, because Jewry has also infiltrated its ranks. After all, the founder of German Social Democracy, Lassalle,[9] was a Semite.

Why are we so surprised? We have among us a flexible, tenacious, intelligent, foreign tribe that knows how to bring abstract reality into play in many different ways. Not individual Jews, but the Jewish spirit and Jewish consciousness have overpowered the world....

All this is the consequence of a cultural history—so unique in its way, so grand that everyday polemics can achieve nothing against it. With the entire force of its armies, the proud Roman Empire did not achieve that which Semitism has achieved in the West and particularly in Germany.

NOTES

1. Wilhelm Marr (1818–1904), German anti-Semite. His pamphlet. *The Victory of Judaism over Germandom: Regarded from a Non-Confessional Point of View*—from which excerpts are presented here—reached its twelfth edition by 1879. As is reflected in its title, this influential pamphlet contrasts the Jew not with the Christian but with the German; the two peoples, Marr holds, are diametrically and irreconcilably opposed to one another. Marr is considered to have introduced in 1879 the word *anti-Semite* into the political lexicon by the founding of the League of Antisemites (*Antisemiten-Liga*) which organized lectures and published a short-lived monthly. The league was the first effort at creating a popular political movement based on anti-Semitism.

2. "Woe to the conquered!" This appeared as the motto of the pamphlet.

3. Léon Gambetta (1838–1882), erroneously considered to be a Jew. A leader of the republicans, he was minister of the interior in the new government of national defense after the defeat of French forces at Sedan in 1870. He organized an unsuccessful resistance to the Germans in 1871. From 1879 to 1882, Gambetta was the president of the chamber of deputies, where he wielded considerable influence.

4. Jules François Simon (1814–1896), born to a Protestant father and a Catholic mother. Marr, however, apparently assumed he was a Jew. Simon was minister of instruction in France's government of national defense. Although himself an opponent of the monarchy, he forced the resignation of Gambetta after the capitulation of Paris in 1870 in order to avoid German retaliation.

5. Isaac Adolphe Crémieux (1796–1880), French lawyer and statesman and leader of French Jewry. He served several times in the chamber of deputies and in 1870 was minister of justice.

6. Jules Favre (1809–1880), leading republican statesman known for his oratorical powers. As foreign minister he was charged with negotiating peace with Germany. On September 6, 1870, he made the ill-considered statement that he "would not yield to Germany an inch of territory nor a single stone of the fortresses." Otto von Bismarck, the German chancellor, quickly responded by declaring that the cession of Alsace and Lorraine was the indispensable condition of peace.

7. Benjamin Disraeli, Earl of Beaconsfield (1804–1881), British statesman and novelist. Although baptized at the age of thirteen, he was proud of his Jewish origins. During his second term as prime minister (1874–1880), he acted to strengthen the British Empire and to check Russian penetration into the Mediterranean. He was a moving force at the Congress of Berlin (1878), where Russia was forced to relinquish her acquisitions in the Balkans.

8. Alliance Israélite Universelle, the first modern international Jewish organization, founded in 1860 (see document 10 of this chapter). The Jewish community of Berlin, supported by the Alliance and the Zion Society of Bucharest, petitioned the chairman of the congress and head of the German delegation, Otto von Bismarck, to raise the question of equal rights for Rumanian Jews at the congress. As a result, the German representatives were instructed to demand equal civil rights for the members of all religions in the Balkan countries and the inclusion in the peace treaty of a special paragraph to this effect explicitly providing for their implementation.

9. Ferdinand Lassalle (1825–1864) German-Jewish socialist leader whose later years were devoted to organizing a political party of the workers of Germany; his efforts culminated in the establishment of the Allgemeiner Deutscher Arbeiter-Verein in 1863.

16. THE QUESTION OF THE JEW IS A QUESTION OF RACE (1881)

KARL EUGEN DUEHRING[1]

A Jewish question would still exist, even if every Jew were to turn his back on his religion and join one of our major churches. Yes, I maintain that in that case, the struggle between us and the Jews would make itself felt as ever more urgent—although the struggle certainly is felt now even when the Jews have yet to convert [in large numbers]. It is precisely the baptized Jews who infiltrate furthest, unhindered in all sectors of society and political life. It is as though they have provided themselves with an unrestricted passport, advancing their stock to those places where members of the Jewish religion [*Religionsjuden*] are unable to follow. Furthermore, several doors are closed to members of the Jewish religion by our legislation, and more particularly, by the principles of our administration. Through these portals the racial Jew [*Racenjude*], who has forsaken his religion, can enter unhindered. A situation similar to the one involving the baptized Jews results as soon as all civic rights and opportunities become available to members of the Jewish religion. Thereupon, they force themselves into all aspects of social and political life, just like those who have converted to Christianity. And, in this way, their contact with the nation in which they live becomes more pronounced. This takes place despite the fact that in society [as opposed to the state] there is never an instance in which the members of the Jewish religion are made completely equal.... I return therefore to the hypothesis that the Jews are to be defined solely on the basis of race, and not on the basis of religion. I dismiss all conclusions hitherto upheld....The Mosaic attempt to locate within the base of our people a Jewish component only makes the Jewish question a more burning issue. The diverse admixture of our modern cultures, or in other words, the sprinkling of racial-Jewry in the cracks and crevices of our national abode, must inevitably lead to a reaction. It is impossible that close contact [between Germans and Jews] will take effect without the concomitant realization that this infusion of Jewish qualities is incompatible with our best impulses.

NOTE

1. Karl Eugen Duehring (1833–1921), German economist and philosopher. One of the initial proponents of modern racial anti-Semitism, he had a seminal influence on the development of German anti-Semitism in the 1880s.

Source: Karl Eugen Duehring, *Die Judenfrage als Racen- Sitten- und Culturfrage* (Karlsruhe and Leipzig: H. Reuther, 1881), pp. 3–4, trans. M. Gelber.

17. JUDAISM: RACE OR RELIGION? (1883)

ERNEST RENAN[1]

I would like to exchange some ideas with you on the difference, which, in my opinion, ought to be made between the religious and ethnographic aspects in regard to Judaism. Judaism is a religion, and a great religion—this much is crystal clear. But ordinarily, people go beyond that: Judaism is considered a matter of race, people actually speak of a "Jewish race"—in short, it is taken for granted that the Jewish nation which originated this religion has always kept it for itself.

It is a well-recognized fact that Christianity detached itself from the Jewish creed at a certain historical moment. Yet, some are willing to believe that this small and creative people has at all times remained so closely identical with itself that being Jewish by faith means necessarily being Jewish by blood. To what extent is this true? And to what degree may such an opinion be modified?…

Beyond doubt, Judaism is the creed of the Bene-Israel, which for centuries did not differ essentially from the beliefs of neighboring tribes such as, for instance, the Moabites….

What was it that transformed that Yahweh cult into the universal religion of the civilized world? It was the work of the Prophets, who lived around the eighth century B.C. They are the very glory that is Israel's. We have no proof of prophets who may have lived among the more or less consanguineous neighbors of Israel such as the Phoenicians. They certainly had their *nabis*—sorcerers, men whom the people would consult when their donkey was lost, or when they wanted secret information.

Israel's *nabis* were of a totally different kind. They were the founders of pure religion. About the eighth century B.C., we find these men appearing, of whom Isaiah is the most illustrious. They are by no means priests, and they say: "Sacrifices are needless. For God takes no pleasure in sacrifices. How can you think so little of the Deity as not to understand that the repulsive odor of burned grease sickens him? Be righteous. Worship God with clean hands—this is the service he asks of you."

I do not believe that such thoughts were usual in the days of King Mesha or King David. In their time religion was a barter, an exchange of good services for adoration. The Prophets, in contradistinction, declare that Jehovah's true servant is he who does good. In this way religion becomes a matter of ethics, something universal, and it is permeated by the idea of justice. And this is why the Prophets of Israel are the most fervent tribunes the world has ever seen, tribunes who are all the more harsh and stern since they do not rely on the concept of another life to comfort themselves but proclaim that here on earth justice must prevail.

This is the unique appearance in the world of pure religion. You can see that such a creed has, in fact, outstripped everything national. In worshipping a God who created heaven and earth, who loves the good and punishes evil …, in proclaiming such a faith, man has surpassed the limitations of his national ideology and has become fully conscious of human values in the broadest sense of the word….

Israel's fundamental idea is the annunciation of a radiant future for mankind, a state where justice will reign on earth, and in which all idolatry and all lower and ruder forms of worship will disappear….

Thus idolatry will perish from the earth, vanquished by the Jews. The Jewish people will then be like "a banner" seen by all nations on the horizon, a pennant around which they soon will rally. This conception indicates that the messianic or sibylline ideal

Source: Ernest Renan, *Le Judaïsme comme race et comme religion* (Paris: Calmann Lévy, 1883). Trans. Robert Pick. *Contemporary Jewish Record. The Cedars of Lebanon. A Series of Judaic Essays*, IV (1943), pp. 436–48.

has been alive long before the Babylonian Captivity. Israel is dreaming of a future of bliss for mankind, a perfect kingdom with Jerusalem as the capital. And all the peoples, so Israel dreams, will go on a pilgrimage to Jerusalem to worship the Eternal. Clearly, such a faith is not national. In its background, it is true, there is a certain amount of pride, but what historical foundation is free from such remnants? The idea as such, however, is, as you can see, basically and profoundly universal....

The light shall rise within the Jewish nation, and this light is to shine over the whole world. This is by no means an ethnic ideology—this is universalism in the highest degree, and the people that proclaims such an idea is obviously called upon to fulfill a destiny far beyond the limits of a nationally determined role....

From all this it becomes crystal clear that originally Judaism represented the tradition of a special race; neither can there be left any doubt that the aboriginal Palestinians contributed racially to the phenomenon of the present-day Jewish race. At the same time, however, it is my conviction that in the Jewish population as it exists today there is a considerable element of non-Jewish blood—even so much as to make this race, which is considered as the very ideal of pure *ethnos* and which has survived the centuries by means of prohibition of mixed marriages, appear as penetrated by foreign blood to only slightly less an extent than all the other races. In other words, in its origin Judaism was a national religion and has become again a closed religious community in our own days. But in the intervening period, the Jewish creed was open to other nations through many long centuries. Actual masses of populations, non-Jewish by blood, have embraced Judaism—which, from the ethnographic point of view, has made thoroughly contestable the meaning of the word "Jewish."

Objection will be made by pointing to what is called the Jewish type. Much could be said on this point. In my opinion, there is no such thing as a Jewish type, although there are Jewish types....

The theory of an ethnic homogeneousness of the Jews has also been supported by the similarity of their customs and habits. But whenever people of whatever race are put together and confined to ghetto life, the outcome is bound to be the same. There is such a thing as a specific mentality of religious minorities, and this mentality is independent of racial conditions. There is much that is analogous in the position of Protestants who live as a minority, as they do in France, and that of the Jews, the reason being that these French Protestants, like the Jews, have been forced to live among themselves for a very long period and that a great many things used to be forbidden to them, as they were to the Jews....

Their peculiar physiognomy and their way of life are results of centuries-old conditions weighing them down rather than of ethnographic phenomena.

Let us be glad that for the everyday life of France these questions, interesting as they may be to the historian and the ethnologist, have no importance whatsoever. In fact, we have done away entirely with their difficult political implications. With us, the racial background is utterly secondary to the question of nationality, and very rightly so.

Ethnic facts, though they constitute the main problem in the early stages of history, gradually lose momentum in proportion to the progress of civilization. Extremely slight attention was paid to the question of race when, in 1791, the National Assembly decreed the emancipation of the Jews. The opinion prevailed that men should not be judged by their blood but by their ethical and intellectual worth.

Such human approach is the glory, which is France. To raze all ghetto walls is the moral obligation of the nineteenth century—I cannot comment on those who try to re-erect them elsewhere. The Jews have rendered the greatest services to the world. Assimilated into the different nations, integrated into the various national units, they will continue to do as they have done in the past, and, by collaboration with the liberal forces of Europe, will contribute greatly to the social progress of mankind.

NOTE

1. One of the great savants of the nineteenth century, Ernest Renan (1823–1892) was a scholar of Semitic languages and cultures. Born into a French Catholic family, he initially regarded himself as destined for the priesthood. Disaffection with what he held to be the oppressive nature of the Church led to a crisis of faith and to the adoption of the ideals of the Enlightenment. The history of Christianity and its roots in biblical Judaism now increasingly engaged his passion. For years he was employed by the department of Hebrew and Semitic Manuscripts at the Bibliothèque Nationale in Paris,

where he met and befriended many Jewish scholars. Increasingly, his scholarship focused on the Hebrew Bible and the history of ancient Israel. In this lecture, delivered before the Saint-Simon Society in Paris on January 27, 1883, he gives expression to his enthusiastic admiration of the biblical prophets, whom he regarded as the founders of a religion of humanity. He also indirectly addresses the antisemitic canard that Jews are a morally degenerate race. The Jews, he underscores, are, in fact, an admixture of many ethnic groups and thus cannot be considered a "pure" race. Nonetheless, Renan has been criticized for contending in his more extensive historical writings that the Jews suffer from a "Semitic mentality," which he characterized as dogmatic and lacking in a cosmopolitan conception of civilization. See Shmuel Almog, "The Racial Motif in Renan's Attitude to Jews and Judaism," in *Antisemitism Through the Ages*, ed. S. Almog, trans. from the Hebrew by N. H. Reisner (New York: Pergamon, 1988), pp. 255–78.

18. THE JEWS: KINGS OF THE EPOCH (1845)

ALPHONSE TOUSSENEL[1]

Critical periods arise in the life of a nation, as they do in the life of an individual. At such times, it seems as if the blood is clotting in your heart. They are times of terrible stagnation, when all of the achievements of the past are undone by one mistake; times when [the forces of corruption], encouraged by a general inertia and torpor of the spirit, usurp the government of a degraded society and consolidate their power for centuries to come. The French nation has come to one of these critical periods.

The parliament is powerless and, one might say, chronically so as of recently. The chamber of deputies, an all too faithful representation of the country, is divided; its factions vote for laws piecemeal. The words *system* and *unity* frighten its members. If, by chance, some miserable question concerning a portfolio [of stocks] or secret funds succeeds in galvanizing [the deputies] from [their] torpor, the majority come together for a moment out of fear, but immediately they scatter when the danger is past. And, every representative, taking up again the harness of local interests, goes back to lining his own pockets with renewed zeal. The law, deprived of any grandiose and national character, is nothing other than a financial transaction among greedy and narrow-minded men. Ministers can only receive a parliamentary majority on the condition, set by the parliament, that they do not govern. The purchase of consciences and catering to villainy—this is the edifying task, and almost the exclusive one, which the spirit of the age assigns to its rulers.

The machinery of the central administration has broken down. The prefect can no longer administrate effectively. Rather, it is the deputy who governs and distributes employment. Ministers have become used to paying for the votes delivered to them by appointing their supporters prefectures and granting them shares in tax collection, so that the highest officers of the government have lost all prestige in the people's eyes, and the holders of those offices have lost their former influence. Accusations of bribery against the highest government officials are daily events: a

Source: Alphonse Toussenel, *Les Juifs, rois de l'époque, histoire de la féodalité finanacière*, 4th ed., 2 vols. (Paris: Libraire de la Sociéte des Gens de Lettres, 1888), vol. 1, pp. 1–6, trans. J. Green.

marshal of France admits before the court that he has *compromised the dignity of his command* by falsifying an account of tribute payments imposed on the enemy; a minister of the navy ingenuously confesses in court that the accounts of his department are not without several *irregularities*. Bankruptcy has become as commonplace among the agents as among notaries and stockbrokers. Some are even being arraigned in criminal court for offenses against decency. Twenty-five Algerian public officials were arraigned at the same time, then dismissed, or simply censured for acts of bribery, indiscipline or incompetence. And, the courts of the mother country are as full as those of Algeria with scandalous cases of bribery and illicit payments. On this topic, one can even say that there is competition between certain military and naval departments. Excisemen participate in the business of the adulteration of beverages. Employees of the mint are accused of having sold the coinage. Fraud, demoralization and contempt for honesty are omnipresent.

The judiciary itself, which has for so long been the last safeguard of our liberty and honor, seems to have forgotten the difference between "just" and "unjust" in the general collapse of public morality and equity. Judges have imprisoned and fined poor workers guilty of joining together *in order to live from their work*. It never occurred to those rigorous executors of the law to blame the employers, who are guilty of having joined together *in order to live from the labor of their workers*. Hardly one judge could be found in the courthouses to find that this coalition of employers had an extenuating circumstance in favor of the poor miners of Saint-Étienne. Even less has French justice, so harsh toward the poor, considered accusing the bankers of Judea, London and Geneva of the crime of ransacking the public treasury, those bankers who brazenly unite every day in order to secure a monopoly of public loans and railroads for a low price.

In foreign affairs, France has fallen to the level of a second-rate power. The absolutist states keep her in quarantine, as the poet said. They deal with questions affecting the balance of power in Europe, without French participation. They banish her from their congresses. And, instead of withdrawing nobly in formidable isolation and making them pay a high price for her return of these congresses (where nothing can be decided without her), France begs shamefully for the favor of resuming her place. In order to

be forgiven, she makes herself humble and modest. She grants the English navy a monopoly in policing the seas. She allows foreign cruisers to inspect her ships. When public opinion has been stirred by these indignities, the French government deceitfully avoids the issue....

Now, favored by this lack of parliamentary power, political inertia and torpor of spirit, economic feudalism advances rapidly to the heart of our institutions. Skillfully taking advantage of the divisions between the royalty and the people that are fomented by the press, this feudalism entrenches itself in the soil more deeply each day, pressing with its two feet the throats of the royalty and of the people. Today, [this feudal clique] is not yet completely organized. But, it will be tomorrow. It already has the producer and the consumer at its mercy. The Jew reigns and governs France.

In [this book], I point out the origin, tendencies and successive invasions of financial feudalism. I expose the dangers of the present situation and indicate the means to remove them. I show that it is still possible to check the insolent power of money. I call upon the king and the people to unite in order to rid themselves of the aristocracy of money—as the king and the people did once before under Richelieu[2] in order to overthrow the aristocracy of caste. I prove that the king must only wish to save the people's freedom one more time and thus be transfigured gloriously in their eyes.

And now, to those who are tempted to ask who I am, I answer: I am one of those you could call "men of the hour," as opposed to those you call "men of tomorrow"; I am one of those devoted and inept people you are always sure to meet in the hottest part of the fighting and in stormy circumstances, but who willingly forget to set conditions on the eve of the battle and to claim their share of the booty on the morrow of the victory. For ten years I served the cause of power with an energetic devotion, which the dangers of battle never weakened for a moment.[3] And I would continue to serve the cause of order and authority, if it were possible for an honorable man to support that degrading policy of continual self-abasement, [euphemistically] called modesty. When I saw that the ministers, who had commissioned me to defend them, betrayed their government and sold France to the Jews, I deserted their camp, so as not to go over to the enemy with them.

NOTES

1. Alphonse Toussenel (1803–1885), French publicist and follower of François Marie Charles Fourier, the French utopian socialist. Toussenel was exceedingly popular as a writer on ornithology and wildlife. In these studies, which earned him the title Balzac of the animal world, he celebrated the pristine majesty of the woods and forests of France—which, alas, he charged, were being destroyed by "Rothschild's railroads." His two-volume work, *Les Juifs, rois de l'époque*, was one of the most vehement attacks on the Jews published in France before the appearance of Edouard-Adolphe Drumont's *La France Juive* (see document 20).

   In this work, first published in 1845 (second edition 1847; republished in 1886–1888), Toussenel paints an apocalyptic picture of France under the July monarchy (1830–1848). He focuses on the parliamentary corruption and social unrest concomitant to the rapid industrial development of this period and on the fact that Jewish financiers were prominent among the ruling oligarchy. In its spiritual and moral torpor, he argues, France had allowed itself to be victimized by "financial feudalism," that is, by usurious Jewry. Toussenel was a pioneer of a literature that linked the medieval image of the Jew as a usurer to the popular contempt for the financier and banker in the age of nascent capitalism: "I wish to point to the popular sense of the word [*Jew*]: banker, usurer" (Toussenel). This dialectic between anti-capitalism and antisemitism was encouraged by the tendency of early socialists, especially in France, to identify the essence of capitalism with high finance and the depiction of this activity as a form of usury. As George Lichtheim observed in his study of socialist antisemitism, "the anti-capitalism and the anti-Jewish themes were intertwined, it took considerable time and trouble before they could be disentangled" ("Socialism and the Jews," *Dissent* [July–August 1968], p. 316).

2. Cardinal-Duc de Richelieu (1585–1642) was appointed Louis XIII's chief minister, a position he held until his death and which allowed him to coordinate the interests of the church with those of the kingdom of France.

3. In the early 1840s Toussenel spent three years in Algeria as a civilian commissioner working with the French army.

19. THE JEWS: OPPRESSED OR OPPRESSORS? (1877)

FYODOR DOSTOIEVSKY[1]

True, it is very difficult to learn the forty-century-long history of a people such as the Jews; but, to start with, this much I know, that in the whole world there is certainly no other people who would be complaining as much about their lot, incessantly, after each step and word of theirs,—about their humiliation, their suffering, their martyrdom. One might think that it is not they who are reigning in Europe, who are directing there at least the stock-exchanges, and therefore also politics, domestic affairs, the morality of the states. . . .

I am fully unable to believe in the screams of the Jews that they are so downtrodden, oppressed and humiliated. In my opinion, the Russian peasant,

Source: Fyodor Dostoievsky, "The Jewish Question" (1877), in *The Diary of a Writer*, trans. Boris Brasol (New York: Charles Scribner's Sons, 1949), pp. 640f., 644f. Copyright 1949 Charles Scribner's Sons; copyright renewed 1976 Maxwell Fassett, Executor of Estate of Boris Brasol. Reprinted with the permission of Charles Scribner's Sons, an imprint of Macmillan Publishing Company.

and generally, the Russian commoner, virtually bears heavier burdens than the Jew....

[Y]ou, too, should remember that at the time when the Jew "has been restricted in the free selection of the place of residence," twenty-three millions of "the Russian toiling mass" have been enduring serfdom which was, of course, more burdensome than "the selection of the place of residence." Now, did the Jew pity them then?—I don't think so: In the Western border region and in the South [of the Russian Empire] you will get a comprehensive answer to this question. Nay, at that time the Jews also vociferated about rights which the Russian people themselves did not have; they shouted and complained that they were downtrodden and martyrs, and that when they should be granted more rights, "then demand from us that we comply with the duties toward the state and the native population."

But then came the Liberator[2] and liberated the native people. And who was the first to fall upon them as on a victim? Who preeminently took advantage of their vices? Who tied them with that sempiternal gold pursuit of theirs? By whom—whenever possible—were the abolished landowners promptly replaced, with the difference that the latter, even though they did strongly exploit men, nevertheless endeavored—perhaps in their own interest—not to ruin the peasants in order to prevent the exhaustion of labor, whereas the Jew is not concerned about the exhaustion of Russian labor: He grabs what's his, and off he goes....

Let it be conceded that I am not firm in my knowledge of the Jewish modes of living, but one thing I do know for sure, and I am ready to argue about it with anyone, namely, that among our common people there is no preconceived, *a priori*, blunt religious hatred of the Jew, something along the lines: "Judas sold out Christ." Even if one hears it from little children or drunken persons, nevertheless our people as a whole look upon the Jew, I repeat, without a preconceived hatred. I have been observing this for fifty years. I even happened to live among people, in their very midst, in one and the same barracks, sleeping with them on the same cots. There were several Jews, and no one *despised* them, no one shunned them or persecuted them. When they said their prayers (and Jews pray with screams, donning a special garment) nobody found this strange, no one hindered them or scoffed at them,—a fact which precisely was to be expected from such a coarse people—in your estimation—as the Russians. On the contrary, when

beholding them, they used to say: "Such is their religion, and thus they pray"; and would pass by calmly, almost approvingly.

And yet these same Jews in many respects shunned the Russians, they refused to take meals with them, looked upon them with haughtiness (and where?—in a prison!) and generally expressed squeamishness and aversion towards the Russian, towards the "native" people....

[H]ow would it be if in Russia there were not three million Jews but three million Russians, and there were eighty million Jews,—well into what would they convert the Russians and how would they treat them? Would they permit them to acquire equal rights? Would they permit them to worship freely in their midst? Wouldn't they convert them into slaves? Worse than that: Wouldn't they skin them altogether? Wouldn't they slaughter them to the last man, to the point of complete extermination, as they used to do with alien peoples in ancient times, during their ancient history?

Nay, I assure you that in the Russian people there is no preconceived hatred of the Jew, but perhaps there is a dislike of him, and especially in certain localities, maybe—a strong dislike. Oh, this cannot be avoided; this exists; but it arises not at all from the fact that he is a Jew, not because of some racial or religious hate, but it comes from other causes of which not the native people but the Jew himself is guilty.

NOTES

1. Fyodor Dostoievsky (1821–1881) was an eminent Russian novelist. He depicted only one Jewish character at any length in his fiction. In *The House of the Dead* (1861–62), Isai Brumstein is an incorrigible criminal who remains faithful to the practices of Judaism. Dostoievsky did, however, often make passing comments, invariably contemptuous, about Jews and Jewishness in his novels and short stories. His contempt of Jews was typical of Russian literature of the nineteenth century, from Pushkin to Chekhov, in which Jews are uniformly portrayed as objects of scorn and derision. In Dostoievsky's case his antisemitism was confounded by his general xenophobia; he was anti-English, anti-French, anti-German and especially anti-Polish.

   In the last two decades of his life, coinciding with the crystallization of his conservative political and religious position, Dostoievsky's antisemitic views became more pronounced and evolved from the traditional Russian antipathy toward the Jews into an ideological anti-Semitism that attributed to them some of the more egregious sins of the modern world. Hence, as has been observed in a study on Dostoievsky's anti-Semitic attitudes, for him the Jew was "initially nothing more than object of scorn or derision, a peddler, a small-time money lender," [indeed] was too ridiculous to be really hated. But, by the end of the 1860s, [the Jew] had become a financier and manipulator, the occult master of the stock exchange and state treasuries dedicated to the destruction of the foundations of Christian civilization. And now [in the 1870s], he had become the nihilist, the driving force behind the revolutionary movement and agent of socialist subversion" (David J. Goldstein, *Dostoievsky and the Jews* [Austin: University of Texas Press, 1981], p. 22). Reflecting on this turn to an ideological anti-Semitism is an essay on "The 'Jewish Question'," included by Dostoievsky in his *The Diary of a Writer*, in which he recorded his thoughts on current affairs and expressed his violent opposition to liberals and revolutionaries. The passage presented here is from his essay "The 'Jewish Question'."

2. The reference is to Alexander II (1818–1881; tsar of Russia 1855–1881), who six years after he ascended the throne published the emancipation law ending serfdom in the Russian empire.

20. JEWISH FRANCE (1886)

EDOUARD-ADOLPHE DRUMONT[1]

The Jews possess half of the capital in the world. Now the wealth of France, with a national budget of close to four million francs, is possibly worth one hundred and fifty billion francs, of which the Jews possess at least eighty billion. In my estimation, however, because one must proceed with circumspection and because of the ease with which finances can be juggled, [the expropriation of Jewish wealth] would produce immediately no more than ten to fifteen billion. I take the figure of ten billion as a minimum: five or six billion francs in cash, and certainly one could also expropriate enough factories. [The latter action] would allow the workers to test their social doctrines in optimal conditions, in that there would be no violent revolution, and no unemployment would be created. All of this, and I do not hestitate to emphasize the point, would be accomplished without violence, without bloodshed; it would, if you will, be accomplished by simple decree, without plunging the country into one of those crises which only benefit the foreigners [viz., the Jews]. The Office of Confiscated Jewish Wealth would function much as the [Revolutionary] Office of National Wealth functioned. And, I do not see very well how anyone could attack the legitimacy of such expropriation, for none of the civics textbooks that are put into the hands of the young dares to condemn revolutionary confiscation.

Actually, the transfer of property which we propose is more legitimate than that which occurred during the revolution. In effect, no one could seriously deny that Jewish wealth has, as we have said, a special character. It is essentially parasitical and usurious. It is not the carefully husbanded fruit of the labor of innumerable generations. Rather, it is the result of speculation and fraud. It is not created by

---

Source: Edouard-Adolphe Drumont, *La France Juive*, 14th ed. (Paris: C Marpon and E. Flammarion, 1885), vol. 1, pp. 520–23, 526, trans. J. Green.

labor, but extracted with marvelous cleverness from the pocket of real workers by financial institutions, which have enriched their founders by ruining their stockholders.

…The obstacles [placed before the workers by the Jews] are indeed considerable. Still they are not insurmountable. A man of French origin may yet arise from among the people, harboring the magnificent ambition of attaching his name to the peaceful solution [I have proposed] of the problem of the proletariat, which has already cost the workers so much blood and which will cost them still more if they follow the old path.[2]

Likewise, a brave officer might appear, who would be acutely struck by the degradation of his country and who would risk his life to raise it up. Given the actual situation, with a government scorned by all and falling apart at the seams, five hundred determined men in the suburbs of Paris and a regiment surrounding the Jewish banks would suffice to carry out the most fruitful revolution of modern times. Everything would be over by the end of the day. After seeing posters announcing that the operations of the Office of Confiscated Jewish Wealth were going to begin in two days, people would embrace in the streets.

Thus, the beautiful saying of Pierre the Venerable, Abbot of Cluny, would be realized: *Serviant populis christians, etiam invitis ipsis, divitiae Judeorum.* "Let the wealth of the Jews even against their will, serve the Christian peoples."

NOTES

1. Edouard-Adolphe Drumont (1844–1917), journalist and leader of the antisemitic movement in France. His *La France Juive*—first published in 1886; subsequently more than a hundred editions were issued—was said to be the most widely read book in France. He followed his success by trying to organize antisemitism as a political and social force; in this effort he was primarily supported by students and lower echelons of the Catholic clergy. In 1892 he founded the *La Libre Parole*, a daily newspaper that reflected both his antisemitism and what has been called his "sentimental socialism," or paternalistic concern for the poor and a repugnance toward capital (as opposed to property), which he defined as wealth illicitly gained through speculation. According to Drumont, property is a Christian value, and capital is Jewish.

His two-volume work of more than a thousand pages purports to depict the historical clash between Jewry and France. This account is prefaced by an effusive discussion of the racial differences between the Aryans of Gaul—an idealistic, chivalrous Christian people—and the Jews. In contradistinction to the Frenchman, the Jew lacks a creative impulse, and he is correspondingly ugly (a hooked nose, contorted fingers, an unpleasant body odor). The Jews, moreover, are by nature spies, traitors, criminals, and carriers of disease. Through their cunning, "the Jewish race" has all but subjugated the benign but careless Aryans of France. The major theme of Drumont's antisemitic canard, however, is the contrast between the poverty of the French workers and peasants and the wealth of Jewish bankers and industrialists. His program for liberating a benighted France from the clutches of a predatory Jewry is presented in this excerpt.

2. The advertisement for an illustrated edition of Drumont's work published in 1887 "portrayed Drumont as a second Charles Martel, clad in shining armor and attacking the nineteenth-century Saracens of the bank and stock exchange, while the cover of this edition showed Drumont, carrying a cross, stamping upon an old man who was holding the tablets of Sinai" (R. F. Byrnes, *Anti-Semitism in Modern France* [New Brunswick: Rutgers University Press, 1950], vol. 1, pp. 139ff.).

21. WHAT WE DEMAND OF MODERN JEWRY (1879)

ADOLF STOECKER[1]

We do not believe the end of the German spirit to be so near. Peoples as well as individuals can be reborn. Germany, and Berlin too, will recover and rid themselves of the foreign spirit. But there are symptoms of the presence of a disease: our national body is plagued by social abuses, and social hostility never exists without reason. Christians as well as Jews should be seriously concerned lest this enmity turn into hatred. For the rumbling of a far-off thunderstorm can already be heard. It is strange indeed that the Jewish liberal press does not have the courage to answer the charges of its attackers. Usually it invents a scandal, even if there is none. It sharpens its poisonous pen by writing about the sermons in our churches and the discussions in our church meetings; but it hushes up the Jewish question and does everything to prevent its readers from hearing even a whisper from these unpleasant voices. It pretends to despise its enemies and to consider them unworthy of an answer. It would be better to learn from the enemy, to recognize one's own defects, and work together toward the social reconciliation which we need so badly. It is in this light that I intend to deal with the Jewish question, in the spirit of Christian love, but also with complete social truthfulness ....

I do indeed consider modern Jewry a great danger to German national life. By this I mean neither the religion of the orthodox nor the enlightenment of the reformed. Orthodox Judaism, this ossification of the Law, the Old Testament without a temple, without priests, without sacrifice, without a Messiah, is neither attractive nor dangerous to the children of the nineteenth century. It is a form of religion which is dead at its very core, a low form of revelation, an outlived spirit, still venerable but set at nought by

Christ and no longer holding any truth for the present. Reformed Judaism is of even less religious significance. It is neither Judaism nor Christianity, but a pitiful remnant of the Age of Enlightenment. Its ideas did not originate on Jewish soil but in a wretched period of the Christian church, a period long since overcome by the church itself. Both factions boast, of course, that the Jews are the bearers of the loftiest religious and moral ideals for mankind and the world and that it is the mission of Jewry, now and in the future, to maintain those ideals, to develop and spread them. On this point the Jewish press, from right to left, stands united ....

Here we wish to make our request. We ask: *please, be a little more modest!* We do not deny that Israel carried the knowledge of the one and only God through ancient times like a sacred flame until Christ came and brought the more perfect faith, the richer conception of God, and the higher truth. But it is a historic fact that the people of Israel time and again relapsed into the grossest idolatry, that God was able to suppress apostasy for short periods only by sending outstanding personalities. It is God's grace rather than Israel's merit that the doctrine of the one God has been preserved for mankind. It is just as indubitable that the ideas of freedom of religion, of tolerance in the modern sense, do not fit into the character of the Old Testament. Whoever violated the Sabbath was stoned, the priests of Baal were slaughtered. This was inherent in the Jewish legal institutions and we are far from blaming the Old Testament for it.

But it is quite out of order when Jews claim as their own ideas which were historically altogether unknown to their religion. And furthermore they are quite aware of the fact that they had a caste of

---

priests—certainly the opposite of equality; that they had slavery—certainly the opposite of freedom; and that they indulged in polygamy—certainly the opposite of ideal family life. Only Teutonic-Christian life put an end to these abuses. It is true, Israel had an enlightened economic legislation, social forms of property ownership, the prohibition of usury, and the greatest charity toward the poor. But we have only to mention these things to realize the fearful chasm between the Old Testament and modern Jewry. It was German law alone that protected the concept of common property, the Christian church alone that decreed the prohibition of usury; it is precisely here that the faults and sins of modern Jewry are plainly revealed.

Even if we presume for once that this lofty mission really is Israel's permanent task, who, then, are those thinkers and poets, who, inspired by the divine spirit, preach, praise and honor the living God? Perhaps the editors of the *Tageblatt*?[2] Or the scholars of the *Kladderadatsch*?[3] Where is the school of the prophets of the Holy Spirit which trains young men for their world mission? Where are the missionary posts? Where are the missionaries? Perhaps at the stock exchanges of Berlin, Vienna and Paris? Alas, the Jews should not be told such foolishness. For it is their ominous fate that, having failed Christ, they have lost their divine course, have abandoned their sublime mission. Confronted with the Lord's sharp-edged alternative—"Thou canst not serve both God and Mammon"—they now worship the idol of gold, having forsaken the path of God....

And in spite of this truth, in spite of their utter lack of religious creativeness, they stick to their delusion of being a religious power. The truth is that modern Jewry is most certainly a power against religion; a power which bitterly fights Christianity everywhere, uproots Christian faith as well as national feeling in the people, in their stead offering them nothing but the idolatrous admiration of Jewry such as it is, with no other content but its self-admiration....

The question is: What shall be done? We believe that Jews and Christians must try to establish a proper relationship with each other. There is no other way. Hatred of the Jews is already flaring up here and there, and this is repugnant to the Gospels. If modern Jewry continues to use the power of capital and the power of the press to bring misfortune to the nation, a final catastrophe is unavoidable. Israel must renounce its ambition to become the master of Germany. It should renounce its arrogant claim that Judaism is the religion of the future, when it is so clearly that of the past. Let not foolish Christians continue to strengthen the self-conceit of this people. Jewish orthodoxy with its circumcision is decrepit, while reformed Judaism is not a Jewish religion at all. Once Israel has realized this, it will quietly forget its alleged mission and stop trying to rob of their Christianity people who offer it hospitality and civil rights. The Jewish press must become more tolerant— that is the first prerequisite for improving the situation. The social abuses which are caused by Jewry must be eradicated by wise legislation. It will not be easy to curb Jewish capital. Only thoroughgoing legislation can bring it about. The mortgage system in real estate should be abolished and property should be inalienable and unmortgageable; the credit system should be reorganized to protect the businessman against the arbitrary power of big capital. There must be new stock and stock-exchange regulations; reintroduction of the denominational census so as to find out the disproportion between Jewish capital and Christian labor; limitation of appointments of Jewish judges in proportion to the size of the population; removal of Jewish teachers from our grammar schools, and in addition the strengthening of the Christian-Germanic spirit—are the means to put a stop to the encroachment of Jewry on Germanic life, this worst kind of usury.

Either we succeed in this and Germany will rise again, or the cancer from which we suffer will spread further. In that event our whole future is threatened and the German spirit will become Judaized. The German economy will become impoverished. These are our slogans: A return to a Germanic rule in law and business, a return to the Christian faith. May every man do his duty, and God will help us.

NOTES

1. Adolf Stoecker (1835–1909), German antisemitic preacher and politician. Imperial court chaplain from 1874, Stoecker was a member of the Prussian diet from 1879 to 1898. In 1881 he was elected to the Reichstag, where he served (except from 1893 to 1898) until 1908. In 1878 he founded the Christian Social Workers' Party, renamed the Christian Social Party in 1881. Through his party Stoecker created a right-wing mass movement of discontented artisans and small shop owners, who were later joined by members of the conservative

educated classes. He was a powerful demagogue who knew how to channel discontent into antisemitism. His inflammatory speeches paved the way for the rampant antisemitic movement in Berlin in the early 1880s, which spread to provincial cities and the countryside. The selection presented here is the text of a speech that

was delivered at a Christian Social Workers' Party rally of September 19, 1879.

2. *Berliner Tageblatt* was a Jewish-owned Berlin daily that had a large proportion of Jews on its staff.

3. *Kladderadatsch* was a weekly of political satire, founded in 1848.

22. A WORD ABOUT OUR JEWRY (1880)

HEINRICH VON TREITSCHKE[1]

Among the symptoms of a great change in mood in the German nation, none appears so strange as the violent movement against the Jews. Until a few months ago, the notorious *reverse* "Hep-Hep call"[2] was still dominant in Germany. About the national shortcomings of the Germans, the French and all other nations, everybody could freely say the worst things; but if somebody dared to speak in just and moderate terms about some undeniable weakness of the Jewish character, he was immediately branded as a barbarian and religious persecutor by nearly all of the newspapers. Today we have already come to the point where the majority of the Breslau voters—obviously not in wild excitement but with quiet deliberation—conspired not to elect a Jew to the diet under any circumstances. Antisemitic societies are formed, the "Jewish question" is discussed in noisy meetings, a flood of antisemitic pamphlets appears on the market. There is only too much of dirt and brutality in these doings, and it is impossible to suppress one's disgust when one notices that some of these incendiary pamphlets obviously come from Jewish pens. It is well known that since Pfefferkorn[3] and Eisenmenger[4] there were always many former Jews among the most fanatical Jew-haters. But is there really nothing but

mob brutality and business envy at the bottom of this noisy activity? Are these outbreaks of a deep, long-suppressed anger really only a momentary outburst, as hollow and irrational as the Teutonic antisemitism of 1819? No, the instinct of the masses has in fact clearly recognized a great danger, a serious sore spot of the new German national life; the current expression "the German Jewish question" is more than an empty phrase. . . .

What we have to demand from our Jewish fellow-citizens is simple: that they become Germans, regard themselves simply and justly as Germans, without prejudice to their faith and their old sacred past which all of us hold in reverence; for we do not want an era of German-Jewish mixed culture to follow after thousands of years of German civilization. It would be a sin to forget that a great number of Jews, baptized and unbaptized, Felix Mendelssohn,[5] Veit,[6] Riesser[7] and others, not to mention the ones now living, were Germans in the best sense of the word, men in whom we revere the noble and fine traits of the German spirit. At the same time it cannot be denied that there are numerous and powerful groups among our Jews who definitely do not have the good will to become simply Germans. It is painful enough to talk about

Source: Heinrich von Treitschke, *A Word About Our Jewry,* ed. Ellis Rivkin and trans. Helen Lederer (Cincinnati: Hebrew Union College—Institute of Religion, n.d.), pp. 1–7. Reprinted by permission of Dr. Ellis Rivkin.

these things. Even conciliatory words are easily mis-understood here. I think, however, some of my Jewish friends will admit, with deep regret, that recently a dangerous spirit of arrogance has arisen in Jewish cir-cles and that the influence of Jewry upon our national life, which in former times was often beneficial, has recently often been harmful. I refer the reader to *The History of the Jews* by Graetz.[8] What a fanatical fury against the "arch enemy" Christianity, what deadly hatred of the purest and most powerful exponents of German character, from Luther to Goethe and Fichte! And what hollow, offensive self-glorification! Here it is proved with continuous satirical invective that the nation of Kant was really educated to humanity by the Jews only, that the language of Lessing and Goethe became sensitive to beauty, spirit and wit only through Boerne and Heine! Is there any English Jew who would dare to slander in such manner the land which guards and protects him? And this stubborn contempt for the German *goyim* is not at all the atti-tude of a single fanatic. There is no German city which does not count many honest, respectable Jewish firms among its merchants. But it cannot be denied that the Jews have contributed their part to the promoting of business with its dishonesty and bold cupidity, that they share heavily in the guilt for the contemptible materialism of our age which regards every kind of work only as business and threatens to suffocate the old simple pride and joy the German felt in his work. In many thousands of German villages we have the Jewish usurer. Among the leading names of art and science there are not many Jews. The greater is the number of Semitic hustlers among the third-rank tal-ents. And how firmly this bunch of literateurs hangs together! How safely this insurance company for immortality works, based on the tested principle of mutuality, so that every Jewish poetaster receives his one-day fame, dealt out by the newspapers immedi-ately and in cash, without delayed interest.

The greatest danger, however, is the unjust influ-ence of the Jews in the press—a fateful consequence of our old narrow-minded laws which kept the Jews out of most learned professions. For ten years public opinion in many German cities was "made" mostly by Jewish pens. It was a misfortune for the Liberals, and one of the reasons of the decline of the party, that their papers gave too much scope to the Jews. The present weakness of the press is the necessary reaction against this unnatural state of things. The

little man is firmly convinced now that the Jews write everything in the newspapers and he will not believe anything they say any longer. Our newspapers owe much to the Jewish talent. The acuteness and nimble quickness of the Jewish mind found the arena of the press always a congenial field. But here, too, the effect was two-edged. Boerne was the first to introduce into our journalism the peculiar shameless way of talking about the fatherland [in an] off-hand [manner] and without any reverence, like an outsider, as if mockery of Germany did not cut deeply into the heart of every individual German.[9] To this was added that unfortu-nate busybody "me-too" attitude, which has to have a hand in everything and does not even refrain from passing judgment on the inner affairs of the Christian churches. What Jewish journalists write in mockery and satirical remarks against Christianity is down-right revolting, and such blasphemies are offered to our people as the newest acquisitions of "German" Enlightenment! The moment emancipation was gained the Jews insisted boldly on their "certificate," demanded literal parity in everything, forgetful of the fact that we Germans are, after all, a Christian nation and the Jews are only a minority. It has happened that the removal of Christian pictures was demanded, and even the celebration of the Sabbath in mixed schools.[10]

If we consider all this—and much more could be added—then the noisy agitation of the moment appears only as a brutal and spiteful but natural reac-tion of the Germanic national consciousness against an alien element which has usurped too much space in our life. It has at least the one involuntary merit of having liberated us from the ban of a tacit false-hood. It is already a gain that an evil which every-body sensed but which nobody wanted to touch is now discussed openly. Let us not deceive ourselves: The movement is deep and strong. A few jokes about the words of wisdom from the mouths of Christian-Socialist soap-box orators will not be sufficient to suppress it. Even in the best educated circles, among men who would reject with horror any thought of Christian fanaticism or national arrogance, we hear today the cry, as from one mouth, "the Jews are our misfortune!"[11]

There can be no talk among the intelligent of an abolition or even of a limitation of the Emancipation. That would be an open injustice, a betrayal of the fine traditions of our state, and would accentuate rather than mitigate the national contrasts. What made the Jews of France and England harmless and often beneficient members of society was at the bottom nothing but the energy of the national pride and the firmly rooted national way of life of these two nations which look back on centuries of national culture. Ours is a young nation. Our country still lacks national style, instinctive pride, a firmly developed individuality; that is the reason why we were defenseless against alien manners for so long. But we are in the process of acquiring these qualities, and we can only wish that our Jews recognize in time the change which is now occurring in Germany as a necessary consequence of the foundation of the German state. In some places there are Jewish societies against usury which silently do much good. They are the work of intelligent Israelites who have recognized that their fellow-Jews must adjust to the customs and ideas of their Christian fellow-citizens. Much remains to be done in this direction. It is not possible to change the hard German heads into Jewish heads. The only way out therefore is for our Jewish fellow-citizens to make up their minds without reservation to be Germans, as many of them have done already long ago, to their advantage and ours. There will never be a complete solution. There has always been an abyss between Europeans and Semites, since the time when Tacitus complained about the *odium generis humani*.[12] There will always be Jews who are nothing else but German-speaking orientals. There will also always be a specifically Jewish education; and, as a cosmopolitan power, it has a historical right to existence. But the contrast can be mitigated if the Jews, who talk so much about tolerance, become truly tolerant themselves and show some respect for the faith, the customs and the feelings of the German people which has long ago atoned for old injustice, and given them human and civil rights. The lack of such respect in many of our Jewish fellow-citizens in commerce and in literature is the basic reason for the passionate anger in our days. It is not a pleasant sight, this raging and quarrelling, this boiling up of unfinished ideas in our new Germany. But we cannot help our being the most passionate of all nations, although we called ourselves phlegmatics so often. New ideas never broke through in our country other than under bad convulsions. May God grant that we come out of the ferment and unrest of these exciting years with a stricter concept of the state and its obligations and with a more vigorous national consciousness.

NOTES

1. Heinrich von Treitschke (1834–1896). In 1879 and 1880 this renowned German historian published a series of articles in the *Preussische Jahrbuecher*—a prestigious academic journal that he edited. These articles, entitled "Ein Wort ueber unser Judenthum," justified the growing hostility toward the Jews in the wake of the unification of Germany. Treitschke held that the core of the problem was Jewry's contradictory desire to preserve its national identity while simultaneously claiming the right to participate fully in the national life of Germany. Accordingly, he urged the Jews to rid themselves of their frivolous arrogance and to pursue a genuine and rapid assimilation into German culture and society. His articles on the Jewish question generated considerable controversy, particularly in educated circles.

2. "Hep! Hep!" A derogatory rallying cry against the Jews common in Germany. It is also the name given to a series of anti-Jewish riots that broke out in August 1819 in Germany and spread to Denmark. See introduction to chapter 5, note 11, and document 3, note 6.

3. Johannes Pfefferkorn (1469–c.1521), German-Jewish convert to Christianity and writer of anti-Jewish tracts. His knowledge of Jewish sources was minimal, and, as a result of a virulent controversy with the humanist scholar Johannes Reuchlin, his name became proverbial for unprincipled denigrators of their own origin and ancestral faith.

4. Johann Andreas Eisenmenger (1654–1704), a German Christian Hebraist who assiduously studied Jewish sources for more than ten years before completing his work denouncing the Jewish religion. Entitled *Entdecktes Judenthum* [Judaism Unmasked], this book, which purports to prove Judaism's intrinsic misanthropy, had a formative influence on modern antisemitic polemics.

5. Jakob Ludwig Felix Mendelssohn-Bartholdy (1809–1847), German composer and grandson of Moses Mendelssohn. Of Jewish birth, Felix was baptized and raised as a Protestant. He showed musical talent at an early age and became a brilliant pianist and an acclaimed composer.

6. Moritz Veit (1808–1864), member of a wealthy Jewish banking family in Berlin. He was a prominent publisher, politician and leader of the Berlin Jewish Community.

7. Gabriel Riesser (1806–1863), German-Jewish political figure and an indefatigable champion of Jewish civil equality. See chapter 3, document 21.

8. Heinrich Graetz (1817–1891), German-Jewish historian and Bible scholar. His monumental *Geschichte der Juden* (*History of the* Jews, 11 volumes) was the first comprehensive attempt to write a history of the Jews from a Jewish viewpoint and to regard the Jews as a living people. Treitschke is referring to the eleventh volume of Graetz's work (1868), in which the author's passionate desire to foster Jewish pride is particularly manifest. Graetz exuberantly celebrates the Jewish contribution to German culture and at the same time denounces German national heroes like Luther and Kant for their antisemitism. He also unhesitatingly discusses Christianity's role in the suffering of the Jews and concludes that Christian ethics would be an inadequate basis for a healthy society. Treitschke viewed Graetz's "Jewish nationalism" as parochial and indicative of his unwillingness to identify with the German nation and culture. In the public debate following Treitschke's attack on Graetz, most Jewish writers, while condemning Treitschke's antisemitic outbursts, nevertheless dissociated themselves from Graetz's brand of Jewish "national pride."

9. See chapter 11, document 8. Treitschke is apparently referring to Boerne's "Letters from Paris," containing ascerbic and radical criticism of German society. Published in a liberal newspaper in Frankfurt am Main, these letters were widely read and debated.

10. Cf. Treitschke's remarks in this paragraph to Bruno Bauer's argument (document 12 of this chapter) that the demand for Jewish emancipation would be valid only if the Jews were to fight for the de-Christianization—as well as the de-Judaization—of the state.

11. This phrase was to become one of the slogans of German antisemitism—it was later adopted by the Nazis. Heinrich Class, a student of Treitschke and later the president of the Pan-German League, once observed that his teacher's "phrase, 'the Jews are our misfortune,' became part of my body and soul when I was twenty years old; it essentially influenced my later political work" (cited in Paul W. Massing, *Rehearsal for Destruction* [New York: H. Fertig, 1967], p. 246, n. 37).

12. "Hatred for the human race" the Roman historian actually attributed to the Christians. On Tacitus, see following document, note 3.

23. ANOTHER WORD ABOUT OUR JEWRY (1880)

THEODOR MOMMSEN[1]

It is the fate of our generation—an opportunity rarely provided by history—that the great goals we thought lay before us have now been reached by our nation. Anyone who still remembers the assemblies in which the Estates held a consulting vote, and the Germany which showed one lone color on the map, will consider no price too high for our parliament and our imperial flag come what may. But one has to be very steadfast and far-sighted in order to be happy under the existing circumstances. The immediate consequences [of the unification] remind one of the saying that fate punishes him whose wishes have come true. While Germany was still in the making, nobody—as befits those who are fighting for a common goal—asked about religious or racial differences, about conflicting interests of rural and urban populations, of traders and industrialists....

How, then, does the status of the Jews within our people differ from that of the Saxons or Pomeranians? It is true that they are neither the descendants of

Source: Theodor Mommsen, *Auch ein Wort ueber unser Judentun* (Berlin: Weidmannsche Buchhandlung, 1880), pp. 1–16, trans. J. Hessing.

Istaevo nor of Hermino and Ingaevo;[2] and our common descent from Noah will certainly not suffice if the genealogy is supposed to make the German. Our nation, however, would have to do without a lot more than just the Children of Israel if its current stock were to be corrected according to Tacitus' *Germania*.[3] Years ago, Mr. Quatrefages[4] proved that only the central states are of truly Germanic descent, while *la race prussienne* is a mass actually made up of depraved slaves and other human refuse; it so happened that *la race germanique* and *la race prussienne* later combined to become the trailblazers for the German nation, and that all those who were retreating before them did not seem to notice any difference between them. Anybody who is really familiar with history will know that the transformation of a nationality is a gradual development with numerous and manifold transitions. Historically as well as practically, only he who is alive is in the right; just as the descendants of the French Colony in Berlin are by no means Frenchmen born in Germany, so our Jewish compatriots are nothing less than Germans....

What does it mean that [Treitschke (see preceding document)] demands that our Jewish compatriots become Germans? They are Germans already, just as I am, and just as he is. He may be more virtuous than they are; but do virtues make a German? What gives us the right to remove our compatriots who are of this or that group from our German ranks? Surely this right is not derived from the few defects which we attribute to this group, even if we do so with a certain amount of justification. However harshly we may judge these defects of our compatriots, however strictly we may deny them any mitigating circumstances—in the last resort, we shall merely come to the conclusion, logically as well as practically, that Jews are Germans who have had to carry more than the normal share of original sin. Serious people who have understood this will have no doubt that harmful results of these defects ought to be met by preventive and punitive legislation. The status of German citizens, however, should not be defined by any supposed quantity of original sin on their part.

This insight, however, is not enough. There is a need for a clearer and more refined conception of the inequality between German Occidentals and Semitic blood. With the war against the Jews, we—whose nation has just been unified—enter upon a dangerous path. Our tribes are very unequal among themselves.

None of them lacks their own specific defects, and our mutual love is not so old that it would not easily corrode. Today we are concerned with the Jews—whether only with the unbaptized or even with the baptized, and, in the latter case, to what degree, nobody cares to define. The question could soon bring about the breakdown of the cordial understanding reached by the liberal and Christian Germanic orthodoxy. Any future regulations concerning the mixture of blood really belongs to the domain of Ernst Dohm.[5]...

By no means do I wish to deny that the peculiarities of the Jews living among us are felt more sharply than those of other tribes or even nations. They are more distinct, and the suppression of the Jews—which for thousands of years has been equally harmful to German Jews and German Christians—has led them to adopt an artificial, and at times gruesome, manner. Our historical and literary development bears the marks of this, and no historian can keep quiet about it. From an international point of view, the history of the Rothschild family is more important than the internal history of the state of Saxony, and does it not matter that this is the history of a German Jew? Our century may not have produced a poet more gifted than Heine; and who could understand his intellectual playing with the blood of his own heart and his creative talent, so powerful in sensuality and fantasy, but devoid of all Shakespearean tragedy, without remembering his origin? Certainly, there are differences; and they are of such a nature that the cult of the Jews during a certain period, or the fear of the Jews—this being the shape which the cult tends to take on nowadays—seems to belong to the most simple-minded confusions of which our nation has loved, and still loves, to avail itself. These failures and defects, however, are balanced by talents and advantages which in turn have partly been acquired under the pressure of the very same agitation directed against the Jews. That the purest and most idealistic philosopher lived and suffered as a Jew was no matter of chance;[6] and Jewish philanthropy, toward Christians as well, may serve the latter as an example. Here as elsewhere, the lights and the shadows are mingled, and nobody will dare to determine the precise degree of the mixture, unless he is a court preacher.[7] Just as the Jews were an element of national decomposition in the Roman state,[8] so they doubtlessly are an element of tribal decomposition in Germany. That is why in the German capital, where the tribes mingle more freely than elsewhere, the Jews hold a position for which they are envied in other places. Such processes of decomposition are often necessary, but they are never pleasant. Their consequences are inevitably negative, in Germany less so than in Rome, because our nation is no pale chimera as the nation of the Caesars used to be. I am not so estranged from my [tribal] homeland, however, that I do not painfully feel the loss of something I used to have and that my children will miss. But the happiness of children and the pride of men do not go together. A certain amount of mutual adjustment on the part of the tribes is necessary, resulting in the formation of a German nationality in which no tribal ingredient will be dominant. The great cities, and first of all Berlin, must become the natural protagonists in this process. I do not consider it at all unfortunate that the Jews have been active in this direction for centuries. It is my opinion that Divine Providence, much more so than Stoecker, has understood very well why a few percent of Israel ought to be added to the Germanic metal....

In conclusion, let me say a word about the way in which the Jews themselves react [to antisemitism]. It is self-evident that our nation, by right and honor, must protect the principle of equality before the law and defend itself from open offence as well as from discrimination by the authorities. This duty, which we first of all owe to ourselves, is by no means dependent on the appropriate conduct of the Jews. We cannot, however, protect the Jews from the estrangement and inequality with which the German Christian still tends to treat them. There is danger in this, as the present moment shows, for the Jews as well as for us—the danger of a civil war waged by a majority against a minority; even the possibility of such a war would be a national calamity. This, in part, is the fault of the Jews as well. The word *Christianity*, in our day no longer means what it used to mean; nevertheless it is the only word which still defines the entire international civilization of our day and which numerous millions of people of our highly populated globe accept as their intrinsic link. It is possible to remain outside these boundaries and yet live within the nation, but it is difficult and fraught with danger. He whose conscience—be it for positive or for negative reasons—does not permit him to renounce his Judaism and accept Christianity, will act accordingly, but he should be prepared to bear the consequences;

issues of this nature can only be resolved in privacy, not in public. It is a notorious fact, however, that a great number of Jews are prevented from conversion not by their conscience; but by quite different emotions which I can understand but not justify. The numerous specifically Jewish societies which have been founded in Berlin, for instance, do not seem—except where they do not serve purely religious ends—to have any positive purpose at all. I should never join a philanthropic institution whose statutes would oblige me to support nobody but the people of Holstein; and while I respect the endeavors and achievements of these societies, I view their separate existence as nothing more than an anachronistic phenomenon from the days of protected Jews [*Schutzjudenzeit*]. If such anachronistic feudal phenomena are to be abolished on the one side, they will have to disappear on the other side as well; and on both sides there is still much to be done. The admission into a large nation has its price. The people of Hanover, Hessen and Schleswig-Holstein are prepared to pay the price, and we all feel that they are giving up a part of themselves. But we make this sacrifice to our common fatherland. The Jews, too, will not be led by another Moses into the Promised Land; whether they sell trousers or write books,[9] it is their duty to do away with their particularities wherever they can do so without offending their conscience. They must make up their minds and tear down all barriers between themselves and their German compatriots.

NOTES

1. Theodor Mommsen (1817–1903), German classical scholar and historian. A staunch liberal member of the Prussian and German parliaments and a luminary of Berlin University, Mommsen was active on behalf of Russian Jewry and consistently opposed all antisemitic manifestations. He was the sole Christian to attack Treitschke publicly. Significantly, Mommsen, despite his liberalism, had no sympathy with the Jews' wish to preserve their cultural identity and religious independence and called upon them to abandon their separateness by assimilating in a more thorough fashion.

2. The three sons of Mannus, son of the god Tuisto, son of Earth, from whom, according to ancient legends, the Germans are descended.

3. Cornelius Tacitus (56 C.E.–c. 120 C.E.), Roman orator and historian. His *Germania*, published in 98 C.E., is a valuable source of ethnographical information regarding the origins of the Germans.

4. Jean Louis Armand Quatrefages (1810–1892), French anthropologist who conducted craniological research.

5. Ernst Dohm (1819–1883), German writer and political satirist.

6. Mommsen is apparently referring to Baruch Spinoza. On Spinoza see chapter 2, documents 1 and 2.

7. The reference is to Adolf Stoecker. See document 21 in this chapter.

8. Mommsen first made his assessment of the Jews' historical role in a passage in his *History of Rome* (3 volumes, 1854–1856). Although Mommsen took a

positive attitude here to the Jewish role in furthering the breakdown of parochial boundaries, anti-Semites frequently cited this very passage as confirming that the Jews were an alien cosmopolitan element in European history.

9. The reference is to Treitschke's statement that "our country is invaded year after year by assiduous pants-selling [Jewish] youth from the inexhaustible cradle of Poland, whose children and grandchildren are to be the future rulers of Germany's stock-exchanges and press."

24. OF THE PEOPLE OF ISRAEL (1882)

FRIEDRICH NIETZSCHE[1]

Among the spectacles to which the coming century invites us is the decision as to the destiny of the Jews of Europe. That their die is cast, that they have crossed their Rubicon, is now palpably obvious: all that is left for them is either to become the masters of Europe or to lose Europe as they once a long time ago lost Egypt, where they had placed themselves before a similar either-or. In Europe, however, they have gone through an eighteen-century schooling such as no other nation of this continent can boast of—and what they have experienced in this terrible time of schooling has benefited the individual to a greater degree than it has the community as a whole. As a consequence of this, the psychological and spiritual resources of the Jews today are extraordinary; of all those who live in Europe they are least liable to resort to drink or suicide in order to escape from some profound dilemma—something the less gifted are often apt to do. Every Jew possesses in the history of his fathers and grandfathers a great fund of examples of the coldest self-possession and endurance in fearful

situations, of the subtlest outwitting and exploitation of chance and misfortune; their courage beneath the cloak of miserable submission, their heroism in *spernere se sperni*,[2] surpasses the virtues of all the saints.

For two millennia an attempt was made to render them contemptible by treating them with contempt, and by barring to them the way to all honors and all that was honorable, and in exchange thrusting them all the deeper into the dirtier trades—and it is true that they did not grow cleaner in the process. But contemptible? They themselves have never ceased to believe themselves called to the highest things, and the virtues which pertain to all who suffer have likewise never ceased to adorn them. The way in which they honor their fathers and their children, the rationality of their marriages and marriage customs, distinguish them among all Europeans.

In addition to all this, they have known how to create for themselves a feeling of power and of eternal revenge out of the very occupations left to them (or to which they were left); one has to say

Source: Friedrich Nietzsche, *DayBreak. Thoughts on the Prejudices of Morality*, trans. R. J. Hollingdale (Cambridge, England: Cambridge University Press, 1997), pp. 205–6.

in extenuation even of their usury that without this occasional pleasant and useful torturing of those who despised them it would have been difficult for them to have preserved their own self-respect for so long. For our respect for ourselves is tied to our being able to practice requital, in good things and bad. At the same time, however, their revenge does not easily go too far: for they possess the liberality, including liberality of soul, to which frequent changes of residence, of climate, of the customs of one's neighbors and oppressors educates men; they possess by far the greatest experience of human society, and even in their passions they practice the caution taught by this experience. They are so sure in their intellectual suppleness and shrewdness that they never, even in the worst straits, need to earn their bread by physical labor, as common workmen, porters, agricultural slaves. Their demeanor still reveals that their souls have never known chivalrous noble sentiments nor their bodies handsome armor: a certain importunity mingles with an often charming but always painful submissiveness.

But now, since they are unavoidably going to ally themselves with the best aristocracy of Europe more and more with every year that passes, they will soon have crafted for themselves a goodly inheritance of spiritual and bodily demeanor: so that a century hence they will appear sufficiently noble not to make those they dominate *ashamed* to have them as masters. And that is what matters! That is why it is still too soon for a settlement of their affairs! They themselves know best that a conquest of Europe, or any kind of act of violence, on their part is not to be thought of: but they also know that at some future time Europe may fall into their hands like a ripe fruit if they would only just extend them.

To bring that about they need, in the meantime, to distinguish themselves in every domain of European distinction and to stand everywhere in the first rank: until they have reached the point at which they themselves determine what is distinguishing. Then they will be called the inventors and signposts of the nations of Europe and no longer offend their sensibilities. And whither shall this assembled abundance of grand impressions which for every Jewish family constitutes Jewish history, this abundance of passions, virtues, decisions, renunciations, struggles, victories of every kind—whither shall it stream out if not at last into great men and great works! Then, when the Jews can exhibit as their work such jewels and golden vessels as the European nations of a briefer and less profound experience could not and cannot produce, when Israel will have transformed its eternal vengeance into an eternal blessing for Europe: then there will again arrive the seventh day on which the ancient Jewish God may *rejoice* in himself, his creation and his chosen people—and let us all, all of us, rejoice with him!

NOTES

1. A trenchant critic of what he perceived to be the hypocrisies of liberal democracy, Friedrich Wilhelm Nietzsche (1844–1900) also scornfully dismissed anti-Semitism as befuddled by stereotypes and crass superficiality. The selection presented here is from a work published in 1883, whose subtitle is significantly "thoughts on the prejudices of morality." His reflections on the Jews' contribution to modern European culture and society may be read as a critique of the antisemitic "contemptuous" evaluation of their place in modern economy and the arts. On Nietzsche's more ambivalent views of Judaism (as opposed to Jews), see Yirmiyahu Yovel, *Dark Riddle. Hegel, Nietzsche, and the Jews* (Cambridge, England: Polity Press, 1998), pp. 103–85.

2. Latin: "despise that one is despised," or answer contempt with contempt.

25. THE RACISTS' DECALOGUE (1883)

THEODOR FRITSCH[1]

1. Be proud of being a German and strive earnestly and steadily to practice the inherited virtues of our people, courage, faithfulness and veracity, and to inspire and develop these in thy children.

2. Thou shalt know that thou, together with all thy fellow Germans, regardless of faith or creed, hast a common implacable foe. His name is Jew.

3. Thou shalt keep thy blood pure. Consider it a crime to soil the noble Aryan breed of thy people by mingling it with the Jewish breed. For thou must know that Jewish blood is everlasting, putting the Jewish stamp on body and soul unto the farthest generations.

4. Thou shalt be helpful to thy fellow German and further him in all matters not counter to the German conscience, the more so if he be oppressed by the Jew. Thou shalt at once take into court any offense or crime committed by the Jew in deed, word or letter, that comes to thy knowledge, lest the Jew abuse the laws of our country with impunity.

5. Thou shalt have no social intercourse with the Jew. Avoid all contact and community with the Jew and keep him away from thyself and thy family, especially thy daughters, lest they suffer injury of body and soul.

6. Thou shalt have no business relations with the Jews. Never choose a Jew as a business partner, nor borrow nor buy from him, and keep your wife, too, from doing so. Thou shalt sell nothing to him, nor use him as an agent in thy transactions, that thou mayest remain free and not become slave unto the Jew nor help to increase his money, which is the power by which he enslaves our people.

7. Thou shalt drive the Jew from thy own breast and take no example from Jewish tricks and Jewish wiles, for thou shalt never match the Jew in trickery but forfeit thy honor and earn the contempt of thy fellow Germans and the punishment of the courts.

8. Thou shalt not entrust thy rights to a Jewish lawyer, nor thy body to a Jewish physician, nor thy children to a Jewish teacher lest thy honor, body and soul suffer harm.

9. Thou shalt not lend ear nor give credence to the Jew. Keep away all Jewish writings from thy German home and hearth lest their lingering poison may unnerve and corrupt thyself and thy family.

10. Thou shalt use no violence against the Jews because it is unworthy of thee and against the law. But if a Jew attack thee, ward off his Semitic insolence with German wrath.

NOTE

1. Theodor Fritsch (1852–1933), German antisemitic publicist and politician and one of the leading early racists. In 1883 he founded the Hammer Publishing House, whose first production was the *Antisemiten-Katechismus* from which the "Decalogue" is taken. Later renamed *Handbuch der Judenfrage*, it was published in more than forty editions, inspiring the Nazis, who honored Fritsch as their *Altmeister*.

26. J'ACCUSE (1898)

ÉMILE ZOLA[1]

Monsieur Le Président,[2]

Permit me, in gratitude for the kind reception which you one day gave me, to be anxious for your just glory, and to tell you that your star, so lucky up to now, is threatened with the most shameful, the most indelible of stains.

You have emerged safe and sound from low calumnies, you have conquered hearts. You appear radiant in the apotheosis of that patriotic festival which the Russian Alliance[3] has been for France, and you are preparing to preside at the solemn triumph of our Universal Exhibition,[4] which will crown our grand century of work, truth and liberty. But what a splash of mud has been cast on your name—I had almost said your reign—by this abominable Dreyfus affair! A court-martial has just dared to acquit an Esterhazy,[5] thus giving a last blow to all truth and justice. It is done; France bears the mark on her cheek, and history will write that it was possible under your Presidency for such a social crime to be committed.

Since they have dared, I also will dare. I will speak the truth, for I have promised to speak it, if justice, regularly informed, should not bring it out full and entire. My duty is to speak out; I do not want to be an accomplice. My nights would be haunted by the spectre of an innocent man who far away, suffering the most frightful tortures, for a crime which he has not committed.

And it is to you, Monsieur le Président, that I will cry out this truth with all my strength.... For your honour's sake, I am convinced that you are ignorant of it. And to whom then, shall I denounce the maleficent mob of real culprits, if not to you, the Chief magistrate of the country?

First of all, the truth about the trial and condemnation of Dreyfus.

An ill-omened person conducted everything. This was Colonel du Paty de Clam,[6] then only a Commandant. He is the Dreyfus affair in its entirety, and this will not be known until a legal inquiry has clearly established his acts and his responsibilities. He appears as the most clouded, the most complicated of minds, haunted by romance-like intrigues, taking delight in stories on melodramatic lines, with stolen papers, anonymous letters, meetings in deserted places and mysterious women who at night retail overwhelming proofs. It was he who conceived the plan of dictating the Memorandum to Dreyfus; it was he who thought of studying his face in a room entirely covered with mirrors; it was he who is described by Commandant Forzinetti as going to the cell of the sleeping accused officer with a dark lantern in order to throw on his face a sudden flood of light, so as to surprise him into a confession in the emotion of an abrupt awakening. I need not say that when one seeks he finds. I simply declare that commandant du Paty de Clam, charged with obtaining information on the Dreyfus case, is in the order of dates and responsibilities, the first culprit in the terrible judicial error which has been committed....

Ah! those first proceedings, a nightmare for those who know their true details! Commandant du Paty de Clam arrested Dreyfus, and subjected him to a secret inquiry. He ran to Madame Dreyfus, and terrorized her by telling her that if she spoke her husband was lost.[7] During this time the unhappy man was tearing his flesh, yelling out his innocence. And so the investigation was conducted in fifteenth-century style, in the midst of mystery, with a complication of savage expedients; all this based on a childish charge, on an idiotic memorandum,[8] which was not only a vulgar treason, but which was also the most impudent

Source: Émile Zola, "'J'accuse...!' Lettre au Président de la République," in L'Aurore (January 13, 1898), trans. in Émile Zola, The Dreyfus Case. Four Letters to France, ed. L. F. Austin (London/New York: John Lane, 1898), pp. 25–45.

of swindles, for the famous secrets betrayed were nearly all valueless. If I dwell on this, it is because the nucleus is here, whence will emerge sooner or later the real crime, the frightful miscarriage of justice that is afflicting France....

But here is Dreyfus before the court-martial. Rigidly closed doors are demanded. If a traitor had opened the frontier to the enemy, to lead the German Emperor to Notre Dame, no more stringent measures of silence and of mystery would have been taken. The nation is stupefied, terrible facts are whispered about, monstrous treasons which shock history; and naturally the nation bowed to the storm. There is no punishment severe enough; it will applaud 'public degradation.' It wishes that the guilty man shall remain on his rock of infamy devoured by remorse. Can all these indescribable things be true; these dangerous matters, capable of setting Europe in flames, which had to be buried carefully behind closed doors? No! there is nothing behind them but the romantic imaginations and untruths of Commandant du Paty de Clam. And all this was only done to hide the most absurd of melodramatic stories. To be assured of this it will suffice to study attentively the indictment read before the court-martial.

Ah! the emptiness of this indictment! That a man could have been condemned on this document is a prodigious iniquity. I defy honest men to read it without their hearts bursting with indignation and crying out in revolt when thinking of the undeserved sentence being served out there on the lle du Diable [Devil's Island].[9] Dreyfus knew several languages, a crime; no compromising papers were found in his house, a crime; he sometimes went to the country of his origin,[10] a crime; he was industrious, he was anxious to know everything, a crime; he was not confused, a crime; he was troubled, a crime. And the ingenuousness of the preparation of the document, the formal assertions of emptiness! We had been told of fourteen counts in the indictment: we found only one after all, that of the memorandum; and we even learn that the experts did not agree.[11]...

These, then, Monsieur le Président, are the facts which explain how a judicial error could be committed; and the moral proofs, the affluence of Dreyfus, the absence of motives, his continual cry of innocence, finish in showing him to have been a victim of the extraordinary imagination of Commandant du Paty de Clam, of the religious circles surrounding

him, of the hunt after "dirty Jews," which dishonours our era....

As I have demonstrated; the Dreyfus case was the affair of the War Office, an officer of the staff, denounced by his comrades on the Staff, condemned through the pressure of the Chiefs of the Staff.... How many people do I not know who, in presence of a possible war tremble with anguish, knowing in what hands the national defence is placed! and what a nest of low intrigues, gossip, distruction and this sacred asylum has become, where the fate of the fatherland is decided! We are scared before the terrible light which the Dreyfus affair has just thrown upon it, this human sacrifice of an unfortunate being, of a "dirty Jew"! All this madness and trickery, the silly imaginations, the practices of a base police, the methods of inquisition and tyranny, the good pleasure of some epauletted individuals, placing their heels on the nation, stifling its cry for truth and justice under the false and sacrilegious pretext of reasons of State!

And it is still another crime to be supported by a vile press, to allow oneself to be defended by all the riffraff of Paris, with the result that this riffraff triumphs insolently in the defeat of justice and simple honesty. It is a crime bringing turmoil to France, those who wish her to be generous, and at the head of free and just nations, whilst hatching oneself an impudent plot to impose this miscarriage of justice on the whole world. It is a crime to mislead public opinion, to utilize for a deadly task this opinion which has been perverted until it becomes delirious. It is a crime to poison the minds of the little and the humble, to exasperate the passions of reaction and intolerance, while seeking refuge behind that odious antisemitism of which great liberal France, France of the rights of man, will die, unless she is cured of her disease. It is a crime to exploit patriotism for works of hatred, and, finally, it is a crime to make of the sword a modern God when all human science is labouring for the coming work of truth and justice.

Such is the plain truth, Monsieur le Président; it is terrible, and will remain a blot on your Presidency. I doubt whether you have any power in this matter, whether you are not the prisoner of the Constitution and of your surroundings. But you have nevertheless the duties of a man, of which you will think, and which you will fulfill. Not that I despair in the least of ultimate triumph. I repeat with the most vehement certainty, truth is advancing, and nothing will stop it. It is only today that the affair is commencing, since today the position is clear—on the one hand, the guilty parties who are unwilling that light should penetrate; on the other hand, agents of justice who will give their lives in order that it may shine forth. When truth is shut in underground, its force becomes concentrated; it assumes there such an explosive power that on the day it breaks out it will blow up everything with it. It will be seen whether there has not just been prepared for a later day the most resounding of disasters.

But this letter is long, Monsieur le Président, and it is time to conclude.

I accuse Lieutenant-Colonel du Paty de Clam of having been the diabolical author of the judicial error, unconsciously I am willing to believe, and of having then defended his pernicious work for three years by the most absurd and culpable machinations.

I accuse General Mercier[12] of having rendered himself the accomplice, at least by mental weakness, of one of the greatest iniquities of the century.

I accuse General Billot[13] of having had in his hands certain proofs of the innocence of Dreyfus, and of having suppressed them, of having rendered himself guilty of the crime of treason to humanity and treason to justice as a political expedient, and in order to screen the compromised Staff.

I accuse General de Boisdeffre[14] and General Gonse[15] of having made themselves accomplices of the same crime, the one doubtless through clerical passion, the other, perhaps, from that esprit de corps which makes the War Office the sacred and unassailable holy ark.

I accuse General de Pellieux[16] and Major Ravary[17] of having made a wicked inquiry, I mean by that an inquiry of the most monstrous partiality, of which we have in the report of the latter an imperishable monument of naive audacity.

I accuse the three experts in handwriting, Sieurs Belhomme, Varinard and Couard of having made lying and fraudulent reports, unless a medical inquiry should prove them to be suffering from diseased sight and judgment.

I accuse the War Office of having carried on in the press, particularly in the *Eclair* and the *Echo de Paris*, an abominable campaign in order to mislead public opinion and screen their error.

Lastly, I accuse the first Court-Martial[18] of having violated the law[19] by condemning an accused person on one document that was kept secret, and I accuse the second Court-Martial of having, in obedience to orders, covered this illegality by committing in its turn the judicial crime of knowingly acquitting a guilty person.

In proffering these charges I do not ignore the fact that I am exposing myself to the penalties of Clauses 30 and 31 of the Press Law of July 29, 1881, which punishes libel. And it is voluntarily that I expose myself.

As to the men whom I accuse, I do not know them. I have never seen them. I have no resentment or hatred against them. They are for me merely entities, spirits of social maleficence. And the act which I am taking here is only a radical means of hastening the explosion of truth and justice.

I have but one passion—that of light. This I ask for in the name of humanity, which has suffered so much, and which is entitled to happiness. My passionate protest is but the cry of my soul: Let anyone who dares bring me before a court of law, and let the inquiry be held in broad daylight.

I am waiting.

Receive, Monsieur le Président, the assurance of my profound respect.

NOTES

1. Emile Zola (1840–1902) was an eminent French novelist. Highly acclaimed for his naturalistic depictions of the social distortions of modern urban life, his voice carried great moral authority. At the height of the Dreyfus affair, he published with great fanfare his novel *Paris*, initially in installments in the daily *Le Journal* in 1897 and 1898. One General Legrand-Girade went abroad in October 1897, just as the first installments of Zola's *Paris* began to appear; when he returned to Paris in mid-November, he noted in his diary that since his departure suddenly "a single matter troubles and fascinates everyone, the question of Dreyfus....Is there something rotten in France?" (Eugene Weber, *France: Fin de Siècle* [Cambridge, Mass.: Harvard University Press, 1986], p. 120f).

   In an open letter to the President of the Republic, published under a banner headline—"J'accuse"—on the first page of a leading Parisian newspaper, Zola unflinchingly declared that in the light of the Dreyfus affair something was indeed rotten in France. He charged that the government and army had conspired in a miscarriage of justice against Captain Alfred Dreyfus (1859–1936), an assimilated Jew and a career officer assigned to the General Staff who in 1894 was tried and found guilty of espionage. Zola implied that the trial was manipulated and that the true facts were suppressed. Further, he accused the government and the army of committing "high treason against humanity" by deliberately diverting popular discontent from their own blatant failures to the fabricated crimes of a hapless, insignificant Jew.

Zola's article made a powerful impression: two hundred thousand copies of the issue of the paper carrying the article were sold in Paris alone. As he anticipated, Zola was placed on trial for libel; the trial was duly covered in the press and thus in effect served to heighten even further the public debate regarding the Dreyfus affair. Zola, who was found guilty, died before he was vindicated. For it was only in 1906 that the High Court of Appeals overruled the verdict of 1894 that sent Dreyfus to Devil's Island and cleared all charges against him.

For more than a decade the Dreyfus affair deeply divided France; the defenders of the democratic principles of the Republic—and of Dreyfus's right to a fair trial—were aligned against a coalition of clerical interests, conservative politicians, and antisemites who were bent more on guarding the honor of the military and the country than on ensuring that justice would prevail.

The Dreyfus affair was a watershed in the history of European antisemitism. It led the socialist parties, which had previously tended to equate Jews with capitalism, to view the "Jewish Question" in a more nuanced fashion. In the wake of the Dreyfus affair proletarian antisemitism weakened, as had organized antisemitism in France. Those most profoundly affected by the affair were the Jews themselves. The confidence of Jews in the liberal order was severely shaken. That such an affair could occur in France, the cradle of modern democracy, stunned many. The fact that a public—and not just the riffraff—schooled for over a century in the principles of "liberty, equality and fraternity"—could still contemptuously regard Dreyfus, an utterly assimilated Jew, as an outsider seemed to prove that assimilation was no defense against antisemitism. This was the somber conclusion drawn by Theodor Herzl, who as a reporter for a Viennese newspaper, witnessed the cries—"death to the Jews"—of the French masses, incited by the antisemitic press, that accompanied the ceremonial degrading of Dreyfus following his initial court-martial.

2. François Félix Faure (1841–1899) served as President of the Republic of France from January 1895 until his unexpected death in February 1899. Despite the new evidence regarding the Dreyfus affair, he was determined to regard it as *chose jugeé* (closed case).

3. Soon after taking office, Faure successfully negotiated what was at the time hailed as an historic Franco-Russian Alliance.

4. The reference is to the Paris Exhibition of 1900.

5. Major M. C. Ferdinand Wallsin-Esterhazy (1847–1923) had worked in the French Intelligence Service during the period when Dreyfus was initially accused of espionage on behalf of Germany. In March 1896, the new head of the Intelligence Service, Lieutenant General Georges Picquart discovered evidence that Esterhazy was a German spy and that the *bordereau* (see note 8), incriminating Dreyfus, was actually in his handwriting. When Picquart brought his suspicions to the attention of his superiors, he was summarily transferred to a post in Africa. Before leaving Paris Picquart entrusted his findings to his lawyer, who then passed them on to a left-wing politician, who in turn declared from the floor of the French Senate that Dreyfus was innocent and that Esterhazy was the true culprit. The French government now had no choice but to place Esterhazy on trial, but he was acquitted and Picquart arrested.

6. Marquis du Paty de Clam (1853–1916) was an officer in the Operations Branch of the French War Office at the time when Dreyfus was accused of espionage. It was he who first analyzed the *leitre-bordereau* indicating that a German spy had infiltrated the General Staff and "confirmed" the suspicions that it was written by Captain Dreyfus. He adamantly refused to countenance his colleagues' reservations concerning patent differences between the handwriting of the *bordereau* and that of Dreyfus. Colonel du Paty de Clam personally arrested Dreyfus, and upon doing so he counseled him to commit suicide in light of the "obvious" evidence against him. What this evidence was, he never told Dreyfus; indeed, he even refused to tell him on what grounds he was being arrested. It was also Colonel du Paty de Clam who prepared the army's brief against Dreyfus, and, since the material gathered was inconclusive to say the least, he constructed the brief on forged documents and on statements by Dreyfus twisted out of context. When Picquart presented him with proof that Esterhazy was a German spy and that the *bordereau* incriminating Dreyfus was actually in Esterhazy's handwriting, Colonel du Paty de Clam dismissed out of hand any thought of reopening the Dreyfus case, remarking "so the Jews have been training someone for a year to imitate [Dreyfus'] handwriting" (quoted in Guy Chapman, *The Dreyfus Case* [London: Rupert, Hart-Davis, 1955], p. 124).

7. When Colonel du Paty de Clam searched Dreyfus's home, he is reported to have threatened Dreyfus's wife that her husband would be killed were she to tell anyone that he had been arrested and was to be tried before a court-martial.

8. The memorandum or *lettre-bordereau* was a secret military document, sent by an unnamed French officer to the military attaché of the German embassy in Paris, that fell into the hands of the French Intelligence Service. On the basis of a certain similarity of handwriting, and probably out of anti-Jewish sentiments, suspicion was directed at Dreyfus. See notes 5 and 6.

9. In March 1895 Dreyfus was exiled for life to the remote and forlorn Devil's Island, off the coast of French Guiana in South America.

10. Dreyfus was born in Mulhausen, Upper Alsace, and moved, with his parents to Paris soon after the area was ceded to Germany as a result of the Franco-Prussian War (1870–71).

11. The various experts who examined the memorandum did not agree that it was in Dreyfus's handwriting. See note 8.

12. General Auguste Mercier (1833–1921) was Minister of War at the time of the initial court-martial of Dreyfus.

13. General Jean-Baptiste Billot (1827–1907) was the French Minister of War at the time Picquart (see note 5) unearthed evidence indicating that Esterhazy was a German spy and the author of the memorandum used to incriminate Dreyfus. General Billot refused to lend credence to Picquart's report.

14. General Raoul François Charles le Moutouton de Boisdeffre (1839–1919) was the French Chief of Staff in 1894. When Picquart determined that the memorandum incriminating Dreyfus was actually written by Esterhazy, he presented his findings to General Boisdeffre. The response of the chief of staff was to ask why the Dreyfus file, including the memorandum, had not been burned earlier; he refused to consider the new evidence and sent Picquart to General Gonse.

15. General Charles Arthur Gonse (1839–1917) also refused to consider the new evidence pointing to Dreyfus's innocence. He likewise forbade Picquart to make the evidence public.

16. Brigadier General Georges-Gabriel de Pellieux (1852–1900) was in charge of the inquiry into the allegations that Esterhazy was a spy and the author of the "Dreyfus" memorandum. After only three days, Pellieux submitted a report stating that Esterhazy was innocent and that there was no cause to reopen the case against Dreyfus. When new evidence against Esterhazy was brought to light, Pellieux was ordered to reopen the investigation. Instead of considering the new materials, he devoted most of his efforts to undermining the credibility of Picquart and once again exonerated Esterhazy.

17. When public pressure forced the army to court-martial Esterhazy, Major Ravary was assigned to prepare the prosecutor's brief. In his brief he not only suggested that the evidence against Esterhazy was flimsy but accused Picquart of illegally showing classified documents concerning Esterhazy to his lawyer. The court-martial, which concluded in September 1898, acquitted Esterhazy, and sentenced Picquart to sixty days' imprisonment.

18. In December 1894 Dreyfus was tried *in camera* before a court-martial, and, contrary to legal procedure, the War Ministry placed a file of secret documents (part of which were forgeries) before the court, concealing this fact even from Dreyfus's attōrney.

19. See note 17.

27. THE FOUNDATIONS OF THE NINETEENTH CENTURY (1899)

HOUSTON STEWART CHAMBERLAIN[1]

Out of the midst of the chaos towers, like a sharply defined rock amid the formless ocean, one single people, a numerically insignificant people—the Jews. This one race has established as its guiding principle the purity of the blood; it alone possesses, therefore, a distinct physiognomy and character. If we contemplate the southern and eastern centers of culture in the world-empire in its downfall, and let no sympathies or antipathies pervert our judgment, we must confess that the Jews were at that time the only people deserving respect. We may well apply to them the words of Goethe, "the faith broad, narrow the thought." In comparison with Rome and still more so with Hellas their intellectual horizon appears so narrow, their mental capacities so limited, that we seem to have before us an entirely new type of being; but the narrowness and want of originality in thought are fully counterbalanced by the power of faith, a faith which might be very simply defined as "faith in self." And since this faith in self included faith in a higher being, it did not lack ethical significance. However poor the Jewish "law" may appear, when compared with the religious creations of the various Indo-European peoples, it possessed a unique advantage in the fallen Roman Empire of that time: it was, in fact, a law; a law which men humbly obeyed, and this very obedience was bound to be of great ethical import in a world of such lawlessness. Here, as everywhere, we shall find that the influence of the Jews—for good and for evil—lies in their character, not in their intellectual achievements. Certain historians of the nineteenth century, even men so intellectually pre-eminent as Count Gobineau,[2] have supported the view that Judaism has always had merely a disintegrating influence upon all peoples. I cannot share this conviction. In truth, where the Jews become very numerous in a strange land, they may make it their object to fulfill the promises of their Prophets and with the best will and conscience to "consume the strange peoples"; did they not say of themselves, even in the lifetime of Moses, that they were "like locusts"? However, we must distinguish between Judaism and the Jews and admit that Judaism as an idea is one of the most conservative ideas in the world. The idea of physical race-unity and race-purity, which is the very essence of Judaism, signified the recognition of a fundamental physiological fact of life; wherever we observe life from the hyphomycetes[3] to the noble horse we see the importance of "race"; Judaism made this law of nature sacred. And this is the reason why it triumphantly prevailed at that critical moment in the history of the world, when a rich legacy was waiting in vain for worthy heirs. It did not further, but rather put a stop to, universal disintegration. The Jewish dogma was like a sharp acid which is poured into a liquid which is being decomposed in order to clear it and keep it from further decomposition. Though this acid may not be to the taste of every one, yet it has played so decisive a part in the history of the epoch of culture to which we belong that we ought to be grateful to the giver; instead of being indignant about it, we shall do better to inform ourselves thoroughly concerning the significance of this "entrance of the Jews into the history of the West," an event which in any case exercised inestimable influence upon our whole culture, and which has not yet reached its full growth.

Nothing is so convincing as the consciousness of the possession of race. The man who belongs to a

Source: Houston Stewart Chamberlain, The Foundations of the Nineteenth Century, trans. John Lees (New York: John Kane Co., 1914), vol. 1, pp. 253–54, 269–73, 330–31.

distinct, pure race, never loses the sense of it. The guardian angel of his lineage is ever at his side, supporting him where he loses his foothold, warning him like the Socratic demon where he is in danger of going astray, compelling obedience, and forcing him to undertakings which, deeming them impossible, he would never have dared to attempt. Weak and erring like all that is human, a man of this stamp recognizes himself, as others recognize him, by the sureness of his character, and by the fact that his actions are marked by a certain simple and peculiar greatness, which finds its explanation in his distinctly typical and superpersonal qualities. Race lifts a man above himself: it endows him with extraordinary—I might almost say supernatural—powers, so entirely does it distinguish him from the individual who springs from the chaotic jumble of peoples drawn from all parts of the world. And should this man of pure origin be perchance gifted above his fellows, then the fact of race strengthens and elevates him on every hand, and he becomes a genius towering over the rest of mankind, not because he has been thrown upon the earth like a flaming meteor by a freak of nature, but because he soars heavenward like some strong and stately tree, nourished by thousands and thousands of roots—no solitary individual, but the living sum of untold souls striving for the same goal. He who has eyes to see at once detects race in animals. It shows itself in the whole habit of the beast, and proclaims itself in a hundred peculiarities which defy analysis; nay more, it proves itself by achievements, for its possession invariably leads to something excessive and out of the common—even to that which is exaggerated and not free from bias. Goethe's dictum, "only that which is extravagant makes greatness," is well known. That is the very quality which a thoroughbred race reared from superior materials bestows upon its individual descendants—something "extravagant"—and, indeed, what we learn from every racehorse, every thoroughbred fox-terrier, every Cochin China fowl, is the very lesson which the history of mankind so eloquently teaches us! Is not the Greek in the fullness of his glory an unparalleled example of this "extravagance"? And do we not see this "extravagance" first make its appearance when immigration from the North has ceased, and the various strong breeds of men, isolated on the peninsula once and for all, begin to fuse into a new race, brighter and more brilliant, where, as in Athens, the

racial blood flows from many sources—simpler and more resisting where, as in Lacedaemon,[4] even this mixture of blood had been barred out? Is the race not as it were extinguished, as soon as fate wrests the land from its proud exclusiveness and incorporates it in a greater whole? Does not Rome teach us the same lesson? Has not in this case also a special mixture of blood produced an absolutely new race, similar in qualities and capacities to no later one, endowed with exuberant power? And does not victory in this case effect what disaster did in that, but only much more quickly? Like a cataract the stream of strange blood over-flooded the almost depopulated Rome and at once the Romans ceased to be. Would one small tribe from among all the Semites have become a world-embracing power had it not made "purity of race" its inflexible fundamental law? In days when so much nonsense is talked concerning this question, let Disraeli[5] teach us that the whole significance of Judaism lies in its purity of race, that this alone gives it power and duration, and just as it has outlived the people of antiquity, so, thanks to its knowledge of this law of nature, will it outlive the constantly mingling races of today.

What is the use of detailed scientific investigations as to whether there are distinguishable races? whether race has a worth? how this is possible? and so on. We turn the tables and say: it is evident that there are such races; it is a fact of direct experience that the quality of the race is of vital importance; your province is only to find out the how and the wherefore, not to deny the facts themselves in order to indulge your ignorance.

Direct experience, however, offers us a series of quite different observations on race, all of which may gradually contribute to the extension of our knowledge as well as to its definiteness. In contrast to the new, growing, Anglo-Saxon race, look, for instance, at the Sephardim, the so-called "Spanish Jews"; here we find how a genuine race can by purity keep itself noble for centuries and tens of centuries, but at the same time how very necessary it is to distinguish between the nobly reared portions of a nation and the rest. In England, Holland and Italy there are still genuine Sephardim but very few, since they can scarcely any longer avoid crossing with the Ashkenazim (the so-called "German Jews"). Thus, for example, the Montefiores of the present generation have all without exception married German Jewesses. But every one who has travelled in the East of Europe, where the genuine Sephardim still as far as possible avoid all intercourse with German Jews, for whom they have an almost comical repugnance, will agree with me when I say that it is only when one sees these men and has intercourse with them that one begins to comprehend the significance of Judaism in the history of the world. This is nobility in the fullest sense of the word, genuine nobility of race! Beautiful figures, noble heads, dignity in speech and bearing. The type is Semitic in the same sense as that of certain noble Syrians and Arabs. That out of the midst of such people prophets and psalmists could arise—that I understand at the first glance, which I honestly confess that I had never succeeded in doing when I gazed, however carefully, on the many hundred young Jews—"bochers"[6]—of the Friedrichstrasse in Berlin....

We live today in a "Jewish age"; we may think what we like about the past history of the Jews; their present history actually takes up so much room in our own history that we cannot possibly refuse to notice them. Herder[7] in spite of his outspoken humanism had expressed the opinion that "the Jewish people is and remains in Europe an Asiatic people alien to our part of the world, bound to that old law which it received in a distant climate, and which according to its own confession it cannot do away with." Quite correct. But this alien people, everlastingly alien, because—as Herder well remarks—it is indissolubly bound to an alien law that is hostile to all other peoples—this alien people has become precisely in the course of the nineteenth century a disproportionately important and in many spheres actually dominant constituent of our life. Even a hundred years ago that same witness had sadly to confess that the "ruder nations of Europe" were "willing slaves of Jewish usury"; today he could say the same of by far the greatest part of the civilized world. The possession of money in itself is, however, of least account; our governments, our law, our science, our commerce, our literature, our art... practically all branches of our life have become more or less willing slaves of the Jews, and drag the feudal fetter, if not yet on two, at least on one leg. In the meantime the "alien" element emphasized by Herder has become more and more prominent; a hundred years ago it was rather indistinctly and vaguely felt; now it has asserted and proved itself, and so forced itself on the attention of even the most inattentive. The

Indo-European, moved by ideal motives, opened the gates in friendship: the Jew rushed in like an enemy, stormed all positions and planted the flag of his, to us, alien nature—I will not say on the ruins, but on the breaches of our genuine individuality.

Are we for that reason to revile the Jews? That would be as ignoble as it is unworthy and senseless. The Jews deserve admiration, for they have reacted with absolute consistency according to the logic and truth of their own individuality, and never for a moment have they allowed themselves to forget the sacredness of physical laws because of foolish humanitarian daydreams which they shared only when such a policy was to their advantage. Consider with what mastery they use the law of blood to extend their power: the principal stem remains spotless, not a drop of strange blood comes in: as it stands in the Torah, "A bastard shall not enter into the congregation of the Lord; even to his tenth generation shall he not enter into the congregation of the Lord";[8] in the meantime, however, thousands of side branches are cut off and employed to infect the Indo-Europeans with Jewish blood. If that were to go on for a few centuries, there would be in Europe only one single people of pure race, that of the Jews, all the rest would be a herd of pseudo-Hebraic mestizos, a people beyond all doubt degenerate physically, mentally and morally.

NOTES

1. Houston Stewart Chamberlain (1855–1927), racist antisemitic author. British by birth, he chose to live in Germany after he married a daughter of Richard Wagner. Influenced by the current antisemitic theories of his time, Chamberlain refined the theory of the "Nordic race" as the born leaders of mankind. Chamberlain's *Die Grundlagen des Neuzehnten Jahrhunderts* (1899) became an important guide for the Nazis. He himself was an admirer and friend of Hitler.

2. Joseph Arthur Gobineau (1816–1882), French diplomat, essayist, and author of *Essai sur l'inégalité des races humaines* (1853–55), in which he argued that the various human races are innately unequal in talent, worth and ability to absorb and create culture. Gobineau placed the white race, in particular its "Aryan" branch, at the top of the hierarchy as the sole possessor of the supreme human values. Gobineau did not, however, associate the Aryans with any particular nation, nor was he an antisemite.

3. A group of simple fungi.

4. Sparta.

5. See this chapter, document 15, note 7.

6. Friedrichstrasse is a boulevard abutting what before the Shoah was a neighborhood with a large population of recent Jewish immigrants from East Europe, many of

whom were traditional. Hence, Chamberlain's snide references to "bochers," which is Yiddish for *yeshivah* students.

7. Johann Gottfried Herder (1744–1803), German philosopher and critic.

8. Deut. 23:2.

28. THE RABBI'S SPEECH: THE PROMISE OF WORLD DOMINATION (1872)[1]

HERMANN GOEDSCHE

Our fathers have bequeathed to the elect of Israel the duty of gathering together once each century around the tomb of the Grand Master Caleb, the holy rabbi Simeon ben Jehuda, whose knowledge gives the elect of each generation power over all the earth and authority over all the descendants of Israel.

For eighteen centuries Israel has been at war with that power which was first promised to Abraham but which was taken from him by the Cross. Trampled underfoot, humiliated by its enemies, living ceaselessly under the threat of death, of persecution, of rape, and of every kind of violation, the people of Israel has not succumbed; and if it is dispersed over the whole earth, that is because it is to inherit the whole earth.

For eighteen centuries our wise men have been fighting the Cross courageously and with a perseverance which nothing can discourage. Gradually our people is rising up and its power increases day by day. Ours is that God of today whom Aaron raised up for us in the desert, that Golden Calf, that universal deity of the age.

The day when we shall have made ourselves the sole possessors of all the gold in the world, the real

power will be in our hands, and then the promises which were made to Abraham will be fulfilled.

Gold, the greatest power on earth...gold, which is the strength, the recompense, the instrument of every power...the sum of everything that man fears and craves...there is the only mystery, the deepest understanding of the spirit that rules the world. There is the future!

Eighteen centuries belonged to our enemies; the present century and future centuries must belong to us, the people of Israel, and they surely will belong to us.

Now for the tenth time, in a thousand years of terrible and ceaseless war against our enemies, the elect of a given generation of the people of Israel are gathered in this cemetery, around the tomb of our Grand Master Caleb, the holy rabbi Simeon ben Jehuda, to take counsel as to how to turn to the advantage of our cause the great errors and sins which our enemies the Christians never cease to commit.

Each time the new Sanhedrin has proclaimed and preached a merciless struggle against the enemies; but in no earlier century were our ancestors able to concentrate in our hands so much gold, and therefore so

---

Source: Norman Cohn, *Warrant for Genocide: The Myth of the Jewish World Conspiracy and the Protocols of the Elders of Zion* (London: Eyre and Spottiswoode, 1967). Reprinted by permission of Peters Fraser and Dunlop Group Ltd.

much power, as the nineteenth century has bestowed on us. We can therefore expect, without any rash illusions, to achieve our aim soon, and we can look with confidence to our future.

Most fortunately, the persecution and the humiliations, those dark and painful days which the people of Israel endured with such heroic patience, are no more with us, thanks to the progress of civilization among the Christians, and that progress is the best shield for us to hide and act behind, so as to cross with firm and rapid strides the space that separates us from our supreme objective.

Let us just look at the material condition of Europe, let us analyse the resources which the Jews have got into their possession since the beginning of the present century simply by concentrating in their hands the huge amount of capital which they control at this moment. Thus, in Paris, London, Vienna, Berlin, Amsterdam, Hamburg, Rome, Naples, etc., and in all the Rothschild branches, everywhere the Jews are the financial masters, simply by possession of so many billions; not to mention that in every town of second or third magnitude it is the Jews who control the currency in circulation, and that nowhere can any financial operation, any major undertaking be carried through without the direct influence of the children of Israel.

Today all reigning emperors, kings, and princes are burdened with debts contracted in keeping up large standing armies to support their toppling thrones. The stock exchange assesses and regulates those debts, and to a great extent we are masters of the stock exchange everywhere. We must therefore study how to encourage borrowing more and more, so as to make ourselves the regulators of all values and, as security for the capital we lend to countries, take the right to exploit their railways, their mines, their forests, their great ironworks and factories, and other kinds of real estate, even their taxes.

In every country agriculture will always be the greatest source of wealth. The possession of large landed property will always bring honours and much influence to the owners. From this it follows that we must concentrate on ensuring that our Jewish brothers acquire landed property on a large scale. So far as possible we must therefore encourage the splitting-up of large estates, so as to help us acquire it more quickly and more easily.

Under the pretext of helping the working classes, we must place the weight of taxation on the great landed proprietors, and when all properties have come into our hands, all the work of the Gentile proletarians will become a source of huge profits for us.

Since the Christian Church is one of our most dangerous enemies, we must work doggedly to diminish its influence; so far as possible; therefore, we must implant in the minds of those who profess the Christian religion the ideas of free thought, of scepticism, of schism, and provoke the religious disputes which are so naturally productive of divisions and sects within Christendom.

Logically, we must begin by disparaging the ministers of that religion. Let us declare open war on them, let us rouse suspicions about their piety, about their private conduct. So, by ridicule and malicious banter, we shall undermine the respect in which the profession and the cloth are held.

Each war, each revolution, each political or religious upheaval brings nearer the moment when we shall attain the supreme aim of our journey.

Trade and speculation, two branches so fertile in profits, must never leave Jewish hands, and once we have become proprietors we shall be able, thanks to the obsequiousness and the shrewdness of our agents, to penetrate to the first source of real influence and real power. It is understood that we are concerned only with those occupations which bring honours, power, or privileges, for those which demand knowledge, work, and inconvenience can and must be left to the Gentiles. The magistrature is for us an institution of the first importance. A career at the bar does most to develop the faculty of civilization and to initiate one into the affairs of our natural enemies, the Christians, and it is in this way that we can get them at our mercy. Why should Jews not become ministers of Education, when they have so often had the portfolio of Finance? Jews must also aspire to the rank of legislators, so that they can work to abrogate the laws which those sinners and infidels, the *goyim*, have made against the children of Israel, who by their unvarying devotion to the laws of Abraham are the truly faithful. But what must be obtained, what must be the object of our ceaseless efforts, is that the law against bankruptcy should be made less severe. Out of that we shall make ourselves a mine of gold which will be far richer than the mines of California ever were.

The people of Israel must direct its ambition towards that height of power which brings esteem and honours. The surest means of attaining it is to have supreme control over all industrial, financial, and commercial operations, while carefully avoiding every trap and temptation which might expose one to legal proceedings in the country's courts. In its choice of speculation the children of Israel will therefore display the prudence and tact which are the mark of its congenital talent for business.

We must be familiar with everything that earns one a distinguished position in society: philosophy, medicine, law, political economy. In a word all the branches of science, of art, of literature, are a vast field where our successes must give us a big part and show off our talent.

These vocations are inseparable from speculation. Thus the performance even of a very mediocre musical composition will give our people a plausible excuse to put the Jewish composer on a pedestal and surround him with a radiance of glory. As for the sciences, medicine and philosophy, they too must be incorporated into our intellectual domain.

A doctor is initiated into the most intimate secrets of the family. The health and life of our mortal enemies, the Christians, are in his hands.

We must encourage marriages between Jews and Christians, for the people of Israel loses nothing by the contact and can only gain from these marriages. Our race, chosen by God, cannot be corrupted by the introduction of a certain amount of impure blood, and by these marriages our daughters will secure alliances with Christian families of some influence and power. It is right that, in exchange for the money we give, we should obtain the equivalent in influence over everything around us. To be related to Gentiles does not imply a departure from the path we have chosen to follow; on the contrary, with a little skill it will make us the arbiters of their fate.

It is desirable that Jews should refrain from taking women of our holy religion as their mistresses and that they should choose Christian virgins for that role. It would be a great gain for us to replace the sacrament of marriage in church by a simple contract before some civil authority, for then Gentile women would stream into our camp!

If gold is the first power in this world, the second is undeniably the press. But what can the second achieve without the first? As the aims listed above cannot be attained without the help of the press, our people must become the editors of all daily newspapers in all countries. Our possession of gold, our skill in devising means of exploiting mercenary instincts, will make us the arbiters of public opinion and enable us to dominate the masses.

So advancing step by step in this path, with that perseverance which is our great virtue, we will push the Gentiles back and undo their influence. We shall dictate to the world what it is to have faith, what it is to honour, and what it is to curse. Perhaps some individuals will rise up against us and will hurl insults and anathemas against us, but the docile and ignorant masses will listen to us and take our side. Once we are absolute masters of the press we will be able to transform ideas about honour, about virtue, about uprightness of character; we will be able to deal a blow against that institution which so far has been sacrosanct, the family, and we shall extirpate all belief and faith in everything that our enemies the Christians have venerated up to the present and, using the allurements of the passions as our weapon, we shall declare open war on everything that people respect and venerate.

Let all this be understood and noted, let every child of Israel absorb these true principles. Then our might will grow like a gigantic tree whose branches will bear the fruits called wealth, enjoyment, power, as compensation for that hideous condition which for long centuries has been the only lot of the people of Israel. When one of our people takes a step forward, let another follow him closely; if his foot slips, let him be picked up and succoured by his co-religionists. If a Jew is summoned before the courts of the country where he lives, let his brothers in religion hasten to give him aid and assistance; but only if the accused has acted in accordance with the Law of Israel, so strictly observed and kept for so many centuries!

Our people is conservative, faithful to the religious ceremonies and the customs bequeathed to us by our ancestors.

It is in our interest that we should at least make a show of zeal for the social questions of the moment, especially for improving the lot of the workers, but in reality our efforts must be geared to getting control of this movement of public opinion and directing it.

The blindness of the masses, their readiness to surrender to that resounding but empty eloquence that fills the public squares, make them an easy prey and a double instrument, of popularity and of credit.

We will have no difficulty in finding as much eloquence among our people for the expression of false sentiments as Christians find in their sincerity and enthusiasm.

So far as possible we must talk to the proletariat, bring it into subjection to those who have the control of money. By this means we will be able to make the masses rise when we wish. We will drive them to upheavals, to revolutions; and each of these catastrophes marks a big step forward for our particular interests and brings us rapidly nearer to our sole aim—world domination as was promised to our father Abraham.

NOTE

1. "The Rabbi's Speech" is from a novel *Biarritz* (1868) by Hermann Goedsche (1816–1878), published under the pseudonym of Sir John Retcliffe. In a chapter entitled "In the Jewish Cemetery in Prague," Goedsche purports to describe a secret nocturnal meeting among thirteen Jews (representing the twelve tribes of Israel and the Jews of the Exile) who report on their activities during the century that has elapsed since their last meeting and who vow to have conquered all of their enemies by the time of the next meeting. This frankly fictional episode was soon treated as an authentic record, appearing as a pamphlet first in Russia (1872) and later in Paris and Prague. In 1887 Theodor Fritsch published the "Speech" together with his "Decalogue" (see document 25 in this chapter), and it received a wide circulation in a number of antisemitic publications, enjoying its greatest vogue in post-World War I Germany. The "Speech" was constantly invoked as proof of the authenticity of the *Protocols of the Elders of Zion* (see the following document).

29. PROTOCOLS OF THE ELDERS OF ZION (c. 1902)[1]

Protocol Number 1: Let us put aside phraseology and discuss the inner meaning of every thought; by comparisons and deductions let us illuminate the situation. In this way I will describe our system, both from our own point of view and from that of the *Goys.*...

Political freedom is not a fact but an idea. One must know how to employ this idea when it becomes necessary to attract popular forces to one's party by mental allurement if it plans to crush the party in power. The task is made easier if the opponent himself has contradicted the idea of freedom, by embracing liberalism, and thereby yielding his power. It is precisely here that the triumph of our theory becomes apparent; the relinquished reins of power are, according to the laws of nature, immediately seized by a new hand because the blind force of the people cannot remain without a leader even for one day, and the new power merely replaces the old, weakened by liberalism.

In our day the *power* of *gold* has replaced liberal rulers. There was a time when faith ruled. The idea of freedom cannot be realized because no one knows how to make reasonable use of it. Give the people self-government for a short time and it will become corrupted. From that very moment strife begins and soon develops into social struggles, as a result of which states are set aflame and their authority is reduced to ashes.

Whether the state is exhausted by internal convulsions, or whether civil wars deliver it into the hands

Source: Protocols of the Meetings of the Zionist Men of Wisdom, translator not indicated (Boston: Small, Maynard & Co., 1920), pp. 11–22.

Russian Secret Police / Ford pays to publish

of external enemies, in either case it can be regarded as hopelessly lost: it is in our power. The despotism of capital, which is entirely in our hands, holds out to it a straw which the state must grasp, although against its will, or otherwise fall into the abyss....

Politics have nothing in common with morals. The ruler guided by morality is not a skilled politician, and consequently he is not firm on his throne. He who desires to rule must resort to cunning and hypocrisy. The great popular qualities—honesty and frankness—become vices in politics, as they dethrone more surely and more certainly than the most powerful enemy. These qualities must be the attributes of *Goy* countries; but we by no means should be guided by them.

Our right lies in might. The word right is an abstract idea, unsusceptible of proof. This word means nothing more than: Give me what I desire so that I may have evidence that I am stronger than you.

Where does right begin? Where does it end?... In laying our plans we must turn our attention not so much to the good and moral as to the necessary and useful. Before us lies a plan in which a strategic line is shown, from which we must not deviate on pain of risking the collapse of many centuries of work.

In working out an expedient plan of action it is necessary to take into consideration the meanness, vacillation, changeability of the mob, its inability to appreciate and respect the conditions of its own existence and of its own well-being. It is necessary to realize that the power of the masses is blind, unreasoning, and void of discrimination, prone to listen to right and left. The blind man cannot guide the blind without bringing them to the abyss; consequently, members of the crowd, upstarts from the people, even were they men of genius but incompetent in politics, cannot step forward as leaders of the mob without ruining the entire nation.... Our motto is Power and Hypocrisy. Only power can conquer in politics, especially if it is concealed in talents which are necessary to statesmen. Violence must be the principle; hypocrisy and cunning the rule of those governments which do not wish to lay down their crowns at the feet of the agents of some new power. This evil is the sole means of attaining the good. For this reason we must not hesitate at bribery, fraud and treason when these can help us to reach our end. In politics it is necessary to seize the property of others without hesitation if in so doing we attain submission and power.

Our government, following the line of peaceful conquest, has the right to substitute for the horrors of war less noticeable and more efficient executions, these being necessary to keep up terror, which induces blind submission. A just but inexorable strictness is the greatest factor of governmental power. We must follow a program of violence and hypocrisy, not only for the sake of profit but also as a duty and for the sake of victory.

A doctrine based on calculation is as potent as the means employed by it. That is why not only by these very means, but by the severity of our doctrines, we shall triumph and shall enslave all governments under our super-government.

Even in olden times we shouted among the people the words *Liberty, Equality and Fraternity*. These words have been repeated so many times since by unconscious parrots, which, flocking from all sides to the bait, have ruined the prosperity of the world and true individual freedom, formerly so well protected from the pressure of the mob. The would-be clever and intelligent *Goys* did not discern the symbolism of the uttered words; did not notice the contradiction in the meaning and the connection between them; did not notice that there is no equality in nature; that there can be no liberty, since nature herself has established inequality of mind, character, and ability, as well as subjection to her laws. They did not reason that the power of the mob is blind; that the upstarts selected for government are just as blind in politics as is the mob itself, whereas the initiated man, even though a fool, is capable of ruling, while the uninitiated, although a genius, will understand nothing of politics. All this has been overlooked by the *Goys*....

In all parts of the world the words Liberty, Equality and Fraternity have brought whole legions into our ranks through our blind agents, carrying our banners with delight. Meanwhile these words were worms which ruined the prosperity of the *Goys*, everywhere destroying peace, quiet and solidarity, undermining all the foundations of their states. You will see subsequently that this aided our triumph, *for it also gave us, among other things, the opportunity to grasp the trump card, the abolition of privileges; in other words, the very essence of the aristocracy of the Goys, which was the only protection of peoples and countries against us.*

On the ruins of natural and hereditary aristocracy we have established this new aristocracy on the qualification of wealth, which is dependent upon us, and also upon science which is promoted by our wise men....

Protocol Number 2: It is necessary for us that wars, whenever possible, should bring no territorial advantages; this will shift war to an economic basis and force nations to realize the strength of our predominance; such a situation will put both sides at the mercy of our million-eyed international agency, which will be unhampered by any frontiers. Then our international rights will do away with national rights, in a limited sense, and will rule the peoples in the same way as the civil power of each state regulates the relation of its subjects among themselves.

The administrators chosen by us from among the people in accordance with their capacity for servility will not be experienced in the art of government, and consequently they will easily become pawns in our game, in the hands of our scientists and wise counselors, specialists trained from early childhood for governing the world. As you are aware, these specialists have obtained the knowledge necessary for government from our political plans, from the study of history, and from the observation of every passing event. The *Goys* are not guided by the practice of impartial historical observation, but by theoretical routine without any critical regard for its results. Therefore, we need give them no consideration. Until the time comes let them amuse themselves, or live in the hope of new amusements or in the memories of those past. Let that play the most important part for them which we have induced them to regard as the laws of science (theory). For this purpose, by means of our press, we increase their blind faith in these laws. Intelligent *Goys* will boast of their knowledge, and verifying it logically they will put into practice all scientific information compiled by our agents for the purpose of educating their minds in the direction which we require.

Do not think that our assertions are without foundation: note the successes of Darwinism, Marxism and Nietzscheism, engineered by us. The demoralizing effects of these doctrines upon the minds of the *Goys* should be already obvious to us....

There is one great force in the hands of modern states which arouses thought movements among the people. That is the press. The role of the press is to indicate necessary demands, to register complaints of the people, and to express and foment dissatisfaction. The triumph of free babbling is incarnated in the press, but governments were unable to profit by this power and it has fallen into our hands. Through it we have attained influence, while remaining in the background. Thanks to the press, we have gathered gold in our hands, although we had to take it from rivers of blood and tears.

But it cost us the sacrifice of many of our own people. Every sacrifice on our part is worth a thousand *Goys* before God.

Protocol Number 3: To-day I can tell you that our goal is close at hand. Only a small distance remains, and the cycle of the Symbolic Serpent—the symbol of our people—will be complete. When this circle is completed, then all the European states will be enclosed in it as in strong claws....

To induce the lovers of authority to abuse their power, we have placed all the forces in opposition to each other, having developed their liberal tendencies towards independence. We have excited different forms of initiative in that direction; we have armed all the parties; we have made authority the target of all ambitions. We have opened the arenas in different states, where revolts are now occurring, *and disorders and bankruptcy will shortly appear everywhere.*

Unrestrained babbles have converted parliamentary sessions and administrative meetings into oratorical contests. Daring journalists, impudent pamphleteers, make daily attacks on the administrative personnel. The abuse of power is definitely preparing the downfall of all institutions and everything will be overturned by the blows of the infuriated mobs.

The people are shackled by poverty to heavy labor more surely than they were by slavery and serfdom. They could liberate themselves from those in one way or another, whereas they cannot free themselves from misery. We have included in constitutions rights which for the people are fictitious and are not actual rights. All the so-called rights of the people can exist only in the abstract and can never be realized in practice. What difference does it make to the toiling proletarian, bent double by heavy toil, oppressed by his fate, that the babblers receive the right to talk, journalists the right to mix nonsense with reason in their writings, if the proletariat has no other gain from the constitution than the miserable crumbs which we throw from our table in return for his vote to elect our agents? Republican rights are bitter irony to the poor man, for the necessity of almost daily labor prevents him from using them, and at the same time deprives him of his guarantee of a permanent and certain livelihood by making him dependent upon strikes, organized either by his masters or by his comrades.

Under our guidance the people have exterminated aristocracy, which was their natural protector and guardian, for its own interests are inseparably connected with the well-being of the people. Now, however, with the destruction of this aristocracy the masses have fallen under the power of the profiteers and cunning upstarts, who have settled on the workers as a merciless burden.

We will present ourselves in the guise of saviors of the workers from this oppression when we suggest that they enter our army of Socialists, Anarchists, Communists, to whom we always extend our help, under the guise of the rule of brotherhood demanded by the human solidarity of our *social masonry*. The aristocracy which benefited by the labor of the people by right was interested that the workers should be well-fed, healthy, and strong.

We, on the contrary, are concerned in the opposite—in the degeneration of the *Goys*. Our power lies in the chronic malnutrition and in the weakness of the worker, because through this he falls under our power and is unable to find either strength or energy to combat it.

Hunger gives to capital greater power over the worker than the legal authority of the sovereign ever gave to the aristocracy. Through misery and the resulting jealous hatred we manipulate the mob and crush those who stand in our way....This hatred will be still more accentuated by the *economic crisis*, which will stop financial transactions and all industrial life. Having organized a general economic crisis by all possible underhanded means, and with the help of gold which is all in our hands, we will throw great crowds of workmen into the street, simultaneously, in all countries of Europe. These crowds will gladly shed the blood of those of whom they, in the simplicity of their ignorance, have been jealous since childhood and whose property they will then be able to loot.

They will not harm our people because we will know of the time of the attack and we will take measures to protect them....

Remember the French Revolution, which we have called "great"; the secrets of its preparation were well known to us, for it was the work of our hands. Since then we have carried the masses from one disappointment to another, so that they will renounce even us in favor of *a despot sovereign of Zionist blood, whom we are preparing for the world....*

NOTE

1. The *protocols* of secret meetings of an international conference of "the learned elders of Zion" is an anti-semitic literary hoax aimed at showing the existence of an international Jewish conspiracy bent on world dominance. As part of this plot the Jews are said to be behind all the egregious forces of modernity: liberalism, parliamentary democracy, finance capitalism, Marxism, anarchism, the press. The term *elders of Zion* is apparently an allusion to the First Zionist Congress, which was held at the time the *Protocols* were written. The *Protocols* were almost certainly concocted in Paris in the last decade of the nineteenth century by an unknown author working for the Russian secret police; in all probability this volume was intended to influence the policy of Czar Nicholas II toward the interests of the secret police. For his purposes the anonymous author adapted a political satire written in 1864 by Maurice Joly (d. 1879). It is ironic that Joly's work—which has nothing to do with the Jews and which seeks to illuminate the tensions of modern society that led to the authoritarian regime of Napoleon III—is a defense of liberalism. Although first published in Russia at the beginning of the twentieth century, the *Protocols* enjoyed wide readership only when they were translated into numerous languages after World War I. In the United States they were distributed principally by Henry Ford under the title *The Jewish Peril*. See chapter 9, document 46.

30. AN EXPERT OPINION IN SUPPORT OF THE RITUAL BLOOD ACCUSATION (1911)

IVAN ALEXEYEVITCH SIKORSKY[1]

May 8th, 1911

PROTOCOL

V. J. FENENKO, Examining Magistrate of the Kiev District for specially important cases, has interrogated at his chambers, with due observance of Art. 443 of the Statute of Criminal Procedure, the person mentioned below in the capacity of an Expert, who deposed as follows:

———————

My name is IVAN ALEXEYEVITCH SIKORSKY, Professor Emeritus of the St. Vladimir University, 68 years of age, Orthodox [i.e., a member of the Eastern Orthodox Church]. I never incurred any penalty, and reside at 15, Yaroslava Wall, Kiev.

In answer to the following questions you have laid before me, Mr. Examining Magistrate:

1. Whether the murder of Yustschinsky[2] had not been committed by a mentally diseased person.
2. Whether the post-mortem examination of Yustschinsky does not show any indications tending to point to the way the murder was executed, as well to the aims and intentions which animated the murderer or murderers.
3. Whether the facts of the case do not supply any indication as to whether the murderers belonged to a certain people, trade and so forth.

After having fully familiarized myself with all the details of the case, and after having examined all the material proofs available in the case, I am able to give the following expert opinion:...

On the strength of psychological considerations, it is also plausible to explain some peculiarities of the technique of the crime. All the lesions and injuries were carried out with a sure and steady hand which did not tremble with fear, nor exaggerate the range and force of the movements, under any influence of anger. It was a precise, heartless, cool piece of work executed, perhaps, by a person in the habit of slaughtering animals. This calm of the murderer or murderers points likewise to the slowness and absence of hurry while at work, which condition had probably been secured by suitable premises, and by a watch having been kept by the accomplices.

To the third question I can give the following answer:

As in the case direct facts pointing to the nationality of the murderers are wanting, one has to confine himself to considerations of an historical and anthropological character, and before everything else, to answer the questions to whether a crime like the assassination of Yustschinsky ought to be regarded as a mere accident, or, on the contrary, as a criminal anthropological type, manifesting itself in different degrees in particular cases. It is imperative to recognize the latter alternative as true, i.e., it must be assumed that murders committed in the same way as that of Yustschinsky recur from time to time in Russia, as well as in other countries that rank high in civilization. The assassination of Yustschinsky appears as a most typical and absolutely complete case, in which three main features, viz., the slow bleeding, the torturing and the subsequent killing of the victim, are distinctly stamped in this case in their full scope and in regular order. In this typical crime the last act, i.e., the killing, only takes place after the victim has been made use of for the two previous acts. An accidental contingency is out of the

———————

Source: "Professor Ivan Alexeyevitch Sikorsky's Expert Opinion in Support of the Ritual Blood Accusation," (Kiev, 1911). Official protocol translated and published apparently by tsarist authorities. Pamphlet in Rosenberger Collection, Regenstein Library, The University of Chicago, file 450 D/5.

question for this crime. Indeed, even such an exact criminological expert as Prof. Hessen,[3] in describing the Velij murder,[4] says: "I am inclined to believe that he was killed 'accidentally'," underlining the word "accidentally." Evidently Hessen would only *like* to believe in an accident. Many other cases of those described exclude the idea of an accident, and confirm, on the contrary, the assumption of intention, and of the typical character of such cases, as it was also quite definitely expressed thus by the surgeon who had performed the judicial postmortem on the boy of Velij: "The boy has been deliberately tortured to death." There is no room for doubts either in the Velij case, or in that of Kiev as to the peculiar kind and the characteristics of the dastardly deed. This criminal anthropological phenomenon must be recognized as an undisputed fact that occurs from time to time in one country or another. One must admit, with the anthropological criminologists, that the psychological basis of crimes of that type is sought in racial revenge or—to use the expression of the well-known opponent of antisemitism, Leroy Beaulieu[5]—in the "Vendetta of the Sons of Jacob." The typical similarity of this vendetta, and of its manifestations in all countries, may be accounted for by the fact that the nationality which produces this crime is interspersed among other nationalities, where it carries with it the traits of racial psychology. It must be admitted in addition to the above that the killing of Yustschinsky as well as the similar murders cannot be explained entirely from the point of view of racial vindictiveness, which only accounts to some extent for the torturing and killing of members of a different race, while it fails to explain the reason why the attempts are directed against infants and juveniles, as well as the evacuating of the blood of the doomed victim. This peculiarity, no doubt, requires other explanations and a special expert investigation, all the more so, as the dastardly murders of children bear the character of a malignant tradition which evidently does not show any tendency to disappear. A careful scientific expert investigation is also required for clearing up the circumstance why Yustschinsky, who was stripped up to the shirt, had a cap put on with the peak to the back, and all the wounds on the head were inflicted across that cap. Seeing that the cap placed on the head could only have rendered more difficult the operation of torturing and evacuating the blood, the question arises, whether these circumstances did not possess some religious or other significance for the assassins.

It transpires from historical instances that in cases in which the perpetrators of the killing were of the Jewish race, and professed the Jewish religion, they put on a garment used for worship for the occasion (Saratov Trial of 1852).[6]

NOTES

1. Ivan Alexeyevitch Sikorsky (1853–1919) was a psychiatrist and professor emeritus of the University of Kiev (St. Vladimir University). He was one of the state's expert witness at the Beilis Trial (cf. chapter 7, document 28.) His opinion on the psychiatric and psychological aspects of the case were introduced as part of the state prosecutor's indictment against Beilis. Professor Sikorsky's reputation as a rabid antisemite as much as his professional stature seems to have recommended him to the prosecutor. Indicatively, the prosecutor allowed Professor Sikorsky to digress and venture "expert" opinion on the allegedly depraved folklore, racial characteristics and demonology of the Jews as well as the history of the Jewish ritual murder. Further, Professor Sikorsky undertook to demonstrate that it was due to Jewish machinations that every case against Jews for this heinous crime had been hitherto dismissed.

   Despite the presiding judge's assurances that it was only Beilis who was on trial and not Judaism—"nobody here accuses Judaism, we are talking of individual fanatics only"—it was manifest that the prosecution was eager to condemn Judaism and the Jewish people.

   The testimony of Professor Sikorsky was of course meant to lend a dimension of scientific credibility to the accusation against the Jew Beilis—and by implication the Jewish people and their religious faith—that he tortured and then murdered a Christian child in order to use his blood for some sinister Passover ritual. The professorial endorsement of the blood libel indicates that it cannot simply be dismissed as a relic of the Middle Ages. Indeed, the nineteenth-century witnessed an increase in the number of blood accusations against Jews, with more than forty such cases throughout Europe. (A list is provided in *The Jewish Encyclopedia*, 2nd edition, 3:777f.) With the growth of the antisemitic movement in Russia in the 1870s, the blood libel (accusation of ritual murder) became a regular motif of the campaign against the allegedly sinister influence of Jewry in contemporary society. Significantly, in many of the trials, both in Russia and elsewhere in Europe, "experts" were called upon to prove that the Jews indeed engaged in such dastardly practices.

The persistence of the medieval canard—the first distinct case of blood libel against the Jews in the Middle Ages was in Norwich, England, in 1144—into the modern era can ultimately be explained by its adaptation by modern political antisemites as a weapon to humiliate the Jews—by pointing to their incorrigible moral depravity—and to incite the uneducated masses against the Jews.

2. Andre Yustschinsky was the twelve-year-old Gentile boy who was allegedly murdered by Beilis in order to use his blood for the Passover ritual. See chapter 7, document 28, for further details.

3. Julius Isidorvich Hessen (1871–1940?) was a historian of Russian Jewry. Active in the struggle for Jewish civil rights in Russia, he saw his scholarship as contributing to that cause. Sikorsky is apparently referring to Hessen's *Is Istorii Ritualnych Protsessov. Velizhskaya Drama* [From the Stories of Ritual Murder Trials. The Velizh Drama] (St. Petersburg, 1905).

4. The reference is to the ritual blood accusation in Velij (Velizh, a city in Belorussia). Toward the end of April 1823 the three-year-old son of a Russian soldier disappeared, and his mutilated body was found in a swamp some days later. Two notables of the local Jewish community were accused of killing the child for the Passover ritual. The subsequent trial exonerated the accused. A group of antisemites prevailed upon Tsar Alexander I to reopen the trial on the suspicion that the Jews had indeed practiced rituals requiring the blood of a Christian. (Alexander thus ignored his earlier edict of 1817 condemning the blood libel as "ancient" prejudice and, accordingly, inadmissable as *prima facie* evidence against Jews accused of murder.) The second trial, which focused as much on the allegedly sinister ritual practices of the Jews as on the actual guilt of the accused, lasted more than ten years and reached the highest tribunal of the land; more than forty Jews of Velizh were arrested as suspected participants in the blood ritual, and all the synagogues of the city were closed for the duration of the trial. Despite the ultimate exoneration in January 1835 of the accused Jews, the protracted trial of Velizh contributed greatly to reviving the ritual murder libel among the Russian masses.

5. Anatole de Leroy-Beaulieu (1842–1912) was a historian who wrote extensively on antisemitism, which he repudiated as a baseless prejudice and insidious doctrine of hatred. A descendant of an old French Catholic family, Leroy-Beaulieu was inspired by his religious faith to fight for individual freedom, regarding it as his principal duty as a scholar to defend the liberty of thought. Among his many activities in behalf of the Jews, stirred by a renewed outbreak of persecutions against the Jews in Russia, he founded in 1894 the "Comité de defense du Progres social." His religious sentiments as well as his intellectual convictions made him one of the great opponents of antisemitism in the nineteenth century.

6. In 1853 in Saratov two Jews and an apostate were found guilty of the murder of two Christian children. Although the Jews were also accused of draining the blood of these children for a secret Jewish ritual, the trial silently ignored this accusation. Thus the prosecutors cleverly avoided a test of the blood libel while allowing it to color the general perception of the Jews' crime.

VII

EAST EUROPEAN JEWRY

Modern East European Jewish history began with the partitions of Poland in 1772, 1793, and 1795; with the incorporation of large numbers of Jews into tsarist Russia; and with the incorporation of a smaller, but not insignificant, number into the Austro-Hungarian Empire, particularly in the province of Galicia. Before the partitions of Poland the tsars had sought to keep the Jews out of Russia, but suddenly millions of Jews were within the borders of the empire. Rather than expelling the Jews, the tsars adopted a three-fold policy which restricted them to certain areas, the so-called Pale of Settlement; the intent was to promote their economic utility and to foster their Russification. Until the February Revolution of 1917 this policy, with various alterations, determined the fate of Jews in the Russian Empire. The tsars attempted to undermine the Jews' traditional way of life, to restructure their communal and social patterns, to direct them into useful "non-Jewish" occupations, and to encourage their assimilation. The execution of this policy alternated between enlightened tact and uninhibited ruthlessness.

Slowly the Jewish community began to crumble, witnessed by the breakdown of traditional leadership and the weakened bonds to traditional Judaism. This was similar to the experience of Western Jewry. But there are crucial differences. Economically, despite some spectacular gains, tsarist Russia was still a stagnant, feudal economy; politically, tsarist Russia had made little progress toward liberalism and democracy; demographically, the Jews of Russia were numerous and confined to large concentrations within the Pale of Settlement, which hindered the possibility of a rapid social and cultural assimilation. The Jews of Russia, therefore, experienced modernity differently from their brethren in the West.

Although they borrowed much from the experience of the German Jews (see documents 6 through 10), the East European Jews, in response to their unique situation, developed cultural and ideological patterns of their own. In the religious sphere, we may mention the modern *yeshivah* movement of Rabbi Haim ben Isaac of Volozhin (see documents 14 and 15) and the Musar movement founded by Rabbi Israel Lipkin Salanter (see documents 14 and 15). The religious denominationalism that characterized Jewish life in Germany and America never took root in Eastern Europe. In the social sphere, both the deracinated intellectuals and the poor urbanized Jewish masses displayed an affinity to socialism and in time developed a socialist ideology specifically adjusted to Jewish needs and aspirations. These needs and aspirations, of course, were variously interpreted. Some felt that the Jewish situation was defined by the oppressive tsarist policies and by the transitional fact that most Jews still spoke Yiddish and had particular cultural sensibilities. To organize the Jewish masses for the cause of socialism, therefore, it was tactically necessary to acknowledge their Jewishness. Others considered the abiding Jewishness of the masses of the Pale to be of an enduring national value and, accordingly, attributed to Jewish secular culture a role independent of or complementary to socialism (see documents 32, 33, and 34).

Secular Jewish culture, based either on Yiddish or Hebrew, was a living reality for millions of East European Jews (see documents 20, 21, 34, and 35). For the majority of Russian Jews secularization was not accompanied by assimilation, as it often was in the West, or even by acculturation. The challenge faced by Russian Jewry was how to foster secular Jewish culture as a viable, creative expression. Given the multiethnic character of tsarist Russia—and the neighboring Austro-Hungarian Empire—national cultural autonomy, distinct from political and economic autonomy, seemed to provide the framework for legitimating a secular Jewish culture without undermining the claim to full civic rights within Russia. The Zionists, although not opposed to cultural autonomy, of course, argued that it would not be sufficient (see document 34).

Another point of contrast between East and West European Jewish history is the nature of the antisemitism encountered by the respective communities. In the West, anti-Semitism, until Nazism, remained mostly on the level of public intellectual discourse or propaganda, whereas in the East it often fell to the level of physical violence. The pogroms of 1880–1881, 1903, and 1905, followed by the Russian Revolution, greatly unsettled Russian Jewry. Despair and panic provoked a massive emigration of Russian Jewry. Faith in the tsar and in Russia waned, and for many Jews the vision of a more dignified and prosperous life was now focused on the West, particularly America, and, for some, on Palestine (see documents 29 through 31).

Fearing that the fleshpots of the West would entice Jewry into assimilation, many Jews remained in Russia (see documents 14, 15, and 29). Still others placed their faith in the revolution. And the Russian Revolution did indeed remove the shackles, granting Jewry full civic rights. "The emancipation of the Jews," Maxim Gorki exclaimed, "is one of the finest achievements of our Revolution. By granting to the Jews the same rights as to Russians, we have erased from our conscience a shameful and bloody stain" (see the articles by Gorki in *Novaya Zhizn*, 1917–1918, and in the French translation in André Pierre, *Écrits de Révolution* [Paris: Stock, 1922]). But to the Bolsheviks, emancipation meant the opportunity to hasten the process of Jewish assimilation, which they viewed as a progressive and desirable solution to the Jewish question. They considered any attempt to foster Jewish identity reactionary. Jewish cultural institutions were merely necessary means to combat clerical and nationalist forces within the Jewish community and to further the cause of communism among Jews (see document 40).

As a result of World War I, Poland, which since the late eighteenth century had been divided and ruled by Austria, Germany and Russia, was reconstituted as a sovereign state. The rebirth of Poland, which many Jews had eagerly anticipated with guarded optimism, was accompanied by a campaign of terror against them. Especially in the period just prior to the reestablishment of Polish independence, Jews often found themselves caught between opposing armies, between Poles and the Ukrainians in the Lvov region, between Poles and Lithuanians in the area of Vilna, between Poles and Bolsheviks during the war of 1920, and the Russian Civil War of 1921, which unleashed pogroms unprecedented in their extent and ferocity. (see documents 41, 42, and 44). The triumph of Polish nationalism created a legacy of bitterness. For the Jews the independence of Poland was associated with renewed persecution, despite the fact that on the surface the legal situation for Jews was excellent. The Treaty of Versailles of 1919, concluded between the victorious powers and the new states that emerged with the defeat of the Ottoman and Austrian-Hungarian empires, included provisions protecting the national rights of minorities; in the Polish treaty Jews were specifically promised their own schools, and the Polish state pledged itself to respect the Jewish Sabbath. The Polish constitution, too, declared that non-Poles would be allowed to foster their national traditions and formally abolished all discrimination based on religious, racial, or national differences. The Jews were recognized by the state as a nationality, something the Zionists and other Jewish nationalists had long sought. There were great hopes that the Jews would be allowed to develop their national institutions on the basis of national autonomy. These hopes were not fulfilled.

1. A PEOPLE THAT DWELLS APART (1892)

HAROLD FREDERIC[1]

Once you cross the Russian frontier, you can tell the Jews at railway stations or on the street almost as easily as in America you can distinguish the Negroes. This is more a matter of dress—of hair and beard and cap and caftan—than of physiognomy. But even more still is it a matter of demeanour. They seem never for an instant to lose the consciousness that they are a race apart. It is in their walk, in their sidelong glance, in the carriage of their sloping shoulders, in the curious gesture with the uplifted palm. [Tsar] Nicholas [the First] ... solidified [the Jews] into a dense, hardbaked and endlessly resistant mass.

NOTE

1. Harold Frederic (1856–1898), London-based correspondent of the *New York Times*. Frederic traveled in Russia in the 1880s on an assignment. A book on the plight of the Jews under the tsars, *The New Exodus*, from which this excerpt is taken, emerged from that journey. The title we have given to this selection refers to Num. 23:9: "There is a people that dwells apart. Not reckoned among the nations."

Source: Harold Frederic, *The New Exodus: Israel in Russia* (London, 1892), pp. 79–80.

2. STATUTES CONCERNING THE ORGANIZATION OF JEWS (DECEMBER 9, 1804)[1]

ALEXANDER I

Numerous complaints have been submitted to us regarding the abuse and exploitation of native farmers and laborers in those provinces in which the Jews are permitted to reside.... The following regulations are in accord both with our concern with the true happiness of the Jews and with the needs of the principal inhabitants of those provinces....

I. EDUCATION AND LANGUAGE

1. Jewish children may study in all the public schools, secondary schools and universities in Russia, on equal terms with other children.

2. Jewish pupils will neither be required to renounce their religion nor will they be compelled to study subjects which are contrary to their religion....

Source: P. Levanda, *Polnyi khronologicheskii sbornik zakonov i polozhenii kasaiuschikhksia evreev* [Complete chronological collection of laws and ordinances relating to Jews] (St. Petersburg, 1874), pp. 53–59. trans. R. Weiss.

6. If the Jews refuse, despite all these encouragements, to send their children to public schools, special schools must be built at their expense. For this purpose a special tax will be levied. The study of either Polish, Russian or German *must* be included in the curriculum....

8. All the Jews residing in the Russian Empire, although free to use their native language in all their religious and domestic affairs, are obliged, as of January 1807, to use the Russian, Polish or German language in all public documents, contracts, and bills of sale. Otherwise these documents will not be registered....

In accordance with these regulations, Jews who are elected as members of the municipal councils in the former Polish province, shall, for the sake of order and uniformity, dress in the Russian or Polish fashion; whereas Jews elected to the municipal councils in those Russian provinces in which they are permitted to reside permanently, shall dress in the German fashion. As of the year 1808, a Jew who cannot read and write either Russian, German or Polish, may not be elected to the municipal councils....

10. As of the year 1812, a person who is not literate in one of the previously mentioned languages, may not be appointed to a communal position or to the rabbinate.

II. THE STATUS, OCCUPATIONS AND RIGHTS OF THE JEWS

11. All the Jews are divided into four classes: (a) farmers, (b) manufacturers and craftsmen, (c) merchants and (d) city dwellers....

13. Jews who are farmers, as well as those who are manufacturers, craftsmen, merchants and city dwellers, are allowed to purchase and own property in the unpopulated areas of the provinces of Lithuania, Belorussia (White Russia), Little Russia, Kiev, Minsk, Volhynia, Podolia, Astrakhan, Caucasus, Ekaterinoslav, Kherson and Tsabaria. They may sell the land, lease it, bequeath it or bestow it as a gift....

18. No Jew will be compelled to engage in agriculture in the aforementioned provinces, but those who do, shall be exempt from payment of taxes for a period of ten years. This exemption, however, does not extend to debts related to the purchase of land. They will receive loans which will be repayable after a few years, on terms under which similar loans are given to settlers from abroad....

20. Jews are permitted to establish factories of all kinds, in those provinces in which they are permitted to settle, with the same freedom and on the same basis as that granted to all subjects of Russia....

23. In the aforementioned provinces, Jewish craftsmen may engage in any craft not prohibited by law. Managers of workshops, or organizations of craftsmen may not interfere in their rights. They [i.e., Jews] are permitted to register as members of a craftsmen's association if it is not in conflict with local regulations....

29. When all the Jews shall evince diligence and industry in agriculture, commerce and manufacturing, the government will take steps to equalize their taxes to those of other Russian citizens.

III. THE DUTIES OF THE JEWS NOT BELONGING TO THE AFOREMENTIONED CLASSES

30. If he is not registered in one of these classes, a Jew will not be tolerated anywhere in Russia. Jews who will not present a written document in standard legal form, certifying their membership in a class will be regarded as vagrants and will be treated according to the full severity of the law....

34. As of January 1, 1807, in Astrakhan, the Caucasus, Little Russia and New Russia, and the other provinces mentioned, no Jew is permitted to hold rented property in any village or settlement. They may not own taverns, pubs or inns, either in their own name or in that of a representative....

IV. THE LEGAL STATUS OF JEWS

44....No persons may coerce [the Jews], or disturb them in matters of their religious practice, and in civilian life generally, either in word or in deed. Their complaints, whatever they may be, will be heard before the courts and will be satisfied according to the strict letter of the law as it applies to all the citizens of Russia....

NOTE

1. From the sixteenth century on, the tsars sought to expel and bar the Jews from Russia. As a result of the various partitions of Poland, by which Russia inherited a Jewish population of some nine hundred thousand, this policy was no longer realistic. The tsars felt that their new subjects presented a grave problem that required a radical solution. Catherine II, who ascended

the throne in 1762, was the first to tackle the "Jewish Problem." In 1772 the tsarina enacted legislation that limited the exercise of the rights granted the Jews under Polish rule to the areas in which they lived prior to the partitions; Polish Gentiles were specifically permitted, by the same legislation, to exercise their former rights throughout the Russian Empire. A decree of 1791 barred the Jews from specific areas in the empire. Thus the Pale of Jewish Settlement began to take shape. Alexander I, who reigned from 1801 to 1825, resolved to find a "humane" solution to the Jewish problem. In 1802 he ordered the creation of a Committee for the Amelioration of the Jews, to consider all aspects of the problem. In their deliberations the committee assumed that the Jews were a parasitic element and that the non-Jewish population, especially the peasants of the territories that formerly belonged to Poland, had to be protected from the allegedly rapacious Jews. The committee's proposals—a mixture of restrictions and "liberal" inducements to Jewish self-improvement— were accepted by the tsar and embodied in the legislation presented here, enacted on December 9, 1804. It was the first comprehensive Russian legislation dealing with the Jewish problem.

3. STATUTES REGARDING THE MILITARY SERVICE OF JEWS (AUGUST 26, 1827)[1]

NICHOLAS I

I. GENERAL RULES APPLYING TO THE JEWISH PEOPLE

1. Upon being called to military service, Jews shall fulfill their obligation in a manner identical to that of other citizens who are members of that class which is required to serve in the armed forces....

II. MANNER OF FULFILLING MILITARY DRAFT OBLIGATIONS

6. If, at the time of the call to service, it is generally permitted to substitute a sum of money for a recruit, this privilege shall be extended to Jews under the following conditions: (a) The Jewish community owes no back taxes to the government; (b) The community is not in debt to other communities or individuals....

8. Jews presented by the community for the purpose of military service must be no younger than twelve and no older than twenty-five years of age....

13. The Jews of each province must fill their quota of recruits independently of the Gentile population thereof....

24. The responsibility for fulfilling the military obligations falls upon the Jewish communities themselves. They shall follow the dictates of the appropriate provincial authority....

EXEMPTIONS:

58. In addition to merchants, rabbis are also exempt from military service. They must show proper documents proving their title....

Source: P. Levanda, *Polnyi khronologicheskii sbornik zakonov i polozhenii, kasaiuschikhksia evreev* [Complete chronological collection of laws and ordinances relating to Jews] (St. Petersburg, 1874), pp. 193–200. trans. R. Weiss.

62. Jewish youths who are enrolled in general schools for a minimum of three years and who perform adequately and those apprenticed to Gentile artisans are exempt from military service for the duration of their studies....

64. Jews who have settled and who work upon land designated for agricultural purposes are exempt....

X. THE ASSIGNMENT OF JEWS TO VARIOUS BRANCHES OF THE MILITARY

74. Jewish minors—those under 18—shall be sent to preparatory institutions for military training [i.e., cantonist units].

75. Jews from the age of eighteen and upwards shall be assigned to active military duty according to their physical condition, as ordered by the military command.

XI. JEWS EVADING THE DRAFT

87. Whoever discloses the names of those who hide a Jew escaping the draft, shall receive a reward in the sum of one hundred rubles from the treasury....

90. For the purpose of release from military service, only time spent in active duty after the age of eighteen shall be taken into account.

91. Jews in active military duty are permitted to observe their religious customs during their *spare time*. This is in accordance with the law of the land concerning accepted religions. Commanding officers shall protect the Jews from disturbances or abuses which may be caused by their religious affiliation.

NOTE

1. The reign of Tsar Nicholas I (1825–1855) is a dark chapter in the history of Russian Jewry. The legislation excerpted here is indicative of his policy for solving the Jewish problem through coerced assimilation or Russification. In addition to a general conscription of Jewish adult males, who served for a period of twenty-five years, the legislation decreed the recruitment of Jewish boys from the ages of twelve to eighteen as cantonists (the Russian term for *juvenile conscripts*). The cantonists underwent a tough regimen of military drill and Russian education; at the age of eighteen they were drafted to the regular army where they served the full twenty-five-year term. The objective of this system was to alienate the Jewish youth from their families and religion; they were forbidden to practice Judaism or speak their native Yiddish and were obliged to attend classes in Christian dogma and ritual. The government imposed on the Jewish communal leaders the task of supplying a quota of cantonists. To meet this quota the leaders—often rabbis—were obliged to dispatch *khapers* (Yiddish for "kidnappers") to seize Jewish children, often as young as eight, from their parents. Needless to say, this institution weakened the moral authority of the traditional leadership—precisely what the government desired. Before the law was rescinded in 1859, it is estimated that between forty and fifty thousand Jewish minors were conscripted into cantonist units.

4. DELINEATION OF THE PALE OF SETTLEMENT (APRIL 1835)[1]

NICHOLAS I

3. A permanent residence is permitted to the Jews: (a) In the provinces: Grodno, Vilna, Volhynia, Podolia, Minsk, Ekaterinoslav. (b) In the districts: Bessarabia, Bialystok.

4. In addition to the provinces and districts listed in the preceding section, a permanent residence is permitted to the Jews, with the following restrictions: (a) in Kiev province, with the exception of the provincial capital, Kiev; (b) in Kherson province, with the exception of the city of Nikolaev; (c) in Taurida province, with the exception of the city of Sebastopol; (d) in the Mogilev and Vitebsk provinces, except in the villages; (e) in Chernigov and Poltava provinces, but not within the government and Cossack villages, where the expulsion of the Jews has already been completed; (f) in Courland province, permanent residence is permitted only to those Jews who have been registered until the present date with their families in census lists. Entry for the purpose of settlement is forbidden to the Jews from other provinces; (g) in Lithuania province, in the city of Riga and the suburb Shlok, with the same restrictions as those applying in Courland province....

11. Jews who have gone abroad without a legal exit-permit are deprived of Russian citizenship and not permitted to return to Russia.

12. Within the general area of settlement and in every place where the Jews are permitted permanent residence, they are allowed not only to move from place to place and to settle in accordance with the general regulations, but also to acquire real estate of all kinds with the exception of inhabited estates, the ownership of which is strictly forbidden to Jews....

23. Every Jew must be registered according to the law in one of the legal estates of the realm. Any Jew not complying with this regulation will be treated as a vagrant.

NOTE

1. This legislation clearly defined the boundaries of the Pale of Settlement, which included fifteen provinces in Western Russia and ten provinces of the former Kingdom of Poland that were incorporated into the Russian Empire in 1815. The Pale included regions beyond those of Poland only where the Jews could serve as a colonizing element. From time to time its boundaries were modified, but on the average the area of the Pale covered one million square kilometers (386,100 square miles), extending from the Baltic Sea to the Black Sea. By 1897, according to an official census, 4,899,300 Jews lived there, forming 11.6 percent of the general population of the area; 82 percent of the Jews lived in towns and villages. They formed 36.9 percent of the urban population. After the February Revolution (1917), the provisional government abolished the Pale of Settlement.

Source: P. Levanda, *Polnyi khronologicheskii sbornik zakonov i polozhenii, kasaiuschikhksia evreev* [Complete chronological collection of laws and ordinances relating to Jews] (St. Petersburg, 1874), pp. 360–63. trans. L. Sachs.

—•—•—•—•—•—• Pale of Settlement. Though there were minor boundary adjustments continually throughout the nineteenth centrury, this map shows the general area of the Pale.

——— • ——— • ——— International boundary between the Russian Empire and Germany, Austria-Hungary, and Rumania.

5. THE MAY LAWS (MAY 3, 1882)

ALEXANDER III[1]

The Council of Ministers, having heard the presentation made by the Minister of Internal Affairs, regarding the execution of the Temporary Regulations regarding the Jews has concluded as follows:

1. As a temporary measure, and until a general re-examination of the laws pertaining to the Jews takes place by set order, it is henceforth forbidden for Jews to settle outside the cities and townships. Existing Jewish settlements which are engaged in agricultural work are exempted [from this ban].

2. The registration of property and mortgages in the name of Jews is to be halted temporarily; the approval of the leasing by Jews of real estate beyond the precincts of the cities and townships is also to be halted temporarily. Jews are also prohibited from administering such properties.

3. It is forbidden for Jews to engage in commerce on Sundays and Christian holidays....

4. The regulations contained in paragraphs one through three apply to those provinces in which the Jews permanently reside.

NOTE

1. Alexander II, who reigned from 1855 to 1881, adopted a milder Jewish policy than his father, pursuing the Russification of the Jews in a more liberal fashion. He abolished the cantonist system and offered special rewards for "useful" Jews, namely, allowing them to reside outside the Pale of Settlement. This right was extended to wealthy merchants in 1859, university graduates in 1861, and certified craftsmen and all medical personnel in 1865. The Jewish communities outside the Pale, which developed in this period, particularly in Moscow and St. Petersburg, became a major factor in Russian Jewish life. Moreover, a great number of Jews now began to participate in Russian intellectual and cultural life. The assassination of Alexander II by revolutionaries in March 1881 led to a sudden shift in Jewish fortunes. In the period of political unrest that followed, widespread pogroms against the Jews broke out. Tsar Alexander III set up a commission to investigate the cause of the disturbances. In its report the commission underscored the alleged failure of the liberal policies of Alexander II and pointed to "Jewish exploitation" as the principal cause of the pogroms. Based on this report, the Temporary Laws were promulgated in May 1882. Excerpts from these so-called May Laws are presented here. In effect they constituted a contraction of the Pale of Settlement. They were repealed in March 1917 by the revolutionary provisional government.

Source: *Nedelnaya kronica voskhoda*, no. 20 (May 15, 1882), pp. 534–35. trans. R. Weiss.

6. THE NEED FOR ENLIGHTENMENT (1840)

S. J. FUENN[1]

You asked, dear friend, for my opinion on the current news and for my judgment on the questions being asked by the governmental commissions with regard to the children of Israel. Now that the good graces of the Tsar have appeared among us to lighten our darkness and he has descended from his lofty throne to lower his gaze on our poverty, to improve our condition, to heal Jacob's misfortune and the bruises of thousands of years—bruises without hope of cure; now that he has ordered that faithful men, lovers of truth, be selected into whose hands and hearts the supervision of our bad situation and station is to be entrusted, so that the source of the evil and the reasons for our fall in wisdom and ethics be known, and the cure and remedy for every fault and fracture be known also; now this question of yours has come my way, and I find myself duty-bound to pour out my thoughts before you. Perhaps they will reach high places, for I dwell among my people, see and know well their station, and have secretly shed not one nor two heartfelt tears for their misfortune. I will, therefore, explain most clearly to you, dear friend, their present condition in all its aspects, good and bad, and the aids and cures which will benefit them, and provide for them a much needed success. After the government has acquired the wisdom to set a good end, to find the general remedy "for improving the station of the leaders of the nation and its rabbis," I too will labor to portray for you details of our brethren's situation, with regard to the teachers and rabbis, for it appears that for the success or ruin of the people we can rely only on them. And I say: The congregation of Israel in this land today compared to the Gentiles of the Christian countries and our brethren in other countries still stands on the lowest rung of the ladder of political and ethical enlightenment. They produce foul fruit but not for a lack of knowledge and readiness to receive the good and useful seed, nor because the soil of their soul is barren rock do they sprout nought but thorns and briar. No, it is because they lack farmers and plowmen for land they have not had, and do not have even today, nor have they had bounteous dew, for several hundred years, not until the days of the good tsars of Russia, may the Lord bless them. The Jew is far from the threshold of the world's ways for he has not yet been granted the right of all men to nourish himself by visiting the halls of wisdom and enlightenment, and because his customs and garments (which he wears not for religious reasons) are a great dividing screen. Because the Christian heads of the country estrange themselves from these Jews, whom they have hostilely rejected, [the Jews] have become the poorest of men, without any land or source of livelihood to support themselves and the members of their household. They have been pushed into one small circle of activity—petty commerce—which tends to be deceitful, and which is based on scheming and contriving that sometimes clashes with the general good of society. Commerce alone is their allotted work; they are far from all that can induce rapprochement with the Christians, far from the spirit of the time which is daily changing, each year growing glorious with wisdom and the splendor of knowledge. They remain at the level of enlightenment where they were hundreds of years ago. Their value diminishes like the house that, having neither prop nor support, grows shaky and collapses. They have not known the language of the people among whom they dwell, except for what is needed for their trade. Wisdom and science cannot take root among them, for these will find neither passage nor currency among men depressed in spirit and soul. What can inculcate itself into [the Jews'] broken-heartedness is hatred of the religions

Source: S. J. Fuenn to Bezalel Stern, Summer 1840, in *Pardes* (Odessa, 1897) vol. 3, pp. 149–56. trans. A. Schwartz.

of other nations. Several generations have passed thus and the Jews of these lands are thought by their neighbors to be harmful members of society. How then can we now amend this sin? What will they do, these impoverished, wretched, depressed exiles who so often have stood before their shearers like mute lambs—not only was their wool shorn but their flesh and skin cut and stripped from them! How many rivers of their blood were spilled as nought throughout history for a libel now known everywhere, as God is in heaven and earth, as an empty lie? How many years of poverty rife with scorn and contempt for the near success of their work in the land of their neighbors? How could they have approached the enemies of their soul, associate with the devourers of their flesh and blood? Does the love of man penetrate the hearts of oppressed and downtrodden Christians? But blessed be you, O Lord, who sees into every broken heart, who rules this world with His mercy, who has placed goodness for a downtrodden people in the heart of our pious king and in the hearts of his advisors. Blessed too be our lord the Tsar who has voiced ideas beneficial to us. We now can hope that the light of deliverance will also fall on the dwellers in darkness, that the iron-bound prisoners chained to slavery and humiliation will also breathe the spirit of freedom, like every man. Now it has begun to be seen that Jacob is man not stone, that his flesh is flesh not wood, that his blood is the blood of mortals not of snakes and scorpions. Our lord the Tsar has now taken upon himself to be farmer and plowman for us; he will uproot each root of ours which sprouts wormwood, will purify the hearts of the children of Israel of every evil scheme, will sprinkle blessed dew on parched thirsty land, and will sow it with the seed of righteousness, wisdom, and mercy. How good and dear is the sentiment that will come to the aid of thousands and thousands of dejected and humiliated people; how fortunate will be the man who raises his hand or engages his mind and soul to consider their welfare; how blessed will be the pen which will inscribe for posterity the remembrance of mercy and truth.

Having spoken about a bit of the corruption of order among the people of Israel, we may add that the government has done well in advising that the leadership of our nation be handed over to several individuals, that all parts of the leadership be united toward one end. The rabbis to be chosen for this task will be the sailors of Israel's ship lashed by the seas of poverty and woe. Their way should first be cleared of stumbling blocks and then these sailors should be instructed in honest and new leadership, that they may bring the storm-tossed ship to port, to the good port desired by the government.

It is apparent to whoever has eyes that the foremost cause of the distance and enmity between the children of Israel and the Christians in our state is the difference of dress. Since the Jew is unwilling to change his dress and is recognizable wherever he goes, this distance will be increased in the heart both of the Jew and the Christian. Before the government takes one step for our welfare it is fitting that we call its attention to having this obstacle removed. The division and difference in dress derive not from reasons of religion, but rather from a corrupted source, the hatred of the nations during the Middle Ages toward Israel. Wanting not to mingle with the children of Israel they placed a seal on the brow of the Jew which established his religion....In the course of time this became a distinguishing mark among the children of Israel, setting them off from their oppressors. From this isolation they took comfort—as do all those who suffer the prohibitions of insolent masters. In the course of time, when the original reason had been forgotten, they claimed it was for their benefit and was freely chosen. Why then should the children of Israel not want to remove their filthy garments which set them off from their neighbors to this very day? Why should they not be willing to erase all traces of the hatred of the forefathers of our present neighbors which they bear on their persons?...

Having set its eyes in particular on the rabbis at the forefront of the people as a means to improve the station of the nation as a whole, the government would be well advised to achieve its goal not only by improving but by thoroughly changing the rabbis' status. Today the rabbi is but a single man standing alone among the assembly of his people, for the most part instructing them with the aid of talmudic hairsplitting to abandon difficult prohibitions concerning forbidden foods, the status of women and the like. He closets himself in his room, has, except for his public lessons on the Talmud, intercourse with no man. The more hallowed among them may also preach on the exalted matters contained in the kabbalah, for in laws of property they have no legal power to give rulings. Today money matters are brought before the government courts, unless the rabbi is chosen by the disputants of their own accord to bring them to compromise. Even then he has no power—not to enforce his decisions, nor to influence the nation's education, nor to guide them toward the government's aim. The nation's leaders are [surely not the rabbis].[2]...

NOTES

1. Samuel Joseph Fuenn (1818–1890), Hebrew writer and educator. Fuenn, an observant Jew, was a respected spokesman of early *haskalah* in Russia. *Haskalah*, the Hebrew term for the enlightenment movement and ideology that began within Jewish society in the 1770s, was introduced into Russia from Western Europe, particularly Germany. Fuenn served as an inspector of the government schools for Jews in his native district of Vilna. He later published and edited the Hebrew periodical *Hakarmel* (1860–81), which included a supplement in German and Russian.

In 1837 Tsar Nicholas I visited a modern Jewish school established by *maskilim* in Odessa. He was greatly impressed and was inspired to consider the creation of a government network of "modern" schools for the Jews. Upon receiving the report of a special study commission in 1844, the government issued a decree establishing a system of modern Jewish schools. The *maskilim* were delighted by the tsar's "enlightened policy." They surely did not know of the secret instructions accompanying the decree, which declared that the purpose of the schools "is to bring the Jews nearer to the Christians and to uproot their harmful beliefs which are influenced by the Talmud." In the letter excerpted here, written during the public debates preceding the government decree of 1844, to Bezalel Stern (1798–1853), the director of the Jewish school in Odessa, Fuenn summarizes the concerns and program of the early Russian *haskalah*.

2. Fuenn proceeds to outline a detailed plan for the reform of the rabbinate and its functions.

7. A JEWISH PROGRAM FOR RUSSIFICATION (1841)[1]

MASKILIM TO THE GOVERNORS OF THE PALE

The Russian government's objectives in the encouragement of enlightenment among the Jewish people [should be]:

1. To establish special schools for Jews in every city and town where Jews live, without, however, preventing any Jew from receiving an education in the general school system.

2. To give greater emphasis to the moral as opposed to the academic aspect in the education of the Jews. To pay special attention to the teaching of Russian history and language, for there is nothing which unites diverse ethnic groups with the dominant nation better than the dissemination of information concerning that nation's history and literature.

3. In order to thwart the harmful influence of the Talmud, without, at this stage, destroying the book which the Jews regard as the Word of God, the rabbis should be empowered to prepare a short religious textbook, to be approved by the director of the General School System. This text should teach the fundamentals of their religion—in accordance with the accepted principles regarding civic responsibilities to

Source: [Memorandum on the organization of the Jewish people in Russia sent by a group of *maskilim* to district governors in the Pale of Settlement (1841)] *Voskhod* Library Pamphlet, no. 5 (1901), pp. 4–5. trans. R. Weiss.

the tsar and the motherland—and guide the students to respectable and useful labor in all branches of the crafts, commerce and agriculture, as is being done in the Jewish schools in Odessa and Uman.[2]

4. The teachers in the Jewish schools shall be selected from among the Jews by the school's governing board. Some of the teachers must be chosen from among those Jews educated in Prussia and Austria. The school at Uman has already demonstrated the success of this method. There, despite opposition from the Jewish community, the teachers trained in Austria have successfully taught the Jewish religion in the spirit of universal principles.

5. Education in the "cottage schools"[3] is to be permitted only where the teachers have passed examinations based on the general requirements for all teachers and instructors [*melamdim*]. Any educational activity outside this approved framework will incur severe punishment....

8. Inasmuch as Jewish dress has no relation whatsoever to religious law, the Jews must be ordered to change their dress for the clothing commonly worn throughout the country, according to the social class to which they belong.

NOTES

1. This document articulates the tendency, typical of the early *maskilim* in Russia, to view the government's Jewish policy favorably and to cooperate with the reform of the social and cultural structure of Jewish life.
2. See document 2 in this chapter.
3. The reference is to the traditional Jewish primary school, the *heder*.

8. AWAKE MY PEOPLE! (1866)

JUDAH LEIB GORDON[1]

Awake, my people! How long will you slumber?
The night has passed, the sun shines bright.
Awake, lift up your eyes, look around you—
Acknowledge, I pray you, your time and your place....

The land in which now we live and are born—
Is it not thought to be part of Europe?
Europe—the smallest of Earth's regions,
Yet the greatest of all in wisdom and reason.

This land of Eden [Russia] now opens its gates to you,
Her sons now call you "brother"!
How long will you dwell among them as a guest,
And why do you now affront them?

Already they have removed the weight of suffering from your shoulder,
They have lifted off the yoke from your neck,

Source: Judah Leib Gordon, "Hakiza ami," *Hakarmel* 7, no. 1 (1866). trans. D. Goldman.

They have erased from their hearts gratuitous hatred and folly,
They give you their hand, they greet you with peace.

Raise your head high, straighten your back,
And gaze with loving eyes upon them,
Open your heart to wisdom and knowledge,
Become an enlightened people, and speak their language.

Every man of understanding should try to gain knowledge;
Let others learn all manner of arts and crafts;
Those who are brave should serve in the army;
The farmers should buy ploughs and fields.

To the treasury of the state bring your strength,
Take your share of its possessions, its bounty.
Be a man abroad and a Jew in your tent,
A brother to your countrymen and a servant to your king....

NOTE

1. Judah Leib Gordon (1831–1892). The foremost Russian Hebrew poet of the *haskalah*, Gordon at first believed that the Jews' isolation was at the root of all the troubles that plagued them. "Be a man abroad and a Jew in your tent"—a line from this poem, "Hakiza ami"—became the motto for a whole generation of maskilim. This poem was composed in 1863, after the liberation of the serfs by Tsar Alexander II. It expressed Gordon's belief in the dawn of a new era for Russian Jewry. For his subsequent beliefs, see following document, note 1.

9. FOR WHOM DO I TOIL? (1871)

JUDAH LEIB GORDON[1]

My enlightened brothers have acquired worldly wisdom,
And are but loosely bound to the language [i.e., Hebrew] of their people;
They scorn the aged mother holding her spindle.
"Abandon that language whose hour has passed;
Abandon its literature, so tasteless, so bland;
Leave it, and let each one use the language of the land."
And our sons? The generation to follow us?
From their youth on they will be strangers to us.
—My heart bleeds for them—
They make progress, year by year they forge ahead:

Source: Judah Leib Gordon, "Lemi ani amel?," *Hashahar* 2 (Vienna, 1871), pp. 353–54. trans. D. Goldman.

Who knows where they will reach, how far they will go?
Perhaps to that place when they shall never return....
Still the Muse visits by night,
Still the heart listens, the hand writes—
Fashioning songs in a tongue forsaken.
What will I hope? To what end travail?
For whom do I toil? To what avail?
The good years wasted,...
Oh, who can foresee the future, who can foretell?
Perhaps I am the last of Zion's poets;
And you, the last readers?

NOTE

1. Judah Leib Gordon, see document 8, note 1, in this chapter. By the 1870s the enthusiasm of the early votaries of the Hebrew *haskalah* began to wane. They showed signs of despair of the possibilities of reforming Jewish culture and life in Russia. They were also disappointed with the young *maskilim*, who exaggerated, in their view, the need to assimilate and impetuously abandoned Jewish values and the Hebrew language. In the poem presented here, Gordon gives bitter protest to the assimilationist trend.

10. THE TIP OF THE *YUD* (1875)

JUDAH LEIB GORDON[1]

Hebrew woman, who knows your life?
You came in darkness and in darkness depart.
Your sorrows and joys, your hopes and desires
Were born within you and die in your heart.
Daughters of other nations
May know comfort and mirth
But the Jewish woman's vocation,
Is endless servitude on earth.
You conceive, bear, nurse and wean in time,
You bake, cook, season and ripen before your prime.

So what if you bear beauty and possess sentiment,
Or if God endowed you with talent and mind!
For you Torah is tasteless, beauty a detriment,
Every gift a flaw, every thought a bind.
Indecent your voice, monstrous your mane,

Source: Judah Leib Gordon, "Kotzo shel Yud." *Ha-Shahar* 7 (1875), no. 10, 565–73, no. 11, pp. 635–45, no. 12, pp. 713–19. The first part of this poem is translated, introduced, and annotated by Rachel Seelig.

You are nothing but a vessel of blood and of bile!
Inside you the filth of the serpent remains.[2]
Your nation sends you like a mourner to exile,
From the school and the house of the Lord you are thrown,
Banished from rejoicing to bear sorrows alone.

It is best that you know not the language of your fathers,
That the door to the house of your Lord is shut tight,
For you hear not the morning blessing of your mockers,
"That He did not make me woman"[3] daily they recite.
They regard you as servile, slave and sinner,
As a hen prepared to raise young chicks.
Why then, milking cow, O burdened heifer,
Why are you required to learn all their tricks?
For naught they continue to teach you well,
Though your disciples are sent directly to hell.

God not only denies you the fruit of your womb
And leaves you a prisoner of grief in your youth,
At so young an age deprived of your bridegroom,
Now his brother's shoe you must also remove.[4]
You weep, unlike your brothers, for your father's demise,
Yet his estate is entrusted to them and not you,
The blessings of earth they steal before your eyes
Depriving you even of the fresh morning dew.
Two hundred and forty-eight commandments these misers obtain,
And for you, wretched female, only three remain.[5]

O Hebrew woman, your heart full of pain!
You long for life and knowledge but end up with none—
Like a sprout of the lord in the desert you wane,
You perceive not the spring and know not the sun,
Like a seedling of fruit crop, a small patch of land,
Your meadow left fallow, now you grow wild;
Before you matured or your mind could expand,
A man took you to bear and nurture his child.
Still a child to your parents, not fully grown,
You were wed and became—mother to your own.

Married—did you know him to whom you were wed?
Did you love him? Did you see him eye-to-eye?
Did you love? Wretched one, long has it been said
Love from a daughter of Israel is a lie.
Forty days before her awaited birth
The matchmaker a match prepares,
Why see him now, what is it worth?
What would love give her but additional cares?
Our mothers knew not the ways to adore—
Shall then our sister be treated like a whore?[6]

Place a kerchief on your head, your face you must hide,
Shear your long tresses and leave your head bald,

Why should you see him who stands at your side,
If he's thin or hunchbacked, youthful or old?
It makes no difference to you! You shall not choose,
Like an object transferred from domain to domain,
Your parents decide—Who are you to refuse?
Like Arameans they should care if the girl shows disdain?[7]
Over your virginity rules your father's firm hand,
Later you submit to your husband's command.

Your husband himself was not properly trained,
He planted no vineyard, no house did he build;
When the dowry and wealth of your parents is drained,
Your time of lodging in their home fulfilled,[8]
Only then will this man lacking reason and heart,
Venture into the world to seek out his wage,
And leave you abandoned, as one kept apart,
A deserted *agunah* to wilt in your cage.
For all Jewish women is this story I share,
The tale of Bat-Shua and her dreadful despair.

NOTES

1. Judah Leib Gordon's epic poem "The Tip of the Yud" (*kotso shel yud*), written in 1875, is an emblem of the Russian *haskalah* and a powerful indictment of the pitiable status of women within traditional Jewish society. The poem offers a scathing portrait of the ill-fated fictional heroine Bat-Shua, who falls victim to parochial societal attitudes and abuses implemented under rabbinic law. A paragon of beauty and virtue, the young Bat-Shua is compelled to marry Hillel, a student of Talmud whose time spent in the Yeshiva has prevented him from learning a trade and supporting his wife and two children. When Hillel departs without a trace, Bat-Shua is relegated to the status of an *agunah* (literally an "anchored" or "chained" woman), the Jewish legal term designating a woman prohibited from remarrying because her husband has not provided a *get* (the official bill of divorce). Hope for redemption arrives with the enlightened and compassionate Fabi, who locates Hillel, now a peddler in Liverpool, and secures the prerequisite *get* in order to take Bat-Shua's hand in marriage. When subjected to the stringent review of the rabbinic authorities, however, the *get* is deemed invalid, for the name Hillel has been misspelled—left off was the miniscule letter *yud*. Playing on the Hebrew expression denoting pedantry, the title of the poem expresses Gordon's disdain for the hairsplitting nature of rabbinic law, which privileges strictness of interpretation over humane concern for the lives it dictates. As Bat-Shua laments in the final stanza, by the "tiny tip of the yud" her fate is sealed. The poem was inspired in part by Gordon's correspondence with Miriam Markel Mosessohn, a highly educated writer and translator who was remarkable for her command of Hebrew during an era when Jewish women were educated—if at all—solely in Yiddish or Russian. Greatly impressed by Mosessohn's Hebrew translations from German, Gordon dedicated the poem to her. Regarded by many as Gordon's finest work, the impact of the poem can be measured by the fact that the opening stanzas, which appear in translation here, "could be recited from memory by hundreds of thousands of Hebrew readers for generations to come." (Michael Stanislawski, "Yehudah Leib Gordon," *Yivo Encyclopedia of Jews in Eastern Europe*, ed, G.D. Hundert, New Haven, 2008, vol. 1, p. 620.)

2. One tradition claims that Eve had sexual intercourse with the serpent in the Garden of Eden.

3. Recited as part of the morning blessings, this verse is intended to express gratitude for the fact that men are obligated to perform more religious commandments than women. Like many contemporary critics, Gordon implies that the verse expresses a quintessential misogyny underlying Jewish ritual life.

4. Levirate law obligates a surviving brother to marry the childless widow of his deceased brother in order to perpetuate his name (Deut 25:5–6). If the surviving brother refuses to marry her, the widow must remove his shoe in a humiliating public ceremony known as *halitzah* ("taking off the shoe").

5. Of the 613 commandments (*mitzvot*) that constitute Jewish law, 248 are considered positive (one for each bone and organ of the male body, according to the Talmud). The only three commandments assigned specifically to women are *halah* (setting aside a portion of the Sabbath ritual bread), *nidah* (observing marital purity), and *hadlakat haner* (lighting Sabbath and festival candles).

6. Gordon ironically invokes the biblical verse in which Jacob's sons Simeon and Levi defend the act of murdering Hamor and his son Shehem, who "defiled" their sister Dinah (Gen 34:31).

7. A reference to Genesis 24:57–58, in which Rebecca's mother and brother ask her whether she wishes to marry Isaac.

8. Traditional Jewish marriage contracts often required the bride's family to feed and house the young couple for an agreed period of time so as to allow the bridegroom the freedom to carry on his religious studies. The term for this arrangement in Yiddish is *kest*. Gordon derides the custom and suggests that it precludes the groom from learning a trade and thus from ever being able to provide for his family.

11. THE NEW HASIDIM (1793)[1]

SOLOMON MAIMON

About this time I became acquainted with a sect of my people called the New Hasidim, which was then coming into prominence. Hasidim is the name generally given by the Hebrews to the pious, that is, to those who are distinguished by the exercise of the strictest piety. From time immemorial men such as these have freed themselves from worldly occupations and pleasures and devoted their lives to the strictest observance of the laws of religion and to penance for their sins. They sought to attain this object, as has been said above, by prayers and other exercises of devotion, by chastisement of the body and by similar means.

But about this time some among them set themselves up as founders of a new sect. They maintained that true piety by no means consists in chastisement of the body, by which the spiritual quiet and inner cheerfulness necessary to the knowledge and love of God are disturbed. On the contrary, they maintained that man must satisfy all his bodily wants and take such enjoyment of pleasures of the senses as may be necessary for the development of our perceptions, inasmuch as God has created all for his glory. True service of God, in their view, consists in exercises of devotion with exertion of all our powers and annihilation of the self before God; for they maintain that man, in accordance with his destiny, can reach highest perfection only when he regards himself not as a being existing and working in and for itself, but as an organ of the Godhead. Instead of spending their lives in separation from the world, suppressing their natural feelings, and deadening their powers, they believed that they acted much more to the purpose in seeking to develop their natural feeling as fully as possible, to bring their powers into exercise, and constantly to widen their sphere of activity.

Those of the first sect [the old Hasidim] press their penitential urge to an extravagant degree. Instead of merely regulating their desires and passions by rules of moderation, they seek to annihilate them; and instead of endeavoring, like the Stoics, to find the principle of their actions in pure reason, they seek it

[handwritten marginal annotation: "Sensual – God wants you to take pleasure in the world"]

Source: The Autobiography of Solomon Maimon, trans. J. Clark Murray (Boston, 1888; reprint, London: East and West Library, 1954), pp. 28, 31–33, 68–70, 126–28. Reprinted with permission of Hebrew Publishing Company.

rather in religion. This is a pure source, it is true; but as these people have false ideas of religion itself, and their virtue has as its basis merely the future rewards and punishments of an arbitrary tyrannical being who governs by mere caprice, their actions in point of fact flow from an impure source, namely the principle of interest. Moreover, in their case this interest rests merely on fantasies; so that, in this respect, they are far below the grossest Epicureans, who have a low, to be sure, but nevertheless genuine interest as the end of their actions. Only when it is itself founded on the idea of virtue can religion yield a principle of virtue.

The ideas of the second sect [the new Hasidim] on religion and morals are indeed better founded; but since their conduct is guided for the most part by obscure feelings rather than distinct knowledge, they likewise necessarily fall into all manner of extravagance. Self-annihilation inevitably cramps their activity or gives it false direction. They have no natural science, no acquaintance with psychology; and they are vain enough to consider themselves organs of the Godhead—which, of course, they are, but to an extent limited by the degree of perfection they attain. The result is that at the charges of the Godhead they perpetrate the greatest excesses; every extraordinary suggestion is to them a divine inspiration, and every lively impulse a divine call.

Those sects were not in fact distinct sects of religion; their difference consisted merely in the mode of their religious exercises. But still their animosity went so far that they condemned each other as heretics and indulged in mutual persecution. At first the new sect held the upper hand and spread over nearly the whole of Poland, and even beyond. The heads of the sect sent regular emissaries everywhere, whose duty it was to preach the new doctrine and win converts. Now the majority of the Polish Jews consist of scholars, that is, men devoted to an inactive and contemplative life; for every Polish Jew is destined from his birth to be a rabbi, and only the greatest incapacity can exclude him from that rank. Moreover, this new doctrine was calculated to make the way to blessedness easier, inasmuch as it declared that fasts and vigils and the constant study of the Talmud are not only useless but even prejudicial to that cheerfulness of spirit which is essential to genuine piety. It was therefore natural that the adherents of the doctrine quickly multiplied. The rapid spread of this sect and the factor with which a great part of the people regarded it may be very easily explained. The natural inclination to idleness and a life of speculation on the part of the majority, who from birth are destined to study; the dryness and unfruitfulness of rabbinical studies; the great burden of the ceremonial law, which the new doctrine promised to lighten and finally, the tendency to fanaticism and the love of the miraculous, which are nurtured by this doctrine—these are sufficient to make this phenomenon intelligible.

I could form no accurate idea of the new sect and did not know what to think of it, till I met with a young man who had already been initiated into the society and had enjoyed the good fortune of conversing with high personages face to face. This man happened to be traveling through the town I lived in, and I seized the opportunity of asking for information on the internal constitution of the society, the mode of admission and so forth. The stranger was still in the lowest grade of membership and consequently knew nothing about the internal constitution of the society and could give me no information on the subject. But for the mode of admission, he assured me that was the simplest thing in the world. Anyone who felt a desire of perfection but did not know how to satisfy it, or wished to remove hindrances to its satisfaction, had only to apply to the superiors of the society, and *eo ipso* he became a member. He need not even tell of his past, as one must do on applying to a medical doctor; he need say nothing to these superiors about his moral weakness, his previous character, and matters of that sort, inasmuch as nothing was unknown to the superiors. They could see into the human heart and discern all that is concealed in its secret recesses; they could foretell the future and bring near things remote.

I could not restrain my astonishment at the exquisite refinement of these thoughts, and consequently I wished nothing so much as the pleasure of becoming a member of this honorable society. Therefore I resolved to undertake a journey to M———,[2] where the superior B———[3] resided. Impatiently I waited for the close of my term of service, which still had some weeks to run. As soon as this was finished, instead of going home (though I was only two miles away), I started at once on my pilgrimage. The journey extended over some weeks.

At last I arrived at M———, and after having rested from my journey I went to the house of the superior with the notion that I could be introduced to him at once. I was told, however, that he could not speak to me at the time, but that I was invited to his table on Sabbath along with the other strangers who had come to visit him: I should then have the happiness of seeing the saintly man face to face and of hearing the sublimest teachings out of his own mouth; although this was a public audience, yet, on account of the individual references which I should find made to myself, I might regard it as a special interview.

Accordingly, on Sabbath I went to this solemn meal, and there found a large number of respectable men who had gathered together from various quarters. At length the great man appeared, his awe-inspiring figure clothed in white satin. Even his shoes and snuffbox were white, this being among the Kabbalists the color of grace. He greeted each newcomer with "Shalom." We sat down to the table, and during the meal a solemn silence reigned. After the meal was over, the superior struck up a solemn inspiring melody, held his hand for some time upon his brow, and then began to call out, "Z——— of H———, M——— of R———, S. M. of N———," and so on. Each newcomer was thus called by his own name and the name of his residence, which excited no little astonishment. Each as he was called recited some verse of the Holy Scriptures. Thereupon the superior began to deliver a sermon for which the verses recited served as a text, so that although they were disconnected verses taken from different parts of Scripture they were combined with as much skill as if they had formed a single whole. What was still more extraordinary, every one of the newcomers believed that he discovered in that part of the sermon which was founded on his verse something that had special reference to the facts of his own spiritual life. At this we were of course greatly astonished....

NOTES

1. The eighteenth century witnessed the rise of a new spiritual and social movement among the Jews of Eastern Europe. Known as Hasidism—or New Hasidism, to differentiate it from an older group practicing an ascetic, mystical piety who also called themselves Hasidim (Hebrew, "the pious ones")—the movement was founded by Israel Baal Shem Tov (1669–1761) in the Ukrainian regions of Volhynia and Podolia. Although Israel Baal Shem Tov (also known by his acronym the Besht) left no writings—his person and teachings are wrapped in legends recorded several generations after his death—it seems that he taught a popular mysticism addressed primarily (albeit not exclusively) to the poorer, less educated masses of Jews. East European Jewry, especially in the Ukraine, was in a depressed state, having still to recover from the traumas of the previous century. Externally, it was battered by the Chmielnicki massacres of 1648, which left in their wake hundreds of thousands of Jewish dead and, according to one witness, 744 Jewish communities destroyed. Internally, Jewish life was also in disarray as a result of the disillusionment that followed the conversion to Islam by Sabbatai Zvi (1626–1676), whom many had believed to be the long-awaited Messiah. The oligarchic leadership together with the scholarly aristocracy of the community seemed inadequate to the task of leading the Jews out of this catastrophic situation. To many the Besht seems to have provided an answer. He taught that all are equal before God and that the ignorant—those for whom wretched circumstances have not allowed the attainment of even the rudiments of rabbinic knowledge—are no less worthy than the learned. For purity of heart was superior to study, and devotion to prayer and the commandments might be pursued through joy and not the prevailing ascetic practices that so heavily weighed on an already burdened people. Communion with God and divine grace were available to all Jews, even the simplest.

The Besht's message led to new and distinctive religious practices and institutions, among them textual innovations and distinctive worship services in which one was encouraged to express personal fervor with intense bodily gestures, shouting, singing, jumping and dance. What primarily distinguished Hasidism was a new type of communal and spiritual leader, called the zadik (or "rebbe" in Yiddish). The zadik (a Hebrew term meaning a "righteous person" but in kabbalistic parlance a term denoting a person of unique mystical virtuosity) is a charismatic leader who serves to facilitate his followers' attainment of holiness and communion with God.

The movement spread rapidly throughout Eastern Europe. Upon the death of the Besht, Rabbi Dov Baer of Mezhirech (d. 1773) assumed the mantle of the movement. He further refined and systematized the teachings of the Besht and succeeded in attracting large numbers of adherents (many from the learned classes) to Hasidism, even from Lithuania, the bastion of traditional rabbinic learning.

This document presents a description of the court of Dov Baer, known as the magid (i.e., preacher). It was written by Solomon Maimon (see chapter 12, document 1) who in his late teens or early twenties spent several weeks in Mezhirech.

2. "M"—Mezhirech.
3. "B"—Baer, i.e., Dov Baer.

12. EXCOMMUNICATION OF THE HASIDIM (APRIL 1772)[1]

THE RABBINICAL LEADERS OF VILNA

Our brethren, sons of Israel, says the manifesto, as you know, new people have appeared, unimagined by our forefathers, who have formed a sect of *hashudim* [i.e., Hasidim; in the text the word *hashudim*—"suspicious ones"—appears, in a play on words with "Hasidim"]...and they associate among themselves and their ways are different from other Children of Israel, in their liturgy.... And in their recitation of the Eighteen Benedictions they roar in abominable words in the vernacular [Yiddish] and they behave in a crazed manner, and say that their thoughts [reach the upper] worlds.... And they belittle the study of the Torah, and repeatedly claim that one should not study much, nor deeply regret one's transgressions.... Every day is a festival for them.... And while standing during their false prayers, [they] voice sounds that are different, and there is a loud commotion in the town,...and they behave like the Vision of the Wheels, upside down and bottom up.[2]...This is just the tip of the iceberg, one of their thousand despicable ways...as the above *hashudim* [Hasidim] have admitted to us,...and praise God that their crime was revealed by Heaven, here among us, that they themselves confessed following a thorough investigation....Therefore we have come to inform our brethren, Children of Israel, from near and far: ... All leaders of our people must wear the mantel of zealotry, zealotry for the Lord of Hosts, to destroy and expunge, and to sound to them the voice of excommunication and banishment. And with God's help we have already uprooted their evil belief from among us, and just as we have uprooted it here, may it be uprooted everywhere.... And though they entreat [you], do not believe them ... for the seven abominations are in their hearts.... Until they themselves repent completely, [they] must be divided and dispersed such that two heretics should not be found together, because two of the same breed are prohibited from everything,...and it befits the world to separate them.

NOTES

1. As Hasidism spread, it sought to establish itself as an alternative to existing forms of Jewish worship and community—the latter being expressed by Hasidism's introduction of its own authority for ritual slaughter, which in addition to enhancing the position of the rabbis who supervised the slaughter of fowl and

Source: Zemir arizim veharvot zurim (Vilna, 1772), reprinted by Simon Dubnow, *Hasidica*, supplement to *Heavar* 2 (Petrograd, 1918): 22–23. trans. G. Svirsky.

cattle was a principal source of income for the community. For no other reason, the traditional leadership had reason to oppose the Hasidim. The opposition was intense and varied; an anti-Hasidic literature appeared, and pamphlets and broadsheets, in acrimonious and bitter language, lampooned the Hasidim. Most famous among these writings was a work published in Vilna in 1772, *Zemir arizim veharvot zurim* (Singing of the tyrants and sharp knives; cf. Isaiah 25:5, Joshua 5:2), which contained many declarations against the Hasidim. Among these is the document presented here, the excommunication of the Hasidim, signed by sixteen leading rabbinic authorities of Vilna, "the Jerusalem of Lithuania," and issued just after the conclusion of the Passover holiday 1772. Circulated in many communities, the ban, calling for the utter

repudiation of the Hasidim, was signed by Rabbi Elijah ben Shlomo, the *Gaon* of Vilna (1720–1797), the most eminent rabbinic authority of his day (see the next document, note 4). The ban of excommunication, together with other statements of the *Gaon* of Vilna, served to crystallize the opposition to Hasidism, which was henceforth known as the *Mitnagdim* (Hebrew, "the opponents"). Scholars are divided on whether the opposition was local, both temporally and geographically. Nonetheless, the emergence of the *Mitnagdim* checked the rapid spread of Hasidism.

2. The Hasidim introduced the practice of standing "upside down," that is, on one's head, during the prayer service, which was intended to break one's pride. The *Goan* of Vilna, however, saw it as clear sign of the frivolity of the Hasidim and their tendency to heresy.

13. HOW I BECAME A HASID (c. 1850)

BARUCH MORDECAI ETTINGER[1]

Rabbi Shneur Zalman's[2] visit to Vilna, in the company of Rabbi Menachem Mendel of Vitebsk,[3] when they came to confront the *Gaon* of Vilna,[4] had left a lasting impression on the Talmudic scholars in the city. They often quoted Rabbi Shneur Zalman's incisive exposition of certain difficult passages in the Talmud, which they were privileged to hear from him on that occasion. This aroused my interest, and I began to study some of Rabbi Shneur Zalman's Hasidic discourses, which were made available to me by local Hasidim. Subsequently, I met young scholars of note, who rehearsed various novellae of Rabbi Shneur Zalman, which singularly clarified complicated passages in the Talmud. I gained a profound respect for the Rebbe's erudition, but I was not sufficiently convinced to become a Hasid of his.

It was not until the year 5553 [1793] that I made my first visit to Liozna.[5] My trip was not the pilgrimage of a Hasid; rather, it was prompted by scholastic curiosity to take a closer look at the teachings of Hasidism as expounded by the Rebbe.

Arriving in Liozna, I discovered that there was a strict routine to be followed by young men desirous of a private audience with the Rebbe. It was first necessary to be interviewed by Rabbi Yehuda Leib, the Rebbe's brother, who was in charge of admissions and arrangements for providing full board for the applicant. If he was satisfied with the sincerity of the applicant, he would recommend him for an examination in Talmudic proficiency. Then followed a period of two or three weeks of intensive Hasidic and talmudic study, upon the completion

Source: Rabbi Baruch Mordecai Ettinger, "Memoir," cited in Nissan Mindel, *Rabbi Shneur Zalman* (New York: Chabad Research Center, 1971), vol. 1, pp. 103–5. (The translation has been altered stylistically by the editors of this volume.)

of which the candidate would be admitted to a private audience with the Rebbe.

The examiners were the Rebbe's other brothers, Rabbi Mordecai and Rabbi Moshe. Rabbi Mordecai excelled himself especially in the Babylonian Talmud and the *Rishonim* [Early Codifiers], while his brother's specialty was the Jerusalem Talmud and the Rambam [Maimonides]. Sometimes one of them was the sole examiner; sometimes both of them gave the examination.

The first Talmudic discussion with these two *geonim*[6] left me completely overwhelmed. I had passed the test, however, and after two weeks' preparation, I was admitted into private audience with the Rebbe.

I had prepared a number of questions pertaining to devoutness, which the Rebbe chose not to answer. Instead, he asked me if I had any questions in the area of Talmudic study.

It so happened that for over a year I had been wrestling with two problems, one in the Jerusalem Talmud and the other in the Rambam. I had discussed them with the *Gaon* of Vilna, who helped me analyze the problems and thus greatly elucidate them but actually gave me no answer to resolve them.

Now, standing before the Rebbe, I put these two questions before him, and I was amazed to receive a clear answer to them, which at once resolved them beyond a doubt.

Upon leaving the Rebbe's room and entering the "Lower *Gan Eden*" [Paradise] (as the Hasidim called the Small Synagogue in the Rebbe's house), I was drawn into the traditional "*yehidut* Dance."[7] This was a lively whirling dance that was introduced by the early Hasidim to celebrate a private audience with the Rebbe. I whirled around with the older Hasidim and younger seminarians, oblivious to what was going on, for I was excited beyond measure by the brilliance of the Rebbe's mind. For years afterward, the impressions of his awe-inspiring countenance and his profound wisdom remained vivid in my mind.

My association with the Rebbe's three illustrious brothers, though only of a few weeks' duration, opened new horizons formed in my Talmudic studies. My conceptual capacity was substantially enhanced. I began to apply myself more assiduously than ever before to the study of both Hasidism and Talmud, and with all the concentration I could muster.

Back home, I had to wait several months for my brother-in-law's, Rabbi Shlomo's, return before I could share with him the excitement of having resolved my two problems. He, too, became very excited and insisted that I go to the *Gaon* [of Vilna] forthwith to hear his opinion about the answers. I agreed and, accompanied by my brother-in-law, went to the *Gaon* [of Vilna].

As soon as I began to speak about the two problems, the *Gaon* reviewed them in a concise manner, adding that he frequently pondered them but as yet had not found a satisfactory clue to the solution. I then advanced the answers without identifying the source of my information. The *Gaon* was visibly moved. Wrapped as he was in his talit and tefilin,[8] he rose to his full height and said reverently: "Such answers could issue only from the Head of the Heavenly Academy [i.e., God Himself]. Whoever the *Gaon*[9] and zadik[10] was who gave these answers, he could only have known the solution by prophetic inspiration. Had I heard it from his mouth, I would have said as Rabbi Jochanan said: 'I would carry his bathing apparel for him to the bathhouse.'"

Later on I greatly regretted not having disclosed to the *Gaon* that it was the Rebbe of the Hasidim who had given me those answers; it might have elicited a better attitude toward the Hasidim, and might have brought the two "giants" together.

Though, in due course, my affiliation with the Hasidim of Rabbi Shneur Zalman was no secret, I still had access to the *Gaon* of Vilna.[11] On one such occasion, soon after the Tanya was publicly burnt in Vilna, I mentioned to the *Gaon* that the author of this book was the one who had told me the answers to the intricate problems, and I reminded the *Gaon* of his reaction at that time and what he had said, quoting Rabbi Jochanan. Unfortunately, the *Gaon* rejected my defense, stating that, according to the law of the Torah, I was an interested party, and consequently my testimony was not worthy.

NOTES

1. Rabbi Baruch Mordecai Ettinger (1767–1857) was the rabbi of Bobruisk, Belorussia, for fifty years before settling in the last year of his long life in the Holy Land. He was the son-in-law of the head of the rabbinic court of Vilna, Rabbi Shmuel ben Avigdor (1720–1793). Thus affiliated with the rabbinic establishment, Rabbi Baruch

was in his own right an acclaimed authority of Talmud and halakhah. Indeed, he was invited to join the prestigious rabbinic court of Vilna, which he declined in favor of the position in Bobruisk. In this document, he relates how he, who was close to the *Gaon* of Vilna and an opponent of Hasidism, became a disciple of Rabbi Shneur Zalman, the founder of Habad Hasidism.

2. Rabbi Shneur Zalman (1745–1813) was the founder of Habad Hasidism. At the age of nineteen he went to study with Dov Baer the *magid* of Mezhirech (c. 1720–1772), then the leader of the Hasidic movement. He soon became a member of the magid's inner circle. In 1774, during the early period of the opposition to Hasidism by traditional Jewry, Shneur Zalman and Menahem Mendel of Vitebsk (see note 3) went to Vilna in an attempt to meet with the Gaon of Vilna (see note 4), who two years earlier had issued a ban of excommunication against Hasidism. They had hoped to seek a reconciliation between Hasidism and its opponents—the *mitnagdim* led by the Gaon, but he did not agree to grant them an audience. After Menahem Mendel went to Eretz Israel with many of his followers, Shneur Zalman succeeded him as the leader of the Hasidic movement in Belorussia.

In time Shneur Zalman created a distinct form of Hasidism, which became known as Habad. In 1797 he published (anonymously) his *Likutei Amarim* [Collected Sayings], more widely known as the *Tanya*—a novel interpretation of the Kabbalah, which became "the written law of Habad." In striking contrast to the popular Hasidism of Volhynia and Podolia—the western regions of the Ukraine where the movement had its origins—Shneur Zalman emphasized the role of the intellect and Torah study; he likewise rejected the doctrine that attributed to the zadik—the charismatic leader of a hasidic community—wondrous and even soteriological abilities. Despite his emphasis on the rational and traditional rabbinic learning, he was decidedly a mystic and deeply emotional. Eventually his influence penetrated the strongholds of the mitnagdim. In 1802 he moved to Liady and became known as the *rebbe* (the zadik) of Liady. Habad is also popularly known as Lubavitch Hasidism after the name of the small town in Belarus that became the center of the movement after Shneur Zalman's eldest son Dov Baer (1773–1827) settled there in 1813.

3. Rabbi Menachem Mendel of Vitebsk (1730–1788) was a disciple of Dov Baer of Mezhirech. In 1777 he left Russia together with three hundred followers and settled in the Holy Land, first in Safed, later in Tiberias.

4. The *Gaon* of Vilna, Elijah ben Shlomo (1720–1797) was a widely acclaimed Talmudic scholar and spiritual leader of Lithuanian Jewry. Although he refused rabbinic office and lived in seclusion, his reputation as a saint and scholar was widespread. The weight of his authority was particularly manifest when he led the opposition to the Hasidim in Lithuania, ordering excommunication and the destruction of their writings. Thereafter, he remained the spiritual leader of the *mitnagdim*, the opponents of Hasidism.

5. Liozna (Polish: Lozniany) was known in Yiddish as Liady. Shneur Zalman was born in this Belorussian town in the province of Vitebsk.

6. *Geonim* is the plural form of the Hebrew *Gaon*, an honorific name given to a great sage and eminent Torah scholar. In the present context, it should be recalled that the spiritual leader of the opponents to Hasidism, Rabbi Elijah ben Shlomo, was popularly acclaimed as the *Gaon* of Vilna.

7. The name of this dance, yehidut (literally: privacy, exclusiveness), is derived from the term for a private audience with a Hasidic master, a zadik or rebbe.

8. Prayer shawl and phylacteries.

9. Cf. note 6.

10. Zadik, here an appellation, meaning a "righteous person," given to an individual of outstanding faith and piety.

11. See note 2.

14. THE VOLOZHIN *YESHIVAH* (1909)

RABBI DAVID MOSES JOSEPH OF KRYNKI[1]

An important announcement concerning the Torah:[2] I have seen with my own eyes that the honor of the holy *yeshivah* of Volozhin—which was founded by our holy master, Rabbi Haim Volozhin. Through prayer and entreaty, and even the shedding of tears—has been brought down and humiliated. There are those who say: What in fact is the importance of the *yeshivah*, are there not other yeshivot in the world? There are others who say that with respect to curricula, the yeshivot in other cities are superior to the *yeshivah* of Volozhin. Everyone seems to feel that there have always been yeshivot in the big cities. I know that this is not the case and that the truth is that the *yeshivah* of Volozhin is the mother and source of all the yeshivot and Talmud Torahs[3] in the world. The latter are as pipes which come from the source and thus in the blessing of the source they too will be blessed....

Therefore I see it as my duty to proclaim the truth to the world, words of truth for he who wants to know, as it is written (Deut. 32:7), "ask your father and he will tell you, your elders and they will say to you." Today I am, with God's help, seventy-eight years old and when our holy rabbi founded the *yeshivah* I was about fifteen or sixteen years old. I was familiar with the ways of the world and I noted that before our holy rabbi founded the "house of God" the world was empty, literally without form; it was void, for even the term *yeshivah* was unknown, let alone what activities took place in one. The term *public study of Torah* was also unknown to a world void of Torah. Holy books, such as volumes of the Talmud, were rare and to be found only in homes of exceptional individuals, such as famous patrons. Even in the communal study halls [*batei midrash*] of large towns, a complete set of the Talmud was not to be found. This was the case because there was no need for these books. When our

holy rabbi founded the *yeshivah*, an appeal was made for volumes of the Talmud and it was necessary to send to the large towns for books. When the rabbi of Slavuta[4] saw that there was a need for volumes of the Talmud, he printed a few hundred sets, in large and small formats, and as a result of their popularity, they spread all over the world. In the first year of the *yeshivah* I noted that many merchants made it their business to travel by way of Volozhin in order to see what this thing called a *yeshivah* was and what was done there. At the sight of dozens of Torah scholars sitting and studying day and night with a wonderful diligence, they were astonished and amazed for they had never seen or even imagined anything like it. Many merchants remained for days and did not want to leave.

After a number of years, one of the students of our holy rabbi went to Minsk—this was Rabbi Mordechai Minsker. He studied with awesome discipline and the sons of the great-patroness Bluma of that city became attached to him. He inspired them and together with their mother they founded a small prayer room and study hall [*kloiz*].[5] She supported all the students of the *kloiz* at her own expense and covered the other expenses of the *kloiz* out of her own pocket as well. This was the very first *kloiz* in the world, for there was no other. A few years later another patron, I think it was Rabbi Haim Michvantzer, founded another and after him Rabbi Samuel Rofe and others. Meanwhile in Vilna there was still no *yeshivah*. I once asked our holy rabbi for permission to give a daily lecture [*shiur*] to students as was done in the *yeshivah* [of Volozhin]. He replied with these words: I get more satisfaction and gratification from the yeshivot of Minsk than from my own *yeshivah*. With regard to the latter I am troubled by all the details necessary for the running of the *yeshivah*, whereas at the yeshivot of Minsk

Source: Moshe Shmuel Schmuckler [*The History of the Rabbi of Volozhin*] (Vilna, 1909), pp. 32–34. trans. S. Stampler.

I have no worries at all and all [the pleasure] is mine! After a few years Mordechai Minsker settled in Vilna and founded a *yeshivah* in the old *kloiz*. Then, with the help of Rabbi Judah Kliatsky he set up a *yeshivah* in the new *kloiz* and after that yeshivot and Talmud Torahs multiplied in a number of towns. Were it not for the fact that our holy rabbi founded his yeshivah, the Torah would have—God forbid—been forgotten in Israel. This I often say about our teacher and holy rabbi, "How great are the deeds of your life." My eyes saw all that is written here and it is not from hearsay. . . .

NOTES

1. Traditional Judaism in Russia was not as desiccated and petrified as the *maskilim* tended to portray it. Throughout the nineteenth century, the leaders of traditional Judaism, aware of the growing disaffection of Russian Jewry, especially of the youth, with the regnant patterns of Jewish life, sought to renew halakhic Judaism. One of the first signs of this renewal was the establishment in 1803 by Rabbi Haim ben Isaac (1749–1821) of the *yeshivah* at Volozhin, a village in Lithuania. Alarmed by the decline of Torah learning among East European Jewry, a process that began in the seventeenth century, Rabbi Haim reintroduced Lithuanian Jewry to the joys of rigorous Torah and Talmudic study, both in terms of method and routine. For six days a week, the more enthusiastic students would commence their studies at 3 A.M., with a break at 8 A.M. for the morning prayers and meal; they would return to the study halls at 10 A.M., continuing to study until 1 P.M.; after a midday recess, study would resume from 4 P.M. until 10 P.M.; some would stay until midnight. The Volozhin *yeshivah* became the prototype and inspiration for the great Talmudic academies of Eastern Europe of the nineteenth and twentieth centuries. The *yeshivah* of Volozhin, which the poet H. N. Bialik was to call "the place where the soul of the nation was molded," profoundly affected the whole intellectual and spiritual character of Lithuanian Jewry. The *yeshivah*, renamed *Ez Haim* (the Tree of Life) in honor of its founder, was closed by the tsarist government in 1879 and was reopened in 1881; it was closed again in 1892 for its refusal to introduce secular studies. In 1899 it was refounded but did not retain its previous position of eminence. The above selection is from a letter, dated Tammuz 25, 5625 (i.e., 1865), by Rabbi David Moses Joseph of Krynki, a former student of the Volozhin *yeshivah*. In the letter he solicits support for a fund-raising campaign on behalf of the Volozhin *yeshivah*, whose building had burned down the previous year.

2. A play of words on a passage in the Babylonian Talmud.

3. Hebrew for a place for "the study of Torah"—a preparatory school for study in the *yeshivah*.

4. Slavuta is a city in the province of Volhynia. During the late eighteenth and the first half of the nineteenth centuries, the Jewish community of Slavuta became renowned for its printing press, founded in 1791 by Rabbi Moses Shapira.

5. "Blumke's *kloiz*" became the largest *yeshivah* in Minsk.

15. THE MUSAR *YESHIVAH* (c. 1910)[1]

HIRSCH LEIB GORDON

A visitor entering the large hall of the Musar *yeshivah* in Slobodka—and there was only one hall—could see the supervisor [*mashgiah*] moving like a shadow among the diligent students. But everyone knew that he and his authority were not of the essence there. The authority of Musar, and the edifier [*mashpia*] who wielded the authority, played the essential role. Rabbi Netta Hirsch Finkel,[2] who at the time of my studies in Slobodka was not yet called "the Grandfather," would go about the *yeshivah* in seeming humility. But all knew that the power and rule were vested in him. The aristocratic figure of the head of the *yeshivah*, Rabbi Moshe Mordecai Epstein,[3] would appear occasionally but it was obvious that he felt a little strange in the spacious hall, where not the Torah held sway but rather "the Method," the special Musar method beside which the Torah was unimportant.

Rabbi Netta Hirsch would look around constantly as if searching for something in the behavior of the students that was not to his liking or taste. Sometimes he would stop beside the desk of a *yeshivah* youth and examine his comportment—his chanting, his movements, his reactions to what was going on around him. The youth upon whom Rabbi Netta Hirsch fixed his stare would shake with fear before the penetrating gaze, uncertain as to whether he had found favor and approval in the eyes of his examiner. Rabbi Netta Hirsch stood in the center of all that went on in the *yeshivah*, and yet stood above it all.

The power and authority of Rabbi Netta Hirsch were at their peak on Sabbath night between *minhah*[4] and *maariv*.[5] Then the hall would be enveloped in shadows and the crowd would surround the chair in the center of the hall on which sat the great *mashpia* like a king in his court. No member of the *yeshivah* would dare be absent from this session. From the day of the great scandal involving the books of the Musar which had been thrown into the public toilet, the relations between the Musar movement and its opponents in Lithuania became increasingly strained; both friend and foe saw in Rabbi Netta Hirsch the chief protagonist in the battle, and my child's heart went out in devotion to this majestic figure.

I began to visit the great *yeshivah* in the evenings, especially at dusk on the Sabbath, when the Grandfather would speak in a low and pleasant voice that dropped sometimes to a secret whisper. Hundreds of youths swarmed around him like bees. Most seemed moved by the preaching and the somber voice, although here and there I could detect an expression of doubt, or a secret smile. On one occasion the Grandfather happened to look at me, and wondering at my relative youth he asked me:

"Who are you, little man?"

"I am the son of Rabbi Komay, and I am studying in the *yeshivah* of Rabbi Hirschel."

"And what are you doing here?"

"I come here in the evenings, that I may gain in piety." (I realized that in my eagerness I was exaggerating a bit.)

The Grandfather smiled and stroked my face affectionately. And whenever he exhorted us in the evenings he would embrace me and hold me in his arms.

The Grandfather would speak in broken phrases, in isolated words and fragments of sentences. I can recall one sermon which he gave in the month of Elul:[6]

> …repentance…repentance and good deeds…difficult to accomplish them…but one must try

Source: Hirsch Leib Gordon [*On the Banks of the Vilija and the Neman*], *Hadoar* 40, no. 8 (1968), p. 207. Cited by permission of *Hadoar*. trans. L. Sachs.

anyway…nothing can stand in the way of true penitents…the Mouth of Hell [*Gehenna*]….He that talks inordinately with women shall inherit Gehenna[7]…anyone who swears obscenely… anyone who gets angry…a flatterer…vulgarities…one who leaves the path of Torah will fall into Gehenna…but one who recites the *Shema*[8] and observes it faithfully, for him Gehenna is cooled…as long as a man lives he has hope…today there is still time, but who can know about tomorrow…anyone who cries in the night, his voice is heard.…

At this point the crowd would burst out weeping. And anyone passing in front of the Holy Ark [in which the Torah scrolls are kept] during the evening prayer after the sermon was like a cantor chanting *Kol nidrei*.[9]

NOTES

1. The Musar movement was a pietistic movement, deriving its name from the Hebrew word for moral instruction (*musar*), which advocated moral earnestness as a necessary supplement to the observance of *mizvot* and Talmudic learning. The movement arose in mid-nineteenth-century Lithuania, becoming by the turn of the century a dominant trend within its yeshivot. Founded by Rabbi Israel Lipkin Salanter (1810–1883), the Musar movement was a response to the increasing laxity in the observance of the halakhah that resulted from the secular influences on Lithuanian Jewry. The problem, as Rabbi Salanter and his disciples understood it, was how to instill a spiritual vitality into the practice of Judaism without attenuating the values of punctilious observance of traditional Judaism. Eventually, the movement developed a distinctive pattern of spiritual and intellectual exercises designed to effect the moral and religious edification of the individual. This program of Musar, directed especially at the young *yeshivah* student, included the reading of classical ethical literature of Judaism, select verses from the Bible, Talmud and midrash. These passages would be recited, preferably in twilight or subdued lighting, to a melody suitable for evoking a pensive mood of isolation and emotional openness to God and His Commandments. The student was also encouraged to continual self-examination; some Musar rabbis recommended that a notebook be kept in which the student would record his moral and personal failings. The Musar *yeshivah* would have a special *mashgiah* or supervisor, who served as a sort of spiritual mentor guiding the moral and religious development of the students. At least once a week the *mashgiah* would hold a *shmues* (Yiddish for "talk"), with all the *yeshivah* students, on either a general moral topic or on a specific incident. In addition to punctilious observance of the *mizvot*, the need for mutual spiritual support, purity of the mind and intention, humility and regard for one's fellow human beings were stressed. The first Musar society was founded by Rabbi Salanter in Vilna in 1842; he later moved to Kovno. After his death, the movement was led, by Rabbi Isaac Blaser (1837–1907) known as Rabbi Itzelle Peterburger, who transformed the *yeshivah* of Slobodka (a suburb of Kovno) into a center of Musar, which influenced the yeshivot throughout Lithuania. The Musar movement—its pride, fraternity and spiritual intensity—helped Lithuanian Jewry resist the secularizing influence of Haskalah, the Bund and other forms of socialism and of Zionism. This selection is from the memoirs of one who studied at the *yeshivah* of Slobodka in the first decade of the twentieth century.

2. Rabbi Nathan Zevi ben Moses Finkel (1849–1927), founder (with the help of Rabbi Isaac Blaser) of the Musar *yeshivah* in Slobodka. As a mark of the deep respect his students had for him, they affectionately called him the Sabba ["grandfather"] from Slobodka.

3. Rabbi Mordecai Epstein (1866–1933) was appointed by Rabbi Finkel as the *rosh yeshivah* ("headmaster") of the *yeshivah* of Slobodka, a position he filled from 1893 until his death.

4. Hebrew term for daily afternoon prayer service.

5. Hebrew term for daily evening prayer service.

6. The twelfth month of the Hebrew calendar, corresponding to August-September. Preceding, the "Days of Awe" (Rosh Hashanah and Yom Kippur), Elul is traditionally a period devoted to preparation for penitence.

7. See Ethics of the Fathers, 1:5.

8. Hebrew designation for the confession of faith, "Hear, O Israel, the Lord our God, the Lord is One." (Deut. 6:4)

9. Opening prayer of the Yom Kippur evening service, which is recited in a very solemn manner.

16. THE MODERN *YESHIVAH* OF LIDA (1907)

ISAAC JACOB REINES[1]

Upon examining the state of Torah learning and Judaism among the people of Israel in Russia today we see before us a heartrending spectacle. The houses of learning, where once flocks of pupils eagerly pursued knowledge of the Torah, now stand vacant and desolate. Instead of young men imbued with the knowledge of God and schooled in the ways of Judaism, we encounter everywhere youths who deny their God and their nation, youths innocent of Torah learning who are as far removed from us in spirit as the moon is from the earth. Our ears are daily assaulted with the sounds of new knowledge and modern opinion such as our forefathers could not have fathomed. In vain do we strain to hear the sweet voice of Jacob. Judaism and tradition, the love of God and Torah learning have grown scarce. We stand besieged by alien thoughts and foreign views. The scholars among us grow fewer and fewer. They are no longer well respected and our sons have ceased to turn to them in their pursuit of knowledge.

Upon the ruins of our world a strange, new world is rising; where once our vineyards flourished we now plant strange fruits. The day is near when not a single scholar will be found among us, and the honor, glory and genius of Judaism will turn to dust. Soon, the vital and vivid Judaism we still find among the Jews of Russia will suffer a fate like that which befell her in France. A dreadful disaster is imminent!

Most regrettably, the fathers, even those who have remained faithful to their God and to the ways of Judaism, are bringing, with their very hands, this disaster upon themselves and upon their sons. They send their sons out at a tender age to face the temptations of the world, to be educated in the secular schools, to earn a living in industry and commerce. What are we to expect then from our offspring who are nurtured upon foreign soil, who are not nourished by a proper study of Judaism? The future awaiting us is grim, indeed. A horrible fate awaits Judaism, the very Judaism which has so valiantly fought for her survival these thousands of years.

Our wise men took this situation to heart, and gathered together to contemplate a solution to the crisis. They understood that the new situation demands a new outlook, that it would be a crime before God and the nation to sit idly while the crisis grows and worsens. They agreed that the present day realities must be reckoned with and may not be ignored, and that one must take into account the changing needs of the people. To this end, they decided to establish a new *yeshivah*, a *yeshivah* which will permit our sons to remain in the temple of the Torah and yet acquire the sort of knowledge and understanding that would assure their future well-being. The *yeshivah* will grant its pupils the moral authority to be rabbis and equip them with enough worldly knowledge to assure their acceptance as leaders of their generation. The *yeshivah* will not only educate Talmudic scholars, but will seek to give a rich Jewish education to those who will find their future in practical, mundane spheres. The *yeshivah* is intended for the good of the Jewish people and for the preservation of Torah learning.

The *yeshivah* is established along the following guidelines: (1) The *yeshivah* will give the students a thorough education in those disciplines required of a rabbi. A special committee will plan the course of studies. The method of study will be based on common sense and intellectual honesty. (2) The *yeshivah* will give the students an adequate education in biblical studies, Hebrew language and its grammar. Jewish history will be taught from the traditional and correct point of view. The pupils will also become familiar with Jewish literature and its bibliography. (3) The *yeshivah* will provide its students with a secular education equal

---

Source: Isaac Jacob Reines [The Mission of the Holy yeshivah of Lida] (Vilna, 1907), pp. 6–7. trans. R. Weiss.

to that of the public schools. They will be taught to speak and write Russian fluently, and will study as well Russian and world history, geography of the five continents, arithmetic, geometry, algebra, and some of the natural sciences. (4) The *yeshivah* will have six grades for the course of studies extending over a period of six years. In order to advance from one form to the next a student will have to pass an examination. Those who fail the examination will repeat the year's study. (5) Four committees shall be in charge of the *yeshivah*. One committee of rabbis will supervise the religious scholars, a second committee will supervise secular studies, a committee of home owners will supervise financial matters and a committee of pupils will concern itself with matters pertaining to the daily life of the pupils.... (6) In matters of scholarship and conduct each student will be supervised individually. The students will be educated to be faithful to God, loyal to their nation and observant of the *mizvot*. They will be expected to be well behaved and civilized. (7) Students of the *yeshivah* will receive financial support which will be increased with each year of study. Students in the upper grades will receive a stipend large enough to support them entirely....

NOTE

1. Rabbi Isaac Jacob Reines (1839–1915). One of the first rabbis to join the Zionist movement, he founded the religious Zionist Mizrahi movement in 1902. (See chapter 10, document 12.) In 1905 he established (after an earlier abortive attempt in the 1880s) the first modern *yeshivah* in Eastern Europe. At the *yeshivah* (founded in Lida, a town in the province of Grodno), secular studies—with an emphasis on the pragmatic—were taught side by side with traditional studies. As is indicated in Reines's statement, the founding of the *yeshivah* of Lida was guided by a desire to strengthen traditional Jewry in the face of the challenge posed by various secular trends. Reines "explained the increase of influence of the *maskilim* as the result of the fact that they were fighting with 'material and practical weapons,' while the leaders of traditional Judaism confined themselves to moral ones. In other words, the *maskilim* provided the needs of this world while [the rabbis] provided only for the next world" (Joseph Salmon, "The *yeshivah* of Lida: A Unique Institution of Higher Learning," *YIVO Annual, 15* [1974], p. 111). Hence, in light of the pressing economic plight of the Jewish masses, Reines held that the youth should be provided with an education that would equip them with the tools to earn a livelihood.

Despite Reines' emphasis on the economic factor in the crisis, he did not wholly overlook the weakening of individual faith in the tradition and its proponents. This clearly implies a process of transformation of values within the [traditional] community. Haskalah is not seen merely as vocational preparation, but as the road to social esteem. A scholar lacking general knowledge was subject [in Reines' words] to "indifference and contempt," on the part of the rank-and-file.... Reines did not see his program as revolutionizing values, but rather as an attempt to find new means to strengthen the basis of traditional society within new social conditions (J. Salmon, op. cit., pp. 113ff.).

17. RUSSIAN MUST BE OUR MOTHER TONGUE (1861)[1]

OSIP ARONOWICH RABINOWICH

In other European countries the Jews speak the pure language of their Christian brothers, and that fact does not hinder them from being good Jews. We in Russia, however, instead of learning the glorious Russian language, persist in speaking our corrupted jargon [i.e., Yiddish], that grates on the ears and distorts. This jargon is incapable in fact of expressing sublime thoughts.... It is our obligation to cast off these old rags, a heritage of the dark Middle Ages.... We believe the time has come for the Russian language to become the Jews' guide on the road to enlightenment and to the widening of their spiritual and material sphere of activity.... The Russian language must serve as the primary force animating the masses, because, apart from divine providence, language is the constitutive factor of humanity. Our homeland is Russia—just as its air is ours, so its language must become ours.

NOTE

1. The *maskilim* were divided regarding which language— Russian, Hebrew, or Yiddish—should be the vehicle to promote social and cultural progress among the Jewish masses. Opinion on this issue reflected differences of generation and ideology. The representatives of the early *haskalah* and the Zionists on the whole favored Hebrew. The socialists by and large preferred Yiddish. Liberals, who believed in the eventual liberalization of the Russian polity and the civil emancipation of the Jews, urged the adoption of Russian. According to a government census of 1897, 96.7 percent of the Jews of the Pale spoke Yiddish as their first language; only 1.3 percent spoke either Russian, Ukrainian, or Belorussian as their mother tongue. Outside the Pale, the latter figure was 72 percent. Hebrew as a written language was known to those Jews who had received a thorough traditional education. The number of Jews who knew Hebrew, although difficult to ascertain, was far greater than the number of those who were literate in Russian.

This selection is from the first Russian Jewish weekly, *Razsvet* [Dawn]. The purpose of this weekly, founded in 1860, was "to assist our government in its constant and sincere efforts to improve the conditions of our people and raise its moral and cultural level." To further this end, *Razsvet* would interpret government decrees for its readers, preach patriotism, genuine piety and morality, and disseminate "useful" knowledge. In the dispute over which language should be used by the "modern" Jew, *Razsvet* advocated the adoption of Russian. Its foremost aim, however, was to champion the cause of Jewish civil rights. This latter position brought the weekly into conflict with the government censor, and it was forced to fold within a year of its first issue.

Source: O. Rabinowich ["Russia—Our Native Land: Just as We Breathe Its Air We Must Speak Its Language"], *Razsvet*, no. 16 (Odessa, 1861), pp. 200–205. trans. R. Weiss.

18. PROGRAM (FEBRUARY 8, 1864)

SOCIETY FOR THE PROMOTION OF CULTURE AMONG JEWS[1]

1. Regarding the dissemination of the Russian language. In accordance with the request of the Deputy Minister of Education we shall endeavor: (a) to publish a new edition of the books originally published by the government in 1857 to teach the Jews to read the Russian language, and to publish an inexpensive Russian primer adapted for the Jewish reader; (b) to print Jewish history texts in Russian, because the contents will surely touch the heart of every Jew; (c) to encourage our brethren who have literary talent and Russian language skills to write material in Russian, by awarding them grants and financial assistance, and to publish their compositions in books, pamphlets and periodicals. This material should deal with Jewish history, literature and other topics of relevance and use to us. This project will have two beneficial results. On the one hand, in the course of time, there will be many Jewish writers of Russian and, on the other hand, such compositions will provide a powerful incentive for the Jewish public to learn Russian. Furthermore, since the books will be published with the help of the Society, it will be possible to sell them at low enough prices to enable all Jews to buy them.

2. Regarding the dissemination of useful knowledge among our brethren. Since the aim of our Society is to care for the masses of our people and their educational needs, to motivate them to acquire an education and to persuade them that enlightenment is not opposed to our faith, it is necessary to distribute among the people books which contain nothing touching on faith and religion. Accordingly, we shall promote only those books dealing with scientific matters which have been edited with good taste and present the material in an appropriate way. Since, as is now the case, the masses of the people do not yet know Russian, the only way to bring this material

to their attention is to publish it in Hebrew and in the traditional rabbinic style of the Talmud, which is most widely understood by the people. Therefore the executive committee of the Society has decided as follows: (a) to attempt to edit for our brethren books written in the aforementioned style and language, dealing with the natural sciences, mathematics, geography and history—especially Jewish history—and other works that the committee will find useful; (b) in order to disseminate information on the natural sciences and mathematics in particular, the committee shall empower [one of its members to speak to the authorities] about renewing the publication of *Hazfirah*,[2] under the conditions approved by the committee; (c) so that Jewish youth shall be informed of all that goes on in the world of Jewry and be acquainted, in addition, with the works of German scholars in the area of the Science of Judaism, the committee will send the relevant German Jewish periodicals to the Talmudic academies, the yeshivot, and to some of the middle-level schools, to libraries and to the *heders* [traditional primary schools]; (d) to attempt to implement the idea of establishing libraries and reading rooms for the Jews in every city, with the assistance of the Society's members in each city. . . .

NOTES

1. The Society for the Promotion of Culture Among Jews was founded in St. Petersburg in 1863 by members of the Jewish upper bourgeoisie; the society was under the supervision of the Ministry of Education. The principal reason for the founding of the society, according to Leon Rosenthal (1817–1887), its first treasurer, was to address a charge made by the government: "whenever Jewish leaders broached the question of civic rights to

Source: [Decisions of the Executive Committee of the Society for the Promotion of Culture Among Jews, February 8, 1864], in Leon Rosenthal, *Toldot hevrat marbei haskalah beyisrael beerez Rusyah* (St. Petersburg, 1885), vol. 1, pp. 4–5. trans. D. Goldman.

government representatives, the latter countered by charging them with the task of educating the masses of Jewry" (Rosenthal, *Toldot hevrat marbei haskalah beyisrael beerez Rusyah*, p. vii). The society accordingly set as its task, as its program reflects, the preparation of its brethren for emancipation and integration into Russian society and culture.

2. Hebrew periodical appearing intermittently in Warsaw from 1862 to 1931. The initial object of the periodical—until 1879, when Nahum Sokolow (1860–1936) joined its editorial staff and changed its direction to emphasize Hebrew literature and Zionist ideology—was to disseminate a knowledge of the natural sciences and mathematics among the Jews of the Pale.

19. YIDDISH IS A CORRUPT JARGON (1828)

ISAAC DOV LEVINSOHN[1]

This language which we speak here in this country, which we borrowed from the Germans and which is called Judeo-German [Yiddish]—this language is completely corrupted. This corruption is a consequence of the eclectic nature of the language, a mixture of corrupted words taken from Hebrew, Russian, French, Polish, as well as from German, and even the German words are mispronounced and slurred. Moreover, this, our language, cannot serve us except for popular usage and simple conversations. If we wish to formulate concepts about higher things, Judeo-German will not suffice....

Why Judeo-German?—From these observations [concerning the shortcomings of Judeo-German] you will readily acknowledge the need to study at least one pure language and know it well. And there is no need to add that the language of the country we live in is doubtlessly the one we are obligated to learn correctly. Thus we can ask: in this country, why speak Judeo-German? Either pure German or Russian. Not only is Russian the language of the country, it is also an especially pure and rich language. It is not lacking in pleasant tones or aesthetic form and it contains all the elements considered necessary for the perfect language (as I have explained at length in the introduction to my book in Hebrew, *The Elements of the Russian Language*, which I wrote for the benefit of Jewish youth and which I hope to publish soon, if God grant me life). We may conclude from our discussion so far that it is a great obligation and necessity to know one of the foreign languages well, especially the language of the country where we live, and that we should know it perfectly so that we can articulate our thoughts in a correct manner.

NOTE

1. Isaac Dov Levinsohn (1788–1860) was the first great protagonist of *haskalah* in Russia. He was hailed by his contemporaries as the Russian Moses Mendelssohn. His works are mainly polemical, excoriating traditional Jewish leadership, particularly Hasidic, and advocating educational reform and the transition to a life of manual labor and agriculture. This selection is taken from his most influential work, *Teudah be-Israel* [Testimony in Israel], written in 1823 but, due to fierce Orthodox opposition, not published until 1828. The Russian government gave him an award for this work.

Source: Isaac Dov Levinsohn, *Teudah be-Israel* (Vilna, 1828), pp. 34–36. trans. D. Goldman.

20. HEBREW—OUR NATIONAL FORTRESS (1868)

PERETZ SMOLENSKIN[1]

When people ask what the renewal of the Hebrew language will give us I shall answer: It will give us self-respect and courage, it will bind us indissolubly to the name Israel. Other peoples may erect stone monuments... and spill their blood like water in order to perpetuate their own name and language.... We have no monument, country or name, and the only memory remaining to us from the destruction of the Temple is the Hebrew language. Many [Jews] despise and scorn it, and those who do, denigrate our entire people...they are traitors to their name and faith. They exhort us: "Let us be like all the other nations." I answer: Let us, like other nations, pursue knowledge and reject evil; let us, like other nations, take pride in our origins and acknowledge our language and national honor. Our faith must not be a source of shame to us.... We are secure if we hold fast to the ancient language which has accompanied us from country to country, to the tongue in which our poets and prophets spoke, in which our forefathers cried aloud with their dying breath.... Our language is our national fortress; if it disappears into oblivion the memory of our people will vanish from the face of the earth.

NOTE

1. Perez Smolenskin (1840–1885), Russian Hebrew novelist and publicist. In 1868 he founded the Hebrew monthly *Hashahar* [The Dawn], which, under his dedicated editorship, became the most significant Hebrew literary platform of the *haskalah* in its late period. Smolenskin sought to steer a path between what he held to be the Scylla of the Orthodox obscurantism and the Charybdis of assimilation. He found this path in Jewish nationalism. Accordingly, he was a passionate advocate of the Hebrew language and literature, which he deemed to be the ground of Jewish nationhood and the surrogate for a national territory.

Source: Perez Smolenskin [Foreword], Hashahar 1 (1868), pp. v–vii. trans. L. Sachs.

21. MY SOUL DESIRED YIDDISH (1862)

MENDELE MOYKHER SFORIM[1]

Here I am, observing the ways of our people and attempting to write for them stories from Jewish sources in the holy tongue, yet most of them do not even know this tongue. Their language is Yiddish. And what life is there for a writer, what profit in his labor, if he is of no use to his people? The question—"for whom do I toil"[2]—has not ceased to trouble me.... The Yiddish language in my day was an empty vessel, containing nothing but slang and trite, meaningless phrases.... The women and the poor would read Yiddish without understanding it, while the rest of the people, even if they didn't know how to read in another language, were ashamed to be caught reading Yiddish, lest this private folly of theirs become public knowledge. And if one of them gave in to temptation and read a Yiddish book and, enjoying it, laughed over it, he immediately justified his deed by saying to himself it was unintentional. Indeed he would justify his reaction by dismissing the book as women's literature, capable of provoking laughter but not thought. Those of our writers who know Hebrew, our holy tongue, and continue to write in it, do not care whether or not the people understand it. These writers look down on Yiddish and greatly scorn it. And if one out of many occasionally remembered the cursed jargon and wrote a few lines in it, he kept his works hidden, so as to escape criticism and ridicule. How perplexed I was then, when I thought of writing in Yiddish, for I feared it would entail the ruin of my reputation—so my friends in the Hebrew literature movement had warned me. But my love for the useful defeated false pride, and I decided to take pity on the much-scorned language and do what I could for my people. One of my friends [Shiye-Mordkhe Lifshits[3]] joined me in persuading the publisher of *Hameliz*[4] to publish a periodical in Yiddish, the language of our people. The publisher agreed and *Kol mevaser*[5] began to appear with great success. I was soon inspired to write my first story in Yiddish: *"Dos kleine Menshele, oder a lebens beshraybung fun Avrom Yitzhok Takif," gedrukt b'hishtadlus Mendele Moykher Sforim.*[6]... And other stories and books followed.

My first story made a big impact on the Jewish masses and was soon published in a third edition... and then in a fourth edition.... That story laid the cornerstone of modern Yiddish literature. From then on, my soul desired only Yiddish, and I dedicated myself entirely to it....

NOTES

1. Mendele Moykher Sforim is the pen name of Russian, Hebrew, and Yiddish author Shalom Jacob Abramowitsch (c. 1836–1917). Beloved for his affectionate descriptions and satires of the Jewish masses of Russia in the late nineteenth century, he was an innovator in artistic prose style in both Hebrew and Yiddish literature; his influence on the latter was particularly marked.
2. Title of a poem by Judah Leib Gordon; see document 9, in this chapter.
3. Shiye-Mordkhe Lifshits (1829–1878) was one of the pioneers of Yiddish literature.
4. *Hameliz* [The Advocate] was a Hebrew periodical that appeared from 1860 to 1904; from 1886 to 1904 it appeared as a daily. Considered the central organ of Russian Jewry, it was moderately conservative and very influential.
5. Hebrew: "The Voice of Good Tidings" from Isaiah 52:7; Yiddish supplement to *Hameliz*.
6. ["The little man, or the life of Abraham Isaac Takif," printed with the assistance of Mendele Moykher Sforim] (Odessa: *Kol mevaser*, 1864).

Source: Mendele Moykher Sforim, "Autobiographical Notes," *The Complete Works of Mendele Moykher Sforim* (Tel Aviv: Dvir, 1947), pp. 4–5. Cited by permission. trans. D. Goldman.

22. EUROPEAN CULTURE DESTROYED MY FAMILY (1909)

PAULINE WENGEROFF[1]

Born at the beginning of the 1830s in Bobryusk [in White Russia] and brought up by strictly observant parents, I was in a position to see the transformation which European education wrought on Jewish family life. I can see how easy it was for our parents to educate us and how hard it was for us, the second generation, to bring up our children. Though we became acquainted with German and Polish literature, we eagerly studied Pentateuch and Prophets, for they gave us pride in our religion and its traditions and bound us to our people. Biblical poetry stamped itself on the untouched childish mind and provided for the days to come chastity and purity, buoyancy and inspiration.

But how hard for us was that great transition period in the sixties and seventies. We had achieved a degree of European education, but we knew of the wide gaps in our knowledge. We did our utmost so that our children would not lack what we had missed. But we overlooked the wisdom of observing moderation. So we have only ourselves to blame for the abyss between us and our children.

We must now obey our children and submit completely to their will, just as once obedience to our parents was inviolable. As once with our parents, so now with our children, we must hold our tongues, and it is harder now than then. When our parents talked, we listened respectfully, as now we listen, in pride and joy, as our children talk about themselves and their ideals. Our submissiveness and admiration allow them to tyrannize us. This is the reverse side of the coin, the negative impact of European culture on the Jews of Russia. No group but the Jews so swiftly and irrevocably abandoned everything for West European culture, discarded its religion, and divested itself of its historical past and its traditions....

A marriage was arranged between me and Hanan Wengeroff, and at eighteen I became the bride of a man I loved deeply but knew not at all. Konotop, where my husband's parents lived, was to be my new home. A small town of ten thousand inhabitants, it yet looked like a village. The inhabitants were mostly Christians; the few Jews were grain merchants and tavern keepers. My father-in-law, the richest man in town, held the government's wine and liquor concession. I remember the way the house was furnished—the large rooms, expensive furniture, beautiful silver, carriages and horses, servants, frequent guests....

I read a lot in Konotop, especially Russian. First, I read the German books I had brought from home....Then I started on the Russian books which stood on the shelves of the Wengeroff library. I read [the German newspaper] *Moskauer Nachrichten* and taught my husband, eager to learn, German. But his chief study was Talmud. Every Monday and Thursday he spent the night with his rabbi, hunched over great tomes.

Since our betrothal, my husband experienced mystical religious moods and devoted himself to the sacred mysteries of the Kabbala. Then, this fervent young man yearned to make a pilgrimage to Lubavich, the seat of the head of the Lithuanian hasidim. The rabbi would surely have the complete answers to disturbing questions and enigmas. Yet barely two years before, my husband had advocated modern ideas which led to conflicts with his parents.

One morning while I was busy at household tasks, my husband came into the kitchen and told

---

Source: Pauline Wengeroff, *Memoiren einer Grossmutter. Bilder aus der Kulturgeschichte der Juden Russlands im 19. Jahrhundert* (Berlin, 1908–10), 2 vols. Selections translated by Lucy S. Dawidowicz, *The Golden Tradition: Jewish Life and Thought in Eastern Europe* (Boston: Beacon Press, 1967), pp.161–66.

me, elatedly, excitedly, that his father had permitted him and his elder brother to go to Lubavich in the company of their rabbi.

What happened there I do not know, for my husband never spoke of this tragic experience. All I know was that this young man, hopeful and inspired, made a pilgrimage to the rabbi, hoping that he would unveil the great mystery, but returned sobered. He continued his religious observances and studied with the rabbi, but the magic and ecstasy had gone. Thereafter, little by little, he began to neglect his religious observances. Then he decided to cut his beard. We had our first quarrel. I begged him not to yield to vanity and let his beard grow. He would not hear of it. He reminded me that he was the man of the house and demanded my obedience and submission.

Four years later we left Konotop and the patriarchal way of life we had led. My husband had obtained the liquor concession in Lubny, where we were to start our own independent life. Now, without having to worry about his parents, my husband organized his life as he desired. Daily prayers, in prayer shawl and phylacteries, ceased, though he continued to study Talmud. He used to discuss it at length with the town rabbi, who was our frequent guest, but his interest was just scholarly. . . .

My wise mother once said: "Two things I know for certain. I and my generation will surely live and die as Jews. Our grandchildren will surely live and die not as Jews. But what our children will be I cannot foresee." The first two parts of this prophecy came true. The third is now coming true, for our generation is some kind of hybrid. Other peoples and other nations have drawn from modern, alien currents and ideas only what is congenial to their own character and thus have preserved their own individuality and uniqueness. But the course that befell the Jews was that they could not acquire the new, the alien, without renouncing the old and repudiating their unique individuality, and their most precious possessions. How chaotically these modern ideas whirled through minds of young Russian Jews! Traditional family ideas disappeared, but new ones did not arise in their stead. These young Jewish men had no sense of moderation nor did they want it. In this transitional period, the woman, the mother, was cruelly brushed aside, for clinging to tradition; she wanted to impart to her children the ethics of Judaism, the tradition of its faith, the sanctity of the Sabbath and the Holy Days, Hebrew, Bible study. She wanted to transmit

this great treasure along with the enlightenment, with the new current of West European culture. But the husbands had the same answer to all pleas: "The children need no religion." In their inexperience, they wanted to take the dangerous leap from the lowest level of education to the highest, without any intermediate step. They demanded not only assent from their wives, but also submission. They preached freedom, equality, fraternity in public, but at home they were despots. . . .

In our family, the struggle to keep the Jewish tradition went on in much the same way as in many other families. First my husband requested, and then demanded, that his wishes be fulfilled. It was not enough for him to have complete freedom over all matters outside our home: I had to "reform" myself and my home. It began with small things, intimate things, dear to me.

As soon as we settled [later] in St. Petersburg I had to discard the *peruke* [wig] which pious Jewish women wore. It was here in Petersburg, after a violent struggle, that I ceased to keep a kosher kitchen. Little by little I had to drive each cherished custom from our home. "Drive" is not the right word, for I accompanied each to the door with tears and sobs. I loved my husband intensely and as faithfully as in the first days of our marriage, yet I could not submit without resistance. I wanted to preserve this cherished tradition for myself and my children, and I fought a battle of life and death.

In Petersburg, a thousand different experiences always seemed to converge on the one problem of Judaism. What a time of heartbreak when my son attended the *gymnasium*! Simon was a fourth-year student. The students were taken to the chapel for religious services. All but Simon kneeled before the icons. When the teacher ordered him to kneel, he refused: "I am a Jew. My religion forbids me to kneel to an image." After the service, the enraged teacher told Simon he was expelled. I went to the school superintendent, imploring and weeping. I wanted to tell him my son had not willfully been disobedient; he wanted only to remain loyal to his own upbringing and religion. I could not speak; my throat was tight and the tears flowed. I foresaw that my son's whole life would be destroyed. The school superintendent reflected. The boy was dismissed from this gymnasium, but he would arrange to have Simon admitted to another. I was relieved and also proud. Simon was the flesh of my flesh. But ought I to expect that my children, growing up under alien influences, would follow the ways of their mother? They understood, in their way, what was happening and often took their father's side. I felt alone and abandoned by my husband and society. I submitted. But no one suspected the tragedy I experienced that day. Only a few yellowed pages to which thirty-eight years ago in an hour of despair I confided my unhappiness are the silent witness of my suffering. These words, which I first wrote, April 15, 1871, I have set down again for they seem to express the woe and despair which so many wives and mothers suffered in that transitional era in Jewish life.

NOTE

1. Born into a pious and wealthy Russian Jewish family, Pauline Epstein Wengeroff (1833–1916) witnessed with consternation the transformation of traditional Jewish life under the impact of secular modernity. In her memoirs, which appeared when she was in her seventies, she gives eloquent expression to what she regards as the tragic disintegration of Jewish tradition and familial bonds; indeed, the tragedy is exemplified by the conversion of several of her own children to Christianity. Significantly, she wrote her memoirs not in Yiddish or Russian, but in German, the language of the European cultural elite. For a translation of her memoirs, see P. Wengeroff, *Remberings of the World of a Russian-Jewish Woman in the Nineteenth Century,* trans. from the German by Henny Wenkart, ed. with an afterword by Bernard D. Cooperman (Potomac: University Press of Maryland, 2000). Also see Shulamit Magnus, "Pauline Wengeroff and the Voice of Jewish Modernity," in *Gender and Judaism: The Transformation of Jewish Tradition,* ed. T. M. Rudavsky (New York: New York University Press, 1995), pp. 181–90.

23. THE JEWISH QUESTION IN EASTERN EUROPE (1877)

AARON LIEBERMANN[1]

In all countries about to acknowledge the dignity of every child of man, the question of Jewish civil rights has, in the context of normal social life, become increasingly important. As of now, however, this question is still out of place in the countries of the East where it has not yet occurred to anyone to consider someone not of his tribe or allegiance as human. [This question has not yet occurred to the] barbaric peoples nor to their yet more barbaric rulers. In America and Western Europe, on the other hand, the question has already been forgotten, for there the concept "man" has dispelled the concepts of nation and faith—at least among the enlightened. Only in those countries bordering the East and the West—the settlements of the Slavic tribes—will some still parley over the Jewish question without resolving the "unsolvable riddle.". . .

[In Eastern Europe] the Jews and their supporters have been compelled to fight for their lives in a defensive war against enemies waging a war of offense, and their stratagems greatly vary depending on the features of the battlefield. In Rumania the Jews seek refuge from persecution and oppression in the protection of the powerful kings. And sometimes they gain satisfaction by hurling insult and abuse back at those who vilify them. It is understandable

Source: Aaron Liebermann, "Sheelat hayehudim," *Haemet* 1 (Summer 1877), pp. 1–5. trans. A. Schwartz.

that they then completely overstep bounds, and seizing upon the doings of their opponents heap scorn and contempt on the entire Rumanian people. For the misdeeds of some, they defame an entire nation with curses of the marketplace.... These strategems may help, but woe to the member of the household who seeks the protection of strangers to defend him from the blows of his father or brother! On most occasions they will manage to break all his bones before his protectors rush to his aid. In the land of Galicia, the Jews are strong enough to defend themselves without outside help. Those Jews with sidelocks as twisted and as long as our exile, who wear cloth pants, stockings, and all the other old Polish garb—now called "Jewish clothing"—those men are politicians and diplomats! Positioned between the Germans and the Poles, they always lean toward that faction whose way seems right to their sight. There, in Galicia, the Jews truly stand on one footing with the other national tribes as far as politics are concerned, and in a time of need they will come here to Vienna with their shoes and stockings, their sidecurls and *zjupitse*[2] to stand before the Kaiser. The Jews of Russia are not like that. Only rarely may their voices be heard speaking of their enemies in the Russian journals. It is not a voice of jubilation but—whoever hears may laugh—a voice of supplication spoken halfheartedly, gravely and in a spirit of utter defeat. We know that our brethren in Russia apologize that they have not been permitted to respond to their enemies as they would like, and we can believe them.... But in fact it is all the same to us if they respond in a tone of jubilation, like the Jews of Rumania, or in a tone of entreaty as they now do. For as we have said from the outset, this is a war of might and guile, lie and deceit—and it is indeed a war! At one end are those who will bring all Jews to trial for every offense committed by individual Jews. The Jews, for their part, will make every effort to drag out their rights and show them off in the bright light of day declaring: Here is the Jewish people! Both will place

individuals in the stead of the collective as a whole. However much the Jew-haters increase their search among us for evil doings, the Jews will strive wherever they can to conceal the blemishes of their brothers from the "desecration of God's name," or they will produce their righteous brothers as having been maligned as sinners. This will sometimes be successful, but most of the time it will fail. For how is it possible to show that all of Israel is a righteous nation or that in all of Jacob's flock there is not even one leprous lamb?

This war over the Jewish question could continue forever, for while both sides are correct concerning details, they have both relied in their arguments on sophistry, both have emphasized *quid pro quo* and both have missed the larger truth. How will it come to an end? When will the fate of the Jews and of the Slavs be joined together in peace? When will each side acknowledge the other's humanity and join hands for the ascent to human perfection?...

NOTES

1. Aaron Liebermann (1845–1880), pioneer of Jewish socialism and Hebrew writer. In 1875 he fled his native Russia in order to avoid arrest for his socialist activities. In London he began to develop a program for a revolutionary socialist organization among the Jews of Russia. He was inspired by the *Narodnik* principle of "going to the masses," which he interpreted as going to the Jewish masses. In 1877 he settled in Vienna and began to publish *Haemet* [The Truth]—the first Hebrew socialist periodical. Only three issues of the periodical appeared; its quick demise was caused by financial difficulties and the need to smuggle the periodical into Russia. Liebermann wrote most of the articles, and in them he criticized organized Jewish life, the exploitation of the poor by the rich Jews, and the unthoughtful hostility of Jewish socialists to Jewish tradition. This selection is taken from the inaugural article of *Haemet*. It describes the plight of various East European Jewish communities.

2. A black overcoat, similar to a caftan.

24. THE PLIGHT OF THE JEWS OF RUMANIA (1878)

CONGRESS OF BERLIN[1]

XLIV. In Rumania the difference of religious creeds and confessions shall not be alleged against any persons as a ground for exclusion or incapacity in matters relating to the enjoyment of civil and political rights, admission to public employments, functions and honors or the exercise of various professions and industries in any locality whatsoever. The freedom and outward exercise of all forms of worship are assured to all persons belonging to Rumania, as well as to foreigners, and no hindrance shall be offered either to the hierarchical organization of the different communions or to their relations with their spiritual chiefs.

The subjects and citizens of all the Powers, traders and others, shall be treated in Rumania without distinction of creed on a footing of perfect equality.

NOTE

1. At the conclusion of the Russo-Turkish War in 1877, the great European powers gathered in Berlin to discuss the problems of the Balkans and the Near East arising from the war. Held between June 13 and July 13, 1878, the Congress of Berlin was attended by representatives of Austria-Hungary, France, Great Britain, Italy, Russia, and Turkey; limited representation was granted the Balkan states themselves: Greece, Montenegro, Rumania, and Serbia. Various Jewish bodies successfully sought to have the position of the Jews in the Balkan states placed on the agenda. To coordinate their efforts, the Jews established a special council consisting of the representatives of the Committee for Jewish Affairs in Berlin, the Alliance Israélite Universelle in Paris, the delegation of Rumanian Jews, and members of the Alliance in Berlin. The committee drew up a memorandum, which was submitted to the Congress, with a second one submitted to the head of the German delegation, Prince Otto von Bismarck. The memoranda described in detail the sorry condition of the Jews in the Balkan countries and called for an international guarantee that members of all creeds and nations in these countries would henceforth enjoy equal civil rights. Individual members of the council, which included some of the leading Jewish figures of the day, were charged with making direct appeals to the delegations of their respective countries. Their coordinated efforts mark an important milestone in the development of a modern Jewish consciousness grounded in a sense of shared social and even political responsibility for one's fellow Jews regardless of country of residence.

   In the deliberations of the Congress, the Jewish question first came up for discussion on June 24, 1878, in connection with the peace treaty to be signed with Bulgaria. The proposal was passed recognizing the independence of Bulgaria, conditioned on its granting equal rights to all its subjects. A similar clause was subsequently introduced into the peace treaty with Serbia. The Russian representative sought to frustrate these efforts by arguing that the Jews of the Balkans and of Russia were different from the Jews of Berlin, London, Paris, and Vienna. Emboldened by the Russian position, the delegate of Rumania, which had the largest Jewish population—about 130,000 at the time—of the Balkan states, put up stiff opposition to efforts to "interfere in its internal affairs." But the great powers had the final say in Rumania, which was still awaiting international recognition of its independence, and passed a special resolution, introduced into paragraph 44 of the peace treaty with Rumania, stipulating that equal rights were to be granted to all its inhabitants. This paragraph, which was also introduced verbatim into the treaties with Greece, Montenegro, and Turkey, is given here.

   Each of the Balkan states complied fully and granted equal rights to all regardless of religion and nationality. Only Rumania balked and refused to meet its obligations under paragraph 44. Indeed, the

Source: Thomas Erskine Holland, ed., *The European Concert in the Eastern Question: A Collection of Treaties and Other Public Acts* (Oxford: Clarendon Press, 1885), p. 301.

year following the treaty it defiantly modified the article of its constitution concerning naturalization to specify that "strangers" could obtain citizenship only on an individual basis; since Jews were legally regarded as "strangers," they were effectively denied Rumanian citizenship. Over the next 38 years, only 2,000 Jews were to be naturalized in Rumania. For a while the great powers withheld recognition of Rumanian independence. In time, however, economic considerations prevailed, and recognition was accorded the country despite its flagrant disregard of the Treaty of Berlin.

25. AWAITING A POGROM IN VILNA (1882)[1]

We expected a pogrom during the Christmas holidays, and the city was in a state of siege. Before the holidays we went to the governor and asked for protection. The Cossacks were called and the stores closed for three days. And now, although the holidays have passed quietly (i.e., there were no riots), our fears have not been allayed and we expect a pogrom at any minute. In brief, we see no end to our anxiety. For ahead of us are the civil New Year, the "Week of Butter," the Holiday of Baptism and Easter. How many threats and curses we heard before the holidays! If someone gets into an argument with a Christian the latter immediately says: "Just wait, soon we'll settle all the scores," or something similar or even worse. What kind of life is this? If I had the courage I would kill all those close to me and then myself, and the farce would be over. If I do not, some drunken riffraff will come along, ravish my wife and daughter and throw my infant Sonia from the third-floor window. Would it not be better for me to kill everyone? What a miserable creature is the Jew? Even when the advantage is clear to him he cannot summon the courage to do a good thing. Death awaits us in any case, so why should we wait?

NOTE

1. *Pogrom* is a Russian word for a violent riot, accompanied by pillage and murder, perpetrated by one group against another. Throughout Russian history, pogroms occurred between various communities in the multinational empire. In the international lexicon, *pogrom* is now a technical term designating the type of attack carried out by the non-Jewish population of Russia—and Eastern Europe in general—against the Jews between 1881 and 1921. Rarely did the police or the army intervene; indeed, they often lent their support to the rioters. The pogroms occurred during periods of severe political crisis and Christian holidays. Three major waves of pogroms took place in Russia: in 1881–1884, 1903–1906 and 1917–1921. The first began in the period of political unrest and confusion that followed the assassination of Tsar Alexander II in March 1881. Starting at the end of April in a Ukrainian town, pogroms spread quickly throughout the region and then erupted in Warsaw, Belorussia and Lithuania. The pogroms of the 1880s had a profound influence on the history of Russian Jewry. The radicalization of Jewish youth, the development of the nationalist and Zionist movement in Russia and the mass emigration of Russian Jewry were all to a great extent prompted by the pogroms. This selection is from letter to the editor of a Russian-language Jewish periodical published in St. Petersburg. The periodical served as the organ of the Russian Jewish intelligentsia, which maintained both a commitment to Judaism and a confidence in the ultimate triumph of liberalism in Russia.

Source: [Unsigned letter to the editor from a Jew in Vilna], *Nedelnaya kronika voskhroda*, no. 1 (February 1882), trans. L. Sachs.

26. THE MASSACRE OF JEWS AT KISHINEV (JUNE 1, 1903)[1]

N. TCHAYKOVSKY

Shortly before Easter, when the Bishop of the Greek Church in the Kishinev province was asked to contradict the absurd rumor that the Jews murdered a young man for their ritual [at Passover], . . . this high priest publicly stated that he himself believed the story of Jews using Christian blood for ritualistic purposes.

The semi-official paper . . . openly preached the extermination of Jews for months . . . All applications for permission to publish a more impartial paper having been repeatedly refused. . . .

And still, when the actual massacres began, the Governor—it is said now—failed for two days to obtain orders from the Ministry and the Tsar at St. Petersburg to use military force against the housebreakers and murderers. Moreover, he refused in the course of those two days any communication with the suffering Jewish population, never left his private quarters, closed all the telephones in the town to the public, and prohibited [the sending of] any private telegrams from Kishinev to St. Petersburg.

The police of the town not only refused to render any efficient protection and assistance to the . . . attacked and murdered Jewish population, but deliberately prevented by force any assistance being rendered to them by those private persons who were willing to do so. The police actually pointed out Jewish houses to the rioters. Whenever Jews themselves attempted to gather to show armed resistance, the police and military instantly attacked, disarmed, and dispersed them.

The results of this terrible circumstance are awful: 118 Jews, men, women and children, have already been buried; over 200 cases of serious injuries are still in the hospitals; and over 1000 cases of lighter injuries [have been] attended [to] in infirmaries; 800 Jewish houses destroyed and demolished; 600 shops and stores broken into and looted; over 4,000 Jewish families have been rendered homeless and destitute. . . .

It has been learned that there were about 12,000 troops in Kishinev at the time, against 200 to 300 active rioters and housebreakers. And as soon as the Government chose to proclaim martial law, after two days of delay, all disorders instantly stopped. . . .

NOTE

1. Kishinev, today the capital of the independent republic of Moldova, was formerly the capital of Bessarabia. At the beginning of the century some fifty thousand Jews lived there, constituting 46 percent of the population. The pogrom, described in this document, took place during Easter on April 6 and 7, 1903. Agents of the Ministry of the Interior and high officials of the Bessarabian administration were apparently involved in the preparation of the pogrom. The pogrom was preceded by a venomous anti-Jewish campaign led by an editor of a local newspaper, who incited the population through a constant barrage of hateful articles. The immediate cause of the pogrom was the death of a Christian child whom the Jews were accused of killing, for the use of his blood in their religious rites. (See chapter 6, document 30.) The pogrom caused a public outcry throughout the world and led to establishment of Jewish self-defense units.

Source: N. Tchaykovsky, "The Massacre of Jews at Kishinyov," *Free Russia: Organ of the Friends of Russian Freedom* 14, no. 6 (June 1, 1903), pp. 62–63. Orthography has been changed to conform with current usage.

27. THE CITY OF SLAUGHTER (1903)

HAIM NAHMAN BIALIK[1]

Arise and go now to the city of slaughter;
Into its courtyard wind thy way;
There with thine own hand touch, and with the eyes of thine head,
Behold on tree, on stone, on fence, on mural clay,
The spattered blood and dried brains of the dead.
Proceed thence to the ruins, the split walls reach,
Where wider grows the hollow, and greater grows the breach;
Pass over the shattered hearth, attain the broken wall
Whose burnt and barren brick, whose charred stones reveal
The open mouths of such wounds, that no mending
Shall ever mend, nor healing ever heal.
There will thy feet in feathers sink, and stumble
On wreckage doubly wrecked, scroll heaped on manuscript,
Fragments against fragmented—
Pause not upon this havoc; go thy way. . . .

Descend then, to the cellars of the town,
There where the virginal daughters of thy folk were fouled,
Where seven heathens flung a woman down,
The daughter in the presence of her mother,
The mother in the presence of her daughter,
Before slaughter, during slaughter, and after slaughter!
Touch with thy hand the cushion stained, touch
The pillow incarnadined;
This is the place the wild ones of the wood, the beasts of the field
With bloody axes in their paws compelled thy daughters yield;
Beasted and swined!
Note also, do not fail to note,
In that dark corner, and behind that cask
Crouched husbands, bridegrooms, brothers, peering from the cracks,
Watching the sacred bodies struggling underneath
The bestial breath,
Stifled in filth, and swallowing their blood!
The lecherous rabble portioning for booty
Their kindred and their flesh!

Source: Haim Nahman Bialik, "City of Slaughter," trans. Abraham M. Klein, in *The Complete Works of Hayyim Nahman Bialik,* ed. Israel Efros (New York: Histadruth Ivrith of America, 1948), vol. 1, pp. 129, 133–34. Copyright 1948 by Bloch Publishing Company. Reprinted by permission of Bloch Publishing Company.

Crushed in their shame, they saw it all;
They did not stir nor move;
They did not pluck their eyes out; they
Beat not their brains against the wall!
Perhaps, perhaps, each watcher had it in his heart to pray:
A miracle, O Lord,—and spare my skin this day!
Those who survived this foulness, who from their blood awoke,
Beheld their life polluted, the light of their world gone out—
How did their menfolk bear it, how did they bear this yoke?
They crawled forth from their holes, they fled to the house of the Lord,
They offered thanks to Him, the sweet benedictory word.
The *kohanim* [descendants of priestly families] sallied forth; to the Rabbi's house
    they flitted:
Tell me, O Rabbi, tell, is my own wife permitted?[2]
The matter ends; and nothing more.
And all is as it was before....

Come, now, and I will bring thee to their lairs
The privies, jakes and pigpens where the heirs
Of Hasmoneans lay, with trembling knees,
Concealed and cowering,—the sons of the Maccabees!
The seed of saints, the scions of the lions!
Who, crammed by scores in all the sanctuaries of their shame,
So sanctified My name!
It was the flight of mice they fled,
The scurrying of roaches was their flight;
They died like dogs, and they were dead!

NOTES

1. Haim Nahman Bialik (1873–1934). Celebrated as the poet laureate of modern Hebrew, Bialik exercised a profound influence on modern Jewish culture. Raised in the Pale of Settlement, he broke with traditional Judaism at the age of eighteen, and he devoted himself to the creation of a national, secular Jewish culture. His attitude to traditional Judaism, however, was ambivalent. On the one hand, he was angered at what he felt to be the moribund state of traditional Jewish society; on the other hand, he was painfully aware of the dilemma of modern Jews whose struggle for the right to determine their own destiny seemed to require a desperate rejection of divine law.

   Bialik was sent to Kishinev on behalf of the Jewish Historical Commission in Odessa in order to interview survivors of the pogrom and to prepare a report on the atrocities. After his visit to Kishinev, he wrote this poem, denouncing neither God nor the Russian mobs but the Jews themselves. This poem became a symbol of the Zionist revolt against traditional Judaism's supine acceptance of Exile and the bi-millennial humiliation of Jewry.

2. The *kohanim* are subject to strict laws of purity.

28. THE BEILIS TRIAL (1913)[1]

NEW YORK TIMES

In Kiev, Russia, yesterday, there was placed on trial behind closed doors one Mendel Beilis, charged with the murder of a Russian lad, Yustschinsky, in 1911. Beilis is a Jew, and is accused of "ritual murder," that is to say of having killed a boy to get his blood for alleged use in the rites of the Jewish religion. There are two elements in this case which make it of great importance and interest to right-thinking persons in all parts of the world.

One is the clear presumption, on all available official Russian testimony, of the entire innocence of the accused. Immediately after the murder of the boy, M. Minschuk, Chief of the Detective Service in Kiev, with several assistants, investigated the case and reported, first, that there was no evidence against Beilis, the accused, and second, that the boy was murdered by a gang of criminals whom he was suspected of betraying. For this report M. Minschuk was accused of manufacturing evidence to hinder the prosecution and to protect Jews, and though acquitted on one trial, was retried and condemned to prison for a year, with his assistants receiving lighter sentences. That fact clearly discredits the whole case of the prosecution.

The second significant fact in the case is the nature of the accusation, the allegation of murder for Jewish ritual purposes. The crime does not and cannot exist. It has been shown over and over again, and long ago, that there is nothing in the religious belief or practice of the Jews that remotely requires or sanctions or suggests the thing charged. Strict and searching inquiry by eminent men of science, theologians, historians, physicians, not Jews, in Great Britain, in Germany, in France, has resulted in the distinct and unqualified verdict that the belief in this crime has not the slightest foundation in fact, and that it is a foolish, blind superstition bred of prejudice upon ignorance.

It has so been held and denounced by the Pope, by the head of the Orthodox Church, by living Bishops of that Church, and by a Tsar of Russia, Alexander I, in 1817, confirmed by Nicholas I in 1835. What renders this base and baseless accusation more revolting at this late day, and by the officials of a Government professedly Christian, is the fact that it is in the twentieth century that a service used by the pagans in the first century is revived to justify the oppression and slaughter of Christians. The Government of Russia, and especially the Tsar of Russia, the authoritative head of a great branch of the Christian Church, in the mad, stupid war on the Jews, is 2000 years behind the times.

For the Russian peasants who are the helpless victims of this superstition, and who accept it like the superstitions accepted by the savage crowds of the Roman Arena, we can have pity, and even with the brutal action inspired by it we can have patience. But for educated men, particularly for Russian officials who deliberately appeal to the superstitious and incite to brutal action, we can have only indignant detestation. And that feeling is in no wise affected by the fact that this outrage is directed to those of one or another race, one or another religion. The outrage is upon humanity.

Every human, every decently human instinct condemns it; it is true that the offense is one that cannot be dealt with in the ordinary ways of international communication, though it is by no means wholly beyond them, as was very properly shown in the case of Rumania as conducted by the late Secretary Hay. But in the court of public opinion such an offense can and must be dealt with. Fortunately there is a large number of educated and fair-minded Russians who not only will recognize the jurisdiction of that court

---

Source: Editorial, "The Czar on Trial," *New York Times*, October 9, 1913, p. 12. Spelling has been changed to conform with current usage.

and respect its verdict, but will contribute to it. And this element in Russia is bound to gain in strength and influence. If the second trial at Kiev results in the conviction of the hapless Beilis, and that is followed by the disorders it is calculated to produce, this element will be not weakened, but reinforced. In view of this fact and of the general protest that has been aroused it may be said the Tsar and the autocracy are now on trial.

NOTE

1. On March 20, 1911, the mutilated body of a twelve-year-old Gentile boy, Andre Yustshchinsky, was found in a cave on the outskirts of Kiev. The right-wing press immediately accused the Jews of killing the child in order to use his blood for ritual purposes. Although the police possessed incontrovertible evidence that a gang of thieves was responsible, the chief district attorney, pressured by antisemitic interests, disregarded the police report and instead insisted on pursuing the blood libel against the Jews. Finally a Jew, Menahem Mendel Beilis (1874–1934), on the basis of circumstantial evidence, was accused of killing the Russian child. On July 21, 1911, Beilis was arrested and sent to prison, where he languished for over two years before being brought to trial. The case attracted world-wide attention. Liberal-minded people throughout the world were shocked that the baseless blood libel, rooted in medieval folklore, still had credence in Russia. An editorial from the *New York Times* is presented here as an example of this protest. The trial of Beilis took place in Kiev in 1913 from the twenty-fifth of September through the twenty-fifth of October. Beilis was acquitted. See also chapter 7, document 30.

29. TO AMERICA OR TO THE LAND OF ISRAEL? (1881)

JUDAH LEIB LEVIN[1]

It is clear that if there were no other proposal for saving tens of thousands of our brothers from their hard and bitter sufferings, if there were no other way in which our people could be reborn and fulfill their destiny, then it would be easier to reconcile ourselves to a thousand sacrifices and to the European spiritual abominations in order to live in tranquility without fear of the wrath of tyrants who threaten to disperse and destroy us, without fear that at any moment our lives and property may be pillaged and plundered. But before us lies the prospect of deliverance from evil and national rebirth in the land of America. The intelligent man will, therefore, choose this path, arguing that... although the ancient memories of our souls are not bound up with the American soil, it is nonetheless a suitable land in which to raise up the remnants of Israel, for it is a country settled by enlightened peoples of culture and civilized behavior. Further, there the Jews, unconstrained by the commandments enjoined upon them concerning their own soil, would be able to lead a good life. And America has a further advantage in connection with the rebirth of our nation and that is: In the Holy Land our dream would be far from realized; there we would be slaves to the Sultan and the Pashas; there, as here, we would bear a heavy burden in the midst of a wild desert people, sustaining

Source: Judah Leib Levin, in *Hamagid* 25, no. 39 (October 6, 1881), pp. 321–22. trans. L. Sachs.

ourselves with the distant hope that if our numbers increase sufficiently we might perhaps, after many years, become another small principality that will, finally, in some ultimate Utopia, . . . achieve its destiny. But in America our dream is closer to fulfillment, for the constitution of that country provides that when the number of colonists reaches sixty thousand they have the right to establish a separate state with a governor, ministers, and a constitution, and to determine their own laws, and our hope of attaining our independence and leading our lives in accordance with our beliefs and inclinations would not be long deferred.

Kindly note, my friend, that I speak not only of the advantages in regard to spiritual rebirth; I have not mentioned the material advantages of America, as they are obvious and require no proof. . . . Our brethren beg for relief from oppression. . . . They must find a safe haven. Our rich and generous must . . . rescue the lost flock of Israel from the dwellings of lions. . . . Let [the rich] find any place which suits them if only they save our wretched brethren.

The eloquence of the Bible, the piteous spectacle of the bereaved daughter of Zion, the emotion aroused by our ancient memories, all these speak for the Land of Israel. The good life recommends America. You know, my friend, that many will yearn for the Holy Land, and I know that even more will stream to America. Let there be no quarrel! Let the writers sharpen their pens, but in the meantime the generous must rise up to rescue their oppressed and persecuted brethren in any way they may choose.

NOTE

1. Judah Leib Levin (acronym *Yehalel*, 1844–1925). Hebrew poet and socialist, he assisted Aaron Liebermann in the publication of *Haemet*. His poems were the first to introduce socialist themes into Hebrew literature. After the pogroms of 1881 he despaired of a solution to the Jewish problem in Russia and advocated emigration to the United States. He presented his position in a letter to David Gordon (1831–1886), editor of the Hebrew weekly *Hamagid* (which was at the time published in Lyck, East Prussia). Excerpts of the letter are presented here. Soon after writing this letter, Levin joined the Hovevei Zion in his native Kiev and became a fervent supporter of emigration to Palestine.

The Jewish masses of the Pale responded to the pogroms with a panicked, spontaneous flight across the borders of Russia westward. Within a decade perhaps 200,000 Jews emigrated. Most were penniless. The Jewish leadership was divided on the question as to whether or not to organize, encourage and regulate the emigration from Russia. The Jewish upper bourgeoisie felt that such endorsement of emigration would be construed as unpatriotic and endanger the cause of Jewish emancipation in Russia. Many rabbinic leaders felt that emigration to the West, especially "materialistic" America, would increase the threat of secularization, a danger worse in their eyes than intermittent pogroms. Only a minority of Jewish leaders favored emigration. The issue was debated in the Jewish press for several years. An estimated 70 to 80 percent of those who emigrated went to the United States; between 1881 and 1890 the number of Russian Jews to enter the United States totaled 135,003 (S. Joseph, *Jewish Immigration to the United States from 1881–1910* [New York, 1914], p. 93). For the Jewish intellectuals who favored emigration the main issue was: America or Palestine?

30. ON THE LATEST WAVE OF EMIGRATION (1891)[1]

HAZFIRAH

With respect to the exodus of Jews from Russia—which has recently gained in momentum—the following letter appeared in the journal *Novoe Vremya*:

Since the spring of this year almost all the Jews living in the southern provinces of Russia have been seized by the urge to leave for abroad. The success of some few Jews who went to America; the false tales spread among the Jews by shipowners' agents about the success and happiness awaiting those who go; and the rumors circulated in anti-Jewish periodicals about the harsh laws soon to be promulgated against the Jews—all these have strengthened the desire of the Jews to leave Russia and go to Palestine or America, with no heed to the danger of this step and no fear of the evil into which they may fall....

Those Jews who wish to go to America make every effort to find the money for the journey, and in anticipation of the success and happiness to come they sell all of their movable possessions. When they are unable to take their families with them, as is frequently the case, they go without them, leaving their wives and children to be a burden on the Jewish community. In most cases the fate of these abandoned wretches is miserable and bitter, for the charity of the Jewish community rarely suffices to meet their needs. And from the husbands and fathers in America come letters full of moans and wails about *their* bitter lot in the new country, for they soon realize there is no chance of success, it is difficult to find work and their pay is sufficient only to buy themselves a few crusts of bread. How then could they save even a penny to send home to their families? Those who leave yearn with all their hearts to return to their homeland, but are unable to find the money for the journey. Many of the refugees who went to America last year are in this miserable state....

[An appeal from a Jewish immigration relief committee in Memel.] May it please you, dear Sir, to publish this letter to all the residents of this city cautioning them against leaving their homes for England or America without sufficient funds to cover the entire cost of the journey and assuming that help will be forthcoming from the committee in this city or in Hamburg. We feel compelled to issue a solemn warning that anyone doing so is bringing a grave disaster upon himself. We are unable to offer any monetary help whatsoever, and the police may seize him and expel him across the border back to his point of origin.... His blood is upon his own head, for we must abide by our warning....

NOTE

1. In 1891 the emigration of Jews from Russia suddenly increased twofold and more. The Jews were spurred by rumors about discriminatory laws, the expulsion of Jews from Moscow and other cities of the interior, and the economic depression that severely affected the Pale. A U.S. commission appointed in 1891 to investigate the causes prompting the wave of emigration to the United States from Europe visited Russia. With regard to the remnants of the Moscow Jewish community, it reported, "Homes are destroyed, businesses ruined, families separated, all claiming that they are not criminal except that they are charged with being Jews; all expressing a willingness and an anxiety to work, begging for the opportunity to begin life [anew] somewhere, where they do not know nor do they care.... We found," the commissioners added with reference to the general situation of Russian Jewry, "that America

Source: Hazfirah, no. 135 (June–July 1891), pp. 548–49. trans. L. Sachs.

was by no means an unknown country to them, and that many of the families have relatives and friends in the United States" (cited in L. Greenberg, *The Jews in Russia: The Struggle for Emancipation* [New Haven: Yale University Press, 1951], vol. 2, pp. 74–75). It is estimated that by 1914 some two million Jews left Russia. This selection is from the Warsaw Hebrew daily newspaper *Hazfirah*; it cites, as a warning against precipitous emigration, a letter to the editor of *Novoe Vremya*, a daily newspaper in St. Petersburg. To strengthen the point of this letter, *Hazfirah* published an accompanying appeal for caution from a Jewish immigration relief committee in Memel, a port city in East Prussia. However, the threat of pogroms exceeded that of poverty as seen by the following figures:

The yearly average of the Russian Jews going to the United States alone was 12,856 for 1881–1886; it reached 28,509 in the next five-year period, rose to 44,829 during 1891–1895 and declined (perhaps affected by an economic slump in America) to 31,278 from 1896 to 1900. The average yearly figures were 58,625 for 1901–1905; 82,223 for 1906–1910 and 75,144 for 1911–1914. Altogether nearly two million Jews left Russia from 1880 to 1914 (Hans Rogger, "Tsarist Policy on Jewish Emigration," *Soviet Jewish Affairs* 3, no. 1 [1973], p. 28. See also W. W. Kaplun-Kogan, *Die juedischen Wanderbewegungen in der neuesten Zeit* [Bonn, 1919], especially pp. 19–25.)

31. APPEAL TO THE JEWS IN RUSSIA (1891)

BARON MAURICE DE HIRSCH[1]

To my co-religionists in Russia: You know that I am endeavouring to better your lot. It is, therefore, my duty to speak plainly to you and to tell you that which it is necessary you should know.

I am aware of the reasons which oblige many of you to emigrate, and I will gladly do all in my power to assist you in your hour of distress. But you must make this possible for me. Your emigration must not resemble a headlong, reckless flight, by which the endeavour to escape from one danger ends in destruction.

You know that properly organised committees are shortly to be established in Russia, with the consent and under the supervision of the Imperial Russian Government. The duty of these committees will be to organise the emigration in a business-like way. All persons desirous of emigrating will have to apply to the local committees, who alone will be authorised to give you the necessary facilities.

Only those persons who have been selected by the committees can have the advantage of the assistance of myself and of those who are working with me. Anyone who leaves the country without the concurrence of the committees will do so at his own risk, and must not count on any aid from me.

It is obvious that in the beginning the number of emigrants cannot be large; for not only must places of refuge be found for those who first depart, but necessary preparations be made for those who follow. Later on the emigration will be able to assume larger proportions.

Remember that I can do nothing for you without the benevolent and gracious support of the Imperial Russian Government.

Source: The Jewish Chronicle (London), September 18, 1891, p. 13.

In conclusion, I appeal to you. You are the inheritors of your fathers, who for centuries, have suffered so much. Bear this inheritance yet awhile with equal resignation.

Have also further patience, and thus render it possible for those to help you who are anxious to do so.

I send you these words of warning and of encouragement in my own name and in the name of thousands of your co-religionists. Take them to heart and understand them.

May the good God help you and me, and also the many who work with us for your benefit with so much devotion.

NOTE

1. Baron Maurice de Hirsch (1831–1896), one of the wealthiest individuals of his time. A German Jewish financier, he devoted the larger portion of his life and vast fortune to philanthropy. He was the benefactor of a variety of Jewish causes, e.g., the Alliance Israélite Universelle; the Baron de Hirsch Fund in New York City, established to assist Jewish immigrants in the United States; and the Jewish Colonization Association, established in 1891 to facilitate and organize the mass emigration of Jews from Russia and to encourage their rehabilitation in agricultural colonies, particularly in Argentina and Brazil. He chose these countries because they contained an abundance of unpopulated land suitable for agriculture and because their governments were eager to receive immigrants. The Baron hoped to divert the flow of Jewish immigration to these areas, for he felt the crowding of hundreds of thousands of pauperized Jews into the cities of North America was bound to lead to antisemitism. A life of farming, even with the Baron de Hirsch's generous assistance, in an unknown distant land, appealed to relatively few immigrants. America continued to be the main destination. Hirsch's letter, which originally appeared in Russian and Yiddish, was addressed to the prospective emigrants from Russia, appealing to them to cooperate with the Jewish Colonization Association.

32. CULTURAL AUTONOMY (1901)

SIMON DUBNOW[1]

Autonomy as a historic claim is thus the firm and inalienable right of each national individuality; only its forms depend on the status which a nationality has within a multinational state.... In view of its condition in the Diaspora, Jewish nationality cannot strive for territorial or political isolation, but only for social and cultural autonomy. The Jew says: "As a citizen of my country I participate in its civic and political life, but as a member of the Jewish nationality I have, in addition, my own national needs, and in this sphere I must be independent to the same degree that any other national minority is autonomous in the state. I have the right to speak my language, to use it in all my social institutions, to make it the language of instruction in my schools, to order my internal life in my communities, and to create institutions serving a variety of national purposes; to join in the common activities with my brethren not only in this country but in all countries of the world and to participate in all the organizations which serve to further the needs of the Jewish nationality and to defend them everywhere."

Source: Simon Dubnow, *Nationalism and History, Essays on Old and New Judaism,* ed. Koppel S. Pinson (New York: Atheneum, 1970), pp. 136–39. Copyright 1958 by the Jewish Publication Society. Reprinted by permission of the Jewish Publication society.

During the "period of isolation" the Jews enjoyed in great measure the right of national autonomy, although in outmoded forms, but they lacked civic and political rights. During the "period of assimilation" they began to participate in the civic and political life of the countries in which they lived, but many became alienated from the chosen inheritance of the nation, from its internal autonomy, which, in their limited view, did not accord with civic emancipation already granted or about to be granted by law. In this manner old Jewry sacrificed its civic rights for its national rights, and new Jewry its national rights for its political or civic rights. The period of autonomy now approaching does not tend to either of the two extremes of the previous epochs, which had rendered the life of the Jewish people defective and impaired. The new epoch must combine our equal civic and political rights with the social and cultural autonomy enjoyed by other nationalities whose historical conditions resemble our own. The Jews must demand simultaneously all civic, political and national rights, without renouncing one for the other as had been the case in the past.

The chief axiom of Jewish autonomy may thus be formulated as follows: Jews in each and every country who take an active part in civic and political life enjoy all rights given to the citizens, not merely as individuals, but also as members of their national groups.[2]

Now that we have succeeded in establishing the principle of autonomy, we must analyze the problem of how it can be realized under the conditions in which the Jewish nationality finds itself. Here we have to differentiate between two kinds of national minorities in a multi-national state: (1) a territorial minority, which is a minority as compared with the total population of the commonwealth, but which constitutes a majority in its own historical state or province; (2) a non-territorial minority, scattered over various provinces without being a majority in any. Nationalities of the first kind require regional autonomy where they are settled, nationalities of the second kind must have communal and cultural autonomy....

The fiction of the "religious community" was bound to be destroyed together with the fiction of the "religious society," not in the sense of a disruption of the religious service, but of a removal of the religious label from secular institutions. It is necessary to reconstruct the shattered autonomy in forms which are adapted to modern social conditions. In countries of German culture, the nationalist Jews must convert their religious communities into national communities [*Volksgemeinden*]. Even before such a change can be effected officially, with the approval of the government, it is possible on the basis of the existing laws guaranteeing freedom of association, to widen perceptibly the circle of activities of the communities, and, at the same time, to wage a parliamentary battle for the recognition of the fullest measures of secular national communal autonomy.... Real and broad autonomy is especially possible in countries in which the principle prevails that the government does not interfere in the private lives of its citizens, and where authoritarian governments or exaggerated concentrations of power do not exist. In such countries, especially in the United States of America, Jews could enjoy a large measure of self-administration even now if they only were willing to advance beyond the confines of the "religious community."...

There is no need to demonstrate that national-cultural autonomy is of singular value to the Jewish masses concentrated in eastern Europe. Here the Jews do not yet have full rights as citizens and, therefore, the extension of the autonomy of their communities meets with external difficulties. Over and against this, however, there are strong inner tendencies in that direction among the Jewish masses which are attracted to the modern national movement....

NOTES

1. Simon Dubnow (1860–1941), Russian Jewish historian, author of the monumental *World History of the Jewish People* (10 volumes, written in Russian but first published in German, 1925–1929; published in English in 1967). From 1897 to 1902 he published a series of articles on the Jewish question in the Russian Jewish journal *Voskhod*. In these articles, drawing upon his study of Jewish history, Dubnow developed a conception of the Jewish people as a "spiritual community," which, despite its dispersion throughout the world, enjoys a national cohesion by virtue of historical, cultural and religious bonds. As such, the Jewish people does not require the material framework of a common territory and of political independence to preserve its national existence. Through spiritual nationhood, the Jewish people, according to Dubnow, have entered a higher stage of history, anticipating the future of all nations. Notwithstanding his historical optimism,

Dubnow recognized the pressures of assimilation in a secular age and accordingly held that although the Jews will remain politically and territorially members of the respective states of their dispersion, they should enjoy cultural autonomy. The historical and theoretical bases of the concept of extraterritorial, cultural (as opposed to political) autonomy were expounded in his fourth article (1901), excerpts of which are presented here. Dubnow sought to realize his program through the political efforts of the Society for Full and Equal Rights of the Jewish People in Russia, an association of nonsocialist Jews founded in 1905, and of the Jewish People's Party, which he helped establish in 1906. Although he was not successful in the sphere of practical politics, Dubnow's theory of autonomism exercised a seminal influence on the Bund's nationality policy (see document 33 in this chapter) and on the Helsingfors Program of the Zionists (see document 34 in this chapter). Also see chapter 5, document 13.

2. Cf. chapter 3, document 2, note 3.

33. DECISIONS ON THE NATIONALITY QUESTION (1899, 1901, 1905, 1910)

THE BUND[1]

The Third Party Convention (December 1899):[2] . . . The Bund has inscribed on its banner the demand for equal civil rights for the Jews. At the Convention the opinion was expressed that Jewish Social Democracy deals with the needs of the Jewish proletariat in too narrow a manner. Many of the most significant rights to be obtained with the fall of the autocratic regime [of the tsar], it was observed, would, as regards the Jewish workers, remain but a dead letter, if complete national emancipation, e.g., freedom to use their own national language, is not also granted them. Accordingly, one comrade[3] insisted that there be a greater emphasis on the national aspect of the Bund's program, for the Jewish proletariat must demand national emancipation as well as equal civil rights. Civil rights, he said, are not enough to enable the Jewish proletariat to protect its own interests. Germany is a prime example of this. Whereas in Germany all citizens enjoy equal civil rights under the law, the Polish workers [residing in Germany and possessing German citizenship] cannot enjoy them to the same extent as the German workers. The Polish worker, like his German comrade, is allowed to convene meetings, but because the commissars who must be present at the meetings do not usually understand Polish, the meetings must be conducted in German. This means that many who are unable to express their thoughts in German or do not understand that language sufficiently, are in practice denied their right to participate in the meetings. If this is the case with regard to the Polish proletariat in Germany, how much more so does this hold for the Jewish workers in Russia? One may ask—what benefit will derive from the Jewish workers' freedom

Source: [Protocol of third convention of the Bund] (Kovno, December 1899), in *Materialy k istorii yevreiskago rabochago dvizhenii* (St. Petersburg, 1906), vol. 1, pp. 74–76. trans. R. Weiss. [Resolution of fourth convention of the Bund] (Bialystok, May 1901), in *Der yidisher arbeter*, no. 2 (1901), pp. 97–102. trans. P. Mendes-Flohr. [Resolution of the sixth convention of the Bund] (Zurich, October 1905), in *Der yidisher arbeter*, ed. M. Rafes (Moscow, 1925), vol. 1, p. 321. trans. D. Goldman. [Resolution of eighth conference of the Bund] (Vienna, October 1910), in M. Rafes, *Ocherki po istorii Bunda* (Moscow, 1923), pp. 393–95. trans. R. Weiss.

of assembly, if in these meetings they must speak Russian, that is to say, a language neither spoken nor understood by the majority of the Jewish workers? Freedom of assembly is thus revealed to be a fine but empty phrase, at least as regards the Jewish workers, as long as Yiddish does not enjoy a status equal to that of Russian. Thus it is necessary to correct the program of the Bund by supplementing the paragraph on equal civil rights with one on equal national rights. It is possible of course to contest this point, continued that comrade, and say that the question of equal national rights is merely of academic interest to us at this time; that the most important task facing us, the task to which we must now devote ourselves fully, is the achievement of political rights. The question of national rights is not likely to become a burning issue for the Jewish worker nor become his battle-cry until there be a democratic regime in Russia, and then only if the democratic character of the Russian constitution be imperfect. Those who present this argument, the comrade continued, forget that every party includes in its program, alongside its short-term demands, demands which may be realized only in the distant future. The Bund should not be an exception in this regard. It must include in its program demands which in all likelihood will be fought for in the more or less distant future.

The paragraph on equal national rights received little support from the convention and aroused a heated debate, involving many of the delegates. Essentially, the discussions focused on the need to avoid making demands which would divert the worker from his class interests by the pull of [spurious or less urgent] national interests. The danger in having the Bund's program include a demand for comprehensive equality of national rights lies in the possibility that it will blur the Jewish proletariat's class consciousness, and, like every nationalism, it could lead to chauvinism.

After lengthy discussion the following decision was passed: (1) The demand for equal civil rights but not equal national rights should be included among the Bund's political demands. (2) To enable comrades to express their opinions on the national question and help clarify the subject, a special section entitled "Arguments" will be set aside for this purpose in the [party's newspaper] *Yidisher arbiter:*[4] there individual authors may express their opinions, on their own responsibility....

The Fourth Party Convention (May 1901):[5]...The Convention recognizes the fact that a state such as Russia, consisting of a great number of disparate nations, will need to be reorganized in the future into a federation of national groups, each enjoying full national autonomy, independent of the territory in which they reside.

The Convention deems that the term "nationality" applies to the Jewish people.[6]

In view of the fact that it is premature under the present conditions [in Russia] to put forth the demand for national autonomy for the Jews, the Convention finds that at the present time it is sufficient to fight for the abolition of all discriminatory laws directed against the Jews and to protest against all forms of oppression of the Jewish people. At the same time, the Bund will refrain from inflating nationalist feelings among the Jews which can only blur the class consciousness of the Jewish proletariat and lead to chauvinism....

The Convention regards Zionism as a reaction of the bourgeois classes to the phenomenon of antisemitism and to the abnormal civil status of the Jewish people in Russia.[7] The Convention views the ultimate goal of political Zionism—i.e., the acquisition of a territory for the Jews—as an objective of little value, because such a territory would be able to contain but a fraction of the whole nation, and thus would be incapable of solving the Jewish question. Hence, to the extent that the Zionists seek to concentrate the whole of the Jewish people, or at least a majority of the Jewish people, in a single land, they pursue a Utopian goal.

Furthermore, the Convention believes that Zionist propaganda inflames nationalist feelings and hinders the development of class consciousness among the Jewish proletariat.

The Sixth Party Convention (October 1905):[8] In accordance with the general principles laid down in the Fourth Convention, the Sixth Convention formulated the program of the Bund regarding the Jewish nationality question as follows: (1) Full civil and political equality for the Jews. (2) The right, guaranteed by law, for the Jews to use their own language in all legal and governmental institutions. (3) National-cultural autonomy [on an extra-territorial basis]: the removal of all functions connected with cultural matters (e.g., popular education) from the administrative responsibility of the state and local government and the transference of these functions to the Jewish nation. [Under the autonomous jurisdiction of the Jewish nation] these functions will be organized in the form of central and local institutions whose officials will be elected in general elections by all those who identify themselves as belonging to the Jewish nation by an honest, secret ballot.

The Eighth Party Conference (October 1910):[9] Whereas the legislation regarding linguistic rights currently being considered by the Duma[10] directly opposes the interests of the proletariat and the masses of the Jewish nation; and whereas this question is of special urgency to the Jewish workers, in that Yiddish is a denigrated, persecuted language, the Conference believes that it is necessary to raise and forcefully pursue the following demands: (1) The division of languages [as proposed in the legislations before the Duma] into two categories, dominant and tolerated, is unacceptable. (2) All governmental institutions—central, regional and local—must use the local language when dealing with the population. (3) This demand must be fulfilled by means of special legislation and legal guarantees. (4) Until the realization of national-cultural autonomy which will transfer responsibility for educational and cultural matters to the nations themselves, it is necessary to work for the establishment of a government school for each national group in the general population in which its own language will be used. (5) All limitations on the use of one's mother tongue in public life, assemblies, the press, business institutions, schools, *et cetera* must be abolished.

In the struggle to achieve these demands, it is necessary to secure the rights of the Yiddish language, which is denied these rights more than any other language and, moreover, is not even officially recognized, while the other non-dominant languages receive at least partial recognition.

While making clear its reservations about those nationalist trends which turn the struggle for Yiddish into an instrument with which to blunt the class consciousness of the proletariat, Jewish Social Democracy, considering the interests and needs of the proletariat, must conduct the struggle against the assimilationists and the Hebraists so that the Yiddish language will acquire in all areas of Jewish public life—especially, in the schools and cultural

institutions—the prominent position it merits as the national language of the Jewish people. (*Adopted unanimously.*)

NOTES

1. The Bund is an abbreviation and popular designation for the *Algemeyner arbeter bund in Poyln un Rusland* (General Jewish Worker's Union in Poland and Russia), a Jewish socialist party founded in Russia in 1897. (Lithuania was later added to the party's name.) The Bund was the result of the merger of several local socialist organizations among the Jews in the northwestern region of the Russian Empire, which was formerly the Lithuanian segment of the old Polish-Lithuanian commonwealth. In this region the Jewish proletariat was a predominant factor in the major cities (viz., Vilna, Vitebsk, Bialystok, and Minsk); moreover, the Jewish intelligentsia in this region "was subject to weaker assimilationist pressures than were its counterparts in the Ukraine and Russian Poland. This combination of a dominant Jewish proletariat and an intelligentsia more likely than elsewhere to be sensitive to its needs made possible the emergence of a specifically Jewish labor movement" (Ezra Mendelsohn, *Class Struggle in the Pale: The Formative Years of the Jewish Workers' Movement in Tsarist Russia* [London: Cambridge University Press, 1970], pp. x–xi). During the 1880s and 1890s the first socialist circles were formed among the Jewish workers of Lithuania. The leaders of these circles were Russified Jews who viewed their task as preparing the Jewish workers for socialism. Initially, these "schools for socialism" concentrated on teaching Yiddish-speaking workers Russian (the language of the vast majority of the empire's proletariat), literature, and natural sciences—the modicum of skills and knowledge deemed necessary for a mature class consciousness. Gradually, these circles evolved into trade unions, concerning themselves with the concrete problems faced by the Jewish proletariat. The struggle of the Jewish proletariat inevitably involved the need to remove the disabilities suffered by the Jewish people as a whole, a battle that the Jewish bourgeoisie, because of their limited class interests, were held to be inherently incapable of waging effectively. This focus of political action, together with the need to employ Yiddish to organize the Jewish workers, led to the formation of a socialist nationalist ideology, in which Yiddish was glorified as the language of the laboring class and national-cultural autonomy for Jewish people was a leading principle. The documents presented here trace the emergence of this ideology. Although the Bund confined its

purview to the Jewish workers of the Russian Empire and opposed collaboration with other Jewish parties (even in matters of self-defense against pogroms), its program was rejected by the Russian Social Democratic Workers' party (RSDWP), of which it was a constituent member. After the final split between the Bolshevik and the Menshevik factions of the RSDWP in 1912, the Bund aligned itself with the Mensheviks, who tended to favor Jewish national-cultural autonomy, while the Bolsheviks stiffened their opposition to this program. By the end of 1917, the Bund had approximately 40,000 members, organized in almost 400 branches. At the twelfth Bund convention held in Moscow in 1920, the majority favored affiliation with the Communists, but on an autonomous basis. Although this condition was rejected by the Communists, the Bund conference of March 1921 decided to join the Communist party. In the parts of Poland not incorporated within the Soviet Union, the Bund remained an independent organization, and it became a major factor in the Jewish life of that country; on the eve of the Nazi invasion of Poland in 1939, the Polish Bund had nearly 100,000 members.

2. At this convention the issue of Jewish national—as opposed to civic and political—rights was broached and debated for the first time in an open forum of the Bund.

3. The reference is to John Mill (1870–1952), one of the founders of the Bund and head of its Committee Abroad. Based in Geneva, the committee served as the party's representative vis-à-vis the international socialist movement, raised funds and printed party literature (which was illegal in Russia). In 1915 Mill emigrated to the United States, where he was active in various Jewish socialist organizations.

4. The *Jewish Worker*, the Yiddish-language organ of the Committee Abroad of the Bund, which was edited at the time by John Mill.

5. At its fourth convention the Bund went beyond its former demand for equal civic and political rights for the Jews and became an advocate of national rights for the Jews of Russia. This was a turning point in Bundist thought; from now on the party's ideology and propaganda would increasingly emphasize the national element. Various factors prompted this change, such as the resonance among the Jewish workers of the positions on Jewish national rights articulated by Simon Dubnow (see document 32), Chaim Zhitlovsky (chapter 9, document 36), and Zionism. The Bund drew Marxist "legitimation" for

its nationalist program from the multinational Austrian Social Democratic Party's Marxist conception of extraterritorial autonomy. In contrast to other Jewish national ideologies, the Bund did not consider the Jews as a worldwide people and thus restricted its concern to the Jews of the Russian Empire. Despite the cautious language of the resolutions of the fourth convention, they quickly aroused the opposition of the RSDWP, of which the Bund was a founding member. The opposition was led by those connected with the magazine *Iskra*, of whom Vladimir Lenin was foremost. Rebuffed, the Bund withdrew from the RSDWP in protest.

6. The formulation of this section of the resolution marked a compromise with the opponents of the proposal. At the sixth party convention the limitation was removed.

7. The RSDWP pilloried the Bund members as crypto-Zionists, "who suffered from sea-sickness" as Georgi Valentinovich Plekhanov (1856–1918), the founder and for many years the leading exponent of Russian Marxism, put it. The Bund for its part regarded Zionism as reactionary and bourgeois, even including the socialist Zionist parties—which had become in this period a political force in the Pale.

8. After the failure of the Revolution of 1905 and the new restrictions on political and trade union activities, the Bund was obliged to concentrate on cultural issues. It became a vigorous advocate of a secular, socialist Jewish culture based on Yiddish. Literary and musical societies, evening courses and drama circles were among the varied activities that the Bund organized. The Bund now even took part in some general Jewish cultural activities. To underscore that its devotion to Jewish culture was solely in the interest of the Jewish proletariat and the class struggle, the Bund formulated the concept of "neutralism"—i.e., it had no principled commitment to Jewish survival, which was a matter for the objective, dialectic laws of history to determine.

9. In addition to conventions, which had full authority to decide party policy, the Bund also held conferences, which had less authority than conventions. The policy outlined by the eighth conference, which included the demand for freedom to rest on the Jewish Sabbath and the establishment of state Yiddish schools, together with the resolutions of the sixth convention, remained the Bund's nationality policy until after the Russian Revolution.

10. The Duma was the Imperial Russian legislature in existence between 1906 and 1917.

34. THE HELSINGFORS PROGRAM (1906)[1]

ALL-RUSSIAN ZIONIST CONFERENCE

The political program includes the following:

1. Full democratization of the regime according to the principles of parliamentary democracy, autonomy of the national territories and guaranteed legal rights for all minority peoples.
2. Full and unconditional [civic and national] rights to the Jewish population.
3. Representation of all national minorities in federal, regional and local elections that shall be conducted by direct secret ballot. The right to vote shall be extended to women.
4. Recognition of the Jewish people in Russia as a single political entity entitled to govern itself in matters of national culture.
5. A national assembly of Russian Jews shall be convened for the purpose of forming the basic structure of a national organization.
6. Jews shall have the right to use the national language (Hebrew) and the spoken language (Yiddish) in schools, courts and public life.
7. Jews shall have the right to observe the Sabbath on Saturday instead of Sunday. This right shall be guaranteed without regard to geographical location.

NOTE

1. The Third All-Russian Zionist Conference, which included various Zionist groups, met in 1906 from December 4 to December 10, in Helsingfors (Helsinki), Finland. In the wake of recent events—the Revolution of 1905, pogroms, the death of Theodor Herzl (who was the founder of political Zionism), the Seventh Zionist Congress (see chapter 10, document 17), the growing influence of competing ideologies among the Jewish masses—the conference dealt with fundamental issues facing the Zionist movement in general and Russian Zionism in particular. Without rejecting the basic Zionist goal of "negating the Diaspora," the conference adopted a program of *Gegenwartsarbeit*, or "work in the "present," that is, political and cultural activities to be undertaken with regard to the immediate needs of Jewish life in the Diaspora. The ideological formulation of this program, which constituted a major revision in Zionist policy, is presented in chapter 10, document 20. The specific proposals for Russia are presented in this document.

Source: Juedische Rundschau 22 (June 8,1917), pp. 190–93. trans. R. Weiss and P. Mendes-Flohr.

35. CZERNOWITZ CONFERENCE OF THE YIDDISH LANGUAGE (1908)[1]

The Conference of the Yiddish Language has the following objectives:

(a) the recognition and attainment of equal rights for the Yiddish language

(b) the advancement and dissemination of culture and art in the Yiddish language

(c) the unification of the Jewish people and its culture in its language

To attain the objectives the Conference will create an organization and an office which will be temporarily stationed in Czernowitz.

Organization: The organization consists of Jews of at least eighteen years of age who are in accord with the objectives of the Conference of the Yiddish Language and contribute at least 1 ruble (2½ crowns, 2 marks, etc.) to it annually.

Agency: The executive organ of the organization is the Agency which it elects. The Agency is to be called Central Agency of the Conference of the Yiddish Language. The Agency must collect the stipulated monetary contributions and execute the decisions of the Conference.

In addition, the Agency will:

(a) solicit members for the organization

(b) establish societies, committees, groups and other units to work on behalf of the objectives of the Conference according to the provisions of the various national laws

(c) publish and support the publication of cultural and artistic materials

(d) establish libraries

(e) organize lectures and public readings

(f) assist in the translation into Yiddish of all the cultural and artistic treasures of the Jewish past and especially of the Bible

(g) assist in the publication of model textbooks

(h) establish and support model Yiddish schools

(i) establish and support a circulating model theater

(j) establish professional unions of writers and artists

(k) arbitrate disputes between writers and artists, on the one hand, and publishers, book dealers and the public, on the other

(l) create a body to serve as an authority in questions of Yiddish orthography, grammar and other language questions

(m) propagandize for the recognition and attainment of equal rights for the Yiddish language, and call periodic conferences.

NOTE

1. The Czernowitz Conference was the first international gathering, embracing virtually all ideological camps within East European Jewry, to consider the role of Yiddish in Jewish life. It was held from August 30 to September 4, 1908, in Czernowitz, the principal Yiddish-speaking center of Bukovina (a region then under Austrian rule and now divided between Rumania and Ukraine). The idea of the conference was first broached by Nathan Birnbaum (see chapter 10, document 28) who quickly gained for it the endorsement of leading Yiddishists in New York City, where he was visiting at the time, namely, the dramatists Jacob Gordin, David Pinski, the publisher A. M. Evalenko and the philosopher Chaim Zhitlovsky. Together with Birnbaum, they formed an organizing committee and issued a call for the conference. Seventy individuals, constituting a pantheon of contemporary Hebrew and Yiddish authors, accepted their invitation. The agenda included problems of Yiddish grammar, orthography,

Source: Emanuel Goldsmith, *Architects of Yiddishism at the Beginning of the Century* (Teaneck, N.J.: Fairleigh Dickinson University Press, 1976), pp. 195–96. Reprinted by permission of Fairleigh Dickinson University Press.

press and theater and a proposed translation of the Bible into Yiddish. The major question, however, was the "national" status of Yiddish. After heated debate, it was resolved to proclaim Yiddish a (as opposed to "the") national language of the Jewish people. The very event of the conference contributed to the prestige of Yiddish; its practical programs, delineated in this document, greatly stimulated Yiddish literary activity and research and laid the foundation for YIVO, the Institute for Jewish Research, founded in Berlin in 1925, with its center in Vilna (see chapter 5, document 13, note 1).

36. WOMEN IN THE BUND AND POALEI ZION (1937)

MANYA SHOHAT[1]

I will speak about the distant past, about a Jewish woman who began to awaken and enter the Russian revolution. I will especially discuss the Bund[2] and Poalei Zion[3] as they were 45 years ago. I did not know the principles of the Bund. I always opposed it, but I knew that its impact on the lives of the masses was enormous. When I was 17, I learned carpentry and lived among workers. In those days there was a great deal of conspiracy. Spying was well developed, and there were many provocateurs. It does honor to the women to note that very few participated in provocations. The status of the woman changed much more among Jews than among Russians. Among us the woman was no more enslaved than the man, and frequently she would support her husband. As a result, she was more independent than the Russian woman. It was actually the intention of Judaism to give respect to the woman. [To be sure], she did not have the freedom of choice in her marriage, but neither did the man. Thus, the Jewish woman was liberated much faster than the Russian, where only the daughters of aristocrats were becoming liberated.

The Bund played an enormous role. It created the ethic of work and inculcated respect for work among the masses. We all know that Jews held an attitude of scorn for manual work. In particular, they scorned a woman's work. Maids were most ashamed of their work. This attitude was a product of the long exile, and the Bund began to fight it. This was its powerful historical contribution, and thus it liberated the woman. Young people were running away from wealthy homes to work in factories. There were also young women among them, and our purpose was to save the entire world. The Bund won the hearts of the youth. I don't understand why it maintained and didn't cut off its ties with Judaism. Most of its members were outsiders. [Yet] they always operated among Jews and felt the burden of [our] history. In fact, they didn't even know the gentiles....

I will [now] discuss the psychological difference between the Bund and the Social Revolutionaries[4] of Russia. I was very close with Breshkovskaya,[5] and her moral personality had a great influence on me. At the beginning of Gershuni's[6] work, I knew about everything that was happening in their party, despite my young age. At that time there was not yet a conspiracy there. I opposed this party because in my opinion they did not defend the masses. Primarily their ideal was

---

Source: Manya Shohat, Hebrew speech before Women Workers' Council, Tel Aviv, June 6, 1937. Pinchas Lavon Archives. trans. G. Svirsky.

revolution at any price, and they would emphasize this during times of imprisonment. The Bund operated in the opposite manner. It was a practical movement, an organization of workers. Breshkovskaya took issue with the Bund. She was [then] 55 years old; the age differences were apparent then between generations of revolutionaries. The Bund sought practical deeds and organizing. During imprisonment [in contrast to the Social Revolutionaries], the Bundists would above all deny everything. This self-defense was, of course, practical. What was important for the Social Revolutionaries was to disseminate their ideas; therefore they did not try to escape punishment. The Bund's propaganda was directed internally. The Jews had their fill of suffering and did not look for more. But the denial of the ideal of suffering affected the entire psyche of the Bund. Its technique was wonderful during this period, such as the following: First, a network of trade unions would be prepared by propagandists and leaders. Then those who would strive to agitate the masses to revolt would take over. I remember a secret gathering of 200 workers in the forest near Minsk. I believe it was Zalkind[7] who persuaded us that we have to become a mass movement. He denied the value of first spreading education among the masses. "Of what use is it to a worker to know that the earth rotates? Can't he bring about the revolution without it?" That was the direction, and the Central Committee of the Bund accepted it. We decided to become an opposition. Forty years ago the worker knew nothing; he could barely read and write. We realized that the decision not to teach a worker is but [his] betrayal. The intelligentsia will lead him astray; he will become mere cannon fodder. Most women joined the opposition, and again we began working with trade unions. In the end came the arrests.

The same phenomena that awakened Zionism also awakened the Bund and Poalei Zion before the Bund. The Bund did not believe in the possibility of a synthesis of Zionism and socialism. And it did not see the need for this, because it believed that eventually there will be fraternity among all the nations of the world. Before Borochov,[8] the situation of Poalei Zion was difficult. There was a certain type among them for whom it was just a name. The constructive Zionist movement did not believe that the socialist movement would bring salvation to the Jews. Among Jews, the Bund succeeded because it organized the workers to strike, carried out practical actions and was a symbol of an ideal

and a wider vision. Youth believed in the Bund. There were many women in Poalei Zion, and they were gifted with feeling for the homeland, together with attraction to socialism. The women would do well in debates; I'll describe one of them. Haya Cohen[9] had almost no education. She was very beautiful and very passionate. Nationalism and class consciousness were both developed in her, and she had considerable organizing skills. At age 18 she would participate in debates with the Bund and electrify her listeners. Her life was difficult—orphaned from her father and daughter to a sickly and irritable mother. Even her material situation was not good. She would sew corsets, her days spent earning a livelihood, her nights devoted to party work. Her power was in her enthusiasm. And one more element. The women members of these movements never felt inferior. No distinction was ever made between jobs for men and jobs for women. There was absolute equality in everything. Women did exceptionally well in the propaganda work, because that demands intuitive intelligence. Organizational work demands a cooler temperament, and they did better there. It was a dedication which trained these women for revolutionary work. The women did not aspire to become party heads. The men competed among themselves to rule, but only very few women wanted to rule. Therefore, women took upon themselves dirty work and dangerous jobs. If the women had not taken part in the revolution in such large numbers, the revolutionary parties would never have attained their major achievements.

I view the tragedy of the woman in this country that she is not allowed to give all that she is able to. This was not the case at that time, when a woman had full satisfaction from her [political] work.

NOTES

1. Manya Shohat (née Wilbushewitz; 1880–1961) was a leading force in Labor Zionism. Emigrating from her native Russia to Palestine in 1904, she was one of the founders of Sejera, the first successful agricultural collective in the country. Together with her husband, Israel Shohat, Rahel Yanait, and Yitzhak Ben Zvi, she founded in 1909 *Hashomer* ("The Watchman"), the defense organization of Jewish workers in Palestine, which through its "labor brigades" also contributed decisively to the establishment of collective settlements during the period of the second *aliyah*. She was also a central figure in the founding of virtually every major institution of the evolving socialist Zionist community

in Palestine, including the Histadrut ("The General Federation of Hebrew Workers in the Land of Israel"), Bank Hapoalim ("The Workers' Bank"), and Hapoel, the workers' sports organization. This document is based on an unedited protocol of a speech she gave in January 1937 at a meeting of the Women Workers' Council, which she was also instrumental in founding. A retrospective account of the role of women in two competing camps within the Jewish workers' movement at its beginnings in tsarist Russia, the speech reflects Shohat's lifelong devotion to securing the equality of women in the struggle to realize socialism; it also laconically records her disappointment with the status of women in Palestine.

2. Bund, see document 33 in this chapter.
3. Poalei Zion, see chapter 10, document 19.
4. The Social Revolutionary Party was founded in 1901. In contrast to the Marxists who regarded the urban workers—the proletariat—as destined by history to overthrow the tsars and to lead the revolution, the Social Revolutionaries believed that the liberation of Russia was the common task of all laboring groups and of the revolutionary intelligentsia. As the spiritual successors of the *Narodniki*, they also adopted terror as a means of overthrowing the hated regime.
5. Yetkaterina Breshkovskaya (Catherine Breshkovsky; 1844–1933) was known as the grandmother (*babushka*) of the Russian Revolution. A daughter of a noble family, she became revolutionary and a source of inspiration to several generations of radical Russian youth. Imprisoned and exiled to Siberia for thirty years, she was released by Alexander Kerensky after the February Revolution of 1917. Returning to Russia, she found herself out of sympathy with the Bolshevik regime under Lenin and went into voluntary exile.
6. Grigori Andreyevich Gershuni (1870–1908) was the charismatic founder and leader of the Social Revolutionary (S.R.) Party. Although completely assimilated into Russian culture, he never denied his Jewish identity.
7. Aaron Zalkind (1874–1942) was a leader of the Bund; he died in the Warsaw Ghetto.
8. Ber Borochov, see chapter 10, document 19.
9. Haya Cohen was a member of Poalei Zion in Minsk.

37. CRITICAL REMARKS ON THE NATIONAL QUESTION (1913)

V. I. LENIN[1]

Whoever wants to serve the proletariat must unite the workers of all nations and unswervingly fight bourgeois nationalism, *home* and foreign. The place of one who advocates the slogan of national culture is among the nationalist philistines and not among the Marxists.

Take a concrete example. Can a Great-Russian Marxist accept the slogan of national, Great-Russian culture? No. Such a man should be placed among the nationalists and not among the Marxists....

The same applies to the most oppressed and persecuted nation, the Jewish. Jewish national culture is a slogan of the rabbis and the bourgeoisie, a slogan of our enemies. But there are other elements in Jewish culture and in the entire history of the Jews. Of the ten and a half million Jews throughout the world, a

Source: V. I. Lenin, *Critical Remarks on the National Question, 1913*, translator not indicated (Moscow: Foreign Language Publishing House, 1954), pp. 19–24. Reprinted by permission of All-Union Agency for Authors' Rights.

little over half live in Galicia and Russia, backward and semi-barbarous countries, which *forcibly* keep the Jews in the position of a caste. The other half live in the civilized world, and there the Jews are not segregated in a caste. There, the great, world-progressive features of Jewish culture have clearly made themselves felt: its internationalism, its responsiveness to the advanced movements of the epoch (the percentage of Jews in the democratic and proletarian movements is everywhere higher than the percentage of Jews in the population as a whole).

Whoever, directly or indirectly, presents the slogan of a Jewish "national culture" is (whatever his good intentions may be) an enemy of the proletariat, a supporter of the *old* and of the *caste* among the Jews, an accomplice of the rabbis and the bourgeoisie. On the other hand, those Jewish Marxists who, in international Marxist organizations amalgamate with the Russian, Lithuanian, Ukrainian, etc., workers, contributing their might (in Russian and in Yiddish) to the creation of the international culture of the working-class movement, such Jews, despite the separatism of the Bund, continue the best traditions of the Jews, fighting the slogan of "national culture."

Bourgeois nationalism and proletarian internationalism—such are the two irreconcilably hostile slogans that correspond to the two great class camps throughout the capitalist world and express the two policies (more than that—two world outlooks) in the national question. By championing the slogan of national culture, building on it an entire plan and practical programme of so-called "cultural-national autonomy," the Bundists *actually* serve as the vehicles of bourgeois nationalism among the workers.

The question of assimilation, i.e., of the loss of national peculiarities, of becoming absorbed by another nation, makes it possible to visualize the consequences of the nationalist vacillations of the Bundists and their like-minded friends....

Developing capitalism knows two historical tendencies in the national question. First: the awakening of national life and national movement, struggle against all national oppression, creation of national states. Second: development and intensification of all kinds of intercourse between nations, break-down of national barriers, creation of the international unity of capital, of economic life in general, of politics, science, etc.

Both tendencies are a world-wide law of capitalism. The first predominates at the beginning of its development, the second characterizes mature capitalism that is moving toward its transformation into socialist society. The national programme of the Marxists takes both tendencies into account, and demands, firstly, equality of nations and languages, prohibition of all *privileges* whatsoever in this respect (and also the right of nations to self-determination, with which we deal separately below); and secondly, the principle of internationalism and uncompromising struggle against the contamination of the proletariat with bourgeois nationalism, even of the most refined kind....

Whoever does not recognize and does not champion equality of nations and languages, does not fight against all national oppression or inequality, is not a Marxist, is not even a democrat. This is beyond doubt. But it is equally doubtless that the alleged Marxist who fulminates against a Marxist of another nation as an "assimilationist" is simply a *nationalist philistine*. In this little-esteemed category of people are all the Bundists....

Those who shout most about Russian orthodox Marxists being "assimilationists" are the Jewish nationalists in Russia in general, and the Bundists in particular. And yet, as is evident from the above-quoted figures, of the ten and a half million Jews in the whole world, *about half* that number live in the *civilized* world, under conditions where there is the *largest* degree of "assimilation," whereas only the unhappy, downtrodden rightless Jews in Russia and Galicia, those who are crushed by the antisemites (Russian and Polish), live under conditions where there is the *least* degree of "assimilation," the largest degree of segregation, right up to "Pale of Settlement," "percentage restrictions," and other charms of Purishkevich [the tsarist bigots'] rule.

The Jews in the civilized world are not a nation, they have become assimilated most of all, say K. Kautsky[2] and O. Bauer.[3] The Jews in Galicia and in Russia are not a nation, they, unfortunately (*not due to their own fault, but to the fault of the [anti-semites]*), are here still a *caste*. Such is the indisputable opinion of people who are undoubtedly familiar with the history of the Jews and who take the above-cited facts into consideration.

What do these facts tell us? That only Jewish reactionary philistines who want to turn back the wheel of history, to compel it not to depart from the conditions prevailing in Russia and Galicia toward the conditions prevailing in Paris and New York, but the opposite way, can shout against "assimilation."

The best Jews of world-historic fame who gave the world advanced leaders of democracy and socialism never shouted against assimilation. Only those who with reverential awe contemplate the "backside" of Jewry shout against assimilation....

NOTES

1. Vladimir Ilyich (Ulyanov) Lenin (1870–1924), Russian revolutionary. He was the leader of the Bolshevik faction within the Russian Social Democratic Workers' Party (RSDWP) and, later, the founder of the Soviet Union. He was very exercised by the Jewish question, and particularly with the Bundist nationality policy and the demand to reorganize the RSDWP on a federated, national basis. He held this proposal to be both an ideological and political threat to the cause of the Russian Revolution. Lenin, as this essay shows, deemed assimilation as the only progressive solution of the Jewish question. It was incumbent upon the Marxist revolutionaries to oppose antisemitism, he held, not only because it was a moral wrong, but because it tended to aggravate Jewish national consciousness and thus inhibit the process of Jewish assimilation. Hence antisemitism was reactionary. Accordingly, Lenin was a consistent and vigorous opponent of antisemitism in both tsarist Russia and later during the founding years of the Soviet Union.

2. Karl Kautsky (1845–1938), the leading Marxist theoretician in the German Social Democratic Party before World War I.

3. Otto Bauer (1881–1938), the leading theoretician of the Austrian Social Democratic Party.

38. THE JEWS ARE NOT A NATION (1913)

JOSEPH STALIN[1]

What is a nation?...*A nation is a historically constituted, stable community of people, formed on the basis of a common language, territory, economic life, and psychological make-up manifested in a common culture.*

It goes without saying that a nation, like every historical phenomenon, is subject to the law of change, has its history, its beginning and end.

It must be emphasized that none of the above characteristics taken separately is sufficient to define a nation. More than that, it is sufficient for a single one of these characteristics to be lacking and the nation ceases to be a nation.

It is possible to conceive of people possessing a common "national character" who, nevertheless, cannot be said to constitute a single nation if they are economically disunited, inhabit different territories, speak different languages, and so forth. Such, for instance, are the Russian, Galician, American, Georgian and Caucasian Highland Jews, who, in our opinion, do not constitute a single nation....

The fact of the matter is primarily that among the Jews there is no large and stable stratum connected with the land, which would naturally rivet the nation together, serving not only as its framework but also as a "national" market. Of the five or six million Russian Jews, only three to four percent are connected with agriculture in any way. The remaining ninety-six percent are employed in trade, industry, in urban

Source: Joseph Stalin, *Marxism and the National Question*, translator not indicated (Moscow: Foreign Language Publishing House, 1934), pp. 9, 16, 64–67, 73–75. Reprinted by permission of All-Union Agency for Authors' Rights.

institutions, and in general are town dwellers; moreover, they are spread all over Russia and do not constitute a majority in a single *guberniia* [district].

Thus, interspersed as national minorities in areas inhabited by other nationalities, the Jews as a rule serve "foreign" nations as manufacturers and traders and as members of the liberal professions, naturally adapting themselves to the "foreign nations" in respect to language and so forth. All this, taken together with the increasing re-shuffling of nationalities characteristic of developed forms of capitalism, leads to the assimilation of the Jews. The abolition of the "Pale of Settlement" would only serve to hasten this process of assimilation.

The question of national autonomy for the Russian Jews consequently assumes a somewhat curious character: autonomy is being proposed for a nation whose future is denied and whose existence has still to be proved!

Nevertheless, this was the curious and shaky position taken up by the Bund when at its Sixth Congress (1905) it adopted a "national programme" on the lines of national autonomy.

Two circumstances impelled the Bund to take this step. The first circumstance is the existence of the Bund as an organization of Jewish, and only Jewish, social-democratic workers. Even before 1897 the social-democratic groups active among the Jewish workers set themselves the aim of creating "a special Jewish workers' organization." They founded such an organization in 1897 by uniting to form the Bund. That was at a time when Russian Social-Democracy as an integral body virtually did not yet exist. The Bund steadily grew and spread, and stood out more and more vividly against the background of the bleak days of Russian Social-Democracy.... Then came the 1900s. A *mass* labour movement came into being. Polish Social-Democracy grew and drew the Jewish workers into the mass struggle. Russian Social-Democracy grew and attracted the Bund workers. Lacking a territorial basis, the national framework of the Bund became too restrictive. The Bund was faced with the problem of either merging with the general international tide, or of upholding its independent existence as an extraterritorial organization. The Bund chose the latter course.

Thus grew up the "theory" that the Bund is "the sole representative of the Jewish proletariat.".…

The second circumstance is the peculiar position of the Jews as a separate national minority within compact majorities of other nationalities in integral regions. We have already said that this position is undermining the existence of the Jews as a nation and puts them on the road to assimilation. But this is an objective process. Subjectively, in the minds of the Jews, it provokes a reaction and gives rise to the demand for a guarantee of the rights of a national minority, for a guarantee against assimilation. Preaching as it does the vitality of the Jewish "nationality," the Bund could not avoid being in favour of a "guarantee." And, having taken up this position, it could not but accept national autonomy. For if the Bund could seize upon any autonomy, i.e., *cultural-national* autonomy, there could be no question of territorial political autonomy for the Jews, since the Jews have no definite integral territory.

Social-Democracy strives to secure for *all nations* the right to use their own language. But that does not satisfy the Bund; it demands that "the rights of the *Jewish language*" … be championed with "exceptional persistence" (see *Report of the Eighth Conference of the Bund*), and the Bund itself in the elections to the Fourth Duma declared that it would give "preference to those of them (i.e., electors) who undertake to defend the rights of the Jewish language."

Not the *general* right of all nations to use their own language, but the *particular* right of the Jewish language. Yiddish! Let the workers of the various nationalities fight primarily for their own language; the Jews for Jewish, the Georgians for Georgian, and so forth. The struggle for the general right of all nations is a secondary matter. You do not have to recognize the right of all oppressed nationalities to use their own language; but if you have recognized the right of Yiddish, know that the Bund will vote for you, the Bund will "prefer" you.

But in what way then does the Bund differ from the bourgeois nationalists?

Social-Democracy strives to secure the establishment of a compulsory weekly rest day. But that does not satisfy the Bund; it demands that *by legislative means* "the Jewish proletariat should be guaranteed the right to observe their Sabbath and be relieved of the obligation to observe another day."

It is to be expected that the Bund will take another "step forward" and demand the right to observe all the ancient Hebrew holidays. And if, to the misfortune of the Bund, the Jewish workers have discarded religious prejudices and do not want to observe these holidays, the Bund with its agitation for "the right to the Sabbath," will remind them of the Sabbath, it will, so to speak, cultivate among them "the Sabbatarian spirit."…

Quite comprehensible, therefore, are the "passionate speeches" delivered at the Eighth Conference of the Bund demanding "Jewish hospitals," a demand that was based on the argument that "a patient feels more at home among his own people," that "the Jewish worker will not feel at ease among Polish workers, but will feel at ease among Jewish shopkeepers."

Preservation of everything Jewish, conservation of *all* the national peculiarities of the Jews, even those that are patently harmful to the proletariat, isolation of the Jews from everything non-Jewish, even the establishment of special hospitals—that is the level to which the Bund has sunk!

Comrade Plekhanov[2] was right a thousand times over when he said that the Bund "is adapting socialism to nationalism."

NOTES

1. Joseph (Dzhugashvili) Stalin (1879–1953), Bolshevik revolutionary, ruler of the Soviet Union, and leader of the world communist movement. During the early factional disputes within the Russian Social Democratic Workers' Party, he sided with Lenin in his opposition to the Bund.

In 1913, with the approbation of Lenin, he published an essay entitled "Social Democracy and the National Question" (later renamed "Marxism and the National Question"), in which *inter alia* the Jewish question and the Bund's "misconceived" policy are analyzed. Excerpts from the essay are presented here. Stalin later became the first commissar of nationalities of the Soviet Union (1917–1923), and, with Lenin, tacitly recognized the Jews of Russia at least as a nationality whose distinct culture and language would have to be considered if effective revolutionary work were to be performed among them. Stalin, especially through the *Yevsektsiya*, fostered Yiddish culture, administrative institutions and agricultural settlements. (See the following document.) In the late thirties, during the great purges of the Communist Party and government, he reversed his attitude toward Jewish national culture. Yiddish schools, publishing houses, theaters, etc., were systematically liquidated. This policy was somewhat suspended during World War II. Moreover, in an effort to dislodge Britain from the Near East, he became a firm supporter of the establishment of a Jewish state in Palestine. From the end of 1948 until his death, however, Stalin's attitude toward Jews and Jewish culture was hostile in the extreme, obsessively linking any positive expressions of Jewish identity with Zionism and U.S. espionage.

2. Georgi Plekhanov, see document 33, note 7, in this chapter.

39. EMANCIPATION BY THE MARCH REVOLUTION (1917)[1]

THE PROVISIONAL GOVERNMENT

Whereas it is our unshakable conviction that in a free country all citizens should be equal before the law, and that the conscience of the people cannot acquiesce in legal restrictions against particular citizens on account of their religion and race:

The Provisional Government has decreed: All restrictions on the rights of Russian citizens which had been enacted by existing laws on account of their belonging to any creed, confession or nationality, shall be abolished.

Source: "Decree of the Provisional Government about the Abolition of Religious and National Restrictions," *Jewish Emancipation, A Selection of Documents,* ed. and trans. Raphael Mahler, Pamphlet Series, Jews and the Post-War World, no. 1 (New York: American Jewish Committee, 1941), pp. 64–65. Reprinted by permission of the American Jewish Committee.

In accordance with this: All laws shall be abolished which have been in force both throughout the entire territory of Russia, as well as in any of her particular localities, and which enacted restrictions depending on the adherence of Russian citizens to any creed, confession or nationality, relating to: (1) settlement, (domicile) and freedom of movement; (2) acquisition of the right of ownership and other property rights on all kinds of movable and immovable goods as well as the disposal, use and administration of those goods and the giving or receiving of them as security;...(6) entering of government services, civil and military alike, the rules and conditions of promotion therein, participation in elections to local self-government bodies and to all kinds of communal bodies, the occupation of all kinds of posts in government and communal institutions and the fulfillment of all duties attached to such offices; (7) entering educational institutions of all kinds, private, community and government owned alike, the attendance of courses therein and benefits from stipends, as well as engaging in instruction and education; (8) fulfillment of duties of guardians, trustees and jurymen; (9) use of languages and dialects other than Russian in the management of private associations, in teaching in educational institutions of any kind and in the keeping of commercial books....

NOTE

1. After the March Revolution (1917) and the dismantling of the tsarist regime, the Provisional Government of Russia headed by Prince Lvov, issued this decree on April 2, 1917, abolishing all restrictions on the rights of Russian subjects, which had been based on national origin and religion.

40. THE LIQUIDATION OF BOURGEOIS JEWISH INSTITUTIONS (1918)[1]

YEVSEKTSIYA

Our Cultural Tasks: Education has always been a powerful means in the hands of the ruling classes. The bourgeoisie claims that schooling and education are beyond class interests and politics. At the same time, however, it makes sure that the broad masses will obtain neither knowledge nor enlightenment.

The Jewish community has hitherto been dominated by the members of the propertied class who want to keep the masses in the dark by superimposing a Hebrew culture upon them. While the upper classes have been sending their own children to public schools, they have provided only dark primary schools [*hadarim*] and synagogues [*shuls*] for the offspring of the proletariat, in which nothing but nonsense is taught.

Only the proletariat, defending the interests of their class, and thus defending the interests of all mankind, will be able to open the treasures of human culture to the broad masses.

Only the proletariat is strong enough to forge the golden chain of human culture, freeing it from the bloody hands of the decadent bourgeoisie.

From now on, the Jewish proletariat will assume the reins of power in the Jewish community.

Source: S. Agurskii, ed., *Di yidishe komisariatn un di yidishe komunistishe sektsies: protokoln, rezolutsies un dokumentn, 1918–1921* (Minsk, 1928), pp. 58–60, 178–81. trans. J. Hessing.

Only the Jewish worker and the Jewish laboring masses will create a free Jewish culture for themselves and arm themselves with the strong weaponry of knowledge.

Our relations with the [Jewish] community and other bourgeois societies: The First Conference of Jewish Communists and Communist *Yevsektsiya* declares that the various institutions which have so far ruled the traditional communal organization, the so-called *kehile*…have no further function in our life.

In the struggle against the organized Jewish community [*kehile*], no compromise can be made with the bourgeoisie. All its institutions are harmful to the interests of the Jewish masses, who are seduced by sweet lullabies of alleged democracy.

Following the proletarian victory in the October Revolution, the Jewish workers have assumed power and have established the dictatorship of the proletariat in the Jewish community. They now call upon the Jewish masses to unite around the Jewish commissariat in order to strengthen its rule.

The first all-Russian conference of Jewish Communists authorizes the members of the Central Commissariat for Jewish Affairs to take steps toward a systematic liquidation of the institutions of the Jewish bourgeoisie….

The Liquidation of the Zionist Party—A Memorandum [Submitted July 4, 1919]: The General Council of the Jewish Communist Union in the Ukraine, in full agreement with the resolution adopted by the conference of Jewish Communist sections of the Russian Communist party in Moscow, has decided to suspend immediately all activities of the Zionist party and its affiliated institutions and organizations.

This decision has been taken for the following reasons: Proclaiming the dictatorship of the proletariat, the Soviet Union has suspended the activities of all bourgeois parties and organizations and discontinued the publication of all their printed periodicals. The free existence of these organs and institutions would merely have interfered with the creative activity of the proletarian power, for they surely would have been used to support the counter-revolution which aims at the reestablishment of the old order. Only a misunderstanding deriving from the incomplete organization of the Soviets can explain, but not justify, the exception that is being made of the Zionists. They are still allowed

to publish their official organ, *Khronik fun yidishen lebn* [Chronicle of Jewish life], and to employ their entire party organization.[2] [But we must not forget that] by its political and social structure, the Zionist party is a Jewish version of the General Russian Cadet party.[3] By forging together the representatives of big and small capital with the Jewish petty bourgeoisie and cementing their union with a nationalistic ideology, this party—in close cooperation with clerical groups—constitutes a natural political center for all Jews who support the counter-revolution and wish to regain their freedom of exploitation and speculation. The pogroms that recently took place in the Ukraine and in Poland[4] have stirred nationalistic tendencies among reactionary Jews and are now being exploited by the Zionist party to strengthen its position. It is natural that in its most recent circular, the central committee of the Zionists in the Ukraine has reported a major increase of its organization, in spite of numerous cases in which local authorities have tried to interfere with this development.

The Zionists often protest their loyalty and pretend to be interested only in their work concerning Palestine. But in reality, their Palestinian agitation is nothing but a nationalistic response to the political events of the day. At the present time when the authorities and the Communist party are trying with all their might to mobilize the laboring masses for the struggle against local and Polish gangs, when they are committing themselves to liberating thousands of Jewish workers from the ideological influence of the petty bourgeoisie and to enlisting them in the revolutionary Red Army—at this time the Zionist agitation, even where it is performed by the Zionist Left, is harmful because it hinders the mobilization of the workers just as it had previously interfered with the attempts to make the Jewish masses a part of the revolutionary movement.

It must further be noted that the Palestinian ideal of the Zionists is in its very content a bourgeois one. Moreover, the current international situation has firmly established the Zionist party in the camp of the international imperialistic counter-revolution.

The Zionist party has linked its fate with the powers of the Entente who, upon dividing the Turkish empire, have made certain promises to the Zionists which force them to support their coalition. The Peace of Versailles, forging chains for the enslavement of the proletariat and for entire peoples, is welcomed by the Zionists. This is a logical consequence of their bourgeois nature. Furthermore, the Zionists are directly interested in a victory of the Entente in Eastern Europe. Only a victory of these powers will get them a little closer to the practical realization of their hopes. Under these circumstances, the continued activity of the Zionist party would be harmful to the interests of the Soviet Union and her international policies. Any protestation on the part of the Zionists that they are not interested in the victory of the reactionary forces cannot be taken seriously if one remembers that the Jewish bourgeoisie, and the Zionists among them, were able to accept even Plehve's regime.[5]

Simultaneously with its political activity, the Zionist party is also engaged in cultural and economic activities which interfere with the cultural and economic policies of the Soviet Union. The Zionists endeavor to defend the vested interests of the petty bourgeoisie, of the middle class, and even of the patricians....

The Zionist party puts special emphasis on its cultural and educational institutions....The Zionist cultural and educational programs, however, do not even pretend to share the liberalism adopted by the Cadet party. All they endeavor to achieve is the strengthening of the clerical spirit in the Jewish *shul*. Furthermore, they support the religious instruction in the [traditional Jewish] schools as the mainstay of their nationalistic education. Their energies are directed toward an artificial revival of the Hebrew language, thereby endangering Yiddish, the daily language of the Jewish laboring masses. The cultural and educational activities of the Zionist party persistently undermine—too often successfully—the budding culture of socialism which has been emerging from within the Jewish proletarian movement throughout the last few decades. In this respect, positive action has already been undertaken in Greater Russia where Hebrew schools are now forbidden....

That is why we must urgently proceed to suspend all activities of the Zionist party, not only where its central and local committees are concerned, but also the economic, cultural and professional organizations centered around the party. In doing so we shall only be taking the steps necessary for the propagation of communistic ideas among the Jewish working class and the younger generation of the Jewish petty bourgeoisie.

NOTES

1. *Yevsektsiya* (plural, *Yevsektsii*) was the Jewish section of the propaganda department of the Russian Communist party from 1918 to 1930 (the singular, *Yevsektsiya*, is commonly used even in reference to many sections). Upon taking power in November 1917, the Communist party was faced with the need to integrate the numerous nationalities and distinct ethnic groups of the Russian Empire into the revolution and ideological structure of the new state. In a radical reversal of Bolshevik policy, special "national" sections were established within the party for this purpose. In January 1918 a Jewish Commissariat was created and Jewish sections (*Yevsektsii*) were formed in order to organize within the revolution the millions of Jews in Russia who spoke their own language and maintained their own social and cultural institutions. The first conference of the Jewish *Yevsektsii*, which were established throughout the Soviet Union, took place in Moscow in October 1918. Some of the resolutions of the conference are presented above. At this conference it was repeatedly emphasized that the *Yevsektsiya* had no other goal than to integrate the Yiddish-speaking masses of the Soviet Union into the revolution; the *Yevsektsiya* was on no account to serve national goals. With the full cooperation of the police and other government agencies, the *Yevsektsiya* dismantled the traditional Jewish communal organization, the *kehilot*, expropriated synagogue buildings, closed yeshivot and other educational institutions and exercised strict control on the publication of books of Jewish interest. At the same time the *Yevsektsiya* attempted to create a Jewish Communist culture: a Communist Yiddish press, publishing houses, a network of primary and secondary schools, Yiddish theaters and other cultural projects. The *Yevsektsiya* even sponsored Jewish settlement projects, the most significant being the proclamation in 1928 of an autonomous Jewish region in Birobidzhan on the Manchurian border (see document 47 in this chapter). The *Yevsektsiya* seemed increasingly committed to preserving the identity of Soviet Jewry. "The Communist party [however] saw the Jewish sections as a transient instrument through which the Jewish masses could be socialized, transformed, and integrated into the society as a whole, and if that integration meant the loss of separate ethnic identity so be it, or even, some argued, so much the better" (Zvi Y. Gitelman, *Jewish Nationality and Soviet Politics: The Jewish Sections of the CPSU 1917–1930* [Princeton: Princeton University Press, 1972], p. 11). In 1930 the Communist party decided to liquidate all national sections, including *Yevsektsiya*. Gradually, the

institutions created by the *Yevsektsiya*, along with many of the section's activities, were liquidated, a process that was completed by the late 1940s.

2. For several years after the revolution the Soviets authorized, for tactical reasons, restricted activities of the Zionists and then only in certain regions of the country; by 1928 Zionism was absolutely banned in the Soviet Union. Many leaders of the movement were imprisoned and sent to labor camps or exiled to outlying districts of Soviet Asia.

3. The popular name of the Constitutional Democratic party, founded in October 1905; it was the principal middle-class party in tsarist Russia.

4. Between 1917 and 1920 (a period of protracted revolutions and civil wars), Eastern Europe, especially Poland and Ukraine, was blighted by devastating pogroms. It has been estimated that 530 communities had been subjected to more than a thousand separate pogroms, in which more than 60,000 Jews were killed and several times that number were wounded. During the pogroms, the Red Army, which adopted strict measures against antisemitism, was generally regarded by the Jews as their protector. Nonetheless, the pogroms strengthened the national consciousness of the Jews and the desire for an independent Jewish homeland.

5. Vyacheslav K. Plehve (1846–1904), Russian politician and leader of reactionary circles during the regimes of Alexander III and Nicholas II. In his post as minister of the interior, he was widely suspected of orchestrating the Kishinev pogroms of April 1903. In August of that year, Herzl met with Plehve and other Russian officials, soliciting their support for the Zionist idea of an organized emigration and resettlement of the Jews in a territory of their own.

41. MINORITIES TREATY (JUNE 28, 1919)[1]

THE ALLIES AND THE REPUBLIC OF POLAND

CHAPTER I

ARTICLE 1

Poland undertakes that the stipulations contained in Articles 2 to 8 of this Chapter shall be recognized as fundamental laws, and that no law, regulation or official action shall conflict or interfere with these stipulations, nor shall any law, regulation or official action prevail over them.

ARTICLE 2

Poland undertakes to assure full and complete protection of life and liberty to all inhabitants of Poland without distinction of birth, nationality, language, race or religion.

All inhabitants of Poland shall be entitled to the free exercise, whether public or private, of any creed, religion or belief, whose practices are not inconsistent with public order or public morals.

ARTICLE 7

All Polish nationals shall be equal before the law and shall enjoy the same civil and political rights without distinction as to race, language or religion.

Differences of religion, creed or confession shall not prejudice any Polish national in matters relating to the enjoyment of civil or political rights, as, for instance, admission to public employments, functions and honours, or the exercise of professions and industries.

Source: Protection of Linguistic, Racial, and Religious Minorities by the League of Nations (Geneva: Publications de la Societé des Nations, I.B. Minorities, 1927), I.B.2, pp. 39–45.

No restriction shall be imposed on the free use by any Polish national of any language in private intercourse, in commerce, in religion, in the press or in publications of any kind, or at public meetings. Notwithstanding any establishment by the Polish Government of an official language, adequate facilities shall be given to Polish nationals or non-Polish nationals of non-Polish speech for the use of their language, either orally or in writing before the courts.

ARTICLE 8

Polish nationals who belong to racial, religious or linguistic minorities shall enjoy the same treatment and security in law and in fact as the other Polish nationals. In particular, they shall have an equal right to establish, manage and control at their expense charitable, religious and social institutions, schools and other educational establishments, with the right to use their own language and to exercise their religion freely therein.

ARTICLE 9

Poland will provide in the public educational system in towns and district in which a considerable proportion of Polish nationals of other than Polish speech are residents adequate facilities for ensuring that in the primary schools the instruction shall be given to the children of such Polish nationals through the medium of their own language. This provision shall not prevent the Polish Government, from making the teaching of the Polish language obligatory in the said schools.

In towns or districts where there is a considerable proportion of Polish nationals belonging to racial, religious or linguistic minorities, these minorities shall be assured an equitable share in the enjoyment and application of the sums which may be provided out of public funds under the State, municipal or other budgets, for educational, religious or charitable purposes.

The provisions of this Article shall apply to Polish citizens of German speech only in that part of Poland which was German territory on August 1, 1914.

NOTE

1. In the wake of World War I, the declared intention of the victorious Allies was to create a new Europe of individual and national liberty. Indeed, as they entered the war, the Allies emblazoned on their banners the cause of national minorities. As the British prime minister Herbert Asquith explained in a statement of August 5, 1914, "We are fighting…that small nationalities are not to be crushed, in defiance of international good faith, by the arbitrary will of a strong…power." With similar sentiments, President Woodrow Wilson of the United States enshrined in his famous "fourteen points" of February 1918 the right of national self-determination. The realization of this objective, however, was enormously complicated by the problem of national minorities in Central and Eastern Europe where there was a plethora of smaller nationalities intermingled among other, nationalities, often without territorial contiguity with other concentrations of their co-nationals elsewhere. Much to the exasperation of the visionary architects of the new Europe, it was often impossible to include large pockets of national minorities within states with a predominant population of another nationality. Thus, the states emerging from the dissolution of the Austrian-Hungarian empire and those states in the western regions of the former tsarist empire asserting their right to self-determination remained multinational societies, containing sizeable national, linguistic and religious minorities. Still preserving their own distinctive culture and language—Yiddish—and often concentrated in large demographic pockets, the Jews were one of these minorities. A Committee of Jewish Delegations (Comité des Délégations Juives), representing, among others, Jewish national assemblies, councils, and committees formed in most Eastern and Southeastern European Jewish communities, attended the Paris Peace Conference and on May 10, 1919, submitted a memorandum petitioning the Allies to ensure that all members of national minorities in each of the newly created or enlarged states would enjoy the full rights of citizenship and that each minority would have the collective right, secured by international law, to preserve and further its own distinctive culture.

   The principle of national minority rights was eventually accepted by the Allies. In addition to signing peace treaties proper, Greece, Czechoslovakia, Poland, Rumania, and Yugoslavia were each signatories to special treaties designed to protect the members of national and religious minorities both as citizens of their respective states and as members of distinct ethnic, religious and linguistic minorities. Later, similar treaties were signed with Austria, Bulgaria, Hungary, and Turkey. Still later, the states of Albania, Estonia, Latvia, Lithuania, Finland, and Iraq (the latter in 1932) pledged themselves to the League of Nations to safeguard the rights of minorities in their respective countries.

The treaty between the principal Allied and associated powers—the United States of America, Great Britain, France, Italy and Japan—and the newly founded Republic of Poland, signed on June 28, 1919, served as a model for similar minority treaties with other nations. With various modifications, articles 10 and 11 of this treaty, which dealt with specifically Jewish cultural and religious liberties, were introduced into the treaties with Czechoslovakia, Greece, Lithuania, and Turkey and into the conventions regarding Upper Silesia and Memel. Significantly, the minority treaty with Rumania included an article (chapter 1, article 7) designed to prevent a repetition of that country's evasion of its obligations under the Treaty of Berlin of 1878 (see document 24 in this chapter). This article reads as follows: "Rumania undertakes to recognize as Rumanian nationals *ipso facto* and without the requirement of any formality Jews inhabiting any Rumanian territory, who do not possess another nationality."

Jews placed great hope in the system of minority rights, guaranteed as it was by international agreement and law. Initially, with all its procedural and substantive imperfections, the system seemed to work. In most states civic equality was achieved while provisions were made, particularly in education, to secure the cultural integrity of national minorities; some minorities, including the Jews, achieved a remarkable measure of cultural and communal autonomy. The great weakness was that the League of Nations, which was charged with supervising the minority rights treaties, had few instruments to enforce compliance. When, for instance, in 1934 the Polish minister of foreign affairs, Colonel Jozef Beck, renounced his country's obligations to its minorities, there was little the international community could do but protest. Whatever was left of the system suffered the fate of the League of the Nations, which met its demise with the outbreak of World War II.

42. HUNGARY VIOLATES THE MINORITIES TREATY (1921)

LUCIEN WOLF[1]

It having been reported in the Press that the Republic of Hungary had made applications to be admitted to membership of the League [of Nations],[2] the Secretary, on November 18, 1920, addressed a protest to the Assembly [of the League] on the ground that Hungary was disqualified by certain violations of the Minority Clauses of the Treaty of Paris signed by her at Trianon on June 4, 1920.[3] The violations were contained in an act passed by the Hungarian National Assembly,

which excluded Jews from Hungarian nationality and imposed upon them educational disabilities.[4] It subsequently transpired that Hungary had not made any application [for membership] to the League, and the Secretary accordingly asked that the protest should not be submitted to the Assembly. It remains, however, on record and it will be renewed if at any future time Hungary should make an application for membership. It should be explained that no other representation

Source: Memorandum by L. Wolf to the Joint Foreign Committee of the Board of Deputies of British Jews, January 12, 1921. Cited by Nathaniel Katzburg, *Hungary and the Jews: Policy and Legislation, 1920–1943* (Ramat Gan: Bar-Ilan University Press, 1981), pp. 239f.

could be made to the League in regard to the treaty default of Hungary because the Minority stipulations of the Treaty of Trianon have not yet received the guarantee of the League. When that happens the Joint [Foreign] Committee will, of course, take appropriate action.

NOTES

1. A highly respected journalist on political affairs, Lucien Wolf (1857–1930) was a long-standing member of the Conjoint [Foreign Affairs] Committee of the Board of Deputies of British Jews. In this capacity, he served effectively as the "Foreign Secretary" of Anglo-Jewry. As part of the Anglo-Jewish delegation to the Paris Peace Conference of 1919, he helped draft the Minorities Treaty, which sought to secure the rights of ethnic, religious, and linguistic minority populations. (Cf. the previous document in this chapter.) In this memorandum, that he dispatched to the Conjoint Committee, he refers to the Republic of Hungary's application for membership in the recently established League of Nations. He explains that the Secretary-General of the League, Sir James Erich Drummond (1899–1974) recommended rejecting the application because Hungary violated the Minorities Treaty with its recently enacted *Numerus Clausus* limiting the number of Jews in institutions of higher learning.

2. On February 12, 1920, Hungary filed a request for membership in the League, but the petition was formally submitted only in May 1921 after the Treaty of Trianon (see note 3) was ratified by the Hungarian parliament.

3. With the conclusion of World War I, the victorious Allies signed on June 4, 1920, a peace treaty with the Republic of Hungary, which was founded subsequent to the dismantling of the Austrian-Hungarian Empire. The treaty, which was negotiated at the Grand Trianon Palace in Versailles, France, determined the international borders of Hungary and committed her to adhere to all the articles of the Treaty of Paris, including the clauses appertaining to minority rights.

4. On July 22, 1920, the Hungarian parliament enacted a law proposed by the Minister of Education and Religious Affairs "About the Entrance Procedures into the Universities, the Technical University, the Budapest School of Economics, and the Law Schools." Although it does not specify Jews, the law sought to limit "overrepresented" national minorities in the institutions of higher education; in effect, this meant the Jews. The law limited the number of Jewish students to 6 percent or their proportion of the general population, whereas prior to the war in some faculties, such as medicine and law, the percentage of Jews, according to some estimates, was as high as 45 percent. The Hungarian *Numerus Clausus* had the dubious renown of being the first anti-Jewish legislation in the twentieth century. It also signified that Hungary was the first country to adopt the draconian policy of tsarist Russia, which, in 1887, introduced the concept of educational quotas based on national and religious affiliation.

43. THE POSITION OF HUNGARIAN JEWRY
(c. FEBRUARY 1939)

THE JEWISH COMMUNITY OF BUDAPEST[1]

The Hungarian Government published on the evening of the 22nd of December the full text of the Second Anti-Jewish Bill, and on the next day, the 23rd of December 1938 a university professor, one of the [country's] most famous ophthalmologists—who was born a Christian [of Jewish converts]—committed suicide; and on the same day one of the most prominent barristers of Budapest, the director of the board of the legal department of the Jewish Community, also committed suicide. The reason of both suicides was the Anti-Jewish Bill.

These two suicides with the symptom-like character illustrate better than any sentimental comments the present and future position of Hungarian Jewry. The first two shots have been fired, and a further 500,000 Hungarian Jews and about 100,000 Christians who according to the new regulations are to be regarded [as] Jews are to face in the coming weeks and months bottomless despair. They are deprived of all hope and can anticipate no other assistance than that of their free co-religionists....

Further restrictions are to be expected. The Second Anti-Jewish Bill, which followed in less than a half a year after the passing of the first, will surely not be the last. They [the Hungarian authorities] say clearly that Hungary, surrounded by a bloc of two hundred million people having anti-Jewish legislation, is forced to follow suit because left behind in the competition, Jews would overflow the country even to a greater extent than up to now. As a consequence, should Germany adopt new restrictions, they would be introduced here [in Hungary] too, and so, alas, the "Arrow-Cross" member of Parliament was perfectly right when he exclaimed at the introduction of the Second Anti-Jewish Bill in the House of Parliament: "The third [anti-Jewish legislation] will come too."

[As a result of the anti-Jewish legislation] Hungarian Jewry is on the way to accelerated economic ruin. And in the background stands the menacing National Socialism, which does not even trouble to conceal what fate they intend to inflict upon Jewry. National Socialism is not to be underestimated. Its strength does not derive as much from its organizations as from the sympathy it encounters among certain groups, though the present representatives of the state demonstrate a certain resistance against it....

The politicians who view with growing anxiety the provisions of the new anti-Jewish Law are afraid to utter their opinion, for if they would do so, they would be accused of being mercenaries of Jews and this imputation might ruin their political careers. In this struggle Jews have no friends or allies. Labor and the remaining liberal minority, though observing with sympathy the tragedy of Jewry, weakened themselves, can do nothing for us but document their sympathy by some touching speeches and gestures, which earn Jewry's full gratitude but could hardly influence the events. The majority of the Gentile middle class hopes for the anti-Jewish Law to improve their financial conditions and even those who are not antisemites approve of the government's action because their own economic supremacy might be weakened by protecting the cause of the Jews, if ever they felt inclined to do so.

We appeal to World Jewry! Hungarian Jewry cannot thus expect assistance from anybody in this country.

Source: Undated memorandum sent by the Jewish community of Budapest to the Secretary of the Board of Deputies of British Jewry. Cited in full by Nathaniel Katzburg, *Hungary and the Jews: Policy and Legislation, 1920–1943* (Ramat Gan: Bar–Ilan University Press, 1981), pp. 266–76. The document was originally written in English. For the sake of clarity, the grammar and diction have been occasionally emened.

It can be rescued only by assistance from abroad. We should not like to be the cause of misunderstanding that may lead to tragic consequences; we do not mean by assistance from abroad any political or economic pressure destined to influence the Hungarian state. Hungarian Jewry expects assistance from abroad only in two respects: on the one hand, they ask for assistance [on behalf] of the aged and infirm who cannot any more leave the country and having become destitute, debarred from the possibility of earning [a livelihood], are facing utter misery, and, on the other hand, they seek a place where our co-religionists who [are in good health and who] have lost the possibilities of earning a livelihood here [in Hungary] could emigrate in order to begin a new life, however hard that may be....

There are but two possibilities for World Jewry. Either to leave their Hungarian fellow Jews to their tragic fate and to resign themselves to watch the starving of half a million Jews, or assist them in the only practicable way [possible] by promoting their emigration. Regarded from our perspective, emigration is a manifold problem. The principal questions relating to it are: 1) How can one leave the country? 2) How to raise the necessary funds for emigration? 3) Which country offers the possibility of emigration? And 4) Which occupations best offer the possibility of earning a livelihood abroad?

The first problem already involves difficulties. To obtain a passport has become very difficult. The neighboring countries refuse even to grant transit visas. Proving one's citizenship is circumstantial. Many ten thousands [of Jews] cannot attest to Hungarian citizenship, even though their ancestors have lived here [for many generations]. The situation of these individuals is most desperate, because of the continuous threat of being deported [to countries under the control of Nazi Germany], and not even the minimal time is accorded them until one of the international Jewish organizations could help them. As a consequence of the revision of [the rules of] citizenship and naturalization, which the new Jewish Law intends, the number of these prospective homeless [Jews] will be immense and, therefore, the first and most urgent requirement is to procure a passport or a transit visa from one of the neighboring states for anyone, whether holding Hungarian citizenship or stateless, who wishes to emigrate. [Something must be done] to prevent a disorganized flight of the masses over the frontier, which can only end in tragedy, in death....

NOTE

1. The confluence of a domestic Fascist movement, the Arrow Cross, and pressure from Nazi Germany led the Hungarian government to institute anti-Jewish laws. The First Jewish Law, submitted on April 8, 1938, limited the number of Jews in the free professions, in administrative positions, and those employed in commercial and industrial companies to 20 percent. The law defined as Jewish those who had converted after 1919 or who were born to Jewish converts after that date. The Second Jewish Law, enacted in 1939, extended the definition of Jewish to a purely racial basis and further limited the economic activities of all those regarded as Jewish. The ratio of 20 percent of Jews set by the First Jewish Law was now reduced to 6 percent. Further anti-Jewish measures soon followed.

44. APPEAL TO JEWISH WORKERS AND TOILERS (1920)[1]

A GROUP OF JEWISH SOLDIERS OF THE RED ARMY

Jewish workers and toilers, we, a group of Jewish Red Army soldiers who are on the Western front in the battle against the Polish lords, turn to you. Do you hear the weeping of the orphans and widows, whose husbands and parents perished at the hands of pogrom-making Polish lords?

Do not the moans and the cries of the thousands who have been tortured and over whom the slaughter knife of the Polish hangman [hovered] reach your ears?

So what have you done to take revenge upon the Polish lords for the blood of the unfortunately perished Jewish workers and toilers?

Jewish worker and toiler! The three years of civil war have clearly shown you that your spiritual and material life can only be secure under the government of the workers and peasants.

Every settlement, every city and town of the Ukraine, White Russia, and Lithuania upon which the boot of the white [i.e. counterrevolutionary] robber had trodden is soaked with the blood of the poor Jewish masses. The thousands of victims who fell in the Ukraine, White Russia and Lithuania at the hands of the bourgeois murderers will always remain in our memory as eternal monuments to the bourgeois world.

The Russian workers' government has inscribed on its banner, among others, the slogan: "Freedom for all nations!"

Jewish workers and toilers!

The Red Army liberates you from your oppressors.

The victory of our Red Army is a harbinger to the Jewish population that they will be liberated from the pogroms they have endured under Polish rule. Therefore you should support the Red Army; every Jewish worker and toiler who can hold a rifle should join the Red Army. Every Jew who runs away from the Red Army has a part in the pogroms that took place in the Ukraine, White Russia and Lithuania.

Jewish workers and toilers!

We Jewish Red Army soldiers who joined the Red Army in order to fight against the capitalist world, which is the cause of the pogroms, call upon you: Help the Red Army! Show that with your blood and sweat you are helping to build a free socialist world.

Long live the Red Army! Long live the battle until victory!

Signed: A group of Jewish Red Army Soldiers. The Press of the Political Department of the 16th Army.

NOTE

1. In the wake of the Bolshevik Revolution of October 1917, the former Russian empire plunged into a civil war that lasted until the beginning of 1921. The Jews were caught in the middle, especially in Ukraine. Various armies and irregular fighting units were at war with each other—the Ukrainian army in alliance with bands of peasants; the Red Army, which came from the north but which incorporated many Ukrainian units with Bolshevik sympathies; the counterrevolutionary so-called White Army; and independent bands under local leaders. These clashing forces often abused and assaulted the large Jewish population of the area. Although in fact the first acts of aggression against the Jews were perpetrated by the

Source: Yiddish leaflet from 1920. Ephemera Collection, Widener Library, Harvard University. Translated for an exhibition of Russian Judaica, December 1–14, 1980, Widener Library, Harvard University. Printed with permission of Harvard College Library.

Red Army, its command soon adopted a clear and decisive policy opposing antisemitism; indeed, the nascent Soviet government declared antisemitism a criminal offense. Further, a systematic program of instruction against antisemitism was conducted throughout the rank and file of the Red Army, and all manifestations of antisemitism were severely punished. Hence, the Jews came to regard the Red Army as their protector. It was otherwise with the other armies. The Ukrainian and White armies, as well as the irregular forces, were unabashedly anti-semitic and often viciously massacred Jews. It is estimated that during the civil war 530 Jewish communities were attacked and subject to more than a thousand separate pogroms, resulting in the deaths of more than 60,000 Jews and many times that number maimed and wounded. In Western Ukraine and Belorussia—areas bordering Poland—it was mainly the Polish army that assaulted the Jews. Although it did not conduct pogroms per se, the Polish army, aided by Ukrainian and Russian "volunteer" units under its command, terrorized the Jewish population it encountered in its battles against the Bolsheviks, apprehending and summarily executing hundreds for suspected Communist affiliation.

Jewish self-defense units were formed in many places in Ukraine and elsewhere. During the last two years of the civil war, as Soviet rule strengthened, these self-defense organizations at first received political and military support from Moscow. The units were later disbanded, however, because the Soviet authorities objected to the nationalist and Zionist elements that tended to dominate them. This document is a reprint of a leaflet issued during the struggle of the Red Army against the Polish army.

45. CONSTITUTION OF THE REPUBLIC OF POLAND (1921)[1]

CHAPTER V

GENERAL DUTIES AND CIVIC RIGHTS

Article 95. The Polish Republic guarantees within its territory full protection for life, liberty and property to all its inhabitants without distinction of origin, nationality, language, race or religion....

Article 100. Every citizen possesses the right of safeguarding his nationality and of cultivating his national language and customs.

Special laws of the State guarantee the full and free development of their national customs to minorities in the Polish State, aided by autonomous federations of minorities, to which statutory recognition may be given within the limits governing general autonomous federations.

In respect of such federations, the State is entitled to control, and if necessary is bound to supplement, their financial resources....

Article 110. Polish nationals belonging to minorities in the nation, whether based in religion or language, have equal rights with other citizens informing, controlling and administering at their own expense charitable, religious and social institutions, schools and other educational establishments, with the full use of their language and practice of their religion therein.

Article 111. Liberty of conscience and religion is guaranteed to all nationals. No one can be restricted

---

Source: Silent Constitutions of the World (Dublin: Stationery Office, 1922), pp. 77–78

in the exercise of rights accorded to other nationals by reason of his religion or of his religious convictions....

Article 114. The Roman Catholic faith, being that of the majority of the Nation, occupies in the State a preponderant position among religions, which all receive equal treatment.

NOTE

1. In consonance with its obligations under the minority rights treaty it signed with the Allied and associated powers (cf. document 41 of this chapter), the constitution of the Republic of Poland, promulgated on March 17, 1921, incorporated the principles of universal civil and political equality and minority rights.

Poland (1921)

46. WHY DID WE CREATE THE MINORITIES BLOC? (1922)[1]

YITZHAK GRUENBAUM[2]

In the founding convention of the Sejm we fought a battle for civil equality and for our national rights. On what power did we rely in this battle of ours? It is clear that a small handful of eleven delegates would be unable to force the majority of delegates of the Sejm to accept our motions. We were isolated and dependent on others in all our actions, especially on the good will of the Polish Socialist Party (P.P.S.).[3]

When we wished to pose a question to the Sejm we were obliged to ask the P.P.S. faction to give us the four additional signatures that we lacked. The leaders of the faction did not in general refuse, but they felt obliged to edit our questions to the government. They refused, for example, to sign the question on the subject of the riots in Kalish,[4] in which workers also participated. They were completely unwilling that a document should exist, with their signatures on it, attesting to riots in Poland against the Jews. At the same time we were accused of fabricating false reports about persecution and rioting against the Jews in order to bring shame upon the Poles in other countries.

Our situation in presenting motions was even worse. A motion would be accepted by the presidency of the Sejm as urgent if it was signed by thirty delegates, and we had only eleven. In order to get the remaining signatures from the P.P.S. we were forced to make serious concessions. Thus, on our motion to rescind the limitations on our civil rights which survived from the days of the tsars,[5] we were forced by the demand of the P.P.S. to remove the section concerning the repeal of the prohibition of the Jews to buy land from farmers.[6] And the Jew Perl,[7] one of the leaders of the P.P.S., demanded that we also remove the section repealing the prohibition against drawing up documents in Hebrew and Yiddish and conferring legal validity to signatures in these languages.[8]

We were freed from the yoke of the P.P.S. faction when six additional delegates joined the two German delegates already present in the founding Sejm. Only then were we able to respond with questions and regular motions to every injustice that was done to us.

The new German delegates who joined the original two thought at the outset that the all-powerful right wing would respond to their demands. At the time the Germans were still reluctant to follow a policy of opposition and hoped to work through behind-the-scenes bargaining. Nevertheless, they understood that they were obliged to give their signatures on our questions and motions, as we did ours on theirs, even though we sat on the benches of the Left and they on the benches of the Right. But even with the Germans we still did not constitute a force that could influence matters effectively.

The power of the Jewish people in Poland was insufficient. It is true that there was a party active in the Jewish community which considered its power almost equal to that of the Poles. Or at least it attempted to lead the Jews into thinking so. But it was not long before it became clear that the power of opposition of the Jews was weaker than we had imagined. On the question of a day of rest on Sundays,[9] which would endanger the Sabbath rest, and on the question of the Law of Citizenship which stripped many Jews of their Polish citizenship[10] (although this had been recognized in the section of the Versailles Treaty concerning minority rights), it became clear that our ability to conduct non-violent opposition—and we did not consider any other kind—was essentially nil.

Source: Yitzhak Gruenbaum, *Milhamot yehudei polin,* 2nd ed. (Jerusalem: Haverim Publications, 1941), pp. 156–61. Trans. by L. Sachs.

Our one support was the power of world Jewry.[11] Only thanks to this support were we able to accomplish anything at all. At the time of the Peace Conference in Versailles the lofty phrases which had brought the various people to war had not yet evaporated. Wilson's demands were still taken seriously. In this atmosphere we too were able to obtain something. For the same reasons the persecutions and pogroms in Poland did not increase particularly in the years 1919–1920. Sections guaranteeing our rights were even incorporated into the Constitution. But this power gradually weakened. World Jewry's power to influence declined.

At the same time the question arose as to whether we should give up our battle and choose another path. But our answer was clear: It is impossible for us to surrender on the issue of our national needs, for the attainment of our civil equality depends on the satisfaction of these needs; it is inconceivable that we give up our just demands. Jews live in Poland in large numbers, and their equal civil rights constitute, of themselves, collective, national rights. If war is waged against the Jews as a nation, if, for example, they are denied the right to establish schools for themselves according to their own needs, to found institutions for their own special purposes, then the war against these rights will of necessity lead to limitations on our civil rights.

From an economic and social point of view a battle is being conducted against the Jewish community, particularly with respect to its legal status, to the advantage of the Polish middle class. The latter is supported in this battle by the apparatus of the state, by legislation and by antisemitism based on blind hatred of the Jews. The Jews are labeled as swindlers, cheaters, traitors and enemies of Poland; horrible pictures are painted of the Jewish monster in order to justify the policy of antisemitism.

Polish leaders have told us more than once that they wish to put the Jews in the same position that they occupy in Western Europe. Our answer to this was that in the countries of Western Europe there are many fewer Jews than in Poland, and their national needs are not the same as ours, or at least not as great. In order that the position of the Jews as citizens be truly equal to that of the Poles, it is necessary to recognize the existence of a Jewish nation, and Jewish nationalism must not be used as an excuse for restrictions, such as occurred in the case of army officers and similar instances. Thus for us to refrain from fighting for our national rights would be interpreted as a surrender on the issue of our civil equality.

Before the peace treaty with Soviet Russia,[12] there were only two national minorities in Poland, the Jews and the Germans. At the time the Jews were the symbol of these national minorities. The Ukrainian, White Russian [Belorussian], Russian and Lithuanian minorities were added after the peace with Russia, but they had no representatives in the Sejm. A decision was taken in the Sejm to hold elections in the territories which were added to Poland in the four months following the signing of the peace treaty. But the elections were not held, and nothing further was heard in the Sejm about the representatives of these peoples. Administrative measures in respect to these national minorities were in many ways reminiscent of those of tsarist Russia, and therefore it was clear that representatives of the new minorities would present their national demands to the Sejm. The national struggle in Poland is just beginning. The common interests of all those peoples whose development is blocked are growing. In this way the power of world Jewry, on which we rely in our struggle, is augmented by the power of the other national minorities whose power of opposition is greater than ours.

Thus we have arrived at the problem: Shall we separate ourselves from these other national minorities, or shall we join them as far as possible? This question is linked to another: Do we wish to serve as an instrument of oppression in the hands of the state, or do we wish to go our special way, the way of the battle for our national rights? This problem was before us in other countries and was answered in a variety of ways; in every case where we became a tool in the hands of the ruling nationality our fate was grim, as happened, for example, in Hungary.[13] Apparently the Jew is not such good cementing material as the rulers of Hungary who granted the Jews full civil equality had thought and turned them into an instrument to be used against the rest of the minority groups. In Poland we do not have rights and status equal to those of the Polish citizens, which we did have in Hungary, and therefore we are not able to play such a role. We must not allow ourselves to be used as a weapon against other national minorities.

Only one way is open to us: We must struggle for a regime in Poland that will guarantee free development to every national minority, which will abolish any exploitation or oppression of such a group. The other national minorities are as interested in this matter as we are. This is the political factor which caused us to consider the creation of a minorities bloc.

NOTES

1. The Minorities Bloc was a political alliance of various national minorities formed in 1922 on the eve of the second parliamentary elections in Poland, held in November 1922. It was founded in response to the government's gerrymandering or mapping of election districts in favor of ethnic Poles; where this was not possible, especially in border areas, the districts were so determined that no one national majority would predominate. This blatant act of discrimination was meant to diminish the parliamentary representation of the national minorities to considerably less than their proportion of the total population of the country, which according to the census of 1921 was 30.8 percent.

Initiated by the leader of the German minority, the Minorities Bloc was, with some exceptions, enthusiastically supported by the Jews led by Gruenbaum. The Ukrainians in Galicia (formerly part of Austria) boycotted the elections because they refused to acknowledge Polish rule; the Zionists in Galicia therefore presented their own national slate. In Congress Poland and in the Belorussian border regions the overwhelming majority of the Jewish public supported the Bloc. Much to the chagrin of the ethnic Poles, the Minorities Bloc gained an impressive victory in the elections, becoming the third largest party in the Sejm with 66 seats (out of 444), including 17 held by Jews. In eastern Galicia 15 Jewish representatives were elected due to the abstention of the Ukrainians, and in western Galicia 2 were elected; the "Jewish club" in the Sejm totaled 34 (in addition, there were 12 Jews in the Senate). The defeat of the Poles was, of course, most dramatic in districts of mixed populations. Needless to say, the Poles regarded the formation of the Bloc as a hostile act, and there was increased antagonism toward the national minorities. During the parliamentary term 1922–1927 only loose links were maintained between the Polish majority and the Bloc.

With the approach of the elections of 1928, a second Minorities Bloc was formed; on this occasion it was joined by the Ukrainians in Galicia. But the political configurations within the constituent minorities had changed such that the Bloc was far less effective. Within the Jewish camp the Galician Zionists decided to run their own national slate; Agudat Israel, the party of ultra-Orthodox Jewry, also ran its own slate, as did the Folkspartei (inspired by S. Dubnow; see document 32 in this chapter); there was also a faction representing Jewish merchants and craftsmen. In addition, many Jews, especially among the Orthodox and the assimilationists, preferred to vote for Polish candidates. These differences led to a sharp decrease in the number of Jewish representatives in the Sejm: seven in the Minorities Bloc, six in the Galician Zionist slate, and none in the other slates. After the third Sejm was abruptly dissolved by the president before the end of its term, new elections were held in 1930. For a variety of reasons, the minority nationalities lost interest in the Minorities Bloc.

The Zionists in Congress Poland under the leadership of Gruenbaum joined forces in six regions of central and western Poland with the German minority. This substitute for the former comprehensive Minorities Bloc received but two seats. The independent Zionist slate in Galicia did only a bit better, gaining four seats. Thus ended the attempt to unite the national minorities of Poland in a common political front; relations between the Jews and other minority groups—not to speak of the uneasy relations with the Polish majority—deteriorated, and the differences, even hostility, arising from divergent economic and political interests increased.

2. Yitzhak Gruenbaum or Greenboim (1879–1970) was one of the principal leaders of Polish Jewry between the world wars. He immigrated to Palestine in 1933, where he later served as the first minister of the interior of the State of Israel. Although an ardent Zionist, he advocated that attention be given to the struggle for Jewish rights and culture in the Diaspora; indeed, he was one of the principal figures in the Helsingfors conference in 1906 and the program of affirming "work in the Diaspora" (see chapter 10, document 20). With the establishment of an independent Poland, he was elected in 1919 to the first Sejm (parliament), and, as a member of that body's commission assigned to draw up the constitution of the nascent republic, he found himself virtually alone in the struggle to guarantee the rights of national minorities. The many frustrations he faced are reflected in this document, a speech he delivered at an election rally in Warsaw on October 20, 1922, in which he outlined the need for the national minorities to form a political alliance and run a common slate of candidates in the forthcoming elections for the second Sejm.

3. The Polish Socialist Party (P.P.S.) had 35 deputies in the first Sejm (out of a total of 394), compared to 13

deputies representing various national minorities. Since the founding of the P.P.S. in Paris in 1892 many Jews were attracted to its ranks.

4. Kalish (Kalisz in Polish) is a city in the province of Poznan, Western Poland. In March 1919, with the establishment of renewed Polish rule in the region, the Endecja (the right-wing and virulently antisemitic Polish National Democratic Party) organized a pogrom in Kalish in which two Jews were killed.

5. Despite its obligations under the Minorities Treaty of June 1919 (cf. document 41 in this chapter), the government of Poland continued to violate Jewish civil rights by adhering to restrictions dating from tsarist rule. It refused to acknowledge the emancipation decreed in April 1917 by the Russian government under Prince Lvov, arguing that it did not apply to Poland since Poland was technically no longer under Russian rule when the emancipation of the Jews was promulgated. Hence, while the Jews in the former regions of Austria and Germany enjoyed civil rights (attained under the previous governments), in Congress Poland (which had been under Russian rule), and especially in the eastern border regions, tsarist limitations on Jewish rights continued (cf. notes 6 and 8). The Polish Constitution of March 1921 included procedures that allowed the government readily to abolish all such restrictions; it needed only to request formally that the Sejm cancel all laws and regulations contrary to the Constitution. Contrary to its treaty obligation, the government lamely argued that although the Constitution promised equality, it did not introduce it. After protracted parliamentary struggle, the restrictions were finally abolished in March 1931.

6. Tsarist law had severely restricted Jewish acquisition and ownership of land.

7. Feliks Perl (1871–1927), a native of Warsaw, played a prominent role in shaping the ideological program of the party, steering it clear of rightist nationalist tendencies and maintaining its firm adherence to socialist principles.

8. Documents written in Hebrew and Yiddish were deemed invalid. In the regions formerly under tsarist rule, Jews were still compelled to pay special taxes and to take the demeaning *more judaico* oath. Further, the *numerus clausus* was maintained at the secondary and university levels. (see this chapter, document 42, note 4.)

9. The Sunday Rest Law, passed by the Sejm in January 1920, which prohibited the operation of all business and commercial enterprises on Sundays, in effect entailed a severe economic burden on religiously observant Jews, whose day of rest was on Saturday.

10. Although obligated by the Minorities Treaty to regard as citizens all inhabitants residing within Poland's reconstituted borders, the government persistently denied citizenship to thousands of Jews, particularly in former Belorussian and Lithuanian areas. Legislation introduced by the government and passed on January 20, 1920, made the acquisition of citizenship subject to stiff administrative formalities, such as provision of proof of length of residence in Poland, that Jews living in the former war zones could not satisfy. Even after the government instructed the local administrative authorities in August 1926 to facilitate the granting of citizenship, many Jews found it difficult to meet the required conditions.

11. Gruenbaum is referring to the Comité des Délégations Juives, which sought to alert the powers gathered at the Paris peace conference to the dire situation of Eastern European Jewry. Apart from British and French Jewries, which maintained separate delegations, the Comité comprised representatives from Jewish communities of most East and Southeast European countries, the American and Canadian Jewish Congresses, the Constituent Assembly of the Jews of Palestine, the World Zionist Organization, the American Jewish Committee and the Bnai Brith, among others.

12. On August 29, 1918, the newly established Union of Soviet Socialist Republics abrogated the partition treaties concerning Poland, concluded by the tsarist regime with Poland and Austria.

13. See Oscar Jászi, *The Dissolution of the Habsburg Monarchy* (Chicago: University of Chicago Press, 1961), 2nd ed., pp. 324–27; also see this chapter document 42.

47. BIROBIDZHAN: A JEWISH AUTONOMOUS REGION (1934)[1]

A. Decision of the Presidium of the Central Executive Committee of the U.S.S.R., March 28, 1928:

Debated: The assignment of the Birobidzhan district in the Far Eastern territory of the Russian Socialist Federative Soviet Republic for the needs of the migration of the toiling Jews [to the jurisdiction of] the Committee for the Settlement of Toiling Jews on Soil (*Komzet*), connected with the Presidium of the Soviet of Nationalities of the Central Executive Committee of the U.S.S.R. Introduced by the *Komzet* and by the All-Union Migration Committee; Protocol of the Secretariat of the Central Executive Committee of the U.S.S.R., No. 41, article 1.

Resolved: To assign to the *Komzet* for the needs of compact settlement by toiling Jews a free land in the Amur zone of the Far Eastern territory, which comprises the Birobidzhan district in the following approximate boundaries: Across the river Amur, west of the city Khabarovsk to the mouth of the river Chingan and along the Chingan to the railway line; further north of the railway zone to the east, to the river Urmi and across the rivers Urmi and Tunguska; and in the east side following the line west of the city Khabarovsk....

Following the favorable results in the compact settlement of the region delimited in article 1, the possibility of the formation of a Jewish national territorial unit on the territory of the said region should be borne in mind.

Secretary of the Central Executive Committee of the U.S.S.R.

A. Enukidze[2]

B. Decision of the Presidium.of the Central Executive Committee of the U.S.S.R., March 7, 1934:

Resolution: After deliberation on the motion of all the Russian Central Executive Committee regarding the transformation of the Jewish National District in Birobidzhan into a Jewish autonomous region, the Central Executive Committee of the U.S.S.R. decided:

To comply with the request and to transform the Jewish National District of Birobidzhan into a Jewish autonomous region as a constituent part of the Far Eastern territory.

President of the Central Executive Committee of the U.S.S.R.

M. Kalinin[3]

Secretary of the Central Executive Committee of the U.S.S.R.

A. Enukidze

NOTES

1. Birobidzhan is the popular name of the region (*oblast*) of the Soviet Union, for which the official designation is the Jewish Autonomous Region (*yevreyskaya avtonomnaya oblast*). Part of the Khabarovsk territory in the Soviet Far East, located on the border with Manchuria, its assigned area is 13,900 square miles, roughly the size of the states of Vermont and Connecticut together.

   Conceived largely as an agriculture settlement, Birobidzhan was part of the Soviet government's effort to alter the economic structure of the Jews. By 1919 the *Yevsektsiya* had already advanced proposals to direct Jews to agriculture, but it was only in 1924

Source: A. Decision of the Presidium of the Central Executive Committee of the Union of Soviet Socialist Republics in support of Jewish colonization in Birobidzhan, March 28, 1928; B. Decision of the Presidium of the Central Executive Committee of the Union of Soviet Socialist Republics to transform the Jewish National District of Birobidzhan into a Jewish Autonomous Region, March 7, 1934. Translated in Raphael Mahler, *Jewish Emancipation. A Selection of Documents* (New York: American Jewish Committee, 1941), pp. 65–66. Reprinted by permission of the American Jewish Committee.

that this idea was pursued in an organized fashion. In that year the government established *Komzet* (Russian initials for the "Committee for Settling Toiling Jews on the Soil"). In January 1925 an allied body, *Ozet*, was founded to assist *Komzet* to marshal public support for the Committee both in the Soviet Union and abroad. Jewish settlement activities quickly gained momentum, and by 1928 more than 220,000 Jews were engaged in agriculture, largely in Ukraine, Belorussia, and Crimea. Concomitantly, the government directed the Jewish masses to all branches of industry. Contrary perhaps to expectations, these developments did not lead to the weakening of Jewish national sentiments; on the contrary, and partially in response to growing nationalism among the Belorussians and the Ukrainians, Jews increasingly expressed a desire for a national territory of their own within the Soviet Union. This demand was undoubtedly strengthened by the fact that Soviet law already recognized the Jews as a nationality and accorded Yiddish official status in five districts of Ukraine and the Crimea where the Jews constituted a significant proportion of the population.

Fear on the part of the Ukrainians and Belorussians that Jewish territorial autonomy would come at their expense, as well as the Soviet government's desire to strengthen the population of its Far Eastern region, led to the Birobidzhan project. In the summer of 1927 a scientific expedition was dispatched to the region to ascertain the feasibility of Jewish settlement there. The expedition's favorable recommendation led to the resolution of the presidium of the Central Executive Committee of the Soviet Union on March 28, 1928, an extract of which is given here, to entrust *Komzet* to facilitate the settlement of Jews in Birobidzhan. On May 7, 1934, by decree of the Central Executive Committee, the Birobidzhan district was granted the status of Jewish Autonomous Region.

Jewish immigration to Birobidzhan began in April 1928; Jewish collective farms were established, Yiddish was recognized as an official language of the region, and the rudiments of a secular Jewish culture (theaters, newspapers, libraries) were set in place. Immigration to the region continued at varying rates throughout the 1930s and again for a brief period after World War II; in the early 1930s fourteen hundred Jewish immigrants arrived from abroad and even from Palestine. At its height the Jewish population of the region, however, never exceeded forty thousand, or twenty-one percent of the total population.

The project failed for a variety of reasons. First, Jewish support for Birobidzhan was essentially limited to those sympathetic to Communism. The harsh conditions of the area were another factor; the majority of the immigrants abandoned the region within a short time. Yet another factor was the abiding attachment of the Jewish masses to Zion and the consequent resistance to Soviet efforts to present Birobidzhan as an alternative to their ancient hopes. The Stalinist purges of 1936–1937 and 1948–1949, which severely affected the Jewish intelligentsia of the region, also played a decisive role in putting an end to the attempt to create an autonomous Jewish life and culture in Birobidzhan.

2. A prominent Bolshevik leader from Azerbaijan, Avel S. Enukidze (1877–1937) became in December 1922 a member and secretary of the Presidium of the Central Executive Committee of the U.S.S.R.; in 1934 he was elected to the Central Committee of the Communist Party of the U.S.S.R.

3. Mikhail Kalinin (1875–1946) was from 1919 to his death the titular head of state of the U.S.S.R. He was an ardent supporter of the Birobidzhan project. Even before the project was conceived, he declared at a meeting of *Ozet* in 1926: "The Jewish people now faces the great task of preserving its nationality. For this purpose a large segment of the Jewish population must transform itself into a compact farming population, numbering at least several hundred thousand souls." He regarded the creation of a Jewish territorial center in Birobidzhan as a way to normalize the national status of the Jews in the Soviet Union and felt, as he put it in a speech of May 28, 1934, that "the transformation of the region into a republic was only a question of time."

48. WE, POLISH JEWS...

JULIEN TUWIM[1]

To My Mother in Poland or to her beloved Shadow

1

And immediately I can hear the question: "What do you mean—WE?" The question, I grant you, is natural enough. Jews to whom I am wont to explain that I am a Pole have asked it. So will the Poles to the overwhelming majority of whom I am shall remain a Jew. Here is my answer to both.

I am a Pole because I want to be. It's nobody's business but my own. I certainly have not the slightest intention of rendering account, explaining, or justifying it to anyone. I do not divide Poles into pure-stock Poles and alien-stock Poles. I leave such classification to pure and alien-stock advocates of racialism, to domestic and foreign Nazis. I divide Poles just as I divide Jews and all other nations into the intelligent and the fools, the honest and the dishonest, the brilliant and the dull-witted, the exploited and the exploiters, gentlemen and cads. I also divide Poles into Fascists and anti-Fascists. Neither of these groups is of course homogeneous; each shimmers with a variety of hues and shades. But a dividing line certainly does exist, and soon will become quite apparent. Shades may remain, but the color of the dividing line itself will both brighten and deepen to a marked degree.

I can say that in the realm of politics I divide Poles into antisemites and anti-Fascists. For Fascism means always antisemitism. Antisemitism is the international language of Fascism.

2

If, however, it comes to explaining my nationality, or rather my sense of national belonging, then I am a Pole for the most simple, almost primitive reasons. Mostly rational, partly irrational, but devoid of any "mystical" flourishes. To be a Pole is neither an honor nor a glory nor a privilege. It is like breathing. I have not yet met a man who is proud of breathing.

I am a Pole because it was in Poland that I was born and bred, that I grew up and learned; because it was in Poland that I was happy and unhappy; because from exile it is to Poland that I want to return, even though I was promised the joys of paradise elsewhere.

A Pole—because, due to some tender prejudice which I am unable to justify by any logic or reason, I desire after death to be absorbed and dissolved into Polish soil and none other.

A Pole—because I have been told so in Polish in my own paternal home, because since infancy I have been nurtured in the Polish tongue; because my mother taught me Polish songs and Polish rhymes; because when poetry first seized me, it was in Polish words that it burst forth; because what in my life became paramount—poetical creation—would be unthinkable in any other tongue no matter how fluent I might become in it.

A Pole—because it was in Polish that I confessed to the quiverings of my first love, and in Polish that I babbled of its bliss and storm.

A Pole—also because the birch and the willow are closer to my heart than palms and citrus trees, and Mickiewicz and Chopin dearer than Shakespeare and

---

Source: Julien Tuwim, "We, Polish Jews...," *Free World. A Monthly Magazine devoted to Democracy and World Affairs,* 8/1 (July 1944), pp. 53–56. Translator of the original Polish, "My, Zydzi Polscy," is not named. Notes 2, 3, and 4 were provided by Antony Polonsky.

Beethoven. Dearer for reasons which again I'd be at a loss to explain.

A Pole—because I have taken over from the Poles quite a few of their national faults. A Pole—because my hatred of Polish Fascists is greater than my hatred of Fascists of other nationalities. And I consider that particular point as a strong mark of my nationality.

Above all a Pole—because I want to be.

3

"All right," Someone will say, "granted you are a Pole. But in that case, why 'we JEWS'?" To which I answer: BECAUSE OF BLOOD. "Then racialism again?" No, not racialism at all. Quite the contrary.

There are two kinds of blood: that inside of the veins, and that which spurts from them. The first is the sap of the body, and as such comes under the realm of physiologists. Whoever attributes to this blood any other than biological characteristics and powers will in consequence, as we have seen, turn towns into smoking ruins, will slaughter millions of people, and at last, as we shall yet see, bring carnage upon his own kin.

The other kind of blood is the same blood but spilled by this gang leader of international Fascism to testify to the triumph of his gore over mine, the blood of millions of murdered innocents, a blood not hidden in arteries but revealed to the world. Never since the dawn of mankind has there been such a flood of martyr blood, and the blood of Jews (not Jewish blood, mind you) flows in widest and deepest streams. Already its blackening rivulets are flowing together into a tempestuous river. *And it is in this New Jordan that I beg to receive the baptism of baptisms; the bloody, burning, martyred brotherhood of Jews.*

Take me, my brethren, into that glorious bond of Innocently Shed Blood. To that community, to that church I want to belong from now on.

Let that high rank—the rank of the Jew Doloris Causa—be bestowed upon a Polish poet by the nation which produced him. Not for my merit, for I can claim none in your eyes. I will consider it a promotion and the highest award for those few Polish poems which may survive me and will be connected with the memory of my name—the name of a Polish Jew.

4

Upon the armbands which you wore in the ghetto the star of David was painted. I believe in the future Poland in which that star of your armbands will become the highest order bestowed upon the bravest among the Polish officers and soldiers. They will wear it proudly upon their breasts next to the old Virtuti Militari. There also will be a Cross of the Ghetto—a deeply symbolic name. There will be the Order of the Yellow Patch, denoting more merit than many a present tinsel. And there shall be in Warsaw and in every other Polish city some fragment of the ghetto left standing and preserved in its present form in all its horror of ruin and destruction. We shall surround that monument to the ignominy of our foes and to the glory of our tortured heroes with chains wrought from captured Hitler's guns, and every day we shall twine fresh live flowers into its iron links, so that the memory of the massacred people shall remain forever fresh in the minds of the generations to come, and also as a sign of our undying sorrow for them.

Thus a new monument will be added to the national shrine.

There we will lead our children, and tell them of the most monstrous martyrdom of people known to the history of mankind. And in the center of this monument, its tragedy enhanced by the rebuilt magnificence of the surrounding city, there will burn an eternal fire. Passersby will uncover their heads before it.

And those who are Christians will cross themselves.

Thus it will be with pride, mournful pride, that we shall count ourselves of that glorious rank which will outshine all others—the rank of the Polish Jew, we who by miracle or by chance have remained alive. With pride? Let us rather say: with contrition and gnawing shame. For it was bestowed upon us for the sake of your torment, your glory, Redeemers!

...And so perhaps I should not say "we Polish Jews," but "we ghosts, we shadows of our slaughtered brethren, the Polish Jews."...

We Polish Jews...We, everliving, who have perished in the ghettos and camps, and we ghosts who, from across seas and oceans, will some day return to the homeland and haunt the ruins in our unscarred bodies and our wretched, presumably spared souls.

We, the truth of our graves, and we, the illusion of living; we, millions of corpses and we, a few, perhaps a score of thousands of quasi non-corpses; we, that boundless brotherly tomb, we, a Jewish burial ground such as was never seen before and will never be seen again.

We, suffocated in gas-chambers and turned into soap—a soap that will not wash clean the stains of our blood nor the stigma of the sin the world has perpetrated upon us.

We, whose brains spattered upon the walls of our miserable dwellings and the walls under which we were stood for mass execution solely because we were Jews.

We, the Golgotha upon which an endless forest of crosses could be raised. We, who two thousand years ago gave humanity a Son of Man slaughtered by the Roman Empire, and this one innocent death was enough to make Him God. What religion will arise from millions of deaths, tortures, degradations and arms stretched wide in the last agony of despair?

We Abies, we Kikes, we Sheenies whose names and nick-names[2] will some day exceed in dignity those of Achilles, Boleslaus the Brave, and Richard Coeur-de-Lion.

We, once more in the catacombs, in the man-holes under Warsaw pavements, splashing in the stink of sewers to the surprise of our companions— the rats.

We, rifle in hand upon barricades, amidst the ruins of our homes bombed from the sky above; we—soldiers of honor and freedom.

"Kike, go and fight!"[3] He did, Gentlemen, and laid down his life for Poland.

We, who made a fortress of every threshold while house after house crashed about us.

We, Polish Jews growing wild in forests, feeding our terrified children on roots and grass; we crawling, crouching, bedraggled and unkempt, armed with an antique shotgun obtained by some miraculous feat of begging and bribing.

"Have you heard the one about the Jewish game-keeper? It's a riot. The Jew fired; and by golly if he didn't wet his pants from fright! Ha! Ha!"

We, Jobs, we Niobes, mourning the loss of hundreds of thousands of our Jewish Urszulkas.[4]...

We, deep pits of broken, crushed bones and twisted, welted bodies.

We—the scream of pain! A scream so shrill that the most distant ages shall hear it. We—the Lament, the Howl, we—the Choir chanting a sepulchral *El Moleh Rachamim*[5] whose echo will be passed from one century to the next.

We—history's most glorious heap of bloody manure with which we have fertilized the Polish soil so that the bread of freedom may be sweeter for those who will survive us.

We, the macabre remnants, we—the last of the Mohicans, the pitiful survivors of slaughter whom some new Barnum may well exhibit throughout the world, proclaiming upon multi-colored billboards: "Super Show! The biggest sensation in the World! Genuine Polish Jews. Alive!" We, the Chamber of Horrors, Schreckenskammer, Chambre des Tourtures! "Nervous persons better leave the audiences!"

We, who sit and weep upon the shores of distant rivers, as once we sat on the banks of Babylon. All over the world does Rachel bewail her children, and they are no more. On the banks of the Hudson, of the Thames, of the Euphrates and the Nile, of the Ganges and Jordan we wander, scattered and forlorn, crying: "Vistula! Vistula! Vistula! Mother of ours! Grey Vistula turned rosy not with the rosiness of dawn but that of blood!"

We, who will not even find the graves of our mothers and children, so deep are the layers, so widely spread all over the country in one huge burial ground. There will be no one sacred plot upon which to lay our flowers; but even as a sower sows grain so shall we fling them in a wide gesture. And, one maybe will find the spot.

We, Polish Jew...We, the legend dripping with tears and blood. A legend, perhaps, fit only to be told in biblical verses "graven with an iron pen and read in the rock forever" (Job 29:24). We—the Apocalyptical stage of history. We—Jeremiah's Lamentations:

..."The young and the old lie on the ground in the streets: my virgins and my young men are fallen by the sword; thou hast slain them in the day of thine anger; thou has killed, and not pitied."...

"They have cut off my life in the dungeon, and cast a stone upon me. Waters flowed over my head, then I said, I am cut off!...I called upon thy name, O Lord, out of the low dungeon.... O Lord, thou hast seen my wrong; judge thou my cause.... Render unto them a recompense, O Lord, according to the work of their hands! Give them sorrow of heart, thy curse unto them. Persecute and destroy them in anger from under the heavens of the Lord!" (Lamentations of Jeremiah, 3)

* * *

A huge and still growing ghost-skeleton looms over Europe. From his empty eyesockets blazes the fire of dangerous wrath, and his fingers are clutched in a bony fist. It is He—our Leader, our Dictator who shall dictate our rights and our demands.

NOTES

1. Julien Tuwim (1894–1953) was one of interbellum Poland's most celebrated poets. He was born into an assimilated Jewish family, which proudly cultivated a Polish cultural identity. His attitude toward his Jewishness was ambivalent; while not denying his ethnic origins, he regarded assimilation to be the most feasible solution to the Jewish question. He was, therefore, particularly troubled by what he eventually realized was Poland's persistent, deeply rooted antisemitism. With the Nazi invasion of Poland, he escaped Warsaw, finding refuge first in France, then in Portugal and Mexico, and finally arriving in the United States in 1941. The New York anti-Fascist journal, *Free World*, published in translation this poem, in which he expresses a deep and unconditional solidarity with the victims of Nazi barbarism.

2. In the original, there is a string of pejorative Polish names for Jews.

3. In the original, "Jojne, idz na wojne!"—Jonah, go to war!—is a well-known Polish rhyme that mocks the Jews for their alleged lack of military aptitude.

4. Urszulka was the daughter of the famous Polish poet Jan Kochanowski (1530–1584), who died in her youth. Her father's collection of elegies upon her death, *Treny* (Dirges, 1580) is famous in the literary and cultural traditions of Poland. In the original English translation, "Jewish Urszulkas" was rendered "little ones."

5. This is a Hebrew verse from the traditional Jewish mourners' prayer.

VIII

SEPHARDI AND MIDDLE EASTERN JEWRY*

For Sephardi and Middle Eastern Jewry,[1] modernization was largely tantamount to westernization, which meant the adoption of European languages, mannerisms, and styles of dress as well as secular notions of citizenship and statehood. Western ideas reached the Ottoman Empire, the Middle East, and North Africa through internal processes of westernization; the activities of colonial powers; and, for Jews, through the cultural and educational reforms introduced by European Jews. The responses of Sephardi and Middle Eastern Jews to political, social, and religious changes were manifold, exhibiting parallels with and divergences from patterns of change in Europe.

Although colonialism profoundly and somewhat swiftly affected the transformation of much of Sephardi and Middle Eastern Jewry, the Eastern Jewish interest in matters Western was born during the eighteenth century. The Sarajevo-born Sephardi David Attias migrated to Italy in 1769 and, within a decade, called upon Ottoman Jews to cultivate European knowledge in his *La Güerta de Oro* (The Garden of Gold), arguably the first secular book printed in Ladino (document 1). Also during the eighteenth century, the sultan of Morocco built the port city Essaouira to engage in trade with Europe, resulting in the influx of European goods, technologies, and ideas.

In 1912, Morocco came under more direct Western influence when the region was divided into two protectorates, one under French and the other under Spanish control. In 1798, Napoleon briefly occupied Ottoman-controlled Egypt, leaving room for the emergence of a state that was independent from the Ottoman Empire until the British occupation of 1882. France occupied Algeria in 1830 and declared Jews (but not others) French citizens in 1870 (document 2). In 1911, Italy conquered Ottoman Libya, creating an occupation that was received by some Jews with ambivalence (document 3); Libya was subsequently lost to the British in World War II. With colonialism came more direct exposure to Western economic, social, and political systems that led many Jews to seek new sources of livelihood and new political and religious identities.

* Jonathan P. Decter wrote the introduction to this chapter and selected and annotated the majority of the documents.

Different patterns of modernization are observed in countries that were not under direct colonial rule. As one of many minority groups in the Ottoman Empire, Jews enjoyed extensive religious, communal, and legal autonomy prior to the mid-nineteenth century. Beginning in the 1830s, a series of Tanzimat Reforms, enacted for the purposes of nationalization and staving off Western encroachment, ultimately granted full citizenship to religious minorities (document 4). Despite this theoretical advancement, the elusiveness of true sociopolitical equality coupled with the erosion of traditional autonomy may have weakened Jews' actual status. Still, as was the case in Western Europe, citizenship inspired fervent nationalism for many Jews. The dismantling of the Ottoman Empire after World War I gave rise to a number of colonial areas under French and British control, a political shift some hoped would bring Jewish naturalization in the colonizing countries (document 5). Nineteenth-century Iran witnessed instances of Jewish persecution, including the mass outward conversion of the Jews of Mashhad in 1839. Toward the end of the nineteenth century, the modernizing Nasir al-Din Shah (1848–1896) met with representatives of the Alliance Israélite Universelle (discussed next) in Europe, leading to the opening of an Alliance school in Tehran in 1898. The enthronement of Reza Khan in 1925 as Shah of Persia several years after a bloodless coup brought about the institution of many secular reforms.

The most ubiquitous force of westernization for Jews in Islamic lands was the educational, cultural, and political activity of the Alliance Israélite Universelle. The consolidation of this network was sparked by the Damascus affair of 1840 and the Mortara affair of 1858. (See chapter 6, documents 9, 10, and11). However, the image of the Eastern Jew as needy of "regeneration" was already entrenched in the minds of European Jews through the sympathetic if paternalistic descriptions reported by travelers as early as the eighteenth century (document 6). Eastern Jews were portrayed as capable and deserving of being lifted from the mire of superstition, ignorance, and poverty that were believed to stem from the corrosive influence of the Islamic environment. The Jew was considered immutably distinct from the Arab (as well as from the Persian and Ottoman), a point that made the westernization of Eastern Jewry seem an attainable task. The image of Eastern Jews as backward was sometimes reinforced by reports sent by indigenous Jews to *haskalah* newspapers that detailed customs and superstitions with contempt (document 7). Western Jewry sought to remake Eastern Jewry in its own enlightened image, an effort that reflected one dimension of the uneasy process of integration in Europe. Ironically, the cultivation of Emancipation and Enlightenment values in the East resulted not in the further integration of Jews within their own environment, as was the case in Europe, but rather in the dissociation of Jews from their Muslim contemporaries.

The foremost vehicle of identity reconstitution brought by the Alliance was education. Usually at the behest of local community officials and often with the approval of religious authorities, the Alliance established schools that taught secular subjects, such as European languages, history, mathematics, and the natural sciences as well as Jewish history and Hebrew. Many of the instructors and directors of the Alliance schools were indigenous women, trained at the École Normale Israélite Orientale in Paris, who not only taught but advocated for educational reform (see document 8). By instructing Jewish boys and girls in a European-oriented curriculum, Eastern Jewry became fit for advancement in a Western-dominated world. Education strove not only to impart knowledge, but to reconstitute the appearance, values, and mannerisms of Eastern Jewry. Some had hoped that the remaking of Eastern Jewry would position Jews to lead their countries into the modern period and deem them worthy of French naturalization (documents 9–13).

In regions where Ladino and Arabic served as Jews' mother tongues, language use (particularly the language of school instruction) was hotly argued. Arabic, especially its colloquial varieties, was considered an embarrassment to be replaced with a cultivated French.

In parts of the Ottoman Empire, Ladino was greatly devalued as Jews embarked on an agenda of Ottomanization; ironically, much of the polemic against Ladino was voiced in that very language in the pages of the nascent Ladino press (documents 14–16).

Ideas of Western science and thought reached Jews of the East through various channels. Mordechai Ha-Kohen (1856–1929) was an inquisitive Libyan rabbi of Italian descent who taught himself foreign languages; he engaged in questions of religious practice but also of linguistics and modern topics, including Darwinian evolution (document 17). Abraham Shalom Yahuda (1877–1951) was born to a Baghdadi family in Jerusalem and became an expert in European languages. He taught in Berlin, Madrid, and New York and wrote works on the Bible in the context of Egyptian language and culture, a critique of Freud's *Moses and Monotheism* based on this expertise (document 18), and a critique on medieval Hebrew and Arabic poetry. Some Jews who were active with the Alliance, such as Avraham Navon (1864–1952), became renowned French novelists, while Egyptian and Iraqi Jews who were aligned with Arab nationalism, such as Murad Faraj (1866–1956), Yaq'ub Sanu' (1839–1912), and Anwar Shaul (1904–84), participated in the flowering of modern Arabic literature.[2] While Jewish participation in the nineteenth- and twentieth-century Arabic *Nahda* (Awakening)—a modernizing Enlightenment-oriented movement—may have been intermittent, it was significant and perhaps proportionate to the size of the Jewish population.

A part of the program of "emancipating" Eastern Jewry entailed the westernization of its women. In the eyes of Western Jews, Eastern Jewish women were seen as shackled in a condition of servitude and disgrace, gravely stunted by the practice of child marriage (document 19). In addition to bringing Sephardi women a basic standard of education, efforts were made by foreign and domestic Jews to westernize their practices in hygiene, diet, and dress. Sephardi rabbis sometimes adopted "progressive" positions on questions of women's status, as illustrated by a responsum of Rabbi Ben-Zion Uzziel (1880–1953) of Jerusalem on women's suffrage (document 20).

Jews of the Middle East never settled upon a taxonomy of Judaism according to Reform and Orthodox categories. New intellectual and cultural trends naturally facilitated movement toward secularization; however, secularism was not formulated as an opposition to rabbinic authority or as a critique of the validity of halakhah. Some welcomed secularization as an antidote for the obstacle to national unity posed by religious difference. Some equated secularization with moral decadence, placing blame squarely on the Alliance schools, whereas others saw the Alliance as a beacon of hope that could *counteract* religious degeneration (documents 21–23).

Sephardi and Middle Eastern Jews adhered to a diversity of (sometimes overlapping) political ideologies in the modern period: communism, socialism, nationalism, and various degrees of allegiance to colonial powers (document 24; see also document 21). As in Europe, the subject of Zionism was one of pronounced debate. Greatly facilitated by the inclusion of Palestine within the borders of the Ottoman Empire, religious emigration to Palestine, largely devoid of nationalist aspirations, was common during the Ottoman period. Rabbi Yehuda Alkalai (1798–1878), born in Sarajevo and educated in Jerusalem, argued for a Jewish Redemption through the creation of Jewish colonies in Palestine and served as a significant precursor to political Zionism (document 25). Soon after the establishment of the First World Zionist Congress (1897), Jews from Eastern communities sent letters of support to Herzl and the World Zionist Organization and formed branches of Zionist organizations (documents 26–27). However, difficulties in attaining power within the European-dominated Zionist movement led to a feeling of marginalization and resentment toward Ashkenazi Jews (document 28). The aims of Zionism were at odds with those of the Alliance, whose agenda was the regeneration of Jews *within* their home countries according to the very model of exilic existence that Zionism disavowed. Although some Jews cultivated the dual values of Zionism and Arab nationalism, nationalist fervor caused others to reject Zionism either because they saw the agendas as incompatible or because they feared ramifications for Jewish stability and security (documents 29 and 30). Some also feared that Arab nationalism would come to exclude non-Muslims, especially as tensions mounted over the issue of Palestine (document 31).

Although World War II was far more devastating for the Jews of Eastern and Western Europe than for Sephardi and Middle Eastern Jewry, it would be an error to suggest that the war was without deleterious effects for Eastern populations. Ladino-speaking populations in the European portions of the former Ottoman Empire were decimated as regions fell under German occupation; the Jews of Serbia and parts of Greece, including the important center of Salonica, were virtually exterminated. In Iraq, Jews were accused of allying with Great Britain, whose colonialist yoke Iraqi nationalists wished to break, and Nazi propaganda took root, which led to anti-Jewish violence in a massacre known as the Farhud (document 32). In French North Africa, the Vichy Regime enacted discriminatory racial laws, confiscating wealth, limiting economic activity, instituting professional quotas, and revoking Jews' French citizenship in the case of Algeria (documents 33 and 34). Axis policies in Italian Libya led to the internment of thousands of Libyan Jews in forced labor camps. Direct Nazi control over Tunisia put some 80,000 Jews at risk; victims of abuse, these Jews were spared death only by the logistical problems involved in bringing them to Europe for execution. The Nazi atrocities and the Allies' use of atomic weaponry left intellectuals such as Moise Ventura, greatly disillusioned with the West (see document 35).

As Zionist and Arab nationalist commitments swelled in the decade after World War II, tensions rose between Middle Eastern Jews and their neighbors. Arab nationalist activities sometimes turned anti-Jewish resulting in the loss of Jewish property, security, and life. The Arab-Israeli war of 1948, which erupted after the establishment of the State of Israel, made Jews in Arab states veritable outsiders however much they may have identified as patriots of their countries. Despite efforts to restore life to a stable and prosperous state, life became largely untenable for Jews in Arab lands. By the late 1950s, the vast majority of Middle Eastern and North African Jews, numbering in the hundreds of thousands, left their countries of domicile and emigrated to Israel, Europe, and the United States (see document 36).

NOTES

1. It is with some hesitation that we treat Sephardi and Middle Eastern Jewry in a single chapter. One categorization defines "Sephardi" Jews as those of Iberian descent who may have lived in places as diverse as North Africa, the Ottoman Empire, the Netherlands, the Americas, and Poland. "Middle Eastern Jews" are those who resided in or derive from Middle Eastern countries whether or not they claim roots from the Iberian Peninsula. According to such a division, Sephardi and Middle Eastern Jews overlap but are not identical. Another method of categorization sees "Sephardi" Jews as those who follow the halakhic school of medieval Iberia (embodied primarily in Joseph Karo's *Shulkhan Arukh*), which is a more expansive definition. The ambiguity is further compounded by the imprecise popular usage of "Sephardi" to designate any non-Ashkenazi Jew, which obscures the great diversity within Sephardi and Middle Eastern Jewry. Even a term like "Middle Eastern Jewry" can be difficult, since the experiences and customs of Arabic-speaking Jews vary significantly between the North African and Asian segments of the Middle East and within these regions. In this chapter, the "Western Sephardim" are not treated

(since their experience is touched on elsewhere in this volume). This chapter focuses on shared and related experiences (such as transformations in language use, styles of dress, and education) among "Eastern" Sephardi and Middle Eastern Jews, however imperfect the elision of these categories may be. The political experiences of the various communities were quite distinct (some were exposed to direct colonial rule, while others were not; some were granted European citizenship, while others were not, and so forth). The terms "Sephardi and Middle Eastern Jews," "Jews of Islamic Lands," and "Eastern Jews" are used somewhat interchangeably.

2. See also documents 21 and 24 for texts by Faraj and Sanu'.

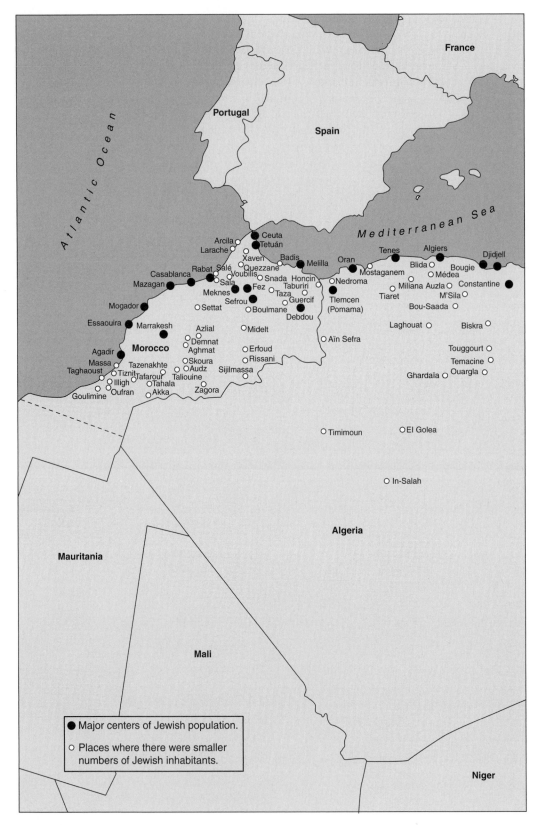

France

Portugal

Spain

Atlantic Ocean

Mediterranean Sea

Arcila
Ceuta
Tetuán
Larache
Xaven
Badis
Melilla
Oran
Tenes
Algiers
Djidjell
Quezzane
Blida
Bougie
Rabat Salé
Voubilis
Snada Honcin
Médéa
Casablanca
Sala
Taburiri
Nedroma
Mostaganem
Constantine
Mazagan
Fez
Taza
Miliana Auzla
Meknes
Guercif
Tlemcen
Tiaret
M'Sila
Sefrou
Boulmane
(Pomama)
Bou-Saada
Mogador
Settat
Debdou
Essaouira
Marrakesh
Azlial
Midelt
Laghouat
Biskra
Demnat
Aïn Sefra
Aghmat
Erfoud
Touggourt
Agadir
Skoura
Rissani
Temacine
Massa
Tazenakhte
Audz
Ghardaïa
Ouargla
Taghaoust
Tiznit
Tafarou
Taliouine
Sijilmassa
Illigh
Tahala
Goulimine
Oufran
Akka
Zagora

Morocco

Timimoun
El Golea

In-Salah

Algeria

Mauritania

Mali

Niger

● Major centers of Jewish population.

○ Places where there were smaller
   numbers of Jewish inhabitants.

North Africa

Tunisia, Libya and the Balkans

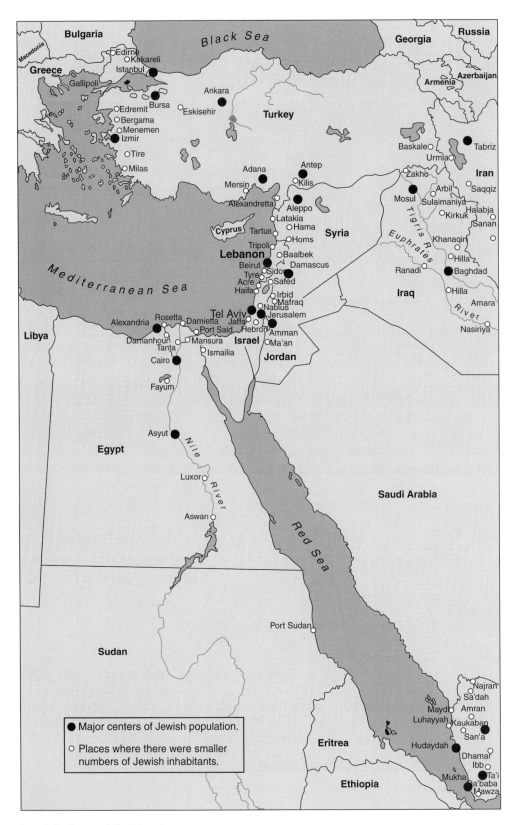

Israel, Turkey and the Near East

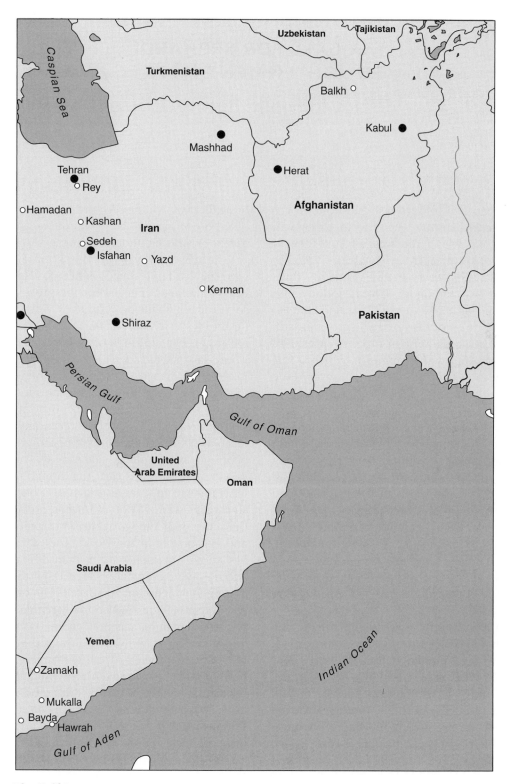

The Gulf States

1. A CALL FOR SEPHARDI ENLIGHTENMENT (1778)

DAVID ATTIAS[1]

I hope that you and [other] wise and honest people will like to read my work and that they will understand that what I did was for your benefit and because of the great desire that was kindled in me when I saw that every nation prints all kinds of books, but that among us, there is nobody who prints any kind of books in our Levantine Spanish language [Ladino]: not history, ancient or modern, nor any book on geography or other sciences. Not even books dealing with commerce, which is the dearest thing to us Jews. Nothing at all—everything there deals with the Law [*la ley*, i.e., Torah] and is in the holy tongue [Hebrew], which only few understand. Our blessed scholars should consider that we live today in a generation that is very different from the old ones. The youngsters of today have a more alert spirit than those in the past, and not all of them are inclined toward [studying] Torah, and to see and hear always the same things repeated and repeated all over again. The old things are annoying for a youngster with a new and alert spirit. They like and enjoy seeing new books that are in a language and script that they understand, in witty and enjoyable language, but are at the same time intelligent....

My intention was none other than to interest and please my above-mentioned friend,[2] i.e., you, as well as everyone who would like to read [this book]. You will see that I tried as much as I could to express myself in the Levantine language [Ladino], so that you and everyone else can understand me, for there are a lot of people who do not understand the real Spanish language, for it has a lot of difficult and complicated words that come from Latin and Italian. Therefore I hope that you will not get angry when you read this, like those who get angry when they read something in a book without understanding it.

The reason why I call this book *La Güerta de Oro* [the Garden of Gold] is because I planted in it things that are beneficial for the purse and for the soul and they will bear fruit for you. I took a little bit of everything, for the world is full of different tastes and all kinds of opinions....Therefore I would say that each person that takes this book into his hands will find something that he will like and that will be useful to read. And he should remember the verse from [the Torah portion] *Va-ethanan* in [the book of] *Devarim* [Deuteronomy]:[3] this is to teach us that it is the desire of the Holy One that his people Israel should be taken by the nations for a wise people, and it is clear that he intended to give wise and sacred rules and laws. But because of our sins, or because of our evil deeds, we are taken by the nations of the world to be the most ignorant and evil people in the world. They say that we do not know any science other than doing commerce and deceiving everyone. Even though there are also among them ignorant and deceitful people: but they respond that there are also many scholars, in astrology, mathematics, algebra, geometry, philosophy, and many other virtuous things and good lessons that serve to open and enlighten people's minds, both in matters relating to this world and in matters relating to the other world. But among us there is nobody who writes or teaches us about the painful journey that one makes in this world. And even more so, there is nobody who would learn from the example of the nations of the world, who the further

Source: David Attias, *La Güerta de Oro* (Livorno, 1778), pp. 32–34a, 35a. Translation and note by Matthias B. Lehmann.

they go, the more refined they are, excelling in sciences and the arts of the ancients. But we, the further we go, the more we fall behind, without going beyond the science that the great sages of former generations left us in writing, like Maimonides and so many others whose writings were known even in the literature of the [gentile] nations. So we live as we are used to, running after our fortune. But the fortune mocks us, and the health fails and the evil pushes, and the good escapes, and the years go by, and prosperity remains elusive, time flies... and life comes to an end....

Since we are dispersed among the nations, we should show them with our deeds the difference between us and them: in everything and every kind of science we need to try to surpass them.

.NOTES

1. David Attias was born in Sarajevo, Bosnia, then part of the Ottoman Empire. In 1769 he moved to Livorno, the foremost port city of Tuscany and home of one of the largest Sephardi communities in Western Europe. In 1778, he published a book entitled *La Güerta de Oro* ("The Garden of Gold"), arguably the first secular book to be printed in Ladino, or Judeo-Spanish, the vernacular language of the Sephardic Jews in the Eastern Mediterranean. The book is ostensibly written for an Ottoman Sephardic audience. Attias tries to promote secular education and the learning of foreign languages among the Ottoman Sephardim, thus anticipating the educational program by the Alliance Israélite Universelle and similar initiatives by more than half a century. The book is of highly varied content, ranging from a seven-page introduction to the Italian language to a short treatise on physiognomy. A constant theme of the book is the juxtaposition of "Europe," which Attias praises as an example of civilization, and the Ottoman "East."

2. Addressed to "a friend in the East," as Attias declares on the title page of his book.

3. "Surely this great nation is a wise and understanding people" (Deut. 4:6): this phrase, cited on the title page of the book, serves as the motto of Attia's book.

2. THE CRÉMIEUX DECREE AND ITS AFTERMATH (1870–1871)[1]

THE CRÉMIEUX DECREE (OCTOBER 24, 1870)

Indigenous Israelites of the departments of Algeria are declared [to be] French citizens. Consequently, their actual status and their personal status shall, from the promulgation of the present decree, be regulated by French law. All rights acquired up to this day shall remain inviolate.

Every legislative provision, sénatus-consulte, decree, regulation, or ordinance to the contrary is abolished.

PROPOSAL FOR ABROGATING THE CRÉMIEUX DECREE (JULY 21, 1871)

EXPLANATION OF MOTIVES

Their presence as jurors in the courts is similarly ruled out. Apart from the fact that the largest number understands or speaks French only most imperfectly, it must be taken into consideration that the Arabs would never patiently bear the sight of native Jews sitting among their judges. The insurrection broke out late in

Source: J. C. Hurewitz, *The Middle East and North Africa in World Politics: A Documentary Record* (New Haven: Yale University Press, 1975), Vol. 1, pp. 376–78.

January 1870 at the very moment when the Muslim peoples saw Jews serving as jurors. Only then did these people, who had not understood the implications of the theoretical declaration of 24 October, understand that they might become defendants before native Jews. If this interpretation of the facts is contested, it will be recalled that the Kalifah of al-Medjana, Si Mokrani [Muqrani], returning his cross [designating him] an officer of the *Légion d'honneur,* made it known that he preferred to die with weapon in hand rather than tolerate the insult to his race in having the Jews placed above it. The conferral on the latter of the right to it among the jurors is therefore premature and dangerous, and it was at least one of the causes of the insurrection.

From the viewpoint of the electorate, the inconveniences are no less serious. They arise from causes analogous to those that have been recorded previously.

One would not expect from the Jews votes dictated by either political considerations or the appreciation of municipal interests, as seen from the perspective of the majority of the local residents. Thus, as has already been said, they form and will continue to form a body apart, considering themselves as having been gifted with a separate existence. Consequently, under their present religious leaders, they will always bring to bear as a united group all the influence at their disposal. This state of affairs can only be serious. For example:

At **Oran** the French population is   8,958
     the Jewish population is   5,653
At.**Constantine** the French population is   7,887
     the Jewish population is   4,396
At **Tlemcen** the French population is   3,264
     the Jewish population is   3,185

It is easy to see that, the Jewish votes not being spread about like those of the French, the municipal councils will be made up wholly of native Jews in their quality as Frenchmen. Alongside them, it is true, there will be foreign and Muslim councillors since the Arabs and foreigners will always keep the number of candidates allowed them. It would therefore not be impossible for native-born Frenchmen to see themselves wholly excluded from a French municipal council.

The same result might be foreseen in the general councils that have at their disposal half of the Arab taxes, the sole resource of the departmental budgets.

Seen from the French viewpoint, this situation is bad. It is even worse from the viewpoint of the traditions, customs, and antipathies of the Muslim populations, which will never understand the relegation of 2.5 million Muslims to the rank of simple subjects, while raising 35,000 Jews to the dignity of French citizens. This inequity is intolerable. It must disappear through the retraction of political rights so imprudently conferred.

Must one on the contrary preserve the decree of 24 October by virtue of which the real status and the personal status of native Jews shall henceforth be regulated no longer by rabbinical but by French law?

We believe that the decree of the delegation of Tours should be abrogated in its entirety.

The civil status of the Jews arises from the same source as their religious status and governs them with an almost equal authority. It follows that to take it from them by a general measure represents in part an attack on their freedom of conscience. With regard to civil rights, it can assuredly occur to no one to prefer rabbinical law to French law. But, in refusing the Jews citizenship rights, it is assuredly just to leave them what pleases them most in their present condition, to know they have the right to settle according to their own traditions all matters relating to marriage, divorce, and inheritance.

Besides, here again it may be said that assimilation cannot be decreed, and that in this regard, in imposing the laws of the metropole, one is liable to create the ever-dangerous conflict between custom and institutions. To avoid this conflict, it is enough to know that time and education will make the Jews seek naturalization which must be offered them individually as a favor.

It must not be forgotten: in Algeria, this favor is still easier to obtain than in France; admission to domicile is not obligatory; seal and registration duties are reduced to one franc, and anyone who has resided in the colony for three years enjoys the right of naturalization without difficulty and expense on the sole condition of proving his morality. It is the continuous and rational application of this liberal legislation that will gradually break up the class of native Jews and assimilate its elements into the overall French unity, while mass naturalization tends only to perpetuate the original distinctions and seems to have had no other aim than to create an instrument in the service of passions and interests against which there can be no sufficient warning.

PROPOSED LAW

Sole Article: The decree issued on 24 October 1870 by the delegation of Tours declaring the native Jews of Algeria [to be] French citizens is abrogated.

PROVISIONAL REINSTATEMENT OF THE CRÉMIEUX DECREE (OCTOBER 7, 1871)

Art. 1. Provisionally, and until the National Assembly has legislated on the maintenance or abrogation of the decree of 24 October 1870, Jews born in Algeria before the French occupation or since that time of parents already established in Algeria shall be considered natives and, in this capacity, shall remain registered on the electoral rolls, if they also fulfill other civil conditions.

Art. 2. Consequently, any Jew wishing to register or remain on the electoral rolls must declare, within twenty days of the promulgation of the present decree, that he has satisfied one of the conditions defined in Article 1.

Art. 3. This declaration shall be made before a justice of the peace at the Jew's place of residence. It shall take the form of either the written declaration or the verbal testimony of seven persons who have been living in Algeria for at least ten years, or any other proof that the justice of the peace may accept as conclusive.

The decision of the justice of the peace shall serve as a certificate for the Jew; he shall immediately be given a copy free of charge. If the Jew has no fixed family and first names, he shall be obliged to adopt them and declare them before the justice of the peace as a preliminary condition for the transfer of this certificate.

For each decision thus taken, a file, which shall be deposited in the town hall of the native's domicile, shall be kept in the form of police records to serve either in the compilation of electoral rolls or as an attested affidavit.

Art. 4. The Jew whose claim is not accepted by the justice of the peace may appeal within three days of the pronouncement of the decision by means of a simple request addressed to the President of the tribunal in the *arrondissement*. The President shall grant a hearing within three days of that date. The tribunal, having heard the Jew or his defense, shall make a final decision. The lodging of an appeal shall not be a bar to later proceedings.

Art. 5. Any Jew presently registered on the electoral rolls who does not carry out the formalities and satisfy the conditions required by the preceding articles shall be struck from [these rolls] and may not be reinstated until the next revision.

Art. 6. All judicial acts entered into under the present decree and in its execution shall be exempt from stamp and registration duties.

Art. 7. The convocation of electoral colleges shall not take place less than a month following the promulgation of the present decree.

Art. 8. The Ministers of Justice and the Interior and the civil Governor General of Algeria are charged, each within his own sphere of responsibility, with the execution of the present decree.

NOTE

1. Isaac Adolphe Crémieux (1796–1880) was a French Jewish lawyer and statesman. He served several times in the chamber of deputies and was appointed minister of justice in 1870. In that year, Crémieux advocated for the full political integration of Algeria into France. He also issued a decree that called for the obligatory enfranchisement of the 32,000 Jews of Algiers, Constantine, and Oran (the optional enfranchisement offered to Jews and Muslims in 1865 was met with only partial acceptance by these communities). The 1870 decree was met with resistance by some segments of the Jewish community that recognized the threat posed by French civil law to traditional autonomy. The decree enhanced the political status of Jews over that of their Muslim compatriots and was rescinded in July 1871 during an insurrection in the Kabylia region only to be reinstituted in October of the same year.

3. THE JEWS UNDER ITALIAN RULE
(c. 1906)

MORDECHAI HA-KOHEN[1]

From the time the Italian soldiers set foot upon the soil of Tripoli, they stimulated economic growth and trade among the general population, particularly among the Jews. This was true not merely because most Jews knew the Italian language,[2] but also because Mohammedan residents took refuge in the desert with the Turkish army. Only the very wealthy were left, those who could not take their possessions with them.

In those days, there were no Mohammedan porters in the city, not even to bring merchandise from the port. However, the Jews who had escaped from the village of 'Amrus and had come with their donkeys to Tripoli as refugees,[3] who had been left without employment, found an opportunity to support themselves. They put their shoulder to the wheel and became porters, and realized a good profit from their efforts.

At the same time, all the hotels were filled from the influx of Italian visitors, merchants, and so forth. Their numbers swelled, and they could find no lodging. The Jews then invented a new business. They crowded themselves in and rented rooms in their homes for a good price. The Italians were overjoyed at this, for they trusted the Jews more than the Mohammedans.

As most of the Italians were not strict or zealous with regard to religion, they became very friendly with the Jews. After a while, however, some hatred developed among a few of the merchants, and they spread it among the masses.[4] This was because the simple merchants among the Italians lost money in business, for two reasons. The first is that they were extravagant in their expenditures. Second, they were not expert in running businesses. It was otherwise with the Jews, who were familiar with business. Sometimes they undersold the Italians, and still they achieved a shining success, making a lot of money. They became well known as businessmen, so much so that Italian customers preferred buying from them over others, saying, "The Jews profit by restricting their consumption."

It appears, moreover, that resentment of the Jews grew elsewhere: among the police, in the courts, and in the hearts of the officials in the customs house. It was as if they were ordered to belittle the Jews and treat them with hostility, and to honor the Mohammedan in his claim, even if he were a simple man arguing against a respected Jewish merchant. The Jews were thus made light of in the eyes of the poor Mohammedan masses.

The Jews could not hold their peace; they complained before God, saying, "What has God done to us? Was it not better for us in former days than now? Even though, during the days of Turkish rule, the Mohammedan majority practiced religious hatred, still a Jew could slyly abate this hatred by appealing to the vanity of the Mohammedan and calling him Lord.[5] Also, the government officials did not treat the claim of a Jew lightly, as they knew very well that in Istanbul there were respected Jews working for liberty and freedom. The words of these Jews were as sharp arrows and were heeded by the government. They would demand redress for an insult to the Jews, and equal treatment from the officials.... How, then, can the Italian government, which is more civilized, allow its officials to act with hostility toward members of other religions,

Source: Harvey E. Goldberg, *The Book of Mordechai: A Study of the Jews of Libya.* (Philadelphia: Institute for the Study of Human Issues, 1980), pp. 190–91.

and to humiliate the Jew for having done nothing except be Jewish?

NOTES

1. Mordechai Ha-Kohen was born in Tripoli, Libya, in 1856, then under Ottoman control, and died in 1929. He worked as a teacher and peddler and eventually became a clerk in the rabbinic court of Tripoli. He was knowledgeable in Hebrew, Jewish law, and customs and was a reformer for a European-style educational system that also safeguarded religious tradition. In 1906, Ha-Kohen met Nahum Slouschz (1871–1966) and served as his guide while Slouschz conducted research on North Africa, culminating in Slouschz's monumental works, *Travels in North Africa* (Philadelphia: Jewish Publication Society, 1927) and *My Travels in Libya*, 2 vols. (Tel Aviv: Vaad Hayavel, 1938–43) (in Hebrew).

Before the two met, Ha-Kohen had completed his *Higgid Mordechai* (Mordechai Narrated), which directly influenced Slouschz's work. In the book, Ha-Kohen detailed the history of the Jews of Libya with special sections on the Jews of Tripoli and the Libyan countryside and a final section on the Italian conquest of Libya. The present selection is taken from the final section and captures the misgivings of Jews concerning the new era of Italian domination.

2. Italian had been taught in schools for several decades. Many adults probably picked up the language through commercial ties with the Italian-speaking population.

3. At the time, Jews constituted about one-third of the Tripoli's population.

4. In 1923, there were disturbances between Jewish and Italian merchants.

5. In Arabic *Sidi*.

4. THE PRIVILEGES AND IMMUNITIES OF THE NON-MUSLIM COMMUNITIES (1856)

SULTAN 'ABDÜLMECID I[1]

Let it be done as herein set forth.

To you, my Grand Vizier Mehemed Emm Aali Pasha, decorated with my imperial order of the medjidiye [honor] of the first class, and with the order of personal merit; may God grant to you greatness and increase your power.

It has always been my most earnest desire to insure the happiness of all classes of the subjects whom Divine Providence has placed under my imperial sceptre, and since my accession to the throne I have not ceased to direct all my efforts to the attainment of that end....

It being now my desire to renew and enlarge still more the new institutions ordained with a view of establishing a state of things conformable with the dignity of my empire, and the rights of my empire [by virtue of the] position which it occupies among civilized nations, and by the fidelity and praiseworthy efforts of all my subjects, and by the kind and friendly assistance of the great powers, my noble allies, received from abroad a confirmation which will be the commencement of a new era, it is my desire to augment its well being and prosperity, to effect the happiness of all my subjects, who in my sight are all equal, and equally dear to me, and who are united to each other by the cordial ties of patriotism, and to insure the means of daily increasing the prosperity of my empire.

Source: J. C. Hurewitz, *The Middle East and North Africa in World Politics: A Documentary Record* (New Haven: Yale University Press, 1975), pp. 315–18.

I have therefore resolved upon, and I order the execution of the following measures:

The guarantees promised on our part by the Hatti-Humayoun of Gulhané, and in conformity with the Tanzimat,[2] to all the subjects of my empire, without distinction of classes or of religion, for the security of their persons and property, and the preservation of their honor, are to-day confirmed and consolidated, and efficacious measures shall be taken in order that they may have their full entire effect.

All the privileges and spiritual immunities granted by my ancestors *ab antiquo*, and at subsequent dates, to all Christian communities or other non-Mussulman persuasions established in my empire, under my protection, shall be confirmed and maintained....

In the towns, small boroughs, and villages where different sects are mingled together each community inhabiting a distinct quarter shall, by conforming to the above-mentioned ordinances, have equal power to repair and improve its churches, its hospitals, its schools, and its cemeteries. When there is question of their erection of new buildings, the necessary authority must be asked for, through the medium of the patriarchs and heads of communities, from my Sublime Porte, which will pronounce a sovereign decision according that authority, except in the case of administrative obstacles.

The intervention of the administrative authority in measures of this nature will be entirely gratuitous. My Sublime Porte will take energetic measures to insure to each sect, whatever be the number of its adherents, entire freedom in the exercise of its religion. Every distinction or designation pending to make any class whatever of the subjects of my empire inferior to another class, on account of their religion, language, or race, shall be forever effaced from administrative protocol. The law shall be put in force against the use of any injurious or offensive term, either among private individuals or on the part of the authorities.

As all forms of religion are and shall be freely professed in my dominions, no subject of my empire shall be hindered in the exercise of the religion that he professes, nor shall he be in any way annoyed on this account. No one shall be compelled to change their religion....

All the subjects of my empire, without distinction, shall be received into the civil and military schools of the government, if they otherwise satisfy the conditions as to age and examination which are specified in the organic regulations of the said schools. Moreover, every community is authorized to establish public schools of science, art, and industry. Only the method of instructions and the choice of professors in schools of this class shall be under the control of a mixed council of public instruction, the members of which shall be named by my sovereign command

All commercial, correctional, and criminal suits between Mussulmans and Christians, or other non-Mussulman subjects, or between Christian or other non-Mussulmans of different sects, shall be referred to mixed tribunals.

The proceedings of these tribunals shall be public; the parties shall be confronted and shall produce their witnesses, whose testimony shall be received without distinction, upon an oath taken according to the religious law of each sect....

NOTES

1. The Islahat Fermani (the Improvement Firman or royal decree) of Sultan 'Abdülmecid I (1823–1861), the first sultan who had a European education, on February 18, 1856, was probably issued in order to undermine the Russian claim to represent the rights of Greek Orthodox Christians in Ottoman territories, a claim that had been a factor in igniting the Crimean War of 1853–1856. In the decree, the sultan reaffirms an existing commitment to "insure the happiness of all classes of subjects" and seeks to expand their rights as equal subjects with full access to civil positions, the repairing of religious and civil buildings, and religious freedom. The reform greatly transformed the traditional status of Jews as *dhimmi*, which had guaranteed physical protection and largely unrestricted religious freedom while limiting their social position and requiring payment of a special tax (*Jizya*). In article 9 of the Treaty of Paris, European powers met the reform warmly and made remote the possibility of political interference between the sultan and his subjects. (See chapter 7, document 41)

2. The Hatti-Humayoun [Imperial Decree] of Gülhané of 1839 launched the Tanzimat or the period of reforms and modernization of the Ottoman Empire under Sultan 'Abdülmecid I.

5. PETITION FOR BRITISH CITIZENSHIP (NOVEMBER 18, 1918)[1]

THE JEWISH COMMUNITY OF BAGHDAD

To: The Civil Commissioner, Baghdad,

Sir,

We have the honor on behalf of the Jewish Community of Baghdad to bring the following to your kind consideration. The Allied Great Powers have triumphantly brought to an end the greatest war that ever scourged mankind to find themselves confronted with a work of pacification and reconstruction of unprecedented magnitude. One of the most important problems which face the Allies is the satisfactory solution of the complicated questions of nationalities.

The Allied Powers have repeatedly proclaimed that they are determined, as regards the small nations to take into account and respect any just aspirations or legitimate claims with the view to precluding any popular friction and eliminating all causes for future wars.

As far as Mesopotamia is concerned, the Allied policy, it is understood, will be to promote indigenous government and encourage the establishment of an autonomous administration. This scheme is excellent in principle and reflects the greatest credit on the Governments of Great Britain and her Allies as a fresh manifestation of the elevation of principles with which this war has been waged. But its immediate execution is coupled with such difficulties as render it hardly recommendable.

It is too early now to have an accurate idea of the exact form of this future government, but the semi-official assurances given suggest the assumption that the local administrative body may be vested with wider powers than perhaps advisable in consideration of the following reasons:

The state of utter unpreparedness of the inhabitants for serious political or administrative responsibilities hardly qualifies them to undertake with success the management of their own affairs.

A local government in accord with the desire of the local majority cannot but bear a very strong theocratical character due to the dominance of religious feelings which are unreconciliable with the idea of giving to alien confessions any sort of privilege or rights. This cannot be consistent with the democratic views of the Allies.

Owing to the absence of scientific institutions, this country cannot furnish men capable to take up any branch of administration. Even the subordinate staff, fresh from the Turkish bureaucratic practices, may be a calamity for the country if freed from control. The higher functionaries under Turkish rule were mostly Turks especially prepared in the Constantinople universities. A small nation abandoned to itself with no adequate preparation for efficient self-government cannot even maintain its rank of small nation but is inevitably destined to be crushed in the great economical strife. It is feared therefore that the results which are to be apprehended might not only be disadvantageous to the progress of the country, but also contrary to the views of the Allied Great Powers and the principles proclaimed by the regretted liberator of Baghdad, the late Lieutenant-General Sir Stanley Maude.[2]

The Jews of Baghdad feel it their duty to declare that their aims in the present juncture would be to have a free opportunity for economic and educational development, these having proved through the ages the two main elements which guaranteed the existence of their race in adversity. Two centuries of active commercial relations with Great Britain have slowly cemented a community of interests which in these days are greatly inspiring in their determination: they wish to submit through the undersigned a request

Source: Norman Stillman, *The Jews of Arab Lands in Modern Times* (Philadelphia: Jewish Publication Society, 1991), pp. 256–58.

that they may be graciously taken under the shield of the British Government and considered true subjects of His Majesty, holding themselves prepared to accept all obligations and rights of true citizens. They are confident that their brethren in all Iraq will formulate the same desire. We may recall on this occasion that since 50 years Baghdad has furnished to the British Empire important colonies of Jewish traders, established mostly in India and England, who enjoy without exception the rights of British citizens. Our Community trust that an agglomeration of 80,000 Jews in a country like Mesopotamia may prove as good subjects to His Majesty as their brethren in England.

This request, however, we fully realize, may raise complicated questions of political and legal character, which we do not propose to examine, this application purporting only to record the desire of the Community and referring to the competent authority the right issues to frame. We beg to request you, Sir, to kindly communicate with the Government at Home on this subject, and solicit your personal assistance in this connection.

We have the honor to be, Sir, Your Obedient Servants.

President of the Jewish Lay Council
Acting Chief Rabbi and President of Religious Council

A. M. Somekh	Heskel Hindee	Sasson Khezam
A. Haim	Ezra M. Bekhor	Saleh M. Cohen
Shoua Bekhor	Shelomo Shooker	Moshi Shashoue
Simon Hay Isac	Manashi Djedda	Isac M. Iny
S. Hougi	M. S. Shashoue	Saleh E. Sasson
Ezra S. Shasoue	Meanshi Sehayek	Murad Djouri
Sasson Murad	Fraim Toeg	M. Jos. Shemtob
Yamen Cohen	Meir H. Gareh	Abr. A. Bashi
Frayem Djedda	Sion E. Dengoor	E. Khezam
Abr. E. Djouri	Sion Is. Mikhael	Daoud Somekh
S. Bekhor	S. Sabha	Saleh F. Haim
Isac Ruben	Sasson H. Toeg	Abr. E. Yehouda
Yamen	A. H. Elikibir	Yehouda Y. Noonoo
E.D. Bassous	Isac Tweina	Ruben Gahtan
Yona M. Yona	Gourji Mokamal	Heskel Ezra Naftali
Ezra A. Salem	Menahem Gahtan	Abraham Denoos
Abdulla S. Ini	Ezra S. Sehayek	
Saleh Y. Naftali	Ezra Abd. Menashi	
S. Birshan	Y. Y. Zelouf	
Sion E. Gourgi	Menahem Daniel	

NOTES

1. World War I brought about the dismantling of the Ottoman Empire and the transfer of its territories to French and British control. This transition triggered doubts among some Jews regarding their fates in the lands of the former empire. The authors of the present document from Baghdad feared that the rise of an indigenous, that is, Muslim, government would have a theocratic character due to the dominance of religious feelings, thus undermining the prospects of democratic principles, particularly with regard to the status of religious minorities. The Jews of Baghdad therefore petitioned the British Civil Commissioner concerning British citizenship.

2. Maude took ill and died of cholera on November 18, 1917, after attending a theatrical performance in his honor at the Alliance school in Baghdad. See Richard Coke, *Baghdad, the City of Peace* (London, 1927), pp. 299–300.

6. TRAVAIL IN AN ARAB LAND (1792)

SAMUEL ROMANELLI[1]

The Israelite community presently living in the Arab territories of Africa's Barbary Coast under the rule of the Emperor of Mauretania, which is called nowadays *Marrakesh* in Arabic and *Maroco* in our languages, is almost entirely hidden from the eyes of the peoples living here in the countries of Europe. How indeed would word of them reach us? . . .

Even though the Jews are mentioned in books on the history of the Maghreb written in Gentile languages, they are only taken into account there as a small part of the whole. For who would be tempted to speak about the Jews without knowing their language? . . .

Who then will prophesy for us? Will it be the Ishmaelite who squats on the ground all day lazy and ignorant, spellbound by his fanatic religion, hating everything that is called by the name of Israel?

Finally, the obstacle to disseminating information about Moroccan Jewry that surpasses all others is the absence of printing. For to this day, it has not been brought there, nor will it ever be.

These, therefore, are a few of the reasons that prompted me to publish these accounts which honestly treat the subject of my brethren and coreligionists in detail. They may also deal in a general way with the foreigners who are with the Jews.

Free of any preconceptions, I allowed myself to seek out and investigate the Jews, their manners and customs. They are good-hearted folk, charitable and hospitable to strangers. They honor the Torah and study it. They hold the European Jews who come there in high esteem and call them "freemen."

The lack of books and news mires their hearts in the mud of ignorance and superstition. They tend to view all new and mysterious things previously unknown to them as miracles. The sciences are too lofty for them. Their ignorance is bliss, for they say that many victims have been thrown into the pits of heresy and atheism by science. The light of knowledge does not shine upon them, nor has it even reached them until now to eradicate their moral feelings and their immature vanities. A veil of obscurantist faith corrupts their hearts and blinds their eyes. They cling steadfastly to their ancestral customs even to the point of transgressing the laws of God, rather than violating their own laws [i.e. practices]. . . .

They do not understand that in so doing they have gone against the intent of the Torah which seeks to set us apart by its laws from the practices of the other nations. With the Moroccan Jews it is the opposite, because they follow their ways completely. . . .

Despite all this, their minds are not entirely blocked from reason, because they comprehend other matters perfectly well. In fact, sometimes their intelligence emits flashes of insight that reveal that it is not thick by nature, but only held down and mired in thick muck, like the sun when it is covered by a very dense cloud.

The women are good looking and have a robust build. However, they are rather like dumb beasts, having no part in science, understanding, or knowledge. They do not know how to speak, read or write Hebrew, Arabic, or Standard Spanish. The women, like the men, speak a mixed language as is common among all Jews in their various diaspora communities who do not make a point of learning properly the language of the peoples among whom they live. Their language is Spanish with a Portuguese accent. The women do not even pray, despite the fact that this was imposed upon them by the sages of the Mishna. The

Source: Samuel Romanelli, *Travail in an Arab Land*, trans. with an Introduction and Notes by Yedida K. Stillman and Norman A. Stillman (Tuscaloosa: University of Alabama Press, 1989), pp. 15–16, 28–30, 131.

Moroccan Jews counter this by citing the Mishnaic dictum: "Whoever teaches his daughter Torah, it is as if he teaches her wantonness." They also contend that a woman is impure during her menstrual infirmity and the days of her menses can fall quite suddenly. This ancient custom has its roots in olden times and was adopted by them from gentile practice, for indeed the Arab women do not pray either. . . .

On Tuesday, I had an urge to see the seashore. It looks rather like the shore at Gibraltar. The latter, however, shows the creative hand of England which adjusted and perfected its beauty. The former expresses the ignorance of the Arabs. For although the hand of Nature is with them to help them and show them the way, they kick its offering and are too lazy to even put one stone next to another. There is not a single ship on the shore, only fishing boats. They have no warships, only pirate vessels on the high seas. . . .

Deceit, injustice, oppression, licentiousness, greed, folly, jealousy, faithlessness, and shamelessness—these are but a bare outline of the Arabs' ways. These characterize all their intentions and acts as I saw them and as I have shown you in the preceding chapters. What about the Jews? Their intellect is muddied, but their hearts are pure. Though wretched, they suffer with hearts humbly open before God. Though their foolishness is deplorable, the object of their hope is commendable. Their sinning is not directed against God, and their righteousness is turned toward their fellow men. Their homes are not full of wealth and riches, but they are happy with their lot. They are not overly clever, but neither are they very mischievous. There is no better than the best of them in their land of bondage; however, you cannot find worse than the worst of them when they go out of it, because when they find themselves free of their oppressors and can cast off their yoke, you can no longer tell them apart. . . .

NOTE

1. Born in Mantua, Italy, to a family of rabbis, teachers, and merchants, Samuel Romanelli (1757–1814) received a broad education that ranged from traditional Jewish sources to European languages and literatures. He wrote poetry in Italian and Hebrew, Hebrew plays, a Hebrew translation of Alexander Pope's *Essay on Man*, and a grammar of the Hebrew language in Italian. He traveled widely in France, Holland, Germany, Poland, and England and affiliated with *haskalah* circles. According to his travelogue *Masa ba'arav (Travail in an Arab Land)*, he was detained in Morocco for a period of four years following a business trip. In Morocco, he worked as a preacher, a teacher of Spanish, a translator, and a secretary and accountant for European consuls, Jewish courtiers, and merchants. He witnessed the turbulence and political chaos following the death of Sultan Sidi Muhammad III in 1790. *Masa ba'arav* was first published in Berlin in 1792 and testifies to the broad interests of its polymath author, to the practices and circumstances of Moroccan Jewry toward the end of the eighteenth century, and to the perception and portrayal of Moroccan Jews by an Italian Jew with value of the *haskalah*. The presentation of Sephardi and Middle Eastern Jews by travelers, such as Romanelli, deeply affected the founders of the *Alliance Israélite Universelle*, who, in the context of a mission statement, cited "travelers who, during the first half of this century, journeyed through Morocco, Turkey and Tunis, were shocked at the very wretched condition of the Jews in those countries, but still more, perhaps, at their intellectual condition, and at the absence of modern culture." (See chapter 6, documents 10 and 11.)

7. A CRITIQUE OF POPULAR MOROCCAN JEWISH CULTURE (1891)

YISHAQ BEN YA'IS HALEWI[1]

Beliefs in idols, charms, amulets, curses, dreams and the existence of spirits is rampant among the Jews of Morocco, and I am going to briefly describe a few of them here. Far from the city, fifteen hours away, is a high mountain called *Iyat Biyavad*. Thirty-two years ago due to a miracle the mountain grew in importance: a woman had an awesome and portentous dream that the excellent and righteous Rabbi Nissim ben Nissim was buried in this holy place. This *tzaddik* [in this context, saint or holy man] who never actually existed nonetheless dazzled the country. The city people come in droves to prostrate on the wonderful *tzaddik*'s mountaintop grave. A man without sons comes along with his wife to ask the *tzaddik* for sons; someone who is ill or mad is bound and brought to the *tzaddik*, in the belief that he will drive out the demon that has a hold on him or the wandering spirit that entered him. Someone stricken by poverty goes up the mountain to ask for the means to live. But this *tzaddik* is no expert in *The Book of Creation*[2] nor a competent doctor. The demon or spirit doesn't leave the body, because what never went in doesn't have to leave; and yet Israel [the Jews] are believers and the sons of believers. In time this amazing mountain will get higher and higher as it fills up with countless *tzaddikim*. Three years ago another woman dreamed that a *tzaddik* of exceptional status was buried at this holy place; the good man's name was Rabbi Yitzhak Halevi; and a woman dreamed last year that (last but not least) another *tzaddik*, Rabbi Abraham Avtain, was buried there. They will go on springing up like grass. How pleasant and how improved is the fate of the Moslems who live on the mountain, getting gifts from everyone who comes to the graves of the *tzaddikim*. Most of the Jews respect and sanctify the *tzaddikim* created by dreams; the Jews give strength to the belief and are thoroughly bound by it. There are those amongst them who say that the *tzaddikim* are buried in Jerusalem and came here by "underground, rolling" to honour the ordinary people. One day I was talking with one of my acquaintances, a scholar, about this strange belief that leads some poor people to sell their clothes so they can visit the dream *tzaddikim*, and he told me that he had had his doubts about it, until one night he merited a tremendous dream where he saw a respected elder appearing as an angel of God who said to him "I am Rabbi Nissim ben Nissim and my family name is Tzarfati [French]," and from that day on he had no more doubts, Heaven forbid.

The holy Arab, Abraham Almagdoli should not be forgotten. A quarter of an hour outside the city in a spacious graveyard is the Moslem grave of Sidi Mogdol, a man who inspired awe in everyone around him; Ishmaelites from all the towns in the sovereign state of Morocco come to prostrate on his grave, bringing sacrifices and donations; Jewish women also come here, with candles and chickens to sacrifice to the holy man and appease him. And since he merited this honor he is undoubtedly a Jew, one of our brethren, and they gave him the title *Rabbi* Abraham Almagdoli. This is what they say in secret so that the ignorant won't know about it. Take note!

Yet another empty custom: When a male child is born they put amulets decorated with foreign names around the house, and paint forms with five extremities on the inside and outside of the house in tar or black paint; and this is good for the evil eye, because

---

Source: Yishaq ben Ya'is Halewi, "Among our Distant Brethen." *Hazfirah* 81, (Warsaw 19 April 1891/11 Nisan 5661), p. 331; and 83–84 (21 April 1891/19 Nissan 5661), p. 341. trans. Mark Joseph.

the number five is a folk remedy against the evil eye, and they draw stars of David high on their backs. Each of the seven nights before the child is circumcised they close the house and pass a big iron knife over all the walls. They bang pieces of iron together so that demons will take fright and not snatch the child, and at the window they hang a chicken neck with its red comb, five buns, a small mat and a piece of iron so that demons will not enter the house, just as crocodiles would be afraid of the shapes of boats.

Another cure for those afflicted by demons is called *Incheria*, where a clairvoyant accompanies a noble woman to an abattoir inhabited by demons, taking with them a black chicken and a clay pot of olive oil, and slaughters the chicken as a sacrifice to the demons, taking some of its blood and mixing it with black ink and olive oil, and writes the name of the ill person on the pot, with the name of his mother and other names and drawings in hieroglyphics. They bring the bowl to the house of the invalid and fill it with water until all the writing is destroyed and using this accursed bitter water they anoint his body and he drinks a little of it, and this is how he is healed.

A man who builds a workshop has to make a feast for his neighbors, the demons, as follows: pious women bring fine flour mixed with olive oil and throw it all around the house; this obligatory feast is called *Lachsim*. Another folk remedy against the evil eye is if a man or woman takes ill and the clairvoyant tells them that the cause of their illness is the evil eye, he or she can be investigated by people who are free of evil, may God protect them, since they have a spark of Balaam ben Peor [the prophet; cf. Numbers 22–25] in them. They do a ruse where they take a small piece of the sick man's clothing and burn it to cinders, and mix them in water and anoint his flesh with it. He also drinks some of it and is thus cured of his illness. People with insight, however, using preventative medicine, hang a horseshoe from a nail at the entrance to their home so the evil eye won't harm them.

There are more diverse and ugly customs that lead Israel into shame and Jacob to spoil. And although these empty methods are of no help to anyone the important thing is faith: if they don't help in this world they will in the world to come. Once at a large gathering of acquaintances I asked them: "how long will we have this foolishness for a hindrance? Why don't we resolve to cut this evil out from amongst us, these chains of idolatry and falsehood?" One of

them responded that it was our fathers' custom both to follow Torah and not to reject our mothers' ways. He added triumphantly that he had seen a statement in the holy book *Likutei Moharan*[3] that goes as follows: it is much better to believe even in nonsense and lies if it also means believing the truth, than to deny everything, in other words to deny principles of faith along with nonsense and lies; and because of this we will perform every kind of clownishness and deny the truth as well.

About twenty *parasangs* [approximately, 124 miles] from our city is the small city of Safi, called in Arabic Asfi. In general characteristics, trade and customs it is like our city, and as I will explain in the rest of this article, most of its trade is in agricultural produce, species of legumes, beans, maize, peas, wheat, barley, more than all the other cities of Morocco. Every day between five hundred and a thousand camels enter the city carrying grain, beans and so on; a camel can carry a load of two hundred and fifty kilos, and every day boats leave fully laden for Europe. The Moslems of Asfi are extremely rich, but they do not have trading relations with Europe. They sell their produce to Jews and Christians who send it to Europe. This city was under the control of the Portuguese until 1781 when it became part of Morocco.

The Jews of Morocco come en masse to prostrate and pray in the city at the graves of the *tzadikkim* who are buried under the name Ola'ad ben Zamiro; these holy ones are seven brothers buried together at the time of the Portuguese, and men commonly help their neighbors and encourage their brothers to come here, with stories and wonders being told about these *tzaddikim*. But even this city does not escape stupidity, emptiness and strange dreams. Not a year goes by that a *tzaddik* isn't created in the city, and the people will not rest until the Tanna[4] Rabbi Yosi Hagalili is buried with them, and there is no convincing them otherwise. "Behold, the former things are come to pass, and new things do I declare:" [Isaiah 42:9] to the dear readers about how the *tzaddikim* came to be born in this city.

In the year 5638 [1853] in the city of Asfi a *tzaddik* was born by a miracle in the home of a wealthy Jew in a hole under the stairs where the people of the house would put their rubbish and filth. One night an old woman dreamed a holy dream where a *tzaddik* by the name of Rabbi David Hazan, may his virtue stand us in good stead, was buried, unknown to the whole city, in that dirty hole, and men and women gathered and stood to pray over the righteous one's grave. This *tzaddik* is no stranger to us, because seventy years ago there was a rabbi and a teacher in our city and he was really a holy man of God and a great rabbi in Israel, wisdom and holiness gathered together. The elders from his generation say that Elijah[5] of blessed memory, was revealed to him. His birthplace was Marrakesh and borne by his illness he went to his city to be buried with his holy fathers, and after some days he ascended to God and was buried in the graves of the righteous ones. In the year 5638 [1853], behold, he turns up having rolled through tunnels to be reincarnated in the city of Asfi to honor the masses, but why did he choose this filthy place instead of the city where he was rabbi?

The children of this rabbi, may his memory be for a blessing, are buried in our city. One of his sons was four years old when he died, and they say he was a prophet. Many hold this belief and swear on the life of the prophet. There was a rabbi from Asfi, righteous and upright, called Sa'adia Raboch, may his virtue stand us in good stead, who was gathered to his people eight years ago and left us bereft. Last year on Lag Ba-Omer[6] some people were in the cemetery where the *tzaddikim* are buried and at the gravesite of Ola'ad ben Zamiro, may his virtue stand us in good stead, celebrating the memory of Rabbi Shimon bar Yochai.[7] During the feasting and festivity a respected Jew told them that in a dream he had seen Rabbi Sa'adia of blessed memory come from his first grave and choose a grave with the *tzaddikim*, and many of our Jewish brethren believed him and made a headstone on the new grave. Now everyone who comes to prostrate oneself on the grave of the rabbi of blessed memory has to go to two graves, the old grave and the new one. Soon the dreams of *tzaddikim* will be immeasurable and numberless as the sand.

The Jews of the state of Susa rest secure, every man under his vine and his fig tree, living in tranquility with the government, pursuing trade in brotherhood and friendship with the locals. But in the rule of one prince called Sidi Mohammad ben Sidi la'Hosain wa Heasam, the lot of the unfortunate Jews is bitter and ugly; they are in difficulty and distress, without legal redress; they and their property are subjected to their ruler, who is afraid of their demand for mercy. He knows nothing about peace and there is no justice around him; in the future he will be completely unrestrained. Most of the soldiers and servants at his command are African slaves who are his property; before he has even finished talking an African jumps to his side. This prince belongs to a family that is holy and revered among Moslems. Twice a year a marketplace in his domain, called Anmogdar de Sidi Hamad u'Musa after a sage, is filled with the people from every Moroccan city and town, bringing wares to sell, and everyone brings sacrifices and gives donations to the prince, and so he becomes very wealthy, and haughty in his wealth. He makes false libels against the Jews, as a way to get their money. The Jews cannot escape his rule and settle in one of the neighboring principalities, as he does not allow them and their households to go. The men go out with their merchandise and [the] women and children stay at home.

NOTES

1. Yishaq Ben Ya'is Halewi (1850–1895) was a modestly successful merchant and bookseller known for his erudition in the *mellah* (Jewish quarter) of Essaouira (Mogador), Morocco. Although relatively powerless in the Jewish community, Halewi advocated for social change using the *haskalah* Hebrew newspaper *Hatzfirah* (see chapter 7, document 18, note 2), published in Warsaw, as a vehicle. (Essaouira was served by French, British, and German steamship companies, and the centrality of Jewish traders allowed for contacts between North African and European Jews.) Beginning in 1891, Halewi became a frequent contributor to the paper in the column "Among our Distant Brothers." The articles are important not only for reconstructing the reality of Moroccan Jewish life at the turn of the twentieth century, but also for studying the reformist and modernizing vision of this Jew of the *mellah*. Halewi aimed criticism at Jewish leadership's misappropriation of funds and its failure to address issues of poverty, housing, medical care, and education, hoping that he could bring pressure to bear through the medium of the press. In this selection, Halewi does not address the leadership but rather critiques practices that were widespread among Moroccan Jewry, such as the use of amulets and spells, exorcisms, and the veneration of saints (*tzaddikim*), all of which he considered deplorable superstitutions contrary to the values of modernity; in doing so, he echoed the view of some European Jews and paralleled the reformist Islamic movement known as the Salafiya. See Daniel Schroeter, "Yishaq Ben Ya'is Halewi: A Moroccan Reformer," in *Struggle and Survival in the Modern Middle East*, ed.,

Edmund Burke III (Berkeley: University of California Press, 1993).

2. Book of Creation (*Sefer Yitzirah*) is a short Hebrew volume containing mystical speculations on the creation of the world. It was probably compiled between the fifth and sixth century C.E.

3. *Likutei Moharan* is a Hebrew collection of the teachings of the Hasidic master Rabbi Nachman of Bratzlav (1772–1811).

4. *Tanna* is the designation of a rabbinic sage from the first two centuries C.E. and whose teachings and opinions are recorded in the Mishnah.

5. The biblical prophet Elijah in the Book of Malachi (3:24) is said to reappear on the future day of judgment.

Accordingly, as is related in the Book of Kings, he did not die but was taken up to heaven in a chariot of fire. Later Jewish thought would thus envision him as returning to earth and heralding the redemption.

6. Lag Ba-Omer is the a minor festival, marking thirty-three days of counting Omer (Leviticus 23:15–21). For many Jewish communities, it is the occasion to celebrate the memory of the past sages of Israel, in particular that of Shimeon bar Yochai.

7. Shimeon bar Yochai was a renowned *Tanna* of the second century C.E. According to Jewish tradition, he is the author of the Zohar, the classical text of Kabbalah. He is said to have died on Lag Ba-Omer (see note 6), when his soul was reunited with its supernal source.

8. LETTER TO THE JEWISH COMMUNITY OF MARRAKESH (1892)

STELLA CORCOS[1]

Lady Corcos wrote a letter to the rabbis and lay leaders [of the Jewish community of Marrakesh] and gave it to the president of the Anglo-Jewish Association[2] who discussed it along with all their other business. She then hastened to tell the Moroccans what the answer was; this is a copy of the letter:

To his honor the distinguished rabbi, our honored Master and teacher Rabbi Josef Harutz, our honored Masters and teachers Rabbi Abraham ibn Miha, Rabbi Jacob ben Haim, Rabbi Yamin Hacohen, May the Lord preserve him and keep him alive, and the honorable Lord Rabbi Joshua Corcos, head of the community, Mr. Samuel Corcos, Mr. Masud Sariki, Mr. Maimon ben Doouch, Mr. Hadan Adrai, Mr. Mordehai Truzman, Mr. Eliyahu/Elijah ben Sisan, Mr. Moses N. Doouch, Mr. David Azulay, et al.

After enquiring after your well-being I ask your forgiveness that I sought the strength and was so bold as to write this letter to your honors which I send to you in all haste with the lord Mr. Reuven Almaliach, president of the Anglo-Jewish Association. Although I did not have the honor of getting to know all of your community, May the Lord preserve you and keep you alive, this is my responsibility and I will do it. You surely know that the Anglo-Jewish Association in London that was founded for the general good of our Jewish brethren in all the lands of their dispersion has as its purpose to be of help and support at all times, to teach morality and an occupation, and all information essential to a human being as a human being, and to spread the light of knowledge over the whole

Source: Y. Ben Ya'is, "Among Our Distant Brethren," *Hatzfirah* (18 May 1892/21 Iyar 5662) vol. 19, no. 99, p. 497; no. 100, p. 411. trans. Mark Joseph.

Earth, as the waters cover the sea. Enlightenment is a jewel raising humanity to the heights of perfection; so that everyone will be regarded as a human being, and those who are now demeaned among the peoples shall be blessed.

Indeed a person can achieve all this if he or she learns to be a writer and knows one world language well, such as, English, French, Spanish, [or] German, and studies everything one will need to know during a lifetime; and to make progress one should also learn to read and write one's national language; [for us] this is our holy Torah, as it is written in the Bible "for this is your wisdom and your understanding..." (Deuteronomy 4:6).

And so we established two progressive organizations according to these fundamentals—the Alliance Israélite Universelle[3] in Paris and the Anglo-Jewish Association in London—thought of as one society and of one purpose in pursuing the general good. The main principle of these two precious societies has been from the beginning to establish schools, such as are found in all countries—Persia, Turkey, India and so on—as well as in our state Morocco. Now that you have the good intention to build new schools in our state, it should preferably be in the capital Marrakesh; that takes precedence because it has been neglected and it is the main city in Morocco, a city where Jewish mothers and their children have intelligence and good sense. So, distinguished Sirs, if you want to help as best you can, [you have as allies] the London society that also wants to open two schools in your cities, where the English language and writing will be taught [in the following way]:

A) In the schools for boys there will be two rabbinic scholars: one to teach the Hebrew Bible, and one to teach the Oral Law and such principles as any Jewish man needs to know. [In addition there should be a teacher of the] English language and writing lectures in Scripture, world history, regional geography of [Morocco], arithmetic and natural sciences.

B) In the schools for young women, there is one teacher for English language and writing, and all requirements for girls: sewing, embroidery, machines, etc. If the august society is known to you and you are satisfied with it, and see that you will help in the near future, send craftsmen from Europe to teach your dear children skills, that will enliven their minds and benefit them and their children after them; our master the king will find satisfaction that the Jews under his protection are happy, and that they turn toward service of the state and the king, openly and publicly. I want to say that all this will be done on the initiative of the king [of Morocco] and in accordance with his desire. The expenses for this lofty scheme need setting out; the salaries for the teachers, the scholar and the rabbis, and rent and so on, amount to the value of ten thousand Francs a year, but you will agree in the goodness of your hearts how much to give for your children and for the good of the poor. The remainder will be given for the poor of the London society, peace on them. I await your precious reply.

NOTES

1. Stella Corcos (1858–1948) was the director of the school for Jewish girls in Marrakesh, Morocco, supported by the Anglo-Jewish Association in London, and was active in educational reform. This selection, excerpted from an article published by Yishaq Ben Ya'is Halewi in his column, "Among Our Distant Brethren" (see the previous document), presents a letter sent by Corcos to the rabbis and communal leaders or the Jewish community of Marrakesh calling for the creation of two schools: one for boys that would teach the Hebrew Bible, Talmud, and Jewish Law (halakhah) as well as English, history, mathematics, and natural sciences, and a school for girls that would teach English and "everything essential for girls, such as sewing and embroidery." By the turn of the twentieth century, there existed three schools in the casbah neighborhood of Marrakesh, home to a small elite of Jewish merchant families (whereas most Jews lived in the cramped *mellah* or Jewish quarter): a French language school of the Alliance Israélite Universelle, an English school for boys supported by the Anglo-Jewish Association, and the school founded by Stella Corcos.

2. Founded in 1871, the Anglo-Jewish Association sought to extend assistance to oppressed and impoverished Jewish communities throughout the world in a manner similar to that of the Alliance Israélite Universelle.

9. NEED FOR ALLIANCE SCHOOLS IN ALGERIA (1901)

MOISE NAHON[1]

The work of the Alliance in Algeria owes its origins to the emotions aroused among world Jewry by the antisemitic outbreaks of 1898. Because its attentions had been focused in the East and in the other countries of North Africa, the Alliance had not considered until then that Algeria should be part of its sphere of activity. Was not that country a French territory; had not our fellow Jews been, in 1870, granted the honorable status of citizens of the Republic? They could not wish for a more certain guarantee for their security, for a more fruitful incentive to regeneration. It was thought that time should run its course and the civilizing contagion would do its work; thus, protected by laws and spurred on by French culture and institutions, a rejuvenated and emancipated Algerian Jewry would soon begin its life of freedom, its head held high. The antisemitic crisis of 1884 and the moral disorder that began to spread through the colony were already reason to give some pause and to temper the optimism. However, it was not until the terrible outbreak of 1898 that the true state of things was made clear. It then appeared that Algeria was the last country in which the Jews could aspire to a normal evolution. The Jews were stripped de facto of almost all the prerogatives of citizenship and slandered; the cynicism with which they were unrelentingly humiliated was like none ever seen before. They were excluded from society, in some cases hunted down and beaten like animals. A spineless magistrature sometimes defended them half-heartedly, sometimes harassed them further. In the end, the question became one of concern for their very right to work, their right to

existence. These Jews, who had achieved so much for the economic development of the colony, saw themselves being trampled by a multitude of schemers anxious to do away with all competitors in their race toward fortune. They had been given their first glimpse of the French spirit, gentle and generous, in the schools. The liberal inroads which had been made at the time of the Revolution and during the nineteenth century had stirred among them the enthusiasm of neophytes. And so, their pain and suffering were compounded with bitterness and disappointment as they saw their ideal slain in its infancy. They were suddenly faced with a brutal alternative: either denounce civilization, at least strip it of all moral content, or denounce the vigor of the Jewish race, curse the religion and the very name "Jewish," which were the cause of all their troubles. It seemed as if this state of confusion had been intentionally prepared over the course of the preceding several years. Religious instruction had been discontinued, education had not been protected from any of the dangers specific to the new environment being created. The mission of enlightening the Jews had been carried out with the methods and institutions which were appropriate and successful for Europeans but of no value in addressing a race held back by history. Snobbery had driven our religious faith, leaving behind only a skeleton of superstition and rote practices. The spirit of solidarity, although not totally extinguished, worked only by fits and starts, like a flickering candle, and was no longer able to create any strong and lasting organization. And so when the fateful day arrived, the people found themselves

Source: Aron Rodrigue, *Images of Sephardi and Middle Eastern Jewries in Transition: The Teachers of the Alliance Israélite Universelle, 1860–1939* (Seattle: University of Washington Press, 1993), pp. 107–110.

with no support whatsoever, no anchoring point between their old society now in a shambles and the new French society, which was suddenly closed to them. The situation called for a vigorous effort; if rapid action were not taken, all hope of success would be lost. For those who had been emancipated and who energetically embraced the modern ideal, in spite of the contradictions modern civilization had demonstrated, there was a need for support. They also had to be shown that their moral being would not be whole until they also looked to the past and to their heritage. For those who had found confirmation for the old superstitions in the acts of crime and violence directed against them, there was a need to make clear that there can be no Jewish faith outside the realm of reason and progress. For those who had abandoned all in their desperation, renouncing both the hope of faith and the promise of science, there was a need to cry out that man cannot live unless he clings to something eternal and immutable. For all there was a need for hope in economic recovery through labor, so that the burdens of some and the poverty of others could be alleviated. Finally, and this was the essential point, there was the need for the creation of a place for peace and labor, a center for solidarity in which all differences would be ignored and from which unity would burn bright. Hence the work of the Alliance was established....

NOTE

1. Moise Nahon (1870–1928) was born in Tangier, where he was educated at the Alliance school before furthering his education in Paris at the École Normale Israélite Orientale. In 1889, he was appointed head of the Alliance boys' school in Fez and was later transferred to teach in Tangier. Nahon built strong relationships with Jewish religious leaders and maintained intellectual bonds with Muslim clergy and intellectuals as well. Like others in the Alliance, he advocated for the Jewish pursuit of the French language and culture. Unlike others, however, he also supported the study of Arabic among Jews and argued that Jews should cultivate Moroccan Arabic, rather than their Judeo-Arabic dialect. He believed that education in the Alliance schools could lead to solidarity among Moroccan Jews of different linguistic backgrounds (Arabic, Berber, and Spanish) and even solidarity between Jews and Christians by encouraging the enrollment of Christian students. During the 1880s, Nahon also called upon Moroccan Jews to aid Russian Jews following the pogroms. In the present document, he discusses the motivations for founding an Alliance school in Algeria. A French territory since 1830, Algeria offered through its state schools the French linguistic and cultural training often brought by the Alliance. According to the document, the Alliance directed its attention toward Algeria only after the antisemitic outbreaks of 1884 (Oran) and 1897–1898 (Algiers).

10. TRADITIONAL SCHOOLS IN CONSTANTINOPLE: A CRITIQUE (1906)

MOISE FRESCO[1]

Any private individual who is without work and knows his prayers passably can bring twenty, thirty, or forty children into the small room which serves as his home, teach them the most basic elements of reading Hebrew, and, lo and behold, a small *Talmud-Torah* [a traditional elementary school] has come into being....

The children spend one or two years learning the Hebrew alphabet, and as many in approaching the mysteries of vowel points; it takes no less time to learn to chant verses of the Bible...in a few of these schools, translation is also taught, a mechanical, word-for-word translation into an archaic, immutable Judeo-Spanish, which is often as little understood by the teacher as by the student. The translation is sung in the same melody as the Hebrew text....

The text and its translation are there to be chanted in singsong, to be whined, not to be understood. There is nothing more strange and more ridiculous than to hear recited in this manner the most vehement prophecies of Isaiah or Ezekiel, the delicious idyll of Ruth, or the fiery pages from the Song of Songs....

I visited three of the large *Talmud-Torah* schools of the Haskeuy.[2]...

Each time one enters one of these places, one's heart sinks, and one is filled with pity and disgust.

In a small room of between eight and ten square meters, on a dirty and greasy floor, there are seated from thirty to forty unclean children. With his stick in his hand, the *hakham*[3] squats upon a foul and grimy pallet in his corner. The children cry out the verses in high shrill tones, each trying to outdo the other. They are accompanied at intervals by the loud, whining voice of their teacher....

On the day of my visit the weather was beautiful and the sun shone in all its splendor; a true spring day. Nonetheless, all doors and windows were shut tight. You can imagine how foul the air was in this building, where the children spend the whole day, from early morning until after sunset. I am certain that the windows are not opened from the end of one summer to the beginning of the next. I was unable to remain more than a few minutes in that oppressive atmosphere, which was rendered all the more fetid by odors coming from poorly maintained toilets.... How happy are those little tramps I have seen idly wandering through the streets or running through nearby fields; they are fortunate their parents did not have what little money as asked to place them in these wretched schools....

NOTES

1. The author of this document, Moise Fresco, was a teacher at the Alliance Israélite Universelle in Constantinople whose manuals were adopted as textbooks in many Alliance schools. In this document, he describes traditional Jewish schools in Haskeuy, a largely Jewish section of Constantinople. The mode of description, which pairs disdain for the curriculum with rebuke for the unhygienic conditions, is typical of such documents whether produced by Western visitors or westernizing indigenous authors. The reproachful tone notwithstanding, such documents can be valuable for reconstructing Sephardi education and the dynamics of modernization.
2. A predominantly Jewish quarter of Constantinople.
3. Hebrew: man of wisdom; title given to rabbis in the Middle East; also the name for the teachers in the traditional schools.

Source: Aron Rodrigue, *Images of Sephardi and Middle Eastern Jewries in Transition:The Teachers of the Alliance Israélite Universelle,* 1860–1939 (Seattle: University of Washington Press 1993), pp. 116–17.

11. GENERAL INSTRUCTIONS FOR TEACHERS (1903)[1]

ALLIANCE ISRAÉLITE UNIVERSELLE

The true goal of the primary schools, especially in the East, is not so much instruction as education. Education includes both intellectual and moral education.

Moral education is provided in part through religious teaching and through the family, but it must be reinforced and developed by the Alliance teachers. Our teaching, on the whole, must be a moral teaching. Through hidden routes and a constant but invisible action, it must strive to elevate the soul and the mind of the student. It must develop a moral attitude within him which will support him and uplift him. One of the principal tasks of the teachers will be to combat the bad habits which are more or less prevalent among Eastern populations: selfishness, pride, exaggerated egotism, lack of original thinking, blind respect for wealth and power, and violent, petty passions. The virtues that one must try to inspire in the children are love of country, love of all men, love and respect for parents, love of truth, honesty, loyalty, dignity of character, uprightness, love of the public good, a spirit of solidarity, a sense of devotion and a spirit of sacrifice for the common good, application and consistency of thought, and the love of work....

What was, what is, the goal of the Alliance in providing the Eastern and African communities with primary schools? First, the goal is to bring a ray of Western civilization into communities which have degenerated as the result of centuries of oppression and ignorance; second, the goal is to give the children the rudiments of an elementary and reasoned instruction, to help them find a way to make a more dependable and less disparaged living than they would through peddling. Finally, the goal is to open their minds to Western ideas and to destroy certain prejudices and antiquated superstitions which have been paralyzing the activity and growth of these communities. But the action of the Alliance also, and primarily, seeks to give to young Jews, and through them to the entire Jewish population, a moral education, which is more important than the strictly technical instruction. The Alliance is less concerned with producing half-learned men than in forming good and tolerant men who feel an attachment to their duties as citizens and as Jews, who are dedicated to the public good and to their brothers, and, finally, who know how to reconcile the demands of modern life with a respect for ancient traditions....

NOTE

1. The teachers of the Alliance Israélite Universelle served as the vanguard for executing the organization's westernizing program. Their training, partly accomplished at the École Normale Israélite Orientale in Paris, was aimed at removing the perceived corrosive influence of their home cultures and at reconstituting their identities as essentially Western. In turn, the teachers were to promote a curriculum that extended far beyond the teaching of language, science, and history into the realm of the "moral," with the hopes of the ultimate "regeneration" and "civilizing" of Eastern Jewry. This document, which consists of instructions for Alliance teachers, calls for the cultivation of certain moral qualities (a work ethic, patriotism, "solidarity," and the like), and starkly contrasts the allegedly deficient qualities of "Eastern populations" with the virtues of the West.

Source: Aron Rodrigue, *Images of Sephardi and Middle Eastern Jewries in Transition: The Teachers of the Alliance Israélite Universelle, 1860–1939* (Seattle: University of Washington Press, 1993), pp. 72–73.

12. BEGINNINGS OF WESTERNIZATION AND REFORM IN THE MELLAH FEZ (1913)[1]

AMRAM ELMALEH

I would also like to mention that in the *Mellah*, European dress is becoming more and more common. It is the young people who set the example. They have admitted to me that since they have had regular contact with the Europeans, they have begun to feel uncomfortable with the difference in dress, especially because their traditional dress sometimes causes them to be treated with a certain disdain. I can but encourage them in this direction. The adoption of European dress means more than just a superficial change. If only they could adopt the style of dress of the Europeans without also imitating them in certain habits and vices, to which our young men are only too inclined, I would be completely satisfied....

...

To conclude this report I must now say a word about the future of the Jewish district of Fez, which I think I can predict with some accuracy. The *Mellah* is located on the outskirts of Fez, between Fez and the probable site of the European city which is to be created—we have this information from General Lyautey[2] himself, who made a public statement to this effect in a meeting with the French community. The *Mellah* will naturally, then, serve as a link between the old city and the new. It will participate in the developing business, commercial, and industrial activities in Fez. The property values have already increased significantly in the *Mellah*, especially for property located on the main road, which we worked to widen and which serves as a main artery between the city of Fez and the [French military] camps.

I expect there will be a better future for our fellow Jews in Fez and I am doing everything in my power to bring it about. I hope that they will reach it more quickly through the instruction we offer them, through the inherent qualities of the Jewish race, which we try to awaken in them, and through a new moral strength.

NOTES

1. By the time of the proclamation of a French Protectorate over Morocco in 1912, Moroccan Jewry had already undergone significant transformations, supported by the Alliance Israélite Universelle, regarding the adoption of Western dress and mannerisms. In this document of 1913, Amram Elmaleh, a rabbi of Essaouira (Mogador) celebrates the adoption of Western dress by residents of the *mellah* of Fez and anticipates the prominent and mediating role that Jews may play when the planned "European city" is developed adjacent to the Jewish quarter in Fez. Because of the rapidity with which Jews adopted Western values and language, they seemed especially poised to associate with colonizing powers.
2. Gen. Louis-Hubert Lyautey (1854–1934) was military governor of French Morocco from April 1907 to April 1912.

Source: Aron Rodrigue, *Images of Sephardi and Middle Eastern Jewries in Transition: The Teachers of the Alliance Israélite Universelle, 1860–1939* (Seattle: University of Washington Press, 1993), pp. 187–88.

13. FRENCH NATURALIZATION OF MOROCCAN JEWS (1923)[1]

Y. D. SEMACH

An employee of the French government sees the current social status of the Moroccan Jew, his particularistic customs, the habits of his family life, and his code of ethics and judges him to be diametrically opposed to the European, tending to confuse the Jew with the Arab. This is not the case. The Arab has a plodding mind and is slow to comprehend; his religion and traditions make him a creature of habit and his ideas are desperately slow in changing. The Jew, on the other hand, now that he has been freed of the chains that had reduced him to the status of pariah through the ages, has suddenly taken flight. Yesterday he was wallowing in his ignorance and humiliation, and here he is today, a free man, capable of keeping step with the European in his dress, manners, and the development of his mind.... He was able to make this transition smoothly and without trauma. The photograph that you published in the most recent issue of *Paix et Droit* is a striking testimony to this power of assimilation in the Jew. Those young girls in shorts preparing to run in a public event, what an impressive example! These are the children of those veiled women who, even ten years ago, did not dare to venture outside the *Mellah*, who lived a cloistered life of silence in their homes, and who in their ignorance and superstition fled at the sight of any foreigner.... The Jew capable of such an awakening may well aspire to a full and complete education within the framework of a European life....

On the other hand, the [French Moroccan] Protectorate, which seeks to instruct and educate the Jew, is not considering that it might one day profit from him in the strengthening of its own political situation; the Protectorate wants the Jew to maintain his native status. In choosing this course of action, it remains haunted by what has quite mistakenly been referred to as the error of the Crémeiux decree. The memory of this past is the dominating influence on policy concerning Moroccan Jews and Tunisian Jews alike. Those who govern us are afraid of the grumbling and protest to which the emancipation of the Jews might give rise. And yet, the patriotism demonstrated by the Algerian Jews should put their minds completely at rest. The Jew who has been given his freedom and raised in the French mentality becomes a true Frenchman; he becomes totally devoted to the development of the strength and power of his country.

In Morocco, where the Muslim population is more dense and more fierce and where the spirit of revolt and independence is stronger even than in Algeria, France must work toward increasing the number of French nationals. While proceeding with prudence and avoiding the displeasure of the Arab population, and even more that of the antisemitic colonies, France must work toward the eventual naturalization of the Jews. This would not happen immediately, of course, and not without certain trials and hardships. The Young Tunisians already create enough worry for the French administration; one need not have particular foresight to predict that in a few years a Young Moroccan party will be formed, a much more dangerous party. When this day comes, France should be able to look for support to the educated and completely liberated Jewish population....

NOTE

1. Unlike the case of Algeria, in which Jews were granted French citizenship in 1870 (see document 2 in this

Source: Aron Rodrigue, *Images of Sephardi and Middle Eastern Jewries in Transition: The Teachers of the Alliance Israélite Universelle, 1860–1939* (Seattle: University of Washington Press, 1993), pp. 218–19, 220–22.

chapter), the creation in 1912 of a French Protectorate in Morocco did not result in the extension of French citizenship to Moroccan Jews because of the unrest generated by the Crémieux Decree and to the fact that Morocco was not officially annexed by France. Jews fell legally within the jurisdiction of local, i.e. Muslim, courts, which was seen as a threat by the Alliance Israélite Universelle. Yomtov David Semach (b. 1869) was director of the Alliance boys' school in Beirut and traveled widely describing the state of Jews in Morocco, Iraq, and Yemen. After 1924, he was inspector of the Alliance schools in Morocco and a representative of Jewish interests before the Protectorate. In the document presented here, Semach argues that the "Jew" is fundamentally distinct from the "Arab" and that Moroccan Jews should not be denied naturalization categorically, but should be considered on an individual basis for sufficient "devotion and merit."

14. FRENCH TO REPLACE THE LOCAL "JARGON": CASABLANCA (1898)[1]

MOISE NAHON

We must not lose sight of the fact that there is nothing more difficult than the study of colloquial French for the children who speak popular Arabic; the very spirit of their maternal dialect is so distant from the European spirit! The sounds, the expressions, and the ideas of the two languages clash when they come into contact. If the idiom popularly spoken here [among the Jews] were even closer to Arabic, our task would be much easier! But it is a jargon, a jumble of expressions from Arabic, Chaldean, Spanish, even Berber, composed without logic, mixed together in a small number of molds so narrowly formed that it is impossible to pour a new idea into them. There is not room enough for thought to function, only a very limited stock of clichés, applied more or less aptly to the diverse circumstances of life. There is no base to work from: ideas, words, and constructions must be created whole. It is a constant struggle to counter the unfortunate deformations of the ear. To our students, *shé*, *zé*, and *ssé* are the same sound; *é*, *i*, and *a* are interchangeable. As it is useless to ask them to listen to the difference in sound, we have to resort to the visual. We are forced to gesticulate, to exaggerate the movements of the mouth, sometimes to physically shape the student's mouth with our hands to get him to imitate the sounds. It is desperately tedious work and it takes up much of our precious time. Once they have learned to distinguish and reproduce sounds more or less accurately, it is time to begin teaching expressions. Here we keep strictly to French from the beginning. It is imperative that their jargon be completely discarded, that translation be forbidden, and that the French form be imposed in its direct relation to the object, the gesture, or the action to be expressed. The methods developed by Mr. Fresco[2] for the teaching of written and spoken French have been invaluable to us in this endeavor.

Our students from Tangier and Tetuan easily surpass their classmates in all subjects because they have a better ear, their articulatory organs are more supple, and their vocabulary is much richer and much closer to French.[3] . . .

Source: Aron Rodrigue, *Images of Sephardi and Middle Eastern Jewries in Transition: The Teachers of the Alliance Israélite Universelle, 1860–1939.* (Seattle: University of Washington Press, 1993), pp. 126–27.

NOTES

1. The most comprehensive element of the Alliance curriculum was the teaching of French to supplement or replace the various languages and dialects of Eastern Jews; specifically Jewish dialects (Judeo-Spanish, Judeo-Arabic, and Judeo-Persian) were regarded as "jargons." Alliance schools often incorporated Hebrew, primarily as a vehicle for teaching the Jewish religion, and the official languages of states (e.g., Turkish and Arabic) in some instances. The teaching of Arabic was regarded with ambivalence, sometimes being viewed as necessary for Jews to function in their host countries or alternatively as a corrosive influence that hindered "regeneration." Arabic exists in different registers, from the highly classicizing Modern Standard Arabic, which is more or less consistent across the Arab world, to the various national, regional, and local dialects. In this document, the author, Moise Nahon, a native of Tangier, fulminates against the "jargon" of Casablanca, having slightly greater regard for the Arabic of Tangier and Tetuan insofar as it is "closer to French." His critique is not only that the Moroccan Jewish dialect is an admixture of several languages, but that its "very spirit" is anathema to the "European spirit," so much so that modernizing ideas cannot be conveyed through it. The need to replace the dialect with French, Nahon argues, goes beyond the need for Moroccan Jews to communicate with colonizers but extends into the very process of regeneration whereby the mind of the Eastern Jew may be infused with concepts for which his own language has no capacity. For further information on the author of this document, see document 9 in this chapter.

2. An Alliance teacher in Constantinople who wrote several manuals that were widely adopted as textbooks by the Alliance schools. See document 10 in this chapter.

3. The mother tongue of most of the Jews of these two cities was Judeo-Spanish.

15. THE SURVIVAL OF JUDEO-SPANISH: CONSTANTINOPLE (1908)[1]

MOISE FRESCO

Judeo-Spanish is the preeminent language of [Ottoman Jewry], and it will remain so for quite some time whatever we might do. Everyone agrees that we should do away with Judeo-Spanish, that there is no reason to preserve the language of our former persecutors...and nevertheless, the lower classes, the bourgeoisie, and even the "aristocracy," as they are called here, everyone still speaks and reads Judeo-Spanish and will continue to do so. In committee meetings where all the members are well educated and everyone knows French, a discussion started in correct, even elegant, French will, often in an instant, inexplicably move into Judeo-Spanish jabbering. The most "select," dignified Jewish ladies when paying a call on a friend will be politely chitchatting in French and suddenly break into jargon. Turkish is like a borrowed suit; French is gala dress; Judeo-Spanish is the worn dressing gown in which one is most at ease....

Source: Aron Rodrigue, *Images of Sephardi and Middle Eastern Jewries in Transition: The Teachers of the Alliance Israélite Universelle, 1860–1939* (Seattle: University of Washington Press, 1993), pp. 130–31.

NOTE

1. In this document, Moise Fresco, a teacher of the Alliance Israélite Universelle in Constantinople, advocates for the abandonment of Judeo-Spanish, referred to as "jabbering," even though it is the language of the Sephardi home and community in the Ottoman Empire. This document is most striking, given that Judeo-Spanish had served impressively as a medium of modernization through the publication of secular books and newspapers (document 1). The document is particularly memorable for the metaphoric comparisons of Turkish, French, and Judeo-Spanish with different types of dress. For further information on the author, see document 10 in this chapter.

16. THE MULTIPLICITY OF LANGUAGES IN AN ALLIANCE SCHOOL IN CONSTANTINOPLE (1913)

A. BENVENISTE

Included in the curriculum are French, as [the] foundation for other studies, Turkish, Hebrew, and German. Here in the East, if we want to begin preparing a child for the future as soon as he begins school, instruction in several languages is absolutely necessary. Yet pedagogues affirm that the study of multiple languages is detrimental to the moral development of the child's mental faculties. Hygienists add that such learning has harmful repercussions on the child's physical faculties by putting too much strain on a frail body and inhibiting the regular growth of its organs.

I do not deny that either of these affirmations is true and certain observations can be cited in support of this thesis.... Some even go so far as to claim that if so few exceptional and brilliant men [are] found among the Jews in Eastern countries, it is due to the fact that, having allowed our mental faculties to grow dull through the course of four hundred years in our *judeiras* [Jewish quarters], where no serious intellectual cultivation has been practiced since our exile from Spain, we are now putting the brains of our young children through intellectual gymnastics to which they are not at all accustomed after several centuries of absolute repose. As a consequence of this sudden, rather than gradual, intellectual development, we are producing young people who speak and write in many languages but who possess neither the maturity of mind nor the logic nor the level of abstraction required to carry out any undertaking of significance or to show any sign of the true intellectual vigor required in the making of men of science and of letters....

[B]ut the unfortunate truth is that we cannot ignore the importance of two significant factors. The first is that we are Ottoman Jews and must therefore satisfy the parents of our students by teaching Hebrew as [the language of our] religion. The second is that we have to fulfill our duty as citizens by teaching our boys, from the moment we can, to speak the official language of the country in which we live. This holds true all the more as our students will be asked later [to] perform their military service,[2] and a knowledge of Turkish becomes, thereby, absolutely indispensable.

Naturally, French remains the very core of our teaching. It is through French culture, eminently

---

Source: Report by A. Benveniste, translated from the French, in Aron Rodrigue, *Images of Sephardi and Middle Eastern Jewries in Transition: The Teachers of the Alliance Israélite Universelle, 1860–1939* (Seattle: University of Washington Press, 1993), pp. 133–34.

suited to the diffusion of liberal ideas, that we can raise our children up from the state of dejection imposed by centuries of oppression and moral stagnation. From a double perspective, French is the language *par excellence* for instruction and education. At the same time it is a powerful tool which permits our students to derive immediate and very lucrative profit from the knowledge acquired in our classrooms.

NOTES

1. This document attests to the various languages contained in the curriculum of the Alliance Israélite Universelle in Constantinople, which placed primary emphasis on French, as would be expected, but also on Hebrew, Turkish, and German. The author supports this emphasis despite what he sees as the likely "harmful repercussions" of education in multiple languages for a child's cognitive *and* physical development. According to the author, Hebrew is taught under pressure of the parents who desire a religious education, and Turkish is taught out of civic duty. Also noteworthy is the author's reference to medieval Spain, which he recalls as a place of "serious intellectual cultivation," and the Sephardi experience of exile.

2. Universal military service was instituted in Turkey in 1909.

17. RESPONSE TO DARWIN[1]

MORDECAI HA-KOHEN

According to our sages, apes were originally human beings who, because of their evil deeds, were cast down by the Creator and turned into apes. The scholar Bondin also demonstrated clearly to the academy in Paris that the ancestors of apes were human beings who, because of their sins and promiscuity, had been cast down and turned into apes. However, according to the scholar Darwin and the scholar La Mettrie, our original ancestors were apes, and we have become civilized over the course of time, while the apes have retained their original form. Each scholar has his reasons and explanations.

Now, we do not rely solely on the tradition of our sages, of blessed memory, if we cannot find conclusive proof. If we take the time to look carefully at the history of nature, whose laws have been constant since the time of creation, wc can bring nature herself as evidence against Darwin and his colleagues.

Nature, which does not change, clearly indicates that our ancestors were not apes. The ape is special in its nature: it does not reproduce in captivity; this is not true of human beings, who reproduce in every habitat. In addition, we witness species of plants and animals which can fertilize related species but which do not reproduce thereafter, except in the case of human intervention, as in the grafting of trees. For example, the horse and the donkey are related and can produce a mule that is similar to both of them, but the mule cannot reproduce. This is not the case, however, with regard to apes and men. Researchers in Australia have already tried to mate a man and an ape and produced nothing, not even a mule. Therefore, if we claim that our ancestors were apes, how did nature change so much that they [men and apes] cannot [mate and] reproduce?

If it is claimed that the time involved is very long, and they have grown apart and therefore cannot

Source: Harvey E. Goldberg, *The Book of Mordechai: A Study of the Jews of Libya* (Philadelphia: Institute for the Study of Human Issues, 1980), pp. 20–21.

cross-fertilize and reproduce, then we can bring an argument from the plants! Everyone is in agreement that plants are older than animals, yet they still function as of old, fertilizing related species and bearing fruit. We thus see that their inner nature has not changed.

However, if we claim that apes were cast down by the Creator, we can also claim that the same act deprived them of the ability to fertilize other related species and reproduce. For there is also the case of the Whites and the Blacks, and according to tradition, "have we not all one father!" They have been separated from one another for hundreds of years, but not through a divine act. Even though Blacks differ from Whites in several respects, the power of reproduction is preserved; they can mate with Whites and yield offspring, and the offspring can yield offspring. They are thus different from the mule, which results from the horse and donkey; because they [Blacks and Whites] all have one father, the seed can yield more seed without outside intervention.

NOTE

1. On the author of this passage, see document 3 in this chapter. In this excerpt, the author reacts to the recent theory of evolution as developed by Charles Darwin. Unsurprisingly, the religiously devout author takes issue with the possibility that humans descend from apes. Indeed, he cites a rabbinic position that apes are the descendents of sinning humans whom God had degraded, a position that was also "demonstrated" by a French scholar. Notable, however, is the reasoned method of Ha-kohen's thought and his position that "we do not rely solely on the tradition of our sages." His method maintains the validity of empiricism over tradition and familiarity with contemporary discourse on race and the development of species.

18. SIGMUND FREUD ON MOSES AND HIS TORAH (1939)

ABRAHAM SHALOM YAHUDA[1]

As with many great sons of our people who have assimilated with non-Jews, Sigmund Freud took no part in our intellectual life or in anything to do with Jewry and its teaching. Like them he thought that emancipation essentially solved the question of the Jews as a people or a community, like those who embraced assimilation hundreds and thousands of years ago—from Samaria in the days of Jeroboam up until the Toledo of Torquemada[2]— those who believed in the right of the world's empires and the righteousness of non-Jewish rule, and the primacy they gave to their teaching and the merits of their morality over our Torah and our morality, which they neither knew nor understood. And like many of them he also thought that what was done in the past in the countries of exile would not be repeated in our generation. And so he lived in a pleasant dream lasting decades that could serve him now, after being woken from his dream by Hitler, to a subject more real than that of his book *Religion: The Future of an Illusion*,[3] that he wrote to prove that religion is nothing but a worthless reverie.

Source: Abraham Shalom Yahuda, "Critique of Freud's *Moses and Monotheism.*" *Bitzaron*, vol. 1 (1939), pp. 455–68; vol. 2 (1940), pp. 6–19, pp. 121–34. trans. Mark Joseph.

Freud grew up and was educated in the period of the Enlightenment which in Catholic Austria was much more hostile to religion and faith than in Protestant Germany that was already more irreligious. This was evident both in the ease with which the framework of religion and its priesthood were set aside, and in the enthusiastic support given to enlightened intellectuals by Jewish youth, who were struggling to be free from the pressure of the religious orthodoxy which dominated the Jewish street.

The Hasid with his long sidelocks and overgrown, uncombed and untrimmed beard was an object of mockery and scorn by the youth who fell into bad ways, just as the exilic balding priest was laughed at by the Austrian enlightenment intellectual; and if he knew that some professor went to church for morning prayers or confession, so he would look on him as especially hypocritical, a fraud unfit for the sanctuary of science. The atmosphere that prevailed in these circumstances influenced Freud's connection to Jewry and its traditions, even if he never estranged himself from the rock whence he was hewn and always longed for his origin in the Jewish People....

In conclusion: I thought it right to leave the domain of literary criticism and to talk in detail about our subject. For the book deals with what I regard to be a central issue, which Freud and all those who he relies on in it, draw out. And in fact it is neither because of the importance of his method nor because of its scientific value that Freud's book is worthy of our consideration, and the only reason for my intervention is that I saw the growth of fear in the camp of Israel and all around me, and those following the Torah and the religion urged me to break apart Leviathan's head and rescue Moses' tarnished reputation. I thought therefore that there was a much greater need to demonstrate the error of the wise men of Egyptian culture in raising one ruler Ikhnaton to the profaned height of faith, than to go to war only against Freud. I also wanted to bring examples to show how much we can learn from Egyptian culture to our credit at precisely the moment when the Egyptologists use it against us.

Before I end I have to say something about the way Freud chose to mention my book *The Language of the Torah and Its Connection to the Egyptians and Their Culture*.[4] He comments on it just twice throughout his whole book, and incidentally only where one could think that my book supports him. Since I show the

Egyptian influence on the Hebrew language it follows that one could think that Moses was Egyptian. But the truth is the opposite: it is indeed the whole point of my research to show that the Hebrew language is the creation of Hebrews, and only of the Hebrews; that it was not found before the Hebrews came to Egypt and that there, under the influence of the Egyptian language, they broadened and developed the Canaanite speech that they spoke when they went down from Canaan to Egypt, and created the Hebrew language in all its refinement and beauty as a literary language in the style and form of the Torah. And since the first books to be written in Hebrew were the books of Moses, it is the case that the main creator of that literary language was Moses himself and that he wrote the Pentateuch. And if so how is it possible to suggest for even one moment that Moses was not Hebrew, by origin and in his power and in all his heart and soul?[5]

NOTES

1. Abraham Shalom Yahuda (1877–1951) was born in Jerusalem to a Baghdadi family and studied Semitics at Heidelberg and Strasbourg. A renowned Orientalist, Yahuda lectured at the Hochschule für Wissenschaft des Judentums in Berlin from 1904 to 1914, the University of Madrid from 1915 to 1922, and thereafter at the New School for Social Research in New York City until 1942. While in Spain during World War I, he advocated on behalf of the Jews of Palestine by petitioning King Alfonso XII to use his influence with the emperors of Germany and Austria; his activities were sharply criticized by Chaim Weizmann, who at the time was the president of the World Zionist Organization. Yahuda published widely on subjects ranging from ancient Egypt and the Hebrew Bible to medieval Jewish thought, medieval Hebrew poetry, the Arabic literature of the Jews, and pre-Islamic poetry. In this selection, he employs his background in the study of Ancient Egypt to pen a critique of Freud's *Moses and Monotheism* (first published in German in 1939) and, more broadly, the psychological approach to the study of religion.
2. Tomas de Torquemada (1420?–98). As the first head of the Spanish Inquisition, he was infamous for the cruelty in his treatment of Jews and *conversos*.
3. Originally published in German in 1927.
4. *Die Sprache des Pentateuch in ihren Beziehungen zum Aegyptischen* (Berlin: Walter de Gruyter Verlag, 1929).

5. [Yahuda's footnote]: I decided to write this article some weeks ago before Freud's death (in 1939) and had to break off because of the many troubles that came my way with the outbreak of war. I put some of my objections directly to Freud before he published his book, but I did not manage to persuade him that none of his opinions about Moses and Egyptian religion stood up to criticism and that it would not bring him honor or enhance his reputation if his book saw the light of day.

19. A "FEMINIST" LOOK AT THE WOMEN OF FEZ (1900)[1]

N. BENCHIMOL

A few words on the women of Fez. You are no doubt aware of the degrading condition of complete servitude which afflicts the feminine sex here in Fez. The man is master here, and his despotism assumes the most cruel of forms in what concerns the woman. A woman is a slave who owes passive obedience to her lord and master. If you entered any home in Fez you have trouble distinguishing the servant from her mistress. They both perform the same household tasks; they both eat in the kitchen. Only his sons are allowed to sit at the master's table. The daughters necessarily share their mother's lot. From the moment of her birth, a woman in Fez feels the weight of her inferiority. Whereas there are cries of joy and endless celebration upon the birth of a son, it is cries of mourning which welcome into the world the young girl, whose only sin is to have been born.

I must confess that as a woman and a feminist, these practices did not fail to revolt me, and I would like to have the power to reform this society, which is deficient in so many respects. Daughters are so loved by their father that as soon as they begin to walk and to talk, a husband is sought for them, a convenient way to get rid of them. This explains the deplorable practice of child marriages.

For a long time I have looked for the origin of this practice, and I can now state with certainty: daughters are married in their earliest childhood so that they may be all the sooner taken off the hands of the father. A daughter is a curse for her family, and the father believes he has more than fulfilled his duty toward her in giving her as a slave to another tyrant, this time with the name of husband.

Was it, then, from this backward population that I was to seek out minds eager for learning and knowledge? Was it likely that a father whose daughter is the least of his concerns would take an interest in my school, trust his children's education to me, [and] make the necessary sacrifices to pay for his daughter's schooling? Such were the questions I asked myself day after day, and ended up with disappointment and a headache.

Today I can consider myself fortunate. The fears that I had have disappeared and I have the pleasure of affirming that these parents, who inspire so little confidence, can nevertheless be reached by means of the good and the useful....

Some parents have already come to see me to tell me proudly that they have turned down several offers of marriage for their daughters so that these girls might continue to come to school. My ardent

Source: Aron Rodrigue, *Images of Sephardi and Middle Eastern Jewries in Transition: The Teachers of the Alliance Israélite Universelle, 1860–1939* (Seattle: University of Washington Press), 1993, pp. 82–84.

desire is to put a stop to these early marriages. This may not be an impossible goal, but it clearly cannot be realized at this time. Only a new generation will be capable of understanding the immorality of these customs; all we can do today is to ready their minds for such an urgently needed reform.

NOTE

1. The letters of women teachers of the Alliance Israélite Universelle share the zeal for westernization characteristic of the letters of male teachers. Their women's letters frequently focus on the specific challenges faced by women in their traditional societies. In this letter, Miss N. Benchimol, an Alliance teacher in Fez, discusses the success of her school and decries the common practice of child marriage, which results in girls' withdrawal from education. The author situates her teaching within a broader mission to "restore dignity to the women of Fez, to give them a place in society, to develop their hearts and minds."

20. RESPONSUM ON WOMEN'S SUFFRAGE (1920)[1]

BEN-ZION UZZIEL

A. THE RIGHT OF WOMEN IN THE LEGISLATURE AND PUBLIC ADMINISTRATION OF THE YISHUV

This question was a point of contention in the Land of Israel and the whole of the Land of Israel was shaken by it. Proclamations and warnings, pamphlets and newspaper articles were ceaselessly published to completely prohibit the participation of women in the elections; some founded their words on Rabbinic law [*din torah*] and some on the notion of guarding the boundaries of morality and modesty, and others on the peace of the family household, but the opinion of all was based on the same Rabbinic dictum: "Novelty is forbidden by the Torah."[2] Regretfully, at this time I am unable to discuss all of the literary material that has accumulated on this question, but may praise reach our companion, "the vessel of the Law,"[3] our great Rabbi and teacher Hayyim Hershenson (*Maharama*),[4] who collected the entire essence of this material in the second part of his book *Malki ba-Qodesh*; this allows me to harken all the proscriptions and discuss them, in accordance with the limits of my comprehension.

This question is itself divided into two parts: a) the active function of the election—to elect [and] b) the (passive) result of the election—to be elected.

On the first, we did not find any clear foundation on which to forbid it, and reason does not accept the denial of this personal right to women, for are we not in these elections assembling the best to be our leaders and giving legal power to our representatives to speak in our name, to arrange the matters of our Yishuv and to levy taxes on our assets? And women, either directly or indirectly, accept the authority of these representatives and obey their orders and their communal and national laws. And how is it possible to grasp the rope at both ends: to impose upon them the disciplinary obligation [required by] the national representatives and deny them the right to elect them? And should they tell us to exclude them from the electorate, because they are irresponsible

Source: Rabbi Ben-Zion Uzziel, Responsum on Women's Suffrage (1920), in *Uzziel be-she'elot ha-zeman* (Jerusalem: Mosad ha-Rav Kook, 1977), pp. 228–34. trans. Adam Stern.

and because they do not know how to elect those fit to stand for the public, then we will say: If this is the case, we will also remove from the electorate those men who are irresponsible, without them ever causing loss to the land. Nevertheless, reality proves us wrong and shows us that in the past, as well as in our time, women are enlightened and their reason is like that of men, negotiating, buying and selling, and managing their affairs in the best manner. And has anyone ever heard of appointing a guardian upon a great woman without her knowledge?...

B. WOMEN AS [POLITICAL] REPRESENTATIVES

The second question is whether or not women can be representatives. And on this we have, indeed, found an apparently explicit prohibition: *"You will surely appoint..."* (Deuteronomy 17:15):[5] Should someone be appointed and die, another is appointed instead of him; a king and not a queen" (*Sifrei Devarim*, Parshat Shoftim, Pisqa 147). And Rambam (Maimonides) understands from this: "Do not place a woman in kingship. As it is said: '[Place] a king upon you, and not a queen.'"[6] And so all the missions in Israel place only a man in charge and not a woman, thus not appointing a female leader over the community. And this befits the *Halakha* that the great Rabbi Shlomo Aharon Wertheimer discovered in the Genizah: *"Do not appoint a foreign man over you:*[7] Therefore they said: a man can be appointed as a community leader, but a woman cannot be appointed as a community leader."[8] However, I am uncertain whether this law stems from the unacceptability of having a woman in a judgeship or from [a concern for] the dignity of the community. This [question] emerges in a place where a court does not appoint her, but a portion of the community chooses her as their delegate and agent. On the one hand, this is also not permissible, just as an individual is not allowed to accept the testimony of a woman in matters of divorce [*gittin*] and marriage [*qiddushin*], and the like, since the Torah disqualifies her. On the other hand, one could say that their election is permissible, that only the entire community or the rabbinical courts are not permitted to appoint her to a communal position, but that a portion of the nation is permitted to choose her as their delegate and agent. And here is what was written in the *Tosafot*[9] in regards to one solution (Tosafot Baba Kama 15a) to the fact that Deborah was a judge

because they accepted her: It is necessary to prove the permissibility of their acceptance even when they all accept her. And even to their solution that she was chosen by the word [of God], one could say, rather, concerning the permissibility of their acceptance, that they are not permitted to do so because of the dignity of the community. And thus one must make evident what is written in the Zohar (see Zohar, Leviticus 3:19b). Here you learn that there is no prohibition against appointing a woman to a public position and that it is permissible to appoint her in a time of need, but that this occurs as the result of an offense to the community, "that there was no one to judge over it except for one woman" (ibid.)

And accordingly, it is clear that the words of Sifrei are also interpreted in this way, such that a queen is not appointed over the community by the members of the court out of a concern for communal dignity. And for this reason, an individual or individuals are permitted and entitled to choose her and it is by the right of her voters that she joins the body of representatives....

NOTES

1. Born in Jerusalem to an illustrious Sephardi rabbinical family, Rabbi Ben-Zion Uzziel (1880–1953) was a highly esteemed rabbinic legal authority, who was positively disposed toward certain European intellectual and cultural trends. The present document is his halakhic opinion on the question of women's suffrage, which had been raised by the ruling of the British Mandatory government's decision to grant women the right to participate in the elections of the governing institutions of the Yishuv (the Jewish community of Mandatory Palestine), which at the time included long-standing traditional Sephardi and Ashkenazi communities as well as recently arrived largely secular Zionists. Most rabbinic authorities—such as Rabbi Abraham Isaac Kook (1865–1935), since 1919 the chief Ashkenazi rabbi of Jerusalem and since 1921 the chief Ashkenazi Rabbi of Palestine—rejected the notion of women's suffrage because of the lack of a precedent and argued that in biblical Israel, women were counted in "neither the *kahal* nor in the *edah*" [that is, women were regarded neither as belonging to the community (*kahal*) as politically constituted nor to the community (*edah*) as religiously constituted and were not counted in the *minyan* or quorum necessary for public prayer; they were, in other words, politically

and religiously nonentities]. Rabbi Uzziel differed and argued that women should be granted suffrage because they are "created in the divine image and endowed with intelligence" no less than men. What is significant is that Rabbi Uzziel wove into his halakhic opinion both theological and sociological judgment. See Zvi Zohar, "Traditional Flexibility and Modern Strictness: A Comparative Study of Halakhic Positions of Rabbi Kook and Rabbi Uzziel on Women's Suffrage," in *Sephardi and Middle Eastern Jewries. History and Culture*, ed. Harvey Goldberg (Bloomington: Indiana University Press, 1996), pp. 119–33.

2. [Translator's note]: Mishnah, 'Orlah 3:9. "*Hadash*—the new cereal crop, before the *omer* offering (on the 16th of Nisan) on the temple altar (v. Hal. 1:1)—*is forbidden by Torah law everywhere*—including lands outside Eretz Israel, thus (Lev. 23:14): 'And you shall eat neither bread nor parched corn, nor green ears until that very day…it shall be a statute forever throughout your generations *in all your dwellings* i.e., wherever you may reside." See *The Mishnah, Seder Zera'im*, Vol. 3, ed. Avraham Tanzer, trans. Rafael Fisch. Commentary: Pinhas Kehati (Jerusalem: Maor Wallach Press, 1994), 48–49. This dictum was enjoined by Hatam Sofer and Ultra-Orthodoxy to justify their utter rejection of all modern innovations to Jewish tradition. See chapter 4, documents 4 and 6.

3. See B. T. Sanhedrin 99b (translator's note).

4. A pro-Zionist rabbinic scholar Hayyim Hirschensohn (1875–1935) wrote a compendious treatise on the laws, which should govern the future Jewish state according to the Torah: *Malki ba Qodesh* (1919–1928), 6 volumes (translator's note.)

5. Deuteronomy 17:15. The verse continues: "whom the LORD thy God shall choose; one from among thy brethren shalt thou set king over thee; thou mayest not put a foreigner over thee, who is not thy brother" (ibid). (translator's note.)

6. Maimonides, *Mishneh Torah*, Sefer Shoftim, Hilchot Melakhim, 5. See also Deuteronomy, 17:15. (translator's note.)

7. Cf. Deuteronomy 1:9–18, which reinterprets two previous accounts (see Exodus, chapter 18) of the creation of a military-juridical system to share in the leadership of the Israelites. This new version not only places the institutionalization of leadership after the exodus from Sinai rather than before, but eliminates the important advisory role of Jethro, a non-Israelite. (translator's note)

8. A Jerusalem rabbinic scholar and collector of rare books and manuscripts, Rabbi Shlomo Aharon Wertheimer (1866–1935) was among the first to recognize the significance of the Cairo Genizah. In the early 1890s, he began to publish manuscripts from this treasure trove of medieval rabbinic and philosophical writings. In 1925 he published a collection of writings on the subject: *Ginze Yerushalayim*, 3 parts (1925). (translator's note)

9. Tosafot are additions to the Babylonian Talmud, namely, glosses, written by French and German rabbinic scholars during the twelfth to the fourteenth centuries. (translator's note)

21. A JEWISH EGYPTIAN PATRIOT CALLS FOR DEEMPHASIZING RELIGION IN HIS COUNTRY'S PUBLIC LIFE FOR THE SAKE OF NATIONAL UNITY (1912)

MURAD FARAJ[1]

I wish to discuss something that has a clear relationship to religion. I wish to speak about the national community, because being a healthy national society requires that there be in its extended national life a complete distancing from anything that might harm it from the realm of religion. Every single nation or kingdom always needs a community, which calls to it the essence of nationhood, especially when it happens that the nation or kingdom belongs to people who are not of a single religion or rite as is the case in Egypt. When the adherents of various religions and rites arm themselves, some of them kill others. I do not mean real killing, but rather the killing of fraternal sentiments and the national feeling in people's hearts. There is no worse slaughter than this because it always bequeaths a legacy of burning fire which cannot be extinguished, or it is a war without end. If a nation has progressed in its conception, the smallest thing from the domain of religion, which might be harmful to it should immediately be considered the greatest thing in proportion to this progress. No one will deny that interfaith relations in Egypt before now were heavier than the Juyushi Mountain or more terrifying than the savage in the wilderness who lies in ambush to assault the passerby on the way. However, the present advance in the concept of the nation, or in the concept of that which is meant to be denoted now by the term "the Egyptian nation," is far more advanced than the actual present state of things. We promote the state in its conception. We do not promote a religious association in accordance with this concept.

Forgive me, my brothers—and all under heaven are my brethren—if I speak, for there is nothing more beneficial than these words nowadays. They are the efficacious medicine for our societal sickness in this country of ours. If we want to improve our condition externally, we must first improve internally. Health begins properly with the internal remedy. We want to have a nation. We want a constitution or a general code. We want to be a sovereign state in our own sight and in the sight of others. It is a duty to work truly and effectively for this goal in a way that there is no doubt as to its efficacy, as it is said in His glorious Book: "Verily, God does not change a people's condition until they change what is in their souls."[2] It is a lofty maxim in language that can almost be grasped with the hand. The power of the work can only come from the will in the soul. When it lacks that will, it does not work, or it performs a false labor. If we want to have a nation, then we must have it in actuality. Moreover, we will have it by transforming ourselves altogether. We must change our souls and make them all into a single soul facing the nation. That is, in order for there to be a single soul, it is necessary for the individual souls to be dedicated to that which they share among one another. This dedication comes from abandoning everything religious which serves as an obstacle on the path to achieving it. I have before me now a palpable witness to this, a witness upon which there is the unspoken consensus of the Ottoman Empire in its entirety, just as there is consensus about it in every kingdom that has progressed before it. That

Source: Norman Stillman. *The Jews of Arab Lands in Modern Times* (Philadelphia: Jewish Publication Society, 1991), pp. 228–30.

witness is what we have seen and are seeing, namely the unity of the Muslims as an entity and marching together in step with their Ottoman brothers on a single path, proclaiming officially at the top of their lungs, "Our condition will only be improved by general, national unity and a lack of discrimination between one religion and another and between one rite and another through mutual association, moral conduct, and good social relations. It is henceforth no longer proper to be called 'Khawaja' or 'Effendi.'[3] Rather everyone, whether Muslim or non-Muslim, should be called 'Effendi,'" in order to unify all the sons of the one nation, to bring their hearts together, and to prevent that antipathy which afflicts human nature when someone addresses someone else as "Khawaja," meaning "O Christian" or "O Jew." . . .

I will not hide from the reader that I was embarrassed and ashamed [when I was addressed as Khawaja]. I returned to my feelings thinking about the incident. It was not the first time, but rather one of a number of times that it had happened to me, while I kept silent and lowered my eyes. However, I did not find in my heart protection from the words; rather I found the words particularly necessary and required. My heart could not bear it any longer. I have retained my composure from it on the one hand, and I serve the national union on the other. I oppose anything of this sort that harms feelings of human brotherhood, let alone national feelings. When people distinguish between people with a greeting, there is in it an alerting of the mind that this is a Muslim or a non-Muslim. What is more than this warning, the person who is giving the greeting is charming every time the "Peace be upon you" is in order, while he almost pays no attention to the fact that non-Muslims are present with Muslims. But we are the people of a single nation who are working for one commonwealth. Seldom is there a gathering of the three—Muslim, Christian, and Jew—without an insult being given as soon as the mental alert is sounded by a simple warning as to who is a Muslim and who is not. Furthermore, [there] is in this warning an indication to the soul that there is some sort of aversion or loathing, or at least a lack of equality in public morals and manners. Every etiquette, like the etiquette of social greeting, requires equalizing. When you are alone with a Muslim there is no harm in saying "Peace be upon you" a thousand times. Similarly, when there is a Christian or a Jew

with him, there is no need for specifying and distinguishing. Then it will never be proper to cut a greeting short after beginning to utter it and to change it to another which distinguishes and specifies even more emphatically than at first. If the Exalted Empire has granted equality between Muslim and non-Muslim in its social policy by prohibiting the term "Khawaja" and by generalizing the use of the title "Effendi" for all, that is equality in its true sense. It is even stronger than according equality in the greeting "Peace be upon you." Is it not fitting, therefore, that we should at least follow the example of that great Islamic Empire which is the possessor of the Prophetic Caliphate with a similar acknowledgement of equality in the greeting "Peace be upon you"?

Murad Farah, *Maqalat Murad*
(Cairo, 1912), pp. 201–8.

NOTES

1. Murad Faraj (1866–1956), born in Cairo, was trained as a lawyer and served as an Egyptian government official between 1892 and 1914. A prominent member of Cairo's Karaite community, Faraj was a frequent contributor of articles and poems to Egyptian and Egyptian-Jewish newspapers. He also edited own journal for the Karaite community, *al-Tahdhib* (Edification), 1901–03. His Arabic poetry is collected in four volumes. He translated several Hebrew works (e.g., the biblical Proverbs) into Arabic and also translated one of his collections of Arabic poems into Hebrew (*al-qudisyyat/ha-qodshiyot*). In addition, Faraj published on Karaite issues, biblical interpretation, Arabic and Hebrew philology, the Arabic literature of the Jews, and legal topics, displaying control of Jewish and Islamic law and jurisprudence. He was an Egyptian nationalist who called for national unity in such books as his *Harb al-watan* (Battle of the Nation) and participated in the drafting of the Egyptian constitution in 1923. He ultimately supported Zionism as well. In this selection, Faraj argues that members of the different religions can participate together in the Egyptian nationalist project and should be treated as equals. It is noteworthy how he employs praise for the Arabic tongue and a quotation from the Qur'an (which he calls "God's glorious Book") within his rhetorical strategy.

2. Sura 13:11. It is interesting that the author, who is Jewish, refers to the Koran as "God's glorious Book."

3. The first title was reserved for non-Muslims, and the latter title was for Muslims.

22. A BAGHDADI RABBI DECRIES THE DECLINE OF TRADITIONAL MORALS (1913)[1]

SIMEON AGASI

As for examining our acts, there is no need for an exhaustive search, because they are clearly manifest and well known. They are heaped up like so many bundles, and the earth reeks from their stench. For in addition to the old misdeeds which we used to commit, new and very serious transgressions have sprung up among us which our forefathers never even considered, such as the public desecration of the Sabbath. You can find it among those of our people who are clerks in the banking houses and other high places. They go there even on the Sabbath and come home to do work, each according to his own occupation. Whatever he does on a weekday, he does on the Sabbath. Not only that, but the riffraff in our midst has developed a craving for forbidden food, seeking to fill their bellies with unkosher carrion and all the rest of the prohibited viands in Gentile restaurants, where they eat the impure and the pure together. May their tables be a snare for them, their food be bitter vipers' venom in their innards, and may the accursed waters come into their intestines to swell their bellies and cause their thighs to sag.[2]

And what can we say about the sin of adultery— God preserve us!—which has spread among us? And what about the brothels that have multiplied among us? "Each man is neighing at his neighbor's wife, and they line up in troops at the harlot's door."[3] They are like dogs that surround a trampled corpse or a stinking carcass without any shame. And what about the sin of homosexuality, which is found among the other peoples in whose midst we live? Has even this come into the House of Israel?

Our heart is also greatly pained by people going to theaters to see women dancing on the stage and to hear erotic songs sung by vile, sensuous women who are like a fire in the chaff—God protect us! It is not only by the youth who have cast aside morals, have transgressed the covenant, and have broken the law, that we are shocked, but by the important people of good repute in the world of commerce, whose position among the leading citizens of the city has been shaken. It is by them that we are taken aback. Even if we were to suppose that they are not concerned by this terrible sin, whom then do they have to care about their honor, because according to general etiquette, going to this sort of despicable show is considered a dishonor, a disgrace, and a shame for a man of stature and nobility. They had to learn from well-mannered people among the Gentiles that they had complained bitterly against the frequenting of these vile houses of entertainment in the city. Satan had so blinded them that they exchanged their honor for hopeless disgrace. Heaven forbid!

And how much more are we heartsick at the immodesty that has arisen of late among women and at their high audacity in modifying their clothing to be like the clothes of wanton Christian women. They have done this despite the fact that we are warned against resembling the Gentiles in dress or in actions, as is clearly stated in the *Shulhan 'Arukh, Yoreh De'a*, Section 178.[4] These women use up their husbands' money to embellish the dresses with decorations and buttons that cost more than the original garment itself. They cause their husbands to go broke and to swallow up the wealth of others. The honor of Israel is lowered in the eyes of non-Jews since most of the bankrupts are Jews.

Worse than this are those women who have cast off the yoke of modesty and go about bareheaded for all to see and are not ashamed. Woe to the eyes that

---

Source: Norman Stillman, *The Jews of Arab Lands in Modern Times* (Philadelphia: Jewish Publication Society, 1991), pp. 243–44.

see such things!…Woe to the generation in which such things have arisen!

This sort of evil which has infected us is the fault of the Alliance schools, those bitter grapes,[5] that have been established in our city. All of the teachers in those schools are deceitful individuals who have shaken off the yoke and do all sorts of evil and abomination. How can students not sin when they see their teacher doing that, and thus they fall upon wicked ways? And thence it extended and spread to the rest of the masses. (The Chief Rabbi and the rabbis and scholars see all this, but they place their hand over their mouth out of weakness. No one demands anything, no one asks anything, even though according to the rules of the Alliance and the rules of etiquette, they have the power to exert oversight upon all of this.)

It was not enough for them until they established schools like these for Jewish girls as well in order to capture precious, pure, and innocent souls. The school mistresses in those institutions are the lascivious wives of the male teachers, and whatever their husbands do, they do as well to separate these daughters of Israel from their God and from the customary religious laws of their pure and modest mothers. Thus, they destroy the world from both ends.

NOTES

1. In this document, originally in Hebrew, the Baghdadi rabbi Simeon Agasi (1851–1914) excoriates the Alliance Israélite Universelle and its teachers for leading Jews to sin. His critiques focus on Sabbath desecration, eating nonkosher food, adultery, attending "erotic" performances, and immodest dress.
2. The imagery is from Num. 5:22.
3. Jer. 5:7–8. However, the verses are cited here in reverse order.
4. The section is entitled "One is not to wear the clothes of idolaters."
5. A play on the Hebrew words *askolot* (schools) and *eshkolot* (cluster of grapes). Cf. Deut. 42:42.

23. DE-JUDAIZATION AMONG THE JEWS OF TUNISIA AND THE STEPS NEEDED TO FIGHT IT (1929)[1]

L. LOUBATON

Hebrew instruction for children, which was highly valued in the time preceding the arrival of the Alliance, can be said to be nonexistent. The *Keter-Torah* [the traditional Jewish school], which had been functioning there for about twenty years, is now completely deserted. Although it is true that on Thursdays and Sundays, as well as during the school holidays, a few children do wander in, they do nothing of value there. This has been attested by the very notables and members of the committee who belong to this society.

The children are ignorant of all that represents the beauty and uniqueness of our doctrine; they have no notion of biblical history or of Jewish history; they are totally unaware that a modern Jewish literature exists. How can these children love and

Source: Aron Rodrigue, *Images of Sephardi and Middle Eastern Jewries in Transition: The Teachers of the Alliance Israélite Universlle, 1860–1939* (Seattle: University of Wahington Press, 1993), pp. 121–24.

practice their religion; how can they form a bond with their past?

I have observed the youth of Sousse in the temples on [*yom*] *Kipur*, which is the only day of the year on which they come to the temple in great numbers. They come only through habit or superstitious fears....

Let us consider the cafés on Saturdays. They are literally invaded by Jews. With few exceptions, all are smoking, gambling—often for large sums of money—at cards or at backgammon, or discussing business.

And let us consider a house in mourning where there is grief over the loss of a respected father or a beloved mother. We first hear a *drashah*[2] delivered by a rabbi who tries to inspire us with an avalanche of citations from the Bible or from the Talmud; the logic with which he strings them together is not always clear. After this, we see the sons form a circle around the preacher as they try to read, or rather mouth the words to the required *Kadish*.[3]

I could provide many more examples, but I have said enough to create a true picture of the situation....

In short, there is a desertion of the synagogues, an almost complete ignorance of the religion and of the Jewish past, a lack of observance of religious practices, an extreme decline in sacred studies, a continual decrease in the number of doctors in the Law, and a decrease in the number of sacrificers and others who hold special functions in our faith.

Can we remain indifferent to these observations? Can we imagine the abyss into which our communities will have been swallowed twenty or thirty years from now if some superior strength is not to intervene energetically in reaction to those erring ways?

Already, mixed marriages are becoming common. The conversion to Protestantism of an entire family still living in Sousse has been registered....

What these failing communities need above all and without delay is the establishment of Alliance schools (for boys, girls, and younger children, as was discussed above). In these schools, where the facilities would be perfectly adapted to their needs, the young Jewish children would receive both a general education, in all respects as good as what they are currently receiving in the public schools, and the moral and religious education of which they are currently almost totally deprived.

NOTES

1. Although the westernizing curriculum of the Alliance Israélite Universelle was sometimes blamed for the decay of traditional Judaism, the author of this document, the Tunisian Leon Loubaton (b. 1884) views the Alliance schools as the antidote for the neglect of traditional values and practices. Although the opening of the document points to the toxic effects of the "French occupation" (in earlier years, the same author looked to colonial rule more optimistically), it is ironically the French-oriented Alliance education that will bring Jews exposure to the "moral and religious education of which they are almost totally deprived." The author also calls for the establishment of other institutions to enhance Jewish religious life and observance.

2. A disquisition on the Holy Scriptures.

3. A traditional prayer to commemorate the dead.

24. THE KORAN AND OTHER SCRIPTURES (1893)

YAAQUB (JAMES) SANU'[1]

You desire me to give you freely my opinion about the Koran.

I shall not speak of its holiness, lest I profane it, and besides I am not an Imam. I shall only show you that the Koran is tolerant, humane and moral. I shall merely quote to you some of its verses, and leave you to judge of its divine precepts.

"Surely those who believe, and the Jews and the Christians and the Sabians, whoever believeth in God and the Last Day, and doeth that which is right, they shall have their reward with their Lord. There shall come no fear on them, neither shall they be grieved." Ch. ii: 59.

I am then not wrong in saying that the Koran is tolerant. Now as to its being moral:

"Good and evil shall not be held equal. Turn away evil for that which is better, and behold, the man between whom and thyself here was enmity shall become, as it were, thy warmest friend." Ch. lxi: 33.

"A fair speech and to forgive is better than alms followed by mischief." Ch. ii: 265.

Observe how humane Mohammed was: "They shall ask thee what they shall bestow in alms. Answer, the good which ye bestow, let it be given to parents and kindred and orphans and the poor and the strangers. Whatever good ye do, God knoweth it." Ch. ii: 211.

Concerning *Hospitality.*—"If any of the idolaters shall demand protection of thee, grant him protection, that he may hear the word of God, and afterwards let him reach the place of security." Ch. ix: 6.

Mercy toward Slaves.—"Unto such of your slaves as desire a written instrument allowing them to redeem themselves on paying a certain sum, write one, if you know good in them, and give them of the riches of God which he has given thee." Ch. xxiv: 33.

Encouragement of Learning.—Mohammed said: "Learned men are the heirs of prophets." "Learning is a divine precept that every Mussulman must fulfill." "Acquire knowledge, even if it were in China." "Expect no good from a man who is neither learned nor student." Moslem writers have said much on this subject.

The Koran's Praise of Women.—"Happy and fortunate is the man who has only one wife, pious and virtuous." "I love three things in your world, woman, perfume and prayer." "The greatest bliss of man after that of his being a faithful believer in God, is his having a pious wife who delights him when he looks at her, obeys him when he commands her, and preserves his honor and his property when he is far from her." "Respect those who have borne you." "If you feel that you cannot act equitably toward many wives, marry one only."

Divorce.—The Apostle says that even if a man has given his wife a talent, if he divorces her, he has no right to take back anything from her.

NOTE

1. Yaaqub Sanu' (1839–1912) was a founding playwright of the Egyptian theater and a prolific journalist and essayist. He directed the Arabic journal *Abu Nazzara Zarqa* (The Man in Blue Glasses), which featured biting political satire directed toward the British colonial authorities and the Khedive Ismail (1830–1895), the ruler of Egypt and Sudan until 1879, in particular. The widely read journal earned him the moniker Abu Nazzara (The Man in Glasses). He was closely associated with early Egyptian nationalists and was a zealous advocate for the national cause. He was the most famous Jewish writer in the Arab world in the nineteenth century and contributed richly to the Arabic *Nahda* (Awakening). His plays mixed classical and colloquial Arabic, the latter being banned in performances in 1872. Born in Cairo, he studied

Source: The World's Parliament of Religions (Chicago: Parliament Publishing Co., 1893), vol. 2, 1146–48.

in Leghorn from 1852–1855 and had a command of several languages, including Arabic, Italian, French, and English. His identity seems to have been primarily Egyptian although he did not deny his Judaism and did not convert to Islam. The present document was delivered at the World's Parliament of Religions, which brought together members of many world religions in Chicago in 1893. Although the morality and tolerance of the Qur'an may seem a curious topic for a Jewish speaker, it fits well with Sanu's vision of himself as an emissary seeking a rapprochement between East and West.

25. THE THIRD REDEMPTION (1843)

YEHUDAH ALKALAI[1]

"And Jacob came in peace to the city of Shechem ... and he bought the parcel of ground where he had spread his tent [Genesis 33:16–18]." We must ask: Why did Jacob buy this land, since being on his way to his father, Isaac, he had not intention of living there? Obviously, he performed this act to teach his descendants that the soil of the Holy Land must be purchased from its non-Jewish owners.

We, as a people, are properly called Israel only in the land of Israel.

In the first conquest, under Joshua, the Almighty brought the children of Israel into a land that was prepared: its houses were then full of useful things, its wells were giving water, and its vineyards and olive groves were laden with fruit. This new Redemption will—alas, because of our sins—be different: our land is waste and desolate, and we shall have to build houses, dig wells, and plant vines and olive trees. We are, therefore, commanded not to attempt to go at once and all together to the Holy Land. In the first place, it is necessary for many Jews to remain for a time in the lands of dispersion, so that they can help the first settlers in Palestine, who will undoubtedly come from among the poor. Secondly, the Lord desires that we be redeemed in dignity; we cannot, therefore, migrate in a mass, for we should then have to live like Bedouins, scattered in tents all over the fields of the Holy Land. Redemption must come slowly. The land must, by degrees, be built up and prepared.

There are two kinds of return: individual and collective. Individual return means that each man should turn away from his evil personal ways and repent; the way of such repentance has been prescribed in the devotional books of our religious tradition. This kind of repentance is called individual, because it is relative to the particular needs of each man. Collective return means that all Israel should return to the land which is the inheritance of our fathers, to receive the Divine command and to accept the yoke of Heaven. This collective return was foretold by all the prophets; even though we are unworthy, Heaven will help us, for the sake of our holy ancestors. ...

The Redemption will begin with efforts by the Jews themselves; they must organize and unite, choose leaders, and leave the lands of exile. Since no community can exist without a governing body, the very first new ordinance must be the appointment of the elders of each district, men of piety and wisdom,

Source: Arthur Hertzberg, *The Zionist Idea: A Historical Analysis and Reader* (New York: Doubleday and Company and Herzl Press, 1959), pp. 103–07.

to oversee all the affairs of the community. I humbly suggest that this chosen assembly—the assembly of the elders—is what is meant by the promise to us of the Messiah, the son of Joseph[2]....

It is not impossible for us to carry out the commandment to return to the Holy Land. The Sultan will not object, for His Majesty knows that the Jews are his loyal subjects. Difference of religion should not be an obstacle, for each nation will worship its own god and we will forever obey the Lord, our God....

NOTES

1. Born in 1798 in Sarajevo, Bosnia and Herzegovina, Yehudah Alkalai was raised in Jerusalem. His father was a rabbi in Sarajevo, and Alkalai was closely associated with Kabbalistic circles in Jerusalem. In 1825, he became rabbi of Semlin, Serbia. As early as 1834, Alkalai called for the creation of Jewish colonies in the Holy Land in order to hasten Redemption. This plan, which rejected the idea that the Messianic age was to be induced by divine grace alone, was also religiously motivated and was argued on the basis of traditional textual interpretation. His program of "self-redemption" gained momentum following the Damascus affair of 1840 and, through Alkalai's own promotional efforts, reached the ears of Western Jewish financiers and dignitaries, such as Moses Montefiore and Adolph Crémieux (See chapter 6, document 9, note 15, note 3). Alkalai died in Jerusalem in 1878. In the present text, Alkalai calls for a "collective return" to be executed through mundane political means, such as purchasing land and establishing a government, which will ultimately cause the "Divine Presence" to rest upon Jews in the Holy Land.

2. According to rabbinic apocalyptic literature, a Messiah, son of Joseph, will appear prior to the Messiah, son of David. He will gather the exiled children of Israel and march on Jerusalem, liberating the city.

26. A LETTER TO THEODOR HERZL (1897)[1]

BAR KOKHBA JEWISH SOCIETY, CAIRO

"Bar Kokhba" Jewish Society
Cairo, Egypt
Founded the 1st of Adar I 5657
February 1897

> Central Headquarters
>   Mr. Theodor Herzl
>   Editor of the "Neue Freie Presse"
>   Vienna

Sir, dear coreligionist in your Jewish State,[2]

Over a year ago, the "Carmel"[3] was not only the first to salute your solemn entry into the Zionist ranks, but also to encourage your project which is as ingenious as it is patriotic. You know, Sir, that it was in Bulgaria[4] that you achieved your first success. Today, still, most of your partisans are the Zionists of Bulgaria.

Well, Sir, you will be happy to learn of the founding in Cairo through patience, perseverance, and action, of a patriotic Zionist society "Bar Kokhba," whose program is the same as that outlined by the "Carmel."

Would you please, Sir, we pray you, bring us up to date about everything that is taking place in the

---

Source: Norman Stillman, *The Jews of Arab Lands in Modern Times* (Philadelphia: Jewish Publication Society, 1991), pp. 305–06.

Zionist world at Vienna and at the same time send your pamphlet "The Jewish State" in French translation if it is possible.

Long live "The Jewish State!"

Please accept, Sir, the assurance of our most distinguished sentiments, together with our warm greetings of Zion.

Joseph Leibovitch   J. Harmalin
Secretary   President

Cairo (Egypt). April 8, 1897

NOTES

1. The activities of the Turkish Jew Joseph Marco Barukh, a colorful and tragic figure who preached Zionism in Algeria, Bulgaria, and Egypt, sparked the creation in Cairo of the first Zionist organization in Egypt, which ultimately became known as the Bar Kokhba Society (which had a largely Ashkenazi following). Zionist organizations sprouted in other Egyptian cities, gaining significant Sephardi participation by 1920. This document, sent to Theodor Herzl from the Bar Kokhba Society in 1897, is notable for its commitment and demonstrates how peripheral Egypt was in Zionist activity. Both the signers of the document are Ashkenazi.

2. The reference is to Herzl's *The Jewish State* (*Der Judenstaat*, 1896), in which he first presented his vision of Zionism.

3. Carmel was the name of both the Zionist society and the newspaper founded by Marco Barukh in Bulgaria. See Jacob Weinschal, *Marko Barukh: Nevi Milhemet ha-Shihrur* (Jerusalem, 1980), p. 20. Barukh was the founder of the Bar Kokhba Society in Cairo.

4. Herzl was hailed by Jewish crowds in Sofia in 1896, while on his way to Constantinople. See G. Hirschler, "Bulgaria, Zionism in," Encyclopedia of Zionism, 1: 169.

27. A CALL TO ALEXANDRIAN JEWRY TO CELEBRATE THE SAN REMO RECOGNITION OF THE BALFOUR DECLARATION (1920)[1]

ZÉIRE ZION SOCIETY, ALEXANDRIA

The hour of deliverance has sounded!

Like the sentiment which our forefathers felt when they saw the walls of Jericho crumbling before them, all of us felt once again a relief, an infinite joy, when the brazen cable transmitted to us, like a song of victory, the San Remo declaration,[2] which consecrated the legitimacy of our rights and aspirations—Palestine as the National Jewish Home....It is indeed the deliverance, the end of our miseries, of bondage, and of exile!

To commemorate this declaration and in order that the Jewish people dispersed over the face of the earth might rejoice together at the same time, the Executive Committee of the World Zionist Organization has decided that the week commencing with the Feast of Shavu'ot will be the "Week of Ge'ula,"[3] in the hope that all Jewish communities, great and small, will find it in their hearts to celebrate it with the greatest possible display.

We Jews of Alexandria join all our brothers in Egypt and abroad in celebrating our deliverance! We who have unfailingly preserved in our hearts a vivifying faith in the justice of our cause, all of us

---

Source: Norman Stillman, *The Jews of Arab Lands in Modern Times* (Philadelphia: Jewish Publication Society, 1991), pp. 309–10.

who have directed ourselves toward the same goal, toward Zion, which shines from afar guiding us as the lighthouse shines over the crests of the waves for the lost navigator, we seize this formal occasion to reunite all of us without distinction and to take part in our celebrations in order to give free rein to our overflowing joy.

…But we must remember the actual situation in our recovered homeland. We left it beautiful and prosperous, the star of the East, shining with the most lively brilliance, and we find it bruised, arid, almost bitter!

Brothers! There is but one solution, and it imposes itself upon us in a most pressing fashion. We must rebuild it and restore its former fertility, splendor, and beauty. This task is not beyond our powers. On the contrary, it is within our means.

Rebuilding Eretz Israel is a sacred duty which no one can evade or shirk.

Jews of Alexandria! We will give all—our money, our work, our health. Our people are sounding the supreme call, and we shall respond to it. We who are on the breach at the frontier of Zion, we perhaps feel more keenly than anywhere else the enormity of the task to be undertaken, but the more formidable the task, the greater will be our sacrifice!

NOTES

1. By 1920, the year in which this document was written, Zionism had been taken up as a cause by many Egyptian Jews. The Pro-Palestine Committee mentioned in the text was founded in 1918 by leading Sephardi families in Alexandria, Egypt; the Zeire Zion Society was an older organization founded by Ashkenazi immigrants. The document calls upon Jews to contribute financially toward the creation of a Jewish homeland and exclaims, "we shall know how to restore our land in order to live in it!"

2. In April 1920 the leaders of the Allied Powers of World War I met at San Remo, Italy. They assigned the mandates of the League of Nations, among them the British Mandate of Palestine, where a "Jewish homeland" would be established.

3. Hebrew for "deliverance."

28. IRAQI ZIONISTS COMPLAIN ABOUT THEIR LACK OF REPRESENTATION IN THE JEWISH AGENCY AND OF ASHKENAZI BIAS (1925)[1]

THE MESOPOTAMIAN ZIONIST COMMITTEE, BAGHDAD

28th Nisan.[2]

From: The Mesopotamian Zionist Committee, Baghdad

To: The Zionist Executive, London

We desire to inform you herewith that we have waited until today for your invitation to the Iraqi Jews, numbering about 150,000, to participate in the Jewish Agency, as you have invited other communities consisting of fewer Jews with whom the Zionist question is not of such political importance as it is with the Jews of Iraq, but we have waited in vain.[3]

We would therefore put the following questions to you:

Source: Norman Stillman, *The Jews of Arab Lands in Modern Times* (Philadelphia: Jewish Publication Society, 1991), pp. 340–41.

a. Is it your intention not to invite the Jews of our country to participate in the Jewish Agency to be composed at the 14th Congress?[4]

b. Is your attitude towards the Sephardim different than towards the Ashkenazim?

Is the article in [the Tel Aviv men's paper] *Haaretz* true that the Executive intends deferring the question of electing Sephardi representatives to the Agency until the general Sephardi Congress will be convened, when two delegates will be elected to the Jewish Agency? If that is so, then it is unjust and offensive, for the question of delegation to the Agency is not connected with the Sephardic Congress, which will not be convened for some years, and the nature of which is unknown.

We cannot refrain from making the following comment: If the Sephardim require a Congress in order to appoint representatives on the Jewish Agency, why should not the Ashkenazim require such a congress too? We therefore wish to say that unless you give us an affirmative reply and an opportunity is given to all Zionist and non-Zionist[5] institutions in Iraq to elect representatives as behooves our standing and the sacrifices we have made for Palestine during the last few years (such as [a] Ezra Sassoon,[6] [b] Elias Kadoorie, deceased,[7] [c] E.S. Kadoorie,[8] and last, [d] Ichezkal Gurgie Shem Tov.[9] It is offensive for us to hear from tourists returning from Palestine that Mr. Sacher[10] belittles the value of the bequest whereby the letter of the illustrious deceased will be refuted), we shall be compelled to sever our connections with the Zionist Organization and to work for Palestine independently.[11]

NOTES

1. Because Zionism was a movement initiated and directed by European Jews, the activity of Middle Eastern Jews was not always recognized or attended to by central Zionist bodies. In this document, Iraqi Zionists complain that they have not yet been granted participation in the Jewish Agency at the 14th Zionist Congress, which was to be held in Vienna in August 1925. The document highlights the sensitivity of the issue in that the Iraqis suspect not mere neglect but discrimination.

2. April 22, 1925.

3. A handwritten note at the top of this draft copy of the translation reads: "*Dr. Lauterbach. Nobody has yet been invited to join.*" (Leo Lauterbach was director of the Organization Department of the World Zionist Organization at the time.)

4. The 14th Zionist Congress was scheduled to meet in August of that year in Vienna.

5. The proposal to expand the Jewish Agency to include non-Zionists had been put forth at the Thirteenth Zionist Congress in Carlsbad in 1923. See Getzel Kressel, "Zionist Congresses: The Thirteenth Congress" Encyclopedia Judaica, 1st ed. EJ 16: 1172.

6. The reference is probably to Ezra Sasson Suheik's gift to the Jewish National Fund in the early 1920s.

7. Sir Ellis Kadoorie of Hong Kong (d. 1922). He left a bequest of 150,000 Palestinian pounds for the establishment of an educational institution in Palestine. The money was used to build two agricultural schools, one for Jews at Mount Tabor, the other for Arabs at Tul Karm. See Abraham Ben-Jacob, *Babylonian Jewry in Diaspora* (Jerusalem, 1985), pp. 382–83 [Heb.]; also Rudolph Loewenthal, "Kadoorie," EJ 10: 667–68.

8. Sir Elly Silas Kadoorie (1867–1944), brother of Sir Ellis. He was an ardent Zionist, was president of the Palestine Foundation Fund in Shanghai, and had contributed a substantial sum of money for the building of the Hebrew University. See Ben Jacob, *Babylonian Jewry in Diaspora*, pp. 378–82 [Heb.]; also Loewenthal, "Kadoorie," EJ 10; 667–68.

9. When this wealthy Zionist from Basra, Iraq, donated all his property, estimated at 140,000 pounds sterling, to the Jewish National Fund, the Zionist Organization in London did not even send him a letter of thanks until prodded by Dr. Ariel Bension. See Hayyim J. Cohen, *ha-Pe'ilut ha-Siyyonit be-'Iraq* (Jerusalem, 1969), p. 141.

10. Harry Sacher (1881–1971), a British lawyer and Zionist activist, who at that time lived in Jerusalem. See Getzel Kressel, "Sacher, Harry," EJ 14: 591–92.

11. This threat was never carried out.

29. DISAVOWAL OF ZIONISM AND PLEDGE OF LOYALTY TO THE ARAB CAUSE (1929)[1]

DAMASCUS JEWISH YOUTH ASSOCIATION

The Association of Jewish Youth has published on Tuesday in the city [of Damascus] as well as in the newspapers the following manifesto:

Certain journals having not distinguished sufficiently between Arab Jews and Zionists, we take this opportunity as Arab citizens from time immemorial to bring the following to the attention of our fellow citizens and Syrians:

The Jews of Syria have no connection with the Zionist question. On the contrary, they share with their Arab fellow citizens all their feelings of joy and sadness. Not long ago *al-Sha'ab* published an article signed by a Jew from Damascus repudiating Zionism and explaining that it was founded by the Jews in Northern Europe and the Jews of Damascus are totally estranged from it.

It is for this reason that we have come to declare by the present note to our Arab fellow citizens and to the members of the press our attitude vis-à-vis the Zionist question, and we ask them to differentiate between the European Zionists and the Jews who have been living for centuries in these lands.

We ask that the population and the press consider the Jews of Damascus to be Arabs sharing completely all of their sentiments in good times and in adversity.

NOTE

1. As in Europe, the association of some Jews with Zionism led to suspicions of disloyalty toward host nations. The issue was exacerbated in Arab lands on account of the Palestine question and the general sentiment of pan-Arabism, which did not have a precise counterpart in Europe. This document from Damascus relates a manifesto of the Association of Jewish Youth, which characterizes Zionism as a solely European-Jewish phenomenon and denounces participation in the movement. Noteworthy in the document is the use of the phrase "Arab Jews," which gained currency during the core years of Arab nationalism and allowed for a religion-neutral construction of Arabness.

Source: Norman Stillman, *The Jews of Arab Lands in Modern Times* (Philadelphia: Jewish Publication Society, 1991), p. 328.

30. AN IRAQI JEWISH NOTABLE EXPRESSES HIS RESERVATIONS ON ZIONISM (1922)

MENAHEM S. DANIEL[1]

Baghdad, 8th September 1922

The Secretary
Zionist Organization
London

Dear Sir,

I have the pleasure to acknowledge receipt of your letter of the 20th July 1922.

It is needless to say that I greatly appreciate and admire your noble ideal, and would have been glad to be able to contribute toward its realization.

But in this country the Zionist Movement is not an entirely idealistic subject. To the Jews, perhaps to a greater extent than to other elements, it represents a problem the various aspects of which need to be very carefully considered. Very peculiar considerations, with which none of the European Jewish Communities are confronted, force themselves upon us in this connection.

You are doubtless aware that, in all Arab countries, the Zionist Movement is regarded as a serious threat to Arab national life. If no active resistance has hitherto been opposed to it, is nonetheless the feeling of every Arab that it is a violation of his legitimate rights, which it is his duty to denounce and fight to the best of his ability. Mesopotamia has ever been, and is now still more, an active center of Arab culture and activity, and the public mind here is thoroughly stirred up as regards Palestine by an active propaganda. At present the feeling of hostility toward the Palestinian policy is more strong, as it is in some sort associated in the mind of the Arab with his internal difficulties in the political field, where his position is more or less critical. To him any sympathy with the Zionist Movement is nothing short of a betrayal of the Arab cause.

On the other hand the Jews in this country hold indeed a conspicuous position. They form one-third of the population of the Capital [Baghdad], hold the larger part of the commerce of the country, and offer a higher standard of literacy than the Moslems. In Baghdad the situation of the Jew is nearly an outstanding feature of the town, and though he has not yet learned to take full advantage of his position, he is nevertheless being regarded by Moslems as a very lucky person, from whom the country should expect [a] full return for its lavish favors. He is moreover beginning to give the Moslem an unpleasant experience of a successful competition in Government functions, which, having regard to the large number of unemployed former officials, may well risk to embitter feeling against him.

In this delicate situation the Jew cannot maintain himself unless he gives proof of an unimpeachable loyalty to his country, and avoids with care any action which may be misconstrued. This country is now trying to build up a future of its own, in which the Jew is expected to play a prominent part. The task will be of extreme difficulty and will need a strained effort on the part of every inhabitant. Any failing on the part of the Jew will be most detrimental to his future....

I hope you will fully understand the point of view which I have tried to set forth. I am the first to regret having to take it, because, I repeat, I have, on principle, great sympathy with your aims and warmly appreciate the devotion of your distinguished leaders of the Jewish cause. But you will realize that in practical policy the Jews of Mesopotamia are fatally bound

Source: Norman Stillman, *The Jews of Arab Lands in Modern Times* (Philadelphia: Jewish Publication Society, 1991), pp. 331–33.

to take for the time being a divergent course, if they are to have a sound understanding of their vital interests. I am not qualified to speak for them. The opinions expressed above are my own personal opinions. The community is unfortunately too helplessly disorganized to have any coordinate opinion, and that is indeed why it is the more exposed....

I again express to you my deepest regrets at being unable to respond to your call, and at the unfortunately difficulty of our position vis à vis your movement.

NOTE

1. Menahem Daniel (1846–1940) was a wealthy leader of Baghdadi Jewry who obtained a position in the Ottoman Parliament and later the Iraqi Parliament in 1924. In 1925, he was appointed representative of Iraqi Jewry in the Senate. In this document, Daniel firmly details his stance against Zionism. The letter demonstrates a strong commitment to the "Arab cause" and a wish to minimize friction with the Muslim population of Iraq. Zionist activity remained fairly subdued in Iraq throughout the 1920s and was officially outlawed in 1929.

31. EVENTS IN THE EAST AND THEIR REPERCUSSIONS ON THE JEWISH COMMUNITIES (1936)[1]

EZRA MENDA

Important events are now taking place in the Near East. Syria, following the example of Iraq, is claiming its right to independence, and the Syrians are hoping that the negotiations that have begun between the Syrian delegation and the French government will conclude in their favor.

I am anxiously wondering:

1. Would it not be more humane for the East to remain subject to the rule of a more civilized people rather than be given its freedom, considering its false conception of civilization and its often primitive instincts?
2. What will be Syria's attitude toward those who will [gain] this freedom?
3. What will then happen to the Jewish communities in Syria?

To give an accurate idea of the repercussions which the change of regime in Syria may have on the future of minorities in general, and of Eastern Jewry in particular, I will try to summarize the impressions, if not the judgments, that I have formed after many years in the East.

The upheaval of the Great War shook the entire world. The East in particular broke out of its lethargy and reclaimed its right to life, to that intense, agitated, and out-of-balance life left by the greatest catastrophe ever to befall humanity. This awakening of the East would have been a most fortunate thing had it been due to the positive forces of civilization—the arts, the sciences, morality, refinement of manners, unselfish ideals—in a word, had it been a kind of humanist renaissance analogous

Source: Aron Rodrigue, *Images of Sephardi and Middle Eastern Jewries in Transition: The Teachers of the Alliance Israélite Universelle, 1860–1939* (Seattle: University of Washington Press, 1993), pp. 279–84.

to the one that shook the Middle Ages [in Europe]. Unfortunately, it is the other side of civilization, that composed of pride, hatred, and national fanaticism, which brought the East out of its thousand-year sleep. If we must place part of the blame for this disastrous awakening on the guns of the Great War, we must still not forget that this monstrous seed could only have grown and flourished in the soil of the East, which has always been rich in hatred and religious fanaticism. Excited Arabs have never hesitated to kill in revenge for the slightest wrongs. Coupled with their sense of vengeance is a cowardice that leads them to attack only when they are certain of impunity. By nature both impulsive and naive, they are easily taken in and enthusiastically join in pillaging and massacring. Religious fanaticism has always been able to keep hatred strong in the Arabs; today's national fanaticism, much more dangerous, has succeeded in arousing and exacerbating that hatred. Today, whether they be believers or atheists, the Arabs have a new religion: nationalism, which translates to hatred of outsiders....

And will the Syrians be content with obtaining their independence? It is certain that they will not. They will have the desire, and will make an effort, to unite. They will seek to form that Arab empire modeled after the Third Reich, the only form of government appropriate for a people in the habit of servitude and permeated with fanaticism. To Arab eyes, Hitler represents the model most in keeping with their ideas. How many swastikas are carved into the desks in secondary schools in Iraq and in the hearts of the young people in school; how much more deeply is Hitler's ideal engraved. This ideal is one of pure hatred: a hatred of Jews, to which is joined a hatred of the colonizers....

What makes the future of the Syrian Jews look even darker is that they have emigrated to Palestine in great numbers. More than a thousand Jews from Aleppo have left over the course of this past year. Many Jewish families in Syria have relatives in Palestine and they will not be forgiven this crime.

The Syrian Arabs thus have serious reason for reproaching the Syrian Jews concerning their Zionism, and for considering them partly responsible for the fate of the Arabs in Palestine....

France is anxious to resolve the Syrian question for the present, but the French must certainly envisage the possibility of Syrian betrayal. They will probably grant independence to Syria, but they must not fail in their eternal and noble duty to protect the weak. The French must not abandon the minorities, who are living in torment and who dearly love France. They must require that Syria make serious guarantees for the protection of its minorities. The presence of *the French army is the only effective guarantee.*

Without French protection, the future of Syrian minorities appears bleak. The Jews especially have the most to fear from this eventuality. In the profound hatred for Zionism shared by the Arabs, the Jew and the Zionist have become fused. The first thing the free and strong Arabs will fight is Zionism, which stands in the way of pan-Arabism. Will the new leaders of a fully independent Syria be equal to the task? Will they be able to neutralize the virus of a new Arab antisemitism and to protect the Jewish communities from the probable persecutions and massacres? Will they be able to find a solution to the economic crisis in a rather poor country? Will they be able to put a stop to the fanatic excesses of the unbridled masses, drunk with their independence?

NOTE

1. The fervor of nationalism that swelled in Arab lands as indigenous populations sought to remove the yoke of colonialism was experienced by Jews in various ways ranging from an embrace of Arab nationalism to fear of what awaits them in the wake of the withdrawal of the European powers from their Middle Eastern mandates. The author of the present document (penned in Aleppo, Syria, on June 9, 1936), Ezra Menda, was extremely apprehensive of the nationalist wave in Syria and perceived a parallel between Syrian nationalism and the Nazi Third Reich that he believed would lead to Jewish exclusion and persecution. The tensions between Jewish and non-Jewish Syrians were greatly compounded by the situation in Palestine, considered by many to be a province of Syria. The author calls for a continued French military presence in Syria to safeguard the welfare of "minorities, who are sitting in torment and dearly love France."

32. THE REPORT OF THE IRAQI COMMISSION OF INQUIRY ON THE *FARHUD* (1941)[1]

The Iraqi Government
Committee for the Investigation of
the Events of June 1 and 2, 1941

In accordance with the resolution of the Council of Ministers issued on June 6,1941, no. 3288, the committee presided over by Mr. Muhammad Tawfiq al-Na'ib and whose members were Mr. 'Abd Allah al-Qassab, representing the Interior Ministry, and Mr. Sa 'di Salih, representing the Ministry of Finance, met in twelve sessions to investigate the events that took place on June 1 and 2,1941. On the basis of the evidence brought before it, it concluded the following:

SUMMARY OF THE AFFAIR

On June 1,1941, it was announced to the public that His Exalted Highness[2] was officially returning, and people rushed to greet him. Some Jewish individuals also went out happy and rejoicing on account of the advent of the Feast of Nabi Shu'a[3] and on account of the easing of the emergency that had resulted from the armed conflict.[4] When they reached the Khurr Bridge,[5] they encountered some soldiers. The latter, seeing them in this state, were not pleased, and their resentment was stirred up. They showered them with blows, punches, and stabbed them with knives. Whoever could, fled. Those who could not were wounded. The soldiers were joined in this incident by some civilians. This assault took place while the civil and military police looked on. Afterward, the police took the wounded and transported them to the central police station in al-Karkh.[6] The number of wounded came to sixteen individuals, and one person was killed. They were sent to the hospital.

A great mob of people gathered in front of the hospital wanting to murder the Jewish medics and nurses. The hospital director, Mr. Jamil Dallali, went out to them and pleaded with them to disperse. But they demanded that he hand over to them the Jewish men and women. When he replied that the women were servants of humanity, they demanded the men, particularly the Jew Heskel, the medic. So the director promised them, but went to tell the police. Then a detachment of the mobile force appeared and broke up that crowd, arresting a number of individuals among them. No investigation was conducted at that time against the soldiers and civilians who had taken part in the assault. News of this spread—as was only natural—among the various social classes, and those with evil in their hearts. Another assault took place in the Rusafa area,[7] where the body of a murder victim was sighted on the pavement of Ghazi Street,[8] near the cinema. The police were informed, and the precinct officer arrived on the scene and found that it was the body of a Jew and that the murderer was unknown. At this time, an injured Jew came, fell down, and died immediately before telling who had killed him. At the same time, word reached the police about a number of murder victims found in the Abu Sayfayn district.[9] So they went and collected the corpses, whose number was eight. It turned out that the perpetrators were individual soldiers who had been joined by civilians....

On the second day, June 2, 1941, at 6:00 A.M., some soldiers began looting, pillaging, and breaking down doors. A military vehicle was seen in al-Amin Street carrying household furniture from Jewish homes....

The total number killed, according to the view expressed in the report of the Investigating Judge,[10] was 110 Jews and Muslims, including 28 women. Many of the victims have not been identified. Two

Source: Norman Stillman, *The Jews of Arab Lands in Modern Times* (Philadelphia: Jewish Publication Society, 1991), pp. 405–17.

hundred four were injured, likewise both Jews and Muslims. The President of the Jewish Community claims that the number of killed and wounded is greater than that.[11]

As to the number of houses looted, no statistics have been made available by the police, even though this committee did request lists of the numbers of looted homes and businesses from the various police stations, but received no reply. The committee concluded that the police did not undertake any accounting. The President of the Jewish Community claims that 586 shops and warehouses were sacked completely and that the value of what was taken came to a total of 271,301 dinars.[12] He claims that 911 houses were looted in which were living 3,395 families, totaling 12,311 souls. This committee doubts the accuracy of these figures since they are not based upon fact. If the government wishes to know with accuracy the extent of the losses, it must form a special committee for that purpose. There were no complaints concerning the outrages against the chastity of families. However, the President of the Jewish Community claims that there were three or four such incidents.

THOSE RESPONSIBLE FOR THE DISORDERS

It is evident from what has been stated above that the disorders started directly with some soldiers who were joined by civilians. This progression of events could have been stopped if the Department of Military Discipline had arrested them on the first day in al-Karkh and held them in check, and if they had deployed their men (the Military Police) to prevent the incidents from reoccurring....

Likewise, had the civil police acted with resolve and done its duty to preserve public safety and prevent danger by arresting those soldiers and civilians who were committing the very first acts of aggression in al-Karkh (since arresting soldiers openly observed in the act of committing crimes is the police's duty)—it would have quashed the movement on the spot and prevented it from spreading to al-Rusafa. Regrettably, however, the police stood by in the role of onlooker....

CAUSES OF THE RIOTS

It is clear to this committee on the basis of the investigations that it conducted that the primary causes

underlying these riots were Nazi propaganda as will be explained in detail below:

1. The German Legation: The German Legation had been spreading Nazi propaganda over a long period of time. It disseminated it among army officers by various ways and means. It employed beautiful and lissome German female agents to advocate this propaganda among the officers and young men, to win their hearts, and to channel their feelings in the direction they intended....

When Germany declared war on England, the Iraqi government broke off relations with it, but not with its ally Italy, which took over the operations of the German Legation. Banco de Roma took over the dispensing of necessary funds to those whom Germany designated. Thus German propaganda activities never ceased within Iraq's borders, but rather continued to inject its venom with all levels of the army and civilian society in the widest fashion....

2. The Mufti of Jerusalem Amin al-Husayni[13] and his entourage which accompanied him to Iraq: This man was received by Iraq with tremendous enthusiasm and he took full advantage of the situation. Once he was firmly established, he began disseminating Nazi propaganda with great cunning, while decrying the injustice done to Palestine and under the guise of Pan-Arabism and the Islamic religion.

NOTES

1. Anti-Jewish activity sharply increased in Iraq circa 1940 with the influx of Nazi propaganda and a coup that overthrew the pro-British government, briefly establishing the regime of Rashid Ali al-Ghaylani in its place. Jews were suspected of harboring pro-British sentiment. The short period of al-Ghaylani's government (only two months) witnessed the significant harassment of the Jewish population. When British troops approached Baghdad in May 1941, Ghaylani and some of his closest associates fled, leaving Yunis al-Sabawi (an economics minister) behind as military governor. Anti-Jewish sentiment erupted into violence and looting over two days in Baghdad in an event known as the *Farhud* (Arabic: "pogrom" "violent dispossession"), which left 179 dead. The present document is the report of the Iraqi Commission established in order to investigate the events of the *Farhud*.

2. The regent 'Abd al-Ilah, who had just returned from exile.

3. The Arabs gave this name to Shavu'ot because many Jews were accustomed to making pilgrimages to the

tomb of Joshua the High Priest (Arabic: Nabi Shu'a) at this time. The tomb was located in the western part of the city, where this attack took place.

4. That is, between the invading British troops and the Iraqi army.

5. The bridge over the Khurr River, which runs through the western portion of the city.

6. The name given to the western portion of the city on the right bank of the Euphrates.

7. The eastern half of the city on the left bank of the Euphrates, where the principal Jewish neighborhoods were located.

8. One of the main streets in Rusafa. Part of Ghazi Street cut through the Jewish Quarter. (The name of the street today is Kifah Street.)

9. A Jewish neighborhood on the eastern edge of the Jewish Quarter that bordered upon Muslim sections of town.

10. Chief Justice Ma'rif Dayyawuq, who headed a separate governmental commission appointed to recommend ways to rehabilitate those who had suffered losses in the disturbances.

11. For its own reasons, the government wanted the casualty figures to be kept down. See 'Abd al-Razzaq al-Hasani, *Ta'rikh al-Wizarat al-'Iraqiyya*, vol. 5 (Sidon, 1953), p. 234, n. 1; and Elie Kedourie, *Arabic Political Memoirs and Other Studies* (London, 1974), p. 298.

12. The Iraqi dinar was more or less equivalent to the pound sterling at that time.

13. Mohammad Amin al-Husayni (c. 1895–1974) served from 1921 to 1948 as the Grand Mufti of Jerusalem. An inveterate opponent of Zionist settlement in Palestine, he forged an alliance with Adolf Hitler and Nazi Germany.

33. ABROGATION OF THE CRÉMIEUX DECREE BY THE VICHY REGIME (1940)[1]

We, Marshall of France, Chief of the French State, with the understanding of the Council of Ministers, decree:

Article 1.—The decree of the Government of National Defense of 24 October 1870[2] regulating the political rights of the Jewish natives of the departments of Algeria and declaring them French citizens is abrogated.

Article 2.—The political rights of the Jewish natives of the departments of Algeria are regulated by the texts defining the political rights of the native Algerian Muslims.

Article 3.—Regarding their civil rights, the civil and personal status of the native Jews of the departments of Algeria continues to be governed by French law.

Article 4.—Those Jewish natives of the departments of Algeria, who have belonged to a combat unit during the war of 1914–1918 or of 1939–1940, and who attained a military Legion of Honor, the Military Medal, or the Croix de Guerre, retain the political status of French citizens.

Article 5.—This status[3] may be retained by a decree countersigned by the Keeper of Seals, the Ministerial Secretary of State for Justice, and the Ministerial Secretary of State for the Interior, by native Jews of the departments of Algeria who have distinguished themselves through services rendered to the country.

Source: Norman Stillman, *The Jews of Arab Lands in Modern Times* (Philadelphia Jewish Publication Society, 1991), p.426.

Article 6.—The present law is applicable to all the beneficiaries of the decree of 24 October 1870 and to their descendants.

Article 7.—The present decree will be published in the *Journal Officiel* and executed as the law of the State.

Done at Vichy, 7 October 1940.[4]

Ph. PÉTAIN

By the Marshal of France,Chief of the French State
The Keeper of Seals,
Ministerial Secretary of State for Justice
Raphaël ALIBERT
The Ministerial Secretary of State for the Interior
Marcel PEYROUTON

NOTES

1. Not long after the fall of France to Germany, the Vichy government extended the racial laws to Jews across North Africa. The transformation in status was most severe in the case of Algerian Jews, who, since the establishment of the Cremieux Decree in 1870, had enjoyed French citizenship.
2. That is, the Crémieux Decree. See document 2, this chapter.
3. Of French citizenship.
4. The final regulation with certain adjustments of this decree was made by Law no. 252 of February 18, 1942, the text of which is published in Michel Abitbol *Les Juifs d'Afrique du Nord sous Vichy* (Paris, 1983), p. 183, Annexe 1.

34. A VICHY OFFICIAL DISCUSSES A GERMAN PROPOSAL TO REQUIRE JEWS TO WEAR THE YELLOW STAR IN TUNIS (1943)[1]

Residency-General of France
at Tunis
and
Secretariat-General of the
Tunisian Government
Office of Judicial and Legislative Affairs

Tunis, March 20, 1943

From the Chief Appeals Attorney
of the Council of State,
Judicial and Legislative Counselor
to the Tunisian Government
to
Admiral Esteva
Resident General of France at Tunis

SUBJECT: Wearing of the yellow star by Jews.

As per his letter of March 17, 1943, the Prefect for General Security has informed you that Colonel Rauff, Chief of the German Police, has advised him that it would be appropriate for the Jews of Tunisia to be required to wear the yellow star, and he has charged him to ask you to make a decision in this regard which would be submitted beforehand for General Von Arnim's approval. He added that the Italian Jews would be subject to a special measure on the part of the German High Command.[2] ...

We have therefore proposed the following preliminary draft of a police ordinance:

The Prefect for General Security of Tunisia

In accordance with the Beylical Decree of October 30, 1941, determining the powers of the Prefect for the General Security of Tunisia, and

---

Source: Norman Stillman, *The Jews of Arab Lands in Modern Times* (Philadelphia: Jewish Publication Society, 1991), pp. 440–42.

In accordance with the Beylical Decree of March 12, 1942, concerning the status of the Jews,

Issues the following ordinance:

Article 1.—In all of the territory of the Regency, all persons of either sex considered Jews under Article 2 of the decree of March 12, 1942, will be obliged as of the age of eighteen to wear a yellow badge representing a six-pointed star.

This badge will be made of lemon yellow fabric and should be 5 cm in diameter. It must be firmly sewn along all its points in the manner that escutcheons are attached to garments on the left side of the chest, and it is to be clearly visible.

Article 2.—Contraventions of the present ordinance will be pursued in conformity with the laws in force. Furthermore, contraventions will be subject to administrative internment.

Article 3.—The police force and the gendarmerie will be charged with the application of the present ordinance, which will go into effect on April 1, 1943.[3]

With regard to the age from which the wearing of the yellow star will be mandatory, it seems to us at the minimum, the age of eighteen should be chosen, after which Jewish workers are required. This will avoid the badge being worn in schools, even secondary schools, where it would present certain inconveniences....

It is up to the German military police to take any special measures that it judges necessary with regard to the Italian Jews. However, in our own opinion, the Protectorate authorities would not be able to make any distinctions according to nationality without violating the decree of March 12, 1942, on Jewish status.

Finally, a certain delay, at least until the end of the month, will be necessary so that those concerned would be able to produce the badges.

(signed) De Font Reaux[4]

NOTES

1. On the history of the Jewish badge, see B. Blumenkranz and B. Ansbacher, "Badge, Jewish," *Encyclopedia Judaica*, 2nd ed. (Detroit: MacMillan Reference USA, 2007), Vol. 3, pp. 45–48.
2. The Germans were constrained to do this by their Italian allies.
3. The ordinance, however, did not go into effect in Tunis.
4. According to Jacques Sabille, *Les Juifs de Tunisie sous Vichy et l'occupation* (Paris, 1954), p. 128, he was "a convinced antisemite, who collaborated with the representatives of the CGQJ [Bureau for Jewish Affairs] at Tunis." Despite their own antisemitism, Vichy officials were becoming more resistant at this time to going along with the Germans on further anti-Jewish measures for reasons discussed by Michael R. Marrus and Robert O. Paxton, *Vichy France and the Jews* (New York: Basic Books, 1981), pp. 326–27.

35. A NEW YEAR'S SERMON (1942)

MOISE VENTURA[1]

After the lamentable failure of Western civilization, the Orient is again called upon to play an important part in the cultural life of Nations. The Orient means Egypt, Palestine, Syria, Iraq; more specifically, the Semites—Jews and Arabs—are again called upon together to play a vital role within the scene of history. Everyone whose mental capacities are in free working order must recognize that today the enemies of the Jews are as well the enemies of the Arabs—that is, the enemies of civilization.

NOTE

1. Moise Ventura (1893–1978) was born in Smyrna, Turkey, and studied at the rabbinical seminary in Istanbul and at the University of Paris. He served as chief rabbi in Alexandria, Egypt (1938–48) and lectured at Yeshiva College, New York (1951–53). Before he settled in Israel in 1955, he also directed Montefiore College, Ramsgate, England. His publications, all in French, deal mainly with medieval Jewish philosophy (books on Saadia Gaon, the logical terminology of Maimonides, a critical translation of Halevi's *Kuzari*, and so forth). Many of Ventura's more presentist sermons are also preserved. This selection, taken from a New Year's sermon of 1942, expresses disillusionment with Europe and hope for a continued civilization in the Orient through the cooperation of Jews and Arabs.

Source: Ammiel Alcalay, "Intellectual Cultural," in *The Jews of the Middle East and North Africa in Modern Times*, Reeva Spector Simon, Michael M. Laskier, and Sara Regeur, eds. (New York: Columbia University Press, 2003), p. 97.

36. THE IRAQI LAW PERMITTING JEWS TO EMIGRATE WITH THE FORFEITURE OF NATIONALITY (1950)[1]

ARTICLE 1

The Council of Ministers is empowered to divest any Iraqi Jew who, of his own free will and choice, desires to leave Iraq for good, of his Iraqi nationality after he has signed a special form in the presence of an official appointed by the Minister of the Interior.

ARTICLE 2

Any Iraqi Jew who leaves Iraq or tries to leave Iraq illegally will forfeit his Iraqi nationality by decision of the Council of Ministers.

ARTICLE 3

Any Iraqi Jew who has already left Iraq illegally will be considered to have left Iraq for good if he does not return within a period of two months from the date of the putting in operation of this law, and he will lose his Iraqi nationality at the end of that period.

ARTICLE 4

The Minister of the Interior must order the deportation of anyone who has lost Iraqi nationality under Articles 1 and 2 unless the Minister is convinced by sufficient reasons that his temporary stay in Iraq is necessary for judicial or legal reasons, or to safeguard someone else's officially testified rights.

ARTICLE 5

This law will remain in force for a period of one year from the date of its coming into effect and may be canceled at any time during that period by a Royal Iradah[2] published in the *Official Gazette*.

ARTICLE 6

This law comes into force from the date of its publication in the *Official Gazette*.

ARTICLE 7

The Minister of the Interior will execute this law.

SUPPORTING AGREEMENTS

It has been noticed that some Iraqi Jews are attempting by every illegal means to leave Iraq for good and that others have already left Iraq illegally. As the presence of subjects of this description forced to stay in the country and obliged to keep their Iraqi nationality would inevitably lead to results affecting public security and give rise to social and economic problems, it has been found advisable not to prevent those wishing to do so from leaving Iraq for good, forfeiting their Iraqi nationality. This law has been promulgated to this end.

NOTES

1. Jewish security was greatly compromised throughout the Middle East following the conclusion of World War II with the issue of Palestine at the core of the tension. Even before the establishment of the State of Israel, anti-Jewish violence erupted in various degrees in Egypt, Libya, and Syria. The Partition plan of 1947 and the establishment of the Jewish state in 1948 made the Jewish presence in Arab countries all but untenable. Violent outbursts were not uncommon and discriminatory legislation was instituted in several places. During the war of 1948, a number of Jews were held in prisons and internment camps, and anti-Jewish violence increased. Prior to the establishment of a law allowing for Jewish emigration out of Iraq, a number of Jews had attempted to leave clandestinely. Those who chose to remain were promised status equal to that of Muslim and Christian Iraqis. By 1953, nearly 90 percent of Iraqi Jewry had emigrated.
2. Arabic: *irada* (decree).

Source: Norman Stillman, *The Jews of Arab Lands in Modern Times* (Philadelphia: Jewish Publication Society, 1991), pp. 525–26.

IX

AMERICAN JEWRY

The Jews of the United States were never legally emancipated. They already enjoyed a large measure of legal equality under the British colonial government (see the Plantation Act of 1740, chapter 1, document 6). In light of the founding ideals of the United States—especially that of the inalienable equality of all human beings and of the absolute separation of church and state—the granting of citizenship to the Jews, along with other (white) minorities of the land, was self-evident and was, in contrast to Europe, never a matter of special legislation. From its very inception religious and ethnic pluralism in the United States, although occasionally challenged, was firmly secured in its Constitution and abiding ethos.

The nation thus became a haven for the dissenters and the persecuted minorities of Europe. Significantly, the inspired poem that graces the Statue of Liberty—"Give me your tired, your poor, your huddled masses yearning to breathe free ..."—was written by a Jewish poet, Emma Lazarus (1849–1887). Lazarus was a descendant of the so-called first wave of Jewish immigration to America, a group of predominantly Spanish-Portuguese Jews who began to arrive on the shores of America in the 1650s (see document 1, this chapter). From 1840 to 1880 large numbers of Jews from German-speaking lands arrived, appreciably augmenting the Jewish population of the United States. From only 4,000 in 1820 the Jewish population increased to about 50,000 in the 1840s and to approximately 280,000 in the 1880s. The largest immigration of Jews, however, came in the period from 1880 to the outbreak of World War I in 1914. Prompted by the pogroms and the increasingly repressive conditions in their native lands, more than two million Russian and other East European Jews left for the United States. In 1914 the Jewish population of the United States had reached three million.

With an expanding industrial, urban economy, America was a land of opportunity, *a goldene medine* (a golden country) as one says in Yiddish. But the immigrants encountered many difficulties, not the least of which was antisemitism. It is crucial to note that the antagonism toward the Jew in America remained largely social in character and that—given America's multi-ethnic character—the Jews were not the only object of discrimination. The blacks, the Catholics, the Irish, the Chinese and others were often, at different times and places, the major focus of group hostility. To be sure, American antisemitism was exacerbated by the influx of large numbers of Jews who represented an alien culture and who were concentrated in the centers of socio-economic stress, that is, the large cities. Nonetheless, with few exceptions the hostility never truly became, as it did in Europe, the focus of a political and ideological struggle. America's strong tradition, indeed, ethos of tolerance and pluralism, confined antisemitism to the social sphere.

Each wave of Jewish immigration developed institutions and patterns of Jewish life that have become distinctive to American Jewry. The German Jews, for instance, founded many of the major national Jewish organizations for charity, mutual aid, and welfare, among them the Bnai Brith (1843), the Young Men's Hebrew Association (1854), and the American Jewish Committee (1906). The German Jews also helped establish Jewish religious denominationalism, which had already begun to emerge in Europe but which crystallized in the more tolerant and innovative United States. Reform Judaism, for instance, was more radical in the United States than it was in its native Germany. Similarly, Conservative Judaism, derivative of Zecharias Frankel's Historical School of Judaism, first took shape in America. Immigrants who arrived after the turn of the century adopted these religious institutions, but they added a vigorous form of "Americanized" Orthodoxy and the Reconstructionism of Mordecai M. Kaplan to the denominational pattern. The East European immigrants also brought with them socialism and various other secular Jewish ideologies, for example, Zionism and Yiddishism, which they sought to implant in America. They established a vital ethnic-national Jewish culture based on these ideologies. This orientation contrasted sharply with the purely confessional and philanthropic Judaism of the older community. At first, these differences engendered considerable conflict between the newer, "ethnic" community and the older, "assimilated" community of Jews. In time, the contrast between the two communities of Jews decreased and they adjusted their institutions and conceptions of Judaism to accommodate one another. Zionism, with its unambiguous affirmation of Jewish nationality, became a touchstone of the older community's accommodation to Jewish ethnicity. Rabbi Judah L. Magnes's sermon, entitled "A Republic of Nationalities," illustrates this adjustment (see document 38). The rabbi's topic was the complementary nature of Americanism and ethnic solidarity, or Jewish national consciousness; the sermon was delivered in 1909 before Temple Emanu-El of New York City, one of America's oldest Reform congregations. Magnes, like Israel Friedlaender, Solomon Schechter, and Mordecai M. Kaplan, used the term *Jewish national consciousness* to express the idea of solidarity with and philanthropic support for one's fellow Jews, in whatever country they may reside. Jewish solidarity so conceived does not contradict allegiance to America. For America's pluralism, this school of thought held, is not only religious but also ethnic, and hence ethnic affections and solidarity are not inimical to American citizenship and patriotism. In a lecture entitled "The Jewish Problem: How to Solve It" given in 1915, Louis D. Brandeis (Supreme Court Justice from 1916 to 1939) summarized this viewpoint when he affirmed that "loyalty to America demands that every Jew become a Zionist" (see document 39 in this chapter). Here ethnic solidarity is extended to include support for those Jews who sought to construct a secure future for themselves in their ancestral homeland, the land of Israel. This pro-Zionism, later pro-Israelism, eventually became the factor that bound, some would say defined, most of American Jewry. It was endorsed, so to speak, in the 1950 agreement between Jacob Blaustein, president of the American Jewish Committee, and David Ben-Gurion, premier of the State of Israel (see document 51 in this chapter).

1. PETITION TO EXPEL THE JEWS FROM NEW AMSTERDAM (SEPTEMBER 22, 1654)

PETER STUYVESANT[1]

The Jews who have arrived would nearly all like to remain here, but learning that they (with their customary usury and deceitful trading with the Christians) were very repugnant to the inferior magistrates,[2] as also to the people having the most affection for you; the Deaconry also fearing that owing to their present indigence they might become a charge in the coming winter, we have, for the benefit of this weak and newly developing place and the land in general, deemed it useful to require them in a friendly way to depart; praying also most seriously in this connection, for ourselves as also for the general community of your worships, that the deceitful race—such hateful enemies and blasphemers of the name of Christ—be not allowed to further infect and trouble this new colony to the detraction of your worships and the dissatisfaction of your worships' most affectionate subjects.

NOTES

1. Peter Stuyvesant (1592?–1672). In May 1645 Stuyvesant was selected by the Dutch West India Company as director of New Netherland; he arrived in New Amsterdam (i.e., New York) on May 11, 1647. A man of autocratic inclinations, he was nonetheless an obedient servant to his employer, the Dutch West India Company, established by the Estates General of the Netherlands as a public company in June 1621. The purpose of the company was to regulate and protect the contraband trade already carried on by the Dutch in the American and African possessions of Spain and Portugal and to establish colonies on both continents and their islands. By the terms of its charter the company was composed of five boards or chambers, established in Amsterdam, Zeeland, Rotterdam, Friesland and Groningen. The general board was endowed with power to negotiate treaties and to make war and peace with native rulers; to appoint its officials, generals, and governors; and to legislate in its possessions subject to the laws of the Netherlands.

   In September 1654, some twenty-three Jewish refugees are said to have arrived in New Amsterdam, after fleeing from Recife, Brazil, where the Portuguese had recaptured several colonies from the Netherlands. (There is some question as to the exact number of refugees.) Although Dutch subjects, these Jewish refugees met with unexpected hostility from Stuyvesant, the governor of New Netherland. Stuyvesant immediately wrote the letter presented here to the directors of the West India Company, requesting permission to bar Jews from the colony.

2. I.e., the sheriff, mayors, and aldermen, who constituted the Inferior Court of Justice of the colony.

Source: Peter Stuyvesant to the Directors of the Amsterdam Chamber of the Dutch West India Company, in Samuel Oppenheim, "The Early History of the Jews in New York, 1654–1664," *Publications of the American Jewish Historical Society* 18 (1909), pp. 4–5. Reprinted by permission of the American Jewish Historical Society.

2. REPLY TO STUYVESANT'S PETITION (APRIL 26, 1655)[1]

DUTCH WEST INDIA COMPANY

We would have liked to effectuate and fulfill your wishes and request that the new territories should no more be allowed to be infected by people of the Jewish nation, for we foresee therefrom the same difficulties which you fear, but after having further weighed and considered the matter, we observe that this would be somewhat unreasonable and unfair, especially because of the considerable loss sustained by this nation, with others, in the taking of Brazil, as also because of the large amount of capital which they still have invested in the shares of this company. Therefore after many deliberations we have finally decided and resolved to apostille [note] upon a certain petition presented by said Portuguese Jews that these people may travel and trade to and in New Netherland and live and remain there, provided the poor among them shall not become a burden to the company or to the community, but be supported by their own nation. You will now govern yourself accordingly.

NOTE

1. Three overriding factors seemed to induce the Amsterdam Chamber to reject Stuyvesant's petition to bar Jews from settling in New Amsterdam: the vigorous intercession on the part of Amsterdam Jewry, some of whom had substantial investments in the Dutch West India Company; an appreciation of the loyalty of the Jews in Brazil; and the imperatives of mercantilism.

Source: Reply of the Amsterdam Chamber of the West Indian Company to Peter Stuyvesant, in Samuel Oppenheim, "The Early History of the Jews in New York, 1654–1664," *Publications of the American Jewish Historical Society* 18 (1909), p. 8. Reprinted by permission of the American Jewish Historical Society.

3. RIGHTS OF THE JEWS OF NEW AMSTERDAM (MARCH 13, 1656)[1]

DUTCH WEST INDIA COMPANY

The consent given to the Jews to go to New Netherland and there to enjoy the same liberty that is granted them in this country was extended with respect to civil and political liberties, without the said Jews becoming thereby entitled to a license to exercise and carry on their religion in synagogues or gatherings. So long, therefore, as no request is presented to you [Stuyvesant] to allow such a free exercise of religion, any consideration relative thereto is too premature, and when later something shall be presented about it you will be doing well to refer the matter to us in order to await thereon the necessary orders.

NOTE

1. This letter was in reply to a letter by Stuyvesant dated October 30, 1655, in which he argued that "to give liberty to the Jews [of New Amsterdam] will be very detrimental, because the Christians there will not be able at the same time to do business. [Moreover], by giving them liberty we cannot refuse the Lutherans and the Papists" (cited in Samuel Oppenheim, "The Early History of the Jews in New York, 1654–1664," *Publications of the American Jewish Historical Society* 18 [1909], p. 20). In a reply to the letter given in this document, dated June 10, 1656, Stuyvesant stated: "[Jews] are not hindered, but trade with the same privilege and freedom as other inhabitants. Also, they have many times requested of us the free and public exercise of their abominable religion, but this cannot yet be accorded to them. What they may be able to obtain from your Honors time will tell."

Source: The Amsterdam Chamber of the West India Company to Peter Stuyvesant, in Samuel Oppenheim, "The Early History of the Jews in New York, 1654–1664," *Publications of the American Jewish Historical Society* 18 (1909), p. 21. Reprinted by permission of the American Jewish Historical Society.

4. THE DECLARATION OF INDEPENDENCE
(JULY 4, 1776)[1]

The unanimous declaration of the thirteen United States of America:

When, in the course of human events, it becomes necessary for one people to dissolve the political bands which have connected them with another, and to assume among the powers of the earth the separate and equal station to which the laws of nature and of nature's God entitle them, a decent respect to the opinions of mankind requires that they should declare the causes which impel them to the separation.

We hold these truths to be self-evident, that all men are created equal, that they are endowed by their Creator with certain unalienable rights, that among these are life, liberty, and the pursuit of happiness. That to secure these rights, governments are instituted among men, deriving their just powers from the consent of the governed. That whenever any form of government becomes destructive of these ends, it is the right of the people to alter or to abolish it, and to institute new government, laying its foundation on such principles and organizing its powers in such form, as to them shall seem most likely to effect their safety and happiness....

We, therefore, the representatives of the United States of America, in general congress assembled, appealing to the Supreme Judge of the world for the rectitude of our intentions, do, in the name, and by authority of the good people of these colonies, solemnly publish and declare, that these united colonies are, and of right ought to be free and independent states; that they are absolved from all allegiance to the British Crown, and that all political connection between them and the state of Great Britain is and ought to be totally dissolved: and that as free and independent states they have full power to levy war, conclude peace, contract alliances, establish commerce, and to do all other acts and things which independent states may of right do. And for the support of this declaration, with a firm reliance on the protection of Divine Providence, we mutually pledge to each other our lives, our fortunes, and our sacred honor....

NOTE

1. Declaration by which the thirteen original colonies broke their allegiance to Great Britain. Its justificatory preamble, presented here, contains idealistic principles largely based on Locke's theory of natural right. The principles of the Declaration were equivalent to a statement of intent. Indeed, although translated into law on the federal level in the Constitution of 1787, New Hampshire extended the right to hold elective public office to non-Protestants only in 1877.

Source: Francis Newton Thorpe, *The Federal and State Constitutions* (Washington, D.C., 1909), vol. 5, pp. 2636–37.

5. THE VIRGINIA ACT OF 1785[1]
(DECEMBER 16, 1785)

The General Assembly, on the sixteenth day of December, seventeen hundred and eighty-five, passed an act in the words following, to wit:

Whereas, Almighty God has created the mind free; that all attempts to influence it by temporal punishment, or burthens [burdens] or by civil incapacitations, tend only to beget habits of hypocrisy and meanness, and are a departure from the plan of the Holy Author of our religion, who, being Lord both of body and mind, yet chose not to propagate it by coercions on either, as was in his Almighty power to do; that the impious presumption of legislators and rulers, civil as well as ecclesiastical, who being themselves but fallible and uninspired men, have assumed dominion over the faith of others, setting up their own opinions and modes of thinking as the only true and infallible, and as such endeavoring to impose them on others, have established and maintained false religions over the greatest part of the world, and through all time, that to compel a man to furnish contributions of money for the propagation of opinions which he disbelieves, is sinful and tyrannical, and even the forcing him to support this or that teacher of his own religious persuasion, is depriving him of the comfortable liberty of giving his contributions to the particular pastor whose morals he would make his pattern, and whose powers he feels most persuasive to righteousness, and is withdrawing from the ministry those temporary rewards which, proceeding from an approbation of their personal conduct, are an additional incitement to earnest and unremitting labors, for the instruction of mankind; that our civil rights have no dependence on our religious opinions any more than our opinions in physics or geometry; that therefore the proscribing any citizen as unworthy the public confidence by laying upon him an incapacity of being called to offices of trust and emolument, unless he profess or renounce this or that religious opinion, is depriving him injuriously of those privileges and advantages to which, in common with his fellow-citizens, he has a natural right; that it tends only to corrupt the principles of that religion it is meant to encourage, by bribing, with a monopoly of worldly honors and emoluments, those who will externally profess and conform to it; that though, indeed, those are criminal who do not withstand such temptation, yet neither are those innocent who lay the bait in their way; that to suffer the civil magistrate to intrude his powers into the field of opinion, and to restrain the profession or propagation of principles on supposition of their ill tendency, is a dangerous fallacy, which at once destroys all religious liberty, because he, being of course judge of that tendency, will make his opinions the rule of judgment, and approve or condemn the sentiments of others only as they shall square with or differ from his own; that it is time enough for the rightful purposes of civil government, for its officers to interfere, when principles break out into overt acts against peace and good order; and finally, that truth is great and will prevail, if left to herself; that she is the proper and sufficient antagonist to error, and has nothing to fear from the conflict, unless by human interposition disarmed of her natural weapons, free argument and debate; errors ceasing to be dangerous when it is permitted freely to contradict them:

Be it enacted by the General Assembly, That no man shall be compelled to frequent or support any religious worship, place or ministry whatsoever, nor shall be enforced, restrained, molested or burthened, in his body or goods, nor shall otherwise suffer on account of his religious opinions or belief; but that all men shall be free to profess, and by argument to

Source: Bill for Establishing Religious Freedom, *Code of Virginia* (Richmond, Virginia, 1904), vol. 1, pp. 770–71.

maintain, their opinions in matters of religion, and that the same shall in no wise diminish, enlarge or affect their civil capacities.

And though we well know that this Assembly elected by the people for the ordinary purposes of legislation only, have no power to restrain the acts of succeeding assemblies constituted with powers equal to our own, and that, therefore, to declare this act to be irrevocable would be of no effect in law; yet we are free to declare, and do declare, that the rights hereby asserted are of the natural rights of mankind; and that if any act shall be hereafter passed to repeal the present, or to narrow its operation, such act will be an infringement of natural right.

NOTE

1. This bill was based on a bill originally framed in 1779 by Thomas Jefferson (1743–1826), the foremost advocate of religious freedom among the founding fathers of the United States. The bill, which was passed by the General Assembly of Virginia on December 16, 1785, served as a precedent for the freedom of religion clause in the Bill of Rights later proposed by Congress and ratified by the legislatures of several states. The Virginia Act also inspired the votaries of Enlightenment and democracy in Europe. Later, the champions of Jewish emancipation in the French National Assembly also used it as an authoritative precedent for the removal of religious restrictions to citizenship.

6. THE CONSTITUTION OF THE UNITED STATES OF AMERICA (1789)

We, the people of the United States, in order to form a more perfect union, establish justice, insure domestic tranquility, provide for the common defence, promote the general welfare, and secure the blessings of liberty to ourselves and our posterity, do ordain and establish this constitution for the United States of America....

Article VI. [Freedom of religion as a basic law of the land.[1]]...The senators and representatives before mentioned, and the members of the several state legislatures, and all executive and judicial officers, both of the United States and of the several states, shall be bound by oath or affirmation to support this constitution; but no religious test shall ever be required as a qualification to any office or public trust under the United States.

Amendment 1. Congress shall make no law respecting an establishment of religion, or prohibiting the free exercise thereof; or abridging the freedom of speech, or of the press; or the right of the people peaceably to assemble, and to petition the government for a redress of grievances.

NOTE

1. The Constitution and its First Amendment guaranteed the legal equality of all citizens of the United States regardless of religion. Although Article VI of the Constitution abolished any religious test "as a qualification to any office," at least two states, Maryland and North Carolina, continued to restrict the right of Jews and Christian dissidents to hold public office, arguing that the Constitution referred only to federal positions. The two states removed these restrictions in 1826 and 1868, respectively. The situation today, under which the First Amendment is explicitly applied to the laws of the various states of the union, did not come about until the twentieth century when the Supreme Court, in the 1940 Cantwell decision, interpreted the Fourteenth Amendment as imposing the Bill of Rights on the states.

Source: Francis Newton Thorpe, *The Federal and State Constitutions* (Washington, D.C., 1909), vol. 1, p. 19.

7. MESSAGE OF WELCOME TO GEORGE WASHINGTON (AUGUST 17, 1790)[1]

THE HEBREW CONGREGATION OF NEWPORT, RHODE ISLAND

Sir:

Permit the children of the stock of Abraham to approach you with the most cordial affection and esteem for your person and merits and to join with our fellow-citizens in welcoming you to New Port.

With pleasure we reflect on those days—those days of difficulty and danger—when the God of Israel who delivered David from the peril of the sword shielded your head in the day of battle. And we rejoice to think that the same Spirit, who rested in the bosom of the greatly beloved Daniel, enabling him to preside over the provinces of the Babylonish Empire, rests, and ever will rest upon you, enabling you to discharge the arduous duties of Chief Magistrate in these states.

Deprived as we have hitherto been of the invaluable rights of free citizens, we now, with a deep sense of gratitude to the Almighty Disposer of all events, behold a government, erected by the majesty of the people, a government which to bigotry gives no sanction, to persecution no assistance, but generously affording to all liberty of conscience and immunities of citizenship, deeming every one, of whatever nation, tongue, or language, equal parts of the great governmental machine. This so ample and extensive federal union whose basis is philanthropy, mutual confidence, and public virtue, we cannot but acknowledge to be the work of the Great God, who ruleth in the armies of heaven and among the inhabitants of the earth, doing whatsoever seemeth him good.

For all the blessings of civil and religious liberty which we enjoy under an equal and benign administration, we desire to send up our thanks to the Ancient of Days, the great Preserver of Men, beseeching him that the angel who conducted our forefathers through the wilderness into the promised land may graciously conduct you through all the dangers and difficulties of this mortal life. And when like Joshua, full of days and full of honor, you are gathered to your fathers, may you be admitted into the heavenly paradise to partake of the water of life and the tree of immortality.

Done and signed by order of the Hebrew Congregation in New Port, Rhode Island.

August 17, 1790.
Moses Seixas, Warden

NOTE

1. When George Washington, who was inaugurated the first president of the fledgling Republic in April 1789, visited Newport on August 17, 1790, the warden of the local synagogue addressed this message of welcome to him. Washington's reply follows in document 8.

Source: Lewis Abraham, "Correspondence Between Washington and Jewish Citizens," *Proceedings of the American Jewish Historical Society* 3 (1895), pp. 90–91. Reprinted by permission of the American Jewish Historical Society.

8. A REPLY TO THE HEBREW CONGREGATION OF NEWPORT (c. AUGUST 17, 1790)

GEORGE WASHINGTON

Gentlemen:

While I receive with much satisfaction your address replete with expressions of affection and esteem, I rejoice in the opportunity of assuring you that I shall always retain a grateful remembrance of the cordial welcome I experienced in my visit to New Port from all classes of citizens.

The reflection on the days of difficulty and danger which are past is rendered the more sweet from a consciousness that they are succeeded by days of uncommon prosperity and security. If we have wisdom to make the best use of the advantages with which we are now favored, we cannot fail, under the just administration of a good government, to become a great and a happy people.

The citizens of the United States of America have a right to applaud themselves for having given to mankind examples of an enlarged and liberal policy, a policy worthy of imitation.

All possess alike liberty of conscience and immunities of citizenship. It is now no more that toleration is spoken of, as if it was by the indulgence of one class of people that another enjoyed the exercise of their inherent natural rights. For happily the government of the United States, which gives to bigotry no sanction, to persecution no assistance, requires only that they who live under its protection should demean themselves as good citizens, in giving it on all occasions their effectual support.

It would be inconsistent with the frankness of my character not to avow that I am pleased with your favorable opinion of my administration and fervent wishes for my felicity.

May the children of the stock of Abraham who dwell in this land continue to merit and enjoy the good will of the other inhabitants, while every one shall sit in safety under his own vine and fig-tree, and there shall be none to make him afraid.

May the Father of all mercies scatter light and not darkness in our paths, and make us all in our several vocations useful here, and, in his own due time and way, everlastingly happy.

G. Washington

Source: Lewis Abraham, "Correspondence Between Washington and Jewish Citizens," *Proceedings of the American Jewish Historical Society* 3 (1895), pp. 91–92. Reprinted by permission of the American Jewish Historical Society.

9. AN OBSERVANT JEWISH WOMAN IN AMERICA (1791)

REBECCA SAMUEL[1]

Petersburg, Virginia
January 12, 1791
Wednesday, 8th [7th] Shebat, 5551

Dear and Worthy Parents,

I received your dear letter with much pleasure and therefrom understand that you are in good health, thank God, and that made us especially happy. The same is not lacking with us—may we live to be a hundred years, Amen.

Dear parents, you complain that you do not receive any letters from us, and my mother-in-law writes the same. I don't know what's going on. I have written more letters than I have received from you. Whenever I can and have an opportunity, I give letters to take, along [with individuals traveling to Germany], and I send letters by post when I do not have any other opportunity. It is already six months since we received letters from you…. The last letter you sent…was received at the beginning of the [Hebrew] month of Ab [July 1790]. Now you can realize that we too have been somewhat worried. We are completely isolated here. We do not have any friends, and when we do not hear from you for any length of time, it is enough to make us sick. I hope that I will get to see some of the family. That will give me some satisfaction.

You write me that Mr. Jacob Renner's son Reuben is in Philadelphia and that he will come to us. People will not advise him to come to Virginia. When the Jews of Philadelphia or New York hear the name Virginia, they get nasty. And they are not wrong! It won't do for a Jew. In the first place it is an unhealthful district, and we are only human. God forbid, if anything should happen to us, where would we be thrown? There is no [Jewish] cemetery in the whole of Virginia. In Richmond, which is twenty-two miles from here, there is a Jewish community consisting of two quorums [*minyanim*], and the two cannot muster a quarter [quorum of ten necessary for Jewish congregational prayer].

You cannot imagine what kind of Jews they have here [in Virginia]. They were all German itinerants who made a living by begging in Germany. They came to America during the War [of Independence] as soldiers, and now they can't recognize themselves.

One can make a good living here, and all live at peace. Anyone can do what he wants. There is no rabbi in all of America to excommunicate anyone. There is a blessing here. Jew and Gentile are as one. There is no *galut* [Hebrew for Exile, but connotes here, rejection of Jews] here. In New York and Philadelphia there is more *galut*. The reason is that there are too many German Gentiles and Jews there. The German Gentiles cannot forsake their anti-Jewish prejudice, and German Jews cannot forsake their disgraceful conduct, and that's what makes *galut*….

[In an undated letter Rebecca informs her parents that they will leave Virginia.] The whole reason we are leaving this place is because of [its lack of] *yiddishkeit* [Jewishness]. Dear parents, I know quite well you will not want me to bring up my children like Gentiles. Here they cannot become anything else. Jewishness is pushed aside here. There are here [in Petersburg] ten or twelve Jews, and they are not worthy of being called Jews. We have a *shohet* [one who performs the slaughter of animals according to Jewish ritual] here who goes to the market and buys *trefah* [unkosher] meat and then brings it home. On Rosh ha-Shanah [New Year] and on Yom Kippur [the Day of Atonement] the people worshipped here without

---

Source: Jacob R. Marcus, *The American Jewish Woman: A Documentary History* (New York: Ktav Publishing House; Cincinnati: American Jewish Archives, 1981), pp. 42–45.

one *sefer torah* [Scroll of the Law], and not one wore a *tallit* [a prayer shawl].... You can believe me that I crave to see a synagogue to which I can go. The way we live now is no life at all. We do not know what the Sabbath and the holidays are. On the Sabbath all the Jewish shops are open, and they do business on that day as they do throughout the whole week. But ours we do not allow to open. With us there is still some Sabbath. You must believe that in our house we all live as Jews as much as we can.

As for the Gentiles, we have nothing to complain about. For the sake of a livelihood we do not have to leave here. Nor do we have to leave because of debts. I believe ever since Hyman [Rebecca's husband] has grown up that he has not had it so good. You cannot know what a wonderful country this is for the common man. One can live here peacefully....All the people who hear that we are leaving give us their blessings. They say that it is sinful that such blessed children be brought up here in Petersburg. My children cannot learn anything here, nothing Jewish, nothing of general culture....

I remain, your devoted daughter and servant, Rebecca, the wife of Hayyim, the son of Samuel the Levite.

NOTE

1. Rebecca, née Alexander, was married to Hyman (Hayyim) Samuel, a silversmith and watchmaker. They had emigrated from Germany to the United States, settling in Petersburg, Virginia. In her letters, written in Yiddish, to her parents in Hamburg, she describes in the most negative terms the quality of Jewish life in their adopted home. In 1796, she and her husband, together with their two young children, moved to Richmond, where there was a more vibrant Jewish community.

10. A COUNTRY WHERE RELIGIOUS DISTINCTIONS ARE SCARCELY KNOWN (1815)

RACHEL MORDECAI LAZARUS[1]

Warrenton, North Carolina
U.S. of America
August 7th, 1815

A young American lady who long felt towards Miss Edgeworth those sentiments of respect and admiration which superior talents exerted in the cause of virtue and morality never fail to excite, ventures, not without hesitation, to indulge a wish formed by months since of addressing her. If such temerity requires more than an ordinary apology, it is to Practical Education[2] she must appeal as her intercessor; it is that, which by lately making her acquainted with the Edgeworth family, has gradually eradicated fear and in its stead implanted confidence....

Relying on the good sense and candor of Miss Edgeworth I would ask, how it can be that she, who on all other subjects shows such justice and liberality, should on one alone appear biased by prejudice: should even instill that prejudice into the minds of youth! Can my allusion be mistaken? It is to the species of character which wherever a *Jew* is introduced is invariably attached to him. Can it be believed that

---

Source: The Education of the Heart: The Correspondence of Rachel Mordecai and Maria Edgeworth, ed. Edgar E. MacDonald (Chapel Hill: University of North Carolina Press, 1977), pp. 3, 6ff.

this race of men are by nature mean, avaricious, and unprincipled? Forbid it, mercy. Yet this is more than insinuated by the stigma usually affixed to the *name*. In those parts of the world where these people are oppressed and made continually the subject of scorn and derision, they may in many instances deserve censure; but in this happy country, where religious distinctions are scarcely known, where character and talents are all sufficient to attain advancement, we find the Jews to form a respectable part of the community. They are in most instances liberally educated, many following honorable professions of the Law, and [medicine], with credit and ability, and associating with the best society that our country affords. The penetration of Miss Edgeworth has already conjectured that it is [a] Jewess who addresses her; it is so, but one who thinks she does not flatter herself in believing that were she not, her opinion on this subject would be exactly what it is now. Living in a small village, her father's the only family of Israelites who reside in or near it, all her juvenile friendships and attachments have been formed with those of persuasions different from her own; yet each has looked upon the variations of the other as things of course—differences which take place in every society. Again and again I beg pardon for thus intruding myself on Miss Edgeworth's notice; yet even now in my temerity about to appear in a new form while I give utterance to a very imperfect hope, that these lines may be honored with a reply, and their author thus taught to be herself not wholly unpardonable,

in the liberty she takes in writing them. Should she be thus highly favored, Miss Edgeworth will have the goodness to direct the letter according to the address, which a brother of the writer's, now in England, will annex.

With sentiments of admiration, esteem, and gratitude, Miss Edgeworth's

> Most respectful and obedient servant
> Rachel Mordecai

NOTES

1. The granddaughter of German Jewish immigrants to the United States, Rachel Mordecai Lazarus (1788–1838) initiated with this letter a ramified correspondence with the Anglo-Irish novelist Maria Edgeworth (1767–1849). Although as in this letter, she staunchly defended the Jews against defamation, especially literary, she herself eventually succumbed to the seduction of Christianity and converted on her deathbed.

2. The reference is to a book written by Maria Edgeworth together with her father Richard Lovell Edgeworth, her stepmother, and her siblings, *Practical Education* (London 1798), 2 vols.; 3 vols. (London 1801). Practical education denoted a rejection of the classical form of education, with its emphasis on memorization, in favor of a pedagogical method of encouragement and an emphasis on the utilitarian and experimental. Rachel's father, Jacob Marcus (1762–1838) was also an educator, having founded and directed the Warrenton Female Academy.

11. PROCLAMATION TO THE JEWS (SEPTEMBER 15, 1825)

MORDECAI MANUEL NOAH[1]

*W*hereas, it has pleased Almighty God to manifest to his chosen people the approach of that period when, in fulfillment of the promises made to the race of Jacob, and as a reward for their pious constancy and triumphant fidelity, they are to be gathered from the four quarters of the globe, and to resume their rank and character among the governments of the earth;

And Whereas, the peace which now prevails among civilized nations, the progress of learning throughout the world, and the general spirit of liberality and toleration which exists together with other changes favorable to light and to liberty, mark in an especial manner the approach of that time, when "peace on earth, good will to man" are to prevail with a benign and extended influence, and the ancient people of God, the first to proclaim his unity and omnipotence, are to be restored to their inheritance, and enjoy the rights of a sovereign independent people;

Therefore, I, Mordecai Manuel Noah, citizen of the United States of America, late Consul of the said States to the City and Kingdom of Tunis, High Sheriff of New York, Counsellor at Law, and by the grace of God, Governor and Judge of Israel, have issued this my Proclamation, announcing to the Jews throughout the world, that an asylum is prepared and hereby offered to them, where they can enjoy that peace, comfort and happiness which have been denied them through the intolerance and misgovernment of former ages; an asylum in a free and powerful country remarkable for its vast resources, the richness of its soil, and the salubrity of its climate; where industry is encouraged, education promoted, and good faith rewarded, "a land of milk and honey," where Israel may repose in peace, under his "vine and fig tree," and where our people may so familiarize themselves with the science of government and the lights of learning and civilization, as may qualify them for that great and final restoration to their ancient heritage, which the times so powerfully indicate.

The asylum referred to is in the State of New York, the greatest State in the American confederacy. New York contains forty-three thousand, two hundred and fourteen square miles, divided into fifty-five counties, and having six thousand and eighty-seven post towns and cities, containing one million, five hundred thousand inhabitants, together with six million acres of cultivated land, improvements in agriculture and manufactures, in trade and commerce, which include a valuation of three hundred millions of dollars of taxable property; one hundred and fifty thousand militia, armed and equipped; a constitution founded upon an equality of rights, having no test-oaths, and recognizing no religious distinctions, and seven thousand free schools and colleges, affording the blessings of education to four hundred thousand children. Such is the great and increasing State to which the emigration of the Jews is directed.

The desired spot in the State of New York, to which I hereby invite my beloved people throughout the world, in common with those of every religious denomination, is called Grand Island, and on which I shall lay the foundation of a City of Refuge, to be called Ararat.

Grand Island in the Niagara river is bounded by Ontario on the north, and Erie on the south, and within a few miles of each of these great commercial lakes. The island is nearly twelve miles in length, and varying from three to seven miles in breadth,

Source: M. J. Kohler, "Some Early American Zionist Projects," *Publications of the American Jewish Historical Society* 8 (1900), pp. 106–13. Reprinted by permission of the American Jewish Historical Society.

and contains upwards of seventeen thousand acres of remarkably rich and fertile land.

Deprived, as our people have been for centuries of a right in the soil, they will learn, with peculiar satisfaction, that here they can till the soil, reap the harvest, and raise the flocks which are unquestionably their own; and, in the full and unmolested enjoyment of their religious rights, and of every civil immunity, together with peace and plenty, they can lift up their voice in gratitude to Him who sustained our fathers in the wilderness, and brought us in triumph out of the land of Egypt; who assigned to us the safekeeping of His oracles, who proclaimed us his people, and who has ever walked before us like a "cloud by day and a pillar of fire by night."

In His name do I revive, renew and *reestablish* the government of the Jewish Nation, under the auspices and protection of the constitution and laws of the United States of America; confirming and perpetuating all our rights and privileges, our name, our rank, and our power among the nations of the earth, as they existed and were recognized under the government of the Judges. And I hereby enjoin it upon all our pious and venerable Rabbis, our Presidents and Elders of Synagogues, Chiefs of Colleges and brethren in authority throughout the world, to circulate and make known this, my Proclamation, and give it full publicity, credence and effect....

Those of our people who, from age, local attachment, or from any other cause, prefer remaining in the several parts of the world which they now respectively inhabit, and who are treated with liberality by the public authorities, are permitted to do so, and are specially recommended to be faithful to the governments which protect them. It is, however, expected that they will aid and encourage the emigration of the young and enterprising, and endeavor to send to this country such as will add to our national strength and character, by their industry, honor and patriotism.

Those Jews who are in the military employment of the different sovereigns of Europe are enjoined to keep in their ranks until further orders, and conduct themselves with bravery and fidelity.

I command that a strict neutrality be observed in the pending wars between the Greeks and the Turks, enjoined by considerations of safety towards a numerous population of Jews now under the oppressive dominion of the Ottoman Porte.

The annual gifts which, for many centuries, have been afforded to our pious brethren in our holy City of Jerusalem (to which may God speedily restore us) are to continue with unabated liberality; our seminaries of learning and institutions of charity in every part of the world are to be increased, in order that wisdom and virtue may permanently prevail among the chosen people....

The Caraite and Samaritan Jews, together with the black Jews of India and Africa, and likewise those in Cochin, China and the sect on the coast of Malabar, are entitled to an equality of rights and religious privileges, as are all who may partake of the great covenant and obey and respect the Mosaical laws.

The Indians of the American continent, in their admitted Asiatic origin, in their worship of God, in their dialect and language, in their sacrifices, marriages, divorces, burials, fastings, purifications, punishments, cities of refuge, divisions of tribes, in their High Priests, in their wars and in their victories, being in all probability, the descendants of the lost tribes of Israel, which were carried captive by the King of Assyria, measures will be adopted to make them sensible of their condition and finally re-unite them with their brethren, the chosen people.

I recommend peace and union among us; charity and good-will to all; toleration and liberality to our brethren of every religious denomination, enjoined by the mild and just precepts of our holy religion; honor and good faith in the fulfillment of all our contracts, together with temperance, economy, and industry in our habits.

I humbly entreat to be remembered in your prayers; and lastly and most earnestly I do enjoin you to "keep the charge of the Holy God," to walk His ways, to keep His statues, and His commandments, and His judgments, and His testimonies, as it is written in the laws of Moses, "That thou mayest prosper in all thou doest, and whithersoever thou turnest thyself."

Given at Buffalo, in the State of New York, this second day Tishri, in the year of the world 5586, corresponding with the fifteenth day of September, 1825, and in the fiftieth year of American independence.

NOTE

1. Mordecai Manuel Noah (1785–1851), editor, politician, and playwright. He was probably the most prominent and influential Jew in the United States in

the early nineteenth century. After serving as U.S. consul in Tunis from 1813 to 1815, he became active in New York State and national politics. For many years he was intrigued by the idea of Jewish territorial restoration, and in 1825 he solicited funds to purchase a tract of land on Grand Island in the Niagara River near Buffalo, New York. He named the territory *Ararat*

(see Genesis 8:4, where it says that Noah's ark came to rest on the mountains of Ararat.) and declared it the future national home of the Jewish people. The project was a fiasco, but it did elicit much discussion both in America and in Europe on the plight of the Jews. It was also one of the first articulations of the concept of America as a haven for oppressed Jewry.

12. AMERICA IS NOT PALESTINE (MARCH 29, 1841)

REBECCA GRATZ[1]

I have not seen the paper you sent containing an account of the Charleston congregation but have heard some passages quoted that are certainly unorthodox. "This is our temple, this our city, this is our Palestine." Is it possible a Jew can write or speak so? Then where is the truth of prophesy? Where the fulfillment of promises? What is the hope of Israel? Of what does the scattered people bear witness? Alas we may hang our harps on the willow and weep for the spiritual destruction of Jerusalem when her own children are content to sing the songs of Zion in a strange land and deny the words of God so often repeated by the prophets. I am afraid the good people of Charleston are paying too much for their organ and allow more important objects to be sacrificed. Certainly the greatest enemies of the Jews never have denied their claims on the country inherited from their fathers, or doubted they would be restored to it in the time God shall appoint. How then can the Charleston congregation sell their birth right for a mess of pottage? But I beg your pardon, as I said before, I speak from hearsay and would fain hope there are watchmen at their posts, scattered among the people who will warn them when they are in danger of falling into error by the spirit of innovation which has been the vice of ages among other religious denominations.

NOTE

1. A prominent Jewish American educator from Pennsylvania, Rebecca Gratz (1781–1869) was also active in Jewish and non-Jewish philanthropic projects, especially on behalf of women and children in need. She is said to have been the inspiration for the heroine Rebecca in Sir Walter Scott's novel *Ivanhoe*. In this letter to her niece, Miriam Gratz Moses Cohen (1824–1864), Gratz, an observant Jew, expresses grave misgivings of a statement ascribed to the cantor of the Reform congregation of Charleston, South Carolina.

Source: Rebecca Gratz to Miriam Gratz Cohen, letter dated March 29, 1841, in Jacob R. Marcus, *The American Jewish Woman: A Documentary History* (New York: Ktav Publishing House; Cincinnati: American Jewish Archives, 1981), p. 101.

13. JEWISH PUBLICATION SOCIETY OF AMERICA (1845)

ISAAC LEESER[1]

The time for action has arrived, not to struggle for political ascendancy, which we do not desire, but to support the noble fabric of our faith, which having stood firm and unshaken during the lapse of centuries, the warfare of an entire world, and the persecutions of mankind, is now threatened by a new danger,—the secret attacks and open assaults, by specious arguments, of those whose darling object it is to break down the landmarks of Judaism. No effort is spared to diffuse false views concerning our faith among the Gentiles; and our own people too are endeavoured to be reached by errors propagated through books, tracts and publications of all kinds; and the mass of erroneous views thus propagated would, if confided in by our brethren, work in silence, but not, the less effectually, the loss to Israel of many precious souls who are now of our communion.

The time, therefore, for counteraction has arrived; and they who are zealous for Israel cannot any longer remain quiet and see the poison scattered far and wide, without endeavouring to do something to arrest its fatal effects.—But how are we to proceed!—We cannot imitate the mode of procedure of our Gentile opponents; we cannot send out missionaries, to assemble around them the young and the old, to preach to them the truth that abides with us; as our people live dispersed over so wide a space of country that we are precluded from waiting upon all individually to speak with them upon the concerns of their immortal souls. But the press is at our service; the thoughts which animate those favored with the knowledge of the Lord can be sent abroad though the writers themselves are unable to travel; the words of peace can be transmitted to every town, to every house, though the speakers themselves may never be seen away from home. —This is, in fact, the plan adopted by our opponents; and shall we not profit by them? Shall they alone be active, whilst we loiter by the way, as though a lion were in the road or a leopard in the streets? —What do we fear? Have we not liberty of conscience? liberty of speech? liberty of the press? And why shall we not labour? Is the object not one of the greatest interest? of the utmost importance? Is not every soul saved unto the Lord a merit in him by whose humble efforts such a result is brought about?

Let us hope that neither any vain idea of fear nor a criminal negligence may prevent us from following the line of duty which both reason and religion mark out as the one which we should pursue. There is surely sufficient enlightenment and knowledge in our brethren to prepare suitable publications to be circulated among all classes of our people, from which they may obtain a knowledge of their faith and proper weapons to defend it against the assaults of proselyte-makers on the one side and of infidels on the other, by which means they may become Israelites in knowledge as well as to be Israelites merely in name.

We, therefore, appeal to all who feel with us the potency of the obligation to unite with us in forming a Jewish Publication Society,[2] whose object it

Source: [Isaac Leeser], "Address of the Jewish Publication Committee to the Israelites of America," preface to *Caleb Ashet,* no. 1 of the series *The Jewish Miscellany* (Philadelphia: Jewish Publication Society of America, 5605 [1845]), p. 1–4. The address, written by Leeser, was unsigned; the anonymous author of this volume is conjectured to be Charlotte Montefiore; cf. Robert Singerman, *Judaica Americana. A Bibliography of Publications to 1900* (New York: Greenwood Press, 1990), vol. 1, p. 181.

shall be to prepare and publish works to be placed in the hands of all Israelites and which shall have the double effect pointed out above. Such a series may embrace tales, sermons, treatises, conversations, all prepared with the sole idea of giving a candid and unprejudiced view of Jews and Judaism, to be distributed by the contributors or sold for the benefit of the general fund.

We address ourselves to all American [Jewish] congregations and individual families and request them earnestly to communicate with their respective friends in the different cities....

The reverend ministers [rabbis], teachers, presidents of congregations and societies are earnestly requested to notice the plan and to urge it upon the serious attention of those who are placed within their sphere of action; and we trust that much good may result, and a strong united effort be made to diffuse light and knowledge among our friends....

NOTES

1. Isaac Leeser (1806–1868) was a *hazan* (cantor), writer, and educator. Born in Germany, he emigrated at the age of 18 to the United States, where he would lay the foundations of many of the central institutions of American Jewish life. In 1829, while serving as a *hazan* of a Sephardic congregation, he was the first to introduce a regular English sermon into the synagogue service. In 1843 he founded the monthly *The Occident*, the first successful Jewish periodical in the United States, which he edited for twenty-five years. He published the first Hebrew primer for children (1838) and the first complete English translation of the Sephardic prayer book (1848); he founded the first Hebrew high school (1849), the first representative defense organization (1859), and the first rabbinical school, Maimonides College (1867) in the United States. His major literary achievement was undoubtedly the first American translation of the Hebrew Scripture from a Jewish perspective.

2. Among Leeser's contributions to the shaping of American Judaism was the creation of the first Jewish Publication Society of America. The immediate stimulus was provided by a decision to combat the heightened activity of Christian missionaries among the Jews of America, many of whom were poorly educated in Judaism and who often lived rather isolated from other Jews. In 1845 Leeser published a manifesto, presented here, calling for a Jewish Publication Society to issue works to further Jewish knowledge and to combat the zealous proselytizers. Leeser soon established his envisioned society, beginning with the publication of a series entitled "The Jewish Miscellany," comprising fourteen booklets of about 125 pages each. Although subscription to the series was poor, Leeser almost singlehandedly maintained the society. Finally, a fire destroyed the building where most of the society's stock was housed. On December 27, 1851, "America's first Jewish Publication Society went up in smoke" (Jonathan D. Sarna, *JPS: The Americanization of Jewish Culture, 1888–1988. A Centennial History of the Jewish Publication Society* ([Philadelphia: Jewish Publication Society, 1989], p. 30).

14. OFF TO AMERICA! (MAY 6, 1848)

L. KOMPERT[1]

"The harvest is past, the summer is ended, and we are not saved" (Jer. 8:20).

The sun of freedom has risen above the fatherland, but for us it is nothing but a bloody northern light. The larks of redemption warble in the sky; for us, however, they are the screaming harbingers of a terrible storm. Shame and rage overcome us when we remember the terrible and hair-raising events of recent weeks! Because slavish hordes and petty merchants have failed to understand the spirit of freedom, we Jews must suffer. Can God really want us to hold out our heads to every cudgel and to tremble before every despot, great or small? We have reached the point where at the very hour which has brought freedom into the land, we have no other wish but to avoid this kind of freedom!

The [Gentiles] apparently do not want it otherwise, and so be it! It will not be the first time that we shall acquiesce to their whims. For centuries, our history has been nothing but a silent acceptance of every torture, agony and restriction they have chosen to impose on us! But should we always accept, always bow our head!...For once, with the permission of the "sovereign people," we want to lose our patience, only once we want to resist—and then we shall move on!

For we shall go to America! Those among you who do not understand the essence of history, should take this as an indication of it—that four centuries ago, at a time when the Jews were persecuted most cruelly, it was a man from Genoa who was haunted by the idea of discovering a new world and did not find peace until Queen Isabella of Spain—whose husband had evoked the dark figure of Torquemada[2] and his thousands of bloodstained Dominican brethren—allowed him [Christopher Columbus] to discover America. It is for this America that we are yearning, thither you shall move! "Off to America!"

We know all your objections and all your answers!...Do you not have any other advice for us, you ask, but to take up once again the wanderer's staff and with wife and child seek a far and foreign land? Shall we leave the native soil which has born and fed us, and in which we have buried our dead? I sense in these words something of Egypt's fleshpots; yes, I, too, smell the flavor of the golden soups and juicy roast—but I also see the people who are stirring the flames and who are extracting their daily bread from the fires of hatred, of prejudice, and of narrow-mindedness. By God, may he who has a penchant for these things stay behind and feed himself!

In our time, two sentences may serve us as points of departure. The first one was said by Moses: "Stand fast and still" [Exodus 14:13–7]. The second one was said by Jeremiah: "The harvest is past, the summer is ended, and we are not saved" [Jeremiah 8:20]. Which of the two sentences do you prefer? To stand still and to wait, to wait patiently, until all who are now opposed to us will make peace with us, until the spirit of humanity is victorious? Or, since "we are not saved," to seek salvation elsewhere— and to move to America?

I think the two sentences can be reconciled easily! May those in our fatherland who wish to "stand fast and still" build their homes upon the sands of the future! We do not want to prevent them from doing so; on the contrary, we shall gladly provide them with bricks for their endeavor. But to all the others, the oppressed and persecuted, those who have been driven from their homes and plundered in the notorious communities, all those who have gained nothing but calamity from this "freedom," all those who feel in their hearts that it will take a long time before there is peace for them in the fatherland...to all those we say: we are not saved. Salvation can only be sought in America!

Source: L. Kompert, "Auf, nach Amerika," *Oesterreichisches Central-Organ fuer Glaubensfreiheit, Cultur, Geschichte und Literatur der Juden* 6 (Vienna, May 6, 1848), p. 77. trans. J. Hessing.

The idea is not new. This we know; but it is practical....The purpose of emigration is the finding of a new fatherland and the gain of immediate freedom!...

Thousands before you have taken this step and are still taking it! And only a disproportionate few have regretted it. The God of your forefathers will watch over you. He will guide you safely across the sea and through the first difficulties of your new life! I am not afraid for you! You have all the necessary qualities and virtues: circumspection, sobriety, frugality, discipline and faith; they will help you in the building of a new life and wealth. Others have perished there, but you will prosper and grow; the God of freedom will be with you.

In my spirit I already greet your children there, the children of those who have become free. *Shalom aleikhem!* [Peace be with you!]

A bright glow fills me as I think of the children born free, and of their mothers.

Therefore, in light of the horrors of the past weeks...I call to you: "Off to America!"

NOTES

1. L. Kompert (1822–1886), German writer celebrated for his descriptions of Bohemian Jewish life. An enthusiastic supporter of the 1848 Revolution, he joined with other Jews in founding a journal (in which this essay was published) advocating Jewish rights or, as Kompert prefered to say, Jewish "right, not rights" (*Recht, nicht Rechte*). The *Oesterreichisches Central-Organ fuer Glaubensfreiheit, Cultur, Geschichte und Literatur der Juden* (An Austrian Journal for Jewish Religious Freedom, Culture, History and Literature), appeared between April and October 1848 in Vienna. In mid-April anti-Jewish riots occurred in Prague, Budapest, and Pressburg; the Jews of Alsace were subject to the fury of the masses in February; and in March, Prussian Poland was the scene of anti-Jewish riots. Kompert was grievously disappointed and responded by urging the Jews to emigrate to the United States. His article presented here was followed by many similar pleas in the *Oesterreichisches Central-Organ* for organized emigration to the United States. Although the editor of the journal, Isidor Bush, himself heeded the call and emigrated to America, Kompert remained in Vienna, where he was active in Jewish affairs.

2. Tomas de Torquemada (1420?–1498), first head of the Spanish Inquisition. At the age of fourteen he entered the Dominican Order where he became the confessor of Queen Isabella and her husband, King Ferdinand. He helped to establish the Inquisition in Spain and was known for his ferocity and cruelty in dealing with Jews and conversos.

15. THE CONFIRMATION OF GIRLS (1854)

ISSAC MEYER WISE[1]

It is well known to our readers that our ecclesiastical code considers a boy of thirteen years and a girl aged twelve years of full age in religious matters. Our fathers have done well in adopting some ceremonial wherewith to impress upon the mind of the young son of Israel that he has reached the age of reflection and responsibility; but as in many other respects they forgot all about our daughters who are not introduced in the synagogue until married, as if the connection between God and the female heart was conditional upon her having a male associate in this life. But no blame can be attached to our fathers, for those views

---

Source: I. M. Wise, "The Confirmation and the Bar Mitzvah. *Asmonean* (New York), 1854; Jacob R. Marcus, *The American Jewish Woman. A Documentary History* (New York: Ktav Publishing House; Cincinnati: American Jewish Archives, 1981), pp. 186–87.

are of an oriental origin and were the product of a bye-gone age. Then, and in the East particularly, an unmarried woman would not leave the house or harem without giving offense to common decency; it would not do for her, of course, under such circumstances to show herself in the synagogue, or in any other public place. We have dispensed with oriental notions; they have been extinguished by the onward march of western civilization, and therefore that class of our people who progress with the time consider it the duty of the synagogue to extend its benevolent influence over the daughters of Israel as well as the sons. The act of confirmation is for the young of both sexes while the ceremony of the *Bar Mitzvah* is for the lads only. We leave to the reader to decide whether this reform was right and good or uncalled for. At the same time we cannot restrain ourselves from entering our complaint on behalf of our female friends. Is it not an insolence that men say in their morning prayers, "Blessed art thou etc. that thou hast not made me a woman"? Is it not an offense to their mothers, wives, sisters, and daughters? And if it should not be said, why is it printed in the prayer books? Is it not a rudeness of the meanest kind that a female is considered as nobody in respect to [her] person in religious affairs not only in the synagogue, but even at the table

in the family circle? This is one of the "established" absurdities—this is evidently the mildest name we could find for it—which serves as arms in the hands of our opponents and which deprives the synagogue of its most devout friends, the most sensible of its devotees. If it was a custom among us that a man with a wife and children should go to the synagogue and occupy their seats together, the whole would be improved, decorum and devotion would be gained, and a ready attendance would be secured....

NOTE

1. One of the principal architects of Reform Judaism in America, Isaac Meyer Wise (1819–1900) was born in Germany, where he received his rabbinical education. Upon his emigration to the United States in 1846, he was appointed rabbi of Congregation Beth El in Albany, New York. The reforms he introduced to the service eventually led to a split in the congregation, obliging him to assume a pulpit in Cincinnati. Upon the founding of Hebrew Union College (see the following document), he was appointed its first president. In this article he justifies the introduction of confirmation because it is gender inclusive, thus righting an ancient wrong with respect to the place of women in Jewish ritual life.

16. DEDICATION OF HEBREW UNION COLLEGE (1875)

DAVID PHILIPSON[1]

The long looked-for day finally dawned. The dream of a quarter of a century began to be realized when on Sunday, the third of October, eighteen hundred and seventy-five, the formal opening of the Hebrew Union College took place in the beautiful temple of

the Bene Yeshurun Congregation, at Eight and Plum Streets [Cincinnati]. The multitude that filled the brilliantly illuminated house of worship little reckoned at how historic an occasion they were assisting. Isaac M. Wise knew it full well but possibly even he did

---

Source: David Philipson, "History of the Hebrew Union College. 1875–1925." *Hebrew Union College Jubilee Volume (1875–1925),* pp. 22–24.

not realize completely the amazing task to which he had set his hand. It was a real work of salvation for Judaism in America. Within the past half-century he has been frequently called the "master builder" of American Judaism. And that in truth he was. His determination, his persistence, his struggle, his faith were finally justified and rewarded. But it was only the beginning. The great tests and trials were still to come. Many doubters and mockers were still in the land. But what of that? Sufficient to the day was the joy thereof. The rung on the ladder of achievement was being ascended. The difficult first step had been successfully taken....

The speakers sensed the epoch-making significance of the event and stressed the responsibility that would lie upon the persons who were blazing the new path in American Israel's onward journey. Bernard Bettmann[2] who served as president of the Board of Governors with singular ability and devotion from the day of its founding until February 1, 1910, when he resigned the office, said in his inaugural address: "Let it be plainly and distinctly understood that while it is hoped that from this college will depart the future rabbis and teachers of the American Israel, not only are its doors open, but a most cordial welcome is extended to any one that may want to seek its benefits, no matter what may be his or her religion, present position or future purpose in life.... We shall be happy to have amongst us the followers of other creeds, not for the purpose of making proselytes of them—for that has always been and still is repugnant to the spirit of Judaism—but that they might understand the parent faith from which their own religion sprang, and enjoy a literature equal to that of Greece and Rome. We confidently count upon the attendance of some of the daughters of Israel, so that in a measure at least may be revived the glory of those ancient days when the *Keter Torah*, the crown of knowledge of the law, encircles many a Jewish woman's brow."

The Reverend Dr. Max Lilienthal[3] who had stood shoulder-to-shoulder with Isaac M. Wise during all these years of preparation and initiatory struggle stressed the American note when in his address he said: "We could have adopted the plan proposed by several good men, of sending those who wish to devote themselves to the Jewish ministry to Germany, where the master minds of Jewish literature and theology are diffusing their store of learning to crowds of Jewish students and where Jewish colleges already are established, thoroughly organized and richly endowed. But we do not want any ministers reared and educated under the influence of European institutions; we intend to have ministers reared by the spirit of our glorious American institutions; men who love their country above all, men who will be staunch advocates of such civil and religious liberty as the men who signed the Declaration of Independence understood it—men who are ready to defend this priceless gem against all and any encroachments, and hence we wish to keep our students at home and raise them as genuine Americans on the virgin soil of America."

When the founder [Isaac M. Wise] rose to speak, a great hush fell on the assembled multitude. There was a feeling that [the] occasion for him was beyond adequate expression in the spoken word. And so it was. Too deeply moved to speak at any length, Isaac M. Wise said that he lacked words to do justice to his feelings. As far as in his power lay he would carry out the hope of Israel *yigdal torah ve-yadir* [that God's law should be magnified and glorified— a refrain from an ancient Hebrew prayer], with all the enthusiasm of his soul and he would strive to raise high the standard of learning and intelligence in this college, to bring down to us the *Shekinah* [God's Presence]. He called the occasion *chag le-Adonai*, a solemn feast of the Lord, which we celebrate. And such indeed it was!

NOTES

1. David Philipson (1862–1949) was born in Wabash, Indiana, to German-Jewish immigrants. A member of the first graduating class (1883) of Hebrew Union College, he became one of the leaders of American Reform Judaism and a guiding spirit of Jewish philanthropy.

2. Bernhard Bettman (1834–1915) immigrated to the United States in 1850 from his native Germany. A successful businessman in Cincinnati, he was a prominent lay leader of the Reform movement and served as the first chairman of the Board of Governors of Hebrew Union College.

3. Upon earning a doctorate at the University of Munich, Germany, Max Lilienthal (1815–1882) accepted the office of principal of a newly established Jewish school in Riga, then part of tsarist Russia. His progressive views led to his appointment by the Russian minister of pubic education to establish a network of

Jewish schools with a "European" curriculum and in which the language of instruction would be Russian. Fearing that these schools would lead to assimilation and even to conversion, the leaders of the Jewish community ostracized Lilienthal. In 1844, he suddenly emigrated to the United States where he served as a rabbi and became one of the leaders of the American Reform movement. He taught Jewish history and literature at Hebrew Union College from its founding until his death.

17. THE PITTSBURGH PLATFORM (1885)[1]

CONFERENCE OF REFORM RABBIS

In view of the wide divergence of opinion and of the conflicting ideas prevailing in Judaism today, we, as representatives of Reform Judaism in America, in continuation of the work begun at Philadelphia in 1869, unite upon the following principles:

First: We recognize in every religion an attempt to grasp the Infinite One, and in every mode, source or book of revelation held sacred in any religious system the consciousness of the indwelling of God in man. We hold that Judaism presents the highest conception of the God-idea as taught in our holy Scriptures and developed and spiritualized by the Jewish teachers in accordance with the moral and philosophical progress of their respective ages. We maintain that Judaism preserved and defended amid continual struggles and trials and under enforced isolation this God-idea as the central religious truth for the human race.

Second: We recognize in the Bible the record of the consecration of the Jewish people to its mission as priest of the One God, and value it as the most potent instrument of religious and moral instruction. We hold that the modern discoveries of scientific researches in the domains of nature and history are not antagonistic to the doctrines of Judaism, the Bible reflecting the primitive ideas of its own age and at times clothing its conception of divine providence and justice dealing with man in miraculous narratives.

Third: We recognize in the Mosaic legislation a system of training the Jewish people for its mission during its national life in Palestine, and to-day we accept as binding only the moral laws and maintain only such ceremonies as elevate and sanctify our lives, but reject all such as are not adapted to the views and habits of modern civilization.

Fourth: We hold that all such Mosaic and Rabbinical laws as regulate diet, priestly purity and dress originated in ages and under the influence of ideas altogether foreign to our present mental and spiritual state. They fail to impress the modern Jew with a spirit of priestly holiness; their observance in our days is apt rather to obstruct than to further modern spiritual elevation.

Fifth: We recognize in the modern era of universal culture of heart and intellect the approach of the realization of Israel's great Messianic hope for the establishment of the kingdom of truth, justice and peace among all men. We consider ourselves no longer a nation but a religious community, and therefore expect neither a return to Palestine, nor a sacrificial worship under the administration of the sons of Aaron, nor the restoration of any of the laws concerning the Jewish state.

Source: Yearbook of the Central Conference of American Rabbis, 45 (1935), pp. 198–200. Reprinted by permission of the Central Conference of American Rabbis.

Sixth: We recognize in Judaism a progressive religion, ever striving to be in accord with the postulates of reason. We are convinced of the utmost necessity of preserving the historical identity with our great past. Christianity and Islam being daughter-religions of Judaism, we appreciate their mission to aid in the spreading of monotheistic and moral truth. We acknowledge that the spirit of broad humanity of our age is our ally in the fulfillment of our mission, and therefore we extend the hand of fellowship to all who cooperate with us in the establishment of the reign of truth and righteousness among men.

Seventh: We reassert the doctrine of Judaism, that the soul of men is immortal, grounding this belief on the divine nature of the human spirit, which forever finds bliss in righteousness and misery in wickedness. We reject as ideas not rooted in Judaism the belief both in bodily resurrection and in Gehenna and Eden (Hell and Paradise), as abodes for everlasting punishment or reward.

Eighth: In full accordance with the spirit of Mosaic legislation which strives to regulate the relation between rich and poor, we deem it our duty to participate in the great task of modern times, to solve on the basis of justice and righteousness the problems presented by the contrasts and evils of the present organization of society.

NOTE

1. German Jews who came to the United States in the first half of the nineteenth century brought with them Reform Judaism, although some congregations, such as the Charleston Reform Movement of 1825, were initiated and led by native-born Jews. By the time of the Civil War, many Reform congregations had been established. The tendency in the practice of Judaism was to radical Reform and by 1885, when the Pittsburgh Conference of Reform Rabbis was convened, it was the dominant position, as is expressed in the platform adopted by the conference. At its founding in 1889, the Central Conference of American Rabbis, the principal Reform rabbinical organization, adopted the Pittsburgh Platform with few reservations. The platform remained the basic statement of the tenets of Reform in America until the Columbus Conference in 1937. See document 49 in this chapter.

18. THE BEGINNING OF THE JEWISH THEOLOGICAL SEMINARY (1886)

H. PEREIRA MENDES[1]

The "Beginnings of the Seminary" must be sought amid the echoes of the Pittsburgh Conference of 1885. The conference, convened by earnest Reform rabbis, adopted resolutions objectionable to the Orthodox and Conservative groups. The resolutions came to be [called] the "Pittsburgh Platform."[2] Fifty-one years have softened the asperities it occasioned.

Be it far from me to revive. But to understand "the Beginnings of the Seminary" we must revert to the atmosphere of Jewish public opinion in those stirring days of fifty years ago.

Today we can well take a calm and reasonable view of the whole situation. Article 3 of that Platform formally rejected "all such ceremonies as are not adapted

---

Source: H. Pereira Mendes, "The Beginnings of the Seminary," in Cyrus Adler, ed., *The Jewish Theological Seminary of America. Semi-Centennial Volume* (New York: Jewish Theological Seminary of America, 1939), pp. 36–38, 41–43.

to the views and habits of modern civilization." That sounded plausible. But it took action pointing to abolition of the ceremony of the Abrahamic rite [of circumcision] for Jewish proselytes. It countenanced Sunday services under certain conditions. It recommended that each rabbi read "only such sections of the Pentateuch as *he* thinks proper, but with regard however to the regulations of the Jewish calendar."...Apart from the clamor of [the] hoi polloi, many calm and thoughtful conservative and Orthodox rabbis belonging to our New York Board of Jewish Ministers met for consultation....One day Dr. [Sabato] Morais,[3] a man whom I had learned to hold in high esteem, a man older than my honored father, called on me in New York to propose changing our action of meetings, debates, press-communications, accusations, recriminations, effervescence and indignation with no tangible result, into action that might mean, under God, something that would advance the cause so dear to us both, namely, the preservation of Historical and Traditional Judaism, with provision for upholding the ethical values of our religion, by establishing a Jewish Institute of Learning, by educating, training and inspiring teachers, rabbis who would stand *le-torah v'le-teudah*, "for the Torah and the Testimony," as cried out by our prophet of old (Isaiah 8:20).

He came with a definite plan of procedure ready. He proposed that he and I, as the head of the oldest congregations in the country, should take immediate action to awaken the two Jewish communities of New York and Philadelphia to the need of the hour, to create a Jewish College or Seminary on the lines indicated above....I eagerly and enthusiastically embraced all his propositions....As for Dr. Morais, I think we are justified in believing that apart from his passionate zeal and intense love *le-torah v'le-teudah*, for our religion and its interests, he was actuated by his conviction that a knowledge of Jewish learning, literature, history, ideals and Jewish science [academic scholarship] in its broadest sense was an absolute essential, if what we understand by the term American Jewry was to live as a power for human uplift and a factor in the evolution of world civilization in both Americas....Naturally Bible and Biblical literature became his special care at the new-born Seminary in New York, now known as The Jewish Theological Seminary of America.

I have now given you "The Beginnings of the Seminary" until the moment of its coming into actual life. Now let me, give you the "Beginnings of the Seminary" in the first years of its existence....As for the material "Beginnings of the Seminary," it is a pleasant personal reflection that the first four-figure check received by the Seminary was from a man whose daughter I was destined to choose as my life-helpmate a few years later. In those first years of our married life her quiet influence for social amenities necessary for modern ministry were felt by those students who came under "the shelter of her roof."

The Seminary became a fact, no longer a dream. It was opened. Dr. Morais naturally became its spiritual head. My own part was to help in the instruction and to interest my congregation in it. My congregation responded wholeheartedly and generously. Mr. Blumenthal, one of our Trustees, became the first President [of the Seminary]. Our Board of Trustees opened our Synagogue-building to the Seminary classes and placed it and all its accommodations at the disposal of the Seminary for its courses and activities. For a whole year all classes were held in our sacred building. It was to my mind a happy augury—that close contact of Seminary and Synagogue.

My own earliest part in its actual work was homiletics and history....Reverence for the Bible and an intimate knowledge of the text of the Bible were thus among "the Beginnings of the Seminary's" actualities.

In history I taught that all history was a palimpsest, a story written on the scroll of time by the hand of man but overwritten by "the finger of God." How mighty were "the hand of God" and "His outstretched arm!" "Is anything too wonderful for me" (Jeremiah 32:27). Therefore would-be rabbis must feel that the mission of Israel, to lead the world to God, would be one day accomplished, despite set-backs, disappointments, hindrances; and therefore they must be rabbis, not for mere vocation and livelihood, but for and because of the inspiration of our idealism. From the very "beginnings of the Seminary" idealism and loyalty to our ideals were stressed. These spiritual urgings were among the beginnings of the Seminary from the spiritual viewpoint.

NOTES

1. A descendant of a distinguished line of Sephardic rabbis, Henry Pereira Mendes (1852–1937) was born in Birmingham, England, where his father Abraham served as a rabbi. He himself officiated as a rabbi in

Manchester. In 1887 he was called to Congregation Shearith Israel (the Spanish-Portuguese Synagogue) in New York City. Together with Rabbi Morais (see note 3), he was a cofounder of the Jewish Theological Seminary in January 1886, of which he became secretary of the advisory board and professor of history. On the death of Rabbi Morais, he was appointed acting president of the seminary until Rabbi Solomon Schechter assumed the position in 1902 (see document 37 in this chapter).

2. The Pittsburgh Platform (see this chapter, document 17) led to a deep split in the American rabbinate. Adherents of traditional Judaism were scandalized by the platform's abolishment of circumcision for male converts to Judaism, the rejection of dietary laws (*kashrut*), the reduction of Hebrew prayers to a bare minimum, and the approval of conducting sabbath services on Sundays. Among those who objected to the Pittsburgh Platform were traditional rabbis, who accepted modified reforms, such as, mixed choirs, family pews, and thus to distinguish themselves from more strictly Orthodox Jews, called themselves "historical" or "conservative" Jews. Eventually in 1913 the United Synagogues of America was formed to unite all Conservative synagogues. The Jewish Theological Seminary, founded in 1886, was adopted by the new organization as the principal seminary to train "conservative" rabbis. Among the founders of the seminary—popularly known by its acronym "JTS"—was Rabbi Mendes, who in this memoir written on the occasion of the institution's fiftieth anniversary recalls its beginnings.

3. Sabato Morais (1823–1897) was born in Leghorn, Italy, to a family that originally came from Portugal to flee the Inquisition. In 1850 he was appointed to the pulpit of the Mikve Israel congregation in Philadelphia. A staunch liberal in social matters, both in Italy and in the United States, he was conservative in religious practice. Among the most ardent proponents of establishing the Jewish Theological Seminary, he was named its first president and professor of the Hebrew Bible, posts he held until his death.

19. THE ORTHODOX JEWISH CONGREGATIONAL UNION OF AMERICA (JUNE 8, 1898)[1]

A convention of Orthodox Congregations met in New York, Wednesday, June 8, 1898. A resolution favouring Zionism was adopted.

The principles of the convention adopted are as follows:

This Conference of delegates from Jewish congregations in the United States and the Dominion of Canada is convened to advance the interests of positive Biblical, Rabbinical and Historical Judaism.

We are assembled not as a synod, and therefore we have no legislative authority to amend religious questions, but as a representative body, which by organization and cooperation will endeavor to advance the interests of Judaism in America.

We favor the convening of a Jewish Synod specifically authorized by congregations to meet, to be composed of men who must be certified Rabbis, and

(a) Elders in official positions (Cf. Numbers 11:16);
(b) Men of wisdom and understanding, and known amongst us (Cf. Deut. 1:13);
(c) Able men, God-fearing men, men of truth, hating profit (Cf. Exodus 18:21).

We believe in the Divine revelation of the Bible, and we declare that the prophets in no way discountenanced ceremonial duty but only condemned the personal life of those who observed ceremonial law,

Source: The American Jewish Year Book 5660 [September 5, 1899 to September 23, 1900] (Philadelphia: Jewish Publication Society of America, 1899), pp. 99–100.

but disregarded the moral law. Ceremonial law is not optative; it is obligatory.

We affirm our adherence to the acknowledged codes of our Rabbis and Maimonides' thirteen principles of faith.

We believe that in our dispersion we are to be united with our brethren of alien faith in all that devolves upon men as citizens; but that religiously, in rites, ceremonies, ideals and doctrines, we are separate, and must remain separate in accordance with the Divine declaration: "I have separated you from the nations to be Mine."

And further, to prevent misunderstanding concerning Judaism, we reaffirm our belief in the coming of a personal Messiah and we protest against the admission of proselytes into the fold of Judaism without *millah*[2] and *tevilah*.[3]

We protest against intermarriage between Jew and Gentile; we protest against the idea that we are merely a religious sect and maintain that we are a nation, though temporarily without a national home, and

Furthermore, that the restoration to Zion is the legitimate aspiration of scattered Israel, in no way conflicting with our loyalty to the land in which we dwell or may dwell at any time.

The following are extracts from the Constitution:

The organization shall be known as the Orthodox Jewish Congregational Union of America.

The objects of this organization shall be the promotion of the religious interests of the Jews in America and the maintenance of the welfare of Orthodox Jewish Congregations in America.

All Orthodox Jewish Congregations in America shall be eligible to membership and entitled to representation in the meetings of the Union, on application for membership to the executive committee....

NOTES

1. The Orthodox Jewish Congregational Union of America (later, Union of Orthodox Jewish Congregations) is the largest organization of Orthodox congregations in the United States and Canada. Founded in 1898, it was originally oriented to the few English-speaking, rather than Yiddish-speaking, Orthodox congregations in the United States. Today it has well over three thousand affiliated synagogues. Among its many activities is national *kashrut* supervision and certification, indicated by its now-famous "U."
2. *Millah* (Hebrew), circumcision required of all males entering the Covenant of Moses.
3. *Tevilah* (Hebrew), immersion in a ritual bath (*mikveh*) required of converts to Judaism.

20. THE CONCORDANCE OF JUDAISM AND AMERICANISM (1911)

KAUFMANN KOHLER[1]

There is no room for Ghetto Judaism in America. Look at any of the creeds and churches in our free land! They are all more tolerant, more liberal, more humane and sympathetic in their mutual relations than those in Europe. Our free institutions, our common school education, our enlightening press and

pulpit, with their appeal to common sense, enlarge the mental and social horizon and render progress the guiding maxim. Least of all could Judaism retain its medieval garb, its alien form, its seclusiveness, in a country that rolled off the shame and the taunt of the centuries from the shoulders of the wandering Jew, to

Source: Kaufmann Kohler, "American Judaism," *Hebrew Union College and Other Addresses* (Cincinnati: Ark Publishing Co., 1916), pp. 198–99.

place him, the former Pariah of the nations, alongside of the highest and the best, according to his worth and merit as *man*, and among a people that adopted the very principles of justice and human dignity proclaimed by Israel's lawgivers and prophets, and made them the foundation stones of their commonwealth. No, American Judaism must step forth, the equal of any church in broadness of view and largeness of scope, as a living truth, as an inspiring message to the new humanity that is now in the making, not as a mere memory of the past and a piece of Orientalism in the midst of vigorous, forward-pressing Occidental civilization.

American Judaism! What a power of inspiration lies in these two words! They spell the triumph of the world's two greatest principles and ideals, the consummation of mankind's choicest possessions, the one offered by the oldest, the other by the youngest of the great nations of history, the highest moral and spiritual and the highest political and social aim of humanity; the God of righteousness and holiness to unite and uplift all men and nations, and the Magna Charta of liberty and human equality to endow each individual with God-like sovereignty. Behold America, the land of the future! When the sun sets on the western horizon of Europe, its effulgent rays gild the hills that herald the dawn to the new world. The land of promise for all the persecuted! God hid it, as it were, in His treasure-house to reserve it for the most glorious chapter of human history, when out of the mingling of races and sects, nay, out of the boldest, the most courageous and most independent elements of society, a new, a stronger, healthier and happier type of men and women should emerge, able to cope successfully with the hardships and problems of life, and bring the world nearer to the realization of its highest and holiest dreams and ideals, social, political and religious. And behold Judaism leaving the ark, because the flood of unrighteousness, of cruelty and inhumanity has ceased, and looking out upon a new earth and a new heaven, wherein justice, liberty and peace reign in fulfillment of its seer's visions. Was not the cry "Land! Land!" that resounded on Columbus' ship, the opening up of a new future for the martyr-race at the very time, when its woe and misery had reached their culmination in the land it had enriched by its own toil? Then the voice of God was heard speaking to the fugitive Spanish Jew, as He afterward spoke to the German, the Galician and the Russian Jew: "Go forth and be a blessing to the multitudes of people, and a light to the many nations and classes that settle in the new hemisphere."

NOTE

1. Kaufmann Kohler (1843–1926), American Reform rabbi and president of Hebrew Union College. Born and educated in Germany, Kohler came to the United States in 1869. He was the principal spirit behind the Pittsburgh Platform, and he was for much of his career a vigorous proponent of the classical Reform point of view, namely, that Judaism is preeminently a religious confession devoted to the mission of leading the world to a genuine, universal faith. Like many Reform leaders, he viewed this mission to be utterly compatible with the ideals of the American Republic, *ergo* there was no contradiction between an abiding loyalty to Judaism and integration into American polity and culture.

The title we have given this excerpt from Kohler is a phrase taken from Emil Gustav Hirsch (1851–1923), another leader of Reform in the United States. The address was delivered before the Union of American Hebrew Congregations on January 8, 1911.

21. THE MANHATTAN BEACH AFFAIR (1879)[1]

NEW YORK HERALD

The war against the Jews, which was carried on at Saratoga two years ago, is apparently to be revived at Coney Island. This time it is in a quarter where the Jewish residents of New York City are particularly aimed at. Several days ago a rumor was circulated to the effect that Austin Corbin, the President of the Manhattan Beach Company, had taken an open stand against admitting Jews to the beach or hotel. This report was on Sunday strengthened by a statement from Mr. P. S. Gilmore, the leader of the Manhattan Beach band, who said that Mr. Corbin told him he was going to oppose the Jews, and that he would rather "sink" the two millions invested in the railway and hotel than have a single Israelite take advantage of its attractions. A representative of the *Herald* called upon Mr. Corbin at his banking establishment in the new Trinity building, No. 115 Broadway, yesterday, to ascertain what foundation there was for these most extraordinary rumors. Mr. Corbin at first exhibited some timidity about talking on the subject, but finally invited the reporter into his private office, where he was joined by his brother and partner, Daniel C. Corbin.

"You see," he began, "I don't want to speak too strongly, as it might be mistaken for something entirely different from its intended sense. Personally I am opposed to Jews. They are a pretentious class, who expect three times as much for their money as other people. They give us more trouble on our railroad and in our hotel than we can stand. Another thing is, that they are driving away the class of people who are beginning to make Coney Island the most fashionable and magnificent watering place in the world."

"Of course, this must affect business?"

"Why, they are hurting us in every way, and we do not want them. We cannot bring the highest social element to Manhattan Beach if the Jews persist in coming. They won't associate with Jews, and that's all there is about it."

"Do you intend to make an open stand against them?"

"Yes, I do. They are contemptible as a class, and I never knew but one 'white' Jew in my life. The rest I found were not safe people to deal with in business. Now, I feel pretty warm over this matter, and I will write a statement which you can publish."

Mr. Corbin sat down at his desk and wrote a few sentences on a slip of paper, as follows:

"We do not like the Jews as a class. There are some well behaved people among them, but as a rule they make themselves offensive to the kind of people who principally patronize our railroad and hotel, and I am satisfied we should be better off without than with their custom."

"There," said he, handing the statement to the reporter, "that is my opinion, and I am prepared to follow up the matter. It is a question that has to be handled without gloves. It stands this way: We must have a good place for society to patronize. I say that we cannot do so and have Jews. They are a detestable and vulgar people. What do you say, eh, Dan?"

This last sentence was addressed to his brother, Mr. Daniel Corbin, who had taken an active part in the conversation. Dan said, with great emphasis, "Vulgar? I can only find one term for them, and that is nasty. It describes the Jews perfectly."

Mr. Austin Corbin then spoke warmly of the loss sustained by the Manhattan Beach Company in consequence of Israelitish patronage.

"Do you mean, Mr. Corbin, that the presence of Jews attracts the element of ruffianism?" asked the reporter.

Source: Stanley McKenna, "Reviving a Prejudice: Jewish Patronage Not Welcomed at Manhattan Beach . . . ," *New York Herald*, July 22, 1879.

"Not always. But the thing is this. The Jews drive off the people whose places are filled by a less particular class. The latter are not rich enough to have any preference in the matter. Even they, in my opinion, bear with them only because they can't help it. It is not the Jews' religion I object to; it is the offensiveness which they possess as a sect or nationality. I would not oppose any man because of his creed."

"Will the other members of the Manhattan Beach Company support you in your position?"

"I expect them to. They know just as much about it as I do, and no reasonable man can deny that the Jews will creep in a place just as it is about to become a grand success and spoil everything. They are not wanted at the Beach, and that settles it."

"Have you spoken to any other members about it?"

"No; but I guess they know my opinions."

Mr. Corbin rose from the chair he had been sitting in and paced the floor. "I'll tell you," said he, running his fingers through his hair, "if I had had my way and there was no one to consult in the matter but myself, I would have stopped the Jews from coming long ago. You just publish my statement. It covers the whole ground, and I mean every word of it."

Mr. Corbin concluded the conversation by telling the reporter to be sure and not give the impression that he was warning against the Jewish religion, but he stigmatized the Jews as having no place in first-class society.

NOTE

1. Beginning in the 1870s, social antisemitism in the United States became increasingly manifest. The much-publicized refusal of accommodations to the Jewish financier Joseph Seligman at the Grand Hotel in Saratoga Springs, New York, symbolized the problem. Seligman was informed that the hotel's manager, Henry Hilton, had "given instructions that no Israelites shall be permitted in the future to stop at this hotel." Jews were barred from private resorts, social clubs, and private schools—institutions of the upper classes. The older social elite were striving to secure their position and to fend off the intrusions of those individuals who had only recently acquired wealth in the post–Civil War industrial boom. This article is an interview with Austin Corbin, president of both the Long Island Railroad and the Manhattan Beach Company. Corbin candidly explains why he wishes to bar Jews from Coney Island, a place that he wants to develop into a fashionable resort.

22. THE JEWS MAKE ME CREEP
(1896, 1901, 1914)

HENRY ADAMS[1]

, Social anti-semitism

[*To Charles Milnes Gaskell*[2]—*July 31, 1896.*]
I am myself more than ever at odds with my time. I detest it, and everything that belongs to it, and live only in the wish to see the end of it, with all its infernal Jewry. I want to put every money-lender to death, and to sink Lombard Street and Wall Street under the ocean. Then, perhaps, men of our kind might have some chance of being honorably killed in battle and eaten by our enemies. I want to go to India, and be a Brahmin, and worship a monkey....

We are in the hands of the Jews. They can do what they please with our values....

For three years I have told you that in my opinion there was only one safe and surely profitable investment, and that is gold, locked up in one's private safe. There you have no risk but the burglar. In any other form you have the burglar, the Jew, the Czar, the socialist, and, above all, the total, irremediable, radical rottenness of our whole social, industrial, financial, and political system....

[*To Elizabeth Cameron*[3]—*August 14, 1901.*]

We arrived here [Warsaw] yesterday afternoon, after a tiresome night and day in what they call an express, through a country flatter than Florida, and less varied. But we had the pleasure of seeing at last the Polish Jew, and he was a startling revelation even to me, who have seen *pas mal de Jew*. The country is not bad; on the contrary, it is a good deal like our plains, more or less sandy, but well-watered. It is the people that make one tired. You would gratify all your worst instincts if you see a dozen women reaping the grain, and one big, clumsy man standing over them, superintending and doing nothing. With what pleasure should I have called your attention to it, knowing your ferocious and evil nature in regard to my sex! While Sister Anne is really so indifferent to masculine crime, wrapped up as she is in the passion for her two hulking boys! I can get very little fun out of her on that account, and she seems to grow worse always. She bore the journey well—better than I expected, for I found it fatiguing; but we've a worse one tomorrow to Moscow, and I shall be glad to see her well over it. Warsaw is a big, bustling city, like all other cities, only mostly Jews, in which it is peculiar to Poland. I see little to remark in the streets; nothing in the shops. The people are uglier than on Pennsylvania Avenue which is otherwise my lowest standard. Like all other cities and places, it is evidently flattened out, and has lost most of its characteristics. The Jews and I are the only curious antiquities in it. My only merit as a curio is antiquity, but the Jew is also a curiosity. He makes me creep....

[*To Charles Milnes Gaskell—February 19, 1914.*]

The winter is nearly over, I am seventy-six years old, and nearly over too. As I go, my thoughts turn to you and I want to know how you are. Of myself, I have almost nothing to tell. It is quite astonishing how the circle narrows. I think that in reality as many people pass by, and I hear as much as I ever did, but it is no longer a part of me. I am inclined to think it not wholly my fault. The atmosphere really has become a Jew atmosphere. It is curious and evidently good for some people, but it isolates me. I do not know the language, and my friends are as ignorant as I. We are still in power, after a fashion. Our sway over what we call society is undisputed. We keep Jews far away, and the anti-Jew feeling is quite rabid. We are anti-everything [Jewish] yet we somehow seem to be more Jewish every day. This is not my own diagnosis. I make none. I care not a straw what happens provided the fabric lasts a few months more; but will it do so? I am uneasy about you. I judge you to be worse than we. At least you are making almost as much howl about it....

NOTES

1. Henry Adams (1838–1918), a grandson of John Quincy Adams, sixth president of the United States, and a distinguished novelist, journalist, and historian.
2. Charles Milnes Gaskell (1842–1919) was an English lawyer and Liberal Party politician, whom Adams befriended in London when he served as a correspondent for the *New York Times*.
3. Elizabeth Cameron was a close friend of Henry Adams and the wife of Pennsylvania senator James Donald Cameron.

23. LEO FRANK LYNCHED (AUGUST 1915)[1]

NEW YORK TIMES

ATLANTA, Ga., August 17—Dangling in a grove within a stone's throw of the hillside birthplace of Mary Phagan, the body of Leo M. Frank, lynched by a mob perfect in its precision and organization, was cut down at Marietta this morning while threats to burn it were being made by the big crowd that gathered after the lynchers had departed.

Hurried to the village square—two miles distant—in an undertaker's dead wagon, the body was then transferred to an automobile, resting lengthwise across the tonneau[2] in a wicker basket, and rushed to Atlanta, followed by a trail of automobiles.

Attempts were made by telephone to intercept the car, but without success, and an undertaker's ambulance met the machine at the outskirts of the city and conveyed the body in safety to Greenburg & Bond's undertaking establishment in Atlanta. It was there embalmed after being viewed by thousands, and about midnight, under a heavy policy guard, was placed aboard a Southern Railway train to be taken to Brooklyn, N.Y., for burial. The funeral party, including Mrs. Frank and several Atlanta friends of the family, who will accompany the body to Brooklyn, was guarded carefully by the police until the train left the terminal station....

No violence other than strangulation was committed upon the body by the lynchers. Despite reports that it had been riddled with bullets, not a mark except upon the throat was visible when it was cut down.

As it fell to the ground the foot of a frenzied onlooker was pushed into the face, badly distorting the features, and adding to the discoloration caused by blood congelation....

The lynching of Frank was the outcome of weeks of deliberate study and planning. It was carried out with clockwork precision. The living victim, fully conscious and aware of his impending fate, was transported more than 100 miles.

As told in long-distance telephone messages to The New York Times early this morning, Frank was taken from the State Prison farm at Milledgeville shortly after 10 o'clock on Monday night, after the prison authorities had been overpowered, was thrown into an automobile and rushed over the country roads with so little disturbance that even in Marietta no one knew of the crime until a voice over the telephone to Deputy Sheriff L. Hicks said:

"Leo Frank's hanging to a limb down here in the Frey's Gin[3] neighborhood. Retribution."

The Deputy Sheriff hastily donned his clothes and, in a buggy, traveled to the spot. He had been preceded by a score of others, one of whom, William Frey, owner and operator of the gin, had seen the procession of lynchers file along the road. They were standing in a circle beneath the body, which swung in the light breeze, still warm.

The story of how Frank passed his last hours and the incidents attending the hanging none but the self-appointed executioners know.

It was the first automobile lynching which Georgia has experienced, and it was carried out with reckless boldness. But few of the twenty-five men who drove up to the State Prison Farm in five automobiles wore masks. The prison was protected by a Warden, a Superintendent, and a score of armed guards, but apparently there was no opportunity given them to resist.

Just before midnight the Superintendent J.E. Burke was summoned to the door of his house and handcuffs were placed on him. Two men with shotguns guarded him and he was told that it was useless to remonstrate, that the men were after Frank and would get him.

Source: "Frank Lynched After 100-Mile Ride; His Face Mutilated by Second Mob, Governor Promises Prompt Action." New York Times, August 18, 1915, p. 1.

A trusty on guard at the penitentiary gate was overpowered and the men rushed up the stairs to Frank's room. Four men seized the prisoner by his arms and legs, a fifth grasped him by the hair. He fought and groaned with pain from the wound, which was inflicted on him a month ago when another convict attempted to assassinate him while he was in the dormitory by cutting his throat. His captors paid no heed to his protests, but dragged him roughly down the stairs. They even put shackles on his wrists.

There were enough men in the lynching party to awe the guards who were aroused and those who had entered the building for Frank were unmolested as they dragged him across the yard and put him in one of the automobiles. Telephone and telegraph wires were cut so that an early warning was impossible and the automobiles started on their way.

The Superintendent said that he did not recognize any of the men, who were believed to be citizens of Marietta, the one time home of Mary Phagan.

NOTES

1. An American-born engineer Leo Max Frank (1884–1915) had come from New York City to work in his uncle's pencil factory in Atlanta, Georgia. When in April 1913 a thirteen-year old girl, Mary Phagan, who was employed at the factory was found murdered, Frank was accused of the crime. During the trial, a leading local newspaper demanded the execution of "the filthy, perverted Jew of New York." On the basis of dubious evidence, Frank was convicted by the Atlanta court; his subsequent appeal to the Supreme Court, which rendered the case a national cause célébre, was turned down. When the governor of Georgia, who was convinced of Frank's innocence, commuted his scheduled execution to a life-term, a mob rushed the prison and dragged Frank out and hung him. More than seventy years later, Frank was vindicated, when an elderly man, Alonzo Mann, came forth and filed an affidavit testifying that as a child of thirteen he saw a one John Conley dragging the body of the murdered child's body. Threatened to keep silent lest he, too, be murdered, Mann guarded his secret until 1983. Encouraged by his testimony, the Anti-Defamation League, which was born in the wake of the Frank affair (see this chapter, document 44), successfully petitioned the State of Georgia's Board of Pardons to grant Frank a posthumous pardon. In March 1986, the governor of Georgia signed the pardon, but without clearing him of the crime. The lynching of Frank pointed to the upsurge of antisemitic feelings sweeping America, especially in the southern and western states, where Jews were identified with the eastern financial establishment and the oppressors of farmers and small businessmen. Numerous organizations were founded to combat the Jews and other putatively pernicious alien elements.

2. A tonneau is an open rear passenger compartment of an automobile.

3. Frank was hanged in an oak grove near a cotton gin owned by William Frey, who was the county sheriff at the time.

24. JEWISH IMMIGRATION INTO THE UNITED STATES: 1881*–1948

1881	8,193†	1899	37,415‡	1916	15,108	1933	2,372
1882	31,807	1900	60,764	1917	17,342	1934	4,134
1883	6,907	1901	58,098	1918	3,672	1935	6,252
1884	15,122	1902	57,688	1919	3,055	1936	6,252
1885	36,214	1903	76,203	1920	14,192	1937	11,352
1886	46,967	1904	106,236	1921	119,036	1938	19,736
1887	56,412	1905	129,910	1922	53,524	1939	43,450
1888	62,619	1906	153,748	1923	49,989	1940	36,945
1889	55,851	1907	149,182	1924	10,292	1941	23,737
1890	67,450	1908	130,387§	1925	10,267	1942	10,608
1891	111,284	1909	57,551	1926	11,483	1943	4,705!
1892	136,742	1910	84,260	1927	11,639	July 1943 to	
1893	68,569	1911	91,223	1928	11,639	Dec. 1945	18,000#
1894	58,833	1912	80,595	1929	12,479	1946	15,535
1895	65,309	1913	101,330	1930	11,526	1947	25,885
1896	73,255	1914	138,051	1931	5,692	1948 (Jan. to Oct.)	
1897	43,434	1915	26,497	1932	2,755		12,300
1898	54,630						

*We have no exact figures for Jewish immigration prior to 1881. Some 50,000 German Jews arrived up to 1848. No statistics are available about arrivals from Central Europe from 1848 to 1869, when greater numbers of Jewish emigrants began to arrive from Russia, through 1880, an estimated total of 30,000 landed in the United States. Of smaller contingents of Jews from Austro-Hungary and Rumania who immigrated up to 1880 we have likewise no statistics.

†For 1881 to 1898 statistics are available only for the number of Jews admitted at the ports of New York, Philadelphia and Baltimore.

‡For 1899 to 1907 figures are available for Jewish immigrants at all ports of the United States.

§Since 1908, statistics of departure as well as of arrivals have been kept on record. For slightly different figures see Simon Kuznets, "Immigration of Russian Jews to the United States: Background and Structure," Perspectives in American History 9 (1975), pp. 35–124.

!That is, the fiscal year July 1942 to June 30, 1943.

#The figure for July 1943 to December 1945 is an estimate.

Source: Mark Wischnitzer, To Dwell in Safety: The Story of Jewish Migration Since 1800 (Philadelphia: Jewish Publication Society, 1948), p. 289. Reprinted by permission of the Jewish Publication Society.

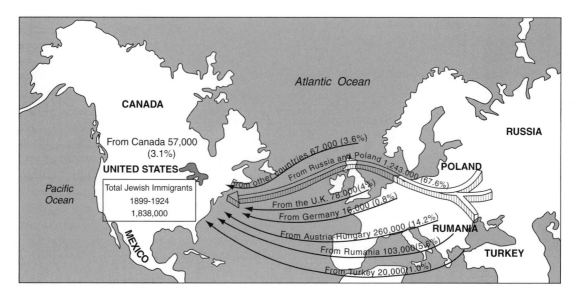

From Canada 57,000 (3.1%)

From other countries 67,000 (3.6%)

From Russia and Poland 1,243,000 (67.6%)

From the U.K. 78,000 (4%)

From Germany 16,000 (0.8%)

From Austria-Hungary 260,000 (14.2%)

From Rumania 103,000 (5.6%)

From Turkey 20,000 (1.0%)

Total Jewish Immigrants 1899-1924 1,838,000

Jewish Immigration to the United States 1899–1924. The percentages indicate the proportions of the total number of immigrants.

25. THE RUSSIAN JEW IN AMERICA (JULY 1898)

ABRAHAM CAHAN[1]

The Jewish population in the United States has grown from a quarter of a million to about one million. Scarcely a large American town does not have some Russo-Jewish names in its directory, with an educated Russian-speaking minority forming a colony within a Yiddish-speaking colony, while cities like New York, Chicago, Philadelphia and Boston have each a Ghetto rivaling in extent of population the largest Jewish cities in Russia, Austria and Rumania. The number of Jewish residents in Manhattan Borough is estimated at two hundred and fifty thousand, making it the largest centre of Hebrew population in the world. The Russian tongue, which twenty years ago was as little used in this country as Persian, has been added to the list of languages spoken by an appreciable portion of the polyglot immigrant population.

Have the newcomers justified the welcome extended to them from Chickering Hall?[2] Have they proved a desirable accession to the American nation?

"Let another man praise thee, and not thine own mouth; a stranger, and not thine own lips," is a proverb current among the people who form the subject of this paper; and being one of them, I feel that it would be better, before citing figures and facts, to

Source: The Atlantic Monthly, July 1898, pp. 130–33.

let Gentile Americans who have made a study of the New York Ghetto answer the question. Here is what Mr. Jacob A. Riis,[3] an accepted authority on "how the other half lives," has to say of Jewish immigrants:

> They (the Jews) do not rot in their slum, but, rising, pull it up after them....As to their poverty, they brought temperate habits and a redeeming love of home. Their strange customs proved the strongest ally of the Gentile health officer in his warfare upon the slum. The death-rate of poverty-stricken Jew-town, despite its crowding, is lower always than that of the homes of the rich....I am a Christian, and hold that in his belief the Jew is sadly in error. So that he may respect mine I insist on fair play for him all around. I am sure that our city has to-day no better and no more loyal citizen that the Jew, be he poor or rich, and none she has less to be ashamed of....

The question of limiting immigration engages the attention of Congress at frequent intervals, and bills aiming at reform in this direction are brought before the Senate and the House. In its bearings upon the Russian, Austrian or Rumanian Jew, the case is summed up by the opinions cited. Now let us hear the testimony of facts on the subject. The invasion of foreign illiteracy is one of the principal dangers which laws restricting immigration are meant to allay, and it is with the illiteracy of the New York Ghetto that we shall concern ourselves first.

The last report of the commissioner-general of immigration gives twenty-eight percent as the proportion of illiterates among the immigrants who came during the past year from Russia. The figure would be much lower, should the computation be confined to immigrants of the Mosaic faith instead of including the mass of Polish and Lithuanian peasants, of whose number only a very small part can read and write. It may not be generally known that every Russian and Polish Jew, without exception, can read his Hebrew Bible as well as a Yiddish newspaper, and that many of the Jewish arrivals at the barge office are versed in rabbinical literature, not to speak of the large number of those who can read and write Russian. When attention is directed to the Russian Jew in America, a state of affairs is found which still further removes him from the illiterate class, and gives him a place among the most ambitious and the quickest to learn both the written and the spoken language of the adopted

country, and among the easiest to be assimilated with the population.

The cry raised by the Russian antisemites against the backwardness of the Jew in adopting the tongue and the manners of his birthplace, in the same breath in which they urge the government to close the doors of its schools to subjects of the Hebrew faith, reminds one of the hypocritical miser who kept his gate guarded by ferocious dogs, and then reproached his destitute neighbor with holding himself aloof. This country, where the schools and colleges do not discriminate between Jew and Gentile, has quite another tale to tell. The several public evening schools of the New York Ghetto, the evening school supported from the Baron de Hirsch fund, and the two or three private establishments of a similar character are attended by thousands of Jewish immigrants, the great majority of whom come here absolutely ignorant of the language of their native country. Surely nothing can be more inspiring to the public-spirited citizen, nothing worthier of the interest of the student of immigration, than the sight of a gray-haired tailor, a patriarch in appearance, coming, after a hard day's work at a sweat-shop, to spell "cat, mat, rat," and to grapple with the difficulties of "th" and "w." Such a spectacle may be seen in scores of the class-rooms in the schools referred to. Hundreds of educated young Hebrews earn their living, and often pay their way through college, by giving private lessons in English in the tenement houses of the district—a type of young men and women peculiar to the Ghetto. The pupils of these private tutors are the same poor overworked sweat-shop "hands" of whom the public hears so much and knows so little. A tenement house kitchen turned, after a scanty supper, into a class-room, with the head of the family and his boarder bent over an English school reader, may perhaps claim attention as one of the curiosities of life in a great city; in the Jewish quarter, however, it is a common spectacle.

Nor does the tailor or peddler who hires these tutors, as a rule, content himself with an elementary knowledge of the language of his new home. I know many Jewish workmen who before they came here knew not a word of Russian, and were ignorant of any book except the Scriptures, or perhaps the Talmud, but whose range of English reading places them on a level with the average college-bred American.

The grammar schools of the Jewish quarter are overcrowded with children of immigrants, who, for progress and deportment, are rated with the very best in the city. At least 500 of 1677 students at the New York City College, where tuition and books are free, are Jewish boys from the East Side. The poor laborer who will pinch himself to keep his child at college, rather than send him to a factory that he may contribute to the family's income, is another type peculiar to the Ghetto.

The innumerable Yiddish publications with which the quarter is flooded are also a potent civilizing and Americanizing agency. The Russian Jews of New York, Philadelphia and Chicago have within the last fifteen years created a vast periodical literature which furnishes intellectual food not only to themselves, but also to their brethren in Europe. A feverish literary activity unknown among the Jews in Russia, Rumania and Austria, but which has arisen here among the immigrants from those countries, educates thousands of ignorant tailors and peddlers, lifts their intelligence, facilitates their study of English, and opens to them the doors of the English library. The five million Jews living under the tsar had not a single Yiddish daily paper even when the government allowed such publications, while their fellow countrymen and co-religionists who have taken up their abode in America publish six dailies (five in New York and one in Chicago), not to mention the countless Yiddish weeklies and monthlies, and the pamphlets and books which to-day make New York the largest Yiddish book market in the world. If much that is contained in these publications is rather crude, they are in this respect as good—or as bad—as a certain class of English novels and periodicals from which they partly derive their inspiration. On the other hand, their readers are sure to find in them a good deal of what would be worthy of a more cultivated language. They have among their contributors some of the best Yiddish writers in the world, men of undeniable talent, and these supply the Jewish slums with popular articles on science, on the history and institutions of the adopted country, translations from the best literatures of Europe and America, as well as original sketches, stories, and poems of decided merit. It is sometimes said (usually by those who know the Ghetto at second hand) that this unnatural development of Yiddish journalism threatens to keep the immigrant from an acquaintance with English. Nothing could be further from the truth. The Yiddish periodicals are so many preparatory schools from which the reader is sooner or later promoted to the English newspaper, just as the several Jewish theatres prepare his way to the Broadway playhouse, or as the Yiddish lecture serves him as a stepping-stone to that English-speaking, self-educational society, composed of working-men who have lived a few years in the country, which is another characteristic feature of life in the Ghetto. Truly, the Jews "do not rot in their slum, but, rising, pull it up after them."

NOTES

1. Abraham Cahan (1860–1953), Russian-born editor, author, and socialist leader. Eluding the tsarist police who sought his arrest because of his revolutionary activities, Cahan arrived in New York City in 1882. There he became a central figure in the Jewish labor movement. In 1897 he helped found the Yiddish-language socialist newspaper the *Forverts* or the *Jewish Daily Forward*, which he edited from 1903 until 1951. (Although published in Yiddish, the front page of the newspaper indicated its title in both English and Yiddish.) Under his editorship, the *Forverts* became America's largest and most influential foreign-language newspaper. See this chapter, document 30.

   In the title of Cahan's article, as in American literature in general, the term *Russian Jew* is a generic designation for all Jewish immigrants from Russia, Rumania, Galicia, Poland, and other countries of Eastern Europe.

2. Chickering Hall was a popular cultural center in New York City.

3. Jacob August Riis (1849–1914) was a Danish-American social reformer who applied his journalistic and photographic talents to advocate for New York City's impoverished.

26. THE BETHLEHEM JUDEA COLONY, SOUTH DAKOTA (1883)[1]

THE AM OLAM MOVEMENT

The colony Bethlehem Judea is founded by the first group of the Kremenchug *Bnei Horin* (Sons of Freedom) to help the Jewish people in its emancipation from slavery and in its rehabilitation to a new truth, freedom, and peace. The colony shall demonstrate to the enemies of our people the world over that Jews are capable of farming. With this as our main premise, we…have adopted the following resolutions:

All members of the colony Bethlehem Judea must engage in farming. Only when all work on the farm is finished may they engage in other productive occupations. Commercial activity is absolutely forbidden. (This point cannot be revised.)

All members of the colony form one family enjoying the same rights and privileges.

Two-thirds of the income of the colony are to be spent on its maintenance and expansion and one-third is to be set aside for a special colonization fund.

The colony considers it its duty to continue the colonization of Russian Jews in America through the establishment of new colonies.

The new colonies thus established form one community with the mother colony and are subject to its regulations.

The scope of the colonization fund is to be determined annually, after the harvest, by the Council of the Colony.

The Council of the Colony, which has also judicial functions, consists of the president, the vice-president, and the judge of the colony.

The Council of the Colony is elected for a period of five years, until such time as the land will become the property of the colony.

The executive powers of the colony are vested in the hands of the president and vice-president. They conclude all agreements in the name of the community, appoint the manager and the agronomist of the community. They bear the responsibility for the financial and social state of the community.

Once a year the president and vice-president shall submit a report to the general assembly of the colony.

The president has the right of veto in all matters pertaining to the colony.

All disputes among members must be brought before the judge of the colony.

Women shall enjoy equal rights with men.…

The colony has unanimously elected the following officers: Saul Sokolovski, president; Isidor Geselberg, vice-president; Shlomo Promislovski, judge. This Council of the Colony is elected for a period of five years, that is from January 1, 1883, to January 1, 1888.

NOTE

1. Am Olam (occasionally referred to in Yiddish as Am Oylom) is the name of a Russian Jewish society, founded in Odessa in 1881, that sought to promote the settlement of Jews in the United States in the form of agrarian communes guided by socialist principles. The movement derived its name from Perez Smolenskin's essay of 1872, "Am olam" (The Eternal People), published in the Hebrew monthly, *Hashahar*, in which he called for the national revival of the Jewish people. Between 1881 and 1882 groups were formed in Yelizavetgrad, Kiev, Kremenchug, Vilna, and Odessa. Although many members of these groups never made

Source: Abraham Menes, "The Am Oylom Movement," *YIVO, Annual of Jewish Social Science* 4 (1949), pp. 26–27. Reprinted by permission of the YIVO Institute for Jewish Research. Orthography has been changed to conform with current usage.

it beyond New York City, four Am Olam communes were established in 1882: one in Louisiana, two in South Dakota, and one in Oregon. Because of debt and other difficulties, these communes disbanded within a few years. After a brief attempt to establish urban communes in San Francisco and in New York, the movement dissolved in 1890. Many of its former members continued to play a significant role in the Jewish labor movement.

The Bethlehem Judea commune, founded in 1883 in South Dakota, initially consisted of twelve young people, all unmarried men, except for one married couple.

They were from Kremenchug and called themselves Bnei Horin ("the sons of freedom"). The aims of the Bnei Horin, which eventually totaled thirty-two members, Menes observes, "were rather ambitious. They dreamed of combining the idea of national revival with a new social order. The members of Bethlehem Judea believed that their enterprise would ultimately prove to be a great material and moral success and that large groups of immigrants would emulate them" (Abraham Menes, The Am Oylom Movement," *YIVO Annual of Jewish Social Science*, 4 [1949], p. 27). Nonetheless, after eighteen months Bethlehem Judea dissolved.

27. WOMEN WAGE-WORKERS (SEPTEMBER 1893)

JULIA RICHMAN[1]

This is an age of progress; and, surrounded as we are to-day by every evidence of the astounding advance that the nineteenth century has carried with in its train, I feel that I am flinging down a challenge that will, perhaps, bring me face to face with a volley of rhetorical bullets, when I assert that in no other country and in no other direction is this progress more noticeable than in the relative position to man and the affairs of the world that woman occupies to-day. This advance has been made in almost every grade in society, in almost every walk in life; but so far as my own personal observations have permitted me to go, so far as my own experiences have enabled me to judge, it is my belief that this change, this revolution, yes, this progress is more noticeable in the position held by the Jewish women of America (notably the descendants of European emigrants driven

from their home forty or fifty years ago), than in that of any other class in our cosmopolitan society.

Many conditions have conspired to bring about this change: the general advance in the education of women; the desire to give children greater educational advantages than the parents enjoyed; the financial value of woman's work; the frequent necessity for women to contribute to the support of families; the growing conviction that there is not a sufficient number of marrying men to supply all the marriageable girls with good husbands—these are but a few, with only one of which it is my privilege to deal, viz., the financial value of woman's work.

Perhaps it is due to custom and tradition, perhaps due to our oriental origin, but notwithstanding the fact that there may have always been among us a certain number of Deborahs, Ruths and Esthers,

Source: Julia Richman, "Women Wage-Workers: With Reference to Directing Immigrants" (1893) in Jacob R. Marcus, *The American Jewish Woman. Documents: A Documentary History* (New York: Ktav Publishers, 1981), pp. 421–27. Reprinted by permission of Ktav Publishing House, Inc.

in general, the wives and daughters of Jews were, and in parts of the world unfortunately still are, regarded as man's inferiors, their chief mission in life being to marry, or rather to be given in marriage, to rear children, to perform household duties and to serve their lords and masters.

This is an age of progress; and thousands of women, many of them good, true, womanly women, have discovered for themselves, or have been led to discover, that there is, at best, only an uncertain chance of real happiness facing the woman who calmly settles down in her parents' home, to perform, in an inane, desultory way, certain little household or social duties, who lives on from day to day, from year to year, without any special object in life, and who sees no prospect of change, unless a husband should appear to rescue her from so aimless an existence. Having made this discovery they try to join, and frequently, in the face of opposition, succeed in joining the ever-increasing army of women wage-workers, striving to lead useful, if sometimes lonely, lives, with the hope of making the world, or that little corner thereof into which their lives have fallen, a little better and a little brighter than they found it....

The Jews of America, particularly the Jews of New York City, are, perhaps, the most charitable class of people in the whole world. Time, labor and money are given freely in some directions. But charity is not always philanthropy; and we have reached a point in the development of various sociological problems which makes it imperative that philanthropy be placed above charity. The need of charity must disappear as we teach the rising generation how to improve its conditions.

Almost all female immigrants who come to this shore, through lack of knowledge as to the means by which they can swing themselves above the discouraging conditions which face them, sink down into the moral and intellectual maelstrom of the American ghettos, becoming first household or factory drudges, and then drifting into one of three channels: that of the careless slattern, of the giddy and all-too-frequently sinful gadabout, or of the weary, discontented wife.

We must disentangle the individual from the mass. We must find a way or several ways of leading these girls, one by one, away from the shadows which envelop them, if not into the sunshine of happiness and prosperity, at least, into the softening light

of content, born of pleasant surroundings, congenial occupations, and the inward satisfaction of a life well spent.

Working girls' clubs are doing a grand work, but these clubs never reach the lower strata. There must be something before and beyond the working girls' clubs, something that shall lay hold of the immigrant before she has been sucked down into the stream of physical misery of moral oblivion, from which depths it becomes almost impossible to raise her.

In this age of materialism, in these days of close inquiry as to the "Why?" of every condition, it has been claimed that the ever-increasing proportion of unmarried women among the Jews of America is largely due to the independent position women make for themselves, first, by becoming wage-earners, and, second, through the development of self-reliance brought about by societies, working girls' clubs and kindred movements. If marriage always meant happiness, and if celibacy always meant unhappiness, to make women independent and self-reliant would be a calamity. But, in the face of so much married unhappiness and so much unmarried discontentment, it is hardly pessimistic to wish that there might be fewer marriages consummated until the contracting parties show more discrimination in their selection of mates.

The saddest of many sad conditions that face our poor Jewish girls is the class of husbands that is being selected for them by relatives. It is the rule, not the exception, for the father, elder brother or some other near relative of a Jewish working girl to save a few hundred dollars, by which means he purchases some gross, repulsive Pole or Russian as a husband for the girl. That her whole soul revolts against such a marriage, that the man betrays, even before marriage, the brutality of his nature, that he may, perhaps, have left a wife and family in Russia, all this counts for nothing. Marry him she must, and another generation of worthless Jews is the lamentable result.

I wish it distinctly understood that there is no desire on my part to disparage matrimony; indeed, happy wifehood and motherhood are to my mind the highest mission any woman can fulfill; but in leading these girls to see the horror of ill-assorted marriages, I intend to teach them to recognize the fact that many of them may never find suitable husbands; and recognizing this fact, they must fill up their lives with useful, perhaps even noble work. Should the possible husband fail to appear, their lives will not have been barren; should he come, will a girl make a less faithful wife and mother because she has been taught to be faithful in other things?

And so I could go on showing how, in every direction, the harm and the evil grow, until the day will come when charity, even with millions at her disposal, will not be able to do good. It is easier to save from drowning than to resuscitate the drowned. Disentangle the individual from the mass; create a new mass of disentangled individuals, who shall become the leading spirits in helping their benighted sisters, and with God's help, the future will redeem the present and the past.

NOTE

1. Julia Richman (1855–1912) was a well-known educator; a university-trained teacher and school principal, in 1903 she was appointed the first woman superintendent of schools in her native New York City. Active on behalf of immigrant children, she organized an employment agency for school dropouts—then a major problem due to economic pressures—while developing various programs to combat truancy and juvenile delinquency. She also pioneered educational reforms and innovative pedagogy; among her many projects were the founding of New York City's Parent-Teacher Association and of medical and social services for pupils as well as special educational programs for mentally retarded children. She was likewise active in specifically Jewish welfare and educational projects; she served as the first president of the Young Women's Hebrew Association, and for many years she was the director of the Hebrew Free School Association in New York City. In recognition of her varied contributions in education and social welfare, a girls' high school in New York City was named in her memory.

In September 1893 she attended the Parliament of Religions, which took place in conjunction with the Chicago's World Fair. At the Jewish Women's Congress, one of the subsessions of the Parliament, she read the paper presented here. She celebrates the comprehensive progress in the status of women in the United States, particularly marked among Jewish women in the urban centers. She, however, also notes the sad plight of immigrant women. The Congress laid the foundation for the establishment of the National Council of Jewish Women, dedicated to promoting the interests and welfare of Jewish working women, especially immigrants. Julia Richman maintained an active role in the leadership of the Council, serving as the chairperson of its committee of religious school work.

28. SWEATSHOPS IN PHILADELPHIA (1905)

CHARLES S. BERNHEIMER[1]

We enter a sweatshop on Lombard, Bainbridge, Monroe or South Fourth Street. It may be on one of several floors in which similar work is going on. The shop is that of the so-called contractor—one who contracts with the manufacturer to put his garments together after they have been cut by the cutter. The pieces are taken in bundles from the manufacturer's to the contractor's. Each contractor usually undertakes the completion of one sort—pants, coats, vests, knee pants or children's jackets. There is

Source: Charles S. Bernheimer, "The Economic Condition of the Russian Jew in Philadelphia," *The Russian Jew in the United States: Studies of Social Conditions in New York, Philadelphia, and Chicago, with a Description of Rural Settlements,* ed. C. S. Bernheimer (Philadelphia: John C. Winston Co., 1905), pp. 124–34.

probably one whole floor devoted to the making of this one kind of garment. It may be that two contractors divide the space of a floor, the one, perhaps, being a pants contractor, and the other a vest contractor, with an entirely distinct set of employees. To his employees the contractor is the "boss," as you find out when you inquire at the shop. Before you have reached the shop, you have probably climbed one, two or three flights of stairs, littered with debris. You readily recognize the entrance to one of these shops once inside the building. The room is likely to be ill-smelling and badly ventilated: the workers are afraid of draughts. Consequently, an abnormally bad air is breathed which it is difficult for the ordinary person to stand long. Thus result the tubercular and other diseases which the immigrant acquires in his endeavor to work out his economic existence.

There are the operator at the machine, the presser at the ironing table, the baster and the finisher with their needles—the latter young women—all bending their backs and straining their eyes over the garments the people wear, many working long hours in [the] busy season for a compensation that hardly enables them to live, and in [the] dull season, not knowing how they will get along at all.

If we apply our ordinary standards of sanitation to these shops they certainly come below such standards. By frequent visits we may grow accustomed to the sights and smells, and perhaps unconsciously assume that such shops must in the nature of things be in bad condition. But a little reflection will readily show the error of such an assumption.

It is all the more harrowing that the workers have a tenacity of life due to a rich inheritance of vitality, and that through sickness and disease, through squalor and filth, they proceed onward, often managing to pull themselves out of the economic slough, though retaining, perhaps, the defects of bad physical development and surroundings....

The shops are chiefly conducted by the contractors, entirely independent of the manufacturers and the various manufacturers for whom they work assume no liability with reference to them or their employees. They merely agree to pay so much per piece for the garments they give out, and expect the garments to be returned to their establishments as agreed upon by the contractors. Few in this city have "inside" shops, that is, shops in which the entire garment is completed inside the establishment, or in

a separate building, under their own supervision. Wherever these inside shops have been established the conditions are very much better; the shop is much cleaner, the light good, the air bearable and the compensation usually more steady.

The last statement requires elucidation. In one clothing manufacturing establishment, there is in the rear a so-called inside shop with a regular contractor in charge. The firm furnishes its first work to this contractor and thus enables him to give, in turn, steady employment, but claims it could not extend such a shop without adding considerably to the expense, as the rental and the assurance of regularity involve a larger outlay than arranging with contractors who compete on the basis of low rentals and the smallest possible expense.

The contractor is usually an operator or other worker who becomes imbued with the desire to set up for himself. Excessive competition among the small contractors has contributed to the bad economic state of affairs in the garment trades. The contractor is between the upper mill-stone of the manufacturer and the nether mill-stone of the workman, forced to take the prices of the one and trying to make the utmost possible out of the other. Some few have saved enough to become manufacturers themselves. Some of the old established manufacturing firms have retired from business as the result of the competition of this new element.

In actual money gains, the contractors whose earnings have been estimated are better off than their workmen. Many said that if they could get their little capital back they would probably return to their former occupation—at least for a time, for the desire to be a "boss" is strong and would doubtless lead to other attempts....

In [the] busy season the employees are required to work long hours, sometimes as high as fifteen, perhaps eighteen, a day. In [the] slack season they must wait for the work that is doled out to them. Where time enters at all into the measurement of the pay, the employers endeavor to stretch it without giving corresponding pay. There seem to be numerous devices by which the workers can be taken advantage of. The character of the work varies so much in any one trade that it seems difficult to regulate the prices unless by the most iron-clad arrangement, backed by the force of strong organization. But the weakness of the organizations has been apparent in the past. Sometimes they have been affiliated with one general labor organization, sometimes with another. They are now welded together under the United Garment Workers of America, into which they have gone during the past few years. With the exception of the Cutters' Union the membership of these organizations is almost entirely composed of Russian Jews.

NOTE

1. Charles Seligman Bernheimer (1868–1960), Philadelphia-born social worker, who was active in Jewish affairs. He edited the pioneer study *The Russian Jew in the United States*, to which he contributed the essay presented here.

Many immigrants found employment in the garment trade. At the time much of the work in this trade was done on a contractual basis. Contractors—middlemen—received cut goods from the manufacturers or merchants, either rented shop space or used their own apartments, bought or hired sewing machines and recruited workers. The minute division of labor permitted the employment of relatively unskilled people. These cramped workshops, with their long working days—a seventy-hour week was not uncommon—became known as "sweatshops."

29. THE ECONOMIC CONDITION OF THE RUSSIAN JEW IN NEW YORK CITY (1905)

ISAAC M. RUBINOW[1]

The Russian Jewish population in New York is far from being the uniform mass that it appears to a superficial observer. It is true that for more than twenty years a uniform stream of poverty-stricken Russian Jews has flowed to New York—but we must not forget that the process began more than twenty years ago and that social differentiation has had time to work upon the early comers. Almost every newly arrived Russian Jew must pay an exorbitant rent to a Russian Jewish landlord. It is almost certain that both have originally come from the same social stratum—for the rich Russian Jewish immigrant was an exception, so rare as to be almost statistically negligible—both at present represent two aspects of the same "economic condition." It is extremely probable that at present the majority of Russian Jewish workers work for Russian Jewish employers....

The years (1898–1903) of unprecedented business activity and "prosperity" for the United States, caused an unusually brisk demand for the products of this Jewish industry; and the growth of Russian Jewish fortunes in New York has been the immediate result of this demand....It certainly is not ready-made clothing and dry goods alone that have brought about this prosperity in a part of the Russian Jewish population. The jewelry business, the liquor business, to a limited extent, and the drug business, to a much greater extent, have all contributed to the same end. New York Jews have come to play a very important part in the theatrical business, but outside of Yiddish theatres and music halls, within the limits

---

Source: Isaac M. Rubinow, "The Economic Condition of the Russian Jew in New York City," *The Russian Jew in the United States: Studies of Social Conditions in New York, Philadelphia, and Chicago, with a Description of Rural Settlements,* ed. C. S. Bernheimer (Philadelphia: John C. Winston Co., 1905), pp. 103–7.

of the Ghetto, the Russian Jews have hardly entered this field.

It is a characteristic phenomenon of Russian Jewish life in New York that professions have formed as important a basis of prosperity as business, and perhaps even a larger one....

Medicine has remained one of the favorite professions...Probably from four hundred to six hundred of the seven thousand physicians in greater New York are Russian Jews. Though of late symptoms of over supply in the market have been noticed, the influx into the profession does not show any signs of abatement. The economic status of the majority is fair—many older members are well-to-do. In the real estate business of the East Side the medical man plays a part by no means unimportant. The dentists, less numerous, are much more prosperous. In the legal profession, on the contrary, the Russians cannot boast of any great success, either financial or otherwise. Pharmacy, on the border line between profession and business, has also attracted a large number of Russian youths, but the returns are far less satisfactory than those of the other occupations.

The teaching profession has probably provided a livelihood for more Jewish families than the others which we have enumerated. For obvious reasons, only the second generation, i.e., those born on the American soil, or those who had emigrated at a very early age, are fit for the profession; but it will certainly be a revelation to many an American to learn how many Russian Jewish young men and girls are doing this work of "Americanization," not only of Jewish, but of Irish, German and Italian children. There is no doubt that the Jews have supplied a greater proportion of public school teachers than either the Germans or the Italians. The profession has never been a road to fortune; yet with the latest salary schedule, a very comfortable living has been provided for several thousands of families.

The important position which the Russian Jew occupies in the professions of New York City is more significant because he entered them but a short time since. Ten years ago, a Russian Jewish journalist found only a few dozen representatives of his race in medicine and law, a few individuals in dentistry, and hardly any in the teaching profession, or in municipal service. These dozens have grown into hundreds, and even thousands, within the following decade. With a remarkable display of energy and enterprise, the Russian Jew was ready to grasp the opportunity whenever and wherever it presented itself....

While the economic significance of the facts passed under review cannot be denied, it is evident that business and professional classes make up only a small percentage of the Russian Jewish population of New York City—much smaller, indeed, than of the German Jews....The vast majority of the Russian Jews are on a much lower economic level. They belong to the "masses," as against the "classes."...

Within these "masses" industrial labor of various kinds is the main source of livelihood. The New York Russian Jew is a wage-worker, notwithstanding the numerous exceptions to the rule. The examples of wage-workers of yesterday changing into employers of labor almost overnight are many. Lately these examples have been rapidly multiplying with the remarkable changes going on within the clothing industry—a process of decentralization, due to the legislative difficulties put in the way of the domestic system, which was the backbone of the clothing industry some years ago. In 1900, New York State had more than 4,000 establishments for [the] manufacture of clothing, most of them in New York City, and a very large proportion in Russian Jewish hands. Yet the number of these proprietors is insignificant in comparison with more than 100,000 workers in this same industry in the same state. The vast majority of the newcomers also join this industrial army in this as well as other branches of manufacturing. The question of the economic condition of the Russian Jew in New York is therefore preeminently the question of wages, hours and conditions of labor in general.

NOTE

1. Isaac Max Rubinow (1875–1936), Russian-born economist and social worker. He was active in Jewish affairs in New York City.

30. THE INTERNATIONAL LADIES' GARMENT WORKERS' UNION AND THE AMERICAN LABOR MOVEMENT (1920)

FORVERTS[1]

In Chicago a convention of the International Ladies' Garment Workers' Union opens to-day at which there will be present about three thousand delegates from the entire length and breadth of the country.

For the first time in the history of this powerful labor organization, the most important trade in the general women's clothing industry comes to the convention one hundred per cent organized. The cloak makers have, during the past two years, captured the last stronghold of the employers, who have always been considered invincible. Cleveland fell; the last factories in Canada were captured; cities in the far West were organized; and the cloak trade comes to the convention entirely under the flag of the union.

Of great significance is the recommendation of the executive committee that the union should organize co-operative shops. This plan reflects the spirit of the new tendencies in the union movement of the world, the spirit which leads workers to control industries themselves.

The I.L.G.W.U. stands now in the foremost ranks of the American labor movement, both materially and spiritually. It is one of the most important unions in the country. It has won for its members such conditions that very few of the real [sic] American unions may compare with it. Spiritually it is in every respect one of the most progressive. It responds to every movement for justice, for light. It is always prepared to help the workers in other trades in their struggles to help the oppressed and the suffering.

The International Ladies Garment Workers' Union is a blessing to its members, a pride to the general labor movement, and a hope for the progress of humanity at large.

NOTE

1. The *Forverts* was a Yiddish-language daily founded in New York City in 1897 as a more moderate offshoot of the militantly left-wing *Abendblatt*. The *Forverts* considered itself to be an educator of the immigrant Jewish community in its transition to American culture. At its peak in the 1920s, the newspaper's circulation, encompassing eleven local and regional editions, surpassed a quarter of a million. The *Forverts* defended the cause of labor, socialism, humanity, and distinguished literature; its articles were published both in Yiddish and in other languages. See document 25, this chapter.

It has been estimated that in 1916 nearly 40 percent of all gainfully employed Jews in New York City were garment workers. It is thus not surprising that organizing the Jewish garment workers was the primary sphere of trade-union activity among the Jews of New York City. The International Ladies Garment Workers' Union (ILGWU), founded in 1900 in New York City, was the largest and most influential of the "Jewish" unions.

Source: "Editorial, *Forverts*, May 3, 1920," trans. in Mordecai Soltes, *The Yiddish Press: An Americanizing Agency* (New York: Teachers College, Columbia University, 1925), pp. 147–48.

31. ZIONISM AND THE JEWISH WOMEN OF AMERICA (1915)

HENRIETTA SZOLD[1]

New York January 17, 1915

Dear Mrs. Julius Rosenwald,[2]

Let me congratulate you and Palestine upon having secured as you tell me in your telegram, a "splendid response from a local" [Chicago Jewish Committee for Palestinian Welfare]. I wish there were a way for Hadassah being kept informed of all you do.... However, the paramount consideration is that you are advancing the cause of Palestine. From my point of view, as I need not tell you, that is the cause of the Jew and, most important of all, of Judaism. In many respects the war catastrophe has left me bewildered and uncertain.[3] In one respect I see more clearly than ever—that is in respect to Zionism. The anomalous situation of the Jew everywhere—the distress, misery, and in part degradation (witness Poland) of seven million, more than half, of our race; the bravery of the Jews who are serving in all armies; the size of the contingent we [are] contributing to every front—means to me that the Jew and his Judaism must be perpetuated and can be perpetuated only by their repatriation in the land of their fathers.

It is a miracle that, though we Zionists were not hitherto able to bring many to our way of thinking, nevertheless many in these days of stress think with pity of our little sanctuary. They have come to us and said: "Even if we do not see eye to eye with you, we are going to help you save the sanctuary you have established." Perhaps they feel that it will yield a sanctuary, refuge, and protection in the days of readjustment soon to dawn, we hope.

If you succeed, in your appeal to the Federation of Temple Sisterhoods, in conveying to the Jewish women of America the need of [a] sanctuary for the Jew, the need of a center from which Jewish culture and inspiration will flow, and if you can persuade them to set aside one day of the year as Palestine Day, on which thoughts and means are to [be] consecrated to a great Jewish world-organizing purpose, you will have accomplished a result that will bring immediate blessing to those now in distress and in terror of life, and a blessing for all future times redounding to the benefit not only of those who will make use of their sanctuary rights in Palestine, but also those who like ourselves, remaining in a happy, prosperous country, will be free to draw spiritual nourishment from a center dominated wholly by Jewish traditions and the Jewish ideals of universal peace and universal brotherhood.

If you and they do not follow us Zionists so far, at least they will respond to the appeal for material help—at least they will recognize that for the sake of Jewish dignity and self-respect, even the purely philanthropic work in Palestine, for which so large a part of Jewry has long felt a keen responsibility, may never again be allowed to relapse into a pauperizing chaos. They may refuse to accept the whole Zionist ideal. But the wonderful vitality shown by the Zionist settlement in the Holy Land—the resourcefulness of the [Zionist] colonists, who could supply the cities with grain and food for months, and the usefulness of the Zionist bank in averting panic and economic distress—they make of me a more confirmed and conscious Zionist than ever. I need not analyze the elements I have enumerated for you. You, who have been in the Holy Land, even if you do not—may I say, not yet?—agree with me, your mind will instinctively

Source: Henrietta Szold to Augusta N. Rosenwald, letter dated January 17, 1915, in Marvin Lowenthal, *Henrietta Szold: Life and Letters* (New York: Viking Press, 1942), pp. 84–88.

understand the leap mine makes in these troublous days to the Zionist conclusion.

Troublous days? I have often wondered during these months how many Jews in America realize that we are living through times comparable only to the destruction of the Second Temple and our commonwealth by the Romans, and exceeding by far the horrors of the exodus from Spain and Portugal, and the abject misery and suffering of the pogrom years 1881, and 1903, and 1905 in Russia.

The Jew speaks of the *Hurban*—the utter ruin of Salomon's Temple. He speaks of the second *Hurban*, the ruin of the second Temple by Titus. I feel that a future Graetz[4] will speak of this war as the Jews' third *Hurban*.

There is only one hope in my heart—the effective aid being rendered to Palestine by all Jews without difference. In the first *Hurban* the Jews could not protect their sanctuary against the hordes of Nebuchadnezzar. In the second *Hurban* the Roman legions destroyed the Temple, leaving only the western wall, the last vestige of glory, now turned into a place of wailing. There is no third Temple on the hill of Zion to be destroyed in this third Hurban; but in Zion, nevertheless, there is a sanctuary, the refuge that has been established by Jewish pioneers, with the sweat, blood, and labor of those who believe. As

American Jewesses they cannot possibly reject the centralized organization of Palestine, an endeavor for which Zionism stands first and last.

With cordial wishes for success, and may I add this only once only, with Zion's greetings, Henriette Szold.

NOTES

1. Born in Baltimore, Maryland, the daughter of a rabbi, Henrietta Szold (1860–1945) was the president of Hadassah, the Women's Zionist Organization of America, which she helped found in 1912. The goal of Hadassah, which is the Hebrew name of the biblical heroine Esther, was to promote the Zionist ideal through education and public health initiatives in Palestine. See also chapter 10, document 24, note 9.

2. Augusta Nusbaum Rosenwald (1869–1929) was the wife of Julius Rosenwald, a Chicago businessman and philanthropist, active in liberal Jewish and non-Jewish causes.

3. The reference is to World War I, which broke out in August 1914. The Jewish masses in Eastern Europe found themselves in the midst of the battles—thus Szold's distress about the plight of the "seven million, more than half, of our race."

4. Heinrich Graetz (1817–1891) was a German-Jewish historian and author of an eleven-volume *History of the Jews* (1853–1875).

32. THE DIVISION BETWEEN GERMAN AND RUSSIAN JEWS (1915)

ISRAEL FRIEDLAENDER[1]

America has, in less than one generation, become the second largest center of the Jewish Diaspora, and bids fair to become the first, instead of the second, within another generation. No other country in the world offers, even approximately, such a favorable combination of opportunities for the development of a Diaspora Judaism, as does America: economic possibilities, vast and sparsely populated territories,

Source: Israel Friedlaender, "The Present Crisis of American Jewry" [1915], in idem, *Past and Present: Collected Essays* (Cincinnati: Ark Publishing Co., 1919), pp. 341–43.

freedom of action, liberty of conscience, equality of citizenship, appreciation of the fundamentals of Judaism, variety of populations, excluding a rigidly nationalistic state policy, and other similar factors. It is no wonder, therefore, that in no other country did Reform Judaism [brought from Germany], as the incarnation of Diaspora Judaism, attain such luxurious growth as it did in America. It discarded, more radically than in Europe, the national elements still clinging to Judaism, and it solemnly proclaimed that Judaism was wholly and exclusively a religious faith, and that America was the Zion and Washington the Jerusalem of American Israel.

On the other hand, the emigrants from Russia brought the antithesis on the scene. They quickly perceived the decomposing effect of American life upon Jewish doctrine and practice, and they became convinced more firmly than ever that Diaspora Judaism was a failure, and that the only antidote was Palestine and nothing but Palestine. The nationalists among them beheld in the very same factors in which the German Jews saw the possibilities of a Diaspora Judaism the chances for organizing Jewry on purely nationalistic lines. Nowhere else, except perhaps in Russia, can be found a greater amount of Palestinian sentiment, as well as a larger manifestation of a one-sided Jewish nationalism, than is to be met with in this country.

This conflict of ideas became extraordinarily aggravated by numerous influences of a personal character. The division between the so-called German Jews and the so-called Russian Jews was not limited to a difference in theory. It was equally nourished by far-reaching differences in economic and social position and in the entire range of mental development. The German Jews were the natives; the Russian Jews were the newcomers. The German Jews were the rich; the Russian Jews were the poor. The German Jews were the dispensers of charity; the Russian Jews were the receivers of it. The German Jews were the employers; the Russian Jews were the employees. The German Jews were deliberate, reserved, practical, sticklers for formalities, with a marked ability for organization; the Russian Jews were quick-tempered, emotional, theorizing, haters of formalities, with a decided bent toward individualism. An enormous amount of explosives had been accumulating between the two sections which if lit by a spark might have wrecked the edifice of American Israel while yet in the process of construction.

NOTE

1. Israel Friedlaender (1876–1920). Polish-born, German and French-educated, from 1904 until his death he was a professor of Semitics and Bible at the Jewish Theological Seminary of America. In addition to many significant scholarly publications, he wrote extensively on contemporary Jewish affairs. He was celebrated for his uncanny ability to appreciate contrasting perceptions of a problem and to offer a Solomonic reconciliation between them; this was particularly true with regard to the tension between the "native" American Jews of German origin and the Jewish immigrants from Eastern Europe.

The masses of Jewish immigrants that began to reach the shores of the United States in the 1880s were greeted by a native Jewish community of some 280,000. The native Jews, mostly of German origin, were economically successful, and, despite some setbacks, liked to think of themselves as culturally and socially integrated into America. As American anti-immigrant sentiments increased in the 1880s and 1890s, the native, class-conscious German Jews were clearly threatened by the influx of Yiddish-speaking, culturally "backward" immigrants (the overwhelming majority of whom came from the poor working classes of East European Jewry). Notwithstanding the antagonism between the "uptown" native Jews and the "downtown" immigrants, the native Jews established an elaborate complex of agencies and philanthropic institutions to aid their co-religionists in their adjustment to the American way of life.

33. THE AMERICAN JEWISH COMMITTEE (JANUARY 12, 1906)

LOUIS MARSHALL[1]

What I am trying to accomplish is to get order out of chaos, and to unite all elements that might possibly seek to father a national movement with the result that union instead of discord would be the rule. Dr. Voorsanger[2] has attempted to organize one movement, Dr. Magnes[3] another, Dr. Mendes[4] a third, the Central Conference[5] a fourth. Mr. Kraus[6] believes that the Bnai Brith[7] affords a panacea for all ills, and the East Side is bristling with organizations, each national in scope and zero in accomplishment.

It has therefore occurred to me and to my associates, that before any scheme is launched, those who have the welfare of Judaism at heart should come together, merely for the purpose of comparing notes, with a view of ascertaining whether or not there is a possibility of promulgating a plan which will be generally acceptable, and which will accomplish the object which all of us have sincerely at heart.

What I am trying to avoid more than anything else is, the creation of a political organization, one which will be looked upon as indicative of a purpose on the part of the Jews to recognize that they have interests different from those of other American citizens. I conceive that there can be but two tenable theories on which the Jews have the right to organize: firstly, as a religious body, and secondly, as persons interested in the same philanthropic purposes.

Obviously, it will be an absolute impossibility for the Jews of this country to unite as a religious body having ecclesiastical and disciplinary powers. It would be impossible to afford to such an organization the authority and sanction which are essential to successfully carry out such a scheme.

We can, however, all unite for the purpose of aiding all Jews who are persecuted, or who are suffering from discrimination in any part of the world on account of their religious beliefs; and we can at the same time, unite for the purpose of ameliorating the condition of our brethren in faith, who are suffering from the effects of such persecution and discrimination directly or indirectly.

Whether it will be wise to go beyond this, I seriously doubt. Whether, if it were attempted, much harm would result, I strongly believe.

As you will see from some of the names which I have mentioned, it is my idea to bring into this organization, everybody who, if outside of it, would be a freelance, and a power for evil. It is better, therefore, to bring into organization men of every shade of opinion.

I do not believe it to be feasible to organize upon the basis of existing organizations. There would be much inequality and injustice if such a plan were adopted. We must, in some way or other, go back to the people and organize on the theory of democracy. While the beginning would be troublesome, I think, in the end, the results accomplished would be most excellent.

NOTES

1. Louis Marshall (1856–1929). U.S. lawyer and Jewish communal leader, Marshall was the chief spokesman of New York City's German Jewish elite. He served as president of the American Jewish Committee, which he helped establish, from 1912 to 1929. Although a non-Zionist, Marshall supported Jewish settlement in

---

Source: Louis Marshall to Rabbi Joseph Stolz, January 12, 1906, in Charles Reznikoff, ed., *Louis Marshall: Champion of Liberty* (Philadelphia: Jewish Publication Society of America, 1957), vol. 1, pp. 21–22. Copyright 1957 by the Jewish Publication Society of America. Reprinted by permission of the American Jewish Committee.

Palestine and sought to cooperate with the Zionists. Through his efforts the governing board of the Jewish Agency for Palestine was expanded to include non-Zionists. In the letter presented here, to Rabbi Joseph Stolz (1861–1941), a Reform rabbi in Chicago and one of Marshall's most intimate friends, Marshall broaches his idea of establishing an organization later to be known as the American Jewish Committee.

The American Jewish Committee, established in 1906, is the oldest still-existing, Jewish defense organization in the United States. In addition to Marshall, its founders included some of the most prominent members of the German Jewish elite in the United States. The organization was their response to pogroms in Russia. The committee conducted its affairs in an oligarchic, noblesse oblige fashion until the 1940s, limiting membership to a select few.

2. Jacob Voorsanger (1852–1908), Reform rabbi in San Francisco. He was considered the foremost rabbi on the West Coast.

3. Judah Magnes (1877–1948), Marshall's brother-in-law. A Reform rabbi, he was the founder and president of the *Kehillah* of New York City from its inception in 1908 until its demise in 1922. Adapting the Kehillah of Eastern Europe as a model, the Kehillah in the United States attempted to be the central organization of their respective communities. Most ambitious was the effort of the New York City Kehillah, which sought to direct community affairs in the fields of education, sociology, religion, industrial problems and general public relations. See document 38 in this chapter.

4. Henry Pereira Mendes (1852–1937), English-born rabbi of New York City's Sephardi congregation, Shearith Israel. He was one of the founders of the Union of Orthodox Congregations in America, the Jewish Theological Seminary of America, and the Federation of American Zionists.

5. The Central Conference of American Rabbis—U.S. association of Reform rabbis founded in 1889.

6. Adolf Kraus (1850–1928). U.S. lawyer and Jewish communal leader, Kraus served as the international president of the Bnai Brith from 1905 to 1925; he also helped found the Anti-Defamation League in 1913.

7. Bnai Brith, founded in New York City in 1843, is the world's oldest and largest Jewish service organization.

34. THE GALVESTON PROJECT (OCTOBER 25, 1907)

JACOB H. SCHIFF[1]

I had a conference yesterday with Messrs. Cyrus Sulzberger,[2] Oscar Straus,[3] and Professor Loeb[4] upon the project about which we have been recently corresponding, and we have reached the conclusion that the Removal Office at New York, with the experience and connections it has already secured, would be well in position to undertake the carrying out of my project, as far as the labor on this side is concerned.

With this in view, it is proposed that the Removal Office create an organization at New Orleans or Galveston, or both, to receive arriving immigrants and at once forward them to their destination, which is to be previously arranged for through the New York organization of the Removal Office. To accomplish this properly, it is thought that the Removal Office should have sixty days' previous notice of the

Source: Jacob H. Schiff to Israel Zangwill, October 25, 1907, in *Jacob H. Schiff: His Life and Letters*, ed. C. Adler (Garden City: Doubleday, 1928), vol. 2, pp. 98–99.

initial embarkation of emigrants for New Orleans or Galveston, and that the first shipment should not exceed 500 persons.

It would be left to the ITO [Jewish Territorial Organization], allied in this, as I hope, with Dr. Paul Nathan's Hilfsverein,[5] to father the movement in Russia, to gather the proposed emigrants, to arrange steamship routes, etc., and for any expense attached to this the funds would have to be found in Europe. On the other hand, I shall undertake to place at the disposal of the Removal Office the $500,000 which it is my intention to devote to the initiation of the project. Based upon the cost per head of carrying on the present removal work, which is steadily going forward, half a million dollars should suffice to place from 20,000 to 25,000 people in the American "Hinterland," and I believe, with the successful settlement of such a number, others would readily follow of their own accord, and that then a steady stream of immigration will flow through New Orleans and Galveston into the territory between the Mississippi River on the east, the Pacific Ocean on the west, the Gulf on the south and the Canadian Dominion on the north.

This project is now to a great extent in your own and your friends' hands, and I shall look forward with deep interest to see what can be done with it....

NOTES

1. Jacob H. Schiff (1847–1920), financier and philanthropist. Born in Germany, Schiff came to the United States in 1865; in 1885 he became head of the banking firm of Kuhn, Loeb, and Company. For many years he was deemed the head of American Jewry and actively and generously supported numerous religious and cultural projects within the Jewish community.

   The Galveston Project, initiated and financed by Schiff, was a project to divert European Jewish immigration to the United States from the big cities of the East Coast to the southwestern states. Established in 1907, the Jewish Territorial Organization (ITO), headed by Israel Zangwill (see chapter 10, document 18), undertook to sponsor and supervise the project. The Galveston Project managed to settle ten thousand Jewish immigrants before it ceased operation during the First World War. In addition to genuine humanitarian motives, the Galveston Project was prompted by a desire to breakup the concentration of the Jews in urban ghettos which the "uptown" Jews deemed to be an inhibiting factor in the Americanization of the immigrants.

2. Cyrus Leopold Sulzberger (1858–1932), prominent New York merchant, philanthropist, and Jewish communal leader.

3. Oscar Solomon Straus (1850–1926), active in Jewish affairs and a U.S. public official. He was a U.S. diplomat and was the first Jew to serve in an American cabinet; he was the secretary of commerce and labor under Theodore Roosevelt from 1906 to 1909.

4. Morris Loeb (1863–1912). Son of Solomon Loeb, the original partner of the banking firm Kuhn, Loeb, and Company, he was a professor of chemistry at New York University and was active in Jewish communal life; he was Schiff's brother-in-law.

5. Hilfsverein der deutschen Juden was the central charitable society of German Jewry to assist Jews in Eastern Europe and oriental countries. Founded in Berlin in 1901, it continued to exist until 1941. Paul Nathan (1857–1927) was a founder of the Hilfsverein and was its general secretary from 1901 to 1914.

35. AMERICAN JUDAISM WILL NOT BE GHETTOIZED (1908)

DAVID PHILIPSON[1]

I hear it said that since the day of the organization of this Conference the face of the American Jewish universe has greatly changed; that, owing to the arrival of masses of immigrants during the past twenty years our religious situation is altogether different from what it was before. Dismay has seized many. The tide of reactionism has swept them off their feet. The optimistic note of the leaders of the nineteenth century has changed in many quarters to a pessimistic wail. The despairers cry that the progressive tendency that this Conference represents cannot possibly hold its own against the overwhelming odds that spell reactionism, ghettoism, romanticism, neo-nationalism and neo-orthodoxy. In spite of many untoward signs I firmly believe that there is no cause for despair, dismay and disheartenment. Ghettoism and reactionism are merely passing phases in the Americanization of our most recently arrived brethren. Let us have no fear; American Judaism will not be ghettoized nor Russianized, but our Russian brethren under the spell of the spirit of our free institutions will be Americanized, and if not this first generation then their children and their children's children will stand with the descendants of the earlier comers to this land as the representatives of that union of progressive modernity and sane conservatism which this Conference symbolizes. In the process of Americanization all the perverted viewpoints that are now distorting the vision of many otherwise excellent people will go the way of all the other extravagant notions wherewith the onward course of civilization has been diverted for a brief spell. Such fads as the glorifying of *Yiddish* as the national language of the Jews, such vain discussions as to whether there is a Jewish art or no, such empty dreams as the political rehabilitation of the Jewish state... will all pass as interesting incidents in the strange medley of this period of transition. And that which shall remain will be the great fundamental ideal of the mission of the Jews... as a people of religion and of Judaism as a religious force through all the world....

NOTE

1. David Philipson (1862–1949), American Reform rabbi. He was a founder of the Central Conference of American Rabbis, serving as its president from 1907 to 1909. He was regarded as a representative spokesman of "classic" Reform Judaism. See this chapter, document 16, note 1.

Source: David Philipson, "Message of the President," Proceedings of the Nineteenth Annual Convention of the Central Conference of American Rabbis, *Yearbook of the Central Conference of American Rabbis* 18 (1908), pp. 145–46. Reprinted by permission of the Central Conference of American Rabbis.

36. YIDDISH AND THE FUTURE OF AMERICAN JEWRY (1915)

CHAIM ZHITLOWSKY[1]

Firstly, we believe that the basis of our life in America will not be the Jewish religion, but rather our Jewish nationality. Actually, this is already the case, as it has always been. Jews in the Diaspora [golus] have always lived as a national minority, indeed everywhere they led the struggle to live as a national minority. Until the era of assimilation we never denied the national character of our existence....

To be sure, religion was the chief weapon in our struggle for a separate existence as a national minority. But it was not religion that constituted us as a people; it is not thanks to religion that we have remained a separate people. We created the Jewish religion: Judaism exists by virtue of the existence of the Jews. We elevated religion to a national duty of every Jew because our people needed it and because religion had the power to maintain us as a nation. In these times, however, religion is being transformed into a private matter of individuals alone, for it is now deemed that every individual has the right to believe as he wishes.

Hence, religious Judaism loses its national value and our existence is now to be reconstituted on a purely secular basis, having no relationship to one's religious belief whatsoever. Nowhere is the secular-national character of our people so manifest as here in America. The so-called congregation—the official religious organization [in America]—performs no effective role in our communal life....

What then can unify the Jewish people, if religion is no longer a factor [in the communal life of the Jew]? What remains, of course, is the national factor, the fact that we are Jews, that we want to live as Jews, that we have national interests. The national Jewish minority in America will therefore have once again to renew its struggle for its national minority existence as it did before the era of assimilation. And if America should not be amenable to our existence as a national minority, we will have to be prepared to bear the sacrifices necessitated by our struggle and to shake off the dust from our feet and once again take the wanderer's staff in our hand.

Fortunately, we have no reason to fear such an eventuality. We are not living in medieval Spain of the Inquisition, nor in contemporary barbaric Poland or Russia. We live in one of the freest countries known in history, a country which will not deny any group the right to live as it wishes, provided, of course, that this group be devoted to the political and social progress of the land, and on the condition that this group love the free nature of America's institutions and laws—provided, of course, that these institutions and laws indeed are free and democratic. We accept these conditions with alacrity, because no other national group appreciates as much as we do political equality and freedom....

We contend that our national cultural existence [in America] will be built on the foundation of the Yiddish language. Through Yiddish we will preserve all the significant treasures of universal culture as well as our own rich Hebrew heritage. We will educate our children in this language. We will establish our own educational institutions, from elementary schools to universities....[These institutions will be the crown of Yiddish culture.]

[In order that the Jewish people be preserved under present circumstances,] we need a power capable of binding all Jews into one entity, while allowing each the freedom of decisions, beliefs, hopes and actions. This power, of course, must be spiritual; it

Source: Chaim Zhitlowsky, "Unzer tsukunft do in land" [1915], *Gezamelte shriftn* (New York: Ferlag Gezelshaft, 1919), vol. 10, pp. 87–91. trans. S. Fuks Fried and P. Mendes-Flohr.

must also be a power that will serve to foster universal human progress. Such a spiritual power can only be the Yiddish language. Hence, our people in America will build its national future on the basis of this language. Nowhere is this being done with such drive and success as here in America.

NOTE

1. Chaim Zhitlovsky (1865–1943), a Russian-born socialist and philosopher of Diaspora (*golus*) nationalism and Yiddishism. In 1893, living in Zurich, he helped found the non-Marxist Russian party of Socialist Revolutionaries in exile and co-edited its journal. At the same time, he founded a Jewish socialist union; which published socialist literature in Yiddish. Although a Jewish nationalist, he opposed Zionism as reactionary and inimical to the interests of the Jewish workers of Eastern Europe. According to Zhitlovsky, the Jews—both as Jews and workers—will be emancipated only under socialism. While continuing the struggle for socialism, the Jewish workers should also seek to develop their own cultural and educational institutions. These opinions were close to those of the Bund, which he joined for a short time. In an article entitled *"Farvos davke yidish?"* (Why Precisely Yiddish?), published in 1900, he introduced his notion of Yiddishism, that is, the cultivation of Yiddish culture as the basis of national Jewish life. In 1904 Zhitlovsky came to the United States for a lecture tour on behalf of the Socialist Revolutionary party. On this occasion he attacked the melting-pot theory and advanced the vision of America as a place of harmony and integrity for separate nationalities. After chairing the Czernowitz Yiddish Conference of 1908 (see chapter 7, document 35), which proclaimed Yiddish to be a national language of the Jews, Zhitlovsky returned to the United States, where he became a leading figure in the burgeoning Yiddish culture and socialist movement.

37. ENGLISH AND HEBREW MUST BE THE LANGUAGES OF AMERICAN JEWRY (1904)

SOLOMON SCHECHTER[1]

I can quite understand the attachment some of us feel toward the German-jargon, or *patois*—call it what you will—in which for so many centuries Jewish mothers wrote their *tehinot* [supplications], and which is still spoken by such a large portion of Jewry. But let us beware lest we attach any sacredness to this dialect [Yiddish]. America, someone rightly remarked, is the grave of languages. No foreign language, be it ever so rich in masterpieces of literature, survives a single generation in this country. The children of the immigrant who visit our public schools soon compel their parents to speak English. It would thus be a sin to attach the fortunes of our great literature to the fortunes of this language, which is a mere accident in our history, doomed to die, and is dying before our very eyes. We cannot, we dare not, endanger the Judaism of our children by making a virtue of what may have once been an unfortunate necessity, but at present, thank God, is becoming an impossibility.

On the other hand, it is not necessary to dwell here at length on the vital importance of Hebrew, the Sacred Tongue. It is the great depository of all that

Source: Solomon Schechter, "Altar Building in America," *Seminary Addresses and Other Papers* (New York: Burning Bush Press, 1959), p. 88. Reprinted by permission of the United Synagogue of America, the Jewish Theological Seminary of America, and the Rabbinical Assembly of America.

is best in the soul-life of the Congregation of Israel. Without it we will become a mere sect, without a past, and without a literature, and without a proper liturgy, and severed from the great Tree which is life unto those that cling to it. Hellenistic Judaism is the only one known to history which dared to make this experiment of dispensing with the Sacred Language. The result was death. It withered away and terminated in total and wholesale apostasy from Judaism. Let us not deceive ourselves. There is no future in this country for a Judaism that resists either the English or the Hebrew language.

NOTE

1. Solomon Schechter (1847–1915). Rumanian-born rabbinic scholar, he served from 1902 until his death as the president of the Jewish Theological Seminary of America. He is considered the chief architect of Conservative Judaism in the United States. See document 40 in this chapter.

38. A REPUBLIC OF NATIONALITIES (FEBRUARY 13, 1909)

JUDAH L. MAGNES[1]

Lincoln believed in freedom. For him an American was a freeman, at liberty to develop his spirit as he chose, so long as he obeyed the law....

Since Lincoln's time, however, a strange phrase has become current. We hear much of Americanization. This is applied particularly to the Americanizing of the immigrant. What Lincoln would have thought of such a phrase is, of course, hard to say; but it is not difficult to see that the term Americanization, as all too often used, is not conceived in liberty and dedicated to the proposition that all men are created free and equal.

It must be accepted as almost axiomatic, that every one living in this land should be a citizen of the land. If Americanization means this, that every inhabitant, native born or foreign, assume the obligations of American citizenship, then Americanization is a process that should be aided by us in every legitimate way. It is, in fact, the very rare exception, that a newcomer refuses to renounce allegiance to his former political sovereign. The newcomers of the past generation and more have equalled their predecessors in the avidity with which they have entered into political partnership with their fellow citizens. There is no force, no compulsion about American citizenship. It is a privilege and a duty. A man is attracted to American citizenship just because this nation was conceived in liberty, and dedicated to the proposition that all men are created free and equal. There is hardly an American citizen who does not love this land, its history, its heroes, its literature, its institutions and its ideals of freedom and equality. That process of Americanization that makes clear the privilege and the duty of American citizenship is something for which we may all be grateful.

For some, however, the process of Americanization goes still further. They would demand of a prospective American that in order to become completely an American, he abandon his traditional religion. This view is, perhaps, more widespread than we imagine...

The phrase Americanization is used in still another sense. To become an American, thus many would have it, it is necessary not that one yield his

---

Source: Judah L. Magnes, "A Republic of Nationalities," *The Emanu-El Pulpit,* February 13, 1909, p. 5.

inherited religion, but that he abandon his traditional nationality. You will understand from what I have already said, that I do not use the word nationality in its political sense. Politically a man can be a member of but one nation at one time. When I speak of nationality here I mean, in particular, such elements of nationality as a man can carry with him when he leaves his old home—his national language, his race, his culture, his history, his traditions, his customs, his ideals. It is such things that a man is asked by some to give up in the name of Americanization. It is held that a man must give up his spiritual nationality in order that he may the better become an American; that is, that he may the better learn the language, the spirit, the ways, the institutions, the ideals of this land....

Now, of course, we must, all of us, accommodate ourselves to our surroundings. Even though we have not the will to do it, the force of life itself modifies us more or less in accordance, with our environment. Everyone must learn the language of the land, everyone must seek to understand the spirit of its history, its laws, its institutions, its ideals. Everyone must, in greater or in less degree, saturate himself with the dominant culture of the land, which is English. Our language is English, our history, our literature, our laws, our institutions, our ideals are almost entirely English....

This does not, however, by any means, imply that therefore a man's traditional national culture must be abandoned. On the contrary, it is possible and it is desirable that parallel with a high appreciation of, and assimilation to English culture, a man cling with reverence to the national culture of his fathers. Such a parallelism is desirable both from the point of view of the individual and for the sake of the developing culture of this country.

Thus there is no reason why, especially in large centers of population, the various nationalities there quartered should not foster their distinctive national culture parallel with the dominant culture of this land. The Italians, the Germans, the Jews, the Irish, the Slavic peoples and others might do this with advantage to themselves and to the whole country. The advantage to themselves would be their development along natural lines. The hiatus between the traditional national culture and the new surroundings is often so great that it leads to degeneracy of many kinds. The children of minority nationalities are all too often not the equals of their parents in

those things that have permanent value, because the chain of tradition has been broken and the accumulated wisdom and beauty of ages is set at nought. A member of a minority nationality is seldom, if ever, caricatured because he is true to himself, because he speaks his own tongue with love and cherishes his inherited spirit. He is most often caricatured and is despised because of his absurd haste to become as English as have those whose traditions reach back into English ways for many generations. For this country, too, the fostering of the national cultures in our midst would mean a richness, a picturesqueness, a variety, which, despite our individualism, we sadly lack. Democracy has the tendency to level all distinctions, to create the average type, most to demand uniformity. If, however, by reason of a variegated, national culture, we might be able to overcome this weakness of democracy, that Americanism which is not yet a finished product, but which is in the making might eventually become like a garden of blossoms of many colors, rather than a vast field of flowers of the same size and color.

Indeed, this recognition of the value to this country of national individualities would help us with many of our problems. I would not have you regard it as a mere pleasantry when I say that the Negroes, for example, may and do lend color to American culture in the making. They have not, by reason of their unfortunate history, attained the dignity of a national entity. But they have a racial individuality possessed of much of beauty and strength and sweetness, and calculated to lend attractiveness and power to the institutions and ideals of this land. The recognition of the same principle would help us in our relations to the Japanese in our midst. It is essential that all of our inhabitants become American citizens. That once accomplished, every one is free to develop his personality as best he can. Have we reached so far beyond barbarism that we can afford to ignore those elements of culture which the Japanese may bring us? Theirs is an ancient and a noble heritage, and it ill becomes us to set our faces against the beauty and the power of a civilization that happens to be oriental. America must, in order to be true to its high conception of liberty and of equality, seek to gather within its borders the representatives of all national cultures and of every civilization.

We Jews in particular have good reason to take this lesson to heart. With us nationality and religion are so inextricably interwoven that it would be dangerous, particularly from the point of view of our religion, to allow the cultivation of our Jewish nationality to fall into neglect or disrepute. . . .

But the cultivation of Jewish nationality in our midst will be of particular benefit to this country if it becomes an element in the development of the Jewish youth. Unfortunately, our main problem lies in the fact that our youth have lost their traditional religion and have not won for themselves an ideal that can even approximately take its place. The cleavage between parents and children presents a tragedy. The children learn (and are very often taught by us) to despise the spiritual heritage of their parents. We are in danger of rearing a godless generation, not because of any unworthiness inherent in our young, but rather because in the name of a spurious Americanization we shout from the housetops that our people give up their national individuality. . . . American culture, American nationality can be made fruitful and beautiful by contact with the culture of the varied nationalities that are among us. America is not the melting pot. It is not the Moloch demanding the sacrifice of national individuality. America is a land conceived in liberty and dedicated to the principle that all men are created free and equal. And a national soul is as precious and as God-given as is the individual soul. . . .

NOTE

1. Judah L. Magnes (1877–1948), American-born rabbi and communal leader. Upon his ordination as a Reform rabbi by Hebrew Union College in 1900, Magnes went to Germany to study. His stay in Germany occasioned several extended trips to Eastern Europe, where he was profoundly impressed by the richness and vitality of Jewish life there. These trips strengthened his sympathy for Jewish tradition, peoplehood, and Zionism. On his return to the United States in 1904, he served as a rabbi of several Reform congregations, most notably Temple Emanu-El (1906–1910). During that time, he was the secretary of the American Zionist Federation (1905–1908) and later became the president of the organized Jewish community of New York City, the so-called Kehillah, from its founding in 1908 until its demise in 1922. He left for Palestine in the same year, where he became the chancellor and, later, first president of the Hebrew University of Jerusalem.

39. ZIONISM IS CONSISTENT WITH AMERICAN PATRIOTISM (JUNE 1915)

LOUIS D. BRANDEIS[1]

Let no American imagine that Zionism is inconsistent with Patriotism. Multiple loyalties are objectionable only if they are inconsistent. A man is a better citizen of the United States for being also a loyal citizen of his state, and of his city; for being loyal to his family, and to his profession or trade; for being loyal to his college or his lodge. Every Irish American who contributed towards advancing home rule was a better man and a better American for the sacrifice he made. Every American Jew who aids in advancing the Jewish settlement in Palestine, though he feels that neither he nor his descendants will ever live there, will likewise be a better man and a better American for doing so.

Source: Louis D. Brandeis, "The Jewish Problem: How to Solve It," *Brandeis on Zionism: A Collection of Addresses and Statements,* foreword by Mr. Justice Felix Frankfurter, ed. Solomon Goldman (Washington, D.C.: Zionist Organization of America, 1942), pp. 28–31.

Note what [the British historian] R. W. Seton-Watson says:

America is full of nationalities which, while accepting with enthusiasm their new American citizenship, nevertheless look to some centre in the old world as the source and inspiration of their national culture and traditions. The most typical instance is the feeling of the American Jew for Palestine which may well become a focus for his *déclassé* kinsmen in other parts of the world.

There is no inconsistency between loyalty to America and loyalty to Jewry. The Jewish spirit, the product of our religion and experiences, is essentially modern and essentially American. Not since the destruction of the Temple have the Jews in spirit and in ideals been so fully in harmony with the noblest aspirations of the country in which they lived.

America's fundamental law seeks to make real the brotherhood of man. That brotherhood became the Jewish fundamental law more than twenty-five hundred years ago. America's insistent demand in the twentieth century is for social justice. That also has been the Jews' striving for ages. Their affliction as well as their religion have prepared the Jews for effective democracy. Persecution broadened their sympathies. It trained them in patient endurance, in self-control, and in sacrifice. It made them think as well as suffer. It deepened the passion for righteousness.

Indeed, loyalty to America demands rather that each American Jew become a Zionist. For only through the ennobling effect of its strivings can we develop the best that is in us and give to this country the full benefit of our great inheritance. The Jewish spirit, so long preserved, the character developed by so many centuries of sacrifice, should be preserved and developed further, so that in America as elsewhere the sons of the race may in the future live lives and do deeds worthy of their ancestors.

But we have also an immediate and more pressing duty in the performance of which Zionism alone seems capable of affording effective aid. We must protect America and ourselves from demoralization which has to some extent already set in among American Jews. The cause of this demoralization is clear. It results in large part from the fact that in our land of liberty all the restraints by which the Jews were protected in their Ghettos were removed and [the] new generation [is] left without [the] necessary moral and spiritual support. And is it not equally clear what the only possible remedy is? It is the laborious task of inculcating self-respect, a task which can be accomplished only by restoring the ties of the Jew to the noble past of his race, and by making him realize the possibilities of a no less glorious future. The sole bulwark against demoralization is to develop in each new generation of Jews in America the sense of *noblesse oblige*. That spirit can be developed in those who regard their people as destined to live and to live with a bright future. That spirit can best be developed by actively participating in some way in furthering the ideals of the Jewish renaissance; and this can be done effectively only through furthering the Zionist movement.

In the Jewish colonies of Palestine there are no Jewish criminals; because everyone, old and young alike, is led to feel the glory of his people and his obligation to carry forward its ideals. The new Palestinian Jewry produces instead of criminals, scientists like Aaron Aaronsohn,[2] the discoverer of wild wheat; pedagogues like David Yellin;[3] craftsmen like Boris Schatz, the founder of the Bezalel;[4] intrepid *shomrim*,[5] the Jewish guards of peace, who watch in the night against marauders and doers of violent deeds.

NOTES

1. Louis D. Brandeis (1856–1941), leader of American Zionism, prominent lawyer, and first Jew to be appointed Supreme Court justice. His espousal of Zionism and intense involvement in the movement marked a significant rapprochement between the native American Jews and the Russian immigrants. In this address, delivered at the conference of the Eastern Council of Reform Rabbis in June 1915, he spoke to the question of divided loyalties.

2. Aaron Aaronsohn (c. 1875–1919), pioneer of scientific agriculture in Palestine. To Brandeis he was the living symbol of the "new Jew."

3. David Yellin (1864–1941), a native of Jerusalem, was an outstanding educator, scholar, and communal leader.

4. The Bezalel School for industrial arts and crafts was founded in Jerusalem in 1906 by the sculptor Boris Schatz (1866–1933).

5. The *shomrim* ("guards") were members of Hashomer, a volunteer organization of Jewish workers who defended the Jewish colonies of Palestine against marauders.

40. CATHOLIC ISRAEL (c. 1896)

SOLOMON SCHECHTER[1]

It is not the mere revealed Bible that is of first importance to the Jew, but the Bible as it repeats itself in history, in other words, as it is interpreted by Tradition. The Talmud, that wonderful mine of religious ideas from which it would be just as easy to draw up a manual for the most orthodox as to extract a *vade mecum* for the most sceptical, lends some countenance to this view by certain controversial passages—not to be taken seriously—in which "the words of the scribes" are placed almost above the words of the Torah. Since then the interpretation of Scripture or the Secondary Meaning is mainly a product of changing historical influences, it follows that the centre of authority is actually removed from the Bible and placed in some *living body*, which, by reason of its being in touch with the ideal aspirations and the religious needs of the age, is best able to determine the nature of the Secondary Meaning. This living body, however, is not represented by any section of the nation, or any corporate priesthood of Rabbi-hood, but by the collective conscience of Catholic Israel as embodied in the Universal Synagogue. The Synagogue "with its long, continuous cry after God for more than twenty-three centuries," with its unremittent activity in teaching and developing the word of God, with its uninterrupted succession of Prophets, Psalmists, Scribes, Assideans, Rabbis, Patriarchs, Interpreters, Elucidators, Eminences, and Teachers, with its glorious record of saints, martyrs, sages, philosophers, scholars, and mystics; this Synagogue, the only true witness to the past, and forming in all ages the sublimest expression of Israel's religious life, must also retain its authority as the sole true guide for the present and the future. And being in communion with this Synagogue, we may also look hopefully for a safe and rational solution of our present theological troubles. For was it not the Synagogue which even in antiquity determined the fate of Scripture? On the one hand, for example, books like Ezekiel, the Song of Songs, and Ecclesiastes, were only declared to be Holy Writ in virtue of the interpretation put upon them by the Rabbis; and, on the other hand, it was the veto of the Rabbis which excluded from the canon the works that now pass under the name of Apocrypha. We may, therefore, safely trust that the Synagogue will again assert its divine right in passing judgment upon the Bible when it feels called upon to exercise that holy office. It is "God who has chosen the Torah, and Moses His servant, and Israel His people." But indeed God's choice invariably coincides with the wishes of Israel; He "performeth all things" upon which the councils of Israel, meeting under promise of the Divine presence and communion, have previously agreed. As the Talmud somewhere expresses itself with regard to the Book of Esther, "They have confirmed above what Israel has accepted below."

Another consequence of this conception of Tradition is that it is neither Scripture nor primitive Judaism, but general custom which forms the real rule of practice. Holy Writ as well as history teaches that the law of Moses was never fully and absolutely put in practice. Liberty was always given to the great teachers of every generation to make modifications and innovations in harmony with the spirit of existing institutions. Hence a return to Mosaism would be illegal, pernicious, and indeed impossible. The norm as well as the sanction of Judaism is the practice actually in vogue. Its consecration is the consecration of general use—or, in other words, of Catholic Israel. It was probably with a view to this communion that

Source: Solomon Schechter, "Introduction," *Studies in Judaism* (Philadelphia: Jewish Publication Society of America, 1896), pp. 17–20. Copyright 1896, 1945 by the Jewish Publication Society of America. Reprinted by permission of the Jewish Publication Society.

the later mystics introduced a short prayer to be said before the performance of any religious ceremony, in which, among other things, the speaker professes his readiness to act "in the name of all Israel."

NOTE

1. Solomon Schechter (1847–1915), president of the Jewish Theological Seminary of America and one of the architects of Conservative Judaism. In this selection, written prior to his immigration to the United States, he develops his idea of "catholic Israel," by which he meant the universally accepted sentiments and practices of devout Jews. This concept exercised a seminal influence on the evolving ideology of Conservative Judaism. See this chapter, document 18.

41. THE RECONSTRUCTION OF JUDAISM (1920)

MORDECAI M. KAPLAN[1]

In the first place, we are intensely desirous of having Judaism play an important role in the spiritual life of mankind, and we therefore refuse to view with equanimity the plight in which Judaism finds itself today. We are not deceived by the few sporadic signs of activity and interest in things Jewish, because we know full well that they represent nothing more than the momentum of Jewish life in the past. If a new synagogue is established, the organizers are not men who have been born and brought up in an American environment, but who immigrated to this country from eastern Europe. If, as a result of strenuous endeavor, a few Jewish student organizations spring up in some of our colleges, in nine cases out of ten the initiative is taken by the foreign-born, or by those who were brought up in the Jewish ghettos of our larger cities. Judaism in America has not given the least sign of being able to perpetuate itself. Very few American Jewish homes, if any, have produced rabbis, or teachers of religion, or communal leaders. Our spiritual poverty is so great that we have not in this country a single Hebrew printing establishment for the publication of books that are essential to the preservation of Judaism. We have not a single original edition of the traditional prayer book, to say nothing of the Bible or post-biblical literature. These and many similar facts go to prove that Judaism under democratic conditions such as obtained in this country has thus far not been able to develop that vitality which could endow it with creative power and make it capable of sustained effort and adaptability....

Secondly we are agreed that the salvation of Judaism cannot come either from Orthodoxy or from Reform. Orthodoxy is altogether out of keeping with the march of human thought. It has no regard for the world view of the contemporary mind. Nothing can be more repugnant to the thinking man of today than the fundamental doctrine of Orthodoxy, which is that tradition is infallible. Such infallibility could be believed in as long as the human mind thought of God and Revelation in semi-mythological terms....

Our dissent from Reform Judaism is even more pronounced than that from Orthodoxy. If we have been content to put up with much in Orthodoxy that we do not approve of, it is that we might not be classed with the "Reformers." The reason for this attitude of ours toward Reform is that we are emphatically

---

Source: Mordecai M. Kaplan, "A Program for the Reconstruction of Judaism," *The Menorah Journal* 6 (August 4, 1920), pp. 181–93.

opposed to the negation of Judaism. The principles and practices of Reform Judaism, to our mind, make inevitably for the complete disappearance of Jewish life. Reform Judaism represents to us an absolute break with the Judaism of the past....

The third point on which we concur, and which therefore gives us reason to believe that we may arrive at conclusions acceptable to all of us, is the fact that we are Zionists. We not only share the aspiration to see Israel restored to his homeland, but also subscribe to the principle that such aspiration is synonymous with the revival of Judaism. The very act of translating the longing for the restoration into practical effort has opened up to us a new vista of Jewish thought. It has helped us to discover the reality of the Jewish soul and the Jewish consciousness behind the system of beliefs and practices identified as Judaism. If we profess a Zionism that is more than merely political, we are largely indebted to Ahad Haam,[2] who was the first to give articulate expression to the spiritual significance of the Zionist Movement. Though practically nothing has been done to develop the larger implications of this profounder view of Zionism, there is a broad basis for cooperation in the conviction common to all of us, that the fate of Judaism is bound up with the success of Zionism....

In view of the fact that existing congregational and rabbinic organizations seem to be insensible to the danger which is threatening Judaism, and spend most of their time either perfecting their machinery or listening to speeches full of smoothing banalities, it is imperative that something be done immediately apart from those organizations to halt the impending disaster to our religion....

In getting to work upon a program for the reconstruction of Judaism we must take care not to miscalculate the magnitude of the task before us. Unless we are prepared to go to the root of the spiritual ills in Jewish life, we had better not begin at all. We must not be like physicians who are content to treat the symptoms of a disease rather than attack the cause, and who, instead of suggesting a real remedy, recommend some patent medicine or incantation. The real issue is not how to render our ritual in keeping with the requirements of modern life, but how to get our people sufficiently interested in religion to want a ritual. If we are not prepared to do much more for Judaism than revise the prayerbook, we should leave the prayerbook alone. We are faced with a problem no less than that of transforming the very mind and heart of the Jewish people. Unless its mythological ideas about God give way to the conception of divinity immanent in the workings of the human spirit, unless its static view of authority gives way to the dynamic without succumbing to individualistic lawlessness, and unless it is capable of developing a sense of history without, at the same time, being a slave to the past, the Jewish people has nothing further to contribute to civilization....

The adoption of the social viewpoint is an indispensable prerequisite to a thoroughgoing revision of Jewish belief and practice. That viewpoint will enable us to shift the center of spiritual interest from the realm of abstract dogmas and traditional codes of law to the pulsating life of Israel. We will then realize that our problem is not how to maintain beliefs or uphold laws, but how to enable the Jewish people to function as a highly developed social organism and to fulfill the spiritual powers that are latent in it. This is not the place to elaborate upon the manner in which the social approach to Judaism would revitalize the fundamental ideas of religion....

In fact, our adherence to the Zionist movement has already paved the way for a common acceptance of the social point of view in Judaism, for the main problem of the Zionist movement is how shall the Jewish people live. As Zionists, the problem of Judaism is to us simply the problem of the spiritual life of the Jewish people, and not a problem of abstract creeds and laws....

In view of these considerations, I believe that a program for the reconstruction of Judaism ought to include the following three items: (1) The interpretation of Jewish tradition in terms of present-day thought. (2) The fostering of the social solidarity of the Jewish people through the upbuilding of Palestine, and the establishment of Kehillahs[3] and communal centers in the Diaspora. (3) The formulation of a code of Jewish practice so that every Jew may know definitely what constitutes loyalty to Judaism.

While all of these activities should be instituted as soon as feasible, the order in which they are mentioned represents the degree of emphasis to be laid upon each at the present time. Thus, any attempt on an extensive scale to change the ritual would be entirely premature just now, before we ourselves have become firmly grounded in this newer outlook upon religion and Judaism, and have developed at least some of the most important implications of that outlook. Even then, I believe that the major part of the energy and time at our disposal will have to be devoted to what might be termed an educational campaign for popularizing the social approach to Judaism.

The achievement of our purpose will be facilitated if our initial activities identify us in people's minds as a new school of thought in Judaism, rather than as a new brand of Reform. If, for example, we come out with a new and revitalized conception of the Jewish duty toward Talmud Torah [Torah study], in its most comprehensive sense, we are less likely to be misunderstood. We must recognize that it is important not only to do right but to appear right. While we do not want to retard unduly the adoption of the much needed changes in our ceremonial practices, we should by all means avoid such a distortion of issues as that which is responsible for making the question of wearing or not wearing the hat the main line of cleavage between diametrically opposed types of Jewish life. We would no doubt be saved from such a fate if our first efforts were aimed at reinstating Jewish study as a religious duty from which no Jew, whether young or old, should be exempt....

The second line of activity, which should consist of efforts to strengthen the social solidarity of the Jewish people throughout the Diaspora, requires as much attention on our part as the work of transforming the mind of the Jewish people. There is at the present time no organized Jewish group that is qualified to foster Jewish communal life in the Diaspora. Both the Orthodox and the Reform Jews have a tendency to concentrate all their efforts upon one limited aspect of Jewish life, the one upon a decorous service, the other upon a kosher meal. The extreme Zionists, who despair of any spiritual life outside of Palestine, certainly have no patience with any attempt to bring order out of the chaos existing in the communal life in the Diaspora. The very existence of that chaos, they believe, will constitute an additional incentive to those who are intensely Jewish to migrate to Palestine. They would, therefore, do nothing to improve the status of Jewish communal life. In the meantime, there has come to the forefront a class which is only too anxious to take control of some of the Jewish communal affairs, in order to guide them away from Judaism. I refer to the class of Jewish philanthropists who are determined to kill Judaism with charity. They are ready to assist the Jew whenever he is in trouble, to heal him in his sickness, to send him relief if he is in want, to supply his children with social facilities and decent amusement,

and, if need be, to distribute him to the four corners of the world. But they systematically oppose anything and everything that might strengthen the Jewish consciousness or promote Jewish solidarity. Their policy has brought into existence a new type of social worker, whose main problem is how to administer an anesthetic to the Jewish people, so as to render its death painless. If, here and there, a social worker is to be found who refuses to contribute towards this solution of the problem, he has a hard time squaring himself with his directorate.

It should be the aim of a movement such as ours to see that the control of Jewish institutions passes over into the hands of those who believe in Judaism and the Jewish future. There is, of course, much more to this second line of activity than merely perfecting the machinery of organization. Jewish organization in the Diaspora must be given a philosophy so as to save it from misunderstanding on the part of either the Jew or the Gentile. Much educational work will have to be done to teach our people to create institutions that are calculated to further Jewish aims. How great an amount of misdirected energy would have been saved if those who have built up synagogues had been shown that the future of many a congregation has been compromised by the failure to provide social and recreational facilities in the synagogue itself. The relation of social and recreational life to spiritual development has only become apparent in recent years, and the truth concerning it is in need of wide diffusion in order that our people may not repeat the mistakes committed in the various Jewish institutions, religious, philanthropic and educational, which they have established....

NOTES

1. Mordecai M. Kaplan (1881–1983), U.S. rabbi and founder of the Reconstructionist movement. Drawing upon traditional Jewish sources, Zionist thought and American philosophical pragmatism, Kaplan developed a program for the creative survival of Judaism in the intellectual, political, and social reality of the twentieth century. The sociologist Charles S. Liebman observed that Reconstructionism is a distinctive "second-generation American Jewish phenomenon" (Charles S. Liebman, "Reconstructionism in American Jewish Life," *American Jewish Year Book*, 71 [1970], p. 4). Reconstructionism, Liebman contends, articulates more authentically than any other religious tendency the

consensus of twentieth-century native-born American Jews. In consonance with Kaplan's premises, "American Jews no doubt are more ethnic, or people-oriented than religion-oriented" (ibid., p. 95). Nonetheless, Reconstructionism has failed to capture the Jewish community, and a relatively small number of synagogues identify themselves with the movement. Many other American synagogues, however, have accepted many innovations suggested by Kaplan, for example, the institution of the comprehensive Jewish communal center. Liebman explains the failure of Reconstructionism to establish itself in the Jewish community as a result of its ideological explicitness. Reconstructionism,

Liebman notes, makes a virtue of its ethnic, folk orientation, and "most American Jews are not quite willing to admit to this virtue publicly. The entire basis of Jewish accommodation to America, of the legitimacy of Jewish separateness, has been that Judaism is a religion, like Catholicism and Protestantism, and that Jews are not merely an ethnic group like the Irish or the Italians" (ibid., p. 96). The article presented here is one of Kaplan's earliest formulations of his philosophy of Reconstructionism.

2. See chapter 10, document 9.
3. Kehillah, Hebrew for community; here democratically structured Jewish community.

42. THE BEGINNINGS OF SECULAR JEWISH SCHOOLS (1918–1920)[1]

At the meeting [of the Workmen's Circle Pedagogical Council and the Educational Committee] the methods to be used in *Arbeter Ring* schools were thoroughly discussed, and the following program was adopted:

THE GOALS OF THE *ARBETER RING* FOLKS-SHUL

1. To teach the children to read, write and speak Yiddish well.
2. To acquaint them with the best specimens of Yiddish literature.
3. To acquaint them with the life of the worker and of the broad Jewish masses in America and other countries.
4. To acquaint them with the history of the Jewish people and with episodes in general history of the struggle for freedom.

5. To develop within them the feelings of justice, love for the oppressed, love of freedom and respect for fighters for freedom.
6. To develop within them the feeling for beauty and physical and moral discipline.
7. To develop within them idealism and the striving to perform noble acts, which are necessary for every child of the oppressed class in making his way through life towards a better order.

THE PROGRAM OF THE *ARBETER RING* SCHOOLS

In the *Arbeter Ring* schools the children will be taught: (a) the Yiddish language: reading, writing and speaking; (b) Jewish history; (c) Yiddish literature; (d) songs, declamations [of poetry] and dances; (e) certain Jewish and general holidays, labor holidays and holidays of freedom will be celebrated.

Source: A. S. Sachs, *Di geshikhte fun arbayter ring. 1892–1925* (New York, 1925, II, pp. 513f., 519–21; trans. in Lloyd P. Gartner, ed., *Jewish Education in the United States. A Documentary History* (New York: Teachers College Press, 1969), pp. 157–60. Reprinted by permission of Lloyd P. Gartner.

Discussions will also be held with the children regarding various manifestations in the child's immediate environment and also regarding the literary selections which the child reads in school. One tells the child and reads to him stories and narratives which develop the imagination and the finest ethical and esthetic feelings. To the same purpose, outings to a park with the children and visits to art museums and other significant institutions which possess educational meaning are arranged from time to time....

A SECULAR YIDDISH SCHOOL CONFERENCE, 1920

The conference recognizes the great poetic value of the ancient Jewish legends of the Bible and *Midrashim* [religious homiletic works], the narrative value of a large proportion of them and their significance as elements of ancient Jewish history; at the same time, it also takes into account that a great many of these legends are permeated with a religious element which does not harmonize with the secularism of the *Arbeter Ring* schools.

The Conference therefore decides that in the curriculum of the *Arbeter Ring* school the legends of the Patriarchs shall be introduced, but only those in which the element of God and religion is not predominant....

ON THE STUDY OF HISTORY

The Conference recommends an attempt to turn over [the study of] history to a special teacher in schools where there is more than one teacher, or [if not] to divide the teaching of history so that children of uniform age and development shall study together.

THE HEBRAIC ELEMENT

The Conference recognizes that (1) In order that the children may know well the Hebrew element in the Yiddish language, of which it is an inseparable and very important part, it is necessary that sufficient time be devoted to this very element, beginning with the second year; (2) In order that the children may consciously adopt and correctly understand all Hebrew words in Yiddish and particularly Hebrew expressions and idioms which are often employed in the Yiddish language, it is necessary in addition that in the last (fourth) class the children be acquainted with the elementary rules of those Hebrew words within Yiddish which are indispensably necessary.

THE FOLLOWING HOLIDAYS TO BE OBSERVED

1. Passover—as the Jewish holiday of freedom
2. *Lag baomer*—in memory of the struggle of Bar Kokhba and Rabbi Akiva
3. The First of May—as the holiday of labor brotherhood and an expression of world peace
4. Hanukkah—as the holiday of emancipation from the Greek yoke
5. March 18—the holiday of labor's struggle for freedom
6. Purim—as a children's holiday (for costuming, exchange of gifts and other amusements)
7. July 4—American freedom
8. February 12 (Lincoln's Birthday)—emancipation of the Negroes
9. Russian Revolution (the Conference leaves to each school the choice of the day).

NOTE

1. The Workmen's Circle (Yiddish: *Arbeter Ring*) is a fraternal society which at its height had more than 60,000 members in more than 400 branches in the United States and Canada. It was founded in 1900 by Jewish immigrant workers with the twofold purpose of providing its members with mutual aid and supporting the cause of socialism. Since 1916 it has also sponsored a wide network of summer and afternoon schools (*folkshule*) to promote a secular, progressive Yiddish education. This document, from a programmatic statement of 1918 and a 1920 conference of the Workmen's Circle, presents the ideology of these schools.

43. THE AMERICAN YESHIVA (1926)

BERNARD REVEL[1]

The Yeshiva ideal of education is based upon the conviction that we serve our country and humanity best by training the growing generation of our youth to live in the ways of Israel's Torah, its moral standards and spiritual ideals.

Not merely does the future of American Jewry depend upon this strengthening in our youth of the bonds of love and understanding of the ideals and eternal truths of Israel, but to a great degree world Jewry is coming to look for its spiritual strength to America. Providence has destined us to play a dominant role in the history of world Jewry and Jewish culture. Many European centers of Jewish learning have suffered greatly from the ravages of the war and the disorganized economic life and spiritual upheaval that have followed it. Russian Jewry, for many centuries the stronghold of Jewish life, learning and idealism, has fallen into temporary confusion and disorganization. The mantle of responsibility is descending upon American Jewry, today the largest single group, as well as the most blessed materially, in the Jewish world. The stream of Jewish learning and idealism from abroad, which has been enriching American Jewish life, is drying up. It is our imperative task to create in this land a Jewish life, inspired and guided by the conceptions and teachings, ideas and ideals, that have ensured the continuity of Israel through all ages and climes, that have been the greatest spiritual force in the history of mankind, and the spirit that guided the minds and inspired the hearts of the Fathers of this Republic. Throughout the ages the historic homes of the Jewish soul, the *Yeshivoth*, have been the centers of intensive Jewish learning, the reservoirs of intellectual energy and spiritual strength, the conscience of Universal Israel,

the instruments for the continued transmission of the divine light of Sinai, to the entire household of Israel. They constitute a glorious chapter in the long history of Israel and, next to the Synagogue, form the most vital institution in the preservation of Judaism. In them the knowledge of and love for the Torah has been cultivated and fostered in the hearts of the Jewish youth. Recognizing that in order to maintain Jewish life and culture in this country as a real and living force, the historic home of the Torah must be transplanted to this land, a small and loyal group of pioneers founded the Yeshiva in America, sanctifying through it the name of the Jewish sage and saint of the last century, Rabbi Isaac Elchanan.

The Yeshiva has sent forth many loyal, spiritually endowed, and mentally equipped rabbis throughout the United States and Canada, who live the life of the Torah, and are constructive forces in their communities for good and for God...But the Yeshiva does not exist merely for the training of rabbis and of teachers. Important as this task is, and carefully as the responsibilities it involves are accepted in its Teachers Institute and in its Rabbinical Department, the Yeshiva looks beyond these fields of service to the general development of Jewish life and culture, to the evolving of a system of Jewish education that will bring harmony into the life of the American Jewish youth and will develop not only his usefulness as a member of his community, but his Jewish consciousness and his will to live as a Jew and advance the cause of Jewry and Judaism; an education through which the human conscience and the Jewish conscience develop harmoniously into the synthesis of a complete Jewish personality, that indicates the guiding laws of life in accordance with the immortal truths of Judaism in

Source: Bernard Revel, "The Yeshiva College" [1926], in Aaron Rothkoff, *Bernard Revel: Builder of American Jewish Orthodoxy* (Philadelphia: Jewish Publication Society, 1972), pp. 256ff. Copyright 1972 by the Jewish Publication Society of America. Reprinted by permission of Yeshiva University.

harmonious blending with the best thought of the age and the great humanitarian ideals upon which our blessed country is founded.

In the fruitful development of the wide field of Jewish learning, which constitutes an integral and vital phase of human knowledge and experience, in the cultivation of the spiritual elements of our faith, harmoniously blended with the general training of high school and college, the Yeshiva and its college will infuse a new note into American education. With the Jewish perspective brought to bear upon the various fields of learning, the Yeshiva will make a lasting contribution to American education, the rich background and point of view that an harmonious Jewish and general training will represent. Thus, in affording the opportunity for this concordant growth, to those American Jewish youth—whatever their future field of activity—who wish to combine the advantages of secondary and higher education with the acquisition of the knowledge of the ideals and truths of historic and living Israel, the Yeshiva at the same time, presents a new force of unique value in American education, the cultural outlook of the educated and Torah-true Jew.

In its high school, the Yeshiva offers an opportunity to those who wish to acquire their general training in a truly Jewish atmosphere while growing in familiarity with the comprehensive sources and the ideals of Judaism. Recognized by the State of New York as of full high school grade, this department of the Yeshiva has established itself prominently among the high schools of New York, being among the first in percentage of State scholarships awarded the graduates, and maintaining an excellent record in the State Regents examinations. During these high school years, while acquiring their general schooling, the students receive, as well, a thorough training in the essentials of Jewish learning, they acquire a living and loving understanding of the tenets and practices of Judaism, and are imbued with love and reverence for knowledge and *idealism* that lead to the formation of character, and are translated into living practice.

In its new home, with adequate facilities and serene academic surroundings, the Yeshiva high school will increase its usefulness, and provide thousands of students with the opportunity of developing their character and preparing themselves in thoroughly Jewish surroundings, for a life of usefulness, bringing them in direct contact with the sources of our faith and culture, deepening their understanding

of and loyalty to the Torah and the ideals of Israel—preparing them for their role of true citizens, bringing our children nearer to the faith of our fathers, and helping to insure the continuity of Israel and his incomparable contribution to human progress.

Promising students of the Jewish religious schools throughout this country and Canada come to the Yeshiva to develop under the combined general and spiritual training of the Yeshiva high school, and the Yeshiva proper. By its very existence, then, the Yeshiva helps raise the standard of the work of these schools throughout the land, whose chosen pupils, insofar as present facilities permit, come to continue their study at the Yeshiva. The Yeshiva encourages the establishment of such schools, and of other secondary schools of Jewish learning, and through this development hopes ultimately to systematize and standardize the education of Torah-true American Jewry. At present many tendencies, especially a concentration upon the secular, national and linguistic aspects of Judaism, are shifting the center of gravity of Jewish education, which is essentially spiritual and religious, to the neglect of its high ideals and values. In such an organized system of Jewish education, the Yeshiva College will stand out as the directing and unifying force. Through its requirements for admission and the courses it will offer, the Yeshiva College will help develop a more Jewishly educated and inspired youth.

At present the Jewish perspective in education ceases at the close of the Yeshiva high school work, or severs itself from the general college training. In order to enable young men of Jewish training and love for the Jewish ideals, who wish to dedicate themselves to the service of Judaism, to continue their complete training in one institution, imbued with the spirit and ideals of true Judaism, the Yeshiva College of Liberal Arts and Science is being organized. Its fundamental purpose is to afford this harmonious union of culture and spirituality, and to bring into the field of American education the contribution of the spiritual values of Judaism, of the Jewish ideals of education, of the Jewish perspective upon the learning and knowledge of our age. It is in no sense a duplicate of the general colleges, a refuge for those who, with real or imagined grievances, consider themselves unwelcome in other institutions. It is dedicated to the service of those Jewish young men of ability and high ideals who have already been imbued with the spirit and sanctity of

Judaism and its teachings, to whom the message of Judaism is of deep significance and who wish to equip themselves fully, as Torah-true Jews.

The Yeshiva College will extend its usefulness to Jewish youth who consider Jewish learning part of the mental and moral equipment they wish to obtain through a college education, and who are equipped for such a higher education as the Yeshiva College will offer, with the standard college curricula combined with courses in Bible, Hebrew Philology, Jewish history and literature, Jewish philosophy and ethics, the Talmud and Rabbinic literature, Jewish archeology, Semitic philology and cognate subjects, offered by eminent scholars of the Yeshiva College Faculty.

In its several departments, the Yeshiva will provide adequate facilities for the education of spiritual leaders, rabbis and teachers who will go forth to continue throughout the Jewish community the work of spreading the spirit and message of Torah, beyond that it will continue the great traditions of scholarship and research that have been a sustaining background to the spiritual and cultural life of Jewry through the ages; and it will bring to ever increasing numbers of American Jewish youth the true perspective of historic Judaism in the complex organization of modern life, combining with the learning of the world today those cultural values and spiritual ideals, the strength of the sustaining faith of our fathers, to the enrichment of the lives of the Jewish community and of America today. The Yeshiva College will in time help span the widening chasm between intellectualism and faith in Jewish life and thought. Throughout the ages the mightiest minds among us have been at the same time our religious guides and our teachers.

It will imbue our Jewish youth with an active and abiding interest in and a spirit of service to the cause of Israel and help cast the eternal truths of Judaism in the mould of true Americanism upon which our country was founded.

In the pattern and design of American culture, in which are interwoven the finest threads of its varied groups, the Jewish strain of religious and moral fervor and steadfastness shall be firm and distinctive. To perpetuate and advance Israel's spiritual and religious heritage, and the proven idealism of steadfast Israel, that has always valued life *sub specie aeternitatis,* to help make it once more a living force in our daily lives, and to aid in the spiritualization of Jewish life in this land, the Yeshiva and its College are dedicated.

NOTE

1. Bernard Revel (1885–1940), U.S. educator, scholar, and leader of modern Orthodoxy in America. Born in Lithuania, where he received a thorough Talmudic education. Revel immigrated to the United States in 1906. In 1915 he was appointed headmaster (*rosh yeshivah*) of the newly reconstituted Isaac Elchanan Theological Seminary—a small institution for advanced study of Talmud founded in 1897 in New York City, which included some secular studies in its curriculum, a radical innovation for an Orthodox institution of that period. In 1916 Revel established the first yeshiva high school, in which both Talmudic and secular studies were taught. Overcoming strong opposition from the Orthodox community, in 1928 he founded Yeshiva College as an extension of the seminary. Yeshiva College represented the first attempt to offer a traditional Talmudic education with a modern curriculum of secular studies on a college level. Yeshiva College, which was elevated to university status in 1945, became the center of a distinctive brand of American Orthodox Judaism.

44. A STATEMENT OF POLICY (MAY 1915)

THE ANTI-DEFAMATION LEAGUE[1]

The Anti-Defamation League of America, founded under the auspices of the Independent Order of Bnai Brith, is the result of a demand by the Jewish people for concerted action against the constant and ever increasing efforts to traduce the good name of the Jew.... For the present the League contemplates the following activities:

Educational: 1. Public and university libraries will be furnished with lists of books on Jewish subjects, which, in the opinion of the League tend to show the facts regarding Jewish ethics, customs, history, religion and philosophy.

Where it is found that the endowment of institutions, either private or public, does not permit the procurement of a fairly comprehensive number of books on these subjects, it will be the aim of the League to supply them. Investigations show that a majority of the public libraries of the country do not even possess a Jewish history written by a Jewish historian.

Investigation will be made of the bibliography on Jewish subjects in libraries. Wherever it is found that books which maliciously and scurrilously traduce the character of the Jew are kept for general circulation—especially in public stackrooms—the proper authorities will be urged to withdraw such books from general circulation, or, at least, to place a restriction on their use.

2. The services of prominent lecturers and publicists, regardless of religious affiliation, will be enlisted for the purpose of delivering lectures on Jewish subjects at universities, public schools and at appropriate gatherings.

The League will provide also for the dissemination of literature designed to give the public a true understanding of the Jew and Judaism.

3. The League recognizes the fact that the mind of the growing child must be safeguarded against even a suggestion of prejudice; therefore, where in our educational system, either public or private, text books are used which tend to pervert the mind of the child and create prejudice, a determined campaign will be waged to eliminate all such books from the curriculum.

Vigilance Work: 1. The services of clipping bureaus have been secured to keep the League advised as to matters of interest affecting the Jewish people. Information regarding defamation and discrimination should be promptly sent to the Executive Committee of the League.

2. The League will secure corresponding representatives in every State, who will submit to the central office in Chicago all matters pertaining to these subjects which come within the scope of the League.

3. We should find our strongest allies in newspapers, periodicals and magazines, the great mediums for expression and exchange of thought. We therefore heartily endorse and commend the action of certain newspapers in adopting the policy of eliminating mention of the religious denomination of malefactors. We shall bend every energy toward making this policy universal.

4. Where articles appear which present the Jew in a false and unworthy light, we shall endeavor to secure correction either by retraction, or by an answer in the next or early issue of the same publication, thereby reaching the same reading public.

5. The League will attempt to secure the co-operation of the Press in eliminating from foreign and domestic news items, all matters which give an untrue impression of the Jew.

Source: Report of the Anti-Defamation League, May 1915. Submitted to the Constitution Grand Lodge Convention, Independent Order Bnai Brith.

Theaters and Moving Pictures: Investigation will be made of all plays which deal with the Jew. If, after careful study, it is apparent that a play gives an untrue or unfair portrayal of the Jew, the League will endeavor to present its production in its offensive form, or if already staged, to secure the elimination of the objectionable matter. Similar measures will be taken in connection with moving picture films.

Legislation: 1. With a view of preventing the presentation, in moving picture theatres, of films which are malicious and scurrilous caricatures, or are objectionable in other respects, the League will endeavor to secure, in the various states of the Union, the enactment of statutes similar to the one recently passed in the State of Ohio, providing for the appointment of a Board of State Censors. Where the passage of such a statute cannot be attained similar relief will be sought from the various municipalities by securing the enactment of appropriate ordinances.

2. The League will endeavor to secure the passage of laws, where the same is practicable, making it unlawful for any hostelry, directly or indirectly, to publish, circulate, issue, display, post or mail any written or printed communication, notice or advertisement, to the effect that any of the accommodations of such places shall be refused, withheld, or denied to any person on account of his creed....

Situation in 1913: When the League was organized in the fall of 1913, an extraordinary situation confronted it. It seemed that whenever film manufacturers desired to depict a hardhearted money-lender, a blackmailer, a fire-bug, a depraved gambler, a swindler, a grafter or a white-slaver, they determined upon a Jewish name for the person in question, and directed the actor to simulate what is popularly regarded as a "Jewish type." There was nothing so unusual in this, as the tendency has been evident since the time of [Christopher] Marlowe's "Barabas."[2] The extraordinary element, however, was that what previously reached the attention of an infinitesimal fraction of the populace, and that fraction a matured and cultured part, was most vividly presented before the eyes of millions of the unmatured, ignorant or the uncultured. A careful survey of the existing situation showed that there were scores of films on the market which were extremely prejudicial to the welfare and happiness of our people. In addition to the criminal characterization, the Jew was often shown in caricature, in a manner similar to that employed on the burlesque and vaudeville stages. These caricaturizations were supposed to be funny, but in many instances the laughter which they stimulated was that which arises from the malicious discomfiture of another. Under the guise of fun, the most sordid, vulgar and unclean characteristics were frequently attributed to Jews in general.

NOTES

1. A U.S. organization founded in 1913 by the Bnai Brith. Its objectives and program are explained in this document. On Bnai Brith, see this chapter, document 33, note 7; and document 50, note 3.
2. Barabas is the title character of Marlowe's play *The Jew of Malta* (1589 or 1590).

45. TEMPORARY SUSPENSION OF IMMIGRATION (1920)[1]

CONGRESSIONAL COMMITTEE ON IMMIGRATION

During the third session of the Sixty-fifth Congress[2] the Committee on Immigration and Naturalization gave thorough consideration to the question of immigration restriction. Several bills were introduced and extended hearings were held. The then chairman of this committee, the late Hon. John L. Burnett, introduced a bill, H.R. 15302, which was reported favorably by the committee January 29, 1919. This bill provided for the prohibition of immigration for a period of four years. The committee was practically unanimously in favor of such a prohibition, and at that time it was thought such a bill could be passed if time for its consideration could be given on the floor of the House. But the House calendars were so congested that the bill did not receive a hearing and therefore failed of enactment....

Since Mr. Burnett's bill ... was reported, January 29, 1919, almost two years have passed. The flood of immigration which was expected when Mr. Burnett's bill was under consideration did not set in until the summer of 1920. This committee is informed that had steamship accommodations been available, this flood of immigration would have set in more than a year ago. But steamship accommodations were not available, due to the necessities of demobilization of the armies, and it was not until the spring and summer of 1920 that the real effects of unsettled conditions in Europe began to evidence themselves in a stream of emigration from European countries.

It is impossible today to estimate the effect which the Burnett bill would have produced had it become a law during the Sixty-fifth Congress. But of this much we can be certain: That countless numbers of persons now coming to the United States would not have left their homes in Europe during the past year. Half of the four-year suspension period proposed in the Burnett bill has elapsed. The flow of immigration to the United States is now in full flood. The need for restrictive legislation is apparent. The accommodations at Ellis Island are not sufficient for the avalanche of new arrivals; larger cities have not houses for them; work cannot be found for them; and, further, the bulk of the newer arrivals are of the dependent rather than the working class....

Members of the committee found the new immigration at Ellis Island to consist practically of all nationalities except Orientals. It found by far the largest percentage of immigrants to be peoples of Jewish extraction. On the steamship *New Amsterdam,* sailing from Rotterdam, the committee found that 80 per cent of the steerage passengers were from Galicia, practically all of Jewish extraction. On the *New Rochelle,* arriving from Danzig, the committee estimated that more than 90 per cent were of the Semitic race. The committee is confirmed in the belief that the major portions of recent arrivals come without funds. It was apparent to the committee that a large percentage of those arriving were incapable of earning a livelihood. These are temporarily detained, causing great congestion, much delay, and pitiful distress, until relatives or others arrive to give bonds that the newcomers will not become public charges.

...The committee has confirmed the published statements of a commissioner of the Hebrew Sheltering and Aid Society of America made after his personal investigation in Poland, to the effect that "If there were in existence a ship that could hold 3,000,000 human beings, the 3,000,000 Jews of Poland would board it to escape to America."

Source: Temporary Suspension of Immigration, Sixty-sixth Congress, Third Session, House of Representatives, Report no. 1109, December 6, 1920.

In the preparation and presentation of this legislation to the House of Representatives the Committee on Immigration and naturalization has disregarded the statements of a Polish labor commissioner to the effect that 225,000 Hebrews have been furnished this year with funds for passage to the United States. The committee has disregarded all statements that might give a religious bias of any kind to the matter under consideration. It is fair to state, however, that the largest number of Jews coming to the United States before the war in a single year was 153,748 (1906); while during the one month of October 1920, it is estimated that of the 74,665 immigrants arriving at Ellis Island, more than 75 per cent were of the Semitic race.

Figures available for the fiscal year ending June 30, 1920, show that a very small number of these peoples gave as their reason for coming to the United States the desire to escape religious or political persecution....

Appendix A
Hon. Albert Johnson
Chairman Committee on Immigration
House of Representatives

Department of State
Consular Service
Washington
December 4, 1920

My Dear Mr. Johnson: In accordance with your request of this morning it gives me great pleasure to send you herewith paraphrases of statements in regard to immigration received from officers of this Government who have visited the countries mentioned. I hope you will find the data of value in connection with the presentation of your bill to Congress.

Very sincerely yours,
Wilbur J. Carr

AUSTRIA: *Vienna*—Sixty per cent of the present emigrants are of the Jewish race, 20 per cent are of the German race, and 20 per cent of other races. The favorite occupation of these emigrants is merchant or clerk.

The committee did not investigate charges of extensive funds from America passing through agencies in Warsaw and elsewhere. The committee does believe, however, that these funds, whether large or small, together with generous contributions made both by government and individuals for the relief of distress in central Europe, combined with the reports which have spread everywhere concerning prospects for certain prosperity and immediate wealth in the United States, all combine to play a part in encouraging the downtrodden of all the war-wrecked countries to sell everything and to pay in their depreciated monies $120 to $130 for steerage passage to the United States in addition to $10 for United States consular visa and registration....

GERMANY: *Berlin*—It is estimated that 2,000,000 Germans desire to emigrate to the United States if passport restrictions are removed.

The Germans who proceed to the United States are not of the most desirable class, due to the fact that military service is at present in most cases an absolute bar. Most of those who receive permission to leave for the United States are the aged parents of American citizens or minor children. The wives of declarants who are now permitted to proceed are almost always of the lower classes. The Poles, Austrians, and nationals of the different Russian States who apply for visas are as a rule of the most undesirable type of emigrant. They are usually traders who only increase the number of middle men or if they work they usually go into sweatshops.

NETHERLANDS: *Rotterdam*—The great mass of aliens passing through Rotterdam at the present time are Russian Poles or Polish Jews of the usual ghetto type. Most of them are more or less directly and frankly getting out of Poland to avoid war conditions. They are filthy, un-American and often dangerous in their habits.

POLAND: *Warsaw*—Concerning the general characteristics of aliens emigrating to the United States from Poland and the occupation or trade followed by them, reports indicate such to be substantially as follows:

1. Physically deficient: (a) Wasted by disease and lack of food supplies, (b) Reduced to an unprecedented state of life during the period of the war, as the result of oppression and want. (c) Present existence in squalor and filth.

2. Mentally deficient: (a) Illy educated, if not illiterate, and too frequently with minds so stultified as to admit of little betterment. (b) Abnormally twisted because of (1) reaction from war strain, (2) shock of revolutionary disorders, (3) the dullness and stultification resulting from past years of oppression and abuse.

3. Economically undesirable: (a) Twenty per cent is given as a round and generous estimate of productive laborers among present applicants for visas. This estimate is meant to include workers or those who may be expected to become workers, from both sexes. The remaining percentage may be expected to be a drain on the resources of America for years. (b) Of the 50 per cent of emigrants from Poland who may be termed efficients, 40 per cent—of the total number of emigrants—will enter a trade as a middleman, not a producer. These will thrive on the efforts of their associates. (c) The productive labor, small percentage as it is, will be found in America, in the sweatshops in the large centers of population. It is decidedly not agricultural, but urban in character. In this report female applicants as housewives, etc., are of course termed as efficients.

4. Socially undesirable: (a) Eighty-five to ninety per cent lack any conception of patriotic or national spirit. And the majority of this percentage is mentally incapable of acquiring it. (b) Seventy-five per cent or upward will congregate in the large urban centers, such as New York or Baltimore, and add to undesirable congestion, already a grave civic problem.

(c) Immigrants of similar class are to be found already in the United States who, taken as a class and not individually, have proved unassimilable. (d) All Europe is experiencing in the reaction from the war a corruption of moral standards. This may even be least noticeable in Germany. The introduction of these lowered standards can not fail but have its evil influence in the United States.[3]

NOTES

1. The 1920s saw a rise in antisemitism that was often expressed in a desire to keep Jews from immigrating to the United States. Jews were seen as an impoverished and racially deficient people who were about to inundate the shores of the United States. Moreover, they were seen as carriers of the Bolshevik revolution, which they intended to use for the purpose of overthrowing Western civilization, It is clear that these views also gained respect in the House of Representatives to whom this report was presented by its Committee on Immigration and Naturalization.
2. From December 1, 1918, to March 4, 1919.
3. Quota laws on immigration were passed by Congress in May 1921 and in May 1924.

46. THE INTERNATIONAL JEW: THE WORLD'S PROBLEM (1920)

HENRY FORD[1]

The Jew is again being singled out for critical attention throughout the world. His emergence in the financial, political and social spheres has been so complete and spectacular since the war, that his place, power, and purpose in the world are being given a new scrutiny, much of it unfriendly. Persecution is not a new experience to the Jew, but intensive scrutiny of his nature and supernationality is. He has suffered for more than 2,000 years from what may be called the instinctive antisemitism of the other races, but this antagonism has never been intelligent, nor has it been able to make itself intelligible. Nowadays, however, the Jew is being placed, as it were, under the microscope of economic observation that the

Source: Henry Ford, "The International Jew: The World's Problem," *The Dearborn Independent,* May 22, 1920, pp. 1–5.

reasons for his power, the reasons for his separateness, the reasons for his suffering may be defined and understood.

In Russia he is charged with being the source of Bolshevism, an accusation which is serious or not, according to the circle in which it is made; we in America, hearing the fervid eloquence and perceiving the prophetic ardor of young Jewish apostles of social and industrial reform, can calmly estimate how it may be. In Germany he is charged with being the cause of the Empire's collapse and a very considerable literature has sprung up, bearing with it a mass of circumstantial evidence that gives the thinker pause. In England he is charged with being the real world ruler, who rules as a super-nation over the nations, rules by the power of gold, and who plays nation against nation for his own purposes, remaining himself discreetly in the background. In America it is pointed out to what extent the elder Jews of wealth and the younger Jews of ambition swarmed through the war organizations—principally those departments which dealt with the commercial and industrial business of war, and also the extent to which they have clung to the advantage which their experience as agents of the government gave them.

In simple words, the question of the Jews has come to the fore, but like other questions which lend themselves to prejudice, efforts will be made to hush it up as impolitic for open discussion. If, however, experience has taught us anything it is that questions thus suppressed will sooner or later break out in undesirable and unprofitable forms.

The Jew is the world's enigma. Poor in his masses, he yet controls the world's finances. Scattered abroad without country or government, he yet presents a unity of race continuity which no other people has achieved. Living under legal disabilities in almost every land, he has become the power behind many a throne. There are ancient prophecies to the effect that the Jew will return to his own land and from that center rule the world, though not until he has undergone an assault by the united nations of mankind.

The single description which will include a larger percentage of Jews than members of any other race is this: he is in business. It may be only gathering rags and selling them, but he is in business. From the sale of old clothes to the control of international trade and finance, the Jew is supremely gifted for business. More than any other race he exhibits a decided aversion to industrial employment, which he balances by an equally decided adaptability to trade. The Gentile boy works his way up, taking employment in the productive or technical departments; but the Jewish boy prefers to begin as messenger, salesman or clerk—anything—so long as it is connected with the commercial side of the business.

The question is, If the Jew is in control, how did it happen? This is a free country. The Jew comprises only about three per cent of the population; to every Jew there are 97 Gentiles; to the 3,000,000 Jews in the United States there are 97,000,000 Gentiles. If the Jew is in control, is it because of his superior ability, or is it because of the inferiority and don't-care attitude of the Gentiles?

It would be very simple to answer that the Jews came to America, took their chances like other people, and proved more successful in the competitive struggle. But that would not include all the facts. And before a more adequate answer can be given, two points should be made clear. The first is this: all Jews are not rich controllers of wealth. There are poor Jews aplenty, though most of them even in their poverty are their own masters. While it may be true that the chief financial controllers of the country are Jews, it is not true that every Jew is one of the financial controllers of the country. The classes must be kept distinct for a reason which will appear when the methods of the rich Jews and the methods of the poor Jews to gain power are differentiated. Secondly, the fact of Jewish solidarity renders it difficult to measure Gentile and Jewish achievements by the same standard. When a great block of wealth in America was made possible by the lavish use of another block of wealth from across the seas; that is to say, when certain Jewish immigrants came to the United States with the financial backing of European Jewry behind them, it would be unfair to explain the rise of that class of immigration by the same rules which account for the rise of, say, the Germans or the Poles who came here with no resource but their ambition and strength. To be sure, many individual Jews come in that way, too, with no dependence but themselves, but it would not be true to say that that massive control of affairs which is exercised by Jewish wealth was won by individual initiative. . . .

"To the victor belongs the spoils" is an old saying. And in a sense it is true that if all this power of control has been gained and held by a few men of a long-despised race, then either they are super-men whom it is powerless to resist, or they are ordinary men whom the rest of the world has permitted to obtain an undue and unsafe degree of power. Unless the Jews are super-men, the Gentiles will have themselves to blame for what has transpired, and they can look for rectification in a new scrutiny of the situation and a candid examination of the experiences of other countries.

NOTE

1. Henry Ford (1863–1947), automobile manufacturer and among America's leading business men. A tsarist emigré in the United States, Boris Brasol, persuaded a group of American business leaders, among them Henry Ford, to publicize the *Protocols of the Elders of Zion*. For several years, Ford's private newspaper, *The Dearborn Independent*, quoted liberally from the *Protocols* and issued repeated warnings against the "Jewish Menace." The article reprinted here was published in his paper. Only in 1927, when a Jewish attorney brought a libel suit against *The Dearborn Independent*, did Ford repudiate his antisemitism and issue a public apology. For further details On the complex relationship between Ford's articles and the *Protocols*, see Leo P. Ribuffo, "Henry Ford and The International Jew," in Jonathan D. Sarna, ed., *The American Jewish Experience* (New York: Holmes and Meier Publishers, Inc., 1986), pp. 175–90.

47. A PROTEST AGAINST ANTISEMITISM (JANUARY 16, 1921)[1]

The undersigned, citizens of Gentile birth and Christian faith, view with profound regret and disapproval the appearance in this country of what is apparently an organized campaign of antisemitism; conducted in close conformity to and co-operation with similar campaigns in Europe. We regret exceedingly the publication of a number of books, pamphlets and newspaper articles designed to foster distrust and suspicion of our fellow-citizens of Jewish ancestry and faith—distrust and suspicion of their loyalty and their patriotism.

These publications, to which wide circulation is being given, are thus introducing into our national political life a new and dangerous spirit, one that is wholly at variance with our traditions and ideals and subversive of our system of government. American citizenship and American democracy are thus challenged and menaced. We protest against this organized campaign of prejudice and hatred, not only because of its manifest injustice to those against whom it is directed, but also, and especially, because we are convinced that it is wholly incompatible with loyal and intelligent American citizenship. The logical outcome of the success of such a campaign must necessarily be the division of our citizens along racial and religious lines, and, ultimately, the introduction of religious tests and qualifications to determine citizenship.

The loyalty and patriotism of our fellow citizens of the Jewish faith is equal to that of any part of our people, and requires no defense at our hands. From the foundation of this Republic down to the recent World War, men and women of Jewish ancestry and faith have taken an honorable part in building up this great nation and maintaining its prestige and honor among the nations of the world. There is not the slightest justification, therefore, for a campaign of antisemitism in this country.

Antisemitism is almost invariably associated with lawlessness and with brutality and injustice. It is also invariably found closely intertwined with other sinister forces, particularly those which are corrupt, reactionary and oppressive.

We believe it should not be left to men and women of Jewish faith to fight this evil, but that it is in a very special sense the duty of citizens who are not Jews by ancestry or faith. We therefore make earnest protest against this vicious propaganda, and call upon our fellow citizens of Gentile birth and Christian faith to unite their efforts to ours, to the end that it may be crushed. In particular, we call upon all those who are molders of public opinion—the clergy and ministers of all Christian churches, publicists, teachers, editors and statesmen—to strike at this un-American and un-Christian agitation.

NOTE

1. This protest against the burgeoning of antisemitic propaganda was signed by President Woodrow Wilson, former President William H. Taft, Cardinal O'Connell of New York City, and 116 other prominent men and women of the Christian faith. It was initiated by the socialist author John Spargo, who emphasized that "all the work connected with the protest and all expenses involved represent the contribution of an individual citizen to the defense of American ideals. Neither directly nor indirectly did any person of Jewish ancestry or faith, or any Jewish organization, contribute as much as a postage stamp to the cost of the undertaking" (*New York Times*, January 16, 1921, p. 30).

48. SOCIAL AND ECONOMIC CHANGE REFLECTED IN JEWISH SCHOOL ENROLLMENT (1936)[1]

Underlying the whole situation is the voluntary character of the Jewish school attendance, the shifting of the Jewish population and difficulty in payment of tuition fees which is indirectly operative in more ways than explicitly stated. We are dealing with an immigrant population in a transitional stage not only geographically, economically and socially, but from the very basic point of view of social patterns. Life is not settled. The parent follows the general impulse of the Jewish tradition to send the child to school. But this traditional force is not certain and begins to break up. The general decline of religion; the desire and necessity of conforming; the multitudinous and harassing attractions of modern life; the state's priority on the child's time for public school; the encroachment of other agencies on the leisure of the child—these and many other features of the modern American scene are undermining the attendance of the traditional intensive Jewish school. The most striking and serious change has been the loss of enrollment in the Cleveland Hebrew Schools.

Fundamental factors in the general American and Jewish situation, associated with the decrease of child population; the cessation of immigration;

Source: Isaac B. Berkson and Ben Rosen, "1936 Jewish Education Survey of Cleveland. Part I—Enrollment and Withdrawals" (mimeographed); cited in Lloyd P. Gartner, *Jewish Education in the United States: A Documentary History* (New York: Teachers College Press, 1969), pp. 174–79. Reprinted by permission of Lloyd P. Gartner.

processes of assimilation, Americanization or modernization; and with the economic depression are to be given due attention in seeking an explanation for the changes.

There is a tendency in all the cities recently studied away from [their] former emphasis on the communal or independent type of school toward the Congregational type of school, where the instruction is, generally speaking, less intensive.

This movement toward Congregational Jewish Centers may be regarded as an adaptation to the methods or needs of organization required by American conditions.

These general trends, characteristic of the United States as a whole, have been accelerated—in some respects modified in Cleveland—by the predominant position held by the Reform Temples in Jewish life in general, and in the educational work in particular.

While the effective school organization of the Reform Temples has undoubtedly been a most valuable contribution to the educational situation, indirectly, however, they have tended to weaken the tradition for intensive week-day instruction by their very success and predominance.

In marked contrast to the social prestige, the magnificent equipment, the variety of cultural opportunities of the Temple Sunday School, stands the poverty of the Hebrew Schools, in buildings, equipment, finances.

In addition to the more general causes noted above, there are several specific factors in the decrease of registrations in the Hebrew Schools:

(a) The schools are situated in immigrant sections from which young parents are steadily moving away. No branches have been opened in the new Jewish neighborhoods. In fact, some of the older branches had to be closed for lack of funds.

(b) Those who remain in the immigrant sections are relatively the poorer element of the population. Forty percent of the children enrolled in the Hebrew Schools are from relief families, the schools thus becoming "schools for the poor," and their social prestige has further been lowered.

(c) As a result of the depression also, private schools have been opened in which unemployed persons—frequently ill-prepared—give instruction in ivris,[2] broches[3] and bar mitzvah, at a pittance, and these schools compete with the Hebrew Schools. Some who

were able to pay formerly, but now cannot, prefer to give their children such "private instruction" rather than to accept what might be termed charity.

In connection with the educational aim of the Jewish schools in Cleveland, a discussion has arisen on the question of "religion" vs. nationalism. It is assumed in some quarters that the Temple schools are mainly "religious" and that the Cleveland Hebrew schools represent the "national" interpretation of Jewish life. When posed in this form of a sharp antithesis, the question can hardly be discussed fruitfully. The difference of emphasis implied is undoubtedly of significance, but the terms mean different things to different people....

When the courses of study in the Sunday schools and Hebrew schools are examined, a striking similarity of subjects will be found.... Both Sunday schools and Hebrew schools include elements which one cannot help referring to as "religious" and "national," using these terms in the usual, not in any forced, sense....

The Temple schools in Cleveland differ significantly from the old-fashioned conventional Reform Sunday schools. They represent new tendencies in Sunday school work which have been developing in recent years. The changes have been in the direction of eliminating anti-Zionist attitudes; more than that, of making full provision for a knowledge of Zionism and the new Palestine....The teaching of history has become normal, a subject in its own right, no longer subordinate to so-called moral lessons. Hebrew is receiving more favorable consideration. Current events and problems of Jewish life are being dealt with in more realistic fashion. In this general movement towards the modernization of the Sunday schools, the Cleveland Temples have marched in the vanguard as far as practical application is concerned.

NOTES

1. This document presents a survey taken in Cleveland in 1936, during the years of the great economic depression. The survey analyzes the changing patterns of enrollment in Jewish schools and the effects of the prevailing economic situation on Jewish education.
2. *Ivris*, the Ashkenazi pronunciation for the Hebrew term for Hebrew, denoting here the mechanical, rote reading of the sacred texts of Jewish tradition.
3. *Broches*, the Ashkenazi pronunciation for the Hebrew term for prayers.

49. THE COLUMBUS PLATFORM (1937)[1]

CONFERENCE OF REFORM RABBIS

In view of the changes that have taken place in the modern world and the consequent need of stating anew the teachings of Reform Judaism, the Central Conference of American Rabbis makes the following declaration of principles. It presents them not as a fixed creed but as a guide for the progressive elements of Jewry.

Judaism and Its Foundations: 1. *Nature of Judaism.* Judaism is the historical religious experience of the Jewish people. Though growing out of Jewish life, its message is universal, aiming at the union and perfection of mankind under the sovereignty of God. Reform Judaism recognizes the principle of progressive development in religion and consciously applies this principle to spiritual as well as to cultural and social life.

Judaism welcomes all truth, whether written in the pages of Scripture or deciphered from the records of nature. The new discoveries of science, while replacing the older scientific views underlying our sacred literature, do not conflict with the essential spirit of religion as manifested in the consecration of man's will, heart and mind to the service of God and humanity....

5. *Israel.* Judaism is the soul of which Israel is the body. Living in all parts of the world, Israel has been held together by the ties of a common history, and above all, by the heritage of faith. Though we recognize in the group loyalty of Jews who have become estranged from our religious tradition, a bond which still unites them with us, we maintain that it is by its religion and for its religion that the Jewish people has lived. The non-Jew who accepts our faith is welcomed as a full member of the Jewish community.

In all lands where our people live, they assume and seek to share loyally the full duties and responsibilities of citizenship and to create seats of Jewish knowledge and religion. In the rehabilitation of Palestine, the land hallowed by memories and hopes, we behold the promise of renewed life for many of our brethren. We affirm the obligation of all Jewry to aid in its upbuilding as a Jewish homeland by endeavoring to make it not only a haven of refuge for the oppressed but also a center of Jewish culture and spiritual life.

Throughout the ages it has been Israel's mission to witness to the Divine in the face of every form of paganism and materialism. We regard it as our historic task to cooperate with all men in the establishment of the kingdom of God, of universal brotherhood, justice, truth and peace on earth. This is our Messianic goal....

9. *The Religious Life.* Jewish life is marked by consecration to these ideals of Judaism. It calls for faithful participation in the life of the Jewish community as it finds expression in home, synagogue and school and in all other agencies that enrich Jewish life and promote its welfare.

The Home has been and must continue to be a stronghold of Jewish life, hallowed by the spirit of love and reverence, by moral discipline and religious observance and worship.

The Synagogue is the oldest and most democratic institution in Jewish life. It is the prime communal agency by which Judaism is fostered and preserved. It links the Jews of each community and unites them with all Israel....

The perpetuation of Judaism as a living force depends upon religious knowledge and upon the Education of each new generation in our rich cultural and spiritual heritage.

Prayer is the voice of religion, the language of faith and aspiration. It directs man's heart and mind

Source: W. Gunther Plaut, *The Growth of Reform Judaism: A Sourcebook of Its European Origins* (New York: World Union for Progressive Judaism, 1965), pp. 96–99. Reprinted by permission of the World Union for Progressive Judaism.

Godward, voices the needs and hopes of the community, and reaches out after goals which invest life with supreme value. To deepen the spiritual life of our people, we must cultivate the traditional habit of communion with God through prayer in both home and synagogue.

Judaism as a way of life requires in addition to its moral and spiritual demands, the preservation of the Sabbath, festivals and Holy Days, the retention and development of such customs, symbols and ceremonies as possess inspirational value, the cultivation of distinctive forms of religious art and music and the use of Hebrew, together with the vernacular, in our worship and instruction.

These timeless aims and ideals of our faith we present anew to a confused and troubled world. We call upon our fellow Jews to rededicate themselves to them, and, in harmony with all men, hopefully and courageously to continue Israel's eternal quest after God and His kingdom....

NOTE

1. The Columbus Platform was adopted by the American Reform movement some fifty years after the Pittsburgh meeting of 1885. By 1937, most Reform Jews had moved away from their anti-Zionist position. Although it avoided a clear-cut pro-Zionist position, the Columbus Platform reflected the fact that Jewish peoplehood and Jewish tradition had come to occupy a more significant role within the movement. Rabbi Felix A. Levy (1884–1963) presided over the conference, the first avowed Zionist to occupy the chair.

50. THE AMERICAN JEWISH CONFERENCE (JANUARY 1943)[1]

In anticipation of the problems that would face the Jewish people in the post-war period in Europe and Palestine, American Jewish citizens of every shade of opinion and affiliation felt the need of organizing a representative body to unite upon a common program of action. The American Jewish Conference, which has been founded for this purpose, is a representative body of American Jews democratically organized to plan the immediate rescue of European Jewry, to take action upon post-war Jewish problems in Europe and to implement the rights of the Jewish people to Palestine.

The Conference came into being as a result of a preliminary meeting held in Pittsburgh of representatives of national Jewish organizations: At that time the purpose and agenda of the American Jewish Conference were formulated.

INVITATION TO THE MEETING

The initiative in calling the preliminary meeting was taken by Henry Monsky,[2] President of Bnai Brith,[3] at whose invitation representatives of thirty-two national organizations gathered at the Hotel William Penn in Pittsburgh, on January 23–24, 1943.

In his letter of invitation, dated January 6, 1943, Mr. Monsky indicated that the purpose of the Pittsburgh Meeting was to reach an agreement among the various organized bodies in the American Jewish community with regard to their responsibilities in

Source: "Proposals Adopted at the Pittsburgh Meeting," *The American Jewish Conference. Its Organization and Proceedings of the First Session* (New York: American Jewish Conference, 1944), pp. 324–26.

representing Jewish demands at the future Peace Table. "American Jewry," he wrote, "which will be required in large measure to assume the responsibility of representing the interests of our people at the Victory Peace Conference, must be ready to voice the judgment of American Jews along with that of the other Jewish communities of the free countries with respect to the post-war status of Jews and the upbuilding of a Jewish Palestine....The purpose of the conference is to bring together the representatives of major national Jewish membership organizations, in order that they may consider what steps should be taken to bring about some agreement on the part of the American Jewish community."

Of the thirty-four organizations that were invited, thirty-two responded favorably and sent to the Pittsburgh Meeting from one to three representatives each, making a total of seventy-eight men and women in attendance. Two of the invited national organizations, the American Jewish Committee and the Jewish Labor Committee, did not participate in this Meeting.

The Pittsburgh Meeting had three sessions, beginning Saturday evening, January 23rd, and ending Sunday late afternoon, January 24th. The first and third sessions were presided over by Mr. Monsky, and the second session, by Eugene B. Strassburger.[4] An invocation was given by Rabbi Solomon B. Freehof[5] on the opening day and one by Rabbi Herman Hailperin[6] on the second day.

As Mr. Monsky pointed out at the opening session, the Meeting was not convened to pass resolutions or make declarations. Its purpose was to allow a free discussion of the problems referred to in the letter of invitation, and to make certain proposals for further procedure. In line with these principles, two committees were appointed, namely, a Committee on Guidance, under the Chairmanship of Judge Louis E. Levinthal,[7] and a Committee on Proposals, under the Co-chairmanship of Robert P. Goldman[8] and Louis Lipsky,[9] which functioned only for the duration of the sessions. The first committee directed the proceedings, while the second formulated the results of the deliberations. The members on each of these committees represented, as far as possible, every major point of view that was reflected among the representatives at this Meeting. A Secretariat was elected consisting of Maurice Bisgyer,[10] Jane Evans,[11] Lillie Shultz[12] and Meyer W. Weisgal.[13]

To allow full and unrestricted expression of opinion, it was ruled by the Chairman, with the concurrence of all the representatives, that a vote cast by a representative in favor of the proposals would not commit his organization. The governing bodies of the respective organizations were free subsequently to accept or reject the proposals of the Meeting, thus expressing their own choice of action.

The discussions that took place in the course of the three sessions revealed not only the extent of the problem confronting American Jewry in relation to post-war Jewish needs, but also the earnest desire on the part of every representative to join in common action.

ADDRESS BY HENRY MONSKY

The keynote of the meeting was sounded by Mr. Monsky in his opening address. "We have come together," he said at the outset, "not to adopt or propagandize for one or another post-war plan; not to issue or publish manifestos or proclamations in reference to the important role of Palestine in any such plan; but rather to take such preliminary steps as will result in a course of action and procedure calculated to accomplish the single objective, devoutly to be desired, of some basis of agreement between the diverse and conflicting groups that constitute the American Jewish community." The speaker then reviewed the events that led to the formation of the American Jewish Congress[14] in the first World War, and how unity of purpose was achieved among the various contending factions at that time. Then, too, there was a division of opinion as to Zionist aspirations (or Palestine and as to the method of safeguarding Jewish rights in certain European countries. When the Congress finally came into being on December 15th, 1918, all factions united on a common program of action. The Congress instructed its delegation to the Peace Conference "to cooperate with representatives of other Jewish organizations [abroad], specifically with the World Zionist Organization...[leading to] the development of Palestine into a Jewish Commonwealth"; and "to suggest that the peace conference insert in the treaty of peace...clauses expressly providing" equal civil, political, religious and national rights to all citizens, without distinction as to race, nationality or creed; minority representation; and national and religious autonomy of the various groups in the management of their communal, religious, educational and charitable institutions.

"Today," the speaker continued, "an even greater emergency than that of twenty-five years ago confronts us. The tragic plight of the Jewish people in Europe is unprecedented in the annals of our history. We have a vital stake in the peace that is to come. Not only have we suffered appalling destruction of Jewish life, but much of what was achieved after the first World War, in respect to the position of the Jew in the afflicted lands, has been lost....There is crucial need for the restoration of that lost position and for its fortification upon enduring foundations of equality and justice. The right of the Jewish people to rebuild their homeland in Palestine, recognized more than a quarter of a century ago, has now again become the subject of controversy. That right may have to be reaffirmed under conditions that will enable Palestine to serve as one of the important factors in the amelioration, if not the solution, of the Jewish problem."

Mr. Monsky called attention "to the state of confusion that exists in the American Jewish community." Dissenting statements have been issued by rabbinical and lay leadership, some opposing, others defending the political aspirations of Zionism. "Meanwhile, many Jews and non-Jews sympathetic with our tragic plight, are so confused, so discouraged and so frightened by the spectacle of conflict as to deem it necessary to withdraw their support from all programs devoted to the welfare of our people....The impact of this struggle for supremacy will affect the accord and the unity in local federations and welfare funds. Cooperation will be replaced by dissension; skepticism and suspicion will take the place of mutual respect and faith of community leaders in each other. The result will be irreparable injury to the whole fabric of Jewish life and activity. The challenge to those of us charged with leadership cannot be ignored."

Mr. Monsky then recommended a plan of procedure for the Meeting, as outlined above, which was adopted by the representatives unanimously. He concluded: "Let our deliberations be characterized by tolerance and a proper perspective of the whole of Jewish life. Let us think in terms of the preservation of the vital spirit of Judaism, the great contemporary Jewish movements, the lessons of Jewish history, a courageous, self-respecting Jewish community and, above all else, the indomitable will to live as Jews."

In the discussion that followed Mr. Monsky's address, many speakers participated, each expressing ideas that emanated from the point of view of his organization. However, all the speakers came to the inevitable conclusion that unity of action on the part of American Jewry was the demand of the hour. Summaries of the remarks made by the various speakers are given herewith in the order of their participation in the discussions.

DISSCUSSION

David Blumberg,[15] recognizing that Jewish survival is "the responsibility of the American Jew more than of any other Jew in the world," felt that this Meeting offered the possibility of forming "a united front for the purpose of presenting to the proper authorities at the proper time a formula that will guarantee this survival." Such a formula, he said, "is not in the nature of a compromise between Jew and Jew, or between one organization and another, but rather an adjustment between the Jewish people and the rest of the peoples of the world." Coming from the West, the speaker said he was expressing the sentiments of many communities in that part of the country in urging that every support be given to a procedure which would lead to the formulation of a program to be heeded "by the proper authorities after the war is over."

Rabbi James G. Heller[16] stressed the importance of a united representation of American Jewry "in the writing of peace." The influence of such a representation here and abroad will be effective only in so far as the participating organizations definitely commit themselves to an agreed policy, and to the extent that the representation speaks in the name of "as large a number of American Jews as possible....It must be realized," Rabbi Heller said, "that this will involve a willingness to subordinate the view of minorities to majorities." It is the task of this gathering to discover a genuine possibility of such unity and to devise the machinery for making it effective. The speaker felt that unity was more imperative now than in the previous war, not only because the suffering of the Jewish people in Europe is infinitely greater now than it was then, but also because of other factors which must not escape attention.

NOTES

1. The American Jewish Conference was established in 1943, in the midst of World War II, to deal with the problems of Palestine and the Holocaust. It was initiated by Bnai Brith (see note 3), which in its letter of invitation to the conference, sent to all major American

Jewish organizations and local Jewish communities, stated: "American Jewry, which will be required...to assume the responsibility of representing the interests of our people at the Victory Peace Conference, must be ready to voice the judgment of American Jews...with respect to the postwar status of Jews and the upbuilding of a Jewish Palestine."

The founding meeting of the Conference took place in Pittsburgh in January 1943; 78 delegates attended, representing 32 major American Jewish organizations. The organizing committee submitted proposals—presented in this document—which were approved, and the Conference was launched. The emphatically pro-Zionist posture adopted by the Conference at a subsequent meeting held in New York City in August 1943 soon alienated some of its constituent members, such as the American Jewish Committee, which eventually seceded from the organization. The Conference dissolved in 1949. The founding of the Conference marked American Jewry's recognition that, in the wake of the destruction of European Jewry, it had been charged by history to assume leadership of world Jewry.

2. Henry Monsky (1890–1947), U.S. communal leader, organization executive, and lawyer. A lifelong Zionist, Monsky was national president of Bnai Brith (see note 3) from 1938 to 1947. He was the principal organizer of the American Jewish Conference.

3. Bnai Brith is the world's oldest and largest Jewish service organization. The organization was established in 1843 by a small group of American Jewish men who originally met to create a fraternal order. In 1882 Bnai Brith became an international organization, with branches in Europe and Palestine.

4. Eugene B. Strassburger (1886–1978), U.S. lawyer and a member of the American Jewish Committee (see document 33 in this chapter). He represented the Union of American Hebrew Congregations (founded in Cincinnati in 1873 and embracing most Reform synagogues) at the American Jewish Conference.

5. Solomon B. Freehof (1892–1990), U.S. Reform rabbi and Judaica scholar. He represented the Central Conference of American Rabbis (see document 17 in this chapter) at the American Jewish Conference.

6. Herman Hailperin (1899–1973), U.S. Conservative rabbi and Jewish educator. He represented the Rabbinical Assembly of America (an association of Conservative rabbis founded in 1940) at the American Jewish Conference.

7. Louis E. Levinthal (1892–1976), prominent U.S. jurist and communal leader. An active Zionist, Levinthal represented the Zionist Organization of America (originally the Federation of American Zionists, founded in 1897) at the American Jewish Conference.

8. Robert P. Goldman (1890–1976), U.S. lawyer and local communal leader. He represented the Union of American Hebrew Congregations at the American Jewish Conference.

9. Louis Lipsky (1876–1963), prominent U.S. Zionist leader, journalist, and author. Lipsky was president of the Zionist Organization of America from 1922 to 1930 and was a founder of the Keren Hayesod, the Jewish Agency, and the American and World Jewish Congresses (see note 14). He represented the American Jewish Congress at the American Jewish Conference.

10. Maurice Bisgeyer (1897–1973), U.S. social worker, author, and executive secretary of Bnai Brith.

11. Jane Evans (1907–2004), executive director of the National Federation of Temple Sisterhoods of the Union of American Hebrew Congregations.

12. Lillie Shultz (1904–1981) administrative director of the American Jewish Congress.

13. Meyer W. Weisgal (1894–1977), U.S. Zionist leader and editor. He represented Poale Zion (see chapter 10, document 19) at the American Jewish Conference.

14. The American Jewish Congress, which met in Philadelphia in December 1918, convened for the purpose of formulating a postwar program for the Jewish people. The Congress elected a delegation of representatives to the Peace Conference held in Versailles.

15. David Blumberg (1911–1989) U.S. merchant. He represented Bnai Brith at the American Jewish Conference.

16. James A. Heller (1892–1971), U.S. Reform rabbi, Zionist leader, and educator. He represented the Central Conference of American Rabbis (see documents 17 and 49 in this chapter) at the American Jewish Conference.

51. A STATEMENT OF POLICY (1944)[1]

AMERICAN COUNCIL FOR JUDAISM

The American Council for Judaism, Inc., was organized to present the views of Americans of Jewish faith on problems affecting the future of their own lives and the lives of world Jewry in the present hour of world confusion.

The Council reaffirms the historic truth that the Jews of the world share common traditions and ethical concepts, which find their derivation in the same religious source....

As Americans of Jewish faith we believe implicitly in the fundamentals of democracy, rooted, as they are, in moralities that transcend race and state, and endow the individual with rights for which he is answerable only to God. We are thankful to be citizens of a country and to have shared in the building of a nation conceived in a spirit which knows neither special privilege nor inferior status for any man.

For centuries Jews have considered themselves nationals of those countries in which they have lived. Whenever free to do so, they have assumed, and will again assume, full responsibilities of citizenship in accordance with the ancient Jewish command, "The law of the land is the law." Those countries in which Jews have lived have been their homes; those lands their homelands. In those nations where political action was expressed through minority groups, the Jew, following the law of his land, accepted minority status, thereby frequently gaining an improvement over previous conditions of inferior citizenship. Such East European concepts, however, have resulted in a misunderstanding, shared by Jews and non-Jews, a misunderstanding which we seek to dispel. American Jews hope that in the peace for which all of us pray, the old principle of minority rights will be supplanted by the more modern principle of equality and freedom for the individual. The interest of American Jews in the individual Jew in countries where the minority right principle prevailed is not to be confused with acceptance of this East European political principle.

As a result of the bigotry, sadism and ambitions for world conquest of the Axis powers, millions of our co-religionists who made homes in and were nationals of other lands have been violently deported and made victims of indescribable barbarism. No other group has been so brutishly attacked and for one reason only—on the false claims that there are racial barriers or nationalistic impulses that separate Jews from other men.

The plight of those Jews together with millions of oppressed fellow men of all faiths, calls for the profoundest sympathy and the unbounded moral indignation of all free men....

We believe that wherever possible the forced emigrés should be repatriated in their original homelands under conditions which will enable them to live as free, upstanding individuals.

For our fellow Jews we ask only this: Equality of rights and obligations with their fellow nationals. In our endeavors to bring relief to our stricken fellow Jews, and to help rebuild their lives on a more stable basis, we rely wholly on both democracy and religion, and which have been declared as the principles which shall prevail in the better world for which the United Nations are fighting....

Palestine has contributed in a tangible way to the alleviation of the present catastrophe in Jewish life by providing a refuge for a part of Europe's persecuted Jews. We hope it will continue as one of the places for such resettlement, for it has been clearly demonstrated that practical colonizing can be done, schools and universities built, scientific agriculture

Source: United States House of Representatives, *Hearings Before the Committee on Foreign Affairs* [February 8–16, 1944] (New York, 1970), pp. 124–26.

extended, commerce intensified, and culture developed. This is the record of achievement of eager, hard-working settlers who have been aided in their endeavors by Jews all over the world, in every walk of life and thought.

We oppose the effort to establish a National Jewish State in Palestine or anywhere else as a philosophy of defeatism, and one which does not offer a practical solution of the Jewish problem. We dissent from all those related doctrines that stress the racialism, the nationalism, and the theoretical homelessness of Jews. We oppose such doctrines as inimical to the welfare of Jews in Palestine, in America, or wherever Jews may dwell. We believe that the intrusion of Jewish national statehood has been a deterrent in Palestine's ability to play an even greater role in offering a haven for the oppressed, and that without the insistence upon such statehood, Palestine would today be harboring more refugees from Nazi terror. The very insistence upon a Jewish Army has led to the raising of barriers against our unfortunate brethren. There never was a need for such an army. There has always been ample opportunity for Jews to fight side by side with those of other faiths in the armies of the United Nations.

Palestine is a part of Israel's religious heritage, as it is a part of the heritage of two other religions of the world. We look forward to the ultimate establishment of a democratic, autonomous government in Palestine, wherein Jews, Moslems and Christians shall he justly represented; every man enjoying equal rights and sharing equal responsibilities; a democratic government in which our fellow Jews shall be free Palestinians whose religion is Judaism, even as we are Americans whose religion is Judaism.

NOTE

1. An anti-Zionist organization founded in 1943, the American Council for Judaism (ACJ) represents the interests of "Americans of Jewish faith." It emphatically maintains that Judaism is a religion of universal values, and not a nationality. Its policy is outlined in this document The ACJ has remained a small group, with very few synagogues and even fewer Jewish organizations endorsing its program. As the following document illustrates, most American Jews, though they adhere to a firm commitment and allegiance to the United States, had—and still largely have—a special relationship of fraternal affection for the Zionist project.

52. AN EXCHANGE OF VIEWS (1950)[1]

DAVID BEN-GURION AND JACOB BLAUSTEIN

ADDRESS OF PRIME MINISTER DAVID BEN-GURION:[2] We are very happy to welcome you here in our midst as a representative of the great Jewry of the United States to whom Israel owes so much. No other community abroad has so great a stake in what has been achieved in this country during the present generation as have the Jews of America. Their material and political support, their warm-hearted and practical idealism, has been one of the principal sources of our strength and our success. In supporting our effort, American Jewry has developed, on a new plane, the noble conception, maintained for more than half a century, of extending its help for the protection of Jewish rights throughout the world and

Source: American Jewish Year Book 53 (1952), pp. 564–68. Copyright 1952 by the Jewish Publication Society of America. Reprinted by permission of the Jewish Publication Society.

of rendering economic aid wherever it was needed. We are deeply conscious of the help which America has given to us here in our great effort of reconstruction and during our struggle for independence. This great tradition has been continued since the establishment of the State of Israel.

It is our great pride that our newly gained independence has enabled us in this small country to undertake the major share of the great and urgent task of providing permanent homes under conditions of full equality to hundreds of thousands of our brethren who cannot remain where they are and whose heart is set on rebuilding their lives in Israel. In this great task you and we are engaged in a close partnership. Without the readiness for sacrifice of the people of Israel and without the help of America this urgent task can hardly be achieved.

It is most unfortunate that since our State came into being some confusion and misunderstanding should have arisen as regards the relationship between Israel and the Jewish communities abroad, in particular that of the United States. These misunderstandings are likely to alienate sympathies and create disharmony where friendship and close understanding are of vital necessity. To my mind, the position is perfectly clear. The Jews of the United States, as a community and as individuals, have only one political attachment and that is to the United States of America. They owe no political allegiance to Israel. In the first statement which the representative of Israel made before the United Nations after her admission to that international organization, he clearly stated, without any reservation, that the State of Israel represents and speaks only on behalf of its own citizens and in no way presumes to represent or speak in the name of the Jews who are citizens of any other country. We, the people of Israel, have no desire and no intention to interfere in any way with the internal affairs of Jewish communities abroad. The Government and the people of Israel fully respect the right and integrity of the Jewish communities in other countries to develop their own mode of life and their indigenous social, economic and cultural institutions in accordance with their own needs and aspirations. Any weakening of American Jewry, any disruption of its communal life, any lowering of its sense of security, any diminution of its status, is a definite loss to Jews everywhere and to Israel in particular.

We are happy to know of the deep and growing interest which American Jews of all shades and convictions take in what it has fallen to us to achieve in this country. Were we, God forbid, to fail in what we have undertaken on our own behalf and on behalf of our suffering brethren, that failure would cause grievous pain to Jews everywhere and nowhere more than in your community. Our success or failure depends in a large measure on our cooperation with, and on the strength of, the great Jewish community of the United States, and, we, therefore, are anxious that nothing should be said or done which could in the slightest degree undermine the sense of security and stability of American Jewry.

In this connection let me say a word about immigration. We should like to see American Jews come and take part in our effort. We need their technical knowledge, their unrivalled experience, their spirit of enterprise, their bold vision, their "know-how." We need engineers, chemists, builders, work managers and technicians. The tasks which face us in this country are eminently such as would appeal to the American genius for technical development and social progress. But the decision as to whether they wish to come—permanently or temporarily—rests with the free discretion of each American Jew himself. It is entirely a matter of his own volition. We need *haluzim*,[3] pioneers too. *Haluzim* have come to us—and we believe more will come, not only from those countries where the Jews are oppressed and in "exile" but also from countries where the Jews live a life of freedom and are equal in status to all other citizens in their country. But the essence of *haluziut* is free choice. They will come from among those who believe that their aspirations as human beings and as Jews can best be fulfilled by life and work in Israel.

I believe I know something of the spirit of American Jewry among whom I lived for some years. I am convinced that it will continue to make a major contribution towards our great effort of reconstruction, and I hope that the talks we have had with you during these last few days will make for even closer cooperation between our two communities.

RESPONSE OF JACOB BLAUSTEIN:[4] I am very happy, Mr. Prime Minister, to have come here at your invitation and to have discussed with you and other leaders of Israel the various important problems of mutual interest....

There is no question in my mind that a Jew who wants to remain loyal to the fundamental basis of Judaism and his cultural heritage, will be in the forefront of the struggle for democracy against totalitarianism.

The American Jewish community sees its fortunes tied to the fate of liberal democracy in the United States, sustained by its heritage, as Americans and as Jews. We seek to strengthen both of these vital links to the past and to all humanity by enhancing the American democratic and political system, American cultural diversity and American wellbeing.

As to Israel, the vast majority of American Jewry recognizes the necessity and desirability of helping to make it a strong, viable, self-supporting state. This, for the sake of Israel itself, and the good of the world.

The American Jewish Committee has been active, as have other Jewish organizations in the United States, in rendering, within the framework of their American citizenship, every possible support to Israel; and I am sure that this support will continue and that we shall do all we can to increase further our share in the great historic task of helping Israel to solve its problems and develop as a free, independent and flourishing democracy.

While Israel has naturally placed some burdens on Jews elsewhere, particularly in America, it has, in turn, meant much to Jews throughout the world. For hundreds of thousands in Europe, Africa and the Middle East it has provided a home in which they can attain their full stature of human dignity for the first time. In all Jews, it has inspired pride and admiration, even though in some instances, it has created passing headaches.

Israel's rebirth and progress, coming after the tragedy of European Jewry in the 1930s and in World War II, has done much to raise Jewish morale. Jews in America and everywhere can be more proud than ever of their Jewishness.

But we must, in a true spirit of friendliness, sound a note of caution to Israel and its leaders. Now that the birth pains are over, and even though Israel is undergoing growing pains, it must recognize that the matter of good-will between its citizens and those of other countries is a two-way street: that Israel also has a responsibility in this situation—a responsibility in terms of not affecting adversely the sensibilities of Jews who are citizens of other states by what it says or does.

In this connection, you are realists and want facts and I would be less than frank if I did not point out to you that American Jews vigorously repudiate any suggestion or implication that they are in exile. American Jews—young and old alike, Zionists and non-Zionists alike—are profoundly attached to America. America welcomed their immigrant parents in their need. Under America's free institutions, they and their children have achieved that freedom and sense of security unknown for long centuries of travail. American Jews have truly become Americans; just as have all other oppressed groups that have ever come to America's shores.

To American Jews, America is home. There, exist their thriving roots; there, is the country which they have helped to build; and there, they share its fruits and its destiny. They believe in the future of a democratic society in the United States under which all citizens, irrespective of creed or race, can live on terms of equality. They further believe that, if democracy should fail in America, there would be no future for democracy anywhere in the world, and that the very existence of an independent State of Israel would be problematic. Further, they feel that a world in which it would be possible for Jews to be driven by persecution from America would not be a world safe for Israel either; indeed it is hard to conceive how it would be a world safe for any human being.

The American Jewish community, as you, Mr. Prime Minister, have so eloquently pointed out, has assumed a major part of the responsibility of securing equality of rights and providing generous material help to Jews in other countries. American Jews feel themselves bound to Jews the world over by ties of religion, common historical traditions and in certain respects, by a sense of common destiny. We fully realize that persecution and discrimination against Jews in any country will sooner or later have its impact on the situation of the Jews in other countries, but these problems must be dealt with by each Jewish community itself in accordance with its own wishes, traditions, needs and aspirations.

Jewish communities, particularly American Jewry in view of its influence and its strength, can offer advice, cooperation and help, but should not attempt to speak in the name of other communities or in any way interfere in their internal affairs.

I am happy to note from your statement, Mr. Prime Minister, that the State of Israel takes a similar position. Any other position on the part of the State of Israel would only weaken the American and other Jewish communities of the free, democratic countries and be contrary to the basic interests of Israel itself. The future development of Israel, spiritual, social as well as economic, will largely depend upon a strong and healthy Jewish community in the United States and other free democracies.

We have been greatly distressed that at the very hour when so much has been achieved, harmful and futile discussions and misunderstandings have arisen as to the relations between the people and the State of Israel and the Jews in other countries, particularly in the United States. Harm has been done to the morale and to some extent to the sense of security of the American Jewish community through unwise and unwarranted statements and appeals which ignore the feelings and aspirations of American Jewry.

Even greater harm has been done to the State of Israel itself by weakening the readiness of American Jews to do their full share in the rebuilding of Israel which faces such enormous political, social and economic problems.

Your statement today, Mr. Prime Minister, will, I trust, be followed by unmistakable evidence that the responsible leaders of Israel, and the organizations connected with it, fully understand that future relations between the American Jewish community and the State of Israel must be based on mutual respect for one another's feelings and needs, and on the preservation of the integrity of the two communities and their institutions.

I believe that in your statement today, you have taken a fundamental and historic position which will redound to the best interest not only of Israel, but of the Jews of America and of the world. I am confident that this statement and the spirit in which it has been made, by eliminating the misunderstandings and futile discussions between our two communities, will strengthen them both and will lay the foundation for even closer cooperation....

NOTES

1. Even before Israel was established, the American Jewish Committee (AJC) received assurances from the Jewish Agency (see document 33, note 1, in chapter 9) that the Jewish State would refrain from interfering in American Jewish internal affairs. Israeli officials continued to assure the AJC on that score after May 1948, when the State was established. However, when in 1949 Ben-Gurion called for large-scale immigration to Israel by American Jewish youth, the committee protested vigorously. The AJC sought to work out with the Israeli government a clear and forceful expression of policy on immigration and on the principle of noninterference. The occasion arose in the summer of 1950 when Jacob Blaustein was a guest of the Israeli government. An agreement was sealed in the form of a statement read at a luncheon by Prime Minister Ben-Gurion and a response by Jacob Blaustein. Both reaffirmed the agreement in April 1961. (See Naomi Cohen, *Not Free to Desist* [1972], pp. 310ff.)

2. David Ben-Gurion (1886–1973), Zionist labor leader, Jewish statesman, architect of the Jewish state, and the first prime minister of Israel.

3. *Haluz* (plural, *haluzim)*, a pioneer, especially in agriculture in the Land of Israel.

4. Jacob Blaustein (1892–1970), associated with his father, Louis, in the founding of the American Oil Company. Jacob Blaustein was director and member of the board of major companies in the fields of petroleum, insurance, and banking; he was reportedly one of the richest individuals in America. Blaustein played an active role in Jewish affairs and had a major commitment to the American Jewish Committee, which he served as president from 1949 to 1954.

X

ZIONISM

The term *Zionism* was most probably coined by Nathan Birnbaum (1864–1937), a leader of the Hovevei Zion, a loose federation of Jewish groups devoted to the national resettlement of the Jews in their ancestral homeland. The Hovevei Zion viewed resettlement as the solution to the Jewish question, which it variously defined as the problem of antisemitism or the problem of Judaism in a modern, secular world. Significantly, the term *Zionism* reflects both traditional sentiment (the longing for Zion) and a modern political orientation. This fact is clearly reflected in the Bilu Program of 1882 (see document 1).

It is frequently assumed that Zionism is a response to modern antisemitism. This is but partially true. As integral to Zionism as its negative reaction to antisemitism is, its positive assertion of belief in the messianic prophecy and the historic destiny of the Jewish people is equally important. The leading precursors of Zionism, Rabbi Zvi Hirsch Kalischer (1795–1874), Rabbi Judah Solomon Hai Alkalai (1798–1878), and even the socialist Moses Hess (1812–1875), were moved to create a Jewish settlement in Palestine not only by sociopolitical considerations but also by a deep religious conviction that the time for the ingathering of the exiles had arrived—the prophecy was to be literally acted upon. Theodor Herzl (see document 6), the founder of the World Zionist Organization, was preeminently concerned with the *Judennot*—the distress or problem of the Jews, viz., antisemitism. But many of the aforementioned Hovevei Zion groups—which preceded Herzl by almost two decades and which constituted a significant element in the World Zionist Organization—were equally concerned with the *Not des Judentums*, the problem of Judaism. They were thus preeminently devoted to securing the future of Jewish culture both in the Diaspora and in Palestine. To this end they sought to foster the revival of the Hebrew language as the basis of a secular national culture (see document 5). This position was best articulated by Ahad Haam (see document 9), who did not withhold his criticism of Herzl's *political* Zionism.

In a certain respect, the differences between Herzl and Ahad Haam reflect the differences between West and East European Jewry, stemming from their contrasting political and cultural situations. In Eastern Europe the secularization that affected the Jews was accompanied neither, as it was by and large in the West, by a jettisoning of national culture and identity nor, most important, by emancipation. The secularized East European Jew, with rare exceptions, continued to live in a ghetto situation—where opportunities for assimilation were limited—and continued to speak Yiddish, read Hebrew, partake in Jewish folkways, and identify ethnically as Jews. In short, secular Jewish culture was already a reality for many East European Jews. Zionists like Ahad Haam merely sought to give it a specific direction in order to assure its vitality and creativity. Moreover, the multiethnic character of some of the states of Eastern Europe theoretically presented the Jews with the possibility of a secular national culture within the context of modern society. However, East European Jewry was forced to face the brutal nature of antisemitism in a much more violent fashion than Western Jewry, and because of the exigency of this problem East European Zionists were pressed to develop a program of immediate, practical solutions that involved alternatives that did not require the restoration of Jewish sovereignty in Palestine. This dual emphasis on "interim" solutions and practical action in both Palestine and the Diaspora is exemplified by the policy of *Gegenwartsarbeit* ("work in the present"; see document 20) and by the fact that East European Jewry provided the vast majority of the earlier, i.e., before 1933, waves of immigration (*aliyot*) to Palestine. The initial *aliyot* were animated by the distinctive ethos and ideals of *haluziut* (pioneering). Dedicated to rebuilding the land of Israel, these *olim* (immigrants) regarded their efforts as the realization of both personal and national renewal (see documents 21, 30). They helped create unique institutions as well (see documents 24 and 41). In contradistinction to East European Zionism, Western Zionism until the rise of Nazism was largely a philanthropic movement devoted to the welfare of the persecuted Jews of Eastern Europe. The Zionism of Western Jews did not necessarily entail a personal commitment to immigrate to Palestine. It did, however, contribute significantly to the intellectual and ideological fermentation of the Zionist movement of the East and the West.

As can be discerned from the documents, the World Zionist Organization embraced a wide spectrum of ideological positions, from Poalei Zion on the Left to Revisionism on the Right (see documents 19 and 38). What unites these divergent ideological positions is the rejection of Exile (*galut* or *golus* in traditional parlance). "The Zionist attitude begins," as the historian Ben Halpern observes, "with a lively awareness and affirmation of Exile as a condition"; this condition is inherently problematic for continued Jewish existence. The analysis of this condition varies, of course, according to one's ideological orientation. "The intellectual substance of Zionism," Halpern emphasizes, "is the rejection of Exile: not the denial of Exile, please note, but its rejection....There were two historical attitudes to which Zionism opposed itself, and in opposing, was defined. The first was the acceptance of Exile as a 'commitment'—the attitude, by and large, of Orthodox Jewry at the time [the nineteenth century]. The other was the 'denial' of Exile as a condition—an attitude that arose in Reform Judaism."[1] Thus, it is not surprising that within the Jewish community Zionism encountered bitter opposition, from assimilationists, liberals, socialists, and traditionalists (see documents 28 and 31).

Zionism acquired a respectability both among Jews and non-Jews with the Balfour Declaration (see documents 32 and 33). This recognition propelled Zionism as a major force not only in Jewish life but also in the international community. This support was not markedly diminished by the seemingly intractable and persistent conflict between the Zionists and the Arabs of Palestine and the region (see documents 38, 43, 50, and 51). Even the gradual erosion of Great Britain's commitment to its Palestine Mandate could

---

[1] Ben Halpern, "Exile," *Jewish Frontier* (April 1954), pp. 6–9.

not stem the mounting political prestige of the Zionist movement. In the aftermath of the Shoah this international recognition of Zionism was reinforced by a groundswell of sympathy for the bereaved Jewish people. On November 29, 1947, the United Nations declared the creation of a Jewish state in Palestine. The following year, on May 14, David Ben-Gurion, on behalf of the Provisional Government formed by the Zionist parties of Palestine, officially proclaimed the creation of an independent State of Israel.

1. MANIFESTO (1882)

THE BILU[1]

To Our Brethren and Sisters in the Exile, Peace be with You!

"If I help not myself, who will help me?" (Hillel.)[2]

Nearly two thousand years have elapsed since, in an evil hour, after an heroic struggle, the glory of our Temple vanished in fire and our Kings and chieftains changed their crowns and diadems for the chains of exile. We lost our country, where dwelt our beloved sires. Into the Exile we took with us, of all our glories only a spark of the fire, by which our Temple, the abode of our Great One, was engirdled, and this little spark kept us alive while the towers of our enemies crumbled to dust, and this spark leapt into celestial flame and shed light upon the faces of the heroes of our race and inspired them to endure the horrors of the Dance of Death and the tortures of the autos-da-fé. And this spark is now again kindling and will shine for us, a true pillar of fire going before us on the road to Zion, while behind us is a pillar of cloud, the pillar of oppression threatening to destroy us. Sleepest thou, O our nation? What hast thou been doing till 1882? Sleeping and dreaming the false dream of Assimilation. Now, thank God, thou art awakened from thy slothful slumber. The pogroms have awakened thee from thy charmed sleep. Thine eyes are open to recognize the cloudy structure of delusive hopes. Canst thou listen silently to the flaunts and the mockery of thine enemies? Wilt thou yield before…? Where is thine ancient pride, thine olden spirit? Remember that thou wast a nation possessing a wise religion, a law, a constitution, a celestial Temple, whose wall[3] is still a silent witness to the glories of the Past, that thy sons dwelt in Palaces and towers, and thy cities flourished in the splendour of civilization, while these enemies of thine dwelt like beasts in the muddy marshes of their dark woods.

While thy children were clad in purple and linen, they wore the rough skins of the wolf and the bear. Art thou not ashamed to submit to them?

Hopeless is your state in the West; the star of your future is gleaming in the East. Deeply conscious of all this, and inspired by the true teaching of our great master Hillel: "If I help not myself, who will help me?" we propose to build the following society for national ends: (1) The Society will be named Bilu, according to the motto: "House of Jacob, come, let us go!" It will be divided into local branches according to the number of members. (2) The seat of the Committee shall be Jerusalem. (3) Donations and contributions shall be unfixed and unlimited.

What we want: (1) A Home in our country. It was given to us by the mercy of God, it is ours as registered in the archives of history. (2) To beg it of the Sultan himself, and if it be impossible to obtain this, to beg that at least we may be allowed to possess it as a state within a larger state; the internal administration to be ours, to have our civil and political rights, and to act with the Turkish Empire only in foreign affairs, so as to help our brother Ishmael in his time of need.

We hope that the interests of our glorious nation will rouse the national spirit in rich and powerful men, and that everyone, rich or poor, will give his best labours to the holy cause.

Greetings, dear brethren and sisters.

Hear, O Israel, the Lord our God, the Lord is one, and our Land, Zion is our one hope.

God be with us!

NOTES

1. The Bilu was a group of young Russian Jews who pioneered the Zionist program of resettlement of the Jewish people in the land of Israel as a solution to the Jewish questions. The group derived its nàme from the Hebrew

Source: Trans. Nahum Sokolow, *History of Zionism* (London: Longmans, Green & Co., 1919), vol. 2, pp. 332–33.

initials of *Beit Yaakov lekhu venelkha* (House of Jacob, come, let us go) (Isaiah 2:5). A reaction to the 1881 pogroms in southern Russia, the Bilu was founded at the beginning of 1882 with Kharkov as its headquarters; later the headquarters was moved to Odessa. The first Bilu contingent arrived in Palestine in mid-1882. After

working in a number of Jewish villages for several years, they founded the settlement of Gederah. The manifesto published here was issued by members of the Bilu in Constantinople in 1882 en route to Palestine.
2. Hillel was a first century B.C.E. rabbinic authority.
3. The Western or Wailing Wall.

2. AUTO-EMANCIPATION (1882)

LEO PINSKER[1]

"If I am not for myself, who will be for me? And if not now, when?"

—*Hillel.*

The misery caused by bloody deeds of violence has been followed by a moment of repose, and baiter and baited can breathe easier for a time. Meanwhile the Jewish refugees are being "repatriated" with the very money that was collected to assist emigration. The Jews in the West have again learned to endure the cry of "Hep, Hep"[2] as their fathers did in days gone by. The flaming outburst of burning indignation at the disgrace endured has turned into a rain of ashes, which is gradually covering the glowing soil. Close your eyes and hide your heads ostrich-fashion as you will; if you do not take advantage of the fleeting moments of repose, and devise remedies more fundamental than those palliatives with which the incompetent have for centuries vainly tried to relieve our unhappy nation, lasting peace is impossible for you.

September, 1882.

I.

The eternal problem presented by the Jewish Question stirs men to-day as it did ages ago. It remains unsolved,

like the squaring of the circle, but unlike it, it is still a burning question. This is due to the fact that it is not merely a problem of theoretical interest, but one of practical interest, which renews its youth from day to day.

The essence of the problem, as we see it, lies in the fact that, in the midst of the nations among whom the Jews reside, they form a distinctive element which cannot be assimilated, which cannot be readily digested by any nation. Hence the problem is to find means of so adjusting the relations of this exclusive element to the whole body of the nations that there shall never be any further basis for the Jewish Question.

We cannot, of course, think of establishing perfect harmony. Such harmony as probably never existed, even among other nations. The millennium in which the "International" will disappear, and the nations will merge into humanity, is still invisible in the distance. Until it is realized, the desires and ideals of the nations must be limited to establishing a tolerable *modus vivendi.*

Long will the world have to await universal peace; but in the interim the relations of the nations to one another may be adjusted fairly well by an explicit mutual understanding, an understanding based upon

Source: Leo Pinsker, *Autoemancipation,* trans. D. S. Blondheim, revised by Arthur Saul Super (New York: Masada Youth Zionist Organization of America, 1935), pp. 4–7, 32.

international law, treaties, and especially upon a certain equality in rank and mutually admitted rights, as well as upon mutual regard.

No such equality in rank appears in the intercourse of the nations with the Jews. In the latter case the basis is lacking for that mutual regard which is generally regulated and secured by international law or by treaties. Only when this basis is established, when the equality of the Jews with the other nations becomes a fact, can the problem presented by the Jewish Question be considered solved. Unfortunately, although such equality existed in reality in days long since forgotten, under present conditions we can hope to see it restored only in so remote a future that the admission of the Jewish people into the ranks of the other nations seems illusory. They lack most of those attributes which are the hall-mark of a nation. They lack that characteristic national life which is inconceivable without a common language, common customs, and a common land. The Jewish people have no fatherland of their own, though many motherlands; they have no rallying point, no centre of gravity, no government of their own, no accredited representatives. They are everywhere as guests, and are nowhere *at home*. The nations *never* have to deal with a Jewish *nation* but always with mere *Jews*. The Jews are not a nation because they lack a certain distinctive national character, possessed by every other nation, a character which is determined by living together in one country, under one rule. It was clearly impossible for this national character to be developed in the Diaspora; the Jews seem rather to have lost all remembrance of their former home. Thanks to their ready adaptability, they have all the more easily acquired the alien traits of the people among whom their fate has thrown them. Moreover, to please their protectors, not seldom did they divest themselves of their traditional individuality. They acquired, or persuaded themselves that they had acquired certain cosmopolitan tendencies which could appeal to others no more than they could bring satisfaction to the Jews themselves.

In seeking to fuse with other peoples, they deliberately renounced, to a certain extent, their own nationality. Nowhere, however, did they succeed in obtaining from their fellow-citizens recognition as native-born citizens of equal rank.

The strongest fact, however, operating to prevent the Jews from striving after an independent national existence is the fact that they do not feel the need for an existence. Not only do they feel no need for it, but they go so far as to deny the reasonableness of such a need.

In a sick man, the absence of desire for food and drink is a very serious symptom. It is not always possible to cure him of this ominous loss of appetite. And even if his appetite be restored, it is still a question whether he will be able to digest food, even though he desire it.

The Jews are in the unhappy condition of such a patient. We must discuss this most important point with all possible precision. We must prove that the misfortunes of the Jews are due, above all, to their lack of desire for national independence; and that this desire must be aroused and maintained in time if they do not wish to be subjected forever to disgraceful existence—in a word, we must prove that *they must become a nation*.

In the apparently insignificant circumstance, that the Jews are not considered an independent nation by other nations, rests in part, the secret of their anomalous position and of their endless misery. The mere fact of belonging to this people constitutes an indelible stigma repellent to non-Jews and painful to the Jews themselves. Nevertheless, this phenomenon has its basis rooted deep in human nature.

II.

Among the living nations of the earth the Jews occupy the position of a nation long since dead. With the loss of their fatherland, the Jewish people lost their independence, and fell into a decay which was not compatible with existence as a whole vital organism. The state, was crushed before the eyes of the nations. But after the Jewish people had yielded up their existence as an actual state, as a political entity, they could nevertheless not submit to total destruction—they did not cease to exist spiritually as a nation. The world saw in this people the uncanny form of one of the dead walking among the living. The ghostlike apparition of a people without unity or organization, without land or other bond of union, no longer alive, and yet moving about among the living,—this eerie form scarcely paralleled in history, unlike anything that preceded or followed it, could not fail to make a strange, peculiar impression upon the imagination of the nations. And if the fear of ghosts is something inborn, and has a certain justification in the psychic life of humanity, what wonder that it asserted itself powerfully at the sight of this dead and yet living nation?

Fear of the Jewish ghost has been handed down and strengthened for generations and centuries. It led to a prejudice which, in its turn, in connection with other forces to be discussed later, paved the way for Judeophobia....

Summary

The Jews are not a living nation; they are everywhere aliens; therefore they are despised.

The civil and political emancipation of the Jews is not sufficient to raise them in the estimation of the peoples.

The proper, the only remedy, would be the creation of a Jewish nationality, of a people living upon its own soil, the auto-emancipation of the Jews; their emancipation as a nation among nations by the acquisition of a home of their own.

We should not persuade ourselves that humanity and enlightenment will ever be radical remedies for the malady of our people.

The lack of national self-respect and self-confidence of political initiative and of unity, are the enemies of our national renaissance.

In order that we may not be constrained to wander from one exile to another, we must have an extensive, productive place of refuge, a *rendezvous* which is our own.

The present moment is more favourable than any other for the plan unfolded.

The international Jewish question must receive a national solution. Of course, our national regeneration can only proceed slowly. *We* must take the first step. Our *descendants* must follow us in measured and not over-hasty time.

A way must be opened for the national regeneration of the Jews by a congress of Jewish notables.

No sacrifice would be too great in order to reach the goal which will assure our people's future, everywhere endangered.

The financial accomplishment of the undertaking can in the present state of the case encounter no insuperable difficulties.

Help yourselves, and God will help you!

NOTES

1. Born in Russian Poland, Leo (Yehudah Leib) Pinsker (1821–1891) was a physician by profession. As a solution to the Jewish Question, he initially advocated the adoption of enlightened Russian culture. While practicing medicine in Odessa, he contributed an article to the Russian-Jewish weekly *Razsvet* (see chapter 7, document 17). His faith in the efficacy of acculturation was undermined by anti-Jewish pogroms in Odessa in 1871 and a palpable shift in official Russian attitudes toward the Jews. The pogroms that swept southern Russia from 1881 to 1884, and the mass emigration—or rather flight—of Jews that followed, led Pinsker to a radical revision of his understanding of antisemitism and its possible solution. He undertook an extensive tour of Western Europe—Vienna, Paris, Berlin, and London—to discuss with various leading Jewish dignitaries the Jewish Question. His suggestion that the most rational solution would be the concentration of the Jews in a country of their own was for the most part dismissed out of hand. One prominent British Jew was less skeptical and encouraged Pinsker to develop his views in writing. And so he did. While in Berlin, he penned a pamphlet in German entitled *Autoemancipation: A Warning of a Russian Jew to His Brethren*. He called upon his fellow Jews to disabuse themselves of the illusion that antisemitism is but a medieval relic and would disappear with the march of progress and the ascendancy of liberal democracy. *Judeophobia*—a medical term he favored to antisemitism, which he regarded a misnomer—is endemic to the Diaspora, for reasons he explored in his pamphlet. When he returned to Russia, he joined the Hibbat Zion movement (see this chapter document 3), which in 1884 named him the chairman of its Central Committee.

2. See chapter 5, document 3, note 6.

3. *HOVEVEI ZION* (1884)[1]

ZALMAN EPSTEIN[2]

The great idea came from the settlement in the Land of Israel like a suckling in the wilderness, like a sapling that is still young and tender. Still full of sap it gives hope that it will send shoots into a great land and bear fruit, blessing the wretched and dispossessed wandering people. In these first days it needs aware and decisive hands to work and keep it. And so God's defeated burst from their holes stricken by the plague of narrow-mindedness, set only on fighting the people and loosening its grip, so that it should not wake from its long sleep: to this end malicious stories are doing harm to those who raise the banner of the great idea. They want to destroy it while still in the bud. To struggle with these traitors and prove that all their phrases and tales are empty, without a grain of truth is a holy duty imposed on all those true to God, His Torah, His people and His land.

An insignificant and narrow-minded man wrote an abhorrent libel against the *Hovevei Zion* in an article saying that "the members of the new sect want to gorge on the destructions of Israel and to achieve their ends by reinforcing wicked and persecutory decrees."—It makes one sad at heart that these words were printed in a respectable organ whose publisher is an important, excellent and highly respected man, and we will not be able to ignore this abhorrent libel without the writer retracting the libel against his name and standing, because of its slanderous language. Firstly this man and all his friends knew that the *Hovevei Zion* are not a sect, and that all of Israel who have reverence and integrity are *Hovevei Zion* except for those who alienate themselves from their origin and want to assimilate, or other twisted hearts who stay ignorant about themselves, whose faces are turned habitually and submissively, like reeds bending to every wind. Their souls are in abhorrent assimilation and their fathers abandoned a place in the land as so many thorns. The whole people love the land of its fathers, desire its settlement and hope for the re-establishment of its fallen *succah*,[3] but do not have the necessary commitment of heart and mind, in the confusion of the times and the development of events: and this slight lack can only last a while, until true teachers are found who love and are faithful to its covenant, opinion makers who will see what the people must do.

And with regard to the libel itself, we ask the writer if he really imagined that the *Hovevei Zion* break out dancing every time our respected brothers from the villages in the Paltava and Tschernigov[4] districts cry out for help? Or if he honestly thinks that Hovevei Zion are "fools" in a dream who think that one sunny morning millions of our brothers will leave their lands of their birth with all their money and possessions that they have gathered by the sweat of their brows, and by a miracle find homes and insurance on the eastern Mediterranean? We ask our critic that he and his like should know that the *Hovevei Zion* do not wish to gorge on the destructions of Israel, because they are deeply connected to the land of Israel and don't wish for any destruction—what will be will be—and because they love their humiliated people no less than him and those who follow his method: because their heartstrings resound thunderously at the sound of our brothers crying, ejected from their homes and livelihoods, and blood and tears fill their eyes. In short they desire and long to see their brothers settled in tranquility wherever they are.—The idea of settling the land of Israel is a great national concern belonging to the whole Jewish people in all the lands of its dispersion, and it will not be in a panic and by rushing, and not in a year or even ten, that it moves from ability to action. For a great and sublime thing like this that is almost alone of its kind in

Source: Z. Epstein, "Hovevei Tziyon," *Hamelitz*, vol 16 (10 Adar 5644/March 7, 1884). Trans. Mark Joseph.

the chronicles, a right mind and abundant caution [are] needed. If, Heaven forbid, Israel's situation will be as bad as it is now and there is no respite from the anger and envy of her mortal enemies, even in such a confusion the possibility of working on this great creation still will not be lost. We are grateful to truth, from the first simple conception in error, and then thinking through substantial concerns one by one. The whole force of the idea of settling the land of Israel was born on the heels of thunder and edicts;[5] therefore at a time when the edicts and storms are quelled the idea of settling the land of Israel also loses strength. Consequently since the *Hovevei Zion* have dedicated themselves to strengthening the fortress of this idea with force and courage, they need to be strong, since the edicts will increase because the two things are interdependent. Contemplation nevertheless convinces us that a perverted law such as this is without foundation, and from beginning to end is built "with a line of chaos and with weights of emptiness" [Isaiah 34:11] as we will explain.

First of all we can say that it is a big error to think that the idea of settlement of the land of Israel came to birth only after the recent events. The best of our writers have already proved decisively that the idea of the revival of the living nation among the people, from the time of its departure for exile, has not left it for even a moment: the new era of national development among the young peoples can help this great conception emerge at last from the world of hopes to the world of practice: but here there was the need for an immense impulse that would with a strong hand awaken the best sons of the people, so they would see that the time is coming for the people's hope to take a substantial form. And since this impulse has already emerged in full force, since the idea of the renewal of the nation has already taken on the form it needed and the best of the people are standing by to assist and support, after all this there is no further need to use artificial means to strengthen the idea of settling the land of Israel. To be sure in the past there was a need for a repellent force to clean the rust that had gathered in dark times, but now that it has come back to purity, it will flourish and flower without cushions and featherbeds, breaking of windows and flowers of May … Our brothers in Ashkenaz [Germany] have not yet rejected these "precious things," though they are "strangers" nevertheless: and we can hope that they too will come round to the view that they can only

be full citizens in the land of their fathers. We too in Russia hope to be left alone a while, that the hard edicts will be annulled, that our possessions won't become the property of any drunken lout: but as for being full and free citizens, it is unthinkable here. The Slavs and the Hebrews are different peoples with particular characteristics, each with its own religion and language, and they will never completely unite.

We, the *Hovevei Zion*, indeed believe with all our hearts that as long as Israel is dispersed and disunited in the lands of their exile they will not find the sought after rest and the honor of citizens in the full sense. Ten, twenty, thirty years will pass peacefully, but suddenly the sky can cloud over and a voice will again be heard: Hep! Hep![6] These cries will be heard everywhere as they have from time immemorial according to language and customs. Whenever Jews succeed in what they turn to, then from among the peoples of the world will be added the scholars' envy and the masses' hatred, and so they will try to restrict their movement on the field of life. The troubles and scandals of any state, civic uprisings, conspiracies, business collapses, unemployment, hunger, anything that goes wrong—it will always be the Jew who is a scapegoat, his haters always found attributing every crime and transgression to him, a son of the unhappy people always compelled to protect himself from the slingshots aimed at him from every direction. To escape from this upheaval there is no advice and no remedy other than a people gradually coming to live in the land of our fathers. All the contemporary and local remedies can bring relief for an hour, but will not eradicate the trouble itself, as long as the bitter roots remain, for we are strangers in the lands of our exile.

If the God of Israel would send us his savior from Zion and in our days we would merit to see thousands of our brothers ascend to build the wastelands of the land of their fathers and lay the very foundation of our future, all the same, multitudes of our brothers would stay in the diaspora, while we would be compelled to do all that we can for their benefit, as much as can be done in a situation where they are strangers in a foreign land. *Hovevei Zion* advise and demand of the people that it consolidate its remaining power and devote itself to the settlement of the Land of Israel, whatever is feasible, and will nevertheless not discourage the people from getting its life in order for its own good here in exile as well. To this end, the *Hovevei Zion* set themselves to work with all their strength on publishing the necessary corrections to the people's way of life, because everything that betters the people's situation will enable it to turn its heart to the great national work to which it is beckoned.

May God grant that the government abolishes in its kindness the harsh decrees, that our brothers living in the villages won't go on being a plaything for every tyrant and orator at a farmers' gathering, and the sound of beatings and looting won't be heard anymore, that the life of Israel will return to its eternal springs, and that the costly experience we acquired in the years of evil when blessed seed returned to the bosom of their people, won't have been in vain. The *Hovevei Zion* and especially the youth have dedicated their best talents to proclaiming that which is highest in their best talents.

NOTES

1. *Hovevei Zion* (or *Hovevei Tziyon*, Hebrew for "Lovers of Zion") is the designation given to the adherents of the *Hibat Zion* (*Hibat Tsiyon*, "Love of Zion") movement, established in Russia and Rumania in the early 1880s. The movement marks the crystallization of Jewish nationalism and its spread from small circles of intellectuals to the masses. Among its founders were Peretz Smolenskin (see chapter 7, document 20), Moshe Leib Lilienblum and Eliezer ben Yehuda (see this chapter, document 5). The movement gained momentum in the wake of the pogroms in the Ukraine in 1880–1882 and the joining of the movement by Leo

Pinsker, who held that antisemitism was not a medieval relic but endemic to Jewish life in the diaspora (see document 2 in this chapter). Under the leadership of Pinsker, the *Hovevei Zion* focused their vision on "auto-emancipation" or liberation of the Jewish nation through settlement in the land of Israel. Conflicting ideological tendencies, especially between religious and secular members, eventually led to the weakening of the movement, although it succeeded in establishing some colonies in Palestine (see the following document). The remnants of *Hovevei Zion* joined Herzl's World Zionist Organization, identifying largely with the cultural Zionism of Ahad Haam and Martin Buber.

2. Zalman Epstein (1860–1936) was a Hebrew essayist and critic. Born in Russia, he was among the founders of the secret Zionist society *Benei Moshe* (The Sons of Moses), headed by Ahad Haam. From 1890 to 1900 he served as the general secretary of *Hovevei Zion* in Odessa.

3. *Succah* is the Hebrew term for the booth in which Jews are commanded to dwell during the festival of Tabernacles (see Leviticus 23:42–45.) Here it simply means shelter.

4. Paltava and Tschernigov are provinces in the Ukraine, where many of the pogroms of 1880 and 1881 took place.

5. The reference is to the anti-Jewish decrees of the Russian authorities and the pogroms that followed in their wake.

6. On the anti-Jewish "Hep! Hep!" riots that broke out in Germany and spread to neighboring countries, see chapter 5, document 3, note 6.

4. RISHON LE-ZION (1882)[1]

JOSEPH FEINBERG

The persecution of the Jews in Russia was getting worse, and there was a need to speed up relief of their heart-rending distress. "Emigration" was the word that went from mouth to mouth, and the only question, so difficult to answer, was "where to?"[2] Many set their sights on America, on the land of freedom, and hoped that they would be safe from persecution there: but they did not know how things were in America. America wants total assimilation from its immigrants: there one has to be an American in body and mind. And the weakness of Jewish settlement in America is simply because Judaism is not suited to a complete blurring of lines that does not stop before the most total assimilation. We have suffered persecution and repeated expulsions for about two thousand years. Peoples and kingdoms rose and fell, while the chosen people alone strengthened its historic watch, preserving the flag and stronghold of Judaism, the holy Torah and its laws. A small part of Russian Jewry reached the decision to go to the holy land. Believing that it really is the pleasant land described in the Torah, and only fell into its current condition because of many generations of neglect; believing that the words of the prophets would be realized, and that redemption was imminent, our community too decided to go up to the Holy Land and establish an agricultural community there and work the holy soil. Experts were sent ahead to assess the fitness of the land for settlement, and their stated opinion was that the land was fertile with a healthy climate and that settlement seemed possible, albeit only with the power of serious labor and strong organization. In accord with this opinion we decided to go up to the land. After much struggle with obstacles that were due to the different circumstances of the Yishuv [the Jewish community of Palestine] and its factions, and also because of the many poor people who came to the land without any plan or support, we had the opportunity, with the help of God may He be blessed, to buy a large piece of land and to lay the corner stone for the first Hebrew settlement in the Holy Land, called "Rishon Le-Zion." It was an hour and twenty minutes' walk to the coastal town of Jaffa from the settlement, which was close to the main Jaffa-Jerusalem and Jaffa-Gaza road. The estate took in 3,340 dunams[3] not including hills, and cost 45,000 francs, that were paid in cash by members of the "Rishon Le-Zion" community. The houses are under construction now, three wells have already been sunk and completed, two of them dug by the settlers, and a road was laid, half an hour's walk in length. Our means were adequate to [do] all this. The residents of the settlement comprise twenty-two families, and of them about fifty souls are ordinary laborers working the land. This number includes six poor families who received land from the community and are obligated in writing to pay off their mortgages over a number of years. These repayments are set aside for the cooperative purposes of the community. Apart from the land these six poor families have nothing and they need work tools and the means to build houses. The rainy season is already in the air and the year of *shmittah* (the sabbatical year of the earth)[4] is nearly over. If help does not arrive then the people will be left without roofs over their heads and they will not be able to work the land. At the moment these six families have fallen back on the community's resources. We are forced to support them and to pay their communal taxes. But we cannot continue to do so. Our material resources were indeed enough at the beginning to include making arrangements for these six families, but the mass of hungry people who immigrated to

Source: Sefer ha-Tzionut. Tekufat Hibat Tzion. Mekorot Veteudot, ed. Shmuel Yavnieli (Jerusalem: Mosad Bialik, 1961), pp. 30–32. Trans. Mark Joseph.

Jaffa needed help if they were not to die of starvation. Support from other sources came only from the most honourable Rabbi Dr Lehmann[5] who donated 1,500 francs, and the honorable Baron Rothschild[6] who gave 605 francs, and we convey to them our heartfelt gratitude. Financial accounts of the monies we have received will be published in the newspapers. Because of the increasing number of immigrants the price of land went up, and we were forced to pay two and a half times more than the asking price of two months before; that is to say 15 francs a dunam, together with outgoings for the bills of sale and state taxes, instead of six and a half francs.

The "Rishon Le-Zion" settlement is the first settlement in the Holy Land. We have the privilege to hope that we will be able to develop it and bring it to prosperity, because its land is fertile, and its climate makes it one of the healthiest places in the Holy Land. We are building our houses on a hill, in the middle of the estate, and we enjoy a view of the sea, as well as sea air. On the other side, overlooking Ramle Valley, we see the mountains of Judah, from where a reparative breeze blows. We have enough labor power, and these are people who believe in working the land and are used to it. The whole community is welded to the idea of reviving our faith on the basis of the words of our holy prophets, and we are all willing to suffer anything to realize our ideals. And since our community is the first to bring sanctity to the land, buy ground and build houses on it, it goes without saying that with the success of the settlement, or with its failure, perish the thought, hangs the success of the whole movement to the Holy Land, at least if the matter is not to be delayed for many years. Because of this all the affairs of the "Rishon Le-Zion" settlement are pursued as concerns of the whole of Jewry; and the more the settlement is improved materially and morally, and the more support multiplies, the more we will be able to prove to opponents that we are truly fit to begin a new life, and can set our brothers an example by having had the faith to come to the land for the purpose of settling it. A word of truth and love, a call as well as thanks from us to you, dear brothers: working for the good of the holy idea of the settlement of the Jews in the Holy Land is holy. The thing itself does not need any defense or apology. It is the obligation of every Jew who feels the urge to do something for the good of Jewry, to be an echo for these events, to call out in the ears of our people and say: "In the land of your fathers, the promised land, that God intended for our people, a soft seedling of Jewry has been planted, "Rishon Le-Zion," which needs nourishment and support, because it is there for the joy of our people. The beautiful and ancient flute sounds its Arab music very softly and a man's generous heart doesn't need wordy entreaties to know what to do. And you are brothers and co-religionists, you are the compassionate sons of compassionate men; and the people's psalm and the congregation's song of praise will proclaim: "Happy are you, who gave a hand at dusk, who made the corner stone ring out the safety of the Jewish people and its peace." God's blessings on you!

At the end of five years the "Rishon Le-Zion" community must return all those donations that were intended especially for the community, in the following way: from these monies a fund will be created to be used for establishing new Jewish settlements. In the name of the community I express true gratitude to the honorable and exalted Rabbi Dr. Lehmann, who made a beginning in this holy matter, and from monies he collected we received the first donation of 600 marks. May this act of generosity be for the benefit of many. Dr. Lehmann also let us know that he can receive individual donations and regular, promissory contributions for the poor, as well as for the whole community's shared purposes, like building a synagogue and a school, obtaining an American wind machine, irrigation of the plantation and vegetables and so on.

Emissary to Europe from the "Rishon Le-Zion" community, Joseph Feinberg. Mainz, 7 September 1882, 23 Elul 5642.

NOTES

1. Founded in 1881 by ten members of Hibat Zion from Russia, Rishon le-Zion (First in Zion; of Isaiah 41:27) marked the beginning of renewed proto-Zionist settlement in the Land of Israel. (In 1878 religious Jews from Jerusalem founded the agricultural settlement of Petah Tikvah, but it was not informed by Zionist sentiments.) The name of the village, located on the coastal plane of the country, is based on Isaiah 41:27: "The first shall say to Zion, Behold I am here. . . ." The leader of the community, Zalman David Levontin (1856–1940), solicited the support of Joseph Feinberg (1855–1902), the son of a wealthy family from the Crimea, to help finance the purchase of the settlement's first parcel of land, approximately 835 acres. During its first year,

one hundred members of the Bilu joined the village. Unanticipated difficulties, especially due to a shortage of water, led to a severe economic crisis that threatened the very existence of the community. Levontin thus decided to send Feinberg to Europe on a fund-raising mission. The document presented here is a report on the beginnings of Rishon le-Zion that Feinberg published in *Der Israelit* September 9,1882), the principal journal of German modern Orthodox Jewry, edited by Rabbi Marcus Lehmann of Mainz, Germany. On Rabbi Lehmann, see note 5.

2. See chapter 7, documents 29 and 30.

3. A *dunam* is a Turkish measurement, the equivalent of a quarter of an acre.

4. Analogous to the Sabbath, every seventh year the earth is at rest; no planting or harvesting may be done during this year. See Leviticus 25:20–21. The fact that the members of Rishone Le-Zion observed the law of *shimtah* is an indication that most were observant Jews, unlike the majority of Zionist pioneers who were soon to follow them.

5. Rabbi Marcus Lehmann (1831–1890) of Mainz, Germany, was a leader of German modern Orthodoxy and, as noted earlier, the editor of its most important journal, *Der Israelit*.

6. Baron Edmond James de Rothschild (1845–1934) responded generously to Feinberg's appeal for assistance. In addition to financial support, he sent agricultural experts to train and instruct the members of Rishon Le-Zion (and other settlements that were soon to be established). Some members found Rothschild's paternalistic patronage overbearing. Indeed, in protest, Levontin would eventually abandon the settlement he had helped found.

5. THE REVIVAL OF HEBREW (1880)

ELIEZER BEN YEHUDA[1]

The days when we Jews could choose which path to take—those happy days have gone.... Since the day we began to pull down the wall dividing us from our Christian brothers we have ceased to walk along a separate path. Whether we like it or not, we follow the ways of the peoples among whom we are scattered, and are powerless to deviate from them. We are enlightened, whether we like it or not, because the nations among whom we dwell are enlightened.[2]... We will speak their language, like it or not.... It is a law of nature, for they are the many and we are the few; they are the ocean and we are but a drop.... Our national-minded authors cry "Teach your children Hebrew": excellent advice, but we are powerless to follow it, because children do not do everything that their parents want them to. The young will not obey our command to learn Hebrew, just as we disobeyed our parents' instructions not to follow the prophets of the Haskalah [Enlightenment mandated through Hebrew]. Time and place influence a man strongly and determine his direction in life. In our days, and in the lands where we dwell, no amount of effort to teach our children Hebrew will succeed. It's a dead language for the new generation, no better than Greek or Latin, and just as pupils abandon these languages when they leave school, so Jewish children will abandon Hebrew....

Let those who have tried to teach their children Hebrew stand up and say whether I'm not right!

Source: Eliezer Ben-Yehuda, "Degel ha-Le'ummiyut," *Ha-Magid* 24 (1, 9, and 16 September 1880), pp. 298, 316. Trans. George Mandel, "Why Did Ben-Yehuda Suggest the Revival of Spoken Hebrew," in *Hebrew in Ashkenaz: A Language in Exile*, ed. Lewis Glinert (New York/ Oxford: Oxford University Press, 1993), pp. 200ff.

Which of our Maskilim and learned men have children who know Hebrew and care about it! Let the learned S.S.[3] testify whether he did not labor in vain to teach his two sons our language and to plant the love our nation in their hearts! . . . Our language and all our heritage are alien to them. Yet who loves his people, and its wisdom, as much as Mr. S. Let Professor Joseph Halévy[4] testify whether the pupils of the Ecole Orientale in Paris didn't tell him that they had no need of the Hebrew language, "for a man can be Israelite without it." Yet . . . the Director [of the Ecole Orientale] reminds his pupils every day that they are Jews, that they have a duty to love their people, to love our language and our learning, that is the only reason for the Alliance's benevolence towards them—and what is the result?[5] . . . Will our language and our literature last much longer if we don't put it into the mouths of descendants, if we don't make it a *spoken* language? And how can we succeed in making it a spoken language other than making it the language of instruction in the schools? Not in Europe, nor in any of the lands of our exile! In all these lands we are an insignificant minority, and no amount of effort to teach our language to our children is going to succeed. But in our land, the Land of Israel, in the schools that we shall found there, we must make it the language of instruction and study.

NOTES

1. The father of modern Hebrew, the Russian-born Eliezer Ben Yehuda (1858–1922) first broached the need to revive Hebrew as the spoken language of the Jews in a series of article he published in *Ha-Magid*, the first Hebrew weekly (see chapter 5, document 11, note 1). In these articles, he argues that because of the nature of secular modernity, assimilation in the diaspora is inevitable. Despite the best efforts of enlightened Hebrew educators and writers, the sociological reality of living as a minority in an open society will draw Jewish youth to the cultural and social world of the majority population. The older generation of *Maskilim*, raised as they were in the insular world of traditional Judaism in which they imbibed a rich and firmly rooted Jewish education and identity, Ben Yehuda reasoned, underestimated the assimilatory pull of modern secular culture. *Maskilim*, such as Perez Smolenskin (see chapter 7, document 20), he held, naively believed that a secular national Jewish identity could be sustained in the Diaspora solely through Hebrew as the literary language of Jews. But a knowledge of written Hebrew is not sufficient to stem the tide of assimilation of a generation bereft of roots in the tradition. A secular Jewish national identity can take root only if Hebrew will once again become the spoken everyday language of the Jews in their ancient homeland. In 1881 Ben Yehuda settled in Jerusalem. Determined to realize his vision, he raised his son, Itamar Ben-Avi (1881–1943), entirely in Hebrew. He would become the first native speaker of modern Hebrew.

2. George Mandel notes that "Ben-Yehuda is using the world 'enlightened' here in the sense of 'familiar with modern secular culture'" (George Mandel, "Why did Ben-Yehuda Suggest the Revival of Spoken Hebrew," in *Hebrew in Ashkenaz: A Language in Exile*, Lewis Glinert, ed., p. 206, n. 9).

3. S.S. is likely a reference to Senior Sachs (1816–1892), a Hebrew scholar who was living in Paris at the time.

4. Joseph Halévy (1827–1917) was a scholar of Semitic languages and a Hebrew writer.

5. "Ben-Yeduda's remarks about the Ecole Normale Israélite Orientale, a school set up in Paris by the Alliance Israélite Universelle to train teachers for the network of Alliance schools in the Orient, were based on his own observation when he had briefly been a pupil there and attended a class taught by Halévy" (Mandel, ibid., p. 201).

6. A SOLUTION OF THE JEWISH QUESTION (1896)

THEODOR HERZL[1]

I have been asked to lay my scheme in a few words before the readers of the *Jewish Chronicle*.[2] This I will endeavour to do, although in this brief and rapid account, I run the risk of being misunderstood. My first and incomplete exposition will probably be scoffed at by Jews. The bad and foolish way we ridicule one another is a survival of slavish habits contracted by us during centuries of oppression. A free man sees nothing to laugh at in himself, and allows no one to laugh at him.

I therefore address my first words to those Jews who are strong and free of spirit. They shall form my earliest audience, and they will one day, I hope, become my friends. I am introducing no new idea; on the contrary, it is a very old one. It is a universal idea—and therein lies its power—old as the people, which never, even in the time of bitterest calamity, ceased to cherish it. This is the restoration of the Jewish State. . . .

Two phenomena arrest our attention by reason of the consequences with which they are fraught. One, the high culture, the other, the profound barbarism of our day. I have intentionally put this statement in the form of a paradox. By high culture, I mean the marvellous development of all mechanical contrivances for making the forces of nature serve man's purposes. By profound barbarism, I mean antisemitism. . . .

The Jewish Question still exists. It would be foolish to deny it. It exists wherever Jews live in perceptible numbers. Where it does not yet exist, it will be brought by Jews in the course of their migrations. We naturally move to those places where we are not persecuted, and there our presence soon produces persecution. This is true in every country, and will remain true even in those most highly civilised—France itself is no exception—till the Jewish Question finds a solution on a political basis. I believe that I understand antisemitism, which is in reality a highly complex movement. I consider it from a Jewish standpoint, yet without fear or hatred. I believe that I can see what elements there are in it of vulgar sport, of common trade, of jealousy, of inherited prejudice, of religious intolerance, and also of legitimate self-defence.

Only an ignorant man would mistake modern antisemitism for an exact repetition of the Jew-baiting of the past. The two may have a few points of resemblance, but the main current of the movement has now changed. In the principal countries where antisemitism prevails, it does so as a result of the emancipation of the Jews. When civilised nations awoke to the inhumanity of exclusive legislation, and enfranchised us—our enfranchisement came too late. For we had, curiously enough, developed while in the Ghetto into bourgeois people, and we stepped out of it only to enter into fierce competition with the middle classes. Historical circumstances made us take to finance, for which, as every educated man knows, we had, as a nation, no original bent. One of the most important of these circumstances was the relation of the Catholic Church to "anatocism."[3] In the Ghetto we had become somewhat unaccustomed to bodily labour and we produced in the main but a large number of mediocre intellects. Hence, our emancipation set us suddenly within the circle of the middle classes, where we have to sustain a double pressure, from within and from without. The Christian bourgeoisie would not be unwilling to cast us as a sacrifice to socialism, though that would naturally not improve matters much. But the Jewish Question is no more a social than a religious one, notwithstanding

Source: The Jewish Chronicle, January 17, 1896, pp. 12–13.

that it sometimes takes on these and other forms. It is a national question which can only be solved by making it a political world-question to be discussed and controlled by the nations of the civilised world in council.

We are one people—One People. We have honestly striven everywhere to merge ourselves in the social life of surrounding communities, and to preserve only the faith of our fathers. It has not been permitted to us. In vain are we loyal patriots, in some places our loyalty running to extremes; in vain do we make the same sacrifices of life and property as our fellow-citizens; in vain do we strive to increase the fame of our native land in science and art, or her wealth by trade and commerce. In countries where we have lived for centuries we are still cried down as strangers; and often by those whose ancestors were not yet domiciled in the land where Jews had already made experience of suffering. Yet, in spite of all, we are loyal subjects, loyal as the Huguenots, who were forced to emigrate. If we could only be left in peace[4]....

We are one people—our enemies have made us one in our distress, as repeatedly happens in history. Distress binds us together, and thus united, we suddenly discover our strength. Yes, we are strong enough to form a state, and a model state. We possess all human and material resources necessary for the purpose....The whole matter is in its essence perfectly simple, as it must necessarily be, if it is to come within the comprehension of all.

Let the sovereignty be granted us over a portion of the globe large enough to satisfy the requirements of the nation—the rest we shall manage for ourselves. Of course, I fully expect that each word of this sentence, and each letter of each word, will be torn to tatters by scoffers and doubters. I advise them to do the thing cautiously, if they are themselves sensitive to ridicule. The creation of a new state has in it nothing ridiculous or impossible. We have, in our day, witnessed the process in connection with nations which were not in the bulk of the middle class, but poor, less educated, and therefore weaker than ourselves. The governments of all countries, scourged by anti-semitism, will serve their own interests, in assisting us to obtain the sovereignty we want. These governments will be all the more willing to meet us halfway, seeing that the movement I suggest is not likely to bring about any economic crisis. Such crises, as

must follow everywhere as a natural consequence of Jew-baiting, will rather be prevented by the carrying out of my plan. For I propose an inner migration of Christians into the parts slowly and systematically evacuated by Jews; if we are not merely suffered to do what I ask, but are actually helped, we shall be able to effect a transfer of property from Jews to Christians in a manner so peaceable and on so extensive a scale as has never been known in the annals of history.

Everything must be carried out with due consideration for acquired rights and with absolute conformity to law, without compulsion, openly and by light of day, under the supervision of authority and the control of public opinion....

Our clergy, on whom I most especially call, will devote their energies to the service of this idea. They must, however, clearly understand from the outset, that we do not mean to found a theocracy, but a tolerant modern civil state. We shall, however, rebuild the Temple in glorious remembrance of the faith of our fathers. We shall unroll the new banner of Judaism—a banner bearing seven stars on a white field. The white field symbolizes our pure new life, the seven stars, the seven golden hours of a working day. For we shall march into the Promised Land carrying the badge of labour....

Let all who will join us fall in behind our flag [and] fight for our cause with voice and pen and deed. I count on all our ambitious young men, who are now debarred from making progress elsewhere....

Thus we also need a "gestor" [manager] to direct this Jewish political cause. The Jewish people are as yet prevented by the Diaspora from undertaking the management of their business for themselves. At the same time they are in a condition of more or less severe distress in many parts of the world. They need a "gestor." A first essential will therefore be the creation of such.

This "gestor" cannot, of course, be a single individual, for an individual who would undertake this giant work alone, would probably be either a madman or an impostor. It is therefore indispensable to the integrity of the idea and the vigour of its execution that the work should be impersonal. The "gestor" of the Jews must be a union of several persons for the purpose, a body corporate. This body corporate or corporation, I suggest, shall be formed in the first instance from among those energetic English Jews to whom I imparted my scheme in London. Let that body be called "the Society of Jews," and be entirely distinct from the Jewish Company[5] previously referred to. The Society of Jews is the point of departure for the whole Jewish movement about to begin. It will have work to do in the domains of science and politics, for the founding of the Jewish state, as I conceive it, presupposes the application of scientific methods. We cannot journey out of *Mizraim* [Egypt] today, in the primitive fashion of ancient times. We must previously obtain an accurate account of our number and strength.

My pamphlet [*The Jewish State*] will open a general discussion on the Jewish question. Friends and enemies will take part in it, but it will no longer, I hope, take the form either of violent abuse or of sentimental vindication, but of a debate, practical, large, earnest and political. The Society of Jews will gather all available information from statesmen, parliaments, Jewish communities and societies, from speeches, letters and meetings, from newspapers and books. It will thus find out for the first time whether Jews really wish to go to the Promised Land, and whether they ought to go there. Every Jewish community in the world will send contributions to the Society towards a comprehensive collection of Jewish statistics. Further tasks, such as investigation by experts of the new country and its natural resources, planning of joint migration and settlement, preliminary work for legislation and administration, etc., must be judiciously evolved out of the original scheme. In short, the Society of Jews will be the nucleus of our public organizations....

Shall we choose [the] Argentine [Republic] or Palestine? We will take what is given us and what is selected by Jewish public opinion. Argentina is one of the most fertile countries in the world, extends over a vast area, and has a sparse population. The Argentine Republic would derive considerable profit from the cession of a portion of its territory to us. The present infiltration of Jews has certainly produced some friction, and it would be necessary to enlighten the Republic on the intrinsic difference of our new movement.

Palestine is our ever-memorable historic home. The very name of Palestine would attract our people with a force of extraordinary potency. Supposing His Majesty the Sultan were to give us Palestine, we could in return pledge ourselves to regulate the whole finances of Turkey. There we should also form a portion of the rampart of Europe against Asia, an outpost of civilisation as opposed to barbarism.[6] We should remain a neutral state in intimate connection with the whole of Europe, which would guarantee our continued existence. The sanctuaries of Christendom would be safeguarded by assigning to them an extraterritorial status, such as is well known to the law of nations. We should form a guard of honour about these sanctuaries, answering for the fulfillment of this duty with our existence. This guard of honour would be the great symbol of the solution of the Jewish Question after nearly nineteen centuries of Jewish suffering....

What form of constitution shall we have? I incline to an aristocratic republic, although I am an ardent monarchist in my own country. Our history has been too long interrupted for us to attempt direct continuity of the ancient constitutional forms without exposing ourselves to the charge of absurdity.

What language shall we speak? Every man can preserve the language in which his thoughts are at home. Switzerland offers us an example of the possibility of a federation of tongues. We shall remain there in the new country what we now are here, and shall never cease to cherish the memory of the native land out of which we have been driven.

People will say that I am furnishing our enemies with weapons. This is also untrue, for my proposal can only be carried out with the free consent of a majority of Jews. Individuals, or even powerful bodies of Jews, might be attacked, but governments will take no action against the collective nation. The equal rights of Jews before the law cannot be withdrawn where they have once been conceded, for their withdrawal would immediately drive all Jews, rich and poor alike, into the ranks of the revolutionary party. Even under present conditions the first official violation of Jewish liberties invariably brings about an economic crisis. The weapons used against us cut the hands that wield them. Meantime, hatred grows apace.

Again, it will be said that our enterprise is hopeless, because, even if we obtain the land with the supremacy over it, the poorest Jews only will go there. But it is precisely the poorest whom we need at first. Only desperados make good conquerors. The rich and well-to-do will follow later, when they will find the new country as pleasant as the old, or even pleasanter....

But we can do nothing without the enthusiasm of our own nation. The idea must make its way into the most distant miserable holes where our people dwell. They will awaken from gloomy brooding, for into their lives will come a new significance. Let each of them but think of himself, and what vast proportions the movement must assume! And what glory awaits those who fight unselfishly for the cause! A wondrous generation of Jews will spring into existence. The Maccabeans will rise again.

And so it will be: It is the poor and the simple who do not know what power man already exercises over the forces of nature, it is just these who will have firmest faith in the new message. For these have never lost the hope of the Promised Land.

This is my message, fellow Jews! Neither fable nor fraud! Every man may test its truth for himself, for every man will carry with him a portion of the Promised Land—one in his head, another in his arms, another in his acquired possessions. We shall live at last, as free men, on our own soil, and die peacefully in our own home.

NOTES

1. Theodor Herzl (1860–1904), father of political Zionism and founder of the World Zionist Organization. While serving as the Paris correspondent for the *Neue Freie Presse* of Vienna, from 1890 to 1895, Herzl—an assimilated Jew of minimal Jewish commitment—was aroused by the growing antisemitism in the birthplace of liberalism and Jewish emancipation. The Dreyfus Case—the trial and the public demand for "Death to the Jew"—prompted Herzl to draw the conclusion that the only feasible solution to the Jewish problem was a mass exodus of the Jews from the countries of their torment and a resettlement in a land of their own. Recent scholarship, however, questions the significance Herzl attached to the Dreyfus Affair and argues that it was rather his reaction to Austrian antisemitism that prompted Herzl's conversion to Zionism. (See Jacques Kronberg, *Theodor Herzl, From Assimilation to Zionism* (Bloomington Indiana University Presss, 1993), 190–93. Herzl devoted the remainder of his life to the realization of this idea. This article, published in the influential London Jewish weekly *The Jewish Chronicle*, adumbrates the main points of his *Der Judenstaat: Versuch einer modernen Loesung der juedischen Frage* [The Jewish State: An Attempt at a Modern Solution of the Jewish Question] (Vienna: M. Breitenstein, 1896), in which he introduced his plan to the world.

2. Herzl arrived in London on November 21, 1895. Through Max Nordau (see document 14), he met Israel Zangwill (see document 18) who introduced him to some influential people and also obtained for Herzl an invitation to a banquet of the Maccabaeans Club, at which Herzl expounded his ideas and where he established important contacts. Herzl met Asher Myers (1848–1902) of The *Jewish Chronicle* at the club. Myers asked Herzl for an article, with the result that his article in *The Jewish Chronicle* preceded by four weeks publication of *Der Judenstaat*.

3. The principle of charging compound interest.

4. This paragraph appears to have been taken verbatim from *The Jewish State*.

5. According to Herzl's plan, the Jewish Company was to be entrusted with the execution of the transfer of the Jews to their own state. The society that Herzl proposed was later to be called the World Zionist Organization.

6. This passage, which also appears in *The Jewish State*, is frequently cited as proof of the colonial, imperialist intentions of Zionism. However, this statement by Herzl must be viewed in light of his vision of the Zionist homeland as an ally of colonized people in their struggle for liberation and restored dignity. See, for example, the passage in his novel *Old-New Land* (1902)—Herzl's romantic vision of the New Society of a sovereign Jewry—in which Professor Steineck, head of the Scientific Institute of the New Society, relates to two foreign visitors, Dr. Loewenberg and Mr. Kingscourt, his hopes for using the institute's knowledge "to open up Africa":

> Yes, Mr. Kingscourt...I hope to find the cure for malaria. We have overcome it here in Palestine....But conditions are different in Africa. The same measures cannot be taken there because the prerequisite—mass immigration—is not present. The white colonist goes under in Africa. That country can be opened up to civilization only after malaria has been subdued. Only then will enormous areas become available for the surplus populations of Europe. And only then will the proletarian masses find a healthy outlet. Understand?"
>
> Kingscourt laughed. "You want to cart off the whites to the black continent, you wonder-worker!"
>
> "Not only the whites!" replied Steineck gravely. "The blacks as well. There is still one problem of racial misfortune unsolved. The depths of that problem, in all its horror, only a Jew can fathom. I mean the Negro problem.

Don't laugh Mr. Kingscourt. Think of the hair-raising horrors of the slave trade. Human beings because their skins are black, are stolen, carried off, and sold. Their descendants grow up in alien surroundings despised and hated because their skin is differently pigmented. I am not ashamed to say, though I be thought ridiculous, now that I have lived to see the restoration of the Jews, I should like to pave the way for the restoration of the Negroes." Theodor Herzl, *Old-New Land*, trans. Lotta Levensohn (New York: Bloch Publishing Company and the Herzl Institute, 1960) pp. 169–70).

7. PROTEST AGAINST ZIONISM (1897)[1]

PROTESTRABBINER

[A]. We recently received from Vienna the new newspaper of the "Zionists," *Die Welt*.[2] It appeared on the eve of the holiday of the Feast of Weeks, which reminds us more than any other holiday that it was Israel's destiny from the start to be a "Kingdom of Priests." This newspaper contains propaganda for a Congress of Jewish Nationals, called for the twenty-fifth of August of this year [1897] in Munich.

Die Welt is a calamity and must be resisted. As long as the Zionists wrote in Hebrew they were not dangerous, but now that they are writing in German, they must be opposed. It is not a question of refuting their claims. For how can one speak with people who on the one hand are fanatics regarding Jewish nationhood and, on the other hand, complain that the Austrian government required a baptismal certificate from the candidate for the position of Secretary of the province of Bukowina. If the Austrian Jews support the efforts of the Zionists, then they should not complain that they are treated by the government like foreigners and are barred from public office.

We, however, can say to our fellow countrymen with complete conviction that we comprise a separate community solely with respect to *religion*. Regarding nationality, we feel totally at one with our fellow Germans and therefore strive towards the realization of the spiritual and moral goals of our dear fatherland with an enthusiasm equalling theirs. Hence, we are permitted to urge the complete implementation of equal rights and to perceive every curtailment of these rights as an injury to our most righteous sensibilities.

What more can one say, if people are so naive as to believe that the West European Jews will hand over their money to purchase Palestine from the Turks and to create a Jewish organization that will reverse the entire development of the Jewish nation? Eighteen hundred years ago, history made its decision regarding Jewish nationhood through the dissolution of the Jewish State and the destruction of the Temple. Recent Jewish scholarship can count among its highest achievements the fact that this conception has gained the widest circulation among the Jews of all civilized countries.

The Zionists want to provide "an internationally guaranteed place to call home" for those Jews "who cannot or do not want to assimilate in their present places of residence." But where are the Jews who do not want to assimilate? The fact that right now they are still unable to assimilate in many countries makes

---

Source: [A] *Allgemeine Zeitung des Judentums*, June 11, 1897. Trans. M. Gelber. [B] *Berliner Tageblatt* (July 6, 1897), trans. in *The Jewish Chronicle*, July 9, 1897, p. 9.

it precisely our duty to fight in common with the most noble and best men of all confessions for the removal of discriminatory laws. Let us protest in the most decisive manner against such a defamation [implied in the claim that there are Jews who do not wish to assimilate] as well as against the insult that the Zionists level at us in that they speak of a "Jewish distress" which they want to eliminate. In this protest, we shall know ourselves to be in complete agreement with all the Jewish communities of the German fatherland.

We ask the Zionists then, in whose name and by what authority do they speak? Who gave them a mandate to call for a congress in Munich, when it would not even be suitable for Przemysl, Grodno, or Jaffa? We are protesting against the organizers who claim to speak for all of Jewry, but behind whom stands not one single Jewish congregation. We are convinced that no Rabbi or Director of a German congregation will appear at the congress. Thus will be demonstrated to the entire world that *German Jewry* has nothing in common with the intentions of the Zionists.

Dr. S. Maybaum[3], Berlin; Dr. H. Vogelstein,[4] Stettin.

[B.] Owing to the convening of a Zionist Congress and the publication of its Agenda, so many erroneous impressions have gone forth respecting the teachings of Judaism and its efforts, that the undersigned Executive Committee of the Union of Rabbis in Germany deem it their duty to make the following Declaration:

1. The efforts of so-called Zionists to create a Jewish National State in Palestine are antagonistic to the messianic promises of Judaism, as contained in Holy Writ and in later religious sources.
2. Judaism obliges its followers to serve the country to which they belong with the utmost devotion, and to further its interest with their whole heart and all their strength.
3. There is no antagonism, however, between this duty and the noble efforts directed towards the colonisation of Palestine by Jewish agriculturists, as they have no relation whatsoever to the founding of a National State.

Religion and Patriotism alike impose upon us the duty of begging all who have the welfare of Judaism at heart, to hold aloof from the before mentioned Zionist Movement, and to abstain from attending the Congress, which in spite of all warnings is yet to be held.

The Executive Committee: Dr. Maybaum, Berlin; Dr. Horovitz,[5] Frankfurt; Dr. Guttmann,[6] Breslau; Dr. Auerbach,[7] Halberstadt; Dr. [Crossman] Werner, Munich.

NOTES

1. At the end of May 1897 news reached the German Jewish community that Herzl intended to convene a Zionist congress in Munich on August fifteenth of that year. A united front of German rabbis—both Reform (liberal) and Orthodox—led a vigorous protest against Herzl's planned congress in Munich. We include here two open letters of the *Protestrabbiner* ("protest rabbis"), as Herzl bitterly dubbed them. The second letter, the more formal protest of the two, was written in the name of the German Rabbinical Association (*Rabbinerverband*). Despite its condemnation by a great number of German Reform and Orthodox rabbis, this letter was endorsed by the general assembly of the Rabbinical Association of Germany convened a year later (July 1–2, 1898), with only one dissenting voice. Due to the storm of protest—not only from the *Protestrabbiner* but also from the Munich Jewish community, the Bnai Brith lodge of Munich and others—Herzl decided to transfer the venue of the First Zionist Congress to Basle, Switzerland.

2. *Die Welt* was a Zionist weekly founded by Herzl and published in Vienna from 1897 to 1905, Cologne from 1906 to 1911 and in Berlin from 1911 to 1914. The first issue of *Die Welt* appeared on June 4, 1897.

3. Sigmund Maybaum (1844–1919), a liberal rabbi in Berlin and a lecturer on homiletics at the Hochschule fuer die Wissenschaft des Judentums in that city.

4. Heinemann Vogelstein (1841–1911), rabbi at Pilsen and Stettin, founder and president of the Association of Liberal Rabbis, and a vice-president of the Association for Liberal Judaism in Germany.

5. Marcus Horovitz (1844–1910). An Orthodox rabbi at Frankfurt am Main, he was a recognized halakhic scholar and a founder of the Rabbinical Association of Germany.

6. Jacob Guttmann (1845–1919). A respected historian of medieval Jewish philosophy, he served as a Liberal rabbi at Breslau.

7. Aviezri Auerbach (1840–1901). A scion of a prestigious German rabbinic family, in 1872 he followed his father as an Orthodox rabbi at Halberstadt.

8. THE BASLE PROGRAM (1897)[1]

THE FIRST ZIONIST CONGRESS

The aim of Zionism is to create for the Jewish people a home in Palestine secured by public law.

The Congress contemplates the following means to the attainment of this end:

1. The promotion, on suitable lines, of the colonization of Palestine by Jewish agricultural and industrial workers.
2. The organization and binding together of the whole Jewry by means of appropriate institutions, local and international, in accordance with the laws of each country.
3. The strengthening and fostering of Jewish national sentiment and consciousness.
4. Preparatory steps towards obtaining government consent, where necessary, to the attainment of the aim of Zionism.

NOTE

1. The historical importance of the First Zionist Congress, convened in Basel, Switzerland, by Herzl in the summer of 1897, was the foundation of the Zionist Organization and the adoption of this official statement of Zionist purpose. While taking into consideration the agricultural achievements of such groups as the Bilu and Hibbat Zion—the movement that constituted the intermediate link between the forerunners of Zionism in the middle of the nineteenth century and the beginnings of political Zionism—the congress endorsed in this statement Herzl's approach, known as political Zionism. According to Herzl, the Jewish problem could be solved only by large-scale migration and the settlement of Palestine, which could be attained only through the political assistance and consent of the community of nations. The solution to the Jewish problem would thus be politically and internationally guaranteed by a Charter granting the Jewish people (through the World Zionist Organization), the right to reestablish an autonomous homeland in Palestine.

Source: The Jewish Chronicle, September 3, 1897, p. 13.

9. THE FIRST ZIONIST CONGRESS (AUGUST 1897)[1]

AHAD HAAM[2]

"The Congress of the Zionists"—the struggle over which filled the vacuum of our small world during the past months—is now past history.

Approximately two hundred members of the House of Israel from all lands and all countries gathered together in Basle. For three days, from morning to evening, they conducted public proceedings before all the nations concerning the establishment of a secure home for the Jewish people in the land of their fathers.

The *national*[3] response to the Jewish question thus broke the barriers of "modesty" and entered into the public realm. With a loud voice, clear language and proud bearing, a message whose like had not been heard since the time of Israel's exile from its land was proclaimed to all the world.

And that was all. This assembly *could* have done no more and *should* have done no more.

For—why should we delude ourselves?—of all the great aims to which *Hibbat Zion*[4] (or, as they say now, "Zionism") aspires, for the time being it is within our powers to draw near in a truly fitting manner to only one of them, namely the *moral* aim. We must liberate ourselves from the *inner* slavery, from the degradation of the spirit caused by assimilation, and we must strengthen our national unity until we become capable and worthy of a future life of honor and freedom. All other aims, are still part of the world of ideas and fantasies. The opponents of the Jewish state doubt whether it will be possible to obtain the consent of the nations, especially Turkey, to the establishment of this state. It appears to me, however, that there is an even more serious question [that must be asked]. Were this consent to be given would we, in our present moral condition, be capable of seizing the opportunity? Moreover, it is also possible to question the very nature of the proposal for a Jewish state. In light of the prevailing situation of the world in general, would the establishment of the Jewish state in our times, even in the most complete form imaginable, permit us to say that "our question" has been solved in its entirety and that the national ideal has been attained? "According to the suffering—the reward." After thousands of years of unfathomable calamity and misfortune, it would be impossible for the Jewish people to be happy with their lot if in the end they would reach [merely] the level of a small and humble people, whose state is a plaything in the hands of its mighty neighbors and exists only by means of diplomatic machinations and perpetual submission to whomever fate is smiling upon. It would be impossible for an ancient people, one that was a light unto the nations, to be satisfied with such an insignificant recompense for all their hardships. Many other peoples, lacking both name and culture, have been able to attain the same thing within a brief period of time without having had to suffer even the smallest part of what the Jews have suffered. It was not in vain that the prophets rose to the aid of Israel, envisioning the reign of *justice* in the world at the end of days. Their *nationalism*, their love for their people and for their land, led them to this. For even in biblical times the Jewish state was caught between two lions—Assyria or Babylonia on the one side and Egypt on the other—so that it had no hope to dwell in tranquility and develop in a suitable fashion. Accordingly, "Zionism" developed in the hearts of the prophets, giving rise to the great vision of the end of days when "the wolf shall dwell with the lamb and nation shall not lift up sword against nation"[5]—and when Israel

Source: *Hashiloah* 2, no. 6 (Elul 5647; August 1897), pp. 568–70. Trans. S. Weinstein.

shall once again safely dwell in its own land. Hence, this *human* ideal was and perforce always will be an integral part of the *national* ideal of the Jewish people. The Jewish state can only find peace when universal justice will ascend to the throne and rule the lives of the peoples and the states.

And so, we did not come to Basle to found the Jewish state today or tomorrow. Rather, we came to issue a great proclamation to all the world: the Jewish people is still alive and full of the will to live. We must repeat this proclamation day and night, not so that the world will hear and give us what we desire, but above all, in order that we ourselves will hear the echo of our voice in the depths of our soul. Perhaps in this way our soul will awaken and cleanse itself of its degradation....

This indeed is what the Basle assembly accomplished at its beginning in a sublime fashion. And for this it would have deserved to have been inscribed in golden letters as a testimony to the generations, were it not for its desire to accomplish even more.

Here, too, rashness—this curse which lies over us and sabotages all our actions—appeared in full force. Had the initiators of the assembly armed themselves with patience and explicitly declared from the beginning that the traces of the messiah are not yet visible and that for the time being our strength lies only in our mouths and hearts—to revive our national spirit and spread the tidings of this renewal among the public at large—then without doubt the list of delegates would have been much smaller. Instead of three days the assembly could have finished its work in one day, but this day would have been the equivalent of entire generations. Those delegates, the elect of our people—for only the elect would have been attracted to an assembly of this kind— would then return, each to his own country, with hearts full of life, will and new energy, to instil this life and energy into the hearts of all the people.

But now...

The initiators of this movement are "Europeans." They are expert in the rules of diplomacy and in the customs of the political sects of our day, and they are bringing these rules and customs with them to the "Jewish state."...Emissaries were dispatched prior to the assembly and various "hints" were distributed orally and in writing in order to awaken among the masses an exaggerated hope for imminent salvation. Hearts were inflamed by an idolatrous fire, a febrile passion, which brought to the Basle assembly a motley crowd of youths, immature both in years and in wisdom. This mob robbed the assembly of its splendor and through their great foolishness turned it into a laughing stock.

Large and small committees, endless commissions, a multitude of imaginary "proposals" concerning the "national treasury" and the rest of the "exalted politics" of the Jewish state—these are the "practical" results of the assembly. How could it have been otherwise? The majority of the delegates, the emissaries of the wretched members of our people waiting for redemption, were sent solely for the purpose of bringing redemption with them upon their return. How, then, could they return home without bearing the tidings that the administration of the "state," in all its various branches, had been placed in trustworthy hands, and that all the important questions concerning the "state" had been examined and solved?...

The delegates will return [from Basle] with the message that redeemers have arisen in Israel and that all we have to do is to wait for "diplomacy" to finish its task. [But] the eyes of the people will quickly be opened and they will realize that they have been led astray. The sudden fire which ignited the hope in their hearts will once again be extinguished, perhaps even to the final spark....

If only I could enter into a pact with the angel of oblivion I would make him vow to obliterate from the hearts of the delegates all traces of what they saw and heard at Basle, leaving them with only one memory. [I am referring to] the memory of that great and sacred hour when they all stood together as brothers—these forlorn men of Israel who came from all comers of the earth—their hearts full of feelings of holiness and their eyes lovingly and proudly directed to their noble brother standing on the platform preaching wonders to his people, like one of the prophets of days of yore. The memory of this hour, had it not been followed by many other hours which deprived the first impression of its purity, could have turned this assembly into one of the most distinguished events in the history of our people.

The deliverance of Israel will come at the hands of "prophets," not at the hands of "diplomats."...

NOTES

1. The First Zionist Congress was held in Basle on August 29–31, 1897.

2. Ahad Haam, pen name of Asher Hirsch Ginsberg (1856–1927), Russian Jew, Hebrew essayist, and leader of Hibbat Zion. He was critical of both political and practical Zionism, the latter because he felt that the mass resettlement of Jewry in Palestine was unfeasible, the former because he held a profound skepticism regarding the efficacy of its diplomatic program and its neglect of Jewish cultural reconstruction, which he held to be of paramount import. Properly considered, he maintained, Zionism could not solve the "problem of the Jews"—their economic, social, and political plight—but it could solve "the problem of Judaism," i.e., assimilation. With the eclipse of religion in the modern period, he observed, Jews were increasingly defecting to non-Jewish secular cultures. Zionist settlement in Palestine should therefore concentrate on fostering a secular Jewish culture based on Jewish national consciousness and the renewal of Hebrew as a means of ensuring the continuity of Jewish creativity. Palestine Jewry would thereby serve as a "spiritual center" nourishing Jewish life in the Diaspora, where most of the Jewish people undoubtedly would continue to exist.

3. All emphases are in the original.

4. Hibbat Zion (Love of Zion), a movement that came into being in 1882 as a direct reaction to the widespread pogroms in Russia in 1881, for the purpose of encouraging Jewish settlement in Palestine and achieving a Jewish national revival there. See this chapter, document 2.

5. Isa. 2:4, 6.

10. THE ZIONISTS ARE NOT OUR SAVIORS (c. 1900)

RABBI ZADOK HACOHEN RABINOWITZ[1]

A voice was heard from on high, a voice of lamentation from the imperial city of Vienna in a matter relating to all of Israel. It concerns the sect that has arisen recently under the name of Zionists. They drag iniquity by cords of vanity and lift up their souls to folly, hoping that in the course of time the sons of Israel will be subdued under their government and subordinated to transgressors. For this my heart grieves exceedingly.

For our many sins, the saying "The face of the generation is as the face of a dog"[2] has been fulfilled among us. We see that their desire to force the whole world to the side of sin, Heaven forbid, is great. Even if in our age the mob will not thank us for uttering words of truth and reproof, I will nevertheless fulfill the commandment "Thou shalt surely reprove"[3] and join in the protest against the Zionists.

For surely this is not a time to hold one's peace. Heaven forbid that one should show respect for persons in this matter. The danger to the community posed by those who are destructive and who dispute with the *Shekhinah* [the Divine Presence] is far too great for that. Concerning them the verse says: "He who observes the wind will not sow and he who beholdeth the clouds will not reap."[4] The Zionists sow wheat and reap thorns and even though the work of Satan should prosper, the end will be, Heaven forbid, what it will be. The House of Israel, the holy and desolate, appears in this hour like a ship sailing without oars in a tempest in the heart of the sea, its helmsmen stricken with blindness.

We surely know that if we were believers and truly trusted in the salvation of the Lord and [were] observers of the commandments of God, we would even

---

Source: Open letter, c. 1900, in *The Transformation: The Case of the Neturei Karta*, ed. I. Domb (London: Hamadfis, 1958), pp. 192–96.

today be dwelling in our holy land. For it is known that the land of Israel, by its very nature and the power of its holiness, was created for Israel alone.

It is said in the Midrash that the Holy One, blessed be He, created the land of Israel only for Israel; but it is also known that because of the power of its holiness the land rejects transgressors in the same way that the stomach vomits forth that which is incompatible with its nature. This matter is not subject to dispute. Yet now there have arisen fools and malicious conspirers whose deeds are born of a bitter poison. They proclaim that the life of Israel is in jeopardy and that they, the Zionists, will hasten salvation by founding a state.

They ask why we have been in exile for so long. But this question has already been asked of the sages and the prophets, and has been explained by the Holy One, blessed be He: "Why did the land perish? Because they abandoned My law which I put before them."[5] It has already been made clear that the Zionists reject all the commandments and cleave to every manner of abomination....

Do we not know that the whole purpose of redemption is to improve our ways so that Israel may observe the Torah with all the restrictions that have been placed upon it by our sages who should not, Heaven forbid, be men of power and influence among us. [Moreover] as the prophets foresaw our redemption, we will not require an army and strategies of war. From this we can see that [the aspiration of the Zionists] is opposed to the spirit of Judaism and to the hope of redemption.

I have heard it said in the name of the Zionists that without a state modeled after other states there would be an end to Judaism, Heaven forbid. To them we would reply that the land of Israel and the people of Israel are above the rules of causality and that, thank God, in our day at least the majority of Jews remains steadfast in their faith.

It may be assumed that if the Zionists gain dominion, they will seek to remove from the hearts of Israel belief in God and in the truth of the Torah. [For] the intention of these inciters and seducers is to cast Israel into heresy, that is, to destruction. Moreover, seeing that the Zionists and those among them who at one time had claims to sanctity say that massacres, Heaven forbid, will follow unless their advice is taken, let us emphasize that we have the Divine promise that even though Israel is in exile, nevertheless the memory of Israel will never be erased.

Jerusalem is the height of heights to which the hearts of Israel are directed. Our soul also pants and yearns to breathe her pure and holy air. In Heaven are my witnesses that I would hasten to go there like an arrow from a bow, without fear of the perils of the roads, or of the misery and poverty in the country, but I fear my departure and my ascent to Jerusalem might appear as a gesture of approval of Zionist activity.

With faith in the Lord, my soul trusts in His word that the day of redemption will come. I stand in expectation of the coming of the messiah. [But before his advent] should three hundred scourges of iron afflict me, I will not budge from my place. I will not go up there [to Jerusalem] and join my name to those of the Zionists.

For me the matter is perfectly plain. The enlightened ones [the *maskilim*] and the reformers who imperil the existence of our people have discovered that through blatant unbelief they will not succeed in driving Israel from its faith and from its religion. Therefore they have thrown off their garment of assimilation and put on a cloak of zeal so that they appear to be zealous on behalf of Judaism. But they are in fact digging a mine beneath our faith and seeking to lead Israel from beneath the wings of *Shekhinah*.

From all that has been said, it emerges that the Zionists and their rabbis are in error when they assert decisively that were it not for the Zionists many of our brethren would have converted. They deceive themselves. The heretics and the transgressors within the camp of Israel do more damage to us than those who have left the community.

Can heretics be regarded as great men? May there not be many like them in Israel! As for us, we need the audacity of holiness and the spirit of self-sacrifice. The counsel to be given to the House of Israel is that they should dissociate from the Zionists and hold themselves apart from this advancing plague. Through the merit of this separation, may we enjoy all the salvations and the comforts and may the Holy One, blessed be He, comfort Zion and build Jerusalem.

NOTES

1. Rabbi Zadok Hacohen Rabinowitz (1823–1900), Hasidic rabbi, known as Zadok Hacohen of Lublin, with a reputation as an outstanding Talmudic scholar.

Although he preferred a secluded life of study and devotion, Zadok Hacohen became the spiritual leader of the Hasidim in Lublin after the death of his friend Rabbi Yehuda Leib Eiger in 1888. In 1890, following the death of his second wife, Zadok Hacohen sought to immigrate to Palestine, but was discouraged from

doing so by his disciples. The letter presented here was written toward the end of his life.

2. Mishnah, tractate *Sotah* 9:15.

3. Lev. 19:17.

4. Eccles. 11:4.

5. Jer. 9:12.

11. WOMEN AND ZIONISM (1901)[1]

THEODOR HERZL

During the French Revolution there lived a very witty revolutionary by the name of Sieyés[2] who played a major role at a later period, too. He was the originator of a fine saying. When someone asked him, "What did you do during the Reign of Terror?" he replied: "I stayed alive." At an earlier date that man had composed an appeal which became very famous.[3] In it there was a reference to the Third Estate which had not yet been liberated. "What is it? Nothing. What should it be? Everything." I should like to apply these words of Abbé Sieyès to our women. What are women to Zionism? I will not say, "Nothing." What could they, what should they be? Perhaps everything. And if our propaganda finds the right way, this is bound to come about.

If we look at the present situation of Jewish women, we will understand why they have been so inactive and so aloof from us up to now. I should like to make a distinction between the women who know the rough and tumble of life and the others. Among the Jews, those women who have been thrust into life's struggles are, at the same time, the poorest. These women may have no husband or other provider who spares them the necessity of going out to earn a living. This is true only of the poorest classes among the Jews.

It goes without saying that no support or enthusiasm can be expected from such women. Coming from Rumania or Galicia or Russia, they show up one day and ask for further transportation for themselves and their meager belongings. They might be good Zionists; they could become good Zionists, if their circumstances improved. But we cannot expect or ask such women to help promote Zionism. The women whom we must win over are those who are shut off as by a wall from the full impact of Jewish misery, bad conditions, and the need for improvement.

Owing to an old tradition, one of the best things in Judaism, the Jewish woman lives in utter seclusion in her home. This tradition has been glorified in the beautiful poem [by Heinrich Heine] "Princess Sabbath";[4] she lives quite remote from the unpleasantness, the storms, and the harshness of life. That is true at least of the old-fashioned kind of Jewish woman, a kind that still exists, though not in great numbers in well-to-do circles. That is the type of woman for whom I have the greatest respect, because in her all the fine qualities, all the great and eternal things that were particularly precious in dark days have been preserved in their purest and

Source: Theodor Herzl, *Essays and Addresses*, trans. Harry Zohn (New York: The Herzl Press, 1975), pp. 159–64. Notes supplied by P. Mendes-Flohr and J. Reinharz.

most beautiful form. But we must reckon with a new breed of Jewish woman whom we lost during the period in which the Jews were well off. These women may be distinguished from old-fashioned Jewish women in that they neither prepare nor observe the Sabbath, a ceremonial filled with the aura of Jewish poetry. But they resemble the old-fashioned Jewish women in that they, too, have no contact with life. That type has a husband who shields his wife completely from the unpleasant things in life. Thus these new Jewesses, the women about whose inactivity we complain so bitterly, are also in a protected position. Just as a man who rides by in a carriage can have absolutely no idea of how the freezing peddler in the street feels, or the trades-man who is buffeted to and fro in the pursuit of his livelihood, so, too, the overprotected woman has learned nothing about Jewish misery, even if she is not a very pampered lady. The good tradition of the Jewish family—a tradition that is a bit of a relic—to keep as far away as possible from the excitements and the noise of the street, has been replaced here by prosperity. This solicitude supplements wealth and explains the inactivity.

Well, how is this to be changed? Do we want these overprotected women to become acquainted with the unpleasant aspects of life? Shall we wish them blight and impoverishment so that their minds might be opened to Zionism, to its greatness and necessity? I would not want to employ such brutal means even if it were in my power to do so. Incidentally, such a woman would then be in the position of those who understand but are not able to do anything. So we have before us a form of this French adagio. You know how the old joke goes:

Si jeunesse savai
si vieillesse pouvait.[5]

[If youth but knew, if old age only could.]
We have to paraphrase this as follows: *Si richesse savait…* [If wealth but knew…]

That is the problem we face. The poor are not able, and the rich do not know.

For our women who are ignorant of the misery it would, therefore, be useful to find a substitute for the hard knocks of life, for the outside experience which is to open their minds to the Zionist movement. I believe that such an expedient could be found. I believe that we can interest the women in this cause, which we

regard as very humanitarian—not by misery of their own, but in another way.

That way would be through poetry and art—in one word, through beauty.

It would be good and effective to draw the atten-tion of those sheltered women to the fact that Zionism contains an element of great beauty and that an old gold mine of Jewish poetry is touched whenever songs of Zion in various forms burst forth from our poets. Women could be shown that, in fact, Zionism, which today appears like a new fashion, harbors a beauty that is imperishable and forever young.

Some of this work will, I believe, be done for us by literature—a literature which has been following in the footsteps of Zionism for years. Inspired by the beauties of Zionism which are much more visible to outsiders, Christian poets have come forward to sing the praises of Zionism. One of the first was the French writer de Bouhélier,[6] the author of a poetic sketch which appeared in *Die Welt* some time ago. In this poem he speaks of the white walls that are mirrored in the Mediterranean and conjures up a vision of a future civilization. There is a cursory treat-ment of Zionism in a novel by Prince Wrede.[7] The beauty of the Jewish renaissance was also glorified in a recent collection of poetry by Börries Baron von Münchhausen; it is entitled *Juda*[8] and was illustrated by a Jew named Moshe (*sic*) Lilien.[9] In the years of our decline (which, strangely enough, are called the years of emancipation, or uplift) we have acquired the habit of paying undue attention to what others say. For this reason I believe that such artistic events can exert some influence. Considering the social cir-cles into which one moves if one regards Zionism as beautiful and great and good, it seems entirely possi-ble to me that snobbishness can be an effective pub-licity vehicle for Zionism among the Jews.

Any woman is the center of a social circle, large or small. Within this small circle she can accom-plish many things. She can raise disciples, propagan-dists who, in snowball fashion, themselves become focal points of other social circles and develop new circles and train more disciples, thus becoming first disciples and then teachers of the Zionist idea. Such women will then be able to tell about the beauties that were inherent in Zionism even at a time when this idea was still young and poor and had only the young and the poor to lean upon. They will be able to point out that a future flowering under more favorable conditions will contribute even more to the enhancement of the idea. The inspired and inspiring activities which Zionism is constantly generating will enable them to demonstrate that one can fill one's leisure time and even one's working hours far more beautifully if one becomes familiar with the Jewish idea and works for it than if women gossip about each other at kaffeeklatsches, relieve each other of their household money at card games, or kill time in all kinds of idle pursuits. This is a form of self-education and uplift which, unlike idle occupations, will benefit the children as well. For a woman who is a good Zionist will also be a very alert and far-sighted mother. I am not saying a "*good*" mother, because there are no "bad" mothers. A mother must understand that if Zionism is great and important, it will be particularly so for the children, because they are the citizens of the future—at any rate, of this future—no matter how soon or how late it comes. Indeed, as we become more and more absorbed in this idea, we have felt this education in our own lives. A mother who understands Zionism will cherish it not only for herself but for her children as well. Thus it is a fine and useful occupation, even if one devotes to it hours formerly given to recreation.

Incidentally, there is every indication that Zionism is meeting with increasing acclaim and that those who keep an eye upon others are less and less shy about espousing a movement which was once misunderstood and regarded as harmful. I can well imagine that as soon as we have some practical, visible, palpable results to show it will suddenly be an honor to have been part of Zionism and to have worked for it. Then it will be useful for one's career; then many people will join the movement in order to get ahead. I ardently desire this, because we certainly don't want to move around in the clouds all the time and the betrothal must some day be followed by the wedding. But I believe that a prolonged engagement will not be harmful to the trial, and you know what a long engagement period the Jews once had to endure before they could enter the Promised Land. You know for how long the wisest of all the Jews led his people through the wilderness in order to purify and cleanse it there.

NOTES

1. In this lecture delivered at the Women's Zionist Association in Vienna in January 1901, Herzl urges his audience to consider how they may enlist "the new breed of Jewish women," the affluent, secular women who, "overprotected," keep a studied distance not only from Jewish tradition but from the misery of their people. He suggests appealing to the aesthetic sensibilities of these "society ladies" as a way of eliciting their engagement in the humanitarian aspect of the Zionist cause.

2. The Abbé Sieyès (born Emmanuel-Joseph Sieyès, 1748–1836) was a Catholic priest and, in time, was appointed to prominent positions in the Church.

3. In the later 1780s, there was a dire financial crisis in the Kingdom of France, and the king conceded in principle to allow the convening of an Estates General at which he would receive submissions from the three Estates of French society (i.e., the aristocracy, the clerics, and the commoners, the so-called Third Estate) as to how the crisis should be resolved. Prior to the actual convening of the Estates General, a Royal minister solicited opinions as to the constitution of the consultative body. In response to this requests Abbé Sieyès penned a pamphlet entitled *Qu'est-ce que le tiers état?* (What Is the Third Estate?). This pamphlet, published in early 1789, attacked noble and clerical privileges. Abbé Sieyès' eloquent appeal for reform begins: "The plan of this book is fairly simple. We must ask ourselves three questions: 1. What is the Third Estate? Everything. 2. What has it been until now in the political order? Nothing. 3. What does it want to be? Something." The pamphlet concludes, "The Third Estate embraces then all that which belongs to the nation; and all that which is not the Third Estate, cannot be regarded as being of the nation. What is the Third Estate? It is everything."

4. In his poem "Princess Sabbath," Heinrich Heine (1797–1856) lauds the traditional way of life.

5. From *Les Prémices* (1594) by Henir Estienne.

6. Saint-Georges de Bouhélier (1876–1947).

7. Friedrich Fürst von Wrede, *Die Goldschilds. Die Geschichte einer jüdischen Familie* (Berlin: Ernst Hoffmann, 1900).

8. Freiherr von Münchenhausen von Börries, *Juda*, with illustrations by E. M. Lilien (Berlin: E. Fleischel, 1900).

9. Ephraim Moses Lilien (1874–1925) was an art nouveau artist, particularly noted for his Jewish and Zionist themes. He was hailed as the "first Zionist artist."

12. MANIFESTO (1902)

THE MIZRAHI[1]

In the lands of the Diaspora the soul of our people—our Holy Torah—can no longer be preserved in its full strength, nor can the commandments, which comprise the entire spiritual life of the people, be kept in their original purity, because the times are besieging us with difficult demands. It is impossible for us to respond to those demands without ignoring the holy treasure entrusted to us at Sinai, without God forbid, turning it into a thing of little value in our eyes, as each of us strays further and further away from the other. Against his will each loses his Jewish self in the [non-Jewish] majority, for only in their midst can he fulfill all those secular requirements which the times demand of him. The people has found one remedy for this affliction—to direct their hearts to that one place which has always been the focus of our prayers, that place wherein the oppressed of our people will find their longed for respite: Zion and Jerusalem. We have always been united by that ancient hope, by the promise which lies at the very roots of our religion, namely, that only out of Zion will the Lord bring redemption to the people of Israel. The emancipation which our German brethren so desired did much to divide us and keep us scattered in the countries of our dispersion. When the limbs are dispersed, the body disintegrates, and when there is no body, the spirit has no place to dwell in this world.

It has therefore been agreed by all those who love the spirit of their people and are faithful to their God's Torah, that the reawakening of the hope of the return to Zion will provide a solid foundation as well as lend a special quality to our people. It will serve as a focus for the ingathering of our spiritual forces and as a secure fortress for our Torah and its sanctity.

NOTE

1. Mizrahi, the religious Zionist movement based on the Basle Program and dedicated to the establishment of the people of Israel in the land of Israel in accordance with the precepts of the Torah. When the Fifth Zionist Congress (Basle, 1901) resolved that the education of the people in the spirit of Jewish nationalism was an important aspect of Zionist activity and an obligation for every Zionist, the religious Zionists felt that there could be no compromise in spiritual matters. They therefore founded in Vilna in 1902 the movement Mizrahi, an abbreviation of the words *merkaz ruhani* ("spiritual center"), adopting the motto "The land of Israel for the people of Israel according to the Torah of Israel." Mizrahi has remained a faction within the World Zionist Organization. This manifesto was distributed as a leaflet announcing in Hebrew the establishment of Mizrahi.

Source: *Kol koreh* (Vilna, 1902). Trans. D. Goldman

13. ZIONISM AND JEWISH ART (1903)[1]

MARTIN BUBER

Honored fellow Zionists! We suffer from theory. Today, in speaking to you about Jewish art I want to stay away from abstract schematic theory and to speak to you of powerful living facts, which are great and overwhelming.

Jewish art is a series of facts.

For thousands of years we were a barren people. We shared the fate of our land. A fine, horrible desert sand blew and blew over us until our sources were buried and our soil was covered with a heavy layer that killed all young buds. The excess in soul power that we possessed at all times expressed itself in the exile merely in an indescribably one-sided spiritual activity that blinded the eyes to all the beauty of nature and of life.

We were robbed of that from which every people takes again and again joyous, fresh energy—the ability to behold a beautiful landscape and beautiful people. The blossoming and growth beyond the ghetto was unknown to and hated by our forebears as much as the beautiful human body. All things, from whose magic the literature spins its golden veil, all things, whose forms are forged through art's blessed hands, were something foreign that we encountered with an uneradicable mistrust. At times only the half-lost sound of a song darted across the dark and narrow alley, rushed by, only to die in the thickness of the night. The very thing in which the true essence of a nation expresses itself to the fullest and purest, the sacred word of the national soul, the artistic productivity, was lost to us. Wherever the yearning for beauty raised itself with tender and shy limbs, there it was suppressed with an invisible, merciless hand. Wherever a young bud stretched toward the sun in fear and expectation, it was suffocated by the existence of the most terrible destiny.

The great transformation became possible when Judaism entered Western civilization. We see its first fruits in our days. I would like to emphasize this because recently a peculiar ghetto sentimentality emerged in some Zionist circles. In remembering the tender, unusual beauty of the unified national life that we led in Europe until the eighteenth century we forget the significant fact that the modern national-Jewish movement, that Zionism, could not have been born without that strange stage in the development of our people that was erroneously called "emancipation." Emancipation usually means the more or less arbitrary actions of individuals and national representatives. But this was only the expression of a great historical transformation that, for the nations, led to the struggle for human rights; for us to an inner move closer to modern civilization. To be sure, due to the character of our *galut* [exile], this move took on an abnormal, leap-like form. It did not create that blind adaptation to modern civilization, which we know by the name assimilation, but to the peculiarities of individual peoples—a sad episode in our history in which we learned the whole seriousness of our degeneration. But when, in the life of Europe, the healthy national self-consciousness stepped into the place of a bloodless ideal of humanity, when the attitude had registered that every person and every nation best serves the public in using their own talents for productive activity, when the social consciousness of that which should be was being fused with the national consciousness of what is, then it was our marriage to Western civilization, after all, that made it possible for us to unfold our ancient

Source: Martin Buber, address before the Fifth Zionist Congress, Basel, Switzerland, December 26–30, 1903; "Address on Art," in *The First Martin Buber: Youthful Zionist Writings of Martin Buber,* ed. and trans. Gilya G. Schmidt (Syracuse, N.Y.: Syracuse University Press, 1999), pp. 47–51.

desire for national existence—a desire that for centuries had expressed itself in dull, yearning waiting or in wild, messianic ecstasies—in the modern form that we call Zionism. And it was also that marriage which allowed our yearning for beauty and action—a yearning that was again and again tortured to death in the ghetto—to mature to a young power in whose unfinished present form we venerate the great future and to which we have given the name "Jewish art." This energy means the rebirth of productivity in our people. We no longer translate the overflowing movement of our soul into isolated intellectualism but into an activity of the entire organism and, through this activity, into lines and sounds, into living being, which again awakens living appreciation.

But the fact alone that we once again have artists—and by artists I understand not only sculptors but also poets and composers—is not enough to confirm the existence of Jewish art. Recently, we have gone beyond this first step, the mere existence of artists of Jewish descent. This happened because an artist here and there paid tribute to the muse of his people and was inspired by it. In the eons of our national life a wealth of fine secret spiritual values accumulated, and our artists began to draw on this treasure. Some went even further; they used what the people had created, themes and material. On the way to a national art this production and utilization will become ever fine and deeper. Even if we are, on the one hand, completely immersed in modern civilization, we cannot, on the other hand, give up the things in which the soul of our people expresses itself: language, customs, naïve folk art of songs and *nigunim* [melodies], of menorahs and *talesim* [prayer shawls]. But we must not see these things as something sacred that we look at with reverent awe but as material from which we build a new beauty—not as statues that we may admire from afar but as a valuable block of marble that waits for our hand and chisel.

But this stage of Jewish productivity, the fact of the national consciousness of our artists, does not yet mean the existence of Jewish art in the strictest sense of the word. If we understand by Jewish art something existing, finished, unified, and not something in the making, developing, unfinished as I do, then I would have to answer the question about the existence of national art with a no. [For a national art] we lack the unifying association of the artists among themselves and with the people and their ideals. A national art needs a soil from which it grows and a sky to strive for. We Jews of today have neither. We are the slaves of many different soils, and our thoughts rise to different skies. In the deepest depths of our soul we have no soil and no sky. We have no homeland that harbors our hopes and that lends support to our steps; we have no national sun that blesses our seeds and brightens our days. A national art needs a unified human community from which it arises and represents. But we only have pieces of community, and only gradually the parts awake to the idea of one body. Only in connection with the continued rebirth can Jewish art come into being and develop. A whole and complete Jewish art will be possible only on Jewish soil, just like a whole and complete Jewish culture as such. But what we have already today are cultural buds, artistic seeds; and we have to nurture these here in the Diaspora with a tender, loving hand until we can plant them into the soil of our homeland where they will be able to unfold fully. What we call Jewish art is not being, but becoming, not fulfillment, but a beautiful possibility, just as Zionism today is becoming a beautiful possibility. Each one of us can contribute to the growth of both in his kind and manner. Each one of us can prepare the way for Zionism and for Jewish art.

There will be some who will not understand why the development of our art is such a big and essential deal for us—surely not those who stress the international nature of art. In a recent letter the Swedish painter Richard Bergh responded in a very sensitive way to the great writer Ellen Key.[2] He admitted that aesthetic appreciation does not care about nationality. "But," he continued, "the momentary bliss is not the most important thing for the human being, rather, his desire to create is, his yearning." In a completed garden one desires to enjoy and to rest, but when we see uncultivated soil, we wish to create new, strange, never before seen gardens, may they be large or small. "*Ubi bene, ibi patria*" [Where there is well-being, there (is your) homeland] is an old lie. Not the land that we enjoy the most is the best but that where we are the most productive. May Jewish art be such a new, strange, never before seen garden. For in artistic creation the specific qualities of the nation express themselves most directly; everything that is particular to this *Volk*, the uniqueness and incomparability of its individuality, finds concrete, living form in its art. Thus, our art is the most beautiful path of our people to ourselves.

As I have already indicated, the rebirth of the Jewish *Volk* is at the same time the form in which this nation participates in the great cultural movement of today's humanity. Zionism and Jewish art are two children of our rebirth....

NOTES

1. Together with young intellectuals who were followers of Ahad Haam's cultural Zionism, such as Leo Motzkin (1867–1933) and Chaim Weizmann (1874–1952) Martin Buber (1878–1965) formed a Democratic Faction. They opposed what they regarded to be Herzl's autocratic leadership and nigh-exclusive emphasis on political objectives. The Democratic Faction, which made its debut at the Fifth Zionist Congress, thus advocated a larger measure of democratic participation in the movement's leadership and the adoption of an educational and cultural program. A student of art history, to which he devoted his never-completed habilitation thesis, Buber had a pronounced interest in art. Concurrent with the congress, he organized with other members of the Democratic Faction an "art exhibition." In his address to the Congress, he explained the rationale of the exhibition and expounded on the vital role that art—in all its expressions—is to play in the spiritual and cultural "rebirth" of the Jewish people. (For a further discussion of Buber and Zionism, see document 29 in this chapter.)

2. Richard Bergh (1858–1919) was a realistic Swedish painter. Ellen Key (1849–1926) was a feminist and respected writer on varied subjects in the fields of family life, education, and ethics.

14. JEWRY OF MUSCLE (JUNE 1903)

MAX NORDAU[1]

Two years ago, during a committee meeting at the Congress in Basle,[2] I said: "We must think of creating once again a Jewry of muscles."

Once again! For history is our witness that such a Jewry had once existed.

For too long, all too long have we been engaged in the mortification of our own flesh.

Or rather, to put it more precisely—others did the killing of our flesh for us. Their extraordinary success is measured by hundreds of thousands of Jewish corpses in the ghettos, in the churchyards, along the highways of medieval Europe. We ourselves would have gladly done without this "virtue" [i.e., the" Christian virtue of corporal mortification]. We would have preferred to develop our bodies rather than to kill them or to have them—figuratively and actually—killed by others. We know how to make rational use of our life and appreciate its value. If, unlike most other peoples, we do not conceive of [physical] life as our highest possession, it is nevertheless very valuable to us and thus worthy of careful treatment. During long centuries we have not been able to give it such treatment. All the elements of Aristotelian physics—light, air, water and earth—were measured out to us very sparingly. In the narrow Jewish street our poor limbs soon forgot their

Source: "Muskeljudentum," *Juedische Turnzeitung* (June 1903). Republished in Max Nordau, *Zionistische Schriften* (Cologne and Leipzig: Juedischer Verlag, 1909), pp. 379–81. Trans. J. Hessing.

gay movements; in the dimness of sunless houses our eyes began to blink shyly; the fear of constant persecution turned our powerful voices into frightened whispers, which rose in a crescendo only when our martyrs on the stakes cried out their dying prayers in the face of their executioners. But now, all coercion has become a memory of the past, and at least we are allowed space enough for our bodies to live again. Let us take up our oldest traditions; let us once more become deep chested, sturdy, sharp-eyed men.

This desire of going back to a glorious past finds a strong expression in the name which the Jewish gymnastic club in Berlin has chosen for itself.[3] Bar Kokhba was a hero who refused to know defeat.[4] When in the end victory eluded him, he knew how to die. Bar Kokhba was the last embodiment in world history of a bellicose, militant Jewry. To evoke the name of Bar Kokhba is an unmistakable sign of ambition. But ambition is well suited for gymnasts striving for perfection.

For no other people will gymnastics fulfill a more educational purpose than for us Jews. It shall straighten us in body and in character. It shall give us self-confidence, although our enemies maintain that we already have too much self-confidence as it is. But who knows better than we do that their imputations are wrong? We completely lack a sober confidence in our physical prowess.

Our new muscle-Jews [*Muskeljuden*] have not yet regained the heroism of our forefathers who in large numbers eagerly entered the sport arenas in order to take part in competition and to pit themselves against the highly trained Hellenistic athletes and the powerful Nordic barbarians. But morally, even now the new muscle-Jews surpass their ancestors, for the ancient Jewish circus fighters were ashamed of their Judaism and tried to conceal the sign of the Covenant by means of a surgical operation,[8]...while the members of the "Bar Kokhba [Association]" loudly and proudly affirm their national loyalty.

May the Jewish gymnastic club flourish and thrive and become an example to be imitated in all the centers of Jewish life!

NOTES

1. Max Nordau (1849–1923), physician, avant-garde literary critic, novelist. One of the most controversial and influential authors of his day, he was among Herzl's earliest supporters.
2. Congress in Basle, i.e., the Second Zionist Congress, held in Basle, Switzerland, during the summer of 1898.
3. At the Second Zionist Congress, Nordau and Max Mandelstamm (1839–1912) (a Russian ophthalmologist and Zionist leader who supported Herzl) proposed a program to promote the physical fitness of Jewish youth. In response, the Bar Kokhba gymnastic club was founded in Berlin in 1898. Similar clubs were soon established throughout Europe.
4. Bar Kokhba (Simeon bar Kosevah) (d. 135 C.E.) led the Jewish revolt against Hadrian that broke out in 132 C.E.
5. According to Josephus (a Jewish historian), Hellenized Jews, who in accordance with Greek custom wrestled in the nude, would often undergo surgery in order to disguise their circumcision.

15. THE UGANDA PLAN (1903)[1]

THEODOR HERZL

Honored members of the Congress: We are assembling for the Sixth Zionist Congress in the good city of Basel which has already earned our gratitude on previous occasions. Again we come together in concern and in hope.

Truly, the situation of the Jews all over the world is no more favorable today than it was in the years of the earlier Congresses. What we have said in this forum about the situation of our people in former years still holds good at the present moment. Here and there a change has taken place, but not a change for the better. Many of us thought that things could not get any worse, but they have gotten worse. Misery has swept over Jewry like a tidal wave. Those who lived in the depths have already been submerged. If the inhabitants of higher, more sheltered places deny this shocking fact, they do no credit either to their insight or to their hearts. Of course, not much is gained by admitting that the Jews are in a pitiable plight. At best such an admission leads to acts of philanthropy which, praiseworthy though they may be in individual cases, must [sic] be censured from a higher, more comprehensive point of view, for, despite their oft-proved inadequacy, they salve the consciences of those who share the responsibility. It is easy to say, "Oh well, we do what we can." There may be people who will feel sufficiently satisfied with themselves if, after reading in their morning paper about a medieval-style massacre of the Jews, they send a modest donation in care of the newspaper, expecting it to be acknowledged in print. But even those who honestly tax themselves in proportion to their means cannot do enough with money alone. Money will not restore life to the dead, health to the maimed, parents to the orphaned. And how can such alms relieve the fears of those who, though they have not been the direct victims of the assault, continue to live under the same conditions? These people are not yet out of danger.

Actually, we Zionists use these arguments only with inner reluctance. It is distasteful to us to make political capital out of disasters and to derive propaganda benefits from the anguish of the unfortunate. But we must state from this platform how great were our pain and our indignation when we learned of the horrible occurrences in Kishinev (see chapter 7, documents 26 and 27), and what sorrow we feel because Jews are living under such conditions. There, poor, careworn existences came to an agonizing end. We will cherish their memory, provide for their survivors, and lose no time in useless demonstrations but devote our living care to the living.

For the bloody days in that Bessarabian city must not cause us to forget that there are many other Kishinevs, and not only in Russia. Kishinev exists wherever Jews are tortured physically or spiritually, where their self-respect is wounded and their property is despoiled because they are Jews. Let us save those who can still be saved!

It is high time. Whoever is not totally blind to visible signs must perceive that there has been a downright disastrous change for the worse in the situation. Even though we Zionists have predicted such a change for years, we were most deeply affected when it actually came to pass.

During the last two decades of the nineteenth century, Jewish communities regarded emigration as a panacea. Even if we disregard all other factors—the misery of the emigrants, the harshness of the new conditions for which they were unprepared, the natural loss caused by these ever-recurring dispersals, and so on—emigration could continue only until the countries of immigrations began to take measures against this influx of a desperate proletariat.

Source: Theodor Herzl, *Zionist Writings: Essays and Addresses,* trans. Harry Zohn (New York: The Herzl Press, 1975), vol. 2, pp. 221–30.

This is the new era which we have entered. The countries of immigration have begun to fight back even though—no, *because*—Jewish misery in Eastern Europe is increasing. And yet only a fool would doubt the high-mindedness of these countries. These countries feel that they have to abandon their general humanitarianism—and I am not saying this ironically—and deal with the Jewish Question, which for them is the question of Jewish immigration, in political terms. Only among us Jews are there some who still nervously refuse to recognize a political element in this. But once we understand this anxiety properly, we shall feel pity rather than anger. It is an agoraphobia which goes back to the narrow streets of the ghetto.

Meanwhile things are inexorably moving forward. In England, hitherto the last place of refuge completely open to us, a Royal Commission was appointed to investigate the immigration of aliens— "aliens," to avoid the use of the word "Jews." The conclusions of the report, however, admit of no doubt as to whose immigration the commission was supposed to discuss. It is plain to see how free, magnanimous England struggled with herself, with what difficulty she brought herself to enact a drastic measure against unfortunate people, how she began a special, protracted investigation before deciding to take final action. There are age-old principles, glorious as banners, which will not remain entirely untarnished if England should no longer grant sanctuary to innocent unfortunates. And the same is true of America, which has become great because it has been a sanctuary.

Each day our work is better understood by the governments that are involved in the migration of the Jews. Our solution, which seeks to provide the Jewish people with a homeland, meets a general need to such a great extent that it is bound to be successful in the end. It is not easy work, of course. There are difficulties which require a great deal of patience and faithfulness. But even this is part of the education we are receiving en route. There are hard days in which we see the disintegration of what has been laboriously achieved, and there are promising beginnings which subsequently collapse. While a movement is still young and weak, its leaders must be concerned about their adherents being demoralized by such setbacks, and on top of one's own disappointment and fatigue we worry about the continuation of the work, the raising of funds, and the endurance of comrades.

But this, too, is to the good. The people we lose are those who are no loss. They leave—some because their vanity has been hurt, others because there was not enough profit in it for them, still others because they like to participate only in successful projects, or for a host of other reasons. But for those who remain the cause is only made more precious by every sacrifice they make. With these people one can go on, and one can also tell them everything. That was our intention when we convened this Congress; we thought that we would have nothing else to announce here but the breakdown of negotiations and the failure of long-prepared attempts. But things developed somewhat differently.

Since we assembled here for the fifth time, I have again had the honor of being summoned to Constantinople on two occasions by his Majesty the Sultan. On both occasions, however, in February and again in August of 1902, the conferences remained without effect. Of course, I could not enter upon any course of action that would have been in conflict with our Basel Program. In particular, scattered, unrelated settlements in various parts of the Turkish Empire could not have satisfied our national needs. The only thing to be revealed by all these troublesome negotiations was that His Majesty the Sultan continues to be kindly disposed toward the Jewish people. This is certainly gratifying and of great value, but it is of no practical help to our movement. Given the kindly sentiments of the sovereign ruler and the indisputable benefits to be gained by the Turkish Empire, the obstacle in our path seemed to be the attitude of the Great Powers interested in the Near East, particularly Russia. That we need not expect any resistance from Germany we know from the memorable interest which was evinced by the German Kaiser. In 1898, when I had the honor of being received, together with a Zionist delegation, in Jerusalem, His Majesty assured us of his sympathetic attitude toward our movement. An emperor's word should not be twisted or subtilized. Nor was there any reason to fear opposition on the part of England, and this is borne out by events which I shall now relate to you.

Given the fruitlessness of the most recent negotiations in Constantinople and in the face of the growing need, we had to cast about for another course of action. Therefore, last October I established contact with several members of the British Cabinet and proposed to them that they grant us a land concession for the Sinai Peninsula so that we might found a settlement for our people there. Not only the Secretaries, to whom I wish to express my warmest thanks on this occasion, but also the high officials of the British government who are concerned with matters of this kind, received me with the greatest good will and readiness to oblige. I was informed that since the territory in question was under Egyptian dominion, it would be necessary to negotiate directly with the Egyptian government. However, the British government generously offered to give me its recommendation and expressed the hope to its representative in Egypt, Lord Cromer, that the plan would be taken into favorable consideration by him and the counselors of His Highness the Khedive. The British government suggested that as a preliminary measure we send out a commission of experts to examine the suitability of the land for settlement purposes and to assess the prospects of such a settlement. In order to obtain the consent of the competent Egyptian authorities for the sending of the commission, and to bespeak their support, our representative, Mr. Greenberg set out for Egypt at the end of October armed with letters of recommendation from the British Foreign Office to the Egyptian government.

Lord Cromer and the Egyptian Foreign Minister gave him a very cordial reception and, after some deliberation, approved the sending of the commission. They also agreed to allow a representative of the Egyptian land surveying department to accompany the commission. Thereupon the commission was organized; it consisted of the following gentlemen: Kessler the engineer, Marmorek the architect, Colonel Goldsmid, Stephens the engineer, Professor Laurent, Dr. S. Soskin, Dr. Hillel Joffe, and Mr. Humphreys, the representative of the Egyptian government.

The commission arrived in Egypt at the end of January and set out for the Sinai Peninsula early in February. In the meantime our representative, Mr. Greenberg, left England and went to Egypt at once again to submit to Lord Cromer and the Egyptian government the draft of a charter covering a tract of land on the Sinai Peninsula. After lengthy negotiations our agent received a note from the Egyptian government in which the latter declared itself to be in accord with the basic provisions of the proposed Charter—namely, Jewish autonomy for the tract of land under consideration and municipal rights for all of the ceded territory, under condition that the report of the commission be favorable and that it convince the government of the feasibility of settling the Peninsula.

Early in March the members of the commission returned to Egypt, and I traveled there myself in order to meet them. I submitted various proposals to Lord Cromer and the Egyptian government, but since I had to return to Europe, I entrusted the further negotiations to a member of the commission.

There ensued protracted negotiations which, I am sorry to say, resulted in a statement by the Egyptian government to the effect that it could not pursue the matter further because, according to the expert evaluation, it would be impossible to supply the Pelusian plain with a sufficient amount of water, which meant that El Arish or any other part of the Peninsula could not be settled. When the officials of the British government with whom I had previously been in touch learned of the expert advice which had been given to the Egyptian government and of the decision which it had been obliged to make, they immediately offered me another tract of land for the purpose of Jewish settlement.

The new territory does not have the historic, romantic, religious, and Zionist value which even the Sinai Peninsula would have had, but I do not doubt that the Congress, acting as a representative of the entire Jewish people, will receive the new offer with the warmest gratitude. The proposal involves an autonomous Jewish settlement in East Africa with a Jewish administration, Jewish local government headed by a Jewish senior official, and, of course, everything under the sovereign supervision of Great Britain. Considering the plight of Jewry and the immediate necessity of finding some way to ameliorate this plight as much as possible, I did not feel justified, when this proposition was made, in taking any steps other than obtaining permission to submit the proposal to the Congress. However, in order that the matter might be of sufficient concrete interest to all of us it was necessary to formulate the proposition in such a way that the national aspirations which are so dear to us all would be taken into consideration. Consequently our representative had several detailed discussions with the members of the British Cabinet and with the various department heads. These conferences proved to be fruitful.

I do not want to anticipate the views of the Congress on the policy which the Zionist movement wishes to pursue with respect to these propositions. But, though it is evident that the Jewish people can have no ultimate goal other than Palestine, and though our views on the land of our fathers are and must remain unchangeable whatever the fate of this proposal may be, the Congress will recognize the extraordinary progress that our movement has made through the negotiations with the British government. I can safely say that our views regarding Palestine have been presented with complete candor and in full detail to other members of the British Cabinet and to the high government officials who are competent in this matter. I believe that the Congress can find a way to make use of this offer. The way in which this offer was made to us is bound to help, improve, and alleviate the situation of the Jewish people without our abandoning any of the great principles on which our movement is founded.

It would not, in my estimation, be practical to present to the full Congress the details of the proposal for which I earnestly bespeak your particular attention. It seems more appropriate to me to ask you to elect a small special committee to deal with this entire matter. Whatever may be decided, I can safely say that in our hearts all of us have nothing but the deepest gratitude for the statesmanlike benevolence which Great Britain has evinced toward the Jewish people in these negotiations.

To be sure, it is not and can never be Zion. It is merely an expedient for settlement purposes, but, be it well understood, on a national and political basis. On the strength of this arrangement we cannot and will not give our masses the signal to start marching. It is and must remain only an emergency measure designed to allay the present helplessness of all the philanthropic undertakings and to keep us from losing scattered fragments of our people.

This was the situation until the most recent turn in events which came only a few days ago, but which is of great significance.

Events which are common knowledge made it necessary for me to travel to Russia in the interests of the Jewish people. I had the welcome opportunity to establish contact with the Russian government, and I can say that I met with some understanding of our Zionist aspirations and heard expressions of good

intentions to do something of decisive importance for us. As a matter of fact, I admit that on this occasion I was not only a Zionist. I know you will not blame me for this. I spoke not only in behalf of the Zionists but for all the Jews in Russia. I took pains to advocate some improvements in their sad plight, and I did receive the assurance that such alleviative measures will be taken into consideration in the near future.

But more important were the assurances which I received concerning the Zionist movement. I am in a position to state that the Russian government will not place any obstacles in the path of the Zionist movement, provided that it retains its accustomed quiet and lawful character. Moreover, the Russian government is ready to cooperate in raising funds for an emigration directed by the Zionists. Finally, and this is the most important fact of all, the Russian government is willing to use its influence with H. M. the Sultan in supporting our efforts to obtain Palestine.

The significance of this statement, which I am authorized to make to the Zionist Congress, is surely evident to all. A promise of this nature from the Russian government means a diplomatic gain that cannot be overestimated. Not only has a tremendous obstacle been removed, but suddenly powerful aid is at hand. Its effects, to be sure, are yet to be seen, but now we can continue to strive for Eretz Israel with renewed courage and with brighter prospects than ever before.

Of course, even now there will be people who will see only the negative side of these benefits. The help of the Powers, they will say, is nothing to cheer about. Either they want to be rid of us or they want to deny us admittance. Fine! If this involves an injustice toward our people, we shall reply to it in the future. In our own future, in our own land! And our answer shall consist in the advancement of human civilization.

NOTE

1. The Sixth Zionist Congress was held in Basel, Switzerland, from August 23 to 28, 1903. The Kishinev pogrom (see chapter 7, documents 26 and 27), which had taken place a few months previously, profoundly affected the Zionist movement and Herzl's activities in particular. Herzl intensified his quest for a territory that would serve as a refuge, even if but provisional,

for the oppressed masses of East European Jewry. In his address to the Zionist Congress, delivered on August 23, 1903, he outlined the proposal made by the British government to provide for the establishment of an autonomous Jewish settlement in Uganda, British East Africa. The proposal came to be known popularly as the "East Africa Scheme" or simply as the "Uganda Plan." While Herzl acknowledged that the Jewish homeland will always be Eretz Israel, he urged the Congress not to reject the British proposal out of hand. At the conclusion of a heated debate, the Congress agreed to send a delegation of experts to British East Africa to ascertain the feasibility of Jewish settlement there.

16. ANTI-UGANDA RESOLUTION (JULY 30, 1905)[1]

SEVENTH ZIONIST CONGRESS

The Seventh Zionist Congress declares:

The Zionist organisation stands firmly by the fundamental principle of the Basle program, namely: "The establishment of a legally-secured, publicly recognised home for the Jewish people in Palestine," and it rejects either as an end or as a means all colonising activity outside Palestine and its adjacent lands.

The Congress resolves to thank the British Government for its offer of a territory in British East Africa, for the purpose of establishing there a Jewish settlement with autonomous rights. A Commission having been sent out to examine the territory, and having reported thereon, the Congress resolves that the Zionist organisation shall not engage further with the proposal. The Congress records with satisfaction the recognition accorded by the British Government to the Zionist organisation in its desire to bring about a solution of the Jewish problem, and expresses the sincere hope that it may be accorded the further good offices of the British Government where available in any matter it may undertake in accordance with the Basle program.

The Seventh Zionist Congress recalls and emphasizes the fact that, according to Article I of the statutes of the Zionist organisation, the Zionist organisation includes those Jews who declare themselves to be in agreement with the Basle program.

NOTE

1. The Seventh Zionist Congress, held in Basle from July 17 to August 2, 1905, was the first congress after Herzl's death in July 1904. The previous congress (August 1903) debated an official offer from the British government which was willing to allocate a territory for Jewish resettlement in Uganda, East Africa. At that congress, Herzl advanced the Uganda scheme for serious examination, while simultaneously emphasizing that "our views on the land of Israel cannot and will not be subject to change; Uganda is not Zion and will never be Zion. This proposal is nothing more than relief measure, a temporary means of allaying distress." By a slim majority, the Sixth Congress voted in favor of the resolution. But those opposed, mostly delegates from Russia, threatened to leave and dissolve the unity of the World Zionist Organization. Only through the personal efforts of Herzl was this prevented. Preserving the fragile unity of the World Zionist Organization was the task of the Seventh Congress. The congress duly reevaluated the Uganda scheme, especially after having received from a commission of inquiry a negative report on the conditions in the proposed territory. After acrimonious debate, this resolution was passed on July 30, 1905.

Source: The Jewish Chronicle, August 4, 1905, p. 21.

17. RESOLUTION ON PALESTINE (JULY 31, 1905)[1]

SEVENTH ZIONIST CONGRESS

The Seventh Zionist Congress resolves that, concurrently with political and diplomatic activity, and with the object of strengthening it, the systematic promotion of the aims of the movement in Palestine shall be accomplished by the following methods: (1) Exploration; (2) Promotion of agriculture, industry, etc., on the most democratic principle possible; (3) Cultural and economic improvement and organisation of Palestine Jews through the acquisition of new intellectual forces; and (4) Acquisition of concessions.

The Seventh Zionist Congress rejects every aimless, unsympathetic and philanthropic colonisation on a small scale which does not conform to the first point in the Basle Program.

NOTE

1. Immediately after the adoption of the anti-Uganda resolution, the Seventh Zionist Congress deliberated upon a statement of policy proposed by Menahem Ussishkin (1863–1941), who was close to the Zionist pioneers (*haluzim*) in Palestine. This proposal reflected the ideas he had developed in a pamphlet, *Our Program* (1905), published on behalf of Russian Zionists opposed to the Uganda scheme. In this pamphlet he laid the foundation for synthetic Zionism: political action, agricultural settlement, and educational and organizational work among the Jewish people in the Diaspora. The last paragraph of the resolution was an amendment framed by Alexander Marmorek (1865–1923), a French Zionist and a close associate of Herzl. He advanced this amendment to prevent the Basle Program, in his words, "from degenerating into a petty Odessa Committee, . . . from drifting back into Hovevei Zionism." The resolution was adopted on July 31, 1905, and represents the policy that thereafter dominated the Zionist movement.

Source: The Jewish Chronicle. August 4, 1905, p. 21.

18. THE JEWISH TERRITORIAL ORGANIZATION (1905)

ISRAEL ZANGWILL[1]

The tragic problem of the Wandering Jew grows daily more insistent. In the language of Dr. [Hermann] Adler, Chief Rabbi of the British Empire, the question of the hour is: *Wohin?* ["Whither?"].

At least a hundred thousand Jews wander forth each year from the lands of poverty and oppression, whether in quest of better life-conditions or actually to escape death by starvation or massacre. The miseries and anxieties of this migration to unknown countries that offer no welcome, the privations and terrors of the journey beset at every turn by harpies and inquisitors, constitute a sum of human misery, of which the extinction, or even the alleviation, would be an immense humanitarian achievement.

This emigration comes principally, and, by an automatic law, from the Russian Pale.... The channels sought are principally the United States and England, but Canada, the Argentine, South Africa, etc., etc., all have their streams of Jewish immigration. In all these centres of refuge, the tendency of the immigrants is to remain near their friends and relatives already in the land, and thus to form great ghettos, unhealthily congesting the already-congested towns, and engendering all the spiritual ills which must inevitably accompany the confusion of atmosphere and ideas attendant on a rapid assimilation with its hopeless alienation of parents and children....

But this immigration into particular centres cannot even go long unchecked. Another law of human nature comes into operation to put the brake upon it—a law formulated by the late Dr. Herzl. The stream of emigration, following the line of least resistance, flows into countries with the least antisemitism, but by its flowing it increases the local antisemitism, till a saturation-point is reached and the immigration is restrained by law.

This point is fast being reached in England, as the Aliens Bill ominously indicates; in America, the just published Report of the Commissioner of the United States Immigration Bureau suggests drastic legislation in the same direction. Is it wise to wait until our hands are forced? Is it wise always to go on hoping that something which we know is bound to occur can be staved off yet a little longer? That is exactly Mr. [Joseph] Chamberlain's[2] definition of absence of statesmanship. Would it not be wiser to face the possibility of all present ports of refuge being dosed to Jewish emigration? And would it not be wiser to prevent by anticipatory action a possibility which would cast a stigma upon all Jewry? Should we not hasten, while the gates are still open, to find a land of refuge of our own?

Thus arises the question with which we began: *Wohin?* But it is now combined with the question whether the new refuge, when found, should be merely a temporary convenience like all the others, or whether it should not rather be a permanent Jewish soil? Philanthropy has proved itself unequal to our emigration problem, or, at least, philanthropy split into national sections. The problem cannot be broken into bits, it must be conceived as a whole. It is an international problem, and must be treated internationally. International philanthropy on so big a scale passes insensibly into the sphere of the political, and can only be handled by statesmanship.

And, here, be it remarked that the stream of Jewish emigration, to which so many peoples object on so many grounds, is not a curse but a blessing to the lands over which it flows. It is a stream to fertilise waste places, to turn mill-wheels, and to move machinery. Really feckless and feeble persons have not the energy to tear themselves out of their native environment, and to adventure themselves in another.

Source: The Jewish Chronicle. August 25, 1905, p. 17.

The Jewish labour-force is, in truth, one of the most potent reservoirs of life and energy in the world. Not its impotency, but its competitive potency, is the true ground of the short-sighted objections to its advent. It is a Nile, which, split into small streams flowing everywhere, loses its force as a Jewish power, though it performs work for other powers in every quarter. In alliance with Jewish capital it has helped to build up many of the greatest cities and states of the world.

The obvious consideration suggests itself: Is it impossible for Jewish labour and capital to create the desired land of refuge? The world still holds—though it will not long hold—vast tracts of comparatively unexploited or neglected territory. British East Africa is only one instance. And the stream of Jewish emigration, though it contains elements that would be useless and even clogging, if turned upon a virgin soil, yet also contains all the elements necessary for pioneer purposes. It includes farmers and artisans, herdsmen and ex-soldiers, miners and rough labourers, and if these elements were sifted and handled by the leaders conversant with Jewish psychology, they could soon prepare the territory for the reception of the general mass of emigrants.

But unless the settlement were made with the full cooperation of the Government of the particular country—and for mutual advantage—the emigration would be attended with great local friction. The territory must be a publicly-recognised, legally-secured home. In this one place of all the world the wanderer must feel himself received not grudgingly, but with the cry of "Peace be to you." Any other form of emigration is, we have seen, inevitably destined to end in local antisemitism. And without a certain measure of self-government the better class of patriotic emigrant will not be attracted. Moreover, we have not the right to burden any other nation with the problem of governing our emigrants—a task with which we ourselves are best fitted to grapple. Of course, should the given territory be in a modern constitutional country, local autonomy could be automatically attained by the mere numerical preponderance of our immigrants in the said territory.

It had been imagined that the establishment of such a settlement fell within the scope of the Zionist movement, but the Seventh Congress having declared itself legally incompetent to work except in Palestine and its neighbourhood—districts that at present offer scant prospect of solving our economic problem—it becomes necessary to create a separate organisation *ad hoc*. This organisation, entitled the Jewish Territorial Organisation, takes as a body no position towards Zionism, its members being left free to determine their individual relations in that movement. Naturally, no land whatever is excluded from our operations provided it be reasonably good and obtainable.

1. The object of the Jewish Territorial Organisation is to procure a territory upon an autonomous basis for those Jews who cannot, or will not, remain in the lands in which they at present live.
2. To achieve this end the Organisation proposes: (a) To unite all Jews who are in agreement with this object; (b) to enter into relations with Governments and public and private institutions; (c) to create financial institutions, labour-bureaus and other instruments that may be found necessary.

NOTES

1. Israel Zangwill (1864–1926), Anglo-Jewish novelist (*Children of the Ghetto*, 1892; *King of the Schnorrrers*, 1894) Among Herzl's earliest followers, Zangwill was one of the most fervent supporters of the Uganda scheme. Upon the rejection of this proposal at the Seventh Zionist Congress, he withdrew from the World Zionist Organization and established the Jewish Territorial Organization (ITO), whose program he delineated in this statement. The ITO endorsed the Basle Program but held that priority should be given to the most suitable territory—which need not, it was emphasized, be Palestine—for Jewish settlement. The ITO investigated the possibility of settling the Jews in various lands (e.g., British East Africa, Australia, Angola, Cyrenaica, Iraq) but without success. Because of this failure and the lack of the emotional appeal among the Jewish masses that Palestine-centered Zionism possessed, the ITO never commanded the support and credibility enjoyed by the World Zionist Organization. Zangwill was the president of the ITO until its dissolution in 1925.
2. Joseph Chamberlain (1836–1914), secretary of state for the colonies from 1895 to 1902 in the cabinet of Lord Salisbury and from 1902 to 1903 in Arthur James Balfour's cabinet. On April 23, 1903, he suggested to Herzl the establishment of a self-governing Jewish settlement in Uganda. Four weeks later he offered a territory in the East Africa Protectorate.

19. PROGRAM FOR PROLETARIAN ZIONISM (1906)

BER BOROCHOV[1]

The Party's General Program: 1. The primary program of the Party is the proletarianization of the means of production and the transformation of the social structure according to the principles of scientific socialism. The only way of achieving these goals recognised by the Party is through the participation of the Jewish proletariat in the class struggle and in the ranks of the world social-democratic movement.

2. The main item in the Party's secondary program, and that which distinguishes it from other social-democratic parties, is the demand for Jewish territorial autonomy based on democratic principles, as a necessary condition for the undisturbed development of the forces of production of the Jewish people.

3. Jewish territorial autonomy can be achieved only in the land of Israel, and the Jewish proletariat must contribute to the realization of this aim....

Party Policy in the Diaspora: 1. In the Diaspora the Party aims to achieve maximal democratization of society by means of the class struggle, and thus shares the secondary program of all social-democratic parties.

2. When relating this aim to the national problem, the Party demands national political autonomy, with wide economic, cultural and financial authority in all internal national matters, for those nations whose interests cannot be satisfied in a suitable manner by territorial or regional autonomy.[2]...

4. Along with the demand for national political autonomy as the leading formulation of Jewish national rights in the Diaspora, the Party emphasizes, however, that the autonomous political institution described above cannot be considered the sole means of achieving the realization of Zionism, and that until territorial autonomy is acquired, no democratic institutions and no national rights can guarantee a solution to the Jewish problem. Until such a time as those national rights attainable in the Diaspora are in fact realized, the Party proposes the implementation of intermediate reforms: freedom in national education, national cultural autonomy, linguistic equality and proportional representation in legislative, executive and judicial institutions.

Guiding principles for the Realization of Zionism: ...2. Since the bourgeois Zionists often tend to use means and methods which are linked with reactionary and degenerate forms of social organization and which in no way lead to the true realization of Zionism, and since the stages in the realization of Zionism are determined by relations based on Realpolitik and the practical interests to which Zionist policy must continually adapt itself, proletarian Zionism believes that part of its task is to support any policy which rests on real interests and to oppose any policy based on philanthropy, other-worldly idealism, obsequious intercession with authorities, and the like.

3. Proletarian Zionism recognizes that historical necessity leads to the strengthening and expansion of the Jewish positions in the land of Israel and to increasing interests by other nations in a solution to the Jewish question along the following lines: (a) the gradual dissolution of the masses of Jewish petty bourgeoisie (a process involving pogroms and impoverishment, the growth of Jewish revolutionary activity and Jewish emigration) has awakened the interest of civilized nations in a territorial solution to the Jewish question; meanwhile the increasing

Source: [Program of the "Poalei Zion—the Jewish Social Democratic Workers' Party in Russia" (1906)], in *Kitvei Borochov,* ed. L. Lavita and D. Ben-Nahum (Tel-Aviv: Hakibbutz Hameuhad—Sifriat Hapoalim, 1955), vol. 1, pp. 383–87. Cited by permission of Sifriat Hapoalim. Trans, by D. Goldman.

national influence of Diaspora Jewry can enlist this awakening international interest to further the cause of Zionism; (b) the strengthening of the Jewish positions in the land of Israel....

4. Jewish capital and Jewish labor are [dialectically] working in the general directions outlined above: (a) in the Diaspora the struggle between labor and capital draws the Jewish proletariat into the worldwide class struggle and allows him to benefit from the democratization of society, which also entails the strengthening of the national character of society in general and the augmentation of Jewish influence in particular; (b) the capital brought by the immigrants to the land of Israel creates the basis for the progressive democratization of society there.

5. Jewish immigration to the land of Israel is a *stychic*[3] process resulting from the growing difficulties Jews face in acquiring positions on the higher forms of production in those large capitalist countries which formerly absorbed Jewish immigration. At the same time the Jews' need to emigrate, rather than weakening, is becoming even more urgent as their economic position is increasingly undermined by intensive national competition. Today, therefore, Jews are forced to turn more and more to the land of Israel, [an underdeveloped] agrarian country and the only one which is capable of absorbing the immigration of Jewish petty bourgeoisie.

6. Proletarian Zionism, unlike preceding utopian trends in Zionism, recognizes that Zionism's primary task is not to find a territory, obtain a charter or initiate settlement. Rather, it consists of the programmatic regulation of the *stychic* process of Jewish immigration to the land of Israel and the achievement of political territorial autonomy in the land of Israel itself....The general Zionist institutions can only facilitate, regulate and rationally organize this *stychic* immigration, by relying on the factors mentioned above: international interest, the democratization of society and the augmentation of Jewish national influence.

The *Party's Relations with the General Zionist institutions:* 1. Proletarian Zionism recognizes the need to coordinate its activities with those of the bourgeois Zionists in matters relating to the practical work in the land of Israel. This must be done in such a way, however, so that the Party will avoid responsibility for activities opposed to proletarian tactics....

7. Given that the bourgeoisie in general have a role to play in the regulation of those factors which produce the *stychic* historical processes of the capitalist regimes, and given that the role of the proletariat lies in the liberation of the conditions of those processes and the introduction of a revolutionary element into them and that the Jewish bourgeoisie, like all other bourgeois groups, needs the liberating power of the proletariat to carry out its regulating functions in the *stychic* process of the realization of Zionism—the proletarian Zionist party formulated its demands regarding Zionist tactics and policies of the bourgeois Zionist institutions in the conviction that, sooner or later, when reality will have forced bourgeois Zionism to recognize its own interests, our demands will be met.

Practical Work in the Land of Israel: ... 2. Even before right of free entry for Jews into the land of Israel has been obtained through the class struggle of the Jewish proletariat, even before the foundations have been laid for obtaining other essential legal guarantees by means of the class struggle in the land of Israel, the proletarian Zionist party demands that the World Zionist Organization undertake immediate practical work in the land of Israel....

4. The Party demands the democratization of the internal administration of the Jewish settlements in the land of Israel, based on principles of municipal autonomy and large-scale participation of workers in the self-governing institutions of the settlements. The Party demands that the settlements themselves regulate the relations between capital and labor within the jurisdiction without the intervention of the Turkish administration....

6. The Party shall organize the Jewish proletariat in the land of Israel and regard the establishment of the World Federation of Jewish Social Democratic Workers, *Poalei Zion*, as a necessary prerequisite to the undertaking of systematic proletarian work in the land of Israel.

NOTES

1. Ber Borochov (1881–1917), leader and foremost theoretician of the socialist Zionists. For a generation of Russian Jews drawn to Marxism, Borochov developed a synthesis of the seemingly irreconcilable demands of the revolutionary class struggle and the devotion to the national needs of the Jewish people. Based on the precepts of Marxist analysis, Borochov's forceful arguments

exercised a commanding influence on the ideology of the emerging socialist Zionist movement.

Borochov was a delegate of the *Poalei Zion* (Workers of Zion) to the Seventh Zionist Congress, where he cooperated closely with Menahem Ussishkin (one of the foremost leaders of Russian Zionism) and the struggle against the Uganda scheme (see document 17, note 1, this chapter). At the time the Poalei Zion was a loose association of socialist Zionist groups in Russia. The deliberations of the Seventh Congress exacerbated the ideological dissension between these groups and left the Poalei Zion in disarray. Some groups felt that continued membership in the World Zionist Organization was intolerable, for it entailed cooperation with the Jewish bourgeoisie; others preferred territorialism; still other groups demanded that Zionism should be abandoned altogether, because it was a utopian ideology that neglected *Gegenwartsarbeit*, i.e., attention to the everyday needs of the Jewish masses in the Diaspora. In early 1906, in the Ukrainian city of

Poltava, Poalei Zion groups loyal to the resolutions of the Seventh Zionist Congress founded, under the leadership of Borochov, the Poalei Zion—Jewish Social Democratic Workers' Party in Russia. In the party's program, written largely by Borochov, the ideological challenges presented by the dissident Poalei Zion groups were met, and the participation of the Jewish proletariat in the World Zionist Organization was justified.

2. The reference is to "extraterritorial" peoples who are not concentrated in a particular region and do not constitute a majority in any single country.

3. A Greek term used by Borochov to designate an "elemental," historically necessary process. The millennial migration of the Jewish people is, according to Borochov, such a process, which will objectively necessitate the territorial concentration of the Jewish masses in Palestine. Zionism appreciates the *stychic* dimension of Jewish history and merely serves it as a "midwife," and it is therefore not a utopian movement.

20. *GEGENWARTSARBEIT* (DECEMBER 1906)[1]

HELSINGFORS CONFERENCE

The third conference of the Zionist Organization in Russia, which took place in Helsingfors, inaugurated a new era in the history of the movement. The conference put an end to the crisis of the last three years.[2] This crisis was not a crisis of objectives but rather one of tactics. The fundamental goal of Zionism was, and remains, *the political revival of the Jewish people in the land of Israel.* The main error committed by our movement was the blind faith that our will and the genius of our leader [i.e., Herzl] were sufficient to obtain almost instantly the land of Israel [for Jewish resettlement]. We expected the Charter[3] to

be granted any day, and this expectation caused us to treat with indifference the mundane problems of the present life.

At the time we thought that we must not waste our energies on matters concerning the Jews in the Diaspora [*golah*], but rather concentrate our entire effort toward the realization of our ideal. Our work during that period consisted of soliciting new members, the sale of shares in the Jewish Colonial Trust[4] and the collection of donations to the Jewish National Fund.[5] The optimism which led us to believe that we would imminently get the Charter,

Source: [Memorandum of the Central Committee of the Zionist Organization of Russia, December 1906], in I. Maor, *Hatnuah hazionit be-Rusyah* [The Zionist Movement in Russia] (Jerusalem: Hasifriyah Hazionit, The World Zionist Organization, 1973), pp. 318–19. Cited by permission. Trans. R. Weiss.

prevented us from performing practical work both in the land of Israel and in the Diaspora. But reality destroyed the dream, and we were forced to recognize the evolutionary and developmental nature of Zionism, and accordingly, to change our tactics. To be sure, our goal remains the same; only our tactics have changed. We now understand that only an organized, unified Jewry is capable of mobilizing the vast material and spiritual resources needed to realize our objectives. But the effective organization of Jewry requires two basic elements: an attention to the daily needs of the Jewish masses and the ongoing work, especially that part which can be carried out already in the present, toward the attainment of the ultimate goal of Zionism.

Zionism must address itself to all aspects of Jewish life and respond to all issues besetting Jewry. [The movement will thereby] tap all the hidden resources of the nation. In consonance with these considerations, it was necessary to prepare an appropriate program. The Conference dealt with this task successfully....

Neither the terrible pogroms [recently perpetrated against our people] nor the shattered hopes that our situation in Russia will change radically in the near future can shake our determination to reach our ultimate goal. On the contrary both the Jewish bourgeoisie and the Jewish proletariat are convinced, now more than ever, that the basic problems of our nation cannot be solved in Exile [*galut*].

NOTES

1. The Third All-Russian Zionist Conference met from the fourth to the tenth of December 1906 in Helsingfors (Helsinki), Finland. In the wake of recent events—the Revolution of 1905, pogroms, the death of Herzl, the Seventh Zionist Congress, the growing influence of competing ideologies among the Jewish masses—the conference dealt with fundamental issues facing the Zionist movement in general, and Russian Zionism in particular. The program endorsed by the conference constituted a major revision of Zionist policy.

The conference is most famous for its resolution on *Gegenwartsarbeit* ("work in the present"). Prior to the conference the Zionist movement in Russia subscribed to the principle of "the negation of the Diaspora" (*galut*) and correspondingly rejected the possibility of Jewish national existence in Russia. But this position suddenly seemed impolitic, if not sterile. After the Seventh Congress, which betrayed the weakness of diplomatic Zionism, the realization of the Basle Program seemed to lie in the remote future; moreover, the Jewish masses of Russia were being successfully organized by movements such as the Bund, which gave priority to the immediate political and economic needs of the masses. The program of *Gegenwartsarbeit* was formulated as a correlate to the policy of "synthetic Zionism" endorsed by the conference. The latter policy postulated that the attainment of the Basle Program objectives was the ultimate end, but not the precondition of Zionist activity, viz., systematic *aliyah* (immigration) and settlement in the land of Israel. Similarly, the basic negation of the Jewish future in the Exile (*galut*), does not preclude participation in the struggles of daily life of the Jews in the existing Diaspora *(golah)*. Accordingly, the Helsingfors Conference advanced a program to work for the democratization of Russia and the reorganization of Russia as a multinational state that would grant wide, autonomous rights to its non-Russian peoples, including the Jewish nation. Such a policy, it was held, would transform Zionism into a dynamic movement of the masses. The document presented here is a memorandum sent by the Central Committee of the Russian Zionist Organization to the local branches in Russia explaining the ideological consideration behind the program.

2. That is, since the Sixth Zionist Congress, at which the Uganda scheme and other "temporary solutions" were first broached.

3. See document 8, note 1, in this chapter.

4. Jewish Colonial Trust, bank established in 1899 in accordance with a decision of the First Zionist Congress. The bank assisted in the colonization of Palestine.

5. Called in Hebrew *Keren kayemet leyisrael*, the Jewish National Fund was founded at the Fifth Zionist Congress (1901) to further the acquisition and development of land in Palestine.

21. OUR GOAL (MAY 1907)

HAPOEL HAZAIR[1]

Conscious of the fact that our national work is of no value as long as there is no measurably large and measurably strong Hebrew[2] workers' party in the land of Israel, we have set ourselves the goal of creating such a party. How to create it and whether indeed it is possible to create such a party under the present conditions is the central question facing us.

The life of the Hebrew worker in the land of Israel is unlike that of the worker in any other country, as almost everyone who deals with this problem understands. Not everyone understands, however, exactly how the Jewish worker's life here differs from that of the worker in other countries. They do not understand what primary factors force him to follow a unique path in his struggle for survival, what laws he must rely upon as he follows that special path and how he must relate to the world around him; in other words, all the questions concerning how to create in the land of Israel a Jewish workers' party worthy of the name, in terms of both quality and quantity.

Some solve the problem with the facile phrase: "Everything will be created by class struggle." Who are these struggling classes within the Jewish people as a whole and, among the Jews in the land of Israel, in particular? To what extent can this class struggle contribute to the development of an undeveloped land and to the growth of a workers' party in it? Such questions they do not bother to raise.

When we propose, therefore, to publish a newspaper our primary goal is to clarify to ourselves our essential nature as workers, the [historical and political] laws which we must follow in different situations, the extent to which we can utilize means applied in other countries and the point beyond which we must make our own way.

We are not so naive as to believe that we can give a final answer to these questions all at once. A land in the process of development cannot be made to follow predetermined laws; as it develops and is transformed, its laws, too, must change. We believe, however, that we can evolve laws suited to the development of the country. If someone comes later and shows us we erred in this or that law, we will not deny it but will readily acknowledge our mistakes. The first part of our newspaper, therefore, will be devoted entirely to the clarification of the questions mentioned above. Study of the conditions of labor and of the life of the worker in the city and village, and careful examination of the development of the country will supply us with the material we need to formulate our answers.

In addition, we will be on constant guard against the use of false or misleading statements for purposes of propaganda, by various public figures and leaders of Zionist institutions. Our national movement is too genuine to require the use of such impure methods which can only do more harm than good. We shall fight against these methods with all our strength. The second part of our newspaper, therefore, will be devoted to a critique of various Zionist institutions and activities in the land of Israel, to an impartial evaluation of the attitudes of the Zionist leadership on different issues and to a presentation of our views on all these matters.

The newspaper must and can fulfill one other need of ours—the need for information. By maintaining constant contact with our comrades in the cities and villages of the land of Israel, we will always be able to give correct information about working conditions in the country and the demand for workers in specific places. The third part of our newspaper will therefore be devoted to the dissemination of such information. Apart from news items, we will also give our comrades an opportunity to express their opinions on various issues related to life in the land of Israel in

Source: "Mataratenu," *Hapoel hazair* (Iyyar 5667; May 1907). Trans. D. Goldman.

general and to their own experiences in particular, in the form of letters to the editor, belletristic essays and popular articles.

At the present time we are unable, both financially and spiritually, to publish a journal that would satisfy all our spiritual requirements. May this modest forum serve our comrades as a central clearing-house for their ideas, and let us hope that it will gradually develop into that larger forum whose lack is so deeply felt here in the land of Israel.

NOTES

1. *Hapoel Hazair* (The Young Worker) was a labor organization active in Palestine from 1905 to 1930 founded by young people who had come to Palestine with the second *aliyah*, 1904–1914, in protest against the Uganda scheme and with the determination to demonstrate the possibility of practical work in country. Unable to identify with any of the existing Hebrew newspapers, the group founded its own organ called *Hapoel hazair*, which quickly became a leading platform for socialist Zionist ideas, mainly non-Marxist. Some of the best Hebrew journalists and authors of the period wrote for its pages. The document presented here was the lead article of the first hectographic pamphlet of *Hapoel hazair*.

2. Indicative of their desire to create a new man, the term *ivri* ("Hebrew") rather than *yehudi* ("Jewish") was employed, as it was—and is—in most Zionist writings.

22. THE HIDDEN QUESTION (AUGUST 1907)

YITZHAK EPSTEIN[1]

Among the difficult issues regarding the rebirth of our people in its homeland, one issue outweighs them all: our relations with the Arabs. This issue, upon whose correct resolution hinges the revival of our national hope, has not been forgotten by the Zionists but has simply gone completely unnoticed by them and, in its true form, is barely mentioned in the literature of our movement. Although in recent years some disconnected words about this issue have appeared in various writings, these, however, have been in the context of claims by the Jews in Palestine (*Eretz Israel*) who deny the possibility of any real Zionist effort, or in accounts of the Arab nationalist movement. The loyal Zionists have not yet dealt with the issue of what our attitude toward the Arabs should be when we come to buy land from them in Palestine, to found settlements and, in general, to settle the country. The Zionists' lack of attention to an issue so basic to their settlement is not intentional; it went unnoticed because they were not familiar with the country and its inhabitants, and, furthermore, lacked a national or political consciousness.

The sad fact that it is possible to ignore a fundamental issue like this, and after thirty years of settlement activity to speak about it as if it were new, virtually proves the irresponsibility of our movement, which deals with issues superficially and does not delve into their core.

Since the emergence of the national movement, Zionist leaders have continuously studied the arrangements and the laws of the land, but the question of the people who are settled there, its workers and its true owners, has not arisen, not in practice and not in theory.... While governmental procedures, the difficulties in purchasing land and constructing homes, the ban against entry of Jews—these and

Source: Yitzhak Epstein, *"Sheelah neelamah," Hashiloah* 17, no. 97 (August 1907), pp. 193–205. Trans. G. Svirsky.

more—have all hampered immigration to Palestine, obstacles related to Arabs do not appear numerous. And if our brothers in Palestine did not entirely grasp the seriousness of the question, it certainly did not occur to the Zionists who live far from the arena of activity. We devote attention to everything related to our homeland, we discuss and debate everything, we praise and criticize in every way, but one trivial thing we have overlooked: In our lovely country there exists an entire people who have held it for centuries and to whom it would never occur to leave.

For a number of years we have been hearing that the population of the country exceeds 600,000. Assuming that this number is correct, even if we deduct from it 80,000 Jews, there are still over half a million Arabs in our land, 80 percent of whom support themselves exclusively by farming and own all the arable land. The time has come to dispel the misconception among Zionists that land in Palestine lies uncultivated for lack of working hands or the laziness of the local residents. There are no deserted fields. Indeed every *fellah* [Arab peasant] tries to add to his plot from the adjoining land, if additional work is not required. Near the cities they even plow the sloped hillsides and, near Metullah,[2] the indigent *fellahin* plant between the boulders, as they do in Lebanon, not allowing an inch of land to lie fallow. Therefore, when we come to take over the land, the question immediately arises: What will the *fellahin* do when we buy their lands from them?...

In general we have made a crude psychological blunder in our relationship with a large, assertive and passionate people. At a time when we are feeling the love of the homeland with all our might, the land of our forefathers, we are forgetting that the people who live there now also have a sensitive heart and a loving soul. The Arab, like any man, has a strong bond with his homeland; the lower his level of development and the more narrow his perspective, the stronger his bond to the land and to the region, and the harder it is for him to part from his village and his field. The Muslim will not abandon his country, will not wander far: he has many traditions which bind him to the soil of his homeland, the most dear to him being respect for the graves of his forefathers. To understand the depth of this feeling, one has to know that these Orientals venerate their dead, they visit their graves and involve their ancestors in the events of their lives, their celebrations and their sorrows. I can still hear

the dirge of the Arab women on the day their families left the village of Ja'una, today Rosh Pina,[3] to settle in Hawran, east of the Jordan. The men rode asses and the women walked behind them, bitterly weeping, and the valley was filled with their keening. From time to time they would stop to kiss the stones and the earth.

Even when the *fellahin* themselves sell some of the village land, the issue of acquisition is not resolved. The *fellah*, in anguish from the burden of heavy taxes, may decide in a moment of despair (and sometimes with the encouragement of the village elders, who receive a hefty sum for this) to sell the field; but the sale leaves him with a festering wound that reminds him of the cursed day that his land fell into the hands of strangers. I have known *fellahin* who, after they sold the land, worked for the Jews together with their wives and who managed to save money. As long as the wages were good, they sealed their lips, but when the work ended, they began to grumble against the Jews and to dispute the purchase.

Can we rely on such a method of land acquisition? Will it succeed and does it serve our goals? A hundred times no. A nation which declared, "But the land must not be sold beyond reclaim,"[4] and which gives preference to the rights of one who cultivates the land over one who buys it, must not and cannot confiscate land from those who work it and settled on it in good faith. We must not uproot people from land to which they and their forefathers dedicated their best efforts and toil. If there are farmers who water their fields with their sweat, these are the Arabs. Who could place a value on the toil of the *fellah*, plowing in torrential rains, reaping in the hot summer, loading and transporting the harvest?...

But let us leave justice and sensitivity aside for a moment and look at the question only from the point of view of feasibility. Let us assume that in the land of our forefathers we don't have to care about others and we are allowed—perhaps even obligated—to purchase all the lands obtainable. Can this type of land acquisition continue? Will those who are dispossessed remain silent and accept what is being done to them? In the end, they will wake up and return to us in blows what we have looted from them with our gold! They will seek legal redress against the foreigners who have torn them from their lands. And who knows, but that they will then be both the prosecutors and the judges....These people are brave, armed, excellent marksmen, have superb cavalry, and are zealous of their nation and most significantly have not yet weakened; they are after all but a fraction of a large nation which controls all the surrounding lands: Syria, Iraq, Arabia and Egypt.

It's easy to dismiss these words and to view them as disloyalty to the ancient and eternal national ideal. But if we weigh the matter disinterestedly, we must admit that it would be folly not to consider with whom we are dealing and the extent of our power and the power against us. Heaven forbid that we close our eyes to what is happening sooner, perhaps, than we imagine. One can definitely say, that *at the present time, there is no Arab national or political movement in Palestine*. But this people has no real need of a movement: It is large and numerous and does not require revival because it never ceased to exist for even a moment. In its physical growth, it exceeds all the nations of Europe.... Let us not make light of its rights, and especially let us not, heaven forbid, take advantage of the evil extortion of their own brothers. Let us not tease a sleeping lion! Let us not depend upon the ash that covers the ember: One spark escapes, and soon it will be a conflagration out of control.

It is not my belief that in our homeland we must be servile and surrender to its [Arab] inhabitants. But we can dwell among them in courage and strength, secure in our settlements; and in the land of sun, we shall also refresh ourselves, renew our blood and be heartened. But we sin against our nation and our future if we facilely cast aside our choicest weapon: the justice and the purity of our cause. As long as we hold to these [principles], we are mighty and need fear no one, but if we abandon them—our strength is in vain and our courage for nought....

The Jewish settlement has already given bountifully to the inhabitants of the land: The situation of the towns and villages near new settlements has improved; hundreds of craftsmen—masons, builders, painters, donkey and camel handlers—and thousands of laborers have found work in the settlements; commerce has increased, as has the demand for dairy products and produce. And yet all this cannot make up for what we have distorted. For the good we shall not be remembered, but the bad will not be forgotten. It is impossible to buy love, but how easy to establish enemies among the simple *fellahin*. Powerful is the passion of those who have been uprooted from their land.

It is time to open our eyes to our methods! If we don't want to ruin our work, we must consider every step we take in our homeland, and we must urgently solve the question of our relations with the Arabs before it becomes a "Jewish question." We must not rest content with the current situation! Heaven forbid that we should digress even momentarily from our act of creation, from the future, but whenever what we believe to be the national good violates human justice, this good will become a national sin from which there is no repentance. Our ideal is so noble that our young people yearn to realize in it the social ideals which throb in humanity these days. But this means that we must distance ourselves from the ugly and from anything which resembles it, i.e., from every deed tainted with plunder.

When we come to our homeland, we must uproot all thoughts of conquest or expropriation. Our motto must be: Live and let live! Let us not cause harm to any nation, and certainly not to a numerous people, whose enmity is very dangerous....

After we own the uncultivated land, we shall turn our attention to the cultivated land. This will be acquired not by expelling the tenants but on condition of having them remain on the land and improving their lot by introducing good agricultural methods. Gradually they will switch from the old ways of extensive farming to intensive farming. When the land yields better returns, it will be sufficient for the Jews and *fellahin* together. As enlightened owners, we will devote a sum of money to improving the lot of the tenants, because their welfare is our welfare. We shall benefit the residents, not furtively with bribes or gold in order to rid ourselves of them but in true material and spiritual ways. Our agronomists will advise them, teaching them the sciences of agriculture, husbandry and cross-breeding, and show them the scientific ways to fight diseases of cattle and poultry and pests of the field, vineyard and garden. They will be able to cheaply purchase medicine against disease and, when in need, will have access to a Jewish doctor. Their children will be accepted to our schools, and when we can relieve the burden of the tithe, they will also be relieved. Although in the early days they will view us with suspicion, not believing the innovations and even less the innovators, but from day to day our integrity will become evident, and they will see the innocence of our aspirations and the benefit of our reforms, which will undoubtedly succeed in the hands of such a diligent, wise and frugal people. The Arab *fellah* is smarter and has more common sense than the farmers of many other countries. And then the Arab tenants will know us at our best, and they will not curse the day the Jews came to settle their land but will remember it as a day of redemption and salvation....

This is not a dream. It is difficult but easy, loyal and more productive than the systems that we used until now. If instead of disinheriting the Druse from Metullah, we would divide the land with them, then we would not have to spend even half of what we spend on bribes to the wicked, with attendant expulsion of indigent families, court cases and lawyers, and untenable compromises. We would not have to enslave ourselves to the butchers, and we would sit in security with our neighbors and work our plots in serenity. Druse respect education, and they would send their sons and daughters to our schools, and in coming generations we could find in them not only honest neighbors but also loyal friends. And this is true of other settlements. We have spent a fortune to gain sworn enemies at a time that we could have spent less—or even more—and acquired friends, enhanced our honor, sanctified the name of Israel and advanced our goals—opening the ports of hearts, which are more important than the ports of the coast.

Our method of land acquisition must be a direct extension of our relations with the Arab nation in general. The principles which should guide us when we settle among this nation are as follows:

(a) The Jewish people, the foremost with regard to justice and law, egalitarianism and the brotherhood of man, respects not only the individual right of every person but also the national right of every nation and ethnic group.

(b) The people of Israel, yearning for rebirth, is in solidarity—in belief and deed—with all nations who are awakening to life and treats their aspirations with love and goodwill and fosters in them *their* sense of national identity.

These two principles must be the basis of our relations with the Arabs....

We must therefore enter into a covenant with the Arabs which will be productive to both sides and to humanity as a whole. We will certainly agree to this covenant, but it also requires the agreement of the other side; and that we shall gain gradually through practical deeds which are of benefit to the land, to us and to the Arabs....

We shall be an angel of peace, who mediates among discordant religious sects, and we can do all this in the purity of our aspirations and our beliefs, we alone, not others.

And when we bring education to our ally and work together with him, let us not forget one principle. Just as the teacher is obliged to know the soul of his pupil and his inclinations, so too it is not enough to hold before us the end goal, but we must also have a proper understanding of the Arab nation, its characteristics, inclinations, hopes, language, literature and especially a deep understanding of its life, customs, pain and suffering....We are entering an environment still living in the sixteenth century, and in all we do we must take into consideration the spiritual condition of this nation today. If we desire to lead someone anywhere, we must take him from where he is right now; otherwise he will not be able to follow us. We must, therefore, study and understand the psyche of our neighbors. It's shameful to say that we have not yet done anything at all about this, that no Jew has yet devoted himself to this study, and that we are absolutely ignorant of everything regarding Arabs and that all that we do know is gleaned at the marketplace. It is time to educate!...

One can object to this lecture on several grounds; but on one thing, the lecturer dares assert with certainty: these words were said in the spirit of our nation, in the spirit of world justice, imprinted on us ever since we became a people.

The prophet of the Diaspora, when he came to speak about the division of the land, said: "You shall divide it by lot for an inheritance unto you and unto the strangers that sojourn among you, which shall beget children among you: and they shall be unto you as native-born children of Israel; they shall have inheritance with you among the tribes of Israel. And in whatever tribe the stranger sojourns, there shall you give him his inheritance, says the Lord God" (Ezekiel, 47:22–23).

And the great prophet from Anatot, who preceded Ezekiel, when he came to prophesize bad tidings to the evil neighbors who threatened the inheritance of Israel, concludes: "And after I have plucked them up, I will again have compassion on them, and I will bring them again each to his heritage and each to his land. And it shall come to pass, if they will diligently learn the ways of my people…then shall they be built up in the midst of my people" (Jeremiah 12:15, 16).

Come let us teach them the right path; we shall build them up and we too shall be built.

NOTES

1. Yitzhak Epstein (1862–1943), Hebrew writer and linguist and pioneer of the instruction of modern Hebrew. Born in Luba, Belorussia, he settled in Palestine in 1886, first as an agricultural laborer, then as an educator. He studied at the University of Lausanne from 1902 to 1908; from 1908 to 1915 he directed the Alliance Israélite Universelle school in Salonika, Greece. After World War I he returned to Palestine, where he resumed his educational activities and his work on Hebrew linguistics. Published in the Hebrew monthly *Hashiloah*, issued at the time in Odessa, Russia, Epstein's essay on the Arab Question—"The Hidden Question"—was introduced by the editor of the journal, the poet Haim Nachman Bialik, with the following note: "Although Epstein's essay was first delivered as a lecture at *Ivriyah* [a society for the renewal of Hebrew as the vernacular of the Jewish people] during the Seventh Zionist Congress in Basel [1905], we regard the matter which it addresses as still of relevance. And precisely now, when the practical issues in *Eretz Israel* have increased it is appropriate that we ponder the issues he has raised."…

2. Metullah, situated at the northernmost point of the Upper Galilee. The land for this Jewish village was purchased in 1896 by Baron Edmond de Rothschild. The name Metullah derives from the original Arabic name of the site.

3. Rosh Pina is a Jewish agricultural village in eastern Upper Galilee, whose land was purchased in 1878 by a group of Jews from Safed, a city in the central Galilee. After a false start, it was resettled in 1882 by members of Hovevei Zion from Romania and Russia. The new settlers gave the village its present name, which means "cornerstone" and which refers to Psalm 188:21: "The stone which the builders refused has become the cornerstone."

4. Cf. Leviticus 25:23f: "But the land must not be sold beyond reclaim, for the land is Mine; you are but strangers resident with Me. Throughout the land that you hold, you must provide for the redemption of the land [by its original inhabitants]."

23. THE FOUNDING OF TEL AVIV: A GARDEN CITY (1906/7)[1]

HOUSING ASSOCIATION OF JAFFA AND ARTHUR RUPPIN

A. Letter to the Jewish National Fund (December, 1906)

We have laid the foundations in Jaffa for an association called Home Estates (*Ahuzat Bayit*) whose purpose is to build cooperatively sixty dwellings for sixty of its members. Establishing our association, intended to meet a most pressing need, was made necessary by the following facts: The immigration of Jews from Russia to the Land of Israel has grown significantly and has brought about a housing crisis in Jaffa, and consequently a rise in rents. In the last two or three years the rent for apartments of

Source: A. Letter of the Founders of Tel Aviv, dated December 1906, to the Jewish National Fund Head Office in Cologne, Germany; B. Letter from Athur Ruppin, dated 21 July 1907, to the Jewish National Fund Head Office. *Sefer Tel Aviv,* ed. Alter Droyanov (Tel Aviv: Va'adat Tel Aviv, 1935), pp. 75–77. Trans. Mark Joseph.

various sizes have nearly doubled. It is the Arabs who benefit, as they own the houses, and consequently they are building more. There is no need to explain that if the situation continues as at present, the Jews will be in great danger and Arab rule will be consolidated.

Our association has already considered a certain plot of land on which it intends to build a neighborhood of 60 houses, install wide and high quality streets, and see to public hygiene, such as sewers, plumbing and so on, and so serve as an example and a guide to the whole urban settlement of Jews in the Land.

The sixty members of the association are from the middle class and need the money they presently have to carry on their businesses. They cannot therefore pay the whole sum that was invested in the building program. In order to see through the whole program 400,000 Francs are needed, and according to the plan that will build:

18 houses at	4,000 Francs each	= 72,000 Francs
16 " "	6,000 Francs each	= 96,000 "
14 " "	8,000 Francs each	= 112,000 "
12 houses at	10,000 Francs each	= 120,000 Francs
60 houses in all		= 400,000 Francs

Deducting what it has already hitherto paid from its initial funds, our association only has at present about 100,000 Francs, and on the basis of this capital it is seeking a loan of three hundred thousand Francs. Since the work of the association can be expected to pave the way for all Jewish urban settlement [in the Land of Israel], and establishing the project is of utmost desirability, the Anglo-Palestine Bank[2] has taken upon itself to assist in securing a loan. Accordingly, it will be the guarantor for the lenders to repay the loan, its capital and interest. The bank is assured that there is no need for concern about the responsibility imposed on it, because the price of the land is constantly rising, and its current price is such that its value can only rise and not fall. The land and the houses to be built will be valued together by the bank against the debt until it is repaid in full. Apart from this the bank is confident about the trustworthiness of every member [of our association] considered as individuals; moreover, the bank has given its agreement to guarantee the loan on condition that it will organize and supervise the construction of the houses.

B. Letter by Arthur Ruppin to the Jewish National Fund (July 1907)

Re: Housing Association of Jaffa

You certainly received a while ago a loan request from this association. I see the great importance of the matter and am therefore again bringing it up. The Home Estates association has 60 members at present, all well-to-do people from Jaffa and its environs. The purpose of the association, according to its statutes, is to build houses for its members in a special quarter. It has already looked at a plot of land of 222 dunams in Jaffa in a well situated place, big enough to build not only the 60 houses for the members of the association, but two hundred houses. From the four hundred thousand Francs, sought for the purchase of the plot of land and for building the sixty houses, the members have already made a deposit of fifty thousand Francs in cash and another fifty thousand Francs in promissory notes. It is a good moment to build in Jaffa, because building has stopped in Jerusalem through lack of water, and consequently the prices of building materials have gone down throughout the country and wages have also gone down.

I attach a high value to the matter of building a Jewish quarter in Jaffa and in Jerusalem, one that will not be put to shame by those of others, and will be in another league in terms of hygiene from the currently existing Jewish neighborhoods in Jaffa and Jerusalem. The narrow streets, the filth and the hideous quality of the buildings in these neighborhoods are a shame and a disgrace to the Jews, and because of them many upper class people hold back from settling in the land. Building good and healthy homes for middle class Jews in Jaffa could not be more important. I believe that without exaggeration a properly built Jewish quarter is the most important step in the economic conquest of Jaffa by the Jews.

I repeat, and it is not only my opinion, but also that of others with whom I have spoken with on the matter, that we have before us an exceptionally important undertaking, and not one of those projects that are born today and buried tomorrow. Therefore I ask you to give the proposal your attention with all the seriousness it deserves.

NOTES

1. Over the centuries, the ancient port city of Jaffa served as the "gate to Zion." It was thus also for the first

Zionist settlers. By the early 1900s, the Jewish population of the city swelled to 8,000 out of a total of 47,000 inhabitants. As a result, there was a severe housing shortage for the ever-increasing number of Jewish immigrants. The idea of establishing a Jewish suburb of Jaffa had been floating about for some time, but it became a concrete proposal only at the initiative of Akiva Aryeh Weiss (1868–1947), who convened a meeting of more than a hundred Jewish residents of Jaffa. At that very meeting an *Agudat Bonei Batim* (Association of House Builders), which was soon changed to an *Ahuzat Bayit* (Housing Estate), was founded. Weiss set forth the vision of the association in its prospectus: "The envisioned suburb will be the First Hebrew city, in which there will live a hundred percent Hebrews, who will speak Hebrew; the city will maintain cleanliness and hygiene.... And like New York City, which symbolizes the main entrance to America, so we must develop our city so that it will be in time the New York of Eretz Israel.... In this city we will arrange the streets with sidewalks and electric lighting. Every house will be supplied with water flowing from the 'fountains of salvation' [Isaiah 12:3] directly into pipes as in every modern city in Europe; similarly, the city will have a proper sewage system for the sake of the health of the city and its residents" (cited in Yaakov Shavit and Gideon Biger, *Historia shel Tel Aviv* [Tel Aviv: University of Tel Aviv Press, 2001], vol. 1, p. 65). The Anglo-Palestine Bank, which had recently opened a branch in Jaffa under the management of Z. D. Levontin (see document 4 in this chapter), offered a loan guarantee. The loan itself, however, would have to be secured from the Jewish National Fund in Cologne, Germany. On behalf of the association, Weiss wrote (in German) a detailed request to the fund. The request was to receive the support of the sociologist Arthur Ruppin (1876–1943). Ruppin had been sent by the president of the World Zionist Organization to study the economic infrastructure and potential of the country. Shortly after his arrival in the country in early 1907, Weiss met him and showed him the site of the future suburb. Ruppin was duly impressed and wrote the letter presented here enthusiastically endorsing the requested loan. His letter, dated July 21, 1907, is the second part of the document. The loan was soon to be approved. On April 11, 1909, sixty housing plots were distributed by lottery. This date marks the founding of the City of Tel Aviv. The name of the city, literally meaning the "Hill of Spring," was actually given a year later; It is based on Ezekiel 3:15, where mention is made of a Babylonian city by that name.

2. The Anglo-Palestine Bank opened its first branch in Jaffa in 1903 under the management of Zalman David Levontin. It was a subsidiary of Bank Leumi, which was founded at the Second Zionist Congress and incorporated in London in 1899 as the financial instrument of the World Zionist Organization.

24. THE COLLECTIVE (1908)[1]

MANYA SHOHAT

I began on my arrival in Palestine with an urban cooperative, for I was more accustomed to city conditions. In Russia I had learned carpentry in the factory of my brother, Gedaliah Wilbushewitz.[2] I raised a loan in order to start a carpenters' cooperative in Jaffa, and I worked out its rules on the basis of the Russian *artels*, which had a communist background. The cooperative existed for three months. When I left for the Galilee internal dissensions broke out and the cooperative fell to pieces.

In the year 1905 Yehoshua Hankin[3] spoke to me about the possibility of buying up the Emek, or Valley of Jezreel, and it was clear to me that only through such a purchase could a Jewish agricultural class be established in Palestine. I was anxious to help Hankin, and I placed before him my plans for collectivist colonization. Meanwhile Jewish immigration into Palestine kept growing....

I realized soon enough that what I had in mind was not to be found anywhere. Indeed, the experts considered agricultural collectivism ridiculous and were ready to prove that the agricultural commune had never been able to succeed.

At about that time a Jewish comrade of mine, arriving from Russia, asked me to help him raise money for the Jewish self-defense in that country. I collected two hundred thousand francs for that purpose—fifty thousand of it coming from Baron Edmond de Rothschild[4]—and helped him, further, to smuggle arms into Russia.

I re-entered Russia illegally. During the pogrom in Siedlce[5] I took an active part in the Jewish self-defense. Later I organized a national group to exact vengeance from the leaders of Russian antisemitism. The police looked for me in St. Petersburg. I changed my lodgings every day, never sleeping twice in the same place. With clockwork regularity the police always searched, too late, the place I had slept in the night before. My name was unknown to them.

I worked for three months with "The Group of Vengeance."[6] The only Jewish party which supported us was the Territorialist,[7] the party which was looking for a Jewish homeland elsewhere than in Palestine. Later, toward the end of 1906, I returned to Palestine via Constantinople.

Once again I turned to my comrades with the old idea of a collective. I wanted to go to America to raise money for collective colonization in Transjordania and in the Hauran, north of Palestine. I also planned to visit the American collectivist colonies.

Early in 1907 I arrived in America and spent nearly half a year there. I became acquainted with Dr. Judah L. Magnes[8] and with Henrietta Szold.[9] I visited South America, too, taking in the collectivist colonies, and convinced myself at first hand that the agricultural commune could succeed. What we needed was a substitute for the religious enthusiasm which had made these settlements possible, and for this substitute I looked to socialism.

In August 1907 I returned to Palestine via Paris. I had one ideal now—the realization of agricultural collectivism. During my absence the idea had taken somewhat deeper root in Palestine.

In the farm of the ICA (Jewish Colonization Association)[10] at Sejera[11] there were comrades of ours working under the direction of the agronomist Krause.[12] Every year this farm showed a deficit. I said to the ICA: "Give us a chance to work here on our own responsibility, and we'll manage without a deficit."

The opportunity was given us. At Sejera, I worked half-days on the books and the other half-days in the cow-barn. I told Krause that he ought to admit

Source: Manya Shohat, "The Collective," in Rachel Katznelson Shazar, ed., *The Plough Woman: Memoirs of the Pioneer Women of Palestine,* trans. Maurice Samuel (New York: Herzl Press, 1975), pp. 22–26. Reprinted by permission of Herzl Press.

women to the work, and the first three women workers there were the sisters Shturman, Sarah (Krigser), Shifra (Betzer) and Esther (Becker). They were all very young, and they followed the plough like real peasants.

When we founded the collective we were eighteen in all who had drifted together gradually toward Sejera.

We worked on our own responsibility. We arranged our own division of labor. Only once a week, when the program was planned, we would have Krause in for a consultation. We also asked him to give regular lectures on agriculture, and no one who lived with us through that time has forgotten those clear and practical expositions.

The workers on the farm did not have a kitchen of their own, and until the coming of the collective they used to eat out. We organized a communal kitchen, and later on we were even able to feed workers not belonging to our commune.

The name we gave ourselves was, simply, "The Collective." The relations between us and the other workers on the farm were excellent. But they had not faith in our plan and did not believe we would come out without a deficit.

The Sejera Collective lasted a year and a half. It ended its work successfully, paid the farm its fifth of the harvest, returned in full the money that had been advanced, and demonstrated once for all that a collective economy was a possibility.

NOTES

1. Manya Shohat (née Wilbushewitz; 1880–1961) was one of the leading figures of the second *aliyah* and the creation of a Jewish workers' culture in Palestine. Born in Grodno, Belorussia, she developed strong political and socialist concerns in her youth. After an unsuccessful attempt to create a Jewish workers' party and participation in revolutionary politics, she responded to an appeal by her brother Nahum Wilbushewitz (1879–1971), who had recently settled in Palestine, to visit him there. For a year she traveled throughout the country, studying its economic and social conditions. Deeply troubled by the fact that Jewish agricultural settlements were based largely on Arab labor, she concluded that the economic vitality of a Jewish society in Palestine would require Jewish labor. She further concluded that such a development would come about only by the establishment of collective agriculture settlements.

Toward that objective she undertook in 1905 a year-long study tour of communal settlements in the United States and South America. Upon her return to Palestine she became affiliated with a group of like-minded Zionist pioneers led by Israel Shohat (1886–1961), whom she married in 1908. This group had been founded a year earlier as a secret society, *Bar-Giora*, to encourage Jews to learn self-defense. In 1908 *Bar-Giora* became *Hashomer*, the Jewish self-defense organization that played a crucial role in the life of the *yishuv* by hiring itself out as guards of Jewish settlements. Earlier, under Manya Shohat's influence, the group had settled on a training farm in Sejera (now Ilaniyah) in the lower Galilee. In 1907–1908 the training farm's director, Eliayahu Krause, adopted Shohat's proposal to incorporate a collective among the farm workers, thus inaugurating a distinctive institution of Zionist settlement in Palestine (i.e., the *kvuzah* and, later, the *kibbutz*). In this memoir Shohat recalls the beginnings of Sejera. (For a complementary statement by Manya Shohat and for additional biographical information on her, see chapter 7, document 36.) (Cf. Shulamit Reinharz, "Toward a Model of Female Political Action: The Case of Manya Shohat, The Founder of the First Kibbutz," *Women's Studies International Forum* 7, no. 4 (1984), pp. 275–87.)

2. Gedalia Wilbushewitz (1865–1945), a mechanical engineer, settled in Palestine in 1882, where he founded a machine and metal-casting factory in Jaffa, the first Jewish enterprise of its kind in the country.

3. Yehoshua Hankin (1861–1945) was one of the principal architects of Zionist settlement policy in Palestine. Having emigrated to Palestine in 1882, he developed very close relations with the Arabs, which allowed him to play a particularly central role in the purchase of land on behalf of the Zionist movement. After many years of negotiations, he successfully purchased in 1920 a large tract of land in the Jezreel Valley, on which many Jewish settlements were established subsequently. Henceforth, he was widely known as the "Redeemer of the Valley."

4. Baron Edmond James de Rothschild (1845–1934) was a philanthropist and the patron of Jewish settlement in Palestine.

5. Siedlce is a city in eastern Poland, then under Russian rule. In September 1906 the tsarist secret police (*Okhrana*) organized a pogrom against the Jewish population (numbering some 10,000) of the city; 26 Jews were killed, and many more were injured. The Siedlce pogrom was part of a huge wave of government-inspired anti-Jewish riots that broke out in tsarist Russia during the years 1903–1906. In response, an extensive Jewish self-defense

movement arose in many cities and towns. Of the 42 known self-defense units, 30 engaged in battles, in which 132 defenders fell, including three women and several Russians who identified with the Jews' struggle (cf. "Self-Defense." *Encyclopaedia Judaica*, 1st ed., 14:1126).

6. Founded following the pogrom in Siedlce, the Group of Vengeance was a Jewish terrorist organization bent on exacting "vengeance against the leaders of Russian antisemitism" (cf. Shulamit Reinharz, "Toward a Model of Female Political Action: The Case of Manya Shohat," *Women's Studies International Forum* 7, no. 4 (1984), p. 283.

7. On Territorialism, see document 18 of this chapter.

8. On Judah L. Magnes, see chapter 9, document 38.

9. Henrietta Szold (1860–1945) was an American educator and social worker. She was one of the most outstanding personalities of the Zionist movement in the United States, where in 1912 she founded Hadassah, the Women's Zionist Organization of America. She settled in Palestine in 1920, where she directed many projects on behalf of Hadassah; with the rise of Hitler to power, she also devoted herself to Youth Aliyah, which sought to facilitate the passage of children and youth from Europe and their settlement in Palestine. See chapter 9, document 31.

10. On the Jewish Colonization Association, see chapter 7, document 31, note 1.

11. See note 1.

12. Eliyahu Krause (1876–1962) emigrated to Palestine from his native Russia in 1892. An agronomist, he was in the employ of the Jewish Colonization Association (ICA), which in 1899 took over the administration of Baron de Rothschild's various projects in Palestine. In 1901 the ICA founded in Sejera a training farm for Jewish settlers and appointed Krause the farm's manager. Without his cooperation, Manya Shohat and her comrades could not have realized their program to establish a collective at Sejera. In 1915 Krause became director of Mikveh Israel Agricultural School, a position he held until his retirement in 1954.

25. FOUNDING PROGRAM (MAY 1912)

AGUDAT ISRAEL[1]

The purpose of *Agudat Israel* is the solution of the respective tasks facing the Jewish collectivity, in the spirit of the Torah. In accordance with this purpose, it sets itself the following goals: (1) the organization, concentration and unification of dispersed parts of Orthodox Jewry, especially of the Jews in Eastern and Western Europe; (2) the generous promotion of Torah studies, and of Jewish education in general, in countries where this promotion is needed; (3) the improvement of economic conditions of the Jewish masses, not only in Palestine, but wherever they suffer want; (4) the organization and promotion of emergency aid in cases of necessity; (5) the advancement of a press and literature in the [traditional] Jewish spirit; (6) a representative forum of all Jews adhering to the Torah; this forum will parry the attacks directed against the Torah and its adherents.

Against this work of unifying Orthodox Jewry, a stock objection is raised in a part of the national [i.e., Zionist] Jewish press which states that Agudat Israel lacks a clear program. In this respect, Agudat Israel is unfavourably compared with Zionism.

Source: "Zum Programm der Agudas Jisroel," in *Agudas Jisroel: Berichte und Materialien*, ed. Provisorischen Comité der Agudas Jisroel zu Frankfurt am Main (Frankfurt am Main: Buero der Agudas Jisroel, 1912), pp. 151–52. Trans. by J. Hessing.

This much is correct: Zionism has not only set up a general program, but is fortunate enough to be able to outline the way in which it hopes to find a definite solution to all Jewish problems. The "national home secured by public law," for which the first battle was fought in Basle, is considered to be the panacea for all national ailments. It is only for this means, transformed into an end, that the Zionists are ready to mobilize and organize their forces.

Agudat Israel, on the other hand—or so they claim—has no program of redemption. And an organization without a program, it is held, is tantamount to an organization without a clear purpose suspended in midair without a foundation and without a supporting pillar.

It can be argued [however] that the general task of Orthodox Jewry has from ancient times been clearly and programmatically defined, and that for its propagation there is no need for any other base than that which has supported and united us through centuries of suffering. New currents and movements must be based on newly created foundations. The work of unification on behalf of Orthodox Jewry does not derive from any new and revolutionary idea. It only wishes to unify, collect and conserve on the basis of our ancient program.

NOTE

1. *Agudat Israel* (Union of Israel) is a world organization of Orthodox Jewry that had learned from the World Zionist Organization that in order to advance the international and political interests of the Jewish people, it must first be organized as a coherent political body. Appreciating the efficacy of politics and mass organization in modern society, Orthodox Jews were alarmed that their secular and assimilated brethren of the World Zionist Organization would assume the mantle of Jewish leadership and the exclusive right to voice the demands and ideals of Jewry before the world. Moreover, modern organizational means had helped the Zionists—and other non-Orthodox and secular trends—to influence Jewish communal and cultural life. The endorsement by the Tenth Zionist Congress (1911) of the cultural program of secular Zionism, which was construed by Orthodox Jewry as lending prestige and legitimacy to secular Judaism, was the immediate spur behind the founding of Agudat Israel. The founding convention, initiated by the Neo-Orthodox community of Germany, met at Kattowitz, Upper Silesia, in May 1912. Attended by 227 Orthodox Jewish leaders from Russia, Austria, Germany, Hungary, and Palestine, the convention reaffirmed in its program the unimpeachable authority of Torah and halakhah in governing Jewish life and priorities. *Agudat Israel* opposed the Zionist program as a profanation of Judaism because it attempted to revive Jewish patrimony in the Holy Land through human agency and because it prompted a secular Jewish society there. On the other hand, Agudat Israel, particularly since the Holocaust, regards the land of Israel as the center—both spiritual and physical—of "Torah-true" Jewry.

26. THE LANGUAGE WAR OF 1913 (JUNE 2, 1913)[1]

HIGH SCHOOL STUDENTS IN *ERETZ YISRAEL*

17 Sivan 5673
[2 June 1913]

The Honorable Board of Directors
The Technion in Haifa
Mr. Asher Ginsberg [Ahad Haam]

We are shocked and astonished to learn that in the Technion, which is about to open in Haifa, Hebrew will not be the language of instruction. It is impossible for us, students in Hebrew schools in Eretz Israel, to acquiesce in this idea.

We have received our Hebrew [i.e., Jewish] knowledge and general development through the medium of the Hebrew language; from our childhood we have been educated on the knees of the language of our people in the land of the patriarchs. We speak, learn and think in Hebrew, and only in Hebrew.

We have demonstrated to the entire world that only the Hebrew language can and should serve as the language of speech and instruction in our land; we have placed so much hope in the only institution of higher learning to be established in our land, we delighted our soul with the hope of continuing directly our development and to receive a complete Hebrew education.

We students, who are about to complete our studies in the secondary schools in Eretz Israel, stand on the threshold of a higher education [and] herewith express the fervent indignation bursting from our hearts against those who dare breach [the position] of the Hebrew language in our land and who thus undermine the foundations of our young culture, the fruit of a gigantic national effort. There is no language in the world that could take the place of Hebrew in our thought and knowledge!

We therefore demand from all those involved in the Technion and concerned that it be a *Hebrew* institution of learning, from those who are creating in the Technion an educational shelter for the youth of our people in general and, in particular, for us, the children of this land, that they give our language its proper place in the Technion.

THE LANGUAGE OF THE TECHNION CAN AND MUST BE HEBREW!

Students of the upper class of the Teachers Seminary and the Commercial High School, Jerusalem. [Followed by 12 signatures]

Students of the eighth grade of "Herzliah" Hebrew Gymnasia in Jaffa. [followed by 23 signatures]

NOTE

1. Since its early settlement in Palestine (Eretz Israel), the Zionist movement sought to assure that Hebrew would be the language of the new *yishuv*. Toward this end, the Hebraization of the educational system became a primary objective. Initially, the various networks of modern schools established by Jewish organizations from abroad—the Alliance Israélite Universelle, the Hilfsverein der deutschen Juden, and the Anglo-Jewish Association—sought to foster the language of their respective countries. Gradually, they gave way to Hebrew. In addition, the Zionist movement established its own system of schools in which Hebrew was naturally the language of instruction. Suddenly, in 1913, the campaign to Hebraize the Jewish educational system seemed to face a serious setback. In October of that year the board of governors of the nascent Technion, an engineering university whose cornerstone had been laid the previous year on the slopes of Mt. Carmel, Haifa, decided that the primary language of instruction

Source: Central Zionist Archives, Jerusalem. Trans. P. Mendes-Flohr.

of what was to be the country's first institution of higher education would be German. Although the sponsoring organization of the Technion, the Hilfsverein, had earlier introduced Hebrew as the language of instruction in a large number of subjects in the schools it operated in Palestine, it reversed its policy, apparently under pressure from the German government.

A "language war" broke out. The Hebrew Teachers Association (*Histadrut Hamorim*) led the battle. Meeting in Jaffa in August 1913, the association issued the following resolution: "The principles of national education demand that all subjects of instruction shall be taught in the Hebrew language, and this meeting pledges that the members of the Teachers Association will fight with all their energy against the teaching of secular subjects in a foreign language." Teachers and prospective students were called upon to boycott the Technion. Protests and student strikes were held. Pressure was placed on the non-Hilfsverein members of the Technion's board of governors. The letter reprinted here, by the graduating seniors of three of the country's leading Hebrew secondary schools, was addressed to Asher Ginsberg (Ahad Haam), who was among the minority of Zionist personalities sitting on the board. The controversy (as well as the outbreak of World War I) delayed the opening of the Technion. When it did open in December 1924, it did so as an all-Hebrew institution.

27. THE HEBREW BOOK (1913)[1]

HAIM NAHMAN BIALIK

Literary-minded Jews have long been perplexed by a strange phenomenon. Our literature, which is thousands of years old, comprises tens of thousands of volumes, and represents the many creative forces of hundreds of generations. It is therefore highly varied in form and content Our modern literature also abounds in excellent talent. There are likewise many important literary works by Jews written in foreign languages. Yet, for all this wealth, we are hardly in a position to indicate to the contemporary Jew with a taste for literature even a limited number of such books as could become sufficiently significant to him and precious enough for him to turn to for spiritual sustenance.

Our wonder is even greater since we know that our people, which is naturally inclined to cherish and ponder over books, has at all times derived spiritual satisfaction from delving into this treasure-house, each individual pursuing his own favorite interest. In all ages there were in our voluminous literature a given number of books of permanent value, whether complete or anthological in nature, which for long periods had graced the Jew's reading-desk. These books deserved to be called, without any reservations, "the books of a people," because they were a source of enjoyment to every class of Jews, the highest as well as the lowest.

There are generally few books of enduring worth that represent the creative powers of a single individual, however great. Yet, a body of literary works which singly appears rather unimportant, in the aggregate forms at times an important literary phenomenon which deserves to be pondered over and delved into by every Jewish reader in every age. There has not been a single period which to some extent, even if it did not produce great works of its own, did not make

Source: Bialik, *The Hebrew Book: An Essay*, trans. Minnie Halkin (Jerusalem: The Bialik Institute, 1951), pp. 5–18.

some permanent contribution to posterity. At its close, each such era of necessity deposited behind it a sort of layer, thick or thin, which finally became the soil for the spiritual crops of the succeeding period. That layer must pass on from father to sons in its original character and essence. And the sons, too, if they do not wish to sow in the wind must constantly turn over that soil, plough and harrow it again and again to the best of their abilities; for without soil there can be no growth; and if a literature lacks tradition and continuity, it is deprived of growth and development and self-renewal.

It is not only impudence and unheard-of ingratitude, but it bespeaks profound ignorance to think that everything in our literature that was created by the nation as a whole and by its spiritual giants over thousands of years is of no value today. What then *is* of value? That which has been written by some certain somebody from a certain year onward?

For thousands of years our people thought and felt as does every speech-endowed organism; in all its metamorphoses it expressed itself in various ways and styles and forms; many men of feeling and thought, great, average and mediocre, appeared who drew their inspiration from the fountain-head of our national life, from its "holy spirit," shedding at the same time their own spirit upon the people. Among these were giants who by virtue of their spiritual strength diverted the whole national train in one sweep onto some new road. The nation has experienced many spiritual revolutions—revolutions which left deep marks upon all its ways of life and upon all its literary pursuits. Is it possible then that all these are of nought when compared with what has been created by one or another given author beginning with this or that given year?

If the term *literature* connotes not merely *belles-letters*, but mainly signifies the sum total of the expression of national thought and feeling in every manner of literary form during the different ages—then our modern literature, when compared with that which preceded it, is no more than a drop in the sea. It suffices merely to indicate the known sub-divisions of the literature: the Bible, the Apocryphal Writings, the Talmud in its two principal aspects—Halakhah and Agadah—Philosophy, Kabbalah, Poetry, Ethics, Homiletics, Chassidism, Folk-literature. Each of these names represents an entire era, with its own special physiognomy, with special content and form, and with its own individual atmosphere; each name testifies to a new turn of the wheel of Jewish thought, and a new scale of emotions. It is enough, I say, to enumerate them one by one in order to comprehend what great wealth is still preserved for us even in these, our ancient treasuries.

If to this we also add the limited number of works produced by our modern literature, which I do not mean to minimize at all—we will have a large, important, literary heritage, of which we need not at all be ashamed, and by which entire generations may be nurtured. Nevertheless, we are aware that we have now arrived at a period of great spiritual distress. Each of us who has "gorged himself" upon the Hebrew literature of all ages, the best as well as the inferior, undoubtedly has more than once experienced the pain similar to the sufferings of Tantalus:[2] one's elder son or friend requests a book or a set of Hebrew books by means of which he may familiarize himself with our national creativity as presented through choice selections from original works; and he, who has been asked, stands there before our mountainous collective heritage and has difficultly in answering. Mountains of books—and not a single book.

Modern Hebrew literature, aside from the fact that to this very day it has not been sanctioned by an important part of the people as its guide and teacher, is in its very nature quantitatively limited. It possesses enough for but slight tasting, just a lick, but not sufficient for one to eat to one's heart's content, to one's fill. There is the old literature? . . . But who of our contemporaries is willing to enter this labyrinth? And should he enter—will he find his way out? Why, it is really impossible honestly and wholeheartedly to advise our contemporary, the mere reader, to dig by himself for days and years in those great piles of ancient and classical literature, in order to extract therefrom some measure of their distilled vitality, the creative element underlying them? Such labor is for professional experts, specially trained for the task and not for a mere reader, no matter how earnest he may be.

There are also creative works by Jews in foreign languages. But these, even if we take them into account as part of our literature—a matter which is at any rate subject to limitations—as long as they remain in their foreign tongues, must be considered as non-existent. Are we to require of every Jew the knowledge of all the languages of the civilized world?

What are we to do then for our contemporary Jew who wants to know the creative literary activity of the Jewish people through the best illustrations culled from all periods? That is, how can we, on the one hand, humanly adjust all that is vital in our old literature, and how, on the other, are we to obtain national approval of our more recent literature?

"The Jewish Encyclopedia" which Ahad Haam conceived of several years ago is not pertinent to the question.[3] A work *on* the knowledge of Judaism is one thing, while actual knowledge in their *original* of the very literary works produced by Judaism is another. For all the national importance of "the Jewish Encyclopedia" it in itself will never satisfy the Jewish reader who wishes to understand Jewish creative works themselves, not only through books and articles written about them—and that is what a Jewish Encyclopedia should consist of—but necessarily from them and through them themselves. The serious searching reader wishes to and must know the "genius" of his people at first hand and not through an intermediary.

The great libraries of collected works that others publish are not likely to relieve the situation either. The best of them deserve praise insofar only as they produce Hebrew books for the market. And for this, of course, we thank them, but they will never, under any circumstances, bring us "*the* Hebrew Book," that book which we are praying for. For that purpose they lack the essential requirement: a supreme idea, a central and basic idea. By merely publishing books, old as well as new, the gaps between the different literary periods have not yet been bridged, and needless to say, they will not produce that perfect literary selection which is our chief concern and which, perhaps, has been far beyond the powers of any private commercial publishing house.

There is only one way, to my mind, in which to extricate ourselves from the aforesaid spiritual straits, an example of which we have in our literary history. Each time that our literature found itself in a situation similar to the present one it necessarily sought a way out in this manner. We must resort to it this time, too—the phenomenon of literary "*ingathering*," that which is known in our literary history by the name of "*canonization*."[4]

The phenomenon of "*canonization*" occurred, as is known, three times in our literature: the canonization of the Holy Scriptures, the canonization of the Mishnah, the canonization of the Talmud. Each time it was accompanied, as if shadowed, by another phenomenon, secondary to it: the "*Genizah*" (concealment of excluded material). An explanation of these two concomitant phenomena is approximately as follows: from among the ancient literary works, which during a certain period accumulated upon the back of the nation like a mountain and became too burdensome, the works which were considered most important and most cherished by that particular generation were collected and arranged. The rest automatically remained outside, or, according to an ancient expression: were "doomed to concealment"—*genizah* (the Apocryphal works and the *Baraitas*[5]). This work, which was carried on (of course not all at once) by a group of representative scholars loyal to the spirit of the people, was a great national undertaking, a sacred task. It not only saved the nation from confusion and distraction, and not only offered it the opportunity of enjoying its spiritual wealth, but it also opened up before it, through the release of great stores of energy, paths by which to enter into a new literary era, an era of different content and new forms.

As long as the process of selection has not been performed with regard to the old literature, the mind of the nation and its individual members cannot be predisposed to the unqualified absorption of new literary values and even less to creating them. Only after a tree has shed its old fruits does it begin to bear new ones. Every canonization announced the close of an old era while at the same time it heralds the dawning of a new one. Moreover, after the exalted essence of the old has safely passed through the new atmosphere and come out of it purified, it becomes itself soil for new plants, providing them with moisture and nourishment and helping them grow and blossom.

The "canonization," with the *genizah* alongside it, is, therefore, simultaneously a process of unloading and loading. On the one hand it removes from the heart of the people the heavy load of ethical responsibility which rests upon it as a voluntary keeper of dead assets. Henceforth it is no longer obliged, against its will, to submit to useless watching over mountains of sand for the sake of the pearls in it—pearls from which it derives no benefit whatsoever. If this responsibility is difficult for a people "settled on its lees," it is infinitely more difficult for an exiled, wandering people which must carry mountains of sand on its back from place to place. From now on the custodianship of these dead assets is turned over to the keepers of the *genizah* and the archives—and the people is free from responsibility. On the other hand, canonization extracts and deposits in the hands of the people the pearls themselves, so that they may reap immediate benefits from them, and that they may hand them down to future generations for their enjoyment.

There are those who fear the word *genizah*. According to conventional opinion, it has caused us great losses. There are also those who will regard this as the imposition of a censorship, decreeing upon the public: "Read this! Do not read that!"—This is a groundless fear, based upon utterly false reasoning. The canonization and the *genizah* are to a certain extent, if not completely, effected automatically, by life itself. Are not entire sections of our literature relegated to *genizah* even in our own days? The people ceases to peruse them—hence *genizah*. Consequently, in our own times, we must regard as consigned to concealment, or excluded, even a large section of our old literature, by which only a generation ago, most of the people were still nourished and lived upon. The work of the scholars responsible for that "canonization" was chiefly of a positive nature, consisting in the preservation of the vital remnant of the past, namely, in gathering, collecting and arranging the best and the finest, the most vital and the most perfect works produced by the literature up to their time and which often lay buried in heaps of worthless material. They intended only to winnow the chaff from the wheat, and if the wind would of itself carry away the chaff—let it carry it! Even conscious *genizah*, if designed against the insignificant and the trite, is good for the literature, just as pruning is for the trees. As a result of it the trunk is strengthened and puts forth new branches and strong roots. And if one is to ask, *who* is to decide? *Who* is to be the one to select and choose?—The views of the people and its taste, or, as the ancient idiom would have it, "the holy spirit" (*ruah ha-kodesh*) of the people? We have no other criterion at the moment. The scholars are but the spiritual representatives of the people and of necessity they submit to the dictates of reality, often even against their own personal inclinations....If we wish to restore to our literature some of its vital force and its influence upon our people, we must, among other things, in the field of literature and education...produce a new "collection," national, of

course, not religious, of the best works in Hebrew literature of all times.

From every field of our literature, from every nook and corner in which there is concealed a bit of the holy spirit of the people, a bit of the creative force of the finest of its personalities—we must draw forth from all of them the sparks which are being lost and driven away, and elevate them and combine them so that they may become one complete unit in the possession of the people. We must not be, of course, dependent in everything upon the anthological methods of the ancients. On the contrary, we shall be absolutely free in this matter. The ancients did their work faithfully in their own way, guided by the views and tastes which prevailed in their own times, and by the spiritual needs of their contemporaries. In our times requirements and thoughts have changed and with them many of the literary values. But the attitude towards this work should be the same in all periods, an attitude imbued with the recognition of the great responsibility which is placed by the people upon all who attempt to deal with its holy of holies, I should say: an attitude of sanctification.

I know that books and literature are profanities in our times. In the eyes of many they are like any other commodity. But true creativity scorns the marketplace and its tumult. Its life is eternal, its sacredness everlasting. Sooner or later, willingly or unwillingly, human beings accept its authority and open their hearts to its influence.

Let the people feel that it has but one place in the world which is all purity, and a receptacle for the spiritual activity of all ages; let it know and recognize that this work, which is being carried out for the sake of the people and its spiritual creativity, has nothing in it of the profane or impure thought and aspiration, but is designed merely at rescuing its own spiritual honor and immortality—and you will see that the people will acknowledge your work and bless your name.

It is unnecessary for me to state that the connotation of the term "canonization" as referred to here is not the traditional one. I have used it only to catch the ear; but substitute for it: "collection," "anthology," or some other similar term. It certainly does not have to be pointed out that this anthological activity is not meant to diminish in the least the creative activity of the present or in any way to deter its progress. Neither exclusion nor retardation is intended. The collection comes to add and not to detract. "When the word went forth"—says the legend—"the whole world stood still and was silent"—perhaps that was true when the Word went forth, but during the process of compilation, the world neither stands still nor is it silent, but conducts itself in its usual manner. Creativity does not cease, its thread spins on beyond all boundaries, and of its own accord joins the web of all the generations. And moreover: we shall recognize the stamp of the age even upon the body of the compilers. The spirit of the age will spontaneously betray itself in the result of their work, in between chapters and in between lines. What is important in this kind of work is the spirit which prevails within the hidden recesses of the heart, and excepting for the concrete contribution of our contemporaries in the form of new "introductions" to old works, and the like, that same hidden spirit will be like a new accretion to the "previous," and unconscious accretion without any intention to add. Everything depends upon the manner of selection of the material, and, above all, the manner of integrating it. New combinations of old material build the world and destroy the world, uproot centers and replant them elsewhere. All the old material, after it has been wrenched out of its environment and passed through the new taste and new spirit of our times—will of itself be lit up from within and from without by an entirely new light. Even our inner attitude to it will be altogether different from that of former eras. It is destined to become a new being.

That "collection" or "compilation," whatever you may wish to call it, which is to be produced by a group of outstanding contemporary scholars and writers, must include, as has been stated, the best of the literary works of all times from the very beginning to the present. And when all the material has been selected and arranged according to a previously set plan and in accordance with a single basic system and idea, with one great national purpose—of necessity, one supreme spirit will hover over that entire work and its results from the beginning to the end. The gap between the ancient and the modern literature will thus be filled in of itself, and from now on there will be but one Hebrew literature. In its details it will, of course, subdivide into periods, gradations, various hues and shades, etc., etc., but in its essence it will be one, its national sacredness will be one, and its name will be one—Hebrew literature.

In the bookcase of the literary-minded Jew there will again appear some important volumes: a new Talmud which will contain the choice essence of the results of Jewish thought and feeling throughout the ages. And he who will drink from it will quench his own spiritual thirst and that of his children.

The Hebrew book will regain its pristine glory—it will become a vital necessity as well as an ornament for every Jewish home. The Jewish heart will cling to its sources and the bond between Hebrew thought and literature will be renewed.

And who knows, perhaps even those who have drifted far away will return and seek paths to the well from which their ancestors drank. Let them not find it choked up with dust and clods. . . .

NOTES

1. The poet laureate of modern Hebrew, Haim Nahman Bialik (see chapter 7, document 27) delivered this essay—*Ha-Sefer ha-ivri*—first as a lecture at the Second Conference on Hebrew Language and Culture that took place in Vienna during the summer of 1913. Published a year later in the monthly review *Hashiloah*, the essay is a manifesto for what he called *"kinus,"* a selective ingathering and anthologizing of the millennial literary resources of the Jewish people in all languages but primarily in Hebrew. The cultural renaissance sponsored by Zionism and the revival of Hebrew as the national idiom of the Jewish people, he insisted, cannot thrive without taking root in the spiritual treasures of Israel's past. "If a literature lacks tradition and continuity, it is deprived of growth and development and self-renewal." The envisioned *kinus* is a form of a new "canonization"—*kinus* is a term Bialik admittedly used only in order "to catch the ear; but substitute for it: 'collection,' 'anthology,' or some similar term"—was meant not only to provide the immense, unwieldy library of Israel's cultural legacy but also to render it through a judicious selection and arrangement that would be accessible to the contemporary Jew. "The essential purpose of *kinus* is to give to all literate Jews the ability to recognize the creative foundation of the literature of Israel from all periods, based on the original text to the extent that it was possible." Bialik exemplified his conception of *kinus* when in 1908 he began to publish (together with Y. H. Ravnitski) *Sefer ha-aggadah*, a three-volume collection of legends and imaginative homiletic literature drawn from the Midrash and Talmud. This monumental project, which underwent numerous editions, served as a wellspring of modern Hebrew

literature. On Bialik's *kinus*, see Adam Rubin, "Like a Necklace of Black Pearls Whose String Has Snapped, and Bialik's *'Aron ha-sfarim'* and the Sacralization of Zionism." *Prooftexts*, 26/2 (Spring 2008), pp. 157–96. On the ramified anthological discourse within Zionism and the twentieth-century Jewish renaissance, see Martina Urban, *Aesthetics of Renewal: Martin Buber's Early Representation of Hasidism as Kulturkritik* (Chicago: University of Chicago Press, 2008), chapter 2.

2. Tantalus was the son of Zeus who was to share in the food of the gods, but because he apparently abused the privilege was punished by being cruelly "tantalized." Suffering from thirst, he was immersed up to his neck in fresh water, but when he bent over to drink, the water was suddenly drained away; desperately hungry he found himself in arms reach of luscious fruit hanging from a tree, but when he reached to grab it, the wind blew the branches beyond his reach.

3. The reference is an ultimately aborted project by Ahad Haam (see document 9 of this chapter) to edit an encyclopedia on Jews and Judaism, *Otzar ha-Yahadut* (the treasure of Judaism). As a presentation of the cultural and national heritage of Judaism in a scholarly and secular perspective, he hoped, the planned encyclopedia would foster the cultural and spiritual orientation that he deemed to be a necessary for the work of Zionism and the settlement of Eretz Israel.

4. For *canonization*, Bialik used the Hebrew term *chatimah*, closure.

5. *Baraita* is an Aramaic term designating a tannaite tradition that was not incorporated into the Mishnah; later it was applied also to collections of such traditions (*Barayata* is the plural of *Baraita*).

28. CONTRA ZIONISM (1919)

NATHAN BIRNBAUM[1]

When Jewish minds first conceived the notion that utter brightness exists in the outside, non-Jewish world, and that Jews live in utter darkness—moreover, that one should introduce this light into that darkness—at that point our oppression by fellow Jews began.

In the beginning, our enlighteners still pitied us, as if we were unfortunate idlers. But soon their pity changed to anger. Can you imagine? *They* want to transform us into "proper human beings": into doctors, salesmen, specialists in innkeeping, movie theaters and saloons—and *we* have the nerve to resist!

The fact is that we intuitively resist this. The fact is that our feelings, our sensitivities will not allow it. The fact is that our ancient faith refuses any credence of these new "triumphs." The fact is that the Gentile peoples are also beginning to tire gradually of these "enlightened" folk with their obscuring "enlightenment."

Such contentions do not suffice for our whole-sale and retail merchants of "light." The Jews of the Enlightenment are not to be trifled with; they sit haughtily and give themselves airs, until a veritable cloud of arrogance surrounds them. After all, haven't they revealed all the secrets of the universe, unraveled all its puzzles? We, however, who are we?: merely paupers who wait empty handed before some purported heavenly throne. They have concluded that one must

Source: Nathan Birnbaum, *In golus bay yidn* (1919), abridged in *Dos yidishe vort* (October 1963), pp. 76–77; trans. in Joshua A. Fishman, *Ideology, Society and Language. The Odyssey of Nathan Birnbaum* (Ann Arbor: Karoma Publishers, 1987), pp. 231–38. Reprinted by permission of Karoma Publishers.

"go with the times," even run with the times, even sin with the times. But we, however, who are we? We are no more than backward folk who subordinate the thought of all generations to the Almighty's commandments. They are modern people, aware of progress. More machines, more politics, more entertainment, more theories, more hypotheses will be the salvation of the world. We, however, who are we? Strange idlers whose souls ask strange questions: How does one spiritually elevate oneself from one level to the next?; how does one become that which God commanded?

It did not suffice to present us with the benefits of their enlightenment; they also felt compelled to bring us other gifts, more "innovations." The first was Justice and Law. The world is all entangled in problems and must be straightened out. There must be no difference between one person and another, between rich and poor. What is yours is mine and, perhaps, just possibly, what is mine is yours.

Apparently, were it not for them, we would never have heard of Justice and Law. Apparently, it is not written in the Torah, "Thou shalt love thy neighbor as thyself." Apparently the Torah pays no attention to the obligations of people toward one another. Apparently the prophets either never lived or never stepped forward against human injustices, never demanded Justice and Law. Apparently there is no ancient Jewish longing, a longing for renewed humanity, with renewed virtuous feelings and renewed consecrated deeds. Apparently there is no ancient Jewish belief, a belief that on Judgment Day, the Messiah will arrive and redeem not only the Jewish people but all peoples and will implant new hearts into one and all.

As for them, not only do they fail to see with whom they are dealing, with whom they are going to renew the world. They do not even look at themselves—at what has become of them. They confront violence with violence. They would build their new wonders on lawlessness, on unchastity and on the infantile megalomania of mortal men. Instead of pulling us out of the mire, they sink us deeper and deeper into it.

We are not deceived, however. We have not forgotten that "the heathen rage and the people imagine a vain thing." We do not make uncertain deals with peoples and nations that are not trustworthy. We know that violence cannot erase violence; that lawlessness, unchastity and megalomania cannot

rectify the world; that only faith in God leads to sanctity. Consequently, we remain with our way—with our Torah, which has rooted out the violent nature within us and directed us to become a people of peace and understanding. Consequently, we remain with our Torah, on whose foundation we will continue to seek self-improvement and spiritual elevation, from one level to another, until the Almighty ordains that the world be filled with understanding, Justice and Law.

They have brought us a third gift, a third tiding, a third discovery: that we are a people. Apparently, if not for them, we would never have become aware of this. It would seem that in the Torah we are never referred to as a nationality, a people, an ethnonational entity. It seems that, until now, we have considered ourselves Tartars, Turks, Germans and Russians.

So what is the difference between their views and ours?

To them a people is a community of individuals who differentiate themselves from other communities only in that they have historically developed a worldliness of a different color. "It is the same woman, but differently veiled." To them, the Jewish people is a people like all other peoples; we must be as foolish as they: learn their ways, their insolence, their materialistic ideals.

We are aware, however, of a higher level of nationhood than that of being merely a "differently veiled woman." A people can and should be a unique creation, with a unique soul and unique content to comprise its peoplehood. And there is no gainsaying that the Jewish people is such a people with a unique nature, with a unique soul, chosen from among all other peoples.

According to them, the Land of Israel is an enlarged city of refuge, a place to which one flees. To them, Israel is terra incognita that, on one fine morning, they declared to be their "fatherland"—and where they want to settle in accord with the usual approach of the nations of the world to their fatherlands—with the maximum "light" possible: enlightened theaters, enlightened cabarets, enlightened conflicts and violence—and without the Jewish religion, without God and without the holy Torah.

For us, Israel is not some terra incognita that only now, in order to rescue ourselves, have we been reminded of our connection to. It had never left our thoughts. We have never ceased to love and to long for it. We want to fulfill the commandment of settling in the Land of Israel and to do so with all our power and love, because of the holiness of sanctity, because of the holiness of that land which must not be desecrated, God forbid.

For them, peoplehood depends primarily on language. Whoever speaks Hebrew or Yiddish is a Jew, in the same way that anyone who speaks Turkish is a Turk. For them, language is a toy. They play with Hebrew in a haughty way and with Yiddish in playboy fashion.

For us, Hebrew is the holy tongue. Our attitude toward the holy tongue is one of amazement and of great love and respect. We regard the Holy Tongue as the tongue in which God's word is written, as the tongue in which the prophets wrote and warned, as the tongue which has become as eternal as the Jewish people—and will never die. Therefore, we want this tongue to remain the Holy Tongue, to remain free of any and all impurity or defilement.

Yiddish is loved and cherished by us because it is the language of our fathers and mothers, the language that the Jews of Eastern Europe have spoken for hundreds of years and into which they have infused their Jewish souls and which they have permeated with their Jewishness.

We love both languages, Hebrew and Yiddish, each with a different love. But we also realize that before this love comes the love of "You shall love the Lord, your God." We realize that "He has lifted us above all languages," indeed, that He has made us higher than language per se.

They approach us with friendly words and with palpable lies, with their temptations to evil, in order to set us upon the European way of life, to transform us into "decent people." They search for slogans by means of which to reach our children, to seize and try to take away our holy Torah and our Jewish way of life for themselves and for their ideologies, for their lawless world. Can there be any greater and more dangerous oppression than this? . . .

We must remain that which we have been until now—those who do not voluntarily open their souls to temptations of evil but who combat it in order to conquer it—those who prefer the unobtrusive holiness of the house of study and synagogue to the modern political and party hustle and bustle. And we must also attempt to ascend, to strive for spiritual improvement. Yes, that is the honest truth!

And if we are reminded of this truth by those who remain distant from unobtrusive holiness and who are drenched in falsehood and partiality up to their necks—then we must be on our guard.

What would happen if their political hustle and bustle were to score a total victory over our people and the destruction, already so great, were to grow and multiply and the unobtrusive holiness were to be totally wiped out as a result?

And what would happen if there were to be no people left among whom our most dedicated could work on behalf of spiritual uplift and improvement, including the very best among us, with the highest apolitical strivings? Is it possible that by maintaining Jewishness as our only treasure we will ever be able to become expert demagogues, such as they are?

Should we try to attain their perfection in banging and noise making? Is it necessary? We are, after all, the mountains, and they the particles of dust. We merely need to collect our forces into a worldwide organization of the religious. Only in this way, and without grand political trickery, will we be able to prevent that which must be prevented and to accomplish that which must be accomplished. And such a worldwide organization of religious Jews need not first be formed at this time. It already exists and its name is well known. It is called *Agudes Yisroel*.

NOTE

1. Nathan Birnbaum (1864–1937) was an author and publicist. His life was marked by a spiritual odyssey leading from Zionism (political, then cultural) to Diaspora nationalism (of which he became one of the leading spokesmen) and Yiddishism (he was among the architects of the Czernowitz Conference of 1908) to an eventual rejection of secular conceptions of Judaism. In the years preceding World War I he gradually turned to religion, embracing in the end Ultra-Orthodox beliefs and practice. Upon the refounding of World Agudat Israel (*Agudes Yisroel* in Yiddish) in 1919 he served as its first secretary-general. It was during his tenure in this position that he issued the statement presented here, in which he condemns the Zionist movement for serving as an instrument to further Jewry's shameless assimilation, thus betraying Israel's pristine vocation to be the People of God. The fact that this erstwhile leader of Zionism and, indeed, the originator—in a pamphlet of 1893—of the very term of the movement reached this conclusion, needless to say, greatly encouraged the Ultra-Orthodox community.

29. A DEBATE ON ZIONISM AND MESSIANISM (SUMMER 1916)[1]

MARTIN BUBER AND HERMANN COHEN

BUBER: Herr Professor Cohen, you state that you view nationality only as a "fact of nature." [It is therefore not surprising] that you use the terms "nationality," "stock" [*Stamm*] and "origin" as synonyms. But how could you, from your viewpoint of a strict pristine monotheism, treat the origin [of the Jewish people] as a mere "fact of nature"? The primeval Jewish concept of "seed" appears everywhere that God makes and renews His covenant with Abraham and Abraham's descendants.... And the principle of covenant, you would agree, is not a "fact of nature," but an expression of God's dynamic purpose and presence in history?...

No, nationality cannot be defined through the concept of "fact of nature." Nationality is a historical reality and a moral duty. To be sure, it also has its roots in the natural, but so too does our humanity. Nevertheless, nature cannot contain us within the borders of its [merely empirical] reality. The idea of humanity can only be realized in the spiritual struggle of mankind, in infinite striving. The same is true for love, art and knowledge. They all have their roots in facts of nature. But we cannot become conscious of their meaning until we change "whence" into "whither" and origin into goal, until the understanding of how they became what they are turns into the insight concerning what should become of them, until that which is given us as fact becomes that which is given us as task. It is then that nature becomes spirit....

Zionism never equated religion with nationality, as you claim. But neither will it ever allow nationhood [*Volkstum*] to be relegated to an anthropological means for the propagation of religion. Rather, every Zionist for whom, as for me, religiosity stands at the core of Judaism will, like me, know and acknowledge that Jewish religiosity is a function, the highest function of the dynamic Jewish nationhood.... This Jewish religiosity is a function that is not merely unable to propagate itself without its bearer, as you suppose. No, in such a case it could not continue to exist. Jewish religiosity thrives on the blood of the nation, is nourished by the nation's natural forces and operates through its will. Without the vitality of the nation, without its ardent and long-suffering power, Jewish religiosity would have no place on earth. What is valid for history is also valid for the life of the individual: the idea [of Judaism] cannot be realized if [Jewish] nationhood is not actualized. But what truly matters is the realization. Nationality, as a simple fact of nature, is a fiction, the same way that humanity as a simple fact of nature is a fiction. Only when we first view nationality as a reality of the spirit and ethos can we also turn it into a reality in our own lives....

[You call for a] clarification of concepts—but are concepts the issue here? Can the question of the Jewish people be settled by terminology? Can the naturalness and sincerity of a national feeling be proven by a definition?...

Zionist literature, you write, "indulges in frivolous derision of the most sublime idea of the Jewish religion," namely, messianism. Where and when? I believe I know Zionist literature well, and I cannot recollect one passage which would substantiate your claim. On the contrary, messianism has been

Source: Martin Buber, "Begriffe und Wirklichkeit, Brief an Herrn Geh. Regierungsrat Prof. Dr. Hermann Cohen," *Der Jude* (July 1916), no. 5, pp. 281ff.; Hermann Cohen, "Antwort auf das Offene Schreiben des Herrn Dr. Martin Buber," *K.-C.-Blaetter*, (July-August 1916), pp. 683ff.; Martin Buber, "Zion, der Staat und die Menschheit," *Der Jude*, no, 7, (October 1916), pp. 425ff. The Buber excerpts are cited by permission of Mr. Rafael Buber. Trans. M. Gelber and S. Weinstein.

depicted, from Moses Hess[2] up until my own writings (to choose a recent example from the present generation) as the dominant idea of Judaism.

Zionism opposes not the messianic idea, but rather the misrepresentation and distortion of this idea found in a considerable part of Liberal-Jewish, anti-Zionist literature. This misrepresentation and distortion glorifies, in the name of messianism, the dispersion, debasement, and homelessness of the Jewish people as something unconditionally valuable and fortunate, as something that must be preserved because it prepares humanity for the messianic age.

Zionism too sees the goal of Judaism as "the redemption of the human spirit and the salvation of the world."[3] But, we see as the means to the realization of this goal "the liberation of a tormented people and its gathering around God's sanctuary."[4] ... In the messianic age, let Jewry merge with mankind. But let us make sure that the Jewish people does not disappear *now* so that the messianic age may perhaps come into being *later*. The Jewish people must persevere in the midst of today's human order—not as a fixed, brittle fact of nature appended to an ever more diluted confessional religion, but as a people pursuing its ideal, freely and unhindered, for the sake of this human order.... The struggle for a "homeland" is a national struggle. The struggle for Jewish communal existence [*juedisches Gemeinwesen*] in Palestine will be a supra-national one. We want Palestine not "for the Jews." We want it for mankind, because we want it for the realization of Judaism.

COHEN: It is characteristic that my opponent irresistably speaks only of people, nation and, if need be, also of religion. He does not mention the state, however, except as it refers to an isolated people. This point of view must be contested. The Jewish question, as it concerns us, deals not with a distinct, cohesive people; but on the contrary, with a people which is dispersed throughout other states and which has to establish and explain its political relationship to each individual state.

I have already referred to the fact that my opposition to Zionism is by no means a matter of apologetics. Rather, I am interested in the general ethical-political problem of preserving nationality. Hence, one may recognize immediately the general reason which led me to attempt to define the difference between nation and nationality. While nationality remains a moral fact of nature, it is only through the state, by virtue of a pure act of political morality, that the nation is constituted....

For us, the state constitutes the hub of all human culture. The "I" of man remains an empirical ambiguity as long as it is not objectified through political self-consciousness. Insofar as I participate in the ideal personality of my state, I may claim a true self-consciousness. Our entire range of feelings is concentrated in our patriotism [*Staatsbewusstsein*]....

The desire of the modern state to be a nation-state presents Judaism and the Jewish people with a dilemma. In that the Jews constitute a distinct ethnic group [*Stamm*], the Jews seem [to non-Jews] to form "a state within a state."[5] In the face of this modern dilemma, all Liberal Jews in every state, without prior agreement, exclaim in self-defense: We do not want to form our own state, or, consequently, to be a separate nation. But we are and shall remain a separate religion, we are and shall remain in principle a distinct ethnic group [*Stamm*], a separate nationality [*Nationalitaet*].

Can one ethicize nationality—that "fact of nature"—with a more cogent claim than that it is needed for the historical preservation of religion?

Whatever Judaism and its adherents have suffered externally and internally derives from this problem. The states, in their delusion, say: There should be no groups among us that under the guise of some fiction or other lead a separate state-like existence. And the Jews, oppressed by the ambiguity of modernity as much as by any general distress of our day, who decide to abandon the faith of their forefathers exclaim: There is an irreconcilable conflict between the Jewish religion and the foundations of modern national experience, namely, the nation-state. Our patriotic consciousness of being members of a state [*Staatsbewusstsein*] thus requires renunciation of Judaism.

Modern Judaism counters these two errors with the following thesis: Our religion is the sole and exclusive difference between us and our state, and, accordingly, between us and our nation [*Nation*].

Can the objection dare be advanced now that this thesis is an evasion of the dilemma or even worse, an expression of a cowardly desire to assimilate? Such an objection offends our conviction that we have a moral obligation to the modern state. With such skepticism, one would not desire to take any part at all in the modern state.... The Zionist rails pitilessly against us Liberal Jews for imagining that we possess a homeland among the cultures of other countries. This [alleged] delusion is contrasted with the [actual] homelessness of the Jewish people. And, only this homeless Jewish people is considered to comprise the Jewish reality. We "pseudo-Jews," on the other hand, are—rightfully, it is thought—separated from the Jewish people.

In this way Jewish reality is tailored by Zionism to suit its preconceived notion. Further, the implementation of this reality becomes ever more exclusive: Only in Palestine, only in the Jewish state, can the "dilapidated," "fictitious" Judaism be overcome and eliminated. The entire past history of Judaism is misrepresented here as mere ideology. The ghetto mentality is not the ghost, but the true spirit of Judaism and of Jewish reality. The verdict has been re-formed regarding all cultural endeavors of Jewish history: these endeavors sow only concepts, but produce nothing real. Furthermore, the modern liberal movement is considered to be merely the continuation of those earlier, illusory endeavors. These illusions, say the Zionists, must be uprooted altogether....

Does my opponent's statement that there are only two directions for authentic Judaism—that of absolute adherence to Jewish Law and that of Zionism—correspond to the reality of our history? Were all the other directions and turns in our history mere aberrations leading to degeneration? What criterion can there be for deciding the question whether the return to Palestine alone will determine the true nature of the future?

Modern Judaism is historical; through historical development it acquires self-consciousness. And, the guide to our religious development is prophetism, the highpoint of which is messianism.

We interpret our entire history as leading toward this goal of messianism. The downfall of the Jewish state is, in our view, the best example of historical theodicy. The same Micha who coined the phrase "God asks of you: only this, to act justly" (6:8), also coined the providential metaphor: "And the remnant of Jacob shall be in the midst of many peoples, like dew from the Lord" (5:6, 7). It is our proud conviction that we are to continue to live as divine dew in the midst of the peoples and to remain fruitful among them and for them. All of the prophets place us in the midst of the peoples and their common perspective is the world mission of the remnant of Israel.

[Modern, Liberal Judaism acknowledges this messianic mission.] Thus we are free of all discord between our Judaism and our Germanism. Moreover, the Jews of every modern state feel free of any such discrepancies caused by religion. In consequence of its messianic conceptions of God, the Jewish religion is thoroughly a world religion. This messianic faith cannot be impaired by historical reality, by misfortune, or even by the auspicious granting of equal rights. "Happy is he that waiteth" (Dan. 12:12). [Messianic] hope alone confirms our [spiritual and moral] reality. Consequently, hope and trust also shape our fundamental political attitudes.

The practical difference between us and the Zionists is to be found in what might be called our political religiosity. While the Zionist believes that he can preserve Judaism only through an all-encompassing, unqualified Jewish nationality, we are of the opposite opinion. It is only, we maintain, the universal humanistic Jewish nationality that can preserve the Jewish religion. All the bitterness of the argument becomes understandable and pardonable in light of this difference, which is not merely one of tactics. Both parties fervently desire the continuation of our religion—that I readily acknowledge. To this end I unconditionally favor the preservation of our nationality. But, just as unconditionally, I favor our political integration into the modern nation-state. Political merger conditions and guarantees the perpetuation of our religion....

Palestine is not just the land of our fathers; it is the land of our prophets, who established and perfected the ideal of our religion. Hence, we do indeed regard Palestine as the Holy Land, however only insofar as it is the land from whence came our eternal, sacred heritage. But just as our present religious reality is increasingly and more exclusively directed to the future, likewise, the moral world, as it evolves in history, is our true promised land....

We do not understand the messianic future in terms of the image which suggests that the Lord will appoint a table on Mt. Zion for all peoples. Instead, we refer to the many imageless pronouncements in which the unique God is proclaimed "Lord of the entire earth." We thereby view the entire historical world as the future abode of our religion. And it is only this future that we acknowledge as our true homeland.

BUBER: Hermann Cohen has published an "Answer to the Open Letter of Dr. Martin Buber to Hermann Cohen." In spite of the title, his essay is not an answer but an evasion of the subjects I raised. He speaks not of my words—which he barely tries to refute—but only of what he perceives to be the easily dismissed, fabricated, slogan-laden argumentation of an imaginary "typical" Zionist....

At one point, however, Cohen does not beat around the bush. He recognizes that the core of the argument between us involves the relationship between state and religion. I might also say between state and spirit, or between state and humanity. For me, religion is not, as it is for him, "one of the concentric, special subjects within the unity of moral culture"; nor do I regard the state as "the hub of all human culture." My views are exactly the opposite. Only in religious life is the unity of humanity truly realized.

But, in applying this basic difference between us to the Jewish problem, Cohen goes astray. "Our argument," he supposes, "centers not so much on the Jewish people as it does on the Jewish state. In reality [Cohen continues], my opponent, for his part accepts my definition that the state first defines a people, but he derives from this a particular state for the Jewish people." What a paradox! For me, just as the state in general is not the determining goal of mankind, so the "Jewish state" is not the determining goal for the Jews. And, the "viable ethnic group's need for power," about which Cohen speaks further, is completely foreign to me. I have seen and heard too much of the results of empty needs for power.

Our argument is about something else entirely. It does not concern the Jewish state, that, yes, were it to be founded today would be built upon the same principles as any other modern state. It does not concern the addition of one more trifling power structure. It does, however, concern the [renewed Jewish] settlement in Palestine, which independent of "international politics," can effect the inner consolidation of the energies of the Jewish people and thereby the realization of Judaism.

[Admittedly, in the contemporary Diaspora] there is an awakening of Jews who have been touched by the spirit. Growing from hour to hour, this awakening is animated by the soul's urge to create.... But this awakening will subside as all soaring expectations have subsided in the Exile, if the energy of the people is not liberated from the fruitless struggle for bare existence.... This then is what I mean by Palestine—not a state, but only the ancient soil which bears the promised security of ultimate and hallowed permanence. Palestine is the firm sod in which alone the seed of the new unity can sprout, not from a "need for power," but solely from the need for self-realization, which is the need to extend God's power on earth.

"The entire history of Judaism," says Cohen, "teaches, in accordance with the vision of the prophets, that the realization of Judaism is grounded in our dispersion among the peoples of the earth." We have learned the opposite lesson from history, namely, that in a life of dispersion not determined by ourselves, we cannot realize Judaism. We can pray here in the Diaspora, but not act; bear witness to God with patience, but not with creativity; praise the jubilee year, but not usher it in....

This, in brief, is our creed: that Zion restored will become the house of the Lord for all peoples and the center of the new world, ... in which "the blood-stained garment of war is burned" and "the swords are turned into plowshares."

The new humanity needs us. However, it needs us not dispersed and working at cross-purposes, but together and united; not befouled by pretences and rumors, but purified and ready; not to acknowledge God with our words while betraying God with our lives, but to serve God faithfully through the establishment of a human community according to His will. Our contribution to the new humanity consists not in explaining and asserting that there is a God, but in showing how God lives in us—how through a true human life, we realize both ourselves and God within us.

NOTES

1. Martin Buber (1878–1965), since the early 1900s a leading figure in German letters. Buber joined the Zionist movement in 1898 and became one of the opponents of Herzl and political Zionism. He favored a shift of priorities from diplomacy and the drive to obtain a charter to a renewal of Jewish culture, with special attention to youth as the fulcrum of this renewal. Buber's understanding of Jewish culture, however, differed from that of other cultural Zionists. For Buber, Jewish culture meant a unique aesthetic and spiritual sensibility, which was ultimately based on what he

called Jewish religiosity (to be distinguished from "religion"), that is, a primal awareness of and longing to realize "the Unconditional" in one's actions. Before the development of his philosophy of dialogue in the 1920s, Buber hesitated to identify the Unconditional as the personal God of traditional faith.

Hermann Cohen (1842–1918). One of Germany's most esteemed professors of philosophy, he taught for more than forty years at the University of Marburg; from 1912 until his death he lectured at the *Lehranstalt fuer die Wissenschaft des Judentums* in Berlin, an institute of advanced Jewish studies associated with Liberal Judaism. His system of philosophical analysis, known as neo-Kantianism, reflects his deep belief in the progress of man as a rational and moral being. He found confirmation for this conviction in the evolution in the modern period of the nation-state, which he viewed as essentially defined by the legal system which aspires to a rational conceptualization of justice and by the tendency of the state to unite within its legal framework and national identity disparate peoples. A world federation of states, Cohen insisted, would be the next and higher stage in the development of man's moral reason; the ultimate goal being an absolute universalism and unity of mankind. Cohen identified this understanding and vision of history with the messianism of the Jewish prophets. He held that the spirit of modern German culture and thought was remarkably consonant with that of prophetic Judaism, and thus as a Jew he felt spiritually at home in German culture. Cohen recognized the Jews as a "nationality" or ethnic group. However, he sharply distinguished nationality from "nation," a designation he reserved for the citizens of a nation-state. Accordingly, since their Exile, Cohen believed, the Jews have ceased to be a nation and are simply a nationality. As a nationality, Jewry is associated with a particular religion. Indeed, Cohen sought to emphasize the religious vocation of the Jews as opposed to their ethnicity. The Jews' nationality is for Cohen but a "fact of nature," or an anthropological means to support Judaism. The religious vocation of Israel, which required the loss of statehood, is to point to the messianic future of mankind by transcending the concerns of everyday concrete reality and those of one's immediate community. This affirmation of the Diaspora occasioned by Israel's messianic mission placed Cohen ideologically close to the Liberal camp of Judaism.

In June 1916 Cohen wrote in the Jewish journal *K.-C.-Blaetter* a critique of Zionism. Buber published, in the July issue of *Der Jude*, a journal that he founded and edited, a response to Cohen, entitled "Begriffe und Wirklichkeit" (Concepts and Reality). The title was an allusion to Cohen's philosophical method which assigned an epistemological role to conceptual constructs. Buber argued in his article that Cohen's understanding of Jewish matters was divorced from reality. Cohen was as deeply hurt by the tenor as by the content of Buber's essay. He responded with a rebuttal in the *K.-C.-Blaetter* issue of July-August 1916. Buber replied to Cohen's rebuttal in an article published in the September 1916 issue of *Der Jude*. Both Buber's and Cohen's arguments were published as separate pamphlets and were widely discussed in Jewish circles throughout Europe; excerpts from their debate are presented here. Although Cohen was not a typical Reform Jew and Buber was hardly a typical Zionist, their debate brought into focus many of the central issues that divided the Liberal Western Jews and the Zionists. These issues were epitomized in their respective understanding of Exile and messianism. Buber advanced the view of Exile as a tragic situation of spiritual and physical homelessness. Cohen denied that the Diaspora was Exile; the Jew was, he affirmed, spiritually, and, since emancipation, politically at home in the Diaspora. By demanding the negation of the Diaspora, Cohen held, the Zionists were negating the messianic vision and task of Israel. Buber countered that Zionism furthers the realization of messianism.

2. Moses Hess (1812–1875), a German-Jewish social philosopher, who at one time was close to Marx and Engels. His work *Rome and Jerusalem* (1862) anticipated many of the major tenets of political and socialist Zionism.

3. Martin Buber, "Renewal of Judaism" [1911], trans. E. Jospe, in Martin Buber, *On Judaism*, ed. N. N. Glatzer (New York: Schocken Books, 1967), p. 51.

4. Ibid., p. 51.

5. See chapter 6, document 4.

30. OUR WORLD-VIEW (JANUARY 17, 1917)

HASHOMER HAZAIR[1]

We believe that the future of the Jewish people is hidden in our youth. We believe that the Jewish people will be revived in the simplest possible way: Youth will renew us.

In bringing out this work-program we are convinced that we can provide a cure for the mortal disease that is consuming our youth. Our meaning is this: We are not complete and healthy men, and we are not complete and healthy Jews; we lack the harmony which should reign between these two fundamental elements of the "I" in us.

Hitherto attention has been paid solely to the lack of Judaism and attempts were made to correct this defect insofar as possible. But no attention whatsoever was paid—or if so then only minimally—to the general human side. For the sake of veracity we must admit that other peoples too, until very recently, worried more about producing good patriotic citizens than about raising whole, healthy men. Only in the last two decades, in fact, has there been a strong movement among the youth—primarily German youth—to break the bonds with which the schools restrained attempts at individual development and to find better forms for the experiences and communality of individuals. But the youth of other peoples have, relatively, a simpler mission to fulfill. For they enjoy a normal national life while we, the children of a people with an abnormal national existence unlike that of any other, have a double task. We wish to save both the man and the Jew together....

Let us look closely at the Jewish youth. Even before he is twenty he is an old man. His soul is shrouded in deep darkness. If he be a superficial man he ultimately becomes an opportunist lacking an independent mind. If he be an intellectual his heart will be eaten by despair and poisoned by pessimism and *Weltschmerz*.

In both cases his soul is bleak and mournful as though in an eternal autumn; he is but a withered flower. Where is the optimism that makes life worth living, that gives strength to bear the sufferings of life and that gives the young man encouragement, joy and vigor? Where is that sincere optimism which imparts a goal and a purpose to life and which every truly young man worthy of the name should profess? Where, we ask, is that fresh and sweet-smelling wind of spring that breathes upon us when we draw close even to a small group of youth?

This and more. In addition to youth, we lack also a pure and true humanity. We stand, therefore, as the miserable inheritors of the faults of our fathers. And these faults are numerous and evil. Truly! Let us not hide within us the words which rise to our lips and demand of expression. Our love for our people is strong and loyal. We wish to see our nation great and noble. But precisely for this reason we have a duty to examine our faults and defects. It pains us greatly but we are forced to admit that those traits of character and that nobility of soul which we possess are obscured by the general appearance of the Jewish community today. The average Jew is but a caricature of a man healthy and normal in body and soul. His whole life is but a procession of irregular and unhealthy acts performed to enable him to survive. He is convinced, nevertheless, that he is the most perfect creature under the sun and this his people are a shining example to the family of nations.

Until now it has been thought that a rule requiring the study of Jewish history, or the acquisition of the Hebrew language was sufficient to give us good Jews, even if their value as human beings was small.

Source: Anonymous [The world-view of the Shomer] (Vienna, January 1917), in *Sefer Hashomer Hazair*, eds. Levi Dror and Israel Rosenzweig, 2nd ed. (Merhavia: Sifriat Poalim, 1956), vol. 1, pp. 40–43. Cited by permission. Trans. L. Sachs.

But the concept of a "human being" is wider and more inclusive than the concept of a "Jew," and it is humanity itself which is the basis of Judaism. It is hard for us to understand how a base human being can be a good Jew.

Until now the individual was not given an opportunity to live a full life in the movement, for the whole system was based on advancing one's studies, on Jewish learning and not on the education of a human being. Therefore, let us establish a new basic element in our program: to give the individual the opportunity to live a full and many faceted life in our organization. We will do this in the form of small associations of members called "troops." We will endeavor to make our organization a second family, for the youths who join us. In some cases we may be the primary family, for as is well known a blood relationship is not always one of spirit or affinity. But the whole organization can be a "spiritual family" to a young member in the most general and inclusive meaning of the term. Therefore, the form of organization should be a small company of members (a troop) which will constitute a little society unto itself.

And if one of the disciples of extreme individualism should come forward with his theories and claim that, in general, communal life with one's fellowman, even with fellowmen of the same psychological disposition, curbs and restrains the individual, we will reply in brief: Man is a social animal and feels the need to live communally with his fellows—that is, of course, with men who are congenial to him. A man can be compared to a flint which will spray off sparks only when it is struck on another flint. Or in our terms: only through confrontations and communal life can the "I" of a man be molded and forged. For a man yearns for the company of men who will love and understand him and with whom he can share his dreams and ideals, his joys and sorrows.

How can we become young and healthy? It should be pointed out that this problem appeared more than ten years ago in modern Hebrew literature, and many different answers were given. The young and the most extreme coined the phrase: "Let us give up books and grasp the sword!" Only the first part of this slogan is acceptable to us. We agree, in fact we strive, for an end to the idolatrous worship of books which is typical of us. Everything we say or write or think gives off the odor of mold on worn-out pages. Our fathers revered ancient books, and their sons admired modern books also, but the latter brought about no change in the state of affairs. But must the need to abandon books lead inevitably to the second extreme, to the sword? We think that there is yet another way—that is, in becoming close to nature. Undoubtedly, there will be people who will see in this idea a desire, sincere or affected, to return to the bosom of nature or to the natural life in the sense that Ruskin and Rousseau used the terms. This is far from our intention. We mean simply a growing intimacy with nature, and we hope that nature will return to us the freshness, the optimism, the love of beauty characteristic of youth, that it will straighten our crooked back, stretch our muscles and strengthen our resolve. Our young man will cast off the urbanized dress of an old man in the city and put on the many-colored garments of youth! He will bathe in the pure springs of nature and his happiness, his freedom, and his innocence will return to him....

Once we define our belief as a first principle (the belief in optimism and idealism), when we say that the value of life lies not only in what it gives us but also in what we give to it, then we will find it easier to define our duty to the Jewish people. The concept of Judaism has become superficial and its content has been removed. We must rescue the concept of a "true Jew" from the disgrace into which it has fallen. We declare openly and clearly: no one will bear the name of a Jew, or will be numbered in our ranks, who has not absorbed the culture of our people to the depths of his soul. All the arguments about the question of language are ended for us since we proclaim that the Hebrew language is our national language, and that, further, anyone wishing to know our people as it now lives, thinks, and speaks must know the language of the people—Yiddish —and the literature in that tongue. But for us the Bible stands above all; we wish to make it our primer, for it is the never-failing source of idealism, and will forever remain the spring from which the thirsty may drink. We wish to remain young Hebrews, and it will be easier for us to do so if we absorb the spirit of the ancient Hebrews, the spirit of the prophets, the spirit of a moral world-view....

This is how we see our educational tasks. Our ideal is a young Jew of strong body and courageous spirit, whose thoughts are healthy and normal, not hair-splitting and sophistic, who is disciplined and knows how to obey, a Jew to the depth of his heart.

His world-view is idealistic; he loves all that is beautiful and noble. We will form a group of such youths—and Zion will be built!

NOTE

1. *Hashomer Hazair* (The Young Guard), world-wide Zionist youth movement founded in Vienna in 1916, merging two groups—*Hashomer*, a British-style scouting organization, and *Zeirei Zion* (Youth of Zion), a cultural association—established somewhat earlier in Galicia, then a province of the Austro-Hungarian Empire. Inspired by the revolutionary ferment of the period but especially by the German youth movement, Hashomer Hazair sought to develop an independent culture and life for Jewish youth. The lifestyle and values of the movement were conceived as an alternative to the life of their parents with its supposed lack of vitality, genuine fellowship, warmth, and ideals. Specifically, the movement prepared its members—physically, culturally, and morally—for pioneering settlement in Palestine and for the "new" Judaism that would arise there. In the twenties, influenced *inter alios by* Borochov (see document 19 in this chapter), Hashomer Hazair evolved a Marxist-Zionist ideology, which stressed class struggle and pioneering settlement in Palestine, particularly within the framework of communal settlements, *kibbutzim*. Together with Blau-Weiss, a German Zionist youth movement, Hashomer Hazair was the forerunner of similar youth movements that were affiliated with virtually every ideological trend to emerge within Zionism. The youth movements were an important force in Zionist recruitment and in the shaping of the ethos of the Zionist movement.

31. AN ANTI-ZIONIST LETTER TO THE *TIMES* [LONDON] (MAY 24, 1917)[1]

CONJOINT COMMITTEE OF BRITISH JEWRY

In view of the statement and discussion lately published in the newspapers relative to a projected Jewish resettlement in Palestine on a national basis, the Conjoint Foreign Committee of the Board of Deputies of British Jews[2] and the Anglo-Jewish Association[3] deem it necessary to place on record the views they hold on this important question....

Two points in [the] scheme [recently published by the Zionist leadership] appear to the committee to be open to grave objections on public grounds.

The first is a claim that the Jewish settlements in Palestine shall be recognized as possessing a national character in a political sense. Were this claim of purely local import, it might well be left to settle itself in accordance with the general political exigencies of the reorganisation of the country under a new sovereign power. The Conjoint Committee, indeed, would have no objections to urge against a local Jewish nationality establishing itself under such conditions. But the present claim is not of this limited scope. It is part and parcel of a wider Zionist theory, which regards all the Jewish communities of the world as constituting one homeless nationality, incapable of complete social and political identification, with the nations among whom they dwell, and it is argued that for this homeless nationality, a political centre and an always available homeland in Palestine are necessary. Against this theory the Conjoint Committee strongly

Source: Times (London), May 24, 1917.

and earnestly protests. Emancipated Jews in this country regard themselves primarily as a religious community, and they have always based their claims to political equality with their fellow-citizens of other creeds on this assumption and on its corollary—that they have no separate national aspirations in a political sense. They hold Judaism to be a religious system, with which their political status has no concern, and they maintain that, as citizens of the countries in which they live, they are fully and sincerely identified with the national spirit and interests of those countries. It follows that the establishment of a Jewish nationality in Palestine, founded on this theory of Jewish homelessness, must have the effect throughout the world of stamping the Jews as strangers in their native lands, and of undermining their hard-won position as citizens and nationals of those lands. Moreover, a Jewish political nationality, carried to its logical conclusion, must, in the present circumstances of the world, be an anachronism. The Jewish religion being the only certain test of a Jew, a Jewish nationality must be founded on, and limited by, the religion. It cannot be supposed for a moment that any section of Jews would aim at a commonwealth governed by religious tests, and limited in the matter of freedom of conscience; but can a religious nationality express itself politically in any other way? The only alternative would be a secular, loose and obscure principle of race and ethnographic peculiarity; but this would not be Jewish in any spiritual sense, and its establishment in Palestine would be a denial of all the ideals and hopes by which the revival of Jewish life in that country commends itself to the Jewish consciousness and Jewish sympathy. On these grounds the Conjoint Committee deprecates most earnestly the national proposals of the Zionists.

The second point in the Zionist programme which has aroused the misgivings of the Conjoint Committee is the proposal to invest the Jewish settlers in Palestine with certain special rights in excess of those enjoyed by the rest of the population, these rights to be embodied in a Charter and administered by a Jewish Chartered Company. Whether it is desirable or not to confide any portion of the administration of Palestine to a Chartered Company need not be discussed, but it is certainly very undesirable that Jews should solicit or accept such a concession, on a basis of political privileges and economic preferences. Any such action would prove a veritable calamity for the whole Jewish people. In all the countries in which they live the principle of equal rights for all religious denominations is vital for them. Were they to set an example to Palestine of disregarding this principle they would convict themselves of having appealed to it for purely selfish motives. In the countries in which they are still struggling for equal rights they would find themselves hopelessly compromised, while in other countries, where those rights have been secured, they would have great difficulty in defending them. The proposal is the more inadmissible because the Jews are, and will probably long remain, a minority of the population of Palestine, and because it might involve them in the bitterest feuds with their neighbors of other races and religions, which would seriously retard their progress, and would find deplorable echoes throughout the Orient....

NOTES

1. The Balfour Declaration (see the next document) was preceded by protracted negotiations initiated by Chaim Weizmann (1874–1952) and Nahum Sokolow (1858–1936) on behalf of the World Zionist Organization. There was much discussion on both the formula and timing of the declaration. Despite the support the Zionists enjoyed from such prominent British Jews as Chief Rabbi Joseph Herman Hertz (1872–1946) and Herbert Samuel (1870–1963) the presidents of the Board of Deputies of British Jews and the Anglo-Jewish Association issued this anti-Zionist statement. This statement is said to have induced the British government to adopt a cautious approach and, accordingly, to modify its endorsement of the Zionist aspirations in Palestine.

2. The Board of Deputies of British Jews, founded in 1760 is the representative, organization of British Jewry. In 1878, the Board and the Anglo-Jewish Association formed a Conjoint Foreign Committee that operated successfully until 1917 when, discredited by its anti-Zionist line, it disbanded.

3. British organization originally founded, in 1871, for the protection, by diplomatic means, of Jewish rights in backward countries.

32. THE BALFOUR DECLARATION (NOVEMBER 2, 1917)[1]

JAMES BALFOUR

Foreign Office
November 2nd, 1917

Dear Lord Rothschild,[2]

I have much pleasure in conveying to you, on behalf of His Majesty's Government, the following declaration of sympathy with Jewish Zionist aspirations which has been submitted to, and approved by, the Cabinet.

His Majesty's Government views with favour the establishment in Palestine of a national home for the Jewish people, and will use their best endeavours to facilitate the achievement of this object, it being clearly understood that nothing shall be done which may prejudice the civil and religious rights of existing non-Jewish communities in Palestine, or the rights and political status enjoyed by Jews in any other country.

I should be grateful if you would bring this declaration to the knowledge of the Zionist Federation.

Yours,
James Balfour

NOTES

1. Chaim Weizmann and Nahum Sokolow, who were instrumental in securing the Balfour Declaration, submitted what they felt to be a moderate formula to the British government to recognize Palestine as "*the* national home of the Jewish people" (emphasis added) and for providing a "Jewish National Colonizing Corporation" for the resettlement and economic development of Palestine. This formula was not accepted. The British government substituted the indefinite article *a* for *the*. The declaration, after having been approved by the British cabinet, was signed by the foreign secretary, Arthur James Balfour (1848–1930) and sent to Lord Rothschild, who was asked to convey it to the World Zionist Organization.

2. Lionel Walter Rothschild, the second Baron Rothschild (1868–1937), honorary president of the Zionist Federation of Great Britain and Ireland at the time of the Balfour Declaration.

Source: "Book of Documents," submitted to the General Assembly of the United Nations by the Jewish Agency for Palestine (New York: Jewish Agency for Palestine, 1947), p. 1.

33. ZIONIST MANIFESTO ISSUED AFTER THE BALFOUR DECLARATION (DECEMBER 21, 1917)[1]

WORLD ZIONIST ORGANIZATION–LONDON BUREAU

To the Jewish People: The second of November, 1917, is an important milestone on the road to our national future; it marks the end of an epoch, and it opens up the beginning of a new era. The Jewish people has but one other such day in its annals: the twenty-eighth of August, 1897, the birthday of the New Zionist Organization at the first Basle Congress. But the analogy is incomplete, because the period which then began was Expectation, whereas the period which now begins is Fulfillment.

From then till now, for over twenty years, the Jewish people has been trying to find itself, to achieve a national resurrection. The advance-guard was the organized Zionist party, which in 1897 by its programme demanded a home for the Jewish people in Palestine secured by public law. A great deal was written, spoken, and done to get this demand recognized. The work was carried out by the Zionist Organization on a much greater scale and in a more systematic manner than had been possible for the Hovevei Zion, the first herald of the national ideal, who had tried to give practical shape to the yearning which had burnt like a light in the Jewish spirit during two thousand years of exile and had flamed out at various periods in various forms. The Hovevei Zion had the greatest share in the practical colonization. The Zionist movement wrestled with its opponents and with itself. It collected means outside Palestine, and laboured with all its strength in Palestine. It founded institutions of all kinds for colonization in Palestine. That was a preface, full of hope and faith, full of experiments and illusion, inspired by a sacred and elevating ideal, and productive of many valuable and enduring results.

The time has come to cast the balance of the account. That chapter of propaganda and experiments is complete, and the glory of immortality rests upon it. But we must go further. To look back is the function of the historian; life looks forwards.

The turning point is the Declaration of the British Government that they "view with favour the establishment in Palestine of a National Home for the Jewish people, and will use their best endeavours to facilitate the achievement of this object."

The progress which our idea has made is so colossal and so obvious that it is scarcely necessary to describe it in words. None the less, a few words must be addressed to the Jewish people, not so much by way of explanation, as to demand the new and greater efforts which are imperative.

The outstanding feature of the Declaration is, that what has been a beautiful ideal— and according to our opponents an empty dream—has now been given the possibility of becoming a reality. The aspirations of 1897 now find solid ground in the British Government's official Declaration of the second of November, 1917. That in itself is a gigantic step forward. The world's history, and particularly Jewish history, will not fail to inscribe in golden letters upon its bronze tablets that Great Britain, the shield of civilization, the country which is preeminent in colonization, the school of constitutionalism and freedom, has given us an official promise of support and help in the realization of our ideal of liberty in Palestine. And Great Britain will certainly carry with her the whole political world.

The Declaration of His Majesty's Government coincides with the triumphant march of the British Army in Palestine. The flag of Great Britain waves over Jerusalem and all Judea. It is at such a moment, while the army of Great Britain is taking possession of

Source: The Jewish Chronicle, December 21, 1917, p. 16.

Palestine, that Mr. Balfour assures us that Great Britain will help us in the establishment of a National Home in Palestine. This is the beginning of the fulfillment.

To appreciate and to understand accurately is the first essential, but it is not all. It is necessary to go further, to determine what is the next step. This must be set forth in plain words.

The Declaration puts in the hands of the Jewish people the key to a new freedom and happiness. All depends on you, the Jewish people, and on you only. The Declaration is the threshold, from which you can place your foot upon holy ground. After eighteen hundred years of suffering your recompense is offered to you. You can come to your haven and your heritage, you can show that the noble blood of your race is still fresh in your veins. But to do that you must begin work anew, with new power and with new means—the ideas and the phrases and the methods of the first period no longer suffice. That would be an anachronism. We need new conceptions, new words, new acts. The methods of the period of realization cannot be the methods of the time of expectation.

In the first place, the whole Jewish people must now unite. Now that fulfillment is displacing expectation, that which was potential in the will of the Jewish people must become actual and reveal itself in strenuous labour. The whole Jewish people must come into the Zionist Organization.

Secondly, a word to our brothers in Palestine. The moment has come to lay the foundations of a National Home. You are now under the protection of the British military authorities, who will guard your lives, your property, your freedom. Be worthy of that protection, and begin immediately to build the Jewish National Home upon sound foundations, thoroughly Hebrew, thoroughly national, thoroughly free and democratic. The beginning may decide all that follows.

Thirdly, our loyal acknowledgment of the support of Great Britain must be spontaneous and unmeasured. But it must be the acknowledgment of free men to a country which breeds and loves free men. We must show that what Great Britain has given us through her generosity, is ours by virtue of our intelligence, skill, and courage.

Fourthly, we must have ample means. The means of yesterday are ridiculously small compared with the needs of to-day. Propaganda, the study of practical problems, expeditions, the founding of new offices and commissions, negotiations, preparations for settlement, relief and reconstruction in Palestine—for all these, and other indispensable tasks, colossal material means are necessary, and necessary forthwith. Small and great, poor and rich, must rise to answer the call of this hour with the necessary personal sacrifice.

Fifthly, we need discipline and unity. This is no time for hair-splitting controversy. It is a time for action. We ask for confidence. Be united and tenacious, be quick but not impatient, be free men, but well-disciplined, firm as steel. From now onwards every gathering of Jews must have a practical aim, every speech must deal with a project, every thought must be a brick with which to build the National Home.

These are the directions for your work to-day.

Worn and weary through your two thousand years of wandering over desert and ocean, driven by every storm and carried on every wave, outcasts and refugees, you may now pass from the misery of exile to a secure home; a home where the Jewish spirit and the old Hebrew genius, which so long have hovered broken-winged over strange nests, can also find healing and be quickened into new life.

N. Sokolow,[2] E. W. Tschlenow,[3] Ch. Weizmann.[4]

NOTES

1. Despite reservations about its ambiguous formulation, the Balfour Declaration—as is reflected in this document—engendered genuine enthusiasm in Zionist circles.

2. Nahum Sokolow (1860–1936). One of the most important figures of post-Herzlian Zionism, he was associated with Chaim Weizmann in the negotiations leading to and following the Balfour Declaration, in connection with which he undertook missions to the French and Italian government and to the Papal Curia. He was president of the Jewish Agency for Palestine and the World Zionist Organization from 1931 to 1935.

3. Yehiel (Echiel) Tschlenow (1863–1918), a leading figure in Russian and in world Zionism.

4. Chaim Weizmann (1874–1952), the most prominent figure in the Zionist movement since the end of World War I. He was president of the World Zionist Organization from 1920 to 1931 and from 1935 to 1946 and the president of the State of Israel from 1949 until his death.

34. PROPOSAL TO THE GENERAL ASSEMBLY OF THE WORKERS OF ERETZ ISRAEL (1919)

AHDUT HAAVODAH[1]

The accompanying proposal includes the main principles of the general union of workers and laborers in the country, as discussed in the meetings of the workers and the brigades, expressed in members' meetings and drafted by the undersigned members of the Unification Committee.

Setting these thoughts in writing should not be viewed as conclusive nor—needless to say—as the final word. The matters are still pending and open to clarification, to additions and to qualifications.

The desire for general unification which has become, after all the stages we went through, the yearning of so many, should not be dependent upon any particular detail. The union must not be contingent upon its clauses; the clauses will be tested as they are, directly, with respect to each issue.

We believe that at the foundation of the desire to unify all the camps of workers in Eretz Israel is the ripening awareness that the labor movement in this country is essentially one, its ways are the ways of unity, and its aim—the creation of the free Hebrew worker, cultured and loyal to his nation—is common to us all.

This belief in the true unity of the movement and its whole internal soul was also the source of the simplicity of the applicable model.

The proper form for arranging the body of workers in Eretz Israel is not unattainable, but is within us, close to and known to us—that is, the form of the general workers' unions according to their professions, trades and daily occupations and the federation of the professional unions into one large movement, substantial in content and aspiration, and a noble enterprise.

As the unification of workers in the country becomes a reality, it will be a prototype and an important clarion call for bringing near those who are far and for rallying the forces of Hebrew workers in the countries of the Diaspora and uniting them with the pioneer workers who are preparing for *aliyah*.

This miracle of unification, which shall be borne on the hills of the homeland, shall become a flag of good tidings that the time has come for creating the large and unified assembly of Hebrew workers.

Members of the Unification Committee:
D. Ben-Gurion,[2] Y. Ben-Zvi,[3] Y. Tabenkin,[4] S. Yavneeli,[5] B. Katznelson,[6] D. Remez[7]

Jaffa, late Shevat, 5679 (1919)

A.

The labor movement in Eretz Israel is a branch of the world socialist labor movement, which aspires to redeem the individual fully from the oppression of the existing order in which private capital rules over the life of the nation, economic and cultural creativity and relations between nations and countries. The prevailing system of government, which consigns the natural resources, the toil of the generations and the fruit of the spirit of man, the sciences and the arts to be the property of individuals, delivers the national economy to the profiteering of the property owners and competition between them; tyrannizes nations; plunders states and calls for wars; necessarily creates a class of "superfluous," impoverished laborers and a class of rulers and their servants who abound in wealth; deprives the worker of his remuneration, his health, his food, his education, his family, his creative strength and his life; and exploits the child and future generations.

Source: Yalkut Ahdut Haavodah (Tel Aviv, 1920), pp. 1–4. Trans. G. Svirsky.

The goal: To base human society—to be a family of free nations, equal in rights—on the foundations of:

—the general labor of all its people;

—transfer of natural resources and property, which were accumulated for generations, from the private to the public domain;

—organization by the working class of all matters related to work and property.

The labor movement in Eretz Israel is a branch of the Zionist movement of the Hebrew nation, which yearns for the redemption of the people of Israel from exile.

Its aspiration: The revival of the nation of Israel, returning to its land in great numbers, clinging to its earth, creating its settlement and its labor and becoming a free nation which rules in its land, speaking in its own Hebrew language, arranging its own life and creating and developing its material and spiritual possessions.

B.

Through pioneering Zionism (*zionut mitgashemet*),[8] the labor movement of *Eretz Israel* aspires, through popular, broad-based, and orderly *aliyah*, to mold the life of the Hebrew nation in *Eretz Israel* as a commonwealth of free and equal workers, which lives on its labor, controlling its property and arranging its own work, economy, [and] culture.

Realizing this goal entails:

(a) transfer of the land of Eretz Israel, its water and natural resources, to the keeping of the nation of Israel for everlasting possession of the entire people.

(b) creation of national capital:

1. for working the land and creating inalienable goods which will belong to the nation (roads, harbors, forests, ships, waterworks, lighting, electricity).

2. for national credit to be devoted to building the national labor, agriculture, and industry, with the aid of free communities of workers.

(c) *aliyah* of pioneers to the country, to live a full working life here, paving the way and creating conditions for a large popular *aliyah* and participating in the creation of a powerful workers' class that will build the future workers' commonwealth.

(d) imparting the Hebrew language and cultural treasures to the entire nation and integrating the workers in the cultural life and its creations.

C.

Ahdut Haavodah encompasses all the workers and laborers in the country and also members of the professions who do not exploit others but who live solely on their own labor.

The Ahdut is composed of autonomous labor unions which federate the members according to their professions.

Ahdut Haavodah organizes the workers' class for economic, cultural and political action; finds work and arranges for its distribution; organizes cooperative supplies, vocational training and general and professional education; protects the workers' dignity and interests; sees to the improvement of working conditions and their modernization; fights to liberate the working class and vigilantly enhances their creative capacity.

Ahdut Haavodah seeks to assist the *haluz* movement[9] abroad by disseminating information and guidance, making its activity more relevant for labor needs in this country; assists in unifying all the national unions of *haluz* into one federation based on mutual aid, group discipline and common labor institutions; and establishes a practical and orderly connection to the labor movement in *Eretz Israel*.

D.

As a national, autonomous body, Ahdut Haavodah participates:

(a) in the World Zionist Federation;

(b) in the Socialist International.

Ahdut Haavodah sees a need and an obligation to help unify all the unions and parties which are in the Hebrew workers' movement and the Zionist movement abroad, which aspire to a workers' society in *Eretz Israel*, to a national Zionist socialist alliance which will work together in economic, cultural and political enterprises for realizing their common goals. With this aspiration, the federation, as a national autonomous union, participates in the world federation of Poalei Zion unions.

E.

The Central Committee of the Ahdut was elected at the General Assembly of the workers of Eretz Israel.

The Labor Department of the Agricultural Workers' Union, with the participation of a member of the Central committee of the Ahdut, shall have the power of attorney of the Ahdut Haavodah regarding every matter related to agricultural settlement.

The central institutions of Ahdut Haavodah which are the first on our agenda (some already exist within several unions and require strengthening, reform, expansion and transfer to the overall workers' camp, and most will be created):

1. An immigrants' transit station—a dining room and organized hotel for welcoming new immigrants as they arrive, receiving their baggage and storing it, and for allowing them rest from the toils of the journey.
2. A labor exchange—for finding jobs, for information and job placement in Eretz Israel and for informational contacts abroad.
3. A sick fund (*Kupat Holim*).[10]
4. A warehouse and goods distribution center (*Hamashbir*).[11]
5. An association of kitchens—Organizing all the workers' kitchens into one cooperative with a central management, which oversees the quality of the food and cooking, hygiene, improvement of systems, arranging dieticians and bookkeepers, reforming working conditions in the kitchen, beautification of the dining rooms, the outdoors and the furniture.
6. A workers' bank (*Bank Hapoalim*)[12]—to be in the hands of the workers, which will be the primary financial institution of the workers' camp, helping in the development of work in the country.
7. A center for cultural work—for disseminating the language, for education in humanities, social studies, and professional studies.
8. A free press[13]—common to all the workers.
9. A publishing house[14]—for the education and enlightenment of the worker.

NOTES

1. Ahdut Haavodah (Unity of Labor) was a Zionist labor party founded in Palestine in 1919 as a result of several

converging currents of the second *aliyah* and developments in the wake of World War I. During the period of the second *aliyah* (1903/4–1914) there evolved in Palestine a unique Hebrew worker's culture, which placed emphasis on collectivist values and, first and foremost, on nonexploitative Jewish labor; the governing ethos was captured by the slogan *kibush haavodah*, the conquest of all branches of work, even the most menial, by Jews. The dependence on non-Jewish (i.e., Arab) labor was to cease. Toward the end of World War I, especially with the Balfour Declaration, there was growing expectation of a large influx of pioneers (*haluzim*). In order to absorb them and to guide them in the ideals which had crystallized during the second *aliyah*, many labor movement leaders felt it necessary to end the rivalry between the two socialist Zionist parties, the Marxist Poalei Zion (which envisaged "an unremitting class struggle") and Hapoel Hazair (which rejected Marxism and the class struggle). A group of unaffiliated workers led by Berl Katznelson and David Remez (see notes 6 and 7, below) appealed for unity so that the movement of new Hebrew workers could exert its full influence on the development of the *yishuv* and absorb the newcomers. They thus called for the establishment of an all-inclusive labor organization that would serve both as a trade union and a framework uniting the rival socialist Zionist parties, as well as various non-party workers' groups.

At a unity conference in February 1919, Poalei Zion and the nonparty groups formed Ahdut Haavodah. Hapoel Hazair refused to join, largely on the ground that Ahdut Haavodah regarded itself as "a branch of the world socialist labor movement." Further, Hapoel Hazair was committed to the ideal of small, closely knit communes, while Ahdut Haavodah sought to develop a mass workers' movement.

To heal the rift Joseph Trumpeldor (1880–1920), a legendary figure of the second *aliyah* and a symbol for pioneer youth, proposed the establishment of a neutral, independent trade union to which both Ahdut Haavodah and Hapoel Hazair would belong. Shortly after advancing this proposal, Trumpeldor was killed in a skirmish with Arab marauders. His initiative, however, bore fruit when, at a conference in Haifa in December 1920, the organization he envisioned was established: *Hahistadrut Haivrit shel Haovdim be-Eretz Israel* (The General Federation of Hebrew Workers in *Eretz Israel*). Ahdut Haavodah became the dominant force in the Histadrut as well as in the Elected Assembly (*Vaad Leumi*) of the *yishuv*. After protracted negotiations Ahdut Haavodah and Hapoel Hazair merged in

1930 to form *Mifleget Poalei Eretz Israel* (Mapai, or the Worker's Party of Eretz Israel).

The proposal to the founding conference of Ahdut Haavodah signed by members of the Unification Committee, representing the various constituent bodies, was actually penned by David Remez (who wrote the introduction) and Berl Katznelson (who composed the body of the text). The proposal, presented here, was ratified by the conference. Many of the proposed institutions, for example, a workers' sick fund, a publishing house, and a newspaper, were actually realized by the Histadrut.

2. David Ben-Gurion (1886–1973) was a Zionist labor leader and the first prime minister of the State of Israel. Born in Poland, he settled in Palestine in 1906 (whereupon he Hebraized his name from Gruen to Ben-Gurion). The same year, he served as chairman of the founding conference of Poalei Zion in Palestine, being elected to its central committee. With the creation of Ahdut Haavodah, he and Katznelson developed a close relationship, grounded in an intimate friendship, that allowed for the emergence of the cooperative leadership so desperately needed by the workers' movement in Palestine. Ben-Gurion served as the first general secretary of the Histadrut from 1921 to 1935.

3. Yitzhak Ben-Zvi (1884–1963) was a Zionist labor leader and, later, the second president of the State of Israel. Born in Ukraine, he emigrated to Palestine in 1907, where he helped organize Poalei Zion. Active in Ahdut Haavodah and the Histadrut, he was the president of the Elected Assembly from 1931 to 1948.

4. Yitzhak Tabenkin (1887–1971) was a labor leader and an ideologue of the kibbutz movement. Born in Belorussia, he was one of the founders of Poalei Zion in Russia. Upon immigration to Palestine in 1912, however, he chose to remain unaffiliated. He was one of the nonparty group that initiated the formation of Ahdut Haavodah. A pioneer of collective settlement in Palestine, he favored—in contrast to the approach of Hapoel Hazair (see note 1)—large collectives (kibbutzim) open to mass membership. A founding member of the Histadrut and, later, of Mapai, he eventually split in 1944 with Ben-Gurion to lead a faction called *Hatnuah Leahdut Haavodah* (Movement for Ahdut Haavodah), which four years later joined with Hashomer Hazair to form *Mifleget Poalim Meuhedet* (Mapam, "United Workers' Party"), a Marxist-oriented Zionist party. Six years later, he withdrew his faction from Mapam, protesting its pro-Moscow leanings, and reestablished Ahdut Haavodah as an independent party. Finally, in 1968 he reunited with Mapai.

5. Shmuel Yavneeli (1884–1961) was born in Ukraine and settled in Palestine in 1905. A founding member of Hapoel Hazair, he undertook several journeys to Yemen, the first as early as 1911, to encourage and organize the immigration of the local Jewish community to Palestine. Prominent in the Histadrut, he was particularly devoted to promoting the cultural and educational activities of the organization.

6. Berl Katznelson (1887–1944) was born in White Russia. He settled in 1909 in Palestine, where he soon became a leading personality and ideologue of the labor movement. He was the moving spirit behind the establishment of Ahdut Haavodah and dominated its inaugural conference, which took place in Petah Tikvah on February 24, 1919. He delivered the keynote address, formulated its resolutions, and supervised the election of its central committee. He was also to play a prominent role in the Histadrut and, later, in Mapai.

7. David Remez (1886–1951) was born in Russia and emigrated to Palestine in 1913, where he became a close associate of Katznelson. He was general secretary of the Histadrut from 1935 to 1945, chairman of the Elected Assembly from 1944 to 1948, and a member of the first and second Knesset (parliament of the state of Israel) representing Mapai.

8. *Zionut mitgashemet*, literally, "Zionism that realizes itself," denoted a Zionism that was true to the ideals of the labor movement: *aliyah*, settlement in the land, the acquisition of a secular, Hebrew culture, and pioneering values. As a personal value, it also implied that in realizing these ideals one fulfills oneself as a Jew. As such, the slogan *"zionut mitgashemet"* embodied the ethos of *haluziut*.

9. *Haluz* movement: see this chapter, document 42, note 2.

10. The sick fund (*Kupat Holim*) was incorporated into the Histadrut.

11. *Hamashbir*; founded during World War I as a cooperative purchasing and consumers' agency of the workers' movement, it became part of the Histadrut.

12. A workers' bank was founded by the Histadrut in 1921. It initially served as a central credit institute for its cooperatives and associated settlements. Eventually it became the full service bank, *Bank Hapoalim*.

13. The idea of a newspaper of the workers' movement was also realized by the Histadrut, which since 1925 has sponsored the daily *Davar* (Word); its first editor was Berl Katznelson, who made it into one of the premier intellectual organs of the *yishuv*.

14. In 1942 the Histadrut founded a publishing house, *Am Oved* (Working Nation); until his death Berl Katznelson served as its editor-in-chief.

35. THE CHURCHILL WHITE PAPER (JUNE 1922)[1]

WINSTON CHURCHILL

The tension which has prevailed from time to time in Palestine is mainly due to apprehensions, which are entertained both by sections of the Arab population and by sections of the Jewish population. These apprehensions, so far as the Arabs are concerned, are partly based upon exaggerated interpretations of the meaning of the Declaration favoring the establishment of a Jewish National Home in Palestine, made on behalf of His Majesty's Government on 2nd November, 1917. Unauthorized statements have been made to the effect that the purpose in view is to create a wholly Jewish Palestine. Phrases have been used such as that Palestine is to become "as Jewish as England is English." His Majesty's Government regard any such expectation as impracticable and have no such aim in view. Nor have they at any time contemplated, as appears to be feared by the Arab Delegation, the disappearance or the subordination of the Arabic population, language or culture in Palestine. They would draw attention to the fact that the terms of the Declaration referred to do not contemplate that Palestine as a whole should be converted into a Jewish National Home but that such a Home should be *in* Palestine. In this connection it has been observed with satisfaction that at the meeting of the Zionist Congress, the supreme governing body of the Zionist Organization, held at Carlsbad in September, 1921, a resolution was passed expressing as the official statement of Zionist aims "the determination of the Jewish people to live with the Arab people on terms of unity and mutual respect, and together with them to make the common home into a flourishing community, the upbuilding of which may assure to each of its peoples an undisturbed national development."

It is also necessary to point out that the Zionist Commission in Palestine, now termed the Palestine Zionist Executive, has not desired to possess, and does not possess, any share in the general administration of the country. Nor does the special position assigned to the Zionist Organization in Article IV of the Draft Mandate for Palestine imply such functions. That special position relates to the measures to be taken in Palestine affecting the Jewish population, and contemplates that the Organization may assist in the general development of the country, but does not entitle it to share in any degree in its Government.

Further, it is contemplated that the status of all citizens of Palestine in the eyes of the law shall be Palestinian, and it has never intended that they, or any section of them, should possess any other juridical status.

So far as the Jewish population of Palestine are concerned, it appears that some among them are apprehensive that His Majesty's Government may depart from the policy embodied in the Declaration of 1917. It is necessary, therefore, once more to affirm that these fears are unfounded, and that the Declaration, re-affirmed by the Conference of the Principal Allied Powers at San Remo[2] and again in the Treaty of Sèvres,[3] is not susceptible of change.

During the last two or three generations the Jews have recreated in Palestine a community, now numbering 80,000, of whom about one-fourth are farmers or workers upon the land. This community has its own political organs; an elected assembly for the direction of its domestic concerns; elected councils in the towns; and an organization for the control of its schools. It has its elected Chief Rabbinate and Rabbinical Council for the direction of its religious affairs. Its business is conducted in Hebrew as

---

Source: Correspondence with the Palestine Arab Delegation and the Zionist Organization. Presented to Parliament by Command of His Majesty, June 1922 (London: Published by His Majesty's Stationery Office, 1922), pp. 18–29.

a vernacular language, and a Hebrew press serves its needs. It has its distinctive intellectual life and displays considerable economic activity. This community, then, with its town and country population, its political, religious and social organizations, its own language, its own customs, its own life, has in fact "national" characteristics. When it is asked what is meant by the development of the Jewish National Home in Palestine, it may be answered that it is not the imposition of a Jewish nationality upon the inhabitants of Palestine as a whole, but the further development of the existing Jewish community, with the assistance of Jews in other parts of the world, in order that it may become a center in which the Jewish people as a whole may take, on the grounds of religion and race, an interest and a pride. But in order that this community should have the best prospect of free development and provide a full opportunity for the Jewish people to display its capacities, it is essential that it should know that it is in Palestine as of right and not on sufferance. That is the reason why it is necessary that the existence of a Jewish National Home in Palestine should be internationally guaranteed, and that it should be formally recognized to rest upon ancient historic connection.

This, then, is the interpretation which His Majesty's Government place upon the Declaration of 1917, and, so understood, the Secretary of State is of opinion that it does not contain or imply anything which need either cause alarm to the Arab population of Palestine or disappointment to the Jews.

For the fulfillment of this policy it is necessary that the Jewish community in Palestine should be able to increase its numbers by immigration. This immigration cannot be so great in volume as to exceed whatever may be the economic capacity of the country at the time to absorb new arrivals. It is essential to ensure that the immigrants should not be a burden upon the people of Palestine as a whole, and that they should not deprive any section of the present population of their employment. Hitherto the immigration has fulfilled these conditions. The number of immigrants since the British occupation has been about 25,000.

It is intended that a special committee should be established in Palestine, consisting entirely of members of the new Legislative Council elected by the people, to confer with the Administration upon matters relating to the regulation of immigration. Should any difference of opinion arise between this committee and the Administration, the matter will be referred to His Majesty's Government, who will give it special consideration. In addition, under Article 81 of the draft Palestine Order in Council, any religious community or considerable section of the population of Palestine will have a general right to appeal, through the High Commissioner and the Secretary of State, to the League of Nations on any matter on which they may consider that the terms of the Mandate are not being fulfilled by the Government of Palestine.

With reference to the Constitution which it now intends to establish in Palestine, the draft of which has already been published, it is desirable to make certain points clear. In the first place, it is not the case, as has been represented by the Arab Delegation, that during the war His Majesty's Government gave an undertaking that an independent national government should be at once established in Palestine. This representation mainly rests upon a letter dated the 24th October, 1915, from Sir Henry McMahon, then His Majesty's High Commissioner in Egypt, to the Sheriff of Mecca, now King Hussein of the Kingdom of the Hejaz.[4] That letter is quoted as conveying the promise to the Sheriff of Mecca to recognize and support the independence of the Arabs within the territories proposed by him. But this promise was given subject to a reservation made in the same letter, which excluded from its scope, among other territories, the portions of Syria lying to the west of the district of Damascus. This reservation has always been regarded by His Majesty's Government as covering the *Vilayet* [provincial administration] of Beirut and the independent *Sanjak* [province] of Jerusalem. The whole of Palestine west of the Jordan was thus excluded from Sir H. McMahon's pledge.

Nevertheless, it is the intention of His Majesty's Government to foster the establishment of a full measure of self-government in Palestine. But they are of opinion that, in the special circumstances of that country, this should be accomplished by gradual stages and not suddenly. The first step was taken when, on the institution of a civil Administration, the nominated Advisory Council, which now exists, was established. It was stated at the time by the High Commissioner that this was the first step in the development of self-governing institutions, and it is now proposed to take a second step by the establishment of a Legislative Council containing a large proportion of members elected on a wide franchise. It was proposed in the published draft that hereof the members of this Council should be non-official persons nominated by the High Commissioner, but representations having been made in opposition to this provision, based on cogent considerations, the Secretary of State is prepared to omit it. The Legislative Council would then consist of the High Commissioner as President and twelve elected and ten official members. The Secretary of State is of opinion that before a further measure of self-government is extended to Palestine and the Assembly placed in control over the Executive, it would be wise to allow some time to elapse. During this period the institutions of the country will have become well established; its financial credit will be based on firm foundations, and the Palestinian officials will have been enabled to gain experience of sound methods of government. After a few years the situation will be again reviewed, and if the experience of the working of the constitution now to be established so warranted, a larger share of authority would then be extended to the elected representatives of the people.

The Secretary of State would then point out the present Administration has already transferred to a Supreme Council elected by the Moslem community of Palestine the entire control of Moslem religious endowments (*waqfs*), and of the Moslem religious Courts. To this Council the Administration has also voluntarily restored considerable revenues derived from ancient endowments which had been sequestrated by the Turkish Government. The Education Department is also advised by a committee representative of all sections of the population, and the Department of Commerce and Industry has the benefit of the co-operation of the Chambers of Commerce which have been established in the principal centers. It is the intention of the Administration to associate in an increased degree similar representative committees with the various Departments of the Government.

The Secretary of State believes that a policy upon these lines, coupled with the maintenance of the fullest religious liberty in Palestine and with scrupulous regard for the rights of each community with reference to its Holy Places, cannot but commend itself to the various sections of the population, and that upon this basis may be built up that spirit of co-operation upon which the future progress and prosperity of the Holy Land must largely depend.

NOTES

1. This document is an official British government "White Paper," (Cmd. 1700), based on a correspondence between the Colonial Secretary, Winston Churchill (1874–1965), a delegation representing the Arabs of Palestine, and the World Zionist Organization concerning the future of Palestine. The Arabs demanded repudiation of the Balfour Declaration as inimical to their interests; moreover, they insisted, Palestine was included in the territory promised the Arabs in the McMahon-Hussein correspondence of 1915–1916 (see note 4). While reassuring the Arabs that Great Britain did not intend to create a wholly Jewish Palestine, Churchill rejected their interpretation of the correspondence as well as the other demands of the Arab delegation. In his principal communication with the Zionists, which is presented here, he reaffirmed His Majesty's commitment to the Balfour Declaration but in so doing offered an interpretation that was deemed by the Zionists as constituting a considerable weakening of the original intent. The Zionists were already distraught by Churchill's earlier detachment from Mandatory Palestine of Transjordan, establishing the region as an Emirate under Abdullah, son of Sheriff Hussein of Mecca; this arrangement was approved by the League of Nations in September 1922. In the present correspondence, Churchill confirmed the Jews' right to immigrate to Palestine but stipulated that immigration would have to be regulated according to the "economic absorptive capacity" of the country—a formulation that struck many Zionists as ominously ambiguous. Nonetheless, the Zionist leadership felt obliged to accept Churchill's White Paper. Acknowledging the geopolitical considerations dictating the shifts in British policy and persuaded that despite these alterations of the original terms of the Mandate, Britain's fundamental support for the establishment of a Jewish home in Palestine remained firm, the Zionist Executive formally accepted Churchill's White Paper in a statement dated June 18, 1922. Many historians believe that the White Paper was actually drafted by Sir Herbert Samuel (1870–1963), the first British High Commissioner for Palestine. A Jew sympathetic to Zionism, Sir Samuel was eager to placate Arab fears of Zionist domination while preserving the spirit of the Balfour Declaration.

2. The Supreme Council of the Paris Peace Conference met at San Remo, Italy, from April 18 to 26, 1920.

Considering various problems arising from that conference, its agenda included the final disposition of Turkey and the territories formely under its rule, including Palestine. The Supreme Council decided to incorporate the Balfour Declaration into the peace treaty with Turkey and to assign the Mandate for Palestine to Great Britain.

3. On August 10, 1920, a treaty between the Allies and Turkey was signed in Sèvres, France.
4. In an exchange of letters in 1915–1916 with Hussein ibn 'Ali, Sheriff of Mecca, Sir Henry McMahon (1862–1949), the British High Commissioner of Egypt, pledged his government's support for the independence of those

Arab countries that would aid the Allied Powers during World War I, especially in the struggle against Turkey. The Arabs were later to cite this correspondence, particularly McMahon's letter of October 14, 1915, in support of their claim to Palestine, thus claiming that the Balfour Declaration, issued subsequent to the correspondence, was invalid. In particular they invoked McMahon's letter of October 24, 1915, although it makes no explicit reference to Palestine. This letter is presented in full in Walter Laqueur, *The Israel-Arab Reader. A Documentary Reader of the Middle East Conflict* (New York: Bantam Books, 1969), pp. 15–16.

36. MANDATE FOR PALESTINE (JULY 24, 1922)[1]

THE COUNCIL OF THE LEAGUE OF NATIONS

Whereas the Principal Allied Powers have agreed, for the purpose of giving effect to the provisions of Article 22 of the Covenant of the League of Nations, to entrust to a Mandatory selected by the said Powers the administration of the territory of Palestine, which formerly belonged to the Turkish Empire, within such boundaries as may be fixed by them; and

Whereas the Principal Allied Powers have also agreed that the Mandatory should be responsible for putting into effect the declaration originally made on November 2, 1917, by the Government of His Britannic Majesty, and adopted by the said Powers, in favour of the establishment in Palestine of a national home for the Jewish people, it being clearly understood that nothing should be done which might prejudice the civil and religious rights of existing non-Jewish communities in Palestine, or the rights and political status enjoyed by Jews in any other country; and

Whereas recognition has thereby been given to the historical connection of the Jewish people with Palestine and to the grounds for reconstituting their national home in that country; and

Whereas the Principal Allied Powers have selected His Britannic Majesty as the Mandatory for Palestine; and

Whereas the mandate in respect of Palestine has been formulated in the following terms and submitted to the Council of the League for approval; and

Whereas by the aforementioned Article 22 (paragraph 8) it is provided that the degree of authority, control or administration to be exercised by the Mandatory, not having been previously agreed upon by the Members of the League, shall be explicitly defined by the Council of the League of Nations;

Confirming the said mandate, defines its terms as follows:

Article 1: The Mandatory shall have full powers of legislation and of administration, save as they may be limited by the terms of this mandate.

Source: Foreign Office, *The Constitutions of All Countries* (London: The British Empire, 1938), vol. 1, pp. 539–45.

Article 2: The Mandatory shall be responsible for placing the country under such political, administrative and economic conditions as will secure the establishment of the Jewish national home, as laid down in the preamble, and the development of self-governing institutions, and also for safeguarding the civil and religious rights of all the inhabitants of Palestine, irrespective of race and religion.

Article 3: The Mandatory shall, so far as circumstances permit, encourage local autonomy.

An appropriate Jewish agency[2] shall be recognised as a public body for the purpose of advising and co-operating with the Administration of Palestine in such economic, social and other matters as may affect the establishment of the Jewish national home and the interests of the Jewish population in Palestine, and, subject always to the control of the Administration, to assist and take part in the development of the country.

The Zionist organisation, so long as its organisation and constitution are in the opinion of the Mandatory appropriate, shall be recognised as such agency. It shall take steps in consultation with His Britannic Majesty's Government to secure the co-operation of all Jews who are willing to assist in the establishment of the Jewish national home....

NOTES

1. The Balfour Declaration was approved by other Allied governments and incorporated in the British Mandate for Palestine on July 24, 1922. The mandate system was created by Article 22 of the Covenant of the League of Nations, which formed part of the Treaty of Versailles of 1919, and then gained the recognition of all states that were members of the League. Article 22 of the Covenant declared that within the ceded territories, inhabited "by people not yet able to stand by themselves under the strenuous condition of the modern world, there should be applied the principle that the well-being and development of such peoples form a sacred trust of civilization," and that the administration of such peoples, "should be entrusted to advanced nations" to be exercised by them on behalf of the League. The mandate system applied to the territories ceded after World War I by Germany and Turkey to the principal Allied Powers. The latter appointed mandatories and approved the mandates, which were subject to confirmation by the League of Nations.

2. Since 1929 the agency established in accordance with this provision was formally known as the Jewish Agency for Palestine.

37. WHAT THE ZIONIST-REVISIONISTS WANT (1926)

VLADIMIR JABOTINSKY[1]

The first aim of Zionism is the creation of a Jewish majority on both sides of the Jordan River. This is not the ultimate goal of the Zionist movement, which aspires to more far-reaching ideals, such as the solution of the question of Jewish suffering [*Judennot-frage*] throughout the entire world and the creation of a new Jewish culture. The precondition for the attainment of these noble aims, however, is a country in which the Jews constitute a majority. It is only after this majority is attained that Palestine can undergo a

Source: Was Wollen die Zionisten-Revisionisten (Paris: Imprimerie Polyglotte, 1926) Trans. S. Weinstein.

normal political development on the basis of democratic, parliamentary principles without thereby endangering the Jewish national character of the country.

"Why proclaim this aim in public?" ask those dreamers who think that Zionism can be turned into a silent conspiracy. They are deceiving themselves. From our standpoint it is first of all useless since all our adversaries not only understand our aims, but also frequently exaggerate them (they say, for instance, that we intend to expel all the non-Jews from Palestine). It is too late to preach a "modified Zionism" [*Kleinzionismus*], for the Arabs have already read Herzl's *The Jewish State* as well as an even more "dangerous" Zionist manifesto—the Bible. Furthermore, the concealment, and particularly the negation of our aims is politically dangerous. It can only lead to the sanction of all preventive measures against Jewish immigration, which, in fact, is what has already happened. [In addition], it provides anti-Zionists with the opportunity to disguise themselves as "cultural Zionists." They argue: "Since the Jews do not wish to form a majority in the country, but rather only intend to create a spiritual center, there is no need to bring tens of thousands of Jews to Palestine annually. For this purpose thousands, and even hundreds, who have been carefully selected and come well-equipped with money, would suffice."...

In order to create a solid Jewish majority within twenty-five years in western Palestine we need an average yearly immigration of 40,000 Jews. If we take the area east of the Jordan into consideration, then we will need from 50,000 to 60,000 Jewish immigrants annually.

The immigration of 1924–1925 demonstrates that we Jews possess adequate human reserves to support immigration of these dimensions over a long period of time.[2] It must not be forgotten, however, that the economic absorption of such masses in a land the size of ours is a quite complicated task and is nearly unprecedented in the annals of modern colonization....

It follows from this that the creation of a Jewish majority in Palestine requires special measures in order to provide economic opportunities for the new settlers. Our enthusiasm, our national funds, our energy and willingness to sacrifice, as great as they may be, are not sufficient for this. The problem of the orderly absorption of such a large annual influx

of people necessitates the direct intervention of governmental authority, that is to say, a whole series of administrative and legislative measures which only a government is in a position to execute.

This is the meaning of the term "political Zionism." No one underestimates the significance of the practical work [being carried out] in Palestine or the importance of our national funds. Zionism is—and must be composed of—90 percent "economics" and only 10 percent "politics." This 10 percent, however, is the precondition, the *conditio sine qua non* of our success. Only a colonization of minor proportions, one which would be capable of creating no more than a minority that is a new ghetto, can be realized without the intervention of the state. The formation of a majority and mass immigration are tasks for a state. Their accomplishment demands the active, benevolent and systematic support of the government.

The precise definition of our political demands is thus the first task of political Zionism. It is not enough to speak in general terms of the "fulfillment of [the conditions of] the mandate" or of the "presentation of our political program." Even the friendliest government in the world would only respond to this with the question: "And so, what and which measures are needed?"...

The opening up of the area east of the Jordan is the first and most important of the reforms [needed to ensure the absorption of mass Jewish immigration]. To be sure, Trans-Jordan is part of the territory of the mandate, but it was subsequently excluded from the Zionist realm of influence within the mandate. This is a practical and historical injustice. Historically, the area east of the Jordan was always considered to be an integral part of Jewish Palestine. From the practical standpoint of mass immigration Trans-Jordan is perhaps even more important than western Palestine. Its land area is nearly the same, but it has two or three times fewer inhabitants. Also, it possesses more fertile land and more streams.... In light of the tremendous Jewish misery in Eastern Europe the exclusion of the best of Palestine from Jewish colonization is also unacceptable from the humanitarian standpoint....

How are these concessions [which we are demanding from the mandatory authority] to be obtained? Suffice it to give a very brief reply to this question: with the same means employed by Herzl, namely, through the instruction, persuasion and organization of public opinion among Jewry, the British and the entire civilized world. This is the sole meaning of the familiar slogan: "political offensive."...We have absolute confidence that every just demand, if it is rationally, energetically and boldly defended, will ultimately find a favourable reception among the British people. This is especially true regarding those demands that are in complete harmony with the obligations that England has taken upon herself and whose fulfillment is indispensable for the relief of frightful human suffering. On the basis of this great trust we call upon the Zionist public to renew the Herzlian tradition, [to pursue] the energetic, systematic and peaceable political struggle for our demands....

Our attitude toward the Palestinian Arabs is determined by the full recognition of an objective fact: even after the formation of a Jewish majority a considerable Arab population will always remain in Palestine. If things fare badly for this group of inhabitants then things will fare badly for the entire country. The political, economic and cultural welfare of the Arabs will thus always remain one of the main conditions for the well-being of the land of Israel. In the future Jewish state absolute equality will reign between residents of both peoples [*Volksstaemme*], both languages and all religions. All measures must be taken to develop the national autonomy of each of the peoples represented in the country with regard to communal affairs, education, cultural activities and political representation. We believe that in this way the Jewish people in Palestine will in the future be able to convince the Arabs inside and outside the country to reconcile themselves to [a Jewish majority in] the land of Israel.

It is a dangerous falsehood, however, to present such a reconciliation as an already existing fact. Arab public opinion in Palestine is against the creation of a Jewish majority there. The Arabs will continue to fight for a long time—sometimes energetically and sometimes apathetically, sometimes with political means and sometimes with other means—against all that which leads to the creation of this majority until the moment that the overwhelming might of the Jews in the country, i.e., the Jewish majority, becomes a fact. Only then will true reconciliation commence. To close our eyes to this state of affairs is unwise and irresponsible. We Revisionists are keeping our eyes open and want to be prepared for every eventuality. With all the sincere goodwill [we feel] toward the Arab people, we nevertheless firmly believe that the transformation of Palestine into a Jewish state is a postulate of the highest justice and that all opposition to it is unjust. One may neither come to terms with injustice or make any concessions to it. In this case especially, namely, the question of the formation of a majority, there is from our side no possibility to concede anything. One can only struggle against injustice, with peaceful means as long as it is not expressed in acts of violence, and with other means when it assumes the form of violence.

We consider the class struggle within Palestinian Jewry to be an unavoidable and even healthy phenomenon. It is to be noted with satisfaction that the pathos of this struggle in Palestine does not express itself in the struggle over already existing values, as it does elsewhere, but rather in the creation of new values. The working class builds [agricultural] collectives and cooperative workshops while the middle class concentrates [on the development of] private enterprise. Revisionism totally rejects the current fashion of taking a position against one or the other of these methods of construction....The Zionist idea of statehood is obliged to make full use of every form of authentic Jewish energy for the creation of a Jewish majority. The energy of these circles of youths who subscribe to the working-class ideology can be expressed only by the establishment of forms of life in keeping with the spirit of socialism. This is a psychological and organic fact which no argument in the world can alter. To this the Zionist idea of statehood can have only one answer: the workers must establish their own presence in Palestine as they deem fit, and the Zionist movement must support their efforts. It is an equally established fact, however, that the more or less well-to-do Jewish bourgeoisie has completely opposing social tendencies and can establish its own presence in Palestine only on an individualistic basis. To this the Zionist idea of statehood has the same answer: build as you deem fit, I will help. This is the sole correct standpoint for Zionism as a sovereign entity and therefore it is the standpoint of Revisionist ideology. Each form of construction has the right to exist. Each merits assistance and where a conflict between them breaks out the representative of the idea of statehood is to play the role of arbiter. All else is useless polemics....

Zionism appeals to the entire Jewish people for help in the reconstruction of the land of Israel. We call upon every Jew not only to give but to come and share the responsibility with us. But—and this must remain absolutely clear for all times—*the extent of responsibility depends on what is given.* From the Diaspora Zionism demands not only money, but belief—belief in the Zionist ideal. He who satisfies both these conditions is called a Zionist and is fully entitled to have a voice in decisions concerning budgetary and political problems in Palestine. However, he who offers his money while openly denying that he acknowledges the Zionist ideal is entitled to participate merely in the purely practical questions concerning our enterprise. The political work, the construction of the Jewish state, is the exclusive prerogative of those who profess to be Zionists.

The Jewish Agency—the sole mouthpiece that officially links the Zionist movement to the mandatory power and the League of Nations—must retain this prerogative. Non-Zionists and even assimilationists can be our co-workers, indeed our brothers in the establishment of new settlements. The political struggle for the future, however, can be led only by those who believe in this future—the solution of the Jewish question through the establishment of the Jewish state—and who [wholeheartedly] embrace this belief, which is called Zionism.

NOTES

1. Vladimir Jabotinsky (1880–1940), Russian Zionist leader who employed his great oratorical and analytical skill in the advocacy of political Zionism. Like Herzl, he regarded the Jewish problem as preeminently the problem of antisemitism and Jewish suffering. Dissatisfied with the acquiescence of the World Zionist Organization to what he believed to be the unsatisfactory policies of the Palestine mandatory administration, Jabotinsky resigned from the Zionist Executive in 1923. As an expression of his opposition to official Zionism, he founded in Paris in 1925 the World Union of Zionist Revisionists.

   The Balfour Declaration, sanctioned by the League of Nations, seemed to fulfil the aspirations laid down in the Basle Program: a home for the Jewish people secured under public law in Palestine. But this formula, like that of the Balfour Declaration, was deliberately vague. To be sure, the Zionists sought territorial sovereignty of the Jewish people in Palestine, but what did this mean concretely? The acquisition of the long-sought charter to establish a "home" for the Jewish people in Palestine now obliged the Zionists to determine whether a "home" was communal autonomy or a political sovereign state for the Jews. Ancillary to this question of the interpretation of Zionist aspirations were tactical issues that were equally pressing: the implementation of the charter, definition of the territorial boundaries of the mandate, the system and tempo of Jewish settlement, and the determination of Zionist policy for dealing with Arab national claims to Palestine. For a variety of considerations the majority of Zionists initially favored retaining the ambiguous formulation of the Basle Program and followed Weizmann's policy of an "organic" approach for slowly building the Jewish national home. Jabotinsky demanded a radical revision of this policy and called upon the Zionist movement to set as its unequivocal objective the establishment forthwith of a sovereign "Jewish State within its historic boundaries," and to prepare for the evacuation of the Jewish masses from the Diaspora to this state. Paradoxically, he made this appeal in the name of Herzl—the author of the Basle Program.

2. In 1924 and 1925 there was a sudden upswing in Jewish immigration to Palestine. In 1924, 14,000 Jews entered the country; in 1925, 30,000.

38. BRITH SHALOM (1925)[1]

ARTHUR RUPPIN ET AL.

STATUTES

§ 1. The name of the Association shall be "The Peace Association" (Brith Shalom).

§ 2. The seat of the Association shall be in Jerusalem. Branches may be established throughout Palestine and abroad.

§ 3. The object of the Association is to arrive at an understanding between Jews and Arabs as to the form of their mutual social relations in Palestine on the basis of absolute political equality of two culturally autonomous peoples, and to determine the lines of their co-operation for the development of the country.

§ 4. Towards this end the Association will promote:

a) The study of the problems arising out of the existence of the two peoples in Palestine, and out of the Mandate under the League of Nations;

b) The spreading of verbal and written information among Jews and Arabs on the history and culture of both peoples, and the encouragement of friendly relations between them;

c) The creation of a public opinion favorable to a mutual understanding;

d) The creation of institutions calculated to advance these ends;

§5. Any person in agreement with the object of the Association and elected by a majority decision of its Committee (§ 8) is eligible for membership.

§6. The membership fee shall be £1 a year. The committee (§ 8) is empowered to reduce this fee for labourers and other persons of limited means.

§7. A General Meeting of the Association shall take place every year. Members shall be advised at least a fortnight in advance by an announcement in three Palestinian papers which appear regularly. The first General Meeting shall be convoked before December 31st, 1927.

§8. The Committee of the Association shall consist of between 7 and 15 members elected by the General Meeting. Branches of the Association in and outside of Palestine shall elect their local Committees on similar lines.

§9. Until the first General Meeting, the founders of the Association shall act as the Committee (§ 8) and shall have the right of co-optation.

NOTE

1. In the spring of 1925, a small group of intellectuals gathered in Jerusalem to establish an association to promote a reconciliation of Zionist and Arab claims to Palestine. Initiated by Arthur Ruppin (1876–1943), the principal architect of Zionist settlement policy, the association was called *Brith Shalom*, in apparent allusion to Ezekiel 34: 25: "I will make with them a covenant of peace (*Brith Shalom*)." The founding members of Brith Shalom included veteran Jewish residents of Palestine; academics; and members of the left-wing Hapoel Hazair, the religious Mizrahi, and liberal Zionists. Gershom Scholem, a founding member who at the time was forging his renown as the preeminent scholar of Jewish mysticism, noted that what united this diverse group was a conviction "that the Land of Israel belongs to two peoples, and these peoples need to find a way to live together...and to work for a common future" (Interview, May 1972, Department of Oral History, Institute of Contemporary Jewry, Hebrew

Source: Martin Buber, *A Land of Two Peoples*, ed. with commentary by P. Mendes-Flohr (New York: Oxford University Press, 1983), p. 74.

University of Jerusalem). For Brith Shalom, it was an incontrovertible fact that the Land of Israel was a land of two peoples—the indigenous Arab population and the Jews who were returning to their ancestral home. As Ruppin succinctly told the Fourteenth Zionist Congress, which met in Vienna in August 1925: "Palestine will be a state of two peoples. Gentlemen, this is a fact, a fact which many of you have not yet sufficiently realized. It may also be that for some of you this is not a pleasant fact, but it nonetheless remains so" (*Protokoll der Verhandlungen des XIV. Zionistenkongress...*, London, 1926, p. 438). Ruppin and his colleagues envisioned a binational state as allowing for a modus vivendi between Zionism and Arab nationalism within the

existing framework of the Mandate, which they tacitly assumed that Britain, because of its imperialistic interests, would tenaciously maintain. The Jewish National Home would somehow have to be realized within the terms of the binational reality of Mandatory Palestine. Accordingly, Brith Shalom proposed, as the most reasonable solution to the problem of Palestine, a constitutional arrangement whereby the Jews and Arabs would enjoy political and civil parity within the unitary framework of the Mandate. Brith Shalom, however, did not view itself as a political party, but, as stated in the statutes of the association, merely as a study circle sponsoring informed and responsible discussion of the Arab question.

39. OPENING OF HEBREW UNIVERSITY (1925)[1]

CHAIM WEIZMANN

We have come together today, on soil steeped in sacred memories, to inaugurate the Hebrew University of Jerusalem. Some of those whom I am happy to see here will cast their minds back to that July afternoon, nearly seven years ago, when we laid the foundation stones. Palestine was still a battlefield. Jerusalem itself was within sound of the guns. The ceremony of 24 July, 1918 was witness to our faith in happier days to come. The intervening years, when throughout the world chaos has been slowly yielding to order, have not been too favourable to our labours. But our faith has been justified. The dreams have already begun to be translated into realities, and the first departments of the Hebrew University have opened their doors.

The university has still a long road to travel before it can realise to the full the hopes of its founders. On that point we are under no illusions. We have made

no attempt to extemporize a pretentious replica of one of the great teaching universities of the West. We have made up our minds that it is for our university to win its spurs and build up its reputation by the distinctive value of its contributions to the common stock of knowledge. We have begun with a group of institutes for advanced research in those branches of science and learning for which Palestine offers a peculiarly congenial soil. The building before which we stand is the modest home of three such institutes devoted respectively to chemistry, to microbiology, and to Jewish and Oriental studies, and before these celebrations are concluded, we shall lay the foundation stone of an Institute of Physics and Mathematics to be associated with the name of Einstein. These various departments are served by the Jewish National Library with its 90,000 volumes and its distinguished collection of Orientalia. A fitting home for the library

Source: The Letters and Papers of Chaim Weizmann, Vol. 1 (Series B: August 1898–July 1931), ed. Barnet Litvinoff (New Brunswick, N. J.: Rutgers University Press; Jerusalem: Israel University Press, 1983), pp. 442–45.

will be built as soon as the architect has made the appropriate plans. Modest, indeed, is our immediate achievement when compared with the towers and the cloisters, the libraries and the museums, the galleries of art, and the magnificent endowments with which the ancient universities of Europe and their younger sisters of America are blessed. But it is not presumptuous on our part if we hold the conviction that in due course the material equipment and the outer garb of our Hebrew University will be worthy of its sisters, worthy of itself, and worthy of this site miraculous in beauty and tradition.

Closely allied to our university, and destined in the course of time to be still more intimately associated with it, are our Agricultural Institute at Tel Aviv and our Technical Institute at Haifa. As Tel Aviv and its hinterland stand for the application of science to agriculture, so Haifa stands for its application to industry. Patient research in the interests of science, combined with practical service to the people of Palestine and its neighbors—these are tasks to which the infant university is dedicated.

What we are inaugurating today is a *Hebrew* University. Hebrew will be the language of its schools and colleges. But a university is nothing if it is not universal. It must stand not only for the pursuit of every form of knowledge which the mind of man embraces, but also for a commonwealth of learning, freely open to all men and women of every creed and race. Within the precincts of these schools political strife and division cease and all creeds and races will, I hope, be united in the great common task of searching for truth, in restoring to Palestine the thriving civilisation which it once enjoyed, and in giving it a place of its own in the world of thought and learning. Our university would not be true to itself or to Jewish traditions if it were not a house of study for all peoples, and more especially for all the peoples of Palestine. Conceived in this spirit, and animated by these ideals, the university has before it, if our hopes are realised, a future pregnant with possibilities not only for the Jews or for Palestine, but also for the awakening of the East and for mankind at large. But we feel in our innermost being that if this university is to express us and, by expressing us, look at the world from our angle and make a distinctive contribution to civilisation, it must be through the medium of Hebrew. The Jewish spirit and the Hebrew tongue have never been separated, and this university must be a witness to their eternal union.

In inaugurating the Hebrew University, we proclaim the fellowship of the Jewish people with the peoples of the world, and the dedication of the Jewish people to the common labour of civilisation. The latest of Jewish academies, it carries on a long tradition of Hebrew learning and of Hebrew striving with the mystery of the universe. It looks back to the schools of the Prophets and the Sages, to those who out of the wreck of the Jewish State constituted the Academies of Jabneh, of Nehardea and of Pumpeditha; to those who in the dark days of the Middle Ages maintained a high and pure standard of intellectual activities in the *yeshivot* and colleges scattered throughout the Diaspora. Deprived of the material props of nationhood, the scattered hosts of Israel found moral unity, and centered their aspirations round the great schools of thought which sprang up in Spain, Italy and France; in Poland and Germany; in Baghdad and Alexandria. These schools were resting-places on the long and weary road of persecuted Israel, and within their walls the Jewish genius, prevented from taking part in the life of the ambient, hostile world, built up a world of its own in which unhampered and unfettered the Jewish genius could express itself.

Our young institutes look also for inspiration and guidance to the many Jewish intellectual workers who, in our day, add their effort to the advancement of science and art the world over.

It now only remains for me to welcome, in the name of the founders, all those who have honoured us today by their presence—His Excellency the High Commissioner for Palestine, representing His Majesty's Government; His Excellency the High Commissioner for Egypt, Lord Allenby, whose name will remain forever associated with the liberation of Palestine and who, in his wisdom, sanctioned the laying of the foundation stones of this university seven years ago; the representatives of the governments; the distinguished delegates of universities and learned bodies in all parts of the world whose fraternal greetings—so generously offered—are deeply appreciated; and the leading members of all sections of the population of Palestine.

It is my special privilege to welcome Lord Balfour, and to welcome him not only as an eminent figure in the world of thought; not only as the Chancellor of an historic university,[4] but also as the statesmen whose name will for all time be associated with the generous act which changed the face of the Jewish world in 1917. The university which Lord Balfour is about to open is the distinctive symbol, as it is destined to be the crowning glory, of the National Home which we are seeking to rebuild.

Humbly and reverently, conscious of what we owe alike to others and to ourselves, we are seeking to make in Palestine our characteristic contribution to the common stock. That is the spirit in which we approach the task to which we have set our hands. That is the spirit in which I shall ask Lord Balfour to inaugurate the Hebrew University.

NOTES

1. In 1920, Chaim Weizmann (1874–1952) was elected the president of the World Zionist Organization, an office he held until 1931 (and then again from 1935 until 1946). It was in this capacity as well as that of the chairman of the Board of Governors of the Hebrew University of Jerusalem, that on April 1, 1925, he presided over the ceremonies inaugurating the realization of an institution of which he was one of the spiritual architects. He was the coauthor (together with Martin Buber and Berthold Feiwel) of a 1902 pamphlet calling for the establishment of a "Jewish college." He continued to advocate for the founding of an institution of higher learning that would meet the needs of Jewish students, especially from Eastern Europe. Finally, his efforts bore fruit when at the 11th Zionist Congress in 1913 a proposal was adopted to take concrete steps to realize the establishment of a Hebrew University in Jerusalem—*Hebrew* because the language of instruction would be Hebrew. As a full-blown secular university, the institution would embody the values of cultural Zionism. Because of World War I, actual work toward realization of the vision was postponed until 1918, when land was purchased on Mount Scopus, overlooking the surrounding hills of Jerusalem, and the foundation stones of the university were laid. Speaking in Hebrew and English, Weizmann—who was later to be the first president of the State of Israel—briefly reviewed the history of the nascent university and its animating vision. He then introduced the first speaker Lord Arthur James Balfour, the author of Great Britain's pledge to support the establishment of a Jewish homeland in Palestine (see this chapter, document 32). Among the many dignitaries, Jewish and non-Jewish, who attended the ceremony were Sir Herbert Samuel, the first High Commissioner of Palestine; Haim Nahman Bialik; and the Chief Rabbi of Palestine, Abraham Isaac Kook.

2. Albert Einstein (1879–1955), who received the Nobel Prize in physics in 1921, became, with the inauguration of the Hebrew University, a member of its Board of Governors, remaining on the board until his death. In 1932, the university opened the Albert Einstein Institute of Physics.

3. Arthur James Balfour (1848–1930) was a senior British statesman, politician, and philosopher. From 1902 to 1905, he was prime minister of England. It was during his premiership that Britain offered Herzl and the Zionist movement a plan to establish a Jewish colony in East Africa (see "the Uganda Plan," document 15 of this chapter). As the British foreign secretary (from 1916 to 1919), he conducted the negotiations with Weizmann and other Zionist leaders that resulted in the issuance of the Balfour Declaration.

4. From 1890 Lord Balfour served as chancellor of the University of Edinburgh.

40. REFLECTIONS ON OUR LANGUAGE[1]

GERHARD SCHOLEM

This country is a volcano: It hosts the [holy] language! One speaks here of many matters that may lead to our failure. One speaks more than ever about the Arabs. But much more disconcerting than the Arab Question is another threat,[2] a threat that the Zionist project has unavoidably had to face: the "actualization" of Hebrew.[3]

Must not the abyss of a holy language, on which we have nurtured our children, once again burst open? To be sure, one does not know what one does. One believes that the language has been secularized, and its apocalyptic thorn [thus] removed. But this is not true at all. The secularization of the language is only a *façon de parler*: a phrase! It is utterly impossible to empty words that are filled to the bursting point [with religious meaning]—lest one sacrifice the language itself. The ghastly gibberish which we hear spoken in the streets [of Jerusalem] is precisely the expressionless language that is possible, indeed is only possible with the "secularization" of the language. If we could transmit to our children that language which was transmitted to us, and if we, a transitional generation, could revitalize the language of the ancient books for them, would it not then reveal itself anew through them? And must not, then, the religious power of this language one day burst forth? But which generation will encounter this power? As for us, we surely live in this language at the edge of an abyss, almost with the surety of the blind, but will not we, or those who come after us, stumble into the abyss when we will regain our sight? And no one knows, whether the sacrifice of those individuals who will perish in the abyss would suffice to close it.

The founders of the movement to revive the [Hebrew] language blindly believed, to the point of pig-headedness, in its miraculous power. That was their good fortune! No one with clear foresight would have mustered the demonic courage to try to revitalize a language in a situation where only an Esperanto could have resulted. They walked and still walk spellbound above the abyss, which remains silent, and have transmitted the language to our youth together with all its ancient names and signs; it often jars us with dread when we hear in a thoughtless conversation a religious term. The Hebrew language is fraught with danger. It cannot remain and will not remain in its present state. Since our children no longer have any other language, they and they alone will have to pay for this predicament, which none other than we have imposed upon them without forethought and without question. The day will come when the language will turn against those who speak it, and on occasion it has already, moments that are difficult to forget, when the audacity of our undertaking has become manifest. When that day will come will our youth be capable of withstanding the [inevitable] revolt of the holy language?

Language is Name. The power of the language is encased within the name; its abyss is sealed within the name. Now that we daily summon up the old names, it is no longer in our power to do so without arousing the forces that they contain. These powers will appear, for we have called upon them, after all, with great violence. *We*, to be sure, speak a rudimentary, ghastly Hebrew: the names go in circles in our sentences, one plays with them in publications and

Source: Gerhard Scholem, "Bekenntnis ueber unsere Sprache: An Franz Rosenzweig," in: *Franz Rosenzweig zum 25. Dezember 1928. Glueckwuensche zum 40. Geburtstag.* [Congratulations to Franz Rosenzweig on this 40th Birthday, December 25, 1928]. Published on the Centenary of Franz Rosenzweig's Birth by the Leo Baeck Institute, New York. Limited facsimile edition with separate booklet of *Transcriptions and Translations*, edited with an introduction by Martin Goldner. The German text and translation of Scholem's "letter" are on pp. 47–49. The letter has been here translated anew by Paul Mendes-Flohr.

in newspapers. One deceives oneself or God, if one claims it is unimportant. And yet out of the spectral degradation of our language, the power of the Holy may spring forth. For the names have their own life! If it were not so, then woe to our children, who would be hopelessly thrust into the void.

Each word that is not newly created, but taken from the "good old" treasures, is ready to burst forth with meaning. A generation that has taken possession of the most fruitful of our holy traditions—our language—cannot simply live without tradition, even if it would most ardently wish to. That moment when the power stored in the language is *released*, when the "spoken word," when the content of the language takes on once again form, our people will find itself confronted with the contemporary [expression of the] tradition as a decisive sign, before which they will only have the strength either to submit to it humbly or to perish. God will not remain silent in the language in which He is entreated a thousand times to enter anew in our lives.

This inevitable revolution of the language, in which the Voice will be heard again, is the only subject that is never discussed in the country. Those who called the Hebrew language back into life did not believe in the Judgment to which they thereby summoned us. May it thus come to pass that their recklessness, which has led us onto an apocalyptic path, not end in disaster.

Jerusalem, 7 Teveth 5687[4]   Gerhard Scholem

NOTES

1. To mark the occasion of the fortieth birthday of Franz Rosenzweig (1886–1929), who was almost totally paralyzed, bedridden, and unable to turn the pages of a book, his friend Martin Buber arranged to send large (39 by 31 centimeters) sheets of specially selected, light-brown paper to forty-six of Rosenzweig's friends and associates. He requested that they use the paper to compose birthday greetings to Rosenzweig in any form they wished. The form of the contributions varied considerably: poems, short stories, translations of ancient texts, philosophical and theological musings, and even a drawing. Most were in German, and a few in Hebrew. They were collected in a portfolio or "*Mappe*" and presented to Rosenzweig on his birthday. Writing in German, Gerhard (Gershom) Scholem (for biographical details, see chapter 5, document 13), who settled in Jerusalem in 1923, recorded his reflections on the project of reviving Hebrew as a spoken secular language.

2. Scholem himself was profoundly exercised by the Arab Question. Indeed, he was one of the founding members of Brit Shalom, which sought to promote the reconciliation of Arab and Jewish claims to Palestine by proposing a binational state. (Cf. document 39 in this chapter.)

3. The reference here is apparently to Rosenzweig's review of Jacob Klatzkin's Hebrew translation of Spinoza's *Ethics*, *Torat Ha-Middot* (Leipzig: Abraham Josef Stiebel Verlag, 1925). Rosenzweig's review, "Classical and Modern Hebrew: A Review of a Translation into the Hebrew of Spinoza's *Ethics*" was published in *Der Morgen* 11/1(1926): 105–109. For an English translation of extensive excerpts of Rosenzweig's review, see *Franz Rosenzweig: His Life and Thought*, presented by Nahum N. Glatzer, 3rd ed. (Indianapolis/Cambridge: Hackett, 1998), pp. 263–71. In the review Rosenzweig questioned the viability of the Zionist project to secularize Hebrew. A Zionist, Klatzkin (1882–1948) advocated the "normalization" of Jewish national existence, and toward that end, the radical secularization of Jewish culture. For Klatzkin, a normal or healthy national life was defined by the purely formal attributes of land and language; the return of the Jews to their land and the renewal of Hebrew as their vernacular, everyday language were thus to be solely formal acts, utterly free of all religious and spiritual content. But as Rosenzweig observes in his review of Klatzkin's translation of Spinoza, which drew upon the vocabulary of medieval Jewish philosophy, which bears the theological presuppositions of traditional Judaism actually discloses the impossibility of a genuine secularization of the Hebrew tongue. Hebrew resists being dislodged from its spiritual moorings. Before emigrating to Palestine Scholem shared this conviction, but after three years of participating in the Zionist project he had his misgivings, which he expressed in his "birthday greetings" to Rosenzweig. He, nonetheless, felt that the secularization of Judaism was dialectically necessary, indeed, urgent. This was the basis of his Zionism. Scholem deemed the rejuvenation of Hebrew as a spoken everyday language and the return of the Jews and their culture to the social realities of secular history to be a necessary condition in order to wrench Judaism from what he regarded to be the deadening grip of a spiritually desiccated Orthodoxy, on the one hand, and a vacuous assimilation, on the other. Although fraught with danger, secularization was the only path leading to the renewal of Judaism as a intellectual and spiritually compelling religious reality.

4. The date according to the Hebrew calendar, which is the equivalent of December 12, 1926.

41. *KIBBUTZ HAKHSHARAH:* A MEMOIR (c. 1935)[1]

DAVID FRANKEL

I was born in a small [Polish] town next to the German border. My parents were very religious and I was sent, of course, to study Torah, first in a *heder* and later at a *yeshivah*. My father, whom everyone called Shmuel the Rabbi, was a fervent *Hasid*, and until the age of eighteen I absorbed the spirit of Hasidism in all its variety. As I matured it became clear to me that there was no future in our town for a Jewish youth, for many of the Christian citizens were antisemitic. I felt that the place was too confining and that the ground was burning under my feet. I decided to join the *Halutz* movement[2] and to strive to immigrate to Israel. When I revealed my ideas to my parents it was a terrible blow to them. My father objected violently but in vain. One bright day I left the house of my parents and went to the *kibbutz hakhsharah* in the city of Lodz.[3]

I arrived at Ugrodova No. 9 at midnight. At the gate of the kibbutz courtyard I was met by the guards, who were accompanied by enormous dogs capable of ripping a man apart. The kibbutz was located on the fifth floor of a large building which belonged to one Trubowitz. A huge hall, with tens of beds arranged on two levels—the sleeping quarters of the kibbutz—made a bad impression on me. The moment I entered, two fellows, Zalman Kirshner and Asher Gabai, jumped from their beds, introduced themselves as members of the kibbutz and began to shower me with questions: Why did I come to the kibbutz? What did I do at home? Was I prepared to suffer? What books had I read? etc. etc. When I heard the whole group burst out laughing I realized that I was being razzed.

My first job was arranging blocks of ice in an empty lot and covering them with sawdust. The work was exhausting and because of this several members left the kibbutz. Some time later I was sent to a unit in Alexander near Lodz.[4] There too the situation was pretty bad. Despite my objections I was forced to stay there. I was chosen to organize the work. This was a difficult task. In this town there were kibbutzim of Mizrahi,[5] Betar,[6] Agudat Israel,[7] and ours, and finding work was the hardest job of all. Fortunately I was lucky. A fellow from my home town was studying in the *yeshivah* of the Rabbi of Alexander,[8] and he advertised the matter of my "family connections," thus winning me the support of the Rabbi. As a result I was able to arrange work for several members who then brought considerable income to the kibbutz. I myself found work in the grain warehouse of one of the members of the Poalei Zion,[9] Yechiel Fein. And of course, where there is bread there is Torah.[10]

In the evenings there were lessons in Hebrew; we had lectures by members of the Secretariat in Lodz who visited us frequently. We had open discussions on Sabbath evenings, we held *oneg shabbat* parties and public singing.[11] We often went to the theatre and the movies. We greatly enjoyed the cultural work of the members of the Poalei Zion party in Alexander. Our unit in Alexander numbered about 30 people at the time. Despite the difficult conditions our life was pleasant.

After some time we received permits to immigrate to Israel. We left for our parental homes to get ready, but because of the lack of certificates[12] we were called back to the kibbutzim. Even I went back to Lodz. The situation improved considerably in this period. The kibbutz moved to Lensho 41, to the large halls belonging to Stein. We had central heating, good quarters, and a spacious and attractive dining room

Source: David Frankel, "By Virtue of My Parentage," in Shlomo Even-Shoshan, ed., *The Story of Kibbutz Hakhsharah: Kibbutz Borochov at Lodz and its Surroundings.* (Tel Aviv: Hakibbutz Hameuchad Press 1970), pp. 59–60 (Hebrew). Trans. by L. Sachs.

with a piano in the corner. A chorus was organized which brought a lot of good cheer to the kibbutz. When I returned to Lodz for the second time I reconciled myself to the prospect of spending several years in this framework.

NOTES

1. This is a memoir of David Frankel, later a resident of Givatayim, Israel, in which he describes his experience in a *kibbutz hakhsharah*, a commune established in the Diaspora to "prepare" or "train" youth for pioneering work in Palestine. During the 1920s and 1930s hundreds of such communes were established throughout the Diaspora. Most of them were oriented to agriculture; others were based on cooperative workshops for the training of members as artisans. The acquisition of agricultural and manual skills, however, was only one aspect of the *hakhsharah* (Hebrew, "preparation"); the prospective pioneers were introduced to communal values, conversational Hebrew, and the secular Jewish culture evolving in Palestine; some *hakhsharot* (pl.) also provided military training, which was particularly stressed by the Revisionists (see this chapter, document 38).

2. Most of the *hakhsharah* centers were maintained by the Halutz (pioneer) movement, which emerged after World War I in Russia. At a conference held in Moscow in January 1919 in which representatives of twenty-three Halutz groups participated, it was decided that the movement should be a nonpolitical body embracing all factions of the Zionist movement dedicated to *aliyah* and to pioneering values. The Soviet authorities soon forbade Zionist activities, and the center of the movement moved to Poland but with branches—and *hakhsharot*—throughout the Diaspora.

3. The kibbutz *hakhsharah* in Lodz was named in honor of Ber Borochov (see this chapter, document 12) and existed from 1931 to 1939.

4. Aleksandrow Lodzki (referred to in Yiddish as Alexander) had a Jewish population in 1939 of 3,500, which was approximately one third of the entire population.

5. See this chapter, document 12.

6. Betar was the youth movement of the Revisionists.

7. The reference is to Poalei Agudat Israel (Workers of Agudat Israel), founded in 1922 in Poland as the workers, organization of Agudat Israel (see this chapter, doc. 25). Initially it was intended primarily to protect the rights of religious Jewish workers. With the deteriorating situation of the Jews in interwar Europe, the movement became increasingly Palestine-centered and established *hakhsharah* centers for the training of pioneers. Although not regarding itself as Zionist, Poalei Agudat Israel cooperated with the secular Zionist movement. In 1960 it seceded from Agudat Israel and established itself as an independent organization.

8. Rabbi Isaac Menahem (1880–1943), who was to perish in Treblinka, was the last of the influential dynasty of the hasidic masters or *zadikim* of Alexander.

9. See this chapter, document 19, note 1.

10. Cf. "If there is no bread [literally "flour"] there is no Torah." *Ethics of the Fathers*, 3:17.

11. *Oneg shabbat* is a gathering held late on Saturday afternoon for lectures and other Jewish cultural events, followed by communal singing. The name, meaning "Sabbath delight," derives from Isaiah 58:13: "and [thou shall] call the Sabbath a delight [*oneg*]." Having its origins in the hasidic "third meal," the institution was developed by the *halutzim* of the second *aliyah* and further refined by the poet Haim Nahman Bialik soon after his arrival in Palestine in the mid-1920s.

12. In 1920 the British Mandatory Government of Palestine issued an Immigration Ordinance, which provided for the admission of Jewish immigrants to the country on the basis of special "certificates" divided into special categories. The system, which was occasionally modified, remained in force for the entire duration of the Mandate and permitted the authorities to regulate and restrict the influx of Jewish immigrants. The Jewish Agency distributed on an individual basis the certificates for the special "labor" category, that is, those for immigrants who were prepared for and assured of gainful employment; naturally, prospective *halutzim* were given preference.

42. "THE WORKER'S WIFE": A PUBLIC TRIAL (FEBRUARY 7, 1937)[1]

ABBA HOUSHI AND ADA MAIMON

ARGUMENTS OF THE PLAINTIFF[2]

1. The aspiration of the Socialist Zionist Workers' Movement—a movement which is building a society of socialist Jewish laborers in their renewed homeland—is to see the woman worker, the working woman, as a partner with equal rights and duties in its labor of construction and creation and in its struggle to achieve its goal.

2. At the basis of our workers' movement stand the principles of freedom and absolute equality for the woman worker.

3. At the outset of the struggle of our movement—during the period of the second *aliyah* and at the beginning of the third *aliyah* [1919–1923]—the woman worker participated fully and as an equal with the man in the labor of building the country, in creating a way of life, in ideological struggle, in defense.

4. With the increased numbers of laborers, with the mass immigration, the numbers of women workers also increased—but the woman worker began to trail behind the man and was pushed aside into family life. The question of the "woman worker" and the question of "deprivation" began to arise in the movement—inequality at the work-place and in political, social and cultural life.

5. The number of women in the Histadrut comes to 40–45 percent [of its membership]; that is, from 40,000 to 45,000. Their [political] weight is not equal to their numbers.

6. And if the woman wage laborer does take part in social life, she leaves it when she has a family, shutting herself off within the confines of the family, breaking her ties with the movement, and when this happens she is gradually alienated from the life of the movement, its aspirations, and its struggle to realize its aims.

7. The proof of this: the number of married members in Haifa (we will limit ourselves to Haifa in order to be sure of the numbers) is at least 5,000–6,000 of which 2,700 are listed in the Histadrut as "workers' wives"—that is, as fictitious members. 300–400 are listed with the Association of Working Mothers[3]—if we are optimistic and add [the suburb Kiryat Haim—the Association of Working Mothers in [greater] Haifa includes perhaps 500–600 members. Of these—again taking an optimistic estimate—100–200 are active. That is, only 10 percent of the married women belong to the association and, of these, only 20 percent are active. The proportion of active members within the total membership comes to 3–5 percent.

8. The great mass of married women devote themselves to the life of the family—which is important in itself—but the family and family life are only part of the life of the society and the movement. And the isolation in family life has negative by-products which endanger the future of the movement, like: the weaving of threads of petty bourgeois life, later anti-social—the woman is concerned with having a nice home, attractive furniture—the rooms turn into furniture warehouses—in workers' neighborhoods we begin to have competition between one woman and another—one decorates a bedroom for 20–30 pounds, and the other tries to outdo her. The laborer's family is over its head in debt—the worker is affected and pulled into the stream of petty bourgeois life, the child—the future of the movement—is brought up in this atmosphere of the desire to have "a modern bedroom."

Source: Abba Houshi Archives, Haifa, translated in Deborah Bernstein, *The Struggle for Equality: Urban Women Workers in Pre-State Israeli Society* (New York: Praeger, 1987), pp. 192–96. We are grateful to Deborah Bernstein for providing us with this document. Reprinted by permission of Deborah Bernstein.

9. The member who is a "worker's wife" does not attend meetings, lectures, does not read the workers' newspapers, does not read books; her thoughts and her horizons narrow and center around the kitchen, the bedroom and at best the garden next to the home.

10. The woman becomes alienated from the questions which are vital to the worker as an individual and from the workers' movement in general, and she cannot extract herself from private concerns—and she calls this "freedom of the individual"—she is alienated from local products and from the products of the Jewish worker, and she runs after the "bargain" which is no "bargain" and she goes to the "market" to buy goods which are not the produce of the Jewish laborer.

11. These phenomena—which are mass phenomena; and few are "exceptions"—endanger the unity of the workers' movement, the righteousness of its struggle, its ability to act and its future (the child, the youth).

12. For these reasons, the panel of judges must come to a verdict which obligates the married woman to cease being simply a "worker's wife" and to live a self-fulfilling and independent life, to organize in associations of working mothers, to take part in the life of society and the movement, to take an active role in its creative work, in its struggles and in its activities, to be active in the Association of Working Mothers, to fight steadily and steadfastly against the petty bourgeois life which is taking root in our lives and to take part in the establishment of social, cultural and educational activities which are specific to women and important to the entire movement.

ARGUMENTS OF THE DEFENSE[4]

1. In every generation women's education has not included creativity, not included preparation for labor and the aspiration to stand on her own two feet—the fruits of this education continue to accumulate in our society, without any resistance against the accepted way of doing things, as if it were natural and there was nothing new under the sun.

2. The new woman, the pioneer who has broken out of the traditional framework and who struggles for the right to work and to support herself without being dependent on others—this pioneer does not find sympathy either in society or in the Histadrut.

And the married woman, the member's wife who sees liberation from the bonds of tradition only in self-support, is often treated with derision and as inconsequential by our members.

3. In the Histadrut, equality regarding the position of the woman in society, at work and in public and political life is an empty platitude. The fact is that even if the woman worker proves that she is productive, she receives daily or monthly wages which are lower than those of a man for the same work and the same output.

4. The worker's wife who is listed as a "helpmate" in her husband's membership card is in fact a fictitious member and this does not, God forbid, affect the integrity of the Histadrut, and it seems that our members are satisfied if the workers' wives can be organized to vote in elections—and no more.

5. The workers' wife does not receive the same Sick Fund services as her husband the member. For the one who pays is viewed as the member and the worker's wife as a "free addition."

6. The property of the family—including the worker's family—is listed only in the name of the man—the lord of the house. And if there is misunderstanding and matters which require separation, it is also acceptable in our society for the property to remain with the man—and if he is a "decent man" he gives something to support the mother and the children.

7. And if the worker's wife also has a vocation and works outside the home, it is clear and well known ahead of time that whatever happens at work—she will be the first to be fired so that justice will be done and two family heads will not be employed. And this is common even in the case where the member's wife earns more than her husband. Leaving the husband at home to take care of the home and the children—that is considered sloth.

8. The fact that 40 percent of Histadrut members are women, yet there are almost no women who actually participate as representatives of the community of workers—this fact leads one to believe that the workers' movement is not making any effort to change the existing situation.

9. It is true that when a woman is a mother she has to stop working for given periods, but that does not mean that she must stop forever, for the part played by women in the settlement of the country and the construction of an independent economy for the workers' movement in Palestine is well known....

10. To summarize the picture, the low wages of the woman worker, her being pushed out of public, economic and political life, the lack of esteem for the hard work of the woman who works in her own home, etc., all these serve to create in the worker's wife a conflict of inferiority and dependence, and she views herself as a second-class citizen and therefore allows herself to break Histadrut prohibitions and no longer has any desire to protest.

In spite of everything, the worker's wife still makes considerable efforts to find a way—on her own—of not leaving the Histadrut.

11. The situation makes it mandatory for us to find ways and means of correcting the defects of our society and, first of all, one must recognize, once and for all, that the basic social problem in our society is to stand the woman on her own two feet. And these are the means of solution:

(a) To reserve those jobs in which the working woman has already proven her capability or will prove her capability—for women.

(b) To establish a network of child-care centers to be operated day and night by the state or the society, in which the family will be able to leave the child with an experienced child-care worker.

(c) To give the woman worker and the working woman job training, for skilled labor is easier than unskilled labor.

(d) To start a campaign the purpose of which is to explain to women as well as to men members the importance of the duty of labor for every person in society, without discriminating between men and women.

(e) To strengthen working women's belief in their own powers, to give them both duties and rights and to strengthen working consciousness.

(f) To repeat day and night that the woman pioneer is a pioneer in a double sense, because she has to inspire confidence in herself and in others that she is capable of work.

(g) And above everything else: to organize all the workers' wives in associations for working mothers, and we must all view this organization as the most reliable means of preserving the values of our movement.

12. And as far as the situation today is concerned—it is not the woman who should be judged but the society and first and foremost our own society, which is a revolutionary society, and we must therefore work for the liberation of women, in every area of life, and not just preach but also practice what we preach. The liberation of the woman is a necessary precondition for the achievement of socialism. Socialism will not liberate the woman, but the liberation of the working woman will bring the realization of socialism closer.

NOTES

1. This document is the protocol of a mock public trial of "the worker's wife"—which, if it actually took place, was presumably in Haifa—concerning the status of women in the Jewish labor movement in Palestine. The idea of the trial was undoubtedly to raise the consciousness of the Histadrut regarding the overall marginality of women, especially married women within the movement, and the problem of gender discrimination within the economy of the *yishuv*. Both the "plaintiff" and the "defense"—represented respectively by two leading figures of the labor movement—acknowledge the inequality of women. The "plaintiff" accuses the "worker's wife" of lacking the initiative and the resolve to correct the situation. The "defense attorney" reverses the accusation, pointing to the hypocrisy of the Histadrut and its ultimate insensitivity to the special problems of working women.

2. The plaintiff was represented by Abba Houshi (Schneller; 1898–1969), who one year later was elected secretary general of the Haifa Labor Council, a position he held until 1951. Born in Galicia, he settled in Palestine in 1920. Among the founders of Kibbutz Bet Alfa, he initially worked on road building, swamp drainage, and agriculture. In 1927 he moved to Haifa, where he worked as a dock worker, gaining prominence as a labor organizer. He was elected to the First Knesset in 1949, representing Mapai; he resigned in 1951 to become mayor of Haifa, a position he held until his death.

3. The Association of Working Mothers (*Irgun Imahot Ovdot*) was founded in 1930 by the Council of Women Workers (see the following note) to address the specific needs of wives of Histadrut members who had no employment outside the home and who as "housewives" saw no role for themselves in public life.

4. The defense was represented by Ada Maimon (née Fishman; 1893–1973), a founder of the women's labor movement in Palestine. Born in Bessarabia, Russia, she settled in Palestine in 1912, where she worked variously

as a teacher and a farmhand. A vigorous advocate of the rights of working women, she was in 1922 among the founders of the Council of Women Workers (*Moetzet Hapoalot*) as part of the Histadrut and served as its secretary from 1921 to 1930. The roots of the council go back to the second *aliyah* and a handful of *halutzot* (pioneer women) who banded together to protest gender discrimination. Their slogan was "Women demand the right to be partners in the revival of our people and

to fulfill (ourselves)…as women and human beings." Maimon was instrumental in the establishment of the Association of Working Mothers.

Maimon held many prominent positions in the Zionist labor movement in Palestine, representing Hapoel Hazair (later Mapai) in the Histadrut, the *Vaad Leumi* (see this chapter, document 48, note 2), Zionist Congresses, and the First and Second Knesset of the State of Israel.

43. ON THE ARAB QUESTION (JANUARY 7, 1937)[1]

DAVID BEN-GURION

DAVID BEN-GURION: A great deal was heard about the benefit which had accrued to this country from Jewish work, the improvement of agriculture in Palestine, the provision of more work, better sanitary conditions, better education and so on. It is not the virtue of the Jews that brought this about and brought benefit to the country, but it is inherent in our work. Our aim cannot be accomplished in Palestine without a creative constructive work in agriculture, industry, education, etc. The welfare of the whole country is our deep concern for moral, economic and political grounds. But I want to remove a possible misunderstanding which may arise in such a discussion. The benefit which is accruing to the country from our work is not the reason and the justification of our being here and of the Jewish National Home. We are here in our own right. We regard the Jewish National Home as an end in itself. We claim to be here and to assure our future here because it is our own right and it is justified in itself, whether it benefits others or not.

…Our right in Palestine is not derived from the Mandate and the Balfour Declaration. It is prior to

that.…The Bible is our Mandate, the Bible which was written by us, in our own language, in Hebrew, in this very country. That is our Mandate. Our right is as old as the Jewish people. It was only the recognition of this right which was expressed in the Balfour Declaration and the Mandate. It is stated in the Mandate that it recognizes the right of the Jewish people to reconstitute their National Home.

We are here as of right and I believe all those people, first of all the British people and then other European nations and the United States of America, which endorsed the action of Great Britain, for them, too, the Jewish National Home was an end in itself. It was not in order that the Jews should benefit Palestine, but it was to solve the Jewish problem. It was to remove a grievance, a historical grievance of the Jewish people against the whole Christian world for many centuries. There were attempts, very worthy and sincere attempts, by civilized people during the last century to remove the grievance of the Jewish people, their persecutions and their sufferings, by giving them equal rights in England and France

---

Source: *Palestine Royal Commission, Notes of Evidence Taken On Thursday, 7 January 1937, Forty-Ninth Meeting* (Public), pp. 288–91.

and other countries; but it proved to be no solution, because it did not take away the root of our troubles, and the root is that we are in every country a minority at the mercy of the majority. This majority may treat us rightly and fairly, as in England and in France, and it may be otherwise, as in Germany, but we are always at the mercy of others.

...We do not intend to create in Palestine the same intolerable position for the Jews as in all other countries. It means a radical change for the Jewish people; otherwise, there is no need for a National Home. It is not to give the Jews equal rights in Palestine. It is to change their position as a people. I want to say one word on why we are here in Palestine. It is not because we once conquered Palestine. Many people have conquered a country and lost it, and they have no claim to that country, but here we are for two reasons unprecedented in history. The first is this—Palestine is the only country in the world that the Jews, not as individuals but as a nation, as a race, can regard as their own country, as their historic homeland, and the second reason is there is no other nation—I do not say population, I do not say sections of a people—there is no other race or nation as a whole which regards this country as their only homeland. All of the inhabitants of Palestine are children of this country and have full rights in this country, not only as citizens but as children of this homeland, but they have it in their capacity as inhabitants of this country. We have it as Jews, as children of the Jewish people, whether we are here already or whether we are not here yet. When the Balfour Declaration was made, there were 60,000 Jews here. It was not only the right of those 60,000. Now we are 400,000, and it is not only the right of these 400,000. It is because we are the children of the Jewish people and it is the only homeland of the Jewish people that we have rights in this country.

We are returning to Palestine, and we gladly and without qualification admit one very essential limit, and that limit is the rights of the inhabitants of Palestine [the Arabs] not to be injured. Nothing shall be taken away from them which they need for their existence and for their well-being. We came to add, not to take away. We came to create. We may and we will come, and we are entitled to come as long as the Jewish problem is not solved, as long as there is need for Jews to come to Palestine, and there is a place for them in Palestine without displacing others. We are

not buying a National Home; we are not conquering it. We are recreating it. This is the great importance which Jewish labor and self-work play in our national movement. As a child cannot be bought of another woman, a mother must give birth to her child, so the people itself must give birth to, must create by its own effort, by its own work, its country, its homeland. That is why we insist that our work in Palestine, the fields which we are ploughing, the factories in which we are working, the houses we are living in, must all be done by ourselves; otherwise we shall not be entitled to call it ours, ours in the sense in which a people calls a land its own land....

If Palestine is our country, it is not to the exclusion of other inhabitants; it is also their country, the country of those who are born here and have no other homeland, and we can come in without any limit except the limit not to displace the existing inhabitants. It means a complete solution of the Jewish problem; it means making the Jewish people masters of their own destiny as any other free independent people—then why a home and not a Jewish State? Sometimes it is also asked. Why does the Balfour Declaration say "in Palestine" and not "Palestine as a National Home"? First of all, I would say the programme of our movement, when it was first formulated—not created, for it existed throughout our history—but when it was first politically formulated at the first Zionist Congress in Basle in 1897—we used almost the same words as are used in the Balfour Declaration, to create in Palestine a homeland for the Jewish people. It was formulated in the German language, *Heimstaette*. ... We did not say "Palestine as a National Home." We did not say to make in Palestine a Jewish State. We did not say it at that time, and we do not say it now, and I will tell you why. There are three reasons. Our aim is to make the Jewish people master of its own destiny, not subject to the will and mercy of others, as any other free people. But it is not part of our aim to dominate anybody else. If Palestine were an empty country wc could say a Jewish State, because the Jewish State would consist of Jews only and our self-government in Palestine would not concern others. But there are other inhabitants in Palestine who are here and, as we do not want to be at the mercy of others, they have a right not to be at the mercy of the Jews. It may be the Jews would behave better, but they are not bound to believe in our goodwill. A state may imply, though not necessarily, it may imply—since there are two nationalities—domination of others, the domination by the Jewish majority of the minority, but that is not our aim. It was not our aim at that time, and it is not our aim now....We take into consideration the fact that there are non-Jews in Palestine, and it was not our aim and we do not need to dominate them. A state may imply a wish to dominate a minority, the wish to dominate others.

The second reason is that a state means a separate political entity not attached to any other state-unit. A Jewish National Home may also mean that, but not necessarily so. On the contrary, we should like this country to be attached to a greater unit, a unit that is called the British Commonwealth of Nations. For the solution of the Jewish problem, for our free national future, it is not necessary that Palestine should constitute a separate State, and we should be only too glad if in the future, when the Jewish National Home is fully established, Palestine shall be eternally and completely free but that it should be a member of a greater unit, that is, the British Commonwealth of Nations.

There is a third reason why we do not use the formula of a Jewish State. There are Holy Places in Palestine which are holy to the whole civilized world, and we are unwilling and it is not in our interest that we should be made responsible for them. We recognize that they should be placed under a higher supervision, under some international control or a mandatory or some other international body, as is laid down in the Mandate.

These are the three reasons why we do not use this term which may be misunderstood, but otherwise there is no difference between a National Home for the Jewish people and what is ordinarily meant by a Jewish State, except that there is one advantage in a National Home. There is something more in a National Home for the Jewish people than in a Jewish State, and I will show you what it is. If we say Jewish State, if those three reasons did not exist—it is an empty country and we do not want to be attached to a greater political unit and there are no Holy Places—and we said a Jewish State, it would be less than a National Home to the Jewish people. Why? A Jewish State, as in the case of any other state, would mean the sovereignty of the people of that state at any given time. They may decide without giving any reasons who shall or shall not come into that state. But when Great Britain and all other European Powers recognized the right of the Jewish people as a whole to return to their country and to reconstitute their National Home here, it was the right of all the Jews—not only the Jews who happened to be here when the Jewish State might be ready and they might refuse arbitrarily to let in other Jews. There is no such right. The Palestinian Jews, however numerous they may be and however they may by virtue of their numbers dominate the country, have no right to refuse to admit other Jews as long as there is a place in this country. A National Home for the Jewish people is, in that respect, a much larger conception than a Jewish State.

The size of the National Home is in no way related to the number of people who are in Palestine. It is related to two things: to the need of the Jewish people in the world, how many Jews are indeed to return to Palestine, and it is related to the objective possibilities of Palestine. As long as there is a Jew in the world who must come back and is willing to come back and as long as a place can be made for him without displacing one of those already here, he can come here. Only these two considerations may, according to our view, determine the size of the Jewish National Home. It may be said that this need is a new one, the need for a large return of Jews to Palestine, that it is a novel fact, created by the present conditions in Germany, Poland and so on. That is not correct historically. As far back as the first Zionist Congress and at all the subsequent Congresses before the war the main feature of our Congresses was a report on the terrible position of the Jews in a great number of countries. The menace to the Jews, even in countries where they enjoyed equal rights, was always taken into consideration by the pre-war Congresses. Their main feature was an address on the Jewish position in the world by the famous Jewish writer Max Nordau. In 1902 a Royal Commission was set up in England to examine the question of alien immigration, and Dr. Herzl was invited to give evidence before that Commission. That was our first contact with a British Royal Commission in the history of our movement. He said at that Commission, which was in 1902, and you will find it in a Command Paper, 'The solution of the Jewish difficulty is the recognition of the Jews as a people and the finding by them of a legally recognized home, to which Jews in those parts of the world in which they are oppressed would naturally migrate," and when the offer was made by

Mr. Chamberlain at that time to settle Jews in Uganda it was also not meant as a spiritual center. Uganda cannot be meant as a spiritual center for the Jews, but it was meant as a place to which Jews who were unable to remain where they were could come. Then when the Balfour Declaration was made, one of the authors of the Balfour Declaration and a member of the War Cabinet, General Smuts,[2] before the new immigration started after the war, made a declaration, "I have no doubt in my mind that, although I may not live to see the day when the whole of Israel will return to Palestine, yet more and more it will become the national home of the Jewish people. From those parts of the world where the Jews are oppressed and unhappy, where they are not welcomed by the rest of the Christian population, from those parts of the world you will yet see an ever-increasing stream of immigrants to Palestine." That was said in 1919.

…This has a bearing on the question of our attitude to our Arab neighbors. We never ignored the existence of the non-Jewish population. We never ignored the existence of the Arab national movement. We believe, and what we have done up to now in Palestine has proved our belief to be true, that our work in Palestine, which was undertaken for the salvation of the Jewish people, will, by its inherent nature, be of great benefit not only to the non-Jewish population of Palestine but to the neighboring countries and to the whole of the Near East. We welcome the fact that the peoples of Iraq, of Egypt and now of Syria have attained their independence, not only on moral grounds, not only because we are Zionists, and so we appreciate a national movement and are able to respect it and to sympathize with it, but also from a deeper sense of self-interest. In order to have a National Home we must have a very strong and numerous Jewish community in Palestine—I am not able to say how many we shall have in the future—and it is essential for our existence and for our development that the countries around us should be happy and developed and prosperous. We believe the benefit we are conferring on the country—and it is only necessary to take a short tour of Palestine to see the benefit of the Jews to the whole country— will also accrue to those peoples in the neighboring countries to Palestine who are now achieving their independence.

It is unfortunate that here among our Arab neighbors there is only a political national movement. I am not blaming anybody, I have no right to blame anybody; every people has the right to arrange its own movement as it likes, but there is a very essential difference between our national movement and the national movement of the Arabs here. Our movement is mainly constructive. We are not engaged in agitation, but in creative work. We had to do it in order to achieve our aim; we had to reclaim land, to increase its productivity, build cities and factories, create artistic and scientific institutions and so on. Our Arab neighbors were engaged in their work, in purely political work. Now we are happy to see that our neighbors in Syria, in Iraq and in Egypt, having achieved their independence, cannot now blame a foreign government for their troubles, and they are also facing constructive problems. They are now responsible for their own country and for their own people, and they cannot put the blame on the British or on the French, but they have themselves to solve their own problems, and they will have also to engage in the same constructive work as we are doing here. I believe that they and, after them, our Arab neighbors in Palestine also will more appreciate the beneficial nature of our constructive work, and they will see that not only is there no conflict of interests between the Jewish people as a whole and the Arab people as a whole but that their interests are complementary.

We need each other. We can benefit each other. I have no doubt that at least our neighbors around us in Syria, Iraq and Egypt will be the first to recognize that fact, and from them this consciousness will also spread in Palestine amongst our Arab neighbors here, because there is no essential conflict. We have never had a quarrel with the Arabs on our side, neither with the Arabs in Palestine nor the Arabs in other countries. On the contrary. We came to this country with the consciousness that, besides saving ourselves and freeing and liberating our own people, we had also a great civilizing task to achieve here and that we could be of great help to our Arab neighbors here and in the surrounding countries, and I believe we have proved it by our work. The stronger we get, the greater our community becomes in Palestine, the greater our colonization work, the more developed our scientific institutions become, the more will be recognized by our neighbors abroad and here the blessing of our work and the mutual interest which exists historically between the Jewish people which is returning to its country, returning with the tradition of European culture, with the blessing of European culture, and the Arab peoples around us, who also want to achieve not only formal political independence but are also interested in achieving an economic, intellectual, spiritual and cultural renaissance, and it is our belief that a great Jewish community, a free Jewish nation, in Palestine, with a large scope for its activities, will be of great benefit to our Arab neighbors, and from the recognition of this fact will come a lasting peace and lasting cooperation between the two peoples.

NOTES

1. David Ben-Gurion, chairman of the Executive of the Jewish Agency, presented this evidence to the so-called Peel Commission in the aftermath of the 1936 Arab riots. The riots, which began in Jaffa in April 1936, sparked a long Arab insurrection, and subsequently the High Commissioner of the League of Nations called for an investigation of the conflict by a Palestine Royal Commission. A month later the Royal Commission, under the direction of Lord Peel, a former Secretary of State for India, and other British notables, examined the claims and grievances of both Arabs and Jews. The commission spent several months collecting information and evidence, and in July 1937 its report, a sizable document, was published. Ben-Gurion's testimony appeared in the commission's final report. See document 45, note 1, in this chapter.

2. Jan Christiaan Smuts (1870–1950) was a South African statesman, soldier, and philosopher. A dominant figure in South African public life. Smuts was a longstanding supporter of the Zionist cause and helped to formulate the Balfour Declaration as well as the British Mandate. He criticized immigration restrictions on Jews in the 1930s, although he himself was deputy prime minister in the South African government in 1937.

44. JEWISH NEEDS VS. ARAB CLAIMS (FEBRUARY 14, 1937)[1]

VLADIMIR JABOTINSKY

The conception of Zionism which I have the honor to represent here is based on what I should call the humanitarian aspect. By that I do not mean to say that we do not respect the other, the purely spiritual aspects of Jewish nationalism, such as the desire for self-expression, the rebuilding of a Hebrew culture, or creating some "model community of which the Jewish people could be proud." All that, of course, is most important; but as compared with our actual needs and our real position in the world today, all that has rather the character of luxury. The Commission have already heard a description of the situation of World Jewry, especially in Eastern Europe, and I am not going to repeat any details, but you will allow me to quote a recent reference in the *New York Times* describing the position of Jewry in Eastern Europe as "a disaster of historic magnitude." I only wish to add that it would be very naive—and although many Jews make this mistake I disapprove of it—it would be very naive to ascribe that state of disaster, permanent disaster, only to the guilt of men, whether it be crowds and multitudes, or whether it

---

Source: Evidence submitted to the Palestine Royal Commission. *Palestine Royal Commission Report.* Cmd. 5479 (London, 1937).

be governments. The matter goes much deeper than that. I am very much afraid that what I am going to say will not be popular with many among my co-religionists, and I regret that, but the truth is the truth. We are facing an elemental calamity, a kind of social earthquake. Three generations of Jewish thinkers and Zionists among whom there were many great minds—I am not going to fatigue you by quoting them—three generations have given much thought to analyzing the Jewish position and have come to the conclusion that the cause of our suffering is the very fact of the Diaspora, the bedrock fact that we are everywhere a minority. It is not the antisemitism of men; it is, above all, the antisemitism of things, the inherent xenophobia of the body social or the body economic under which we suffer. Of course, there are ups and downs; but there are moments, there are whole periods in history when this "xenophobia of life itself" takes dimensions which no people can stand, and that is what we are facing now. I do not mean to suggest that I would recognize that all the governments concerned have done all they ought to have done; I would be the last man to concede that. I think many governments, East and West, ought to do much more to protect the Jews than they do; but the best of governments could perhaps only soften the calamity to quite an insignificant extent, but the core of the calamity is an earthquake which stands and remains. I want to mention here that, since one of those governments (the Polish government) has recently tried what amounts to bringing to the notice of the League of Nations and the whole of humanity that it is humanity's duty to provide the Jews with an area where they could build up their own body social undisturbed by anyone, I think the sincerity of the Polish government, and of any other governments who, I hope, will follow, should not be suspected, but on the contrary it should be recognized and acknowledged with gratitude.—Perhaps the greatest gap in all I am going to say and in all the Commission have heard up to now is the impossibility of really going to the root of the problem, really bringing before you a picture of what that Jewish hell looks like, and I feel I cannot do it. I do hope that the day may come when some Jewish representative may be allowed to appear at the Bar of one of these two Houses just to tell them what it really is and to ask the English people: "What are you going to advise us? Where is the way out? Or, standing up and facing God, say that there is no way

out and that we Jews have just to go under." But unfortunately I cannot do it, so I will simply assume that the Royal Commission is sufficiently informed of all this situation, and then I want you to realize this: the phenomenon called Zionism may include all kinds of dreams—a "model community," Hebrew culture, perhaps even a second edition of the Bible—but all this longing for wonderful toys of velvet and silver is nothing in comparison with that tangible momentum of irresistible distress and need by which we are propelled and borne. We are not free agents. We cannot "concede" anything. Whenever I hear the Zionist, most often my own Party, accused of asking for too much—Gentlemen, I really cannot understand it. Yes, we do want a State; every nation on earth, every normal nation, beginning with the smallest and the humblest who do not claim any merit, any role in humanity's development, they all have States of their own. That is the normal condition for a people. Yet, when we, the most abnormal of peoples and therefore the most unfortunate, ask only for the same condition as the Albanians enjoy, to say nothing of the French and the English, then it is called too much. I should understand it if the answer were, "It is impossible," but when the answer is, "It is too much" I cannot understand it. I would remind you (excuse me for quoting an example known to every one of you) of the commotion which was produced in that famous institution when Oliver Twist came and asked for "more." He said "more" because he did not know how to express it; what Oliver Twist really meant was this: "Will you just give me that normal portion which is necessary for a boy of my age to be able to live?" I assure you that you face here today, in the Jewish people with its demands, an Oliver Twist who has, unfortunately, no concessions to make. What can be the concessions? We have got to save millions, *many millions.* I do not know whether it is a question of re-housing one third of the Jewish race, half of the Jewish race, or a quarter of the Jewish race; I do not know; but it is a question of millions. Certainly the way out is to evacuate those portions of the Diaspora which have become no good, which hold no promise of any possibility of a livelihood, and to concentrate all those refugees in some place which should not be Diaspora, not a repetition of the position where the Jews are an unabsorbed minority within a foreign social, or economic, or political organism. Naturally, if that process of evacuation is allowed to develop, as it ought to be allowed to develop, there will very soon be reached a moment when the Jews will become a majority in Palestine. I am going to make a "terrible" confession. Our demand for a Jewish majority is not our maximum—it is our minimum: it is just an inevitable stage if only we are allowed to go on salvaging our people. The point when the Jews will reach a majority in that country will not be the point of saturation yet—because with 1,000,000 more Jews in Palestine to-day you could already have a Jewish majority, but there are certainly 3,000,000 or 4,000,000 in the East who are virtually knocking at the door asking for admission, i.e., for salvation.

I have the profoundest feeling for the Arab case, in so far as that Arab case is not exaggerated. This Commission have already been able to make up their minds as to whether there is any individual hardship to the Arabs of Palestine as men, deriving from the Jewish colonization. We maintain unanimously that the economic position of the Palestinian Arabs, under the Jewish colonization and owing to the Jewish colonization, has become the object of envy in all the surrounding Arab countries, so that the Arabs from those countries show a clear tendency to immigrate into Palestine. I have also shown to you already that, in our submission, there is no question of ousting the Arabs. On the contrary, the idea [is] that Palestine on both sides of the Jordan should hold the Arabs, their progeny, *and* many millions of Jews. What I do not deny is that in that process the Arabs of Palestine will necessarily become a minority in the country of Palestine. What I do deny is that *that* is a hardship. It is not a hardship on any race, any nation, possessing many National States now and so many more National States in the future. One fraction, one branch of that race, and not a big one, will have to live in someone else's State: well, that is the case with all the mightiest nations of the world. I could hardly mention one of the big nations, having their States, mighty and powerful, who had not one branch living

in someone else's State. That is only normal and there is no "hardship" attached to that. So when we hear the Arab claim confronted with the Jewish claim; I fully understand that any minority would prefer to be a majority, it is quite understandable that the Arabs of Palestine would also prefer Palestine to be the Arab State No. 4, No. 5, or No. 6—that I quite understand; but when the Arab claim is confronted with our Jewish demand to be saved, it is like the claims of appetite versus the claims of starvation. No tribunal has ever had the luck of trying a case where all the justice was on the side of one Party and the other Party had no case whatsoever. Usually in human affairs any tribunal, including this tribunal, in trying two cases, has to concede that both sides have a case on their side and, in order to do justice, they must take into consideration what should constitute the basic justification of all human demands, individual or mass demands—the decisive terrible balance of Need. I think it is clear.

NOTE

1. On February 14, 1937, Jabotinsky testified in the British House of Lords before the so-called Peel Commission on Palestine (see the following document, note 1). Representing the Zionist-Revisionist movement, he delineated its position on the Mandate, explaining that from the larger perspective of the calamity facing the Jews in Europe, it would be morally amiss for the Commission to consider the question of Palestine only in terms of its immediate demographic and political context and merely to seek to reconcile the interests of the existing Jewish and Arab populations of the country. The Commission, Jabotinsky insisted, must realize that the real question facing it is "the Jewish demand to be saved." In the light of the magnitude and the urgency of the Jewish people's "need" for a sovereign state of their own in Palestine, the Arab claim, as justified and understandable as it was, "is like the claims of appetite versus the claims of starvation."

45. THE PEEL COMMISSION REPORT (JULY 1937)[1]

To foster Jewish immigration in the hope that it might ultimately lead to the creation of a Jewish majority and the establishment of a Jewish State with the consent or at least the acquiescence of the Arabs was one thing. It was quite another to contemplate, however remotely, the forcible conversion of Palestine into a Jewish State against the will of the Arabs. For that would clearly violate the spirit and intention of the Mandate System. It would mean that national self-determination had been withheld when the Arabs were a majority in Palestine and only conceded when the Jews were a majority. It would mean that the Arabs had been denied the opportunity of standing by themselves: that they had, in fact, after an interval of conflict, been bartered about from Turkish sovereignty to Jewish sovereignty. It is true that in the light of history Jewish rule over Palestine could not be regarded as foreign rule in the same sense as Turkish; but the international recognition of the right of the Jews to return to their old homeland did not involve the recognition of the right of the Jews to govern the Arabs in it against their will....

An irrepressible conflict has arisen between two national communities within the narrow bounds of one small country. About 1,000,000 Arabs are in strife, open or latent, with some 400,000 Jews. There is no common ground between them. The Arab community is predominantly Asiatic in character, the Jewish community predominantly European. They differ in religion and in language. Their cultural and social life, their ways of thought and conduct, are as incompatible as their national aspirations. These last are the greatest bar to peace. Arabs and Jews might possibly learn to live and work together in Palestine if they would make a genuine effort to reconcile and combine their national ideals and so build up in time a joint or dual nationality. But this they cannot do. The War [World War I] and its sequel have inspired all Arabs with the hope of reviving in a free and united Arab world the traditions of the Arab golden age. The Jews similarly are inspired by their historic past. They mean to show what the Jewish nation can achieve when restored to the land of its birth. National assimilation between Arabs and Jews is thus ruled out. In the Arab picture the Jews could only occupy the place they occupied in Arab Egypt or Arab Spain. The Arabs would be as much outside the Jewish picture as the Canaanites in the old land of Israel. The National Home, as we have said before, cannot be half-national. In these circumstances to maintain that Palestinian citizenship has any moral meaning is a mischievous pretense. Neither Arab nor Jew has any sense of service to a single State....

NOTE

1. Peel Commission is the name commonly given to the Royal Commission on Palestine, under the chairmanship of William Robert Wellesley Peel, Earl Peel, (1867–1937). The Commission, appointed by the British government on August 7, 1936, was established in response to the outbreak of violent Arab riots, climaxing many years of tension, protesting Zionism and its increasingly palpable progress in Palestine. The Commission was charged with ascertaining "the underlying causes of the disturbances...; to inquire into the manner in which the Mandate for Palestine is being implemented in relation to the obligations of the Mandatory towards the Arabs and Jews respectively; to ascertain whether upon a proper construction of the terms of the Mandate either the Arabs or Jews have any legitimate grievances on account of the way in which the Mandate has been or is being implemented for their removal and for the prevention of their recurrence." The commission arrived in Palestine on November 11, 1936, and stayed for two months, conducting 66 meetings in which 113 witnesses were heard; the Commission also conducted several meetings upon its return to London. The report, a 400-page volume, was issued in July 1937.

Source: Palestine Royal Commission Report. Cmd. 5479 (London, 1937).

The report, acclaimed for its judicious and balanced nature, concluded that the recurrent and often violent Arab opposition to the Zionist project in Palestine was principally due to national aspirations of the Arabs of the country and their concomitant fear that the establishment of the Jewish National Home would usurp their political rights. The Commission, accordingly, found that Arab and Jewish interests were not to be reconciled under the terms of the Mandate. As a solution to this impasse, it recommended the partition of Palestine into two sovereign states, Jewish and Arab. The Jewish state was to comprise the Galilee, the Jezreel Valley, and part of the coastal plain; the Arab state would include all remaining parts of Palestine and Transjordan. The holy cities of Jerusalem and Bethlehem, as well as a corridor to the sea, however, were to remain under British Mandatory rule; the mixed cities of Acre and Haifa were to be placed under temporary Mandatory rule. The Arab leadership summarily rejected the plan; the Zionists reluctantly accepted it. Initially responding favorably to the Commission's proposal, the British government issued a statement in November 1938 rejecting the envisioned partition as "impracticable."

46. WHITE PAPER OF 1939 (MAY 1939)[1]

MALCOLM MACDONALD

In the Statement on Palestine, issued on the ninth of November, 1938, His Majesty's Government announced their intention to invite representatives of the Arabs of Palestine, of certain neighbouring countries and of the Jewish Agency to confer with them in London regarding future policy. It was their sincere hope that, as a result of full, free and frank discussion, some understanding might be reached.... Certain proposals were laid before the Arab and Jewish delegations as the basis of an agreed settlement. Neither the Arab nor the Jewish delegations felt able to accept these proposals, and the conferences therefore did not result in an agreement. Accordingly His Majesty's Government are free to formulate their own policy....

3. The [Peel] Commission and previous Commissions of Enquiry have drawn attention to the ambiguity of certain expressions in the Mandate, such as the expression "a national home for the Jewish people," and they have found in this ambiguity and the resulting uncertainty as to the objectives of policy a fundamental cause of unrest and hostility between Arabs and Jews. His Majesty's Government are convinced that in the interests of the peace and well-being of the whole people of Palestine a clear definition of policy and objectives is essential. The proposal of partition recommended by the Royal Commission would have afforded such clarity, but the establishment of self-supporting independent Arab and Jewish States within Palestine has been found to be impracticable. It has therefore been necessary for His Majesty's Government to devise an alternative policy which will, consistently with their obligations to Arabs and Jews, meet the needs of the situation in Palestine. Their views and proposals are set forth below under the three heads, (I) The Constitution, (II) Immigration, and (III) Land.

I. THE CONSTITUTION

4. It has been urged that the expression "a national home for the Jewish people" offered a prospect that

Source: British Statement of Policy. Cmd. 6019 (May 1939).

Palestine might in due course become a Jewish State or Commonwealth. His Majesty's Government do not wish to contest the view, which was expressed by the Royal Commission, that the Zionist leaders at the time of the issue of the Balfour Declaration recognised that an ultimate Jewish State was not precluded by the terms of the Declaration. But, with the Royal Commission, His Majesty's Government believe that the framers of the Mandate in which the Balfour Declaration was embodied could not have intended that Palestine should be converted into a Jewish State against the will of the Arab population of the country.

5. The nature of the Jewish National Home in Palestine was further described in the Command Paper of 1922 as follows:

> ...When it is asked what is meant by the development of the Jewish National Home in Palestine, it may be answered that it is not the imposition of a Jewish nationality upon the inhabitants of Palestine as a whole, but the further development of the existing Jewish community, with the assistance of Jews in other parts of the world, in order that it may become a centre in which the Jewish people as a whole may take, on grounds of religion and race, an interest and a pride. But in order that this community should have the best prospect of free development and provide a full opportunity for the Jewish people to display its capacities, it is essential that it should know that it is in Palestine as of right and not on sufferance. That is the reason why it is necessary that the existence of a Jewish National Home in Palestine should be internationally guaranteed, and that it should be formally recognised to rest upon an ancient historic connection.

6. His Majesty's Government adhere to this interpretation of the Declaration of 1917 and regard it as an authoritative and comprehensive description of the character of the Jewish National Home in Palestine. It envisaged the further development of the existing Jewish community with the assistance of Jews in other parts of the world....

8. His Majesty's Government are charged as the Mandatory authority "to secure the development of self-governing institutions" in Palestine. Apart from this specific obligation, they would regard it as contrary to the whole spirit of the Mandate system that the population of Palestine should remain forever under Mandatory tutelage. It is proper that the people of the country should as early as possible enjoy the rights of self-government which are exercised by the people of neighbouring countries. His Majesty's Government are unable at present to forsee the exact constitutional forms which the government in Palestine will eventually take, but their objective is self-government, and they desire to see established ultimately an independent Palestine State. It should be a State in which the two peoples in Palestine, Arabs and Jews, share authority in government in such a way that the essential interests of each are secured....

10. In the light of these considerations His Majesty's Government make the following declaration of their intentions regarding the future government of Palestine: (1) The objective of His Majesty's Government is the establishment within ten years of an independent Palestine State in such treaty relations with the United Kingdom as will provide satisfactorily for the commercial and strategic requirements of both countries in the future. This proposal for the establishment of the independent State would involve consultation with the Council of the League of Nations with a view to the termination of the Mandate. (2) The independent State should be one in which Arabs and Jews share in government in such a way as to ensure that the essential interests of each community are safeguarded....

II. [IMMIGRATION]

12. If immigration has an adverse effect on the economic position in the country, it should clearly be restricted; and equally, if it has a seriously damaging effect on the political position in the country, that is a factor that should not be ignored. Although it is not difficult to contend that the large number of Jewish immigrants who have been admitted so far have been absorbed economically, the fear of the Arabs that this influx will continue indefinitely until the Jewish population is in a position to dominate them has produced consequences which are extremely grave for Jews and Arabs alike and for the peace and prosperity of Palestine. The lamentable disturbances of the past three years are only the latest and most sustained manifestation of this intense Arab apprehension. The methods employed by Arab terrorists against fellow-Arabs and Jews alike must receive unqualified condemnation. But it cannot be denied that fear of

indefinite Jewish immigration is widespread amongst the Arab population and that this fear has made possible disturbances which have given a serious set-back to economic progress, depleted the Palestine exchequer, rendered life and property insecure, and produced a bitterness between the Arab and Jewish populations which is deplorable between citizens of the same country. If in these circumstances immigration is continued up to the economic absorptive capacity of the country, regardless of all other considerations, a fatal enmity between the two peoples will be perpetuated, and the situation in Palestine may become a permanent source of friction amongst all peoples in the Near and Middle East. His Majesty's Government cannot take the view that either their obligation under the Mandate, or considerations of common sense and justice, require that they should ignore these circumstances in framing immigration policy.

13. In the view of the Royal Commission, the association of the policy of the Balfour Declaration with the Mandate system implied the belief that Arab hostility to the former would sooner or later be overcome. It has been the hope of British Governments ever since the Balfour Declaration was issued that in time the Arab population, recognizing the advantages to be derived from Jewish settlement and development in Palestine, would become reconciled to the further growth of the Jewish National Home. This hope has not been fulfilled. The alternatives before His Majesty's Government are either (1) to seek to expand the Jewish National Home indefinitely by immigration, against the strongly expressed will of the Arab people of the country; or (2) to permit further expansion of the Jewish National Home by immigration only if the Arabs are prepared to acquiesce in it.... His Majesty's Government, after earnest consideration, and taking into account the extent to which the growth of the Jewish National Home has been facilitated over the last twenty years, have decided that the time has come to adopt in principle the second of the alternatives referred to above.

14. It has been urged that all further Jewish immigration into Palestine should be stopped forthwith. His Majesty's Government cannot accept such a proposal. It would damage the whole of the financial and economic system of Palestine and thus affect adversely the interests of Arabs and Jews alike. Moreover, in the view of his Majesty's Government, abruptly to stop further immigration would be unjust to the Jewish National Home. But, above all, His Majesty's Government are

conscious of the present unhappy plight of large numbers of Jews who seek a refuge from certain European countries, and they believe that Palestine can and should make a further contribution to the solution of this pressing world problem. In all these circumstances, they believe that they will be acting consistently with their Mandatory obligations to both Arabs and Jews, and in the manner best calculated to serve the interests of the whole people of Palestine, by adopting the following proposals regarding immigration: (1) Jewish immigration during the next five years will be at a rate which, if economic absorptive capacity permits, will bring the Jewish population up to approximately one-third of the total population of the country. Taking into account the expected natural increase of the Arab and Jewish populations, and the number of illegal Jewish immigrants now in the country, this would allow of the admission, as from the beginning of April this year, of some 75,000 immigrants over the next five years....

15. His Majesty's Government are satisfied that, when the immigration over five years which is now contemplated has taken place, they will not be justified in facilitating, nor will they be under any obligation to facilitate, the further development of the Jewish National Home by immigration regardless of the wishes of the Arab population.

III. LAND

16.... The reports of several expert Commissions have indicated that, owing to the natural growth of the Arab population and the steady sale in recent years of Arab land to Jews, there is now in certain areas no room for further transfers of Arab land, whilst in some other areas such transfers of land must be restricted if Arab cultivators are to maintain their existing standard of life and a considerable landless Arab population is not soon to be created. In these circumstances, the High Commissioner will be given general powers to prohibit and regulate transfers of land. These powers will date from the publication of this statement of policy and the High Commissioner will retain them throughout the transitional period....

18. In framing these proposals His Majesty's Government have sincerely endeavoured to act in strict accordance with their obligations under the Mandate to both the Arabs and the Jews. The

vagueness of the phrases employed in some instances to describe these obligations has led to controversy and has made the task of interpretation difficult. His Majesty's Government cannot hope to satisfy the partisans of one party or the other.

NOTE

1. As it faced the political exigencies of administering its mandate in Palestine, Great Britain's commitment to the Balfour Declaration underwent continuous reevaluation. These shifts in policy were largely prompted by the growing Arab opposition to Zionism. In a series of White Papers it was made clear that "a Jewish National Home" did not mean a sovereign Jewish state; moreover, restrictions were imposed on Jewish immigration and areas of settlement. The Arabs, however, were not appeased, and their opposition intensified. From 1936 to 1939 the Arabs of Palestine were in veritable revolt. The Peel Commission's recommendation, published in July 1937, to partition Palestine into separate Jewish and Arab states was reluctantly accepted by the Zionists; the Arab leadership rejected it. In the search for a mutually agreeable solution, further commissions and conferences were held, but to no avail. Exasperated, Colonial Secretary Malcolm MacDonald issued, in the name of his Majesty's government, this White Paper. It amounted to a repudiation of the Balfour Declaration, a "death sentence," as Weizmann put it.

47. STATEMENT ON THE MACDONALD WHITE PAPER OF 1939 (MAY 17, 1939)[1]

THE JEWISH AGENCY FOR PALESTINE

1. The effect of the new policy for Palestine laid down by the Mandatory Government in the White Paper of May 17, 1939, is to deny to the Jewish people the right to reconstitute their National Home in their ancestral country. It is a policy which transfers authority over Palestine to the present Arab majority, puts the Jewish population at the mercy of that majority, decrees the stoppage of Jewish immigration as soon as the Jewish inhabitants form one third of the total [population], and sets up a territorial ghetto for the Jews in their own homeland.

2. The Jewish people regard this breach of faith as a surrender to Arab terrorism. It delivers Great Britain's friends into the hands of those who are fighting her. It must widen the breach between Jews and Arabs, and undermine the hope of peace in Palestine. It is a policy in which the Jewish people will not acquiesce. The new regime announced in the White Paper will be devoid of any moral basis and contrary to international law. Such a regime can only be set up and maintained by force....

5. It is in the darkest hours of Jewish history that the British Government proposes to deprive the Jews of their last hope, and to close the road back to their homeland. It is a cruel blow; doubly cruel because it comes from the Government of a great nation which has extended a helping hand to Jews, and whose position in the world rests upon foundations of moral authority and international good faith. This blow will not subdue the Jewish people. The historic bond between the people and the land of Israel will not be broken. The Jews will never accept the closing against

Source: "An Official Communique Issued by the Jewish Agency for Palestine on May 17, 1939," in "Book of Documents," submitted to the General Assembly of the United Nations by the Jewish Agency for Palestine (New York: Jewish Agency for Palestine, 1947), pp. 137–38.

them of the gates of Palestine, nor let their national home be converted into a ghetto. Jewish pioneers, who in the past three generations have shown their strength in the upbuilding of a derelict country, will from now on display the same strength in defending Jewish immigration, the Jewish home, and Jewish freedom.

NOTE

1. The authority and functions of the Jewish Agency prior to the establishment of the State of Israel were outlined in Article 4 of the British Mandate for Palestine, which provided that "an appropriate Jewish agency shall be recognized as a public body for the purpose of advising and cooperating with the administration of Palestine in such…matters as may affect the establishment of the Jewish National Home and the interests of the Jewish population in Palestine," and that "the Zionist Organization…shall be recognized as such agency." With the establishment of the State of Israel in May 1948. the Jewish Agency automatically ceased to be the spokesman for the interests of the Jewish population in that country whose internal and external affairs were now conducted solely by its sovereign government, but it continues as an international nongovernmental body that functions as the coordinator of all Jewish overseas efforts for Israel.

48. THE BILTMORE PROGRAM (MAY 1942)[1]

1. American Zionists assembled in this Extraordinary Conference reaffirm their unequivocal devotion to the cause of democratic freedom and international justice to which the people of the United States, allied with the other United Nations, have dedicated themselves, and give expression to their faith in the ultimate victory of humanity and justice over lawlessness and brute force.

2. This Conference offers a message of hope and encouragement to their fellow Jews in the Ghettos and concentration camps of Hitler-dominated Europe and prays that their hour of liberation may not be far distant.

3. The Conference sends its warmest greetings to the Jewish Agency Executive in Jerusalem, to the *Vaad Leumi*,[2] and to the whole *yishuv* in Palestine, and expresses its profound admiration for their steadfastness and achievements in the face of peril and great difficulties. The Jewish men and women in field and factory, and the thousands of Jewish soldiers of Palestine in the Near East who have acquitted themselves with honor and distinction in Greece, Ethiopia, Syria, Libya and on other battlefields, have shown themselves worthy of their people and ready to assume the rights and responsibilities of nationhood.

4. In our generation, and in particular in the course of the past twenty years, the Jewish people have awakened and transformed their ancient homeland; from 50,000 at the end of the last war, their numbers have increased to more than 500,000. They have made the waste places to bear fruit and the desert to blossom. Their pioneering achievements in agriculture and in industry, embodying new patterns of cooperative endeavor, have written a notable page in the history of colonization.

5. In the new values thus created, their neighbors in Palestine have shared. The Jewish people in its own work of national redemption welcomes the economic, agricultural and national development of the Arab peoples and states. The Conference reaffirms the stand previously adopted at the Congress of the

Source: New Palestine, May 11, 1942. p. 6.

World Zionist Organization, expressing the readiness and the desire of the Jewish people for full cooperation with their Arab neighbors.

6. The Conference calls for the fulfillment of the original purposes of the Balfour Declaration and the Mandate which recognizing *"the historical connection of the Jewish people with Palestine"* was to afford them the opportunity, as stated by President Wilson [of the United States] to found there a Jewish Commonwealth.

The Conference affirms its unalterable rejection of the White Paper of May 1939 and denies its moral or legal validity. The White Paper seeks to limit, and in fact to nullify, Jewish rights to immigration and settlement in Palestine, and, as stated by Mr. Winston Churchill in the House of Commons in May 1939, constitutes "a breach and repudiation of the Balfour Declaration." The policy of the White Paper is cruel and indefensible in its denial of sanctuary to Jews fleeing from Nazi persecution; and at a time when Palestine has become a focal point in the war front of the United Nations, and Palestine Jewry must provide all available manpower for farm and factory and camp, it [the White Paper] is in direct conflict with the interests of the allied war effort.

7. In the struggle against the forces of aggression and tyranny, of which Jews were the earliest victims, and which now menace the Jewish National Home, recognition must be given to the right of the Jews of Palestine to play their full part in the war effort and in the defense of their country, through a Jewish military force fighting under its own flag and under the high command of the United Nations.

8. The Conference declares that the new world order that will follow victory cannot be established on foundations of peace, justice and equality, unless the problem of Jewish homelessness is finally solved.

The Conference urges that the gates of Palestine be opened; that the Jewish Agency be vested with control of immigration into Palestine and with the necessary authority for upbuilding the country, including the development of its unoccupied and uncultivated lands; and that Palestine be established as a Jewish Commonwealth integrated in the structure of the new democratic world.

Then and only then will the age-old wrong to the Jewish people be righted.

NOTES

1. An extraordinary conference was convened in May 1942 at the Biltmore Hotel, New York City. Since no Zionist congress could be held because of the war, this conference was in effect invested with the authority of a congress. Delegates from every American and Canadian Zionist organization were joined by all European and Palestinian leaders able to attend. Chaim Weizmann, the president of the World Zionist Organization, and David Ben-Gurion, the chairman of the Jewish Agency, were in attendance. The conference set a strategy to combat the White Paper of 1939. Ben-Gurion, the main force of the conference, explained that Jewry could no longer depend on Great Britain to advance the establishment of a Jewish national home in Palestine and that, given the catastrophe currently facing the Jewish people in Europe, it was imperative that the mandate be transferred to the Jewish Agency. Some delegates felt that the demand was premature; others urged the adoption of a proposal for a binational Jewish Arab state; some recommended the transference of the mandate to the United Nations. Ben-Gurion's position prevailed. The Biltmore program was more a symbol than a policy; it was "a slogan, reflecting the radicalization of the Zionist movement as the result of the war and the losses suffered by the Jewish people. It foreshadowed the bitter postwar conflict with the British government" (Walter Laqueur, *A History of Zionism* [New York: Schocken Books, 1976]. pp. 548ff.)

2. The *Vaad Leumi*, or National Council constituted by representatives of almost all the major Jewish factions of Palestine was established in 1920 in order to conduct the affairs of the *Yishuv*. It would later form the provisional government of the nascent State of Israel upon its founding in May 1948.

49. THE SERMON (1942)

HAIM HAZAZ[1]

"You've already heard that I'm opposed to Jewish history".... "I want to explain why. Just be patient a little while....First, I will begin with the fact that we have no history at all. That's a fact. And that's the *zagvozdka*. I don't know how to say it in Hebrew....In other words, that's where the shoe pinches. Because we didn't make our own history, the *goyim* made it for us. Just as they used to put out our candles on Sabbath, milk our cows and light our ovens on Sabbath, so they made our history for us to suit themselves, and we took it from them as it came. But it's not ours, it's not ours at all! Because we didn't make it. we would have made it differently, we didn't want it to be like that, it was only others who wanted it that way and they forced it on us, whether we liked it or not, which is a different thing altogether....In that sense, and in every other sense, I tell you, in every sense, we have no history of our own. Have we? It's clear as can be! And that's why I'm opposed to it, I don't recognize it, it doesn't exist for me! What's more, I don't respect it, although 'respect' is not the word, still I don't respect it....I don't respect it at all! But the main thing is, I'm opposed to it. What I mean is, I don't accept it....

"I don't accept it!" he repeated, with the stubborn insistence of one who has come to a final, fixed opinion. "Not a single point, not a line, not a dot. Nothing, nothing...nothing at all! Will you believe me? Will you believe me? You can't even imagine how I'm opposed to it, how I reject it, and how...how...I don't respect it! Now, look! Just think...what is there in it? Oppression, defamation, persecution and martyrdom. And again oppression, defamation, persecution and martyrdom. And again and again and again, without end....That's what's in it, and nothing more! After all, it's...it's...it bores you to death, it's just plain dull! Just let me mention one fact, just one little fact. It's well known that children everywhere love to read historical fiction. That's where you get action, see, bold deeds, heroes, great fighters and fearless conquerors. In a word, a world of heroism. Now, here now, in Palestine, our children love to read, unless they're stupid. I know this for a fact. I've looked into it, Yes, they read, but historical novels about *goyim*, not about Jews. Why is that so? It's no accident. It's simply because Jewish history is dull, uninteresting. It has no glory or action, no heroes and conquerors, no rulers and masters of their fate, just a collection of wounded, hunted, groaning and wailing wretches, always begging for mercy. You can see for yourselves that it can't be interesting. The least you can say is it's uninteresting. I would simply forbid teaching our children Jewish history. Why the devil teach them about their ancestors' shame? I would just say to them: 'Boys, from the day we were driven out from our land we've been a people without a history. Class dismissed. Go out and play football....' But that's all in passing. So, let me proceed. I'm sure you won't take me wrong. I know that there is heroism in the way we stood up to all that oppression and suffering. I take it into account....But...I don't care for that kind of heroism. Don't laugh....I don't care for it! I prefer an entirely different kind of heroism. First of all, please understand me, it's nothing but the heroism of despair. With no way out, anyone can be a hero. Whether he wants to or not, he must be, and there is no credit or honor in that. In the second place, this heroism after all amounts to great weakness, worse than weakness, a kind of special talent for corruption and decay. That's how it is! This type of hero sooner or later begins to pride himself on his 'heroism' and brags about it: 'See what great torments I withstand! See what untold shame and

Source: Haim Hazaz, "Hadrashah." *Luah Haaretz Lishnat 5703 (1942/3)* (Tel Aviv: Haim Publishing, 1942), pp. 82–96. Trans. Ben Halpern and reprinted here with permission of Mrs. Gertrude Halpern.

humiliation I suffer! Who can compare with me!' See, we don't merely suffer torments. It's more than that, we love the torments too, we love torment for its own sake....We want to be tortured, we are eager, we yearn for it....Persecution preserves us, keeps us alive. Without it, we couldn't exist. Did you ever see a community of Jews that was not suffering? I've never seen one. A Jew without suffering is an abnormal creature, hardly a Jew at all, half a goy. That's what I mean; it's just such 'heroism' that shows our weakness...suffering, suffering, suffering! Everything is rotten around suffering....Please notice, I said around, not in suffering. There's a tremendous difference....Everything, everything around it rots: history, life itself, all actions, customs, the group, the individual, literature, culture, folk songs...everything! The world grows narrow, cramped, upside down. A world of darkness, perversions and contradiction. Sorrow is priced higher than joy, pain easier to understand than happiness, wrecking better than building, slavery preferred to redemption, dream before reality, hope more than the future, faith before common sense, and so on for all the other perversions....It's horrible! A new psychology is created, a kind of moonlight psychology....The night has its own special psychology, quite different from the day's. I don't mean the psychology of a man at night, that's something separate, but the psychology of night itself. You may not have noticed it, perhaps, but it's there, it's there. I know it. I feel it every time I stand guard. The whole world behaves quite differently too in the day, nature moves in a different way, every blade of grass, every stone, every smell, all different, different....

"I've already told you, and I beg you to remember that a special, perverted, fantastic psychology has grown up among us, if I may say so, a moonlight psychology, altogether different in every way from other people's....We love suffering, for through suffering we are able to be Jews; it preserves us and maintains us, it proves we are bold and heroic, braver than any people in the whole world. I admit, I am forced to admit that this is heroic indeed, in a way. People, you know, abuse many fine and noble words. ... In a certain sense suffering is heroic. And in a sense even decay is heroic and degradation is heroic....That is exactly the kind of people we are. We don't fight, or conquer, or rule. We have no desire, no will for it. Rather, we submit, we suffer without limit, willingly, lovingly. We actually say: You shall not conquer us,

nor break us, nor destroy us! There is no power on earth strong enough for that...because power has its limits, but there is no limit, no end to our suffering....In fact, the more we are degraded, the greater we think is our honor; the more we are made to suffer, the stronger we become. For this is our staple food, it is our elixir of life....It's all so beautifully arranged! A character like that, imagine it, a nature so perfected...and that explains everything: Exile, martyrdom, Messiah...these are three which are one, all to the same purpose, the same intention....Doesn't it say somewhere: The threefold cord?'...

"The Exile, that is our pyramid, and it has martyrdom for a base and Messiah for its peak. And...and...the Talmud, that is our Book of the Dead....In the very beginning, as far back as the Second Temple, we began to build it. Even that far back we planned it, we laid the foundations....Exile, martyrdom, Messiah....Do you grasp the deep cunning hidden in this wild fantasy, the cold moonlight with which it flames?...Do you grasp it? Just think, just think! Millions of men, a whole people plunging itself into this madness and sunk in it for two thousand years! Giving up to it its life, its very existence, its character, submitting to affliction, suffering, tortures, agreed that it is foolish, a lunatic dream. But a dream, that is, a vision, an ideal....What an uncanny folk! What a wonderful, awful people! Awful, awful to the point of madness! For look, it scorns the whole world, the whole world and all its fighters and heroes and wise men and poets all together! Fearsome and blind! A bottomless abyss....No, one could go mad!

"...A single myth, all that is left of the whole past, the closing speech of all that great drama, after the Judges, the Prophets and the Kings, after the First Temple and the Second, after the wars and wonders— and all the rest of it....And that's what we are left with—a single, simple legend, and no more. Not much, you say? You are mistaken. On the contrary, it is a great deal. It is far too much. You might think it's no more than a trifle, a kindergarten legend. But it's not so. It's by no means so innocent. It has such a cunning, do you know, like that of well-tried, ancient men, a cunning of the greatest subtlety, so fated, so *podlaya*—that is, so corrupt a cunning....Let me add, by the way, it's a wonderful legend, a tale of genius, although—apart from the philosophy and symbolism in it—not free of caricature, you know, not without a biting Jewish wit and humor; he comes on an ass! A great, a colossal, a cosmic image—not on a snorting steed, but precisely on a donkey, on the most miserable and insignificant of animals....And this was enough to determine a people's fate and chart its course in the world for endless ages, for all eternity, this, and not the disputes of the schools of Shammai and Hillel. I'm not familiar with these things, 1 never learned Talmud, but it's quite clear....It's an obvious thing, a certainty that if not for this myth it would all have been different. For then, they would finally have had to go right back to Palestine or somehow or other pass on out of the world. At any rate, they would have had to think of something or do something, somehow or other, to bring it all to an end...."

NOTE

1. Haim Hazaz (1898–1973) was a Hebrew writer. Born in Ukraine, he escaped pogroms that erupted in the wake of the Russian Revolution, settling first in Constantinople, then Paris and Berlin. In 1931 he immigrated to Palestine. He began his literary career in Russia and is regarded as one of the major authors of modern Hebrew fiction. In his novels, stories, and plays he often explored inner conflicts of a generation beholden to revolutionary ideals—socialism and Zionism—especially as they faced the inevitable frustrations and disappointments in seeking to realize their ideals. In "The Sermon," perhaps the most famous of his shorter works, Hazaz somewhat ironically depicts the Zionist ideal of the "negation of *galut*"—the rejection of Jewish life in the Diaspora as fundamentally untenable—through the sermonic soliloquy of his protagonist Yudka. who declares at a general assembly of his kibbutz his "opposition to Jewish history." Free of the debilitating and debasing quietism of *galut* Judaism, he explains, Zionism is bent on returning the Jewish people to history as heroic masters of their fate. In this tale Hazaz deftly captures one of the most pervasive themes of classical Zionism.

50. THE CASE FOR A BI-NATIONAL PALESTINE (NOVEMBER 1945)

HASHOMER HAZAIR[1]

The subject of this memorandum is an attempt to outline a policy for Palestine which, while providing for the ultimate fulfillment of the respective Jewish-Zionist and Arab aspirations is the only one, in our opinion, likely to lead to Jewish-Arab cooperation and to peace and prosperity in this country....

[We hold that] a state is not an end in itself. In its political implications it is only an instrument whereby a people seeks to ensure its national welfare and felicity. Assuming that millions of Jews could be saved from their present distress, enabled to build "their own body social in Palestine undisturbed by anyone," yet in no way affect or violate either the Palestine Arabs' "profound attachment to their soil and culture" or their motive of "self-preservation and self-determination"; assuming, furthermore, that adequate safeguards to that effect could be agreed upon and their practicality demonstrated, we fail to

Source: Executive Committee of the Hashomer Hazair Workers' Party in Jerusalem, "Memorandum Submitted to the Anglo-American Inquiry Commission" (Jerusalem, 1946), pp. 7, 49, 59ff, 71ff, 126–29, 131, 136.

see what meaning the controversy of a Jewish *versus* an Arab State would then still possess and why it could not be resolved instead in a form which might be termed a Jewish-Arab State....

We [therefore] suggest that the logical and realistic way out of the situation is an Arab-Jewish State or a Palestinian State which would merit the appellation "Jewish" or "Arab" as little as Belgium deserves to be called Walloon or Flemish, or South Africa—Boer or English....It must be fully grasped and appreciated once and for all that neither in justice nor in practice can either Jews or Arabs maintain exclusive sovereignty over the country. Sovereignty can, however, be exercised *jointly and equally* to the benefit of all concerned. It is this *joint sovereignty* which we have laid down as an essential principle in our efforts to formulate a solution. It is, in fact, the core and substance of binationalism....

Parity in Government has been offered as the practical concept for implementing non-domination in terms of constitution and administration....The essence of parity is in the equality of numerical representation it grants the component units of a state notwithstanding any differences in the numerical voting strength of their electors. It is thus intended as a means of preserving the equality of rights of smaller units against the weight of population enjoyed by the bigger ones....Parity should be regarded as the indispensable constitutional and administrative form of regulating the relations between Jews and Arabs in any system of self-government that may be set up in Palestine. Both peoples are entitled to the maximum amount of safeguards: Any constitution adopted for the country in the future will, in our opinion, have to take special care to provide both communities with adequate means of preventing effectively the enactment of measures designed to encroach upon their vital, legitimate interests. Parity in a legislative body possessing the final vote in passing the important legislation of the country seems to us the most far-reaching of guarantees to either party against eventual domination by the other.

The possibility for constitutionally implementing the principle of joint sovereignty and parity seems to us to lie in a form which we choose to term "Communal Federalism." By this is meant the setting up of a system of government to be constituted as a federation not of territories but of two organized national communities. The territory would remain undivided and as such would be administered by the Central Government. But this Central Government would, again be set up by two component units jointly administering the country's sovereignty and between them maintaining a state of parity; the demarcation between them, be it noted, would run along national and not along geographical lines.

...The successful operation, however, of any bi-national constitution would require a suitable economic foundation. As long as there continued to exist two distinct national economies within the one country—a Jewish economy and an Arab economy—the functioning of a bi-national state would meet with numerous obstructions. Separate economies tend to become competitive; and economic competition between two races must lead to grave political complications.

Now, the merging of the two existing economies into one broad economic system would depend on an increasing measure of economic cooperation between Jews and Arabs in all walks of life. But this, in turn, would require a greater similarity in their respective living standards as well as in their general social and intellectual levels. Hence, it would be essential to the satisfactory solution of the Palestine problem that the Arab standard of living should be raised as quickly as possible to the present Jewish standard and that simultaneously corresponding changes in the social and educational level should be effected. We have no doubt that it is on the manner in which economic activities in Palestine will affect the Arabs during the next five years that removal of the last vestiges of Arab intransigence depends.

With this in mind, we propose that for the next twenty or twenty-five years Palestine should be placed under the administration of a Special Development Authority the specific objective of which would be:

1. To promote the settlement in Palestine of at least two to three million Jews during the next twenty or twenty-five years by developing the economic possibilities of the country to full capacity.
2. To raise the standard of living and education of the Palestinian Arabs to approximately the present Jewish level during the same period.
3. To promote and actively encourage Jewish-Arab cooperation in every field and by every legitimate means available as well as to encourage

the gradual development of self-governing institutions, local and national, on bi-national lines, until the stage of full independence within the framework of a bi-national constitution is reached.

No doubt, it is far from easy to accomplish such a threefold undertaking in a comparatively short time. But, equally we have no doubt that it could be done, given the proper conditions, authority, and leadership....

The other alternative, often spoken of, and advanced with vigour and persuasion by the Royal Commission,[2] is to partition Palestine between the Jews and the Arabs. The Royal Commission started from the assumption that the Jews and the Arabs could not live together. "Half a loaf is better than no bread,"—so let's give each one half the loaf—was the underlying idea behind the Royal Commission's recommendation. It seems simple, it seems easy, it seems plausible. It seems just for an occasion where there *is* "a conflict of right with right."...

The protagonists of the partition plan cherish the illusion that certain Jewish and Arab circles favour partition as the "lesser evil" so that their support, or at least their acquiescence, might be gained. They overlook the fact that what these Jews and Arabs respectively have in mind is a "good" partition—"good" meaning favourable to their own point of view. But there is no partition that would be "good" for Jews and Arabs at one and the same time. If it were "good" for the Jews, it would rally *all* the Arabs against it, and *vice versa*. Most probably, it would rally both sides against it. The problem would be further complicated by the additional interests bearing on the situation, such as strategic, cultural, commercial, or religious considerations....

[Moreover] these carved out portions of a small country, which would be arbitrarily designated as "states" would be absolutely untenable either economically or politically. Trade and commerce would be strangled. The normal flow of goods and services in a country which naturally presents a single geographic and economic unit would be prevented. It must always be remembered that the reason for any partition would be that "Jews and Arabs will not cooperate." If they could not cooperate in a single Palestine, how would they ever do so across frontiers which each would regard as the burning wounds in their national life?...The premise, then, if it is at all

a true one, that conflict between Jews and Arabs is inevitable, would not be removed by partition. On the contrary, partition would only project it into the future by fixing and amplifying its causes.

By eliminating the unpromising alternatives, once more we reach our original conclusions: that there is no other way out of the deadlock save through a system calculated to bring the Jews and the Arabs together. No matter how much this idea may be criticised as unrealistic by people unable to see beyond a particular, though temporary, situation, we have no doubt that any, or every, other settlement is much more unrealistic....

[A bi-national solution] cannot hope to be carried into effect if Jews, Arabs and British alike each persist in maintaining that they have always been right while only the others were in the wrong. A thorough heart-searching on the part of all concerned is what is needed. Previous mistakes should be acknowledged. And we hope that the greatness of the cause at stake will not suffer on account of petty considerations. We hope that faith in humanity, in the better qualities of mankind, in progress and the victory of the masses will be the inspiring force in the solution of this grave problem. It is not only Palestine that stands at the cross-roads. The issue affects the entire Middle East. The choice is between friction and harmony, between Balkanization and cooperation, between fascist reaction and democratic progress. Now is not the time to set the clock back. A wise decision on Palestine will start us off in the right and glorious direction.

NOTES

1. Hashomer Hazair (The Young Guard)—a Palestinian political party associated with a Zionist youth movement of the same name (see document 30 in this chapter). In Palestine its members established numerous kibbutzim. In 1946 the party received 20 percent of the votes cast in the Histadrut (General Federation of Jewish Labor in Palestine). After the establishment of the State of Israel, Hashomer Hazair participated in the formation of Mifleget Poalim Meuhedet (Mapam, "United Workers' Party").

Since the 1920s various Zionist groups advocated as a solution to the Palestinian conflict the establishment of binational state in which both the Jewish and Arab communities would govern on a parity basis while enjoying communal autonomy. Foremost among the proponents of bi-nationalism was the Brit Shalom, founded in 1926 by Arthur Ruppin (see this chapter, document 38); the Ihud, organized in 1942 by *inter alios* J. Magnes and M. Buber; and Hashomer Hazair, which submitted the above proposal to the Anglo-American

Inquiry Commission appointed in November 1945 to reconsider the Palestine problem in light of the plight of Jewish survivors of the Holocaust.

2. That is, the Royal Commission appointed in 1936 and headed by Lord Peel.

51. BI-NATIONALISM IS UNWORKABLE (JULY 17, 1947)

MOSHE SHERTOK[1]

The [Arab-Jewish conflict in Palestine] can certainly not be met by the adoption of a bi-national solution based on parity. Such a solution, to be operative, presupposes two collective wills acting, by and large, in unison.

It is not a question of individuals combining on some minor matters. Individuals may combine across the barriers of race or community or religion, but on major matters, what one would have to face for a considerable time—heaven knows for how long—would be two national entities, each with a collective will of its own. And to imagine that such a state would be something workable is to presuppose a willingness to walk together on the part of those two national entities.

These prerequisites do not exist, and therefore the issue, I am afraid, is a purely academic one. If, for the sake of argument, I am to assume that it may be practical politics—which I do not—then I would have to say that it would either lead to a state of permanent deadlock on major matters, or that it would lead to the virtual abolition of independence. For in this case again, in order to save the situation from a state of perpetual deadlock, a third party would have to be introduced either as a result of foresight or as a result of an *esprit d'escalier*.

I do not think I am fully competent to judge the subject from the point of view of comparative constitutional law, but I am not aware of any precedent for such an arrangement. There are bi-national and multinational states in the world, and in all of them, I believe, sovereignty in the ultimate resort is vested in the majority of the population or the majority of some elected assembly. In the last resort the majority prevails, and nowhere do you find two equally balanced communities set against each other. It would have been more logical to expect such an arrangement in those countries than in a country like Palestine, because in those countries there are no such fundamental cleavages and no such diametrical divergencies as we have to face in Palestine. It is not a workable solution.

I must stress again and again that the question is not whether Jews and Arabs can live together within the framework of one state. They can. They do. They will. The question is whether they can operate a state machinery by pulling an equal weight in its councils. They will pull apart. The problem in this country is not how to compose the differences between two static sections of the country's population. If that were the case, it would not be so difficult. The problem is how to reconcile independence with the dynamic

Source: Oral testimony given on July 17, 1947, to the United Nations Special Committee on Palestine, in "The Jewish Plan for Palestine: Memoranda and Statements Presented by the Jewish Agency for Palestine to the United Nations Special Committee on Palestine" (Jerusalem, 1947), pp. 511–13.

development of the Jewish section and of the country as a whole. Perhaps I could formulate it a little differently, and that perhaps would be more correct. The problem is how to make of independence an instrument of development and not a stranglehold on development. But if you assign equality to both statics and dynamics, then the statics will have the advantage. Equality of veto will mean Jewish defeat. What can a Jewish veto do to the Arabs, vitally, crucially? The Arabs are here. Nobody in his senses would try to eradicate them; anyhow you won't do it by a veto. What positive act can doom the hopes of the Arabs to live here, to enjoy prosperity? But an Arab veto could and would prevent Jewish immigration and that is the most fundamental issue for the Jews.

You do not solve the problem by taking immigration out of the context and entrusting it to some ad hoc authority. It cannot be taken out of the context. The problem of immigration is bound up with the whole machinery of Government, with economic policy, with fiscal policy. It is not merely a question of issuing visas and letting people in. It means absorbing those people, providing for them, so shaping the country's economic policy as to enable us to absorb immigrants. If there is harmony between the ad hoc immigration authority and the state machinery, then it is all right. But if there is complete discord, the possibility of it, the certainty of it, then it will not work, and the immigration powers which you might grant to the ad hoc authority would prove a delusion....Again, in a bi-national state...we shall be irresistibly driven to the installation of a third party wielding real power with all the negative results—primarily, no independence.

NOTE

1. Moshe Shertok (1894–1965). From 1933 to 1948 he was the secretary of the Jewish Agency's political department, a position equivalent to the foreign minister of the nascent Jewish National Home. Indeed, with the establishment of the State of Israel in 1948 Shertok (who then hebraized his name to Sharett) was appointed foreign minister of the Provisional Government.

52. RESOLUTION ON PALESTINE (NOVEMBER 29, 1947)[1]

UNITED NATIONS GENERAL ASSEMBLY

The General Assembly,...Considers that the present situation in Palestine is one which is likely to impair the general welfare and friendly relations among nations;

Takes note of the declaration by the mandatory power that it plans to complete its evacuation of Palestine by August 1, 1948;

Recommends to the United Kingdom, as the mandatory power for Palestine, and to all other Members of the United Nations the adoption and implementation, with regard to the future government of Palestine, of the Plan of Partition with Economic Union set out below;

Source: New York Times, November 30, 1947, p. 1. Copyright 1947 by the New York Times Company. Reprinted by permission.

Requests that (a) The Security Council take the necessary measures as provided for in the plan for its implementation; ...

PART I

A. TERMINATION OF MANDATE, PARTITION AND INDEPENDENCE

1. The Mandate for Palestine shall terminate as soon as possible but in any case not later than August 1, 1948.

2. The armed forces of the mandatory power shall be progressively withdrawn from Palestine, the withdrawal to be completed as soon as possible but in any case not later than August 1, 1948.

The mandatory power shall advise the Commission, as far in advance as possible, of its intention to terminate the Mandate and to evacuate each area.

The mandatory power shall use its best endeavours to ensure that an area situated in the territory of the Jewish State, including a seaport and hinterland adequate to provide facilities for a substantial immigration, shall be evacuated at the earliest possible date and in any event not later than February 1, 1948.

3. Independent Arab and Jewish States and the Special International Regime for the City of Jerusalem, set forth in part III of this plan, shall come into existence in Palestine two months after the evacuation of the armed forces of the mandatory power has been completed but in any case not later than October 1, 1948....

D. ECONOMIC UNION AND TRANSIT

1. The Provisional Council of Government of each State shall enter into an undertaking with respect to Economic Union and Transit....

PART III—CITY OF JERSUALEM

A. SPECIAL REGIME

The City of Jerusalem shall be established as a *corpus separatum* under a special international regime and shall be designated to discharge the responsibilities of the Administering Authority on behalf of the United Nations.

NOTE

1. On February 14, 1947, His Majesty's government announced that, given the anarchy reigning in Palestine, the mandate could no longer be properly administered and that Britain would thus seek to return the mandate to the United Nations (which had replaced the League of Nations). On November 29, 1947, the United Nations General Assembly approved, by a vote of thirty-three to thirteen, of the partition plan for Palestine recommended by the United Nations Special Committee on Palestine. Among the states voting in favor of the plan were the United States and the Soviet Union—Britain abstained. The plan was accepted by the Jews and rejected by the Arabs, who declared that they would do all in their power to prevent its implementation. Britain stated it would do nothing to enforce the plan.

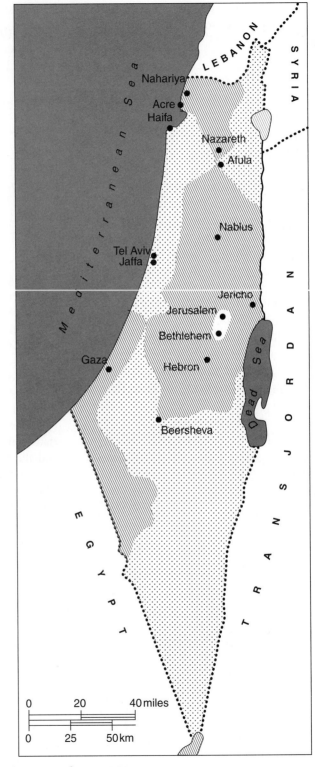

Jewish state

Arab state

International zone

Partition of Mandatory Palestine, November 29, 1947

53. PROCLAMATION OF THE STATE OF ISRAEL (MAY 14, 1948)[1]

The Land of Israel was the birthplace of the Jewish people. Here their spiritual, religious and national identity was formed. Here they achieved independence and created a culture of national and universal significance. Here they wrote and gave the Bible to the world.

Exiled from Palestine, the Jewish people remained faithful to it in all the countries of their dispersion, never ceasing to pray and hope for their return and the restoration of their national freedom.

Impelled by this historic association, Jews strove throughout the centuries to go back to the land of their fathers and regain their Statehood. In recent decades they returned in their masses. They reclaimed the wilderness, revived their language, built cities and villages and established a vigorous and evergrowing community, with its own economic and cultural life. They sought peace yet were prepared to defend themselves. They brought the blessings of progress to all inhabitants of the country.

In the year 1897 the First Zionist Congress, inspired by Theodor Herzl's vision of the Jewish State, proclaimed the right of the Jewish people to national revival in their own country.

This right was acknowledged by the Balfour Declaration of November 2, 1917, and reaffirmed by the Mandate of the League of Nations, which gave explicit international recognition to the historic connection of the Jewish people with Palestine and their right to reconstitute their national home.

The Nazi holocaust, which engulfed millions of Jews in Europe, proved anew the urgency of the reestablishment of the Jewish State, which would solve the problem of Jewish homelessness by opening the gates to all Jews and lifting the Jewish people to equality in the family of nations.

The survivors of the European catastrophe, as well as Jews from other lands, proclaiming their right to a life of dignity, freedom and labor, and undeterred by hazards, hardships and obstacles, have tried unceasingly to enter Palestine.

In the Second World War the Jewish people in Palestine made a full contribution in the struggle of the freedom-loving nations against the Nazi evil. The sacrifices of their soldiers and the efforts of their workers gained them title to rank with the peoples who founded the United Nations.

On November 29, 1947, the General Assembly of the United Nations adopted a Resolution for the establishment of an independent Jewish State in Palestine, and called upon inhabitants of the country to take such steps as may be necessary on their part to put the plan into effect.

This recognition by the United Nations of the right of the Jewish people to establish their independent state may not be revoked. It is, moreover, the self-evident right of the Jewish people to be a nation, like all other nations, in its own sovereign state.

Accordingly, we, the members of the National Council, representing the Jewish people in Palestine and the Zionist movement of the world, met together in solemn assembly today, the day of the termination of the British Mandate for Palestine, and by virtue of the natural and historic right of the Jewish people and of the resolution of the General Assembly of the United Nations, hereby proclaim the establishment of the Jewish State in Palestine, to be called Israel.

We hereby declare that as from the termination of the Mandate at midnight, this night of the fourteenth to the fifteenth of May, 1948, and until the setting up of the duly elected bodies of the State in accordance with a Constitution, to be drawn up by a Constituent Assembly not later than the first

Source: *Palestine Post*, May 16, 1948, pp. 1–2.

day of October 1948, the present National Council shall act as the Provisional State Council, and its executive organ, the National Administration, shall constitute the Provisional Government of the State of Israel.

The State of Israel will be open to the immigration of Jews from all countries of their dispersion; will promote the development of the country for the benefit of all its inhabitants; will be based on the precepts of liberty, justice and peace taught by the Hebrew Prophets; will uphold the full social and political equality of all its citizens, without distinction of race, creed or sex; will guarantee full freedom of conscience, worship, education and culture; will safeguard the sanctity and inviolability of the shrines and Holy Places of all religions; and will dedicate itself to the principles of the Charter of the United Nations.

The State of Israel will be ready to cooperate with the organs and representatives of the United Nations in the implementation of the Resolution of the Assembly of November 29, 1947, and will take steps to bring about the Economic Union over the whole of Palestine.

We appeal to the United Nations to assist the Jewish people in the building of its State and to admit Israel into the family of nations.

In the midst of wanton aggression, we yet call upon the Arab inhabitants of the State of Israel to return to the ways of peace and play their part in the development of the State, with full and equal citizenship and representation in all its bodies and institutions, provisional or permanent.

We offer peace and amity to all the neighboring states and their peoples, and invite them to cooperate with the independent Jewish nation for the common good of all. The State of Israel is ready to contribute its full share to the peaceful progress and development of the Middle East.

Our call goes out to the Jewish people all over the world to rally to our side in the task of immigration and development and to stand by us in the great struggle for the fulfillment of the dream of generations—the redemption of Israel.

With trust in the Rock of Israel, we set our hand to this Declaration, at this Session of the Provisional State Council, in the city of Tel Aviv, on this Sabbath eve, the fifth of Iyar, 5708, the fourteenth day of May, 1948.

NOTE

1. At eight o'clock on the morning of May fourteenth, the British lowered the Union Jack in Jerusalem. By midafternoon the Arabs launched a full-scale attack against the Jews. At 4:00 P.M. despite great pressure from the government of the United States and the doubts of many of his colleagues, David Ben-Gurion, chairman of the Jewish Agency Executive, read the Declaration of Independence of the State of Israel. The Jewish population of Palestine, except for Jerusalem, which was without electricity, heard the proclamation ceremonies as they were broadcast by radio from the Tel Aviv Museum.

54. ADDRESS TO THE KNESSET ON THE LAW OF RETURN (JULY 3, 1950)[1]

DAVID BEN-GURION

The Law of Return and the Law of Citizenship that you have in front of you are connected by a mutual bond and share of common conceptual origin, deriving from the historical uniqueness of the State of Israel, a uniqueness vis-à-vis the past and the future, directed internally and externally. These two laws determine the special character and destiny of the State of Israel as the state bearing the vision of the redemption of Israel.

The State of Israel is a state like all the other states. All the general indications [of statehood] common to the other states are also to be found in the State of Israel. It rests on a specific territory and a population existing within this territory, it possesses sovereignty in internal and external affairs, and its authority does not extend beyond its borders. The State of Israel rules only over its own inhabitants. The Jews in the Diaspora, who are citizens of their countries and who want to remain there, have no legal or civil connection to the State of Israel and the State of Israel does not represent them from any legal standpoint. Nevertheless, the State of Israel differs from the other states both with regard to the factors involved in its establishment and to the aims of its existence. It was established merely two years ago, but its roots are grounded in the far past and it is nourished by ancient springs. Its authority is limited to the area in which its residents dwell, but its gates are open to every Jew wherever he may be. The State of Israel is not a Jewish state merely because the majority of its inhabitants are Jews. It is a state for all the Jews wherever they may be and for every Jew who so desires.

On the fourteenth of May, 1948 a new State was not founded *ex nihilo*. Rather, the crown was restored to its pristine splendor 1,813 years after the independence of Israel was destroyed, during the days of Bar Kokhba and Rabbi Akiba....

The establishment of the Jewish state was not an event limited to the place and time of its emergence. Rather, it is a world event, in the sense of time as well as place, an event summarizing a prolonged historical development. This event has introduced radical reforms and itself serves as a source for alterations and changes exceeding its temporal and spatial framework....

It is not accidental that the Proclamation of Independence began with cogent and succinct passages concerning the perpetual link between the Jewish people and its ancient homeland. Neither is it accidental that as a primary and essential principle governing the direction of the state it was declared before anything else that "the state of Israel shall be open to Jewish immigration and the ingathering of exiles."...Just as it was clear that the renewal of the State of Israel is not a beginning, but a continuation from days of yore, so, too, was it understood that this renewal is not an end and conclusion but another stage in the long path leading to the full redemption of Israel.

The Diaspora has not ceased with the foundation of the state. In fact, this Diaspora is not a recent phenomenon, having preceded by a long period of time the destruction of our independence. Already in the seventh century B.C.E., simultaneous to the destruction of the First Commonwealth, we find Jews in foreign lands....

In the last meeting of the Zionist Executive in Jerusalem a debate arose concerning the question:

Source: "Debate on the law of return and law of citizenship," July 3, 1950, *Proceedings of the Knesset* 6 (Jerusalem, 1951), pp. 2035–37. Trans. S. Weinstein.

ingathering of exiles[2] or ingathering of *all the* exiles? This debate will not be decided by ideology or by political resolutions; only Jewish history can offer a solution. Nevertheless, it is a fact worth noting that foreign volunteers from fifty-five countries representing all five continents of the world served in the Israel Defense Force [during the War of Independence]. Further, with respect to its scope, dimensions, pace and diversity the return of the exiles taking place in our days has no precedent, even in the annals of the Jewish nation. This is the great, decisive event of our generation that will determine the fate of the State of Israel and fashion the image of the Hebrew nation for many generations; no event in our life from our emergence as a people until the present has been so decisive.

The motives at work in the Jewish immigration [to the land of Israel] in all the generations, including our own, have been many and varied. Longings for redemption, ancient memories, religious feelings, love of homeland and above all, distress—economic, political and spiritual distress. With the foundation of the state a new factor has been added whose strength will continually increase: the power of appeal and attraction of the State of Israel. The pace and scope of the return of the exiles will in no small part be dependent upon our capacity to augment this appeal and to turn the State of Israel into the center for the realization of the longings of the nation and for the satisfaction of its material and spiritual needs. In addition, this capacity may very well be the primary factor in attracting immigration from the countries of the new world.

The Law of Return is one of the Basic Laws of the State of Israel. It comprises the central mission of our state, namely, ingathering of exiles. This law determines that it is not the state that grants the Jew from abroad the right to settle in the state. Rather, this right is inherent in him by the very fact that he is a Jew, if only he desires to join in the settlement of the land. In the State of Israel the Jews have no right of priority over the non-Jewish citizens. The State of Israel is grounded on the full equality of rights and obligations for all its citizens. This principle was also laid down in the Proclamation of Independence....The right to return preceded the State of Israel and it is this right that built the state. This right originates in the unbroken historical connection between the people and the homeland, a connection which has also been acknowledged in actual practice by the tribunal of the peoples.

NOTES

1. David Ben-Gurion (1886–1973). Chairman of the National Council (*Vaad Leumi*) and of the Jewish Agency, 1935 to 1948, he also served as the first prime minister of the State of Israel. During the Knesset's deliberations on the Law of Return (see the next document) proposed by the government, Ben-Gurion outlined in this address the rationale of this legislation that would define the infant slate as legally committed to the Zionist idea of the repatriation of the "exiled" Jewish people to their ancestral homeland.

2. This ancient expression (in Hebrew, *kibbutz galuyot*). conceptually originating in the Book of Ezekiel, is found in the Talmudic literature and in some of the central prayers of the traditional liturgy. The "ingathering of the exiled communities" to the land of Israel was linked with the messianic idea, an association that Ben-Gurion acutely appreciated.

55. THE LAW OF RETURN (JULY 5, 1950)[1]

1. Every Jew has the right to immigrate to the country.

2. (a) Immigration shall be on the basis of an immigrant's visa, (b) An immigrant's visa shall be granted to every Jew who has expressed his desire to settle in Israel, unless the minister of immigration is convinced that the applicant (1) is acting against the Jewish people, (2) is likely to endanger public health or the security of the state.

3. (a) A Jew who comes to Israel and after his arrival expresses his desire to settle there, is entitled, while he is still in Israel, to obtain an immigrant certificate. (b) The reservations detailed in section 2(b) will also be in force regarding the granting of an immigrant certificate, but a person will not be considered as endangering the public health as a result of an illness he contracted after his arrival in Israel.

4. Every Jew who immigrated to Israel before this law entered into effect, and every Jew born in the country, whether before or after this law entered into effect, shall be considered as having immigrated according to this law.

5. The minister of immigration is responsible for the enforcement of this law, and he is empowered to enact regulations in all matters concerning its implementation as well as the granting of immigrant visas and immigrant papers to minors under the age of eighteen.

NOTE

1. This law was passed unanimously by the Knesset on July 5, 1950.

Source: Reshumot [Official record of the laws of the State of Israel] (Jerusalem, 1951), vol. 51, p. 159. Trans. S. Weinstein.

XI

THE SHOAH

Holocaust is a term that has come to designate the destruction of European Jewry during World War II. The term derives from the Septuagint, the Jewish translation of the Hebrew Scripture into Greek from the third century B.C.E., in which *Holokaustos* ("totally burnt") is the Greek rendering of the Hebrew *olah,* the burnt sacrificial offering dedicated *exclusively* to God.[1] Later the term lost its theological nuance and simply denoted sacrifice or vast destruction, especially by fire. Nonetheless, one now tends to prefer the less ambiguous Hebrew term *Shoah* (catastrophe).

As numbing as it is, the decimation of six million Jews by the Nazis is not an inexplicable, mysterious cataclysm. Although scholars still debate the causes of the Holocaust, all point to a confluence of economic, psychological, political, and social factors, among them a history in Germany of political and racial antisemitism, a dictatorship, an obedient and disciplined bureaucracy, and the technological means for industrial mass murder.

The Nazis initiated their war against the Jews with the rescission of emancipation through the systematic removal of Jewish civic rights and through the legislated deassimilation of the Jews (see documents 4, 5, 7, 8–10, 17, and 18). The Jews were forced back into the ghetto—occupational, cultural, social, and, in some of the occupied areas, also residential. The ghettoization and induced emigration of the Jews of Europe did not satisfy the demands of the Nazi ideology. By the end of 1941, a policy of extermination of Jewry—the so-called Final Solution—was formulated.

The Final Solution was dutifully and systematically carried out. For the most part it was not executed by rioting mobs and pogroms; rather the Nazis employed the most advanced industrial and organizational means of Western civilization to ensure efficiency and thoroughness (see documents 24 and 35). Puzzling to the student of the Holocaust is the unique morality that guided those who were responsible for carrying out the Nazi program of genocide (see documents 25, 31, and 36). Also baffling is the apathetic response of the bystanders in the free world. The lack of moral resolve to aid the victims of the Nazi atrocities invites reflection on Goebbels's cynical observation in his diary that the silence of the churches and of the Western democracies indicated implicit approval of Nazi antisemitism. In every respect, the Holocaust revealed a profound weakness in the moral conscience of Western humanity.

---

[1] The term *olah qua holokaustos* first appears in the Septuagint, Exod. 18:17. For the meaning of *olah,* see Lev. 1:9.

1. A LETTER ON THE JEWISH QUESTION (SEPTEMBER 16, 1919)[1]

ADOLF HITLER

Antisemitism as a political movement should not and cannot be determined by emotional factors, but rather by a realization of the facts. And these facts are:

First, Jewry is clearly a racial and not a religious group....All that which is for men a source of higher life—be it religion, socialism or democracy—is for the Jew merely a means to an end, namely, the satisfaction of his lust for power and money.

His actions will result in a racial tuberculosis of peoples [*Rassentuberkulose der Voelker*].

Hence it follows: Antisemitism based on purely emotional grounds will find its ultimate expression in the form of pogroms [which are capricious and thus not truly effective]. Rational antisemitism, however, must pursue a systematic, *legal* campaign against the Jews, by the revocation of the special privileges they enjoy in contrast to the other foreigners living among us. But the final objective must be the complete removal of the Jews [*die Entfernung der Juden ueberhaupt*].

NOTE

1. Adolf Hitler (1889–1945), Austrian-born leader of the National Socialist German Workers' Party (the Nazi Party) from 1920 and chancellor of the German Reich from 1933 until his suicide on April 30, 1945. Hitler inspired—and was the one ultimately responsible for planning and implementing—the Nazis' "war against the Jews," which culminated in the extermination of European Jewry. He felt himself called upon by Providence to lead the struggle against the Jews. In 1919 he joined a small nationalist, antisemitic political circle, the Deutsche Arbeiterpartei (German Workers' Party) and in 1920 he became the Führer of the party, which had been renamed the National-Sozialistische Deutsche Arbeiterpartei (National Socialist German Workers' Party—Nazi). Upon the assumption of the leadership of the nascent Nazi Party, he declared, "It is our duty to arouse, to whip up and to incite in our people the instinctive repugnance for the Jews." Hitler's antisemitism is an eclectic weave of motifs from Austrian and German political and racial antisemitism; his obsession with the worldwide Jewish conspiracy is apparently derived from the *Protocols of the Elders of Zion*, which was translated into German in 1920. (See document 29 in chapter 6.) With the Nazis' accession to power in January 1933, Hitler's impassioned call for the Aryan peoples to gather together in an apocalyptic effort to check the insidious schemes of Jewry—whom he perceived as the incarnation of absolute evil—gained expression in the policy of "racial purification" and the systematic exclusion of the Jews from German society.

In this letter, which is his earliest extant political statement in print, Hitler outlined his views on the Jewish question. At the time he was employed as a secret agent of the Press and Propaganda Office of the political department of the Reichswehr (National Defense), which was charged with checking the inroads of revolutionary politics within the ranks of the demobilizing troops. A certain Adolf Gemlich addressed an inquiry to this office regarding the place of the Jewish question within the Wehrmacht's anti-revolutionary propaganda. Hitler was asked to write the reply to Gemlich and used the occasion to adumbrate his conception of a rational antisemitism (*Antisemitismus der Vernunft*), viz., a two-stage policy of first systematically and legally rescinding the emancipation of the Jews and then bringing about their total "removal" (*Entfernung*) from German life. (The exact nature of this "final objective" remained for the time being unspecified.) This emphasis on a two-stage solution to the Jewish question continued to characterize Hitler's policy.

Source: Adolf Hitler to Adolf Gemlich, September 16, 1919, Hauptstaatsarchiv Muenchen, in Ernst Deuerlein, "Hitlers Eintritt in die Politik und die Reichswehr," *Vierteljahreshefte fuer Zeitgeschichte 7* (1959), pp. 203–5. Trans. P. Mendes-Flohr.

2. MEIN KAMPF (1923)[1]

ADOLF HITLER

Today it is difficult, if not impossible, for me to say when the word "Jew" first gave me ground for special thoughts. At home I do not remember having heard the word during my father's lifetime. I believe that the old gentleman would have regarded any special emphasis on this term as cultural backwardness. In the course of his life he had arrived at more or less cosmopolitan views which, despite his pronounced national sentiments, not only remained intact, but also affected me to some extent.

Likewise at school I found no occasion which could have led me to change this inherited picture....

Not until my fourteenth or fifteenth year did I begin to come across the word "Jew," with any frequency, partly in connection with political discussions. This filled me with a mild distaste, and I could not rid myself of an unpleasant feeling that always came over me whenever religious quarrels occurred in my presence.

At that time I did not think anything else of the question.

There were few Jews in Linz.[2] In the course of the centuries their outward appearance had become Europeanized and had taken on a human look; in fact, I even took them for Germans. The absurdity of this idea did not dawn on me because I saw no distinguishing feature but the strange religion. The fact that they had, as I believed, been persecuted on this account sometimes almost turned my distaste at unfavorable remarks about them into horror....Then I came to Vienna. [Gradually], I encountered the Jewish question....

My views with regard to antisemitism thus succumbed to the passage of time, and this was my greatest transformation of all.

It cost me the greatest inner soul struggles, and only after months of battle between my reason and my sentiments did my reason begin to emerge victorious. Two years later, my sentiment had followed my reason, and from then on became its most loyal guardian and sentinel.

At the time of this bitter struggle between spiritual education and cold reason, the visual instruction of the Vienna streets had performed invaluable services. There came a time when I no longer, as in the first days, wandered blindly through the mighty city; now with open eyes I saw not only the buildings but also the people.

Once, as I was strolling through the Inner City, I suddenly encountered an apparition in a black caftan and black hair locks. Is this a Jew? was my first thought.

For, to be sure, they had not looked like that in Linz. I observed the man furtively and cautiously, but the longer I stared at this foreign face, scrutinizing feature for feature, the more my first question assumed a new form:

Is this a German?

As always in such cases, I now began to try to relieve my doubts by books....

I could no longer very well doubt that the objects of my study were not Germans of a special religion, but a people in themselves; for since I had begun to concern myself with this question and to take cognizance of the Jews, Vienna appeared to me in a different light than before. Wherever I went, I began to see Jews, and the more I saw, the more sharply they became distinguished in my eyes from the rest of humanity....

The cleanliness of this people, moral and otherwise, I must say, is a point in itself. By their very exterior you could tell that these were no lovers of water, and to your distress, you often knew it with your eyes closed. Later I often grew sick to my stomach from the smell of these caftan-wearers. Added to this, there was their unclean dress and their generally unheroic appearance.

All this could scarcely be called very attractive; but it became positively repulsive when, in addition to their physical uncleanliness, you discovered the moral stains on this "chosen people."

In a short time I was made more thoughtful than ever by my slowly rising insight into the type of activity carried on by the Jews in certain fields.

Was there any form of filth or profligacy, particularly in cultural life, without at least one Jew involved in it?

If you cut even cautiously into such an abscess, you found, like a maggot in a rotting body, often dazzled by the sudden light—a kike!

What had to be reckoned heavily against the Jews in my eyes was when I became acquainted with their activity in the press, art, literature and the theater. All the unctuous reassurances helped little or nothing. It sufficed to look at a billboard, to study the names of the men behind the horrible trash they advertised, to make you hard for a long time to come. This was pestilence, spiritual pestilence, worse than the Black Death of olden times, and the people was being infected with it! . . .

And I now began to examine my beloved "world press," from this point of view.

And the deeper I probed, the more the object of my former admiration shriveled. The style became more and more unbearable; I could not help rejecting the content as inwardly shallow and banal; the objectivity of exposition now seemed to me more akin to lies than honest truth; and the writers were—Jews.

A thousand things which I had hardly seen before now struck my notice, and others, which had previously given me food for thought, I now learned to grasp and understand.

I now saw the liberal attitude of this press in a different light; the lofty tone in which it answered attacks and its method of killing them with silence now revealed itself to me as a trick as clever as it was treacherous; the transfigured raptures of their theatrical critics were always directed at Jewish writers, and their disapproval never struck anyone but Germans. . . .

The development was accelerated by insights which I gained into a number of other matters. I am referring to the general view of ethics and morals which was quite openly exhibited by a large part of the Jews, and the practical application of which could be seen.

Here again the streets provided an object lesson of a sort which was sometimes positively evil.

The relation of the Jews to prostitution and, even more, to the white-slave traffic, could be studied in Vienna as perhaps in no other city of Western Europe, with the possible exception of the southern French ports. If you walked at night through the streets and alleys of Leopoldstadt, at every step you witnessed proceedings which remained concealed from the majority of the German people until the War gave the soldiers on the eastern front occasion to see similar things, or, better expressed, forced them to see them.

When thus for the first time I recognized the Jew as the cold-hearted, shameless and calculating director of this revolting vice traffic in the scum of the big city, a cold shudder ran down my back.

But then a flame flared up within me. I no longer avoided discussion of the Jewish question; no, now I sought it. And when I learned to look for the Jew in all branches of cultural and artistic life and its various manifestations, I suddenly encountered him in a place where I would least have expected to find him.

When I recognized the Jew as the leader of the Social Democracy, the scales dropped from my eyes. A long soul struggle had reached its conclusion. . . .

Only now did I become thoroughly acquainted with the seducer of our people.

A single year of my sojourn in Vienna had sufficed to imbue me with the conviction that no worker could be so stubborn that he would not in the end succumb to better knowledge and better explanation. Slowly I had become an expert in their own doctrine and used it as a weapon in the struggle for my own profound conviction.

Success almost always favored my side.

The great masses could be saved, if only with the gravest sacrifice in time and patience.

But a Jew could never be parted from his opinions. . . .

For me this was the time of the greatest spiritual upheaval I have ever had to go through.

I had ceased to be a weak-kneed cosmopolitan and become an antisemite.

Just once more—and this was the last time—fearful, oppressive thoughts came to me in profound anguish.

When over long periods of human history I scrutinized the activity of the Jewish people, suddenly there rose up in me the fearful question whether inscrutable Destiny, perhaps for reasons unknown to us poor mortals, did not with eternal and immutable resolve, desire the final victory of this little nation.

Was it possible that the earth had been promised as a reward to this people which lives only for this earth?

Have we an objective right to struggle for our self-preservation, or is this justified only subjectively within ourselves?

As I delved more deeply into the teachings of Marxism and thus in tranquil clarity submitted the deeds of the Jewish people to contemplation, Fate itself gave me its answer.

The Jewish doctrine of Marxism rejects the aristocratic principle of Nature and replaces the eternal privilege of power and strength by the mass of numbers and their dead weight. Thus it denies the value of personality in man, contests the significance of nationality and race and thereby withdraws from humanity the premise of its existence and its culture. As a foundation of the universe, this doctrine would bring about the end of any order intellectually conceivable to man. And as, in this greatest of all recognizable organisms, the result of an application of such a law could only be chaos, on earth it could only be destruction for the inhabitants of this planet.

If, with the help of his Marxist creed, the Jew is victorious over the other people of the world, his crown will be the funeral wreath of humanity and this planet will, as it did thousands of years ago, move through the ether devoid of men.

Eternal Nature inexorably avenges the infringement of her commands.

Hence today I believe that I am acting in accordance with the will of the Almighty Creator:, *by defending myself against the Jew, I am fighting for the work of the Lord.*

NOTE

1. In 1923 the National Socialist German Workers' Party attempted a political coup in Munich. Their intention had been to set out from the Bavarian capital to conquer the whole of Germany. The *putsch* ("uprising") failed, and Hitler and several of his comrades were brought to trial, a trial which Hitler cleverly used as a forum to publicize the Nazi cause. During the short period he spent in prison, Hitler wrote his autobiography, *Mein Kampf* [My Struggle], in which he outlined the program of his movement. The first volume of the book was published in 1925 and volume two in 1926.

2. In the 1920s Linz, the capital of Upper Austria, had a population of just under 100,000. Less than one percent of this were Jews. Hitler actually lived with his parents in various villages in the vicinity of Linz.

3. WEAR THE YELLOW BADGE WITH PRIDE (APRIL 4, 1933)

ROBERT WELTSCH[1]

The first of April, 1933, will remain an important date not only in the history of German Jewry, but in that of the entire Jewish people. For the events of the boycott day have not only their political and economic but their moral and spiritual aspects....

It has never been our fashion to lament. To react to happenings of such catastrophic force and sentimental babble we leave to the Jews of that generation which learned nothing and forgot everything. What is needed in the discussion of Jewish affairs is an entirely new tone. We live in a new time. A whole world of ideals and concepts has crashed to ruin. That may give pain to many. But none will be able to sustain himself from now on who shirks realities. We are in the midst of a complete transformation of our intellectual and political, social and economic life. Our gravest concern is this: How does Jewry react?

The first of April, 1933, can be a day of Jewish awakening and Jewish rebirth. If the Jews will it so! If the Jews have the inner maturity and magnanimity. If the Jews are not as their enemies represent them.

Embattled Jewry must affirm itself....

In the midst of all the bitterness that fills us at the reading of the National-Socialist calls to boycott our people and at the false accusations contained therein, for one regulation we are not ungrateful to the boycott committee, which states in paragraph 3: "It goes without saying that we mean business concerns owned by members of the Jewish race. We are not concerned with religion. Jews who have submitted to Catholic or Protestant baptism or have seceded from their religious community remain Jews within the meaning of the order."

That is a sound reminder to all *our* traitors. He, who slinks away from his community in order to improve his personal position shall not earn the reward of his treason. In this attitude toward our renegades there may be the faint beginning of a clarification. The Jew who denies his Judaism is no better a citizen than he who affirms it uprightly. To be a renegade is shameful enough. So long as the world seemed to reward this shame, it seemed profitable. The profit is swept away. The Jew is rendered recognizable as such. He wears the yellow badge.

That the boycott committee ordered shields "showing on a black background a yellow spot to be attached to the shops in question," is a terrific symbol. For this shield was supposed to brand us and to render us contemptible in people's eyes. Very well. *We accept the shield and shall make of it a badge of honor.*

Many Jews underwent last Saturday [the first of April] a gruelling experience. Not for an inner conviction, not for loyalty to their people, not for their pride in a magnificent history and in noblest human achievement were they suddenly forced to admit their Jewishness, but by the affixing of a red placard or a yellow badge, sticking their placards to doors and windows and painting the window-panes. For four-and-twenty hours the whole of German Jewry stood, so to speak, in the pillory. In addition to other signs and inscriptions the troopers frequently painted upon windows the *Magen David*. They meant to dishonor us. *Jews, take it upon yourselves, that shield of David, and honor it anew.*

For—at this point begins our duty of self-recollection—if this escutcheon is defiled today, think not that our enemies alone have done it. How many Jews were there among us who could not seem

Source: Robert Weltsch, [Editorial], *Juedische Rundschau* (April 4, 1933) in Ludwig Lewisohn, *Rebirth* (New York, 1935), pp. 336–41. Copyright 1935 by Behrman House, Inc. Reprinted by permission of Behrman House, Inc.

to get their fill of undignified self-irony. Judaism was held to be a thing outdated; it was regarded without seriousness; men and women sought to flee from its tragic implications by a grin. But let it not be forgotten that today and for long there has existed a new type, that free and proud Jew, whom the non-Jewish world does not yet know. . . .

Less than thirty years ago it was considered scandalous even to mention the Jewish problem among educated people. The Zionists were regarded as disturbers of the peace haunted by a mania. Today the Jewish problem is such a burning one that every child, every schoolboy, every simple man in the street is ceaselessly preoccupied with it. On April the first every Jew in Germany was stamped as such. According to the latest regulations of the boycott committee it has been determined that, in case of renewal, only two uniform signs are to be employed: "German house" and "Jew." The Jew is known. Evasion or hiding is at an end. The Jewish answer must be clear. It must be that briefest of sentences that Moses spoke to the Egyptians: IVRI ANOCHI, I am a Jew.[2] We *must affirm our Jewishness*. That is the moral meaning of this hour in history. The time is too agitated for argument. . . . But we, the Jewish people, can defend our honor by a moral act. We remember all those who in the course of five thousand years have been called Jews and have been stigmatized as Jews. The world reminds us that we are of them, that we are Jews. And we answer: Yes, it is our pride and glory that we are!

NOTE

1. Born in Prague, Robert Weltsch (1891–1982) served from 1919 to 1938 as the chief editor of the *Juedische Rundschau*, a respected Zionist newspaper in Berlin. During the Nazi period, the *Juedische Rundschau*, under Weltsch's inspired editorship, sought to instill pride in a humiliated people and to foster Jewish cultural and national consciousness. Later he was a highly respected correspondent for the Tel Aviv daily *Haaretz*. From 1956 to 1978 he edited the *Leo Baeck Institute Year Book*. He died in Jerusalem.

   On January 30, 1933, Hitler, as head of the single largest party in the Reichstag, was appointed chancellor of Germany. One of the first acts of the new regime was a program to intimidate its political adversaries, primarily the Socialists and Communists. On March 21, 1933, a concentration camp was established, and within ten days more than 15,000 individuals in Prussia alone were taken into "protective custody." The worldwide protest that ensued was construed by the Nazis as a Jewish plot. This provided them with the pretext to initiate their campaign against the Jews. In retaliation for instigating foreign misunderstanding of their policy to control the intractable opponents of orderly government, the Nazis proclaimed for April 1, 1933, a general boycott of Jewish shops, enterprises, and professionals. This boycott was backed by the full weight of the Nazi propaganda machine. On the appointed day, uniformed Nazi pickets appeared in front of Jewish shops, attacked their clients, and wrote anti-Jewish slogans on their windows. Students prevented their Jewish classmates and Jewish instructors from entering the universities. Some troops surrounded the courthouses to keep Jewish judges away. The offices of Jewish doctors, lawyers, and other professionals were also picketed. In his editorial in the *Juedische Rundschau*, presented here, Robert Weltsch urged the bewildered Jewish community of Germany to respond with inner fortitude and renewed Jewish pride. Weltsch did not, of course, foresee the Final Solution.

2. This proud declaration—literally "I am a Hebrew"—is actually ascribed to Jonah 1:9. In fact, according to the rabbis, it was because of Moses' failure to assert before pharaoh *ivri anochi* that God forbade him to enter the Promised Land. Cf. the Midrash in Mekhilta on Deut. 31.

4. FIRST RACIAL DEFINITION (APRIL 11, 1933)[1]

On the basis of paragraph 17 of the Law Regarding the Restoration of Professional Service of April 7, 1933, the following decree is issued:

Addendum paragraph 3. (1) A person is to be regarded as non-Aryan, who is descended from non-Aryan, especially Jewish parents or grandparents. This holds true even if only one parent or grandparent is of non-Aryan descent. This premise especially obtains if one parent or grandparent was of Jewish faith. (2) If a civil servant was not already a civil servant on August 1,1914, he must prove that he is of Aryan descent, or that he fought at the front, or that he is the son or the father of a man killed during the World War. Proof must be given by submitting documents (birth certificate and marriage certificate of the parents, military papers). (3) If Aryan descent is doubtful, an opinion must be obtained from the expert on racial research commissioned by the Reich Minister of the Interior [*Sachverstaendiger fuer Rasseforschung*].

NOTE

1. The ultimate objective of Nazi policy was to rescind the emancipation of the Jews. The Nazis did not, however, summarily deny the Jews citizenship. They pursued their policy cautiously through the legislature, enacting laws that gradually withdrew Jewish civil rights. The initial legislative stage (from April 1933 to September 1935)—which sought to eliminate the Jews from public office and from economic and cultural life—began immediately after the general boycott of April 1. On April 7, 1933, the first anti-Jewish ordinance was passed. The Law for the Restoration of the Professional Civil Service dismissed from the civil service opponents of the regime and non-Aryans. This law included teachers and university lecturers and professors. Similar legislation from the same day prohibited non-Aryans from practicing law. Within the next few months laws were enacted that barred non-Aryans from serving as patent lawyers, lay assessors, jurors, commercial judges, tax consultants, editors, publishers as well as physicians and dentists in the state social insurance institutions. A *numerus clausus* was also introduced in all public educational institutions. The Defense Law of May 21, 1935, excluded non-Aryans from military service. The term *non-Aryan*—used in legal documents until the Nuremberg Laws as a circumlocution for Jews—was defined in the above decree reprinted here that was issued on April 11, 1933.

Source: First Decree for the Execution of the Law of Restoration of the Professional Civil Service, in Bernard Dov Weinryb, *Jewish Emancipation Under Attack* (New York: American Jewish Committee, 1942), pp. 41–42. Reprinted by permission of the American Jewish Committee.

5. DECREES EXCLUDING JEWS FROM GERMAN CULTURAL AND PUBLIC LIFE (1933–1942)[1]

"In the future Jewish lawyers and notaries may no longer handle the legal affairs of the City of Berlin."

Municipal Government of Berlin, March 18, 1933

"The City Health Insurance Institute will as of April 1, 1933 no longer reimburse the costs for treatment by Jewish physicians."

Berlin Commissioner of Health, March 31, 1933

"Jews are no longer to be employed in the public services of the City of Cologne. This prohibition applies also to baptized Jews and non-Jews who are married to Jews."

Municipal Government of Cologne, April 1, 1933

"All district offices of Berlin are instructed to dismiss immediately all teachers who have Jewish blood (*sic*)."

Superintendent of Berlin Public Schools, April 1, 1933

"1) Civil servants, who are not of Aryan descent, are to be pensioned; honorary civil servants are to be dismissed. 2) This [ordinance] does not hold for civil servants who are employed since before August 1, 1914, or who fought for the German Reich at the front in the World War or whose father or sons fell in the war."

Chancellor's Office, the Interior Ministry of the Reich, Finance Ministry of the Reich, April 7, 1933

"An 'Aryan clause' is to be introduced into the by-laws of all German sports and gymnastic clubs. It is not to be applied to those who fought at the front in the First World War or lost someone in the war."

Sports Commissioner of the Reich, April 25, 1933

"Jews may change their names only to other Jewish names."

Prussian Interior Minister, May 13, 1933

"Membership in the Greater German Chess Association, which from now on will be the [country's] sole chess organization, is to be determined in accordance with an Aryan paragraph."

German Chess Association, July 9, 1933

"Farmers of the district of Bütow are forbidden to sell the products to Jewish dealers."

Governor of the District of Bütow, July 18, 1933

"Membership in choral associations will be determined according to the regulations of the Reich [prohibiting] the employment of non-Aryans in public positions."

Chairman of the German Choral Associations, August 18, 1933

"Jews are forbidden to bathe at the following public beaches: Berlin-Wannsee, Fulda, Beuthen, Speyer [et cetera]."

Interior Ministry of the Reich, August 22, 1933

"The performance of Jewish actors is not permitted."

Directive of the Ministry of the Reich for Popular Enlightenment and Propaganda, March 5, 1934

"Non-Aryans and those married to non-Aryans are no longer permitted to have pharmacies."

Ordinance of the Prussian Ministry of the Interior, April 17, 1934

"Theater directors must register and prove their Aryan origins."

The Reich's Chamber of Theater, May 3, 1934

"Non-Aryan students will not be permitted to take the examination to become teachers of dance."

President of the Reich Chamber of Theater, July 27, 1934

"It is forbidden in the cattle market to speak Yiddish or Hebrew."

Bavarian Ministry of the Interior, August 2, 1934

Source: Joseph Walk, ed., *Das Sonderrecht fuer Juden im NS-Staat. Eine Sammlung der gesetzlichen Maßnahmen und Richtlinien. Inhalt und Bedeutung.* (Heidelberg/Karlsruhe: G. F. Mueller, 1981), passim. Trans. Paul Mendes-Flohr.

"Jews are forbidden to display on their shops or homes flags with the Swastika or black-white-red flag [of the Reich]."

Order of the Gestapo, February 12, 1935

"Work permits for non-Aryan musicians will not be renewed."

The Reich's Chamber of Music, March 31, 1935

"All Jewish authors are to be notified by the President of the Reich Chamber of Writers that they are not permitted to engage in any literary activity in Germany."

President of the Reich's Chamber of Writers,
March 1935

"Jews can no longer be trained as book dealers, since membership in the Reich Chamber of Writers is required for such training. Exception: Jews can be accepted who intend to work as booksellers in the Jewish community and sell only to Jews."

Breslau City Council, December 27, 1934

"Non-Aryans can be engaged as foreign exchange consultants. The law from May 6, 1933, expressly states that non-Aryans are forbidden from acting as tax consultants. The prohibition is thus not valid for representatives in foreign exchange concerns, foreign exchange consultants and the like."

The Reich's Bureau for Foreign Exchange,
January 22, 1935

"Meetings of Jewish organizations, which seek to dispel fears of staying in Germany, are forbidden. The advisory does not apply to Zionist activities, for the Zionists seek to encourage emigration."

Karlsruhe Gestapo, February 26, 1935

"Entrance of Jews to public bathing and swimming facilities is forbidden."

The City Council of Augsburg, July 19, 1935

"Jews are forbidden from entering public bathing facilities, sports halls and the like."

Mayor of Dortmund, July 25, 1935

"§ 1: Marriage between Jews and citizens of German or related blood is forbidden. Such marriages that have already taken places are void.

§ 2: Extramarital intercourse between Jews and citizens of German or related blood are forbidden.

§ 3: Jews are not permitted to engage in their homes female citizens of German or related blood under forty-five years old.

§ 4: Jews are not permitted to fly the flags of the Reich and Nation, or the Display of the Colors of the Reich. They are permitted 'the Display of Jewish Colors.'

§ 5: Penalties: Violation of § 1 imprisonment; of § 2, for men imprisonment; § 3 and 4, imprisonment and/or a fine." The Führer, Chancellor of the Reich, the Minister of Interior of the Reich, the Minister of Justice of the Reich, and the Vice Führer.

Law for the Protection of German Blood and
German Honor, The Reich Party Rally for Freedom,
September 15, 1935.

"To avoid giving foreign visitors a bad impression, all signs with extreme content are to be removed. It should suffice to have signs such as "Jews are unwanted here."

Municipal Council of Frankfurt am Main,
January 29, 1936

"It is prohibited to engage the service of a veterinarian, who because of his or his spouse's racial origin, is not a civil servant."

The Führer, Chancellor of the Reich, the Minister of
the Interior of the Reich, April 3, 1936

"Members of the Reich Press Chamber must prove their and their spouses' descent from persons of German or related blood back to the year of 1800."

President of the Reich's Press Chamber,
April 15, 1936

"Conversion of Jews to Christianity has no bearing on their racial status. As soon as the officials of the Racial Research Institute assume their functions, the possibility of camouflage of one's racial origins through the change of one's religious confession must be brought to an utter end."

The Minister of the Interior of the Reich,
October 4, 1936

"1. Jews with German citizenship will no longer be admitted to doctoral examinations; the issuance of doctoral diplomas [for Jews] shall cease forthwith.

2. Those of mixed race (*Mischlinge*) will be permitted to earn a doctorate.

3. No consideration will be made for Jews who have already fulfilled the requirements for their doctorate; exceptions to the rule will require the consent of the Minister.

4. Jews of mixed race can earn a doctoral degree in medicine and dentistry if they commit themselves to leaving Germany immediately thereafter."

Directive of the Reich's Minister of Science,
April 15, 1937

"Post office workers who or whose spouse are not of pure Aryan descent are obliged to retire."

Directive of the Reich's Minister of Posts,
June 8, 1937

"Jews can no longer be members of the German Red Cross."

Employment Instructions of the German Red Cross,
January 1, 1938

"As of September 30, 1938, Jewish physicians will no longer be allowed to practice. The Minister of Interior of the Reich can grant permission to Jewish physicians to treat Jews as well as their wives and children. Jews, whose license has expired, and who have not received such permission, are absolutely forbidden to practice medicine. Those Jews who have received permission to treat their fellow Jews may not use the title "Doctor," but the title "health care worker."

Addendum to the Reich's Law of Citizenship, decreed
by the Führer, Vice Führer, the Chancellery of the
Reich, the Minister of the Interior of the Reich,
the Reich's Minister of Justice, the Reich's
Minister of Finance, July 27, 1938

"To the degree it has yet to happen, all streets named after Jews and Jewish *Mischlinge* of the first degree are to be immediately renamed. The old street signs are to be removed forthwith and exchanged with new signs.

Minister of the Interior of the Reich, July 27, 1938

"Jews who do not have first names, which are on the list to be circulated on August 18, 1938, by the Ministry of the Interior, must as January 1, 1939, have an additional first name, 'Israel' for men, or 'Sara' for women."

Minister of Interior of the Reich, Minister of Justice of
the Reich, August 17, 1938

"All German passports belonging to Jews are invalid. They must be returned and new ones marked with the letter J will be given for foreign travel."

Ministry of the Interior of the Reich, October 5, 1938

"Jews are not permitted to leave their apartments and to be on the streets after eight in the evening (in the summer after nine)."

By order of the Police, September 1, 1939

"Jews holding German citizenship and stateless Jews are forbidden to possess radios. The prohibition holds also for Aryans who live in Jewish houses, and for *Mischlinge*."

Headquarters of the Reich Security Service,
September 20, 1939

"Jews in Berlin are only permitted to buy food between four and five o'clock in the afternoon."

President of the Berlin Police, July 4, 1940

"As of September 30, 1940, all telephone lines used by Jews will be cut off. Jewish health and dental workers, and Jewish organizations are exempt [from this order]."

The Reich's Ministry of Posts, July 29, 1940

"Jews are no longer allowed to possess soap and shaving cream. Jewish men are, therefore, to grow beards as a sign that they are Jews."

Director of the Bureau of the National Socialist Party,
June 26, 1941

"Jews are not permitted to use public libraries."

President of the Reich's Chamber of Writers,
August 2, 1941

"As of September 15, 1941, all Jews over the age of six are forbidden to appear in public without wearing a Jewish Star; without written police permission they are not allowed to leave their residential district and to wear military decorations, honorary badges and the like."

Ministry of the Interior of the Reich,
September 1, 1941

"Jews require the permission of the police to leave their residential district and to travel on designated means of transportation; [upon boarding] they must show the certificate of permission. Jews may not use a sleeping wagon of a Reich train nor dine in a train restaurant; they may not use excursion buses or ships. Jews are entitled to use other means of public transportation only if there is a free place, and at no means during peak travel hours, when non-Jews cannot find a place. Jews may travel only in lower class trains and take a seat only when no other travelers are standing. The use of waiting rooms and other public facilities is strictly limited."

Reich's Ministry of Transport,
September 18, 1941

"Bakeries and cafés must display signs that indicate that Jews and Poles will not be served cake."

Director of the Bureau of the National Socialist Party,
February 14, 1942

"Jews are no longer allowed to have household pets."

Ordinance published in Juedisches Nachrichtenblatt,
Berlin, February 15, 1942

"Jews are not permitted to purchase newspapers, journals, and other documents from newsstands, neither through the post nor directly from the publishers. Permission to do so will be given only in special cases."

Headquarters of the Reich Security Service,
February 17, 1942

"Further restrictions of the Jews' use of public transportation: 1) Jews, who are required to wear the Jewish Star, also need permission from the police to use local transportation in their residential district; 2) Jews may only use public transportation if their place of work is more than 7 kilometers from their residence; Jewish school children may only use public transportation if the school is more than five kilometers from their residence; the same limitation applies to health care workers, nurses, and midwives. Violation of these regulations will be dealt with by the police."

Ministry of the Interior of the Reich, March 24, 1942

"Jews, who are obliged to wear in public the Jewish Star, may not be served by non-Jewish barbers."

Headquarters of the Reich Security Service,
May 12, 1942

"Jews are to receive coupons to purchase tobacco products."

Deutscher Reichs und Preussischer Staatsanzeiger,
June 11, 1942

"Jews are required to surrender immediately electric appliances, optical appliances, bicycles, cameras, binoculars et cetera in their possession....Refusal to do so will meet with the severest measures by the state police."

Headquarters of the Reich Security Service,
June 12, 1942

"Jews are no longer to be given coupons to purchase eggs."

Ordinance published in Deutscher Reichs und
Preussischer Staatsanzeiger, *June 6, 1942*

"Jews are not to receive fresh milk."

Director of the Bureau of the National Socialist Party,
July 10, 1942

"Jews may no longer purchase meat, meat products, eggs, milk and other rationed foods. Food rations for Jewish children will be reduced. Ration coupons for Jews will be specially marked."

Reich Ministry for Food and Agriculture,
September 18, 1942

NOTE

1. With Hitler's ascension to power, the federal government and local authorities issued in the course of the twelve years of the Third Reich more than two thousand separate by-laws, directives, laws, and ordinances intended to exclude Jews, racially defined, from the economic, social, and cultural life of Germany. The above selection of these regulations attests to the intent both to re-ghettoize and demoralize the Jews.

6. PROCLAMATION OF THE (NEW) *REICHSVERTRETUNG* (SEPTEMBER 17, 1933)[1]

REICHSVERTRETUNG DER DEUTSCHEN JUDEN

At a time that is as hard and difficult as any in Jewish history, but also significant as few times have been, we have been entrusted with the leadership and representation of the German Jews by a joint decision of the State Association of the Jewish Communities (*Landesverbande*),[2] the major Jewish organizations and the large Jewish communities of Germany.

There was no thought of party interests, no separate aims in this decision, but solely and wholly the realization that the lives and future of the German Jews today depend on their unity and cooperation. The first task is to make this unity live. There must be recognition of the vitality and aims of every organization and association, but in all major and decisive tasks there must only be one union, only the totality of the German Jews. Anyone who goes his own way today, who excludes himself today, has committed a wrong against the vital need of the German Jews.

In the new State the position of individual groups has changed, even of those which are far more numerous and stronger than we are. Legislation and economic policy have taken their own authorized road, including [some] and excluding [others]. We must understand this and not deceive ourselves. Only then will we be able to discover every honorable opportunity to continue to exist. The German Jews will be able to make their way in the new State as a working community that accepts and gives work.

There is only one area in which we are permitted to carry out our own ideas, our own aims, but it is a decisive area, that of our Jewish life and Jewish future. This is where the most clearly defined tasks exist.

There are new duties in Jewish *education*, new areas of Jewish *schooling* must be created, and existing ones must be nurtured and protected, in order that the rising generation may find spiritual strength, inner resistance and physical competence. There must be thoughtful selection in order to develop and re-direct our youth toward professions which offer them a place in life and prospects of a future.

All there is now, all that has been begun, all that has been attempted must be joined together here to give aid and support. All that is destructive must be opposed, and all our strength devoted to reconstruction on the religious base of Judaism.

Much of our former economic security has been taken from us German Jews, or at least reduced. Within the area that remains to us the individual must be drawn away from his isolation. Occupational connections and associations, where permissible, can increase existing strength and give support to the weak, can make experience and contacts useful for all. There will be not a few who will be refused a place of work or the exercise of their profession on German soil. We are faced by the fact which can no longer be questioned or opposed, of a clear, historic necessity to give our youth new [living] space. It has become a great task to discover places and open roads, as on the sacred soil of *Palestine*, for which Providence has decreed a new era, as everywhere where the character, industry and ability of the German Jews can prove themselves, robbing none of their bread, but creating a livelihood for others.

For this and all else we hope for the understanding assistance of the Authorities, and the respect of

Source: "Kundgebung der neuen Reichsvertretung der deutschen Juden." *Juedische Rundschau* (September 19, 1933); in Y. Arad, Y. Gutman and A. Margaliot, eds., *Documents on the Holocaust*, trans. Lea Ben Dor (Jerusalem: Yad Vashem, 1981), pp. 57–59. Reprinted by permission of Yad Vashem.

our Gentile fellow citizens, whom we join in love and loyalty to Germany.

We place our faith in the active sense of community and responsibility of the German Jews, as also in the willingness to sacrifice of our Brothers everywhere.

We still stand united and, in confidence in our God, labor for the *honor of the Jewish Name.* May the nature of the German Jews arise anew from the tribulations of this time!

Reichsvertretung der deutschen Juden

Leo Baeck[3]
Otto Hirsch[4]—Stuttgart
Siegfried Moses[5]—Berlin
Rudolf Callmann[6]—Cologne
Jacob Hoffman[7]—Frankfurt
Leopold Landenberger[8]—Nuremberg
Franz Meyer[9]—Breslau
Julius L. Seligsohn[10]—Berlin
Heinrich Stahl[11]—Berlin

NOTES

1. *Reichsvertretung der deutschen Juden* (National Representation of German Jews) was German Jewry's central organization during the period of the Nazi rule. It was established on September 17, 1933, through the initiative of several Jewish communities in western Germany, joined by the Berlin Jewish community and the *Landesverbaende* (state unions) of German Jewry; its proclamation, presented here, was endorsed by leading figures of German Jewry representing a wide spectrum of ideological—Zionist and anti-Zionist—and religious factions in German Jewry. The demonstration of unity was an expression of pride and a defiant determination to gather the organizational and moral strength to endure degradation. Practically, its task was to deal with the myriad problems facing Jewry under the ignominious conditions of the Nazi regime.

   Rabbi Leo Baeck (see note 3) was elected president and became the moving spirit of the organization; Otto Hirsch (see note 4) was elected executive chairman. Objecting to the appellation "German Jews," the Nazi authorities in 1935 ordered the organization to change its name to *Reichsvertretung der Juden in Deutschland* (National Representation of Jews in Germany).

   The main achievement of the Reichsvertretung was to mount a "spiritual resistance" to Nazi efforts to humiliate and deprive German Jewry of its dignity. Jewish education was strengthened; a renaissance of Jewish culture was vigorously promoted; general cultural life of the German Jew, increasingly excluded from "Aryan" society, was supported with all the resources of the Jewish community. "In brief, it did everything within its power to encourage the creative faculties, to restore a sense of self-respect and to enhance the stature of the remaining [Jewish] community on the eve of its extinction" (Max Gruenewald, "The Beginning of the Reichsvertretung" *Leo Baeck Institute Year Book* 1 [1956]: 67).

   In July 1939 the government issued an order disbanding the organization and in its stead established the *Reichsvereinigung der Juden in Deutschland* (National Association of the Jews in Germany), which was a compulsory organization of all Jews, as defined by the Nuremberg Laws, in Nazi Germany (except for those in Austria and the Protectorate of Bohemia-Moravia). Supervised by the Ministry of the Interior, i.e., the secret police, the Reichsvereinigung was to help the regime facilitate the ghettoization of the Jews and their eventual emigration. On June 10, 1943, the *Reichsvereinigung* was dissolved and its remaining leadership arrested and deported to Theresienstadt.

2. There existed previously in the Weimar Republic a *Reichsvertretung der juedischen Landesverbaende* (National Representation of Jewish State Unions) which was a loose federation established in January 1932 and which did not lend itself to a unified representation of all German Jews.

3. Leo Baeck (1873–1956) was one of the preeminent rabbis and theologians of German Jewry. From 1912 to his deportation in 1943 to Theresienstadt, he served as a Liberal Rabbi in Berlin. From 1922 he was chairman of the General Rabbinical Council of Germany; he was a leading member of the board of the *Central Verein,* the Central Union of German Citizens of Jewish Faith, the largest association of German Jews, which while seeking to improve the civic and social status of Jews, affirmed their loyalty to Germany and German culture. Upon his election to the presidency of the Reichsvertretung, he devoted himself to defending the dignity of German Jewry. Rejecting repeated opportunities to leave Germany, he elected to stay with the last *minyan* (prayer quorum) of Jews in Germany, thus earning the sobriquet "shepherd of German Jewry." Surviving the war, he settled in 1945 in London, where he became the president of the Council of Jews from Germany and the chairman of the World Union for Progressive Judaism.

4. Otto Hirsch (1885–1941) was from Stuttgart, where he held various positions in the municipal administration and later occupied a senior post in the Ministry of

Interior of the State of Hesse. He was also a member of the executive board of the Central Verein, belonging to its pro-Zionist wing. He was executive chairman of the Reichsvertretung. In 1941 he was deported to Mauthausen death camp, from which he never returned.

5. Siegfried Moses (1887–1974) was a leading German Zionist; from 1931 to 1936 he was a member of the executive board of the Berlin Jewish community; from 1933 to 1937 he was the chairman of the Zionist Federation of Germany and a member of the Executive of the Reichsvertretung. In 1937 he emigrated to Palestine, where he later served as the first State Comptroller of the State of Israel.

6. Rudolf Callmann (1892–1976) was a lawyer in Cologne and at the time a member of the board of the Central Verein. From 1933 to 1936 he was a member of the presidential council of the Reichsvertretung. He emigrated to the United States in 1936.

7. Jacob Hoffmann (1891–1956) was a Hungarian-born Orthodox Rabbi in Frankfurt active in Mizrahi, the movement of religious Zionists. In 1937 he emigrated to the United States, settling in Israel a year before his death.

8. Leopold Landenberger (1888–1967) was a lawyer in Nuremberg. From 1922 to 1938 he was a member and the executive chairman of *Reichsbund juedischer Frontsoldaten*, the association of German Jews who fought in the front during World War I, which defended the rights of Jewish veterans while affirming the patriotism of German Jewry. He was also the president of this organization in Bavaria. He was a member of the presidential council of the Reichsvertretung. In November 1938 he emigrated to England, thence to the United States.

9. Franz Meyer (1897–1972) was a leading Zionist and a member of the executive board of the Jewish community of Breslau; from 1933 to 1939 he was the executive director of the Zionist Federation of Germany. He emigrated to Palestine in 1939.

10. Julius L. Seligsohn (1890–1942) was until 1933 a lawyer in Berlin. A senior officer in the German army in World War I, he was a leading member of *Reichsbund juedischer Frontsoldaten*. At the time he was a representative of Liberal Judaism on the board of the Berlin Jewish community. He was a member of the presidential council of the Reichsvertretung and later the Reichsvereinigung. In 1940 he was deported to Sachsenhausen, from which he did not return.

11. Heinrich Stahl (1868–1942) was the president of the Berlin Jewish community during the Third Reich. He was the vice president of the Reichsvertretung. He later served as the executive chairman of the Reichsvereinigung until his deportation to Theresienstadt, where he died.

7. WHY THE NUREMBERG LAWS (SEPTEMBER 15, 1935)[1]

ADOLF HITLER

[With respect to the recent attempts to sabotage German interests in the international arena,] we must point out that we are speaking, almost without exception, of the action of Jewish elements, who stand revealed as the agents of this incitement and subversion against [our] people [*Traeger dieser Voelkerverhetzung und Voelkerzersetzung*].

Unfortunately it appears that this international ferment in the world has aroused among the Jews of Germany the idea that perhaps the time has come

Source: Adolf Hitler, [Speech before the Reichstag, September 15, 1935], in *Hitler: Reden und Proklamationen, 1932–1945*, ed. Max Domarus (Munich: Sueddeutscher Verlag, 1965), p. 537. Trans. L. Sachs and P. Mendes-Flohr.

to oppose outright the interests of the Jews to the national interests of Germans in the Reich. Bitter complaints have come in from countless places citing the provocative behavior of individual members of this people. On the basis of the striking increase in the number of these occurrences and the similarities among them we may conclude that a certain amount of planning was involved....

Lest these occurrences lead to the outbreak of vigorous defensive actions on the part of the [Aryan] population, we have no choice but to contain the problem through legislative measures. The government of the German Reich is guided in this by the idea that it may nonetheless be possible, through the agency of a definitively secular solution, to create a basis upon which the German people can have a tolerable relation with the Jews. Should this hope not be realized, and Jewish incitement within Germany and outside her borders continue, the situation will be reviewed.

I hereby propose to the Reichstag the adoption of laws which will be read to you by Party Member and President of the Reichstag Goering.[2] ...

This law is an attempt to find a legislative solution to the Jewish problem; in the event that this attempt fails it will be necessary to transfer the problem, by law, to the National Socialist Party for a final solution [*endgueltige Loesung*]. The National Socialist Party supports all three laws and is in turn supported by the entire German people.

I ask you to adopt these laws.

NOTES

1. In this speech before the Reichstag, Hitler outlined the ideological objectives of the so-called Nuremberg Laws. For a comprehensive analysis of this speech, see Otto Dov Kulka, "The 'Jewish Question' in the Third Reich" (Ph.D. diss., Hebrew University, 1975), vol. 1. part 1, pp. 200ff.

2. Hermann W. Goering (1893–1946) was Hitler's designated successor, President of the Reichstag, and commander of the *Luftwaffe* (German Air Force).

8. LAW FOR THE PROTECTION OF GERMAN BLOOD AND HONOR[1]

THE NUREMBERG LAWS (SEPTEMBER 15, 1935)

Imbued with the conviction that the purity of the German blood is the pre-requisite for the future existence of the German People, and animated with the unbending will to ensure the existence of the German nation for all the future, the Reichstag has unanimously adopted the following law, which is hereby proclaimed.

Paragraph 1. (1) Marriages between Jews and state members [*Staatsangehoerige*] of German or cognate blood are forbidden. Marriages concluded despite this law are invalid, even if they are concluded abroad in order to circumvent this law. (2) Only the State Attorney may initiate the annulment suit.

Paragraph 2. Extra-marital relations between Jews and state members of German or cognate blood are prohibited.

Paragraph 3. Jews must not engage female domestic help in their households among state members of

---

Source: Bernard Dov Weinryb, *Jewish Emancipation Under Attack* (New York: American Jewish Committee, 1942), p. 45. Reprinted by permission of the American Jewish Committee.

German or cognate blood, who are under forty-five years [of age].

Paragraph 4. (1) The display of the Reich and national flag and the showing of the national colors by Jews is prohibited. (2) However, the display of the Jewish colors is permitted to them. The exercise of this right is placed under the protection of the state....

Paragraph 7. This law goes into effect on the day following promulgation, except for Paragraph 3, which shall go into force on January 1, 1936.

NOTE

1. Despite the discriminatory legislation, all Jews, with the exception of those who were naturalized after September 1918, remained German citizens. Moreover, many Jews were granted extraordinary status, permitting them to practice their professions. By September 1935, however, the Nazi leadership concluded that Germany had reached the political juncture that would allow the full rescission of emancipation. This policy was implemented by the Nuremberg Laws, so-called because they were promulgated at the Nazi Party Congress that met at Nuremberg in September 1935.

9. THE REICH CITIZENSHIP LAW[1]

THE NUREMBERG LAWS (SEPTEMBER 15, 1935)

Paragraph 2. (1) A Reich citizen [*Reichsbuerger*] is only the state member [*Staatsangehoeriger*] who is of German or cognate blood, and who shows through his conduct that he is both desirous and fit to serve in faith the German people and Reich.... (3) The Reich citizen is the only holder of full political rights in accordance with the provisions of the laws.

NOTE

1. In effect, the Jews were by virtue of this law and its various amendments deprived of citizenship and all civil and political rights.

Source: Bernard Dov Weinryb, *Jewish Emancipation Under Attack* (New York: American Jewish Committee, 1942), p. 46. Reprinted by permission of the American Jewish Committee.

10. FIRST DECREE TO THE REICH CITIZENSHIP LAW (NOVEMBER 14, 1935)

Paragraph 4. (1) A Jew cannot be a citizen of the Reich. He cannot exercise the right to vote on political matters; he cannot hold public office. (2) Jewish officials are to be retired on December 31, 1935. In case these officials served either Germany or her allies at the front in the World War, they shall receive as a pension, until they reach their age limit, the full salary last received; they are not, however, to be promoted according to seniority. After they reach the age limit, their pension is to be calculated anew according to the salary last received, on the basis of which their pension was to be computed. (3) Affairs of religious organizations are not affected therewith. (4) The conditions of service of teachers in public Jewish schools remain unchanged until the forthcoming regulation of the Jewish school system.

Paragraph 5. (1) A Jew is anyone who is descended from at least three full Jewish grandparents. (2) A Jewish state member of mixed descent [*Staatsangehoeriger juedischer Mischlinge*] who is descended from two full Jewish grandparents is also considered a Jew, if (a) He belonged to the Jewish religious community at the time this law was issued or [he] joined the community later; (b) He was married to a Jew at the time when the law was issued, or if he married a Jew subsequently; (c) He is the offspring of a marriage with a Jew within the meaning of clause 1, which was contracted after the Law for the Protection of German Blood and Honor of September 15, 1935 went into effect; (d) He is the offspring of extra-marital intercourse with a Jew, within the meaning of clause 1, and will be born out of wedlock after July 31, 1936.

Source: Bernard Dov Weinryb, *Jewish Emancipation Under Attack* (New York: American Jewish Committee, 1942), p. 46. Reprinted by permission of the American Jewish Committee.

11. THE RESPONSE OF THE CHRISTIAN POPULATION IN GERMANY TO THE NUREMBERG LAWS (SEPTEMBER 1935)[1]

A PUBLIC OPINION SURVEY

KOENIGSBERG: In Allenstein, a town with a predominantly Catholic population, it must be stated that many purchases are still made in Jewish shops. It should also be mentioned that a certain part of the Catholic population displays a friendly attitude toward the Jews and shows little consideration for the race laws.... Therefore, no actual success of the antisemitic endeavors and no real reduction of the numbers of Jews can be sensed in Allenstein itself. On the other hand, the picture is entirely different in the [predominantly Protestant] cities of the district.

AACHEN: The new laws promulgated in Nuremberg did not meet with unanimous public approval.... The church circles do not quite approve of the Jew-legislation, as might have been expected considering the well-known mentality of the local Catholic population.... Only the fact that the Jew-legislation would prevent extreme manifestations of antisemitic propaganda and riots is received with satisfaction. It would indeed be desirable to stop such antisemitic excesses, which are condemned by the greater part of the population.

NOTE

1. Upon their rise to power, the Nazis developed an elaborate system to monitor the public's response to their various deeds and programs. Secret periodical reports—so-called *Lageberichte* or *Stimmungsberichte*—on the mood and attitude of the public were prepared by the security services and various government and party authorities. The picture that these reports reveal, as Otto Dov Kulka observes, "differs from that projected in the daily press and in the official organs and contradicts the image of nation-wide monolithic identification with the regime and its doctrines...." (Kulka, "Popular Christian Attitudes," p. 252). We herein present two *Lageberichte* from September 1935, which survey the response of Christian laity to the Nuremberg Laws. The first is from the East Prussian district of Koenigsberg, the second from the district of Aachen in the western part of the country. These similar reports indicate that the response varied, although it had a discernible pattern. "In some areas, we can see that responses denouncing the anti-Jewish policy of the regime came forth from a Catholic minority in a Protestant area or vice versa; in certain sectors, especially in the western part of the Reich, reactions in this spirit were characteristic of the mood of the predominantly Catholic population of these areas" (Kulka, "Popular Christian Attitudes.") For an abridged English version of this article under the same title, see *The Jerusalem Quarterly* 25 [Fall 1982]: 121–44; 26 [Winter 1982]: 35–45.) For an extensive study of German public opinion as revealed by the secret *Lageberichte*, see Otto Dov Kulka, and Eberhard Jaeckel, eds., *The Jews in Secret Nazi Reports on Popular Opinion in Germany, 1933–1945* (New Haven/London: Yale University Press, 2010).

Source: Report prepared by the Gestapo, September 1935, in Otto Dov Kulka, "Popular Christian Attitudes in the Third Reich to National Socialist Policies Towards the Jews," *Judaism and Christianity Under the Impact of National Socialism, 1919–1945,* Otto Dov Kulka and Paul Mendes-Flohr, eds. (Jerusalem: Historical Society of Israel, 1987), p. 256.

12. GERMAN ECONOMIC GOALS AND THE JEWISH QUESTION (AUGUST 1936)[1]

ADOLF HITLER

The Political Situation. Politics are the conduct and the course of the historical struggle for life of the peoples. The aim of these struggles is the assertion of existence. Even the idealistic ideological struggles [*Weltanschauungskaempfe*] have their ultimate cause and are most deeply motivated by nationally [*volklich*] determined purposes and aims of life. Religions and ideologies are, however, always able to impart particular harshness to struggles of this kind, and therefore are also able to give them great historical impressiveness. They leave their imprint on the content of centuries. In such cases it is not possible for people and States living within the sphere of such ideological or religious conflicts to dissociate or exclude themselves from these events. . . .

Since the outbreak of the French Revolution, the world has been moving with ever increasing speed towards a new conflict, the most extreme solution of which is called Bolshevism, whose essence and aim, however, is solely the elimination of those strata of mankind which have hitherto provided the leadership and their replacement by worldwide Jewry.

No State will be able to withdraw or even remain at a distance from this historical conflict. *Since Marxism, through its victory in Russia, has established one of the greatest empires in the world as a forward base for its future operations, this question has become a menacing one.* . . .

Germany. Germany will, as always, have to be regarded as the focal point of the Western world in face of the Bolshevist attacks. I do not regard this as an agreeable mission but rather as a handicap and encumbrance upon our national life regrettably resulting from our position in Europe.

We cannot, however, escape this destiny. . . .

It is not the aim of this memorandum to prophesy the time when the untenable situation in Europe will become an open crisis. I only want in these lines, to set down my conviction that this crisis cannot and will not fail to arrive and that it is Germany's duty to secure her own existence by every means in the face of this catastrophe, and to protect herself against it, and that from this compulsion there arises a series of conclusions relating to the most important tasks to which our people have ever been set. *For a victory of Bolshevism over Germany would not lead to a Versailles Treaty but the final destruction, indeed to the annihilation of the German people.*

The extent of such a catastrophe cannot be foreseen. How, indeed, would the whole of densely populated Western Europe (including Germany) after a collapse into Bolshevism [*nach einem bolschewistischen Zusammenbruch*] live through probably the most gruesome catastrophe for the people which has been visited upon mankind since the downfall of the States of antiquity? *In face of the necessity of defense against this danger, all other considerations must recede into the background as being completely irrelevant.* . . .

I consider it necessary for the Reichstag to pass the following two laws: (1) A law providing the death penalty for economic sabotage, and (2) A law making the whole of Jewry liable for all damage inflicted by individual specimens of this community of criminals upon the German economy, and thus upon the German people. . . .

Source: Unsigned Memorandum on the Four Year Plan, August 1936, *Documents on German Foreign Policy, 1918–1945*, Series C (1933–37) (Washington, D.C., n.d.), vol. 5, pp. 853–62.

NOTE

1. Antisemitism was central to Hitler's political vision and strategy. In this document, an unsigned memorandum on the Four Year Plan of 1936—a plan that was to strengthen the German economy and military preparedness—Hitler presented the ideological rationale of this plan as the "apocalyptic" struggle against Bolshevism and world Jewry. On Hitler's authorship of the memorandum, see *Documents on German Foreign Policy, 1918–1945*, Series C (1933–37) (Washington, DC, n.d.), vol. 5, pp. 853ff., n. 1.

13. *KRISTALLNACHT*—A PRELIMINARY SECRET REPORT TO H. W. GOERING (NOVEMBER 1938)

R. T. HEYDRICH[1]

Re: Action Against the Jews. The reports so far received from the stations of the State Police give the following picture until November 11, 1938:

In numerous cities the plundering of Jewish shops and firms has taken place. In order to prevent further plundering, severe measures were taken everywhere. One hundred seventy-four plunderers were arrested.[2]

The number of pillaged Jewish shops and apartment houses cannot yet be confirmed. The following numbers appearing in the reports—815 destroyed shops, 29 warehouses set on fire or otherwise destroyed, 171 apartment houses set on fire or otherwise destroyed—reflect only part of the actual damage. The urgency with which the reports had to be prepared made it necessary to restrict them to general statements, such as "numerous" or "most shops destroyed." The reported numbers, therefore, will greatly increase.

One hundred ninety-one synagogues were set on fire, another 76 completely demolished. Also, 11 community houses, cemetery chapels and the like were set on fire and another 3 completely destroyed.

About 20,000 Jews were arrested,[3] also 7 Aryans and 3 foreigners. The latter were taken into protective custody.

Thirty-six fatalities were reported, as well as 36 seriously wounded. All fatalities and the seriously wounded are Jews. One Jew is still missing. Among the Jewish fatalities there was one Polish citizen; among the wounded there were 2 Polish citizens.[4]

NOTES

1. Reinhard Tristan Heydrich (1904–1942). In 1931 Heydrich joined the SS (Schutzstaffeln), the private army of the Nazis, as chief of its Intelligence Service. He later became chief of the Gestapo—the German State Secret Police. He was also to play prominent roles in the design and execution of the Final Solution (see document 24 in this chapter).

  After the Nuremberg Laws and certain amendments that followed, there was a lull in anti-Jewish legislation. After the *Anschluss*, or the occupation of Austria on March 13, 1938, the pace of legal measures against the Jews suddenly gained momentum. In that year, as a prelude to confiscation, registration of Jewish

---

Source: Leon Poliakov and Josef Wulf, eds., *Das Dritte Reich und die Juden: Dokumente und Aufsaetze* (Berlin: Arani-Verlag, GmbH, 1955), pp. 41–42. Copyright 1955 by Arani-Verlag, GmbH. Cited by permission. Trans. by J. Hessing.

properties was ordered; the exclusion of Jews from the professions was completed; Jews were issued new passports and identity papers stamped with a red *J* for *Jude*; they were compelled to adopt Jewish names; special taxes were imposed on the Jews; they were required to obtain special permission to open up a new industry or commercial enterprise. Also in that year the Jews of Polish origin who lived in Germany were expelled en masse. The Polish governmment refused to accept the refugees, and they were obliged to live in congested transit camps on the Polish frontier. On November 7, 1938, Herschel Grynszpan (1921–c. 1943/1945), whose family was among the unwanted refugees, assassinated Ernst vom Rath, the third secretary of the German Embassy in Paris. This act provided the Nazis with the pretext to launch the next stage of their Jewish policy: liquidation. Two days later, on the night of November 9, a wave of anti-Jewish pogroms swept through Germany and Austria. Although the German government sought to present the *Aktion* against the Jews as a spontaneous protest on the part of the Aryan population, it was clearly orchestrated by the Nazi leadership. Because of the many shop windows broken, the pogroms became known as the *Kristallnacht* or "Night of the Broken Glass." The extent of the pogroms is indicated in this matter-of-fact "provisional" report made by the head of the Gestapo, Heydrich, to Goering.

Hermann Wilhelm Goering (1893–1946), was an intimate friend of Hitler from the days of the founding of the Nazi party. With the accession of Hitler to power, he was appointed prime minister of Prussia and President of the Reichstag. In 1936 he was appointed plenipotentiary for the Four Year Plan to prepare the German economy for war. For this purpose he devised a scheme to expropriate Jewish property and wealth.

2. It is hardly to be expected that police intervened in order to protect Jewish property. Goering himself, at a meeting on November 11, 1938, put it very bluntly and cynically: "...Look, gentlemen, I'm quite fed up with the demonstrations. In the end they will not harm the Jews but myself who, in the last resort, is responsible for the economy...." (cited in Leon Poliakov and Josef Wulf, eds., *Das Dritte Reich und die Juden* [Berlin: Arani-Verlag, GmbH, 1955], p. 41).

3. These Jews were sent to concentration camps at Sachsenhausen, Buchenwald, and Dachau. Early in 1939 many were released.

4. In Austria major pogroms broke out on November 10, during which 42 synagogues were destroyed in Vienna alone. A total of 7,800 Jews were arrested in Vienna; 4,600 Jews from all of Austria were sent to Dachau, of whom 4,000 were later permitted to emigrate. According to the Security Service of the SS, 680 Jews committed suicide; 27 Jews were reported killed.

14. THE OPERATION AGAINST THE JEWS (NOVEMBER 9–10, 1938)[1]

SECURITY SERVICE REPORT ON THE *KRISTALLNACHT*

The foundations of Jewish life and their internal organization were completely altered as a result of the operation mounted against Jewry in all parts of the Reich in the wake of the murder of the Counsel [of the German Embassy in Paris] Ernst vom Rath by Herschel Grynszpan, a Jew of Polish nationality.

In general the operation took the form of destruction or burning of synagogues, and the destruction of almost all Jewish shops, which were thereby forced to discontinue business. Some Jewish apartments were damaged. Due to lack of attention or ignorance on the part of those involved in the incidents archival materials and valuable art treasures were destroyed.[2] Several Jews were killed or wounded attempting to resist. At the same time, in order to intensify the pressure on emigration, 25,000 Jewish men were brought to concentration camps, in some cases temporarily.

After the conclusion of the operation further steps were taken against the Jews in the form of laws and administrative orders....

Thus the order concerning the arrangement about Jewish property of December 3, 1938, prescribes that the owner of a Jewish business—industrial, agricultural or forestry—can be forced to transfer the business or to close it within a specified period of time....Further decrees were issued forbidding Jews from possessing weapons, and they were decisively excluded from participating in German culture and education.

In addition, a collective fine of one billion marks was imposed upon the Jewish population to compensate for the damages caused by the operation.

Hence, in conclusion it can be stated that Jewry—in so far as German citizens and stateless persons are concerned—has finally been removed from all areas of life of the German people, and Jews, therefore, have only one way to insure their continued existence and that is emigration.

NOTES

1. In its annual report for 1938, the SD (the Security Service of the SS) provided a lengthy discussion of the *Kristallnacht* and the ensuing legislation against the Jews. In this report the SD not only clearly stated the motivations behind the anti-Jewish riots (and later legislation) but also that the SD and the SS had orchestrated the "popular demonstrations against the Jews." This thesis, based on an analysis of previously unpublished materials, is advanced by Otto Dov Kulka ("'Public Opinion' in National Socialist Germany and the 'Jewish Question'" [Hebrew with documents in German], *Zion: Quarterly for Research in Jewish History* 40, nos. 3–4 [Jerusalem, 1975], pp. 46–47. See also *The Jerusalem Quarterly* 25 (Fall 1982), pp. 135ff.

2. The report ascribes this "excess" to the unsupervised actions of forces "who lacked the professional training in dealing with the Jewish Problem." On the night of the riots, Reinhard Heydrich (1904–1942), chief of the SD and the Gestapo, issued specific orders instructing the SD and the Gestapo to protect Jewish archives and art treasures, and generally to observe the "proper" limits of the demonstrations. See Kulka, "Public Opinion," p. 231, n. 114.

Source: "Die Aktion gegen die Juden am November 9–10, 1938," *Jahreslagebericht des Sicherheitshauptamtes,* vol. 1, pp. 33ff., in Otto Dov Kulka, "'Public Opinion' in National Socialist Germany and the 'Jewish Question'" (Hebrew with documents in German), *Zion: Quarterly for Research in Jewish History* 40, nos. 3–4 (Jerusalem, 1975), pp. 283–86. Trans. by P. Mendes-Flohr. Cited with permission of Otto Dov Kulka.

15. DECREE REGARDING ATONEMENT FINE OF JEWISH STATE SUBJECTS (NOVEMBER 12, 1938)[1]

H. W. GOERING

The hostile attitude of Jewry toward the German nation and Reich, an attitude which does not even shrink from cowardly murder, demands determined resistance and severe punishment.

On the basis of the Decree of October 18, 1936 for the Execution of the Four Year Plan, I therefore order the following:

Paragraph 1. The payment of an atonement of one billion Reichsmarks to the German Reich is imposed on all Jewish subjects of the State.

Paragraph 2. The Reich Minister of Finance in cooperation with the competent Reich ministers shall issue the regulations for the execution of this decree.

NOTE

1. Following the *Kristallnacht*, Goering (see this chapter, document 7, note 2) convened a conference on November 12 of Nazi officials to deliberate what punitive action to take against the Jews for the assassination of vom Rath and for thus provoking the "just wrath" of the Aryan masses. The conference decided upon the decree presented here. The same conference also issued a decree compelling Jewish store owners to repair at their own cost the damage incurred to their properties; insurance claims were also nullified. On November 28, 1938, a police order empowered the local authorities to "prevent Jews from entering certain districts or from appearing in public at certain times."

Source: Bernard Dov Weinryb, *Jewish Emancipation Under Attack* (New York: American Jewish Committee, 1942), p. 53. Reprinted by permission of the American Jewish Committee.

16. PUBLIC RESPONSE TO THE *KRISTALLNACHT* (DECEMBER 1938)

[A] The actions against Jewry in November have been received very badly....The destruction of the synagogues was declared an irresponsible act. ... It could be observed that the opposition to the anti-Jewish actions was much stronger in the south (with the exception of Ostmark) and in the west of the Reich (with a dense Catholic and mostly urban population) than in the north (with a Protestant, less dense, and rural population).

[B] Dear Sirs:

The events that occurred amongst our people on and after November ninth of this year [1938] force me to take a clear stand. Far be it from me to disregard the sins that many members of the Jewish people have committed against our Fatherland, especially during the last decades; also, far be it from me to deny the right of orderly and moderate proceedings against the Jewish race. However, not only will I by no means justify the numerous excesses against Jewry that took place on and after November ninth of this year (it is unnecessary to go into details), but I reject them, deeply ashamed, as they are a blot on the good name of the Germans.

First of all, I, as a Protestant Christian, have no doubt that the commitment and toleration of such reprisals will evoke the wrath of God against our people and Fatherland, if there is a God in heaven. Just as Israel is cursed and on trial because they were the first who rejected Christ, so surely the same curse will fall upon each and every nation that, by similar deeds, denies Christ in the same way.

I have spoken out of the ardent concern of a Christian who prays to his God everyday for his people and their rulers [*Obrigkeit*]. May God harken to my voice, [I hope] not the only one of this kind. With due respect to the authorities [*Obrigkeit*]....

Source: [A.] Summary statement of a nation-wide *Lagebericht* on the *Kristallnacht* prepared by the S.D., [B.] A Protestant clergyman from Berlin to Hitler, Goering, Goebbels, et al., December 1938. The sender's full name and address were given in the letter. Section A is in Otto Dov Kulka, "'Public Opinion' in National Socialist Germany and the 'Jewish Question,'" *The Jerusalem Quarterly* 25 (Fall 1982), p. 141. Section B, German facsimile included in Otto Dov Kulka, "Popular Christian Attitudes in the Third Reich to National Socialist Policies Towards the Jews," Papers Presented at the International Symposium on Judaism and Christianity Under the Impact of National Socialism, 1919–1945, June 1982 (Jerusalem: Historical Society of Israel, 1982), p. 252. Trans. P. Mendes-Flohr.

17. DECREE FOR THE ELIMINATION OF THE JEWS FROM GERMAN ECONOMIC LIFE (NOVEMBER 12, 1938)

On the basis of the Decree of October 18, 1936 for the Execution of the Four Year Plan, the following is decreed:

Paragraph 1. (1) From January 1, 1939, Jews are forbidden to own retail stores, mail order houses, or commission houses [*Bestellkonttore*] and to engage independently in a trade. (2) They are further forbidden, from that day on, to offer for sale, goods or trade services, to advertise them or to accept orders at markets of all sorts, fairs or exhibitions. (3) Jewish enterprises which violate this decree are to be closed by the police.

Paragraph 2. (1) From January 1, 1939, a Jew can no longer be head of an enterprise within the meaning of the Law of January 20, 1934 for the Regulation of National Work. (2) If a Jew is employed in an enterprise in an executive position, he may be given notice to leave within six weeks. At the expiration of the term of the notice, all claims of the employee, based on the contract, especially such pertaining to maintenance and compensation, expire.

Paragraph 3. (1) A Jew cannot be a member of a cooperative. (2) Jewish membership in cooperatives expires on December 31, 1938. No special notice is necessary.

Source: Bernard Dov Weinryb, *Jewish Emancipation Under Attack* (New York: American Jewish Committee, 1942). p. 53–54. Reprinted by permission of the American Jewish Committee.

18. *NUMERUS NULLUS* IN SCHOOLS (NOVEMBER 16, 1938)

After the ruthless murder of Paris,[1] German teachers no longer can be expected to give instruction to Jewish pupils. It is also self-evident that German students find it unbearable to share classrooms with Jews.

Racial segregation in schools has been carried out in general during the past years, but a small number of Jewish pupils have remained, who can no longer be permitted to attend schools together with German boys and girls. Reserving additional regulations by law, Reich Minister of Education [Bernard] Rust has decreed the following which goes into effect immediately.

1. Jews are forbidden to attend German schools. They are permitted to attend Jewish schools only. Insofar as it has not yet happened all Jewish school boys and girls still attending German schools are to be dismissed immediately.

Source: Bernard Dov Weinryb, *Jewish Emancipation Under Attack* (New York: American Jewish Committee, 1942). p. 53–54. Reprinted by permission of the American Jewish Committee.

2. Paragraph 5 of the First Decree to the Reich Citizenship Law of November 14, 1935, specifies who is Jewish.[2]

3. This regulation extends to all schools under the supervision of the Reich Minister of Education, including continuation schools.

NOTES

1. The "murder of Paris" refers to the shooting of Ernst vom Rath, the third secretary of the German Embassy in Paris, by Herschel Grynszpan, a Jewish Polish refugee, on November 7, 1938.
2. See this chapter, document 10.

19. GHETTO DECREED FOR BERLIN (DECEMBER 5, 1938)

On the basis of the Police Decree Regarding the Appearance of the Jews in Public of November 28, 1938, the following is decreed for the police district of Berlin.

Paragraph 1. Streets, squares, parks and buildings, from which the Jews are to be banned, are to be closed to Jewish subjects of the State and stateless Jews, both pedestrians and drivers.

Paragraph 2. Jewish subjects of the State and stateless Jews who at the time when this decree goes into effect still live within a district banned to the Jews, must have a local police permit for crossing the banned area.

By July 1, 1939, permits for Jews living within the banned area will no longer be issued.

Paragraph 3. Jewish subjects of the State and stateless Jews who are summoned by an office within the banned area, must obtain a local police permit for twelve hours.

Paragraph 4. The ban on Jews in Berlin comprises the following districts: (1) All theatres, cinemas, cabarets, public concert and lecture halls, museums, amusement places, the halls of the Fair, including the Fair grounds and broadcasting station on the Messedamm, the Deutschlandhalle and the Sport Palace, the Reich Sport Field, all athletic fields including ice skating rinks; (2) All public and private bathing places....

Source: Bernard Dov Weinryb, *Jewish Emancipation Under Attack* (New York: American Jewish Committee, 1942), p. 56. Reprinted by permission of the American Jewish Committee.

20. A PROPHECY OF JEWRY'S ANNIHILATION (JANUARY 30, 1939)[1]

ADOLF HITLER

In connection with the Jewish question I have this to say: It is a shameful spectacle to see how the whole democratic world is oozing with sympathy for the poor tormented Jewish people, but remains hard-hearted and obdurate when it comes to helping them—which is surely, in view of its attitude, an obvious duty.[2] The arguments that are brought up as an excuse for not helping them actually speak for us Germans and Italians.

For this is what they say:

1. "We," that is the democracies, "are not in a position to take in the Jews." Yet in these empires there are not even 10 people to the square kilometre. While Germany, with her 135 inhabitants to the square kilometre, is supposed to have room for them![3]

2. They assure us: We cannot take them unless Germany is prepared to allow them a certain amount of capital to bring with them as immigrants.

For hundreds of years Germany was good enough to receive these elements, although they possessed nothing except infectious political and physical diseases. What they possess today, they have by a very large extent gained at the cost of the less astute German nation by the most reprehensible manipulations.

Today we are merely paying this people what it deserves. When the German nation was, thanks to the inflation instigated and carried through by the Jews, deprived of the entire savings which it had accumulated in years of honest work, when the rest of the world took away the German nation's foreign investments, when we were divested of the whole of our colonial possessions, these philanthropic considerations evidently carried little noticeable weight with democratic statesmen.

Today I can only assure these gentlemen that, thanks to the brutal education with which the democracies favoured us for fifteen years, we are completely hardened to all attacks of sentiment. After more than eight hundred thousand children of the nation had died of hunger and undernourishment at the close of the War, we witnessed almost one million head of milking cows being driven away from us in accordance with the cruel paragraphs of a dictate which the humane democratic apostles of the world forced upon us as a peace treaty.[4] We witnessed over one million German prisoners of war being retained in confinement for no reason at all for a whole year after the War was ended. We witnessed over one and a half million Germans being torn away from all that they possessed in the territories lying on our frontiers, and being whipped out with practically only what they wore on their backs. We had to endure having millions of our fellow countrymen torn away from us without their consent, and without their being afforded the slightest possibility of existence. I could supplement these examples with dozens of the most cruel kind. For this reason we ask to be spared all sentimental talk. The German nation does not wish its interests to be determined and controlled by any foreign nation. France to the French, England to the English, America to the Americans, and Germany to the Germans. We are resolved to prevent the settlement in our country of a strange people which was capable of snatching for itself all the leading positions in the land, and to oust it. For it is our will to educate our own nation for these leading positions. We have hundreds of thousands of very intelligent children of peasants and of the working class. We

Source: Adolf Hitler, "Speech before *Reichstag,* January 30, 1939," in Norman H. Barnes, ed., *"The Speeches of Adolf Hitler, April 1922–August 1942* (London: Oxford University Press for the Royal Institute of International Affairs, 1942), I, pp 737–41.

shall have them educated—in fact we have already begun—and we wish that one day they, and not the representatives of an alien race, may hold the leading positions in the State together with our educated classes. Above all, German culture, as its name alone shows, is German, not Jewish, and therefore its management and care will be trusted to members of our own nation. If the rest of the world cries out with a hypocritical mien against this barbaric expulsion from Germany of such an irreplaceable and culturally eminently valuable element, we can only be astonished at the conclusions they draw from this situation. For how thankful they must be that we are releasing these precious apostles of culture, and placing them at the disposal of the rest of the world. In accordance with their own declarations they cannot find a single reason to excuse themselves for refusing to receive this most valuable race in their own countries. Nor can I see a reason why the members of this race should be imposed upon the German nation, while in the States, which are so enthusiastic about these "splendid people," their settlement should suddenly be refused with every imaginable excuse. I think that the sooner this problem is solved the better; for Europe cannot settle down until the Jewish question is cleared up. It may very well be possible that sooner or later an agreement on this problem may be reached in Europe, even between those nations which otherwise do not so easily come together.

The world had sufficient space for settlements, but we must once and for all get rid of the opinion that the Jewish race was only created by God for the purpose of being in a certain percentage a parasite living on the body and the productive work of other nations. The Jewish race will have to adapt itself to sound constructive activity as other nations do, or sooner or later it will succumb to a crisis of an inconceivable magnitude.

One thing I should like to say on this day which may be memorable for others as well as for us Germans: In the course of my life I have very often been a prophet, and have usually been ridiculed for it. During the time of my struggle for power it was in the first instance the Jewish race which only received my prophecies with laughter when I said that I would one day take over the leadership of the State, and with it that of the whole nation, and that I would then among many other things settle the Jewish problem. Their laughter was uproarious, but I think that for some time now they have been laughing on the other side of their face. Today I will once more be a prophet: If the international Jewish financiers in and outside Europe should succeed in plunging the nations once more into a world war, then the result will not be the bolshevization of the earth, and thus the victory of Jewry, but the annihilation of the Jewish race in Europe!

…The nations are no longer willing to die on the battlefield so that this unstable international race may profiteer from war or satisfy its Old Testament vengeance. The Jewish watchword "Workers of the world unite" will be conquered by a higher realization, namely, "Workers of all classes and of all nations recognize your common enemy!"

NOTES

1. In this speech, delivered to the Reichstag in Berlin on the occasion of the sixth anniversary of the Nazi rise to power, Hitler in effect declared war on Jewry, lifting for the first time in public the veil on his ultimate plan for the Jews: "Annihilation of the Jewish race in Europe." To be sure, the speech did not reflect the policies followed at the time, but it was a clear declaration of what he intended if war were to break out in Europe. As Hitler put it, it was a "prophecy," an apocalyptic vision of the horror that was to come. When the Final Solution was officially formulated and set into motion, Hitler would return to the speech, repeating almost verbatim on at least three separate occasions the same three prophetic sentences, indicating that once again he had indeed been a prophet whom only myopic fools would ridicule. See Saul Friedlaender, Introduction to Gerald Fleming, *Hitler and the Final Solution* (Berkeley: University of California Press, 1982), p. xxxiv.

2. Hitler is referring to the worldwide outrage at the *Kristallnacht* pogroms against German Jewry. He found the protests hypocritical, since the relatively modest influx of German Jews—since the ascension of the National Socialists to power only slightly more than 100,000 had until that date emigrated—into those countries protesting so vociferously had clearly met with resistance; the United States, France, Holland, and Norway each persisted in severely restricting the number of emigrants they would allow into their respective countries (cf. documents 21 and 33 in this chapter). Hitler was well aware of the comment made by the Australian delegate at the opening session of

the international Evian Conference, held in July 1938, to consider the problem of German Jewish refugees: "Since we have no racial problem, we are not desirous of importing one."

3. Together with the struggle against "international Jewry," the effort to find *Lebensraum* for the German people was the focal point of Hitler's ideological world-view.

4. The reference is to the terms of the Treaty of Versailles of 1919, which concluded World War I and in which the victorious allies exacted humiliating punishment on Germany.

21. THE PLIGHT OF THE REFUGEES (JUNE 1939)[1]

NEW YORK TIMES

[A] "German Jews Attempt Suicide After Being Barred in Three Lands" (Cairo, Egypt). After wandering six weeks from port to port in the Mediterranean, eight German Jews attempted suicide by taking poison while their steamer was anchored in Alexandria harbor today. They are six men and two women who left Hamburg by steamer April 22 en route to Alexandria.

They were not allowed to enter Egypt and proceeded with the steamer to Palestine, where their efforts were again unsuccessful. Continuing to Turkey, they were again barred and returned to Alexandria, where their second plea was refused, so no alternative was left but to return to Germany.

When a steward went to their cabins to call them for breakfast he found them writhing in pain, apparently having taken poison. The Alexandria Governor's office was notified, which in turn asked the Ministry of the Interior to be allowed to take them to shore for treatment.

The Ministry ordered a government doctor to examine the victims to determine whether they could be treated aboard ship. The doctor replied that he could not treat them without proper diagnosis, so the refugees were taken to the Jewish Hospital in Alexandria, where they are being cared for.

It is understood the Ministry of Interior has ordered that if they recover they shall again be placed aboard the steamer and deported. How serious their condition is, is still undisclosed.

[B] "The Refugee Ship *St. Louis*." The saddest ship afloat today, the Hamburg-American liner *St. Louis*, with 900 Jewish refugees aboard, is steaming back towards Germany after a tragic week of frustration at Havana and off the coast of Florida. She is steaming back despite an offer made to Havana yesterday to give a guarantee through the Chase National Bank of $500 a piece for every one of her passengers, men, women and children, who might land there. President Laredo Bru [of Cuba] still has an opportunity to practice those humanitarian sentiments so eloquently expressed in his belated offer of asylum after the refugee ship had been driven from Havana harbor. His cash terms have been met. But the *St. Louis* still keeps her course for Hamburg.

No plague ship ever received a sorrier welcome. Yet those aboard her had sailed with high hopes. About fifty of them, according to our Berlin dispatch, had consular visas. The others all had landing permits for which they had paid; they were unaware that these

---

Source: [A] *New York Times*, June 7, 1939, p. 11. [B] "Editorial," *New York Times*, June 8, 1939, p. 24. Copyright 1939 by the New York Times Company. Reprinted by permission.

permits had been declared void in a decree dated May 5. Only a score of the hundreds were admitted. At Havana the *St. Louis's* decks became a stage for human misery. Relatives and friends clamored to get aboard but were held back. Weeping refugees clamoring to get ashore were halted at guarded gangways. For days the *St. Louis* lingered within the shadow of Morro Castle, but there was no relaxation of the new regulations. Every appeal was rejected. One man reached land. He was pulled from the water with slashed wrists and rushed to a hospital. A second suicide attempt led the captain to warn the authorities that a wave of self-destruction might follow. The forlorn refugees themselves organized a patrol committee. Yet out of Havana the *St. Louis* had to go, trailing pitiful cries of "Auf Wiedersehen." Off our shores she was attended by a helpful Coast Guard vessel alert to pick up any passengers who plunged overboard and thrust them back on the *St. Louis* again. The refugees could even see the shimmering towers of Miami rising from the sea, but for them they were only the battlements of another forbidden city.

It is useless now to discuss what might have been done. The case is disposed of. Germany, with all the hospitality of its concentration camps, will welcome these unfortunates home. Perhaps Cuba, as her spokesmen say, has already taken too many German refugees. Yet all these 900 asked was a temporary haven. Before they sailed virtually all of them had registered under the quota provisions of various nations, including our own. Time would have made them eligible to enter. But there seems to be no help for them now. The *St. Louis* will soon be home with her cargo of despair.[2]

Her next trip is already scheduled. It will be a gay cruise for carefree tourists.

NOTES

1. After the *Kristallnacht* there was absolutely no place for the Jews in the German economic and cultural life; with the banning of the Jewish press and the dissolution of most Jewish cultural and communal bodies, the possibilities of an independent Jewish life also vanished. The pressure on the Jews to emigrate was thus greatly increased. This, of course, was in accordance with Nazi policy. When the Jews still bore German passports emigration was relatively easy. Later, when the deprivation of German citizenship rendered the Jewish emigrants refugees, they increasingly encountered obstacles. For the most part, the existing immigration regulations of such countries as the United States, Britain, Canada, and Australia were not eased to accommodate the refugees. Except for Britain in 1938–1939 no entry visas were issued by these countries beyond the scope of the existing emigration quotas. According to estimates of the League of Nations' high commissioner for refugees, 329,000 Jews fled Nazi persecution in the years 1933–1939, of whom 315,000 left Germany proper. In June 1933 there were 503,000 Jews by religion in Germany; six years later there were 214,000. The desperate situation of many of these refugees is reflected in these two items from the *New York Times*.
2. Denied entrance to Cuba and the United States, the *St. Louis* returned to Europe, docking at Antwerp, Belgium on June 12, 1939. The United Kingdom agreed to take 288 of the German-Jewish refugees. The remaining passengers found refuge in Belgium, France, and the Netherlands.

22. THE JEWISH REFUGEE COMMUNITY OF SHANGHAI (1941)

YEHOSHUA RAPOPORT

INTRODUCTION BY IRENE EBER

In the fall of 1939, after Germany invaded Poland, a group of Jewish intellectuals, writers, journalists, actors, and students of yeshivot, including nearly the entire Mir Yeshiva, fled to Lithuania. The country was neutral at the time, conquered neither by the Germans nor the Soviets, and the Jews believed they had found a safe haven. Indeed, the Jewish community in Vilna and Kovno had received the refugees hospitably and many were able to support themselves with jobs. Little did they expect that less than a year later, in June 1940, the Red Army would march into Lithuania.

Faced with having to accept Soviet citizenship, some three to four thousand Jews desperately searched for other countries of escape. A solution presented itself when the businessman, now acting Dutch consul in Lithuania, Jan Zwartendijk (1896–1976), began to issue visas for the Dutch Caribbean colony of Curacao, even though no visas were required for the colony. Between July 24 and August 3, 1940, Zwartendijk issued 2,345 visas.[1] With the all important "Curacao" visas in hand and hoping somehow to make their way to North America via Japan, they next approached the Japanese consul in Kovno, Chiune Sugihara (1900–1986) for Japanese transit visas. This they needed in order to obtain a Soviet exit and transit visa for travel to Moscow and the Trans-Siberian Railway to Vladivostok. Once in Vladivostok, they boarded a ship for Tsuruga on the Japan coast and then a train to Kobe where there was a Jewish community.

Similar to Lithuania, they were received hospitably in Kobe and the refugees, secular and religious, liked the city very much. Money for their support was sent by the American Joint Distribution Committee, and those who were unable to obtain visas for other countries hoped once more to weather the war in friendly surroundings. But it was not to be. When, due to the gathering war clouds, American money ceased to be forthcoming, the Japanese authorities decided that they had overstayed their welcome and shipped them off to Shanghai.

Their arrival by stages throughout the summer and early fall of 1941 was not greeted enthusiastically. Nor were the newcomers happy with the Shanghai scene. According to the few accounts left by the Polish contingent, whereas the religious members among them were immediately attended to, the secular refugees barely found accommodations. A number of reasons accounted for this, among which the most important was that Shanghai was, for all practical purposes, inundated by destitute refugees. Aside from the Chinese refugees, resulting from the outbreak of the Sino-Japanese War in mid-1937, the vast majority of Central Europeans had arrived in 1939 and 1940. Businessmen of the established Baghdadi Jewish and Russian Jewish communities were responsible for their upkeep, and they could barely cope. Nearly 20,000 refugees had found a haven from Nazi persecution and the majority of these required shelter and sustenance. The more than 1,000 Polish Jews who came in 1941 were in many ways the last straw for the harassed Jewish businessmen whose responsibility they had become.

Yehoshua Rapoport (1895–1971), whose essay is translated here,[2] was one of the Polish group. He

Source: Y. Rapoport, "Ot azoy hoibt zikh dos on…(Yidishe kulturarbeit in Shanghai)," *In veg,* zamelheft, (November 1941), pp. 9–14. Translated from Yiddish and annotated by Irene Eber. This selection is also introduced by Professor Eber, who discovered this memoir in the course of her research on the Jewish refugee community of Shanghai.

recorded the indifferent reception [that] he and others suffered in his unpublished diary.

> I remember now my first meeting with Jewish Shanghai. Such a disappointment, such a blow to my hopes....I had so longed for [even] a small Jewish population where I can work again. When fate brought us to Shanghai, which was to be the solution to my spiritual imprisonment, I rejoiced: a city with a Jewish population!...The Jewish community in Shanghai did not receive the...refugees in their homes, [they] sent us to the Jewish Club where we were to sit for the night....for the writers and the simple Jews there was no place....[3]

The essay, which Rapoport wrote some months thereafter, must be understood within the context of his perception of Jewish life in Shanghai. There was in Shanghai, he and others believed, no viable Jewish and certainly no Yiddish life. Therefore, the only way to continue some kind of spiritual and intellectual existence was to create anew a Jewish life. The harbingers of this new Judaism were he and other like-minded men like the poet Yosl Mlotek (1918–2000) and the writer Yankel Fishman (1891–1965). As a result Rapoport devoted himself heart and soul for the next five to six years to writing, translating, and publishing.

Rapoport, born in Bialystok, spent most of his adult life in Warsaw where he was a respected and widely known essayist, translator, and literary critic. He translated from as many as five languages into Yiddish. In Shanghai he became a frequent contributor to the Russian paper *Nasha Zhizn* (Our Life) and to its Yiddish page, *Undzer Lebn* as well as to other Yiddish periodicals. Despite enormous difficulties, he published in Shanghai a book on literary criticism. As testimony to his persistence and dedication to Jewish letters, he tells his readers in the introduction that the manuscript of this work was left behind in Warsaw when he fled to Vilna. Its reconstruction was once more left behind when he traveled to Kobe, and the reconstruction in Shanghai had to be carried out without the necessary books.[4] Rapoport, his wife and son, were able to leave Shanghai for Australia in 1946. He settled in Melbourne where he was finally able to pursue again a fruitful literary career as a Yiddish writer and literary critic.

"AND SO IT BEGINS . . . (JEWISH CULTURAL WORK IN SHANGHAI)"

BY YEHOSHUA RAPOPORT

A bee flies about [looking] for sweet material for her honey production and on the way fertilizes flowers and tree blossoms.

People run from destruction and pogroms and plant on the way a settlement here, a little spiritual [content] there with which to animate an atrophied limb. But the present human characteristic has almost become as if second nature to Jews: who else has run as much from destruction as we Jews? And who has so many times like us planted our spiritual goods and new settlements in all corners of the world?

* * *

A quarter century ago the dual storm of war and revolution brought a few Jews to East Asia. Jewish life began to breathe weakly and anemically in Harbin, Tianjin, and Shanghai. There were Jewish libraries, clubs, lectures, and performances. There was even a Yiddish newspaper in Harbin.

The Jewish pulse, however, grew ever weaker. No transfusions of new blood were available; a part of the Jewish blood that had been brought along dried up due to emigration; the rest atrophied due to anemia. The red corpuscles of Jewish blood lost their resistance, although one might have thought that once there had been an attempt at Jewish life to strike roots in East Asia. However, as it turned out, it was still too early to say kaddish....Storm no. 2 again drove a small Jewish community to East Asia. And perhaps we are witnessing the timid beginnings of a miracle: Jewish life in East Asia begins again; it shows signs of Jewish strength and resistance.

It is told that when one of the pyramids was opened [by archeologists] a few wheat kernels were found that had dried out in the thousands of years they were buried. But a little earth and sunshine were enough for the dry kernels to sprout.[5] Their inner vitality sufficed to preserve them for centuries. The Jewish seed contains no less vitality. No matter how dried out it is on the outside, within lies dormant Jewish vitality that is prepared to [come to life].

We came to Jewish Shanghai as if to a dead kingdom, as if an evil power had transformed into stone everything that was truly Jewish. Still, our despairing screams, our spiritual pitying glance were enough to remove from this stone the evil [curse]. There, where it was assumed all was waste, stone, and cold, something began to move, and to thaw.... Like in the fairy tale, the promised one only has to prove himself for the destined one to awaken.

* * *

Thus the miracle simply begins.
And so it begins.

A Jewish journalist comes to Shanghai and naturally wants to continue his journalistic career. He wanders about town and writes eleven pages in Russian in order to have one small page in Yiddish. The page looks poor, almost ridiculous, as if harking back to destruction. One would like to cry out in a bitter moment: better nothing! It is understandable, one can empathize, but it is not right. Injustice would be done.

That small page looks as if superfluous, it is not read much, but there are the few in number for whom it is meant among the other twelve pages. Readers turn the pages over, the single small page, and dream of more [pages] . And those who yell that a Yiddish page is not needed become accustomed [to its existence]. It becomes a fact for which room must be made, a little room, a life.

How was this possible in Shanghai?

God, they say, heals before the scourge. Two weeks before the outbreak of war, the Jews here received some Yiddish written material from Warsaw. The writing remained unpacked until the embarrassing Yiddish content was unpacked in front of the embarrassing Yiddish page. According to a popular saying misfortune has a way of growing. The written material did not rest a minute. A four-page Yiddish newspaper was soon typeset and an essay in Hebrew as well as a pamphlet of sixty-four pages and a collection [zamelheft] of thirty-two pages.

How was this possible in Shanghai? Again, the same: God heals before the scourge. How does a tree or a flower grow in a mountain of stone? The wind brings a little soil, the soil collects, and together with the soil accumulate seeds of various plants.

The storm that brought to Shanghai a fragmented host, also brought Jewish writers, cultural activists and with these the natural coworker of writers, a Yiddish typesetter. He dismissed the Chinese who had busied himself with the Yiddish page and began to work. Already more typesetters are being searched for! Jews

are insatiable! Together with the written word one can hear now also in Shanghai spoken Yiddish words. In the beginning there was the Shanghai ditty:

A new sensation in Shanghai
Listen, listen, be astonished.
It seems that Jews have arrived
and they even speak Yiddish.

In the beginning Shanghai Jews could not suffer this. It was much harder to extract from their mouth a word in Yiddish than from the wallet a hundred cash. They were forever afraid that nobody would come to hear a lecture in Yiddish because no one understands the language. And those who could understand were not ashamed to admit that it did not concern them. [Another claim] was to give a Yiddish lecture in Shanghai was as difficult as splitting the Red Sea.

But the effort was not in vain. After the first [lecture] came a second and third, and now there is already a forum of three hundred with the attendance growing. The Yiddish word is now no longer only spoken, people sing and recite in Yiddish. We even grabbed a radio station and we have Yiddish broadcasts three times a week. To Shanghai came a lively Yiddish element and Jewish life breathes more strongly and is growing. Different sounds are heard, the Jewish Club is happy, because its first cultural offering in its new location was in Yiddish and the club's culture committee hopes that its activities will increasingly include Yiddish offerings.

To tell the truth, all this was said in Russian, but we have heard a strangely submerged call, "Hear O Israel in Every Language that You Can Hear,"[6] which means "Hear O Israel" can be said in every language one can say it in. It is better to say every Yiddish "Hear O Israel" in a foreign language before uttering it in rather plain Yiddish.

The spoken Yiddish word has [however] become accepted in Shanghai. [Moreover] people who insisted they don't know Yiddish suddenly discovered extraordinary linguistic abilities and in a short time learned to speak Yiddish! And those who usually rejected Yiddish because in Shanghai [they said] Yiddish is not needed, is not known, are now intent on publishing a Yiddish newspaper or a Yiddish book.

One must not be blind: there is in this still too much philanthropy and good-natured consent. All right, if the crazies want it they are welcome to it! And get to know with whom you are dealing! But with good deeds it is the same as with transgressions: in the beginning one does not derive pleasure from them, one simply wants to show off, to emulate daring men. Still, such men do favors by satisfying a taste and [after a time] good deeds become a personal matter.

* * *

Regarding Jewish culture, it would be very unjust to suspect me of blind enthusiasm about that which is being done in Shanghai. My requirements are too great, for Shanghai, no matter what its effort, can only satisfy me partially. But it would be unfair if Shanghai's efforts were not evaluated according to the facts, namely that the ice has melted more rapidly and faster than one might have expected. Each cultural undertaking in Shanghai could be much criticized, but this should not interfere with acknowledging the importance of all the steps undertaken. Somehow Shanghai has allowed itself to be seduced by Yiddish, for there was only a semblance of resistance. Deep and warm streams must have been in Jewish Shanghai for the ice to move that quickly. We must look for these streams. All our cultural attempts serve and must serve the one purpose: to discover where the present streams are and to free and direct them toward us.

And one more thing must be said clearly and openly for us and for you, Shanghai people: nobody does anything for someone else. Whatever one does is for oneself. Our cultural work that we want to do here is also in accordance with our need. We are not doing you [Shanghai people] a favor because what for you is merely refreshing is for us like the air we breathe. A work environment, collective existence, is the highest and probably the only alternative to live humanly like human beings. But don't do us a favor either because you need [Yiddish culture] as much as we, maybe even more than we. We feel uncomfortable in your cultural environment, but we feel within ourselves the cultural ties to our tortured home. You have far less [anguish] about this than we. We still feel sharply our new uprooted condition and we are no longer nourished by the roots [of our homes]. However, we have brought along sufficient nourishment for our severed and displaced lives. You may no longer feel the pain of being uprooted. But I cannot believe you are unfeeling, that you have no roots, and that the stem [of your tree] is dry. I cannot believe it—I see the worry in your eyes. When you look at your children, or when you talk about them, I see that you still value stray Yiddish books [even if] such books are not living nourishment that you need every day and are more like relics that one values but no longer uses.

You now have a chance to abandon, at least, a small portion of your orphaned state. You have the chance to expose your children to an electric shock through contact with a still wriggling limb from a damaged, but living folk organism. We don't want favors from you, nor do we want to do you favors. We only long for mutual work [with you] because it is a mutual necessity. That is our aim and that is the meaning of our modest work.

So it always begins.

And this is how it began.

NOTES

1. This figure is according to Jonathan Goldstein, "Motivation in Holocaust Rescue: The Case of Jan Zwartendijk in Lithuania, 1940," in Jeffry M. Diefendorf, ed., *Lessons and Legacies VI, New Currents in Holocaust Research* (Evanston, Ill.: Northwestern University Press, 2004), p. 71.
2. A somewhat abridged version is in Irene Eber, *Voices from Shangha, Jewish Exiles in Wartime China* (Chicago and London: University of Chicago Press, 2008), pp. 65–69.
3. Arc. 4°, 410, Yehoshua Rapoport Diary, The Jewish National and University Library, Jerusalem. Entry May 12,1941, pp. 44–45.
4. Y. Rapoport, *Der mahut fun diktung un ir sotsiale funktsy* [The very essence of poetry and its social function] (Shanghai: Elberg, 1941), pp. 2–5.
5. In various versions this story must have been told and retold many times. It is repeated by Avraham Sutzkever in a poem of March 1943. Quoted by David E. Fishman, *The Rise of Modern Yiddish Culture*, Pittsburgh: University of Pittsburgh Press, 2005, pp. 152–53.
6. Rapoport wrote this sentence in Hebrew.

23. "WE MUST FINISH WITH THE JEWS" (DECEMBER 16, 1941)

HANS FRANK[1]

One way or another—I will tell you quite openly—we must finish off the Jews. The Fuehrer put it into words once: Should united Jewry again succeed in setting off a world war, then the blood sacrifice shall not be made only by the people driven into war, but then the Jews of Europe will have met their end. I know that there is criticism of many of the measures now applied to the Jews in the Reich. There are always deliberate attempts to speak again and again of cruelty, harshness, etc; this emerges from the reports on the popular mood. I appeal to you: before I now continue speaking, first agree with me on a formula: We will have pity, on principle, only for the German people, and for nobody else in the world. The others had no pity for us either. As an old National-Socialist I must also say that if the pack of Jews (*Judensippschaft*) were to survive the war in Europe while we sacrifice the best of our blood for the preservation of Europe, then this war would still be only a partial success. I will therefore, on principle, approach Jewish affairs in the expectation that the Jews will disappear. They must go. I have started negotiations for the purpose of having them pushed off to the East. In January there will be in Berlin a major conference[2] on this question to which I shall send State Secretary Dr. Buehler.[3] The conference is to be held in the office of SS *Obergruppenführer* Heydrich[4] at the Reich Security Main Office *(Reichsicherheitshauptamt)*. A major Jewish migration will certainly begin.

But what should be done with the Jews? Can you believe that they will be accommodated in settlements in the *Ostland?*[5] In Berlin we are told: Why are you making all this trouble? We don't want them either, not in the *Ostland* nor in the [other] *Reichskommissariate;*[6] liquidate them yourselves, Gentlemen, I must ask you to steal yourselves! against all considerations of compassion. We must destroy the Jews wherever we find them, and wherever it is at all possible, in order to maintain the whole structure of the Reich.... The views that were acceptable up to now cannot be applied to such gigantic, unique events. In any case, we must find a way that will lead us to our goal, and I have my own ideas on this.

The Jews are also exceptionally harmful consumers of food. In the Government-General we have approximately 1.5 million [Jews], and now perhaps 3.5 million together with persons who have Jewish kin, and so on.[7] We cannot shoot these 3.5 million Jews, we cannot poison them, but we will be able to take measures that will lead somehow to successful destruction; and this in connection with the large-scale procedures which are to be discussed in the Reich. The Government-General must become as free of Jews as the Reich. Where and how this is to be done is the affair of bodies which we will have to appoint and create, and on whose work I will report to you when the time comes....

NOTES

1. Hans Frank (1900–1946) was an early follower of Hitler, joining in 1927 the National Socialist German Workers' Party. He quickly rose in the ranks of the party, attaining the position of chairman of the National Scoialist federation of lawyers. He was minister without portfolio in 1934 and in 1939 became head of the "General Government for the occupied territories of Poland"—that is, Poland bereft of the areas ceded to

Source: Hans frank, "From a Speech by [Hans] Frank on the Extermination of the Jews, December 16, 1941." Yad Vashem Archives, Jerusalem, trans. in Y. Arad, Y. Gutman, and A. Margaliot, eds. *Documents on the Holocaust*, trans. Lea Ben Dor (Jerusalem: Yad Vashem, 1981), pp. 247–49. Reprinted by permission of Yad Vashem.

the Soviet Union as a result of the Ribbentrop-Molotov Pact and the western provinces annexed to the Third Reich after the *Blitzkrieg*. The Nuremberg Tribunal in 1945–1956 sentenced him to death for his atrocities against the Polish people.

This document is an excerpt from a speech Frank gave during a session of the administration *(Regierungssitzung)* of the General Government. On the agenda of that session were the question of security arrangements for the transport of Polish workers to Germany and the policies regarding the Jews. In his address Frank, the highest Nazi official in Poland, intimates the policy of extermination that would first be broached officially at the Wannsee Conference a few weeks later. Frank's speech is thus highly significant, since it seems to indicate that plans for the physical liquidation of European Jewry were already well advanced before the conference. Frank seems to speak with a knowledge of such plans, which he himself did not have the authority to initiate, thus indicating that were he, indeed, speaking on the basis of classified information, it came from the highest authorities of the Nazi regime.

2. The reference is to the Wannsee Conference (see the following document).
3. Josef Buehler (1904–1948) served as State Secretary of the General Government of Poland from 1939 to January 1945. Buehler represented the General Government at the Wannsee Conference, where he urged the immediate initiation of the Final Solution in the occupied territories.
4. Reinhard Heydrich (1904–1942), who as head of the Gestapo (the secret police in Nazi Germany) was entrusted with the "final solution" of the Jewish Question. He presided over the Wannsee Conference. On May 27, 1942, he was assassinated by the Czechoslovak resistance.
5. *Ostland*; The *Reichskommissariat Ostland*, one of the two major administrative units of the German civil administration in the occupied territories of the Soviet Union, headed by Alfred Rosenberg (1893–1946).
6. *Reichskommissariate* were administrative units of German-occupied Europe. Due to the failure of the Russian campaign, only two eastern *Reichskommissariate* could be established.
7. These figures are fanciful.

24. PROTOCOLS OF THE WANNSEE CONFERENCE (JANUARY 20, 1942)[1]

Chief of the Security Police Security Service Lieutenant General Heydrich opened proceedings by addressing the executive charged by the Reich Marshal [Goering] with the preparation of the Final Solution of the European Jewish question, and pointed out that invitations to the conference in progress had been issued to elucidate some questions of principle. The Reich Marshal's wish to obtain an outline of the organizational material and financial aspects involved in the Final Solution of the European Jewish Question, called for preliminary consultations of all the central authorities directly affected by these problems, in order to develop action on parallel lines.

Concerning elaboration of a final solution to the Jewish Question, he stated that regardless of geographical borders, the decision rested centrally with [Himmler], the SS *Reichsführer* and Chief of the German Security Police.

Then the Chief of the Security Police and Security Service [Himmler] gave a brief survey of the battle waged up to the time of the meeting against the

Source: Jeno Levai, ed., *Eichmann in Hungary: Documents* (Budapest: Pannonia Press, 1961), pp. 24–28.

adversary. The essential stages were: (a) removal of Jews from the various walks of life of the German people; (b) removal of the Jews from the *Lebensraum* [living space] of the German people.

To accomplish these endeavours, acceleration of the emigration of Jews from Reich territory was to be intensified and supported by planned activity as the only means of solution for the time being....

The work of emigration had become a problem not only to Germany but also to the authorities in the countries of destination, i.e., a problem that had to be dealt with also by the immigration countries. Financial difficulties, increased visa and landing fees exacted by various foreign governments, and lack of shipping space presented growing obstacles, while strict limitation of immigration or complete embargo rendered efforts at emigration extremely difficult. Despite these difficulties, altogether 537,000 Jews had nevertheless been brought to emigrate from the day of the assumption of power [by Hitler in January 1933] until the day of October 31, 1941; of these, 360,000 left the Old Reich after January 30, 1933; 147,000 left Austria after March 15, 1938; 30,000 left the Protectorate of Bohemia and Moravia after March 15, 1939.

Emigration was financed by the Jews and the Jewish political organizations themselves. In order to avoid the stay of indigent Jews, the principle was established and acted on that wealthy Jews had to finance the emigration of the poor ones; a certain amount, commensurate to financial circumstances, was exacted from rich Jews as a contribution to emigration funds employed to cover the emigration costs of needy Jews.

In addition to Reichsmark expenses, foreign currency was required for visa and landing fees. In order to spare German foreign-currency holdings, Jewish financial institutions abroad were approached through inland Jewish organizations and requested to provide for adequate amounts of foreign currency. Up to October 30, 1941, the donations of foreign Jewry put at our disposal the sum of exactly 9,500,000 dollars.

In the meantime, with a view to the dangers of wartime emigration and the possibilities offered by the East, emigration of the Jews was prohibited by the SS *Reichsführer* and Chief of the German Police [Himmler].

Instead of emigration, evacuation of the Jews to the East had then been taken into consideration as another possibility of solution, after previous approval by the Führer.

These actions are, however, to be regarded as temporary expedients; practical experience was nonetheless accumulated here, which are of outstanding importance for the Final Solution of the Jewish question in the future.

This Final Solution of the European Jewish question is estimated to apply to exactly eleven million Jews, distributed over various countries as follows:[2]

Country	Number
A. Old Reich	131,800
Ostmark (Austria)	43,700
Eastern Areas	420,000
Generalgouvernement[3]	2,284,000
Bialystok	400,000
Protectorate of Bohemia and Moravia	74,000
Estonia—Free of Jews	
Latvia	3,500
Lithuania	34,000
Belgium	43,000
Denmark	5,600
France, occupied territory	165,000
France, unoccupied territory	700,000
Greece	69,600
Netherlands	160,800
Norway	1,300
B. Bulgaria	48,000
England	330,000
Finland	2,300
Ireland	4,000
Italy, including Sardinia	58,000
Albania	200
Croatia	40,000
Portugal	3,000
Rumania, including Bessarabia	342,000
Sweden	8,000
Switzerland	18,000
Serbia	10,000
Slovakia	88,000
Spain	6,000
Turkey (European part)	55,300
Hungary	742,000
USSR	5,000,000
Ukraine	2,994,685
White Russia (without Bialystok)	446,484
Total	over 11,000,000

The figures quoted for various countries refer to Jews of Jewish religion, since the definition of Judaism by racial principles is not yet practiced everywhere....

With adequate management the Final Solution is expected to result in Jews being put to appropriate work in the East. In large groups of workers, the sexes separated, able-bodied Jews should be made to build roads in these areas, which would doubtlessly lead to the natural diminution of numbers at a considerable rate.

The final remnant, doubtlessly consisting of the toughest and most resistant individuals, would have to be treated accordingly, since they would have survived by natural development.

When it [comes] to the practical execution of the Final Solution, Europe would have to be combed from West to East; Reich territory, including the Protectorate of Bohemia and Moravia, would have to be exempted, for reasons of housing problems and other socio-political necessities.

The evacuated Jews should be taken in successive trainloads first to so-called transit ghettos, to be transported from there to the East.

An essential precondition, continued SS Lieutenant General Heydrich, for carrying out the evacuation at all, was an accurate basis of criteria concerning the group of persons involved.

It was intended that Jews over 65 years of age should not be evacuated, but transferred to old-age ghettos—presumably Theresienstadt.[4]

In addition to old-age groups—out of the approximately 280,000 Jews living in the Old Reich and Austria, about 30 per cent were over 65 years on October 31, 1941—the old-age ghettos would also take in badly incapacitated Jewish war veterans and Jews holding medals for distinguished military services (Iron Cross First Class). This expedient solution should effectively neutralize the basis for many (foreign) interventions....

Initiation of the several major actions of evacuation would greatly depend on military development. In connection with the handling of the Final Solution in European countries under our occupation of influence, it has been proposed that available experts in this field attached to the Foreign Ministry should discuss matters with the competent executives of the Security Police and the Security Service.

In Slovakia and Croatia the situation had grown less difficult, since the essential and crucial problems have already been solved there in this respect. Also in Rumania, an executive of Jewish affairs has been installed in the meantime. To regulate the question in

Hungary it was necessary to force on the Hungarian government a counsellor on Jewish questions without delay.

As concerns the initiation of preparations for settling the problem in Italy, Lieutenant General Heydrich thought it advisable to establish contact with the Chief of Police [Himmler].

In occupied and unoccupied France alike, rounding up Jews for evacuation should in all probability be carried out without any serious difficulties.

Deputy State Secretary [Hans] Luther [of the Foreign Office] thereupon informed the conference that, upon thorough tackling of the problems, difficulties would arise in several countries, for instance in the northern countries; therefore it appeared desirable to omit these countries for the time being. Owing to the small number of Jews in question, their omission would by no means constitute a noteworthy limitation. On the other hand, the Foreign Ministry did not anticipate too great difficulties in the countries of South-East and South-West Europe....

Efforts to bring about a Final Solution should be based mainly on the Nuremberg Laws, while solution of the problem of mixed marriages and Mischlinge continue to form a precondition for clearing up the [Jewish Question] completely....[5]

NOTES

1. On September 1, 1939, the armies of Germany invaded Poland. World War II had commenced. By June 1941, the beginning of the campaign against Russia, the Germans had succeeded in conquering most of Europe, inheriting millions of Jews. The Nazis desired an expeditious and radical solution to the Jewish Question. But it was soon realized that the policy of forced emigration was no longer a feasible solution. The vast number of Jews in question, the general unwillingness of the prospective countries of refuge to accept these Jews, and the fact that most of these countries were now engaged in war against Germany or its allies obliged the Nazis to search for an alternative solution.

   In July 1938 an international conference on the Jewish refugee problem was convened at Evian-les-Bains, France. After nine days of deliberation, the delegates of the thirty-three participating countries did little more than express sympathy for the refugees. The restrictions on immigration remained in place. In effect the failure of the Evian confrence was interpreted by the Nazis as a green light for the Final Solution.

Sometime in the late spring or early summer of 1941, Hitler issued an oral order for "a Final Solution of the Jewish Question." In Nazi parlance the Final Solution become a euphemism for the physical liquidation of the Jews. In the summer of 1941 construction on the first *Vernichtungslager*, ("annihilation camp") was begun. The camp at Chelmno, some twenty-five miles from the Polish city of Lodz, commenced operation on December 8, 1941. The Chief of the Gestapo, Reinhard Heydrich, was designated to supervise the overall operational aspects of the Final Solution. On January 20, 1942, he convened a conference of representatives of the various state bureaucracies that would be involved in the Final Solution. The Conference, which met at Wannsee, a suburb of Berlin, was of utmost importance, for it set and coordinated the plans for the extermination. The minutes of the conference are presented here.

2. These figures, far from accurate, suggest that Heydrich believed that all of Europe would fall to the Nazis, extending the purview of the Final Solution.

3. The partition and occupation of Poland gave Hitler the opportunity to carry out his racial policies. On October 12, 1939, he issued a decree establishing a civil administration in Poland, called *Generalgouverenment*, with Hans Frank as governor general.

4. Theresienstadt, near a town in Bohemia of that name, was to become a "model camp," the only one into which the Nazis would permit foreign observers.

5. The conference went on to discuss in detail the status of the *Mischlinge*, i.e., persons of mixed German-Jewish blood. Second-degree *Mischlinge*, for instance, being only a quarter Jewish, were in principle to be regarded as Germans. Should these *Mischlinge*, however, have "an exceptionally poor racial appearance" or should "they feel and behave like Jews," they were to be treated as Jews. Regarding the *Mischlinge*, sterilization was proposed by one of the delegates as the most humane alternative to evacuation. This proposal was endorsed by the representative of the Ministry of the Interior, because it would ease the "endless administrative task" of determining the exact status of *Mischlinge*. A representative of the Four Year Plan urged that Jews employed in war industries not be evacuated until replacements were found. The military governor of Poland welcomed the Final Solution, because the Jews constituted "a substantial danger as carriers of epidemics." Moreover, the majority of the Jews in Poland, he held, were useless and not capable of working.

25. THE NAZI RESPONSE TO RESISTANCE (MAY 1942)

JOSEPH GOEBBELS[1]

*M*ay 27, 1942....An alarming news item has come from Prague. In the suburbs of Prague an attempt has been made to assassinate Heydrich with a bomb....We must be clear about this, such an assassination would become a model for others unless we proceed to take brutal measures....

I shall now likewise complete my war against the Berlin Jews. At the moment I am having a list drawn up of the Jewish hostages to be followed by many arrests. I have no desire to put myself into a position to be shot in the belly by a twenty-two-year-old Jew from the East—such types are to be found among the

---

Source: Diary of Joseph Goebbels, May 27, 29 and 30, 1942, in Ernest K. Bramsted, ed., *Goebbels and National Socialist Propaganda, 1925–1945* (East Lansing: Michigan State University Press, 1965), pp. 396–97. Reprinted by permission of Michigan State University Press.

assassins at the Anti-Soviet Exhibition. Ten Jews in a concentration camp or under the earth are better than one going free. We are engaged today in a fight for life and death and he will win who most energetically defends his political existence. Surely we are the one.

May 29, 1942. [A few days later Goebbels jotted down further details of the new anti-Jewish drive after noticing that Heydrich's condition was very disquieting.[2]] We still don't know the background of the plot.... In any case, we are making the Jews pay. I am having my planned arrest of 500 Jews in Berlin carried out, and am informing the leaders of the Jewish community that for every Jewish plot or attempt at revolt 100 or 150 Jews whom we are holding are to be shot. As a consequence of the attempt on Heydrich a whole group of Jews, against whom we have evidence, were shot in Sachsenhausen. The more of this rubbish we get rid of the better for the security of the Reich.

May 30, 1942. The Germans [the Führer recently told me] take part in the subversive movements only when Jews have tricked them into it. For this reason the Jewish danger must be liquidated, cost what it may.

NOTES

1. The Reich's Minister of Propaganda, Joseph Goebbels (1897–1945) was also the *Gauleiter* (district head) of Berlin. As these excerpts from his diary indicate, the Nazi response to armed resistance was swift and brutal. Goebbels refers to two separate incidents of resistance: the first, the assassination on May 27, 1942, of the SS leader Reinhard T. Heydrich by the Czechoslovakian underground; the second, a sabotage attempt on an anti-Soviet exhibit in Berlin on May 15, 1942. (Of the twelve saboteurs captured, seven were Jews.) In retaliation the Nazis razed the Czech village of Lidice, executing all of the male inhabitants. At the same time 152 Jews in Berlin were killed in a "special action," and more than 3,000 Jews in the Theresienstadt ghetto were deported to various death camps. The extermination of Polish Jewry was designated by the Nazis *Aktion Reinhard*, in memory of Heydrich.

2. Heydrich died of his wounds on June 4, 1942.

26. A WARSAW GHETTO DIARY (MARCH 10 AND OCTOBER 2, 1940)

CHAIM A. KAPLAN[1]

March 10, 1940

The gigantic catastrophe which has descended on Polish Jewry has no parallel, even in the darkest periods of Jewish history. Firstly—the depth of the hatred. This is not hatred whose source is simply in a party platform, invented for political purposes. It is a hatred of emotion, whose source is some psychopathic disease. In its outward manifestation it appears as physiological hatred, which sees the object of its hatred as tainted in body, as lepers who have no place in society.

The masses have accepted this sort of objective hatred. Their limited understanding does not grasp ideological hatred; psychology is beyond them, and

Source: Chaim A. Kaplan, *Scroll of Agony, Warsaw Ghetto Diary* (Tel Aviv/Jerusalem: Am Oved with Yad Vashem, 1966), pp. 201f., 350 (Hebrew), in Y. Arad, Y. Gutman and A. Margaliot, eds., *Documents on the Holocaust*, trans. Lea Ben Dor (Jerusalem: Yad Vashem, 1981), pp. 201–04. Reprinted by permission of Yad Vashem.

they are incapable of understanding it. They have absorbed their masters' teaching in a concrete bodily form. The Jew is filthy; the Jew is a swindler and evil; the Jew is the enemy of Germany and undermines its existence; the Jew was the prime mover in the Versailles Treaty, which reduced Germany to a shambles; the Jew is Satan, who sows dissension between the nations, arousing them to bloodshed in order to profit from their destruction. These are easily understood concepts whose effect on day-to-day life can be felt immediately.

But the founders of Nazism and the party leaders created a theoretical ideology with deeper foundations. They have a complete doctrine which represents the Jewish spirit inside and out. Judaism and Nazism are two attitudes to the world that are incompatible, and for this reason they cannot coexist side by side. For 2,000 years Judaism has left its imprint, culturally and spiritually, on the nations of the world. It stood fast, blocking the spread of German paganism, whose teaching was different and whose culture was drawn from a different source. Two kings cannot wear one crown. Either humanity would be Judaic, or it would be pagan-German. Up until now it was Judaic. Even Catholicism is a child of Judaism, and the fruit of its spirit, and thus afflicted by all the shortcomings inherited from its mother. The new world which Nazism would fashion would be pagan, primordial, in all its attitudes. It is therefore ready to fight Judaism to the finish....

It is our good fortune that the conquerors failed to understand the nature and strength of Polish Jewry. Logically, we are obliged to die. According to the laws of nature, our end is destruction and total annihilation. How can an entire community feed itself when it has no grip on life? For there is no occupation, no trade which is not limited and circumscribed for us.

But even this time we did not comply with the laws of nature. There is within us some hidden power, mysterious and secret, which keeps us going, keeps us alive, despite the natural law. If we cannot live on what is permitted, we live on what is forbidden. That is not disgrace for us. What is permitted is no more than an agreement, and what is forbidden derives from the same agreement. If we do not accept the agreement, it is not binding on us particularly when this forbidden and permitted comes from a barbarous conqueror, who limits life to one made in his image and his murderous and larcenous views.

...The Jews of Poland—oppressed and broken, shamed and debased—still love life, and do not wish to leave this world before their time. Say what you like, the will to live amidst terrible suffering is the manifestation of some hidden power whose nature we do not yet know. It is a marvelous, life-preserving power that only the most firmly established and strongest of the communities of our people have received as a blessing.

The fact that we have hardly any suicides is worthy of special emphasis. We have remained naked. But as long as that secret power is concealed within us, we shall not yield to despair. The strength of this power lies in the very nature of the Polish Jew, which is rooted in our eternal tradition that commands us to live....

October 2, 1940
Eve of the New Year, 5701

We have no public prayers even on the High Holy Days....

Even for the High Holy Days permission was not received for public prayers, although I do not know whether the Community [Council] tried to get it. And if it did not try that is only because it knew that its request would be refused. Even in the darkest days of our exile we did not suffer this trial....

The wonder is that despite all this we go on living. Our life is one of scorn and debasement as it is seen from outside, but our human emotions have become so numbed that we no longer feel, and the awareness of insult that is concealed within every human being no longer rises up in protest against even the most barbarous and cruel of such insults.

To what can this matter be compared? To a vicious dog who does treat you with respect; would you, then, be insulted? Is not that why he is a dog?

Again: everything is forbidden to us; and yet we do everything! We make our "living" in ways that are forbidden, and not by permission.

It is the same with community prayers: secret *minyanim*² in their hundreds all over Warsaw hold prayers together and do not leave out even the most difficult hymns. Neither preachers nor sermons are missing; everything is in accordance with the ancient traditions of Israel. Where there is no informer the enemy does not know what is going on. And surely no member of the Community of Israel, even if he was [not] born in Poland, will go to lay information against Jews standing before their Maker.

Near the central synagogue some side room is chosen with windows facing the courtyard, and there hearts are poured out to the God of Israel in whispered supplications. This time it is without cantors and without choirs; there are only whispered prayers, but the prayers comes from heart; even tears may be wept secretly, and the gate of the tears cannot be locked....

NOTES

1. Chaim A. Kaplan (1880–1942) was a Hebrew educator. In 1902 he founded in Warsaw an innovative Hebrew elementary school, which he directed for 40 years. In 1933 he began a diary, which prepared him for the mission he was later to undertake: to record with meticulous detail all that he witnessed in the Warsaw Ghetto. Just before he was to be deported in late 1942 to Treblinka, he entrusted the diary, written in Hebrew, to a friend to be smuggled out of the ghetto. After the war the diary was discovered almost intact in a kerosene can and was published in 1966 under the title *Megalat yisurim* (Scroll of Agony) and edited by A. I. Katsh and N. Blumental. The volume was published in English as the *Warsaw Diary of Chaim A. Kaplan*, trans. and ed. A. I. Katsh (New York: Macmillan, 1965, 1978).

2. *Minyanim*: plural for the Hebrew term for the quorum of ten males necessary for Jewish communal prayer.

27. WARSAW GHETTO MEMOIRS (MAY TO AUGUST 1942)

JANUSZ KORCZAK[1]

The city discards for me children like little sea shells and I do nothing. I am just good to them. I ask neither where they come from nor for how long, nor whither they are going, for benefit or harm to man.

The "Old Doctor" doles out candy, tells stories, answers questions. Peaceful, quiet, lovable years removed from the market-place of life.

Sometimes a book or a visit by a friend and always some kind of a patient requiring over the course of long years the greatest of care.

The children recover, die—as it happens in a hospital.

I did not play the philosopher. I did not try to go deeper into a subject which was already known to me in depth. Indeed, for the first seven years I was really a sort of modest resident doctor in a hospital.

Afterwards, for all the remaining years I was tormented by the unpleasant feeling of having been a deserter. That I betrayed the sick child, the medical profession, the hospital. I got carried away by a false ambition: physician and sculptor of the child's soul. Soul. No more and no less. (Oh, you old fool, you have made a mess of your life and your cause! You got what you deserved!)...

For that I went around hungry, down-at-the-heels in clinics of three European capitals. Better not to talk about this though.

* * *

I don't know how much of this autobiographical stuff I have already scribbled. I don't have the pluck to read all that baggage. And I'm in danger that

Source: Janusz Korczak, *The Warsaw Ghetto Memoirs of Janusz Korczak*, trans. from the Polish with an introduction by E. P. Kulawiec (Washington, D.C.: University Press of America, 1979), pp. 34–37, 39–41, 43, 98–99, 109–12. Reprinted by permission of Edwin P. Kulawiec.

more and more increasingly will I repeat myself. What is even worse, the facts and experiences may, must, and will be differently told as regards the details.

No matter. It only proves that the events to which I return were important, were deeply experienced.

And it proves, too, much that reminiscences depend on our immediate experience. In recalling we unconsciously prevaricate. This is obvious, and I say it only for the benefit of the most naive reader.

The frequent daydream and plan was a trip to China.

That could have happened, even quite easily.

My poor four-year-old Iuo-ya from the times of the Japanese war. I wrote her a dedication in Polish.

Painstakingly she tried to teach her dull pupil Chinese.

Of course, there ought to be institutes of oriental languages. Certainly, professors and lectures.

But everyone must spend a year in such a village in the Orient, and pass such an introductory course under a four-year-old.

I was taught German by Erna. Walter and Frieda were already too old for that, already grammatical, influenced by novels, hand-books, schooling.

Dostoievsky says that in time all our dreams materialize, only in such a degenerated form that we don't recognize them. I can recognize those dreams of my pre-war years.

Not that I went to China but that China came to me. Chinese famine, Chinese orphan misery, Chinese mass and child mortality.

I don't want to pursue this subject. To describe someone else's pain is like stealing, preying upon misfortune, as if what he already had wasn't enough.

The first newsmen and officials from America did not conceal their disappointment: it wasn't all that terrible. They were even looking for corpses, and in the orphanage, skeletons.

While they visited the Children's Home, the boys were playing soldiers. Paper caps and sticks.

"Apparently, the war hasn't upset them," said one, ironically.

"That's so now. But their appetites have increased and their nerves have become numb. Things are beginning to improve. Here and there even toys are to be seen in shops and plenty of candy, from a single pence to a whole zloty's worth.

"I saw with my own eyes: a small child scrounged up ten groszy by begging and then promptly spend it on candy."

"Don't write that in your paper, friend."

I once read: Nothing is easier to get used to than another's misfortune....

* * *

Five shots of raw alcohol mixed half and half with hot water gives me inspiration.

Then comes a delicious feeling of lassitude, utterly painless, for the old scar doesn't count then, nor the stiffness in my legs, nor even the aching eyes and the burning in the scrotum.

I draw inspiration from the awareness that I am lying in bed and will continue to do so till morning. That means that for twelve hours the heart and muscles will function normally.

After a hard day....

The day began with the weighing of the children. The month of May showed a marked decline. The earlier months of this year were not too bad and even May isn't yet alarming. But we still have two months or more before pre-harvest. This is certain. And the restrictions imposed by official regulations and new interpretations ought to make the situation still worse.

The children's weighing hour on Saturday is one of strong emotions.

After breakfast, the school meeting.[2]...

After breakfast, on the run, *à la fourchette*—the toilet (just in case, therefore, with some difficulty), and a meeting to discuss the school's summer program, vacations, replacements.

It would be convenient if it could all be arranged as it was last year. But a lot has changed since then, a different situation in the dormitories, many new arrivals and departures, new promotions. Things are—but why keep on about it—different. And we would like things to be better.

After the meeting, the school newspaper and court decisions. Abuses have appeared. Not everyone is willing to listen carefully for a good hour to the subject of who has managed well and who badly, what has been, received and what lost, what should be expected, what accomplished. The school newspaper will be a revelation to the new children.

But the older ones know they will discover neither this way nor that what is most important for them. In fact, no one is interested, no one listens, and so if it is possible to save some bother, then why not?

Right after the newspaper, tiring for me personally as one who acquiesces and skillfully avoids seeing that which is more convenient not to see, when one doesn't want to use force if persuasion is not possible—right after the newspaper a longer conversation with a woman who is using her influence in trying to get a child admitted; this is an intricate affair requiring caution, tact and firmness; one can go absolutely crazy. But about this some other time. Because the dinner bell has sounded. . . .

A dead boy is lying on the sidewalk. Near-by three boys are fixing something with some rope. At a certain moment they glanced at the body and moved away a few steps, not interrupting their game.

Anyone who is better off must help the family. The family—that's his brothers and sister and wives, their brothers, sisters, old parents, children. Help with from five to fifty zlotys—and so from dawn to late at night.

If someone is starving to death and finds relatives who are willing to acknowledge kinship and to ensure two meals a day, he is happy for two or three days, not more than a week. Then he asks for a shirt, shoes, a human place to live, a little coal, then he wants to treat himself, his wife, children—finally, he resists being a beggar, demands employment, wants a steady job.

It cannot be otherwise. And yet, it arouses such anger, discouragement, fear and resentment that even a decent and sensitive person becomes an enemy of his family, others, himself.

I wish that I had nothing at all so that they would see this for themselves, so that then there would be an end to it.

Tomorrow I'll be sixty-four or sixty-five years old. My father put off making out my birth certificate for several years. I suffered several trying moments because of this. Mama called it criminal negligence; as a lawyer, father should not have put off the matter of the birth certificate.

I was named after my grandfather, his name being Hersz [Hirsz]. Father had every right to name me Henryk: he himself was given the name Jozef. And to the rest of his children grandfather gave Christian names: Maria, Magdalena, Ludwick, Jakub, Karol. Yet father vacillated and procrastinated.

I ought to devote a lot of a space to my father: I achieve in life that which he strove for, for what my grandfather strove for painfully over so many years.

And my mother. Later perhaps. I am both a mother and a father. I know and understand a great deal thanks to this. My great-grandfather was a glazier. I'm pleased about this: Glass gives warmth and light.

It is a splendid thing, this, to be born and to learn to live. A much simpler problem lies ahead of me: to die. After death, it may again be difficult, but I don't think about that. The last year, or month, or hour.

I should like to die in full consciousness and with presence of mind. I do not know what I should say to the children by way of a farewell. I should want to make clear to them only this—that they have complete freedom as to what path they choose.

Ten o'clock. Shots: two, several, two, one, several. Maybe it is my own poorly blacked out window.

But I do not interrupt my writing.

On the contrary: Thought soars higher (a single shot).

* * *

22 July 1942[3]

Everything has its limits. Only brazen shamelessness is limitless.

The authorities have ordered the hospital in Stawka Street to be cleared[4] and the directress has to accept all critical cases in Zelazna Street.

What's one to do? A hasty decision, like a spring action.

X and Z have one hundred and seventy-five convalescent children. They have decided to place a third of them with me. There are our fifteen institutions, but ours is near by.

And the fact that for over a period of six months the lady in question stooped to every conceivable outrage against the patients for the sake of convenience, through obstinacy or stupidity; that she fought with devilish cunning against my humane and uncomplicated plan—that means nothing. . . .

In my absence Mrs. K. gave her consent and Mrs. S. proceeded to carry out the shameless demand—shameless to the last degree, both to their own children as well as ours. . . .

Spit on the floor and leave! I've been thinking this a long time now. Any longer—a noose, lead on one's feet.

(It again came out incomprehensibly. But I feel too exhausted to write more fully.)

Azrylewicz[5] died this morning. Oh, how hard is life, how easy death!

* * *

4 August 1942[6]

1.

I was watering the flowers, poor orphanage plants, Jewish orphanage plants. The parched earth revived.

A guard watched me as I worked. I wonder, does this peaceful work of mine at six o'clock in the morning annoy or move him?

He stands and looks on, legs planted wide apart.

2.

All efforts to get Miss Esther released came to nothing. I was not quite sure whether, in the event of success, I would be doing her a favor or whether I would be harming and hurting her.

"Where did she get caught?" someone is asking.

Perhaps it is not she but we who have gotten caught (for remaining).

3.

I have written to the police asking that they send Adzio away: mentally underdeveloped and maliciously undisciplined. We cannot risk exposing the Home to his outbursts. (Collective responsibility.)

4.

For Dzielna Street a ton of coal for the time being—for Roza Abramowicz.[7] Someone asks if the coal will be safe there.

In reply—a smile.

5.

A cloudy morning,. It is five-thirty. An apparently ordinary beginning of the day. I say to little Hannah:

"Good morning!"

She answers with a look of surprise.

I plead: "Smile."

They are unhealthy, pale, lung-sick smiles.

6.

You drank, Sirs, Officers, you drank plenty and with gusto for your blood; dancing, you jingled your medals, honoring the infamy which you were too blind to see, or, rather pretended not to see.

7.

My share in the Japanese war. Defeat—disaster.

In the European war. Defeat—disaster.

In the world war . .. .

I don't know how or what a soldier of a victorious army feels. . . .

8.

The journals to which I contributed were usually shut down—went bankrupt.

One publisher, ruined, committed suicide.

And all this not because I am a Jew but because I was born in the East.

It might be a sad consolation that the haughty West is not so well off either.

It might be, but it isn't. I don't wish anyone any harm. I don't know how. I don't know how that is done.

9.

Our Father who art in heaven . . . .

Hunger and misery have carved this prayer.

Our daily bread.

Bread.

Why, this very thing which I am now experiencing was. It existed.

They were selling furniture, clothing for a liter of lamp oil, a kilogram of groats for a glass of vodka.

When a plucky, young Pole kindly asked me at the police station how I managed to run the blockade, I asked him whether he couldn't possibly do "something" for Miss Esther.

"You know very well that I can't."

I said quickly:

"Thanks for the kind word."

This expression of thanks is the bloodless child of poverty and degradation.

10.

I am watering my flowers. My bald head is at the window—what a good target it is. He has a gun. Why is he standing and looking on so calmly? He's not under orders. And maybe as a civilian he was a village school teacher, or a public notary, or a street-cleaner in Leipzig, or a waiter in Cologne? I wonder what he would do if I nodded to him, or waved my hand at him in a friendly way? Maybe he doesn't even know that things are as they are here. He may have arrived only yesterday from afar.

NOTES

1. Janusz Korczak (pen name of Henryk Goldszmit; 1878 or 1879–1942) was a physician, writer, and educator. Born in Warsaw to an assimilated Jewish family, he studied medicine at the University of Warsaw, where he was drawn to circles of liberal educators and writers. Upon graduating medical school, he served as a physician in the Russian army during the Russo-Japanese War of 1905. After the war he continued his studies in Berlin. He returned to Warsaw in 1911 to become the director of the Jewish orphanage.

   He developed a distinctive philosophy of education and wrote more than twenty books, primarily about children, many directly addressed to children. The overarching theme of his work was his respect and appreciation of children and their world, trust and belief in their wisdom. Korczak firmly believed that the improvement of child-bearing and the lot of children led to the betterment of the world.

   An idealist by disposition, even as a medical student he gave free medical care to the poor and indigent in Warsaw's old town. Upon receiving his medical degree he was appointed director of an orphanage for Jewish children in Warsaw; in 1920 he assumed the co-directorship of a similar institution for Polish children. When the Nazis established a ghetto in Warsaw, Korczak and the entire personnel of the Jewish orphanage, together with its children, were relocated to a building within the ghetto walls:

   > Caring daily for the fate of some two hundred children assumed monumental proportions. Yet schooling continued as of old, work assignments went on, the children's court functioned, the newspaper was printed, the bulletin board attended to, games and diversions organized—all continued as before under the increasing hardship of sickness, hunger, and fright. Korczak's days were filled with constant rounds to all possible quarters of the ghetto, to groups and institutions, to organizations and committees, to individuals and even to successful smugglers operating within the ghetto, asking for food for his home, begging, pleading, demanding, threatening for help for his children. With the children he tried to be the same as they had known him—a person of great warmth, kindness and humor, a trusted friend and confidant, a task master, organized, in control....At night, surrounded by sleeping children...he lost himself to his jottings, his musings, trying to find reason where all reason appeared lost (Kulawiec, Introduction, Warsaw Ghetto Memoirs, p. ix).

   Korczak's diary covers a very brief period, from May through August 1942. The last entry was written four days before Korczak, rejecting the possibility of escape, led a long, orderly line of children from the ghetto through the streets of Warsaw on a three-mile march to the Gdansk, railway station. A train took him and his children to the Treblinka death camp, where they perished in the crematoria.

   Before departing, Korczak entrusted the memoirs to his long-time personal secretary from before the war, the writer Igor Newerly, who duly hid the manuscript. It was published for the first time in 1958 in its original Polish.

2. At the post-breakfast meeting, Korczak announced that the flag of the Orphans' Home—made of green silk (since green is the color of all that grows)—would be dedicated on June 1, the anniversary of the death of Dr. I. Eliasberg, the founder of the institution. At the ceremony at the grave of Eliasberg, Korczak and the children dedicated the flag and pledged to live and labor peaceably for truth and justice. A year later, Korczak and his children would march, under the flag, from the ghetto to the freight trains transporting them to the Treblinka death camp.

3. On July 22, 1942, Korczak's birthday, the very day the so-called liquidation of the Warsaw Ghetto began.

4. The hospital on Stawka Street was emptied because it was located on the site of the *Umschlagplatz*, or embarkation square, from which the ghetto population would be dispatched to extermination camps. The patients from the Stawka hospital were transferred to the Children's Hospital in Zelazna Street, and some of the convalescent children from the latter hospital were sent to Korczak's Orphans' Home.

5. Hemryk Arzylewicz was the brother of a worker in the office of the Orphans' Home.

6. This is the last entry in the diary.

7. An alumna of the Orphans' Home, Roza Abramowicz was later a coworker of whom Korczak was particularly fond.

28. CALL TO RESISTANCE (JANUARY 1943)

JEWISH FIGHTING ORGANIZATION[1]

On January 22, 1943, six months will have passed since the deportations from Warsaw began. We all remember well the days of terror during which 300,000 of our brothers and sisters were cruelly put to death in the death camp of Treblinka. Six months have passed of life in constant fear of death, not knowing what the next day may bring. We have received information from all sides about the destruction of the Jews in the Government-General, in Germany, in the occupied territories. When we listen to this bitter news we wait for our own hour to come, every day and every moment. Today we must understand that the Nazi murderers have let us live only because they want to make use of our capacity to work to our last breath. We are slaves. And when the slaves are no longer profitable, they are killed. Everyone among us must understand that, and everyone among us must remember it always.

During the past few weeks certain people have spread stories about letters that were said to have been received from Jews deported from Warsaw, who were said to be in labor camps near Minsk or Bobruisk. *Jews in your masses, do not believe these tales. They are spread by Jews who are working for the Gestapo.* The blood-stained murderers have a particular aim in doing this: to reassure the Jewish population in order that later the next deportation can be carried out without difficulty, with a minimum of force and without losses to the Germans. They want the Jews not to prepare hiding-places and not to resist. Jews, do not repeat [the reports of] these lying [Nazi] agents. The Gestapo's dastardly people will get their just deserts. *Jews in your masses*, the hour is near. You must be prepared to resist, not to give yourselves up like sheep to slaughter. *Not even one Jew must go to the train. People who cannot resist actively must offer passive resistance, that is, by hiding.* We have now received information from Lvov that the Jewish Police there itself carried out the deportation of 3,000 Jews. Such things will not happen again in Warsaw. The killing of Lejkin[2] proves it. Now our slogan must be: *Let everyone be ready to die like a human being!* January 1943

NOTES

1. The Jewish Fighting Organization (*Zydowska Organizacja Bojowa*, or ZOB) was formed at the beginning of the first mass deportation of Jews from the Warsaw Ghetto to the Treblinka extermination camp in July 1942. When the deportations suddenly stopped in mid-September 1942, only some 70,000 out of a population of 370,000 inhabitants of the ghetto were left. The ZOB was a coalition of fighting units from socialist Zionist youth movements, joined a bit later by the Bund and the Communists; the Revisionists maintained their own separate fighting unit, "Swit" (ZZW). In October 1942, Mordecai Anielewicz (cf. this chapter, document 29) was named the commander-in-chief of the ZOB.

The second wave of deportations began on January 18, 1943, Nazi troops entered the ghetto, surrounded many buildings, and rounded up the inhabitants; they even liquidated the hospitals, shot the patients, and deported the personnel. The underground organizations offered armed resistance, and four days of street battles ensued. This was the first case of urban armed resistance in occupied Poland. Fearing the impact of this outburst on other parts

---

Source: Archives of the Jewish Historical Society in Poland; cited in Y. Arad, Y. Gutman and A. Margaliot, eds., *Documents on the Holocaust*, trans. Lea Ben Dor (Jerusalem: Yad Vashem, 1981), pp. 301–02. Reprinted by permission of Yad Vashem.

of Poland, the Germans stopped the deportations and decided to carry out their program to liquidate the ghetto by "peaceful" means, namely, by "voluntary" registration for alleged work camps. The underground in turn conducted an intensive information campaign about the real intentions of the Nazis. This document, a leaflet distributed by ZOB, was part of that campaign.

2. Yaakov Lejkin was the head of the Jewish police in the Warsaw Ghetto. Because of his collaboration with the Nazis, he was assassinated by the Jewish Fighting Organization on October 29, 1942.

29. HIS LAST COMMUNICATION AS GHETTO REVOLT COMMANDER (APRIL 23, 1943)

MORDECAI ANIELEWICZ[1]

Dear Antek,[2] ... It is impossible to put into words what we have been through. One thing is clear, what happened exceeded our boldest dreams. The Germans ran twice from the Ghetto. One of our companies held out for 40 minutes and another—for more than 6 hours. The mine set in the "brush-makers" area exploded. Several of our companies attacked the dispersing Germans. Our losses in manpower are minimal. That is also an achievement. Y [Yechiel] fell. He fell a hero, at the machine-gun. *I feel that great things are happening and what we dared to do is of great, enormous importance....*

Beginning from today we shall shift over to the partisan tactic. Three battle companies will move out tonight, with two tasks: reconnaissance and obtaining arms. Do remember, short-range weapons are of no use to us. We use such weapons only rarely. What we need urgently: grenades, rifles, machine-guns and explosives.

It is impossible to describe the conditions under which the Jews of the Ghetto are now living. Only a few will be able to hold out. The remainder will die sooner or later. Their fate is decided. In almost all the hiding places in which thousands are concealing themselves it is not possible to light a candle for lack of air.

With the aid of our transmitter we heard a marvelous report on our fighting by the "Swit" radio station.[3] The fact that we are remembered beyond the Ghetto walls encourages us in our struggle. Peace go with you, my friend! Perhaps we may still meet again! *The dream of my life has risen to become fact. Self-defense in the Ghetto will have been a reality. Jewish armed resistance and revenge are facts. I have been a witness to the magnificent, heroic fighting of Jewish men and women of battle.*

M. Anielewicz

NOTES

1. Mordecai Anielewicz (1919–1943) was the commander-in-chief of the underground Jewish Fighting Organization [ZOB] (see document 28 of this chapter). He led the Warsaw Ghetto uprising, which began on April 19, 1943. At the height of the revolt,

---

Source: M. Anielewicz, letter to Yitzhak Cukierman [Zuckerman], Warsaw Ghetto, April 23, 1943; cited in *Na oczach swiata* (Warsaw, 1943). Written anonymously, this Polish work, whose title means "In the Eyes of the World," was published by Jewish members of the Polish underground in Warsaw in 1943. It is translated in Y. Arad, Y. Gutman and A. Margaliot, eds. *Documents on the Holocaust*, trans. Lea Ben Dor (Jerusalem: Yad Vashem, 1981), pp. 315f. Reprinted by permission of Yad Vashem.

he wrote the letter reprinted here. He fell on May 8, 1943, together with scores of his fellow fighters, in the command bunker at 18 Mila Street. Soon after his death, Hashomer Hazair, of which he was a member, founded a kibbutz, Yad Mordecai, in Palestine in his memory. The kibbutz maintains a museum of the ghetto resistance.

2. "Antek" was the code name of Yitzhak Cukierman (Zuckerman; 1915–1982), a member of the command of the ZOB. During the uprising, he was on an assignment on the Polish side beyond the walls of the ghetto. When the Polish uprising in Warsaw broke out

on August 1, 1944, he led the remnants of the ZOB in the battle. Surviving the war, in 1947 he emigrated to Palestine, where he was a founder of Kibbutz Lohamei Hagetaot (Fighters of the Ghetto). At the Eichmann trial in 1961, he read to the court this letter he received from Anielewicz.

3. Swit was the name of the Polish radio in exile. The Polish underground transmitted news of events in Poland to Swit in London, which in turn broadcast the news back to Poland in Polish, creating the illusion that there was a local radio station of "Free Poland." Swit reported the Warsaw Ghetto uprising.

30. LAST LETTER FROM WARSAW (MARCH 1, 1944)

EMANUEL RINGELBLUM[1]

Dear Friends:[2]   Warsaw, March 1, 1944

We write to you at a time when 95 per cent of the Polish Jews have already died in the throes of horrible tortures in the gas chambers of the annihilation centers in Treblinka, Sobibor, Chelmno, Oswiecim [Auschwitz] or were slaughtered during the numberless "liquidation campaigns" in the ghettos and camps. The fate of the small number of Jews who still vegetate and suffer in the few concentration camps has also already been determined. Perhaps there will survive a small group of Jews who are hidden in the "Aryan districts" in the constant fear of death or who wander through the woods like hunted animals. That any of us, the community workers, who carry on under conditions of twofold secrecy, will outlive the war, we greatly doubt. We, therefore, want to take this means to tell you in brief about those activities which link us most closely to you.

At the moment when the Polish Jews fell under the horrible Hitlerite yoke, the more active elements of the Jewish population began conducting a program of broad scope and with the rallying-call of self-help and struggle. Through the active and generous aid of the American Joint Distribution Committee,[3] a large net of institutions for communal welfare was spread throughout Warsaw and in the country, conducted by the Jewish Society for Social Welfare (ZTOS), the Central Organization for the Protection of Children and Orphans (CENTOS) and the Society for the Protection of the Health of the Jewish Population (TOZ). The ORT,[4] too, carried on considerable work. Tens of thousands of adults and children were able to survive for a longer period because of the help of these institutions and of the ramified network of house committees which cooperated with them. These organizations conducted their self-sacrificing work up to the

Source: Emanuel Ringelblum, Letter to various institutions and communal leaders (cf. note 1, below), dated March 1, 1944, translated from Polish in *Jewish Frontier* 12, no. 2 (February 1945), pp. 14–15. Reprinted by permission of *Jewish Frontier*.

last minute, as long as even the slightest spark of life still burned in the Jewish group. Under their cloak all the political parties and ideological trends conducted their clandestine activities. Under their cover practically all the cultural activities were organized.

The watchword of the organized groups of the Jewish community was "To live with honor and die with honor!" We made every effort to carry out this watchword in the ghettos and concentration camps. An expression thereof was the wide scope of the cultural work which was undertaken notwithstanding the horrible terror, hunger and poverty and which grew and spread until the martyr death of Polish Jewry.

At the time when the Warsaw Ghetto was hermetically sealed, a clandestine cultural organization was formed with the name Jewish Cultural Organization (YIKOR). It conducted broad educational work, organized series of lectures, literary anniversaries (in honor of I. L. Peretz, Sholem Aleikhem, Mendele [Moykher Sforim], Borokhov, etc.) and literary and dramatic programs. The spirit of the YIKOR was the young scholar Menakhem Linder, an economist, murdered by the Germans as early as April 1942.

Under the cloak of the children's kitchen and homes of the CENTOS, a net of underground schools of various ideological trends was spread (CISHO, Tarbut, Shul-Kult, Yavne, Horeb, Beth Jacob, etc.). The secular schools using Yiddish as the language of instruction were particularly active. They were organized by the unforgettable leaders Shakhne Zagan and Sonia Nowogrudzki, both of whom were sent to death in Treblinka.

Clandestine central Jewish archives were formed under the innocent name of *Oneg Shabbat* [Society for the Delight of the Sabbath]. Under the direction of Dr. Emanuel Ringelblum, the founder of the archives, and with the active cooperation of [six names are listed here], the archives amassed materials and documents relating to the martyrology of the Jews in Poland. Thanks to the intensive work of a large staff, tens of crates were collected with extraordinarily valuable documents, diaries, memoirs, reportages, photographs, etc. All of these materials were buried in [...]; we have no access to them. Most of the material sent abroad originates from our archives. We raised a cry to the world with exact information about the greatest crime in history. We are still continuing the archival work. Notwithstanding the terrible conditions we are still collecting memories and documents about

the martyrdom of the Jews, their struggle and the present living conditions of the remnants of the Polish Jews. In 1941 and 1942 we were in contact with [...] in Vilna, who, under [the shadow of] German control classified the materials of the Yiddish Scientific Institute-YIVO[5] and secretly hid a good deal of them. Now there are no more Jews left in Vilna. The great center of Jewish culture and of modern research work has been completely destroyed.

Lively, underground educational activities were conducted by almost all parties and ideological groups, particularly youth organizations. During almost the entire time in which the Ghetto existed, an underground press issued newspapers, journals and miscellaneous volumes. An especially stimulating press was maintained by the following organizations: Jewish Workers Alliance—Bund (*Bulletin, Tsayt-Fragn, Yugnt-Shtime, Za Nasza; Wasza Wolnose, Nowa Mlodziez*), Left-Wing Poalei Zion (*Proletarisher Gedank, Yugnt-Ruf, Avangard, Nasze Hasla*), Hashomer Hazair (*Przedwiosnie, Jutrznia, Oifbroiz* and a number of miscellanies), Dror (*Dror-Yedies, Hamadrikh, Gvure un Payn*), Right-Wing Poalei Zion (*Bafreiung*); the anti-fascist bloc (*Der Ruf*); the Communists (*Morgen Freiheit*) and others. Some of these periodicals published in Warsaw were circulated in all the ghettos, despite the overwhelming contact and communication difficulties.

The center for child welfare, CENTOS, conducted many cultural activities among the great masses of children and youth under the leadership of [...] and the unforgettable Rosa Sinchowicz (who died of typhus which she caught during her work among the street urchins). Hundreds of children's projects in boarding schools, nurseries and clubs were undertaken with the assistance of a group of teachers, educators and artists. A central library for children was created under the direction of [...] and a theatre under the leadership of [...] with the cooperation of [four names are given]. Courses were given in the Yiddish language and literature. Especially impressive were the cultural and artistic performances given during the "Children's Month," when the audience, consisting of thousands of weary spectators, came to spend a few carefree hours with the children and thus, for a short time, escape from the nightmare of reality. Hundreds of children from the CENTOS homes and from the schools participated in these performances which rose to a high artistic level.

Today there are no more Jewish children in Poland! Ninety-nine percent of them were murdered by the Hitler criminals.

Within the Ghetto, a symphony orchestra was formed, conducted by Szymon Pullman. Beautiful symphonic and chamber music concerts were given, bringing moments of rest and oblivion. Pullman and almost all the other members of the orchestra, including the first violinist, Ludwig Holzman, were put to death in Treblinka. The young concert master, Marian Neeteich, was slaughtered in the camp of Trawniki. New young talents sprang to the fore and expressed themselves in the ghetto. The phenomenal young singer Maryla Eisenstadt, the "nightingale of the Ghetto," shone like a meteor; she was the daughter of the conductor of the synagogue at Tlomackie Street in Warsaw. She was killed by the SS men during the liquidation action. Excellent choral groups were formed; the children's choir, led by J. Fevishis, was a great success; Fevishis was killed in the camp of Poniatow. Other choir leaders like Gladstein Zaks were murdered in Treblinka. The Jewish artists and sculptors who lived in dire need occasionally displayed their masterpieces; Felix Friedman was one of the organizers of these exhibits. All the Jewish sculptors were sent to Treblinka, where they were put to death.

Our social and cultural committee kept on with its vital work even in the concentration camps of the SS where a certain number of Jews from Warsaw and other cities were deported. It was not discontinued. Its members stood at their posts and served the people. Underground self-help committees arose in Trawniki, Poniatow and other camps. From time to time, secret cultural projects, entertainments, etc., were carried out. Communal and cultural work persisted as long as life pulsated in the Jewish collectivity. Remember that our workers were ever faithful to the ideals of our culture until their dying moments. The flag of culture and of struggle with barbarism was clenched in their hands until death.

When the period of murderous deportations began, the slogan of self-help was abandoned for the idea of active resistance. Our youth of all the movements, especially of the pro-Palestine organizations, revealed its indomitable courage; it was the onset of the colossal epic by the armed Jewish battle in Poland; the heroic defense of the Warsaw Ghetto, the illustrious battle in Bialystok, the destruction of the extermination dens in Treblinka and Sobibor, the battles in Tarnow, Bendzin, Czestochowa and other places. The Jews showed the world that they could fight, weapon in hand, that they know how to die honorably in the battle against the deadly enemy of the Jewish nation and of all humanity.

This is all we wanted to tell you, dear friends. Not many of us survived. Among the writers […] live, write and work with us [Here ten names are given. Then follow three names of well-known writers who were transported beyond the Polish border by the Germans.] We do not know whether or not they are alive. The International Red Cross cares for them. A list of the members of the Culture Committee who were killed is enclosed.

Whether we shall have the opportunity to meet with you is doubtful. To all the workers for Jewish culture, writers, journalists, musicians, sculptors and all the contributors to modern Jewish culture and fighters for national liberation and the cause of mankind, we send our warmest greetings.

Dr. E. Ringelblum

NOTES

1. Emanuel Ringelblum (1900–1944) is known as the "historian of the Warsaw Ghetto." A university-trained historian, he taught at a Jewish high school in Warsaw while publishing articles on Jewish history. Soon after the establishment of the Warsaw Ghetto, he established a secret historical and literary society under the code name *Oneg Shabbat* (Sabbath Delight), a Hebrew term designating a Sabbath cultural gathering; Ringelblum's society would meet on the Sabbath. The society also maintained secret archives chronicling the life and martyrdom of Polish Jewry under the German occupation. These archives, hidden in several places in Warsaw, were discovered after the war; they constitute the most extensive documentary source about Jewish life in Poland during the Holocaust.

    The letter reprinted here, dated March 1, 1944, was received by the YIVO (cf. note 5, below) through the good offices of the Ministry of the Interior of the Polish Government in Exile, then seated in London. The letter, written in Polish government code, was signed by Ringelblum and one of his associates. Ringeblum, who had escaped the ghetto and lived in a hideout in the "Aryan" section of Warsaw, was killed on March 6, 1944—five days after posting the letter—along with 35 others when the Nazis discovered their clandestine abode.

2. The letter was addressed to YIVO, the Yiddish PEN Club, the Yiddish writers Sholem Asch (1880–1957), Haim Leivick (1886–1962), Joseph Opatoshu (1886–1954) and the historian Raphael Mahler (1899–1977), each of whom then resided in the United States.

3. The American Joint Distribution Committee (popularly known as the "Joint" or JDC) was created in 1914 to extend relief and rehabilitation services to Jews throughout the world in distress. The committee was founded "jointly" by the American Jewish Committee, several Reform, Orthodox Jewish groups, Jewish labor elements, and socialist organizations.

4. ORT (initials of Russian: *Obshtchestvo Remeslenovo Truda*: "Society for the Encouragement of Handicrafts") was founded in Russia in 1880 at the initiative of several Jewish leaders to provide Jews with skilled trades and agricultural knowhow. To this end it established a network of vocational school and cooperative workshops in Russia and, after World War I, elsewhere in Eastern and Central Europe. In 1933 the head office of the organization moved from Berlin to Paris, and thence to Geneva in 1943.

5. YIVO (initials of Yiddish: *Yidisher Visenshaftlikher Institut*, or Institute for Jewish Research) was founded at a conference of Jewish scholars and social scientists that took place in Berlin in August 1925. Vilna was selected as the center of this society devoted to promoting the scientific study of Jewry throughout the world, with particular emphasis on Eastern European and Yiddish-speaking Jewry. By the beginning of World War II more than thirty branches of YIVO had been established throughout the world. Ringelblum was a leading member of the Warsaw branch. When the Nazis occupied Vilna in 1940, the New York branch assumed the role of the central office of the institute. See chapter 5, document 13.

31. THE JEWISH RESIDENTIAL AREA OF WARSAW IS NO MORE (MAY 16, 1943)

JUERGEN STROOP[1]

The number of Jews taken out of the buildings and arrested was relatively small during the first days [of the operation against the Warsaw Ghetto]. It transpired that the Jews had taken to hiding in the sewers and in specially erected dug-outs. Whereas we had assumed during the first days that there were only scattered dug-outs it transpired in the course of the large-scale action that the whole Ghetto was systematically equipped with cellars, dug-outs and passages. In every case these passages and dug-outs were connected with the sewer system. Thus, the Jews were able to maintain undisturbed subterranean traffic.... Through posters, handbills and whisper propaganda, the communistic resistance movement in the former Jewish residential area brought it about that the Jews entered the dug-outs as soon as the large-scale operation started. How providently the Jews had worked can be seen from the fact that the dug-outs had been skillfully installed and equipped with furnishings for entire families, washing and bathing facilities, toilets, arms and munition stores, and large food supplies for several months. There were special

Source: The Report of Juergen Stroop Concerning the Uprising in the Ghetto of Warsaw and the Liquidation of the Jewish Residential Area, ed., B. Mark, trans., B. Dabrowaka (Warsaw: Jewish Historical Institute, 1958), pp. 22–26. Reprinted by permission of Jewish Historical Institute.

dug-outs for rich and for poor Jews. To discover the individual dug-outs was exceedingly difficult for the acting forces, as they had been camouflaged, and in many cases it was possible only through betrayal on the part of the Jews.

Just after the first days it became apparent that the Jews no longer had any intention to resettle voluntarily,[2] but were determined to defend themselves by all means and by using all weapons at their disposal. So-called battle groups had been formed, under Polish and Bolshevistic leadership; they were armed and paid any price asked for available arms.

During the large-scale action we succeeded in catching some Jews who had already been evacuated to Lublin or Treblinka, but had broken out from there and returned to the Ghetto, equipped with arms and ammunition. Time and again Polish bandits found refuge in the Ghetto and remained there almost undisturbed, since we disposed of no forces to penetrate into this maze. Whereas it had first been possible to catch considerable numbers of Jews, who are cowards by nature, it became more difficult during the second half of the large scale action to capture the bandits and Jews. Over and over again battle groups, consisting of 20 to 30 or more Jewish fellows, 18 to 25 years of age, accompanied by a corresponding number of women, kindled new resistance. These battle groups were under orders to put up armed resistance to the last and if necessary to escape arrest by committing suicide. One such battle group (about 30 to 35 bandits) succeeded in mounting a truck by ascending from a sewer hole in the so-called Prosta [street on the Aryan side of the city] and in escaping with it. One bandit who had arrived with this truck exploded two hand grenades, which was the signal for the bandits waiting in the sewer to climb out of it. The bandits and the Jews— there were over and over again Polish bandits among them armed with carbines, firing hand arms and one light machine gun— mounted the truck and drove away in an unknown direction....

During this armed resistance the women belonging to the battle groups were equipped the same as the men; some were members of the Haluzim movement.[3] Not infrequently, these women fired pistols with both hands. It happened time and again that they had pistols or hand grenades (Polish "pineapple" hand grenades) concealed in their bloomers up to the last moment to use them afterwards against the men of the Waffen-SS, Police and Wehrmacht.

The resistance put up by the Jews and bandits could be broken only by energetically and relentlessly using our raiding parties by day and night....I therefore decided to destroy completely the Jewish residential area by setting every block on fire, including the blocks of residential buildings belonging to the armament works. One factory after the other was systematically evacuated and subsequently destroyed by fire. The Jews then emerged from their hiding places and dug-outs in almost every case. Not infrequently, the Jews stayed in the burning buildings until, because of the heat and the fear of being burned to death, they preferred to jump down from the upper stories after having thrown mattresses and other upholstered articles into the street from the burning buildings. With their bones broken, they still tried to crawl across the street into blocks of buildings which had not yet been set on fire or were only partly in flames. Often Jews changed their hiding places during the night, by moving into the ruins of burnt-out buildings, taking refuge there until they were found by our raiding parties. Their stay in the sewers also ceased to be pleasant after the first eight days. Frequently from the street, we could hear loud voices coming through the sewer shafts. Then the men of the Waffen-SS, the Police or the Wehrmacht Engineers courageously climbed down the shafts to bring out the Jews, and not infrequently they then stumbled over Jews already dead, or were shot at. It was always necessary to use smoke candles to drive out the Jews. Thus one day we opened 183 sewer entrance holes and at a fixed time lowered smoke candles into them, with the result that the bandits fled from what they believed to be gas to the center of the former Jewish residential area, where they could then be pulled out of the sewer holes there. A great number of Jews who could not be counted, were finished in the sewers and dug-outs by blowing them up.

The longer the resistance lasted, the tougher the men of Waffen-SS, Police and Wehrmacht became; here, too, they fulfilled their duty indefatigably in faithful comradeship and [fought] as model and exemplary soldiers. The work often lasted from early morning until late at night. At night, search patrols with rags wound round their feet remained at the heels of the Jews and gave them no respite. Not infrequently they caught and killed Jews who used the night for supplementing their stores from abandoned dug-outs or for contacting neighboring groups, exchanging news with them. . . .

Only through the continuous and untiring work of all forces we succeeded in catching a total of 56,065 Jews whose extermination can be proved. To this figure should be added the number of Jews who lost their lives in explosions, fires and so on, but whose numbers could not be ascertained. . . .

The Polish population for the most part approved the measures taken against the Jews. Shortly before the end of the large-scale operation, the Governor [General of Poland] issued a special proclamation which he submitted to the undersigned for approval before publication, to the Polish population; in it he informed them of the reasons for destroying the former Jewish residential area. . . . .

The large-scale action was terminated on May 16, 1943 with the blowing up of the Warsaw synagogue at 20:15 hours.[4] . . .

NOTES

1. Juergen Stroop (1895–1951), SS general who was dispatched to Warsaw on April 19, 1943, to crush the ghetto revolt. After the war he was extradited to Poland, where he was sentenced and hanged for his criminal actions in suppressing the Warsaw Ghetto uprising.

   German forces entered Warsaw on September 29, 1939. On October 2, 1940 an area of approximately 840 acres was designated as the Jewish ghetto. Within six weeks all Jews residing in Warsaw were to move into the ghetto, while the Aryan inhabitants of the designated area had to leave. Initially some 400,000 Jews lived within the ghetto. With the influx of refugees from the provinces of Poland, the ghetto population reached 500,000. Mass deportations to the Treblinka death camp started on July 21, 1942. Between July and September 13, 1942, the ghetto population was reduced to an estimated 60,000 Jews. In the meantime, the Jewish Fighting Organization was established to prepare for armed resistance (see document 26 in this chapter). On January 18, 1943, the Nazis began a second wave of deportations. They were met with armed resistance, which led to four days of street fighting. The deportations were suspended, but on April 19, 1943, a German force equipped with tanks and artillery entered the ghetto in order to resume the deportations. Again, armed resistance thwarted their plan of action. General Stroop took over the command of the German forces and ordered his troops to avoid further street combat with the Jews. Instead, he planned systematically to burn down the ghetto and gas and flood the sewers, which the Jewish fighters used as bunkers. Major resistance continued until May 8, 1943, although sporadic resistance actually lasted until May 16, when Stroop issued the report reproduced here to his superiors. The title introducing this document is taken from the subtitle Stroop gave his report.

2. After the suspension of forced deportations in January 1943, the Nazis tried to carry out their objectives through "peaceful" means, namely, by voluntary registration for alleged labor camps in the East.

3. Haluz movement, the Zionist movement promoting pioneering settlements in Palestine.

4. To celebrate his victorious suppression of Jewish resistance Stroop blew up the Great Synagogue of Warsaw.

32. GOING UNDERGROUND IN HOLLAND[1]

MAX M. ROTHSCHILD

My own decision to go into hiding came in the course of an afternoon in August of 1942. It must have been a Sunday, for my farmer would not have given me half a day off otherwise. Shushu[2] arrived early in the afternoon. It was still possible for a Jew with good identity papers to use a train. We started to go for a walk, just the two of us, since we didn't want anybody else to share our secret concerning what action to take. Shushu told me that he had come to visit his old farmer, where he had worked for a few months immediately after our arrival in Holland, fresh from Buchenwald. He would, so he said, ask this former boss of his whether he could go into hiding on his homestead. Shushu was also looking around in the neighborhood for other hiding places for many youngsters from Loosdrecht, a Youth Aliyah training center where he worked at the time. Some of those children had already been placed.

Shushu was quite secretive during that part of our conversation. When I pressed him for details, he said that he had just listened to the BBC, and for a few days in a row their official lines had been that the war would be over in three to four months at most. For that reason, he said, it would be much wiser not to report for "harvest help" but to go into hiding right away. We should prepare ourselves for the work of rebuilding the Zionist youth movement after the collapse of Germany which, according to the British broadcasts, was just around the corner.

Large-scale deportations had already begun from Amsterdam, but not even he himself was aware that these transports were anything but roundups for help in the harvest, perhaps as far away as in Germany itself, which of course was short of manpower. What's the sense of risking our lives in Allied bombardments, which now occurred on a daily basis, he argued.

Shushu's reasoning sounded plausible to me. He influenced me decisively during that afternoon's conversation, our last one. I made up my mind then and there not to report for the work camp should the call-up arrive.

I started immediately to contact my Dutch friends. One of our friends, H. te Riet, gave me a promise that very evening that he would help me when the time came. He would not tell me with whom I would hide, nor where, nor under what circumstances. My first concern—again a reflection of our shortsightedness and total lack of information—was money! I had perhaps fifty Dutch guilders saved up, sufficient for about three to four weeks of food supplies, and I had some clothes and books in a big trunk. I started figuring our how much their sale would bring in to sustain me. If I would stretch it and eat very little, perhaps even if I could do some clandestine work, I might get through those coming three to four months until liberation time! He said not to worry. Money was not the big question—and, as it turned out, he was right. The main thing was to disappear right now, and not to answer the call-up.

Two weeks after that memorable last walk with Shushu, I received the official notice in the mail: you must report for harvest help in a labor camp. By that time I had already made all my preparations. I cannot stress often enough that at the time, nobody, not even the worst pessimist, had any inkling about the true nature of the deportations, or the so-called "harvest help." This was truly the fault of Allied intelligence.

What grieves me sometimes is the total lack of understanding of the motivations of those of my many friends who, at that time in the very early stage of the deportations, resolved to obey the German call. I remember so many of them. I recall the conversations we had, the arguments back and forth.

Source: Max M. Rothschild, unpublished memoirs. All the notes but the first are by Max Rothschild.

Where are they now, those dear ones, who tried to convince me and others like me that we, as *chalutzim*[3], had a special task towards our Jewish people, that we would have to set an example, that we ought to impress the Germans with our will to work, our ability to do physical labor, and that we should show them our skill as farmhands. Above all, however, their argument was that we ought to go along for the harvest in order to support the elderly and the sick. Yes, that idea to help the weak while we were still young and strong, and well fed because of our stay at the farm—all of these thoughts moved quite a number of our group, and certain many others as well, to obey the German orders! I bow my head even today when I think of those good people, boys and girls who were highly motivated. They were greater heroes than many of us. My heart aches for them. They were so young, so idealistic. Where, where was Allied intelligence then? Where was the Jewish Agency? One word from the BBC, one word from our leaders who by now were in safe lands, would have sufficed to save those beautiful people. They would all have gone into hiding and most of them would have survived, just as we did. Instead, the BBC continued to speak of an early end to the war, and it would intersperse this political wisdom with reports of the Shakespeare festival somewhere in August of 1942! Even if those authorities in England did not yet know the true meaning of Auschwitz, they could at least have warned us not to go voluntarily to the German labor camps, not to participate in their "resettlement" programs, not to help with their harvest. All they had to do—as they indeed did later on—was to declare it a crime to cooperate with the enemy, and many more of us would have been convinced that going into hiding was the right thing to do.

Half a year later, the decision was no longer one to be made. It became purely academic. The die was cast, and even the most idealistic among us would not go out of their free will to a labor camp to help the old and the weak. By that time, word had already gotten around about the true nature of Auschwitz, the real meaning of "harvest help." And surely everybody by that time saw that the war was going to last quite a bit longer than the BBC had predicted.

I felt apologetic, especially towards those of our group who had so steadfastly considerd it their moral and Zionist duty to help other Jews; I felt uneasy in the family of farmer Gast when arguments about obedience to the Germans went back and forth. To my boss, resistance people and those who went into hiding were outlaws who made it bad for all the other Hollanders and who caused the Germans to issue ever-stricter regulations week after week. When some of the brave guerillas were sentenced to the firing squad, Gast would say that they got what they had coming to them. It was stupid enough of me, up to the very last moment of leave-taking from the Gast family to take an opposite view in those discussions. Looking at the situation in retrospect, my attitude seems to me unforgivable. I could never know whether my farmer wouldn't actually betray me to the authorities for planning to go into hiding, or at least engage in loose talk about me. And not only about myself, but about a number of my Dutch contacts who came to visit me on the farm during those last critical weeks. How easy it would have been for Gast just to mention the names of those who had come to visit me! Yes, instead of keeping my mouth shut, I had said several times during the family meals that, if I were to receive the call-up, I would surely not go. The boss would then get annoyed with me and point out that Gerd who was a *chulutz* on the farm of the boss's father and brothers, would of course go, because he was a good and law-abiding fellow. Gerd was indeed a good soul. I prayed many times that he and his friend would be able to give each other support and go to their death in dignity.

In early August of 1942, during those last weeks of my stay at the farmer's, the reports of razzias[4] and call-ups for labor camps increased by the day. I made my preparations. Everything had to be done during daylight, unfortunately, because there was already a curfew in force for us Jews after nightfall. In addition, we had to turn in our bicycles. Rumors, radio, messages, all kinds of stories filled the air in that intensely charged period of 1942. But, in the last analysis, we were terribly alone, alone with our decision to go underground, and we could not reveal that decision to our friends, except a very few. What family was there for us to lean on? I do not think that I ever felt as lonesome as during those few days preceding my going into hiding.

And then the feared notice arrived in the mail, just a mimeographed slip sent first class, forwarded, if I am not mistaken, by the Dutch police, and ordering me, with my name typed in, to report for harvest help in a certain place. I had to appear the day after receipt of the notice. How bizarre—you receive your death notice on a mimeographed slip in the mail. If I remember well, that reporting place, a collection center for our part of Holland, was quite a distance away from Almelo. It seems that the Germans expected us to walk there on foot, some 30 or 40 miles! It takes a convicted murderer in the United States a dozen years of appeals and injunctions to be, perhaps, finally executed. For us it was an order, delivered by the mailman, and mimeographed at that....

When I received my notice, I did another of my foolish things. I became so furious that I tore it in two or three pieces, put it back in the envelope, sealed it and put the return address on it! I walked to the mailbox half a mile from the farm during the noon meal, and I sacrificed a few pennies for the stamp to be able to feel some sort of victory. Nothing could have been more stupid, or more frivolous, of course. Others had received their "slips" and either answered them, or applied for a postponement, or just ignored it and went into hiding. Again, as I look back upon my attitude at that time, I did not understand in the slightest the true nature of the catastrophe. I approached the situation, so to speak, with an air of "normalcy," as though I were arguing with the proper authorities for a bicycle license or some extra food coupons. I did not dispute the authority of the government at all, as though I were merely arguing with them about their mistakes, their bureaucratic inanity. Then, adding frivolity to foolishness, I told the farmer's family that I had indeed received my slip but that I had absolutely no intention to answer the call-up and that I would go into hiding the next day! As expected, they strongly disapproved. You have to obey the law, they said, and now especially, and it was no wonder that the Jews were hated by the Germans because they always tried their own tricks to slip out from under the law.... G.,[5] in father's farm, would never do such a thing.

I was lucky that they did not betray me, or that the children did not babble to their friends about my plans. I asked for my big trunk to be kept by them, gave them a few of my belongings (my good bike they had already appropriated and turned an old one in as ordered); I took a small handbag and said goodbye. I walked through the fields on that beautiful August day—it was the sixteenth—but I did so with a heavy heart and close to tears—something I had to try to camouflage by my brashness with the farmer's family. I wore several layers of clothes, sweating profusely,

My Jewish star, I was sure of it, protected me. If I were stopped I could always say that I was en route to follow the call-up.

A young fellow waited at a crossroads. He said goodbye to me, and repeated last-minute instructions. I had fifty guilders on me. That would surely be enough to last me through the few remaining weeks of the war.

It was that night that things began to dawn upon me in all their seriousness. H. and I bicycled back to Almelo.[6]

The house where he deposited me that night stood in a section of Almelo which I had not known before. My new host was a middle-aged, single man, somewhat evasive about his occupation, but fiercely anti-German. He put me up in the attic. There were a few small cubicles there, each with a bed. My own bed was full of stains, about whose origins there could be little doubt....

The main danger here was noise, extra noise made by myself as an additional resident, because the house was attached on both sides to neighboring dwellings of exactly the same construction, with very thin dividing walls separating them. Even flushing the toilet was a problem. Mr. F., my new host, taught me to cook vegetables. He went out a great deal, including one long weekend. That, I remember, was a particularly difficult time, not only because of my loneliness, but because I had to keep absolutely quiet, since the neighbors had seen F. go out. They might have suspected a burglar, had they heard anything unusual, and of course, if the police had come to investigate, it would have been the end. But somehow I did manage. When F. returned, we both agreed that my stay in his house could only be temporary. F. was very good about it, though. He wanted to help me, a total stranger. When I offered him the few guilders I had on me, he refused and actually was a bit offended. H. had not taken my money either. So, once again I thought I would be able to manage for the few weeks until war's end. In the meantime, I gave F. a note for E. V. in Almelo, my central contact, following my original instructions. I briefly described my situation, and shortly afterwards F. brought a note back from her in which she praised me for not having panicked in a situation which had not exactly worked out as planned. Here was already the beginning of an organization of underground work. Friends would soon come and pick me up, but first they would have to find a more permanent hiding place for me. Also, E. said in the note, it did not look as though the war would be over so soon after all!

When we got to the B.'s house, I found a fellow *chalutz* there, one of my buddies! I had no idea that he had gone into hiding. He had just arrived at the B.'s place through his own contacts, and neither of us had known the B. family. How could we, anyway? They lived in one of a hundred little semi-detached houses, which a former progressive Dutch government had built for working people before the war. G.S. and I were together in the attic room of the B.'s house for close to two years.

A strange thing happened after we settled down in that attic. We began to feel free, free at last. I remember that this was my first notation in a diary which—stupidly and without regard to safety considerations—I had begun at the time. "For the first time I feel free!" Free from the farmer, free from the constant fear of a call-up, free from all the small and large pressures and uncertainties of my everyday life as farmhand or Palestinian-trainee. I know that this will sound again paradoxical, but I also know today as though it were but yesterday, that these were my true feelings at that time. Finally, at long last, having made my decision to go into hiding, not being pushed around any longer, finally I felt free. This no Nazis could take away from me. I had made my choice. It was my decision, and nobody else's, not to go to a work camp to help with the harvest. Even when it dawned upon me the next day that the troubles had only begun, that there was always the chance of being betrayed, always the threat of sweeping razzias, I felt free at last.

By the time G. and I were down to our routine in the hiding place of the B. family, i.e., toward the end of September 1942, the deportations and call-ups were in full swing. Going into hiding was no longer something extraordinary by that time, as we heard from our visitors, who told us who among people we knew, had "disappeared." Unfortunately, for some the decision had been made too late. For that, I place such blame on the Allied information program. We were lucky—and this is a very important point to consider—that we were young in the first place, and that we lived in the country and not in Amsterdam where chances to hide were much more limited. In addition, it had become quite obvious by September that the war would not be over so quickly,

and that the "harvest help" was actually something much more serious, although nobody had as yet any inkling about the true nature of those camps. In our thoughts we would compare it to earlier experiences, such as Buchenwald in 1938, and the individual razzias later on.

So—our life began to become routine. We had to be absolutely silent, of course, in the little worker's house that looked like all the others, attached so closely on both sides that you could hear the neighbors snoring. At first, the B.'s were not sure whether those neighbors could be trusted, and so we took great pains not to raise our voices above a whisper. Our friends would visit us mostly after dark. Going outside was out of the question during the first months. When we wanted to air our room, we would lie on the floor with the windows open, so that we could not be seen from across the street. If we wanted to look outside, the curtains had to be tightly shut. One day I stared into the street and saw an old Jew, a gentlemen I had known before, wandering about aimlessly, his big yellow star on his overcoat. He wept as he crossed in front of our house. Our hosts told us that all his children and grandchildren had followed the call-up, their house had been confiscated, and now he had no place to go, waiting to be picked up himself by the Germans. Nobody would take that old man into his home as a hideaway. It was bitter for G. and me to see this fellow Jew so totally lost, and we were not able to do anything for him.

Food was brought upstairs to us at set times. We would do some light chores in between reading, such as peeling potatoes, cleaning vegetables, disentangling wool. Of course we had to be constantly on the lookout for German soldiers and police, and listen for unfamiliar noises. I suffered particularly from the frequent air raid alerts, which made me terribly nervous. It so happened that Almelo and surroundings were situated on the main bombing route between England and the Northwestern German industrial area. This corridor was also used quite often for diversionary tactics. As time went on, we became accustomed to the deep, humming noise in the evening, which grew louder and louder until the German flak [anti-aircraft guns] which were placed in residential locations all around us, began to pop off. As the war progressed, the Allied planes flew over our houses during daylight as well. Now and then, after a big explosion, we would see an allied airman slowly drifting down, hanging in his parachute. We would peek out from behind our curtains to watch him sway back and forth, and we would pray that his legs would not freeze.

Those overflights were scary. On the other hand they gave us a great morale boost, notwithstanding the facts that now and then a miss would occur. After all, Almelo was so close to the German border that an occasional bomb released a few seconds too soon would hit a Dutch dwelling. This we dreaded at least as much as we feared the German roundups and searches. Mom's[7] hiding place in the home of Miss V. was damaged in that fashion, and she had to leave in a hurry. In the nearby town of Hengelo a number of people in hiding were caught as they ran from the ruins of their houses, which had been hit by mistake.

Rumors were the order of the day during all the years of the years of the war. We lived on rumors, we cultivated them, they were food for our soul. A few people still had access to a radio and could listen to the BBC clandestinely. This was of course a capital offense, and those who were caught were usually shot on the spot. At least the Germans threatened it. All of this has been described in the many war stories, and I need not elaborate on it here. What concerned us, however, was the news about the fate of Jewish deportees and all those who had responded to the call-ups. Reports about the camps in the East became more and more frightful. After several months of hiding away in our shelter at the B. home, we, finally knew the truth. But it took at least a full year for this truth to be disseminated over the BBC. We had then no illusions left anymore. Now and then, during a moment of utter misery, we would ask ourselves whether it was fair to impose upon good people such as our various helpers when all that was involved for us was a few months of hard labor in a work camp. But these feelings were now stilled, once and for all. I knew then that I had done the right thing in every respect by going underground.

NOTES

1. Max Michael Rothschild, Ph.D., was born in Gunzenhausen, Germany, in 1921 and grew up in a religious Zionist home. Following Kristallnacht in 1938, he was sent to Buchenwald and was released after six weeks when he received a permit to enter Holland as a member of a Zionist youth group ultimately headed for Palestine. Unable to get a certificate to Palestine, he was trapped in Holland when the Nazis entered in May 1940. He escaped capture and deportation by going into hiding as an *Onderdiker*—literally someone who "dives under" to disappear. He initially hid in farming villages, then in Amsterdam, and finally in Rotterdam. During the final year of the war, he joined the resistance movement and operated a clandestine printing press. He spent one year after the war in Holland and then moved to the United States where he worked for the United Synagogue of America and served numerous congregations as a rabbi.

2. Shushu is the nickname of Joachim Simon, a German Jewish refugee in his early twenties, who had been in the Zionist youth movement in Germany with Max Rothschild and was later imprisoned with him in Buchenwald after Kristallnacht. Once they escaped to Holland, Shushu joined the underground group of Joop Westerweel, a Dutch Gentile. Together these two extraordinary men saved Dutch Jews by smuggling them over the French border and on to neutral Spain. Both Westerweel and Simon were caught. Westerweel was executed in the concentration camp of Vught, Holland, and Simon took his own life in a Dutch prison in the city of Breda. Because of his underground activities, Shushu understood the dangers facing the Jews of Holland and tried to persuade them to go into hiding rather than cooperate with the German call-up for assistance with the harvest.

3. *Chalutzim* (Hebrew: pioneers)—Jewish youth throughout the world who were trained to work in pioneer settlements in Palestine. Some Jews were trained on collective farms established by Zionist youth movements; others were placed as individual laborers on Dutch farms; in his case, Max Rothschild was placed with a farmer named Gast.

4. Razzias—raids by the Dutch police or the Nazis, designed to round up Jews in the particular areas, especially those in hiding.

5. "G" refers to Gerd, a friend of Max Rothschild, who was placed on another farm.

6. Almelo is a Dutch town, surrounded by farms, close to the German border.

7. Mom is Ilse Strauss, later Rothschild.

33. BERMUDA CONFERENCE JOINT COMMUNIQUÉ (MAY 1, 1943)[1]

The United States and United Kingdom delegates examined the refugee problem in all its aspects including the position of those potential refugees who are still in the grip of the Axis powers without any immediate prospect of escape. Nothing was excluded from their analysis and everything that held out any possibility, however remote, of a solution of the problem was carefully investigated and thoroughly discussed. From the outset it was realized that any recommendation that the delegates could make to their governments must pass two tests: Would any recommendation submitted interfere with or delay the war effort of the United Nations and was the recommendation capable of accomplishment under war conditions? The delegates at Bermuda felt bound to reject certain proposals which were not capable of meeting these tests. The delegates were able to agree on a number of concrete recommendations which they are jointly submitting to their governments and which, it is felt, will pass the tests set forth above and will lead to the relief of a substantial number of refugees of all races and nationalities. Since the recommendations necessarily concern governments other than those represented at the Bermuda conference and involve military considerations, they must remain confidential. It may be said, however, that in the course of discussion the refugee problem was broken down into its main elements. Questions of shipping, food, and supply were fully investigated. The delegates also agreed on recommendations regarding the form of intergovernmental organization which was best fitted, in their opinion, to handle the problem in the future. This organization would have to be flexible enough to permit it to consider without prejudice any new factors that might come to its attention. In each of these fields the delegates were able to submit agreed proposals for consideration of their respective governments.

NOTE

1. As word of the concentration and extermination camps reached the outside world, there was a mounting cry that the Allied governments should work against the diabolical scheme of the Nazis. Under pressure from Jewish organizations, parliaments, churches, and humanitarian groups, the British Foreign Office, on January 20, 1943, proposed a joint consultation between Britain and the United States to examine the problem and discuss possible solutions. The ensuant Anglo-American Conference on Refugees was held in Bermuda from April 19 to April 30, 1943. The only positive decision of the conference was to extend the mandate of the Inter-Governmental Committee on Refugees, set up at the Evian Conference of 1938 to organize the emigration and settlement of refugees from Nazi persecution. But clearly the problem was no longer one of refugees. See this chapter, document 24, note 1.

Source: *Department of State Bulletin* (Washington, D.C.), May 1, 1943.

34. WHERE IS THE WORLD'S CONSCIENCE?
(JUNE 1943)

SHMUEL ZYGELBOYM[1]

I take the liberty of addressing to you my last words and through you the Polish government and people of the Allied States and the conscience of the world.

From the latest information received from Poland, it is evident that without doubt the Germans with ruthless cruelty are now murdering the few remaining Jews in Poland. Behind the walls of the ghettos the last act of a tragedy unprecedented in history is being performed.

The responsibility for the crime of murdering all the Jewish population in Poland falls in the first instance on the perpetrators, but indirectly also it weighs on the whole of humanity, the peoples and governments of the Allied States which so far have made no effort toward a concrete action for the purpose of curtailing the crime. By passive observation of this murder of defenseless millions and the maltreatment of children and women, the men of those countries have become accomplices of criminals.

I have also to state that although the Polish government [in exile] has in a high degree contributed to stirring the opinion of the world, yet it did so insufficiently, for it did nothing extraordinary enough to correspond to the magnitude of the drama now being enacted in Poland.

Out of nearly 350,000 Polish Jews and about 700,000 Jews deported to Poland from other countries, there still lived in April of this year, according to the official information of the head of the underground Bund organization sent to the United States through a delegate of the government, about 300,000. And the murders are still going on incessantly.

I cannot be silent and I cannot live while the remnants of the Jewish people of Poland, of whom I am representative, are perishing.

My comrades in the Warsaw Ghetto perished with weapons in their hands in their last heroic impulse.

It was not my destiny to perish as they did together with them but I belong to them and their mass graves.

By my death, I wish to express my strongest protest against the inactivity with which the world is looking on and permitting the extermination of Jewish people. I know how little human life is worth, especially today. But as I was unable to do anything during my life, perhaps by my death I shall contribute to destroying the indifference of those who are able and should act in order to save now, maybe at the last moment, this handful of Polish Jews who are still alive from certain annihilation.

My life belongs to the Jewish people in Poland and therefore I give it to them. I wish that this handful that remains of the several million Polish Jews could live to see with the Polish masses the day of liberation—that it could breathe in Poland and in a world of freedom and in the justice of socialism in return for all its tortures and inhuman sufferings. And I believe that such a Poland will arise and that such a world will come.

I trust that the President and the Prime Minister [of Poland] will direct my words to all those for whom they are destined and that the Polish government will immediately begin appropriate action in the diplomatic and propaganda fields in order to save from extermination the Polish Jews who are still alive.

I bid farewell to all and everything dear to me and loved by me.

Source: Shmuel Zygelboym to the President and the Premier of the Polish Government-in-Exile, *New York Times*, June 4, 1943. Copyright 1943 by the New York Times Company. Reprinted by permission.

NOTE

1. Shmuel Zygelboym (1895–1943), a leader of the Polish Bund (the General Jewish Workers' Union). When the Germans entered Warsaw and demanded from the mayor twelve hostages, Zygelboym volunteered to be one of these hostages. He was later appointed to represent the Bund on Warsaw's *Judenrat*, the Jewish council established by the Nazis. In January 1940, he managed to escape Poland in order to report to the executive council of the Socialist International in Brussels on the conditions of German-occupied Poland. From there he reached the United States. From the spring of 1942 he resided in London, where he was the Bund's representative at the national council of the Polish government-in-exile. Zygelboym received information about the Nazi program for a Final Solution and implored the Polish, British, and other authorities to take retaliatory and rescue action. He was profoundly depressed by the irresoluteness of the Anglo-American Conference on Refugees, held in Bermuda on April 19–30, 1943, and by the brutal suppression of the Warsaw Ghetto revolt. As a protest to the world's indifference to the sufferings of his people, Zygelboym committed suicide on May 11, 1943. The letter he left in explanation is reprinted here.

35. A SECRET SPEECH ON THE JEWISH QUESTION (OCTOBER 8, 1943)[1]

HEINRICH HIMMLER

May I now, in this most intimate circle, touch upon a question which all of you, members of the Party, have accepted as self-evident, but which for me has become the hardest question of my life: The question of the Jews. You will accept it as self-evident and gratifying that in your districts there are no Jews any more. All German people—a few exceptions notwithstanding—have also understood that we could not have endured the Allied bombardment, nor the hardships of the fourth—and, perhaps, the coming fifth and sixth—year of war with this destructive pestilence still in the body of our people. The sentence, "The Jews must be exterminated," is a short one, gentlemen, and is easily said. For the person who has to execute what this sentence implies, however, it is the most difficult and hardest thing in the world. Look, of course they are Jews, it is quite clear, they are only Jews, but consider how many people—members of the Party as well—have sent their famous petitions to me or to the authorities, declaring that all Jews, naturally, were pigs, but that so-and-so was a decent Jew and should not be touched. I dare say that, according to the number of petitions and opinions expressed in private, there were more decent Jews in Germany than the number of Jews that actually were to be found in the entire country. In Germany we have so many millions of people who have their famous decent Jew....I am only saying this because, from your own experience within your districts, you will have learned that respectable and decent National Socialist people all know their decent Jews.

Source: Bradley R. Smith and Agnes F. Peterson, eds., *Heinrich Himmler, Geheimreden, 1933 bis 1945 und andere Ansprachen* (Frankfurt am Main, Berlin and Vienna: Propylaen Verlag, 1974), pp. 169–71. Copyright by Verlag Ullstein, GmbH. Cited by permission. Trans. by J. Hessing.

I must ask you only to listen and never to speak about what I am telling you in this intimate circle. We had to answer the question: What about women and the children? Here, too, I had made up my mind, find a clear-cut solution. I did not feel that I had the right to exterminate the men—that is, to murder them, or have them murdered—and then allow their children to grow into avengers, threatening our sons and grandchildren. A fateful decision had to be made: This people had to vanish from the earth. For the organization in charge of the mission, it was the hardest decision we have had to make so far. It has been executed—as I believe I may say—without damage to the spirit and soul of our men and leaders. This danger was very real. The path between the two existing possibilities, either to become too brutal and to lose all respect for human life, or else to become too soft and dizzy and suffer from nervous breakdowns—the path between this Scylla and Charybdis was frightfully narrow.

All Jewish fortunes that were confiscated—a property of infinite value—were transferred, up to the last penny, to the Treasury of the Reich. I have always insisted on this: if we want to win the war we are obliged to our people and to our race—and obliged to our Fuehrer who is now, once in 2,000 years, given to our people—not to be petty in these matters and to be consistent. From the outset I decided that should a member of the SS take only one single Mark, he would be sentenced to death. In recent days I have therefore signed a number of death warrants—I might as well say it, approximately a dozen. Here one has to be relentless, lest the Party and Nation suffer.

I feel most obliged to you—who are the highest commissioners, the highest dignitaries of the Party, of this political order, of this political instrument in the hands of our Fuehrer. By the end of this year, the Jewish question in the countries occupied by us will be solved. There will only be remnants of isolated Jews who went into hiding. The question of the Jews married to Gentiles, and the question of half-Jews, will be investigated logically and rationally, decided upon, and solved.... With this I wish to conclude my remarks concerning the Jewish question. Now you know all about it, and you will keep silent. In the distant future, perhaps, one might consider if the German people should be told anything more about it. I believe it is better that we—all of us—who have taken this upon ourselves for our people and have taken the responsibility (the responsibility for the deed, not merely for the idea), should take our secret to our graves....

NOTE

1. Heinrich Himmler (1900–1945), head of the SS. A close associate of Hitler from the days of the Munich *putsch* in 1923, Himmler created the SS, from an elite guard of the party into a huge "Nordic" army in the service of Nazi ideological goals. Accordingly, Hitler charged Himmler and the SS with the implementation of the Final Solution. Following Himmler's arrest by British troops in May 1945, he committed suicide. This speech was given by Himmler at a secret meeting of state and district leaders in Posen on October 8, 1943.

36. COMMANDANT OF AUSCHWITZ (c. 1945)

RUDOLF HOESS[1]

By the will of the Reichsfuehrer SS (Himmler), Auschwitz became the greatest human extermination centre of all time.

When in the summer of 1941 Himmler himself gave me the order to prepare installations at Auschwitz where mass extermination could take place, and personally to carry out these exterminations, I did not have the slightest idea of their scale or consequences. It was certainly an extraordinary and monstrous order. Nevertheless the reasons behind the extermination program seemed to me right. I did not reflect on it at the time: I had been given an order, and I had to carry it out. Whether this mass extermination of the Jews was necessary or not was something on which I could not allow myself to form an opinion, for I lacked the necessary breadth of view.

If the Fuehrer had himself given the order for the "final solution of the Jewish question," then for a veteran National-Socialist and even more so for an SS officer, there could be no question of considering its merits. "The Fuehrer commands, we follow" was never a mere phrase or slogan. It was meant in bitter earnestness....

But outsiders simply cannot understand that there was not a single SS officer who would disobey an order from the Reichsfuehrer SS, far less consider getting rid of him because of the gruesomely hard nature of one such order.

What the Fuehrer, or in our case his second-in-command, the Reichsfuehrer SS, ordered was always right....

Before the mass extermination of the Jews began, the Russian *politruks* and political commissars were liquidated in almost all the concentration camps during 1941 and 1942......

While I was away on duty, my deputy, [Karl] Fritzsch, the commander of the protective custody camp, first tried gas for these killings. It was a preparation of prussic acid, called Cyclon B, which was used in the camp as an insecticide and of which there was always a stock on hand. On my return Fritzsch reported this to me, and the gas was used again for the next transport.

The gassing was carried out in the detention cells of Block 11. Protected by a gasmask, I watched the killing myself. In the crowded cells death came instantaneously the moment the Cyclon B was thrown in. A short, almost smothered cry, and it was all over. During this first experience of gassing people, I did not fully realise what was happening, perhaps because I was too impressed by the whole procedure. I have a clearer recollection of the gassing of nine hundred Russians which took place shortly afterwards in the old crematorium, since the use of Block 11 for this purpose caused too much trouble. While the transport was detraining, holes were pierced in the earth and in the concrete ceiling of the mortuary. The Russians were ordered to undress in an anteroom; they then quietly entered the mortuary, for they had been told they were to be deloused. The whole transport exactly filled the mortuary to capacity. The doors were then sealed and the gas shaken down through the holes in the roof. I do not know how long this killing took. For a little while a humming sound could be heard. When the powder was thrown in, there were cries of "Gas!," then a great bellowing, and the trapped prisoners hurled themselves against both the doors. But the doors held. They were opened several hours later, so that the place might be aired. It was then that I saw, for the first time, gassed bodies in mass. It made me feel uncomfortable and I shuddered, although I had imagined that death by gassing would be worse

Source: Rudolf Hoess, *Commandant of Auschwitz*, trans. C. Fitzgibbon (London: Weidenfeld and Nicolson, 1953), pp. 144–50, 153–55. Copyright 1953 by George Weidenfeld and Nicolson, Ltd. Reprinted by permission.

than it was. I had always thought that the victims would experience a terrible choking sensation. But the bodies, without exception, showed no signs of convulsion. The doctors explained to me that the prussic acid had a paralyzing effect on the lungs, but its action was so quick and strong that death came before the convulsions could set in, and in this its effects differed from those produced by carbon monoxide or by a general oxygen deficiency.

The killing of these Russian prisoners-of-war did not cause me much concern at the time. The order had been given, and I had to carry it out. I must even admit that this gassing set my mind at rest, for the mass extermination of the Jews was to start soon and at that time neither Eichmann[2] nor I was certain how these mass killings were to be carried out. It would be by gas, but we did not know which gas or how it was to be used. Now we had the gas, and we had established a procedure. I always shuddered at the prospect of carrying out exterminations by shooting, when I thought of the vast numbers concerned, and of the women and children. The shooting of hostages, and the group executions ordered by the Reichsfuehrer SS or by the Reich Security Head Office had been enough for me. I was therefore relieved to think that we were to be spared all these blood-baths, and that the victims too would be spared suffering until their last moment came. It was precisely this which had caused me the greatest concern when I had heard Eichmann's description of Jews being mown down by the Special Squads [*Einsatzkommandos*] armed with machine-guns and machine-pistols. Many gruesome scenes are said to have taken place, people running away after being shot, the finishing off of the wounded and particularly of the women and children. Many members of the *Einsatzkommandos*, unable to endure wading through blood any longer, had committed suicide. Some had even gone mad. Most of the members of the *Kommandos* had to rely on alcohol when carrying out their horrible work....

In the spring of 1942 the first transports of Jews, all earmarked for extermination, arrived from Upper Silesia.

They were taken from the detraining platform to the "Cottage"—to Bunker I—across the meadows where later Building Site II was located. The transport was conducted by [Hans] Aumeier and [Gerhard] Palitzsch and some of the block leaders. They talked with the Jews about general topics, enquiring

concerning their qualifications and trades, with a view to misleading them. On arrival at the "Cottage," they were told to undress. At first they went calmly into the rooms where they were supposed to be disinfected. But some of them showed signs of alarm, and spoke of death by suffocation and of annihilation. A sort of panic set in at once. Immediately all the Jews still outside were pushed into the chambers, and the doors were screwed shut. With subsequent transports the difficult individuals were picked out early on and most carefully supervised. At the first signs of unrest, those responsible were unobtrusively led behind the building and killed with a small-calibre gun that was inaudible to the others, The presence and calm behaviour of the Special Detachment[3] served to reassure those who were worried or who suspected what was about to happen. A further calming effect was obtained by members of the Special Detachment accompanying them into the rooms and remaining with them until the end.

It was most important that the whole business of arriving and undressing should take place in an atmosphere of the greatest possible calm. People reluctant to take off their clothes had to be helped by those of their companions who had already undressed, or by men of the Special Detachment.

The refractory ones were calmed down and encouraged to undress. The prisoners of the Special Detachment also saw to it that the process of undressing was carried out quickly, so that the victims would have little time to wonder what was happening.

The eager help given by the Special Detachment in encouraging them to undress and in conducting them into the gas chambers was most remarkable. I have never known, nor heard, of any of its members giving these people who were about to be gassed the slightest hint of what lay ahead of them. On the contrary, they did everything in their power to deceive them and particularly to pacify the suspicious ones. Though they might refuse to believe the SS men, they had complete faith in these members of their own race, and to reassure them and keep them calm the Special Detachments therefore always consisted of Jews who themselves came from the same districts as did the people on whom a particular action was to be carried out.

They would talk about life in the camp, and most of them asked for news of friends or relations who had arrived in earlier transports. It was interesting to hear the lies that the Special Detachment told them with such conviction, and to see the emphatic gestures with which they underlined them.

Many of the women hid their babies among the piles of clothing. The men of the Special Detachment were particularly on the lookout for this, and would speak words of encouragement to the woman until they had persuaded her to a take the child with her. The women believed that the disinfectant might be bad for their smaller children, hence their efforts to conceal them.

The smaller children usually cried because of the strangeness of being undressed in this fashion, but when their mothers or members of the Special Detachment comforted them, they became calm and entered the gas chambers, playing or joking with one another and carrying their toys.

I noticed that women who either guessed or knew what awaited them nevertheless found the courage to joke with the children to encourage them, despite the mortal terror visible in their own eyes.

One woman approached me as she walked past and, pointing to her four children who were manfully helping the smallest ones over the rough ground, whispered:

"How can you bring yourself to kill such beautiful, darling children? Have you no heart at all?"

One old man as he passed by me, hissed:

"Germany will pay a heavy penance for this mass murder of the Jews."

His eyes glowed with hatred as he said this. Nevertheless he walked calmly into the gas-chamber, without worrying about the others.

I remember, too, a woman who tried to throw her children out of the gas-chamber, just as the door was closing. Weeping she called out:

"At least let my precious children live."

There were many such shattering scenes, which affected all who witnessed them.

During the spring of 1942 hundreds of vigorous men and women walked all unsuspecting to their death in the gas chambers, under the blossom-laden fruit trees of the "Cottage" orchard. This picture of death in the midst of life remains with me to this day.

This mass extermination, with all its attendant circumstances, did not, as far I know fail to affect those who took a part in it. With very few exceptions, nearly all of those detailed to do this monstrous "work," this

"service," and who, like myself, have given sufficient thought to the matter, have been deeply marked by these events.

Many of the men involved approached me as I went my rounds through the extermination buildings, and poured out their anxieties and impressions to me, in the hope that I could allay them.

Again and again during these confidential conversations I was asked: is it necessary that we do all this? Is it necessary that hundreds of thousands of women and children be destroyed? And I, who in my inner most being only fought them off, attempted to console them by repeating that it was done on Hitler's order. I had to tell them that this extermination of Jewry had to be, so that Germany and our posterity might be freed for ever from their relentless adversaries.

There was no doubt in the mind of any of us that Hitler's order had to be obeyed regardless, and that it was the duty of the SS to carry it out. Nevertheless we were all tormented by secret doubts.

I myself dared not admit to such doubts. In order to make my subordinates carry on with their task, it was psychologically essential that I myself appear convinced of the necessity for this gruesomely harsh order.

Everyone watched me. They observed the impression produced upon me by the kind of scenes that I have described above, and my reactions. Every word I said on the subject was discussed. I had to exercise intense self-control in order to prevent my innermost doubts and feelings of oppression from becoming apparent.

I had to appear cold and indifferent to events that must have wrung the heart of anyone possessed of human feelings. I might not even look away when afraid lest my natural emotions get the upper hand. I had to watch coldly, while the mothers with laughing or crying children went into the gas-chambers.

On one occasion two small children were so absorbed in some game that they quite refused to let their mother tear them away from it. Even the Jews of the Special Detachment were reluctant to pick the children up. The imploring look in the eyes of the mother, who certainly knew what was happening, is something I shall never forget. The people were already in the gas-chamber and becoming restive, and I had to act. Everyone was looking at me. I nodded to the junior noncommissioned officer on duty and he picked up the screaming, struggling children in his arms and carried them into the gas-chamber, accompanied by their mother who was weeping in the most heart-rending fashion. My pity was so great that I longed to vanish from the scene; yet I might not show the slightest trace of emotions.

I had to see everything, I had to watch hour after hour, by day and by night, the removal and burning of the bodies, the extraction of the teeth, the cutting of hair, the whole grisly, interminable business. I had to stand for hours on end in the ghastly stench, while the mass graves were being opened and the bodies dragged out and burned.

I had to look through the peep-hole of the gas-chambers and watch the process of death itself, because the doctors wanted me to see it.

I had to do all this because I was the one to whom everyone looked, because I had to show them all that I did not merely issue the orders and make the regulations but was also prepared myself to be present at whatever task I had assigned to my subordinates.

The Reichsfuehrer SS sent various high-ranking party leaders and SS officers to Auschwitz so that they might see for the themselves the process of extermination of the Jews. They were all deeply impressed by what they saw. Some who had previously spoken most loudly about the necessity for this extermination fell silent once they had actually seen the "final solution of the Jewish problem." I was repeatedly asked how I and my men could go on watching these operations, and how we were able to stand it.

My invariable answer was that the iron determination with which we must carry out Hitler's orders could only be obtained by a stifling of all human emotions. Each of these gentlemen declared that he was glad the job had not been given to him.

I had many detailed discussions with Eichmann concerning all matters connected with the "final solution of the Jewish problem," but without ever disclosing my inner anxieties, I tried in every way to discover Eichmann's innermost and real convictions about the "solution."

Yes, every way. Yet even when we were quite alone together and the drink had been flowing freely so that he was in his most expansive mood, he showed that he was completely obsessed with the idea of destroying every single Jew that he could lay his hands on. Without pity and in cold blood we must complete this extermination as rapidly as possible. Any compromise, even the slightest, would have to be paid for bitterly at a later date.

In the face of such grim determination I was forced to bury all my human considerations as deeply as possible.

Indeed, I must freely confess that after these conversations with Eichmann I almost came to regard such emotions as betrayal of the Fuehrer.

There was no escape for me from this dilemma.

I had to go on with this process of extermination. I had to continue this mass murder and coldly to watch it, without regard for the doubts that were seething deep inside me.

I had to observe every happening with a cold indifference. Even those petty incidents that others might not notice I found hard to forget. In Auschwitz I truly had no reason to complain that I was bored.

NOTES

1. Rudolf Hoess (1900–1947). A member of the SS, in May 1940 he was appointed first commandant of Auschwitz. At the end of 1941 Himmler ordered him to adapt the camp for the Final Solution. In November 1943 he was transferred to the inspection authority of the concentration camps. In 1944, however, he returned to Auschwitz for a two-month period to supervise the extermination of 400,000 Hungarian Jews. After the war the Polish government tried him, condemning him to death. While in prison Hoess wrote his autobiography, from which this except is taken. He was hanged at Auschwitz in 1947. Auschwitz, the Nazis' largest concentration and extermination camp, was located near the small Polish town Oswiecim (in German, Auschwitz) in Galicia. Estimates of the victims of Auschwitz's gas chambers vary from 1,000,000 to 2,500,000. In addition to Jews, tens of thousands of gypsies and other prisoners were killed at Auschwitz.

2. Adolf Eichmann (1906–1962), head of the Gestapo Section IV B 4, which dealt with Jewish affairs and the deportation of the Jews to the death camps. See this chapter, document 41, note 1.

3. These *Sonderkommandos*—popularly known as *kapos*—were recruited from among the camp inmates. See this chapter, document 38, note 4.

37. ON THE DEPORTATION OF CHILDREN FROM THE LODZ GHETTO (SEPTEMBER 4, 1942)

MORDECAI CHAIM RUMKOWSKI[1]

The ghetto has been struck a hard blow. They demand what is most dear to it—children and old people. I was not privileged to have a child of my own and therefore devoted my best years to children. I lived and breathed together with children. I never imagined that my own hands would be forced to make this sacrifice on the altar. In my old age I am forced to stretch out my hands and to beg: "Brothers and sisters, give them to me!—Fathers and mothers, give me your children.... [Bitter weeping shakes the assembled public.] Yesterday, in the course of the day, I was given the order to send away more than 20,000 Jews from the ghetto, and if I did not—"we will do it ourselves." The question arose: "Should we have accepted this and carried it out ourselves, or left it to others?" But as we were guided not by the thought: "how many will be lost?" but "how many can be saved?" we arrived at the conclusion—those closest to me at work, that is, and myself—that however difficult it was going to be, we must take upon ourselves the carrying out of this decree. I must carry out this difficult and bloody operation, I must cut off limbs in order to save the body! I must take away children, and if I do not, others too will be taken, God forbid.... [Terrible wailing]

I cannot give you comfort today. Nor did I come to calm you today, but to reveal all your pain and all your sorrow. I have come like a robber, to take from you what is dearest to your heart. I tried everything I knew to get the bitter sentence canceled. When it could not be canceled, I tried to lessen the sentence. Only yesterday I ordered the registration of nine-year-old children. I wanted to save at least one year—children from nine to ten. But they would not yield.

I succeeded in one thing—to save children over ten. Let that be our consolation in our great sorrow.

There are many people in this ghetto who suffer from tuberculosis, whose days or perhaps weeks are numbered. I do not know, perhaps this is a satanic plan, and perhaps not, but I cannot stop myself from proposing it. "Give me these sick people, and perhaps it will be possible to save the healthy in their place." I know how precious each one of the sick is in his home, and particularly among Jews. But at time of such decrees one must weigh and measure who should be saved, who can be saved and who may be saved.

Common sense requires us to know that those must be saved, who can be saved and who have a chance of being saved and not those whom there is no chance to save in any case....

NOTE

1. Mordecai Chaim Rumkowski (1877–1944) was a Jewish communal leader and, before the war, a director of an orphanage near Lodz, Poland. Upon their occupation of Lodz—a city of 665,000 residents, a third of whom were Jews—in September 1939, the Germans disbanded all Jewish communal organizations, as was their policy throughout Poland. A single Jewish Council (*Judenrat*), called in Lodz a Council of Elders, was then established, beholden to the occupying authorities. On October 13, 1939, they appointed Rumkowski the Elder of Jews (*Aelteste der Juden*), the official title of the chairman of the Lodz *Judenrat*. With the establishment of the Lodz ghetto in March–April 1940, Rumkowski was charged with organizing life in the ghetto from establishing factories, medical care,

Source: M.C. Rumkowski, Speech of September 4, 1942, stenogram cited in Isaiah Trunk, *Lodz Ghetto* (New York; Marstin Press, 1962), pp. 311–12 (Yiddish). Trans. in Y. Arad, Y. Gutman and A. Margaliot, eds. *Documents on the Holocaust*, trans. Lea Ben Dor (Jerusalem; Yad Vashem, 1981), pp.283f. Reprinted by permission of Yad Vashem.

and housing to ensuring "law and order"—for the more than 160,000 Jews remaining in Lodz. In his position as Elder of the Jews, he had often to make tragically difficult and inevitably controversial decisions. At the end of 1941, when the Chelmno extermination camp was completed, Rumkowski was forced to organize the deportations of part of the ghetto population, ostensibly for resettlement elsewhere. He and his staff had the task of deciding who was to be deported. The document presented here reflects one such decision. It is an address that Rumkowski delivered in Yiddish at a hastily called public meeting held on September 4, 1942, at a central square in the ghetto before an assembly of several thousand; the stenographer also dutifully recorded the responses of the audience. (The document is from Rumkowski's personal archives found after the war in the ruins of the ghetto.)

The day following the speech, the Germans initiated the notorious 'Gehsperre' Aktion in which German troops stormed the ghetto, and, without reference to the lists prepared by Rumkowski, seized 16,000 Lodz Jews, including children under ten years of age, persons over sixty, and the sick and the emaciated and deported them to death camps.

More than any other *Judenrat* leader, Rumkowski is cast as a damnable collaborator and traitor. Others view his leadership as one of heroic pragmatism, which through a calculated cooperation with the Nazis sought to render life under the appalling conditions prevailing in the ghetto a bit more tolerable and to save as many of his brethren as possible. He held his position until September 1944, when the Lodz Ghetto was liquidated and he was dispatched with the last transport to Auschwitz to meet his death.

38. INSIDE AUSCHWITZ—A MEMOIR (C. 1970)

FRANZI EPSTEIN[1]

KONZENENTRATIONSLAGER A I FRAUENLAGER[2]

The camp was much larger, more crowded than Birkenau,[3] the barracks built of stone, the roads in better shape, although the base was the same ochre loam, but here they were dotted with rough stones. Instead of the SS guards, SS women were very much in evidence. The prisoners here wore raggedy striped uniforms and generally looked much more decimated than the girls from Birkenau. The exception were the *kapos*[4] and their deputies who looked positively well fed, clean with their long hair worn in pony tails caught with neat black bows. The same could be said about the young teenage runners who

were the exact counterpart of [those] in Birkenau. It was almost impossible not to be reminded of a pet Pekingese or poodle when observing them. Most of the rank and file had shaven heads or very short hair just beginning to grow in. Walking was seemingly VERBOTEN since everybody was constantly running. Counted off by groups of five hundred, the newcomers were herded into low Russian-style barracks with tiny windows. Inside, instead of bunks there were long shelves about five feet deep against the walls and another similar construction running through the center. There were no pallets, no blankets and no straw. They were chased up into these cage-like contraptions with a flood of curses and shoves from the

---

Source: Franzi Epstein (born Franziska Paulina Margaret Rabinek). Excerpts from an unpublished memoir, entitled *Round Trip*. Printed with the permission of the author's daughter, Helen Epstein.

Polish *kapos* and strictly admonished to stay there or else. The *kapos* seemed to be absolutely incapable of speaking in a normal tone much less to be talked to or asked a question. Every shouted sentence was preceded with a curse. "You Czech whores who think that you are different, or dirty Jew bitches who deserve to drown in their own shit, we will teach you what Auschwitz is all about. You haven't seen anything yet." All this in Polish which many understood, few spoke but all got the meaning anyway. No sooner were they packed in, than they were chased out in the same fashion to stand *Appell*.[5] This time a number of individuals were called out by their numbers and taken away for reasons no one quite understood until later. Twins were taken out for medical experiments. Dr. [Josef] Mengele[6] was running the camp hospital, also some nurses and others who were supposed to stay in A I for reasons they certainly did not know. Various SS women came and went inspecting the rows of women standing at attention. Talking was strictly VERBOTEN. One of the SS caught a girl whispering to her neighbor and made her kneel on the stony ground her arms lifted above her head and then placed a heavy rock in each hand. Every time her arms relaxed a little the guard or *kapo* would yell at her to stretch them out or else. This went on for hours. Finally when *Appell* was over the girl had to be held up on both sides by her friends. Her knees would not carry her. Next a dozen stools were brought in and hair was cut. It came as a pleasant surprise that it was not shaven, but just cut short to the ears which seemed like a good omen considering that it is easier to shave a live body than a dead one. If they would have been destined for the gas, the reasoning went, all of it would have come off for the German arts and crafts shop. There was a good deal of scuttling and regrouping during the relatively less guarded period of the haircutting with the effect that a few girls including [my bunkmate] Dime and "A-4116" succeeded not only in saving their manes but also managed to form a cluster that vowed to stay together come what may....

After all these hours everybody had the desperate need to go to the latrine and groups of ten were escorted by the *kapos* in relays. The time to spend there was strictly rationed and whoever took too long in the view of the escort was poked in the buttocks with pitchforks. This again was accompanied by a stream of profanities utilizing every [conceivable]

filthy word....With the echo of the favorite curse: "Cholera should take you" [the women] were chased back to their barracks to stand another long *Appell*. At last they were given a mugful of black liquid called coffee and a slice of bread and locked inside the barracks. With darkness another kind of assault materialized in the form of the biggest bedbugs ever seen by anyone present. They were the size of a fully grown cockroach and they attacked without giving quarter. The shelves [for sleeping] were so overcrowded that sleep was only possible...sandwiched between one's neighbors so that when one turned the whole row of some fifty people had to turn as well. "A-4116" had always been an irresistible attraction for bugs of any kind and was now so bitten up that she could not sleep at all. Disregarding the orders not to leave the bunks she slid down in the darkness to the stone floor where she felt behind her a barrel covered by a blanket. This she pulled over herself and feeling warm and comfortable dozed off in a few seconds. The next morning she slept so soundly that Dime and a few others had to spend considerable time to bring her back to consciousness. The barrel contained chlorine and the blanket was soaked full of its gases.

With the next days things really got going. The group was taken under armed guard to a different section where the other Birkenauers were already assembled in front of a building marked as a SAUNA. This immediately revived all old anxieties since it was well known that the gas chambers were camouflaged under this title. There were flower beds all around and to "A-4116" the bright red of the begonias looked positively obscene against the dismal gray of the windowless building. Still outside in full view of the escorting SS men they were ordered to strip and throw their clothes and shoes on two separate piles. Hysteria flared up here and there....Two by two they were slowly let into the bathhouse and came first to a room where a big, fat SS woman stood in front of an old dirty surgical table with stirrups, a white coat thrown over her uniform. Brutally she inspected every single orifice without once changing her rubber glove. One of the girls determined to save a souvenir from her beloved clutched a few buttons of his coat in her hand. Realizing that there was absolutely no place to hide them she finally swallowed the keepsakes. The next stop in the processing were the showers. Groups of one hundred were let in at a time. The orders were: one minute of water, one minute of soaping with a piece of ersatz distributed to each foursome, one minute to rinse and NO NOISE. Hesistantly the herd entered the shower room, prodded by guards and *kapos* with unspeakable horror at the showerheads reputed to carry gas as well as water.

"Shema yisrael adonai eloheinu," was heard in a whisper. An eternity seemed to pass and then a hissing sound from overhead: WATER. Boiling hot water. A shout of relief went up and the whole scene changed to a mad ballet in an effort to avoid the scalding streams. Coming out on the other side each one was given a pair of under pants and a gray prisoner shift and later ordered to pick shoes from the pile outside. This was practically impossible for how could anyone find her shoes in a mixed-up pile of 2,000 pairs? The result was too ridiculous for words but the fights that broke out when one found her shoes on someone else were not.

Another long *Appell* and the *Lagerkommandant* Ilse Koch arrived for inspection....The command ACH-TUNG was given but "A-4116," who had already recovered some of her natural sass neglected to take her hands out of her pockets. The Kommandant stopped in front of her: "Hands out of your pockets Jewbitch." A blow flat across the face with back of her ringed hand followed almost simultaneously. The prisoner's hand flew forward to go for her throat but Dime and another girl in back of her already had her elbows in a tight grab so that she could not move. With a nod from Frau Koch the group was ordered a right turn and marched off out of A I in the direction of the ramp.

After each being provided with a piece of bread for the trip, they were loaded into rather clean cattle cars with fresh straws. To their delight and surprise the doors remained open about a foot wide and after some more delays and shouted commands, the train started to move slowly. Gathering speed, it took at least twenty minutes of travel to get out of the Auschwitz installations. The administration buildings formed a little town in itself. Only now in broad daylight did one get an idea of the immensity of this death factory. Countless square compounds separated by barbed wire fences were dotted with watch towers and the inmates seemed like crawling ants as seen from the train.

Quite suddenly the view changed. Moving in a western direction the train passed through flowering meadows with bubbling brooks. Lush, green, totally unbelievable. The sight of farmers working in the field, grazing cattle and ordinary people just going about their business brought a sudden awareness that there was a life to be lived after all and that maybe some day one would be part of it again.

It was the fourth of July, the sun brilliant in the sky, the smoke of Auschwitz receding in the distance. Someone started to sing:

> The world is ours
> There's room for everyone
> and on the ruins of the ghetto we will laugh.

It was a song from a prewar avant-garde revue that had been adapted for Theresienstadt and a favorite among all Czech prisoners. The scene was reminiscent of a youth hostel trip. Song followed song and after running through the repertory of Czech pop and folksongs, "Old Man River" and "Anchors Away" followed. Empty stomachs were forgotten, they laughed, teased and tickled each other like an exuberant bunch of kids intoxicated with sheer joy of living. Even the armed escorts riding in the cabin of each car could not suppress a smile.

At nightfall the doors of the cars were locked when the train neared the more industrial regions of Germany. But not even this could dampen the girls' high spirits. The box car "A-4116" and Dime rode in contained almost only girls from Prague with a sprinkling from the provinces. All belonged to the same generation and had known each other long before the emergence of Adolf Hitler. Thrown together again and bound by the recent common experiences, they swore to try to stay together and help each other.

NOTES

1. Franziska Paulina Margaret Rabinek [Franzi Epstein] (1920–1989). Born in Prague, she was baptized by her father, an engineer and himself a baptized Jew; her mother, raised in an observant Jewish home in Kolin, Bohemia, was a dress designer, a profession Franziska also acquired when she left school at the age of fifteen to work in her mother's business. On August 10, 1942, she was deported from Prague to Theresienstadt; in May 1944 she was transferred to Auschwitz. Finally she was sent to Bergen-Belsen and was liberated by the British in April 1945, the sole surviving member of her family. In 1946 she married Kurt Epstein, and two years later she emigrated to the United States, where she worked as a dress designer. At the behest of her children, she wrote

her memoirs. She completed the hitherto-unpublished English manuscript in the mid-1970s.

2. A I was the designation of the main camp (*Stammlager*) at Auschwitz. Female inmates at Auschwitz were kept in a special section (*Frauenlager*) in this camp.

3. Birkenau was one of the three component camps of Auschwitz.

4. *Kapo* is a term of unknown origin. Some scholars believe it is derived from the Italian word *capo*, or chief or boss; another hypothesis is that the word is based on the German *Kameradschaftspolizei*, "community police". The term was used in the concentration camps to designate those inmates who were appointed by the authorities to head a work gang made up of fellow prisoners.

By extension the term was derisively applied to any inmate regarded as a collaborator with the Nazis.

5. *Appell*, German term for roll call, military inspection.

6. Josef Mengele (1911–1978?) was a physician and an SS officer. In may 1943 he was appointed to Auschwitz, where he conducted notorious medical experiments on the inmates; he was also charged with examining the arriving inmates, stripped naked, and making the *Selektion* (selection) of who was fit for labour in Auschwitz's factories and plants and who was expendable and thus to be dispatched forthwith to the gas chambers. Making his selection with a casual flip of the finger, Mengele became a symbol of the sadistic cynicism of the Nazi machinery of mass murder.

39. ESTIMATED NUMBER OF JEWS KILLED BY THE NAZIS[1]

Country[2]	Jewish population September 1939	Number of Jews murdered[3]	Percentage of Jews murdered
1. Poland	3,300,000	2,800,000	85.0
2. USSR, occupied territories	2,100,000	1,500,000	71.4
3. Rumania	850,000	425,000	50.0
4. Hungary	404,000	200,000	49.5
5. Czechoslovakia	315,000	260,000	82.5
6. France[4]	300,000	90,000	30.0
7. Germany[5]	210,000	170,000	81.0
8. Lithuania	150,000	135,000	90.0
9. Holland[4]	150,000	90,000	60.0
10. Latvia	95,000	85,000	89.5
11. Belgium[4]	90,000	40,000	44.4
12. Greece	75,000	60,000	80.0
13. Yugoslavia	75,000	55,000	73.3
14. Austria[6]	60,000	40,000	66.6
15. Italy[4]	57,000	15,000	26.3
16. Bulgaria	50,000	7,000	14.0
17. Others[7]	20,000	6,000	30.0
Total	8,301,000	5,978,000	72.0

Source: Leon Poliakov and Josef Wulf, eds., *Das Dritte Reich und die Juden: Dokumente und Aufsaetze* (Berlin: Arani-Verlag GmbH, 1955),p. 229. Copyright 1955 by Arani-Verlag GmbH, Reprinted by permission. For alternative estimates (differing slightly), see *Encyclopedia of the Holocaust*, ed. Israel Gutman (New York: Macmillan, 1990), vol. 4, p. 1799.

NOTES

1. With few exceptions there are no exact statistics on Jews who were killed. Thus all statistics are estimates.
2. Within its prewar boundaries.
3. The survivors did not always remain in their countries of origin.
4. The numbers for France, Holland, Belgium, and Italy include emigrants from Germany and Austria.
5. The percentage of victims is for the Jewish population of September 1939. Between 1933 and 1939 an estimated 300,000 German Jews emigrated.
6. Again, the percentage of victims is for the population of September 1939. From the *Anschluss* (the German annexation of Austria in March 1938) to September 1939, it is estimated that 110,000 Jews left Austria.
7. Danzig, Denmark, Estonia, Luxemburg, and Norway.

40. SIX MILLION ACCUSERS (1961)

GIDEON HAUSNER[1]

When I stand before you here, Judges of Israel, to lead the Prosecution of Adolf Eichmann, I am not standing alone. With me are six million accusers. But they cannot rise to their feet and point an accusing finger towards him who sits in the dock and cry: "I accuse." For their ashes are piled up on the hills of Auschwitz and the fields of Treblinka, and are strewn in the forests of Poland. Their graves are scattered throughout the length and breadth of Europe. Their blood cries out, but their voice is not heard. Therefore I will be their spokesman and in their name I will unfold the awesome indictment.

The history of the Jewish people is steeped in suffering and tears.... Yet never, down the entire blood-stained road travelled by this people, never since the first days of its nationhood, has any man arisen who succeeded in dealing it such grievous blows as did Hitler's iniquitous regime, and Adolf Eichmann as its executive arm for the extermination of the Jewish people. In all human history there is no other example of a man against whom it would be possible to draw up such a bill of indictment as has been read here.... Murder has been with the human race since the days when Cain killed Abel; it is no novel phenomenon. But we have had to wait till this twentieth century to witness with our own eyes a new kind of murder: not the result of the momentary surge of passion or mental black-out, but of calculated decision and painstaking planning; not through the evil design of an individual, but through a mighty criminal conspiracy involving thousands: not against one victim whom an assassin may have decided to destroy, but against an entire people....

This murderous decision, taken deliberately and in cold blood, to annihilate a nation and blot it out from the face of the earth, is so shocking that one is at a loss for words to describe it. Words exist to express what man's reason can conceive and his heart contain, [but] here we are dealing with actions that transcend our human grasp. Yet this is what did happen: millions were condemned to death, but only because they belonged to the Jewish people. The development of technology placed at the disposal of the destroyers efficient equipment for the execution of their appalling designs. This unprecedented crime, carried out by Europeans in the twentieth century,

---

Source: Shabatai Rosenne, ed., *Six Million Accusers: Israel's Case Against Eichmann* (Jerusalem: *The Jerusalem Post*, 1961), pp. 29–33, 37–38, 43. Reprinted by permission of *The Jerusalem Post*.

led to the definition of a criminal concept unknown to human annals even during the darkest ages—the crime of Genocide....

Hitler, his regime and crimes, were no accidental or transient phenomenon. He did not come to power as a result merely of a unique combination of circumstances. Historical processes are usually the product of many developments, like many streams flowing each in its own channel until they combine into a mighty river. They will come together only if their flow is in the same general direction.

No doubt various events contributed to the rise of Nazism: the defeat of Germany in World War I; the subsequent economic difficulties; lack of leadership and futile party divisions; fratricidal strife and disunion—all these impelled the German people, disoriented and groping, to turn its eyes towards the false prophet. But Hitler would not have been able to remain in power, and to consolidate in his support among all the strata of the German people, including most of the intellectuals—to win the support of so many university professors and professional men, the civil service and the whole army—if the road to his leadership had not already been paved. Not even the oppressive regime of the concentration camps, and the atmosphere created by the terror so rapidly activated against all opposition by the hooligans of the SS and SA, are adequate alone to explain the enthusiastic and devoted support he received from the majority of the nation, unless it had been preceded by an extensive spiritual preparation. When we read today the declarations of the scientists, authors, and journalists—including many who had not been among his adherents before—who chanted his praises and willingly gave him their support and backing, how they willingly and joyfully accepted his yoke, we must reach the conclusion, however reluctantly, that the people were ready and prepared to crown him as their leader.

Hitler [freed] the hatred of the Jew which was latent in the heart of large sections of the German people, intensified it and stimulated it into greater activity. The germ of antisemitism was already there; he stimulated it and transformed it into the source of an epidemic. For the purpose of Nazi Germany's internal policy, the Jew was a convenient object of hatred; he was weak and defenseless. The world outside remained silent when he was persecuted, and contented itself with verbal reactions that did

little harm. The Jew was pilloried as a supporter of Communism—and therefore an enemy of the German people. In the same breath he was accused of being a capitalist—and therefore an enemy of the workers. National-Socialism had found in the Jew an object of hostility appropriate to both halves of its name, and it set him up as a target for both national enmity and class hatred. The Jew was also a ready target through which the attention of the public could be diverted from other problems. This too was an age-old weapon; which had been used by many antisemites down the ages.....

A confused and blinded world was not alarmed by this campaign of hatred and the denial of human rights. It did not understand that the persecution of the Jew was only the beginning of an onslaught on the entire world. The man whose henchmen howled the infamous words: "When Jewish blood spurts from the knife/Then all goes doubly well!" ("*Wenn Judenblut vom Messer spritzt/Dann geht's nochmal so gut!*")—the same man would soon, by a natural development and led by the same master-feeling of hate, proclaim that all the cities of England would be subjected to the same fate as bombed Coventry.

In order to complete the picture, we should point out that there were in Germany tens of thousands of scientists and ecclesiastics, statesmen and authors and ordinary people, who dared to help the Jews, to raise their heads in opposition to the iniquitous regime, and even to rebel against it, and among these were men whose names were famous in German science and culture. Thousands of opponents of the bloody regime were imprisoned and were later destined to suffer greatly in concentration camps before the Nazi monster was brought low. Thousands of these died without seeing the day of liberation. Hundreds of ecclesiastics were arrested and imprisoned. There were also examples of personal bravery—like that of a priest who was sent by Eichmann to a concentration camp for intervening openly on behalf of the Jews. There were Germans who hid Jews and shared their rations with them and who at the risk of their lives helped them to hide or to obtain "Aryan" papers, and there were others who maintained an anti-Hitler underground. During the war there were Germans who even protested to Hitler at the disgrace the Gestapo was bringing on the German people by acting like beasts of prey, as they described the extermination of the Jews. There were also soldiers who tried to frustrate the killings by direct intervention.

But after all is said and done, these were a very small minority. The decisive majority of the German people made peace with the new regime, and were phlegmatic witnesses of the most terrible crime ever perpetrated in human history.…

There is a Hebrew saying: "The wicked, even at the gate of Hell, do not repent." In April 1945, at the moment of his death agonies, when the Soviet cannons were thundering in the streets of Berlin, when Hitler sat imprisoned in the cellar of the *Reichskanzlei*, his entire world in ruins and his country stricken, over the corpses of six million Jews—at that moment, the Führer wrote his political last will and testament. He bequeathed to his people the injunction of eternal hatred for the Jews, and he concluded:

> Above all, I enjoin the leadership of the nation to uphold the racial laws and to resist mercilessly the poisoners of all peoples, international Jewry.

Even from beyond the grave, Hitler was still trying to sow the seeds of hatred and destruction for the Jewish people.

NOTE

1. Gideon Hausner (1915–1990). The attorney general of Israel from 1960 to 1963, Hausner was the chief prosecutor in the Adolf Eichmann trial. This selection is taken from his speech at the trial, which took place before the Jerusalem District Court and which lasted from April to December 1961. Adolf Eichmann (1906–1962)—who was the Gestapo officer in charge of organizing the deportations of the Jews to the death camps—was charged with "crimes against the Jewish people and humanity." He had been brought to Israel by Israeli security agents who had abducted him from Argentina, where he had been hiding since 1950. The Jerusalem court found Eichmann guilty of the charges against him and condemned him to death. In May 1962 he was hanged in an Israeli prison.

41. JEWISH CULTURAL RECONSTRUCTION, INC. (1950)[1]

HANNAH ARENDT

Jewish Cultural Reconstruction, Inc., founded in 1947,[2] for the recovery and redistribution of the Nazi looted cultural treasures of European Jewry, under the chairmanship of Professor Salo W. Baron and with the late Dr. Joshua Starr as Executive Secretary, was preceded and prepared by the Commission on European Jewish Cultural Reconstruction. In 1947, this small body of eminent Jewish scholars[3] started to gather all available data on Jewish libraries, museums and archives in European countries prior to their occupation by the German armies, and at the same time tried to ascertain the new needs of post-war Jewry. Subsequent developments justified the initiative and foresight of the Conference on Jewish Relations, which under the leadership of Salo W. Baron had set up the Commission and prepared the ground for future action.

Source: Hannah Arendt, Jewish Cultural Reconstruction, Inc., unpublished document, Department of Special Collections, Stanford University Library, Salo W. Baron Papers, M0580, Box 81, Folder 20; discovered, introduced and annotated by Elisabeth Gallas.

When at the end of the war the Allied Armies occupied Germany, they found in the vicinity of Frankfurt huge caches containing almost exclusively Judaica and Hebraica. This was the material with which Alfred Rosenberg had planned to equip a central anti-Jewish research center in Frankfurt.[4] There were other centers: Gestapo headquarters in Berlin had established a tremendous collection of German Jewish institutional libraries and smaller Nazi officials among them Julius Streicher, had started Jewish collections of their own confiscating and looting wherever they happened to have power to do so.

Among the books found in Frankfurt and eventually housed in Offenbach by the American military authorities[5] were the famous collections of the Alliance Israélite Universelle of Paris, the Collegio Rabbinico of Rome, the Jewish Division of the Amsterdam University Library, and other precious holdings. But such identifiable and easily restitutable collections formed only part of the accumulated Jewish books. 250,000 volumes, looted or confiscated from Jewish private or public libraries in all European countries, had no ownership marks. Only 50,000 came from the great German Jewish institutional libraries and less than 50,000 bore the marks of private libraries.

As the huge volume of ownerless or heirless cultural property was gradually accumulated, it became apparent that no other Jewish organization existed which had taken the preparatory steps necessary to deal with this unique situation. In 1947 the Commission was therefore in a position to organize Jewish Cultural Reconstruction, Inc., a corporation whose members include the great international Jewish organizations and represent all larger Jewish communities in the world. From the beginning JCR worked in close cooperation with the Israeli institutions, notably the Hebrew University Library in Jerusalem. When in 1947 the Joint Distribution Committee and the Jewish Agency for Palestine formed a Jewish Restitution Successor Organization for all heirless Jewish property in the American zone, it was only natural that JCR should become its cultural agent.

JCR could start its operations only after the occupation authorities had restituted all identifiable property and it was not until the early months of 1949 that the Monument and Fine Arts Division of HICOG[6] turned over the first 250,000 Judaica and Hebraica to

Jewish Cultural Reconstruction, as the trustee for the Jewish people.[7]

The job with which the late Dr. Starr[8]—who went to Germany to supervise these operations—was confronted was tremendous. In a few months these books had to be sorted and redistributed among Jewish Communities all over the world. First choice was given to the Hebrew University in Jerusalem. Its librarian, Dr. Shunami,[9] made the selection for Israel while he was in Germany as the leading librarian for JCR. During the same year 50,000 more books from the German Jewish institutional libraries were turned over to JCR as heirless property and this was followed by 45,000 volumes of identifiable, heirless private property in 1950.

JCR's German depot, first in Offenbach and them in Wiesbaden, has been part of the American Collection Point and some of its staff consists of workers paid by the government. 350,000 books were processed in less than two years and shipped to Jewish communities all over the world. JCR's Board of Directors, following expert opinion of its Advisory Committee, redistributed this material according to the following key: 40% went to Israel, 40% to the Western Hemisphere and 20% to all other countries. At the end of this year, when JCR expects to close its activities in Germany, Israel will have received more than 125,000 books and the United States approximately 100,000. The chief beneficiaries in Europe were Great Britain and Switzerland, the latter having received 7,000 volumes of the famous collections of the Breslau Theological Seminary. France, Belgium and the Netherlands were able to replenish their old and famous libraries, while the new refugee community in Sweden received a well-selected first nucleus of a community library. Approximately 5,000 books went to the survivors of Jewish communities in Germany. South Africa and Morocco, too, were among the recipients from the beginning, while Latin America recently acquired more than 10,000 books, 5,000 of which went to Argentina. Canada received a first shipment of 1,500 books and will get more during the next few months. Negotiations are now under way to give the Australian Jewish community their share, so that at the end of this year four out of five continents will have received their share of the Nazi loot as a result of the activities of Jewish Cultural Reconstruction.

These are dry figures. Their actual meaning for Jewish communities and libraries will be better understood from comments such as these made by a Latin American country: "…we wish to express to you our sincerest gratitude for the invaluable treasures our library has received and to assure you that the best use shall be made of them for the benefit of the cultural reconstruction of our people…we have received such a valuable gift that words cannot express it." Or like the following, expressing the gratitude of an important Jewish New York library: "The volumes are in excellent condition and are just the ones we needed to complete our sets of these titles. We are very happy to have been able to get these and we will always feel grateful to JCR and you for helping us."

Such response, more often expressed orally as a spontaneous reaction to the unexpected "windfall," can be heard almost daily in JCR's New York depot, where books are sorted, selected and distributed to libraries in the United States. 37 libraries in the United States have been recognized as recipient institutions, while a great part of the Rabbinic literature—more than 10,000 volumes—were distributed among 44 Yeshivoth. The Yeshiva University received the real unicum of this material: 6,000 volumes, mostly Rabbinics and other Hebraica, collected by Julius Streicher in the hope of finding proof for ritual murder, Jewish world conspiracy and what not.[10] Each of these volumes has a sticker prepared by Nazi "scholars," which sometimes gives a rather picturesque translation and short description of the volume. This unit will be kept intact and will certainly be of great interest to future historians and scholars.

Many librarians of the more important libraries have come to the depot and picked hundreds and sometimes thousands of books from the shelves, where they are arranged according to categories. Not only the great libraries of all Jewish institutions of higher learning, but also the Jewish divisions of general libraries have been invited to participate, in view of the generous help accorded to JCR by the American occupation authorities. The Library of Congress thought this unique offer important enough to send its librarian to New York, who spent several days in the depot selecting 1,700 books. At the present time JCR is distributing periodicals—perhaps the most valuable single category—and many libraries, Jewish, as well as the famous university libraries of Yale, Columbia, Harvard and New York University, are happy about this opportunity to complete their sets or to acquire complete runs of periodicals they never would be able to buy on the market.

This heritage of European spiritual tradition, constituting as it probably does, the last remnants of an era which has ended, contains a great deal of material which is no longer available anywhere else. Not only did we recover more than 6,000 books, which were classified as rare and among which there are incunables and other early prints, but we also unearthed tens of thousands of items which either have not been reprinted for many decades or were printed on the eve of the Second World War and never reached the market.

Books—their sorting and redistribution—have constituted our greatest task, in view of the quantity as well as the quality of this material. But these were not the only cultural treasures found among the Nazi loot. In addition to books, JCR received more than 10,000 ceremonial objects, nearly 500 Torah Scrolls and fragments and some archival material. The ceremonial objects and Torah Scrolls were evidently looted from Central European synagogues, although they show no signs of their origin. Unlike the books which had been pretty well preserved by the Nazis, the Torah Scrolls and ritual objects bear the all too visible marks of willful destruction. More than 3,000 of the 10,000 objects can no longer be regarded as objects at all; they are merely fragments, not only beyond repair, but sometimes even beyond recognition.

All ceremonial objects were carefully sorted and catalogued with the help of Dr. Narkiss,[11] the Director of the Jerusalem Bezalel Museum. Here again Israel received first choice and selected more than 2,600 objects, almost 2,000 of which went to the Bezalel Museum. France and other Western European countries received nearly 400 of these treasures, Great Britain more than 300, South Africa more than 200, Canada 150 and Argentina 250. Allocations are now being made to other Latin American countries. Almost 3,000 have been distributed in the United States. Of these 1,700 were given to eleven Jewish and non-Jewish museums because of their artistic value. The remainder will go to United States' synagogues, not so much to fill a need, but as a token of remembrance.

The problem presented by the Torah Scrolls, many of which were torn and had to be repaired, was a particularly difficult one. It was fortunate that JCR could enlist the help of the Religious Department of JDC in Paris, which found among Eastern European refugees, a team of highly qualified scribes and scholars who were able to put fragments together, do repairs and discard all those Scrolls which could no longer be regarded as kosher. Because of the great amount of work involved, the distribution of these Torah Scrolls has just started, but a number of [them have] already been shipped to Israel for numerous newly constituted congregations. Some 30 Scrolls were given to Great Britain, [which] lost a number of Torah Scrolls through Nazi bombing, and a small number went to Western European countries in general.

JCR was never satisfied with being the mere recipient of material discovered and entrusted to it by the American authorities. We knew from the beginning that many more Jewish cultural treasures must be hidden away somewhere in Germany. A special investigation was therefore made not only in the American zone, but in all the three Western zones of Germany. As a result of these investigations, we have today a pretty reliable picture of what has survived in the French and British as well as the American zone.[12] Moreover, due to JCR's special status in the American zone, more than 60,000 additional books, some of particularly high value, approximately 60 Torah Scrolls and fragments, several hundreds of ceremonial objects and a great number of archival material has been recovered from German institutions. The famous collection of the Frankfurt Jewish Museum, or rather the remnants of this collection—artistically probably the most precious part of our ceremonial objects—was discovered in Frankfurt and all the Jewish community archives of Bavaria were located in the Bavarian state municipal archives.

JCR hopes to terminate its activities during the coming year.[13] It knows that the job which it has done has not yet been completed because material conditions in Germany at the present time do not allow for a satisfactory inventory of all former Jewish property. However, the main job has been done. More than 400,000 books will have been redistributed to the Jewish people through its efforts. More than 7,000 ceremonial objects and at least 800 Torah Scrolls will have found new homes in Jewish museums and synagogues. Jewish scholarship everywhere in the world will have received that heritage of European Jewry to which it can rightly lay claim and many

countries, especially Latin America and Israel, but also the United States, have received new and inspiring sources of learning.

The Conference of Jewish Relations has demonstrated how much can be achieved by a small and independent organization which does not form part of a big machine. Not only did it take the initiative and display the courage required to change foresight into action, it was also able, limited as its facilities are, to offer a home for the offices of JCR's headquarters, giving it office space, typewriters, telephone service, files, desks, chairs, and thus made it possible for JCR to carry out this great service to the Jewish people.

November 29, 1950

NOTES

1. The political philosopher and refugee from Nazi Germany, Hannah Arendt (1906–1975) wrote this paper as an initial draft of an article on the history of the Jewish Cultural Reconstruction, Inc. (JCR), which she never managed to complete. At the time she served as executive secretary of the JCR, in which she had been active since 1947. The draft article, written in a period when the activities of the JCR had yet to be terminated, reviews the conception, achievements, and significance of this small but far-reaching organization. The JCR was closely allied to the Commission on European Jewish Cultural Reconstruction, which was founded in 1944 as an offshoot of the New York Conference on Jewish Relations. Under the directorship of the historian Salo W. Baron (1900–1980), the Commission's main tasks were the documentation of the Jewish cultural treasures that had been systematically looted and destroyed by the German National Socialists, as well as to prepare the procedure for the restitution of these objects after the war. The JCR, Inc. was established in 1947 and later authorized to act as the formal trustee for heirless Jewish cultural treasures that were found and assembled in the American Zone of Occupation in Germany. It was formally approved as the cultural agent of the earlier authorized Jewish Restitution Successor Organization (JRSO), which had already acted as the general trustee for Jewish property in the American Zone. The JCR's membership included representatives of the most important Jewish institutions and organizations worldwide. Between 1945 and 1952, American officials as well as Jewish representatives in Europe carried out one of largest operations in cultural restitution ever. Over 5 million books and thousands of Jewish ritual objects were salvaged and

either returned to their owners and heirs or were taken into custody by the JCR. Associated with JCR's mission were important intellectuals of the time, such as Hannah Arendt, Salo Baron, Lucy Dawidowicz, Morris Cohen, Koppel Pinson, Cecil Roth, Max Weinreich, and Gershom Scholem.

2. The JCR was supported by the following organizations: the American Jewish Committee, the American Jewish Conference, the Commission on European Jewish Cultural Reconstruction, the Council for the Protection of the Rights and Interests of Jews from Germany, the Hebrew University of Jerusalem, the Synagogue Council of America and the World Jewish Congress. In 1949 it was enlarged by addition of the following members: Agudath Israel World Organization; The American Jewish Joint Distribution Committee; the Anglo-Jewish Association; the Board of Deputies of British Jews; the Committee on Restoration of Continental Jewish Museums, Libraries and Archives; Interessenvertretung der juedischen Gemeinden und Kultusvereinigungen in der US-Zone; and the Jewish Agency of Palestine.

3. To name only the most important ones: Hannah Arendt, Maurice Finkelstein, Aaron Freimann, Horace Kallen, Adolf Kober, Alexander Marx, Jerome Michael, Koppel Pinson, Max Weinreich, Bernard Weinryb, and Rachel and Mark Wischnitzer.

4. The "Institut zur Erforschung der Judenfrage" [Institute for the Research of the Jewish Question] was founded by Alfred Rosenberg (one of the highest Nazi officials in charge of ideology and education within the National Socialist German Workers' Party) as a part of the planned National Socialist University "Hohe Schule," which was to be set up by the end of the war. The institute gathered book collections from all over Europe, which were looted by the notorious "Einsatzstab Reichsleiter Rosenberg" including millions of Jewish-owned books.

5. In March 1946 the American Military Government in Germany established the Offenbach Archival Depot, which served as the central collecting point for library collections and archival materials as well as ritual objects looted by the Nazis and found in the American zone of occupation.

6. The Monuments, Fine Arts and Archives unit (MFA&A) of the American Forces was established in 1943 by the U.S. War Department at the suggestion of the American Commission for the Protection and Salvage of Artistic and Historical Monuments in War Areas. Its tasks were the preservation of cultural treasures that were damaged within the combat operations and a systematic search for all hidden looted cultural material in Germany and the formerly occupied territories. The units were at that time supervised by the U.S. High Commissioner for Germany.

7. In February 1949, through the so-called Frankfurt Agreement, the JCR, Inc. was officially recognized as the authorized trustee for heirless Jewish cultural treasures in the American zone of Occupation.

8. Joshua Starr (1907–1949), historian and editor, worked as executive secretary for the Conference on Jewish Relations and later the JCR, Inc., and in 1948 served as one of its so-called field directors working in the Offenbach Archival Depot (cf. note 5).

9. Shlomo Shunami (1897–1984), head librarian of the Jewish National and University Library in Jerusalem and a key figure in the process of salvaging Jewish book collections from Europe within the *Otzrot HaGola* (Treasures of the Diaspora) initiative of the Hebrew University.

10. The Julius Streicher Collection counted about 15,000 volumes as property of the "Stuermer" publishing house. The looted collection of Jewish provenance was assembled in Nuremberg and after 1945 was passed on to the Offenbach Archival Depot as well as the Nuremberg municipal library and the Jewish community, which after its emigration to Palestine also transferred the books to the Offenbach Archival Depot.

11. Mordechai Narkiss (1898–1957), art historian and one of the first directors of the Bezalel Museum (later the Israel Museum) in Jerusalem.

12. Encouraged by the JRSO and the JCR, Inc., the authorities in the British and the French zones established similar bodies. The British Jewish Trust Corporation was set up in 1949, and its French counterpart, the Branche Française, was set up in 1952.

13. JCR terminated its activities around 1955 but existed formally until 1977. Most of its activities were continued by the Cultural and Education Reconstruction Program of the Conference on Jewish Material Claims Against Germany.

XII

JEWISH IDENTITY CHALLENGED AND REDEFINED

In the accelerated process of acculturation and assimilation that characterized the Jews' entrance into the modern world, a large number of Jews were to varying degrees estranged over time from their primordial community. Their bonds—social, cultural, spiritual, and psychological—with the community of their birth were weakened, while at the same time Jewish self-identify became problematic. The readings in this chapter represent various types of response to the problems of Jewish identify in the modern period: alienation (Solomon Maimon, Karl Emil Franzos, Franz Kafka); conversion (Joseph Michael Edler von Arnsteiner, Abraham Mendelssohn, Heinrich Heine); cosmopolitanism (Ludwig Boerne, Rosa Luxemburg, Rahel Levin Varnhagen, Eduard Bernstein, Isaac Deutscher); and Jewish self-hatred (Walter Rathenau, Otto Weininger, Theodor Lessing). In contradistinction to these responses, from the midst of assimilation, there is a dialectical affirmation of Jewish identity and Judaism. Four varieties of this affirmation are represented here: national-Zionist affirmation (Moses Hess); affirmation of Jewishness *qua* unique sensibility (Gustav Landauer, Sigmund Freud); *Trotzjudentum* ("defiant Judaism"), an affirmation of Jewish identity in defiance of the antisemites and as an expression of solidarity with one's oppressed brethren (Emma Lazarus, Arthur Koestler); and the affirmation of Jewish religious faith (Franz Rosenzweig, Jeri Langer, Arthur A. Cohen). A fifth, and perhaps *sui generis* category—the "Holocaust Jew"—is represented by the testimony of Jean Amery. A Jew solely by virtue of the racist definitions of the Nuremberg Laws, Amery affirmed what was for him "the [existential] necessity and impossibility of being a Jew."

The special inflections of the identity of modern Jewish women are represented by selections by from Bertha Pappenheim, Ernestine Louise Rose, Emma Lazarus, Regina Jones (the first female rabbi), Rochel Frank, Rachel Adler, and the voice of a convert to Judaism, Martha C. Nussbaum. The varied identities of Sephardi Jewry are documented by statements by a member of the Donme Judeo-Islamic sect; by Elias Canetti; and Albert Memi. The challenge of Zionism to a post-Holocaust Jewish identity is explored by Daniel Bell, Ben Halpern, George Steiner, and A. B. Yehoshua.

1. MY EMERGENCE FROM TALMUDIC DARKNESS (1793)

SOLOMON MAIMON[1]

The subjects of the Talmud, with the exception of those relating to jurisprudence, are dry and mostly unintelligible to a child—the laws of sacrifice, of purification, of forbidden meats, of feasts and so forth—in which the oddest rabbinical conceits are elaborated through many volumes with the finest dialectic, and the most far-fetched questions are discussed with the highest efforts of intellectual power, for example, how many white hairs a *red cow* may have, and yet remain a red cow; what sorts of scabs require this or that sort of purification; whether a louse or a flea may be killed on the Sabbath—the first being allowed, while the second is a deadly sin—whether an animal should be slaughtered at the neck or tail; whether the high priest puts on his shirt or his socks first; whether the *Yibbun*, that is, the brother of a man who dies childless, being required by law to marry the widow,[2] is relieved of his obligation if he falls off a roof and sticks in the mire. *Ohe iam satis est:* ["Alas, it is enough already!"] Compare these glorious disputations, which are served up to young people and forced on them even to their disgust, with history, in which natural events are related in an instructive and agreeable manner, and with a knowledge of the world's structure, by which the outlook into nature is widened, and the vast whole is brought into a well-ordered system; surely my preference will be justified....

I must now say something of the conditions of the Jewish schools in general. The school is commonly a small smoky hut, and the children are scattered, some on benches, some on the bare earth. The master, in a dirty blouse sitting on the table, holds between his knees a bowl, in which he grinds tobacco into snuff with a huge pestle like the club of Hercules, while at the same time he wields his authority. The ushers give lessons, each in his own corner, and rule those under their charge quite as despotically as the master himself. Of the breakfast, lunch and other food sent to the school for the children, these gentlemen keep the largest share for themselves. Sometimes the poor youngsters get nothing at all; and yet they dare not make any complaint on the subject, if they will not expose themselves to the vengeance of these tyrants. Here the children are imprisoned from morning to night, and have not an hour to themselves, except on Friday and a half-holiday at the New Moon.

As far as study is concerned, the reading of Hebrew is regularly taught. On the other hand, very seldom is any progress made towards the mastery of the Hebrew language. Grammar is not taught in the school at all, but has to be learnt by translation of the Holy Scriptures, very much as the ordinary man learns imperfectly the grammar of his mother-tongue by social intercourse. Moreover, there is no dictionary of the Hebrew language. The children therefore begin at once with the explanation of the Bible. This is divided into as many sections as there are weeks in the year, in order that the books of Moses, which are read in the synagogue every Saturday, may be read through in a year. Accordingly, every week some verses from the beginning of the section of the week are explained in school, and those with every possible grammatical blunder. Nor can it well be otherwise. For the Hebrew must be explained by means of the vernacular. But the vernacular of the Polish Jews is itself full of defects and grammatical inaccuracies; and so the Hebrew language, which is learned by its

Source: The Autobiography of Solomon Maimon, trans. J. Clark Murray (London: East and West Library, 1954), pp. 28, 31–33, 68–70, 126–28. Reprinted by permission of the Hebrew Publishing Company.

means, must be of the same stamp. The pupil thus acquires just as little knowledge of the language, as of the contents of the Bible.

In addition to this the Talmudists have attached all sorts of curious fancies to the Bible. The ignorant teacher believes with confidence, that the Bible cannot in reality have any other meaning than that which these expositions ascribe to it; and the pupil must follow his teacher's faith, and so the right understanding of words necessarily becomes lost...

Thanks to the instruction received from my father, but still more to my own industry, I had got on so well, that in my eleventh year I was able to pass as a full rabbi. In addition I possessed some disconnected knowledge in history, astronomy and other mathematical sciences. I burned with desire to acquire more knowledge, but how was this to be accomplished, lacking guidance, scientific books and all other means for the purpose? I was obliged therefore to content myself with making use of any help that I could by chance obtain, without plan or method.

In order to gratify my desire for scientific knowledge, there were no means available but that of learning foreign languages. But how was I to begin? To learn Polish or Latin with a Catholic teacher was for me impossible, on the one hand because the prejudices of my own people prohibited all languages but Hebrew, and all sciences but the Talmud and the vast array of its commentators; on the other hand because the prejudices of Catholics would not allow them to give instruction in those matters to a Jew. I was obliged to support a whole family by teaching, by correcting proofs of the Holy Scriptures, and by other work of a similar kind. For a long time therefore I had to sigh in vain for the satisfaction of my natural inclination.

At last a fortunate accident came to my aid. I observed in some stout Hebrew volumes, that they contained several alphabets, and that the number of their sheets was indicated not merely by Hebrew letters, but that for this purpose the characters of a second and a third alphabet had also been employed, these being Latin and German letters.... [I] gradually learnt the Latin and German characters.

By a kind of deciphering. I began to combine various German letters into words; but as the characters used along with the Hebrew letters might be quite different from these, I remained doubtful whether the whole of my labour would not be in vain, till

fortunately some leaves of an old German book fell into my hands. I began to read. How great were my joy and surprise, when I saw from the connection, that the words completely corresponded with those which I had learnt....

I still felt a want I was not able to fill. I could not completely satisfy my desire for scientific knowledge. Up to this time the study of the Talmud was still my chief occupation. With this, however, I found pleasure merely because of its form, for this calls into action the higher powers of the mind; but I took no interest in its subject matter. It affords exercise in deducing the remotest consequences from their principles, in discovering the most hidden contradiction, in hunting out the finest distinctions, and so forth. But as the principles themselves have merely an imaginary reality, they cannot by any means satisfy a soul thirsting after knowledge....

[Maimon eventually obtained some old German books on the natural sciences.] I pocketed these few books, and returned home in rapture. After I had studied these books thoroughly, my eyes were opened. I believed that I had found a key to all the secrets of nature, as I now knew the origin of storms, of dew, of rain, and such phenomena. I looked down with pride on all others who did not yet know these things, laughed at their prejudices and superstitions, and proposed to clear up their ideas on these subjects and to enlighten their understanding. But this did not always succeed. I laboured once to teach a Talmudist that the earth is round...

[Having made his way to the centers of the Enlightenment in Germany, and after great travail, Maimon acquired the rudiments of German secular culture.] I had received too much education to return to Poland, to spend my life in misery without rational occupation or society, and to sink back into the darkness of superstition and ignorance, from which I had delivered myself with so such labour. On the other hand, I could not reckon to succeed in Germany owing to my ignorance of the language, as well as of the manners and customs of the people to which I had never been able to adapt myself properly. I had learnt no particular profession. I had not distinguished myself in any special science, I was not even master of any language in which I could make myself perfectly intelligible. It occurred to me, therefore, that there was no alternative left but to embrace the Christian religion and get myself baptised in

Hamburg. Accordingly I resolved to go to the first clergyman I should come across and inform him of my resolution, we well as of my motives for it, without any hypocrisy in a truthful and honest fashion. But as I could not express myself well orally, I put my thoughts into writing in German with Hebrew characters, went to a schoolmaster, and got him to copy it in German characters. The purport of my letter was in brief as follows:

> I am a native of Poland, belonging to the Jewish nation, destined by my education and studies to be a rabbi; but in the thickest darkness I have perceived some light. This has induced me to search further after light and truth and to free myself completely from the darkness of superstition and ignorance. As this could not be attained in my native place, I went to Berlin, where through the support of some enlightened men of our nation I studied for some years—not indeed with any plan, but merely to satisfy my thirst for knowledge. But as our nation is unable to use, not only such planless studies, but even those based on the most perfect plan, it cannot be blamed for becoming tired of them, and pronouncing their encouragement to be useless. I have therefore resolved, in order to secure temporal as well as eternal happiness, which depends on the attainment of perfection, and in order to become useful to myself as well as to others, to embrace the Christian religion. The Jewish religion, it is true, comes in its articles of faith, nearer to reason than Christianity. But in practical use the latter has an advantage over the former; and since morality, which consists not in opinions but in actions, is the aim of all religion, clearly the latter comes nearer than the former to this aim. Moreover I esteem the mysteries of the Christian religion for that which they are, that is, allegorical representations of the truths that are most important for man. Thus I make my faith in them harmonise with reason, but I cannot believe them literally. I beg therefore most respectfully an answer to the question, whether after this confession I am worthy of the Christian religion or not. If I am, I am prepared to carry my proposal into effect; but if not, I must give up all claim to a religion which enjoins me to lies, that is, to deliver a confession of faith which contradicts my reasons....

I went then to a prominent clergyman, delivered my letter, and asked for a reply. He read it with great attention, was equally astonished, and on finishing began to converse with me.

"So," he said, "your intention is to embrace the Christian religion merely in order to improve your temporal circumstances."

"Excuse me, Herr Pastor," I replied, "I think I have made it clear enough in my letter that my object is the attainment of perfection. For this, it is true, the removal of all hindrances and the improvement of my external circumstances are an indispensable condition. But this condition is not the chief end".

"But", said the pastor, "do you not feel any inclination to the Christian religion without reference to any external motives?"

"I should be telling a lie if I were to give you an affirmative answer."

"You are too much of a philosopher," replied the pastor, "to be able to become a Christian. Reason has taken the upper hand with you, and faith must accommodate itself to reason. You hold the mysteries of the Christian religion to be mere fables, and its commands to be mere laws of reason. For the present I cannot be satisfied with your confession of faith. You should therefore pray to God, that He may enlighten you with His grace and endow you with the spirit of true Christianity; and then come to me again."

"If that is the case," I said, "then I must confess, Herr Pastor, that I am not qualified for Christianity. Whatever light I may receive, I shall always make it luminous with the light of reason. I shall never believe that I have fallen upon new truths, if it is impossible to see their connection with the truths already known to me. I must therefore remain what I am—a stiff-necked Jew. My religion enjoins me to *believe* nothing, but to *think* the truth and to *practice* goodness. If I find any hindrance in this from external circumstances, it is not my fault. I do all that lies in my power."

With this I bade the pastor goodbye....

NOTES

1. Solomon Maimon (c.1753–1800). Born in Sukoviboeg, Poland, he received a traditional Talmudic education. In search of secular learning Maimon abandoned his family and rabbinic office and went to Germany, where he gradually acquired a profound knowledge of German culture and philosophy. Kant noted that of all his critics nobody

understood his work as well as Maimon. In his auto-biography, published in German in 1793, Maimon describes his estrangement from traditional Judaism. Although he presents it as a process immanent to his experience of Judaism, his estrangement undoubtedly gained articulation and self-consciousness from

his contact with non-Jewish culture. His autobiography was widely read throughout the nineteenth and twentieth centuries by German intellectuals—non-Jewish and Jewish— who derived their conception of traditional Judaism from it.

2. See Deuteronomy 25: 5–6.

2. EVERY COUNTRY HAS THE JEWS THAT IT DESERVES (1877)

KARL EMIL FRANZOS[1]

When I took up my pen four years ago, I strongly felt the necessity of making my work as artistic as possible. I wished to write stories, and strove to give them poetic value. For this very reason, it seemed necessary that I should describe the kind of life with which I was best acquainted. This was essentially the case with regard to that of the Podolian Jews. I therefore became the historian of the Podolian Ghetto, and it was my great desire to give these stories an artistic form; but not at the cost of truth. I have never permitted my love of the beautiful to lead me into the sin of falsifying the facts and conditions of life, and am confident that I have described this strange and outlandish mode of existence precisely as it appeared to me. If in my first published volume my efforts to portray men and manners needed the assistance of my powers as a novelist, so in this book my knowledge of men and manners has to help me in my labors as a novelist. Sometimes the one side of my character takes the upper hand, and sometimes the other; but still they are at bottom inseparable, and it has always been my endeavor to describe facts artistically. However the novelist may be judged, the portrayer of men and manners demands that his words should be believed.

This request is not superfluous, for it is a very strange mode of life on which I am about to introduce the reader.... I have kept before my eyes, while penning these stories, that I am writing for a Western reader. If he will only trust to my love of truth, and regard the separate stories in combination with each other, he will gain a clear idea of the kind of life I describe without any further particulars. Every country has the Jews that it deserves—and it is not the fault of the Polish Jews that they are less civilized than their brethren in the faith in England, Germany, and France. At least, it is not entirely their fault....

NOTE

1. Karl Emil Franzos (1848–1904), Austrian-Jewish novelist and journalist. He was born in Czortkow, Galicia, which he later fictionalized as Barnow. His collections of sketches and tales about life in the Podolian Ghetto—most notably *Halb-Asien* [Semi-Asia] (1876) and *The Jews of Barnow* (1877)—reveal Franzos's ambivalent feelings.

   On the one hand he is compassionate; on the other he is self-consciously critical about the superstitions and the backward, "Asiatic" ways of the ghetto. Franzos's popular stories did much to disseminate a negative image of the "unassimilated" Jews of Eastern Europe.

Source: Karl Emil Franzos, "Preface," *The Jews of Barnow*, trans. M. W. Macdowall (New York: D. Appleton & Co., 1883), pp. xix–xxi.

3. MY FATHER'S BOURGEOIS JUDAISM (1919)

FRANZ KAFKA[1]

I found little means of escape from you in Judaism. Here some escape would, in principle, have been thinkable, but more than that, it would have been thinkable that we might both have found each other in Judaism or even that we might have begun from there in harmony. But what sort of Judaism was it I got from you? In the course of the years I have taken roughly three different attitudes to it.

As a child I reproached myself, in accord with you, for not going to the synagogue enough, for not fasting, and so on. I thought that in this way I was doing a wrong not to myself but to you, and I was penetrated by a sense of guilt, which was, of course, always ready at hand.

Later, as a young man, I could not understand how, with the insignificant scrap of Judaism you yourself possessed, you could reproach me for not (if for no more than the sake of the piety, as you put it) making an effort to cling to a similar insignificant scrap. It was indeed really, so far as I could see, a mere scrap, a joke, not even a joke. On four days in the year you went to the synagogue, where you were, to say the least, closer to the indifferent than to those who took it seriously, [you] patiently went through the prayers by way of formality, [you] sometimes amazed me be being able to show me in the prayer book the passage that was being said at the moment, and for the rest, so long as I was in the synagogue (and this was the main thing) I was allowed to hang about wherever I liked. And so I yawned and dozed through the many hours (I don't think I was ever again so bored, except later at dancing lessons) and did my best to enjoy the few little bits of variety there were, as, for instance, when the Ark of the Covenant was opened, which always reminded me of the shooting galleries where a cupboard door would open in the same way whenever one got a bull's eye, only with the difference that there something interesting always came out and here it was always just the same old dolls with no heads. Incidentally, it was also very frightening for me there, not only, as goes without saying, because of all the people one came into close contact with, but also because you once mentioned, by the way, that I too might be called up to read the Torah. That was something I went in dread of for years. But otherwise I was not fundamentally disturbed in my state of boredom, unless it was by the bar mizvah, but that meant no more than some ridiculous learning by heart, in other words, led to nothing but something like the ridiculous passing of an examination, and then, as far as you were concerned, by little, not very significant incidents, as when you were called up to read the Torah and came well out of the affair, which to my way of feeling was purely social, or when you stayed on in the synagogue for the prayers for the dead, and I was sent away, which for a long time, obviously because of being sent away and lacking, as I did, any deeper interest, aroused in me the more or less unconscious feeling that what was about to take place was something indecent.—That was how it was in the synagogue, and at home it was, if possible, even more poverty-stricken, being confined to the first evening of Passover which more and more developed into a farce, with fits of hysterical laughter, admittedly under the influence of the growing children. (Why did you have to give way to that influence? Because you brought it about in the first place.) And so there was the religious material that was handed on to me, to which may be added to most the outstretched hand pointing to "the sons of the millionaire Fuchs," who were in the synagogue with their father at high holidays. How one could do anything better with this material than get rid of it as fast as possible was something I could not understand; precisely getting rid of

Source: Franz Kafka, *Dearest Father: Stories and Other Writings*, trans. E. Kaiser and E. Wilkins (New York. Schocken: 1954), pp. 171–72. Copyright 1954 by Schocken Books Inc. Reprinted by permission of Pantheon Books.

it seemed to me the most effective act of "piety" one could perform....

NOTE

1. Franz Kafka (1883–1924), Czech-born German-Jewish novelist. Although estranged from the bourgeois Judaism of his father, Kafka identified positively with Judaism, shown by his interest in secular Jewish culture and Zionism, which provided a counter-Jewish identity for many middle-class Jewish youths of his day. Kafka wrote at the age of thirty-six this autobiographical letter to his father in 1919, which he never actually sent.

4. MEMOIRS OF A BALKAN JEW

ELIAS CANETTI[1]

The biggest cleaning in the house came before *Pesakh* (Passover). Everything was moved topsy-turvy, nothing stayed in the same place, and since the cleaning began early—lasting about two weeks, I believe—this was the period of the greatest disorder. Nobody had time for you, you were always underfoot and were pushed aside or sent away, and as for the kitchen, where the most interesting things were being prepared, you could at best sneak a glance inside. Most of all, I loved the brown eggs, which were boiled in coffee for days and days.

On the seder evening, the long table was put up and set in the dining room; and perhaps the room had to be so long, for on this occasion the table had to seat very many guests. The whole family gathered for the seder, which was celebrated in our home. It was customary to pull in two or three strangers off the street; they were seated at the feast and participated in everything.

Grandfather sat at the head of the table, reading the Haggadah, the story of the exodus of the Jews from Egypt. It was his proudest moment: Not only was he placed above his sons and sons-in-law, who honored him and followed his directions, but he, the eldest, with his sharp face like a bird of prey, was also the most fiery of all; nothing eluded him. As he chanted in a singsong, he noticed the least motion, the slightest occurrence at the table, and his glance or a light movement of his hand would set it aright. Everything was very warm and close, the atmosphere of an ancient tale in which everything was precisely marked out and had its place. On seder evenings, I greatly admired my grandfather; and even his sons, who didn't have an easy time with him, seemed elevated and cheerful.

As the youngest male, I had my own, not unimportant function; I had to ask the *Ma-nishtanah*. The story of the exodus is presented as a series of questions and answers about the reasons for the holiday. The youngest of the participants asks right at the start what all these preparations signify: the unleavened bread, the bitter herbs, and the other unusual things on the table. The narrator, in this case my grandfather, replies with the detailed story of the exodus from Egypt. Without my questions, which I recited by heart, holding the book and pretending to read, the story could not begin. The details were familiar to me, they had been explained often enough; but throughout the reading I never lost the sense that my grandfather was answering me personally. So it was a great evening for me too, I felt important, downright

Source: The Memoirs of Elias Canetti (New York: Farrar, Straus and Giroux, 1996), pp. 25–28.

indispensable; I was lucky there was no younger cousin to usurp my place.

But although following every word and every gesture of my grandfather's I looked forward to the end throughout the narrative. For then came the nicest part: The men suddenly all stood up and jigged around a little, singing together as they danced: "*Had gadya, had gadya !*"—"A kid! A kid!" It was a merry song, and I was already quite familiar with it, but it was part of the ritual for an uncle to call me over when it was done and to translate every line of it into Ladino.

When my father came home from the store, he would instantly speak to my mother. They were very much in love at that time and had their own language, which I didn't understand; they spoke German, the language of their happy schooldays in Vienna. Most of all, they talked about the *Burgtheater*; before ever meeting, they had seen the same plays and the same actors there and they never exhausted their memories of it. Later I found out that they had fallen in love during such conversations, and while neither of them had managed to make their dream of the theater come true—both had passionately wanted to act—they did succeed in getting married despite a great deal of opposition.

Grandfather Arditti, from one of the oldest and most prosperous Sephardic families in Bulgaria, was against letting his youngest, and favorite, daughter marry the son of an upstart from Adrianople. Grandfather Canetti had pulled himself up by his bootstraps; an orphan, cheated, turned out of doors while young, he had worked his way up to prosperity; but in the eyes of the other grandfather, he remained playactor and a liar, "*Es mentiroso*" (He's a liar), I heard Grandfather Arditti once say when he didn't realized I was listening. Grandfather Canetti, however, was indignant about the pride of the Ardittis, who looked down on him. His son could marry any girl, and it struck him as a superfluous humiliation that he wanted to marry the daughter of that Arditti of all people. So my parents at first kept their love a secret, and it was only gradually, very tenaciously, and with the active help of their older brothers and sisters and well-disposed relatives, that they succeeded in getting closer to making their wish come true. At last, both fathers gave in, but a tension always remained between them, and they couldn't stand each other. In the secret period, the two young people had fed their love incessantly with German conversations, and one

can imagine how many loving couples of the stage played their part here.

So I had good reason to feel excluded when my parents began their conversations. They became very lively and merry, and I associated this transformation, which I noted keenly, with the sound of the German language. I would listen with utter intensity and then ask them what this or that meant. They laughed, saying it was too early for me, those were things I would understand only later. It was already a great deal for them to give in on the word "Vienna," the only one they revealed to me. I believed they were talking about wondrous things that could be spoken of only in that language. After begging and begging to no avail, I ran away angrily into another room, which was seldom used, and I repeated to myself the sentences I had heard from them, in their precise intonation, like magic formulas; I practiced them often to myself, and as soon as I was alone, I reeled off all the sentences or individual words I had practiced—reeled them off so rapidly that no one could have possibly understood me. But I made sure never to let my parents notice, responding to their secrecy with my own.

I found out that my father had a name for my mother which he used only when they spoke German. Her name was Mathilde, and he called her Maedi. Once, when I was in the garden, I concealed my voice as well as I could, and called loudly into the house: "Maedi! Maedi! That was how my father called to her from the courtyard whenever he came home. Then I dashed off around the house and appeared only after a while with an innocent mien. My mother stood there perplexed and asked me whether I had seen father. It was a triumph for me that she had mistaken my voice for his, and I had the strength to keep my secret, while she told him about the incomprehensible event as soon as he came home.

It never dawned on them to suspect me, but among the many intense wishes of that period, the most intense was my desire to understand their secret language. I cannot explain why I didn't really hold it against my father. I did nurture a deep resentment toward my mother, and it vanished only years later, after his death, when she herself began teaching me German.

NOTE

1. Elias Canetti (1905–1994) was a Nobel Prize-winning German author, playwright, and essayist. He

was born in Rustschuk, Bulgaria, to a Ladino—Judeo-Spanish—speaking family. His parents also spoke German, which, as he describes in the passage from his memoir, they used as a "secret language." The family emigrated to Manchester, England, in 1911, and following the death of his father in 1912, to Lausanne, Switzerland, in 1913. It was here that Canetti began to learn German from his mother, soon moving to Vienna, Zurich (Canetti's favorite city), Frankfurt, and again to Vienna, where he largely remained until 1938. In 1929 he completed a Ph.D in chemistry at the University of Vienna. He associated with literary circles in Vienna and wrote voluminously, publishing in the 1930s several plays and a novel, *Die Blendung* (The Blinding), which was translated into English as *Auto de Fe* (1946). Needless to say, the novel was banned in Nazi Germany. In 1938 he fled Vienna and the persecution of the Jews and settled in Paris and later in England; he spent his final years in his beloved Zurich. He is also well-known for his multi-disciplinary study of mass movements and mob violence, a work inspired by his witnessing the burning of the Palace of Justice in Vienna in 1927 and the mass murder by the Nazis.

5. I HAVE CONVERTED (1785)

JOSEPH MICHAEL EDLER VON ARNSTEINER[1]

My venerable parents!

Believe me, dearest parents, since I have last opened my heart to you I was ready for the daring step a hundred times; now, finally, I am going to take it. (I herewith inform you that I have adopted the Catholic faith.)

Only respect—and fear, lest you look harshly upon my [decision]—have kept me from writing to you. I wanted first to prove to you... that your son is not unworthy of you. I wanted to show you that neither ulterior motives, nor desire for the easy life, nor innate licentiousness have led me to forgo your religion, but rather a conviction that I will find salvation and peace of mind on a different road. Ever since [my conversion], I have tried everything, and have used every means, to gain your permission to meet with you and to kiss the hand of my venerable parents; but, alas, all these efforts were in vain!

Either my entreaties have not reached your ears or, even worse, have not reached your heart. I am your son, dearest father! I—formerly, your most beloved son—challenge anybody to point out one single fact by which I have [deservedly] forfeited the love and the affection of my parents; were it so, were I conscious of any offence against you, I would be able to bear my predicament more easily; I would patiently wait for the softening of your heart; I would seek to expiate my crimes, and [deem it proper] that an appropriate punishment precede our reconciliation. But mine, unfortunately, is the case of the melancholic individual who is most depressed because he cannot find an objective reason for his depression, for I do not know of any personal defect for which I should deserve such painful chastisement.

I certainly appreciate, dearest parents, the attitudes usually inculcated by upbringing and a

---

Source: Hilde Spiel, *Fanny von Arnstein oder die Emanzipation: Ein Frauenleben an der Zeitenwende, 1758–1818* (Frankfurt am Main: S. Fisher Verlag, 1962), pp. 86–89. Copyright 1962 by S. Fischer Verlag GmbH, Frankfurt am Main. Cited by permission of S. Fischer Verlag GmbH. Trans. by J. Hessing.

misconceived religion, but are you really capable of hating your son just because he adheres to principles of belief other than your own? In our age of enlightenment, under the government of our most gracious monarch, whose every action creates a singular example of general tolerance for each of his subjects, who lets everyone *believe* in whatever he wishes as long as he *acts* as he should? Under such a government which grants you, who abide by Jewish law, the same protection, and the same rights, as every other fellow citizen? Where you can collect your riches and live off them without the slightest fear of pressure and coercion? Under a tolerant government such as ours, could you really be capable of hating an innocent, blameless son, and of rejecting his request for permission to meet with you and to receive your blessing, only because he does not share your religious principles? Could you banish your grandchild from your countenance, an innocent minor who could do nothing but follow the well-meant advice of his father? In this case, may I refer to my brother and sister-in-law who are still Jewish and who, on their many excursions into the world, are met with all due love and respect by the members of the numerically dominant religion, while you, out of religious hatred, banish an erstwhile beloved son from your eyes! Your very religion, dearest parents, does not condemn anybody forever, and yet even in our temporal life, you have chosen to be inexorably severe!

Once again, therefore, venerable parents, I implore you to accept my entreaties which do not stem from my self-interest and do not pursue any secondly object: allow me and my dear child, your grandchild, to approach you and even to come and see you daily, so that we may kiss you hands and receive your blessing. We are human beings, dearest parents! Human beings who are flourishing today and may fade away tomorrow! It is a dreadful thought to me—and, I daresay, should be one to you, as well—that one of us might leave this temporal world without having achieved a complete and cordial reconciliation and reunification. I therefore implore you to think all this over once more, and to take the words of wise Solomon into consideration: *He who lives within the boundaries of the laws is the son of a wise man; but he who follows the squanderer brings disgrace upon his father.*

Please fix an hour when I and my child shall be allowed to appear before you, our parents. Believe me that I shall remain until the final breath of my life,

Your dearest son, . . .

NOTE

1. Joseph von Arnsteiner (d.1811), son of Adam Isaac Arnsteiner (1721–1785), purveyor to the court of Austrian Empress Maria Theresa. Joseph Michael converted to Catholicism in 1778; he was ennobled in 1783 after his second marriage into Austrian aristocracy. Despite his impassioned plea for parental forbearance, his father disowned him for having abandoned Judaism.

6. WHY I HAVE RAISED YOU AS A CHRISTIAN: A LETTER TO HIS DAUGHTER (c. JULY 1820)

ABRAHAM MENDELSSOHN[1]

My Dear Daughter,

You have taken an important step, and in sending you my best wishes for the day and for your future happiness, I have it at heart to speak seriously to you on subjects hither to not touched upon.

Does God exist? What is God? Is He a part of ourselves, and does He continue to live after the other part has ceased to be? And where? And how? All this I do not know, and therefore I have never taught you anything about it. But I know that there exists in me and in all human beings an everlasting inclination towards all that is good, true, and right, and a conscience which warns and guides us when we go astray. I know it, I believe it, I live in this faith, and this is my religion. This I could not teach you, and nobody can learn it; but everybody has it who does not intentionally and knowingly cast it away. The example of your mother, the best and noblest of mothers, whose whole life is devotion, love and charity, is like a bond to me that you will *not* cast it away. You have grown up under her guidance, ever intuitively receiving and adopting what alone gives real worth to mankind. Your mother has been, and is, and I trust will long remain to you, to your sister and brothers, and to all of us, a providential leading star on our path of life. When you look at her and turn over in your thoughts all the immeasurable good she has lavished upon you by her constant self-sacrificing devotion as long as you live, and when that reflection makes your heart and eyes overflow with gratitude, love and veneration, then you feel God and are godly.

This is all I can tell you about religion, all I know about it; but this will remain true, as long as one man will exist in the creation, as it has been true since the first man was created.

The outward form of religion your teacher has given you is historical, and changeable like all human ordinances. Some thousands of years ago the Jewish form was the reigning one, then the heathen form, and now it is the Christian. We, your mother and I, were born and brought up by our parents as Jews, and without being obliged to change the form of our religion have been able to follow the divine instinct in us and in our conscience. We have educated you and your brothers and sister in the Christian faith, because it is the creed of most civilized people, and contains nothing that can lead you away from what is good, and much that guides you to love, obedience, tolerance, and resignation, even if it offered nothing but the example of its founder, understood by so few, and followed by still fewer.

By pronouncing your confession of faith you have fulfilled the claims of *society* on you, and obtained the *name* of a Christian. Now *be* what your duty as a human being demands of you, *true, faithful, good*; obedient and devoted till death to your mother, and I may also say to your father, unremittingly attentive to the voice of your conscience, which may be suppressed but never silenced, and you will gain the highest happiness that is to be found on earth, harmony and contentedness with yourself.

I embrace you with fatherly tenderness, and hope always to find in you a daughter worthy of

---

Source: Abraham Mendelssohn to Fanny Mendelssohn, c. July 1820, in S. Hensel, *The Mendelssohn Family (1729–1847): From Letters and Journals*, 2nd rev. ed., trans. C. Klingemann (New York, 1882), vol.1 pp. 79–80.

your, of our, mother. Farewell, and remember my words.

NOTE

1. Abraham Mendelssohn (1776–1835), son of Moses Mendelssohn. A deist and a rationalist by conviction, Abraham brought up his children—Fanny and Felix—as Protestants in order to improve their social opportunities. In 1822 he and his wife also embraced Christianity "because it is the religious form acceptable to the majority of civilized human beings." He wrote this letter to his daughter Fanny (1805–1847) upon her confirmation into the Lutheran church.

7. A TICKET OF ADMISSION TO EUROPEAN CULTURE (1823, c. 1854)

HEINRICH HEINE[1]

September 1823

From the nature of my thinking you can deduce that baptism is a matter of indifference to me, that I do not regard it as important even symbolically, and that in the circumstances in which it will be carried out in my case, it will have little significance for others likewise. For me perhaps its significance will be that I can better devote myself to championing the rights of my unfortunate brethren. And yet I hold it beneath my dignity and a stain on my honor to undergo conversion in order to obtain a position in Prussia. Dear old Prussia! I really do not know what course to take in this bad situation. I'll turn Catholic yet for spite, and hang myself.

c.1854

We are living in sad times. Scoundrels become our "best," and the best must turn scoundrel. I understand well the words of the psalmist: "Lord, give us our daily bread, that we blaspheme not Thy name…"

The baptismal certificate is the ticket of admission to European culture…

My becoming a Christian is the fault of those Saxons who suddenly changed saddles at Leipzig,[2] or of Napoleon, who really did not have to go to Russia, or of his teacher of geography at Brienne, who did not tell him that Moscow winters are very cold.

NOTES

1. Heinrich Heine (1797–1856), German-Jewish poet and essayist. In 1825 he was baptized a Lutheran, with the hope that his conversion would facilitate the gaining of a doctorate and the pursuit of a career as a civil servant or academic. His repeated attempts to secure a position were, however, futile. Finally, after having failed to obtain a promised chair at the University of Munich and fearing police action against himself because of his political satire, he left Germany for Paris in 1831.

   He spent the remainder of his life in exile. His attitude to Judaism was complex. He deemed it "a misfortune," but he also wrote warmly and proudly of Judaism. To a friend he once declared, "I make no secret of my Judaism, to which I have not returned, because I never left it."

2. At the battle of Leipzig, October 1813, the Saxon troops fighting with the French defected to the allies, and thus ensured the defeat of Napoleon.

Source: Hugo Bieber, *Heinrich Heine: A Biographical Anthology*, trans. M. Hadas (Philadelphia: Jewish Publication Society of America, 1956), pp. 157, 196. Reprinted by permission of the Jewish Publication Society.

8. BECAUSE I AM A JEW I LOVE FREEDOM (1832)

LUDWIG BOERNE[1]

My well-meaning friend in the *Deutsche Allgemeine Zeitung* says: no one should forget that I am a Jew. Unlike others, however, he does not mean this as a reproach; on the contrary, he recalls the fact as an excuse for me, or even in praise of me. He says: I am justified in being resentful of the Germans who have oppressed and disgraced my people; not hatred, but love has distorted my view.... It is miraculous! I have experienced it a thousand times, and yet it is always new to me. Certain people object to my being a Jew; others forgive me; still others even praise me for it; but everybody remembers it. The Jewish mystique seems to have cast its spell on them, they are unable to free themselves from it. And I know fairly well where this evil spell comes from. The poor Germans! Living on the first floor, and oppressed by the seven stories of the higher classes, it relieves them of their anxiety to speak of people who live even further down, in the basement. That they are not Jews consoles them for the fact that they are not even court counselors. No, that I was born a Jew has never made me bitter against the Germans and has never distorted my perspective. I would not be worthy of the sunlight if I repaid with base ingratitude the grace which God has bestowed upon me by making me a German and a Jew at the same time—just because of the scorn which I have always despised, or because of the pain which I have long since forgotten. No, I know how to value the undeserved fortune of being a German and also a Jew, thus being able to strive for all virtues of a German without having to share any of his faults. Yes, because I was born a slave I love freedom more than you do. Yes, because I have learnt all about servitude, I understand more about freedom than you do. Yes, because I was born to no fatherland, I yearn for a fatherland more fervently than you. And because my birthplace was no bigger than the *Judengasse* and beyond its locked gate foreign territory began for me, neither city nor even country or province will suffice me as a fatherland.... I have built the house of my freedom on strong foundations; do as I have done, do not content yourselves with putting new tiles on the roof of the dilapidated building of your state. I beg you, do not despise my Jews. If you were as they are you would be better off; were they as many as you are they would be better than you. You are thirty million Germans and you count only as thirty in the world; were there thirty million Jews, the world would count as nothing in comparison. You have deprived Jews of air but this saved them from decay. You have strewn their hearts with the salt of hatred; but this has kept their hearts fresh. During the entire long winter you have shut them up in a deep cellar and stuffed the cellar hole with dung; but you yourself, exposed to the cold, are half frozen to death. When spring comes we shall see who blossoms earlier, the Jew or the Christian.

NOTE

1. Ludwig Boerne (1786–1837), German-Jewish political essayist, born into a prominent banking family and raised in *Judengasse* in the Frankfurt ghetto. After the defeat of France at Waterloo in 1815, the anti-Jewish restrictions of the pre-Napoleonic era were reimposed in Germany. As a result Boerne lost his

---

Source: Ludwig Boerne, *Briefe aus Paris*, in *Gesammelte Schriften*, ed. Alfred Klaar (Leipzig, 1899), vol.6, pp. 62–64. Trans. By J. Hessing.

position as an official in the Frankfurt police department. He converted to Lutheranism in 1818 so that he could reassume the position, but then decided to become a political journalist instead. Because of his radical views, he was obliged to leave Germany in 1830; he fled to Paris, where he was regarded as the leader of the political émigrés. His *Briefe aus Paris* [Letters from Paris] (1930–33), from which this selection is taken, was a milestone in the struggle for liberalism and democracy in Germany. Although he was greatly concerned with the Jewish question, he insisted that the cause of Jewish emancipation should not be divorced from that of the freedom of humanity as a whole.

9. O HOW PAINFUL TO HAVE BEEN BORN A JEWESS! (1795–1833)[1]

RAHEL LEVIN VARNHAGEN

A.

I imagine that just as I was thrust into this world some supermundane being plunged these words into my heart with a dagger. "Yes, have sensibility, see the world as only a few see it, be great, noble; nor can I free you of incessant, eternal thought. But I add one thing more: Be a Jewess!" And now my whole life is a slow bleeding to death. But keeping still I can prolong it. Every attempt to stop the bleeding is to die anew, and immobility is only possible for me in death itself.... I can ascribe every evil, every misfortune, every vexation that has befallen me from that.

B.

"What a history!" she exclaimed [on her death-bed] with deep emotion. "Here I am, a fugitive from Egypt and Palestine, who has found your help, love, attention! Divine guidance has led me to you, dear August, and you to me! With sublime rapture I am contemplating my origins and this fateful nexus between the oldest memories of mankind and the latest developments linking poles far apart in time and space. What for a long period of my life has been the source of my greatest shame, my most bitter grief and misfortune—to be born a Jewess—I would not at any price now wish to miss. Will it be the same with my illness, shall I once find delight in it, never wanting to miss it again? O dear August, what consoling insight, what a meaningful parable! Let us continue on this way!" And then, weeping, she went on: "Dear August, my heart is refreshed in its innermost depths; I thought of Jesus and cried over his passion. I have felt, for the first time in my life, that he is my brother. And Mary, how she must have suffered! She witnessed the pain of her beloved son, and did not succumb, but kept standing at the cross! I could not have been able to do that; I would not have been strong enough. May God forgive me, I confess how weak I am."

Source: A. Rahel Levin to David Veit, 1795, in *Briefwechsel zwischen Rahel und David Veit*, ed. Ludmilla Assing (Leipzig, 1861), vol.2, pp. 79–80. Trans. by P. Mendes-Flohr. B. Statement by Rahel on her deathbed as recorded by Karl August Varnhagen von Ense, in *Rahel, Ein Buch des Andenkens fuer Ihre Freunde* (Berlin, 1834), vol. 1, p. 34, Trans. by J. Hessing.

NOTE

1. Rahel Levin Varnhagen (1771–1833). Born into a prospeperous Jewish merchant family in Berlin, she was raised in Orthodox Jewish surroundings. She was noted for her scintillating intelligence, and her home became the informal center of literary, social and political luminaries of her day. In 1814, after repeated romantic disappointments, she married a man fourteen years her junior, a minor Prussian diplomat named Karl August Varnhagen von Ense, and she converted to his religion, Protestantism.

10. NO ROOM IN MY HEART FOR JEWISH SUFFERING (1916)

ROSA LUXEMBURG[1]

But look, girl, if you so rarely find the opportunity to take a book into your hand, at least make a point of reading *good* books, not such *kitsch* as the Spinoza novel you have just sent me. Why do you come to me with your particular Jewish sorrows? I feel equally close to the wretched victims of the rubber plantations in Putumayo, or to the Negroes in Africa with whose bodies the Europeans are playing a game of catch. Do you remember the words elicited by the General Staff's work on Trotha's campaign in the Kalahari desert[2]: "....The rattling in the throats of the dying, and the mad screams of those who were withering from thirst, faded away into the sublime stillness of the infinite." Oh, this "sublime stillness of the infinite" in which so many screams fade away unheard—it reverberates within me so strongly that I have no separate corner in my heart for the ghetto: I feel at home in the entire world wherever there are clouds and birds and human tears.

NOTES

1. Rosa Luxemburg (1871–1919), Marxist theoretician and politician. Born into a Jewish family in Zamosc, Russian Poland, she helped found the Social Democratic Party of Poland and Lithuania. In 1898 she immigrated from Switzerland to Germany, where she became a leading figure in the revolutionary left wing of the German Socialist movement. With Franz Mehring and Karl Liebknecht she founded the Spartakusbund (the Spartacus Party), which at the end of 1918 was transformed into the Communist Party of Germany. She and Liebknecht were arrested in Berlin on January 15, 1919, for their involvement in the Spartacist uprising. While they were being transported to prison, both were murdered by army officers. A consistent internationalist, she found national particularism inimical to socialism—an attitude that is reflected in the letter presented here, in which she rebukes her friend for her Jewish national sentiments.

2. A revolt of Herero and Nama peoples of the German colony of Southwest Africa was brutally supressed by Lt. Gen. Lothar von Trotha in 1904–1907. Trotha's campaign is said to be the first genocide of the twentieth century.

Source: Rosa Luxemburg to Mathilda Wurm, February 16, 1916, in Rosa Luxemburg, *Briefe an Freunde*, ed. B. Kautsky (Hamburg: Europaeische Verlagsanstalt GmbH, 1950), pp. 48–49. Cited by permission of Europaeische Verlagsanstalt GmbH. Trans. By J. Hessing.

11. HOW I GREW UP AS A JEW IN THE DIASPORA (1918)

EDUARD BERNSTEIN[1]

My parents were Reform Jews, but Jews nevertheless. To which degree my father believed in God I cannot tell; we never discussed the question in depth. He approached the Bible as a rationalist, and I can still remember his critical remarks about it. This critical thinking, to be sure, accounts for the fact that my surname is not David. According to Jewish family tradition I should have been named thus. But my father held David in particular disdain, for as a king, David was a villain, and, therefore, my father was not going to have his son bear the name of such a man. My father, in any case, was not a pious man. But he knew much about Judaism, he could explain the Jewish customs and knew all the old songs by heart, which he sang at times. My mother, on the other hand, although not religious by the letter, was of a more pious nature and would have preferred, had the situation allowed it, to keep a Jewish household. She did not actually contradict my father, but did not share his rationalistic aloofness. During the High Holy Days, both my parents liked to attend the service at the Reform congregation in Berlin....

Upon leaving my parents' home [for boarding school] I entered a house, a street, and a school of completely Gentile character. This Gentile world seemed to me the normal, the Jewish world the anomalous one, and children, more gregarious than adults, tend to respect greatly what seems normal to them. Moreover, the Gentiles I met were Protestants, which made them very sympathetic to me. Which childish soul is not touched by the stories of Jesus, his mother, his suffering, and his great love of mankind? I heard of this in the dormitory and read of it in the spelling-book while I attend the first grades of boys' school. For a while, although as a Jew I was not obliged to do so, I even attended religious [Protestant] classes and enjoyed them more than the majority of my Christian schoolmates.

I still remember quite a few Christian chorals; some of them arouse feelings in me as strong as those associated with the ardent Jewish songs I heard in my parents' home, and later in the Reform temple. Emotionally, I accepted Judaism and Christianity, too, as long as Christian dogma was not discussed. My father praised Christ's Sermon on the Mount, and my mother used to say that Jesus, although he was not God's son, surely was a very noble human being. Nor did they mind when we children—on Christmas Eve, while father, in the living room, was spreading out the gifts under the Christmas tree—sat down in the dark adjoining room and sang assorted Christmas chorals to our edification.... Christmas actually was the main feast in my parents' home, my father's favorite holiday. Always short of money, he gladly put in a bit of work in order to transform a young, unhewn, cheaply bought conifer into a beautiful Christmas tree and, being a plumber by training, to prepare many a present for us children with his own hands....

[At the age of eleven] I decided to be a proper Jew, at least. Accordingly, in my opinion, I had to refrain first of all from eating pork. Whereupon I revealed to my parents one day that, in the name of Judaism, I would touch pork no more. Surprisingly, there was no opposition. "If you don't want to, my son, don't eat pork," replied my father. This absolute tolerance was poison to my intention. A bit of opposition would certainly have strengthened it, but now it lacked the attraction of a conquered right and consequently did not last very long. Without pork, to be sure, I could have done for quite a while. But since the

Source: Eduard Bernstein, "Wie Ich als Jude in der Diaspora aufwuchs", *Der Jude* 2 (1917–18), pp. 186–95. Trans. by J. Hessing.

law also prohibited all food prepared with lard, my decision was actually much more far-reaching than I had thought. I soon found out, moreover, that even a strict adherence to my decision would be of little avail, because to an Orthodox Jew many other things besides the eating of pork were forbidden. After a few weeks I gave in and admitted that observance of the dietary laws did not yet make a Jew.

When I was fifteen, a fatal illness befell a beloved member of my family, and I remember the prayer I sent to heaven: "If you exist, good Lord, please help my cousin." This help, however, was not extended. To be brief, my belief in the world to come finally broke down three years later, the night after the death of my mother, whom I had loved very much. I wondered for a long while whether I might hope to meet my dear mother again in the next world. The longer I thought about it, the more clearly I felt that it was impossible that I should ever meet my mother again as I had known and loved her, with all her virtues and weaknesses, with all her human attributes; she would live on for me only as long as I could keep her image in my mind. With the loss of my belief in the world to come, however, I lost the last vestige of my belief in a personal God as well.

There was no trace of Jewish faith in me, and for the Jewish ritual I only felt the contempt of the rationalist who was not influenced by any tradition. And yet, not all Jewish interest had died within me. I had a certain, albeit not pronounced, concern for the Jewish people. On the Sunday after my confirmation, walking home from the temple, I told my father that I would like to study the history of Judaism after the advent of Christianity, and especially during the Middle Ages. I was interested in finding out how the Jewish people had survived and developed throughout centuries of strife and suffering. But the vicissitudes of life never allowed me to realize my plan. There was no relevant literature in my home, and my evenings belonged to endeavors which led me into very different fields.

My formative years, moreover, overlapped the time when liberalism seemed to dominate the public scene in Germany and Jews played an ever-growing part in politics. To be sure, the Jews had enemies, but there was [as yet] no antisemitic movement; civil service was gradually opening up to them. Even in countries where the Jews had not yet gained equality, a spreading liberalism tended to improve their lot. In short, there was nothing to involve me, who had broken with the Jewish faith, in any way with the Jewish cause.

I felt thoroughly German, although a German of the liberal-democratic school. As many others, the national movement for German unification in the sixties held me in its spell. Black-Red-Gold, the democratic tricolor of German unity, was my flag: at times I even carried it on my breast, in the shape of an artfully designed heart of pasteboard. I bemoaned the suffering of the Schleswig Holsteiners under Danish rule, whose situation was idyllic, compared to the life of Jews in Russia and Poland to whom I remained indifferent. I composed jubilant verses when the Danes were defeated in 1864 and later, with young people of my age, I secretly sang the "Wacht am Rhein" and "Deutschland ueber Alles," [patriotic songs] which at the time were officially forbidden in Prussia. When war broke out between Germany and France in 1870, I decided that if Germany was going to suffer defeat I would volunteer, despite my weak health. "Napoleon, who has in cold blood provoked this war, must not be victorious, " I wrote to my best friend, who was vacationing with relatives at a village in the Mark Brandenburg. But he, a "pure" German, wrote back that I should not exaggerate, that no one really knew what was going on in the world of diplomacy. At the end of the war, neither he nor I were flushed by the victory, and when, after the battle at Sedan, the capture of Napoleon III did not bring the coveted peace, I lost all interest in the war. A year and a half later my friend and I joined the Socialist party, which sided with the International.

The early years after the establishment of the new German Empire were ill-suited to awaken my Jewish sympathies. The part played by Jewish capital on the stock exchange; Jewish wheeling and dealing with billions in the period known as the "foundation era" [of the German Empire]; The [opportunistic] participation of Jewish liberal newspapers in the struggle against the Catholic Church; the shallow opposition of these papers to socialism—all this repelled me, a socialist and a democrat, so much that at times it aroused anti-Jewish feelings within me. The first signs of antisemitism, which appeared in Germany during the second half of the seventies, seemed to me to be a logical reaction against the improper intrusion of the Jews and it did not greatly excite me. It was my mistake not to realize that these obtrusive Jews were but a small minority compared with the large numbers of Jews who quietly pursued their livelihood. Only as antisemitism turned from accusation to persecution, my attitude gradually changed. But in fighting against it, I always considered the question in terms of democratic equality. I have never thought of the Jewish question as one in which Jewish national rights or interests were involved.

In the light of my personal development, could it have been different? I do not want to make too much of the fact that until a very advanced age all of my more intimate friends were Gentiles. In this, chance has played no small part. I very much loved most of my Jewish relatives, felt attracted to a number of my Jewish fellow-students in high school, and met many a Jew whom I esteemed for his personal qualities and admired for his intellect. Circumstance, not prejudice, prevented an intimacy with Jewish contemporaries. I had no inherent affinity for a Jew *qua* Jew in favor of a Gentile. Eight years after the Franco-German war I once used the words "we Jews" in a conversation with a friend who was completely taken aback. "Never before," he said, "have you drawn a line between yourself as a Jew and the rest of us. Do you really want to start doing this now?" I had never intended anything of the sort. I had used the phrase as one might say "we traders," or "we non-smokers." But it made a strong impression on me that he should have taken offense at the phrase.

With this friend, as I have said already, I had joined the International in 1872, enthusiastically embraced its principles and program. As much as I felt myself a German, I was never possessed by national prejudices. In 1864, during the Prusso-Danish war, a high school teacher forbade the recitation of a poem by [Karl Joseph] Simrock, "Half the Bottle," because

its protagonist was a Dane; this, my patriotism and respect for the teacher notwithstanding, seemed rather tasteless to me. On two occasions in 1870 in the early stages of the [Franco-German] war, I barely escaped lynching when I publicly rebuked individuals who had insulted the French people. Now at last my thoughts—which a pure feeling for humanity had bred within me, and whose roots surely go back to my upbringing, free as it was of all religious prejudice—had found political expression. And when the Jewish question began to take on a more aggressive character, I believed that the solution would be found in the Socialist International. To this belief I still adhere, and it is more important to me than any separatist movement. After the experience of this world war, more than ever before, I wish to work for this belief with undivided devotion.

NOTE

1. Eduard Bernstein (1850–1932), German-Jewish socialist theoretician, identified with the so-called revisionist school within Marxism. In this book, *The Task of Jewry during the World War* (*Die Aufgabe der Juden in Weltkrieg*, 1917), he argued that because of their dispersion and universalist values, the Jews were uniquely qualified to lead the world to internationalism which would unite nations and put an end to war. Toward the end of his life, Bernstein lent Zionism his moral support through his participation in the international Socialist Pro-Palestine Committee.

   After the publication of his book in 1917, the Zionist journal, *Der Jude*, edited by Martin Buber, invited Bernstein to set forth his views on Zionism. Rather than giving an ideological statement, he offered this autobiographical explanation of his attitude toward Judaism and Jewish identity.

12. THE NON-JEWISH JEW (1958)

ISAAC DEUTSCHER[1]

There is an old Talmudic saying: "A Jew who has sinned still remains a Jew." My own thinking is, of course, beyond the idea of "sin" or "no sin"; but this saying has brought to my mind a memory from childhood which may not be irrelevant to my theme.

I remember that when as a child I read the Midrash, I came across a story and a description of a scene which gripped my imagination. It was the story of Rabbi Meir, the great saint and sage, the pillar of Mosaic orthodoxy and coauthor of the Mishnah, who took lessons in theology from a heretic, Elisha ben Abuyah, called *Akher* (The Stranger). Once on a Sabbath Rabbi Meir was with his teacher, and as usual they became engaged in a deep argument. The heretic was riding a donkey, and Rabbi Meir, as he could not ride on a Sabbath, walked by his side and listened so intently to the words of wisdom falling from his heretical lips that he failed to notice that he and his teacher had reached the ritual boundary which Jews were not allowed to cross on a Sabbath. The great heretic turned to his orthodox pupil and said; "Look, we have reached the boundary—we must part now; you must not accompany me any father—go back!" Rabbi Meir went back to the Jewish community, while the heretic rode on—beyond the boundaries of Jewry.

There was enough in this scene to puzzle an orthodox Jewish child. Why I wondered, did Rabbi Meir, that leading light of orthodoxy, take his lessons from the heretic? Why did he show him so much affection? Why did he defend him against other rabbis? My heart, it seems, was with the heretic. Who was he? He appeared to be in Jewry and yet out of it. He showed a curious respect for his pupil's orthodoxy, when he sent him back to the Jews on the Holy Sabbath; but he himself disregarding cannon

and ritual rode beyond the boundaries. When I was thirteen, or perhaps fourteen, I began to write a play about *Akher* and Rabbi Meir, and I tried to find out more about *Akher's* character. What made him transcend Judaism? Was he a Gnostic? Was he an adherent of some other school of Greek or Roman philosophy? I could not find the answers, and did not manage to get beyond the first act.

The Jewish heretic who transcends Jewry belongs to a Jewish tradition. You may, if you like, see *Akher* as a prototype of those great revolutionaries of modern thought: Spinoza, Heine, Marx, Rosa Luxemburg, Trotsky, and Freud. You may, if you wish, place them within a Jewish tradition. They all went beyond the boundaries of Jewry. They all found Jewry too narrow, too archaic and too constricting. They all looked for ideals and fulfillment beyond it, and they represent the sum and substance of much that is greatest in modern thought, the sum and substance of the most profound upheavals that have taken place in philosophy, sociology, economics, and politics in the last three centuries.

Did they have anything in common with one another? Have they perhaps impressed mankind's thought so greatly because of their special "Jewish genius"? I do not believe in the exclusive genius of any race. Yet I think that in some ways they were very Jewish indeed. They had in themselves something of the quintessence of Jewish life and of the Jewish intellect. They were *a priori* exceptional in that as Jews they dwelt on the borderlines of various civilizations, religions, and national cultures. They were born and brought up on the borderlines of various epochs. Their minds matured where the most diverse cultural influences crossed and fertilized each other. They lived on the margins or in the

---

Source: Isaac Deutscher, *The Non-Jewish Jew and Other Essays* (London: Oxford University Press, 1968), pp. 25–27. Reprinted by permission of the Merlin Press Ltd.

nooks and crannies of their respective nations. Each of them was in society and yet not in it, of it and yet not of it. It was this that enabled them to rise in thought above their societies, above their nations, above their times and generations, and to strike out mentally into wide new horizons and far into the future.

NOTE

1. Isaac Deutscher (1907–1967). A Marxist theoretician and historian, born in Cracow, Poland, he was raised in the strictly Orthodox tradition of Hasidism. In his youth he was renowned for his mastery of the Talmud and of the Hebrew language. In 1926 he became a member of the illegal Communist Party of Poland. However, because of his Trotskyite sympathies, he was expelled from the party in 1932. In 1939 he emigrated to London, where he devoted himself to journalism and historical research. His political biographies of Stalin and Trotsky earned him wide acclaim. His tender feelings for the Jewish masses of Eastern Europe and for the Yiddish and Hebrew languages did not compromise his commitment to internationalism.

13. HEAR, O ISRAEL! (1897)

WALTER RATHENAU[1]

Let me confess from the outset that I am a Jew. Need I any justification if I write in a spirit other than that of defending the Jews? Many of my fellow tribesmen [*Stammesgenossen*] know themselves only as Germans, not as Jews. A few, especially those who by profession and inclination meet native Germans [*Stammesdeutsche*] more often than with one another, and whose external features, therefore, have ceased to differ greatly from those of the Germans, have sufficient integrity not to follow the banners of their philo-Semitic protectors any longer. I am gladly joining their ranks.

The philo-Semites are wont to proclaim, "There is no Jewish Question. If Jews harm their country, they do so through the reprobate actions of individuals. To counter such actions one creates laws or tightens existing ones." They are indeed right. The response to the economic question is a matter for legislation. But I do not wish to address the economic question.

Far more menacing is the social question, the cultural question. Whoever wishes to comprehend its language should go to the *Tiergartenstraße* at noon on Sunday or to the foyer of one of Berlin's theatres in the evening, and look about. What a strange sight! In the midst of German life an isolated, alien human tribe, fitted out in resplendent and ostentatious attire, and with hot-blooded, animated gestures. An Asiatic horde on the soil of Mark Brandenburg. The forced cheerfulness of these people does not betray how much old, inexhaustible hatred rests on their shoulders. They seem to have no inkling that only an age that keeps all natural forces at bay is able to protect them from what their fathers had to suffer. In close association with each other, strictly isolated from the outside—they thus live in a semi-voluntary, invisible Ghetto, not as living members of the [German] people, but as an alien organism in its body.

It is of no avail to investigate how this has come about and which side is at fault. Life asks about what is; and history regards only the vanquished to be wrong.

Source: Walter Hartenau [pseud.], "Höre Israel!" *Die Zukunft*, XVIII (March 6, 1898), pp. 452–62. Trans. by Jacob Hessing and P. Mendes-Flohr.

It is incontestable truth that the best Germans harbor a deep antipathy toward the Jewish character (*juedisches Wesen*) and activities, and above all those who don't say much about it and who acknowledge numerous exceptions—as strange phenomena of nature, so to speak. And although Jews try to deceive themselves about the breadth and depth of this current—they cannot shake off the uneasy feeling of being hemmed in and abandoned. The old idea of glory is spent and with more longing than they are prepared to admit, they look for reconciliation. But the sea of seclusion will not part before any magical decree.

I repeat: I will not here deal with the economic question, which is the actual sphere of so-called antisemitism. As I see it, the heart of the social question does not lie in the economic interests of circles of individuals, no matter how extensive these circles may be, but rather in the almost passionate antipathy of the disinterested majority. And this social question threatens all corners of the Reich. It buzzes through the classrooms and university lecture halls; it careens through the streets and figures in shop signs; it rumbles in the business offices and in workshops; it discreetly walks up the front steps of the houses and giggles its way down the backstairs; it nests in the cushions of the trains compartments and presides at the tavern tables; it spreads out into the barracks squares and knocks on the doors of the courtrooms.

Who is today looking seriously for an answer [to this question]? To the ethnic German the question is as repugnant as its subject. He is satisfied if the swarthy people leave him alone. He has no reason to concern himself with its future.... And what is Israel doing to free itself from the curse? Less than nothing....

For all that, I do acknowledge that there are individuals among you who are pained and ashamed to be strangers and half-citizens in the country, and who long to leave the sweltering Ghetto for the air of the German forests and mountains. I speak to you alone. May the others, however few or many may hear me, remember their thousand year law right to punish and persecute those who wish to help them. You, however, who are counted among the minority of Jews, have the difficult task to placate the aversion of your fellow countrymen [*Landesgenossen*]—you who have, after all, hitherto made little effort—you will forgive me—to make friends among them. Nonetheless, your efforts in this regard will succeed, and the grandchildren of today's apathetic [Jews] will follow you.

You may ask if I am trying to convert you [my fellow Jews to Christianity]. Certainly not!

> To the preacher in the desert,
> As we read in the Gospels,
> Came also the soldiers running
> Repented and let themselves be baptized.

When I recently laid hands on the membership registry of Berlin's Jewish community, it pleased me to come across old, familiar names. Yes, the old friends are still alive; the orthodox zoological, mineralogical, and botanic families are fully accounted for.[2] But among the younger generation I found nobody whom I knew. They have all been baptized—not as soldiers, but even prior to that—and each and every one would now like to be a civil servant or lieutenant.[3]

And why not? There is no difference between the Deism of a liberal Protestant clergyman and that of an enlightened rabbi. Christian ethical teachings are so self-evident to today's educated Jewry that one can convince oneself that they can be deduced from the Old Testament. Conversion in most cases is no longer a matter of religion or conscience. Among the oldest and wealthiest families of Jewish descent, it in part already took place decades ago. Often the only reminder of the faith of their forefathers is a certain ironic atavistic externality, Abraham's malicious act [i.e., circumcision.].

But baptism is not the end of the Jewish question. An individual, perhaps, could improve the conditions of his existence through breaking away; the Jewish collectivity could not. For if half of all Israel would convert, nothing would come of it but a passionate "antisemitism against the baptized"' whose effect wold be even more unhealthy and immoral than the contemporary [antisemitic] movement by virtue of prying and suspicions on the one hand, and mendacity and hatred for the renegades on the other. The half left-behind, however deprived of its elite, will be crumpled together into an uneducated mass. By this kind of extraction much good metal, perhaps the best, would be cast off as dross and waste matter, for precisely those of the most refined sentiments will have the hardest time to decide whether to take the ideal step [i.e., conversion], [especially] so long as material advantage is often inseparably attached to it.

What then ought to be done? Something without historical precedent: the conscious self-education and adaptation of the Jews to the expectations of the Gentiles. Adaptation not as "mimicry" in the Darwinian sense—namely, the art of certain insects to take on the coloration of their environment—but a shedding of tribal attributes which, whether they be good or bad in themselves are known to be odious to our countrymen, and a replacement of these attributes by more appropriate ones. If such a metamorphosis also brought about an improvement in the balance of our moral values, this would be all for the better. The final result of the process should not be German by imitation, but Jews of German character and education. At first, it is necessary for an intermediate condition to develop, which recognized by both sides, will act as a dividing and connecting link between Germans and typical Jews (*Stockjudentum*): Jewish patricians not of property, but of spiritual and physical culture. From below, this estate will imbibe more and more nourishment through its roots, until in due time all material capable of transformation has been digested.

Few outsiders may know that there are already such Jewish patricians who because of the conservatism inherent in the Jewish people are readily accepted. Far less than it is generally believed can the traditional concept of the "good family" be blurred by either old or new wealth. While many very poor families are highly esteemed, many extremely wealthy families are fairly detested despite their contacts with the genuine gentry. The intermediary class, experienced in the task of self-education, would exert a greater influence on the masses below, were it for not the [apostasy] of individuals from this class. But fortunately, even among the masses a new self-awareness can now be detected and fortunately they are beginning to be cognizant of certain attitudes and traits as typically "Jewish". I once overheard a conversation about a man who, for reasons of his career, had himself baptized. It was a fellow Jew who pronounced the verdict: "Lord, how Jewish!"....

Look at yourselves in the mirror! This is the first step toward self-criticism. Nothing, unfortunately, can be done about the fact that all of you look frighteningly alike and that your individual vices, therefore, are attributed to all of you. Neither will it console you that in the first place your east Mediterranean appearance is not very well appreciated by the northern tribes. You should therefore be the more careful not to walk about in a loose and lethargic manner, and thus become the laughingstock of a race brought up in a strictly military fashion. As soon as you have recognized your unathletic build, your narrow shoulders, your clumsy feet, your sloppy roundish shape, you will resolve to dedicate a few generations to the renewal of your outer appearance. During that time you will refrain from donning the costumes of the lean Anglo-Saxons, in which you look like a dachshund dressed up like a a greyhound. You will not offend nature by wearing a sailor's dress on the beach, or half-stockings in the Alps. I do not know what the people of Israel looked like in Palestine—their contemporaries do not seem to share their beauty— but two thousand years of misery cannot but leave marks too deep to be washed away by eau-de-cologne. During all this time your women have forgotten their smile; their laughter has become shrill and unhappy, and their beauty has become melancholy. If you understood their strange and exotic beauty you would never choke it under bales of satin, clouds of lace, and nests of diamonds....

You rarely find a middle course between wheeling subservience and vile arrogance. Self-confidence without presumption cannot be learned, of course; only he who feels himself to be neither creditor nor debtor to anyone will gain it. Furthermore, all of you labour under the extreme obligation to keep up appearances. If you could only observe yourselves through the eyes of others, you sportsmen on the coach-box, you patrons of the studios, you directors of the board, standing on your platforms! You masters of observation and sarcasm—what striking analogies you would find! But, surely dear reader and fellow Jew! all this may be true for the others, but the two of us are completely different, aren't we?....

NOTES

1. Walter Rathenau,(1867–1922), German-Jewish writer, industrialist, and statesman. In February 1922 he was appointed foreign minister of the Weimar Republic, the first Jew to hold such a position in Germany. A target of antisemitic attacks, he was assassinated by extreme right-wing youths on June 24, 1922.

   "Hear, O Israel!" was first published under a pseudonym in *Die Zukunft*, an influential political weekly published by the German-Jewish journalist Maximilian Harden. When it later became apparent that his essay, with its severe critique of his fellow Jews, abetted the cause of antisemitism, Rathenau withdrew from circulation the volume of his collected works, in which the essay was reprinted. The Nazis, however, made "Hear, O Israel!" required reading in German schools. Although he did not revise his views favoring complete assimilation, toward the end of his life Rathenau expressed pride in the intellectual, ethical, and economic achievements of Jewry.

2. Rathenau is alluding to the practice of German-speaking Jews to adopt—and often to be simply assigned by the bureaucrats of the modern state—family names derived from names of animals, plants, or minerals, for example, Wolf, Rosengarten, and Goldberg.

3. Rathenau is pointing to the fact that, at the time, to attain a position in the German civil service and to achieve the rank of a commissioned officer in the German military, in practice, one had to be a Christian.

14. THE JEW MUST FREE HIMSELF FROM JEWISHNESS (1903)

OTTO WEININGER[1]

I must make clear what I mean by Judaism; I mean neither a race nor a people nor a recognised creed. I think of it as a tendency of the mind, as a psychological constitution which is a possibility for all mankind, but which has become actual in the most conspicuous fashion only amongst the Jews. Antisemitism itself will confirm my point of view.

The purest Aryans by descent and disposition are seldom antisemites, although they are often unpleasantly moved by some of the peculiar Jewish traits; they cannot in the least understand the antisemite movement, and are, in consequence of their defence of the Jews often called philosemites; and yet these persons writing on the subject of the hatred of Jews, have been guilty of the most profound misunderstanding of the Jewish character. The aggressive antisemites, on the other hand, nearly always display certain Jewish characteristics, sometimes apparent in their faces, although they may have no real admixture of Jewish blood.

The explanation is simple. People love in others the qualities they would like to have but do not actually have in any great degree; so also we hate in others only what we do not wish to be, and what notwithstanding we are partly. We hate only qualities to which we approximate, but which we realise first in other persons.

Thus the fact is explained that the bitterest antisemites are to be found amongst the Jews themselves. For only the quite Jewish Jews, like the completely Aryan Aryans, are not at all antisemitically disposed; amongst the remainder only the commoner nature are actively antisemitic and pass sentence on others without having once sat in judgment on themselves in these matters; and very few exercise their antisemitism first on themselves. This one thing, however, remains none the less certain: whoever detests the Jewish disposition detests it first of all in himself; that he should persecute it in others is merely his endeavour to separate himself in this way from Jewishness; he strives to shake it off and to localise it in his fellow-creatures, and so for a moment to dream himself free of it. Hatred, like love, is a projected phenomenon; that person alone is hated who reminds one unpleasantly of oneself.

Source: Otto Weininger, *Sex and Character,* translator not noted (London: William Heinemann, 1906), pp. 303–12.

The antisemitism of the Jews bears testimony to the fact that no one who has had experience of them considers them lovable—not even the Jew himself; the antisemitism of the Aryans grants us an insight no less full of significance; it is that the Jew and the Jewish race must not be confounded....

That these researches should be included in a work devoted to the characterology of the sexes may seem an undue extension of my subject. But some reflection will lead to the surprising result that Judaism is saturated with femininity, with precisely those qualities the essence of which I have shown to be in the strongest opposition to the male nature. It would not be difficult to make a case for the view that the Jew is more saturated with femininity than the Aryan, to such an extent that the most manly Jew is more feminine than the least manly Aryan.

This interpretation would be erroneous. It is most important to lay stress on the agreements and differences simply because so many points that become obvious in dissecting woman reappear in the Jew.

Let me begin with the analogies. It is notable that the Jews, even now when at least a relative security of tenure is possible, prefer moveable property, and, in spite of their acquisitiveness, have little real sense of personal property, especially in its most characteristic form, landed property. Property is indissolubly connected with the self, with individuality. It is in harmony with the foregoing that the Jew is so readily disposed to communism. Communism must be distinguished clearly from socialism, the former being based on a community of good, an absence of individual property, the latter meaning, in the first place a co-operation of individual with individual, of worker with worker, and a recognition of human individuality in everyone. Socialism is Aryan (Owen, Carlyle, Ruskin, Fichte). Communism is Jewish (Marx). Modern social democracy has moved far apart from the earlier socialism, precisely because Jews have taken so large a share in developing it. In spite of the associative element in it, the Marxian doctrine does not lead in any way towards the State as a union of all the separate individual aims, as the higher unit combining the purposes of the lower units. Such a conception is as foreign to the Jew as it is to the woman.

For these reasons Zionism must remain an impracticable ideal, notwithstanding the fashion in which it has brought together some of the noblest qualities of the Jews. Zionism is the negation of Judaism, for the concept of Judaism involves a worldwide distribution of the Jews. Citizenship is an un-Jewish thing, and there has never been and never will be a true Jewish State. The State involves the aggregation of individual aims, the formation of obedience to self-imposed laws; and the symbol of the State, if nothing more, is its head chosen by free election. The opposite conception is that of anarchy, with which present-day communism is closely allied. The ideal State has never been historically realised, but in every case there is at least a minimum of this higher unit, this conception of an ideal power which distinguishes the State from the mere collection of human beings in barracks. Rousseau's much-despised theory of the conscious co-operation of individuals to form a State deserves more attention than it now receives. Some ethical notion of free combination must always be included.

The true conception of the State is foreign to the Jew, because he, like the woman, is wanting in personality; his failure to grasp the idea of true society is due to his lack of a free intelligible ego. Like women, Jews tend to adhere together, but they do not associate as free independent individuals mutually respecting each other's individuality.

As there is no real dignity in women, so what is meant by the word *gentleman* does not exist amongst the Jews. The genuine Jew fails in this innate good breeding by which alone individuals honour their own individuality and respect that of others. There is no Jewish nobility, and this is the more surprising as Jewish pedigrees can be traced back for thousands of years.

The familiar Jewish arrogance has a similar explanation; it springs from want of true knowledge of himself and the consequent overpowering need he feels to enhance his own personality by depreciating that of his fellow-creatures. And so, although his descent is comparably longer than that of the members of Aryan aristocracies, he has an inordinate love for titles. The Aryan respect for his ancestors is rooted in the conception that they were *his* ancestors; it depends on his valuation of his own personality, and in spite of the communal strength and antiquity of the Jewish traditions, this individual sense of ancestry is lacking.

The faults of the Jewish race have often been attributed to the repression of that race by Aryans, and many Christians are still disposed to blame themselves in this respect. But the self-reproach is not justified. Outward circumstances do not mould a race in one direction, unless there is in the race the innate tendency to respond to the moulding forces; the total result comes at least as much from the natural disposition as from the modifying circumstances. We know now that the proof of the inheritance of acquired characteristics has broken down, and, in the human race still more than the lower forms of life, it is certain that individual and racial characteristics persist in spite of all adaptive moulding. When men change, it is from within, not outwards, unless the change, as in the case of women, is a mere superficial imitation of real change, and is not rooted in their natures....

Orthodox or unorthodox, the modern Jew does not concern himself with God and the Devil, with Heaven and Hell. If he does not reach the heights of the Aryan he is also less inclined to commit murder or other crimes of violence. So also in the case of the woman; it is easier for her defenders to point to the infrequency of her commission of serious crimes than to prove her intrinsic morality. The homology of Jew and woman becomes closer the further examination goes. There is no female devil, and no female angel; only love, with its blind aversion from actuality, sees in woman a heavenly nature, and only hate sees in her a prodigy of wickedness. Greatness is absent from the nature of the woman and the Jew, the greatness of morality, or the greatness of evil. In the Aryan man, the good and bad principles of Kant's religious philosophy are ever present, ever in strife. In the Jew and the woman, good in strife. In the Jew and the woman, good and evil are not distinct from one another.

Jews, then, do not live as free, self-governing individuals, choosing between virtue and vice in the Aryan fashion. They are a mere collection of similar individuals each cast in the same mould, the whole forming as it were a continuous plasmodium. The antisemite has often thought of this as a defensive and aggressive union and has formulated the conception of a Jewish "solidarity." There is a deep confusion here. When some accusation is made against some unknown member of the Jewish race, all Jews secretly take the part of the accused and wish, hope for and seek to establish his innocence. But it must not be thought that they are interesting themselves more in the fate of the individual Jew than they would do in the case of an individual Christian. It is the menace to Judaism in general, the fear that the shameful shadow may do harm to Judaism as a whole, which is the origin of the apparent feeling of sympathy. In the same way, women are delighted when a member of their sex is depreciated, and will themselves assist, until the proceeding seems to throw a disadvantageous light over the sex in general, so frightening men from marriage. The race or sex alone is defended, not the individual.....

I desire at this point again to lay stress on the fact, although its should be self-evident, that, inspite of my low estimate of the Jew, nothing, could be further from my intention than to lend the faintest support to any practical or theoretical persecution of Jews. I am dealing with Judaism, in the Platonic sense, as an idea. There is no more an absolute Jew than an absolute Christian. I am not speaking against the individual, whom, indeed, if that had been so, I should have wounded grossly and unnecessarily. Watchwords, such as "Buy only from Christians," have in reality a Jewish taint; they have a meaning only for those who regard the race and not the individual, and what is to be compared with them is the Jewish use of the word "Goy," which is now almost obsolete. I have no wish to boycott the Jew, or by any such immoral means to attempt to solve the Jewish question. Nor will Zionism solve that question; as H.S. Chamberlain has pointed out, since the destruction of the Temple of Jerusalem, Judaism has ceased to be a nation, and has become a spreading parasite, straggling all over the earth and finding true root nowhere. Before Zionism is possible, the Jew must first conquer Judaism.

To defeat Judaism, the Jew must first understand himself and war against himself. So far, the Jew has reached no further than to make and enjoy jokes against his own peculiarities. Unconsciously he respects the Aryan more than himself. Only steady resolution, united to the highest self-respect, can free the Jew from Jewishness. This resolution, be it ever so strong, ever so honourable, can only be understood and carried out by the individual, not by the group. Therefore the Jewish question can only be solved individually; every single Jew must try to solve it in his own person.

NOTE

1. Otto Weininger (1880–1903), Austrian-Jewish psychologist and philosopher. On the day he received his Ph.D., he converted to Protestantism—an expression of his desire to become a "non-Jew" His major work, *Sex and Character* [*Geschlecht und Character*, 1903] was a very popular book enjoying some thirty editions. It advances the thesis of a fundamental relationship between sex and character. Man, a Platonic typology, is a positive, productive, logical, conceptual, ethical, and spiritual force; Woman is a negative force, incapable of any of these virtues. Woman is either interested purely in sexual pleasure (the Prostitute) or in procreation (the Mother). Accordingly, Woman depends on Man, on the Phallus, and Man's emancipation as well as his spiritual progress is contingent upon the ending of coitus. Judaism is a force that is even more delecterious than Woman; the Jew believes in nothing and thus is drawn to the spiritual vacuities of communism, anarchism, naturalism, empiricism, and atheism. Every individual is a combination of Male and Female elements. As a Platonic idea, Judaism is also a tendency of the psyche to which every individual is subject in varying degrees. There are thus Germans who are more Jewish than Jews and vice versa. (Just as there are males who are more female than women and vice versa.) This conception of Judaism provided Weininger with the mechanism to transcend the "tragedy" of his Jewish birth. However, a few months after the publication of *Sex and Character*, he rented a room in the house in which Beethoven had died and solemnly put a bullet in his heart. It was surmised by his friends that this desperate act was prompted by his failure to convince the world that he had overcome the Judaism within himself and had become an authentic Aryan.

15. JEWISH SELF-HATRED (1930)

THEODOR LESSING[1]

I should like to…put a few question to the non-Jewish world:

Do you know how it feels to curse the soil on which one lives? To draw poison from one's roots instead of nourishment? Do you know what it means to be ill-born, begotten in the nuptial bed of calculation and superficial selfishness? To be ill-protected, neglected, pampered, effeminate and thrashed? And now to hate, senselessly and for an entire lifetime, your father, your mother, your teachers and all those others who have bred and shaped you in their own disgusting image?….

If it is true that most individuals of all peoples have to suffer an unhappy fate and that the perfect and successful only come about in rare cases, it is also true that a *people* resembles a large stream which can absorb all dark tributaries and yet, finally, carry them into the clear and pure surge.

Thus even the most wretched individual breathes like a leaf in a verdant forest. His national identity [*Volkstum*] supported him. A revered history receives him. A legitimate culture accepts his voice into the choir of a great community.

With the Jew, alas, it is otherwise. For centuries, his national identity has been like a small and calm pond, constantly endangered by an underlying swamp. He has had only the company of his dead, and he has forgotten their language. No soil has

Source: Theodor Lessing, *Der juedische Selbsthass* (Berlin: Juedischer Verlag, 1930), pp. 45–51. Trans, by J. Hessing.

supported him, no history relieved him of his sins, no cultural heritage [*Bildung*] has been *his own*; his hero is the sufferer.

We all love to use the beautiful phrase: "Happy is he who gladly remembers his forefathers." But what is left for a child who must turn away in shame from his forefathers because they have played their irresponsible games with the energies peculiar to their race and have thrown him, the grandchild, into the world as though he were an *accident*? Such a child, surrounded by a base and unsatisfactory environment, spends his feeble answers on a hateful tearing against unbreakable chains.

We are always taught about "community." One should teach about loneliness. The community, in one way or another, is sought by everyone. Loneliness is a matter for the few. It is possible for a man to *hate* deeply the community into which he was born, in which he was reared, and in which he spends his entire lifetime. But he will nevertheless not be able to separate his individual fate from that of the community.

There are countless Jews who constantly quarrel with *kehile un mish poke* [Yiddish: community and family] and yet live according to the awful proverb: "Bind my hand and bind my feet, and throw me into the family." How can this be explained ?

What could they who are uprooted expect when they find themselves in another community? Secretly, he would have to live with the humiliating consciousness: "I do not belong here, actually. They may be no better than I am, and they may not achieve more than I do. But they have something which I, obviously, lack: *They love themselves*". . . .

What alternatives are left to him who hears this? I discern three:

First: It is possible that he who was born with a defect will become a judge of the world. He becomes a castigator, a zealot, a moralist who delivers penitential sermons. There is an ethical power which can arise only from corrupt blood. This moralism torments those who are nearest (and at the same time, the farthest away) with sublime demands which cannot be fulfilled; and, in most cases, are not even fulfilled by the prophet himself. His spirit carries him beyond himself and beyond the unloved world. This is possible as long as he lives in his *spirit*. But woe! should he fall. He is nothing but a moving ball, thrown about by fate. The more often he touches earth, the weaker he becomes until he remains grounded on the most hated spot. His spirit is used up, and he is full of doubt and despair. And then he discovers what he never wanted to see: "I have no innate equilibrium, I have merely kept myself balanced. I am a priest who has turned his fault into a virtue. A liar who has covered up his empty holes with ideals. A broken man who has turned his own discontent against others. A fraud who has been living in the air because he did not know of any place on earth whose people and soil did not disgust him."

This way, then, leads to the death of the *soul*.

Second: A greater and more noble way than the way of the prophet and the judge of the world—he directs his torment exclusively again himself. He exempts all others. He is his own judge and hangman. He loves others more than himself. He dedicates himself completely and selflessly to his friend, to his lover. . . . Woe to him!

He has made himself into a footstool to be stepped upon by anyone. The more he gives the more surely he will be abused. . . . Be a tormentor of men, and men will adore you. Be truculent, and they will honestly love you. But turn yourself into a lamb, and the wolves will devour you.

Offer yourself up for sacrifice—good and well! They will kiss your hands and then proceed to celebrate the feast of immolation. Those whom you have loved the most will butcher you. And they will never realize what they are doing. And never repent. . . .

They will always find reasons to bless themselves. They sacrifice you in good faith. He who does not love himself sufficiently is not loved by anyone. And no one will have mercy on him.

This is the end of the second way, worse than the death of the soul.

Third: Now the great transformation succeeds, all mimicry succeeds. You become "one of the others" and look marvelously genuine. Perhaps a little too German in order to be completely German. Perhaps a little too Russian to be completely Russian. And precisely because Christianity is a little new to you, you tend to over-emphasize it a bit. But still: Now you are protected. Really?

Your corpse is protected. You are dead. Your duality has died, and so have you. You went the way of suicide in order to gain happiness and fame. But deep down in your soul a million dead are crying, and the dead are more powerful than your happiness and fame.

All ways, then, seem to be useless. What ought to be done?...

Be whatever you *are*, and bring to perfection whatever potential you find within yourself. But do not forget that by tomorrow, you and this entire world of human beings will have wasted away. Fight, yes—fight incessantly. But do not forget that *every* life, even the defective one, even the criminal one, is in need of love....

We all tend to take our existence much too seriously.

Who *are* you? The son of the slovenly Jewish pedlar Nathan, would you think, and of lazy Sarah whom he had accidentally slept with because she had brought enough money into their marriage? No! Judan Maccabee was your father, Queen Esther your mother. From you, and you alone, the chain goes back—via defective links, to be sure—to Saul and David and Moses. They are present in every one of you. They have been there all the time and tomorrow their spirit could be revived.

You carry an oppressive legacy. So what! Free yourself from it. Your children will forgive you that you were the child of your parents. Do not betray your fate. Love it. Accept it. Accept it even unto death. Be firm! You will surely endure your personal hell and attain deliverance in your true self in your eternal people.

NOTE

1. Theodor Lessing (1872–1933), German-Jewish philosopher. As a student he converted to Lutheranism. He later, however, embraced Zionism and returned to Judaism. His *Der Juedische Selbsthass* [Jewish self-hatred] is a psychological analysis of Jewish intellectuals who suffered self-hatred, a malady that had once afflicted Lessing himself. He viewed the Jews as an exiled Asiatic people forced to live an unnatural life in Europe. Once a peasant people, the Jews were cut off from the soil and became overspiritualized. Their return to the Land of Israel promised the renewal of both the land and the people. A stauuch and widely-read critic of National Socialism, in 1933 he was assassinated by Nazi agents in Marienbad, Czechoslovakia.

16. RETURNING HOME (1862)

MOSES HESS[1]

After an estrangement of twenty years, I am back with my people. I have come to be one of them again, to participate in the celebration of the holy days, to share the memories and hopes of the nation, to take part in the spiritual and intellectual warfare going on within the House of Israel, on the one hand, and between our people and the surrounding civilized nations, on the other; for though the Jews have lived among the nations for almost two thousand years, they cannot, after all, become a mere part of the organic whole.

A thought, which I believed to be forever buried in my heart, has been revived in me anew. It is the thought of my nationality, which is inseparably connected with the ancestral heritage and the memories of the Holy Land, the Eternal City, the birthplace of

Source: Moses Hess, *Rome and Jerusalem: A Study in Jewish Nationalism,* trans. Meyer Waxman (New York: Bloch Publishing Company, 1945), pp. 40–41. Reprinted by permission of Bloch Publishing Company.

the belief in the divine unity of life, as well as the hope for the future brotherhood of men.

For a number of years this half-strangled thought stirred within my breast and clamored for expression. I lacked the strength to swerve suddenly from my beaten track, which seemed to be so far from the road of Judaism, to a new path which had unfolded itself before me in the hazy distance, in vague and dim outline....

It was only when I saw you* [the Jewess, symbol of our nation's piety] in anguish and sorrow that my heart opened and the cover of my slumbering, national feeling was thrown off. I have discovered the fountain whence flows your belief in the eternity of the spirit.

Your infinite soul-sorrow, expressed on the death of one dear to you, brought about my decision to step forth as a champion of the national renaissance of our people. Such love which, like maternal love, flows out of the very lifeblood and yet is as pure as the divine spirit; such infinite love for family can have its seat only in a Jewish heart. And this love is the natural source whence springs the higher, intellectual love of God which, according to Spinoza, is the highest point to which the spirit can rise. Out of this inexhaustible fountain of family love have the redeemers of humanity drawn their inspiration.

"In thee," says the divine genius of the Jewish family, "shall all the families of the earth be blessed."[2] Every Jew has within him the potentiality of a Messiah and every Jewess that of a Mater dolorosa.

---

* "The Talmud, as well as the Midrash, ascribes the redemption of Israel from Egypt to the chastity of the Jewish women and their faithfulness to the Jewish nationality. It is especially emphasized that the Jews in Egypt retained their national names and language and did not adopt the names and language of the Egyptians and were thus more worthy of redemption than the exiles of later generations, when this form of assimilation was a frequent phenomenon....

NOTE

1. Moses Hess (1812–1875), German-Jewish socialist and precursor of Zionism. Until the age or fourteen, Hess was raised in the Orthodox Jewish home of his grandfather. During his student days he was fervently committed to socialism and cosmopolitan values. He is said to have won Friedrich Engels to communism and to have exercised a seminal influence on Karl Marx's thought. In his twenties he declared that the Jews had already accomplished their mission in history and should therefore assimilate into more historically relevant nations, such as Germany. In this respect, he claimed himself to be thoroughly German. Although the suffering of his fellow Jews occasionally did affect him, it was not until the publication of *Rome and Jerusalem* in 1862 that he owned a genuine identification with Jewry. This *volte-face* was effected, he claimed, by the Austro-Italian War of 1859, which witnessed the emergence of the movement of Italian national liberation as a vigorous, democratic, progressive force. He now viewed the struggle of oppressed peoples as of equal significance to the class struggle. In *Rome and Jerusalem* he developed the thesis that the regeneration of these peoples would be an essential component of the ultimate liberation of humanity for which socialism strives; hence, he focused on the exigent need for the national and political rehabilitation of the Jewish people.

2. Gen. 12:8.

17. I AM A CHILD OF ISRAEL AND A FEMINIST (1852)[1]

ERNESTINE LOUISE ROSE

Speaking before the Women's Right Convention, Ernestine L. Rose was introduced as "a Polish lady, educated in the Jewish faith"

It is of very little importance in what geographical position a person is born, but it is important whether his ideas are based upon facts that can stand the test of reason, and his acts are conducive to the happiness of society. Yet, being a foreigner, I hope you will have some charity on account of speaking in a foreign language. Yes, I am an example of the universality of our claims; for not American women only, but a daughter of poor, crushed Poland, and the down-trodden and persecuted people called the Jews, "a child of Israel," pleads for the equal rights of her sex. I perfectly agree with the resolution, that if woman is insensitive to the wrongs [perpetrated against her], it proves the depth of her degradation. It is a melancholy fact, that woman has worn her chains so long that they have almost become necessary to her nature—like the poor inebriate, whose system is so diseased that he cannot do without the intoxicating draft, or those who are guilty of the pernicious and ungentlemanly practice of using tobacco until they cannot dispense with the injurious stimulant. Woman is in a torpid condition, whose nerves have become so paralyzed that she knows not that she is sick, she feels no pain, and if this proves the depth of her degradation, it also proves the great wrong and violence done to her nature....

Woman is a slave, from the cradle to the grave. Father, guardian, husband—master still. One conveys her, like a piece of property, over to the other. She is said to have been created only for man's benefit, not for her own. This falsehood is the main cause of her inferior education and position. Man has arrogated to himself the right to her person, her property, and her children; and so vitiated is public opinion, that if a husband is rational and just enough to acknowledge the influence of his wife, he is called "hen-pecked." The term is not very elegant, but it is not of my coining; it is yours, and I suppose you know what it means; I don't. But it is high time these irrationalities are done away, for the whole race suffers by it. In claiming our rights, we claim the rights of humanity: It is not for the interest of woman only, but for the interest of all. The interest of the sexes cannot be separated—together they must enjoy or suffer—both are one in the race.

NOTE

1. Ernestine Louise Rose (neé Polozsky; 1810–1892) was an outspoken feminist, social reformer, abolitionist, and freethinker. Born and raised in Russian Poland as the daughter of a patriarchal rabbi, she developed already as a young teenager a rebellious, independent spirit. Rejecting an arranged marriage, she left home and eventually made her way to England, where she joined a circle of social reformers and utopian socialist. Through these activities she met her future husband, a non-Jewish silversmith, William Ella Rose. In 1836, the couple emigrated to the United States Ernestine soon became a prominent figure in various progressive causes, but especially the women's rights movement. This selection is a speech she delivered on September 8, 1852, at the Third National Woman's Convention, which met in Syracuse, New York. Introduced as a Polish

Source: E. L. Rose, *Proceedings of the Woman's Rights Convention held at Syracuse [New York], September 8th, 9th and 10th, 1852* (Syracuse: J. E. Masters, 1852), pp. 63–64.

Jew, she affirmed her origins in such a manner as to highlight the universal significance of the struggle for the rights of women. Although she never denied her Jewish origins and, indeed, unflinchingly opposed antisemitism, Ernestine Rose, true to her atheistic convictions, often vented harsh criticism of Judaism as a religion. See Paula Doress-Worters, ed., *Mistress of Herself. Speeches and Letters of Ernestine L. Rose. Early Women's Rights Leader* (New York: Feminist Press, 2007), pp. 311–33.

18. AN EPISTLE TO THE HEBREWS (1882)

EMMA LAZARUS[1]

It is a singular fact that the contemporary student of Jewish life and character derives chiefly from Christian sources a faith in the regenerating powers of Judaism. The Jews themselves, especially those of America, seem rarely imbued with that vivid sense of the possibilities and responsibilities of their race, which might result in such national action as to justify the expectations (and in some cases the ignoble fears) of their Gentile critics. When one turns glowing with enthusiasm from the pages of George Eliot, of Gabriel Charmes, of Ernest Havet, of Laurence Oliphant, to the actual Jewish community amidst which we live, one is half tempted to believe that it is necessary to be born outside of Judaism in order to appreciate the full beauty and grandeur of her past, the glory and infinite expansiveness of her future. The unworthy desire on the part of many Jews to conceal their lineage, evinced in the constant transmutation of family-names, and in the contemptible aversion and hostility manifested between Jews of varying descent, painfully prove the absence of both the spirit and the training essential to a higher national existence. Fancy a self-respecting American, Englishman, Frenchman, etc., endeavoring to impose upon his neighbors the idea that he belongs to a race other than his own! Yet nothing is more common (and, we may add,

more futile) among the Jews. As long as every man respects the virtues and achievements of his ancestors, he is proud to claim his rightful lineage. Only when a deep and abiding sense of national humiliation has taken root, is it possible for men of ordinary honesty and intelligence to repudiate or shrink from acknowledgment of their descent. Nor have we in America the excuse for such national weakness as has been elsewhere afforded up to our own day by the brutal Jewish-baiting of European countries. A century of civil and religious equality has removed every extenuating circumstance that could be pleaded for it. Firmly convinced as I am of the truth of the axiom that a study of Jewish history is all that is necessary to make a patriot of an intelligent Jew, and I shall undertake from time to time to bring before the Jewish public such facts and critical observations gathered in the course of my studies as I think calculated to arouse a more loyal spirit and a more intelligent estimate of the duties of the hour. If I speak with occasional severity of the weakness or the degeneracy in certain points of my people, I promise that I do with full appreciation of the heroic martyrdom of ages that has in great part engendered their national defects. Not for the sake of those who have mainly begotten in us the faults inseparable from long subjection to

---

Source: Emma Lazarus, "An Epistle to the Hebrews" (Letter One). *The American Hebrew* (November 3, 1882); reprinted in E. Lazarus, *An Epistle to the Hebrews* (New York: Philip Cowen, 1900), pp. 7–10.

oppression and contempt, but for our own sakes, for the sake of the coming generation, I shall endeavor to impress upon my readers the urgent necessity for reform along the whole line of Jewish thought and Jewish life, and for a deepening and quickening of the sources of Jewish enthusiasm.

During the last two or three years we have been passing through what the meteorologists call a "storm-centre" in our history; nor, although we happily hear no more of riot and murder in Russia, or of active antisemitism in Prussia, have we yet handily emerged from the skirts of tempest. The immediate danger is over, but it will be long before the evil effects of the cruelties inflicted, the violent passions aroused, and the seeds of mutual mistrust, discord and rancor that have been sown, shall have disappeared. We are no longer, as before the French Revolution, minors and bondsmen, the chattels of mercenary sovereigns and the prey of lawless mobs. In nearly all so-called civilized countries, we control our own destinies, and we have no need to fawn upon the returning of impotent sophists, fanatics, bullies and tyrants, who begin to renounce, or at least to intermit the hopeless task of crushing an indomitable people. But none the less should we profit, to the full extent of our intellectual and moral capacities, by the bitter experience of our recent adversity. It is not a theme to be lightly forgotten or dismissed. In the universal discussion which it has excited, we have opportunities such as are afforded to few nations, for self study, introspection and retrospection. Let us profit by all the blunders and vices of our foes; let us take to heart the wise counsels, and study how best to realize the auspicious predictions of our friends. It behooves us to look into the mirror held up to us by well-wishers and enemies alike; to investigate coolly, rationally and impartially our situation and the nature of the reproaches that are cast upon us. Wherever a show of justice be found for these reproaches, we must shrink from no single or united effort to remove it. Wherever (as I am persuaded will more frequently be the case) these strictures prove to have no other foundation than ignorance and malice, we must confront them with that steadfastness of concerted action, that moral dignity and that calm logic of intellectual superiority which in themselves will promote the speedier advent of the larger truth and humanity destined to supersede the already enfeebled power of Christendom. Only with the breaking of that brighter dawn whose harbingers are

the scientists and philosophers of our own day shall we be absolutely secure from the possibility of such outrages as have been perpetrated upon us by the Christianity of 1880, '81 and '82. But the light is slow to dawn, and in the meantime we must ourselves take such measures of re-enforcement and self-defence as will render the recurrence of these crimes less and less probable. To foster a spirit of union and nationality, and at the same time to reform the internal abuses of our present social condition, should be, then, our first and most imperative duty.

Is the education of our young conducted on such principles as to revive and develop the honorable love of manual arts and of wholesome outdoor pursuits inculcated by the Bible and the Talmud, and so long crushed out by cruel foreign legislation that its absence is supposed to be a racial characteristic? We, who should be the pioneers of intellectual progress, do we in our own free schools even keep abreast with the reforming spirit of the age? Does the language in which the synagogue service is conducted appeal to the worshipper's springs of religion and poetry, or keep alive in their breasts the spirit of prophetic exaltation? Such are some of the questions for consideration, to which I shall endeavor to fine the reply. The persistence of the Jewish type, and the extremes of animosity and admiration which it still persistently excites, make it idle to repeat the hackneyed question whether Judaism be a race or a religion. *It is both*, and instead of shirking the responsibilities which a full acknowledgement of our nationality entails, let us "choose our full heritage, claim the brotherhood of our nation, and carry into it a new brotherhood with the nations of the Gentiles."

NOTE

1. Born in New York City to a Sephardic father and an Ashkenazic mother, Emma Lazarus (1849–1887) was a poet who is best known to posterity for her sonnet of 1883, "The New Colossus," whose final verse is engraved on the bronze plaque at the pedestal of the Statue of Liberty: "Give me your tired, your poor, your huddled masses yearning to breathe free, The wretched refuse of your teeming shore. Send these, the homeless, tempest-tost to me, I lift my lamp beside the golden door!"

   Although her parents were members of New York City's venerable Sephardic congregation Shearith Israel, the family's degree of observance and of Jewish involvement were minimal. Lazarus's interest in Jewish affairs was initially aroused by George Elliot's novel *Daniel Deronda* and news of the Russian pogroms of the early 1880s. Resolved to promote Jewish solidarity, she wrote a series of fifteen "epistles" to her fellow "Hebrews" that were published in the *American Hebrew*, from November 1882 to February 1883. She is often regarded as a proto-Zionist because of her passionate expression of Jewish national consciousness and her advocacy for the establishment of a Jewish homeland in Palestine for the persecuted Jewish masses of Eastern Europe. The first of her "epistles to the Hebrews," presented here, testifies to her defiant Jewish pride and embryonic Zionism.

19. JEWISHNESS IS AN INALIENABLE SPIRITUAL SENSIBILITY (1913)[1]

GUSTAV LANDAUER

A.

No true human being can consider himself merely as a bridge for coming generations, as a preface, as seed and fertilizer. He wants to be somebody and to accomplish something. The mother tongue of some of my offspring will perhaps be Hebrew, perhaps; it does not affect me. My language and the language of my children is German. I feel my Judaism in the expressions of my face, in my gait, in my facial features, and all these signs assure me that Judaism is alive in everything that I am and do. But much more than the Frenchman Chamisso was a German poet—if there can be a "more" in such matters—am I, the Jew, a German. The expressions "German Jew" or "Russian Jew" sound odd to me, just as would the terms "Jewish German" or "Jewish Russian." The relationship indicated by these terms is not one of dependency and cannot be described by means of an adjective modifying a noun. I take my fate as it is, and live accordingly: My being a Jew and a German at the same time does not do me any harm, but actually a lot of good, just as two brothers, a first-born and a Benjamin, are loved by their mother—not in the same way but with equal intensity. And just as these two brothers can live in peace with one another whenever their paths cross and whenever they go their different ways—just so I experience this strange and yet intimate unity in duality within myself as something precious and do not distinguish one element of this relationship within myself as primary, and the other, secondary. I have never felt the need to simplify myself or to create an artificial unity by way of denial; I accept my complexity and hope to be an even more multifarious unity than I am now aware of.

But since it is now that I am alive and active, now that I exist and act as a Jew, I cannot inwardly prepare for a thing, cannot find the will within me for a new decision that would extinguish part of my being, or at least hinder it....

Only that is alive which has developed through time and is still in the process of developing. Only he who, in his own time and reality, simultaneously recognizes his past and his future, and only he who takes himself, his true and complete self, on the journey

Source: A. Gustav Landauer, "Sind das Ketzergedanken?" in *Vom Judentum: Ein Sammelbuch,* ed. Verein Juedischer Hochschueler Bar Kochba in Prag (Leipzig, 1913), pp. 250–57. Trans. J. Hessing. B. Gustav Landauer [Review of Martin Buber], *Die Legende des Baal Schem* in *Das Literarische Echo* (Berlin, October 1, 1910), pp. 148-49. Trans. J. Hessing.

to his promised land—only he, it seems to me, cherishes his Judaism as a living possession. The [Gentile] nations have drawn political boundaries around themselves and have neighbours beyond their borders who are their enemies; the Jewish nation has its neighbours in its own breast; and this friendly neighbourliness creates peace and unity within anyone who is complete within himself, and who acknowledges this friendly neighbourliness creates peace and unity. Is not this a sign of the mission which Judaism ought to fulfill in relation to humanity and within humanity?

B.

In the thought and poetry of Martin Buber more than anywhere else, a Jew can learn what many nowadays no longer learn in their homes, but often find within themselves by way of an impulse from the outside: That Judaism is not an external contingency, but an inalienable inner property which transforms a number of individuals into a single community. This is the common ground on which the reviewer and the author of the book meet one another—a common spiritual sensibility [*Seelensituation*] which cannot *a priori* be assumed to be existent in other readers [of Martin Buber]. And yet, many among the Germans do perceive the authenticity and beauty, the depth and truth in the poetry, fairy tales and legends of the Greeks, Indians, Chinese, and Finns. In like manner, the myth of the Jews...has become part of popular culture in Germany, and this latest product of Jewish myth [viz., Hasidim], reborn in the spirit of the German language, must therefore sound familiar to many....

Everywhere [in Martin Buber's *The Legend of the Baal Shem*] we are faced with the struggle of the soul to grasp the incomprehensible and ultimate, the experience beyond the life of the senses,...the realization of God.... At the same time, however, this God is the Messiah who will raise the poor and persecuted Jews in the Diaspora out of their agony and oppression. Here, more than anywhere else, the legend, the fairy tale of God [*Gottesmaerchen*], is steeped in a melancholy made of earthly depression and heavenly yearning....

NOTE

1. Gustav Landauer (1870–1919), German-Jewish philosopher, literary critic, novelist, and anarchist. Like many other Jewish intellectuals of his day who sought to identify themselves as Jews, Landauer was estranged from the Jewish religion and communal institutions on the one hand, and yet was not satisfied with merely ethnic identification on the other. He was inspired by Martin Buber (1878–1965) and his concept of a primal Jewish religiosity or spiritual sensibility that is independent of doctrine and ritual prescriptions. His indebtedness to Buber is indicated in the two complimentary articles presented here. The first is an essay Landauer published in a volume sponsored by the Bar Kochba Society of Prague, a Zionist student circle close to Buber; the second is a review of Buber's *The Legend of the Baal Shem* (1908).

   When the Bavarian Soviet Republic was proclaimed in 1919, Landauer became the minister of public instruction. In May of that year he was bludgeoned to death by antirevolutionary troops. Buber, whom he named in his will the executor of his literary estate, compiled his scattered articles into several volumes and edited his voluminous correspondence. Their close relationship is also expressed in the seminal influence Landauer had on Buber's social philosophy.

20. THE DONME AFFAIR: A LETTER ON ASSIMILATION (1925)[1]

A SABBATIAN FROM SALONICA, GREECE[2]

Dear Sir,

I read the articles on the Donmes in your precious journal. Some of the articles were dictated by Mrs. Meziyet Hanim and penned by a respectable author, Esat Mahmut. Despite his good intentions, however, Esat Mahmut Bey was misled by Meziyet Hanim's irrational and illogical fabricated stories.

Do not understand that I am uncomfortable with the articles published in your journal. On the contrary, they make me happy. Initiated by Rustu Karakas Bey, this process [of discussing the subject of the Donmes openly] was continued by Meziyet Hanim, and now, I wish to complete it.

The reason why this publication pleases me is as follows: Based on what I say, you may think that I am an enemy of the Donmes. I cannot be an enemy of them, since I myself am of Donme origin. Nevertheless, I am not happy to bear this inescapable identity. I am so uncomfortable by the fact that the Salonican Donmes have been living in isolation practicing their own customs, and not mixing with Turkish society. Because of this, we lead a double life. Turks are right when they consider the Donmes to be a separate ethnicity and community. I and some other people believe it would be best were the Donmes to be dissolved in Turkish Society. What pleases me is that these publications began to further such a mission. And I want to help to further this process, by presenting—but not in the way of Meziyet Hanim's absurd explanations—the essences, facts and traditions of the Donmes to the larger Turkish public.

Since I was confident about the good intention and objectivity of your journal, I had the courage to send this letter to you. If you publish it in one of the corners of your journal, you would do a great service both to the Turkish community and to the new generation of the Donmes.

The following customs and traditions that I will report have almost disappeared among some segments of the Donme and the new generation. Even if these rites and rituals have influence on the older generations, the new generation reacts against them and detaches itself from this tradition.

It was during the time of Sultan Mehmed the Hunter that a Jewish messiah named Sabbatai Sevi appeared in Edirne and claimed that there was no need for religion. He claimed that believing in God and acting in accordance with one's conscience was sufficient. In other words, religion is nothing but conscience. It seems that what Sabbatai Sevi argued in those days was essentially the philosophy of today's world.

Naturally Sabbatai's sayings had a negative influence on the Jewish people. Jewish rabbis convened and excommunicated Sabbatai Sevi. Since he was not able to remain there [in Edirne] he moved to Izmir where he not only managed to attract people to his ideas but also made messianic claims. Jewish scholars were upset and issued a decree for the murder of Sabbatai. He had to leave Izmir for Istanbul. He disseminated his message for a short period in Istanbul, but because of the rumors concerning him, he had to move to Salonica. He continued to make the same messianic claims in Salonica.

Whenever he was offered marriage he said that he was married to the Torah. This greatly upset the rabbis, who considered it blasphemy and began to work against him. Finally he had to flee to Egypt but ultimately had to flee from there as well due to the same reason. Upon the invitations of the Izmir Jews,

Source: *Resimile Duenza*, Istanbul (15 Tesrinisani 1341/November 1925), pp. 3-4; translated from the Turkish by Cengiz Sisman, and annonated by Jouthan P. Dector.

he returned to Izmir. He continued to make the same claims in Izmir, and committed further transgressions until the Ottoman authorities became aware of the problem and arrested him. He was brought to Istanbul and was imprisoned in the Yedikule citadel. After a while he was imprisoned in the Aydos castle [of the Dardanelles]. However, he did not stop disseminating his message and while he was there his fame continued to grow. His fame, ultimately reached the ears of the Sultan Mehmed the Hunter in Edirne, who ordered that Sabbatai be brought into his presence.

Because of his fear of the Sultan and his council, the coward Sabbatai immediately converted to Islam and took the name, Mehmed Aziz. He was exiled from Istanbul to Salonica, then to Ulgun[3] where he died. His shrine still exists today. His house in Izmir has been preserved by the Cikurel family until recently.[4] He must have been such a charismatic figure that he attracted many people in such a short period of time.

Today it is thought that the Donmes live only in Salonica, but that is not true. In Albania, Hungary, Montenegro, [and] Jerusalem, there are Donme communities converted by the Sabbatian missionaries. These people belong to the same Salonican denomination, and they practice the same rites and rituals. Thus far, I have mentioned things that are known to everyone. But what I really want to talk about is the essence of the Donme.

After the death of Sabbatai, there remained 200–300 [Sabbatian] families. A struggle broke out as to who would replace the messiah. Those who partook in the struggle divided into two camps, the second of which also divided, creating three groups, which continue to exist today.

The first group is called Yakubi or Hamdi Beyler. The second half was divided into two again, and one group was called Karakass or, as the Donme would say, Komsu Agalar, and the other are called Kapancis.[5] The Yakubis are journalists, professors, teachers and governmental officials. The number of businessmen and tradesmen among them is quite few. One of the Yakubis, whose name I cannot disclose, is a professor in Istanbul University. These is also a famous journalist. Komsu Agalar or Karakass are strong in business. There was one Karakass, professor in Istanbul University before it was reorganized. The Yakubis still practice ancient beliefs and rituals. But as opposed to other groups, they do not practice solidarity or provide help to the needy.

Karakass were called Komsu Agalar as well as Onyollu (lit., "ten-strands") or in a more corrupted form, Honyolar. Because the [Karakass] elders believed that Sabbatai Sevi was going to be resurrected, but it was not clear in which religious garb he would appear, the group became mixed with ten groups (Gypsies, Greeks, Poles, Jews, Albanians, Turks, Russians, Hungarians, Montenegrians, and Bulgarians) in order to attract the Messiah's attention. The relations of the Karakass remained strong with these ten groups so that they became mixed with them. Among the Karakass, there are people whose ancestors are Polish, Russian and Albanian.

The Karakass are the most conservative and religious group among the Donmes. Now they practice moderate rituals. Since the most interesting practices belong to this group, I will explain them in detail. Here I have to tell that although I am of the Kapanci origin, I know the rites and rituals of other groups, and by writing these things, I do not intend to insult anyone, nor do I harbor negative feelings toward anyone. With all my objectivity, I analyze their rites and rituals. Therefore, neither Donmes broadly nor the Karakass in particular have a right to hold any negative feelings toward me.

The Karakass worship a man who was once the leader of the community. His name is Osman Baba [Baruhia Russo]. They have a statue of Osman Baba, made out of limestone. Like the Zoroastrians, they worship the statue. Leaders were called Aga and leadership [is] passed from father to son. Now the leadership is in the hands of the Misirli family, and currently the leader is Misirli Aga. They have utmost respect for this person.

While they were in Salonica, the statue of Osman Baba was located in a house called Orta Evi, a special prayer house, located in the basement of the Aga. It was a secret place. Brides and grooms, before they married, visited the statue of Osman Baba under the guidance of Misirli Baba. First the bride and then the groom knelt before the statue and kissed its hands and feet. Following this, they were sanctified by the Misirli Aga.

I was exposed to this information by interacting with them for years, or by overhearing when two Karakass were speaking in school. These things cannot be revealed by anyone else in any case.

I cannot imagine that Meziyet Hanim was correct when she claimed that the newlywed bride slept with the Misirli Aga on her wedding night. All the Agas I knew had reached the age of 80 or 90. Also, I do not think that the bride or her husband would accept such a thing.

Their marriage customs are also strange. They became engaged at the age of one or two, without being aware of it. Even if they do not like each other, they have to get married. I knew people at school at the age of 15, 16 or 17, or even at the age of 6 or 8, who were engaged. The statue of Osman Baba in Salonica was transferred here, and now it is housed in one of the houses in Makrikoy (Istanbul). But, of course, I do not know where that house is. Even if I did know, I would not have the right to disclose this secret.

When the Karakass wake up they do not greet anyone else before they greet one another. Otherwise it is a sin.

As I explain later, the prayers, beliefs and holidays are the same for all the [Donme] groups. The Kapancis are the people who are the most open minded, modern, and stripped of their superstitions. I am saying this, not because I am one of them or am proud of them, but because it is simply the truth.

Now, those who have reached the age of 70 or 80 naturally preserve ancient rites, rituals and customs. But they cannot perform their rituals as freely as in earlier times. Because of new conditions,[6] and the fact that the young generation mocks them, they have become reserved about their customs. The old generation calls the new generation freemasons.

Some of the Donmes are so detached from their tradition that neither ancient customs nor solidarity remains a part of their life. Although the previous generation, namely that of our fathers, still observes some of the ancient rituals, those things will gradually disappear. The young generation has no time to deal with such matters.

Thanks to the unity of the people, they have a school, called the Terakki Mektebi. Most of the Donmes go to this school. Now let's talk about their beliefs and practices, which are shared by the three groups.

Donmes believe in the existence of one God who is the creator of the universe. After God, Sabbatai Sevi ranks second. Although Sabbatai Sevi became a Muslim out of fear, he preserved his religion inside.

In other words, although Donmes are in the guise of Muslims and Turks, they are in fact Jews. The Jews call them *ma'minkino*.

Like Jews, their prayers are in Hebrew. Unlike the Jews, however, they follow additional holidays and customs. But like members of all other religions, the Donmes too have superstitions. On special nights, the Donme religious leaders and eligible Donmes—except children—meet at the Orta Evi, and perform special prayers.

Donmes do not separate men and women in their meetings. When someone dies, they pray seven nights consecutively. Also, on the 40th night and once a year, they commemorate the date of the deceased and hold a prayer ceremony.

I suspect that the tradition of the "extinguishing the candle" ceremony still exists among the Karakas community, having existed among the Kapancis previously also, but I have never witnessed it myself.[7] Let me explain the meaning of the "extinguishing the candle" ceremony: Donmes do not eat lamb meat until they hold a Lamb Festival every spring on the same night. On that infamous night, the lamb meat is cooked while prayers are recited. After cooking, the lamb meat is divided into pieces and sent to other Donme families. After they eat the lamb meat, they are allowed to buy lamb meat from butchers. On this night, they perform other rituals as well. On this night, only married couples can attend the meetings. The reason that they do not allow non-married individuals, I believe, is they do not want anyone to derive benefit from another person's partner without offering their own. However much I tried to learn more about this, I was told that I could learn more about it when I got married.

Nevertheless, none of these customs are followed anymore. Everyone buys lamb meat from Turkish, Greek, or Armenian butchers [and] eats it before the Lamb Festival.

The Donmes also have some holidays that are based on superstitious beliefs. These holidays are Hinali Balik,[8] Purim, [Yom] Kippur, Mi shibirah,[9] Ta'ani[yt], and the Lamb Festival. On these holidays and on some other special days, they fast. Smoking is allowed during the fasting. There is no need to give the full list of holidays in detail, since it is a waste of time. They are based on silly traditions in any case.[10]

Now I contemplate what I have written here. I am sure that there will be many people who would like to excommunicate, denigrate, or censure me because I disclosed many of their secrets.

But as I told you previously, I am in the opinion that the Donme tradition should come to an end. Therefore, I will not be intimidated by anyone. As a small precaution, however, I do not disclose my name. I hope that this will be excused by you.

Respectfully Yours Forever,
A Young Donme from Salonica

NOTES

1. Following the conversion of the purported Jewish Messiah Sabbatai Sevi (1626–1676) in 1666 to Islam (see chapter 7, document 11, note 1), some of his believers also converted and formed an idiosyncratic Judeo-Islamic community known as the Donme, most of whom settled in Ottoman Salonika (modern-day Greece). During the population exchange of Christians and Muslims between Greece and Turkey in 1924, the Salonikan Donmes were considered to be Muslim Turks and were resettled in different parts of Modern Turkey. During the first quarter of the twentieth century, a series of debates emerged among the Donmes regarding whether they should give up their traditional Donme beliefs and practices and adopt a modern, secular Turkish identity. The following letter, sent to the editor of a newspaper in Istanbul, is one of the most important documents and presents the main points of the debate among the Donmes. It is also one of the earliest internal reports, disclosing some of the Donme "secrets." However, the letter should be read with caution because it was composed within the context of this heated debate. Today, although there are still some Donme believers in Turkey, most of them gave up their traditional identities following this debate.

2. A Sabbatian man, named Karakas Rütstü, sent a petition to the Turkish Grand National Assembly on January 1, 1924, claiming that his coreligionists were neither ethnically nor spiritually nor "morally" Turkish, and it was time to bring this "hypocrisy" of their alleged Turkish identity to an end. This petition triggered a ramified debate, which manifested itself in different newspapers and journals. For a short summary of the debate, see Paul Bessemer, "Who Is a Crypto-Jew? A Historical Survey of the Sabbataean Debate in Turkey". *Kabbalah: Journal for the Study of Jewish Mystical Texts* (Fall 2003).

3. Present-day Ulçin/Ulcinj/Dulcingno in Montenegro.

4. The house is in ruins today. For a contemporary account of the house, see Cengiz Sisman, "Saving Sabbatai Sevi's House from Oblivion," *International Journal of Middle Eastern Studies*, Vol. 40/, no.1 (2008):9–11.

5. For the naming practices of the Donmes, see Cengiz Sisman, "In Search of the Name: A History of Naming Ottoman/Sabbatian Communities," in *Studies on Istanbul and Beyond: The Freely Papers*, ed. Robert G. Ousterhout (Philadelphia: University of Pennsylvania Press, 2007), pp. 37–53.

6. "New conditions" refer to the period after the population exchange between Turkey and Greece when the Donmes were uprooted from Salonica and brought to the newly established Turkish republic.

7. The reference is to an infamous allegation that the Donmes had a special night, corresponding to the 22nd of Adar in the Hebrew calendar, at the end of which they extinguish the lights and swap their partners. Some claim that this sexual practice or spiritual orgy was added to the Sabbatian festival during the time of Judah Levi Tovah, or Dervish Efendi, at the end of the eighteenth century, but was abandoned at the end of the nineteenth century.

8. *Cuna* means cradle in Ladino, and *balik* means fish in Turkish. It was believed that Sabbatai Zevi put a fish into a cradle and said that emancipation of the Jews would come from the Zodiac sign, Pisces, a fish. *Hinali Baluk* is a corrupted pronunciation of *Cunali Balik*.

9. This particular phrase is contained in a special eulogy for Sabbatai Zevi. The eulogy begins, "Bless our Signor, King, Saint, the Just, Sabbatai Zevi, the Messiah of the God of Jacob."

10. For a full list of Sabbatian festivals, see Cengiz Sisman, *A Jewish messiah in the Ottoman Court: The Sabbatian Movement and the Emergence of the Messianic Judeo-Islamic Sect in the Ottoman Empire*, unpublished Ph.D. dissertation (Harvard University, 2005), pp. 344–57.

21. ADDRESS TO THE SOCIETY OF BNAI BRITH (MAY 6, 1926)

SIGMUND FREUD[1]

Most honourable Grand President, honourable Presidents, dear Brethren,—

I thank you for the honors you have paid me today. You know why it is that you cannot hear the sound of my own voice. You have heard one of my friends and pupils speak of my scientific work; but a judgment on such things is hard to form, and for a long while yet it may not be reached with any certainty. Allow me to add something to what has been said by one who is both my friend and the physician who cares for me.[2] I should like to tell you shortly how I became a B.B. and what I have looked for from you.

It happened that in the years from 1895 onwards I was subjected to two powerful impressions which combined to produce the same effect on me. On the one hand, I had gained my first insight into the depths of the like of the human instincts; I had seen some things that were sobering and even, at first, frightening. On the other hand, the announcement of my unpleasing discoveries had as its result the severance of the greater part of my human contacts; I felt as though I were despised and universally shunned. In my loneliness I was seized with a longing to find a circle of select men of high character who would receive me in a friendly spirit in spite of my temerity. Your society was pointed out to me as the place where such men were to be found.

That you were Jews could only be agreeable to me; for I was myself a Jew, and it had always seemed to me not only unworthy but positively senseless to deny the fact. What bound me to Jewry was (I am ashamed to admit) neither faith nor national pride, for I have always been an unbeliever and was brought up without any religion though not without a respect for what are called the "ethical" standards of human civilization.[3] Whenever I felt an inclination to national enthusiasm I strove to suppress it as being harmful and wrong, alarmed by the warning examples of the peoples among whom we Jews live. But plenty of other things remained to make the attraction of Jewry and Jews irresistible—many obscure emotional forces, which were the more powerful the less they could be expressed in words, as well as a clear consciousness of inner identity, the safe intimacy of a common mental construction. And beyond this there was a perception that it was to my Jewish nature alone that I owed two characteristics that had become indispensable to me in the difficult course of my life. Because I was a Jew I found myself free from many prejudices which restricted others in the use of their intellect; and as a Jew I was prepared to join the Opposition and to do without agreement with the "compact majority."[4]

So it was that I became one of you, took my share in your humanitarian and national interests, gained friends among you and persuaded my own few remaining friends to join our society. There was no question whatever of my convincing you of my new theories; but at a time when no one in Europe listened to me and I still had no disciples even in Vienna, you gave me your kindly attention. You were my first audience.[5]

For some two thirds of the long period that has elapsed since my entry I persisted with you conscientiously, and found refreshment and stimulation in my relations with you. You have been kind enough today not to hold it up against me that during the last third of the time I have kept away from you. I was overwhelmed with work, and demands connected

---

Source: Sigmund Freud, "Address to the Society of Bnai Brith," trans. James Strachey, *in The Standard Edition of the Complete works of Sigmund Freud,* ed. James Strachey in collaboration with Anna Freud and assisted by Alix Strachey and Alan Tyson (London: Hogarth Press, 1959), vol. 20, pp. 273–74.

with it forced themselves on me; the day ceased to be long enough for me to attend your meetings, and soon my body began to rebel against a late evening meal. Finally came the year of my illness, which prevents me from being with you even today.

I cannot tell you whether I have been a genuine B.B. in your sense. I am almost inclined to doubt it; so many exceptional circumstances have arisen in my case. But of this I can assure you—that you meant much to me and did much for me during the years in which I belonged to you. I ask you therefore to accept my warmest thanks both for those years and for today.

Yours in W.B.& E.[6]

Sigm. Freud.

NOTES

1. Sigmund Freud (1856–1939) was the founder of psychoanalysis. Born in Moravia, he was raised in Vienna, where he attended university, earning a degree in medicine. His interest in neurology led him to psychiatry and the eventual development of the theory and therapeutic technique of psychoanalysis. His career was constantly buffeted by antisemitism, which he felt frustrated a balanced and objective reception of his novel and admittedly radical perspective on human mental life. He nonetheless persisted, and slowly psychoanalysis gained respectability, exercising a wide influence on both psychology and general culture. Soon after the Nazi occupation of Austria in 1938, he hastily left Vienna and settled in London, where he died the following year.

   The address presented here was written by Freud on the occasion of a celebration of his seventieth birthday by the Bnai Brith Society of Vienna on May 6, 1926. Founded in New York in 1843, Bnai Brith (Sons of the Covenant) is the oldest and largest Jewish service organization with branches throughout the world. Joining Bnai Brith in 1885 (some scholars say in 1887), Freud for many years regularly attended the meetings of the Viennese lodge of the organization, which were held on alternate Tuesdays. Occasionally he gave lectures there on various themes (see note 5).

   Illness prevented him from attending the festive meeting to mark his seventieth birthday; his address was read on his behalf. Freud expresses his gratitude to Bnai Brith for providing him with supportive friendship during the long years when he was virtually ostracized. His remarks also record his understanding of his own, emphatically secular, Jewish identity.

2. The reading of Freud's address was preceded by a laudatory speech by his physician, Professor Ludwig Braun (1867–1936). In his speech, titled "Freud's Personality and His Importance as a [Bnai Brith] Brother," Braun described Freud, despite his lack of Jewish religious belief and observance, as "genuinely Jewish" and rhetorically asked, "Can anyone even imagine Freud as not Jewish?" Cited in Dennis B. Klein, *Jewish Origins of the Psychoanalytic Movement* (New York: Praeger, 1981), p. 85.

3. It has been argued that Freud's Jewish upbringing was actually more traditional than he claimed. See Yosef Hayim Yerushalmi, *Freud's Moses: Judaism Terminable and Interminable* (New Haven: Yale University Press, 1992).

4. The reference is to a theme in Henrik Ibsen's *Enemy of the People* (1882), which deals with the insidious intrusions of society and its conventions into the personal affairs of individuals.

5. Freud's occasional lectures before the Bnai Brith of Vienna are discussed in detail in Klein, op. cit., pp .69–102, 155–65.

6. The abbreviation "W.B. & E" stands for "*Wohlwollen, Bruderliebe und Eintracht*," the motto of the Bnai Brith: "Benevolence, Brotherly Love and Harmony."

22. A VALEDICTORY MESSAGE TO THE JEWISH PEOPLE (1949)

ARTHUR KOESTLER[1]

In the Proclamation of Independence of the new State [of Israel] there is a paragraph which says:

> Exiled from the Land of Israel. The Jewish people remained faithful to it in all the countries of their dispersion, never ceasing to pray and hope for their return and the restoration of their national freedom.

It is the kind of phrase which has been so often said before that one hardly realizes what momentous implications it carried on that specific occasion for the seven or eight million Jews outside Palestine. For it was the occasion on which their prayer had been fulfilled; and the logical consequence of the fulfillment of a prayer is that one ceases to repeat it. But if prayers of this kind are no longer repeated, if the mystic yearning for the return to Palestine is eliminated from the Jewish faith, its very foundations and essence will have gone.

Towards the end of the Passover meal which commemorates the Exodus from Egypt, Jews all over the world lift their glasses and exclaim: "To next year in Jerusalem." For nearly twenty centuries this was a moving ritual symbol. Now that no obstacles bar any longer the fulfillment of the wish, the alternative before the faithful is either to be next year in Jerusalem, or to cease repeating a vow which has become mere lip-service.

In fact, the greater part of the formulae and vocabulary of Jewish ritual has become meaningless since May 15, 1948. The Proclamation of Independence affirms that "the State of Israel will be open to Jews from all the countries of their dispersion." In the future, Jews can no longer refer to themselves with the ritual stock phrase of living in the Diaspora, or in Exile—unless they mean a self-imposed exile, which has nothing to do with religion or tradition.

The existence of the Hebrew State—that is, a State whose language and culture are Hebrew, not Yiddish, Polish or American—puts every Jew outside Israel before a dilemma which will become increasingly acute. It is the choice between becoming a citizen of the Hebrew nation and renouncing any conscious or implicit claim to separate nationhood.

This dilemma is not derived from abstract speculation, nor from the claims of logical consistency; it is imposed by hard historical circumstances. Antisemitism is once more on the increase. In his address to the Anglo-American Committee of Enquiry,[2] the aged leader of Zionism, Dr. Chaim Weizmann, summed up a lifetime of experience:

> I am worried, but I don't see how I can stop it or what can be done. [Antisemitism] is a sort of disease that spreads apparently according to its own laws. I only hope that it will never reach the terrible dimensions which it reached in Europe. In fact, I somehow think that the Anglo-Saxon countries may be immune from it. But that is a hope, a pious wish—and when I look at Canada, South Africa, even Great Britain, even America, I sometimes lose my freedom from fear.... I believe the only fundamental cause of antisemitism—it may seem tautological—is that the Jew exists. We seem to carry antisemitism in our knapsacks wherever we go....

It is the twenty-first installment of a twenty-century-old story. To expect that it will come to a

Source: Arthur Koestler, "Epilogue," *Promise and Fulfillment: Palestine. 1917–1949* (London: Macmillan, 1949), pp. 332–35. Copyright 1949 by Arthur Koestler, renewed 1977 by Arthur Koestler and reprinted by permission of the Macmillan Press Ltd.

spontaneous end is to go against historical psychological evidence. It can only be brought to an end by Jewry itself.

Before the prayer was fulfilled by the rebirth of Israel this was difficult if not impossible. To renounce being a Jew meant in most cases to deny solidarity with the persecuted, and seemed a cowardly capitulation. Apart from pride, there was the consciousness of an old heritage which one had no right to discard, of a mission uncompleted, a promise unfulfilled. Jewry could not vanish from the scene of history in an anticlimax.

Now the climax is reached, the circle closed. It is no longer a question of capitulation, but of a free choice. The proclamation of the Hebrew State is a signal to Jewry to pause on its long journey, review its situation with sincerity towards itself, and face facts which some time ago it was excusable and even honourable to shun.

The dilemma would not arise if being a Jew were merely a matter of religion like being a Protestant, or merely a matter of racial descent like being a French-Canadian. But both these comparisons are fallacious. The Jewish religion is not merely a system of faith and worship, but implies membership of a definite race and potential nation. The greater part of the sacred texts is national history. To be a good Catholic or Protestant it is enough to accept certain doctrines and moral values which transcend frontiers and nations; to be a good Jew one must profess to belong to a chosen race, which was promised Canaan, suffered various exiles and will return one day to its true home. The "Englishman of Jewish faith" is a contradiction in terms. His faith compels him to regard himself as one with a different past and future from the Gentile. He sets himself apart and invites being set apart. His subjective conviction creates the objective fact that he is not an English Jew, but a Jew living in England....

The conclusion is that since the foundation of the Hebrew State the attitude of Jews who are unwilling to go there, yet insist on remaining a community in some way, apart from their fellow-citizens, has become an untenable anachronism. The true orthodox believers must draw the consequences, now that the opportunity is offered to him, otherwise his creed will become lip-service. But orthodox Jewry is a vanishing minority. It is the well-meaning but confused majority which, through inertia, perpetuates the anachronism by clinging to a tradition in which it no longer really believes, to a mission which is fulfilled, a pride which may become inverted cowardice. Such honest sentimentalists should stop to think whether they have the right to place the burden of the ominous knapsack, now void of contents, on their children who have not asked for it.

To break the vicious circle of being persecuted for being "different," and being "different" by force of persecution, they must arrive at a clear decision, however difficult this may be. They must either follow the imperative of their religion, the return to the promised Land—or recognize that that faith is no longer theirs. To renounce the Jewish faith does not mean to jettison the perennial values of Judaic tradition. Its essential teachings have passed long ago into the main stream of the Judeo-Christian heritage. If a Judaic religion is to survive outside Israel, without inflicting the stigma of separateness on its followers and laying them open to the charge of divided loyalty, it would have to be a system of faith and cosmopolitan ethics freed from all racial presumption and national exclusivity. But a Jewish religion thus reformed would be stripped of all its specifically Jewish content.

These conclusions, reached by one who has been a supporter of the Zionist movement for a quarter-century, while his cultural allegiance belonged to Western Europe, are mainly addressed to the many others in a similar situation. They have done what they could to help to secure a haven for the homeless in the teeth of prejudice, violence and political treachery. Now that the State of Israel is firmly established, they are at last free to do what they could not do before: to wish it good luck and go their own way, with an occasional friendly glance back and a helpful gesture. But, nevertheless, to go their own way, with the nation whose life and culture they share, without reservations or split loyalties.

Now that the mission of the Wandering Jew is completed, he must discard the knapsack and cease to be an accomplice in his own destruction. If not for his own sake, then for that of his children and his children's children. The fumes of the death chambers still linger over Europe; there must be an end to every calvary.

NOTES

1. Arthur Koestler (1905–1983), British author. Born into an assimilated Jewish family in Budapest, Hungary,

Koestler joined the Zionist movement at the age of nineteen, and from 1926 to 1929 he lived in Palestine. In 1931 he became a Communist, but the Stalinist purges of the later thirties and the Stalin-Hitler pact disillusioned him, and he left the party. With the spectre of Nazi antisemitism over Europe, he once again passionately devoted himself to the Zionist cause and the establishment of a Jewish state as a refuge for European Jewry. However, when this objective was realized, he withdrew—as he explains in the epilogue to his history of the Zionist struggle for Palestine presented here—from the Zionist movement and the Jewish community.

2. See chapter 10, document 50, note 1.

23. JEWISH LEARNING AND THE RETURN TO JUDAISM (1920)

FRANZ ROSENZWEIG[1]

Learning—there are by now, I should say, very few among you unable to catch the curious note the word sounds, even today, when it is used in a Jewish context. It is to a book, the Book, that we owe our survival—that Book which we use, not by accident, in the very form in which it has existed for millennia: it is the only book of antiquity that is still in living use as a scroll. The learning of this Book became an affair of the people, filling the bounds of Jewish life, completely. Everything was really within this learning of the Book.

Then came the Emancipation. At one blow it vastly enlarged the intellectual horizons of thought and soon, very soon, afterwards, of actual living. Jewish "studying" or "learning" has not been able to keep pace with this rapid extension. What is new is not so much the collapse of the outer barriers; even previously, while the ghetto had certainly sheltered the Jew, it had not shut him off. He moved beyond its bounds, and what the ghetto gave him was only peace, home, a home for his spirit. What is new is not that the Jew's feet could now take him farther than ever before—in the Middle Ages the Jew was not an especially sedentary, but rather a comparatively mobile element of medieval society. The new feature is that the wanderer no longer returns at dusk. The gates of the ghetto no longer close behind him, allowing him to spend the night in solitary learning. To abandon the figure of speech—he finds his spiritual and intellectual home outside the Jewish world.

The old style of learning is helpless before this spiritual emigration. In vain have both Orthodoxy and Liberalism tried to expand into and fill the new domains. No matter how much Jewish law was stretched, it lacked the power to encompass and assimilate the life of the intellect and the spirit. The *mezuzah* may have still greeted one at the door, but the bookcase had, at best, a single Jewish corner. And Liberalism fared no better even though it availed itself of the nimble air squadron of ideas rather than trying to master life by engaging it in hand-to-hand combat with the Law. There was nothing to be done apparently, except dilute the spirit of Judaism (or what passed for it) as much as possible in order to stake off the whole area of intellectual life; to fill it in the true sense was out of the question....

Source: Franz Rosenzweig: His Life and Thought, ed. Nahum N. Glatzer (New York: Schocken, 1953), pp. 228–29, 231–32, 234. Copyright 1953, 1961 by Schocken Books Inc. Reprinted by permission of Pantheon Books.

There is no one today who is not alienated, or who does not contain within himself some small fraction of alienation. All of us to whom Judaism, to whom being a Jew, has again become the pivot of our lives—and I know that in saying this here I am not speaking for myself alone—we all know that in being Jews we must not give up anything, not renounce anything, but lead everything back to Judaism. From the periphery back to the center, from the outside, in....

It is not a matter of apologetics, but rather of finding the way back into the heart of our life. And of being confident that this heart is a Jewish heart. For we are Jews.

That sounds very simple. And so it is. It is really enough to gather together people of all sorts as teachers and students. Just glance at our prospectus. You will find, listed among others, a chemist, a physician, a historian, an artist, a politician. Two-thirds of the teachers are persons who, twenty or thirty years ago, in the only century when Jewish learning had become the monopoly of specialists, would have been denied the right of teaching in a Jewish House of Study. They have come together here as Jews. They have come together in order to "learn"—for Jewish "learning" includes Jewish "teaching." Whoever teaches here—and I believe I may say this in the name of all who are teaching here—knows that in teaching here he need sacrifice nothing of what he is. Whoever gathers—and all of us are "gatherers"—must seize upon that which is to be gathered wherever he finds it. And more than this: he must seize upon himself as well, wherever he may find himself. Were we to do otherwise, we should continue in the errors of a century and perpetuate the failure of that century: the most we could do would be to adorn life with a few "pearls of thought" from the Talmud or some other source, and—for the rest—leave it just as un-Jewish as we found it. But no: we take life as we find it. Our own life and the life of our students; and gradually (or at times, suddenly) we carry this life from the periphery where we found

it to the center. And we ourselves are carried only by a faith which certainly cannot be proved, the faith that this center can be nothing but a Jewish center.

This faith must remain without proof. It carries further than our word. For we hail from the periphery. The oneness of the center is not something that we possess clearly and unambiguously, not something we can be articulate about. Our fathers were better off in that respect. We are not so well off today. We must search for this oneness and have faith that we shall find it....

It is in this sense that now, at the opening of the new term in this hall, I bid you welcome. May the hours you spend here become hours of remembrance, but not in the stale sense of a dead piety that is so frequently the attitude toward Jewish matters. I mean hours of another kind of remembrance, an inner remembering, a turning from externals to that which is within, a turning that, believe me, will, and must become for you a returning home. Turn into yourself, return home to your innermost self.

NOTE

1. Franz Rosenzweig (1886–1929), German-Jewish philosopher and theologian. Overcoming a philosophical agnosticism, Rosenzweig affirmed a faith in the traditional God of Creation, Revelation, and Redemption. Initially, he felt that this faith could be realized only within the Church. But on the threshold of the baptismal font, he returned to Judaism and discovered therein the possibility of living faith. Thereafter he devoted himself totally to the study and practice of Judaism. This approach was expressed in the Freies Juedisches Lehrhaus, a house of Jewish study, which he founded in 1920 in Frankfurt am Main. The Lehrhaus became the center and source of inspiration for a growing number of Jews, many from assimilated backgrounds, seeking to rediscover Jewish religious spirituality. This statement is taken from Rosenzeig's inaugural address at the Lehrhaus.

24. FROM PRAGUE TO BELZ (1937)

JERI LANGER[1]

It is an impassable road to the empire of the Hasidim[2]. The traveler who pushes his way through the thick undergrowth of virgin forests, inexperienced and inadequately armed, is not more daring than the man who resolves to penetrate the world of the Hasidim, mean in appearance, even repellent in its eccentricity.

Only a few children of the West have accomplished this journey, hardly as many—when I come to think of it—as there are fingers on the hand that writes these lines.

One summer's day in 1913, a nineteen year-old youth, brought up like all the youth of his time in the dying traditions of the pre-war generation, left Prague inspired by a secret longing which even now after the passage of so many years he still cannot explain to himself, and set out for the east, for strange countries.

Had he a foreboding of what he was losing on that day?

European civilization with its comforts and achievements, its living successes called careers? Had he a foreboding that his soul would no longer be capable of feeling poetry which up to that time he had been so fond of quoting, that, from the first moment when he heard the rhythms of the Hasidic songs, all the magic charms of music would be swamped once and for all, and all beautiful things which his eye had ever conceived would in the future be half hidden by the mystic veil of the knowledge of good and evil?

He hardly suspected that, at the very moment when he believed he had reached his goal, the most impassable part of his journey was only beginning. For the gate to the empire of the Hasidim never opens suddenly for anyone. It is closed by a long chain of physical and spiritual suffering. But he who has once looked inside will never forget the riches he has seen.

The rulers of this empire are hidden from the eyes of the world. Their miraculous deeds and all-powerful words are only, as it were, of secondary importance—they are merely the hem of the veil in which their being is wrapped, while their faces are turned away from us towards the distant calm of the Absolute. Only a faint reflection of their souls falls on our too material shadows. Yet, even today, years afterwards, these shapes haunt me one after the other. Not only those I knew personally but also those I have heard so much about and read about in the old Hebrew books; they rise again before me in all their greatness and strength. I feel overcome. Something compels me to take up my pen and faithfully write down everything as best I can.

It is Friday afternoon. The small town of Belz, the Jewish Rome, is preparing to welcome the Sabbath. Small towns in eastern Galicia have all had the same character for centuries. Misery and dirt are their characteristic outward signs. Poorly clad Ukrainian peasant men and women, Jews wearing side-whiskers, in torn caftans, rows of cattle and horses, geese and large pigs grazing undisturbed on the square. Belz is distinguished from other places only by its famous synagogue, its no less famous House of Study and the large house belonging to the town rabbi. These three buildings enclose the square on three sides. They are simply constructed. But in this poor, out-of-the-way region of the world they are truly memorable. Belz has somewhat more than three thousand inhabitants, half of whom are Jews.

It is a long summer afternoon. There are still six or seven hours before dusk, when the Sabbath begins and even the lightest work is strictly forbidden. In

Source: Jeri Langer, *Nine Gates to the Chassidic Mysteries*, trans. Stephen Jolly (New York: James Clarke & Co. Ltd., 1961), pp. 3–5, 12ff., 18. Copyright 1961 by James Clarke & Co Ltd. and Stephen Bagster Jolly, trans. Reprinted by permission of Jason Aronson Inc., Publishers.

spite of this, the shops are already shut, the tailors are putting away their needles, and the casual labourers—wearing side-whiskers like the rest—their hoes and spades. The housewives in the cottages are adding the last touches to their preparations for the festival.

The men hasten to the baths. After a steam bath we dive—always several of us at the same time—into a small muddy swimming pool, a *mikveh*, or special ritual bath. As thought in mockery of all the rules of hygiene, a hundred bodies are "purged" from the spirit of the working day. The water, like all the water in Belz, smells of sulphur and petroleum....

Although everybody is in a tearing hurry on this day, the whole community already knows that a *boher*, or young lad, has come to Belz all the way from Prague. A hundred questions are fired at me from every side. I am embarrassed because I do not understand a single word. I have never heard "Yiddish" spoken before, that bizarre mixture of mediaeval German and Hebrew, Polish and Russian. It was only later that I gradually began to learn it....

From the window of the [House of Study's] entrance hall to the saint's apartment one can see far out across the Ukrainian steppe. For miles round there is nothing but a flat plain, without a single tree or hill to be seen. It is a fen with a narrow path made of boards running across it. In the distance a small bridge leads into a barren little field; then the path leads on across the bog into the unknown. When I am weary of the House of Study, I cross this bridge and lie down in the little field. This is the only bit of nature where on can find spiritual refreshment in all this wilderness!

I can endure it no longer. This life of isolation form the rest of the world is intolerable. I feel disgusted with this puritanism, this ignorance, this backwardness and dirt. I escape, I travel back to my parents in Prague. But not for long. I must perforce return to my Hasidim.

[In Prague] one night I cannot sleep. I am lying down, facing the kitchen door, which looks towards the East. I have left the door ajar. I have just been reading some holy Hebrew book in the kitchen. The kitchen windows are open, open towards the East, the East where Belz lies at the end of a train journey of a few hours more than a day and a night.... It is useless for me to close my eyes to induce sleep. Suddenly I am dazzled by a bright light penetrating into my dark bedroom through the half-open door. What is

it?—I know that I have put out the lamp, and there is no one in the kitchen. I stare at the light, and in the middle of it a few steps in front of me, I can see quite clearly through the half-open door—*the saint of Belz!* He is sitting in his room at Belz looking fixedly at me. On his expressive countenance shines that barely recognizable, sublime smile of his, full of wisdom. I have no idea how long the apparition lasts, but it is long enough to shake me.

So I travel to Belz a second time, this time firmly resolved. I am no longer alone as on my first pilgrimage. This time I have a companion, a Prague lad like myself, who has also decided for Hasidism.

My vision for the saint of Belz that night was a great favour. So the Hasidim said when I told them about it. To behold a living saint from far away and, moreover, while still awake is not indeed an absolutely isolated phenomenon among the Hasidim, but it is a greater expression of God's favour than, for instance, a conversation with someone who is dead or with the prophet Elijah....

I am still a foreigner. People are very polite and full of respect when they talk to me, but they are mistrustful. The mere fulfillment of religious injunctions, however precise and conscientious, is as little adequate to inspire confidence here as is the utmost zeal over one's study. Excessive religiosity is not welcomed. But now that my beard and side whiskers are well grown, now that I am able to speak some Yiddish and have begun wearing a long *shipits* [an overcoat similar to a caftan] instead of a short coat, and ever since I have started wearing a black velvet hat on weekdays, as all the other Hasidim do, this ice-wall of mistrust has gradually begun to thaw. But why, even now, am I not completely like the others? For example, why am I not gay, all the time, as a true Hasid ought to be?....

At last, when my face is pallid from undernourishment and illness, and my emaciated body has acquired a stoop, it is clear to nearly all of them that "I am really in earnest". No longer will the gates of Hasidism be closed in front of the youth from Prague.

NOTES

1. Jeri Mordecai Langer (1894–1943), Czech poet and writer. Raised in an acculturated upper middle-class Jewish family, in 1913, prompted by vague mystical

longings, he left his native Prague for the Hasidic community of Belz. In Belz, the center of Galician Hasidim, he discovered his spiritual roots and calling and adopted the Hasidic mode of Jewish piety. Langer eventually returned to Prague, but he retained his loyalty to Hasidism. He wrote extensively in Czech and German on Hasidism and Kabbalah. His Freudian interpretations of Jewish mystical literature and piety in particular generated great excitement among students of religion. A friend of Kafka, whom he taught Hebrew, Langer displayed his literary interests in two volumes of Hebrew poetry and in his rendition of Hasidic tales into Czech, *Nine Gates to the Chassidic Mysteries* (1937), from whose introduction this except is taken. Upon the Nazi invasion of Czechoslovakia, Langer fled to Palestine.

2. Hasidim, members of a religious and mystical revival movement that originated in southern Poland and Ukraine in the eighteenth century and spread to other parts of Eastern Europe (Poland, Russia, Rumania, Hungary). Hasidism is now found mainly in the State of Israel and the United States.

25. THE JEWISH WOMAN (c. 1930)

BERTHA PAPPENHEIM[1]

The wife of the Jew was to carry bricks for family life as a beast of burden, her spirit was to remain dull. But how she was praised and exalted—*Esches Chajil*[2] (a love song with *gefuelte* fish)—how were all male commentaries turned against her, whose spirit was certainly also open and willing! This official attitude brought on a serious revenge. What people do not know—or know only as unattractive or a burden—without ethical value, is not highly esteemed, and I see the logical and tragic consequence in that women and mothers of the recent past were not able to raise their children with respect for the spirit of tradition. The thread had been torn and the house was emptied which today is completely blamed on emancipation.... Precisely the lack of interest in what women and girls were learning (in the period of early marriage there was scarcely girlhood in our present sense), indifference to the interest in what the boys and men were supposed to learn and to know, brought a slow and in the beginning, not noticeable movement into Jewish womanhood. The most evident reaction to this centuries-old attitude was seen without question and symptomatically in the attendance of the Baron Hirsch[3] schools in Galicia, with its predominantly strictly Orthodox people. In the beginning, these schools were violently attacked by the *Cheder*; boys were not to attend them; there were also serious mistakes in the management. What Jewish girls were learning was not taken seriously, they frequently attended the Baron Hirsch schools or the Polish schools with great eagerness and growing resistance against their own families and circle which seemed less educated in their religious and outward forms as the "Fraeulein" as they were called with respect even by their own parents. I, myself, could watch, in Austria, Hungary, Rumania, Bohemia, Moravia, Poland, Galicia, Russia, in three generations—as Yiddish, the women's German, developed, how the middle generation spoke its respective country's language, less than German, scarcely fluent, and could not write it. (It is characteristic that in well-to-do families the Jewish cook also spoke German; the other servants, the language of the country.) A definitely German interest in

---

Source: Dora Edinger, *Bertha Pappenheim: Freud's Anna O.* (Highland Park, Ill.: Congregation Solel, 1968), pp. 78–80. Reprinted by permission of Congregation Solel. The original transliteration of Hebrew and Yiddish has been retained.

education within Jewish womanhood developed, an interest which in bilingual and, in educated families, often trilingual women (if they spoke French) met new cultural elements which neglected the Jewish ones in form and essence. Beginning with the prominent families of the Pressburg ghetto and its influence through the waiting rooms of the rabbi of Sadarora and other citadels of "classic" Orthodoxy until the circle of the families Schmelkes, Ringelheim, Ginsburg, Lilien, Buber, Nussbaum, Mandelstamm, Motzkin, I could observe with great reverence the influence of German language and German spirituality, but at the same time among the women less interest in Jewish consciousness, for instance, in Hungary, Poland and Bohemia (today the Czech Republic). Women naturally attended synagogue on the High Holy Days, older ones also on Saturdays, but they could not follow the service. Here begins a break which in later days affected Liberal and Reformed liturgy. It would have been more sensible if women—and, of course, not only women—had been educated to understand the service than later to construct a service which was unhistoric and without tradition adjusted to the lagging understanding of the congregation. Yet it was a fact that most of the women did not understand the mixed language of the sermons with Hebrew quotations, nor did they understand the Torah reading, nor the words of the prayers, though they would follow the service with *kewonoh* (devotion). The old women with their head-bands and *scheitels*,[4] I saw cry bitterly over their big prayer books in Rashi script;[5] the next generation gossiped over prayerbooks printed in square Hebrew type, mostly with a German translation.

According to my own observations, which I can only quote briefly in this context, I must say that the Jewish women of all countries and all the social strata to whom I could talk occasionally understood my suggestions and recommendations on social problems. To men, they were not of interest, or they found them a nuisance. Woman, with tradition in their blood and brains, showed a ready understanding to relate the command to love your neighbor to modern times. I found in the unknown Jewish women of Diaspora Judaism the ability to perform great tasks. This conviction I took back to Germany from travels to my daily work which I did not consider in narrow context.

To show my experience of the development of German Jewish women, it was necessary to sketch this background....[The spiritual life of Jewish women began to change with] the understanding of the necessity to adjust the *Mizwah* (religious commandment)—to help your neighbor in changing times—from overblown philanthropy and blind, senseless spending of money to sensible and conscientious action. The congregation of Frankfurt-on-the-Main fifty years ago offered a rich and challenging place for such an effort.

If was therefore only a relatively small group of unknown women (Orthodox and Liberal) who, in Frankfurt, understood the work of welfare by women in different ways and in modest, tireless, sacred little work prepared the soil of the *Kehillos Kodaushim* (holy communities), to serve the old culture and to start a new one. Gratefully, one must remember the generation of unknown women who followed these ideas, while men resisted them stubbornly. It is an interesting and strange fact that male resistance against organization of social work resulted in hypertrophy of organization, an "idée fixé" of a Federation which kills all personal social action. Social work, which grew in the religious soil in Frankfurt, would not have had any importance outside the city if it had not found help and encouragement from the German feminist movement. Out of a new congruence of German cultural elements and Jewish civilization grew a spiritual substance of greatest importance, both for the German feminist movement and for Jewish life.... These women who did not know how Jewish they were through their inherited spirituality became strong pillars of the feminist movement, which movement brought to the timid uncertain steps of Jewish women a goal and determination. This confluence of Jewish civilization could not be eliminated from the German, nor from Jewish life. All women, whatever their position and philosophy may be today, are, even if they do not know it themselves, the disciples of the fighters for equal rights for women in everything....

NOTES

1. Bertha Pappenheim (1859–1936) was a social worker and a leader of the Jewish feminist movement in Germany. Born in Vienna to a traditional family, she underwent analysis with a colleague of Sigmund Freud, who acclaimed her case ("Anna O") as a decisive breakthrough in psychoanalysis. She subsequently moved to Frankfurt am Main where she directed an

orphanage. In 1904 she founded in the same city the *Juedischer Frauenbund* (Society for Jewish Women), to combat white slavery, especially of Jewish girls from East Europe; the society soon expanded its purview to promote the cause of women's rights. She was tirelessly devoted both to Jewish social causes, particularly refugee relief, and to the general plight of women drawn to prostitution and crime. She translated into German Yiddish classics, among them the memoirs of her ancestor Glueckel of Hameln. In 1936, soon after being interrogated by the Gestapo, she died.

2. The reference is to the concluding passages of the biblical book of Proverbs, which speaks of "a valorous woman" (*esches chajil*, in the Ashkenazi pronunciation of the Hebrew). These passages are traditionally cited at the Sabbath evening meal by the husband addressing his wife: "What a rare find is a valorous woman...."

3. Baron Maurice de Hirsch (1831–1896) was a German-Jewish banker and philanthropist. Among his many projects to relieve the economic hardships of East European Jewry, he founded in 1891 the Hirsch Fund for agricultural and crafts schools in Galicia.

4. *Sheitl* is a Yiddish term for the wig worn by strictly Orthodox Jewish married women as a covering for their hair as required by Jewish religious law.

5. *Rashi* is the acronym for Rabbi Solomon Yitzhak (1040–1105), a French rabbinical scholar. Rashi script is a semicursive form of Hebrew letters, used principally for writing and printing rabbinical commentaries, especially those of Rashi himself.

26. WHAT I WOULD DO IF I BECAME A RABBI (1890)[1]

RAY (RACHEL) FRANK

If I were one of the elect, one who deemed myself worthy to expound the law to men created like myself with an understanding, and a small but mighty organ termed by physiologists the heart, why, then I would not, if I were a rabbi, endeavor to impress the nature of my calling by loud and shallow words, not by a pompous bearing unbecoming the man of God. I would not say to my fancied inferiors, "*I am a rabbi!*," and you must therefore do this or that; but I would reach their actions through their hearts.

I would try and remember that example is better than precept: I would not imagine myself a fixed star around which lesser lights must move.

I would try the effect of a gentle demeanor, a quiet voice, an earnest will, and a helping hand. I would learn if an unfailing courtesy and a positive sincerity were not sufficient to announce and impress my high vocation to the stranger and to the sinner.

I would not, if I were a rabbi, consider a stylish residence, fine garments, including a silk hat, not any of the jewels representing the original twelve tribes, as absolutely essential to keeping up my position as a "priest of the temple." I would not make a business matter of my calling other wise than for the good of my congregation or humanity in general.

I would not say my services are worthy a salary of so much per annum because I do this or that, or because I preach oftener or more learnedly than Mr. A or Rev. B.; but, after satisfying my own wants in a modest way, I would use amounts expended on "high living," on cigars, cards, and other pleasantries toward enlightening the ignorant of my people—If

Source: Jacob R. Marcus, *The American Jewish Woman, A Documentary History* (Cincinnati: American Jewish Archives, 1981), pp. 380–83.

not in my own town, where perhaps they are blessed with both intelligence and wealth, then I would use it for the poor and oppressed abroad. I would be more like Judah Asheri;[2] less like one type of Hebrew satirically mentioned as "Solomon Isaacs."[3] It is, indeed, difficult nowadays to note the difference between the rabbi and his friend the clothier, or the broker, his dress, his diamonds, his language, his very walk is not bookish but business; is not piety but pecuniary display.

I would not, if I were a rabbi, attempt to be a politician, for religion and politics do not and cannot under existing circumstances walk hand-in-hand. I would not degrade my holy office by assuring any ward political "boss" that for a consideration I would capture the votes of my co-religionists, "because being the rabbi, they will do as I tell them," as one rabbi of my acquaintance is said to have remarked.

If I were a rabbi and holidays were at hand, I would not make "stock" of my seats in schul [Yiddish for synagogue]; or in other words, I would not sell religion in the form of pews and benches to the highest bidder.

I would not treat disdainfully the moneyless fellow who comes on Rosh Hashanah, Yom Kippur, or Pesach to drink at the fountain of our faith, but alas! finds that unless he can pay for his drink of religion he must either go thirsty or beg it.

During the last holiday season a poor but faithful son of Israel travelled many miles afoot (he was a peddler) that he might reach a certain city before the morning services for Rosh Hashanah began. Weary and dusty he hastened to the synagogue, drawn thither by the teachings of childhood and an undoubted sincerity to be in God's holy temple.

When our shabby countryman entered, the *schul* was crowded almost to the doors by those who had *bought* religion at so much a seat; with difficulty the fellow found a resting place but no sooner was he in it than the rabbi's aide-de-camp, the *shames* [sexton], requested him to pay two dollars and a half for the privilege of saying his prayers in the place dedicated to God. Now it so happened [that] this poor peddler had not the amount, so after having the attention of scores of more fortunate brethren called to his case, he was finally refused a *seat*—no, not in Heaven, but in a fashionable *schul*. I'm glad, very glad, that *schuls* are depots in one of the big way stations on the road to Paradise. Yet one cannot but regret that the ticket agents are not more thoughtful.

If I were a rabbi, I would not refuse any man a ticket for Heaven.

If I were a rabbi, I would not frequent such public places as street corners, cigar stands, nor business houses, until I was conspicuous only when absent.

I would not, were I a rabbi, canvass the town with tickets for a party if the funds went toward my own high salary. I would prefer less salary and have no soliciting to do.

If I were a rabbi of what is termed the Reform type, I would not be funny or sarcastic at the expense of my Orthodox brother. If I were Orthodox in my ideas, I would not apply harsh names nor deny a state of future bliss to my brother of modern opinions.

If I were a rabbi, I would not direct my sermon to the costliest sealskin, handsomest bonnet, and smallest brain, but I'd divine my attention, as my remarks, among my audience.

If I had a Sabbath school, I would so conduct it that each boy and girl should see in my conduct that which I preached in my sermon.

I would not correct evil-doers among children by physical pain, inflicted because "they do so in the old country". I would not, while an incumbent of one position, be on the "lookout" for another with a bigger salary, unless I felt I could do more good in the one than in the other.

I would not, at a wedding, be the first at the feast and the last to leave the wine; it looks too carnal for a rabbi.

There are many other things, too numerous to mention, which I would not do.

One thing more, and I am done. Were I a rabbi, none should insult my manhood by offering to pay me for praying at a funeral nor would I dare accept money, unless for charity's cause, for any service I might do the living in memory of the dead.

Were I worthy to offer up a prayer for the departed, the consciousness that I was an ambassador to the court of courts, the thought of pleasing the afflicted, would all be ample pay.

Would that the spiritual mantle of Elijah was more often donned, or at least thrown over the very material broadcloth of our modern rabbis.

Women are precluded from entering the Holy of Holies; but it is a great satisfaction to contemplate *what we would not do* were the high office not denied us.

NOTES

1. Rachel "Ray" Frank (1861–1948) was born in San Francisco to Orthodox parents. Her father, a peddler who worked among the Indians, was said to be a descendant of the Gaon of Vilna (see chapter 7, document 12).Although she made no claim to rabbinic office, she was popularly called the "girl rabbi of the Golden West" because of her passionate and learned engagement in Jewish religious life. Dedicated to securing religious observance among the scattered Jewish communities of the Pacific coast, she was often invited to deliver sermons. On one occasion she arrived in Spokane Falls, Washington, on the eve of the Jewish New Year (Rosh ha-Shanah) and, to her dismay, learned that the town had no synagogue because the small Jewish community was divided between Orthodox and Reform Jews who adamantly refused to join forces. A local acquaintance, who shared her feelings, organized a service at which she gave a sermon. It was said that she thus became the first Jewish woman to preach formally at a synagogue in the United States. Thereafter her reputation as a lay religious leader grew throughout the Northwest. More significantly, her acclaim as a preacher and lecturer on Jewish issues provoked a debate on the position of women in the religious life of the American Jewish community. Frank's views about women's emancipation were complex and seemingly contradictory. Although Frank advocated broader roles for women within the synagogue and Jewish community, she was ambivalent about ordination for women. When she married Simon Litman in 1901, she largely gave up her career as a journalist, insisting that a woman's place is at home. The selection presented here is from an article she wrote for a newspaper in response to the question, "What would you do if you were a rabbi?"

2. Judah Asheri (d. 1349), chief rabbi of Toledo, Spain was renowned for his philanthropy.

3. In late nineteenth century American "Solomon Isaacs" was a scornful epithet for a frugal Jew.

27. WHY I BECAME A RABBI (1938)[1]

REGINA JONAS[2]

Dear Fraeulein Laaser,

After I struggled with all my might "again" writing something for you about myself and my chosen rabbinical career (actually, it chose me, not the reverse), some of your reasons in the end won me over; I won't confess which they were: official secret! So for the first time I take up the pen to express myself on the question so often put to me: Why have I as a woman become a rabbi? You have given me a difficult task. I do not enjoy writing; and besides, I must report about hardship and disappointment, and who enjoys doing that? In addition, I have to speak about *myself* and *my* struggles, because it is my fate to be the first woman in this field. That is not my style. I find any romanticization of the human sense of duty to be repulsive. In speaking, I can more easily address myself to other women than in writing; for tone, gesture, expression, and posture enliven whatever I want to say. What I am writing gets stuck in my attempt to express myself. But what I was going to say is that I hope a time will

---

Source: Letter from Regina Jonas to Mala Laser in response to the survey, "Was haben Sie zum Thema 'Frau' zu sagen?" [What Do You Have to Say on the Theme of 'Woman'?] *Central-Verein Zeitung*, XVII. Jhrg./Nr. 25 (June 23, 1938): 6. Trans. Elisa Klapheck, *Fraeulein Rabbiner Jonas: The Story of the First Woman Rabbi*, trans, from the German by Toby Axelrod (San Francisco: John Wiley & Sons, 2004), p. 59.

come for all of us in which there will be no more questions on the subject of "woman": for as long as there are questions, something is wrong. But if I must say what drove me as a woman to become a rabbi, two elements come to mind: My belief in the godly calling and my love for people. God has placed abilities and calling in our hearts, without regard to gender. Thus each of us has the duty, whether man or woman, to realize those gifts God has given. If you look at things this way, one takes woman and man for what they are: human beings.

With best wishes,
Rabbi Regina Jacobs

NOTES

1. The Berlin Liberal Jewish weekly, *Central-Verein Zeitung*, invited the writer and novelist Mala Laaser (d. 1953) to edit a special section on Jewish women, in which she organized a symposium in which six prominent German-Jewish women addressed the question of how they understood the category "woman." They were expressly instructed not to respond in an academic fashion but "simply to tell what [thoughts and feelings] the question evoked."

2. Born in Berlin, Regina Jonas (1902–1944) was the first Jewish woman to be ordained as a rabbi (although there had been a few previous women who served in the role; see the previous document in this chapter). She studied at the *Hochschule fuer die Wissenschaft des Judentums*, a seminary in Berlin for training liberal rabbis and educators, where she wrote a dissertation that addressed the question, "Can a Woman be a Rabbi according to Halachic Sources?" On the basis of a thorough review of the relevant texts, she concluded that the rabbinic law permits the ordination of women, whereupon she petitioned to be ordained as a Liberal Rabbi. Fearing that the ordination of women would cause a rift with the Orthodox rabbinate at a time when, because of Nazi persecution, Jewish solidarity was an overarching imperative, her request was initially rejected. Although, in 1935 she was ordained, she did not serve as pulpit rabbi but was employed as a teacher in Jewish schools, lectured widely, gave occasional guest sermons, and served as a chaplain in the Berlin Jewish hospital, an institute for the blind, and at homes for senior citizens. In 1942 she was arrested by the Gestapo and deported in 1942 to Theresienstadt and two years later to Auschwitz, where she was murdered.

28. PORTRAIT OF A JEW (1962)

ALBERT MEMMI[1]

I was born in Tunisia, in Tunis, a few steps from that city's large ghetto. My father, a harness maker, was somewhat pious, naturally somewhat so, as were all men of his trade and his station in life. My childhood was marked by the rhythms of the weekly Sabbath and the cycle of Jewish holidays. At a fairly early age, after first attending *yeshivah* and then the Alliance Israèlite, I became associated with various Jewish youth movements—scouts, cultural groups, political groups—so that, though I had profound doubts about religion, I did not stray from Jewry. On the contrary, I found it secured me and even deepened a certain continuity for me. For a number of years I pursued a course of studies that dispensed Jewish culture both traditional and reformed, open to the most immediate problems and yet solidly anchored to the

Source: Albert Memmi, *Portrait of a Jew.* Trans. Elisabeth Abbott. (New York: Orion Press, 1962), pp. 3–8.

past. I took up collections, among the flat graves in the Jewish cemetery or in front of old synagogues, on behalf of various community works, for the poor, for Polish refugees, for German refugees. Without too much embarrassment, illegally or not, I went from door to door trying stubbornly to convince my co-religionists of the beauty, importance and necessity of the Zionist movement at a period when that movement appeared to be nothing but an adventure. I even thought of going to Israel, or rather, to the romantic, pioneer Palestine of those days. In other words, I was sufficiently involved in all Jewish activities for my emotions, my mind and my life to become identified with the lot of all Jews over a fairly long period.

A moment came, however, which actually had its roots in the French lycée, when that intense ardor seemed to stifle me, and the rest of the world suddenly became more important. That was the period of the war in Spain, of the French *Front Populaire,* and of my own departure for the university. While the physical break with the clan and the community, then with the city, and the contact with the non-Jews whom I admired and liked, did not make me forget I was a Jew, it did cause me to consider that aspect of myself as part of a nobler and more urgent problem. The solution to that large body of ills from which all men suffered would in a way automatically solve my personal difficulties. Exchanging one enthusiasm for another, I came to consider anyone who did not think in universal terms as narrow-minded and petty.

It is necessary to bear in mind what that extraordinary period meant to our generation. We believed, finally, that for the first time humanity had perceived the light that could and must disperse darkness once and for all: oppressive measures, differences that separated us from each other, would be shattered, they were already being shattered. . . . Paradoxically, that universal light bore the clearly defined face of Europe—and more specifically, of France; but that did not trouble us; on the contrary, we were doubly grateful to the privileged for relinquishing their privileges and identifying themselves with freedom and progress. After all, it was they who had invented remedies after the ills; equality after domination, socialism after exploitation, science, techniques and promises of abundance. And by the time I left Tunis to continue my studies—soon to be interrupted, however—I thought no more about Palestine but only of returning to my native land, a universalist and

non-denominational, reconciled to everything and everybody, Tunisians, French and Italians, Moslems and Christians, colonizers and colonized. . . . "The Jewish problem" had been diluted with the honey of that universal embrace which, though not fully realized, was so near, so obvious, because so necessary.

We know what came of it: the sequel belongs to world history: it was war. Our youthful hopes of universalism and brotherly love were destroyed. The Europe we admired, respected and loved assumed strange faces: even France, democratic and fraternal, borrowed the face of Vichy. Afterwards they explained that Vichy was not their only face, nor even the true one, that behind that mask, clandestine and noble. . . . So greatly did I hope it was true that I almost believed it, but I was no longer so enthusiastic or naive. On the whole, it was better to make allowances for a dual personality and hope for a change of roles, which was always possible on the revolving stage of history. In any case, I had learned the harsh lesson that *my* destiny did not necessarily coincide with the destiny of Europe. And when peace came and, after numerous vicissitudes, I returned to Tunisia, I envisioned, for the first time but of my own accord and without anxiety, that separate destiny.

What it was to be, I had no idea when suddenly the event presented itself. My Moslem fellow citizens, having made the same discoveries, were beginning to develop their own history. Sensitive to mass enthusiasms when I considered them legitimate, I naturally shared in theirs: the Tunisians aspired to become a nation; in a world composed essentially of nations and oppressed minorities, what could be fairer?

This time, however, I did not altogether overlook the fact that I was a Jew. Moreover, mistrust, hesitancy, blunders forced me to remember it constantly. But, I was assured, Jews would certainly have their place in the future nation; had they not suffered the same lot and the same insults as other Tunisians? Why would they not benefit from the same liberation? I wanted to believe this. In any case, how could I, who applauded so wildly the struggle for freedom of other peoples, have refused to help the Tunisians in whose midst I had lived since birth and who, in so many ways, were my own people? In short, I did not believe I had any right to think of a separate Jewish destiny. Thus, having ceased to be a universalist, I gradually became, in some ways, a Tunisian nationalist. . . . though I failed to see that, on my part, there was still a great deal of hidden, abstract universalism in it, and perhaps even escapism.

Justice done to the Tunisians, I quickly found myself faced with that strange destiny which was still unchanged. Events that followed would force me to recognize that its singularity was still unimpaired, that it decidedly could not be overpowered by any other. To take only one example: the young states, formerly under colonial rule, were in urgent need of all sorts of personnel: technicians, administrators, intellectuals. That formidable vacuum could be partially filled by Tunisian Jews. But, as I had feared, the new states preferred to do without them. I hasten to add that it was difficult to picture a fifty percent Jewish personnel at the head of the new state; such a situation would have raised dangerous problems of domestic, and perhaps foreign, policies. But it was soon equally apparent that our distinctness as Jews was by no means resolved by our new status as citizens. Neither for non-Jews, nor for that matter, for Jews. When the war over Suez broke out, the Tunisian newspaper to which I was contributing and which I had helped to found printed on the front page: "Whoever sheds the blood of Egypt, sheds our blood!" At that time the hearts of all Jews beat as one for the Israeli army: their sons and grandsons were there and the sons and grandsons of their friends. I did not approve of that expedition, but how could one reconcile those two conflicting loyalties! When the Tunisian Constitution appeared, it established the Moslem religion among its essential provisions. For a number of reasons that have nothing to do with my subject, I did not find that too shocking; but why would I, who had rebelled against my own religion, accept, under compulsion, the Moslem religion which was now official? Each step, in short, had to be carefully reviewed and put in order.

It will be said that this is no different from the situation of Jews in Europe, in a Catholic country, for example. Of course, I know that! I have now been around the world enough to realize that precisely the same situation exists everywhere. But does that make it any the less difficult? The end of colonization in Tunisia and Morocco has almost restored the condition of those Jews to the level of the condition of all Jews, a notable and decisive step forward. But where has the common Jewish lot ever been simple and without trouble?

In short, I must admit that I had only postponed attacking my problem seriously; it was time for me to tackle it directly and, if possible, finally. Not that I regret or repudiate anything leading up to this; neither my Jewish childhood and adolescence, my Western and French culture and experiences which played such an essential part in my development, nor the aid and backing I gave to the just cause of the Tunisians.

NOTE

1. Albert Memmi (b. 1920) is a novelist and sociologist. A native of Tunisia and a scion of an old North African Jewish family, he fought with the Free French during World War II. After completing his studies in France, he returned to Tunis, the city of his youth, to become a director of a psychological institute. In 1959 he joined the Centre de la Recherche Scientifique in Paris, where he also taught at the Ecole Pratique des Hautes Etudes. His research focuses on the sociopsychological effects of colonization; he has discerned parallels between the situation of the Jews of the Diaspora and colonized peoples. In recent years he has given increasing attention to the experience of North African Jewry, a theme that he already explored in his early novels.

   In *Là statue de sal* (1953; *Pillar of Salt*, 1955), Memmi deals within the initial encounter of Maghreb Jewry, taking its first, hesitant steps beyond the protective precincts of tradition, with French culture and Western civilization. He also tells of its eventual disillusionment with an idealized Western humanism. The isolation of the North African Jew, rejected by both the French and the Arabs, is the theme of *Agar* (1955; *Strangers*, 1958). These issues are further considered in two volumes of autobiographical essays, *Portrait d'un Juif* (1962; *Portrait of a Jew*, 1963) and *La liberation du Juif* (1966; *The Liberation of the Jew*, 1966). Inspired by the teachings of Jean-Paul Sartre, his close friend, he seeks to portray the existential anguish of the contemporary Jew who is torn between the assimilatory imperatives of Western culture and an abiding desire to retain a distinctive identity, drawing the conclusion that the State of Israel "is our only solution, our one trump card, our historical opportunity."

29. REFLECTIONS OF A "HOLOCAUST JEW" (1966)

JEAN AMERY[1]

Not seldom, when in conversation my partner draws me into a plural—that is, as soon as he includes my person in whatever connection and says to me: "We Jews..."—I feel a not exactly tormenting, but nonetheless deep-seated discomfort. I have long tried to get to the bottom of this disconcerting psychic state, and it has not been very easy for me. Can it be, is it thinkable that I, the former Auschwitz inmate, who truly has not lacked occasion to recognize what he is and what he must be, still did not want to be a Jew, as decades ago, when I wore white half socks and leather breeches and nervously eyed myself in the mirror, hoping it would show me an impressive German youth? Naturally not. The foolishness of my masquerading in Austrian dress—although it was, after all, part of my heritage—belongs to the distant past. It is all right with me that I was not a German youth and am not a German man. No matter how the disguise may have looked on me, it now lies in the attic. If today discomfort arises in me when a Jew takes it for granted, legitimately, that I am part of his community, then it is not because I don't want to be a Jew but only because I cannot be one. And yet must be one. And I do not merely submit to this necessity but expressly claim it as part of my person. The necessity and impossibility of being a Jew, that is what causes me indistinct pain....

To be who one is by becoming the person one should be and wants to be: for me this dialectical process of self-realization is obstructed. Because being Something, not as metaphysical essence, but as the simple summation of early experience, absolutely has priority. Everyone must be who he was in the first years of his life, even if later these were buried under. No one can become what he cannot find in his memories.

Thus I am not permitted to be a Jew. But since all the same I must be one and since this compulsion excludes the possibilities that might allow me to be something other than a Jew, can I not find myself at all? Must I acquiesce, without a past, as a shadow of the universal-abstract (which does not exist) and take refuge in the empty phrase that I am simply a human being? But patience, we haven't reached that point yet. Since the necessity exists—and how compelling it is!—perhaps the impossibility can be resolved. After all, one wants to live without hiding, as I did when I was in the underground, and without dissolving into the abstract. A human being? Certainly, who would not want to be one? But you are a human being only if you are a German, a Frenchman, a Christian, a member of whatever identifiable social group. I must be a Jew and will be one, with or without religion, within or outside a tradition, whether as Jean, Hans, Yochanan. Why I must be one is what will be told here.

It didn't begin when schoolmates said to the boy: You're Jews anyway. Nor with the fight on the ramp of the university, during which, long before Hitler's ascent to power, a Nazi first knocked out one of my teeth. Yes, we are Jews, and what of it? I answered my schoolmate. Today my tooth, tomorrow yours, and the devil take you, I thought to myself after the beating, and bore the gap proudly like an interesting dueling scar.

It didn't begin until 1935, when I was sitting over a newspaper in a Vienna coffeehouse and was studying the Nuremberg Laws, which had just been enacted

Source: Jean Amery, *At the Mind's Limits: Contemplations by a Survivor on Auschwitz and its Realities.* Trans. Sidney and Stella P. Rosenfeld (New York: Schocken, 1986), pp. 82, 84f., 86, 91, 94–96. Reprinted by permission of Indiana University Press.

across the border in Germany. I needed only to skim them and already I could perceive that they applied to me. Society, concretized in the National Socialist German state, which the world recognized as the legitimate representative of the German people, had just made me formally and beyond any question a Jew, or rather it had given a new dimension to what I had already known earlier but which at that time was of no great consequence to me, namely, that I was a Jew.

What sort of new dimension? Not one that was immediately fathomable. After I had read the Nuremberg Laws I was no more Jewish than a half hour before. My features had not become more Mediterranean-Semitic, my frame of reference had not suddenly been filled by magic power with Hebrew allusions, the Christmas tree had not wondrously transformed itself into the seven-armed candelabra. If the sentence that society had passed on me had a tangible meaning, it could only be that henceforth I was a quarry of death. Well, sooner or later it claims all of us. But the Jew—and I now was one by decree of law and society—was more firmly promised to death, already in the midst of life. His days were a period of false grace that could be revoked at any second. I do not believe that I am inadmissibly projecting Auschwitz and the Final Solution back to 1935 when I advance these thoughts today. Rather, I am certain that in that year, at that moment when I read the Laws, I did indeed already hear the death threat— better, the death sentence....

To be a Jew, that meant for me, from this moment on, to be a dead man on leave, someone to be murdered, who only by chance was not yet where he properly belonged; and so it has remained, in many variations, in various degrees of intensity, until today. The death threat, which I felt for the first time with complete clarity while reading the Nuremberg Laws, included what is commonly referred to as the methodic "degradation" of the Jews by the Nazis. Formulated differently: the denial of human dignity sounded that death threat. Daily, for years on end, we would read and hear that we were lazy, evil, ugly, capable only of misdeeds, clever only to the extent that we pulled one over on others. We were incapable of founding a state but also by no means suited to assimilate with our host nations. By their very presence, our bodies—hairy, fat, and bow-legged—befouled public swimming pools, yes, even park benches. Our hideous faces, depraved and spoilt by protruding ears and hanging noses, were disgusting to our fellow men, fellow citizens of yesterday. We were not worthy of love and thus also not of life. Our sole right, our sole duty was to disappear from the face of the earth....

To be a Jew meant the acceptance of the death sentence imposed by the world as a world verdict. To flee before it by withdrawing into one's self would have been nothing but a disgrace, whereas acceptance was simultaneously the physical revolt against it. I became a person not by subjectively appealing to my abstract humanity but by discovering myself within the given social reality as a rebelling Jew and by realizing myself as one....

In my deliberations I am unable to consider Jews who are Jews because they are sheltered by tradition. *I* can speak only for myself—and, even if with caution, for contemporaries, probably numbering into the millions, whose being Jewish burst upon them with elemental force and who must stand this test without God, without history, without messianic-national hope. For them, for me, being a Jew means feeling the tragedy of yesterday as an inner oppression. On my left forearm I bear the Auschwitz number; it reads more briefly than the Pentateuch or the Talmud and yet provides more thorough information. It is also more binding as a basic formula of Jewish existence. If to myself and the world, including the religious and nationally minded Jews, who do not regard me as one of their own, I say: I am a Jew, then I mean by that those realities and possibilities that are summed up in the Auschwitz number.

But since being a Jew not only means that I bear within me a catastrophe that occurred yesterday and cannot be ruled out for tomorrow, it is—beyond being a duty—also *fear*. Every morning when I get up I can read the Auschwitz number [branded] on my forearm, something that touches the deepest and most closely intertwined roots of my existence; indeed, I am not even sure if this is not my entire existence. Then I feel approximately as I did back then when I got a taste of the first blow from a policeman's fist. Every day anew I lose my trust in the world. The Jew without positive determinants, the Catastrophe Jew, as we will unhesitatingly call him, must get along without trust in the world....

Without trust in the world I face my surroundings as a Jew who is alien and alone, and all that I can manage is to get along within my foreignness. I must accept being foreign as an essential element of my personality, insist upon it as if upon an inalienable possession. Still and each day anew I find myself alone. I was unable to force yesterday's murderers and tomorrow's potential aggressors to recognize the moral truth of their crimes, because the world, in its totality, did not help me to do it. Thus I am alone, as I was when they tortured me. Those around me do not appear to me as antihumans, as did my former torturers; they are my co-humans, not affected by me and the danger prowling at my side. I pass them with a greeting and without hostility. I cannot rely on them, only on a Jewish identity that is without positive determinants, my burden and my support.

NOTE

1. As he explains in this memoir, Jean Amery (1912–1978) was, in his own words, a "Holocaust Jew." Born Hans Maier in Vienna, the only child of a Catholic mother and a Jewish father, he was raised without an active Jewish identity. It was only with the ascendancy of the Nazis to power that he began to consider his Jewish provenance, acknowledging it fully only after the proclamation of the Nuremberg Laws in 1935, which of course defined him unambiguously as a Jew.

(See chapter 11, document 7.) Upon the incorporation of Austria into the German Reich in 1938, he fled with his wife—an East European Jewish woman whom he had married the previous year—to Belgium, where he adopted his French name. His wife died of a heart ailment, and he was eventually apprehended by the Nazis at first on the suspicion that he was a German military deserter. When it was realized that he was "racially" a Jew, Amery was summarily dispatched to Auschwitz.

Surviving the death camp, he returned to Belgium where he remarried and assumed a career as a freelance writer. For twenty years he refused to visit Germany or to publish his writings in Germany. He wrote exclusively for Swiss publications. Then in 1964 he met the German poet and critic Helmut Heissenbuettel, who persuaded him to deliver a radio talk to a German audience on his experience at Auschwitz. Thus were sown the seeds of the book *At the Mind's Limits*—five autobiographical essays published in Germany in 1966—from which this excerpt is taken.

Our selection is from a chapter significantly titled "On the Necessity and Impossibility of Being a Jew." A Jew neither by rabbinic law nor by cultural attachments, he found it inauthentic and thus impossible to acquire a Jewish heritage that was not part of his upbringing; on the other hand, by virtue of the Holocaust he was existentially a Jew.

30. A PARABLE OF ALIENATION (1946)

DANIEL BELL[1]

"Woe to a man who has no home."
Friedrich Nietzsche

American Jewish life, both in the ghetto and in the greater polis, has had a dialectical quality that shapes its basic expressions: the personal environment of the immigrant generation was defined by a pervasive love that emerged out of the concreteness of family experience, since ritual and social life were one. As he grew up, the young Jew confronted with the pressure of secularization gradually detached himself from this source. But the secular world, stripping him

Source: Daniel Bell, "A Parable of Alienation," *Jewish Frontier* 13, no. 11 (November 1946), pp. 12–19. Reprinted by permission of *Jewish Frontier*.

of his kinship, could offer no other unity of purpose in its place. Today the Jew feels the loss of his concreteness of love so necessary for all moral life. As a result, he turns back into himself, creating either pride or resentment in an empty status. It is the loss of communal love which is the source of the self-love and the self-hate, the arrogant chauvinism so characteristic of Jewish life in our time....

The deepest impulses urge us home. But where are we to go? Our roots are a Yiddish immigrant world from which we ventured forth each day to return at night. It was a home that had, in its best moments, a warmth and quality of selfless sacrifice which shaped our ethics and defined our lives. It is a world that has faded and cannot be recreated. All that is left is the hardness of alienation, the sense of otherness. And with it a special critical faculty, an unwillingness to submerge our value completely into any "cause" because of the germ cells of corruption which are in the seeds of organization.

Superficially, this may seem to be a retreat to personal-identification or nihilism. Yet we cannot accept philosophical nihilism, for if each man's values are exclusively his own, then no universe of discourse is possible, mediation between peoples is inconceivable, and the only method of persuasion open is force. The assumption of alienation is a positive value, fostering a critical sense out of a role of detachment; it is, if you will, the assumption of the role of the prophet, the one who through an ethical conscience indicts the baseness of the world, the one of whom the Hebrew essayist Ahad Haam has written: "[H]e is a man of truth. He sees life as it is with a view unwarped by subjective feelings; and he tells you what he sees just as he sees it, unaffected by irrelevant considerations. He tells the truth not because he wishes to tell the truth, not because he has convinced himself, after inquiry, that such is his duty, but because he needs must, because truth telling is a special characteristic of his genius—a characteristic of which he cannot rid himself, even if he would...."

Alienation does not mean deracination. It means the acceptance of the Jewish tradition—its compulsion to community—and the use of its ethical precepts as a prism to refract the codes and conduct of the world. As long as moral corruption exists, alienation is the only possible response. A dialectic of action accelerates this course; the tragic

gesture of the Bundist leader Shmuel Zygelboym[2] is a relevant answer. Zygelboym had been smuggled out of the Nazi-encircled Warsaw ghetto to plead for help for the doomed Jews. When the world refused to listen, he took his own life. For, as he wrote in his suicide note, he felt he had no right to live while his comrades lay buried in the Warsaw rubble. We are told that it is the mass death of thousands that has failed to stir the world. But precisely because this act had no effect do we recoil even more sharply at the lack of conscience and callousness of the world.

What of the relation of this position to Zionism? The stand outlined is a personal one, fused out of inheritance and experience, creating its own life and destiny. It is not meant as a political program, although it is an attitude, I feel, which is shared by others of the homeless radical generation. This "otherness," for us, is a special role. It cannot exist within a territorial demarcation. It can exist, and with it the special historical quality of being Jewish, the quality of alienation, only as the attitude of an eternal stranger in a foreign land. This does not mean that alienation is a solution for the "Jewish problem." For most people, undoubtedly Zionism is. But for those like us who have grown out of the peculiar radical ghetto soil, it is the only path. Emotionally and morally, we identify ourselves as Jews, the definition being derived from our specific immigrant roots. From this position, Zionism and nationalism, paradoxically, have intellectual, not emotional, appeal, with no roots in our living. Thorstein Veblen[3] in a prescient essay defined the special quality which would disappear in a Zionist world:

> "In short, he [the Jew] is a skeptic by force of circumstances over which he has no control....Intellectually he is likely to become an alien; spiritually he is more likely to remain a Jew; for the heart string of affection and consuetude are tied early, and they are not readily retied in after life. Nor does the animus with which the community of safe and sane gentiles is wont to meet him conduce at all to his personal incorporation in that community, whatever may befall the intellectual assets which he brings. Their people need not become his people nor their god his gods, and indeed the provocation is forever and irritably present all over the place to turn back from following

after them....One who goes away from home will come to see many unfamiliar things, and to take note of them; but it does not follow that he will swear by all the strange gods whom he meets along the road."[4]

The plight—and glory—of the alienated Jewish intellectual is that his role is to point to the need of brotherhood, but as he has been bred, he cannot today accept any embodiment of community as final. He can only live in permanent tension and as a permanent critic. The Zionist message is extremely strong. Like migratory terns we need to make our way back, and the Zionists offer a haven for prodigal sons. But the whole world is our world; we were born in ghettos and have a special place. Each man has his own journey to make, and the land we have to travel is barren. Out of this emerges the tragic sense of life: that we are destined to waste it.

NOTES

1. Daniel Bell, born in New York City in 1919, is professor emeritus of sociology at Harvard University. At the time he wrote this "celebration" of exile (*galut*) as a graced condition of alienation—of a spiritual and moral destiny to be forever estranged from the prevailing foibles of society—he was an instructor in social sciences at the University of Chicago. Published in *Jewish Frontier*, the organ of Labor Zionism in America, it was addressed to Zionists and their view that the Diaspora is an intolerable condition of "exile" that must be "negated."
2. Shmuel Zygelboym, see chapter 11, document 34.
3. Thorstein Veblen (1857–1929) was an American sociologist and economist.
4. Thorstein Veblen, "The Intellectual Preeminence of Jews in Modern Europe," in *The Political Science Quarterly* 34 (March 1919); reprinted in Veblen, *Essays in Our Changing Order*, ed. Leon Ardzrooni (New York: Viking, 1934), pp. 229–30.

31. LETTER TO AN INTELLECTUAL: A REPLY TO DANIEL BELL (1946)

BEN HALPERN[1]

Dear Dan Bell,

In your essay "The Parable of Alienation" you speak for—how many people? Five or ten who have said their say on the meaning of their Jewishness? A hundred who are still silent? In any case they are certainly few. Yet neither you nor I can feel that this gauges the importance of the matter. You have written what amounts to a manifesto, and you express (in a way of your own which need not commit the others) the existence of a type (it does not matter how stable) which is becoming self-conscious: Shall we call it the type of the alienated Jewish intellectual? The question you raise is thus one of considerable significance, for "intellectuals" like me as well as for "intellectuals" like you. (Since I need a catchword to distinguish between us—only for the purposes of this letter—will you permit me to call your type the "alienated" and my type simply the "Jewish intellectual," leaving aside the question in what sense we too may be alienated? By this usage I wish merely to indicate we are not alienated from our Jewish community in the same way as you profess to be.) My reason for

Source: Jewish Frontier 13, no. 12 (December 1946), pp. 13–18. Reprinted by permission of Mrs. Gertrude Halpern.

considering your essay important may surprise you. It is, you may feel, quite a "parochial" reason: it is simply that the "intellectual" in the past has played an unusual and even a decisive role and, in the future, may still have an important role to play in the mysterious history of Israel....I know that you...are a perceptive and true and at the same time objectively benign observer of your community of origin. What you see must be, in your experience, the fact. When you say that Jewish affective life (or the "concreteness of love") inheres almost exclusively in the family, *I must accept it as true.*

But that is the very source and root of the disintegration. A "community" whose common values are rooted exclusively in the family is hardly worthy of the name; and if it exists on this basis, it is exposed to the menace of swift and practically certain decay. It is a commonplace of contemporary thought that the family is the arena of deep and basic conflicts, which almost inevitably turn the generations against one another. This is not a special feature of our own "neurotic civilization," for it is found in greater or smaller measure, in one or another form, in a society which exists on the basis of underlying values. But, despite his alienation from the family, the individual reaching maturity can usually maintain a hold on traditional values and a place in the community, because both transcend the family. This was certainly true of the Jewish community and of Jewish values, else they could never have survived so long. If you today claim that Jewish values inhere only in the family—and as I say, I am bound to accept your analysis as a report on extensive experience by a perceptive and sincere observer—then it is small wonder that the Prodigal Son finds that there is no Return. For there never is *such* a return. The reconciliation with the family must always make its way through the community, finding there again threads of the same tradition that had been woven into family ties now irrevocably cut.

How to find the community: that, you recognize, is the dilemma of the Jewish intellectual of our day—but not only of the Jewish intellectual! And in this fact that you think you may have discovered a way out. That way is through the community of all the disinherited—the "alienated," those who see the world "as disenchanted."

But you are too much the sociologist and, as an intellectual, too much the modern man—that is to say, a psychologist—not to understand that through the incoherent "community" of the disinherited there is no return to the family, to the "concreteness of love," or to any historic continuum. Every member of the academy of alienated intellectuals must regard himself, in a sense, as the last of his tribe. There are some, indeed, who may welcome this condition, feeling that only at the heights of individuality, where the intellectual frees himself finally and completely from the orbit of the community, is the highest culture created. "*Après moi, le déluge*" might be the motto not only of the absolute monarch but of the absolute intellectual. But you, who are seeking new ways to brotherhood and not roots for community, cannot write off history, either past or future, as easily as this....

It is the extraordinary distinction of Jewish existence in the Diaspora that it *permanently* maintained not a mythological but an ideological opposition to the ruling ideas. Jews had their own scale of values: their historic time reckoning was their own—alongside the year count of the Christians and the Moslems, and later the French and Russian and Fascist Revolutions; their sacred calendar of festivals and fast days was their own marking out a different rhythm from the saint-days of the Christians; in spatial terms, they faced east towards Jerusalem to pray, like Judah Halevi, they regarded the Land of Israel, not Rome or Greenwich, as the earth's heart and reference point; and in sacred history they referred all events to the Revelation at Mount Sinai and the future return to Zion, rather than to Calvary or the revelation of Mohammed, or to the Italian Renaissance, the Lutheran Reformation, the British Glorious Rebelling, the American, French or Russian revolutions. In short, the Jew, afflicted of God, and without the least chance or impulse to bring about a revolution or secular change in their environment, maintained in oppression the ideological independence of a Chosen People.

It is because of this that, as you note in your essay, the Jews were so plainly seen to be *whole*, though radically alienated: because of this strong ascendancy of the intellectuals and their close integration with the people. And this, too, no doubt, was a reason why we were so hated and resented.

Nothing so clearly indicates how this integral "alienation" of the past has been breached and shattered as the findings of your essay-confession: that the values of Jewish life today inhere exclusively in the family. At one blow this reduces the whole ideological alienation of the Jews, which constituted us a Chosen People, into the mere mythological rebelliousness of an oppressed group. The Jews then accept the scale of values of the Gentiles—including the dubious position assigned to Jews even on the most generous understanding of this criterion.

There then arises a serious problem: How can one love such a tribe? All efforts to "reconstruct" the Jewish community in the United States are fundamentally derived from this tension—even though they are often signally misdirected in their attempt to resolve it. Seeing that most who try to flee the Jewish community explain that they cannot tolerate it because it is so "parochial," some architects of "Reconstruction" propose to *naturalize* Judaism, to divest it of its alienness: specifically, to drop the Chosen People concept and so reinterpret ancient themes that they appear to be identical with the contemporary values of Democracy and Progressivism.[2] This may pass quite well with those who are satisfied to be Jewish chiefly by virtue of the fact that society offers them no way out. For the time that they are forced to reside in the precincts of Israel, a reconstructed Judaism may offer them a halfway house, modishly redecorated in the style of the Castle which it is the historic propensity of these Jews to attain. They need not love it as a home. But the estranged intellectual needs precisely love; he will not be won over to a community whose value-trappings are not its own. It is the derivative quality of these ideas which will most repel him as "parochial." If, as your article suggests, there is really a reawakening of an interest in the Jewish community among alienated Jewish intellectuals, I would gladly wager that it will take quite a different direction: like the Buber-Rosenzweig group in Germany, the alienated American Jewish intellectuals will, I imagine, return to the *integrally alienated*, the highly *individual* Judaism of our literature and of the remaining Jewish communities which have retained their wholeness. (I do not, of course, assume that they would choose as their lodestar the same aspects of our tradition or the same existing community as did German Jewish intellectuals.)

But even this would be an incomplete return, subject to the reproach of romanticism. A community with which one communes by way of literature cannot sustain the "concreteness of love."

There is a much more direct access to the Jewish community, and a much more immediate call upon our love. The struggle of Israel for life is a spectacle that must enlist the concern and sympathy of any man who can view it directly, without the distortions of special interest. For any Jew who does not resist his natural tendency to become engaged by its powerful current, it offers an identification which will open the floodgates of his love.

It is easy to understand the inhibitions which paralyze the will of an intellectual of your particular background in the face of such a powerful pull and attraction. The straining of the Jewish people to live bears the name of a movement—Zionism; and toward all political movements the alienated intellectual of the post-Bolshevik school feels the horror of the burnt child. He dreads the cynicism with which his experience has indissolubly associated the very idea of an organization, a political movement. It is only a spiritual trauma of this sort that could force any Jew of our time to face Zionism on a merely intellectual plane.

Obviously, it would be idle to argue a point of this nature. However, I should like to conclude this discourse with a few observations, mostly relating to certain premature crystallizations of attitude.

Dan, first, let me suggest that you are driving into a blind alley when you flirt with the idea that it is necessary to live in a physically defined state of alienation, like the Jews in the Ghetto, in order to be a prophet. I assure you that many prophets lived in Israel and Judea and felt alienated from the false idols which the people set up even in the very Temple.

Then, a second point: May I suggest, Dan, that it might be a fruitful exercise if you were to ponder all over again the question of love and social organization, of community and the pitfalls of romanticism and cynicism. We have gone through a very purgatory of social education in our century, and one of the chief devils stoking the fires has been the demon of intellectual theocracy—the Ideocrat. Movements have been organized around ideas with a ruthless consistency and single-mindedness quite equal to anything in the history of the Church Militant. Appalled by the consequences of the adventures of the intellectual as Apostle and Pope, a new generation of intellectuals shrinks from *any* commitment to action, because it dreads the corruptions of romanticism and cynicism. But it is a little hard to believe that action *as such* must lead to falsehood, that any commitment must involve the lapse into romanticism or cynicism. Should we not still explore the possibility that there are ways of action and types of commitment by which the independence of the spirit need not be sold out?

As a first modest contribution towards the quest, let me propose the thesis that loyalty to a dogma is a tyranny which suffers only slaves in its realm; but loyalty to one's fellowmen—and, first of all, to the concrete, particular aggregation of fellowmen who have the precise responses which meet the acts and fill the deeper expectations by which each of us defines his true personality—can be a compact of love and freedom, preserving the independence of the individual and of the spirit.

NOTES

1. Ben Halpern (1912–1990) was a leading American Zionist thinker and writer. At the time he wrote this reply to Daniel Bell (see the previous document), he was the managing editor of *Jewish Frontier*. From 1968 to his retirement in 1980, he served as professor of modern Jewish history at Brandeis University.
2. The reference is to Mordecai Kaplan's program of Reconstructionism. See chapter 9, document 41.

32. WHY I CHOOSE TO BE A JEW (1959)

ARTHUR A. COHEN[1]

Until the present day, the Jew could not *choose* to be a Jew—history forced him to accept what his birth had already defined.

During the Middle Ages he was expected to live as a Jew. He could escape by surrendering to Islam or Christianity, but he could *not* choose to remain anonymous. In the nineteenth century, with the growth of nationalism, Christianity became the ally of patriotism. The Jews of Europe were compelled to prove that their religion did not compromise their loyalty to king, emperor, kaiser, or tsar. But no matter how desperately they tried to allay suspicion by assimilation or conversion, the fact of their birth returned to plague them. Finally, in the Europe of Nazism and Communism, the Jew could not choose—on any terms—to exist at all.

In the United States today, it is at last possible to choose *not* to remain a Jew.

Given the freedom to choose I have decided to embrace Judaism. I have not done so out of loyalty to the Jewish people or the Jewish state. My choice was religious. I chose to believe in the God of Abraham, Isaac, and Jacob; to acknowledge the law of Moses as the Word of God; to accept the people of Israel as the holy instrument of divine fulfillment; to await the coming of the Messiah and the redemption of history.

Many Jews will find my beliefs unfamiliar or unacceptable—perhaps outrageous. The manner in which I arrived at them is not very interesting in itself, but I think two aspects of my experience are worth noting because they are fairly common: I come from a fundamentally unobservant Jewish home and my first religious inclination was to become a Christian.

My parents are both second-generation American Jews whose own parents were moderately religious, but, newly come to America, lacked either the education or the opportunity, patience, and time to transmit to their children their own understanding of Judaism. My parents went to synagogue to observe

Source: Arthur A. Cohen, "Why I Choose to Be a Jew," *Harper's Magazine* 218, no. 1307 (April 1959), pp. 63–66.

the great Jewish holidays—Passover, the New Year, and the Day of Atonement—but worship at home, knowledge of the liturgy, familiarity with Hebrew, concern with religious thought and problems, did not occupy them. Their real concern—and they were not unique—was adjusting to American life, achieving security, and passing to their children and those less fortunate the rewards of their struggle.

It would be ungrateful to deny the accomplishment of my parents' generation. They managed to provide their children with a secular education and security. But although the flesh was nourished, the spirit was left unattended. When I had finished high school and was ready to leave for college I took with me little sense of what my religion, or any religion, involved. I knew only that in these matters I would have to fend for myself.

When an American Jew studies at an American university, it is difficult for him not to be overwhelmed—as I was at the University of Chicago—by the recognition that Western culture is a Christian culture, that Western values are rooted in the Greek and Christian tradition. He may hear such phrases as "Judaeo-Christian tradition" or "the Hebraic element in Western culture," but he cannot be deluded into thinking that this is more than a casual compliment. The University of Chicago, moreover, insisted that its students study seriously the philosophic sources of Western culture, which, if not outspokenly Christian, were surely non-Jewish. I soon found myself reading the classics of Christian theology and devotion—from St. Augustine and St. Anselm through the sermons of Meister Eckhart.

It was not long before my unreligious background, a growing and intense concern with religious problems, and the ready access to compelling Christian literature all combined to produce a crisis—or at least my parents and I flattered ourselves that this normal intellectual experience was a religious crisis. The possibility of being a Christian was, however, altogether real. I was rushed, not to a psychoanalyst, but to a rabbi—the late Milton Steinberg, one of the most gifted and profound Jewish thinkers of recent years. Leading me gently, he retraced the path backward through Christianity to Judaism, revealing the groundwork of Jewish thought and experience which supported what I have come to regard as the scaffolding of Christian "unreason."

It was extremely important to me to return to Judaism through the medium of Christianity—to choose after having first received the impress of Western education and Christian thought. Since it would have been possible to become a Christian—to accept Christian history as my history, to accept the Christian version of Judaism as the grounds of my own repudiation of Judaism, to believe that a Messiah had redeemed me—I could only conclude that Judaism was not an unavoidable fate, but a destiny to be chosen freely.

My own conversion and, I suspect, the conversion of many other Jews to Judaism, was effected, therefore, through study, reflection, and thought. What first seized my attention was not the day-to-day religious life of the Jewish community around me, but rather principles, concepts, and values. I had first to examine the pressing theological claims of a seemingly triumphant Christianity, before I could accept the ancient claims of a dispersed, tormented, and suffering Jewry.

This may sound reasonable enough to a gentile, but I must point out that it is an extremely unconventional attitude for a Jew. Historically, Judaism has often looked with disfavor upon theology....

Why this distrust of theology? I suspect that some Jewish leaders fear—perhaps not unjustifiably—that theological scrutiny of what they mean by God, Israel, and Law might reveal that they have no theology at all. Others no doubt fear—again not unjustifiably—that their unbending interpretations of Jewish Law and life might have to be revised and rethought. Theology often produces a recognition of insufficiency, an awareness that valid doctrine is being held for the wrong reasons and that erroneous doctrine is being used to rationalize right action. But the major Jewish argument against Jewish theology is that it is a Christian pastime—that it may, by insinuation and subtle influence, Christianize Judaism. In this view, Christianity is a religion of faith, dogma, and theology and Judaism is a religion which emphasizes observance of God's Law, not speculation about it.

For me this argument is a vast oversimplification. Christianity is not without its own structure of discipline, requirements, and laws—the Roman sacraments and the Lutheran and Anglican liturgy, for example—and this structure does not move with the Holy Spirit as easily as St. Paul might have wished. Judaism, on the other hand, is not tied to the pure act. It has matured through the centuries a massive speculative and mystic tradition which attempts to explain the principles upon which right action is founded. Judaism need not, therefore, regret the renewal of theology. It already has one. It is merely a question of making what is now a minor chord in Jewish tradition sound a more commanding note.

As a "convert" who thinks that theology must come first, what do I believe?

The convert, I must point out, is unavoidably both a thinker and a believer—he thinks patiently and believes suddenly. Yet belief, by itself, cannot evict the demons of doubt and despair. As a believer I can communicate my beliefs, but as a thinker I cannot guarantee that they are certain or will never change. As all things that record the encounter of God and man, beliefs are subject to the conditions of time and history, and pitiable limitation of our capacity to understand such enormous mysteries. . . .

First, I chose to believe in the God of Abraham, Isaac, and Jacob. This is to affirm the reality of a God who acts in history and addresses man. Although this God may well be the same as the abstract gods formulated by philosophers, he is still more than these—he is the God who commanded Abraham to quit the land of the Chaldeans and who wrestled with Jacob throughout the night. . . .

For me then to believe in the biblical God, the God of the Patriarchs, the smoking mountain, the burning bush, was not to surrender reason, but to go beyond it. More than accepting the literal words of the Bible, it meant believing in the Lord of History—the God who creates and unfolds history, and observes its tragic rifts and displacements—from the Tower of Babel to the cold war; who, in his disgust, once destroyed the world with flood and later repented his anger; who, forgoing anger, gave to the world counsels of revelation, commencing with the gift of Torah to Moses and continuing through the inspired writings of the ancient rabbis; and who finally—through his involvement with the work of creation—prepares for redemption.

It may seem difficult—indeed for many years it was—to consider the Bible, which is the source of this belief, as more than the unreliable account of an obscure Semitic tribe. But gradually I came to discover in it an authentic statement of the grandeur and misery of man's daily existence—a statement which I could accept only if I believed in a God who could be addressed as "Lord, Lord."

My second belief is an acknowledgement that *the Law of Moses is the word of God.* The Bible tells us that the Word of God broke out over the six hundred thousand Hebrews who assembled at the foot of Sinai. That Word was heard by Moses—he who had been appointed to approach and receive. The word became human—in its humanity, it undoubtedly suffers from the limitation of our understanding—but it lost none of its divinity.

The Law is always a paradox: it is both the free Word of God and the frozen formality of human laws. But the Law of Moses was vastly different from what we usually understand law to be. It is true that in the days before the temple was destroyed by Titus in 70 A.D. divine law was the enforceable law of the judge and the court; but later the great rabbis who interpreted it conceived of the revelation of God to Israel, not as law in its common usage, but as *Torah*—teaching.

Torah is a fundamental concept for the Jew. Narrowly conceived, it refers to the Pentateuch—the first five books of the Bible which are the pristine source of all Jewish tradition. In them are the laws of the Sabbath and the festivals; the foundations of family and communal morality; and the essentials of Jewish faith—the unity of God, the election of Israel, and the definition of its special mission. But, broadly conceived, Torah refers to *any* teaching with brings man closer to the true God, who is the God of Israel and the Lord of History.

Torah has two aspects—the actual way of law and observance (the *halakhah* as it is called Hebrew) and the theology of the rabbis which interpret that way (called the *aggadah*). By means of both, according to Jewish tradition, God proposes to lead *all* of his creation to fulfillment, to perfect its imperfections, to mend the brokenness of his creatures. The Jewish people—the guardian of the *halakhah* and the *aggadah*—has been elected to be the pedagogue to all the nations of the world, to become on its behalf "a kingdom of priests and a holy people."

Jews can achieve holiness—the primary objective, I believe, of their religion—neither by prayer nor mediation alone. Judaism values prayer only in conjunction with the act; it praises study only in relation to life.

God does not propose or suggest ways to achieve holiness; he commands them. According to Torah, he places upon each Jew "the yoke of the commandments." To observe the Sabbath is as much a commandment as is the obligation to daily prayer; the grace which accompanies eating is as essential as the study of sacred literature. Although tradition distinguishes between practical and intellectual commandments, it considers both to be equally the expressed will of God. The arbitrary and the reasonable—the dietary laws and the prohibition of homosexuality for example—both proceed from God.

Judaism begins with an explicit fact: the revelation of Torah. Many of its commandments may seem trivial. But it should not be expected that God will leave the trivial to man and concern himself only with the broad, general, and universal. The corruption of man takes place not only in the province of principle, but in the small and petty routine of life. The Torah is therefore exalted and picayune, universal and particular, occupied equally with principle and the details of practice. It tolerates no separation between the holy and the profane—all that is secular must become sacred, all that is profane must be kept open to the transforming power of God.

The exact degree to which Jews should fulfill all the commandments of the Law is one of the most difficult and perplexing dilemmas for modern Jews. Orthodox Jews are in principle obligated to observe all of Jewish Law. Reform Jews have cut observance to a minimum (though there is a movement to increase it). Conservative Jews stand somewhere in between. I will not attempt it in this space, but I believe it is possible to show that the fundamental question is not whether the Jew performs the required acts of observance, but whether he is truly aware of the sacred intention of these acts. One can, for example, recite the blessings over the food one eats and feel nothing of the sanctity of food; on the other hand one can silently acknowledge the holiness of eating, and fulfill the command of God. Both are needed—the blessing and the inner acknowledgement, but the former is surely incomplete without the latter.

The third of my beliefs is, as I have indicated, simply an element of God's revelation in Torah—that *the Jewish people has been chosen as a special instrument of God....*

This tradition of election should not be confused with racial pride or an attitude of arrogant exclusion towards others. The Jew believes neither that the truth flows in his blood nor that the gentile cannot come to possess it. Judaism is exclusive only in the sense that we affirm [that] we possess important truth which is available to all—everyone can join but only on our terms.

The election of Israel is not a conclusion drawn from history—the survival and endurance of the Jews through twenty centuries of destructive persecution could be no more than blind accident. At best it could be construed as a compliment to the resiliency and stubbornness of the Jewish people. Judaism has insisted, however—not as a declaration after the fact, but as a principle of its very existence—that it is both a holy nation chosen by God to be his own and a suffering nation destined to ensure martyrdom for his sake. God announces not only that "Ye shall be holy unto me; for I the Lord am Holy, and have separated you from the peoples, that ye should be mine" (Leviticus 20:26) but that "You only have I known of all the families of the earth: therefore I will visit upon you all your iniquities" (Amos 3:2).

Israel is thus called not only to be the example to the nations, but, being the example, is tried all the more sorely for its transgressions. To be sure, this is not a doctrine for the uncourageous. No one even slightly familiar with the agonies of Jewish history could claim that the election of Israel has brought with it particular reward and security. It is however precisely the fact of Jewish suffering which makes its election and mission all the more pertinent to the modern world. To have believed and survived in spite of history is perhaps the only evidence which Judaism can offer to the accuracy of its conviction that it is called to be a holy community.

In the face of Christendom and the obvious success which its claims have enjoyed, it may seem foolish or presumptuous for Judaism—a small and insignificant community of believers—to assert my fourth belief: that *Jesus is not the Messiah of which the Bible speaks*, that Christianity has conceived but one more imperfect image of the end, and that a *Messiah is yet to come who will redeem history*.

But there are enduring reasons why Jews cannot accept Jesus as the Messiah. Both Christian and Jew begin with the conviction of the imperfection of man. The Christian argues, however, that creation has been so corrupted by man as to be saved only through the mediation of Jesus. The Jew considers creation imperfect but, rather than corrupt, he finds it rich with unfulfilled possibility. The role of man is to bring creation to that point at which the Messiah can come to glorify man by bringing him the praise of God—not to save him from self-destruction, as Christianity would have it. According to Jewish tradition, Moses died from the kiss of God. It would be fitting to conceive the advent of the Messiah and the Kingdom of God as the bestowal of a kiss.

This does not mean that God congratulates man for his good works but rather that he shares both in the agony of history and in its sanctification. Judaism does not imagine that every day we are getting better and better, and that finally we will reach a point where the Messiah will come. As likely as not, it seems to be, history is coming closer each day to suicide. The mission of Judaism is not to stave off disaster but to enlarge man's awareness of the Divine Presence.

Jews believe, if they are to remain Jews, that the Messiah has not come. They can accept Jesus of Nazareth as little more than a courageous witness to truths to which his own contemporaries in Pharisaic Judaism by and large subscribed. Jesus was, as Martin Buber has suggested, one in the line of "suffering servants" whom God sends forth to instruct the nations. It is to the dogmatization of St. Paul that one must ascribe the transformation of "prophet" into "Christ"—and it is therefore St. Paul who severs Jesus from the life of Israel. The rejection of Jesus must now stand to the end of time.

The role of Israel and Judaism, until the advent of the true Messiah, is to outlast the world and its solutions—to examine its complacencies, to deflate its securities, to put its principles to the test of prophetic judgment. This is an aristocratic and painful mission, for though Judaism may address the world and lay claim to it, it does not seek to convert it.

Judaism does not say "The world is not changed—therefore we do not believe in the Messiah." This is only partially true, for the coming of the Messiah will mean more than a reformed world in which the wolf and the lamb shall share bread together and war shall cease. This social image of salvation is true as far as it goes, but it does not go far enough. The Messiah is not a handyman or a plumber—his task does not consist in "mending" a world that is temporarily faulty but is essentially perfect. The world is to be transformed—not reformed—by the Messiah.

This transformation will come to pass, Judaism believes, only when the world wishes it so deeply that it cannot abide itself more a single moment. At that moment the Messiah may come. This moment of expectancy has not yet arrived. The rabbis have taught us that I, and all of the House of Israel, prevent him

from coming. Of this there is no question, but we cannot avoid concluding that he has not come.

For the Jew who comfortably repeats the rituals of his religion without confronting the principles of faith which they express, and for the Jew who was not aware that Judaism had any principles of faith at all, this personal statement may seem shocking. But I do not think my position or my background are by any means unique. If, as I have argued, the present generation of American Jews is indeed the first generation of Jews in centuries who are free to choose to believe as Jews, then, in my terms at least, my argument is important. Now as never before it will be possible for the Jewish people and the State of Israel to survive, but for Jewish religion to perish. For me, and for other believing Jews, it is crucial for mankind that Judaism survive. The mission of Judaism is not completed nor the task of the Jewish people fulfilled. If the Jewish people is an instrument sharpened by God for his own purposes, it must go on serving that purpose, sustaining its burden, and keeping that trust which alone can bring all men to redemption.

NOTE

1. Arthur A. Cohen (1928–1986) was, as he recurrently declared, a theological Jew. To him, theology had an existential urgency borne of a need to be a Jew by faith and religious commitment. As an American Jew, relatively free of the fear of antisemitism and feeling secure within the social and cultural fabric of his country, he was faced with the possibility of indifference to his ancestral identity and religion and even the option of adopting another religion. Finding the imperatives of sentiment and primordial loyalty not sufficiently compelling, he understood his abiding attachment to Judaism—as a system of religious discourse and practice—to be one of choice. Yet as a conscious choice it required sustained intellectual clarification and justification. It required theology. As an ongoing project, Cohen's theology had varied expressions: learned theological disquisitions, exegetical studies of Jewish religious thinkers, and fiction. He wrote five novels exploring the religious quest and quandaries of the modern Jew. In the present selection, he sketches his initial path to religious faith and explains why his affirmation of Judaism was a matter of theological choice.

33. A KIND OF SURVIVOR (1969)

GEORGE STEINER[1]

For Elie Wiesel

Not literally. Due to my father's foresight (he had shown it when leaving Vienna in 1924), I came to America in January 1940, during the phony war. We left France, where I was born and brought up, in safety. So I happened not to be there when the names were called out. I did not stand in the public square with the other children, those I had grown up with. Or see my father and mother disappear when the train doors were torn open. But in another sense I am a survivor, and not intact. If I am often out of touch with my own generation, if that which haunts me and controls my habits of feeling strikes many of those I should be intimate and working with in my present world as remotely sinister and artificial, it is because the black mystery of what happened in Europe is to me indivisible from my own identity. Precisely because I was not there, because an accident of good fortune struck my name from the roll.

Often the children went alone, or held the hands of strangers. Sometimes parents saw them pass and did not dare call out their names. And they went, of course, not for anything they had done or said. But because their parents existed before them. The crime of being one's children. During the Nazi period it knew no absolution, no end. Does it now? Somewhere the determination to kill Jews, to harass them from the earth simply because *they are*, is always alive. Ordinarily, the purpose is muted, or appears in trivial spurts—the obscenity daubed on the front door, the brick through the shop window. But there are, even now, places where the murderous intent might grow heavy: in Russia, in parts of North Africa, in certain countries of Latin America. Where tomorrow? So, at moments, when I see my children in the room, or imagine that I hear them breathing in the still of the house, I grow afraid. Because I have put on their backs a burden of ancient loathing and set savagery at their heels. Because it may be that I will be able to do no more than the parents of the children gone to guard them.

That fear lies near the heart of the way in which I think of myself as a Jew. To have been a European Jew in the first half of the 20th century was to pass sentence on one's own children, to force upon them a condition almost beyond rational understanding. And which may recur. I have to think that—it is the vital clause—so long as remembrance is real. Perhaps we Jews walk closer to our children than other men; try as they may, they cannot leap out of our shadow.

This is my self-definition. Mine, because I cannot speak for any other Jew. All of us obviously have something in common. We do tend to recognize one another wherever we meet, nearly at a glance, by some common trick of feeling, by the darkness we carry. But each of us must hammer it out for himself. That is the real meaning of the Diaspora, of the wide scattering and thinning of belief.

To the Orthodox my definition must seem desperate and shallow. Entire communities stayed close-knit to the end. There were children who did not cry out but said *Shema Yisroel* and kept their eyes wide open because his kingdom lay just a step over the charnel pit (not as many as is sometimes said, but there *were*). To the strong believer the torture and massacre of six million is one chapter—one only—in the millennial dialogue between God and the people He has so terribly chosen. Though Judaism lacks a dogmatic eschatology (it leaves to the individual the imagining of transcendence), the Orthodox can mediate on the camps as a forecourt of God's house, as an almost intolerable but manifest mystery of His will. When he teaches his children the prayers and

Source: George Steiner, "A Kind of Survivor," *Commentary*, 39/2 (February 1965), pp. 32–38.

rites (my own access to these was that of history, not of present faith), when they sing at his side at the high holidays, the pious Jew looks on them not with fear, not as hostages that bear the doom of his love, but in pride and rejoicing. Through them the bread shall remain blessed and the wine sanctified. They are alive not because of a clerical oversight in a Gestapo office, but because they no less than the dead are part of God's truth. Without them history would stand empty. The Orthodox Jew defines himself (as I cannot) in the rich life of his prayer, of an inheritance both tragic and resplendent. He harvests the living echo of his own being from the voices of his community and the holiness of the word. His children are like the night turned to song.

The Orthodox Jew would not only deny me the right to speak for him, pointing to my lack of knowledge and communion; he would say, "You are not like us, you are a Jew outwardly, in name only." Exactly. But the Nazis made of the mere name necessary and sufficient cause. They did not ask whether one had ever been to synagogue, whether one's children knew any Hebrew. The antisemite is no theologian; but his definition is inclusive. So we would all have gone together, the Orthodox and I. And the gold teeth would have come out of our dead mouths, song or no song.

Two passages from Exodus help the mind grasp the enormity. Perhaps they are mistranslations or archaic shards interpolated in the canonic text. But they help me as does poetry and metaphor, by giving imaginative logic to grim possibility. Exodus 4:24 tells how God sought to kill Moses: "And it came to pass by the way in the inn, that the Lord met him and sought to kill him." I gloss this to mean that God suffers gusts of murderous exasperation at the Jews, toward a people who have made Him a responsible party to history and to the grit of man's condition. He may not have wished to be involved; the people may have chosen Him, in the oasis at Kadesh, and thrust upon Him the labors of justice and right anger. It may have been the Jew who caught Him by the skirt, insisting on contract and dialogue. Perhaps before either God or living man was ready for proximity. So as in marriage, or the bond between father and child, there are moments when love is changed to something very much like itself, pure hatred.

The second text is Exodus 33:22–3. Moses is once more on Sinai, asking for a new set of tablets (we have

always been nagging Him, demanding justice and reason twice over). There follows a strange ceremony of recognition: "And it shall come to pass, while my glory passeth by, that I will put thee in a cleft of the rock, and will cover thee with my hand while I pass by: And I will take away mine hand, and thou shalt see my back parts: but my face shall not be seen." This may be the decisive clue: God can turn His back. There may be minutes or millennia—is our time His?—in which He does not see man, in which He is looking the *other way*. Why? Perhaps because through some minute, hideous error of design the universe is too large for His surveillance, because somewhere there is a millionth of an inch, it need be no more, out of His line of sight. So He must turn to look there also. When God's back parts are toward man, history is [Bergen] Belsen.

If the Orthodox Jew cannot allow my definition, or this use of the holy word as metaphor and paradox, neither can the Zionist and the Israeli. They do not deny the catastrophe, but they know that it bore splendid fruit. Out of the horror came the new chance. The state of Israel is undeniably a part of the legacy of German mass murder. Hope and the will to action spring from the capacity of the human mind to forget, from the instinct of necessary oblivion. The Israeli Jew cannot look back too often; his must be the dreams not of night but of day, the forward dreams. Let the dead bury the mounds of the dead. His history is not theirs; it has just begun. To someone like myself, the Israeli Jew might say: "Why aren't you here? If you fear for the lives of your children, why not send them here and let them grow up amid their own kind? Why burden them with your own perhaps literary, perhaps masochistic, remembrance of disaster? This is their future. They have a right to it. We need all the brains and sinews we can get. We're not working for ourselves alone. There isn't a Jew in the world who doesn't hold his head higher because of what we've done here, because Israel exists."

Which is obviously true. The status of the Jew everywhere has altered a little, the image he carries of himself has a new straightness of back, because Israel has shown that Jews can handle modern weapons, that they can fly jets, and turn desert into orchard. When he is pelted in Argentina or mocked in Kiev, the Jewish child knows that there is a corner of the earth where he is master, where the gun is his. If Israel were to be destroyed, no Jew would escape unscathed. The shock of failure, the need and harrying of those seeking refuge, would reach out to implicate even the most indifferent, the most anti-Zionist.

So why not go? Why not leave the various lands in which we still live, it seems to me, as more or less accepted guests? Many Russian Jews might go if they could. North African Jews are doing so even at the price of destitution. The Jews of South Africa might before too long be forced to the same resolve. So why don't I go, who am at liberty, whose children could grow up far from the spoor of the inhuman past? I don't know if there is a good answer. But there is a reason....

The sense I have of the Jew as a man who looks on his children with a dread remembrance of helplessness and an intimation of future, murderous possibility, is a very personal, isolated one. It does not relate to much that is now alive and hopeful. But it is not wholly negative either. I mean to include in it far more than the naked precedent of ruin. That which has been destroyed—the large mass of life so mocked, so hounded to oblivion that even the names are gone and the prayer for the dead can have no exact foothold—embodied particular genius, a quality of intelligence and feeling which none of the major Jewish communities now surviving has preserved or recaptured. Because I feel that specific inheritance urgent in my own reflexes, in the work I try to do, I am a kind of survivor.

In respect of secular thought and achievement, the period of Jewish history which ended at Auschwitz surpassed even the brilliant age of co-existence in Islamic Spain. During roughly a century, from the emancipation of the ghettoes by the French Revolution and Napoleon to the time of Hitler, the Jew took part in the moral, intellectual, and artistic noon of bourgeois Europe. The long confinement of the ghetto, the sharpening of wit and nervous insight against the whetstone of persecution, had accumulated large reserves of consciousness. Released into the light, a certain Jewish elite, and the wider middle-class circle which took pride and interest in its accomplishments, quickened and complicated the entire contour of Western thought. To every domain they brought radical imaginings; more specifically, the more gifted Jews re-possessed certain crucial elements of classic European civilization in order to make them new and problematic. All this is commonplace; as is the

inevitable observation that the tenor of modernity, the shapes of awareness and query by which we order our lives are, in substantial measure, the work of Marx, Freud, and Einstein.

What is far more difficult to show, though it seems to me undeniable, is the extent to which a common heritage of fairly recent emancipation, a particular bias of rational feeling—specialized in origin but broadening out to become the characteristic modern note—informs their distinct, individual genius. In all three, we discern a mastering impulse to visionary logic, to imagination in the abstract, as if the long banishment of the Eastern and European Jew from material action had given to thought a dramatic autonomy. The intimation of an energy of imagination at once sensuous and abstract, the release of the Jewish sensibility into a world dangerously new, unencumbered by reverence, is similarly at work in the subversion of Schoenberg and Kafka, and in the mathematics of Cantor. It relates Wittgenstein's *Tractatus* to that of Spinoza.

Without the contribution made by the Jews between 1830 and 1930, Western culture would be obviously different and diminished. At the same time, of course, it was his collision with established European values, with classic modes of art and argument, which compelled the emancipated Jew to define his range and identity. In this collision, in the attempt to achieve poise in an essentially borrowed milieu, the converted Jew or half-Jew, the Jew whose relation to his own past grew covert or antagonistic—Heine, Bergson, Hofmannsthal, Proust—played a particularly subtle and creative role.

Those who helped define and shared in this *Central European humanism* (each of the three terms carrying its full charge of implication and meaning) showed characteristic traits, characteristic habits of taste and recognition. They had a quick way with languages. Heine is the first, perhaps the only great poet whom it is difficult to locate in any single linguistic sensibility. The habits of reference of this European Jewish generation often point to the Greek and Latin classics; but these were seen through the special focus of Winckelmann, Lessing, and Goethe. An almost axiomatic sense of Goethe's transcendent stature, of the incredible ripeness and humanity of his art, colors the entire European-Jewish enlightenment and continues to mark its few survivors (Goethe's fragment *On Nature* converted Freud from an early interest in law to the study of the biological sciences). The Central European Jewish bourgeoisie was frequently intimate with the plays of Shakespeare and assumed, rightly, that the performance of Shakespearean drama in Vienna, Munich, or Berlin (often acted and staged by Jews) more than matched what could be found in England. It read Balzac and Stendhal (one recalls Leon Blum's pioneer study of Beyle [Stendhal]), Tolstoy, Ibsen, and Zola. But the Jews often read them in a special, almost heightened context. The Jews who welcomed Scandinavian drama and the Russian novel tended to see in the new realism and iconoclasm of literature a part of the general liberation of spirit. Zola was not only the explorer of erotic and economic realities, as were Freud, Weininger, or Marx: he was the champion of Dreyfus.... *almost nothing* of it survives. This is what makes my own, almost involuntary, identification with it so shadowy a condition....

The humanism of the European Jew lies in literal ash. In the accent of survivors—Hannah Arendt, Ernst Bloch, T. W. Adorno, Erich Kahler, Levi-Strauss—whose interests and commitments are, of course, diverse, you will hear a common note as of desolation. Yet it is these voices which seem to me contemporary, whose work and context of reference are indispensable to an understanding of the philosophical, political, aesthetic roots of the inhuman; of the paradox that modern barbarism sprang in some intimate, perhaps necessary way, from the very core and locale of humanistic civilization. If this is so, why do we try to teach, to write, to contend for literacy? Which question, and I know of none more urgent, or the idiom in which it is put, probably puts the asker thirty years out of date—on either side of the present.

Men are accomplices to that which leaves them indifferent. It is this fact which must, I think, make the Jew wary inside Western culture, which must lead him to re-examine ideals and historical traditions that, certainly in Europe, had enlisted the best of his hopes and genius. The house of civilization proved no shelter.

But then, I have never been sure about houses. Perforce, the Jew has often been wanderer and guest. He can buy an old manse and plant a garden. An anxious pastoralism is a distinctive part of the attempt of many American middle-class and intellectual Jews to assimilate to the Anglo-Saxon background. But I wonder whether it's quite the same. The dolls in the attic were not ours; the ghosts have a rented air. Characteristically, Marx, Freud, [and] Einstein ended their lives far from their native ground, in exile or refuge. The Jew has his anchorage not in a place but in a time, in his highly developed sense of history as personal context. Six-thousand years of self-awareness are a homeland.

The rootlessness of the Jew, the "cosmopolitanism" denounced by Hitler, by Stalin, by Mosley, by every right-wing hooligan, is historically an enforced condition. The Jew finds no comfort in "squatting on the window sill" (T. S. Eliot's courteous phrase). He would rather have been *echt Deutsch* or *Francais de vieille souche* or Minuteman. At most times he has been given no choice. But though uncomfortable in the extreme, this condition is, if we accept it, not without a larger meaning.

Nationalism is the venom of our age. It has brought Europe to the edge of ruin. It drives the new states of Asia and Africa like crazed lemmings. By proclaiming himself a Ghanaean, a Nicaraguan, a Maltese, a man spares himself vexation. He need not ravel out what he is, where his humanity lies. He becomes one of an armed, coherent pack. Every mob impulse in modern politics, every totalitarian design, feeds on nationalism, on the drug of hatred which makes human beings bare their teeth across a wall, across ten yards of waste ground. Even if it be against his harried will, his weariness, the Jew—or some Jews, at least—may have an exemplary role. To show that whereas trees have roots, men have legs and are each other's guests. If the potential of civilization is not to be destroyed, we shall have to develop more complex, more provisional loyalties. There are, as Socrates taught, necessary treasons to make the city freer and more open to man. Even a Great Society is a bounded, transient thing compared to the free play of the mind and the anarchic discipline of its dreams.

When a Jew opposes the parochial ferocity into which nationalism so easily (inevitably) degenerates, he is paying an old debt. By one of the cruel, deep ironies of history, the concept of a chosen people, or a nation exalted above others by [a] particular destiny, was born in Israel. In the vocabulary of Nazism there were elements of a vengeful parody on the Judaic claim. The theological motif of a people elected at Sinai is echoed in the pretense of the master race and its chiliastic dominion. Thus there was in the obsessed relation of Nazi to Jew a minute but fearful grain of logic.

But if the poison is, in ancient part, Jewish, so perhaps is the antidote, the radical humanism which sees man on the road to becoming man. This is where Marx is most profoundly a Jew (while at the same time arguing for the dissolution of [a] Jewish identity). He believed that class and economic status knew no frontiers, that misery had a common citizenship. He postulated that the revolutionary process would abolish national distinctions and antagonisms as industrial technology had all but eroded regional autonomy. The entire socialist Utopia and dialectic of history is based on an international premise.

Marx was wrong; here, as in other respects, he thought too romantically, too well of men. Nationalism has been a major cause and beneficiary of two world wars. The workers of the world did not unite; they tore at each other's throats. Even beggars wrap themselves in flags. It was Russian patriotism, the outrage of national consciousness, not the vision of socialism and class solidarity, which enabled the Soviet Union to survive in 1941. In Eastern Europe, state socialism has left national rivalries fierce and archaic. A thousand miles of empty Siberian steppe may come to matter more to Russia and China than the entire fabric of Communist fraternity.

But though Marx was wrong, though the ideal of a non-national society seems mockingly remote, there is in the last analysis no other alternative to self-destruction. The earth grows too crowded, too harassed by the shadow of famine, to waste soil on barbed wire. Where he can survive as [a] guest, where he can re-examine the relations between conscience and commitment, making his exercise of national loyalty scrupulous but also skeptical and humane, the Jew can act as a valuable irritant. The chauvinist will snarl at his heels. But it is in the nature of a chase that those who are hunted are in advance of the pack.

That is why I have not, until now, been able to accept the notion of going to live in Israel. The State of Israel is, in one sense, a sad miracle. Herzl's Zionist program bore the obvious marks of the rising nationalism of the late 19th century. Sprung of inhumanity and the imminence of massacre, Israel has had to make itself a closed fist. No one is more tense with national feeling than an Israeli. He must be if his strip of home is to survive the wolfpack at its doors.

Chauvinism is almost the requisite condition to life. But although the strength of Israel reaches deep into the awareness of every Jew, though the survival of the Jewish people may depend on it, the nation-state bristling with arms is a bitter relic, an absurdity in the century of crowded men. And it is alien to some of the most radical, most humane elements in the Jewish spirit.

So a few may want to stay in the cold, outside the sanctuary of nationalism—even though it is, at last, their own. A man need not be buried in Israel. Highgate or Golders Green or the wind will do.

If my children should happen to read this one day, and if luck has held, it may seem as remote to them as it will to a good many of my contemporaries. If things go awry, it may help remind them that somewhere stupidity and barbarism have already chosen them for a target. This is their inheritance. More ancient, more inalienable than any patent of nobility.

NOTE

1. Francis George Steiner was born in Paris in 1929 and emigrated with his parents to the United States in 1940. A citizen of multiple cultures and languages, Steiner is widely regarded as one of the twentieth century's premier literary and cultural critics. Steiner is professor emeritus of English and comparative literature at the University of Geneva (1974–1994), professor of comparative literature and fellow at the University of Oxford (1994–1995), and professor of poetry at Harvard University (2001–02). He makes his home in Cambridge, England, where he has been Extraordinary Fellow at Churchill College at the University of Cambridge since 1969. A prolific author, his writings reflect an unbending commitment to European high culture as the fulcrum of the cosmopolitan ideal that challenges what he regards as the insidious barriers of territory, ethnicity, and language. In his many essays and lectures on a post-holocaust Jewish identity, he insists that the promotion of the cosmopolitan ethic so conceived is the true mission of the Jews. While expressing a sympathetic understanding of Zionist commitments, he nonetheless feels that *his* Judaism can be realized and cultivated only in the Diaspora, beyond the delimiting boundaries of a homeland. This selection, dedicated to the author and holocaust survivor Elie Wiesel, is one of Steiner's earliest essays on his Jewish identity as a "kind of survivor."

34. THE MEANING OF HOMELAND (2006)

A. B. YEHOSHUA[1]

Just before I entered the hall for the symposium in Washington that inaugurated two days of discussion on the future of the Jewish people in light of the century that has passed since the founding of the host organization (American Jewish Committee), my youngest son phoned from Israel and told me about how moved he was by the memorial ceremony, in which he and his wife and toddler daughter had just taken part, for the fallen of Israel's wars. I made a brief comment to the panel's moderator about the fact that the symposium was taking place on the eve of Yom Hazikaron, Israel's Memorial Day, and I hoped that, amid the many congratulatory speeches at the start of the evening, this would be noted and that we might also all be asked to honor the Israeli Memorial Day, as customary, with a minute of silence. But this didn't happen. And Yom Ha'atzmaut, Israel's Independence Day, due to be marked the following day, received only faint and brief mention from the speakers.

I do not cite this as a grievance, but rather as a symptomatic example that may also explain my gloomy state of mind at that symposium, given that the deep and natural identification that a large portion of American Jewry once felt with Israeli life has been steadily and seriously weakening in recent years. All of the participants in the subsequent discussion agreed that, for some years now, a slow process of disengagement of American Jewry from Israel has been intensifying. The reasons are numerous and complex, and related both to the fact that the "Israeli drama" has lost many of its attractive features for American Jews, and to the accelerated processes of assimilation occurring to varying degrees within America itself.

MISSED OPPORTUNITY

Even though the title of the symposium was "The Future of the Past: What Will Become of the Jewish People?" I may have been the only one to begin by talking about the failure of most of the Jewish people to foresee in the twentieth century the depth and vehemence of the hostility towards it, which eventually led to an annihilation unprecedented in human history. "The Jewish texts," which many Jews today consider to be the core of their identity, did not help us to understand better the processes of the reality around us. The Jews were too busy with mythology and theology instead of history, and therefore the straightforward warnings voiced by [Ze'ev] Jabotinsky[2] and his colleagues in the early twentieth century—"Eliminate the Diaspora, or the Diaspora will surely eliminate you"—fell on deaf ears.

After Palestine was taken over by the British, the Balfour Declaration of 1917 promised a national home for the Jews, and if during the 1920s when the country's gates were open wide, just a half million Jews had come (less than 5 percent of the Jewish people at that time) instead of the tiny number that actually did come, it certainly would have been possible to establish a Jewish state before the Holocaust on part of the Land of Israel. This state not only would have ended the Israeli-Arab conflict at an earlier stage and with less bloodshed—it also could have provided refuge in the 1930s to hundreds of thousands of Eastern European Jews who sensed the gathering storm, and thus would have significantly reduced the number of victims in the Holocaust.

The Zionist solution, which was proven as the best solution to the Jewish problem before the

Source: A. B. Yehoshua, "The Meaning of Homeland," in *The A. B. Yehoshua Controversy: An Israel-Diaspora Dialogue on Jewishness, Israeliness, and Identity,* eds. Noam Marans and Roselyn Bell (New York: Dorothy and Julius Koppelman Institute on American Jewish-Israeli Relations, American Jewish Committee, 2006), pp. 7–13. And A. B. Yehoshua, "An Apology to Those Who Attended the Symposium," *Ha'aretz,* May 14, 2006. Reprinted with permission of *Ha'aretz* and the author.

Holocaust—when the Communist revolution cut off Soviet Jewry, the gates of America were closed because of the Depression, and European democracies were destroyed by fascism and Nazism—was tragically missed by the Jewish people. And if it weren't for those few (less than half of 1 percent of world Jewry) people who, a hundred years ago, believed and actually sought the fulfillment of the need for the sovereign normalization of the Jewish people in its ancient homeland, the Jewish people could have found itself after the horrors of World War II just wandering among Holocaust museums without even that piece of sovereign homeland that still offers some solace for the disaster that occurred.

But such a tough and piercing reckoning, coming from such an old-fashioned Zionist premise about our painful and tragic missed opportunity in the past century, is not welcome at the festive opening of a convention of a Jewish organization that, like many other Jewish organizations at the start of the twentieth century, shunned, if not actively opposed, the Zionist solution. Better to talk about all the Nobel Prizes and prestige garnered by Jews in the past century, about the intellectual achievement of Freud and Einstein, and about the tremendous contribution that Jews have made to Western Culture. Therefore, right from the start, I felt like I was spoiling the nice, pleasant atmosphere with my anger. And instead of joining in the celebration of the wonderful spirituality of the Jewish identity, and of the cultural renaissance in America, and instead of extolling the texts that we must learn and the Jewish values that we must inculcate, I tried nevertheless to outline at least a fundamental boundary between Jewish identity in Israel and Jewish identity in the Diaspora.

This is no easy task nowadays. Many Israelis would disagree with me as well. The basic concepts of Zionism have either been pulverized beyond recognition with the normality of sovereign life, or usurped in a distorted and grotesque way by fascist rightist ideologies or radical postmodernism.

And this is where the conflict between myself and my listeners arose. (Not with all of my listeners, actually. Some, mainly Jews who had some Israeli experience, came up to me after the discussion was over to express deep solidarity with what I'd said.)

I did not talk about "the negation of the Diaspora." The Jewish Diaspora has existed ever since the Babylonian exile, about 2,500 years ago, and it will

continue to exist for thousands more years. I have no doubt that in the future when outposts will be established in outer space, there will be Jews among them who will pray "Next year in Jerusalem" while electronically orienting their space synagogue toward Jerusalem on the globe of the earth. The Jew has a wonderful virtual ability to express his identity with consciousness alone. The lone Iraqi Jew in Baghdad after the American conquest or the two Jews sitting in Afghanistan are no more or less Jewish in their foundational identity than the chief rabbi of Israel or the president of the Jewish community in America. The Diaspora is the most solid fact in Jewish history; we know its cost, and we are aware of its accomplishments and failures in terms of Jewish continuity. In fact, the most harshly worded statements concerning its theological negation are to be found scattered in the "core" religious texts; there is no need for an Israeli writer to come to Washington to talk about the negation of the Diaspora.

All of the reports suggesting that I said that there can be no Jewishness except in Israel are utterly preposterous. No one would ever think of saying such an absurd thing. It is Israel and not the Diaspora that could be a passing episode in Jewish history, and this is the source of compulsion to reiterate the old and plain truths that apparently need to be repeated again and again. Not just to Diaspora Jews, but to Israelis, too.

Jewish identity in Israel, which we call Israeli identity (as distinct from Israeli citizenship, which is shared by Arab citizens who also live in the shared homeland, though their national identity is Palestinian)— this Jewish-Israeli identity has to contend with all the elements of life via the binding and sovereign framework of a territorially defined state. And therefore the extent of its reach into life is immeasurably fuller and broader and more meaningful than the Jewishness of an American Jew, whose important and meaningful life decisions are made within the framework of his American nationality or citizenship. His Jewishness is voluntary and deliberate, and he may calibrate its pitch in accordance with his needs.

We in Israel live in a binding and inescapable relationship with one another, just as all members of a sovereign nation live together, for better or worse, in a binding relationship. We are governed by Jews. We pay taxes to Jews, are judged in Jewish courts, are called up to serve in the Jewish army, and compelled by Jews to defend settlements we didn't want or, alternatively, are forcibly expelled from settlements by Jews. Our economy is determined by Jews. Our social conditions are determined by Jews. And all the political, economic, cultural, and social decisions craft and shape our identity, which, although it contains some primary elements, is always in a dynamic process of changes and corrections. While this entails pain and frustration, there is also the pleasure of the freedom of being in your own home.

Homeland and national language and a binding framework are fundamental components of any person's national identity. Thus, I cannot point to a single Israeli who is assimilated, just as there is no Frenchman in France who is an assimilated Frenchman—even if he has never heard of Molière and has never been to the Louvre, and prefers soccer matches and horse races. I am sure, for example, that some of the British pilots who risked their lives in defense of London during World War II knew the names of the Manchester United players better than Shakespeare's plays, and yet no one would dare call them assimilated Britons.

IDENTITY AS A GARMENT

What I sought to explain to my American hosts, in overly blunt and harsh language perhaps, is that, for me, Jewish values are not located in a fancy spice box that is only opened to release its pleasing fragrance on Shabbat and holidays, but in the daily reality of dozens of problems through which Jewish values are shaped and defined, for better or worse. A religious Israeli Jew also deals with a depth and breadth of life issues that is incomparably larger and more substantial than those with which his religious counterparts in New York or Antwerp must contend.

Am I denouncing their complete identity? I am neither denouncing nor praising. It's just a fact that requires no legitimating from me, just as my identity requires no legitimating from them. But since we see ourselves as belonging to one people, and since the two identities are interconnected, and flow into one another, the relation between them must be well clarified.

As long as it is clear to all of us that Israeli Jewish identity deals, for better or worse, with the full spectrum of the reality and that Diaspora Jewry deals only with parts of it, then at least the difference between the whole and part is acknowledged. But the moment that Jews insist that involvement in the study and interpretation of texts, or in the organized activity of Jewish institutions, are equal to the totality of the social and political and economic reality that we in Israel are contending with—not only does the moral significance of the historic Jewish grappling with a total reality lose its validity, there is also the easy and convenient option of a constant flow from the whole to the partial.

Not by chance do more than half a million Israelis now live outside of Israel. If Jewish identity can feed itself on the study of texts and the mining of memories, and some occasional communal involvement—and as long as all those capable Chabad emissaries are supplying instant Jewish and religious services everywhere on the planet—what's the problem, in the global age, with taking the Israeli kids and exiling the whole family to some foreign high-tech mecca? After all, the core of the identity is eternal and accessible anywhere.

This is how Israeliness in the homeland will also become a garment that is removed and replaced with another garment in times of trouble, just as Romanian-ness and Polish-ness were replaced by English-ness and American-ness, and Tunisian-ness and Moroccan-ness were replaced by French-ness and Canadian-ness. And in the future, in another century or two, when China is the leading superpower, why shouldn't some Jews exchange their American-ness or Canadian-ness for Chinese-ness or Singaporean-ness? Just think about it: Who would have believed in the sixteenth century that within 200 or 300 years, the Jews would be concentrated in an unknown land called America?

The Jews have proven their ability to live anywhere for thousands of years without losing their identity. And as long as the *goyim* don't cause too many problems, Jewish perseverance will not falter. If Israeliness is just a garment, and not a daily test of moral responsibility, for better or worse, of Jewish values, then it's no wonder that poverty is spreading, that the social gaps are widening, and that cruelty toward an occupied people is perpetrated easily and without pangs of conscience. Since it will always be possible to escape from the reality to the old texts, and to interpret them in such a way that will imbue us with greatness, hope, and consolation.

The national minority among us of the Palestinian Israelis, who share Israeli citizenship with us, could also make a contribution to this identity, just as American Jews contribute to the general American identity, and the Basques to the Spanish identity and the Romanian minority in Hungary to the Hungarian identity, and the Corsicans to the French, and so on. The more Israeli we are, the better the partnership we have with them. The more we concentrate solely on Jewish spirituality and texts, believing this to be of chief importance, the more the alienation between us grows.

THE SIMPLE TRUTH

I keep bringing up the matter of texts, because in liberal Jewish circles this has recently become the most important anchor of identity, as evidenced by the return of manifestly secular people to the synagogue—not in order to find God, but to clutch onto identity. The struggle for Soviet Jewry is over; the Security Council will deal with Iran; there is nothing left but to return to the familiar and the known. As someone who has spent his whole life dealing with texts—writings, reading and analyzing—I am incensed by the increasingly dangerous and irresponsible disconnection between the glorification of the texts and the mundane matters of daily life. Instead, I propose that we continue to nurture the concrete and living value of "the homeland" rather than the dull and worn-out value of Jewish spirituality.

In all the Bible, the word *moledet* (homeland) is mentioned just twenty-two times, and many of these times in reference to other nations. The first sentence spoken to the first Jew is, "Go for yourself from your land, from your *moledet*, and from your father's house to the land that I will show you." And throughout their long history, the Jews obeyed the first part of this imperative with great devotion, moving from one *moledet* to another with surprising ease. And the terrible end to these wanderings needs no further mention.

If we don't want this kind of Jewish mindset (with the help of our Palestinian rivals for the homeland) to pull the rug out from under our feet, we ought to reiterate the basic, old concepts to Israelis just as much as to American Jews who, though they were offended by me, treated me with exemplary courtesy, perhaps because deep down, they felt that I was speaking the simple truth.

AN APOLOGY TO THOSE WHO ATTENDED THE SYMPOSIUM

Reverberations from the first evening of the conference have made me realize to my distress that a not insignificant portion of the audience was offended by the tone of my remarks, as well as by part of their content. I wish, therefore, to express to them my deepest apologies. Everything I said about the partial nature of Jewish life in the Diaspora as opposed to the all-inclusive nature of Jewish life in Israel has been said by me over the course of many years in the past, both in print and in addressing numerous Diaspora Jews. Never before did this lead to such an angry reaction as it did this time. Presumably, there was something in my tone [of] an imprecise formulation that insulted part of the audience. I say "part," because there were also those who came up afterward to thank me—which does not, of course, compensate for the feelings of the others.

The debate between us is a basic one that goes to the root of things. But we are one people, and I have never ceased to stress this cardinal principle. Nor was there anything in what I said at the conference that called it into question. I am appending an article [see the previous document] that I have written for the weekly magazine of the Hebrew newspaper *Ha'aretz*, in which I deal with my opinions on the matter in greater detail. And once again, permit me to apologize to anyone whose feelings I have hurt.

A. B. Yehoshua
May 2006

A BRIEF EPILOGUE

The storm that arose in the wake of my comments—scores of articles that were published, for and against, in the Diaspora and in Israel—testifies truthfully that my words roused (albeit without particular intention) a raw and dormant nerve. Everyone—those who objected and those who agreed with my comments—repeatedly asserted that: a) What I expressed was not new. I have repeated and publicized these views for many years in many places and have expressed them scores of times to the Jews of the Diaspora and Israel. (As Alfred Moses, the past president of the American Jewish Committee and Centennial chair, said, "I heard A. B. Yehoshua say the same things thirty years ago, and so I invited him . . . because I wanted to debate."); b) There was complete agreement among supporters and detractors of my views that it was very good that the debate on this age-old subject was rekindled.

Why the debate reignited with such force now calls out for a sociological and ideological study both of the changes that have occurred in the concept of national identity in the world and how the importance and meaning of Zionism have lessened among the Jewish people. And here I wish to make one observation:

Two events of world importance took place during the twentieth century, only three years apart: A) the Holocaust, an event that has no parallel in human history, and B) the return of the Jewish people to its homeland after 2,000 years, also an unparalleled event in human history. In my estimation, the Jewish people have not yet fully digested the deep meaning of the failure of the Diaspora outlook as it was experienced during the Holocaust. And the Jewish people, including many Israelis, have not grasped the qualitative change that has occurred in Jewish identity with the return to complete sovereignty. Since the Diaspora mode of Jewish identity existed for more than 2,000 years, the qualitative change that has occurred within this identity with the establishment of the state of Israel has not yet been fully internalized.

Nevertheless, the fact that during the last seventy years the Jewish community in Israel has been transformed from less than 2.5 percent of world Jewry to almost 50 percent of that whole proves that, despite all, the trend from partial Jewishness to complete Jewishness is natural and true.

A.B. Yehoshua
August 2006

NOTES

1. Abraham B. ("Bulli") Yehoshua was born in 1936 to a Sephardi family that has lived in Jerusalem on his father's side for five generations. He is one of Israel's most acclaimed novelists and playwrights. Since 1972 he has taught comparative and Hebrew literature at Haifa University. He subscribes to the classical Zionist position that a viable national Jewish identity is no longer possible in the *galut* (exile), as Zionists are wont (in consonance with traditional Judaism) to refer to the Diaspora. He often asserts this position, especially in public forums, in a provocative and acerbic manner. This was particularly the case in a dialogue between Israeli and American Jews sponsored by the American Jewish Committee in May 2006. At this symposium he made such comments as "[Diaspora Jews] change [their] nationalities like jackets. Once they were Polish and Russian; now they are British and American. One day they could choose to be Chinese or Singaporean....For me, Avraham Yehoshua, there is no alternative....I cannot change my identity outside Israel. [Being] Israeli is my skin, not my jacket." Such comments evoked a heated controversy that echoed far beyond the walls of the Library of Congress where the symposium took place on the evening of May 1, 2006. A. B. Yehoshua's statement is given in full in this selection.
2. See chapter 10, document 37.

35. A CONVERT'S AFFIRMATIONS (2003)

MARTHA C. NUSSBAUM[1]

I am an Enlightenment Jew. My Judaism is marked by a commitment to the primacy of the moral, to the authority of truth and reason, and to the equal worth of all human beings. That this Judaism is both feminist and cosmopolitan follows from its commitment to these three great organizing values. Like the intellectual leaders who gave rise to Reform Judaism in Germany, I conceive of God's kingdom as the kingdom of ends, a virtual polity, containing both true autonomy and true community, that organizes our moral hopes and efforts in this world of confusion, herdlike obedience, and unenlightened self-interest....

But because I am a convert to Judaism, and have thus, already a rationalist, *chosen* Judaism, I shall also have to face the question: if your religion is this rationalist, why do you call yourself religious at all?...

I was raised as an Episcopalian, in Bryn Mawr, Pennsylvania, on Philadelphia's fashionable "Main Line." It was fashionable to be an Episcopalian; the Presbyterians down the street were regarded as slightly less fashionable, although they did everything in their power to emulate the Episcopalians. Methodists and Baptists were thought to be very low-class; one would not ordinarily wish one's child to visit such a church. Catholics were not permitted to buy houses in this community. My father's explanation for this policy was that their large family size would drive up property taxes because of the stress on the school system, and thus property values would be lowered. Like so many economic explanations, this one was both irrational (ignoring parochial schools) and a screen for darker motives.

Jews, of course, were nowhere to be seen. The year I graduated from high school, a house on my street was sold to a Jewish doctor by the widow who had owned it. The received interpretation of this act of betrayal was that the owner had had a nervous breakdown after the death of her husband and had become insane. Two years after that, when my parents sold our house, Bill Cosby made an offer for it. My father rejected the offer, saying to me that he had never liked our neighbors, but he did not want to take revenge on them to that extent. (I thought that Cosby, who already seemed an admirable person, had had a lucky escape.)

But in my early childhood, the harmony of Bryn Mawr was undisturbed. Episcopalians and Republicans ruled the land, and they were one and the same. (When I worked for local candidates, I noted that the only registered Democrats in Bryn Mawr were the teachers at my school) The Church of the Redeemer was a fine church, with three very dedicated ministers and one of the best organs in Pennsylvania. Nonetheless, it increasingly struck me, as I moved from childhood into adolescence, as a smug bastion of hypocrisy and unearned privilege, to which people came in order to be seen and to avoid seeing those whom they would rather not see.

It was possible for a child to ignore, for a time and up to a point, these social features of the Church. I believe I was only dimly aware of them until I was in my teens. I was very serious about Christianity between the ages of ten and sixteen. My deepest connection to the Church was through music: I sang in both the child and the adult choirs, thus going to two services every Sunday, and I took organ lessons from the choir director, a gifted musician. The emotions of joy and pain and longing that were embodied in the music we performed were my route to an understanding of religious ideas, and I had a very deep longing for the salvation that I heard figured there. Because my mother was an alcoholic, my home was an unhappy one, and I believe my search for salvation was motivated, above

Source: Martha A. Nussbaum, "Judaism and the Love of Reason," in Marya Bower and Ruth Groenhout, eds., *Philosophy, Feminism, and Faith* (Bloomington: Indiana University Press, 2003). Other than the first note, the annotations are supplied by the author.

all, by my fear of my own anger at her, and a desire to be forgiven for the terrible cauldron of emotions that I felt in myself every time I came home from school and smelled bourbon in the kitchen air.

I therefore went not only to the two services, but also to the Sunday School classes for high school students. I conceived the plan of becoming an Episcopalian minister. Our assistant minister, a timorous character, told me that women would never be ordained; I doubted this because I had little confidence in the man's judgment....

It seemed to me that there was a synergy between Republican libertarianism and Christianity: it was morally permissible to believe either only if there were no extremely urgent issues of earthly justice that took priority over the next world (or, what came to the same thing, the Utopian fantasy of voluntary individual compliance with norms of racial justice). During a summer on a student exchange program in Wales, I lived with a family of factory workers, and saw how real poverty grinds down the human spirit. I therefore finally rejected the libertarian idea that we could allow justice to depend upon individual choice. Nor was I prepared to leave justice for the life after death. It seemed to me that Jesus encouraged complacency about poverty and indignity in this world, telling people that they could wait for the next to receive their due reward. I preferred the idea of the Jews, that the Messiah should do his work for the downtrodden here and now. I went off to college with many doubts in my heart, and I went to church less often. I preferred outsiders and underdogs. I looked for anyone who would not be invited to the Junior Dance Assembly.

After two years at Wellesley College, one year as an actress, and two years at NYU (during which I sang in one of the best Episcopal church choirs in New York, but with religious skepticism), I found myself in love with a Jewish man whose family was reluctant to accept a non-Jewish spouse. At this point, all the doubts about Christianity that had for a long time pushed me from the Church crystallized in a preference for Judaism. Here I found a this-worldly religion, a religion in which the primacy of the moral, and of this-worldly justice, informed not only the judgments but also, or it seemed to me, the entirety of a tradition. I felt a passionate sympathy for my future husband's family, refugees from the Holocaust and dedicated social democrats of the sort who read I. F. Stone and *The Nation*. I had an intense desire to join the underdogs

and to fight for justice in solidarity with them. I read Martin Buber and understood that virtually every relationship I had observed in Bryn Mawr had been an I-it relationship, involving no genuine acknowledgement of humanity. And I saw, I think, that the best solution to the problem of personal anger and guilt lay in some form of "reparation," a dedication to good deeds that seemed well embodied in Jewish ethical norms.

At this time in the U.S., the strong and traditional affiliation between Judaism and socialism made it easy to think of Judaism as centrally about the search for social justice, the resistance to oppression. Writer Grace Paley put it this way:

> *What was your sense of what it meant to be Jewish when you were growing up?*
>
> Well, it meant to be a socialist. Well, not really. But it meant to have social consciousness....It was a normal sense of outrage when others were treated badly, and along with that the idea that injustice not be allowed to continue. Blacks, for example. When I was a little kid, I said the word "nigger," my big sister hauled off and socked me. When I tell her this, she's absolutely amazed. She really doesn't remember it. But those are the feelings that seemed to me very important, that seemed to me for some peculiar reason connected to being Jewish.[2]

As I shall later argue, this connection is not at all accidental or peculiar, but a central part of the history of Judaism in general, and Reform Judaism above all. This sense of outrage, and the combination of joy and relief I found in entering a community in which outrage at injustice was normal, propelled me strongly toward conversion.

I therefore embarked on the conversion process. A rabbi in Passaic, New Jersey, a friend of my future husband's family, agreed to instruct me. He was Orthodox, but he understood that the family was not, and he never expected me to keep a kosher home. Nor, however, did he introduce me directly to the ideas of the great Reform leaders—that I had to discover much later, on my own, finding a confirmation of ideas to which I had already come in my own thinking. Rabbi Weinberger was, himself, however, in some crucial respects a Mendelssohnian:[3] he believed firmly in the priority of the practical, and he understood the biblical revelation as (essentially moral) legislation that demanded performance, rather than as metaphysical dogma demanding belief, or as mystical experience demanding faith. He taught me in the spirit of Mendelssohn's interpretation of Mosaic law:

> Among all the prescriptions and ordinances of the Mosaic law, there is not a single one that says: *You shall believe or not believe.* They all say: *You shall do or not do.* Faith is not commanded. All the commandments of the divine law are addressed to man's will, to his power to act.[4]

Weinberger believed this, I think, for Mendelssohn's reasons: he saw belief as something that could not be commanded. For Rabbi Weinberger himself, as for Mendelssohn, the commandments to do were both ritual and moral. But knowing from the start that my practice was highly unlikely to be Orthodox, he presented ritual practice to me not in Mendelssohn's way—as legislation binding on a specific historical group—but, rather, in a manner consistent with the practice of nineteenth-century German reformers such as Abraham Geiger—as options I should consider, pondering the wisdom that might be encompassed in tradition, but recognizing that the choice to adopt or reject resided with my own conscience.

In consequence of this commitment to the primacy of the moral, our discussions focused almost entirely on the tradition of Jewish ethics. Because Rabbi Weinberger, long accustomed to a rather non-intellectual congregation in Passaic, New Jersey, was pleased to have a philosophical discussion partner, we increasingly focused on *Pirke Avoth* and other great writings on moral matters. In the process, I learned too little Hebrew (studying on my own from a wretched phonetic text from which my husband had learned at age 10), something that still inhibits my participation in services. I came to see Judaism as a religion of argument, with a profound faith in the worth of reason. In great contrast to my Christian education, focused on catechism and professions of faith, I discovered that in a Jewish conversion process it was possible to dispute about everything. Always I was asked what I had learned and what I was resolved to do, never what I believed.

My gender was never a problem in the process. I knew that everyone involved respected me as an equal, and indeed admired my intelligence and dedication. I thought it somewhat ridiculous to go to the *mikvah* during the conversion ceremony, I found it embarrassing and extremely uncomfortable to go to that dark run-down cold building in Paterson and

immerse myself, while three rabbis sat on the other side of a screen. I had already told Rabbi Weinberger in no uncertain terms that I found the idea of ritual sexual abstinence during menstruation and ritual female cleansing after a menstrual period degrading. He responded by simply saying, softly and tentatively, that sometimes in a marriage it is good for the parties to get away from one another. Rabbi Weinberger's wife was unstable and had repeatedly been hospitalized for mental illness. Sometimes she interrupted our tutorials to express intense anger about some matter, in a violent and scary way. So I sympathized with his statement, but saw it as having no bearing on my actions. He understood my views, and made no objection to my flat rejection of menstrual custom. Thus my arrival at the conversion *mikvah* was surrounded by an agreement that the aspect of the *mikvah* I found degrading was already repudiated by me on the basis of good reasons.[5] I quickly got out of the slimy cold water, and emerged to be shown off in discussion with the Rabbis as Rabbi Weinberger's prize pupil. Nobody involved suggested that my intelligence and ambition were other than great assets in this process.

Shortly after the *mikvah* came the marriage ceremony, performed by Rabbi Weinberger in a Reform temple near my mother's home in suburban Philadelphia. My sister, a professional organist and choir director (in Christian churches), played the organ, and we marched out to the Coronation March from Meyerbeer's *Le Prophète*.

We moved to Cambridge, where, for the next twenty-five years (attending more and less regularly, most regularly during the three years before my daughter's *bat mitzvah*) I belonged to a Conservative *minyan* at Harvard, the Worship-Study congregation, among the first Conservative congregations to be fully egalitarian in sex roles. Reform Judaism was not strong at Harvard; this Conservative group, led by the remarkable and deeply inspiring Ben-Zion Gold, a survivor of Auschwitz and a profound scholar, had all the points that I value in Reform now: sex equality, a passion for argument, a deep concern for social justice. It also had traditional ritual observances [and] traditional melodies, which I found and find deeply satisfying. On Saturday mornings we would argue about Israel and Palestine; about Hellenism and Judaism; about racial justice; about sex equality.

Also, importantly, about whether God acted rightly in asking Abraham to kill his son. I firmly believe that he did not: i.e., that this is a morally heinous myth that does not accurately represent the actions of any being whom I could call God. That either the Bible is wrong in portraying God this way, or else the myth is to be interpreted as that of a test that Abraham fails, when he chooses obedience over morality. The fact that I can say this and not be tossed out of the group is one of the crucial factors that keeps me within Judaism today. I note that even our most fundamentalist citizens, both Christian and Jewish, do not hold that laws against homicide impose a substantial burden on any individual's free exercise of religion. I infer from this silence that they agree with me about the real world, judging that no human being can claim exemption from these laws on account of a belief in a divine command. I see no reason to think that things were different several thousand years ago. I am not enamored of Kierkegaardian leaps, nor yet of obedience, where the death of a child is at issue. The moral law is the moral law, and any mystery that is incompatible with it is a snare and a delusion. I do believe that serious moral dilemmas exist; once given God's command, Abraham, a man of deep faith, had just such a dilemma. The myth in that way invites us to meditate on the plurality of moral values that are not always harmoniously situated in our lives. But that, to me, does not morally justify the command itself, nor would I concede that it is inappropriate to raise questions of moral justification about it. My view is by no means isolated: it is one of the interpretations that my congregation is asked to ponder, and it has been defended by Jewish thinkers in both remote and modern times.

Many Jews find these views objectionable; there are many views of many Jews that I find objectionable. I knew from the beginning of my conversion, however, that I was entering a religion in which disagreement about fundamental matters was invited and seen as a part of religion itself. (This I believe to be true of Conservative Judaism, and indeed of many strands in Orthodox Judaism, as well as of Reform.) My awareness of the prominence of contestation and argument in the recent history of Judaism made it easier for me to conclude that I could pursue my own political and moral concerns within Judaism.

I have officially been a Reform Jew only since moving to Chicago, where I found that temple more passionate about social justice and more committed to debate than the local Conservative temple. I was also delighted by the even more thoroughgoing sex equality, which extends to the language of the ritual itself: we speak of the (four) mothers as well as the (three) fathers, and address God as "you" rather than "he." And it is consequently only recently that I have become fascinated by the ideas of the founders of Reform, and have read their eloquent articulations of belief that I held in a more inchoate form....

NOTES

1. Martha Nussbaum (née Craven; b. 1947) is a distinguished philosopher with particular interests in ancient Greek and Roman philosophy, political philosophy and ethics. She is currently the Ernst Freud Professor of Law and Ethics at the University of Chicago, a chair that included appointments in the Philosophy Department, the Law School, and the Divinity School. She converted to Judaism in 1969 and had her *bat mitzvah* in 2008, at which she was blessed by the late Rabbi Arnold Jacob Wolf (1924–2008).

2. Melanie Kay/Kantrowitz and Irena Klepfisz, "An Interview with Grace Paley," in *The Tribe of Dina: A Jewish Women's Anthology* (Montpelier, Vt.: Sinister Wisdom Books, 1986). In a similar vein, Abner Mikva tells me that Rabbi Harold Kushner quoted a female friend as saying: "When I was young, I was taught that being Jewish meant: you don't cross picket lines, you work for peace, you fight for social justice, you never forget the suffering of your people as a link to the suffering of others."

3. Mendelssohn himself was orthodox in practice, as were most of the Enlightenment Jews of this period. For the best overall account of Mendelssohn's views, see David Sorkin, *Moses Mendelssohn and the Religious Enlightenment* (Berkeley: University of California Press, 1996); the best biography is Alexander Altmann, *Moses Mendelssohn: A Biographical Study* (London: Routledge and Kegan Paul, 1973).

4. Moses Mendelssohn, *Jerusalem*, trans. Allan Arkush, Introduction and Commentary by Alexander Altmann (Hanover, N.H.: University Press of New England, 1983), p. 100. Mendelssohn points out that the Hebrew term that is standardly translated "faith" is better rendered as "trust" or "confidence."

5. See, in this connection, the discussion of feminist reinterpretation of the *mikvah* in Sylvia Barack Fishman, *A Breath of Life: Feminism in the American Jewish Community* (New York: Free Press, 1995), p. 116; understandings include a general idea of purification from daily inattention and from corroding resentment and an idea of oneness with a source of physical and spiritual energy.

36. THE JEW WHO WASN'T THERE: HALACHA AND THE JEWISH WOMAN (1971)

RACHEL ADLER[1]

It is not unusual for committed Jewish women to be uneasy about their position as Jews. It was to cry down our doubts that rabbis developed their pre-packaged orations on the nobility of motherhood; the glory of childbirth; and modesty, the crown of Jewish womanhood. I have heard them all. I could not accept those answers for two reasons. First of all, the answers did not accept *me* as a person. They only set rigid stereotypes, which defined me by limiting the directions in which I might grow. Second, the answers were not really honest ones. Traditional scholars agree that all philosophies of Judaism might begin with an examination of Jewish law, Halacha, since, in the Halacha are set down the ways in which we are expected to behave, and incontestably our most deeply engrained attitudes are those which we reinforce by habitual action.

Yet scholars do not discuss female status in terms of Halacha—at least not with females. Instead, they make lyrical exegeses on selected *Midrashim* and *Agadot* which, however complimentary they may be, do not really reflect the way in which men are expected to behave toward women by Jewish law. I think we are going to have to discuss it, if we are to build for ourselves a faith, which is not based on ignorance and self-deception. That is why I would like to offer some hypotheses on the history and nature of the "woman problem" in Halacha.

Ultimately our problem stems from the fact that we are viewed in Jewish law and practice as peripheral Jews. The category in which we are generally placed includes women, children, and Canaanite slaves. Members of this category are exempt from all positive commandments which occur within time limits.[2]

These commandments would include hearing the *shofar* on Rosh ha-Shanah, eating in the *Sukkah*, praying with the *lulav*, praying the three daily services, wearing *tallit* and *t'fillin*, and saying the *Sh'ma*.[3] In other words, members of this category have been "excused" from most of the positive symbols, which, for the male Jew, hallow time, hallow his physical being, and inform both his myth and his philosophy.

Since most of the *mitzvot* not restricted by time are negative, and since women, children, and slaves are responsible to fulfill all negative *mitzvot*, including the negative time-bound *mitzvot*, it follows that for members of this category, the characteristic posture of their Judaism is negation rather than affirmation.[4] They must not, for example, eat non-kosher food, violate the Shabbat, eat *chametz* [breads, grains, and leaven products that are forbidden to eat] on Pesach, fail to fast on fast days, steal, murder, or commit adultery. That women, children, and slaves have limited credibility in Jewish law is demonstrated by the fact that their testimony is inadmissible in a Jewish court.[5] The *minyan*—the basic unit of the Jewish community—excludes them, implying that the community is presumed to be the Jewish males to whom they are adjuncts. Torah study is incumbent upon them only insofar as it relates to "their" mitzvot. Whether women are even permitted to study further is debated.[6]

All of the individuals in this tri-partite category I have termed peripheral Jews. Children, if male, are full Jews *in potentia*. Male Canaanite slaves, if freed, become full Jews, responsible for all the *mitzvot* and able to count in a *minyan*.[7] Even as slaves, they have the *b'rit mila*, the covenant of circumcision,

---

Source: "The Jew Who Wasn't There: *Halakha* and the Jewish Woman," *Davka* (Summer 1971), pp. 7–11. Aside from note 1, all the notes are in the original article.

that central Jewish symbol, from which women are anatomically excluded. It is true that in Jewish law women are slightly more respected than slaves, but that advantage is outweighed by the fact that only women can never grow up, or be freed, or otherwise leave the category. The peripheral Jew is excused and sometimes barred from the acts and symbols which are the lifeblood of the believing community, but this compliance with the negative *mitzvot* is essential, since, while he cannot be permitted to participate fully in the life of the Jewish people, he cannot be permitted to undermine it either.

To be a peripheral Jew is to be educated and socialized toward a peripheral commitment. This, I think, is what happened to the Jewish woman. Her major *mitzvot* aid and reinforce the life-style of the community and the family, but they do not cultivate the relationship between the individual and God. A woman keeps kosher because both she and her family must have kosher food. She lights the Shabbat candles so that there will be light, and hence, peace, in the household. She goes to the *mikva* [ritual purificatory bath] so that her husband can have intercourse with her and she bears children so that, through her, he can fulfill the exclusively male mitzvah of increasing and multiplying.[8]

Within these narrow confines, there have been great and virtuous women, but in several respects the *tzadikot* (saintly women) have been unlike the *tzaddikim* (saintly men). Beruria, the scholarly wife of Rabbi Meir, the Talmudic sage, and a few exceptional women like her stepped outside the limits of the feminine role, but legend related how Beruria came to a bad end, implying that her sin was the direct result of her "abnormal" scholarship.[9] There is no continuous tradition of learned women in Jewish history. Instead there are many *tzadikot* (righteous women), some named, some unnamed, all of whom were pious and chaste, outstanding and charitable, and, in many cases, who supported their husbands. In contrast, there are innumerable accounts of *tzaddikim*, some rationalists, some mystics, some joyous, some ascetic, singers, dancers, poets, halachists, all bringing to God the service of a singular, inimitable self.

How is it that the *tzaddikim* seem so individualized and the *tzadikot* so generalized? I would advance two reasons. First of all, the *mitzvot* of the *tzadikah* [saintly woman] are mainly directed toward serving others. She is a *tzadikah* to the extent that she sacrifices herself in order that others may actualize themselves

spiritually. One has no sense of an attempt to cultivate a religious self built out of the raw materials of her unique personality. The model for the *tzadikah* is Rachel, the wife of Rabbi Akiva, who sold her hair and sent her husband away to study for twenty-four years, leaving herself beggared and without means of support; or the wife of Rabbi Menachem Mendel of Rymanov (her name incidentally, goes unremembered) who sold her share in the next world to buy her husband bread.

Frequently there is a kind of masochism manifest in the accounts of the acts of *tzadikot*. I recall the stories held up to me as models to emulate, of women who chopped holes in icy streams to perform their monthly immersions. A lady in the [Orthodox] community I came from, who went into labor on Shabbat and walked to the hospital rather than ride in a taxi, was acting in accordance with this model. Implicit is the assumption that virtue is to be achieved by rejecting and punishing the hated body which men every morning thank God is not theirs.

Second, as Hillel says, "an ignoramus cannot be a saint."[11] He may have the best of intentions, but he lacks the disciplined creativity, the sense of continuity with his people's history and thought, and the forms in which to give Jewish expression to his religious impulses. Since it was traditional to give women cursory religious educations, they were severely limited in their ways of expressing religious commitment. Teaching, the fundamental method of the Jewish people for transmitting religious insights, was closed to women—those who do not learn, do not teach.[12] Moreover, expressions of spiritual creativity by women seem to have been severely limited. Religious music written by women is virtually non-existent. There are no prayers written by women in the liturgy, although there were prayers written in Yiddish by women for women who were unable to pray in Hebrew.

It was, perhaps, most damaging that the woman's meager *mitzvot* are, for the most part, closely connected to some physical goal or object. A woman's whole life revolved around physical objects and physical experiences—cooking, cleaning, childbearing, meeting the physical needs of children. Without any independent or spiritual life to counterbalance the materialism of her existence, the mind of the average woman was devoted to physical considerations; marriages, deaths, dinners, clothes, and money. It was, thus, natural that Jewish men should have come to identify women with *gashmiut* (physicality) and men with *ruchaniut* (spirituality).

The Talmudic sages viewed the female mind as frivolous and the female sexual appetite as insatiable.[13] Unless strictly guarded and given plenty of busywork, all women were potential adulteresses.[14] In the Jewish view, all physical objects and experiences are capable of being infused with spiritual purposes; yet it is equally true that the physical, unredeemed by spiritual use, is a threat. It is therefore easy to see how women came to be regarded as semi-demonic in both [the] Talmud and Kabbalah. Her sexuality presented a temptation, or perhaps a threat which came to be hedged ever more thickly by law and custom.[15] Conversing with women was likely to result in gossip or lewdness.[16] Women are classed as inadmissible witnesses in the same category with gamblers, pigeon-racers, and other individuals of unsavory repute.[17]

Make no mistake: for centuries, the lot of the Jewish woman was infinitely better than that of her non-Jewish counterpart. She had rights that other women lacked until a century ago. A Jewish woman could not be married without her consent. Her *ketubah* (marriage document) was a legally binding contract which assured that her husband was responsible for her support (a necessity in a world in which it was difficult for a woman to support herself), and that if divorced, she was entitled to a monetary settlement. Her husband was not permitted to abstain from sex for long periods of time without regard to her needs and her feelings.[18] In its time, the Talmud's was a very progressive view. The last truly revolutionary ruling for women, however, was the Edict of Rabbenu Gershom forbidding polygamy to the Jews of the Western world. That was in 1000 C.E. The problem is that very little has been done since then to ameliorate the position of Jewish women in observant Jewish society.

All of this can quickly be rectified if one steps outside of Jewish tradition and Halacha. The problem is how to attain some justice and some growing room for the Jewish woman if one is committed to remain *within* the Halacha. Some of these problems are more easily solved than others. For example, there is ample precedent for decisions permitting Jewish women to study Talmud, and it should become the policy of Jewish day schools to teach their girls Talmud. It would not be difficult to find a basis for giving women *aliyot* to the Torah [i.e. "going up" to bless the Torah as it is read before the congregation]. Moreover, it is both feasible and desirable for the community to begin educating women to take on the positive time-bound *mitzvot* from which they are now excused; in which case, those mitzvot would eventually become incumbent upon women. The more difficult questions are those involving *minyan* and *mechitza* (segregation of men and women at prayers). There are problems concerning the right of women to be rabbis, witnesses in Jewish courts, judges, and leaders of religious services. We need decisions on these problems which will permit Jewish women to develop roles and role models in which righteousness springs from self-actualization, in contrast to the masochistic, self-annihilating model of the post-Biblical *tzadikah*. The halachic scholars must examine our problem anew, right now, with open minds and with empathy. They must make it possible for women to claim their share in the Torah and begin to do the things a Jew was created to do. If necessary we must agitate until the scholars are willing to see us as Jewish souls in distress rather than as tools with which men do *mitzvot*. If they continue to turn a deaf ear to us, the most learned and halachically committed among us must make halachic decisions for the rest. That is a move to be saved for desperate straits, for even the most learned of us have been barred from acquiring the systematic halachic knowledge which a rabbi has. But, to paraphrase Hillel, in a place where there are no *Menschen* [decent human beings], we may have to generate our own *Menschlichkeit*. There is no time to waste. For too many centuries, the Jewish woman has been a golem, created by Jewish society. She cooked and bore and did her master's will, and when her tasks were done, the Divine Name was removed from her mouth. It is time for the golem to demand a soul.[19]

Postscript: The sort of *piskei halacha* [halakhic rulings] requested in the text of this article are *genuine* decisions based on sources and understanding of the halachic process made by people who understand and observe the Torah. Rationalizations will not do.

NOTES

1. When Rachel Adler (b. 1943) wrote this article, she was a young Orthodox woman who was torn by what she perceived to be the disjunction between her religious commitments and secular sensibilities. With an unflinching honesty, she scrutinizes both the theological and practical implications of the status of women within the bounds of Jewish religious law, the *halakhah*. Her protest that *halakhah*

cast women in a "peripheral" position in the spiritual life of traditional Judaism is widely held to have played a seminal role in launching Jewish feminism. Despite her misgivings about the halakhic attitude toward women, Adler does not abandon rabbinic law. Rather she reinterprets in order to create a constructive Jewish theology that is inclusive and honors women in the fullness of their humanity and thus allows them to participate fully in the religious life of Judaism. Adler presently serves as professor of Jewish religious thought and feminist studies at the Los Angeles campus of Hebrew Union College–Jewish Institute of Religion. She now finds her spiritual home in Reform Judaism.

2. Babylonian Talmud, Kiddushin 29a.

3. Ibid.; also Mishna Sukkah 2:9, and Mishna Brachot 3:3.

4. Kiddushin 29a.

5. Babylonian Talmud, Shavuot 30a. See also Babylonian Talmud, Rosh ha-Shanah 22a.

6. Babylonian Talmud, Sotah 20a.

7. It must be admitted that Canaanite slaves were only to be freed if some overriding *mitzvah* would be accomplished thereby. The classic case in which Rabbi Eliezer frees his slave in order to complete a *minyan* is given in the Babylonian Talmud, Gittin 38b.

8. Attending the *mikvah* is not itself a *mitzvah*. It is rather a prerequisite to a permitted activity, just as *schitah* [the ritual slaughter of animals] is a prerequisite to the permitted activity of eating meat. See *Sefer ha-Chinuch, Mitzvah* 175.

9. Babylonian Talmud, Avoda Zara 18b. See Rashi on this passage.

10. See in the traditional prayer book the morning blessing: "Blessed are You, Lord our God, King of the Universe, who has not created me a woman."

11. Mishnah Avot 2:6.

12. Exactly this expression is used in the Babylonian Talmud, Kiddushin 29b, where it is asserted that the *mitzvah* of teaching one's own offspring the Torah applies to men and not to women.

13. Kiddushin 80b contains the famous statement, "The rational faculty of women weighs lightly upon them." Interestingly enough, the Tosafot illustrate this with an ancient misogynistic fabliau whose written source is the Satryicon of Petronius Arbiter. See also Babylonian Talmud, Sotah 20a.

14. Mishnah Ketubot 5:5.

15. This is the context in which one may understand the statement of the *Kitzur Shulchan Arukh*, "A man should be careful not to walk between two women, two dogs, or two swine." Solomon Ganzfried, *Codes of Jewish Law*, trans. Hyman E. Goldin, 2nd ed. (New York, Hebrew Publishing Co., 1961), p. 7.

16. Mishna Avot 1:5. See also the commentaries on this passage by Rashi, Rambam, and Rabbenu Yonah.

17. Babylonian Talmud, Rosh ha-Shanah 22a.

18. Mishnah Ketuboth 5:6.

19. There is a famous folk tale that the Scholar Rabbi Loewe of Prague created a *golem* or robot, using Kabbalistic formulae. The robot, formed from earth, came to life and worked as a servant when a tablet engraved with the Divine Name was placed in its mouth. When the tablet was removed, the *golem* reverted to mindless clay.

APPENDIX

The Demography of Modern Jewish History

The transformations that characterize the modern period in Jewish history are in part reflected in dramatic demographic changes: a sudden and rapid increase in the population of the Jews, paralleled by major shifts in geographic distribution and by far-reaching changes in social, economic, and educational patterns.[1]

Whereas in the classical world the Jewish people was comparatively numerous—at the time of the destruction of the Second Temple in 70 C.E., according to various estimates, there were between four and a half and seven million Jews in the world[2]—the numbers declined drastically during the Middle Ages. The eclipse of commerce and urban life which followed the dismantling of the Roman Empire, together with the restrictions and persecutions which marked the feudal period, led to a sharp reduction in the size of the Jewish population. Thus, by the fifteenth century "on the entire European continent there were probably fewer than 300,000 Jews; in the entire world there were fewer than a million, most of whom were concentrated in the Near East."[3] With the dawn of mercantilism—the revival of commerce and urban life and the concomitant relaxation of Jewish disabilities—there was a gradual increase in the population of European Jewry, reaching by the end of the eighteenth century an estimated million and a half, the world Jewish population totaling two and a half million.

Until the beginning of the modern period, the Jews were predominantly a Near Eastern people; with the numerical ascendancy of European Jewry, the Jews became largely European, as is noted in tables 1 and 2.

The Jews shared in the general increase of Europe's population which resulted from a marked improvement of economic conditions, sanitation and medical care, extension of

---

[1] Employing varying criteria and sources, demographers differ, sometimes radically, in their statistical estimates. Our selections in this appendix are based not only on the reliability of a given set of statistics but also on their value in illuminating what we deem to be salient trends and patterns.

[2] Adolf Harnack, *Die Mission und Ausbreitung des Christentums* (Leipzig: J. C. Hinrichs, 1923), vol. 1, pp. 5–19; Arthur Ruppin, *Soziologie der Juden* (Berlin: Juedischer Verlag, 1930), vol. 1, p. 69; Uriah Zevi Engelman, "Sources of Jewish Statistics," in *The Jews: Their History, Culture, and Religion*, ed. L. Finkelstein (Philadelphia: Jewish Publication Society of America, 1966), vol. 2, p. 1517; *Encyclopaedia Judaica*, 2nd ed., s.v. "Population [Jewish]," vol. 16, p. 385. In the Roman Empire the Jews, according to various estimates, were between 8 and 10 percent of the population.

[3] Engelman, "Sources of Jewish Statistics," p. 1519.

TABLE I   APPROXIMATE WORLD JEWISH POPULATION 1700

Continent and Region	
Europe	
Eastern and Balkans (excluding Asian areas of Russia and Turkey)	570,000
Central and Western	146,000
Total	716,000
Near East	
Asia	205,000
Palestine	5,000
Rest (including Asian areas of Russia and Turkey)	200,000
North Africa	165,000
Total	370,000
America	
North America	–
Caribbean and Latin America	4,000
Total	4,000
Rest of the world	10,000
Total	1,100,000

Source: Adapted from Jacob Lestschinsky, "Die Umsiedlung und Umschichtung des juedischen Volkes im Laufe des letzten Jahrhunderts," *Weltwirtschaftliches Archiv*, vol. 30, pt. 2 (Jena, 1929), p. 155; and Sergio DellaPergola, "Major Demographic Trends of World Jewry: The Last Hundred Years," in Batsheva Bonne-Tamir and Avinoam Adam, eds., *Genetic Diversity Among Jews* (New York: Oxford University Press, 1992), p. 7.

life expectancy and a sharp decrease of infant mortality. In the nineteenth century the growth of both the Jewish and non-Jewish populations of Europe was astronomical, as is noted in tables 2 and 3.

It has been observed that political emancipation was an insignificant factor in the expansion of the Jewish population. For "the major increase . . . occurred in eastern Europe, which remained politically unemancipated." The western countries that granted the Jews civil equality "shared only indirectly in the growth of the Jewish population by accepting the population overflow from eastern Europe."[4] It was this latter area—comprising Ukraine, White Russia, Lithuania, Poland, Rumania, Galicia, and Hungary—that supplied virtually all of the natural increase of the Jewish population in the nineteenth century. In this period, East European Jewry had "a higher rate of natural increase, and a lower standard of living than any of the other Jewish population groups of western and central Europe, or America."[5] Moreover, the increase in East European Jewry exceeded the average growth of the region's non-Jewish population.

This rate of growth is not to be explained by a higher Jewish fertility—indeed, the Jews were less fertile[6]—but a higher life-span of the Jews.[7] This fact is generally attributed to Jewish religious and cultural traditions. "There can be no doubt that greater stability of the family, the smaller number of illegitimate children, the infrequency of venereal diseases, the higher status of woman within the family, the care lavished on babies and small children, abstinence from alcohol, the readiness of the individual and the community to undergo considerable economic sacrifice in order to help others and the lengthy tradition of charitable deeds combined, among Jews, to serve as the basis for their demographic development."[8] It may also be noted that East European Jewry lived in far greater proportion than non-Jews in cities where medical care was much more readily available than in rural areas. Moreover, the Jews tended to have a greater trust in medical science, and, accordingly, availed themselves of medical care to a much greater degree than the non-Jewish population.[9]

Propelled by acts of discrimination and persecution, the impoverished Jews of Eastern Europe began to emigrate westward to more prosperous and enlightened European countries and especially to the Americas. It is estimated that between 1840 and 1947 there were some four million Jewish immigrants, the vast majority from East Europe.[10]

The United States became the principal focus of Jewish immigration. In the first seven decades of the nineteenth century, some 50,000 Jews from Central Europe came to the United States. In the wake of the pogroms of 1881 in Russia, East European Jewry began to emigrate en masse. From 1881 to 1900 more than 500,000 Jews emigrated to the United States; smaller numbers went to other countries in the Americas, and others settled in South Africa. But this mass emigration was but a prelude. Between 1900 and 1914 nearly two million Jews left Eastern Europe,

---

[4] Engelman, "Sources of Jewish Statistics," p. 1521.

[5] Engelman, "Sources of Jewish Statistics," p. 1522.

[6] See Ruppin, *Soziologie der Juden*, vol. 1, pp. 175–77; Engelman, "Sources of Jewish Statistics," pp. 1524–25.

[7] See Ruppin, *Soziologie der Juden*, vol. 1, pp. 237–44.

[8] Shmuel Ettinger, "The Modern Period," in *A History of the Jewish People*, ed. H. H. Ben-Sasson (London: Weidenfeld and Nicolson, 1976), pp. 790–91.

[9] See Ruppin, *Soziologie der Juden*, vol. 1, pp. 238–41.

[10] Jacob Lestchinsky, *Tfuzat yisrael leahar hamilhamah* (Tel Aviv, 1948), p. 31.

TABLE II GEOGRAPHIC DISTRIBUTION OF WORLD JEWRY: 1850–1939

Place	Year	Number of Jews	Percentage of World Jewry	Year	Number of Jews	Percentage of World Jewry	Year	Number of Jews	Percentage of World Jewry	Year	Number of Jews	Percentage of World Jewry
Eastern Europe	1850	3,420,000	72.0	1880	5,812,500	75.0	1939	7,328,000	45.6	1969	4,019,000	29.2
Rest of Europe	1850	688,750	14.5	1880	1,046,250	13.5	1939	1,876,000	11.3	1969		
Americas	1850	71,250	1.5	1880	271,250	3.5	1939	5,556,000	33.4	1969	6,952,000	50.4
Near East	1850	570,000	12.0	1880	620,000	8.0	1939	1,445,000	8.7	1969	2,750,000	19.9
Total		4,750,000	100.0		7,750,000	100.0		16,205,000	99.0		13,721,000	99.5

Source: Compiled on the basis of data presented in Jacob Lestschinsky, "Die Umsiedlung und Umschichtung des Juedischen Volkes im Laufe des letzten Jahrhunderts," *Weltwirtschaftliches Archiv*, vol. 30, pt. 2 (Jena, 1929), p. 155; Arthur Ruppin, *The Jews in the Modern World* (London: Macmillan, 1934), pp. 23–25; Arthur Ruppin, "The Jewish Population in the World," in *The Jewish People: Past and Present* (New York: Central Yiddish Culture Organization, 1946), vol. 1, pp. 350–51; and *Encyclopaedia Judaica*, s.v. "History [of the Jews]: Modern Times," vol. 8, p. 730.

TABLE III   GROWTH OF EUROPE'S POPULATION IN THE MODERN PERIOD: 1580–1880

	1580	1680	1780	1880
England	4,600,000	5,532,000	9,561,000	35,002,000
Prussia	1,000,000	1,400,000	5,460,000	45,260,000
Russia	4,300,000	12,600,000	26,800,000	84,440,000
France	14,300,000	18,800,000	25,100,000	37,400,000

Source: Uriah Zevi Engelman, "Sources of Jewish Statistics," in *The Jews: Their History, Culture, and Religion*, ed. Louis Finkelstein. (Philadelphia: Jewish Publication Society of America, 1949), vol. 4, p. 1184. Reprinted by permission of Jewish Publication Society.

TABLE IV   GROWTH OF JEWISH POPULATION IN THE NINETEENTH CENTURY

	1825	1850	1880	1900
Western and Central Europe	458,000	693,500	1,044,500	1,328,500
Eastern and South eastern Europe	2,272,000	3,434,000	5,726,000	7,362,000
Europe (Total)	2,730,000	4,127,500	6,770,500	8,690,500
America	10,000	65,000	250,000	1,175,000
Asia	300,000	320,000	350,000	420,000
Africa	240,000	250,000	280,000	300,000
Australia	1,000	2,000	12,000	17,000

Source: Jacob Lestschinsky, "Di entviklung fun yidishen folk far die letzte 100 yor," in *Yidisher visnshaftlekher institut. Ekomomish-statistishe skezie* (Berlin, 1928), vol. 1, p. 6.

75 percent of whom settled in the United States. It is important to note that this mass emigration of Jews was part of a general wave of emigration from Europe in the period. It is estimated that in the decade prior to the outbreak of World War I, approximately one and a half million Europeans left the continent annually, immigrating chiefly to North America but also to South America, South Africa and Australia. A tenth of these emigrants were East European Jews. See tables 5 and 6.

As a result of immigration new centers of Jewry emerged, most notably in the Americas. See table 7.

Jewish destiny in the modern period was to a large measure guided by the emergence of the liberal, democratic institutions, and by the expansion of industry and commerce. Not surprisingly, the Jews were drawn to the focus of these revolutionary economic and political developments—the city. Thus, it may be said that modern Jewish history is associated with the rise of the cities in nineteenth and twentieth century Europe and America. It has been calculated that in 1925, 45 percent of world Jewry resided in cities with more than 100,000 inhabitants

and that 23 percent lived in cities with more than a million residents. Thus, close to one-fourth of Jewry lived in large cities, nearly one-eighth in New York City alone.[11] In several instances the majority of the Jews of a particular country was concentrated in the capital or largest city of that country, as is noted in tables 8 and 9.

As they became urbanized, the Jews also became increasingly middle class, as indicated by their transition from petty trade and handicrafts—typical occupations of the Jews in agrarian and semi-urban societies—to modern urban vocations in commerce and the free professions.[12]

The transformation of the occupational structure of the Jewish community corresponds to its secularization, as is reflected in the remarkable and disproportionate increase of Jews seeking a secular, general education. See table 12.

The embourgeoisment and secularization of the Jews parallel their unprecedented assimilation in the modern period. In 1904 Arthur Ruppin, a pioneer of Jewish demography and sociology, schematically correlated the adoption of modern education and urban vocations to the degree of assimilation as indicated by four factors: distance from traditional Judaism, decline of birthrate, increase in intermarriage and conversion. (See tables 14 and 15.) Ruppin's scheme, which sought to delineate the prevailing pattern as it emerged in 1900, was, as he admitted, ambitious. Nonetheless, the scheme is illuminating, for as Ruppin explained, "to anyone who has studied

---

[11] Jacob Lestschinsky, "Die Umsiedlung und Umschichtung des juedischen Volkes im Laufe des letzten Jahrhunderts," *Weltwirtschaftliches Archiv*, vol. 30, pt. 2 (Jena, 1929), p. 147.

[12] "In the countries where there has been no marked development of industry, and where the percentage of Jews has remained comparatively high, say, about 10 percent, their occupational distribution has changed little. Thus in Galicia it is now [1934] practically the same as it was a hundred years ago, while in late Russian Poland, which before the War had become an important industrial area working for export to Russia, many Jews have entered industry.... In Central Europe, where their percentage in the total population was much smaller, there was a marked change: they have entered industry and the professions...." Arthur Ruppin, *The Jews in the Modern World* (London: Macmillan, 1934), pp. 137ff. See tables 10 and 11.

TABLE V   JEWISH MIGRATIONS, 1881–1930

To	From					
	Russia	Austria-Hungary (since 1920 from Poland)	Rumania	Great Britain	Other Countries	Total
United States	1,749,000	597,000	161,000	114,000	264,000	2,885,000
Canada	70,000	40,000	5,000	…	10,000	125,000
Argentina	100,000	40,000	20,000	…	20, 000	180,000
Brazil	6,000	10,000	4,000	…	10,000	30,000
Other South and Central American Countries	5,000	10,000	5,000	…	10,000	30,000
Total for Americas	1,930,000	697,000	195,000	114,000	314,000	3,250,00
Great Britain	130,000	40,000	30,000	…	10,000	210,000
Germany	25,000	75,000	…	…	…	100,000
France	40,000	40,000	…	…	20,000	100,000
Belgium	15,000	30,000	…	…	5,000	50,000
Switzerland, Italy, Scandinavian Countries	30,000	…	…	…	…	30,000
Total for Western and Central Europe	240,000	185,000	30, 000	…	35,000	490,000
South Africa	45,000	10,000	…	…	5,000	60,000
Egypt	20,000	10,000	…	…	5,000	35,000
Total for Africa	65,000	20,000	…	…	10,000	95,000
Palestine	45,000	40,000	10,000	…	25,000	120,000
Australia and New Zealand	5,000	10,000	…	…	5,000	20,000
Total	2,285,000	952,000	235,000	114,000	389,000	3,975,000

Source: Arthur Ruppin, *Soziologie der Juden* (Berlin: Juedischer Verlag, 1930), vol. 1, p. 157

TABLE VI   JEWISH AND GENERAL IMMIGRATION INTO THE UNITED STATES FROM 1899 TO 1944

Fiscal Years*	Absolute Numbers		Percentage of Jewish Immigrants	Fiscal Years*	Absolute Numbers		Percentage of Jewish Immigrants
	Jews	Total			Jews	Total	
1899	37,415	311,715	12.0	1923	49,719	522,919	9.5
1900	60,764	448,572	13.5	1924	49,989	706,896	7.1
1901	58,098	487,918	11.9	1925	10,292	294,314	3.5
1902	57,688	648,743	8.9	1926	10,267	304,488	3.4
1903	76,203	857,046	8.9	1927	11,483	335,175	3.4
1904	106,236	812,870	13.1	1928	11,639	307,255	3.8
1905	129,910	1,026,499	12.7	1929	12,479	279,678	4.5
1906	153,748	1,100,735	14.0	1930	11,526	241,700	4.8
1907	149,182	1,285,349	11.6	1931	5,692	97,139	5.9
1908	103,387	782,870	13.2	1932	2,755	35,576	7.7
1909	57,551	751,786	7.7	1933	2,372	23,068	10.3
1910	84,260	1,041,570	8.1	1934	4,134	29,470	14.0
1911	91,223	878,587	10.4	1935	4,837	34,956	13.8
1912	80,595	838,172	9.6	1936	6,252	36,329	17.2
1913	101,330	1,197,892	8.5	1937	11,352	50,244	22.6
1914	138,051	1,218,480	11.3	1938	19,736	67,895	29.0
1915	26,497	326,700	8.1	1939	43,450	82,998	52.3
1916	15,108	298,826	5.1	1940	36,945	70,756	52.2
1917	17,342	295,403	5.9	1941	23,737	51,776	45.8
1918	3,672	110,618	3.3	1942	10,608	28,781	36.9
1919	3,055	141,132	2.2	1943	4,705	23,725	19.8
1920	14,292	430,001	3.3	1944	…	28,551	…
1921	119,036	805,228	14.8				
1922	53,524	309,556	17.3	Total	2,082,136	20,059,957	10.4

Source: L. Hirsch, "Jewish Migrations During the Last Hundred Years," *The Jewish People: Past and Present* (New York: Central Yiddish Culture Organization, 1946), vol. 1, p. 409.
*From July 1 of the preceding year to June 30 of the year stated.

TABLE VII   THE EMERGENCE OF NON-EUROPEAN CENTERS OF JEWRY

Approximate Number of Jews in the Year	United States	Canada	Argentina	Palestine	South Africa	Brazil	Uruguay	Cuba	Mexico	Egypt	Australia and New Zealand
1800	2,000	...	...	10,000	...	...	...	...	...	...	...
1850	50,000	500	...	12,000	1,000	...	...	1,000	...	...	...
1880	230,000	2,400	...	25,000	...	...	...	...	...	...	...
1890	500,000	6,400	1,000	35,000	...	...	...	...	...	...	...
1900	1,000,000	16,400	30,000	55,000	30,000	3,000	...	3,000	1,000	27,000	16,000
1910	2,200,000	70,000	90,000	80,000	50,000	5,000	...	...	2,000	40,000	18,000
1920	3,200,000	120,000	130,000	75,000	60,000	7,000	1,000	4,000	...	60,000	24,000
1930	4,400,000	150,000	220,000	170,000	...	40,000	10,000	9,000	12,000	65,000	...
1933	4,500,000	170,000	240,000	220,000	80,000	45,000	12,000	9,000	12,000	70,000	33,000

Source: Arthur Ruppin, *The Jews in the Modern World* (London: Macmillan, 1934), p. 52.

TABLE VIII   THE URBANIZATION OF EUROPEAN JEWRY: THE SIX MOST POPULOUS JEWISH CITIES IN EUROPE

	Warsaw*		Lodz		Budapest†		Vienna		Berlin‡		Odessa	
	Number Jews	Percent of total pop.	Number Jews	Percent of total pop.	Number Jews	Percent of total pop.	Number Jews	Percent of total pop.	Number Jews	Percent of total pop.	Number Jews	Percent of total pop.
1860	41,000	25.0	3,000	...	...	...	6,217	2.2	18,953	3.5	25,000	...
1870	89,318	32.6	...	...	44,747	16.6	40,227	6.1	36,105	4.4	...	...
1880	127,917	33.4	...	...	70,277	19.7	72,588	10.1	53,916	4.8	...	...
1890	151,076	33.1	...	...	102,377	21.0	118,495	8.6	79,286	5.0	...	...
1900	219,128	34.3	96,671	31.4	166,198	23.6	146,926	8.8	92,206	4.9	138,935	34.4
1910	306,061	39.2	...	...	203,687	23.1	175,318	8.6	144,007	3.9	...	...
1920	310,334	33.1	156,155	34.5	215,512	23.2	200,000	12.8	...	...	...	...
1925	...	...	...	...	207,015	21.5	201,513	10.8	172,672	4.4	153,194	36.4
1929	...	...	195,000	32.7	...	...	201,513	10.8	172,672	4.3	153,194	36.4

Source: Compiled on the basis of data presented in Arthur Ruppin, *Soziologie der Juden* (Berlin: Juedischer Verlag, 1930), vol. 1, pp. 114–15; J. Kreppel, *Juden und Judentum von Heute: Ein Handbuch* (Zurich: Amalthea Verlag, 1925), pp. 301, 323–24, 349; and S. Dubnow, *Die neuste Geschichte des juedischen Volkes* (Berlin: Juedischer Verlag, 1920–23), vol. 2, p. 121.

* In 1813 there were circa 8,000 Jews in Warsaw, constituting 12 percent of the city's total population.
† In 1789 there were only 114 Jews in Budapest; in 1833, 6,730; and in 1849, 19,148 Jews. In the nineteenth century Budapest grew faster than any other European capital. The Jews were demographically so prominent in the Hungarian capital that it was pejoratively called "Judapest."
‡ In 1816 there were 3,373 Jews in Berlin, constituting 1.7 percent of the general population. Whereas the total population of Berlin increased twelvefold in the period between 1811 and 1910, the Jewish population of the city increased twenty-sevenfold in the same period.

TABLE IX   THE JEWISH POPULATION IN THE LARGEST CITY OF VARIOUS COUNTRIES

		Number of Jews in country		Number of Jews in city	Percentage of country's Jews in largest city
1921	Denmark	5,946	Copenhagen	5,482	92.2
1926	France	200,000	Paris	140,000	70.0
1923	Austria	300,000	Vienna	201,513	67.3
1926	England	300,000	London	200,000	66.6
1920	Holland	115,229	Amsterdam	68,758	59.7
1917	Egypt	59,581	Cairo	29,207	49.0
1926	United States	4,000,000	New York	1,800,000	45.0
1921	Hungary	473,310	Budapest	212,736	44.9
1920	Bulgaria	43,232	Sofia	17,038	39.4
1925	Germany	564,379	Berlin	172,672	30.6
1921	Poland	2,829,456	Warsaw	310,334	10.9
1921	Czechoslovakia	354,342	Prague	31,751	9.0

Source: Adapted from Arthur Ruppin, *Soziologie der Juden* (Berlin: Jüdischer Verlag, 1930), vol. 1, p. 117.

TABLE X   OCCUPATIONAL DISTRIBUTION OF JEWS IN VARIOUS COUNTRIES: PERCENTAGE OF GAINFULLY EMPLOYED PERSONS, EXCLUDING AGRICULTURAL LABOR

	Year	Industry and Trade		Commerce and Credit		Communications and Transport		Public Service and Liberal Professions		Domestic and Personal Service		Others*	
		Jews	Non-Jews	Jews	Non-Jews	Jews	Non-Jews	Jews	Non-Jews	Jews	Non-Jews	Jews	Non-Jews
Poland	1931	45.4	44.0	38.2	9.3	3.5	7.3	6.1	12.0	3.3	10.9	3.5	11.5
U.S.S.R.	1926	41.5	38.9	23.8	7.9	3.3	10.8	17.5	16.1	...	...	13.9	26.3
Ukraine	1926	43.5	41.7	24.2	5.6	3.5	10.5	14.1	15.2	...	...	14.3	27.0
Central Russia	1926	33.4	38.6	24.4	8.4	2.6	10.8	27.2	16.2	...	...	12.4	26.0
White Russia	1926	49.6	26.1	20.2	4.2	4.0	2.9	11.1	22.6	...	...	15.1	34.2
Germany	1933	18.7	45.6	49.8	15.1	0.3	5.5	9.4	8.3	1.3	5.3	20.5	20.2
Rumania	1930	34.8	47.5	51.5	18.1	2.6	10.1	2.9	13.4	...	...	8.2	10.9
Hungary	1930	32.8	49.5	46.2	10.0	2.0	6.2	8.4	10.4	1.5	11.6	9.1	12.3
Czechoslovakia: Slovakia and Carpatho-Ruthenia	1930	24.8	41.3	46.2	7.4	2.9	8.0	8.3	11.1	2.5	11.1	15.2	21.1
Czechoslovakia: Bohemia, Moravia and Silesia	1930	19.0	53.2	47.1	10.5	1.3	5.8	8.4	6.0	0.9	6.3	23.3	18.2
Canada	1931	33.3	27.1	39.0	12.4	2.9	11.3	5.7	10.4	6.0	13.4	13.1	25.4

Source: Adapted from Jacob Lestschinsky, "The Economic and Social Development of the Jewish People from the Beginning of the Nineteenth Century to the Second World War," in *The Jewish People: Past and Present* (New York: Central Yiddish Culture Organization, 1946), vol. 1, pp. 378–80.

*Includes those living on income not derived from personal labor, such as pensions, welfare, charity, and inherited wealth.

TABLE XI   THE OCCUPATIONAL DISTRIBUTION OF WORLD JEWRY: 1929

Occupation	Number	Percent
Commerce (including transport, entertainment, trade, and banking)	6,100,000	38.6
Industry (including mining and handicrafts)	5,750,000	36.4
Professions and civil service	1,000,000	6.3
Agriculture	625,000	4.0
Casual laborers and domestic servants	325,000	2.0
Unemployed (living on private means, pensions, charity, welfare)	2,000,000	12.7
Total number of Jews	15,800,000	100.0

Source: Adapted from Jacob Lestschinsky, "A Century's Changes in Jewish Numbers and Occupations," *The Menorah Journal* 20, no. 6 (1932), p. 177.

the conditions of the Jews in the large European cities [of the nineteenth century], this process [illustrated by the scheme] is as familiar as it is clear."[13] See table 13.

It should be emphasized that this scheme is only a statistical description of certain characteristic phenomena of modern Jewish history; it is not an explanation of these phenomena. In themselves, statistics do not provide an explanation; at most they alert the scholar to certain correlations and patterns that require independent sociological and historical analysis. What is indeed clear from the statistics is that as the Jews became increasingly middle class and urban, intermarriage and voluntary conversion increased to an unprecedented degree.

The Zionist movement sought to redirect the course of modern Jewish history. Drawn to the ideals of Zionism, a relatively small but ever increasing number of Jews immigrated to Palestine—the land of Israel—in order to create alternative forms of *modern* Jewish life. Zionist-inspired immigration to the land of Israel was called *aliyah* (plural, *aliyot*), the Hebrew term meaning "ascent" and also traditionally denoting the spiritual elevation associated with permanent settlement in the Holy Land. Initially, Zionist *aliyot* were highly selective groups of pioneers (in Hebrew, *haluzim*) who were pledged to the revival of Hebrew as a spoken language and to the realization of various Zionist social ideals. In the course of time, Jewish refugees joined the *halutzim*. There were seven distinct waves of Zionist-sponsored *aliyot* to the land of Israel. See table 16.

With the proclamation of the State of Israel in May 1948, hundreds of thousands of Jews from the four

---

[13] Arthur Ruppin, *The Jews of Today*, (New York: H. Holt, 1913), p. 14.

TABLE XII ATTENDANCE OF JEWS AT ADVANCED ACADEMIC INSTITUTIONS AND UNIVERSITIES

Country or city	Types of Schooling	Period	Number of Jewish students		The Percentage of Jewish Students Exceeds Percent of Jews in the Population
			Absolute No.	Percentage	
Germany*	Universities	Winter Session 1929–1930	2,970	3.4	3.7 times
	Technical Institutes	"	264	1.3	1.4 times
	Art Academies	"	73	1.6	1.8 times
	Together	Winter Session 1929–1930	3,307	2.9	3.2 times
Czechoslovakia	Universities	Winter Session 1927–1928	2,414	14.5	5.6 times
	Technical Institutes	"	1,314	12.2	4.7 times
	Art Academies	"	50	2.2	0.8 times
	Together	Winter Session 1927–1928	3,778	12.8	4.9 times
Vienna	Universities	1928–1929	2,377	21.3	2.0 times
	Technical Institutes	"	328	10.7	1.0 times
	Art Academies	"	239	9.6	0.9 times
	Together	1928–1929	2,944	...	...
Hungary	All Universities and Advanced Academic Institutions	Winter Session 1930	1,350	10.5	1.8 times
Poland	All Universities and Advanced Academic Institutions	Winter Session 1929–1930	8,711	19.3	1.9 times
Soviet Russia	All Universities and Advanced Academic Institutions	1926–1927	23,699	13.4	5.9 times
Latvia	Universities	1930–1931	744	8.7	1.8 times
Lithuania	Universities	1926	756	31.4	4.1 times
United States	Universities	1918–1919	14,837	9.7	3.2 times

Source: Adapted from Arthur Ruppin, *The Jews in the Modern World* (London: Macmillan and Co., 1934), p. 313.

* These figures do not include the many East European Jews who attended German universities.

TABLE XIII THE FOUR STRATA OF EUROPEAN JEWRY IN 1900

Numbers		Typical Representatives	Economic Conditions	Religious Outlook	Education	Birth-rate per 1,000 souls	Percentage of Mixed Marriages	Conversions Annually per 10,000 souls
First Stratum	Six million	The great mass of Jews in Russia and Galicia	Workmen, artisans and shopkeepers without means—and of uncertain livelihood	Orthodox	Heder	30–40	0–2	0–2
Second Stratum	Three million	Settlers in England and America, Rumanian Jews	Artisans and merchants with modest but settled income	Liberal	Jewish elementary schools	25–30	2–10	2–5
Third Stratum	Two million	The mass of German Jews	Well-to-do bourgeoisie	Free-thinking	Christian elementary and secondary schools	20–25	10–30	5–15
Fourth Stratum	One million	Rich Jews and Jews of university education In all the big towns	Wealthy bourgeoisie	Agnostic	Public School and University	15–20	30–50	15–40

Source: Arthur Ruppin. *The Jews of Today* (New York: H. Holt, 1913), p.15.

TABLE XIV INTERMARRIAGE

		Percentage of Jews Marrying Non-Jews		
	Year or Period	Jewish Males	Jewish Females	Total
Germany	1901–1904	8.48	7.41	7.95
	1910–1911	13.49	10.37	11.96
	1928	25.15	16.79	21.19
	1929	27.16	17.82	22.79
	1930	26.60	17.60	22.36
Prussia	1875–1884	4.60	4.98	4.79
	1885–1889	8.29	7.33	7.81
	1905–1908	11.81	10.57	11.19
	1925	23.56	13.97	19.05
	1928	26.06	17.65	22.08
	1929	27.81	18.46	23.47
Berlin	1876–1880	15.69	11.99	13.88
	1901–1904	17.89	12.02	15.06
	1925	30.53	17.90	24.75
	1926	29.19	18.63	24.52
	1929	35.31	21.95	29.21
Hamburg	1886–1890	16.50	9.30	13.10
	1906–1910	26.40	22.20	24.30
	1925	31.82	24.53	28.83
	1928	39.86	26.45	33.83
Bavaria	1876–1880	1.54	2.08	1.82
	1901–1905	4.47	4.o4	4.25
	1926–1927	16.90	9.52	13.36
Hungary	1895–1899	2.68	2.73	2.70
	1907–1908	4.12	4.55	4.33
	1925	11.90	10.90	11.40
	1927	11.93	12.06	12.00
	1928	12.50	11.60	12.05
	1929	12.04	11.90	11.97
Budapest	1896–1900	6.71	7.22	6.97
	1925	17.96	15.27	16.64
	1927	16.74	16.18	16.46
	1929	16.61	16.43	16.52
Vienna	1926	12.68	11.71	12.20
	1927	12.16	9.93	11.06
	1928	12.83	10.06	11.47
	1929	13.86	12.02	12.95
Amsterdam	1899–1908	--	--	5.00
	1921–1925	12.66	9.56	11.14
	1926–1927	13.79	12.60	13.20
	1928–1930	17.03	12.49	14.83
Copenhagen	1880–1889	--	--	21.84
	1900–1905	--	--	31.76
Trieste	1887–1890	--	--	14.30
	1900–1903	--	--	17.90
	1927	60.87	50.00	56.10
Galicia	1929	1.02	0.64	0.83
Central Russia	1924–1926	20.68	12.47	16.77
White Russia	1924–926	1.87	3.73	2.81
Ukraine	1924–1926	4.19	4.90	4.55
Total European Russia	1924–1926	7.41	6.21	6.80

Source: Adapted from Arthur Ruppin, *The Jews in the Modern World* (London: Macmillan, 1934), pp. 318–19.

TABLE XV   JEWISH CONVERSIONS TO CHRISTIANITY IN THE NINETEENTH CENTURY

	Protestant	Roman Catholic	Greek Orthodox	Total
Prussia	13,128		...	
Bavaria	330	5,000	...	
Saxony	770		...	22,520
Wuerttemberg	115		...	
Rest of Germany	3,177		...	
Great Britain	28,830	...	...	28,830
Netherlands	1,800	...	...	1,800
Sweden and Norway	500	...	...	500
Denmark	100	...	...	100
Switzerland	100	...	...	100
France	600	1,800	...	2,400
Austria	6,300	28,200	200	44,756
Hungary	2,056	8,000		
Tsarist Russia (including Poland)*	3,136	12,000	69,400	84,536
Italy	...	300	...	300
Rumania	...	...	1,500	1,500
Turkey	...	...	3,300	3,300
Balkan Countries	...	...	100	100
Asia and Africa	100	500	...	600
Australia	200	...	...	200
North America	11,500	1,500	...	13,000
Total	72,742	57,300	74,500	204,542

Source: J. de le Roi, "Judentaufen im XIX. Jahrhundert. Ein statistischer Versuch." *Nathanael, Zeitschrift für die Arbeit der Evangelischen Kriche an Israel* 5, nos. 3–4 (Berlin. 1899), pp. 65–118.

* This figure includes Frankists. The majority of Jewish conversions in Russia were under one form or another of coercion, the most outrageous being the forced baptism of the cantonists. (See chapter 7, document 3.) Strictly voluntary conversion in tsarist Russia was relatively rare.

TABLE XVI   ZIONIST ALIYOT TO THE LAND OF ISRAEL: 1882–1948

	Origin	Motivation	Number
First *aliyah*, 1882–1903	Russia Rumania	Hibbat Zion and Bilu	25,000
Second *aliyah*, 1904–1914	Russia	Labour and Social Zionism	40,000
Third *aliyah*, 1919–1923	Russia Poland Rumania (Smaller numbers from Germany, Lithuania, United States, and Other places)	Hehaluz and Hashomer Hazair	35,183
Fourth *aliyah*, 1924–1932	Poland	Mainly middle-class refugees who left Poland because of anti-Jewish economic measures; four-fifths settled in cities	81,613
Fifth *aliyah*, 1932–1938	Poland, Germany, and Central Europe	Youth aliyah, refugees from Nazi Persecution	197,235
Sixth *aliyah*, 1939–1945	All of Europe	Refugees from Nazi Europe	81,808
Seventh *aliyah*, 1946–1948	All of Europe	Survivors of the Holocaust, many of whom entered Palestine "illegally"	56,467

Source: Compiled on the basis of data presented in the *Statistical Abstract of Israel* (Israel: Central Bureau of Statistics, 1992), no. 43, p.170.

corners of the earth—among them displaced persons, survivors of the Holocaust, and Jewish communities animated by a messianic enthusiasm—settled in their ancestral homeland.

The establishment of the State of Israel was preceded by the Nazi nightmare in which a third of Jewry was murdered. From close to seventeen million people, Jewry was reduced to eleven million. (Sergio DellaPergola estimates that had the Holocaust not occurred, the world Jewish population might have reached some thirty million, [*Haaretz*, April 19, 2009].)In the generations since the Holocaust, Jewry has not grown appreciably. Intermarriage and a low fertility rate have contributed to the virtual demographic stagnation of the Jewish people. Table 17 presents the world Jewish population at the beginning of 2008, as calculated by the demographer Sergio DellaPergola of the Hebrew University of Jerusalem. These statistics are, of course, but estimates. In computing the size of the Jewish population, as DellaPergola explains, demographers must contend with seemingly intractable definitional and methodological problems. First and foremost, they must decide who is to be deemed a Jew? Are the children of mixed marriages to be regarded as Jews? If they are, then by what criteria? By matrilineal descent, as designated by rabbinic law? Or should demographers follow the ruling by the American Reform movement to honor patrilineal descent as well? Second, the principal challenge is how to collect the relevant demographic data. In most countries in the Diaspora where Jews currently dwell in large numbers, official population statistics remain imprecise because of legal and cultural restrictions on soliciting information about one's religious and ethnic affiliation. Are the demographers thus confined to consulting the membership rosters of synagogues and Jewish organizations? But, then, what about the presumably large number of unaffiliated Jews? In a word, how is one to determine the composition and size of a given Jewish population?[14] Demographers have

---

[14] On the complex definitional and methodological problems that beset the scientific study of the Jewish

developed sophisticated methods to estimate contemporary Jewish populations. Nonetheless, depending on the methodologies employed, the demographic estimates may still differ, as in the case of determining the Jewish population of the United States.[15] Whereas DellaPergola estimates the Jewish population of the United States (as of January 1, 2008) to be 5,275,000, the definitional criteria and statistical methodologies that were used in a report prepared by the Steinhardt Social Research Institute of Brandeis University yield an estimate between 6 million and 6.5 million U.S. citizens who identify themselves as Jews.[16] Table 19 presents the results of the latter study according to various categories of self-identification, namely, of individuals who consider themselves Jews.

Table 17 also reflects the fact that following the collapse of the Soviet Union in the early 1990s, the distribution of the world Jewish population has shifted considerably. Primarily as a result of

---

population, see Paul Ritterband, Barry A. Kosmin, and Jeffrey Scheckner, "Counting Jewish Populations: Methods and Problems." *American Jewish Year Book* (New York: American Jewish Committee, 1988), vol. 88, pp. 204–21; Sergio DellaPergola, "Demography," *Oxford Handbook of Jewish Studies*, ed., Martin Goodman (Oxford, England, and New York: Oxford University Press, 2002), pp. 797–823.

[15] Cf. Laurence Kotler-Berkowitz, Steven M. Cohen, Joanathan Ament, Vivian Klaff, and David Marker, *The National Jewish Population Survey 2000–2001: Strength, and Diversity in the American Jewish Population* (New York; United Jewish Communities, 2003); for a critical analysis of this latter study, see Charles Kadushin, Benjamin Phillips, and Leonard Saxe, "National Jewish Population Survey, 2000–01: A Guide for the Perplexed." *Studies in Contemporary Jewry*, vol. 25, ed., Samuel Heilman (New York: Oxford University Press, 2005), pp. 1–32; and Sergio DellaPergola, "Was It the Demography? A Reassessment of U.S. Jewish Population Estimates, 1945–2001, "in *Studies in Contemporary Jewry*, vol. 25, pp. 85–131.

[16] Leonard Saxe, Elizabeth Tighe, Benjamin Philipps, and Charles Kadushin, *Reconsidering the Size and Characteristics of the American Jewish Population: New Estimates.* (Waltham, Mass.: Steinhardt Social Research Institute, Brandeis University, 2007). This report is based on a synthesis of government-sponsored surveys conducted between 1998 and 2004 and establishes that 1.9 percent of American adults identify themselves as Jews by religion. Including those who identify themselves as Jews by nonreligious criteria and children who are being raised as Jews, the report concludes that the Jewish population of the United States is between 6 million and 6.5 million individuals. Cf. Table 18.

emigration, the Jewish population of the former Soviet Union (FSU) in Europe had declined from an estimated 780,400 to 328,300; the Jewish population of the FSU in Asia has dwindled from 108,100 to some 20,000. In the wake of the so-called Dirty War of the 1980s in Argentina and the attendant economic crisis, the Jewish population of that country declined from 210,000 to 183,000. Developments in South Africa since the dismantling of apartheid have led to the depletion of the country's Jewish population through emigration by more than 25 percent, namely, from 100,000 to 71,300. The Jewish population in the State of Israel, on the other hand, continues to increase because of the relatively high birth rate (certainly in comparison to the Jewish communities

---

TABLE XVII   WORLD JEWISH POPULATION: JANUARY 1, 2008

The Americas	Total Population	Jewish Population	Jews per 1,000 Population
Canada	33,300,000	375,000	11.4
United States	304,500,000	5,275,000	17.5
Total North America[a]	**337,927,000**	**5,650,000**	**16.9**
Baharnas	300,000	300	1.0
Costa Rica	4,500,000	2,500	0.6
Cuba	11,200,000	500	0.0
Dominican Republic	9,900,000	100	0.0
El Salvador	7,200,000	100	0.0
Guatemala	13,700,000	900	0.1
Jamaica	2,700,000	300	0.1
Mexico	107,700,000	39,600	0.4
Netherlands Antilles	215,000	200	0.9
Panama	3,400,000	8,000	2.4
Puerto Rico	4,000,000	1,500	0.4
Virgin Islands	115,000	500	4.4
Other	26,070,000	300	0.0
Total Central America	**191,000,000**	**54,800**	**0.3**
Argentina	39,700,000	183,000	4.6
Bolivia	10,000,000	500	0.1
Brazil	195,100,000	96,000	0.5
Chile	16,800,000	20,600	1.2
Colombia	44,400,000	2,800	0.1
Ecuador	13,800,000	900	0.1
Paraguay	6,200,000	900	0.1
Peru	27,900,000	2,000	0.1
Suriname	500,000	200	0.4
Paraguay	3,300,000	17,700	5.4
Venezuela	27,900,000	12,500	0.5
Total South Americaa	**386,600,000**	**337,100**	**0.9**
Total	**915,527,000**	**6,041,900**	**6.7**

Source: Adapted from Sergio DellaPergola, "World Jewish Population 2008," *American Jewish Year Book 2008*, ed. Stephen Massil (New York: American Jewish Committee, 2008), p. 586.

[a] Including countries not listed separately.

TABLE XVII   (CONTINUED)

Europe	Total Population	Jewish Population	Jews per 1,000 Population
Austria	8,400,000	9,000	1.1
Belgium	10,700,000	30,500	2.9
Bulgaria	7,600,000	2,000	0.3
Czech Republic	10,400,000	3,900	0.4
Denmark	5,500,000	6,400	1.2
Estonia	1,300,000	1,900	1.5
Finland	5,300,000	1,100	0.2
France[a]	62,000,000	488,000	7.9
Germany	82,200,000	120,000	1.5
Greece	11,200,000	4,500	0.4
Hungary	10,000,000	48,800	4.8
Ireland	4,500,000	1,200	0.3
Italy	59,900,000	28,500	0.5
Latvia	2,300,000	10,100	4.3
Lithuania	3,400,000	3,500	1.1
Luxembourg	500,000	600	1.2
Netherlands	16,400,000	30,000	1.8
Poland	38,100,000	3,200	0.1
Portugal	10,600,000	500	0.0
Romania	21,500,000	9,800	0.5
Slovakia	5,400,000	2,600	0.5
Slovenia	2,000,000	100	0.1
Spain	46,500,000	12,000	0.3
Sweden	9,200,000	15,000	1.6
United Kingdom	61,500,000	294,000	4.8
Other[b]	1,500,000	100	0.1
Total European Union	**497,900,000**	**1,127,300**	**2.3**
Gibraltar	28,000	600	21.4
Norway	4,800,000	1,200	0.3
Switzerland	7,600,000	17,700	2.4
Total other West Europe[c]	**12,898,000**	**19,500**	**1.5**
Belarus	9,700,000	17,000	1.8
Moldova	4,100,000	4,300	1.1
Russia[d]	141,900,000	215,000	1.5
Ukraine	46,200,000	76,500	1.6
Total FSU Republics	**201,900,000**	**312,800**	**1.5**
[Total FSU in Europe][e]	**208,900,000**	**328,300**	**1.6**
Bosnia-Herzegovina	3,800,000	500	0.1
Croatia	4,400,000	1,700	0.4
Macedonia	2,000,000	100	0.1
Serbia	7,400,000	1,400	0.1
Turkey[d]	74,800,000	17,700	0.2
Total other East Europe and Balkans[c]	**98,400,000**	**21,500**	**0.2**
Total	**811,098,000**	**1,481,100**	**1.8**

Source: Ibid., pp. 602–3.

[a] Including Monaco.
[b] Cyprus and Malta.
[c] Including countries not listed separately.
[d] Including Asian regions.
[e] Including Baltic countries.

TABLE XVII   (CONTINUED)

Asia	Total Population	Jewish Population	Jews per 1,000 Population
Israel[a]	6,968,400	5,209,200	747.5
West Bank and Gaza[b]	3,775,200	269,000	71.3
Total Israel and Palestine	**10,743,600**	**5,478,200**	**509.9**
Azerbaijan	8,700,000	6,600	0.8
Georgia	4,600,000	3,500	0.8
Kazakhstan	15,700,000	3,700	0.2
Kyrgyzstan	5,200,000	800	0.2
Turkmenistan	5,200,000	200	0.0
Uzbekistan	27,200,000	4,800	0.2
Total former USSR in Asia[c]	**77,000,000**	**19,600**	**0.3**
China[d]	1,332,300,000	1,500	0.0
India	1,149,300,000	5,000	0.0
Iran	72,200,000	10,600	0.1
Japan	127,700,000	1,000	0.0
Korea, South	48,600,000	100	0.0
Philippines	90,500,000	100	0.0
Singapore	4,800,000	300	0.1
Syria	19,900,000	100	0.0
Taiwan	23,000,000	100	0.0
Thailand	65,700,000	200	0.0
Yemen	22,200,000	200	0.0
Other	932,156,400	200	0.0
Total other Asia	**3,888,356,400**	**19,400**	**0.0**
Total	**3,976,100,000**	**5,517,200**	**1.4**

Source: Ibid., p. 611.

[a] Total population of Israel, including Jews in West Bank, 1/1/2008:7,243,600.
[b] Total Palestinian population in West Bank and Gaza, 1/1/2008: 3,500,000 (our revised estimate).
[c] Including Armenia and Tajikistan. Not including Asian regions of Russian Republic.
[d] Including Hong Kong and Macao.

TABLE XVII   (CONTINUED)

Africa	Total Population	Jewish Population	Jews per 1,000 Population
Egypt	74,900,000	100	0.0
Ethiopia	79,100,000	100	0.0
Morocco	31,200,000	2,900	0.1
Tunisia	10,300,000	1,000	0.1
Total North Africa[a]	**276,400,000**	**4,100**	**0.0**
Botswana	1,800,000	100	0.1
Congo D.R.	66,500,000	100	0.0
Kenya	38,000,000	400	0.0
Namibia	2,100,000	100	0.0
Nigeria	148,100,000	100	0.0
South Africa	48,300,000	71,300	1.5
Zimbabwe	13,300,000	400	0.0
Other	372,500,000	300	0.0
Total other Africa	**690,600,000**	**72,800**	**0.1**
Total	**967,000,000**	**76,900**	**0.1**

Source: Ibid., p. 615.

[a] Including countries not listed separately.

TABLE XVII (CONTINUED)

Oceania	Total Population	Jewish Population	Jews per 1,000 Population
Australia	21,300,000	107,000	5.1
New Zealand	4,300,000	7,500	1.8
Other	9,400,000	100	0.0
Total	**35,000,000**	**114,600**	**3.3**
World Total	**6,705,000,000**	**13,231,700**	**1.97**

Source: Ibid., p. 615.

TABLE XVIII UNITED STATES JEWISH POPULATION: 2007

Adult Jews who regard themselves as Jewish by religion	3.5 million
Adult Jews who regard themselves as Jewish not by religion	920,000
Unenumerated adult Jews*	250,000 to 350,000
Children being raised as Jews	1.1 million to 1.7 million
Total	6.0 million to 6.4 million

Source: Based on Leonard Saxe, Elizabeth Tighe, Benjamin Philipps, and Charles Kadushin, *Reconsidering the size and Charateristics of the American Jewish Population: New Estimates.* (Waltham, Mass.: Steinhardt Social Research Institute, Brandeis University, 2007).

*Unenumerated Jews refers to individuals who were not included in the surveys upon which this table is based because they were in jail, military dormitories, aged care facilities, and long-term care facilities.

TABLE XIX JEWISH EDUCATION IN THE UNITED STATES BY DENOMINATIONS OF PARENTAL HOME, AGE, AND GENDER

Denomination in which Raised		Men		Women	
		% Ever had formal Jewish education grades 1–12	Mean years of Jewish education grades 1–12	% Ever had formal Jewish education grades 1–12	Mean years of Jewish education grades 1–12
Orthodox	18–24	100.0	9.5	97.5	10.1
	25–44	100.0	9.0	96.3	8.5
	45–64	98.1	7.9	82.9	5.6
	65+	96.0	5.7	78.3	3.9
	Total	**97.8**	**7.4**	**85.2**	**6.0**
Conservative	18–24	97.8	7.1	97.2	7.5
	25–44	97.4	6.6	92.0	6.0
	45–64	96.3	5.7	81.5	4.7
	65+	92.7	5.0	72.0	3.5
	Total	**96.0**	**5.9**	**82.6**	**4.9**
Reform/ Reconstructionst	18–24	97.8	6.5	90.2	5.6
	25–44	93.9	5.5	85.0	5.4
	45–64	91.3	5.2	80.7	4.9
	65+	86.5	4.2	69.6	4.2
	Total	**92.6**	**5.4**	**81.3**	**5.0**
Unaffiliated (with mainstream denomination)	18–24	81.0	3.8	55.6	2.5
	25–44	60.6	2.6	50.4	1.6
	45–64	63.4	2.6	43.3	1.2
	65+	68.0	2.0	48.7	1.4
	Total	**65.0**	**2.5**	**48.1**	**1.5**

Source: Table supplied by Harriet Hartman, based on 2000–01 National Jewish Population Survey, *unweighted data.* Adapted from Harriet Hartman and Moshe Hartman, *Gender and American Jews: Patterns in Work, Education, and Family in Contemporary Life* (Waltham, Mass.: Brandeis University Press, 2009).

of the West) and immigration (mainly from the FSU and France). Primarily due to immigration from the FSU, the Jewish population of Germany has grown rapidly from an estimated 50,000 to over 120,000. The Jewish population of Canada has also benefited from an influx of former citizens of the Soviet Union. The Australian Jewish community has been strengthened by immigrants, particularly from South Africa as well as the FSU.[17]

---

[17] On migration as a factor in modern Jewish history, see Sergio DellaPergola, "Migrations," *Encyclopedia Judaica*, 2nd. ed, vol. 14, pp. 207–19.

INDEX